HANDBOOK OF COMMUNICATION SCIENCE

HANDBOOK OF COMMUNICATION SCIENCE

EDITORS

Charles R. Berger &- Steven H. Chaffee

SAGE PUBLICATIONS
The Publishers of Professional Social Science
Newbury Park   Beverly Hills   London   New Delhi

For information address:

SAGE Publications, Inc.
2111 West Hillcrest Drive
Newbury Park, California 91320

SAGE Publications Inc.
275 South Beverly Drive
Beverly Hills
California 90212

SAGE Publications Ltd.
28 Banner Street
London EC1Y 8QE
England

SAGE PUBLICATIONS India Pvt. Ltd.
M-32 Market
Greater Kailash I
New Delhi 110 048 India

Printed in the United States of America

Library of Congress Cataloging-in-Publication Data

Main entry under title:

Handbook of communication science.

Includes index.
1. Communication.   I. Berger, Charles R.
II. Chaffee, Steven H.
P90.H294   1987   001.51   87-9783
ISBN 0-8039-2199-3

CONTENTS

To the memory of Jerry Kline,
who brought so many of us together

PREFACE

THIS *Handbook* represents possibly the most ambitious undertaking in our field since Wilbur Schramm pulled together the first set of papers on mass communication research more than 30 years ago. Schramm's original vision was to bring under one cover contributors from every social science field that had something to add to the problem of studying human communication behavior: psychology, sociology, political science, anthropology, linguistics, and so on. This was the spirit of his original *Process and Effects of Mass Communication* (1954), and of the *Handbook of Communication* (Pool, Schramm, Frey, Maccoby, & Parker, 1973).

Our purpose is almost the converse. We have primarily sought contributions to this volume from scholars who make their academic homes somewhere *within* the field of communication rather than in surrounding disciplines. We are able to do so because a large entity we might call communication research proper has grown up on the foundations laid some years back by Schramm and other pioneers. It is housed today not only in traditional departments of speech and journalism, but increasingly in university programs with the more generic term "communication" in their titles. Most of the authors of the pages that follow find their strongest professional affiliation in the International Communication Association (ICA), even though many remain active in the older organizations of journalism, psychology, speech, political science, and other fields of origin.

This project would not, however, have posed any special challenge if communication were an integrated and stable academic discipline. The fact is, it is not close to that stage in its development, which is precisely why we feel such a *Handbook* is needed at this time. We have consciously tried here to bring together what has up to now been quite separate, by imposing a common theoretical framework on active scholars who have looked at different aspects of communicatioin at different levels of analysis—and reported them to different academic bodies and taught them to students in different departments even within the same university.

The plan of this book was developed at a meeting following the 1983 ICA convention in Dallas. We assembled a number of leaders from the interpersonal, organizational, mass communication and other divisions of ICA, many of whom were unfamiliar with one another's work. As they sought common ground, they began to find it in a conception of communication study as cutting across many levels of analysis. After much discussion we agreed—in some cases grudgingly—upon the four levels that are outlined in Part II of this book, and that form the basic outline for almost all our other chapters. The list is as follows: individual, interpersonal, network/organizational, and macrosocietal. The reader will encounter it so often as to consider it a cliché after even a few chapters.

The concept of "communication science" as the overall label for this activity was even more difficult to choose. The study of communication is approached from many perspectives, as many of our contributors point out. No one of our acquaintance is sufficiently experienced in all of them to cover the whole of communication study. Our own work, like that of most of our colleagues in ICA and the departments we and our students have taught in, follows the general tradition of American social and behavioral science. This, we decided, had grown into a sufficiently diverse and fragmented field for one *Handbook,* so, after considering a number of alternative titles that struck us as more objectionable, we added the limiting term "science" to the broad commitment implied in "communication."

Quite a few of our contributors note some difficulty with the title, as with the four levels of analysis we asked them to consider. We did not fully recognize until after much of the writing was underway just how demanding the task of contributing to this book would become. With only two or three exceptions, none of these authors—all of whom have been quite prominent in the production of original scientific research on communication—has worked at all four levels of analysis. A specialized researcher normally knows intimately the main lines of inquiry at one or two levels, but has no need for more than passing familiarity with other levels. Students of the field, on the other hand, ought to know something about every level if they are to make informed choices in planning new studies. So we asked busy social and behavioral scientists who study interpersonal communication to look also at more macroscopic levels of analysis, just as we asked scholars of mass communication to explore the literature on their assigned subjects at the interpersonal level. A number of our contributors complained that this was the hardest synthesizing task they had taken on since they were themselves students.

We will not pretend that this volume contains an absolutely balanced

synthesis across levels. Each of us has his own specialty, Berger in interpersonal communication and Chaffee in mass communication, although
both of us have maintained interests and done some original research at
other levels and have edited journals and topical books that cut across all
levels. We have divided editorial responsibilities to take advantage of our
specializations, even as we have found many commonalities between us.
We know that our authors have not freed themselves—and we would not
want them to do so—from their own specializations either. In matching
editor to author, Berger has taken principal editing responsibility for
Chapters 6, 7, 12, 13, 15, 16, 18, 19, 23, and 27; Chaffee for Chapters
8, 9, 11, 14, 20, 21, 22, 24, 25, and 26. Responsibility for overall editing and the chapters in Part I, as of course with all jointly authored chapters, is shared equally. Order of our names as editors and authors has, in
the finest tradition of behavioral scientists who don't know what else to
do, been determined by the flip of a fair coin.

Not all of the people responsible for this book appear as authors of the
chapters that follow. In particular, it was Sara Miller McCune, then
President (and now Chairman) of Sage Publications, who came to us
originally with the idea of such a *Handbook,* and who has been both the
driving administrative force and a welcome source of substantive ideas
throughout the project. If a third Editor were to be listed, it should
be her. Just as Sara represents the "sa" of Sage, the "ge" is George
McCune, originally Chairman (and now President) of the publishing
house and a constant referent for intellectual good sense in our editing.
Although George may not have seen any of these chapters, in selecting
the material that is represented here we have repeatedly asked ourselves
the hard questions he asks us.

Two other leaders of the field, in addition to authors of many of these
chapters, participated most helpfully in the original 1983 meeting at
which the book was planned. One is Karl Erik Rosengren, the noted
Swedish scholar, whose comments, writings, and research have had a
clear influence on this volume and on the field at large. The other was
the late F. Gerald Kline of the University of Minnesota (for a time at the
University of Michigan), to whom this book is dedicated. It was Jerry
Kline who initiated most of the communication research series of Sage
Publications, which is by far the most active publishing house in this
field. He was also to have written a chapter for Part I, on the intersection
of technology, policy, and human values. Fatal illness intervened, but
some of the spirit of our discussions with Jerry is reflected in observations we make in the concluding Chapter 28.

We wish to acknowledge Mark Wright for the index preparation. A
number of generic acknowledgments are also due, especially to those

who have assisted us in both clerical and professional tasks, and to family, friends, and associates who have suffered our foibles during a time of singular concentration on our part.

—Charles R. Berger
Steven H. Chaffee
Wawona Valley
Yosemite National Park
California

PART I
OVERVIEWS

1   The Study of Communication as a Science

CHARLES R. BERGER
Northwestern University

STEVEN H. CHAFFEE
Stanford University

A generation ago, in a volume entitled *The Science of Human Communication,* Wilbur Schramm noted that as of that time communication was not a discipline on the model of psychology or mathematics, but "an academic crossroad where many have passed, but few have tarried" (1963, p. 2). In the years since he wrote, so many have tarried at the crossroad that a relatively large urban center has developed. There has been much construction—of communication departments, research traditions, and journals. If these indicators can be taken as measures of the construct "disciplinicity," communication is acquiring the trappings of a discipline.

Not only has a figurative city grown up at the crossroad of which Schramm wrote, but the people in it are considerably more heterogeneous than were the interdisciplinary wayfarers of those more bucolic times. The conceptual domain of communication science was narrower then than it is today. Schramm's 1963 explanation of the nature of communication, like many of that time (e.g., Berlo, 1960), conceived of it as a process in which sources encode messages and then send them through channels to be decoded and acted upon by receivers. This linear conceptualization fit easily into the *Zeitgeist* of message effects, which dominated the field then. Most of the contributors to the 1963 *Science* volume were concerned with persuasive uses of communication within the context of either mass media or interpersonal situations. The study of communication was largely the study of persuasion.

Today the limitations of that linear conceptualization of communication are recognized by researchers in most subareas of communication science (see especially Cappella, Chapter 7, and Rogers & Storey, Chapter 26). Concentration upon persuasive impact has given way to such concerns as the ways people use media information and how they develop *mutual definitions* of their social relationships with others. Communication is no longer viewed as simply a way to change others' attitudes and actions.

Several other features of communication science have also changed since the 1960s. Schramm asserted that communication research in the United States is "quantitative, rather than speculative" (1963, p. 5). Communication science was equated with the use of the quantitative tools of the social sciences. Few then argued with his relegation of non-quantitative approaches to the intellectual backwater of "speculation." This rather narrow view of the scientific enterprise has been replaced by one that recognizes that communication also needs to be studied using methodologies that do not rely upon a statistical approach.

The attributes that define communication science have shifted from methodological to theoretical ones. The central preoccupation of a science is conceptual explanation. Given this view, it is possible to employ quantitative methodologies in unscientific ways. It is all too common, for example, to evaluate information about program outcomes in statistical terms that do not contribute to more general theory. Much early quantitative communication research was both atheoretical and applied, not scientific in the sense of testing a theory or building a body of knowledge.

Another aspect that has changed is the locus from which research ideas are generated. Schramm (1963) noted the contributions made to the study of communication by psychologists (Hovland and Lewin), sociologists (Lazarsfeld), and political scientists (Lasswell). In the past decade or two, however, an increasing number of communication researchers have advanced their own theories for testing instead of relying upon work in allied disciplines. While communication researchers still look to other fields for ideas, the degree of dependence on outside disciplines is considerably less. In that way too, communication is becoming a discipline itself.

THE PLAN OF THIS BOOK

This first section of the handbook explores some broad features of communication science. Chapter 2, by Delia, presents a history of the evolution of the field to about the time Schramm wrote the statements we have quoted above. In Chapter 3 we outline some of the basic assumptions underlying the scientific study of human communication. Then in Chapter 4 Farrell discusses humanistic approaches to communication study. His analysis marks, in a way, the boundaries of communication science, which are constantly expanding; although we use the term "science" to distinguish the main concerns of this handbook from humanistic scholarship, the reader will note in several of the later chapters questions raised in philosophical writings that are now being addressed by communication scientists.

In the remainder of this chapter we begin to map the intellectual domain of communication science; because subsequent chapters deal with this problem in specific detail, this initial presentation will be painted with broad strokes. Our main purpose is to present the general framework within which this volume has been conceptualized.

WHAT IS COMMUNICATION SCIENCE?

Although there are a number of possible ways to define both "communication" and "science," the following working definition of communication science is a useful one:

> Communication science seeks to understand the production, processing, and effects of symbol and signal systems by developing testable theories, containing lawful generalizations, that explain phenomena associated with production, processing, and effects.

This definition is sufficiently general to embrace various communication contexts, including the production, processing, or effects of symbol or signal systems (including nonverbal) in interpersonal, organizational, mass, political, instructional or other contexts.

Most scholars in the discipline should see a relatively close fit between their research and the view our definition advances. But we also have colleagues engaged in communication inquiry whose research activities *cannot* be subsumed under our definition. Intellectuals who criticize the symbolic output of individuals or the media, for example, are not doing communication *science*. Those involved in these critical efforts ordinarily employ a set of idealized aesthetic standards that are not derived from any scientific theory. Researchers whose job it is to make ethical or moral judgments about the communicative conduct of persons or institutions are not communication scientists by our definition. Neither are reformists who seek to change public policies concerning communication institutions, even when they gather social scientific data to support their arguments. Finally, there are analysts who seek to explain individual communication events in their own terms, without recourse to broader theoretical principles; we would not classify their work, valuable though it often is, as communication science.

For instance, studying the speaking style of Dr. Martin Luther King, Jr., in an attempt to understand how he was able to become the leader of the civil rights movement is not, in our terms, an activity of communication science. But when the same scholar examines a large number of leaders of social movements in the hope of drawing a generalization about the relationship between communication style and effectiveness, the scholar is acting in the role of scientist. The key issue here is that science seeks to explain by developing general principles that can be used to account for specific events or classes of events. We ourselves are only engaged part of the time in communication science; much of our work is devoted to extrascientific concerns about communication activities and institutions in society.

As we have pointed out, we do not believe that the critical attribute defining communication science is the use of quantitative techniques. But these methods do give communication scientists a set of powerful tools and a systematic logic for evaluating hypotheses. The use of mathematics as a way of representing communication theory forces theorists to think more carefully about what they mean; mathematics is less ambiguous than natural language. Throughout the history of communication research criticisms have been lodged to the effect that "People aren't numbers." This truism has been advanced as if it were a sufficient argument to establish that quantitative approaches to the study of human communication should be abandoned in favor of unspecified qualitative techniques. We offer two replies to this old saw.

First, while people surely are not mere numbers, it is equally true that people are not mere words. Attempts to code human action in any symbolic form suffer from inherent limitations. A verbal description of, say, a person's emotional reaction in a situation may be no more—and no less—informative than judges' ratings on scales.

A second and more critical point is that in the absence of well-articulated theory, neither qualitative nor quantitative data have much meaning. Research findings, no matter how counterintuitive or intriguing, have little value in a scientific sense when they are presented outside the context of a theory. One cannot build a scientific discipline solely upon descriptive accounts; scientists seek to predict and explain phenomena in addition to describing them. To accomplish the objective of explanation, theory is necessary. The concept of "theory" is not one we can outline briefly in this chapter. It is a central concern of our Chapter 3 and, indeed, appears throughout virtually every chapter of this book.

Levels of Analysis in Communication Science

Obviously, it would be desirable to have a general theory of human communication that would explain a wide range of communication phenomena. It is equally obvious, however, that at this point in history no such theory is available. Instead, the field has been growing in separate directions, as if communication in, say, interpersonal and organizational and intercultural contexts is so different that these areas of inquiry should be the provinces of different academic departments, organizations, and journals. Such a mind-set runs counter to the spirit of general theory development.

We have tried to address this problem in our organization of this *Handbook*. In Part II our contributors present a scheme for analyzing communication phenomena at four different levels: (1) intrapersonal, (2) interpersonal, (3) organizational and social network, and (4) macrosocietal. These presentations address a number of common issues and problems concerning the analysis of communication within each level. In the remainder of the book other authors attempt to show how a specific function or context of communication is related to these four levels of analysis. Our general purpose is to encourage integration of theory by asking authors to consider how these different levels are related to one another.

The titles of Parts III and IV ("Functions" and "Contexts," respectively) reflect the organization of communication science subfields at the present time. Part III separates analysis into a number of functions communication serves, and Part IV looks at some important contexts in which communication takes place. What is most unique is the application of our four-level outline to each of these topics.

Our hope is that in the not too distant future, we will see a reduction in the number of chapters that a volume like this contains. While such a development might be viewed by some with great alarm—growth is, after all, highly valued in a science—we would consider it a sign that synthetic forces had produced some degree of integration in our discipline. This integrative activity is the precursor of general theory, which would be a welcome development toward a mature science.

REFERENCES

Berlo, D. K. (1960). *The process of communication.* New York: Holt, Rinehart & Winston.
Schramm, W. (1963). *The science of human communication.* New York: Basic Books.

2   Communication Research: A History

JESSE G. DELIA
University of Illinois, Urbana-Champaign

AS the study of communication has taken shape over the past decades, some of the field's most significant scholarship has been historical: studies in the history of rhetorical theories; historical analyses of public discourse; histories of communication technologies; studies of communication institutions and their social, economic, and political effects; histories of literacy; studies in the history of journalism and publishing; and historical scholarship on communication education. However, until recently there has been almost no serious scholarship on the history of communication study itself, perhaps because it has only been in the past 35 years or so that the field has begun to be well enough defined to be seen as having its own history (examples of the recent turn to serious historical scholarship on communication research include Chaffee & Hochheimer, 1985; Czitrom, 1982; Rowland, 1983; Wartella & Reeves, 1985).

The present chapter, like some other recent efforts (e.g., Benson, 1985; Rogers & Balle, 1985), locates the field of communication study historically, particularly as an organized institutional domain. My aim is not to write a complete history of communication research, but to provide a general understanding of the sources and themes that have contributed to the development and institutionalization of communication study within the system of American higher education. While concentrating on the central research traditions in America, attention is directed to the development of communication research within a wider perspective, including its relationship to European developments.

My general thesis emphasizes the importance of the initial coalescence of the field as a distinct domain in the 1940s. In this my focus is similar to that of Rowland (1983), though unlike him I do not treat this coalescence simply in terms of the emerging dominance of administrative research. Both prior to that coalescence and following it, a significant feature of communication research has been its fragmentation as a topical concern across virtually all the disciplines and fields of the social sciences and humanities. The coalescence in the 1940s of a distinct, discipline-like domain led quickly to a particular construction of the history of communication research that was itself a significant event in the consolidation of the field.

The most important source of this construction of communication study's history was, I have come to believe, Katz and Lazarsfeld's (1955) account of the relationship of their research to the past. The view advanced there was subsequently propagated through important retellings in various forms in the field's basic textbooks (DeFleur, 1966, was particularly influential). As an embodiment and focusing of those aspects of communication research that had coalesced in the 1940s, this received view was articulated within several parameters. These included (1) an identification of communication research with the study of the media of mass communication, (2) a presumption that the methods of communication research were the methods of social scientific research, (3) the treatment of communication research as an exclusively American research tradition, and (4) identification of the core concern of communication research as the processes by which communication messages influence audience members. Against the backdrop of these parameters, the received view constructed the history of communication research as reflecting a shift from a conception of direct, undifferentiated, and powerful effects to an understanding of effects as highly limited because of processes of psychological and social mediation within the audience. In addition, for many it also privileged a particular model of scientific practice.

Most commentaries on the received view have concentrated on the interpretation of this last point, including both those who have accepted the essential outline of the received view while emphasizing its political roots (e.g., Gitlin, 1978; Rowland, 1983) and those who have found general fault with the received view's adequacy as a historical account (e.g., Chaffee & Hochheimer, 1985; Wartella & Reeves, 1985). I will argue, however, that the received view has most profoundly affected the assumptions defining the parameters of the field. A similar point has been intimated by recent commentaries that emphasize the extent to which the received view marginated explorations of the relationship between culture and communication, particularly those not fitting the prevailing quantitative model of social science in the 1940s (e.g., Czitrom, 1982; Hall, 1982). Unfortunately these recent efforts do not come to terms adequately with the fragmentation of early communication research. Moreover, in providing penetrating critical understandings of communication research, they frequently overweigh those strands of work tied to commercial interests and fail adequately to map other historical forces shaping the development of communication research in twentieth-century America.

I will emphasize several general influences on the development of communication research. Most important is the fragmentation of con-

cern with communication across diverse disciplines and fields of interest as a fundamental fact that must be taken into account in understanding
the history of communication research. Communication as a topic of
research has not been limited to any societal domain (government, education, etc.), discipline, or field of specialized focus within disciplines.
In fact, across the century communication has been fractured into
myriad conceptual fragments and research practices (propaganda, significant symbols, radio research, interaction ritual, effects assessment,
intelligibility, cultural analysis, egocentric speech, etc.). This fragmentation has been widely, if implicitly, recognized, but its deeper implications for the development of research in communication has, to my
knowledge, never received emphasis. In redressing this omission, I
give particular attention in the present chapter to conflicts embedded in
American cultural understandings of science and the evolving patterns
of practice within various social science domains.

Three other recurrent sources of influence on the development of
communication research in twentieth-century America will be emphasized throughout the discussion. First, communication research has
largely (though not exclusively) been identified with the study of the
media of mass communication. Despite their pervasiveness in contemporary life, it must be kept in mind that these "agencies of mass
impression" (Wiley & Rice, 1933) are essentially twentieth-century
phenomena. Silent motion pictures, radio broadcasting, talking movies,
and television have evolved as social institutions in successive waves
across the century. Since these communication media emerged as commercial ventures and attained enormous popularity quickly (e.g., see
Barnouw, 1966, 1968, 1975; Czitrom, 1982; Jowett, 1976) their growth
and audiences have been objects of considerable research—much of
which has reflected commercial or regulatory interests.

A second recurrent source of influence is the concern with the role of
public communication media in social and political life. The perceived
significance of the media as agencies of social change made them the
object of public controversy in a society offering considerable avenues
of democratic expression. This was intensified by the development of
the new media during periods when a meliorist and reformist spirit was
prominent, particularly among many American social scientists (e.g.,
see Fleming, 1963). Concern over the impact and control of the media
by liberals and conservatives alike served to focus commentary and
scholarship on communication's role in social and political life (see
Davis, 1985; Jowett, 1976; Wartella & Reeves, 1985). But even this
work was fragmented, scattered, and largely unconnected. Each medium
generated its own cadre of researchers as it emerged. In the most
ground-breaking historical analysis to date of research on communication, Wartella and Reeves (1985) have shown, for instance, that in

research on media and children virtually all of the research before 1960 involved study of one medium at a time and was not cumulative. Systematic tracking of research and citations across research groups was uncommon.

A third general development shaping the history of communication research that will be emphasized is the evolution of professional practices within and across the social science disciplines. The social sciences and humanities have diverged as the professional authority of science has been embraced within the social sciences. Issues of professional status and authority in disciplines and within groups of research clients have shaped research styles and agendas. Reform-focused research has declined, and since the 1920s has been brought progressively under the control of disciplinary canons of research practice. The overall effect by late midcentury was the ravishing of the social sciences by "objectivist" methodologies. Moreover, the fusion of scientific practice and professional authority became foundational to the American educational system and promoted a general social commitment to technical competence, efficiency, and control (Bledstein, 1976).

Of particular importance for communication research, the rise of methodological behaviorism in psychology and quantitative research orientations in sociology and political science spawned increasing attention in those disciplines to issues of objectivity, measurement, operational procedure, and the development of theoretical concepts tied closely to research. Works such as Bridgeman's (1927) theory of operationalism had a strong impact on these fields; and the generation of psychologists and social scientists coming of age in the late 1920s and 1930s increasingly embraced operationalism, even if they continued to use concepts emphasizing interpretation and individual difference (Schultz, 1969). I will emphasize, however, that developments in research practices were far from monolithic within or across disciplines. In addition, I will seek to turn aside the mistaken assumption that increasing commitment to scientific canons in pre-World War II research was accompanied by a denial of the role of interpretive psychological and social processes in communication.

This chapter thus provides an overview of twentieth-century American communication research both as a topical interest within a panoply of disciplines and research fields and as a set of evolving traditions moving toward disciplinary status. The discussion is organized in three sections. The first treats communication research from 1900 to roughly 1940. The second section discusses the coalescence of communication research into a distinct domain, its consolidation within the received view, and the relationship of the tradition so defined to the broader scope of scholarship on communication. The final major section treats the relocation of this communication research tradition into journalism

schools and speech departments. The latter two sections concentrate on
the post-World War II period through the 1960s.

AMERICAN COMMUNICATION RESEARCH
1900 TO 1940

American society, like that of other western industrial nations, was
transformed from agrarian life into modernity during the nineteenth
century. The expansion of newspaper circulation and the ready availability of other reading material created the context for expansion of the
literacy demanded by the rising industrial order, which relied more
heavily on skilled labor. With the development of statewide public
schools literacy increased rapidly; increased education and literacy
fed and were sustained by the growing industries of communication,
commerce, and production. Expanding transportation and communication spurred the rapid growth of cities, whose demand for wider commerce and easier access accelerated the pace of change. Expanded
commerce swelled the middle class who, with newly acquired leisure
time, demanded more conveniences, products, and materials for relaxation, thus promoting the spread of mass-distributed magazines and books.
The more visible signs of change in the nineteenth century—industrialization, urbanization, and literacy—were thus inexorably intertwined
with developments furthering the possibilities of communication. (For
general histories of American social change in the late nineteenth and
early twentieth centuries see Hays, 1957; Hofstadter, 1955; Wiebe,
1967.) The most prominent social movement spawned by the rapid
changes in American society was progressivism, which took as its task
building a new social system to replace lost community. A major paradox of progressive thought was its effort to recapture community with
the very tools of its destruction—science, technology, and bureaucracy
(see Noble, 1958).

A useful point of departure for understanding this aspect of progressive thought and its paradox is the work of John Dewey (1922, 1927).
Dewey's conceptions of communication, intelligence, education, and
social reform each combined the instrumentalism of science and the participation of community. His psychological theory treated intelligence
as an organism's adaptation to its milieu through anticipation and interpretation (see Woodworth & Sheehan, 1964). Likewise communication
was seen as growing out of the capacity for empathy, the instrument of
social foresight. Dewey saw empathy as expanding with participation
in community and the acquisition of shared symbols. Consequently,
Dewey took the tasks of education and social reconstruction to be the
same. Through participation the individual is given the opportunity to
acquire and exercise control over the tools of life, intelligence and empa-

thy. In education this meant learning by doing to acquire the structures of foresight, sensitivity, and adaptation. In social reform, it meant changing social institutions to provide understanding, prediction, and participation. Thus in his lengthiest statement on communication, Dewey (1927) argued for restoring the consensus-building capacity of mass communication systems through the institution of a free and unfettered press vividly transmitting the products of a reformed social science to provide understanding of the forces that controlled modern life. Science was wed to communication, foresight to participation.

Dewey is taken as a point of departure to underscore the drama of change and the authority of science in twentieth-century American communication research. Dewey also expresses well the spirit of meliorist reform and democratic control that has been the impetus for much twentieth-century American social and communication research. The development of American communication research has, I believe, been influenced in basic ways by the tenets of pragmatism and progressivism reflected in Dewey's general philosophy (see Lewis & Smith, 1980). We will see, however, that progressivism was not monolithic, and that conflicting concepts clothed in similar language shaped developments and fed unseen contradictions.

It is also appropriate to use Dewey's work in framing this chapter since my discussion emphasizes a pragmatist conception of disciplinary traditions and practices. I will present an appreciation of communication research in its American social and institutional context. Kuhn's (1970) pragmatist conception of science as a system of evolving practices is basic to my approach, but I will enlarge on the Kuhnian vision to examine the connection between science and society. Among the goals of this approach are providing points of connection between American and European understandings of this research tradition and between its mass communication and speech communication variants.

It is, of course, impossible to treat the conduct of research on communication during the first four decades of this century in detail here. However, it is possible to give the varied flavor of the work and to deepen understanding of important themes. These general goals are pursued through discussing five fields of research. These are (1) work on communication and political institutions, (2) research concerned with the role of communication in social life, (3) social-psychological analyses of communication, (4) studies of communication and education, and (5) commercially motivated research.

Communication Research and Political Issues

Propaganda analysis. The first lines of work to be discussed are those concerned primarily with public communication and politics. Most recountings of the received history of mass communication research begin with the post-World War I study of propagandistic political communication (though it will be shown later that a good deal of research predated the rise of propaganda analysis). I will have more to say about this particular starting point, but it can serve as a convenient entry way because government-based propaganda in the world war resulted in a host of exposés, memoirs, commentaries, and studies that heightened interest in communication (e.g., Creel, 1920; Lasswell, 1927b; Lumley, 1933). (A later, thoughtful history, of the principal American agency of information control, the Creel Committee, is Mock & Larson, 1939.)

Lasswell's *Propaganda Technique in the World War* (1927a) is the pivotal work in this early group. The focal concern of the book is with the strategies and conduct of the wartime propaganda efforts of the conflicting principals. Lasswell emphasizes the power of mass political communication to shape national consciousness. It is fair to read Lasswell's work as an undifferentiated and direct-effects conception of mass communication. The viewpoint expressed is reminiscent of the nineteenth-century European conservative tradition that had emphasized a concept of group mind and processes of imitation, suggestion, and, as in LeBon's widely read theory of the crowd, "irresistible impetuosity" (LeBon, 1920, p. 35). It is important to note, however, that American psychology and social theory were never very fertile ground for European mass society concepts, and by the 1920s the European theories were not much in vogue among American social scientists (just as biological instinct psychologies, such as McDougall's, were not; see Karpf, 1932). American social science was influenced by Darwinian biological thinking, but this was filtered through the functionalism of pragmatism (see Boring, 1950). Lasswell turned toward a variety of concepts that emphasized individual psychological processes (including psychoanalytic concepts), and by the 1930s was focusing on his lifelong project of understanding the symbols of power (e.g., Lasswell, 1935). His persistent research focus from the 1930s on was the description and content analysis of propaganda and symbols (e.g., Lasswell, 1938; Lasswell & Blumenstock, 1939; Lasswell et al., 1949; also see Berelson, 1954).

Analysis of political and social themes in public communication. Domestic conditions and world events sustained concern with propaganda throughout the period between the world wars. Indeed, during this period one has to cut through a massive popular literature on propaganda to find the work of scholarly significance. Some of that work reflected Lasswell's influence. However, the work was scattered across disciplines and subfields, and most analysts started the research task afresh. Included among the analysts were political scientists, social psychologists, professors of literature, sociologists, historians, educational psychologists, journalism scholars, and speech professors. Cross-citations were infrequent, as each researcher attended more to the topical focus of the analysis than to the fact that it involved communication or content description. Some work employed an interpretive approach that anticipated contemporary rhetorical analyses utilizing speeches or media messages as entry points into understanding the values and symbolic inducements of a message's source.

This now mostly forgotten work included a wide range of investigations of newspaper content, including many of the standard space-measurement studies (e.g., Kingsbury et al., 1937). However, there also were descriptive and interpretive studies employing qualitative modes of analysis. Studies ranged from investigations of the treatment by high school history texts of wars and of Blacks (Carpenter, 1941; Walworth, 1938) to studies of movies and newsreels and political speeches (e.g., Dale, 1935a, 1937; Lee & Lee, 1939; McDiarmid, 1937); from social interpretations based on analyses of classified advertising and sermons (Hamilton, 1942; Severson, 1939) to investigations of war themes in magazine fiction and the history of cartoons (Johnson, 1937; McKenzie, 1941). Some of the work offered penetrating social criticism, including, for example, studies of racial attitudes in the American South discerned from newspaper treatments (e.g., Ames, 1938). Contrary to what would be expected from a 1980s perspective, several of the interpretive and critical studies appeared in the *Public Opinion Quarterly,* which was launched in 1937 as the flagship of scientific public opinion research (e.g., Ames, 1938; Hamilton, 1942).

Content analysis and the quantitative analysis of messages. There also was clearly visible by the late 1930s and early 1940s a turn, particularly in Lasswell's work, to a search for the tools of systematic content analysis. Technical issues of coding and reliability took on greater importance (e.g., Geller, Kaplan, & Lasswell, 1942; Janis & Fadner, 1943; Lasswell, 1938). Again, however, there was fragmentation across fields as researchers in diverse areas developed techniques for dealing with content analysis (e.g., Britt & Lowry, 1941; Wilson, 1938). Moreover, many other researchers took a broader approach to propaganda and political communication, considering frequently the entire institutional apparatus by which messages were developed and shaped (e.g., Lavine & Wechsler, 1940; Stoke, 1941). Interestingly the independent development of quantitative techniques within English departments (Rickert, 1927) stimulated many speech professors to pursue quantitative analysis of various rhetorical devices and stylistic features of speeches (e.g., Barnard, 1932; Hayworth, 1930). This line of work was accompanied by a significant body of humanistic scholarship analyzing speeches in their historical contexts. Most of this latter work employed historical research and the canons of classical and modern rhetorical theory to describe and interpret important speeches as responses to their individual situations (see Gregg in Benson, 1985).

Studies of propaganda for the most part focused on the content of mass communication and on issues surrounding the institutional management of information rather than directly on communication processes and effects (see Lasswell, Casey, & Smith, 1935). Consequently, propaganda analysis was not seen as central to post-World War II effects-focused communication research; one clear sign of this is the complete absence of citations to Lasswell in Klapper's (1949, 1960), and Hovland's (1954) summaries of mass communication effects research.

Public opinion research. The connection between propaganda and opinion and attitude processes, however, was made early in the 1920s, and a line of scholarly development was launched in subfields of political science, psychology, and sociology. (Aspects of the histories of these disciplines important to the development of communication research are noted in other sections; it is important here simply to trace the emerging field of opinion research). Walter Lippmann, the noted progressivist journalist, set the agenda for the field's development in his broadly influential analysis of public opinion in contemporary society (e.g., Lippmann, 1922). Democracy was endangered, Lippmann believed, because the agencies of modern mass communication could mold a society's knowledge by appealing to its "stereotypes"—beliefs rooted not in facts, but in myths, dreams, ancient traditions, and personal wishes. Lippmann believed that systems of public communication, including the press and forms of popular entertainment, served to reinforce stereotypic opinions and that the hope for democracy was in the development of the social scientist's capacity to assess and interpret public opinion objectively and to work through organizations of independent experts to make "the unseen facts intelligible to these who have to make decisions" (Lippmann, 1922, p. 18).

Lasswell also promoted the link between propaganda and investigations of attitudes and opinions. Even in the 1920s, Lasswell (1927b) defined propaganda as "the management of collective attitudes by the manipulation of significant symbols" (p. 627). This encapsulated the already generally accepted view that a principal mechanism underlying social behavior was the functioning of "attitudes." An attitude was, Lasswell (1927b) said, a "tendency to act according to certain patterns of valuation" (p. 627). By the mid-1930s, firmly established research traditions focused on the experimental analysis of attitude creation and change through propaganda and the measurement of public attitudes and opinions.

From their beginnings propaganda analysis and public opinion studies were suffused with political commitments; and until the end of World War II, domestic and international conditions led many researchers to characterize their work as directly motivated by the aims of liberalism and rationalism (e.g., Albig, 1939; Childs, 1936; Lasswell, 1941). However, as is discussed later, aspects of this fusion of political and research interest were to conflict with developments shaped by dominant research traditions and status issues within the evolving disciplines of the social and behavioral sciences.

The 1930s witnessed the transformation of public opinion study into a quantitative, scientific field. In fact, there are few areas of the social sciences in which canons of quantitative scientific practice were more clearly or more pervasively adopted. Influenced by the emergence of strong quantitative orientations in political science and sociology, a significant scientific literature on polling was developing by the mid-1930s (e.g., see the summary of Droba, 1931). Even greater strides had been taken within psychology with the development of refined techniques for attitude assessment (e.g., see the summary of Droba, 1932; also see Likert, 1932; Thurstone & Chave, 1929). The volume of scientific public opinion studies was to rise even more dramatically after 1935, however. This reflected both continuation of the general trend and the dramatic demonstration of scientific polling's superiority in out-predicting the *Literary Digest* straw poll in the 1936 presidential election (see Gosnell, 1937).

The development of scientific public opinion research was greatly facilitated by the formation of the American Association for Public Opinion Research and the launching in 1937 of the *Public Opinion Quarterly.* This journal immediately became the primary outlet for research on polling and public opinion, and published considerable research on political communication as well. The direction of disciplinary development toward more refined methods of sampling, questionnaire construction, and polling precedures was evident in the sharp upturn in methodologically focused research (e.g., Blankenship, 1940; Gosnell & DeGrazia, 1942; Mosteller & McCarthy, 1942).

The broader landscape of political communication. While scientific public opinion research developed toward a unified perspective, other aspects of the broad concern with communication and politics remained largely fragmented and dispersed. The work was both diverse and significant, and most of the fragments have evolved within different disciplinary traditions. The most important clusters of work represented historical, philosophical, and legal frameworks for analyzing political issues in communication. Works appeared during the decades between the world wars that extended and deepened the ongoing philosophical debate in Western societies concerning the nature and role of public opinion in democratic action (e.g., Dewey's 1927 statement was at least in part a reply to Lippmann). Among the works receiving scholarly attention were Childs (1936), Ickes (1941), and Lasswell (1941). Important general works were published on freedom of speech and of the press and on journalism law (e.g., Chaffee, 1941; Jones, 1940; Siebert, 1934), along with many focused studies (e.g., Feinberg, 1940; Mock, 1941; Nafziger, 1937). The international situation also stimulated a number of studies comparing aspects of different media systems, particularly at the level of press law (e.g., Barlow, 1936; Harley, 1941; Kiefer, 1942). Other work focused on regulation and the government's role in the mass communication industries (e.g., Herring & Gross, 1936) and accompanying issues of industry responsibility and ethics (e.g., Crawford, 1924; Pollard, 1937).

Work in the broad areas of political communication thus was visible, developing, and scattered across a host of disciplines by the outbreak of World War II. Only the research in public opinion seemed to be converging in disciplinary terms. Even work on the press, which one might assume would be largely identified with journalism programs, in fact reflected the interests and orientations of several disciplines.

Communication and Social Life

The need to understand and shape the great changes that were overtaking American society in the second half of the nineteenth century was accompanied by a breakdown in the traditional organization of higher education and the beginnings of modern department structures (see Veysey, 1965). The first generations of scholars who occupied many of the newly formed departments faced the task of defining the direction work would take. The boundaries of many fields were uncertain, and issues of legitimacy in the academy and the desire to establish professional standards were salient. Thus the last decades of the nineteenth century and the first decades of this century were witness to the definition in standards of professional certification and practice and the consolidation of legitimating disciplinary identities (see Bledstein, 1976; Furner, 1975). Professionalism reconciled the need for difference in a nation whose "fundamental fact," de Tocqueville had observed, was "the general equality of conditions." Education and the neutrality of science provided the institutional vehicle and ideology for consolidating "a social faith in merit, competence, discipline, and control" (Bledstein, 1976, p. x). It is in this context that the makers of the modern social science disciplines were to play out their commitment to science.

Communication research in the Chicago school of sociology. In approaching the development of research on communication and social life, I will emphasize the work of the "Chicago school" of sociology. This is appropriate because the Chicago school developed a general approach to social theory that emphasized the role of communication in social life (the most important general statements were Cooley, 1902, 1909; Dewey, 1927; Mead, 1934).

For the first decades of the century the University of Chicago was the American center of the search for the meaning of democracy in urban life (see Duncan, 1962). Moreover, the sociology department was dominant in its discipline from its—and the university's—founding in 1892 into the 1920s, and maintained considerable influence through the 1930s (Matthews, 1977). The department instigated the founding of the American Sociological Association, edited its only journal, the *American Journal of Sociology*, until 1935, and produced the two most influential texts across a 40-year period (Park & Burgess, 1921; Small & Vincent, 1894). Supported by Dewey and Mead in the combined department of philosophy, psychology, and education, the sociology department counted among its early members Albion Small, W. I. Thomas, Robert Park, Ellsworth Faris, and Ernest Burgess. Strauss (in Mead, 1964) writes, "Although Sumner was at Yale, Ross at Wisconsin, Cooley at Michigan, Giddings at Columbia, and Sorokin at Minnesota and Harvard, the massed graduate faculty at Chicago, along with its former students, was the major influence on prewar sociology" (p. viii).

The Chicago sociologists influenced the development of communication study in several important ways. First, collectively they were a major force in the establishment of scientific sociology (and thus, indirectly, of communication science). Faris (1967) remembers that the most characteristic thing about the Chicago department by the 1920s was the surging pace of research under Park's leadership, particularly on urban social life. From the beginnings of empirical research at Chicago, investigations were tied to general analyses of the social process: Mead's analysis of social interaction (Mead, 1934); Thomas's considerations of the inner psychic life in social change (Thomas & Znaniecki, 1918-1920); Park's interpretation of Simmel's interactionist stance (Park & Burgess, 1921); and Park and Burgess's emerging "ecological" perspective (e.g., Park, Burgess, & McKenzie, 1925). Park in particular pressed to shift the goal of social research from almost exclusive concern with the interests of reform and social service toward attention to theory development (see Matthews, 1977). As Matthews (1977) emphasizes, Chicago sociology "hoped to integrate field research with general theory and produce, not philosophical systems, or random information, but a sound body of 'scientific' knowledge" (p. 104).

The methods of research encouraged at Chicago were highly eclectic, but there was a characteristic openness to them. The emphasis was upon richness of description and sensitivity to the interrelation of persons' experiences and the social contexts of their lives. This general "documentary" approach was expressed in Thomas and Znaniecki (1918-1920). Park and Burgess extended the documentary approach to include the use of census data, surveys, and observation. Park in particular insisted that his students get out into the city itself. Thus he fostered the development of methods of systematic observation and of participant observation. When collecting data by survey, he demanded that detailed life histories be collected through a series of questions allowing the respondents to express their feelings and attitudes (see Madge, 1962, pp. 88-125). However, it was emphasized first and foremost that scientific sociology must be objective. For example, although Park was himself a lifelong laborer for improved race relations, he could tell a group of students who wished to wed sociology and social activism that the world is "full of crusaders." The role of the sociologist, he contended, is to be "the calm detached scientist who investigates race relations with the same objectivity and detachment with which the zoologist dissects the potato bug" (quoted by Turner in Park, 1967, p. xvi).

Chicago sociology has a second important continuity with later communication research through its promotion of theory-based applied sociological research. Its research wed theory to concern with social problems and work for a wide range of clients. This is the essential fusion of applied social research, and the development of such research was to have considerable importance in later communication research. Thus at Chicago, as Matthews (1977) puts it, the concerns of sociology "were enclosed within the strategic assumption that sociology, even in its most theoretical moods, was a practical science oriented toward action and reform" (p. 91).

The final general connection of Chicago sociology to the development of communication research is in the general impetus given social psychological research in sociology (the development of social psychology within psychology is discussed below). Some of this work directly concerned communication, but as important to later communication research was the Chicago school's attention to concepts that contributed generally to the analysis of societal processes in social psychological terms and its furtherance of the development of social psychology as a distinct subfield. Louis Wirth (1953) comments that "the emergence of social psychology as a more or less autonomous discipline" was the "most significant" development in twentieth-century American social science because it assured that methods would be developed for studying the relationship of individual and social processes (p. 62). In his history of the origins of American social psychology, Karpf (1932) reveals that from 1915 on the major efforts to develop unified perspectives in social psychology were largely derivative from the Chicago viewpoint. In addition to the seminal contributions of Dewey, Mead, Cooley, and Thomas, Ellsworth Faris, Park and Burgess, Emory Bogardus, Kimball Young, Charles Ellwood, and L. L. Bernard all wrote field-defining texts and papers during the 1920s that expressed the social interactional and functionalist psychological emphases of the Chicago school. In fact, Floyd Allport's *Social Psychology* (1924) was the only highly influential text of the 1920s not to reflect the domination of the Chicago viewpoint.

The most important general effect of the Chicago school's influence on social psychological thought was to turn aside instinct-based thinking and its emphasis on the concepts of imitation and suggestibility. In place of biological instincts, the Chicago theorists followed Mead and emphasized the social origins of personality and life-organizing attitudes (see Lewis & Smith, 1980, on Mead's influence). They gave considerable attention to processes of interaction; they stressed concepts such as empathy, social distance, and forms of conflict and communication relevant to understanding group life and intergroup relations. By the mid-1920's social psychology took understanding the individual as a social being as its focus and broadly embraced a view of persons as relating to the world through processses of interpretation, primary group connections, and functional adaptations. Social psychology was to be a discipline founded on concepts of social influence, individual difference and group process.

The focal concern of Chicago sociology and social psychology, at least by the 1920s, was the effects of urbanization on everyday life and the urban ecology of the city. Communication was given attention within this focus in Burgess and Park's studies of communication, transportation, and social change (e.g., Park et al., 1925). Park also contributed analyses of the foreign-language immigrant press (Park, 1922, 1925), an approach to the history of the newspaper (Park, 1923), and discussions of the nature, forms, and social and political functions of contemporary news (e.g., Parks, 1940). Almost a quarter of the dissertations completed at Chicago prior to World War II were social or institutional analyses of the news and the press (see the listings of Fleming, F. Park, Kawaabe, Jensen, Detweiler, Clark, Hughes, and Johns, in Lunday, 1969). And Herbert Blumer authored two of the twelve volumes of the classic Payne Fund studies of movies and their effects on children (Blumer, 1933; Blumer & Hauser, 1933).

The broader practice of "Chicago-style" research. There also were many important Chicago-style studies of the social significance of communication conducted outside the Chicago sphere. These included most notably the attention given to communication media and leisure in Lynd and Lynd's (1929, 1937) classic studies of "Middletown," but also major studies of journalism and film (Desmond, 1937; Lee, 1937; Rosten, 1937, 1941; Thorpe, 1939). These studies suggested that mass communication was having broad impact on patterns of everyday life and the creation of a national culture. They also showed the importance of understanding media institutions as parts of a larger social process. Many smaller studies reflected similar perspectives (e.g., Prugger, 1941; Punke, 1937). Although most researchers focused on communication institutions and their effects on society, the influence of society on the communication media also was recognized (e.g., Harris, 1933).

Most of the research on the social impact of communication grew out of concern with the effects of mass communication, particularly on children and youths. The early studies directly expressed the concerns of the researchers, as in Healey's (1915) highly biased "case studies" of movies and delinquency and Phelan's (1919) survey of movie attendance and effects in Toledo. The 1920 study of the Chicago Motion Picture Commission, which was directed by Chicago's Ernest Burgess, only sent questionnaires to school principals and teachers to assess the effects of movie attendance (see Jowett, 1976; Young, 1922). Discipline-based canons of research method were evolved to address such questionable practices and promote greater detachment and objectivity. As research methods were increasingly defined by these disciplinary canons, the research evolved toward practices similar to those of contemporary researchers (e.g., see Mitchell, 1929; and the Payne Fund studies, which are discussed below).

There was also a good deal of effort to establish historical understanding of the developing media of communication. In his dissertation in sociology at the University of Pennsylvania, Donald Young (1922) discussed the problems caused by the lack of social control on the film industry's growth and surveyed local efforts at censorship. Many other historical studies of the media did not have this "social problems" orientation, however. These included a number of historical works, of which Mott's (1938, 1941) histories of American newspapers and magazines are the most distinguished. Less notable works included histories of film (Hampton, 1931; Jacobs, 1939) and radio (Archer, 1938, 1939).

The Chicago school, neopositivism, and standard research practices. Before leaving discussion of communication and social life, the relationship of the Chicago school to later developments in sociological and communication research should be discussed. By the end of the 1920s, academic sociology was a discipline committed to empirical social science. Moreover, the discipline was rapidly evolving in the direction of canons of science that placed a premium on standard methods (a limited set of research designs, random sampling, standardized measurement procedures, quantification, and statistical analysis). Such developments were grounded in disciplinewide desires to make research serve theoretical issues and to limit the intrusion of bias into research. Research shifted in the 1920s toward a "more detached program of scientific inquiry, characterized by the development of scientific method and more long-range empirical research" (Wirth, 1953). Even highly interpretive sociologists such as Cooley turned their attention to issues of method and standard practice (e.g., Cooley, 1928).

Frequently the turn toward standard methods (and particularly toward statistical procedures) has been seen as reflecting the needs of corporate and bureaucratic agencies for data that serve administrative ends. However, it is essential not to lose sight of the extent to which the adoption of such practices reflected evolving goals of the social scientific community. In sociology these goals were promoted by the pragmatic temper and empirical orientation of the Chicago faculty, though their work also exemplified the interpretation of social phenomena in local contexts. Unfortunately, in their repetitive, frequently rote, application, the practices adopted to elevate research and limit capriciousness also restricted judgment and devalued creativity. These interwoven advantages and limitations continue to define major metatheoretical and metamethodological issues in the social sciences (e.g., in communication research, see Delia, O'Keefe, & O'Keefe, and Pearce, Cronen, & Harris in Dance, 1982).

The historical development of methods of standard practice in American social science is connected to the emergence of the "neopositivist" movement in sociology (see Timasheff, 1967). The leaders of this movement were George Lundberg, Stuart Dodd, Read Bain, and Franklin Giddings. The movement, which was centered at Columbia University, did not reach its pinnacle in sociology until after World War II, but its influence was already clearly evident by 1930. As we have seen, this was particularly the case in the development of survey methods and public opinion measurement. At the theoretical level, thinking shifted toward approaches such as that of Giddings, who argued for analyzing alternative response patterns in different social aggregates (political party, sex, social class, etc.).

After World War II the center of sociological communication research was to shift from the Chicago school to Columbia. Two differences between the work of the Chicago school and later mainstream communication research are noteworthy since they illuminate the general forces shaping the disciplinary movement toward methods of standard practice. First, as Coleman (1980) has emphasized, the particular conception of communication and social process nurtured at Chicago was less well suited to the easy analysis of national problems than were subsequent views. The focal social concern of Chicago sociology had been the integration of immigrants into the fabric of individual American communities. Issues of culture, conflict, and consensus were central. However, new issues presented themselves that were associated with economic dislocations and marketing problems of national scope. As the problems shifted, control of the way they would be studied passed to other increasingly powerful research traditions that emphasized standardized research practices and methods of quantification.

A second and equally important difference between the Chicago school and Columbia quantitative sociology is to be found in their divergent implicit models of science. Matthews (1977), notes, for example, that while Park called for a more "scientific" sociology, his implicit definition of "science" seems to have been adequate explanation of external reality through direct observation and then classification within a set of interrelated concepts; the "adequacy" of explanation would be measured subjectively, not through a very explicit and precise method of inference and verification. (p. 179)

Near the end of his career, Park railed against statistics as "parlour magic" and a substitute for thought (Matthews, 1977, p. 179). "The question of methods of investigation is important," Park maintained,

> but it is distinctly secondary. I think we should assume that we can study anything in regard to which we need knowledge. It is important that we employ the best methods such as they are . . . if we succeed in getting a more accurate, objective, intelligible statement about the matter than anyone else, we may count the results of our investigations as science. (quoted in Matthews, 1977, p. 179)

Even in sociology at Chicago, however, the research models began to shift markedly after 1930. The juxtaposition of the Chicago school to later standard communication research thus reveals the paradox of the tradition. The school was anchored by a deep and seemingly unshakable optimism in the application of scientific understanding to the problems of community and social life. Its members were, in Quandt's (1970) terms,

> squarely in the tradition of Edward Bellamy, Andrew Carnegie, and Henry Ford, the tradition in American thought which attributed progress to invention, mechanization, and efficiency. The technological bias also gave them common cause with later representatives of this tradition . . . for whom science, efficiency and technology gave the best answers to social problems. (p. 66)

Given their commitment to science, the Chicago sociologists were not antagonistic to the developments of more systematic and quantitative approaches within the discipline. Park supported the use of a diversity of methods. Emory Bogardus developed his systematic measurement of social distance at Park's urging. Burgess made important uses of survey and census data. Samuel Stouffer, who completed his dissertation on the statistical analysis of attitudes in 1930, was kept on the faculty, and the statistically oriented sociologist from Columbia, William Fielding Ogburn, was recruited to Chicago in 1930.

That the decline in importance of the Chicago perspective thus resulted because of the evolving meaning of social scientific practice presents a striking irony. The goals of limiting bias and securing objective knowledge nurtured by the spirit of scientific social research at Chicago were not abandoned, but absorbed and expanded in the disciplinary pursuit of changing problems. Seen in historical context, it appears that time and different practices appropriated the mantle of science and overtook the Chicago school. Its call for the development of scientific sociology having been appropriated, Chicago's course became not so much a path not taken as one merging into a wider trail whose beginning it had shared.

The continuing presence of Chicago-style research. Chicago-style research went forward as part of empirical sociological research. The development of more refined and systematic methods for the conduct of naturalistic research was vigorously pursued. Different schools emerged within the continuing tradition (Meltzer & Petras, in Manis & Meltzer, 1972) and increasingly took interpersonal symbolic interaction as their focus (see Manis & Meltzer, 1972; Stone & Farberman, 1970). Symbolic interactionism was joined in this pursuit by Goffman's (1959) dramaturgical approach and social phenomenological perspectives (e.g., Douglas, 1970).

Social histories and institutional analyses of communication reflecting concerns similar to Chicago sociology also continued to be written, though their production became increasingly dispersed across disciplines (e.g., Innis, 1951, came to communication from an obscure branch of economic history, bringing McLuhan, 1965, with him from English literature). Issues concerning public communication's role in shaping mass society and culture also reasserted themselves in the post-World War II era (e.g., see Rosenberg & White, 1957).

Linguistics and anthropology generated research traditions that emphasized the cultural foundations of language and the relationship of language to society. These included studies of American Indian languages that gave attention to the relationship of language, culture, and thought, as did the famous Whorf-Sapir hypothesis (e.g., Whorf, 1957), as well as studies of the relationship between language variation and social organization. A historical overview connecting these developments to the later emergence of substantial lines of work in sociolinguistics and the ethnography of communication spawned by European linguistic and anthropological traditions can be found in Gumperz and Hymes (1972; also see Harris, 1968, for historical positioning of such work within the development of anthropology).

Social Psychological Analyses of Communication

The development of social psychology in psychology. Developments in psychology have left a powerful impress on communication research from the late 1920s forward. This influence came primarily through the areas of social and educational psychology. These areas, even more than psychology generally, were influenced by the functionalist tradition. That tradition, grounded in pragmatism, was advanced forcefully at Chicago by Dewey and Angell (see Dewey, 1922, for his social psychology). While advancing an instrumentalist and adaptational theory of intelligence and action, the functionalists embraced the experimentalism imported into American psychology from Germany and promoted comparative and animal studies (e.g., Watson, the founder of behaviorism, took his Ph.D. under Angell and remained at Chicago for several years). As was noted earlier, Mead's functionalist "social behaviorism" was incorporated into the social psychological theories being developed among Chicago-trained sociologists.

The interest in social psychology within psychology was also fed by strands of psychological thinking that were largely independent of those influencing sociology (see Karpf, 1932). The interest in social psychology expanded rapidly among psychologists during the 1920s, particularly after the publication of Allport's (1924) text. There are three features of the development of social psychology within psychology that need to be emphasized here: its methodological proclivities; its eclecticism; and its concern with individual differences, attitudes, and processes of social influence.

Allport's *Social Psychology* (1924) set the study of individual social behavior on a clear and unequivocally experimental course. While not behavioristic, Allport's orientation was decisively on the side of precise measurement and experimentation. From the early 1920s objective measures, particularly in the form of refined questionnaires, were routinely employed in social psychology. The use of statistical techniques also spread rapidly and were standardly employed by the end of the 1920s. Attitude measurement shifted from interview-based assessments to assessments based on the application of scaling procedures (e.g., see Droba, 1932; Likert, 1932; Sherman, 1932; Thurstone & Chave, 1929). Social psychology within psychology also followed the general pattern in the discipline at large of preferring experimental approaches. Indeed, the preference for experimental studies can only be understood by appreciating the disciplinary value placed on the experiment by American psychology following the importation of the approach from Germany in the late nineteenth century (see Woodworth & Sheehan, 1964). Where sociologists employed the documentary method, naturalistic observation, and questionnaires, social psychologists in psychology from the beginning placed special value on experimental or quasi-experimental approaches and the synthesis of research findings. In *Experimental Social Psychology,* Murphy and Murphy (1931) listed over 800 references in integrating research on influences on the socialization of the individual; another 300 were included in the revised edition (Murphy, Murphy, & Newcomb, 1937).

The second important characteristic of social psychology was its eclecticism. Gordon Allport (1954) discusses this characteristic of the field at length in his historical overview: "The student of social psychology has no choice but to learn many maps, realizing that the master chart is not yet available" (p. 51). The field had, and continues to have, no narrow theoretical or topical boundaries. Moreover, although experimentation, psychometrically based assessment, and quantification were preferred by psychologists, there was no strict methodological boundary on the field as a whole. The domain, therefore, brought together work that would otherwise remain within the province of psychology, sociology, political science, or other specialized corners of the behavioral sciences.

A final important characteristic of social psychology as it developed within psychology was its adoption of concepts treating communication reception and effects in complex mediational terms. Regardless of the particular theoretical vocabulary chosen, social psychologists within psychology by and large saw communication as grounded in complex mediational processes. In this, they appropriated, in part, the terms of the sociologists who dominated the field in the 1920s. However, their own historical vocabulary of concepts provided terms that were open to merger with the sociological tradition (for example, see Allport's 1935 discussion of the attitude concept). Consequently, social psychological studies of communication were inclined to demonstrate individual differences in interpretation and response rather than dramatic direct effects.

Social psychological research on communication began to appear before the end of World War I, but reached a cascade by the mid-1930s. The Payne Fund studies of movies and children, studies of persuasion and attitude change, and studies of group processes and interpersonal communication will be considered here.

Social psychological studies of movies and children. The Payne Fund studies were published separately in 12 volumes along with an overview volume; the overview volume is Charters (1933); the Payne Fund studies are reviewed and placed in historical context by Jowett (1976; also see Wartella & Reeves, 1985). The individual volumes are Blumer (1933), Blumer & Hauser (1933), Dale (1935a, 1935b, 1937), Dysinger & Ruckmick (1935), Holaday and Stoddard (1933), Peters (1933), Peterson and Thurstone (1933), Renshaw, Miller, and Marquis (1933), and Shuttleworth and May (1933). The studies were conducted under the auspices of the Motion Picture Research Council, a group founded for the purpose of promoting research on movies and society, with funding from the Payne Fund. The goal of the research was to provide dispassionate, objective data concerning the influence of movie attendance on children. The movies had developed rapidly and were a major entertainment activity, particularly for adolescents, before World War I (see Czitrom, 1982; Jowett, 1976). Consequently, they were an object of both heated social controversy and significant research by the early 1930s (the best early scholarly work includes Lashley & Watson, 1922; Mitchell, 1929; Munsterberg, 1916; Thurstone, 1931).

The Payne Fund studies are striking in their embodiment already in the early 1930s of multifaceted social psychological approaches to studies used a range of research methods: physiological measures and experimental methods; rating scales; attitude and information-acquisition scales; questionnaires; interviews and life history elicitation; and content analysis. Diverse aspects of potential effects were assessed, including effects on emotions, sleep loss, attitudes and information about a wide range of issues, school performance, ratings by teachers, sociometric choice, delinquent conduct, and general attitudes and "schemes of life." Content analyses of the themes of hundreds of feature films were made, and ratings were made of the relationship of depicted behaviors to societal mores.

The Payne Fund studies are striking in their embodiment already in the early 1930s of multifaceted social psychological approaches to research on communication, of multiple and complex ways of conceptualizing the question of effects, and of efforts to deal with communication as a social and psychological process. The results of the studies provided in the early 1930s the essential understanding of communication effects that three post-World War II decades of similar social psychological research would later support—namely, that effects are mediated by a host of individual and situational characteristics (age, sex, predispositions, perceptions, past behavior patterns and experiences, social background and parental influence, viewing mates, etc.). Although there would be steady refinements in methodological and measurement procedures, it would be a very long time before communication research developed beyond these studies; and in many ways the dominant research trend that was to emerge out of marketing and political campaign contexts would represent a significant retreat in complexity (see Chaffee & Hochheimer, 1985).

The theme of the Payne Fund studies was reiterated by other social psychological researchers, most notably Paul G. Cressey (1934, 1938; Cressey & Thrasher, 1934). Cressey argued against taking simple direct effects as the criterion of a movie's impact. He noted the importance of making "clear the methodological distinction between a study of the cinema as *a source* for patterns of thought, feeling and behavior and a study of its *net contribution* in terms of the total social situation, or 'configuration,' in which it is experienced" (Cressey, 1938, p. 517). A film's effect lay, he concluded, in the experience of an individual audience member, with his or her particular mood, personality, and response to the total situation. Sometimes and for some issues the effects of motion pictures will be minimal, Cressey reasoned; for other matters, particularly those involving informal education, fashion, and the like, the movies are likely to make a much greater contribution to the overall conditions of change. Hence, in searching for direct effects, Cressey cautioned, the researcher must be careful not to overlook the extent to which "the cinema is an important social and educational force contributing directly and incidentally" to both social disorganization and social amelioration (p. 518).

Wartella and Reeves (1985) have shown that in studies of children and the media, successive waves of research have followed the introduction of each new medium. Responding to the significance of the medium and public controversy surrounding it, each wave of research follows a similar course. My own research supports their conclusion—though I would add that the research has, with each wave, come increasingly under the control of the canons of research practice embodied in dominant disciplinary research traditions.

Social psychological studies of propaganda and persuasion. One finds much the same patterns in surveying research of the 1920s and 1930s on the persuasive effects of communication (usually termed "propaganda"). Many of the studies were summarized in Murphy and Murphy's survey of experimental social psychology (see Murphy et al., 1937, pp. 946-980, for the summary and citations). Taken together, the studies demonstrate the difficulty of changing attitudes with brief messages and show the important role of prior attitude in the communication reception process. Social psychological research on persuasion continued to be published in the years after the Murphys' second edition appeared (e.g., Asher & Sargent, 1941; Bateman & Remmers, 1941; Menefee, 1938). Related studies applied the experimental method to such topics as the analysis of radio and responses to different information channels (e.g., Cantril & Allport, 1935), judgments of language intensity in persuasive messages (Sargent, 1939), and assessments of the persistence of persuasive effects (e.g., Reemers, 1938). Research began to pursue increasingly focused and more theoretically motivated questions with more precise methods and designs. An independent line of persuasion research was going on in applied psychology and advertising.

Social psychological studies of interpersonal and group communication. Several lines of research, taken together, reflect the pre-World War II development of work that would enter the field of communication study in the 1950s and 1960s with the coalescence of interpersonal communication as a research specialization. In the 1920s and 1930s this work encompassed several, largely unrelated, lines of work on social interaction and group processes.

Social interaction processes received extensive coverage in Murphy et al.'s (1937) review of empirical social psychological research. Much of this research involved studies of children's social interactions using methods of controlled observation, rating instruments, and sociometric analysis (see Murphy et al., 1937, chap. 5). Patterns of cooperation, competition, aggression, and submission in interaction were given particular attention (e.g., Dawe, 1934; Goodenough, 1928). Much of this work concerned the development of stable interactional styles, though there was already growing realization that situational factors influence the expression of interpersonal styles and traits (see Murphy et al., 1937, pp. 872-888). Research stimulated by Piaget's (1926/1965) *Language and Thought of the Child* investigated the characteristics of children's conversations and social role-taking in communication (e.g., Baker, 1942). Studies of adult social interaction gave attention to the general problem of interaction analysis (e.g., Chapple, 1940) and in particular to the impact of social interaction on individual attitudes and performance (see Dashiell, 1935). However, the research terrain was very broad and ranged across topics as diverse as sex differences in conversational content (e.g., Landis & Burtt, 1924); analysis of cooperation, competition, decision making, and interpersonal leadership as social processes (e.g., Carr, 1929; Cowley, 1931); individual differences in response to verbal humor (e.g., Landis & Ross, 1933); the nature of interaction in personal and psychiatric interviews (e.g., Bingham, 1929); and the nonverbal communication of emotion (see Murphy et al., 1937, chap. 2).

Research on group dynamics also emerged within social psychology following World War I and was later to be defined within the scope of communication research. Cartwright and Zander (1968) provide an overview of the historical development of this area. They note that the rapid development in the area in the late 1930s and early 1940s reflected the orientation to social issues and group life characteristic of the Chicago school, the emergence of attention within a host of disciplines to the problems of professions in which group processes were central (social work, group psychotherapy, education, corporate administration and management), and theoretical concern with the general question of social facilitation. Among the early studies were investigations of the effects of the presence of others on performance (e.g., see Dashiell, 1935); research comparing individual and group problem solving (e.g., Shaw, 1932); studies by Mayo and others showing the importance of interpersonal relations and social norms to performance in the work place (Mayo, 1933; Rothlisberger & Dickson, 1939); systematic observational studies of interpersonal interaction in adults and children (see discussion above); studies of sociometric choice and social networks (e.g., Moreno, 1934); Sherif's integration of thought from anthropology, sociology, and experimental psychology as the basis for his investigations of the origins of social norms in groups (Sherif, 1936); studies of the social anchorage of attitudes (e.g., Newcomb, 1943); investigations of natural social groups in the tradition of interactionist sociology (e.g., Whyte, 1943); and Lewin and his coworkers' research on group leadership and the experimental study of group atmosphere and decision making (e.g., Lewin, Lippitt, & White, 1939). These lines of research, initially not thought of as "communication" research, would come in the decades following World War II to be incorporated into both the analysis of the flow of mass communications to individual receivers and the study within speech communication of interpersonal interaction, social relationships, and group decision making.

Social psychological research in the speech departments. Some work similar to that in social psychology was generated in speech departments before World War II. Psychology appears to have been the dominant influence on experimental research in these departments; the influence came through such figures as Charles Woolbert at Illinois and Franklin Knower at Ohio State, who had taken their degrees in psychology. The standard summary of this research is Thompson (1967). Among the lines of work are studies of oral persuasion (e.g., Gilkinson, 1942), comparisons of logical and emotional persuasive appeals (Knower, 1935), judgments of speakers from messages (e.g., Fay & Middleton, 1942), the effects of group discussion on attitude change and decisions (e.g., Robinson, 1941; Simpson, 1939), the accuracy of nonverbal communication of affect (Dusenbury & Knower, 1938), and factors influencing the learning of oral messages (e.g., Woolbert, 1920; Knower, Phillips, & Keoppel, 1945).

Communication and Education

Basic communication skills have been a persistent concern of educators and researchers throughout the twentieth century. In addition, every major new technology of communication introduced in this century has stirred the educational community. In this section, some aspects of early educational research on communication are briefly discussed. Attention is given to four areas of work: (1) the educational use of new technologies, (2) research on communication skills, (3) investigations of communication strategies and instructional outcomes, and (4) research on reading and listening.

Educational uses of new communication technologies. Much of the early educational literature on new technologies of communication consists of little more than arguments about the usefulness of the technology. Considerable journal space was spent informing teachers about the nature, sources, and possible applications of the technology. Some raised concerns about each new medium and its effect on the schools (e.g., Greene, 1926); others saw great potential in the same technology (e.g., Cressey, 1934); yet others reflected on the causes for the lack of penetration and use of the new instructional tools (e.g., Koon, 1935). Even the less pedagogically concrete publications often consisted of little more than reports of the diffusion of new audio and visual technologies (e.g., Koon & Noble, 1936), explorations of their applications (e.g., Thrasher, 1937), or surveys and analyses of institutional policies governing their use (e.g., Frost, 1937). Tracking diffusion and use frequently involved international comparisons (e.g., Mason, 1939). The progress in applying new technologies such as radio to take information to those hard to reach or to receive it from those far away also was the subject of regular reporting (e.g., Atkinson, 1942). Also prominent by World War II in the education literature was standard experimental research that assessed learning from instruction using the new communication technologies (e.g., Barr, Ewbank, & McCormick, 1942; Westfall, 1934).

Research on basic communication skills. In the last major section of this chapter, the relationship of communication research to speech departments is explored at some length. It is important here, however, to note that the formation of speech departments during the first decades of the century provided the vehicle for significant developments in oral communication education (see Wallace, 1954). Given the presence of experimentalists in the speech departments and the disciplinary concern with teaching basic communication skills for the public platform, radio, and a host of other arenas, speech departments generated a good deal of work on modes of instruction (e.g., Borchers, 1935, 1936). Communication skills relevant to new communication technologies, particularly radio, also were investigated (e.g., Ewbank, 1932). Other communication skills research focused on the value of democratic group discussion in promoting effective decision making (e.g., Timmons, 1941). A brief flurry of pedagogical work was stimulated in speech and English departments and education schools by the Institute for Propaganda Analysis's promotion of educational programs intended to help students learn to recognize and resist propaganda techniques (for a history of the Institute for Propaganda Analysis, see Sproule, 1983). The tests of the instructional programs largely failed to find the expected effects (e.g., Osborn, 1939).

Speech departments gave considerable attention to the development of pedagogical principles for speaking through analysis of classical and modern rhetorical theories. During the 1930s English departments also rediscovered the rhetorical tradition as a communication-centered basis for writing instruction and the critical analysis of literature and language. This rediscovery of rhetoric led to some research on writing (for a history of English education and composition research, see Applebee,

1974; Moran & Lunsford, 1984). Even more important, the English departments spawned major new theories of rhetoric and rhetorical analysis, including most notably those of I.A. Richards (1936) and Kenneth Burke (1962, 1966). Work in oral communication education, writing research, and studies in rhetorical analysis were all later to come under the umbrella of communication.

Communication strategies and instructional outcomes. Much contemporary work in communication education focuses on instructional strategies and their effects. Research anticipating this later focus appeared in the 1920s and 1930s. The most interesting of this work assessed the effects on learning of such communication tactics as threats, praise, reprimands, sarcasm, and ridicule, and considered such mediating factors as whether the communication occurred in public or private or was immediate or delayed (e.g., Benton, 1936; Brenner, 1934; Briggs, 1927; Laird, 1923). Methods of systematic observation were introduced into study of the learning environment (e.g., H. Anderson, 1939) and later evolved into a major approach to research on the classroom (e.g., see Simon & Boyer, 1967). Other research analyzed the classroom instructional process as a persuasive event creating and changing beliefs and attitudes (e.g., Caldwell & Lundeen, 1933; Kroll, 1934).

Educators regularly noted one of the effects of mass communication—its competition with reading. Consequently, both in education colleges and in library schools, research was stimulated comparing usage levels of the communication media, and attempts were made to assess the impact of the new modes of mass communication on reading. Among the most prominent scholars to come to communication through this route were Douglas Waples and Bernard Berelson from the University of Chicago library school and Lyman Bryson of Columbia University Teachers College. A representative study charting statistics on the production and consumption of reading matter is Waples (1937).

Waples also was involved in a number of studies that sought to determine the basis of reading tastes and preferences and the effects of reading. In line with the general social psychological mediationalism of the 1930s, Waples, Berelson, and Bradshaw (1940) argued, for example, that reading leads to a variety of responses—facilitating the achievement of instrumental goals, enhancing self-esteem or prestige, reinforcing existing positions on controversial issues, enriching aesthetic experience, and providing for escape from problems and worries. The kind of response obtained, they argued, results from an interaction between the material read and the reader's orientation and predispositions. They stressed that the predispositions brought to reading are significant determinants of which communications will be selected and the effect those communications will have.

Other studies of reading developed simplified algorithms for determining "readability"; of these the most notable were those of Gray and Leary (1935) at Chicago and Flesch at Columbia (1944). The easy availability of these statistical tools stimulated considerable research on the difficulty level of written materials. The procedures and their variants were applied widely in journalism (e.g., English, 1944), and also attracted considerable favor within market-conscious segments of the publishing industry. The presence of radio naturally led to comparisons across the communication modes (e.g., Goldstein, 1940). Speech departments also pursued parallel lines of work, including statistical analysis of speaking styles (e.g., J. Anderson, 1939; Barnard, 1932) and comparisons of platform and radio speaking (Ewbank, 1932).

Commercially Focused Communication Research

Understanding the development of commercially focused research necessitates appreciation of a complex of more general matters, including the social and industrial developments supporting the rise of national brands and national marketing, general developments in applied psychology and social science as a field, the rise of professionalism in advertising, and the deeper connection of these developments to some of the roles of science in twentieth-century American culture. In this section, the development of scientific concern with advertising and Paul Lazarsfeld's applied sociological research are discussed in the context of issues reflecting these more general developments.

Research on advertising. Advertising began to increase significantly in America immediately after the Civil War. However, it remained at a relatively low absolute level until the last decades of the nineteenth century. The first great surge in advertising came in the decades from 1880 to 1910 with the fivefold increase in America of both the value of manufacturing output and the volume of advertising (see Borden, 1942). Changes in the character of advertising reflected the merging of the economic interests of national advertisers, large agencies, and major publishers with the professional desires and aspirations of local advertising agents who formed clubs and associations during the decades around 1900 (Schultze, 1978).

The first vehicles for large-scale advertising were national magazines, which rose to prominence in America after the Civil War. Although many magazines resisted the effort to use their pages for advertising, Wood (1958) reports that by 1900 "the magazine had become the medium par excellence for the newer kind of advertising in which manufacturers of branded merchandise sought wide national markets for their products" (p. 193). This development was spurred through the creation of national advertising agencies that bought magazine space and then marketed it to advertisers. J. Walter Thompson, the first of these national agents, achieved a near monopoly and forced some magazines to set up their own advertising departments (Schultze, 1978). As magazines with their own advertising departments and other large agencies grew, intense competition emerged. One result of this competition was the birth of research within advertising agencies and the progressive incorporation of "scientific" advertising.

This development was greatly accelerated by the commercialization of radio following World War I (see Czitrom, 1982). Broadcasting developed initially in America almost wholly without regulatory control. As commercial interests discovered the possibility of securing audiences through broadcasting entertainment, marketing and advertising interests demanded data documenting the sizes and compositions of audiences. Industry-sponsored research developed to meet this need. A good deal of the voluminous publication on communication from outside the industry also has involved efforts to track the diffusion of the new media and forms of communication. The most notable study of this kind is the Hoover administration-sponsored study by Wiley and Rice (1933).

Broadcasting's commercialization has been of enormous importance to the development of broad aspects of communication research. Here I will concentrate on the shaping of academic specialties tied to commercial interests (see Baritz, 1960; Ewen, 1977; Noble, 1977). Broadcasters needed evidence concerning their audiences and advertisers needed information concerning the effectiveness of the media and of their advertisements. Consequently, the modest efforts in research on communication and consumer behavior were greatly expanded after World War I with the development of commercial broadcasting.

Nineteenth-century advertising was largely based on a philosophy of providing information (e.g., see Rowell, 1906). Curti (1967) argues that this philosophy changed in the early twentieth century to one of persuasion (also see Kuna, 1976). America was shifting toward an industrial economy based on expanding production. Advertising's role became not only influencing choices among similar competing products but also among alternative desires (see Buckley, 1982). Many progressives saw business culture as closely linked to the expansion of democracy. For example, to the progressivist founder of "scientific advertising," Northwestern University psychologist Walter Dill Scott, advertising was "a secular gospel that would usher in a democracy of consumption for the common man by streamlining the distribution of goods and uplifting the standard of living" (Schultze, 1978, p. 102; see Scott, 1931). Scott's scientific advertising amounted to little more than promise, however, and prior to World War I the influence of scientific advertising was limited to the development of a new language of description and to the invention of statistical techniques for completing circulation and market analyses.

Notions of scientific advertising appealed mostly to professional advertising agents who embraced the authority of science in hopes of securing the professionalism of their craft (Schultze, 1980). At the same time, little status in academic psychology was associated with commercial research. Indeed, Baritz (1960) notes that many of the earliest academics to apply social scientific methods to business problems were forced by fears of losing status to keep their work secret. Consequently, much of the development of applied social science shifted to business schools where writing textbooks and working with industry provided status (see Schultze, 1978). However, some major converts were won to applied research in the pre-World War I psychological community, most notably Thorndike at Columbia, Munsterberg at Harvard, and Watson at Johns Hopkins (e.g., Munsterberg, 1913; Thorndike, 1911).

The aims of applied psychologists were greatly advanced by America's entry into World War I and the enlisting of psychologists in personnel selection and management processes (for a general history of psychologists' role in the war see Camfield, 1969). Walter Dill Scott headed the Army's Committee on Classification of Personnel, which instituted systematic intelligence testing and procedures for personnel classification and training. The attention given the work of the Scott Committee greatly enhanced the prestige and promise of applied psychology and sharply increased the business community's demand for the services of psychologists after the war. The Scott Company and the Psychological Corporation were formed as visible signs of the new alliance (for histories of these companies see, respectively, Ferguson, 1962, and Sokal, 1981). Researchers in these organizations and others directly in the employ of agencies and companies solidified psychology's and social science's role in advertising during the two decades between the world wars (for a history of psychology's development after World War I see Napoli, 1980). The most important of these individuals was the founder of psychological behaviorism, John B. Watson (for a perceptive analysis of Watson's role in the development of scientific advertising see Buckley, 1982).

By 1920 Watson had achieved international recognition from his academic position at Johns Hopkins. However, he left academia to join the J. Walter Thompson advertising agency (see Buckley, 1982). Watson secured a position with the Thompson agency in part through the offices of Chicago's W. I. Thomas (see Matthews, 1977). The move to the corporate world provided a vehicle for Watson's pursuit of his dream of a psychology that could serve the needs of social control in urban society (for a discussion of the relationship of behaviorism and urbanism, see

Bakan, 1966). Buckley (1982) argues that the notion of control is one of the underlying themes

> connecting the growth of science, technology, and the emerging professions with the expansion of an industrialized urban society. The shift of authority from older institutions such as the church, the family, and the local community to a bureaucracy of experts that provided services to corporations, public institutions, and social agencies gave rise to a demand for methods of behavior control, to which Watson directed his energies.

In this Watson shared much with important elements of the progressive movement. The contrast with the Chicago school's alternative formulation of progressivism's spirit reveals the deep contradictions in the meanings of science and of modern America's relationship to them. In the Chicago formulation the instrumentalism of science was seen as rooted in the capacity of all organisms to functionally adapt to their worlds. Neither environment nor organism were believed to be controlling. Hence for the Chicago School the problem of modern society was not control, but participation.

The role of someone like Watson at the Thompson agency was to legitimize the turn to scientific advertising both as an approach within the industry and as an area of research inquiry into the influence process. Although Watson's first job for the agency was as a road salesman of Yuban coffee, his functional role from the start was important both practically and symbolically. As Buckley (1982) has observed, national advertising grew as a response to the development of a system of industrial production geared toward the national marketing of goods. Advertisers looked to psychology for principles and techniques that would rationalize the distribution and marketing process and permit them to sustain the claim that they could deliver to industry a predictable group of consumers. Thus, as Buckley (1982) says,

> Within the Thompson agency, Watson served a dual role. Watson was proof to the business community that the Thompson agency was serious in its commitment to find scientific solutions to marketing problems. In addition, his task as an advertising psychologist was to develop campaigns of mass appeal that would create reliable markets for goods created by mass production. (p. 211)

Under Watson's leadership behavioristic psychology was embraced as a model to rationalize and legitimate the application of quantitative and experimental methods to the advertising process.

Studies of consumer behavior and advertising appeals increased significantly as areas of study among applied psychologists. The typical research involved tightly controlled experiments focused on effects (e.g., the psychological effects of a trade name change, see Blankenship & Taylor, 1937; attention and recall value of visual and auditory advertisements, see Dewick, 1935; Elliott, 1937). Other studies sought to demonstrate the level of advertisements' effects (e.g., Likert, 1936; Stanton, 1940) or to discern listeners' evaluations of programs (as in Longstaff's, 1936, 1937, studies of children's programs). During this period the academic journals also caught the shadow of the industry research programs designed to develop improved methods of audience measurement and program ratings (for histories of audience research see Hurwitz, 1983; Meehan, 1983). In addition, after 1938 public relations—the application of advertising to corporate identity—became an increasingly visible topic of commentary and research (e.g., see Childs, 1940; Ettinger, 1945).

Lazarsfeld and the institutionalization of applied research. The significance of the commercially focused research tradition for American academic communication research comes from its institutionalization within American universities. There is no figure more important to this development than Paul F. Lazarsfeld. Lazarsfeld came to the United States in 1932 as a travelling scholar sponsored by the Rockefeller Foundation, but stayed, given the political situation in his native Austria (see Lazarsfeld's memoir in Fleming & Bailyn, 1969).

From his applied social research background in Austria, Lazarsfeld brought two commitments that were to leave an indelible stamp on American mass communication research. First, he had a characteristic research style. In his memoir, he describes his research policy as one of "improvisation guided by available material and personal interests and contacts" (in Fleming & Bailyn, 1969, p. 317). Most often the available material reflected some commercially sponsored administrative question. For example, while still being sponsored as a fellow by the Rockefeller Foundation, he undertook a study with David Craig at the University of Pittsburgh's Retail Research Institute. The following passage from that report has been described as distinctively Lazarsfeldian:

> Like other theories, the generalizations here to be set forth were derived originally from a specific problem. A department store raises the question "why do our customers run away when we label our merchandise 'Rayon?' And what can we do about it that is honest?" This question was asked, one day, of the staff of the Research Bureau for Retail Training. On the following day, by accident, the two authors of this paper happened to meet. One was an Austrian with a method, seeking an opportunity. The other was an American with a problem, seeking a solution that appeared

attainable through the Austrian's method. The result was a happy collaboration, a three-month cooperative arrangement involving a thousand organized interviews and innumerable experimental calculations, summarized briefly herewith. (Craig & Lazarsfeld, 1934, p. 1)

A commercial question was combined with questions concerning buyers' motivations and experiences, and the trivial question was turned into one of potential academic interest.

It is interesting that Lazarsfeld came to be associated almost exclusively with the survey research approach to mass communication (e.g., Berelson, 1959; Schramm, 1985). However, seeing Lazarsfeld in this way reflects the general drift in mass communication and public opinion research toward this kind of work more than close attention to the voluminous output from Lazarsfeld and his coworkers. It requires ignoring broad ranges of the studies undertaken under Lazarsfeld's sponsorship. Many investigations employed just a few subjects who answered open-ended questions probing their perceptions, attitudes, and motives (e.g., Herzog, 1941; Wolf & Fiske, 1949); others applied the open-ended questionnaire approach to studies of a focal case (e.g., Cantril, Gaudet, & Herzog, 1940; Merton, 1946). In addition, Lazarsfeld and his coworkers frequently relied upon archival information (e.g., Lazarsfeld & Wyant, 1937). The key to Lazarsfeld's own research was not his very real comfort with the survey, but his customary adoption of the marketer's concern for understanding the factors related to discrete, individual choices (see Chaffee & Hochheimer, 1985).

Lazarsfeld's second enduring commitment was to the institutionalization of applied research within the university through the creation of centers along the lines of one he had helped create in Vienna. He realized his goal through the creation of the much-duplicated Bureau of Applied Social Research at Columbia.

The passion of Lazarsfeld's life thus was not the study of communication. He came to the area through need of a job, and the good offices of Columbia's Robert Lynd. With Princeton psychologist Hadley Cantril and CBS research director Frank Stanton as codirectors, Lazarsfeld set about creating an Office of Radio Research under a Rockefeller Foundation grant. This happenstance turn in Lazarsfeld's career was to shape profoundly the course of communication research in America.

More so than any other individual or group, Lazarsfeld cemented the emerging bridge between academic and commercial interests in communication research and established the theoretical relevance of communication research based on applied problems. Cantril and Stanton had originally envisioned the Rockefeller project as emphasizing precise experimental studies of radio's effects. However, Lazarsfeld directed investigations toward the general questions of the sort he had worked with in Vienna and in his freelance commercial and foundation research in America. Since Lazarsfeld operated the radio project out of his office in Newark, it was never clearly differentiated from the ongoing commercially sponsored projects that he continued to pursue. The wholly unsympathetic reaction of the German critical theorist Theodore Adorno (in Fleming & Bailyn, 1969) pinpoints the applied interests that dominated the Rockefeller project:

> My first impression of the researches already in progress there was not exactly marked by any great understanding. . . . But this much I did understand: that it was concerned with the collection of data, which were supposed to benefit the planning departments in the field of the mass media, whether in industry itself or in cultural advisory boards and similar bodies. For the first time, I saw "administrative research" before me.

Lazarsfeld was convinced, however, that his approach was not inconsistent with the pursuit of theoretical understanding. He staunchly defended applied research to the end of his career with considerable success within the sociological community (see, for example, Lazarsfeld & Reitz, 1975).

One important avenue to understanding Lazarsfeld's research practices is appreciation of the way they were shaped by the interests of administrative and marketing research. Indeed, it is common in recent critical readings of the American empirical research tradition to weight this influence to the exclusion of others (e.g., Rowland, 1983). Lazarsfeld's place in communication research calls for a more complex understanding, however. In particular, it is important to recognize that the success of his approach within sociology depended heavily upon establishing its theoretical significance. It is surely the case that sociologists' receptiveness to Lazarsfeld's arguments for the importance of applied research is to be understood partly in terms of the position that funded research came to secure for its principal investigators within American universities. But a more complete understanding will also address the means by which the products of the research were made to fit within disciplinary goals. In this vein, Lazarsfeld's arguments for the theoretical role of applied research become quite important (e.g., see Lazarsfeld & Reitz, 1975) because by World War II and increasingly thereafter the contribution of research to the development of sociological theory was a central value defining the goals of sociology as a discipline. At the disciplinary level, there was a shift across the 1920s and 1930s in sociology away from service-oriented research, unprogrammatic research, and research yoked to grand theoretical structures. A central movement of the discipline was toward valuing, in Merton's (1957) formulation, "theories of the midrange." These developments are of great significance to understanding the success of the Lazarsfeld program (see Chaffee & Hochheimer, 1985). Such disciplinary developments should be seen as in part shaped by the needs to rationalize the products of administrative research, but one must also look at the context shaping broader development of these disciplinary commitments and to the ways the canons of research practice and theory building were worked out within the particular discipline. For example, although both sociology and psychology were beneficiaries of enormous corporate and government sponsorship, their research models and implicit structures of theory development reflected accommodations and practices responsive to their own disciplinary histories (e.g., as in social psychology's accommodation to psychology as an experimental science and its preference for hypothesis testing as a standard research practice).

Lazarsfeld also occupied a crucial role in the purely "sociological" development of communication research. By sociological development here I mean simply who knew and read whom. Lazarsfeld was an organizer, and the Rockefeller radio project quickly became a center of activity for many interested in communication research. At various times, Lazarsfeld enlisted various European intellectuals he had known in the study of communication (e.g., Herta Herzog, Theodore Adorno, Rudolf Arnheim). He established contact with Samuel Stouffer in sociology and Harold Lasswell in political science at the University of Chicago and briefly drew them into Rockefeller projects. Those in the library school at Chicago were also brought into the circle (including Douglas Waples and Bernard Berelson). In addition, he promoted contact between mainstream sociologists (e.g., Robert Lynd, Robert Merton) and established connections with those studying propaganda and public opinion in other disciplines (e.g., Hadley Cantril, Gerhard Wiebe, and Daniel Katz in psychology and associates of Lasswell such as Alexander George and Daniel Lerner in political science).

Lazarsfeld had an even more substantial impact on the sociology of communication, however, through the establishment of a unit for applied social research at Columbia. The Office of Radio Research was transferred from Princeton to Columbia in 1940. Lazarsfeld succeeded in translating the office into a general center for applied research that became an integral part of the university structure. Lazarsfeld's applied research institute evolved into a model that was duplicated in many other universities (most notable was the Institute for Social Research at the University of Michigan).

The voluminous publication output of the Columbia researchers similarly channeled the development of the field. As has already been suggested, the research projects served to organize and unify a core group of scholars concerned with communication. But far beyond the role for these involved scholars, many of the studies were to become the exemplars defining concretely what doing communication research meant. Among the major publications associated with Lazarsfeld and the Princeton/Columbia research shops were such classic works as Lazarsfeld (1940); Cantril et al. (1940); Lazarsfeld and Stanton (1941, 1944, 1949); Lazarsfeld, Berelson, and Gaudet (1944); Merton (1946); Berelson, Lazarsfeld, and McPhee (1954); Katz and Lazarsfeld (1955); and Klapper (1960).

Other research on the communication industries. Before leaving the topic of commercially focused communication research, I want to return to the general theme of fragmentation and dispersal. Although scientific advertising research and Lazarsfeld's administrative research have much in common, they represent distinct traditions of work. Each was shaped not only by the commitment to serve both the interests of science and commercial clients, but also by the research practices and models sanctioned within disciplinary subfields. Moreover, there was much other communication research that addressed the corporate side of American communication from very different traditions. Most notable among these were economic analyses, of which Borden's (1942) analysis of advertising's place in the economy is perhaps the best example. But there were many others, from many academic orientations (e.g., Cherington, 1913; Huettig, 1944; Lee, 1937; McCarry, 1939).

COMMUNICATION SCIENCE 1940 TO 1965:
CONSOLIDATION

This section traces the consolidation of the interdisciplinary study of communication after World War II. The first two parts address the impact of World War II on the study of communication and the coalescence of communication research as a self-consciously defined domain in the immediate postwar years. The third part then discusses the major research programs in communication science during the 1950s. A final part discusses the relationship of the communication research consolidation in the late 1940s and 1950s to the broader landscape of academic concern with communication.

World War II and Communication Research

World War II had a tremendous impact on the development of communication research. Just as had the first world war, the second advanced the interest of applied social science generally. Indeed, Napoli (1980) argues that it was their contributions in World War II that finally won for applied social scientists, particularly psychologists, the professional standing they had sought throughout the century. Increased attention to communication problems was a major result of this emphasis on applied issues. The war played a much more concrete role for communication research, however, by drawing a number of researchers to the topic. Some of the researchers completed a few studies dealing with communication and then took up other issues when they returned to the universities; others, however, were attracted to the field and stayed.

The most important in the former group is another European emigre, Kurt Lewin. Lewin was a German social psychologist; after coming to America he and his colleagues launched a research program on group dynamics (e.g., Lewin, 1945). Although Berelson (1959) and Schramm (1985) count him as one of the major figures in the development of communication research, Lewin's influence in America was primarily in the areas of general social psychology and small group processes. His influence within the growing community of communication researchers was relatively insignificant (e.g., Smith, Lasswell, & Casey, 1946, list only one obscure general paper of Lewin's in their bibliographic handbook; Klapper, 1960, does not cite Lewin at all). Lewin's general influence in social psychology was considerable, however. He had significant impact on the study of group dynamics and (indirectly through Heider and Festinger) on attitude studies. Work in these areas entered the communication field in the 1950s and 1960s as speech departments gave increased attention to group discussion and decision making, and speech and mass communication programs pursued studies of persuasion and attitude change.

Among the researchers who took up wartime communication research and came to have a major impact on the field the most important was Carl Hovland. Hovland was a Yale University experimental psychologist and colleague of the learning theorist, Clark Hull. During the war Hovland was involved in research on mass communication for the War Department. Upon his return to Yale after the war, he continued the kinds of studies undertaken during the war. Hovland's work, which is discussed below, placed the methods of experimental social psychology in the mainstream of communication research.

One concrete source of the war's influence on the course of American communication research was the development of interpersonal contacts among leading researchers. Samuel Stouffer, who had left Chicago for Harvard, became the research director for the Army's Information and Education Division (originally called the Morale Division). Hovland directed the mass communication program within this division. Through Stouffer, the Lazarsfeld group was tied into the war research; a number of projects were farmed out to the Columbia research center. After the war, much of the data collected by the researchers under Stouffer were reanalyzed with an eye to theoretical issues; the result was an important milestone in the development of American empirical social psychology (see Madge, 1962; the Information and Education Division volumes are

Hovland, Lumsdaine, & Sheffield, 1949; Merton & Lazarsfeld, 1950; Stouffer et al., 1949a, 1949b, 1950). The connections made through Stouffer and the Army Information and Education Division thus placed the communication researchers in the mainstream of American sociology and social psychology. Similar connections were established through Harold Lasswell's role as Director of War Communications Research for the Library of Congress. Even though he had lost his academic position at Chicago before the war, Lasswell remained broadly connected among scholars interested in communication and propaganda. He had already been drawn into the Columbia group. Lasswell also had personal ties with Daniel Lerner, Ithiel deSola Pool, Irving Janis, Morris Janowitz, and was, in addition, connected with such communication researchers at the University of Chicago as Berelson and Waples.

As communication study began to take shape as a defined field of study, it reflected in no small measure the particular intersection of viewpoints and interests brought together through these personal contacts, particularly those built up around Lazarsfeld at Columbia, Stouffer and Hovland in the Division of Information and Education at the War Department, and through Lasswell's ties. At the end of the 1940s Lazarsfeld and Stanton (1949) would speak of the field's pioneers as a "closely knit group" (p. xiii).

A final influence on the development of communication research indirectly spawned by the second world war was the unparalleled expansion of American higher education in the postwar period. As educational opportunities were opened through government support, the universities became engines of social and economic transformation fueled increasingly by the national government (see Lyons, 1969). It is doubtful that communication study would have emerged as it has had it not been consolidated as a field of study during a period of wholesale expansion of American higher education, for that expansion created a context that strongly supported the formation of new departments and programs.

The Consolidation of Communication Science

"Communications research" emerges. The years following World War II were witness to the emergence and consolidation of communication research as a distinct domain of investigation. Our examination of research up to 1940 has shown the enormous range of interests and approaches to communication across the developing disciplines of the social sciences. The war years saw an intensification of these research interests; and after the war, publications literally burst forth across the range of disciplines and topics.

This period is best known by contemporary communication scholars, however, for a few classic works, among the most important of which are Lazarsfeld et al. (1944); Merton (1946); Smith et al. (1946); Bryson (1948); Schramm (1948, 1949); Hovland et al. (1949); Lasswell et al. (1949); Lazarsfeld and Stanton (1949); Berelson and Janowitz (1950); Hovland, Janis, and Kelley (1953); Berelson et al. (1954); Katz and Lazarsfeld (1955). These and related works were taken as central by the particular network of scholars who were to exercise direct influence in the decade from 1945 to 1955 in defining communication research as a field of study, including most notably those associated with Lazarsfeld, Lasswell, Hovland, and Schramm.

The terms "mass communication" and "communications research" appeared in print only occasionally before the middle years of the 1940s, though their arrival was evident from the early 1940s (see Lazarsfeld & Stanton, 1941; Waples, 1942). Previously the dominantly employed terms for describing the aspects of communication science were "propaganda and public opinion," "radio research," "print research," "reading research," "audience research," "motion picture research," and so forth. However, with the publication of Smith et al.'s (1946) bibliographic guide entitled *Propaganda, Communication, and Public Opinion,* the term "communication" rapidly entered the vocabulary of media and persuasion researchers. Two volumes based on papers presented around the theme of communication were published in 1948: *The Communication of Ideas* (Bryson, 1948) and *Communications in Modern Society* (Schramm, 1948). The 1949 report of research initiated under the Rockefeller radio research grant was issued under the title *Communications Research, 1948-1949* (Lazarsfeld & Stanton, 1949). Within a year, two collections of readings that defined the parameters of the field displayed the term in their titles: *Mass Communications* (Schramm, 1949) and *Reader in Public Opinion and Communication* (Berelson & Janowitz, 1950). A new sense of unity and coherence was visible among the community of researchers.

The development of a center: Behavioral science, theory development, and the flow and effects framework. The first unity that was evident among the scholars most involved in the coalescence of communication research during the late 1940s was a shared sense of the history of the field. The most involved scholars came with focal interests in the scientific analysis of public opinion, propaganda, and the uses and effects of communication. From their perspectives an emerging field with a shared historical orientation was evident. Again and again, individuals at the core of the emerging network pictured their work as part of a new scientific turn in the analysis of the systems of public communication. Lazarsfeld and Stanton (1949) noted that the shift to "communications research" reflected the conviction that "the whole field of communications research should be covered simultaneously" (p. xi).

The longstanding desire to understand communication as a vehicle of democratic life also continued to motivate many communication researchers. For example, Berelson (in Schramm, 1948) described the development of academic interest in public opinion and communication as tied closely to the "urgency of the problem" of modern public persuasion. Schramm (1948) likewise elaborated the goal of the new researchers as being "how they might make their efforts more than the sum of their individual efforts, and of how they might use those efforts toward the better understanding of communications and toward the maximum use of communications for the public good" (p. 6). Scientific solutions were to be found to the problems facing democratic life; the task was, in Lasswell's (1948) terms, to contribute to the development of efficient communication, where efficiency is defined by "the degree that rational judgments are facilitated" (p. 46). Even the most committed experimentalist stressed that although scientific studies themselves must "try to be objective and uninterested in *values*," research "can provide . . . objective data basic" to those "evaluating the effect of various communication policies" (Hovland in Schramm, 1948, p. 183). Those who brought forth communication science thus inherited traditions of thought emphasizing the centrality of communication in political life and the importance of science to social understanding and informed political action (interestingly, Louis Wirth, the remaining spokesperson of the Chicago school, reiterated, though more soberly, the familiar Chicago themes on consensus and mass communication in his 1947 presidential address to the American Sociological Association; see Wirth, in Schramm, 1949).

There was, however, an intrinsic conflict for many of the researchers drawn to communication research between the demands of science as practiced within their maturing disciplines and the political commitments implicit in much of the work on communication. This tension is evident in the above quotation from Hovland stating that science must strive to be free of values. The adoption of such an attitude toward the practice of science reflected a general development across the social sciences to which we have already called attention. As social scientists sought to secure objectivity and authority for their work, they increasingly focused on "empirical investigations of problems that were normally defined by the state of knowledge in their fields rather than by the state of society" (Furner, 1975, p. 8).

In retrospect, it is evident that this attitude to locate research problems within the matrix of disciplinary values rapidly entered communication research after World War II, so that for most communication researchers, the commitment to science became detached from—and thereby made invisible—the commercial and political interests that had generated the basic research models in the first place. (Chaffee & Hochheimer, 1985, have presented a convincing case for the role of this attitude in contributing to the adoption of the "limited effects" conception of mass communication's role in society; I would also point, however, to the deep roots of the limited effects view in the social psychological conceptions of the 1920s and 1930s.)

Thus the shared historical commitment to pursue scientific understanding of mass communication's practical and policy aspects was transformed by the achieved professionalism of social scientists into pursuits defined by the conduct of research within the questions and canons of established social science disciplines. Within many of the disciplines, the accepted canons of professionalism defined theoretical questions as of principal significance and sustained the bracketing of overtly value-centered questions. This attitude was particularly strong among psychologists committed to the experimental method and hypothesis testing and was taken over as a central research value by many communication researchers, particularly those in speech communication whose research problems were more likely to test theoretical hypotheses than assess the social effects of public communication. By the end of the 1950s this attitude was firmly fixed as a core commitment among the majority of communication researchers.

The change even from the immediate pre-World War II period was dramatic, and is nicely represented in the views of Yale's Leonard Doob. Doob had authored the most influential social psychological text on propaganda in the 1930s (Doob, 1935) and had served as an adviser to the reform-oriented Institute for Propaganda Analysis in the late 1930s and early 1940s. Sproule (1983) interviewed Doob concerning his work on propaganda analysis:

> He [Doob] notes that an academician could not serve both the causes of social reform and a theoretical social psychology. . . . In . . . universities such as Yale, theoretical research is more prestigious than applied work. Further, Doob indicates, the very term "propaganda" began to lose favor as the more objective . . . concepts of communication, persuasion, and public opinion replaced it in the lexicon of social science. Indeed, Doob reports he would not have dreamed of using propaganda as a significant theoretical term in his 1961 study of *Communication in Africa*. (p. 495)

Concepts of propaganda analysis "were obsolete" and were "superseded by the new knowledge and methods in academic social science" (Sproule, 1983, p. 495, summarizing Doob).

Communication research thus sprang forth as a distinct domain of study in part as a rejection of the atheoretical, politically suffused work of the past. The organizing commitment that clearly asserted itself in the postwar period was to a social science of communication aimed at theory development. Lazarsfeld and others, it will be recalled, had long argued that theoretical advance should come out of applied research.

However, in my judgment Hovland (and the experimental social psychological establishment) and Berelson were to have the most dramatic effect in establishing theory development as the principal goal of communication research. In doing this, they were aligning communication research with the conceptions of the maturing disciplines of experimental social psychology and neopositivist sociology.

Hovland had been trained in Hull's laboratory and before the war had worked as an experimental psychologist extending Hullian learning theory. Hovland's orientation naturally led him to advance (for the first time, so far as I can discern) that the primary goal of communication research is theory development, not the analysis of applied problems. Hovland (1948) noted,

> The problem confronting us currently is no . . . lack of ideas and hypotheses. These . . . are available on every side. What are primarily lacking are two things: (1) lack of a comprehensive theoretical structure to embrace the diverse ideas and hunches . . . and (2) systematic experimental work to check and verify or refute the hypotheses obtaining. (p. 374)

The Yale persuasion and attitude research program was established as a long-term project to wed experimental social psychological research on communication to theory development.

Lazarsfeld and many of his coworkers—particularly Berelson—also made theory development a principal goal of communication research. Chaffee and Hochheimer (1985) note Berelson's fondness for summarizing empirical relationships in a particular study as "empirical generalizations" or "laws" of behavior (this was taken to its extreme in Berelson & Steiner, 1964). In the postwar years, Berelson put forth the development of such laws of communication behavior as the goal of the new science. The job of researchers, he said, was working out empirical generalizations describing the relationship between five sets of variables interacting in the communication process: communications, issues, people, conditions, and effects. Berelson (in Schramm, 1948) offered a vision for communication science that transcended past concerns with pragmatic issues:

> The interrelationships of these variables constitutes the subject-matter of a scientific theory in this field. . . . Whatever the method of investigation . . . propositional organization of statements presenting interrelationships among variables should be considered the framework of study. In this way, a scientific theory of communication and public opinion can be developed. (pp. 184-185)

Schramm (1963) continued 15 years later to identify theory development as the field's principal goal.

The crystallization of the core of the emerging field as a social-scientific domain concerned with theory development was facilitated by three factors: (1) the adoption of a vocabulary of organizing terms, (2) the establishment of a core subject matter with the appearance of field-defining books, and (3) the embracing of a standard conception of the "basic communication process." A standard organizing framework for approaching communication was rather quickly overlaid on the commitment to scientific understanding. The organizing vocabulary expressed the well-known "model of flow" (Tunstall, 1970, p. 4). The outlines of this framework were visible in Smith et al. (1946); however, the framework had already been developed before the war and appears as the organizing terms in an unpublished memorandum on mass communication research developed by Lazarsfeld, Lasswell, and others at a conference sponsored by the Rockefeller Foundation (see Czitrom, 1982, pp. 131-132). In organizing research in the field, Smith et al. (1946) focused on the question they took to be "central in the minds of scientific students of the communication process: 'If *who* says *what*, through what *channels* (media) of communication, to *whom*, what will be the *results*? and how can we *measure* what is said and its results?'" (p. 121) Thus their major categories for organizing research were communicators, communications institutions and their control, contents, channels, effects, and measurement procedures (also see Lasswell's question "Who says what . . . ?" in Schramm, 1948). A field of study, previously fragmented, was thereby given structure and the semblance of coherence.

The influence of Lasswell's framework was enshrined through its adoption as the central organizing structure in the text-oriented readers that were to establish the field's parameters (Berelson & Janowitz, 1950; Schramm, 1949, 1954). It is important to note that the flow-and-effects framework did not describe the vast terrain of communication research even in the late 1940s, but it and the first field-defining texts did leave a permanent mark. The effect of the texts was to define a range of relevant content, with the language of flow from communication source to audience effects providing an organizing structure. It is significant, however, that the parameters of the field as defined were neither clear nor coherent. The scope of inclusion was selective, with only apparent integration.

Even given the connection between Smith et al.'s (1946) bibliographic survey and their earlier volume on propaganda (Lasswell et al., 1935), a wealth of the material included in that survey fits a linear flow framework only by arbitrary classification. Moreover, though they emphasized that work was becoming increasingly scientific, the vast majority of Smith et al.'s references are to nonscientific commentaries or studies. Similarly, Schramm's (1949) edited reader, *Mass Communications,* strongly embraced Lasswell's organizing framework, but included a section on the historical development of mass communication and a variety of papers reflecting the perspectives of scholars with backgrounds and interests far removed from those of the Lazarsfeld, Lasswell, or Hovland groups. The more narrowly cast reader of Berelson and Janowitz (1950) likewise embraced the Lasswellian organizational structure, but included a range of readings that did not embody the viewpoint that the flow-and-effects framework came to represent.

The Lasswellian organizing framework also was transformed into an implicitly accepted conceptual description of the communication process. There had been no explicit argument for this fusion, but it was clearly evident by the mid-1950s. *The Mathematical Theory of Communication* (Shannon & Weaver, 1949) was given wide distribution among communication researchers both by Weaver's general essay translating Shannon's technical theory of information transmission to human communication and by Schramm's reliance on the information theory framework in his overview of the communication process (Schramm, 1954, pp. 3-26). The source/message/channel/destination terms integrated naturally with both the Lasswellian language and the essential structure of communication as conceptualized within studies of communication effects. By its organization and coverage Schramm's (1954) reader, *The Process and Effects of Mass Communication,* argued implicitly for a source-to-receiver effects model as describing *the* core process of communication. In the foreword, Schramm (1954) made this view explicit:

> One must understand how the communication process works, how attention is gained, how meaning is transferred from one subjective field to another, how opinions and attitudes are created or modified, and how group memberships, role concepts, and social structure are related to this process. . . . What is said about these subjects is equally applicable to any of the great laboratories in which social communication can be examined—for example, advertising, or domestic political campaigns, or adult education through the mass media. (p. iii)

By the time Klapper's (1960) *The Effects of Mass Communication* and Berlo's (1960) *The Process of Communication* were published, the linear flow-and-effects framework had become a conceptual description of the core of the communication process. The Lasswellian organizational structure, the conceptual understanding of communication as a mediated-effects process, and the view that the science of communication involved the formation of empirical generalizations all combined to exert a strong hold over the center of the field. Research variables involved in the communication process (source attributes, message features, channel variables, receiver characteristics, operational definitions of effect, etc.) were accepted as both organized and integratable within a framework that served theory development.

The Hovland and Lazarsfeld Traditions in the 1950s

Given this history in the two decades following World War II, it is not surprising that the study of communication found its greatest exemplars in the voting studies of Lazarsfeld and Berelson and the experimental persuasion studies of Hovland. By the mid-1950s, *theoretically focused* communication study was concerned with issues of effects. This work recreated the general mediational framework in social psychology that was already evident in the 1930s in the Payne Fund studies, the work of the Chicago library school group, and the studies conducted by the Princeton and Columbia researchers associated with Cantril and Lazarsfeld. Those lines of work had emphasized the mediating roles in communication of recipient predispositions and social processes, and had acknowledged the possibility of differential effects. As Berelson (in Schramm, 1948) summarized the shared conception, it was the belief that "some kinds of *communication* on some kinds of *issues,* brought to the attention of some kinds of *people* under some kinds of *conditions,* have some kinds of *effects*" (p. 172).

The two great traditions of communication effects research that dominated the 1950s, those of Hovland and Lazarsfeld, fit comfortably under the umbrella of this general outlook. Together these traditions provided the primary threads that were woven into the mediational process-and-effects orientation that defined the center of theoretically directed communication research. However, the two traditions emphasized different concepts and approaches and, hence, communication effects research tended to be defined more broadly in the emerging communication research field than in the primary disciplines.

Hovland and the Yale attitude change studies. Hovland's group recognized the role social norms and group influences could play on persuasion, but as a psychologist Hovland focused on the individual and the psychological mediation of the persuasion process. The most important theoretical influence on Hovland was Hullian learning theory. That perspective provided a broad mediational behaviorist outlook that served to organize the Yale research efforts. However, the important influences that were to come from the Hovland program reflected its research practices rather than its general theory. It is instructive in this regard that Hovland et al. (1953) largely ignore previous persuasion research.

Hovland's most important research decision was the selection of attitude change as the dependent variable of greatest interest. As early as 1935, Gordon Allport described attitude as "probably the most distinctive and indispensable concept in American social psychology" (p. 798). The concept had entered American social psychology from both sociological and psychological sources and was initially a very diffuse and general construct reflecting various aspects of an individual's predisposition to act in certain ways. Over the years the concept was refined, particularly by psychometricians and experimental social psychologists; and by the early 1950s referred to a construct with cognitive, affective, and behavioral overtones conflated into operational measures emphasizing evaluation. The 1950s and 1960s saw intense interest in attitude theory and research in social psychology (particularly in the development of work on the change of attitudes under conditions of cognitive inconsistency; see, for example, Festinger, 1962; Heider, 1958; Osgood, Suci, & Tannenbaum, 1957). Hovland's emphasis on attitude change through communication, in combination with the expanding work in social psychology on attitude change processes, served to bring these topics to center stage for communication researchers.

The second imprint the Yale researchers made on communication research grew out of their standard research paradigm. This paradigm reflected Hovland's basic model of the communication process. Hovland (in Schramm, 1948) defined communication as "the process by which an individual (communicator) transmits stimuli (usually verbal symbols) to modify the behavior of other individuals (communicatees)" (p. 59). As we have seen the behavior of the communicatee was translated into the assessment of attitudes, the presumed principal behavior-mediating mechanism. The other aspects of the communication process were studied by adapting the experimental paradigm to manipulate source and message cues presented to the communicatee (e.g., source credibility, fear appeals, order of arguments, channel of presentation). Such a paradigm adapts the standard behavioral learning framework of the day to the study of communication, and indeed, Hovland was quite explicit in his view that communication was simply a special case of learning (see Hovland et al., 1953). The standard model of source, channel, message, and receiver was thus at once wed to general learning theory and instantiated as the organizational structure for experimental variable analysis (this viewpoint was elaborated in Berlo, 1960).

During the decade of the 1950s and for a time afterward, Hovland's students and associates were among the guiding forces in communication research. The core output of the group was the "Yale volumes": Hovland et al. (1953), Hovland et al. (1957); Hovland et al. (1959); Hovland & Rosenberg (1960); Sherif & Hovland (1960). With Hovland's death in 1961, the Yale program went into immediate decline.

However, the first three volumes in the series were the exemplars that many were to use as research models for decades.

Seen in historical perspective, the Hovland tradition has had two broad, enduring effects on communication research. First, experimental social psychology was moved into the center of communication research, with an influence far transcending the two-decade-long flurry of research on attitude change. The experimental model of research was broadly adopted and applied to different problems. For example, as television grew in importance as a new media force fed by an expanding consumer culture, the experiment was turned on it. Hundreds of experimental studies of television have been conducted since the 1950s, with studies of televised portrayals of violence being particularly important (e.g., see Comstock & Fisher, 1975; also see Rowland's 1983 critical analysis). By 1960 the social psychological experiment was firmly entrenched as the preferred methodology in the arsenal of American communication science. Second, the movement of social psychology into the center of communication science led to a wholesale importation of constructs and research problems going beyond the problem of persuasion and attitude change. By 1970, American communication research was utterly dominated by social psychological approaches.

Katz, Lazarsfeld, and the social-mediation effects framework. While Hovland's research program was going strong, developments within the Lazarsfeld research tradition, in combination with more general developments in sociological research, led to a reassertion of the connections between social organization and mass communication. This line of development is most strongly associated with Katz and Lazarsfeld's (1955) description of the movement of information and influence from media to recipient as a "two-step flow" mediated by group networks and opinion leaders. In presenting their theory, Katz and Lazarsfeld outlined its relationship to the general history of research on mass communication. In the process they constructed what would become the received history of communication research. Hence in discussing the development of sociological analyses of mass communication, I wish here also to address in passing the reconstructed history of communication research advanced by Katz and Lazarsfeld.

Katz and Lazarsfeld (1955) asserted that early traditions of communication research reflected either concern with the media of public communication as instruments of clandestine manipulation or hope for them as the agencies of social integration. However, it is worth observing that they continued a general pattern in the Lazarsfeld research tradition—namely, working largely independent of past scholarship (fewer than 10% of their references are to works appearing before World War II, even though their research was carried out in the mid-1940s; their attention to early work on communication appears to be based largely on excerpts reprinted in readers of the day). Katz and Lazarsfeld connected the two traditions, the one emphasizing manipulation and the other integration, to a common conception of society and the *process* of mass communication:

> Their image, first of all, was of an atomistic mass of millions of readers, listeners and movie-goers prepared to receive the Message; and secondly, they pictured every Message as a direct and powerful stimulus to action which would elicit immediate response. In short, the media of communication were looked upon as a new kind of unifying force—a simple kind of nervous system—reaching out to every eye and ear, in a society characterized by amorphous social organization and a paucity of interpersonal relations. (p. 16)

As I have said before, this instantiation of the field's history was broadly, if implicitly, accepted, particularly the ideas of direct effects and the role of the mass society concept. Bauer and Bauer (1960) argued, for example, that "'the theory of mass society' must . . . be taken as the point of departure in a discussion of the role of the mass media in America" (p. 430); and DeFleur (1966) in his highly influential text treated early mass communication theories as tied directly to mass society theory. Shils (1957), Bramson (1961), Bell (1960), and others reconstructed similar versions of a monolithic mass society theory. However, as Czitrom (1982) notes, such a reconstruction is at best a convenient fiction.

There is considerable diversity to the analyses of modern society advanced by Toinnes, Durkheim, Weber, Dewey, and others that are simply not captured in the monolithic reconstructions, and the failure of the more pessimistic ideas of mass society to take hold in the American context is almost uniformly ignored among those who use the concept in discussing the history of mass communication (however, see Bramson, 1961, who in using mass communication research to refute the conception of the mass society also discusses how unfertile the American soil was for European mass society theories). The late nineteenth- and early twentieth-century American intellectual climate was dominated by a sense of progress—of possibility for the positive reformation of society and promotion of opportunities for the individual; major American social theorists were overwhelmingly unreceptive to the conservative European conceptions of the "mass" (Lippmann is something of an exception).

The interpretation advanced by Katz and Lazarsfeld also ignores the history of sociological concern with mass communication. As was discussed earlier, the Chicago school had firmly established the idea that society is constituted in group life. Urban life was recognized as organized by "a mosaic of little worlds" (Park et al., 1925, p. 40). Public communication was seen as serving the social function of consensus not through direct effects, but (in Park's conception) through establishing "the rules by which interdependent but dissimilar groups played the game of urban life" (Quandt, 1970, p. 69). This view was the standard stuff of many sociology and social psychology texts of the 1920s and after and was centrally displayed in Park and Burgess (1921), the most influential general sociology text of the interwar period.

It should be noted, however, that the notion of the audience as atomistic, as consisting of disparate and independent individuals, is in general harmony with the research practices of many early mass communication researchers and became progressively more accepted with the shift to survey and marketing research methods (see Chaffee & Hochheimer, 1985). The study of a question focused on a specific item or choice using samples drawn from a universe of individuals implicitly supports the development of such a view. In fact, Katz (1960) was later to suggest that the general idea of the audience held among many mass communication researchers in the Columbia tradition was of "aggregates of age, sex, social class, and the like" without thought for "the relationships implied thereby or to more informal relationships" (p. 436).

A general revision in this line of thinking led during the 1940s and 1950s to a much more social-centered conception of mass communication. Lazarsfeld and his coworkers stumbled on the mediating role of interpersonal relations in the mass communication process almost by accident. In their papers in Lazarsfeld and Stanton (1941), both Robinson and Suchman noted the effects of friendship and interpersonal relationships in mediating aspects of media influence. Then Lazarsfeld et al. (1944) reoriented the report of the 1940 election study in part to call attention to what they called "molecular leaders," individuals who were influential among their acquaintances even though they were not necessarily prominent within the overall community. Merton (in Lazarsfeld & Stanton, 1949) explicitly focused on the issue of interpersonal influence in the use of magazines, and brought forward his distinction between "locals" and "cosmopolitans" as two distinct orientations to magazines (orientations that were related to different patterns of influence). The study of interpersonal relations in the mass communication process that was to be published as Katz and Lazarsfeld (1955) was also undertaken in the mid-1940s, and the study of the 1948 presidential election focused in part on the question of interpersonal influence (Berelson et al., 1954). Klapper (1949) gave considerable attention to the role of interpersonal influence in his widely distributed summary of mass media effects research, and a major panel was held on the topic at the 1950 meeting of the American Association of Public Opinion Research (see Riley & Riley, 1951). Sociological researchers in other areas were also calling attention to the importance of group ties (e.g., Shils & Janowitz, 1948).

Thus Katz and Lazarsfeld (1955) served less to establish than to crystallize the turn to investigation of social connections in mass communication. The year following the publication of *Personal Influence* the special twentieth-anniversary issue of *Public Opinion Quarterly* (1956) had as a recurring theme the "new" vision of the mass communication audience as a social network (see especially the papers of Katz, Lerner, and Pool; also see Bauer & Bauer, 1960).

Across the 1950s and into the 1960s the social analysis of mass communication grew in importance. The social-mediation framework was important to the expanding work on international communication, especially that in developing countries (e.g., Lerner & Schramm, 1967). Work was undertaken on the social networks by which news moves from event to the media institutions and through them to the public, including attention to the role of "gatekeepers" who decide which stories are forwarded (e.g., Gieber, 1956; White, 1950). The two-step flow hypothesis was joined with a similar tradition of research in rural sociology concerned with the diffusion of innovations (see Katz, 1960; Rogers, 1962). Research on small group processes in sociology and social psychology was made relevant to the study of communication, and the field's parameters were expanded to encompass this new subject matter.

For the most part, however, the dominant linear model of flow from the media to the audience was maintained. In 1959 John and Matilda Riley could still set "the development of a sociological view of mass communication as the most pressing need facing . . . this field" (p. 538). By this they meant that even though the two-step flow idea suggested revision of the idea of the audience as a mass of isolated individuals, still it was a one-directional model of flow and so did not represent a fundamental break with the linear model of the Lasswellian formulation. Nor did it recognize, they argued, "the ongoing processes of social interaction of which the communicative act is merely one component" (p. 543). A genuinely sociological view of the mass communication process would require, the Rileys asserted, locating "both mass communication and recipient in their respective social groupings," connected by communication in both directions, and linked "in a chain of communication which extends over time" (pp. 568-569).

Such a sociological view giving attention to the movement of messages from audience to media, while little researched, was recognized by some researchers (e.g., Westley & McLean, 1955). However, well into the 1960s the sociological tradition in communication research remained dominated by a relatively narrow concern with effects. As in Klapper's (1960) culminating summary of this research tradition, the work of the Lazarsfeldian tradition was seen by broad numbers of those involved in the field as harmoniously meshing with the narrower focus of the social-psychological persuasion research tradition. In the following section, attention is turned to the relationship of the linear-effects tradition that was consolidated between 1945 and 1955 to the broader landscape of communication studies.

The Communication Science Core and the Broader Field

As noted above, communication research emerged in the 1940s as an area encompassing study of the mass communication media and by the mid-1950s had been consolidated around a core that took theory development as its principal goal and a linear-effects perspective as its organizing framework. In this section, the relationship of the field's early organization to the broader domain of communication study from the 1940s through the 1960s will be discussed. The essential point is that the particular set of individual and professional interests that gave rise to the field's initial organization served to narrow it in important ways and to create unseen internal tensions that would shape the field's later history. An extensive development of this thesis is beyond the scope of the present chapter. I have already discussed the effect of the consolidation in reconstructing the relationship of the field to its past. Here I will discuss the exclusion or margination of several areas and approaches to communication studies: European research was largely excluded, historical research and cultural research were made peripheral, nonstatistical approaches to communication science were given marginal treatment, mass communication research was divorced from interpersonal communication studies, and professional and basic education in communication was by and large ignored.

The historical relationship between American and European communication research has been highlighted by a number of commentators over the years, particularly recently with the growing contact between the traditions (e.g., see Blumler, 1985; Carey, 1979; Rogers & Balle, 1985). At its inception communications research was an almost exclusively American enterprise despite the role of Lazarsfeld and the involvement of other European scholars such as Adorno, Lowenthal, and Lewin. Curiously, probably the strongest European influence on 1950s communication science was that of Lewin and other gestaltists through the indirect route of their impact on general social psychology (important concepts concerning group process and the cognitive organization of attitudes entered the field through this route). On the whole, however, the European influence on communication research was minimal. Indeed, even where European work converged with American research, it was not given attention. Brouwer (1964) notes, for example, that the German-Dutch communication specialist Kurt Baschwitz advanced in 1938 a concept similar to the two-step flow hypothesis, but the similarity went unnoted.

This separation has contributed importantly to the course of developments on both the European and North American continents. In America, strands of communication research coalesced quickly within the flow model, later to confront and come to terms with European traditions reflecting radically different orientations. On the European side, communication research and other social sciences were influenced by American developments, but the imported perspectives were organized within dominant national strands of work that were quite distinct from the American framework. Rogers and Balle (1985) report, for example, that work in France following World War II was dominated by the legalist orientation of Fernand Terrou and the development of a theory of democratic state regulation of the press and broadcasting. The American empirical research tradition provided the overarching organizational structure à la Lasswell and channeled the conduct of what little quantitative research was undertaken. Germany and England also were to see the development of research following the imported American line, but that research stood alongside indigenous traditions that sought to understand the media as agencies of cultural formation and gave extensive consideration to political and social interests in analyzing the processes and institutions of mass communication.

By the 1960s Europeans identified American communication research almost entirely with the Lazarsfeld and Hovland traditions (e.g., see Brown in Tunstall, 1970). Blumler (1985) suggests that this resulted in part from the great increase in the number of European scholars becoming concerned with mass communication in the 1960s, just after Klapper (1960) forwarded his integrative summary of communication effects research. This surge of European development in communication study came, however, just as European "social science . . . was hit by a wave of revived interest in Marxism, as well as hosting certain other less specialized schools of thought, such as semiotics, structuralism, interactionism, sociolinguistics, contemporary cultural studies, and others" (Blumler, 1985, p. 187). The result was the development of lines of work that, when imported into the American context, have been the source of much of the "ferment in the field" of recent years (see the special issue of the *Journal of Communication,* 1985).

The uneasy relationship of American communication research to European communication studies in part reflects another result of the terms on which the American field was organized. Although the American communication studies field was seen initially as bringing diverse work on communication media under a single umbrella, the particular scientific commitments of the centrally involved figures in the communication research coalition quickly pushed historical, cultural, and critical studies to the periphery. This is well represented in the uneasy relationship between the mass communication researchers and the members of the Frankfurt school of critical theory who were in exile in America (see Jay, 1972, 1973; also see Czitrom, 1982; Rowland, 1983). Lazarsfeld had brought some of the Frankfurt group into the Rockefeller project (e.g., see Adorno in Lazarsfeld & Stanton, 1941; Lowenthal in Lazarsfeld & Stanton, 1944), but they felt bridled by the quantitative marketing research style encouraged in the project. The critical theorists wanted to address issues of cultural values with historical and critical tools. Both Adorno (in Fleming & Bailyn, 1969) and Lowenthal (in Rosenberg & White, 1957) were later to criticize the largely ahistorical and uncritical stance of empirical mass communication research (also see Lazarsfeld, 1941). As Lowenthal (in Rosenberg & White, 1957) said, "social research takes the phenomena of modern life, including mass media, at face value. It rejects the task of placing them in an historical and moral context" (p. 52). By contrast critical theorists "first ask: What are the functions of cultural communication within the total process of society? Then we ask such specific questions as these: What passes the censorship of the socially powerful agencies? How are things produced under the dicta of formal and informal censorship?" (p. 56).

A deep tension was thus built into the mass communication field from its inception. It aimed to organize the whole scope of concern with the mass media under a single, encompassing umbrella, while its focus on scientific research placed historical and critical studies on the margin. After World War II, film and popular culture studies would evolve in essential independence of communication research, even though this was not the expectation of many of the founders of communication research (e.g., see Lazarsfeld & Stanton, 1949, p. xviii). Even the mass culture debate of the 1950s was carried on largely outside the newly defined field of communication research.

The concentration upon survey and experimental research and the preference for quantitative data and statistical analysis also created a clear hierarchy of methods that squeezed nonquantitative social science approaches to the margin. This is not to say that there was no qualitative analysis in communication research during the 1950s and 1960s. It is instructive, however, that the leading research methods text designed to train the new generation of communication researchers concentrated almost entirely on survey, experimental, and statistical techniques (Nafziger & White, 1963; part of the chapter on field research treats observation). The coalescence of American communication research was founded on the hegemony of quantitative social science. This preemption of the field would be challenged in the 1970s with the reassertion of the Chicago school tradition, the turn to perspectives employing the methods of linguistics, anthropology, and other largely nonquantitative social sciences, and the appropriation of European traditions and research models.

Communication research also was consolidated on terms that identified communication research primarily with mass communication, thereby driving a wedge between studies of public and interpersonal communication. The divorce of mass communication and interpersonal communication restricted access to concepts of language and sociality that are foundational to communication and precluded the development of viable general and comparative frameworks for investigating communication. The token redress of the separation of mass and interpersonal communication with the turn of the Lazarsfeld group to the social mediation of mass communication effects still failed to incorporate most of the work on group dynamics as well as the traditions of research on social interaction and interpersonal processes, communication in childhood, language and culture, nonverbal communication, and organizational communication, among others. The separation of interpersonal and mass communication was continued with the movement of communication research into journalism and speech departments, which were themselves already founded on the separation. As is traced below, this separation continues to hinder both theoretical development in the field and its evolution toward disciplinary status.

A related, and implication-laden, characteristic of the terms within which communication research was initially consolidated is tension between its tightly knit consensus on scope and methods and its apparent interdisciplinary character. The founding members of the communication research coalition came from several established disciplines, and the field clearly seemed constituted on interdisciplinary terms (for example, Schramm, 1949, p. vii, notes "by bringing together anthropologists, psychologists, sociologists, political scientists, economists, and media men, [this volume] has attempted to combine diversity of approach with unity of target"). However, interconnections among the early researchers and their sense of unity clearly pointed toward the formation of an autonomous area of study not unlike political science, which treats a single domain at many levels and with various methods. Lazarsfeld and Stanton (1949), for example, saw it "no longer necessary today either to justify communications research as a special discipline or to outline its general scope" (p. xiii). Was the field to be interdisciplinary or autonomous; and if autonomous, on what terms? Communication study in the late 1940s embraced divergent and contradictory attitudes that leave this question unresolved after 40 years.

A special difficulty for the growth of the field as an autonomous domain grew out of the development of communication research essentially independent of those fields concerned with professional and undergraduate education in communication. As is discussed below, communication research was to be appropriated by departments of speech and journalism, which had long traditions of concern with instruction in communication practice. Despite its roots in applied research, communication research was remarkably insulated from the needs and interests of students. The inclusion of only a few journalism researchers at the 1948 University of Illinois conference on communication research, hence, could lead Lazarsfeld and Stanton (1949) to describe its product as "oriented toward the practical ends which communications can serve" (p. xiii; see Schramm, 1948; seen in its historical context the Illinois conference, in fact, strongly emphasized research). Despite the divergence of backgrounds and goals among communication scientists, professional journalism educators, and speech faculties, the journalism schools and speech departments were to face the task of working out terms of connection with communication research, and in many cases with one another. That process was to change profoundly both them and the new science of communication research.

RELOCATION AND TRANSFORMATION: COMMUNICATION SCIENCE IN THE JOURNALISM SCHOOLS AND SPEECH DEPARTMENTS

Past the original consolidation of communication research into a distinct domain of scholarship, no process has been more important to the development of the field than its integration into journalism schools and speech departments. The process was to broaden the scope of communication research and to transform the departments that have evolved into the principal homes of communication study within American colleges and universities.

Communication Science and the Journalism Schools

Communication research developed with little connection to the professional schools and departments committed to basic education in communication practice. There were, however, some individuals in such programs who from the 1930s and early 1940s made contributions to communication research. For example, we have already confronted the name of Ralph Casey of the University of Minnesota School of Journalism, who coedited the field's major bibliographic works with Lasswell and Smith. W. G. Bleyer in journalism at Wisconsin had earlier in the century promoted a scientific approach to his field and was instrumental in establishing a joint Ph.D. program with social science departments (Troldahl, 1980). Ralph Nafziger, who received a political science Ph.D. through Bleyer's program, advanced the goals of communication research at Minnesota and returned to journalism at Wisconsin after World War II. However, the most important figure in the development of mass communication within the journalism tradition—and arguably in the history of communication research—was Wilbur Schramm. Schramm's influence came not so much from his research, which was considerable, but from his role in institutionalizing communication research in American higher education (see Chaffee, 1974; Rowland, 1983). In this regard Schramm's influence is similar to that of Lazarsfeld in sociology. Schramm's (1985) own recollections of the development of communication research should be consulted.

Schramm's greatest contributions to communication research were made at the University of Illinois and Stanford University. He came to Illinois from the journalism program at the University of Iowa. Although he had a Ph.D. in American literature, he had been drawn to a scientific orientation, and was influenced by his exposure to Lewin during his Iowa days. Schramm migrated to Illinois after World War II and organized the Institute of Communications Research in 1947. The institute quickly became a leading center of graduate education in communication. In 1956 Schramm founded a parallel institute (the Institute of Communication Research) at Stanford. Influenced by the success at Illinois, research units were also formed within journalism departments at other major midwestern universities. Most notable among the early efforts were those at Minnesota, Wisconsin, and Michigan State. In the mid-1950s communication and coordination among the increasing numbers of research-oriented faculty and programs were facilitated by the formation of a "theory and method" division within the major professional association in the field, the Association for Education in Journalism (see Troldahl, 1980). Other influential programs developed, including those at the Universities of Washington, North Carolina, Iowa, and Indiana. Journalism programs began to change their names to include "communication" or "communications" in their titles. Illinois organized a College of Communications; Stanford changed to the Department of Communication and absorbed broadcasting and film units; Wisconsin and Minnesota joined "journalism" and "mass communication" in the names of their departments (see Schramm, 1985). The Annenberg School of Communication was organized at the University of Pennsylvania.

The rapid expansion of the social scientific approach to communication research within journalism schools and newly organized mass communication programs was fed both by the desire for increased professional status and by the needs for faculty with graduate training to meet the increasing demands for higher education in journalism, broadcasting, and advertising. As was mentioned earlier, the post-World War II period was one of great expansion for American higher education. It was also a period during which many schools evolved from teaching institutions into major nationally oriented research universities fed by government grants and contracts (e.g., see Lyons, 1969). This was particularly true of many of the large midwestern universities in which communication first entered journalism programs in substantial ways. In the status politics of university life, contributions to undergraduate education were accorded less significance; the emphasis shifted to graduate education and research contributions. Schramm (1985) comments that in such a context

> there was also a very strong feeling . . . that journalism and speech, broadcasting and film, should be made more active in research. Looking at the products of Lazarsfeld's Columbia Bureau, Hovland's Yale organization, and Lewin's Iowa program, journalism leaders admitted somewhat ruefully that these social science organizations were doing the work journalism ought to be doing. (p. 209)

The desire to secure academic status through a more vigorous research orientation within journalism coincided with the demand that faculty have research, not just professional, credentials. The doctorate became a requirement for hiring in many journalism programs where it had not been before. Schramm (1985) is again worth quoting:

> A great deal of the pressure for these new institutes came from the communication skills departments of universities—first from journalism, then from speech, broadcasting, film, and the like. The doctorate had become a common requirement for heads of journalism schools and departments, and it substituted for long and distinguished news careers in the case of many new young faculty members. As the doctorate became more necessary, more and more journalism schools began to offer their own doctorates, so that a prospective teacher or researcher in journalism could earn a doctorate in communication rather than political science, sociology, psychology, or history. That meant that graduate courses developed for journalism had to be subjects like the theory of communication, history of communication, research methods in communication, and the like. (p. 208)

The incorporation of the interdisciplinary communication research tradition within journalism was facilitated by an openness of journalism publication outlets to a variety of work. Until after World War II, for example, the main journal of professional journalism educators, *Journalism Quarterly,* covered the full range of journalism research as well as pedagogical concerns. Humanistic scholarship was accompanied by a wide range of readership and content studies (which frequently would include simple descriptive statistical summaries; e.g., Gallup, 1930). There were also reports on such topics as readability measurement and effects (e.g., English, 1944), media professionals (e.g., Prugger, 1941),

and newspaper ownership (e.g., Nixon, 1945). Researchers who turned
to quantitative methods in the 1950s found no difficulty in securing
space in the *Journalism Quarterly.* Schramm (1963) noted that by the
end of the 1950s more than half the studies being published there were
quantitative, although "a very large proportion of journalism research
has been descriptive, and the analysis that accompanied the description
has not often been of the kind to contribute to theory" (Schramm, 1963,
p. 10). However, work was evolving rapidly in the journalism schools
and by the late 1960s communication research was consolidated as a
theoretical research enterprise in the schools.

The process of integrating communication research into the journalism schools presented fundamental conflicts. Journalism was concerned
with professional education for a career in the press and had evolved a
scholarly tradition grounded largely in qualitative research (largely historical, legal, and interpretive). The 1950s and early 1960s saw increasing tension and conflict between the aims of professional journalism
educators and communication researchers (commentaries and editorials
in professional magazines explored the collision in vivid terms: "Chi-
Square vs. Green Eye Shades," "My Stand Against Chi-Square," etc.)
Communication researchers such as Schramm (1963, pp. 25-28) would
go to considerable length to establish the relevance of the social scientific research tradition to the needs of professional education. For the
most part, however, coexistence was the norm, with communication
research kept at the margin of undergraduate and professional education
in journalism.

Penetration to these levels of the curriculum was most notable in
advertising and in broadcasting and television. In fact it is probably the
case that work in communication research significantly promoted attention to broadcasting and television within the print-dominated journalism schools. Schramm (1963) notes that where journalism study was
almost entirely restricted to newspaper and magazine research before
World War II, by the early 1960s the schools of journalism supported
work in radio, television, photography, and advertising, and were pursuing interests ranging "over the entire field of communication" (p. 3).
Thus "the communication research interests of journalism" were maintained on terms "broader than those of the other behavioral sciences.
For whereas communication research is a small part of psychology, of
economics, of anthropology, of law, of sociology, of political science, it
is the main part of journalism research" (Schramm, 1963, p. 5).

Indeed, within the journalism schools communication research not
only maintained the broad umbrella of inclusion evident within its original consolidation as a social science of media studies, but was actually
extended to encompass the existing tradition of humanistic scholarship
in journalism. The traditions of historical scholarship on the press and

analyses of freedom of the press and press responsibility were particularly well developed. Hence, the history of the press and communication, along with journalism's traditional concern with responsibility, were integrated into the fabric of the flow-and-effects organizing framework in Schramm's (1948, 1949) earliest field-defining books. Notable examples of work in these traditions were included in Schramm's (1948) recommended set of 100 readings on communication. Among these were Chafee (1947), Cooper (1942), Desmond (1937), Hocking (1947), Inglis, (1947), Mott (1938, 1941), Nafziger (1940), Rosten (1937, 1941), Shurick (1946), Siebert (1934), and White and Leigh (1946).

Although some programs would single-mindedly embrace the behavioral science model, familiarity with both humanistic and social scientific scholarship was an unescapable part of life in most journalism schools. The development of programs that legitimated a range of methodological approaches and levels of analysis was the norm, and the door was opened to integrating traditional humanistic scholarship on the press and electronic media with social scientific communication research. Schramm's (1963) comment is representative:

> In a communication research organization which knows its business there is a close relationship between studies of mass media responsibility and mass media effect, although one is necessarily qualitative and the other quantitative. And because this kind of relationship exists throughout the spectrum of communication study, expectation is not that quantitative research will crowd out qualitative or that the two will necessarily live in worlds of their own, but rather they will go forward together on the road to an adequate theory of communication. (p. 12)

By the mid-1960s one could find field-defining introductory texts reflecting such an integration of journalism's humanistic scholarship with that of mass communication research (e.g., Peterson, Jensen, & Rivers, 1965).

Communication Research and Speech Departments

Speech departments, like journalism schools, have been reshaped by their absorption of communication research. However, the course of change has been different in important ways from that in journalism. The differences reflect the different histories and missions of the programs.

Speech instruction in American colleges reaches back to the colonial period (Wallace, 1954, remains the best source of historical discussion). Speech departments per se began to emerge near the turn of the century, for the most part out of English departments. The domination of the English departments by the literary tradition provided little support for those who saw language as a tool of social and political life or wished to give literature life in performance. During a time when the basic composition of the American university was becoming fixed, there were strong interests motivating the formation of independent departments. The movement toward autonomy of speech departments took its most dramatic turn shortly before World War I when university speech teachers broke with English and founded an independent association, the National Association of Academic Teachers of Public Speaking. A journal was founded that would later become the *Quarterly Journal of Speech,* to be followed over the years by *Speech Monographs* (now *Communication Monographs*), *The Speech Teacher* (now *Communication Education*), and (quite recently) *Critical Studies in Mass Communication.*

The association changed its name in a few years to the Speech Association of America (SAA) in the process of working out the alliance that would constitute the scope of most departments until the 1950s and 1960s. That alliance was between all those academic elements concerned with speech production and performance. This "orality alliance" included those committed to basic speech communication education, theatre, the oral interpretation of literature, and speech pathology. Broadcasting joined the alliance in many departments in the 1930s.

One course of development within speech has been the evolving relationships among the parties to the orality alliance. Many faculty worked across the areas; but divisions developed in larger departments, and independent developmental trajectories for subareas were fostered by the formation of separate associations in theatre, speech pathology, and the tremendous fragmentation in broadcasting education. By the late 1950s and 1960s this course of development was resulting in reorganization with independent departmental status being given to theatre and speech pathology, although many departments even today continue to operate with divisions under the umbrella of the original alliance (very useful perspectives on the historical development of speech departments are presented in Bochner & Eisenberg's and Pearce's chapters in Benson, 1985; also consult Wallace, 1954, and the chapters on the histories of subject matter subareas in Benson, 1985).

Our concern here is with that central part of the orality alliance that today forms the core of most departments of speech communication. The roots of contemporary speech communication research reach back in many instances to areas of basic communication education. Speech communication from the first decades of the century took teaching as its principal mission. As in journalism, graduate study and research came slowly; at the end of the 1920s only a handful of universities offered the Ph.D. (O'Neill, 1935). The basic pedagogic areas included public speaking, persuasion, group discussion, business and professional communication, and radio. Instruction in most areas was utilitarian and concerned with practice in fitting with the commitments of the founders and the midwestern settings of most of the leading departments (for a useful discussion of the values of utilitarian education in turn-of-the-century midwestern and western universities consult Veysey, 1965).

As we have noted at various points earlier, there were several emerging research traditions in speech similar to those in social psychology. The speech pathologists also pursued scientific research, though they turned to the natural sciences of physiology and acoustics for research models. A significant emphasis had been placed on science in the speech departments from their founding—in part to make room for the speech pathologists, but as well to smooth the break with English (see Bochner & Eisenberg in Benson, 1985). The most important of the founding members of the profession with scientific leanings was Illinois's Charles Woolbert, who had taken his Ph.D. in psychology. The use of standard social scientific methods was thus present in speech departments from their beginnings. However, research was never focused on central theoretical issues, and for the most part the early research involved the application of standard methods to problems concerned with various aspects of speech instruction (see Thompson, 1967).

In part the slow development of social scientific research reflected the utilitarian and pedagogical focus of the speech departments. However, scientific development also was restricted by the emerging dominance of historical and critical research through the "rediscovery" of the classical and modern rhetorical traditions (a useful discussion of the effect of the rhetorical tradition on the development of science in speech departments is presented in Pearce's chapter in Benson, 1985). The renaissance in rhetorical studies was centered at Cornell (Windt, 1982). The Cornell tradition emphasized Aristotelian rhetorical theory, directed attention to scholarship on the history of rhetorical theories, and advanced an approach to the study of public addresses that called for studying speeches historically in their fully reconstructed contexts. By the 1930s, rhetoric and public address constituted a central part of graduate curricula and had become the area of the field's most sustained and serious scholarship (for histories of this work see the chapters of Enos and Gregg in Benson, 1985). Though present from the founding of the profession, scientific approaches were thus made secondary (see Pearce's chapter in Benson, 1985).

There was a general surge in scholarly activity following World War II across all areas of speech, including social scientific studies. A "behavioral sciences" interest group within the SAA became the hub of professional connections for the new generation of researchers. The increasing incursion of science was fed by three sources. First, the indigenous tradition of empirical research increased under the rapid expansion of graduate education in speech. Through the 1950s this work overwhelmingly reflected traditional concerns of the field, including studies of public speaking instruction, speech anxiety and stage fright, variables influencing persuasion, factors affecting group discussion, variables influencing the comprehension and learning of information through oral messages, and the use and role of speech communication in business (see the historical surveys of Gouran; Putnam & Cheney; Pearce; and Rawlings in Benson, 1985; also see Thompson, 1967). The research programs of some department members, particularly those in speech pathology and speech science, also were greatly stimulated by government support during and after World War II, as had been the case for many mass communication researchers. For example, concern with the problem of speech intelligibility in voice transmissions of instructions resulted in a minor research explosion on the topic (e.g., see Black, 1946).

Second, a number of faculty associated with speech departments joined in forming the National Society for the Study of Communication (NSSC) in the late 1940s. The NSSC, which was later to become the International Communication Association, founded the *Journal of Communication* in 1950, to be followed later by *Human Communication Research*. At the outset the NSSC included mostly professionals with applied and pedagogical interests. The group included educators committed to the unified communication instruction model (writing, speaking, reading, and listening), personnel specialists from the corporate sector, a few individuals with various roles and interests in the media, a scattering of faculty from around the social sciences and humanities, and a host of speech faculty, mostly with diffuse social scientific learnings. The mix of participants in the association in the 1950s served to promote the development of interests in business and organizational communication, semantics and social aspects of language, group communication and human relations, and the role of communication in social integration, along with more traditional areas. The association also was one conduit through which the coalesced lines of communication research reached speech departments.

The discovery of that already well-developed body of research was the third, and I believe the most important, influence on the development of social scientific research in the speech departments. A new brand of faculty member emerged in the years around 1960 with one foot in speech and the other in communication research. The University of Illinois was a major point of diffusion where many students worked in both speech and communication research (e.g., David Berlo, Erwin Bettinghaus, Roger Nebergall). The speech department at the University of Iowa also sent forth a group of behaviorally trained researchers at about the same time (e.g., Samuel Becker, Gerald Miller, Robert Bostrom, John Bowers). And these were joined by individuals from other programs as the leaders of the new generation of researchers (e.g., Theodore Clevenger, Thomas Scheidel, Fredrick Williams). This new generation of researchers expanded the traditional areas of empirical research in speech to include expanded concern with persuasive communication, the role of psycholinguistic processes in speech, and interaction processes in group decision making, while continuing to give attention to problems of speech performance and speech education.

As had been the case in journalism, the expansion of scientific research was met with opposition. However, in speech the conflict was more basic and its ramifications more far-reaching. In most journalism programs the commitment to professional education led to the restriction of communication research to the graduate curriculum and a few undergraduate courses. In speech, however, the conflict of values and aims of scientific and humanistic research reached deep into the curriculum. This was intensified by what many took to be the similarity between the rhetorical theory that underlay much humanistic work and the persuasion model in communication research. Rhetoric approached communication as public discourse; it analyzed the forms and contexts of public persuasion; it emphasized audience analysis and the schemes for constructing an appropriate verbal response to the rhetorical situation; it sought to instill rhetorical understanding so that intelligent and responsible verbal choices might be made. Many communication researchers saw their task as developing a "new scientific rhetoric," whose principles would be verified rather than prescriptive (Maccoby, 1963). Rhetorical critics, whose work was grounded in concepts of choice and systems of evaluation, recoiled from this reduction of the act of speaking to the process of communication (see, for example, Wallace, 1970).

The prolonged "joint custody" of speech departments by social scientists and by rhetorical critics and theorists appears to have been a major source of recent changes in the field, although we are not yet distanced enough for historical understanding. It is nonetheless perhaps worth noting that many rhetorical critics have become very much like qualitative and interpretive social scientists. No doubt part of this comes from the deep impression made on the field in recent decades by Kenneth Burke (e.g., 1962, 1966). Under the influence of Burke and other contemporary theorists, there has been a general drift away from concern with the pursuit of narrow rhetorical purposes to the more general analysis of rhetoric as symbolic action (e.g., see Ehninger, 1972; and Gregg in Benson, 1985). Concepts such as Burke's gave rhetorical critics the freedom to analyze a host of symbolic forms and events. Rhetorical approaches to the analysis of protest rhetoric (e.g., Scott & Brockreide, 1969), films, and broadcast media (e.g., Medhurst & Benson, 1984) have become commonplace. Readily at hand from colleagues, social and psychological theories also have found their way into the work of critics. And social scientists in speech communication appear to have become more receptive to qualitative modes of research than have social scientists in many fields. Moreover, the level of theoretical activity and the attention to rhetorical theories emphasizing the symbolic construction of reality has been a major source of the seeming preoccupation in speech communication with metatheoretical issues (e.g., Benson & Pearce, 1977; Cronkhite & Liska, 1977).

The concrete historical context created by joining the Hovland-Lazarsfeld communication research tradition with that of the speech departments also has shaped the speech communication research agenda. Again we are too close for much historical perspective, but I will offer some tentative thoughts. One conclusion I have reached is that in speech communication, communication research did not achieve status simply through the appeal of scientific method. Rather, a general convergence in the essential model of communication presented in the Hovland-Lazarsfeld research meshed with a particular understanding of the rhetorical act. This fusion captured the imagination of many social scientists and rhetorical critics alike. Hence, for example, the rhetorical theorist Douglas Ehninger (1972) noted,

> a new functional terminology is gradually replacing the older and less precise language by which many of the variables in the rhetorical transaction traditionally have been identified. Even in elementary textbooks on writing and speaking one finds the maker of a speech or essay described as a "sender-encoder," *ethos* called "source credibility." (p. 7)

At a deeper level, communication was identified with persuasion and the psychological process of learning and behavior change. For a time many speech communication researchers used rhetoric, communication, and persuasion interchangably (e.g., note the fusion of learning, persuasion, and communication in Berlo, 1960).

Many speech communication researchers immediately embraced Hovland-style research, and for a time the communication-as-persuasion framework dominated the research agenda. But this view was to face crisis in speech communication in the late 1960s. The issue of whether all communication was persuasion became one surface manifestation of the search for a broader perspective (e.g., see Miller, 1966; Nielsen, 1970). Another, more widely argued issue was whether and in what way communication is a process. The identification of communication research with the model of the single, persuasive event presented at best a highly static picture severed from interaction and mutual influence. Some researchers sought to address the question of process within the single-event framework itself (e.g., Brooks & Scheidel, 1968), but most turned to basic issues concerning the nature of communication and possible objects of communication research (Smith, 1970; Smith, 1972). The issue of process was a major focus of the conference on directions for communication theory and research that spurred action to change of the association name from the Speech Association of America to the Speech Communication Association (SCA; Kibler & Barker, 1969). The compromise in the name change well captured the profession's uneasy balance of traditional interests with a broader concern with communication.

This search for a more adequate understanding of communication was reflected in and carried out through efforts from the mid-1950s into the 1970s to develop a suitable model of the communication process. Many of the models followed mass communication scholars' formulations, which outlined and altered the basic mediated flow and information-theoretic frameworks (e.g., Gerbner, 1956; Schramm, 1954; Westley & MacLean, 1955). However, there were a variety of other efforts, all of which were summarized by Johnson and Klare (1961) in a paper that became standard reading in communication theory seminars. Within speech communication the concern with model building continued throughout the 1960s, with increasingly complex deviations from the early linear formulations (e.g., Barnlund, 1970; Dance, 1967). The preoccupation with models in speech communication addressed simultaneously the desires for a general, if superficial, orientation to understanding communication as a process and the need for a pedagogical vehicle adaptable to the undergraduate classroom (for a representative survey of models given attention in speech communication, see Mortensen, 1972).

Simultaneous with this search for an expanded general orientation to communication, the waning of persuasion's dominance also led teachers and researchers to search for different research problems. Social psychology presented itself as one ready source of orientation; many areas of the field, such as group discussion and the newly coalescing areas of organizational communication and interpersonal communication, drew heavily upon the literatures of social psychology (for orientations to speech communication work in these areas see historical surveys by Gouran, Putnam & Cheney, and Rawlings in Benson, 1985). The depth of the incursion of social psychology into speech communication is evident in the *Handbook of Rhetorical and Communication Theory* (Arnold & Bowers, 1984) in which many of the chapters are largely reviews of social psychological theory and research refracted through analysis of the functions of communication.

Social psychology was not the only source of conceptual change and direction in the field, however. Three other aspects of speech communication study in the late 1960s seem to have importantly shaped the subsequent development of speech communication research. The first of these factors has already been mentioned—namely, the influence on communication researchers of expanded conceptions of rhetoric and rhetorical action. The amalgamation of rhetoric and communication in graduate programs and the concentration of attention on general theoretical issues during the 1960s and 1970s were facts of life in most speech communication departments. The knowledge and orientation of many speech communication researchers thus reflects the influence of theories of rhetoric and symbolic action.

Rhetorical theory's direction of attention to general theoretical frameworks and issues was strongly influenced by a second aspect of speech communication's history during the late 1960s and early 1970s. Speech communication faculty interested in addressing questions of communication process and the adequacy of the persuasion framework found a range of authors from across the social sciences who presented highly disparate general orientations to the analysis of communication. Among the most important of these were Wiener (1948), Ruesch and Bateson (1968), and Watzlawick, Beavin, and Jackson (1967), who transmitted systems-theoretic views into the field. The importation of viewpoints embracing fundamentally different theoretical assumptions and conceptions combined with the juxtaposition of the rhetorical and communication traditions have focused continuing discussion in speech communication on metatheoretical and metamethodological issues.

The final aspect of speech communication study in the 1960s that has significantly shaped the subsequent development of the field is the consolidation of interpersonal communication as the field's core research area. The waning persuasian framework presented one way to define interpersonal communication. The general concern with analyzing communication as a temporal and interactional process presented another. The turn in social psychology from primary concern with interpersonal and social attitudes to perceptual and cognitive processes offered a third direction. Systems theories presenting communicational analyses of interpersonal relationships constituted a fourth. These were joined by a general importation into speech communication in the late 1960s of humanistic psychology and its celebration of the development and liberation of the individual (see Rawlings's chapter in Benson, 1985). Interpersonal communication thus came together defined by the strands of thought that were prominent at a particular historical moment and social location.

The subsequent research agenda in interpersonal communication has been influenced by studies of various fields: persuasion, interaction, self-disclosure in communication, compliance-gaining strategies, cognitive processes in message interpretation, communication in relationships, and so on. The more enduring development in speech communication research, however, appears to be the reach beyond the methodological boundaries of the Hovland-Lazarsfeld tradition to an openness to a wide range of research approaches and methods; but that is a possibility for contemporary discussion rather than historical reflection.

EPILOGUE

Communication research had expanded greatly by the beginning of the 1960s. Where only a few dozen books of real merit had appeared in the first half of the century, research and scholarship cascaded across the 1950s. However, despite this productivity and corresponding hopes for the science of communication, an odd sort of pessimism began to appear. In the twentieth-anniversary issue of the *Public Opinion Quarterly,* Daniel Lerner (1956) found it necessary to snipe at the critics of communication research by telling a story "of mice and mousery." Mousery is a behavioral science, Lerner said, but it is a science that is becoming beset by problems just when it was thought that a General Theory of Mouse Behavior was in the offing. It has been found that "the caught mice stay caught, but fewer are coming into the traps at all. Moreover, a high proportion of those caught are underweight mice of the shorthaired species—whose past records indicate relatively poor vision and olfaction, extreme fear of superior power (cats), and subnormal maze performance" (p. 200). While Lerner expressed his faith that better mousetraps would solve these difficulties, others began to wonder about the ease with which the big mouse of communication would be caught.

At the close of the 1950s, Berelson (1959) delivered his famous autopsy on a field he found to be "withering away." The great research traditions that he thought had given rise to the communication field were "playing out: the innovators have left or are leaving the field, and no ideas of comparable scope and generating power are emerging" (p. 4). Most researchers in the established disciplines of psychology, sociology, and political science who had entered the field with those who fashioned the hope of the 1940s had departed by the 1960s.

As we have seen, however, a new generation of scholars was to take up the study of communication. The center of research was shifting from the established disciplines into departments for whom it really was the central subject matter of their concern. The study of communication was being adopted, albeit with reluctance by some. Perhaps those who were reluctant understood the changes that would follow. These adoptive homes—journalism schools and speech departments—have been remade by the study of communication. But in the process communication study also is being remade.

The change from the pessimism of 1960 to the expansive possibilities seen for communication research in the 1980s involves developments too vast to yield to simple accounts. Among the differences, however, are changes in the attitudes toward communication scholarship and the tasks of communication science. The post-World War II consolidation of communication science was built upon a restricted base and narrow aims. I have endeavored to put the constriction of communication in perspective by describing the broader scope communication study had and has been reconstituting. In part, I think, the pessimism of 1960 and the optimism of 1987 are grounded in tacit recognitions of a field with limited goals and restricted avenues for productive work as against one with a complex and varied past and manifold pathways to understanding its central phenomena. The constriction of communication research was built on a spurious view of its history. My hope is that a future historian of a mature discipline of communication will be able to write that a part of the remaking of the field was in turning aside that limited and limiting construction of history.

REFERENCES

Albig, J. N. (1939). *Public opinion.* New York: McGraw-Hill.
Allport, F. H. (1924). *Social psychology.* New York: Houghton Mifflin.
Allport, G. W. (1935). Attitudes. In C. C. Murchison (Ed.), *A handbook of social psychology.* Worchester, MA: Clark University Press.
Allport, G. W. (1954). The historical background of modern social psychology. In G. Lindzey (Ed.), *Handbook of social psychology* (Vol. 1). Reading, MA: Addison-Wesley.
Ames, J. D. (1938). Editorial treatment of lynchings. *Public Opinion Quarterly, 2,* 77-84.
Anderson, H. H. (1939). Domination and social integration in the behavior of kindergarten children and teachers. *Genetic Psychology Monographs, 21,* 287-385.
Anderson, J. (1939). Man of the hour or man of the ages? The honorable Stephen A. Douglas. *Quarterly Journal of Speech, 25,* 75-93.
Applebee, A. N. (1974). *Tradition and reform in the teaching of English.* Urbana, IL: National Council of Teachers of English.
Archer, G. L. (1938). *History of radio to 1926.* New York: American Historical Co.
Archer, G. L. (1939). *Big business and radio.* New York: American Historical Co.
Asher, R., & Sargent, S. (1941). Shifts in attitude caused by cartoon caricatures. *Journal of General Psychology, 24,* 451-455.
Atkinson, C. (1939). *Development of radio education policies in American public school systems.* Edinboro, PA: Edinboro Education Press.
Atkinson, C. (1942). *Public school broadcasting to the classroom.* Boston: Meador.
Bakan, D. (1966). Behaviorism and American urbanization. *Journal of the History of the Behavioral Sciences, 2,* 5-28.
Baker, H. V. (1942). Children's contributions in elementary school discussion. *Child Development Monographs,* No. 29.
Baritz, L. (1960). *The servants of power.* New York: John Wiley.
Barlow, R. R. (1936). French and British schools of journalism: A comparative analysis. *Journalism Quarterly, 13,* 157-169.

Barnard, R. H. (1932). An objective study of the speeches of Wendell Phillips. *Quarterly Journal of Speech, 18,* 571-584.

Barnland, D. C. (1970). A transactional model of communication. In J. Atkin, A. Goldberg, G. Meyers, & J. Stewart (Eds.), *Language behavior.* The Hague: Mouton.

Barnouw, E. (1966). *A tower in Babel.* New York: Oxford University Press.

Barnouw, E. (1968). *The golden web.* New York: Oxford University Press.

Barnouw, E. (1975). *Tube of plenty.* New York: Oxford University Press.

Barr, A. S., Ewbank, H. L., & McCormick, T. C. (1942). *Radio in the classroom.* Madison: University of Wisconsin Press.

Bateman, R. M., & Remmers, H. H. (1941). A study of the shifting attitudes of high school students when subjected to favorable and unfavorable propaganda. *Journal of Social Psychology, 13,* 395-406.

Bauer, R. A., & Bauer, A. (1960). America, mass society and mass media. *Journal of Social Issues, 16,* 3-66.

Bell, D. (1960). *The end of ideology.* New York: Collier Books.

Benson, T. W. (Ed.). (1985). *Speech communication in the 20th century.* Carbondale: Southern Illinois University Press.

Benson, T. W., & Pearce, W. B. (Eds.). (1977). Alternative theoretical bases for the study of human communication: A symposium. *Communication Quarterly, 25,* 1-73.

Benton, A. L. (1936). Influence of incentives upon intelligence test scores of school children. *Journal of Genetic Psychology, 49,* 494-497.

Berelson, B. (1954). Content analysis. In G. Lindzey (Ed.), *Handbook of social psychology.* Reading, MA: Addison-Wesley.

Berelson, B. (1959). The state of communication research. *Public Opinion Quarterly, 23,* 1-6.

Berelson, B., & Janowitz, M. (1950). *Reader in public opinion and communication* (2nd ed.). New York: Free Press.

Berelson, B., Lazarsfeld, P. F., & McPhee, W. (1954). *Voting.* Chicago: University of Chicago Press.

Berelson, B., & Steiner, G. (1964). *Human behavior.* New York: Harcourt Brace Jovanovich.

Berlo, D. K. (1960). *The process of communication.* New York: Holt, Rinehart & Winston.

Bingham, W. V. (1929). The personal interview studied by means of analysis and experiment. *Social Forces, 7,* 530-533.

Black, J. W. (Ed.). (1946). Studies in speech intelligibility. *Speech Monographs, 9,* 1-68.

Blankenship, A. B. (1940). Choice of words in poll questions. *Sociology and Social Research, 25,* 12-18.

Blankenship, A. B., & Taylor, H. R. (1937). Psychological effects of changing a trade name. *Journal of Applied Psychology, 21,* 94-101.

Bledstein, B. J. (1976). *The culture of professionalism.* New York: Norton.

Blumer, H. (1933). *Movies and conduct.* New York: Macmillan.

Blumer, H., & Hauser, P. (1933). *Movies, delinquency and crime.* New York: Macmillan.

Blumler, J. (1985). European-American differences in research. In E. M. Rogers & F. Balle (Eds.), *The media revolution in America and western Europe.* Norwood, NJ: Ablex.

Borchers, G. L. (1935). Speech without work? *Quarterly Journal of Speech, 21,* 376-378.

Borchers, G. L. (1936). An approach to the problem of oral style. *Quarterly Journal of Speech, 22,* 114-117.

Borden, N. H. (1942). *The economic effects of advertising.* Chicago: Irwin.

Boring, E. C. (1950). *A history of experimental psychology* (2nd ed.). New York: Appleton-Century-Crofts.

Bramson, L. (1961). *The political context of sociology.* Princeton, NJ: Princeton University Press.

Brenner, B. (1934). Effect of immediate and delayed praise and blame upon learning and recall. *Teachers College Contributions to Education,* No. 620.

Bridgeman, P. (1927). *The logic of modern physics.* New York: Macmillan.

Briggs, T. H. (1927). Praise and censure as incentives. *School & Society, 26,* 596-598.

Britt, S. H., & Lowry, R. L. (1941). Conformity behavior of labor newspapers with respect to the AFL-CIO conflict. *Journal of Social Psychology, 14,* 375-387.

Brooks, R. D., & Scheidel, T. M. (1968). Speech as process: A case study. *Speech Monographs, 35,* 1-7.

Brouwer, M. (1964). Mass communication and the social sciences: Some neglected areas. In L. A. Dexter & D. M. White (Eds.), *People, society, and mass communications.* New York: Free Press.

Bruner, J. S. (1941). The dimensions of propaganda: German shortwave broadcasts to America. *Journal of Abnormal and Social Psychology, 36,* 311-337.

Bryson, L. (Ed.) (1948). *The communication of ideas.* New York: Harper & Row.

Buckley, K. W. (1982). The selling of a psychologist: John Bordus Watson and the application of behavioral techniques to advertising. *Journal of the History of the Behavioral Sciences, 18,* 207-221.

Burke, K. (1962). *A grammar of motives and a rhetoric of motives.* New York: World Publishing.

Burke, K. (1966). *Language as symbolic action.* Berkeley: University of California Press.

Caldwell, O., & Lundeen, G. E. (1933). Changing unfounded beliefs—a unit in biology. *School & Society, 33,* 394-413.

Camfield, T. (1969). *Psychologists at war: The history of American psychology and the first World War.* Ph.D. dissertation, University of Texas at Austin.

Cantril, H., & Allport, G. W. (1935). *The psychology of radio.* New York: Harper & Row.

Cantril, H., Gaudet, H., & Herzog, H. (1940). *The invasion from Mars.* Princeton, NJ: Princeton University Press.

Carey, J. W. (1979). Mass communication research and cultural studies: An American view. In J. Curran et al. (Eds.), *Mass communication and society.* Newbury Park, CA: Sage.

Carpenter, M. E. (1941). *The treatment of the Negro in American history school textbooks.* Menasha, WI: Banta.

Carr, L. J. (1929). Experimental sociology: A preliminary note on theory and method. *Social Forces, 8,* 63-74.

Cartwright, D., & Zander, A. (Eds.). (1968). *Group dynamics* (3rd ed.). New York: Harper & Row.

Chafee, Z., Jr. (1941). *Free speech in the United States.* Cambridge, MA: Harvard University Press.

Chafee, Z., Jr. (1947). *Government and mass communication.* Chicago: University of Chicago Press.

Chaffee, S. H. (Ed.). (1974). Contributions of Wilbur Schramm to mass communication research. *Journalism Monographs,* No. 36.

Chaffee, S. H., & Hochheimer, J. L. (1985). The beginnings of political communication research in the United States: Origins of the "limited effects" model. In E. M. Rogers & F. Balle (Eds.), *The media revolution in America and western Europe.* Norwood, NJ: Ablex.

Chapple, E. D. (1940). Measuring human relations: An introduction to the study of interaction of individuals. *Genetic Psychology Monographs, 22,* 3-147.

Charters, W. W. (1933). *Motion pictures and youth.* New York: Macmillan.

Cherrington, P. T. (1913). *Advertising as a business force.* Garden City, NY: Doubleday.

Childs, H. L. (Ed.). (1936). *Propaganda and dictatorship.* Princeton, NJ: Princeton University Press.

Childs, H. L. (1940). *An introduction to public opinion.* New York: John Wiley.

Coleman, J. S. (1980). The structure of society and the nature of social research. *Knowledge: Creation, Diffusion, Utilization, 1,* 333-350.

Comstock, G., & Fisher, M. (1975). *Television and human behavior.* Santa Monica, CA: Rand Corporation.

Cooley, C. H. (1902). *Human nature and the social order.* New York: Scribner.

Cooley, C. H. (1909). *Social organization.* New York: Scribner.

Cooley, C. H. (1928). Case study of small institutions as a method of research. *Publications of the American Sociological Society, 22,* 133-143.

Cooper, K. (1942). *Barriers down.* New York: Farrar & Rinehart.

Cowley, W. H. (1931). The traits of face to face leaders. *Journal of Abnormal and Social Psychology, 26,* 304-313.

Craig, D. R., & Lazarsfeld, P. F. (1934). *Some measurement of the acceptance and rejection of rayon by Pittsburgh women: An experimental study of 800 women.* Paper presented to the American Society for Testing Materials.

Crawford, N. A. (1924). *Ethics of journalism.* New York: Knopf.

Creel, G. (1920). *How we advertised America.* New York: Harper & Row.

Cressey, P. G. (1934). The motion picture as informal education. *Journal of Educational Psychology, 7,* 504-515.

Cressey, P. G. (1938). The motion picture experience as modified by social background and personality. *American Sociological Review, 3,* 516-525.

Cressey, P. G., & Thrasher, F. M. (1934). *Boys, movies and city streets.* New York: Macmillan.

Cronkhite, G., & Liska, J. (Ed.). (1977). Symposium: What criteria should be used to judge the admissibility of evidence to support theoretical propositions regarding communication research? *Western Journal of Speech Communication, 41,* 3-65.

Curti, M. (1967). The changing concept of "human nature" in the literature of American advertising. *Business History Review, 41,* 337-345.

Czitrom, D. J. (1982). *Media and the American mind.* Chapel Hill: University of North Carolina Press.

Dale, E. (1935a). *The content of motion pictures.* New York: Macmillan.

Dale, E. (1935b). *How to appreciate motion pictures.* New York: Macmillan.

Dale, E. (1937). Need for study of the newsreels. *Public Opinion Quarterly, 1,* 122-125.

Dance, F.E.X. (1967). A helical model of communication. In F.E.X. Dance (Ed.), *Human communication.* New York: Holt, Rinehart & Winston.

Dance, F.E.X. (Ed.). (1982). *Human communication theory.* New York: Harper & Row.

Dashiell, J. F. (1935). Experimental studies of the influence of social situations on the behavior of individual human adults. In C. C. Murchison (Ed.), *Handbook of social psychology.* Worchester, MA: Clark University Press.

Davis, R. (1985). *Response to innovation: A study of popular arguments about new mass media.* Doctoral dissertation, University of Iowa.

Dawe, H. C. (1934). An analysis of two hundred quarrels of pre-school children. *Child Development, 5,* 139-157.

DeFleur, M. L. (1966). *Theories of mass communication.* New York: David McKay.

Desmond, R. W. (1937). *The press and world affairs.* New York: Appleton-Century-Crofts.

Dewey, J. (1922). *Human nature and conduct.* New York: Holt, Rinehart & Winston.

Dewey, J. (1927). *The public and its problems.* New York: Holt, Rinehart & Winston.

DeWick, H. N. (1935). Relative recall effectiveness of visual and auditory presentations of advertising material. *Journal of Applied Psychology, 19,* 245-64.

Doob, L. W. (1935). *Propaganda.* New York: Holt, Rinehart & Winston.

Douglas, J. D. (Ed.). (1970). *Understanding everyday life.* Chicago: Aldine.

Droba, D. D. (1931). Methods used in measuring public opinion. *American Journal of Sociology, 37,* 410-23.

Droba, D. D. (1932). Methods for measuring attitudes. *Psychological Bulletin, 29,* 309-324.

Duncan, H. D. (1962). *Communication and social order.* New York: Bedminster Press.

Dusenbury, D., & Knower, F. H. (1938). Exceptional studies of the symbolism of action and voice—I: A study of the specificity of meaning in facial expression. *Quarterly Journal of Speech, 24,* 424-36.

Dysinger, W. S., & Ruckmick, C. A. (1935). *The emotional responses of children to the motion picture situation.* New York: Macmillan.

Ehninger, D. (Ed.). (1972). *Contemporary rhetoric.* Glenview, IL: Scott, Foresman.

Elliott, F. R. (1937). Attention effects from poster, radio, and poster-radio advertising of an exhibit. *Journal of Applied Psychology, 21,* 365-71.

English, E. (1944). A study of the readability of four newspaper headline types. *Journalism Quarterly, 21,* 217-229.

Ettinger, K. E. (Ed.). (1945). *Public relations directory and yearbook.* New York: Public Relations Directory and Yearbook.

Ewbank, H. L. (1932). Studies in the techniques of radio speech. *Quarterly Journal of Speech, 18,* 560-71.

Ewen, S. (1977). *Captains of consciousness.* New York: McGraw-Hill.

Faris, R.E.L. (1967). *Chicago sociology, 1920-32.* San Francisco: Jossey-Bass.

Fay, P. J., & Middleton, W. C. (1942). Judgment of introversion from the transcribed voice. *Quarterly Journal of Speech, 28,* 226-228.

Feinberg, I. R. (1940). Picketing, free speech, and "labor disputes." *New York University Law Review, 17,* 385-405.

Ferguson, L. W. (1962). *The heritage of industrial psychology.* Hartford, CT: Findlay.

Festinger, L. (1962). *A theory of cognitive dissonance.* Palo Alto, CA: Stanford University Press.

Fleming, D. (1963). Social Darwinism. In A. M. Schlesinger, Jr., & M. White (Eds.), *Paths of American thought.* Boston: Houghton Mifflin.

Fleming, D., & Bailyn, B. (Eds.) (1969). *The intellectual migration.* Cambridge, MA: Harvard University Press.

Flesch, R. F. (1944). *Marks of readable style: A study in adult education.* Ed.D. dissertation. Columbia University, New York.

Frost, S. E., Jr. (1937). *Education's own stations.* Chicago: University of Chicago Press.

Furner, M. O. (1975). *Advocacy and objectivity.* Lexington: University of Kentucky Press.

Gallup, G. (1930). A scientific method for determining reader-interest. *Journalism Quarterly, 7,* 1-13.

Geller, A., Kaplan, D., & Lasswell, H. D. (1942). An experimental comparison of four ways of coding editorial content. *Journalism Quarterly, 19,* 362-371.

Gerbner, G. (1956). Toward a general model of communication. *Audio-Visual Communication Review, 4,* 171-199.

Gieber, W. (1956). Across the desk: A study of 16 telegraph editors. *Journalism Quarterly, 27,* 383-390.

Gilkinson, H. (1942). Social fears as reported by students in college speech classes. *Speech Monographs, 9,* 141-160.

Gitlin, T. (1978). Media sociology: The dominant paradigm. *Theory and Society, 6,* 205-253.

Goffman, E. (1959). *The presentation of self in everyday life.* Garden City, NY: Doubleday.

Goldstein, H. (1940). *Reading and listening comprehension at various rates.* New York: Columbia University Press.

Goodenough, F. L. (1928). Measuring behavior traits by means of repeated short samples. *Journal of Juvenile Research, 12,* 230-235.

Gosnell, H. F., & DeGrazia, S. (1942). A critique of polling methods. *Public Opinion Quarterly, 6,* 378-390.

Gosnell, H. F. (1937). How accurate were the polls? *Public Opinion Quarterly, 1* (1), 97-105.

Gray, W. S., & Leary, B. E. (1935). *What makes a book readable, with special reference to adults of limited reading ability.* Chicago: University of Chicago Press.

Greene, N. L. (1926). Motion pictures in the classroom. *Annals of the American Academy of Political and Social Science, 217,* 122-130.

Gumperz, J. J., & Hymes, D. (Eds.). (1972). *Directions in sociolinguistics.* New York: Holt, Rinehart & Winston.

Hall, S. (1982). The re-discovery of "ideology": Return of the repressed in media studies. In M. Gurevitch et al. (Eds.), *Culture, society and the media.* London: Methuen.

Hamilton, T. (1942). Social optimism and pessimism in American protestantism. *Public Opinion Quarterly, 6,* 280-283.

Hampton, B. B. (1931). *History of the movies.* New York: Covici, Friede.

Harley, J. E. (1941). *World-wide influences of the cinema.* Los Angeles: University of Southern California Press.

Harris, F. (1933). *The presentation of crime in newspapers.* Hanover, NH: Sociological Press.

Harris, M. (1968). *The rise of anthropological theory.* New York: Crowell.

Hays, S. P. (1957). *The response to industrialism.* Chicago: University of Chicago Press.

Hayworth, D. (1930). An analysis of speeches in presidential campaigns from 1884-1920. *Quarterly Journal of Speech, 16,* 35-42.

Healey, W. (1915). *The individual delinquent.* Boston: Little, Brown.

Heider, F. (1958). *The psychology of interpersonal relations.* New York: John Wiley.

Herring, J. M., & Gross, G. C. (1936). *Telecommunication: Economics and regulation.* New York: McGraw-Hill.

Herzog, H. (1941). On borrowed experience: An analysis of listening to daytime sketches. *Studies in Philosophy and Social Science, 9,* 65-95.

Hocking, W. E. (1947). *Freedom of the press.* Chicago: University of Chicago Press.

Hofstadter, R. (1955). *The age of reform.* New York: Knopf.

Holaday, P. W., & Stoddard, G. D. (1933). *Getting ideas from the movies.* New York: Macmillan.

Hovland, C. I. (1948). Social communication. *Proceedings of the American Philosophical Society, 92,* 371-375.

Hovland, C. I. (1954). The effects of the mass media of communication. In G. Lindzey (Ed.), *Handbook of social psychology* (Vol. 2). Reading, MA: Addison-Wesley.

Hovland, C. I., Janis, I. L., & Kelley, H. H. (1953). *Communication and persuasion.* New Haven, CT: Yale University Press.

Hovland, C. I., Lumsdaine, A. A., & Sheffield, F. D. (1949). *Experiments on mass communication.* Princeton, NJ: Princeton University Press.

Hovland, C. I., & Rosenberg, M. J. (Eds.). (1960). *Attitude organization and change.* New Haven, CT: Yale University Press.

Huettig, M. D. (1944). *Economic control of the motion picture industry.* Philadelphia: University of Pennsylvania Press.

Hurwitz, D. L. (1983). *Broadcast "ratings": The rise and development of commercial audience research and measurement in American broadcasting.* Ph.D. dissertation, University of Illinois, Champaign-Urbana.

Ickes, H. L. (1941). *Freedom of the press today.* New York: Vanguard.

Inglis, R. A. (1947). *Freedom of the movies.* Chicago: University of Chicago Press.

Innis, H. (1951). *The bias of communication.* Toronto: University of Toronto Press.

Jacobs, L. (1939). *The rise of the American film.* New York: Columbia University Teachers College Press.

Janis, I. L., & Fadner, R. H. (1943). A coefficient of imbalance for content analysis. *Psychometrica, 8,* 105-19.

Jay, M. (1972). The Frankfurt school in exile. *Perspectives in American History, 6,* 339-385.

Jay, M. (1973). *The dialectical imagination.* Boston: Little, Brown.

Johnson, F. C., & Klare, G. R. (1961). General models of communication research: A survey of the developments of a decade. *Journal of Communication, 11,* 13-26.

Johnson, I. S. (1937). Cartoons. *Public Opinion Quarterly, 3,* 21-44.

Jones, R. W. (1940). *Law of journalism.* Brooklyn, NY: Metropolitan.

Jowett, G. (1976). *Film: The democratic art.* Boston: Little, Brown.

Karpf, F. B. (1932). *American social psychology.* New York: McGraw-Hill.

Katz, E. (1960). Communication research and the image of society: Convergence of two traditions. *American Journal of Sociology, 65,* 435-440.

Katz, E., & Lazarsfeld, P. F. (1955). *Personal influence.* New York: Free Press.

Kibler, R. L., & Barker, L. L. (1969). *Conceptual frontiers in speech-communication.* New York: Speech Association of America.

Kiefer, A. F. (1942). Government control of publishing in Germany. *Political Science Quarterly, 57,* 72-97.

Kingsbury, S. M., et al. (1937). *Newspapers and the news.* New York: G. P. Putnam.

Klapper, J. T. (1949). *The effects of mass media.* New York: Columbia University Bureau of Applied Social Research.

Klapper, J. T. (1960). *The effects of mass communication.* New York: Free Press.

Knower, F. H. (1935). Experimental studies of changes in attitudes: I. Study of the effect of oral argument on changes of attitude. *Journal of Social Psychology, 6,* 315-344.

Knower, F. H., Phillips, D., & Keoppel, F. (1945). Studies in listening to informative speaking. *Journal of Abnormal and Social Psychology, 40,* 82-88.

Koon, C. M. (1935). Motion pictures in education in the United States. *International Review of Educational Cinematography, 6,* 476-477.

Koon, C. M., & Noble, A. W. (1936). *National visual education directory.* Washington, DC: American Council on Education.

Kroll, A. (1934). The teacher's influence upon the social attitude of boys in the twelfth grade. *Journal of Educational Psychology, 25,* 274-280.

Kuhn, T. S. (1970). *The structure of scientific revolutions* (2nd ed.). Chicago: University of Chicago Press.

Kuna, D. P. (1976). *The psychology of advertising, 1896-1916.* Ph.D. dissertation, University of Texas at Austin.

Laird, D. A. (1923). How the college student responds to different incentives to work. *Pedagogical Seminar, 30,* 366-370.

Landis, M. H., & Burtt, H. E. (1924). A study of conversation. *Journal of Comparative Psychology, 4,* 81-90.

Landis, M. H., & Ross, J.W.H. (1933). Humor and its relation to other personality traits. *Journal of Social Psychology, 4,* 156-175.

Lashley, K. S., & Watson, G. B. (1922). *A psychological study of motion pictures in relation to venereal disease campaigns.* Washington, DC: Interdepartmental Social Hygiene Board.

Lasswell, H. D. (1927a). *Propaganda technique in the world war.* New York: Knopf.

Lasswell, H. D. (1927b). Theory of political propaganda. *American Political Science Review, 21,* 627-631.

Lasswell, H. D. (1935). *World politics and personal insecurity.* New York: McGraw-Hill.

Lasswell, H. D. (1938). A provisional classification of symbol data. *Psychiatry, 1,* 197-204.

Lasswell, H. D. (1941). *Democracy through public opinion.* Menasha, WI: Banta.

Lasswell, H. D., & Blumenstock, D. (1939). *World revolutionary propaganda.* New York: Knopf.

Lasswell, H. D., Casey, R. D., & Smith, B. L. (1935). *Propaganda and promotional activities.* Minneapolis: University of Minnesota Press.

Lasswell, H. D. et al. (1949). *Language of politics.* New York: Stewart.

Lavine, H., & Wechsler, J. (1940). *War propaganda and the United States.* New Haven, CT: Yale University Press.

Lazarsfeld, P. F. (1940). *Radio and the printed page.* New York: Duell, Sloan, and Pearce.

Lazarsfeld, P. F. (1941). Remarks on administrative and critical communications research. *Studies in Philosophy and Social Science, 9,* 2-16.

Lazarsfeld, P. F., Berelson, B., & Gaudet, H. (1944). *The people's choice.* New York: Duell, Sloan, and Pearce.

Lazarsfeld, P. F., & Reitz, J. G. (1975). *An introduction to applied sociology.* New York: Elsevier.

Lazarsfeld, P. F., & Stanton, F. N. (Eds.). (1941). *Radio research, 1941.* New York: Duell, Sloan, and Pearce.

Lazarsfeld, P. F., & Stanton, F. N. (Eds.). (1944). *Radio research, 1942-1943.* New York: Duell, Sloan, and Pearce.

Lazarsfeld, P. F., & Stanton, F. N. (Eds.). (1949). *Communications research, 1948-1949.* New York: Harper & Row.

Lazarsfeld, P. F., & Wyant, R. (1937). Magazines in 90 cities—who reads what? *Public Opinion Quarterly, 1* (4), 29-41.

LeBon, G. (1920). *The crowd.* London: Unwin.

Lee, A. M. (1937). *The daily newspaper in America.* New York: Macmillan.

Lee, A. M., & Lee, E. B. (1939). *The fine art of propaganda.* New York: Harcourt Brace Jovanovich.

Lerner, D., & Schramm, W. (Eds.). (1967). *Communication and change in developing countries.* Honolulu: East-West Center Press.

Lewin, K. (1945). The Research Center for Group Dynamics at Massachusetts Institute of Technology. *Sociometry, 8,* 126-136.

Lewin, K., Lippitt, R., & White, R. (1939). Patterns of aggressive behavior in experimentally created "social climates." *Journal of Social Psychology, 10,* 271-299.

Lewis, J. D., & Smith, R. L. (1980). *American sociology and pragmatism.* Chicago: University of Chicago Press.

Likert, R. (1932). *A technique for the measurement of attitudes.* New York: Columbia University Archives of Psychology, No. 140.

Likert, R. (1936). Method for measuring the sales influence of a radio program. *Journal of Applied Psychology, 20,* 175-182.

Lippmann, W. (1922). *Public opinion.* New York: Harcourt Brace Jovanovich.

Longstaff, H. P. (1936). Effectiveness of children's radio programs. *Journal of Applied Psychology, 20,* 208-220.

Longstaff, H. P. (1937). Mother's opinions of children's radio programs. *Journal of Applied Psychology, 21,* 265-279.

Lumley, F. E. (1933). *The propaganda menace.* New York: Century.

Lunday, A. (1969). *Sociology dissertations in American universities 1893-1966.* Commerce: East Texas University.

Lynd, R. S., & Lynd, H. M. (1929). *Middletown.* New York: Harcourt Brace Jovanovich.

Lynd, R. S., & Lynd, H. M. (1937). *Middletown in transition.* New York: Harcourt Brace Jovanovich.

Lyons, G. M. (1969). *The uneasy partnership.* New York: Russell Sage.

Maccoby, N. (1963). The new "scientific" rhetoric. In W. Schramm (Ed.), *The science of human communication.* New York: Basic Books.

Madge, J. (1962). *The origins of scientific sociology.* New York: Free Press.

Manis, J. G., & Meltzer, B. N. (Eds.). (1972). *Symbolic interaction* (2nd ed.). Boston: Allyn & Bacon.

Mason, J. B. (1939). Germany's leadership in school films. *California Journal of Secondary Education* (January), 46-49.

Matthews, F. H. (1977). *Quest for an American sociology.* Montreal: McGill-Queen's University Press.

Mayo, E. (1933). *The human problems of an industrial civilization.* New York: Macmillan.

McCarry, J. L. (1939). *Government publicity.* Chicago: University of Chicago Press.

McDiarmid, J. (1937). Presidential inaugural addresses: A study in verbal symbols. *Public Opinion Quarterly, 3,* 79-82.

McKenzie, V. (1941). Treatment of war themes in magazine fiction. *Public Opinion Quarterly, 5,* 227-232.

McLuhan, M. (1965). *Understanding media.* New York: New American Library.

Mead, G. H. (1934). *Mind, self, and society.* Chicago: University of Chicago Press.

Mead, G. H. (1964). *On social psychology* (rev. ed; A. Strauss, Ed.). Chicago: University of Chicago Press.

Medhurst, M. J., & Benson, T. W. (Eds.). (1984). *Rhetorical dimensions in media.* Dubuque, IO: Kendall/Hunt.

Meehan, E. R. (1983). *Neither heroes nor villains: Towards a political economy of the rating industry.* Ph.D. dissertation, University of Illinois, Champaign-Urbana.

Menefee, S. C. (1938). Experimental study of strike propaganda: The Pacific Northwest lumber strike of 1935. *Social Forces, 16,* 574-582.

Merton, R. K. (1946). *Mass persuasion.* New York: Harper & Row.

Merton, R. K. (1957). *Social theory and social structure* (rev. ed.). New York: Free Press.

Merton, R. K., & Lazarsfeld, P. F. (Eds.). (1950). *Studies in the scope and method of "The American Soldier."* New York: Free Press.

Miller, G. R. (1966). On defining communication: Another stab. *Journal of Communication, 16,* 88-98.

Mitchell, A. M. (1929). *Children and the movies.* Chicago: University of Chicago Press.

Mock, J. R. (1941). *Censorship.* Princeton, NJ: Princeton University Press.

Mock, J. R., & Larson, C. (1939). *Words that won the war.* Princeton, NJ: Princeton University Press.

Moran, M. G. & Lunsford, R. F. (Eds.). (1984). *Research in composition and rhetoric.* Westport, CT: Greenwood Press.

Moreno, J. L. (1934). *Who shall survive?* Washington, DC: Nervous and Mental Diseases Publishing.

Mortensen, C. D. (1972). *Communication.* New York: McGraw-Hill.

Mosteller, F., & McCarthy, P. J. (1942). Estimating population proportions. *Public Opinion Quarterly, 6,* 452-458.

Mott, F. L. (1938). *History of American magazines.* Cambridge, MA: Harvard University Press.

Mott, F. L. (1941). *American journalism.* New York: Macmillan.

Munsterberg, H. (1913). *Psychology and industrial efficiency.* Boston: Houghton-Mifflin.

Munsterberg, H. (1916). *The photoplay.* New York: Appleman.

Murphy, G., & Murphy, L. B. (1931). *Experimental social psychology.* New York: Harper & Row.

Murphy, G., Murphy, L. B., & Newcomb, T. M. (1937). *Experimental social psychology* (rev. ed.). New York: Harper & Row.

Nafziger, R. O. (1937). World War correspondents and the censorship of the belligerents. *Public Opinion Quarterly, 14,* 226-243.

Nafziger, R. O. (1940). *Internatonal news and the press.* New York: Wilson.

Nafziger, R. O., & White, D. M., (Eds.). (1963). *Introduction to mass communication research* (rev. ed.). Baton Rouge: Louisiana State University Press.

Napoli, D. S. (1980). *The architects of adjustment.* Port Washington, NY: Kennikat.

Newcomb, T. M. (1943). *Personality and social change.* New York: Dryden.

Nielsen, T. R. (1970). On defining communication. In K. K. Sereno & C. D. Mortensen (Eds.), *Foundations of communication.* New York: Harper & Row.

Nixon, R. B. (1945). Concentration and absenteeism in daily newspaper ownership. *Journalism Quarterly, 22,* 97-114.

Noble, D. F. (1977). *America by design.* New York: Knopf.

Noble, D. W. (1958). *The paradox of progressive thought.* Minneapolis: University of Minnesota Press.

O'Neill, J. M. (1935). The professional outlook. *Quarterly Journal of Speech, 21,* 60-72.

Osborn, W. W. (1939). An experiment in teaching resistance to propaganda. *Journal of Experimental Education, 8,* 1-17.

Osgood, C. E., Suci, G. J., & Tannenbaum, P. H. (1957). *The measurement of meaning.* Urbana: University of Illinois Press.

Park, R. E. (1922). *The immigrant press and its control.* New York: Harper & Row.

Park, R. E. (1923). The natural history of the newspaper. *American Journal of Sociology, 29,* 273-289.

Park, R. E. (1925). Immigrant community and immigrant press. *American Review, 3,* 143-152.

Park, R. E. (1940). News as a form of knowledge: A chapter in the sociology of knowledge. *Journal of Sociology, 45,* 669-686.

Park, R. E. (1967). *On social control and collective behavior* (R. H. Turner, Ed.). Chicago: University of Chicago Press.

Park, R. E., & Burgess, E. W. (1921). *Introduction to the science of sociology.* Chicago: University of Chicago Press.

Park, R. E., Burgess, E. W., & McKenzie, R. D. (1925). *The city.* Chicago: University of Chicago Press.

Peters, C. C. (1933). *Motion pictures and standards of morality.* New York: Macmillan.

Peterson, R., & Thurstone, L. L. (1933). *Motion pictures and the social attitudes of children.* New York: Macmillan.

Peterson, T., Jensen, J. W., & Rivers, W. L. (1965). *The mass media and modern society.* New York: Holt, Rinehart & Winston.

Phelan, J. J. (1919). *Motion pictures as a phase of commercialized amusement in Toledo, Ohio.* Toledo, OH: Little Book Press.

Piaget, J. (1965). *The language and thought of the child* (3rd ed.). New York: Humanities Press. (Original work published 1926)

Pollard, J. E. (1937). Advertising copy requirements of representative newspapers. *Journalism Quarterly, 14,* 259-266.

Prugger, F. V. (1941). The social composition and training of the Milwaukee *Journal* newstaff. *Journalism Quarterly, 19,* 231-244.

Punke, H. H. (1937). Sociological factors in the leisure-time reading of high school students. *Library Quarterly, 7,* 332-342.

Quandt, J. B. (1970). *From the small town to the great community.* New Brunswick, NJ: Rutgers University Press.

Reemers, H. H. (1938). Propaganda in the schools—do the effects last? *Public Opinion Quarterly, 2,* 197-210.

Renshaw, S., Miller, V. L., & Marquis, D. P. (1933). *Children's sleep*. New York: Macmillan.

Richards, I. A. (1936). *The philosophy of rhetoric*. London: Oxford University Press.

Rickert, E. (1927). *New methods for the study of literature*. Chicago: University of Chicago Press.

Riley, M. W., & Riley, J. W., Jr. (1951). A sociological approach to communication research. *Public Opinion Quarterly, 15*, 444-460.

Riley, J. W., & Riley, M. W. (1959). Mass communication and the social system. In R. K. Merton, L. Broom, & L. S. Cottrell, Jr. (Eds.), *Sociology today*. New York: Basic Books.

Robinson, K. F. (1941). An experimental study of the effects of group discussion upon the social attitudes of college students. *Speech Monographs, 8*, 34-57.

Rogers, E. M., & Balle, F. (Eds.). (1985). *The media revolution in America and in western Europe*. Norwood, NJ: Ablex.

Rogers, E. M. (1962). *Diffusion of innovations*. New York: Free Press.

Rosenberg, B., & White, D. M. (Eds.) (1957). *Mass culture*. New York: Free Press.

Rosten, L. C. (1937). *The Washington correspondents*. New York: Harcourt, Brace.

Rosten, L. C. (1941). *Hollywood*. New York: Harcourt Brace Jovanovich.

Rothlisberger, F. J., & Dickson, W. J. (1939). *Management and the worker*. Cambridge, MA: Harvard University Press.

Rowell, G. P. (1906). *Forty years as an advertising agent*. New York: Printers' Ink Publishing Co.

Rowland, W. D., Jr. (1983). *The politics of TV violence*. Newbury Park, CA: Sage.

Ruesch, J., & Bateson, G. (1968). *Communication: The social matrix of psychiatry*. New York: Norton.

Sargent, S. S. (1939). Emotional stereotypes in the Chicago *Tribune*. *Sociometry, 2*, 69-75.

Schramm, W. (Ed.). (1948). *Communications in modern society*. Urbana: University of Illinois Press.

Schramm, W. (Ed.). (1949). *Mass communications*. Urbana: University of Illinois Press.

Schramm, W. (Ed.). (1954). *The process and effects of mass communication*. Urbana: University of Illinois Press.

Schramm, W. (1963). The challenge to communication research. In R. O. Nafziger & D. M. White (Eds.), *Introduction to mass communications research*. Baton Rouge: Louisiana State University Press.

Schramm, W. (1985). The beginning of communication study in the United States. In E. M. Rogers & F. Balle (Ed.), *The media revolution in America and in western Europe*. Norwood, NJ: Ablex.

Schultz, D. P. (1969). *A history of modern psychology*. New York: Academic Press.

Schultze, Q. J. (1978). *Advertising, science and professionalism 1985-1917*. Ph.D. dissertation, University of Illinois, Champaign-Urbana.

Scott, R. L., & Brockreide, W. E. (1969). *The rhetoric of black power*. New York: Harper & Row.

Scott, W. D. (1931). *The psychology of advertising*. New York: Dodd, Mead.

Severson, A. L. (1939). Nationality and religious preferences as reflected in newspaper advertisements. *American Journal of Sociology, 44*, 540-545.

Shannon, C. E., & Weaver, W. (1949). *The mathematical theory of communication*. Urbana: University of Illinois Press.

Shaw, M. E. (1932). A comparison of individuals and small groups in the rational solution of complex problems. *American Journal of Psychology, 44*, 491-504.

Sherif, M. (1936). *The psychology of social norms*. New York: Harper & Row.

Sherif, M., & Hovland, C. I. (1960). *Social judgment*. New Haven, CT: Yale University Press.

Sherman, M. (1932). Theories and measurement of attitudes. *Child Development, 3,* 15-28.

Shils, E. A., & Janowitz, M. (1948). Cohesion and disintegration in the Wehrmacht. *Public Opinion Quarterly,* 12, 300-315.

Shurick, E. P. J. (1946). *The first quarter-century of American broadcasting.* Kansas City, MO: Midland.

Shuttleworth, F. K., & May, M. A. (1933). *The social conduct and attitudes of movie fans.* New York: Macmillan.

Siebert, F. S. (1934). *The rights and privileges of the press.* New York: Appleton-Century-Crofts.

Simon, A., & Boyer, E. G. (Eds.). (1967). *Mirrors for behavior.* Philadelphia: Research for Better Schools.

Simpson, R. H. (1939). The effect of discussion on intra-group divergencies of judgment. *Quarterly Journal of Speech, 25,* 546-552.

Small, A. W., & Vincent, G. E. (1894). *Introduction to the study of society.* New York: American Book Company.

Smith, D. H. (1972). Communication research and the idea of process. *Speech Monographs, 39,* 174-182.

Smith, D. R. (1970). The fallacy of "communication breakdown." *Quarterly Journal of Speech, 56,* 343-346.

Smith, B. L., Lasswell, H. D., & Casey, R. D. (1946). *Propaganda, communication, and public opinion.* Princeton, NJ: Princeton University Press.

Sokal, M. M. (1981). The origins of the Psychological Corporation. *Journal of the History of the Behavioral Sciences, 17,* 54-67.

Sproule, J. M. (1983). The Institute for Propaganda Analysis: Public education in argumentation, 1937-1942. In D. Zarefsky, M. O. Sillars, & J. Rhodes (Eds.), *Argument in transition.* Annandale, VA: Speech Communication Association.

Stanton, F. (1940). Commercial effects of radio: A two-way check on the sales influence of a specific radio program. *Journal of Applied Psychology, 24,* 665-672.

Stoke, H. W. (1941). Executive leadership and the growth of propaganda. *American Political Science Review, 35,* 490-500

Stone, G. P., & Farberman, H. A. (Eds.). (1970). *Social psychology through symbolic interaction.* Waltham, MA: Ginn-Blaisdell.

Stouffer, S. A., et al. (1949a). *The American soldier: Adjustment during army life.* Princeton, NJ: Princeton University Press.

Stouffer, S. A., et al. (1949b). *The American soldier: Combat and its aftermath.* Princeton, NJ: Princeton University Press.

Stouffer, S. A., et al. (1950). *Measurement and prediction.* Princeton, NJ: Princeton University Press.

Thomas, W. I., & Znaniecki, F. (1918-1920). *The Polish peasant in Europe and America* (Vols. 1-5). Boston: Badger.

Thompson, W. N. (1967). *Quantitative research in public address and communication.* New York: Random House.

Thorndike, E. L. (1911). Psychology and advertising: The scientific appeal to human nature. *Scientific American, 105,* 250-251.

Thorpe, M. F. (1939). *America at the movies.* New Haven, CT: Yale University Press.

Thrasher, F. M. (Ed.). (1937). Educational aspects of motion pictures. *Journal of Educational Sociology, 11,* 130-192.

Thurstone, L. L. (1931). Influence of motion pictures on children's attitudes. *Journal of Social Psychology, 2,* 291-305.

Thurstone, L. L., & Chave, E. J. (1929). *The measurement of attitudes.* Chicago: University of Chicago Press.

Timasheff, N. S. (1967). *Sociological theory* (3rd ed.). New York: Random House.

Timmons, W. M. (1941). Sex differences in discussion. *Speech Monographs, 8,* 68-75.

Troldahl, V. C. (1980). *The social scientific roots of the mass communication tradition.* Paper presented at the annual convention of the International Communication Associaton, Acapulco, Mexico.

Tunstall, J. (Ed.). (1970). *Media sociology.* Urbana: University of Illinois Press.

Veysey, L. R. (1965). *The emergence of the American University.* Chicago: University of Chicago Press.

Vold, L. (1940). Defamatory interpretations in radio broadcasts. *University of Pennsylvania Law Review, 88,* 249-296.

Wallace, K. R. (Ed.). (1954). *History of speech education in America.* New York: Appleton-Century-Crofts.

Wallace, K. R. (1970). *Understanding discourse.* Baton Rouge: Louisiana State University Press.

Walworth, A. (1938). *School histories at war.* Cambridge: Harvard University Press.

Waples, D. (1937). *People and print.* Chicago: University of Chicago Press.

Waples, D. (Ed.) (1942). *Print, radio and film in a democracy.* Chicago: University of Chicago Press.

Waples, D., Berelson, B., & Bradshaw, F. R. (1940). *What reading does to people.* Chicago: University of Chicago Press.

Wartella, E., & Reeves, B. (1985). Historical trends in research on children and the media: 1900-1960. *Journal of Communication, 35,* 118-133.

Watzlawick, P., Beavin, J., & Jackson, D. D. (1967). *Pragmatics of human communication.* New York: Norton.

Westley, B., & MacLean, M. (1955). A conceptual model for communication research. *Audio-Visual Communication Review, 3,* 3-12.

White, D. M. (1950). The "gate-keeper": A case study in the selection of news. *Journalism Quarterly, 27,* 383-390.

White, L. W., & Leigh, R. D. (1946). *People speaking to peoples.* Chicago: University of Chicago Press.

Whorf, B. L. (1957). *Language, thought, and reality* (J. B. Carroll, Ed.). Cambridge: MIT Press.

Whyte, W. F., Jr. (1943). *Street corner society.* Chicago: University of Chicago Press.

Wiebe, R. H. (1967). *The search for order.* New York: Hill & Wang.

Wiener, N. (1948). *Cybernetics.* Cambridge: MIT Press.

Wiley, M. W., & Rice, S. A. (1933). The agencies of communication. In President's Research Committee on Social Trends, *Recent social trends.* New York: McGraw-Hill.

Wilson, L. (1938). Newspaper opinion and crime in Boston. *Journal of Criminal Law and Criminology, 29,* 202-215.

Windt, T. O., Jr. (1982). Hoyt H. Hudson: Spokesman for Cornell school for rhetoric. *Quarterly Journal of Speech, 68,* 186-200.

Wirth, L. (1953). The social sciences. In M. E. Curti (ed.), *American scholarship in the twentieth century.* Cambridge, MA: Harvard University Press.

Wolf, K. F., & Fiske, M. (1949). In P. F. Lazarsfeld & F. N. Stanton (Eds.), *Communications research, 1948-1949.* New York: Harper & Row.

Wood, J. P. (1958). *The story of advertising.* New York: Ronald.

Woodworth, R. S., & Sheehan, M. R. (1964). *Contemporary schools of psychology* (3rd ed.). New York: Ronald.

Woolbert, C. (1920). The effects of various modes of public reading. *Journal of Applied Psychology, 4,* 162-185.

Young, D. R. (1922). *Motion pictures.* Philadelphia: Westbrook.

3   What Communication Scientists Do

STEVEN H. CHAFFEE
Stanford University

CHARLES R. BERGER
Northwestern University

T HE question this chapter addresses is, What sets communication scientists apart from others who study communication, or indeed from everyone else? It would be hard to live as a human being without developing some expectations—we could even call them implicit theories—about how we and others communicate. Our answer lies in the way communication scientists *think,* more than anything else; so we will review here some key features of thought that are common among communication scientists but rare in everyday life. Many of the principles we will discuss are shared with other social and behavioral sciences, but some are peculiar to communication science and are points of contention between it and other forms of communication study.

BACKGROUND ASSUMPTIONS

The concept of a science of human communication rests upon the optimistic assumption that behavior can be both understood and improved through systematic study. Further, it assumes that improvement must be based upon understanding, which is the primary goal of a science. Like all assumptions, these beliefs are not tested within the science itself. Instead they provide a working point of view, which derives its validity in the long run from the value of the knowledge produced. If we did not believe that we could understand human communication, and so perhaps improve upon it, we would not undertake scientific study with those goals in mind. Still, we know that there are limits beyond which communication is not subject to further understanding or improvement through scientific research.

These limits do not concern us when we are acting in the role of communication scientist. The working assumptions of a scientist are called into question only after the research is done. If it fails to produce the

99

hoped-for understanding or improvement, we might consider approaching the communication problem through methods other than science (see Farrell, Chapter 4 in this volume).

Besides explanation, basic goals of science include prediction and control. By control we do not mean that communication scientists want to manipulate individuals or institutions for their own purposes; scientific control means that we would know how to produce a phenomenon in which we are interested by setting up the conditions that account for it. Understanding those conditions is the essence of prediction.

Whether the phenomenon we produce has a positive or a negative impact is a question that lies beyond scientific discourse. For example, the ability of physicists to produce atomic reactions has led to both nuclear weapons and nuclear medicine. Theories of communication are used both to sell people cigarettes and to persuade them not to smoke. As citizens we can certainly oppose nuclear weapons or cigarette smoking. That has little to do with our work as scientists, except that our selection of research topics might reflect our personal values. Whether knowledge about nuclear fission or how to market cigarettes should be suppressed "for the good of society" is not a question to take up here. But communication scientists know that our explanations and predictions could be used to produce effects we would not want.

THEORY

Communication scientists think and talk about theory a lot. They work toward development of theory, and they bemoan the fact that there is not more good theory in the field. This raises two basic questions: What is "theory"? And what makes a theory "good"?

We will spend some portion of this chapter describing what theories are and how they can be evaluated. We will also present a way of thinking about communication at four levels of analysis, which we believe can promote more useful theoretical work. This effort is not itself a theory, but a way to integrate many disparate domains of communication inquiry. The world offers an incredible variety of communication phenomena begging for explanation, so there is ample room for the development of communication theories.

What Is a Communication Theory?

This entire book is filled with examples of communication theory. Behind them lies an ongoing debate over the proper approach. We cannot possibly deal with the full variety of positions here. Some advocate rule-governed approaches, in which communication acts would be interpreted as the result of people following certain rules for behavior; research would seek to find out what those rules are (Cushman, 1977). Others hold to a classically scientific law assumption; that is, that there are general laws of human behavior as there are in, say, biology or chemistry, and that research should test predictions from general propositions to see if they hold up (Berger, 1977; Hempel, 1965). Another position is to assume that a general form of theory cuts across all sciences and will be equally applicable to communication, such as the general systems approach (Monge, 1973, 1977). A decade ago this kind of debate occupied an entire issue of *Communication Quarterly* (1977, Vol. 25). These meta-theoretical issues are important because they influence the directions researchers take. But overemphasis on them can discourage researchers from developing *substantive* theories to explain communication.

A useful working definition of a theory is *a set of constructs that are linked together by relational statements that are internally consistent with each other.* *Constructs* are concepts that are formed inductively by generalizing from particulars. An example is "interpersonal influence," which is a name that has gradually developed to refer to a variety of observations of human activity. Constructs are abstractions; they are given meaning through theoretical definitions. Interpersonal influence may be defined conceptually as a change in one individual that is produced by another individual or a group.

Constructs vary in levels of abstraction. The more abstract they are, the more of a particular domain they cover. Interpersonal influence is more abstract than "salesmanship" but less abstract than "persuasion."

Constructs may also be thought of as theoretical *variables,* which means they may take on different values. The relational statements in theories of communication are about two or more variables. For example, we may theorize that there is more interpersonal influence between people of great "empathy." This is the most common kind of theoretical statement: a prediction that two constructs will *covary* together.

Not all relationships are so simple; in human communication few are. There are a number of types other than the *positive* relationship exemplified by empathy and interpersonal influence. Relationships can also be *inverse* or *negative,* which means that increases in one variable are associated with decreases in another. For example, increases in self-disclosure produce decreases in one's attractiveness. Other, more complex relational statements can be used to link constructs. *Nonlinear* relationships are common in communication. For example, it may be that increases in empathy heighten interpersonal influence up to a certain level, but beyond that make no further improvement; this is called an *asymptotic* function. Or perhaps very high levels of empathy are associated with a decline in interpersonal influence, in which case the relationship is *curvilinear*. It is very important to know about asymptotic or curvilinear effects in communication so that extensive effort is not put into activity that is useless or counterproductive. For example, in political advertising a candidate can gain support by simply having his name repeated several times—but lose support if it is mentioned so often that people get tired of hearing it (Becker & Doolittle, 1975). It is rarely the case that the more communication, the better.

Most theories have more than two constructs in them, and relationships can become complex. They should, because human communication is quite complex. A three-variable theory may involve an *interaction,* where the relationship between two variables depends upon values of other variables. For example, self-disclosure might be positively related to attractiveness for females, but for males these two variables might be negatively related. In this example, sex, the third variable, determines the relationship between the other two. Again, interactions are the rule rather than the exception in communication. The most defensible answer to many questions about relationships between communication constructs is "It depends."

Theories also contain boundary conditions. Boundary conditions specify the domain of events the theory explains, and what lies outside it. A theory constructed to explain communication in work groups might not apply to family groups. Or a theory about media use based on the middle class might not successfully predict what very wealthy or very poor people do. Boundary conditions can be introduced a priori as part of the theory, but more often they grow out of empirical research findings when it turns out that the theory does not work under some conditions.

Scientific theories are useful to the extent that they can be tested to assess their validity. To test theoretical relationships, it is necessary to measure theoretical variables. The move from the theoretical level to that of empirical research is accomplished by *operationally defining* theoretical constructs. Operational definitions specify how constructs are measured. For example, self-disclosure might be measured by a set of questions asking the person how much she provides others with information about herself. Or alternatively, the researcher might observe people in interactions and keep track of how often they say things about themselves. Finally, one might manipulate self-disclosure by having people interact with a confederate who systematically varies the amount of disclosure. In fact, all three of these ways of operationalizing self-disclosure have been used.

Several important points should be made about operational definitions. First, no one operational definition can possibly capture the full meaning of a theoretical construct. Second, it is difficult to create an operational definition that represents *only* the construct intended. There is always some slippage between constructs and what is done in a specific study. Therefore, multiple operations of a construct are preferable to singular operations. If we operationalize a construct several different ways, and get approximately the same result each way, we have much more confidence that the research represents the construct intended. There have been strong arguments for a multiple operations procedure (Blalock, 1984; Webb, Campbell, Schwartz, & Sechrest, 1966) but it is rarely used in studies of communication. Somewhat the same purpose is served by *replication* of a study, when the second study uses different operational definitions. This presumes, however, that the comparison of the two studies will be made by someone in a *review of the literature;* examples can be found in many chapters of this book, frequently pointing up discrepancies between studies that lead to reformulated theories.

While many theories contain constructs that are not amenable to operationalization ("nominal" constructs), a theory with too many is hard to test. Psychoanalytic theory is an example. A theory that cannot be tested may contain valuable insights, but it is difficult to evaluate. Often in communication research we use operational measures to represent dispositional constructs that may not exist. For example, the notion of "attitude" originated from observing consistencies in behavior, but no one has ever seen an attitude. The term is deeply entrenched in our literature, but the validity of the measures rests upon the success with which they enter into relationships specified in theories.

Once theoretical constructs are operationally defined, we can test specific hypotheses deduced from the more general theory. Since operational definitions never fully represent their theoretical constructs, there is always some degree of doubt about the theoretical significance of a particular hypothesis test. Even when specific hypotheses are supported by research findings, one cannot be confident that the general theoretical proposition tested is fully supported. Replications with different operational definitions under varying conditions are needed. For example, if we postulated a positive relationship between exposure to violent media content and propensity to act aggressively, we would want to test this proposition using a number of measures of the two constructs, as well as a number of people and situations. Corroboration of each specific prediction would increase our confidence in the general proposition. This is not often the case, however. For example, the predicted positive relationship between media violence and aggressiveness is usually found when the operational measure concerns what is actually watched, but not when it concerns the persons's "favorite programs"; it is also more often found in junior high school samples than at other ages (Chaffee, 1971). Communication scientists spend a great deal of effort trying to adjudicate such conflicts between studies. Are they due to faulty operations, or to poorly specified boundary conditions, or is the theory simply inadequate? These possibilities are discussed in detail by Blalock (1984).

Theories typically contain a number of theoretical relationships, and it is not unusual for some propositions to be better supported than others. Assuming that the lack of empirical support for a proposition is not due to faulty operationalizations or an inappropriate test domain, the theorist may be forced to abandon a theoretical proposition. Because theories are internally consistent systems of propositions, the deletion of one proposition will most probably entail changes in those that remain. Such modifications are commonplace in communication, as in any science. The theories of many of the most venerated names—Galileo, Newton, Einstein—contained errors.

Evaluating Theories

In discussing how communication scientists think about and develop theories, we have also used many of the criteria for evaluating theories. It is time to specify these. The following list of attributes of a good theory is similar to those most communication scientists—who are typically professors—outline for their beginning graduate students. We summarize our own list here to help theory builders (and borrowers) be critical of theory construction efforts they encounter or undertake.

(1) *Explanatory power:* Here we are concerned with the theory's ability to provide plausible explanations for the phenomena it was constructed to explain. Also considered here is the range of phenomena that the theory explains; the greater the range, the more powerful the theory.

(2) *Predictive power:* This criterion assesses theoretical adequacy by measuring the theory's ability to predict events. It is, however, possible for theories to predict but not be able to provide plausible explanations.

(3) *Parsimony:* Simple theories are preferred to more complex ones, assuming that both predict and explain equally well. The complexity of a theory is directly related to the complexity of the reality it seeks to explain.

(4) *Falsifiability:* Theories should be capable of being proved false. If a theory is not, it cannot be said to have survived a test even if research is consistent with it. Popper (1963) suggests that theoretical propositions be attacked from a variety of angles to see whether they can withstand efforts to disprove them. If there are numerous nominal constructs in a theory, it may be difficult to falsify since negative evidence can be explained away.

(5) *Internal consistency:* The internal logic of a theory can be assessed independently of empirical tests. Theoretical propositions should be consistent with each other. If they are not, empirical findings may be difficult to interpret within the theory.

(6) *Heuristic provocativeness:* Good theories generate new hypotheses, which expand the range of potential knowledge.

(7) *Organizing power:* Useful theories not only generate new knowledge, they are able to organize extant knowledge.

Theory at Work: Agenda-Setting

A good example of how communication scientists use theory can be found in the study of "agenda setting" by the news media. Cohen (1963) wrote that the media may not be successful much of the time in telling people what to think, but they are "stunningly successful in telling people what to think *about*." McCombs translated this comment into a prediction that topics emphasized in the press would be the topics people think are important. This was first tested in the 1968 election campaign; the researchers found that coverage of issues by a newspaper corresponded fairly strongly with the issues voters used in deciding how to vote (McCombs & Shaw, 1972).

The hypothesis has not always been suppported in subsequent research. Weaver (1977) showed that it applies only to people with a high "need for orientation," and other researchers found the results hard to replicate in a two-newspaper city (McLeod, Becker, & Byrnes, 1974) or for local television (Palmgrccn & Clarkc, 1977). But the theory held up well in a field experiment where people watched TV newscasts that had been purposely altered to emphasize different political issues (Iyengar, Peters, & Kinder, 1982). Their preferences among candidates were strongly affected by the issues stressed in the experimental news programs.

Agenda setting meets some of the tests we have outlined better than others. As a simple two-construct prediction it is certainly parsimonious, and in its matching of the orders of two sets of issues it is internally quite consistent. Most important to researchers, it has been heuristically provocative; many studies have been organized around the idea. So it has fairly strong predictive power. It is falsifiable, in that several studies have searched for agenda-setting effects and not found them, although there is some tendency for the term "agenda-setting function" to survive data that seem to falsify its prediction. On the other hand, it is a relatively narrow theory, not very useful for organizing knowledge beyond the studies specifically directed at it. Its explanatory power is limited, although it was improved by adding the "need for orientation" proviso. We know how to look operationally for agenda-setting effects, and we can recognize them clearly when they occur; but we do not know much yet about how or why they occur—or why they often do not.

This brief example illustrates how theory relates to research in communication science. There is an ongoing dialectic between the two. Initially, one scholar thought of a way of operationalizing the constructs, tested the theory, and found encouraging results. Then, as this scholar and others tried to expand on the original findings, they discovered some of its limitations and trimmed back the theory accordingly. In the absence of a theory, this research would have had little point. Even when it turns out to be incorrect in some ways, a theory is indispensable to a communication scientist trying to formulate new directions for study.

Theories of the Middle Range:
Limited Effects

Scholars sometimes lament the absence of a grand theory, such as the atomic table or evolution, in communication science. We have many specific hypotheses; but typically when many implications of a general postulate are tested, the results include quite a few falsifications. Lazarsfeld's pioneering group at Columbia University (see Delia, Chapter 2) suggested that we should be aiming instead to develop "theories of the middle range." Their idea was that specific findings from replicated studies would cumulate into empirical generalizations.

Unfortunately, communication scientists can be an impatient lot. Many broad generalizations were drawn *without the necessary replications,* on the basis of one study or perhaps a couple of studies that used very similar operationalizations. McLeod and Blumler (Chapter 9) discuss some premature conclusions about limited media effects that were advanced by the Columbia group in the 1940s and 1950s. These propositions have not stood the tests of time and replication under different operational conditions.

These theories of the middle range have not held up well partly because they were not sufficiently modest in the scope claimed for them— they might better have been labeled "upper-middle-range" theories— but perhaps more because they were seized upon for their organizing power rather than for predictive power or falsifiability. That is, the limited-effects view of media was advanced as *general knowledge* about communication, written into books (Berelson & Steiner, 1964; Klapper, 1960) and soon after into introductory textbooks. That is not the main purpose of theory for a communication scientist, who is instead looking for ideas *to guide research.* The precepts of the limited-effects model were later used to organize research presentations demonstrating their falsity. For example, Chaffee (1978) derived a series of predictions about the effects of the presidential debates of 1976 from the limited-effects model, and then showed how they had mostly been falsified by various studies. The heuristic value of this middle-range theory was considerable, even as its organizing power was being reduced.

This example illustrates the important point that the criteria for evaluating a theory are not all consistent with one another. A communication scientist must make some choices, emphasizing one criterion or another.

Early proponents of middle-range theory were anxious to demonstrate that their research was producing knowledge, and they built theories to organize what had been found to that time. When a theory is framed for that purpose, it is not being designed with falsifiability and further empirical testing in mind.

LEVELS OF COMMUNICATION ANALYSIS

As we pointed out at the beginning of this chapter, the paucity of theory in communication science is often bemoaned by its practitioners. In this section we present a pretheoretical conceptual scheme meant to help promote interrelated theory-building efforts. Communication scientists assume they can find important patterns in social behavior through observations of many similar actions. No one instance of communication, in this view, is especially important, although sometimes a single event produces significant consequences. People are rarely conscious that they are communicating and often have difficulty recalling details of their communication after the event. Everyday activities such as talking, reading road signs, or listening to the radio are not important enough for us to mark carefully in time or space so that we can later reconstruct them. The researcher faces a difficult task in imposing order upon communication because it is taken so casually by the people involved in it.

One valuable approach to ordering the study of communication is to think of several *levels of analysis* of communication events (Cushman & Craig, 1976; Wright, 1959). Part II of this book is broken down by the levels at which research is conceived and conducted. There is not total agreement within the field on the precise definitions of levels, but most of our colleagues are comfortable with a four-level breakdown.

The four levels of analysis we employ here are (1) the intraindividual level, of processes that occur within the person in relation to communication activities; (2) the interpersonal level, where communicatory relationships involving two or a slightly larger number of persons are studied; (3) the network or organizational level, where larger sets of persons are studied in the context of a set of ongoing relationships; and (4) the macroscopic societal level, where the communication properties and activities of large social systems are studied, often without immediate reference to the people in those systems.

There is more than a heuristic value in organizing our presentation of communication science in this way. These different levels tend to involve different researchers, in pursuit of different goals. Research methods vary widely across levels, as do the kinds of theories tested.

Levels of analysis should not be confused with topics of communication. Many communication scientists are drawn to their work by a concern for a specific communication function or context, such as the socialization of new members to society or the conduct of political communication. These substantive topics may be studied at several levels— and often at all four. For example, in socialization there are individual processes (learning), interpersonal (parent-child interaction), network and organizational influences (peer groups, schools, churches), and macrostructural factors (cultural influences of mass media). Each level needs to be considered for a full picture of communication in the overall process of socialization. Similarly, in political communication we find studies of opinion formation (intraindividual), family influence (interpersonal), reference groups and ethnic groups (network/organizational), and campaign broadcasting policies (macrosystemic).

Just as a research topic cuts across levels, there are generic issues and questions about communication at each level. These questions may receive different answers in the hands of researchers faced with different theoretical problems. But they must be resolved in some fashion by each researcher.

ANALYTIC AND SYNTHETIC ISSUES
FOR RESEARCH

An important function of our levels scheme is to demonstrate how general questions about communication can be asked at each level, and how questions can foster *integration* of levels. Communication scientists typically confine a research effort to one level. This means that, for example, those who study informal interactions could overlook influences of individual cognitive mechanisms or wider social networks. Their theories in turn would have only limited explanatory power.

Analytic Issues Within Levels

In this section we consider questions and issues to be dealt with at each level. These questions are general, and responses to them are considered in each level chapter of Part II.

Structural issues. "Structure" refers to ways in which units of a communication system are linked. First, what units make up the communication structure? At the individual level, the unit of analysis is often a person's behavior, belief, or cognition; at the macro level, the units might be communication institutions. The problem of specifying units at any level can be difficult. For example, some interpersonal communication researchers argue that interactions are best understood from an intraindividual cognitive perspective (Planalp & Hewes, 1982); others (Millar & Rogers, 1976), however, insist that interpersonal communication needs to be examined at the level of the "interact" rather than the individual act. Our point is that only after an investigator has settled upon a unit of analysis is it possible to specify what *linkages* exist among units.

Early theories of social cognition (Festinger, 1957; Harvey, Hunt, & Schroder, 1961; Rokeach, 1960; Schroder, Driver, & Streufert, 1967) were concerned with the ways cognitions are linked. Models of semantic memory emphasized linkages among memory nodes and how these linkages influence recall, as in Anderson and Bower's (1973) and Anderson's (1976) model of human associative memory (HAM). Models of discourse comprehension and processing also concern themselves with linkage issues (Abelson, 1981; Schank & Abelson, 1977; van Dijk, 1980; van Dijk & Kintsch, 1983).

Similar questions can be raised at the other three levels. In dyadic communication systems we can look at linkages between persons, which can have attributes such as reciprocity. Analysis of different linkage patterns is an active area of organizational communication research (Farace, Monge, & Russell, 1977; Rogers & Agarwala-Rogers, 1976). Institutions can be linked too. The broadcast networks in the United States are linked by competition with one another in the marketplace, but in mutually supportive ways in their collective opposition to public regulation. Some mass media institutions are controlled by corporate conglomerates, making it difficult for the media to be critical of capitalist institutions (Golding & Murdock, 1977).

Once linkages are specified, we can ask how *active* they are in relationship to each other. Network analysts of formal organizations focus on this variable, asking, "What units of the system are highly active information processors?" or, "What units are relative isolates?" Directional studies distinguish information "receivers" from "givers." A related issue is *complexity*. A communication system becomes more complex with more links. How does complexity influence communication in the system? What does increasing complexity do to the units? Can a system be "too complex"?

We can also consider the *organization* of a system. Are the units linked as a hierarchy? Or in a linear fashion? Many models of individual cognition and of formal organization favor a hierarchical structure. Before the 1940 voting study (Lazarsfeld, Berelson, & Gaudet, 1948), academics assumed that influential people were of higher social status than their followers. On many topics, though, "opinion leaders" are a lot like the people they influence (Katz & Lazarsfeld, 1955).

Other kinds of organization are possible too. Some cognitive psychologists argue that sometimes people process information in a relatively linear fashion, by "scripts" (Abelson, 1976, 1981; Schank & Abelson, 1977). Scripts are expectations for event sequences that people encounter repeatedly. In a restaurant, for example, we expect a series of events to unfold because the restaurant script is structured in about the same order every time. A script represents a linear-order organization principle that can occur at many levels of abstraction (Abelson, 1976). In social or institutional relations, nonhierarchical forms of organization can develop. Nations maintain elaborate formal protocols for diplomacy (and even war).

For the communication scientist, the structural organization of communication systems affects such variables as communication frequency and time, direction of influence, message content, communicator style, and who interacts with whom. These parameters may be related to the evolution of structural organization. For example, forming a task-oriented group whose members vary in communicative style can affect the power structure that evolves. Once formed, that structure influences people who later join the group. Similarly, at the individual level the structure of prior knowledge influences processing of new information; current information may in turn alter knowledge structures.

Communication goals. In the 1970s some social psychologists (especially Harré & Secord, 1973) raised philosophical issues about dominant theories and methodologies. One criticism was that social psychology is based on a mechanistic conception of behavior, as if humanity is at the mercy of powerful environmental influences that shape behavior through stimuli, reinforcements, and punishments. Harré and Secord (1973) charged that by searching for *causes* of behavior in laboratory experiments, social psychologists make the same assumptions about human actions as do radical behaviorists. They proposed instead that social behavior should be viewed as emanating from the person, as an actor capable of making choices. They contended that people specify goals in social situations and take action to achieve those goals.

Current theory in cognitive science and artificial intelligence allows for both kinds of explanations. System units, either persons or groups, do formulate and pursue goals. In some contexts, such as family communication, individual members may not have well-articulated goals, and yet the family as a unit may have goals. A number of questions can be asked within each level concerning these goals.

The "uses and gratifications" approach to mass media suggests that *individuals* may consume media content to gratify such needs as passing time, acquiring information, arousal, and companionship (Blumler & Katz, 1974; Greenberg, 1974). A person might also generate symbols in order to persuade, inform, or entertain an audience. At the level of social and group interaction, Bales (1950) suggested that communication can serve either task or socioemotional group goals. Parsons (1955) distinguished between instrumental and socioemotional goals in families. It is questionable whether persons, groups, or institutions can give adequate verbal descriptions of their goals. Norman's (1981) activation-trigger-schema (ATS) model of cognitive processes and human action argues that people may be aware of their general goals but not of the many specific subgoals that must be reached to accomplish the main goal.

Another problem is the multiplicity of goals in many situations. When individuals, groups, or institutions act, they may be pursuing several goals with a single action. Researchers on natural language processing recognize this problem in their attempts to develop computer programs that understand and produce natural language (Wilensky, 1983). The utterance, "I like you very much," might be an attempt to induce the recipient to like the person making the statement (ingratiation), or to make the recipient more receptive to future requests for favors, or both. It is difficult to design computer programs to understand such statements.

Individuals, groups, and institutions may intentionally mislead their constituents. Statements about one's communicative goals may in turn mislead the researcher. Goffman (1969) analyzed the moves and countermoves individuals and governments make to mislead observers about their true intentions. There is a considerable literature on deception in interpersonal communication (Knapp, Hart, & Dennis, 1974; Miller, de Turck, & Kalbfleisch, 1983; also see Knapp, Cody, & Reardon, Chapter 13), but the practice is certainly not limited to this level. There is evidence, for example, that television advertisements are regarded as deceptive by many people, including grade school children (Ward, Wackman, & Wartella, 1977).

Unintended effects. While communicative goals are being pursued, unanticipated effects may be produced. Such effects have been observed in public information campaigns and diffusion studies, but are not confined to these settings. A person may produce messages for one purpose only to find that they have also produced outcomes that were both unanticipated and undesired. Unintended effects can also occur at the group and organizational levels. Communication scientists are especially attentive to "side-effects" or "latent functions" of communication.

Unintended effects can occur simply because the creator of a message is unaware of the usual effects it might have. An example is television violence, which has the primary purpose of attracting large audiences but can also have the unintended effect of stimulating aggressive behavior (National Institute of Mental Health, 1982). Or, a non-native speaker of English might utter a statement in a way that produces a humorous or angry response. The receiver's noncompliance may stem from the foreign speaker's lack of knowledge about appropriate communication. For example, an employee does not "give orders" to the boss.

A second source of unintended effects is unanticipated contingencies in the communication episode. During a conversation, a person may disclose information related to other issues so that the emotional tone of the conversation changes quickly. For example, two interactants may intend an amiable conversation, but end up in an argument due to sensitive comments. Information from mass media is especially prone to unintended effects; once a message is sent via the media, it is difficult to "take it back." In face-to-face encounters, retractions can often prevent major damage.

Predispositions of message receivers can also cause unintended effects. While a given communicator may know what is appropriate to say in a situation, individual differences in the audience may interact with incoming messages in unforeseen ways. In persuasion, influence agents may overgeneralize about their audiences, imagining for example that they are more (or less) hostile than they actually are. Often people in everyday interactions are surprised to find that others disagree (or agree) with them on an issue.

Unintended effects are not always "bad," of course. Sometimes people who initially interact to solve a problem become close friends. Influence agents might not only persuade their audiences, they may inform and entertain them as well. However, unintended effects are probably negative as often as not. People who influence others may also induce those others to dislike them, for example.

Processing capacity. Miller (1956) noted that humans are limited to the perception of about seven ("plus or minus two") items at one time, which he took to be an individual's maximum information processing capacity. This work spawned an enduring interest among experimental psychologists in information processing. Individuals can process only a fraction of the information available in a given situation; they rely on internal knowledge structures to help "fill in the gaps" due to these limitations. Taylor and Fiske (1978) demonstrated how judgments can be inordinately affected by a salient stimulus in the environment. Target persons who are made more salient than other group members are judged by observers to be most influential in the group, even when their contributions do not exceed those of the other members. People erroneously "recall" actions from stereotyped sequences they have observed, although the recalled action did not actually occur. What is being accessed is the scripted expectation that the action should have occurred, not the action itself (Bower, Black, & Turner, 1979). Nisbett and Ross (1980) and Kahneman, Slovic, and Tversky (1982) have documented several biases among people making judgments about others. These biases arise, in part, because of various "heuristics" we use to overcome our inability to process all relevant information.

Communication scientists have developed some evidence on limitations of social systems. Allport and Postman's (1947) classic studies of rumor transmission concluded that messages sent in sequence through a communication system become distorted. Bartlett's (1932) demonstrations of memory distortion in serial transmission suggests memory limitations are a primary cause. But later authors (e.g., Shibutani, 1966) questioned the serial nature of rumor transmission, asserting that rumors are frequently generated by groups trying to construct an explanation for events they cannot otherwise explain. He argues that when people do not get adequate information from the mass media about causes of various events, they will concoct a plausible explanation. Rumors arise, in this view, not because an original story gets distorted as it passes from person to person, but because people combine their individual explanations to form an overall story. Coleman (1957) notes the limits of the media, when rumor and slander circulate rapidly during a community controversy. The information-processing limitations of organizations and institutions have also been studied (March & Simon, 1958).

New technologies. Communication scientists are highly alert to the introduction of new communication technologies, which have major impact on the capacities of communication systems to process large amounts of information. Widespread use of computers in institutional, organizational, and individual settings expands the abilities of these systems to process, store, and retrieve messages. Current emphasis in discussions of computer technologies is on the *quantity* of information that can be handled. Less attention has been paid to the issue of information *quality* (Lester, 1981). Similarly, promoters of cable television stress the number of channels available rather than programming quality.

Some communication scientists become so enamored with the quantitative aspects of new technologies that they overlook more important questions connected with their widespread adoption. There is not much healthy skepticism concerning the future impact of these technologies. For example, advertising for home computers emphasizes that tasks such as balancing a checkbook and finding recipes and telephone numbers can be facilitated by home computers. But these mundane tasks can usually be handled faster, more easily, and more economically using what might in reaction be called "low technology" (e.g., pocket calculators, index cards). The home computer may still be a technology in search of uses (and gratifications) for most consumers, despite the enthusiasm of some academics.

The expanding memory capacity of computers raises issues of individual and institutional privacy. With the increased use of computers by government and commercial agencies, many groups have become concerned about the kinds of information the government collects, security of stored information, and possible invasive uses. Instances of home computers being used to "break in" to data storage systems raise issues about the status of information stored in government, hospital, and business computers. As personal use of computers expands *beyond* playing computer games, which was the main early use of home computers

(Rogers, 1986), problems of social management proliferate. So do negative societal side-effects that stem from socioeconomic inequalities.

System constraints. At each level of analysis there are other constraints on communication systems that limit their capacities to achieve certain goals. At the individual level, the way human sense organs are arrayed determines how well people can adapt to changes in their environments. Because our eyes are set the way they are and because we do not have a very well-developed ability to localize sound (i.e., to determine its direction), it is difficult for us to respond in a discriminating manner to events that occur behind us. People can make considerably finer adjustments in their actions when stimuli are within their view and when both the eyes and the ears can help to locate things.

At the dyadic and social network levels, there are additional constraints too. People meeting for the first time are expected to converse in pleasant ways rather than unpleasant ones. In dating relationships, individuals may be especially careful to observe norms of politeness and social appropriateness in order to make themselves attractive. Conformity to these conventions can prevent people from knowing one another as *individuals* (Jones & Davis, 1965). One of the few things conformity tells an observer is that the person is like many others; it thus prevents leakage of information that might give one insight into the other's personality. Social norms and rules may make interactions in public places more congenial, but these interactions may be vacuous when it comes to learning about the people in them.

A similar problem occurs in the context of interactions in formal organizations. When people perform organizational roles, those roles may be functional for task accomplishment but dysfunctional for emotional satisfaction or the development of friendships. This is a problem if people expect work not only to provide them with material rewards but with socioemotional rewards as well. The same difficulties occur in interactions between parents and children; parental role demands (e.g., supervision, training) may preclude the parents from some behaviors (e.g., play) they might want to share.

At the level of social institutions there is at least one rather glaring institutional constraint that makes achievement of goals difficult. The American public has demanded progressively more services from government at all levels. Various sectors of the public have looked to government to solve social problems concerned with education, health care, poverty, and the like. But even with massive infusions of tax money, government cannot ameliorate many of these problems. Most likely, the government could not solve these problems no matter how much money it has. It is not so much a matter of size ("big government") as it is the organizational structure of government agencies and the "top-down" problem-solving approach it fosters. Perhaps a structure that encourages a "bottom-up" approach to problem solving would be more satisfying. It has been noted that government authorities who live in the environs of Washington, D.C., have little awareness of issues confronting other social classes and regions of the country. Some communication scientists think this isolation might be remedied by strategic use of new communication technologies, which could enable more people to have direct access to political elites (e.g., Siune & Kline, 1975).

System change. Natural communication systems evolve over time, but some changes are more rapid and dramatic than others. Human anatomy might very gradually evolve so that the eyes would be repositioned to increase the width of the visual field, or the internal structure of the eye might be altered. But technologies could much more quickly be developed to compensate people for evolutionary shortcomings. Examples include optical instruments that allow people to see for long distances in the dark, or devices to project voices far away (amplifiers).

In contrast to the slow pace of human anatomy and physiological evolution are the sometimes rather rapid changes in people's beliefs, attitudes, and behaviors. One of the most extensively researched areas in communication has been persuasion. The early genres of persuasion research were cast at the individual level; almost all the studies viewed influence as a one-way process in which a source induced change in individual audience members. It has become apparent to communication scientists that persuasion can be more fruitfully studied in the context of interpersonal influence. Most probably, a majority of persuasive attempts occur in situations where the person being influenced can resist the influence and try to exert counterinfluence. While the early persuasion research paradigms concerned themselves with resistance issues, little attention was paid to counterinfluence. Investigators of communication at the relational level (Ericson & Rogers, 1973; Millar & Rogers, 1976) have explicitly incorporated counterinfluence into their coding schemes.

Despite considerable interest in effects of organizational and institutional changes on productivity and satisfaction, little attention has been paid to organizational and institutional change itself. Like individuals, large formal social entities undergo both evolutionary and revolutionary changes. Some are purposely induced and some are unintentional. Communication scientists seek to find conditions that produce these changes. That is, what variables are responsible for producing change and what conditions trigger these causal variables? We also need to understand how and why changes are *resisted* by individuals, groups, organizations and institutions. System goal conflicts are important to change and resistance, but information-processing capacity, constraints, and structure are also involved.

Outcome evaluation issues. A critical issue in public communication is "communication effectiveness." Whether one is concerned with the individual or the institutional level, communication practitioners are deeply concerned with promoting effective communication. This notion is variously offered as a panacea for marital problems, voter apathy, and corporate image difficulties. Criteria of effectiveness obviously vary with these different situations. Effects sought in communication may be to inform, to persuade, to be liked, to resolve a dispute, and so forth. A journalist or teacher may be "effective" if their efforts are informative, while a salesperson must sell, a mediator must resolve disputes, and a public health campaign must reduce morbidity and mortality. Most organized communication programs are undertaken to achieve many proximal, intervening, and ultimate mission-determined goals (see Rogers & Storey, Chapter 26). Evaluation research, the measurement of communication effectiveness, usually involves matching the criterion measures to this complex set of pragmatic goals. Communication scientists often shy away from these "mundane" questions. But this attitude may be doing their research enterprise a disservice in the name of intellectual purity. There are many examples of healthy collaborations between "pure" physical sciences and engineering. Communication science has yet to develop an identifiable cadre of "communication engineers," but mission-oriented agencies see communication problems at the root of many social evils and seek solutions.

Who should be the judge of communication effectiveness? Some argue that judgments of communication experts or critics should be employed, rather than the impact a communication has on its audience. In this view, the message and its presentation would be judged effective or not on its own merits. The alternative view, which is shared by most communication scientists, is that communication should be evaluated in terms of goal achievement. Messages that accomplish their goals are effective; those that do not are ineffective. Most people appear to understand the importance of effective communication; perhaps what the public does not understand are the conceptual complexities that arise when effectiveness indicators are examined critically. It is a responsibility of communication scientists to analyze these complexities and develop theories and research programs that examine them in detail.

Designing communication systems. Given that communication systems have goals, can systems be designed to assure that their goals will be realized in an efficient manner? We noted earlier individuals often process information in ways that produce judgmental biases. Nisbett and Ross (1980) suggest that one way to ameliorate these information processing deficits is to train people in statistical inference. (Unfortunately, elsewhere in their book they cite evidence that persons with extensive training in statistics are almost as likely as naive subjects to make inferential errors.)

At the interpersonal level, there is some interest in redesigning various kinds of relational arrangements. The 1970s saw considerable attention to redefinition of marriage arrangements (O'Neill & O'Neill, 1972) and gender relationships. Kramarae (1981) argues that because males were primarily responsible for development of language, most languages contain biases that prevent females from expressing themselves as they wish. Some minor linguistic changes have been effected, but languages are notoriously resistant to significant change.

Organizations have a longstanding concern for design of "optimal" communication systems to achieve goals. In businesses, the profit motive has a lot to do with this interest, but it is also true that effectiveness criteria are less ambiguous in organizations than at the individual or interpersonal levels. McClelland (1961), in his work on achievement motivation, pointed out that money earned is a rather unambiguous index of success, whereas emotional outcomes of interpersonal relationships are considerably more difficult to evaluate.

There has been some interest in redesigning certain institutions to optimize their performance. Proposals for reorganization of the federal government are often made, and there has been significant change in religious institutions because of decreases in church membership across many denominations. But threat of extinction may be necessary before some institutions will initiate internal modification. In any event, communication scientists are often involved in redesign of communication systems at all levels.

Synthetic Issues Among Levels

Our previous discussion has dealt with questions *within* each level of analysis; we now consider relationships *between and among* levels. We are *not* advocating a reductionist position that argues for the explanatory primacy of any one level of analysis. For example, we would reject the position that all other levels can ultimately be explained by individual cognitive processes or, at the other extreme, by social structure. But in some instances one level may offer a better explanation of a communication phenomenon than does another level. Research at one level is sometimes more satisfactorily explained by theory at another level.

Interlevel effects. A number of questions can be raised regarding interlevel effects. For example, we can ask how interactions between individuals and institutions influence individuals' cognitive development, as in Newcomb's (1947) classic Bennington College study. Research has demonstrated how individual attitudes and cognition can be changed by different organizational milieux (Lieberman, 1956). Large formal organizations consist of interrelated smaller work groups, and these smaller units have an impact upon the entire organization; in turn, organizationwide actions influence each group.

For many of the phenomena communication scientists study, events at one level of analysis may be at least partially explained by recourse to events at another level of analysis. But at this point in the history of communication science it is difficult to say that any one level is most likely to provide satisfying explanations. Our more modest hope is that communication scientists will become sensitive to the influences that phenomena at each level can exert.

Transcendent principles. Finally, let us consider the search for principles that operate in a similar fashion across all levels. This kind of "horizontal" integration of levels is akin to the basic objective of general systems theory (GST; von Bertalanffy, 1968). While the vocabulary of systems has made a strong impact upon communication science (e.g., Monge, 1973, 1977), actual implementations of systems approaches are rare. The systems approach has been at most a stimulating metaphor.

This does not, however, mean that the global objective of GST is not a reasonable one to pursue in communication science. We could well explore such questions as, Are there similarities between the ways individual cognitive systems are organized and the structure of formal organizations? Both models of human cognition and models of formal organization stress that superordinate units exert influence over subordinate units. Given this isomorphism, do the systems operate in any similar ways? Rokeach (1960) discusses the organization of belief systems that are open to discrepant information from the environment and those which are less permeable. We should expect to find structural parallels between the openness of belief systems and the openness of groups, organizations, and institutions to outside information.

It is most unlikely that we could find a communication scientist who would undertake to test such a relationship across all four levels. Moreover, given the current structure of communication science, even if individual researchers were investigating our hypothesized relationship at each level, they would probably be unaware of one another's research efforts, or would not recognize the similarities. We have in the later sections of this chapter shifted somewhat from describing what communication scientists do to discussing what we feel they ought to do in order to advance the discipline. We have continually stressed the different levels because few communication scientists are used to thinking across levels. There may indeed be principles that transcend our analytic levels, and which have already been verified by research. But the relative isolation of research literatures may prevent us from discerning these transcendent generalizations.

CONCLUSION

We have addressed a number of issues surrounding the conduct of communication research and the building of communication theory. Not all communication scientists will subscribe to the assumptions we have presented, the issues we have raised, or our blandishments to consider multiple levels of analysis. The concept of communication science is not yet an established, operating reality. We have noted many more discontinuities between levels of analysis than commonalities. Still, we have been able to locate and describe the heart of what appears to be an emergent, unified discipline. In addition to a central core of assumptions and issues, a field of study must also have its outer boundaries. Not all communication phenomena are studied by scientific methods. Our purpose here has been to outline the work of those who are within the scientific tradition.

REFERENCES

Abelson, R. P. (1976). Script processing in attitude formation and decision making. In J. S. Carroll & J. W. Payne (Eds.), *Cognition and social behavior*. Hillsdale, NJ: Lawrence Erlbaum.

Abelson, R. P. (1981). Psychological status of the script concept. *American Psychologist, 36*, 715-729.

Allport, G. W., & Postman, L. J. (1947). *The psychology of rumor*. New York: Henry Holt.

Anderson, J. R. (1976). *Language, memory, and thought*. Hillsdale, NJ: Lawrence Erlbaum.

Anderson, J. R., & Bower, G. H. (1973). *Human associative memory*. Washington, DC: V. H. Winston.

Bales, R. F. (1950). *Interaction process analysis*. Reading, MA: Addison-Wesley.

Bartlett, F. C. (1932). *Remembering: A study in experimental and social psychology*. Cambridge: Cambridge University Press.

Becker, L., & Doolittle, J. (1975). How repetition affects evaluations of and information seeking about candidates. *Journalism Quarterly, 52*, 611-617.

Berger, C. R. (1977). The covering law perspective as a theoretical basis for the study of human communication. *Communication Quarterly, 25*, 7-18.

Berelson, B. R., & Steiner, G. A. (1964). *Human behavior*. Orlando, FL: Harcourt Brace Jovanovich.

von Bertalanffy, L. (1968). *General systems theory*. New York: Braziller.

Blalock, H. M. (1984). *Conceptualization and measurement in the social sciences*. Newbury Park, CA: Sage.

Blumler, J. G., & Katz, E. (1974). *The uses of mass communications*. Newbury Park, CA: Sage.

Bower, G. H., Black, J. B., & Turner, T. J. (1979). Scripts in memory for text. *Cognitive Psychology, 11*, 177-220.

Chaffee, S. H. (1971). Television and adolescent aggressiveness (overview). In G. Comstock & E. Rubinstein (Eds.), *Television and social behavior: Vol. III, Tele-*

vision and adolescent aggressiveness (pp. 1-34). Washington, DC: Government Printing Office.

Chaffee, S. H. (1978). Presidential debates—are they helpful to voters? *Communication Monographs, 49,* 330-346.

Cohen, B. (1963). *The press and foreign policy.* Princeton, NJ: Princeton University Press.

Coleman, J. (1957). *Community conflict.* New York: Free Press.

Cushman, D. P. (1977). The rules perspective as a theoretical basis for the study of human communication. *Communication Quarterly, 25,* 30-45.

Cushman, D. P. & Craig, R. T. (1976). Communication systems: Interpersonal implications. In G. R. Miller (Ed.), *Explorations in interpersonal communication.* Newbury Park, CA: Sage.

Ericson, P. M., & Rogers, L. E. (1973). New procedures for analyzing relational communication. *Family Process, 12,* 245-267.

Farace, R. V., Monge, P. R., & Russell, H. M. (1977). *Communicating and organizing.* Reading, MA: Addison-Wesley.

Festinger, L. (1957). *A theory of cognitive dissonance.* Stanford, CA: Stanford University Press.

Goffman, E. (1969). *Strategic interaction.* Philadelphia: University of Pennsylvania Press.

Golding, P., & Murdock, G. (1977). Theories of communication and theories of society. *Communication Research, 5,* 339-356.

Greenberg, B. S. (1974). Gratifications of television viewing and their correlates for British children. In J. G. Blumler & E. Katz (Eds.), *The uses of mass communications.* Newbury Park, CA: Sage.

Harre, R., & Secord, P. F. (1973). *The explanation of social behavior.* Totowa, NJ: Littlefield, Adams & Co.

Harvey, O. J., Hunt, D. E., & Schroder, H. M. (1961). *Conceptual systems and personality organization.* New York: John Wiley.

Hempel, C. G. (1965). *Aspects of scientific explanation.* New York: Free Press.

Iyengar, S., Peters, M., & Kinder, D. (1982). Experimental demonstrations of the "not so minimal" consequences of television news programs. *American Political Science Review, 76,* 848-858.

Jones, E. E., & Davis, K. E. (1965). From acts to dispositions: The attribution process in person perception. In L. Berkowitz (Ed.), *Advances in experimental social psychology* (Vol. 2, pp. 219-266). New York: Academic.

Kahneman, D., Slovic, P., & Tversky, A. (1982). *Judgment under uncertainty: Heuristics and biases.* Cambridge: Cambridge University Press.

Katz, E., & Lazarsfeld, P. F. (1955). *Personal influence.* New York: Free Press.

Klapper, J. T. (1960). *The effects of mass communication.* New York: Free Press.

Knapp, M. L., Hart, R. P., & Dennis, H. S. (1974). An exploration of deception as a communication construct. *Human Communication Research, 1,* 15-29.

Kramarae, C. (1981). *Women and men speaking.* Rowley, MA: Newbury House.

Lazarsfeld, P. F., Berelson, B., & Gaudet, H. (1948). *The people's choice.* New York: Columbia University Press.

Lester, R. E. (1981, February). *Embedding network constructs in a theoretical framework: A preliminary formulation of a model of intraorganizational communication behavior.* Paper presented at the Western Speech Communication Association, San Jose, CA.

Lieberman, S. (1956). The effects of changes in roles on the attitudes of role occupants. *Human Relations, 9,* 385-402.

March, J. G., & Simon, H. A. (1958). *Organizations.* New York, Wiley.

McClelland, D. C. (1961). *The achieving society.* New York: Van Nostrand.

McCombs, M., & Shaw, D. (1972). The agenda-setting function of mass media. *Public Opinion Quarterly, 36,* 176-187.

McLeod, J., Becker, L., & Byrnes, J. (1974). Another look at the agenda-setting function of the press. *Communication Research, 1,* 131-166.

Millar, F. E., & Rogers, E. (1976). A relational approach to interpersonal communication. In G.R. Miller (Ed.), *Explorations in interpersonal communication.* Newbury Park, CA: Sage.

Miller, G. A. (1956). The magical number seven plus or minus two. *Psychological Review, 63,* 81-97.

Miller, G. R., deTurck, M. A., & Kalbfleisch, P. J. (1983). Self-monitoring, rehearsal, and deceptive communication. *Human Communication Research, 10,* 97-117.

Monge, P. R. (1973). Theory construction in the study of communication: The system paradigm. *Journal of Communication, 23,* 5-16.

Monge, P. R. (1977). The systems perspective as a theoretical basis for the study of human communication. *Communication Quarterly, 25,* 19-29.

National Institute of Mental Health. (1982). *Television and behavior: Ten years of scientific progress and implications for the Eighties.* Rockville, MD: National Institute of Mental Health.

Newcomb, T. M. (1947). Some patterned consequences of membership in a college community. In T. M. Newcomb, E. L. Hartley, et al. (Eds.), *Readings in social psychology* (pp. 345-357). New York: Henry Holt.

Nisbett, R., & Ross, L. (1980). *Human inferences: Strategies and shortcomings of social judgment.* Englewood Cliffs, NJ: Prentice-Hall.

Norman, D. A. (1981). Categorization of action slips. *Psychological Review, 88,* 1-15.

O'Neill, N., & O'Neill, G. (1972). *Open marriage: A new life style for couples.* Philadelphia: Lippincott.

Palmgreen, P., & Clarke, P. (1977). Agenda-setting with local and national issues. *Communication Research, 4,* 435-452.

Parsons, T. (1955). Family structure and the socialization of the child. In T. Parsons & R. F. Bales, *Family, socialization and interaction processes.* New York: Free Press.

Planalp, S., & Hewes, D. (1982). A cognitive approach to communication theory: Cogito ergo dico? In M. Burgoon (Ed.), *Communication yearbook 5.* New Brunswick, NJ: Transaction Press.

Popper,K.R. (1963). *Conjectures and refutations: The growth of scientific knowledge.* London: Routledge & Kegan Paul.

Rokeach, M. (1960). *The open and closed mind.* New York: Basic Books.

Rogers, E. M. (1986). *Communication technology: The new media in society.* New York: Free Press.

Rogers, E. M., & Agarwala-Rogers, R. (1976). *Communication in organizations.* New York: Free Press.

Schank, R. C., & Abelson, R. P. (1977). *Scripts, plans, goals and understanding.* Hillsdale, NJ: Lawrence Erlbaum.

Schroder, H. M., Driver, M. J., & Streufert, S. (1967). *Human information processing.* New York: Holt, Rinehart & Winston.

Shibutani, T. (1966). *Improvised news: A sociological study of rumor.* New York: Bobbs-Merrill.

Siune, K., & Kline, F. G. (1975). Communication, mass political behavior, and mass society. In S. Chaffee (Ed.), *Political communication* (pp. 65-84). Newbury Park, CA: Sage.

Taylor, S. E., & Fiske, S. T. (1978). Salience, attention, and attribution: Top of the head phenomena. In L. Berkowitz (Ed.), *Advances in experimental social psychology* (Vol. 11, pp. 249-288). New York: Academic Press.

van Dijk, T. A. (1980). *Macrostructures.* Hillsdale, NJ: Lawrence Erlbaum.

van Dijk, T. A., & Kintsch, W. (1983). *Strategies of discourse comprehension.* New York: Academic Press.

Ward, S., Wackman, D., & Wartella, E. (1977). *How children learn to buy.* Newbury Park, CA: Sage.

Weaver, D. (1977). Political issues and voters' need for orientation. In D. Shaw & M. McCombs (Eds.), *The emergence of American political issues.* St. Paul, MN: West.

Webb, E. J., Campbell, D. T., Schwartz, R. D., & Sechrest, L. (1966). *Unobtrusive measures: Nonreactive research in the social sciences.* Chicago, IL: Rand McNally.

Wilensky, R. (1983). *Planning and understanding: A computational approach to human reasoning.* Reading, MA: Addison-Wesley.

Wright, C. (1959). *Mass communication: A sociological perspective.* New York: Random House.

4 Beyond Science: Humanities Contributions to Communication Theory

THOMAS B. FARRELL
Northwestern University

T HE phrase "beyond science" should be understood in a nontranscendental sense. There is no doubt a version of the term "science," as it was employed by Hegel and Vico, in which we can never be "beyond" science so long as we are engaged in some aspect of knowing. While I endorse this larger usage, that is not the way the term is employed here. It is my challenge to address scholarly work that brings special competencies to the study of communication—competencies that are not "scientific" in the usual empirical sense of that term. Perhaps it is one sign of advancement in the study of communication that increasing specialization and reflective speculation can exist side by side. Even if aesthetic, historical, and philosophical inquiries into communication practice never quite yield the empirical confirmation that "normal" science has sought, there is some agreement that nonscientific approaches still admit to tests of rigor, insight, and heuristic value that might benefit the discipline generally.

Some additional qualifiers may help clarify the intent of this chapter. First, I will argue that theory in human communication is a sufficiently underdeveloped enterprise as to require the concerned reflection of communication scholars from many different perspectives. But this does *not* imply that scientific theory may properly be debunked on purely aesthetic or political grounds alone, any more than a criticism of communication may be cast aside as unscientific. The price of intradisciplinary detente has been to grant that standards of adequacy, while communicable across perspectives, are—at least for now—incommensurable. Second, the categories I will use for interpretation are designed to distinguish among certain levels of analysis in the *nonscientific* study of communication. They are not intended to be exhaustive; there are no doubt many nonscientific approaches to this topic that are outside my range of familiarity. Third, I am not a scientist; this means that actual ranges of application to scientific research must be confined to a layperson's intuitions.

I will be confining my attention to touchstone studies that either typify a perspective or break new ground. The works discussed here should invite closer attention to the many worthy studies that have been left out.

At least three large clusters of research type offer important alternative perspectives to social science scholarship in communication. These include *philosophical* approaches, which would ground or extend understanding of some critical feature of communication through an identifiable school of thought. There are also *aesthetic-allegorical* approaches. Here we may find the closest fit to actual communicative form: how the process works. Suppositions about structure, explanation, and performance are guided by traditions of taste and judgment. Theory in this area is rich with implications for scientists as well as aestheticians. Finally, there are *interpretative and critical* approaches, in which the experience of communication, as discourse and text, tends to be framed, recreated, and qualified in light of certain derived or invented norms. There is a great deal of literature here, of highly variable quality. For the most part, this chapter will focus on work from the first category (i.e., philosophical approaches) that clearly intersects with investigations on other conceptual levels of analysis.

How is this work best evaluated? In keeping with the enlightened pluralism discussed earlier, I would dismiss out of hand the supposition that it *cannot* be evaluated. We invoke nonempirical standards of gradation all the time when it comes to our scholarly enterprises. When a would-be scholar's research program is confronted with the question "Why?" more than once, it is probably time to return to the drawing board. Among the standards we might wish to consider are the following:

(1) Analytic consistency: Does the work derive from a consistently formulated theoretical position?

(2) Methodological rigor: Is the method of investigation formulated precisely, and applied carefully? Could others employing the method find approximately the same things?

(3) Intuitive credibility: This standard addresses the pertinence of humanistic research to actual communicative practice. The issue is whether there might ever be sufficient discrepancy between research formulations and actual practice as to require revising the formulations.

(4) Heuristic value: Here we would be concerned with the generalizable implications of research for a host of other inquiries, scientific and otherwise. It is not usually the aim of humanities research in communication to formulate comprehensive laws or universal principles. Still, such research should at least allow for some additive insight about the object of study. But the best answers to this last question must come from others.

CONCEPTUALIZING COMMUNICATION
NONSCIENTIFICALLY

There is a stage in experimental research where the investigator is instructed to "operationalize" the constructs, so that these might be tested in a controlled setting. We all know that when constructs are reduced to empirical components other nonempirical features of their definition are set aside. It is difficult to determine whether the end result, in each case, is an improvement (rigor triumphing over fuzzy thinking) or a corruption (ideas replaced by things). One justification for a broad nonempirical construal of communication is that it might allow us to attend more closely to this definitional process, to see what is gained and lost in the search for empirical grounding.

Central to my own approach is the idea that human communication is simultaneously a *process* and a *practice*. It is, as the old saw goes, the transformation of matter into energy with symbolic significance. It is something that happens involuntarily, and something that we do, with malice and wisdom aforethought. This double aspect of communication becomes apparent whenever we are reminded of something we habitually do in conversation or in public settings (e.g., play with our tie, punctuate utterances with some familiar verbal crutch). When these things are drawn to our attention, we are likely to react with embarrassment or annoyance. Here is something we should be able to control and monitor, but have not. And now we are on our guard, anticipating and screening our every thought, until the habit is purged. In this example, communication has never abandoned its status as a process; but through the phenomenon of self-reflection, we are able to attend to aspects of the process as a form of conduct.

From the perspective I am sketching, it would be pointless to consider one side of this vision to be more advanced or sophisticated than the other. To the extent that interests are reflected in all forms of inquiry, there is bound to be some strain between method and object of study where communication is concerned. Since communication is something that all of us, in practical experience, *do,* we will always be actors and spectators simultaneously. If certain aspects of our communicative behavior are open to the explanations afforded by lawlike regularities, higher-order communicative skills are only acquired through the mastery of rules and pragmatic competencies. Certain broader interpersonal and even cultural communication patterns may ultimately reduce to constructs localized in intrapersonal, perhaps physiological components. But equally sound is the intuition that there is an emergent dimension of communicative meaning—a dimension that may contextualize the most idiosyncratic behavioral traits, that could be larger than the sum of its parts. To hold communication accountable as a *process* is to subscribe to generalizable standards for adequacy of explanation in the scientific community. To hold communication accountable as a *practice* is to ask equally pertinent questions about the fidelity, reliability, and quality of what we are saying.

Since we are actors and spectators at the same time, there will always be a reflective domain of our own communication practice that will be—in principle—outside our purview of explanation. This reflective domain involves our own communicative performances as scientists and scholars. This is one of the things Weimer (1977) and Campbell (1975) are up to when they analyze rhetorical characteristics of the scientific enterprise. More "radical" versions of the same approach (Cohen, 1972; Gouldner, 1973; Weimer, 1983) announce that *all* scholarly investigations of any kind ("pure" science, social science, whatever), involve certain language-bound aspects of subjectivity in their very attempt to establish foundations and first principles, select objects of study, and so forth. When practicing scientists are met with this allegation, however, their usual response is, "Yes, that is correct . . . and now, what were we talking about?"

The response is one with which I sympathize. While it may be helpful to remind ourselves that we are, after all, choosing to look at things a certain way when we do science (or art, for that matter), this revelation is far from a conclusive debunking of the enterprise. All that is learned is that science is itself a practice that often finds it most useful to look at things a certain way, to bracket the practical aspects of its subject, to treat communication—in short—as a process. To that extent, the science of communication commits to the paradox of employing technical means and interests to study a social subject. Communication science is therefore a line of inquiry that will always be leaving something out. Rigor and regularity of explanation, the "view from nowhere" described by Nagel (1986), is always obtained at a price: that we are, in actuality, somewhere doing something all the while. We need to be reminded of this fact every now and again, but once reminded there is not much more to be said. The contributions of science to our understanding of communication need no further defense from me. And once we have realized that communication will always have aspects that elude full scientific elucidation, perhaps the momentous implications of this fact may be set aside in favor of asking our central question: How may nonscientific research paradigms help to enrich and deepen our overall picture of communication?

THE MAIN APPROACHES

The primary category of research that is useful to my own overview includes what I would call philosophical approaches. Since Western philosophy traces its modern origin to a sense of "dialogue," the philosophical investigation of communication would seem a natural union of method and object. However, the term "philosophy" these days is no clearer a mark of commonality than is the nomenclature of our own discipline. Not only is there the much-discussed cognitivity paradox concerning what philosophy itself is *about,* there is also the tendency of philosophers themselves to announce, with something akin to exhilaration, the "end of philosophy." Whatever branches and tributaries of the humanities remain are, if anything, further from a language of discussion than before. To expect approaches such as these to enrich our subject, then, requires that we look beyond what they actually do and reflect somewhat on what they say.

The general areas that seem most fruitful to our overview are hermeneutics and phenomenology, semiotics and structuralism, Marxism and social theory, and nonrational philosophy (or deconstruction). Bluntly put, what most of these approaches *do* is to establish certain foundational principles (or postulates) about communication on more or less a priori grounds, and then jump directly to one of the several levels of analysis overviewed in this volume. The level of analysis (whether intra-, inter-, network, or system structure) is then interpreted or read almost entirely through the lens afforded by the postulates. Through such an inference practice, philosophies of communication are able to appear internally consistent to fellow adherents, but more or less unintelligible not only to communication scientists but to other philosophies of communication. This, at any rate, is what they do. What they say is something else again.

HERMENEUTICS AND PHENOMENOLOGY

While not technically the same thing, both hermeneutics and phenomenology offer themselves as interpretive methods designed to expand upon the ways in which any object of inquiry comes to acquire meaning. From this deceptively simple beginning, however, come a host of differing lines of development and "doctrines" for each root method. From classical to religious to ontological to critical hermeneutics; from radical empirical to transcendental to Heideggerian phenomenology to whatever is left thereafter. (This is not the place for a whirlwind tour.) It is worth noting first that both hermeneutics and phenomenology have fastened upon some aspects of communication as primary objects or illustrations of their philosophical quest. Second, while it may not always seem to be worth the price of understanding, both branches of inquiry have something important to say to the scientific study of communication.

A perceptive essay by Sloan (1971) traced the origin of the concept of hermeneutics from Biblical scholarship to what he had hoped would be a prominent place in the interpretation of literature. Since that ground-breaking essay scholars in a variety of disciplines have found hermeneutics to provide a particularly useful means for highlighting neglected features of communication. Specifically, hermeneutics draws our attention to the problem of meaning as two or more actors leave the subjectivity of self to encounter the "worlds" of another. Gadamer's monumental *Truth and Method* (1975) initiated this line of influence by applying the metaphor of conversation to the interpretation of literature. His correlate had more interest, however, for students of the neglected art of conversation. Among Gadamer's insights about conversation was that we are "less the leaders of it than the led," that conversation is not something that we plan, but rather something that we "fall into." What Gadamer is after, it seems, is a theory of critical interpretation that is not cut short by the use of judgment as an arbitrary instrument. In at least three respects, Gadamer's paradigm of conversation may be valuable to interested communication scientists:

(1) His notion of "text" is communicative in ways that may help enrich our concepts of message analysis.
(2) He allows for the possibility of an agent-centered theory of communication, without presupposing that the stages of communication are all tactically controlled.
(3) He does not rule out any contextual layer of meaning, as a possible dimension of understanding (Gadamer, 1976).

This much having been said, Gadamer's intent and method are surely alien to the traditional social science precepts of prediction and control. Also, this formidable contemporary thinker has a disconcerting habit of presenting what theorists of social cognition regard as active attribution processes in the passive voice. So, we "are led," meaning "speaks itself through us," and so forth. Ultimately, Gadamer begins with some foundational principles of communication and *is led* to the destination he had in mind all along: the comforting refuge of contemplative aesthetics. For rhetoricians, the book on Gadamer is too easily closed. What he finds comforting in the real setting of interactants, others may find unsettling and unfinished. For all the difficulties of application, or perhaps because of them, the work of Gadamer remains a distinctive "counter-statement" to the intrapersonal and public domains of communication.

Schutz (1964) brings a more practical marriage of interpretative hermeneutics and phenomenology to the world of communication practice. In a wide-ranging series of studies using classic literature, pragmatic philosophy, and social research, Schutz helped make a critical transition from the interpretive domain of the individual to the interpersonal and social aspects of knowledge. While many of Schutz's studies seem to be framed according to "social types" (the "stranger," the "well-informed citizen," the "homecomer"), these types really coalesce as recurring problems of communication. Moreover, Schutz brings to his subjects a wealth of insight that may be applicable to the current interest in patterns of relational development, friendship networks, and even political communication.

A host of contemporary scholars have reasserted the importance of hermeneutics and phenomenology to the understanding of communication practice: Apel's "The A'Priori of Communication" (1972), Edie's *Speaking and Meaning* (1976), Ricoeur's studies of interpretation, textuality, time, and action (1974, 1976, 1977, 1984, 1985), and Schrag's *Communicative Praxis and the Space of Subjectivity* (1985). These works raise fascinating questions about the meaning and comprehension of communication practice. There is, of course, an understandable bias throughout much of this literature toward the subjective *intra*personal domain of communication. But since a great many constructs and variables in the scientific study of communication are derived from this same intrapersonal realm, this bias should not reduce the literature's value to communication research.

Much of the best scholarship employs its own heuristic test of phenomenological and hermeneutic sources. Hyde and Smith's "Hermeneutics and Rhetoric: A Seen But Unobserved Relationship" (1979) documents the influence of Heideggerian phenomenology upon the whole problem of creating and discovering "meaning" in communication texts. Hyde's work with the study of anxiety (1980) and recent problems in communication technology (Hyde, 1982) offer powerful heuristic examples of how philosophical method may enrich construct definition in communication science. Stewart's (1981) work in the study of dialogic communication owes much to a variety of phenomenological influences, and yet manages to be compatible with a range of practicing social sciences. The extensive research programs in constructivism have been much influenced by the various generations of Schutzian phenomenology. This research relies on a basic phenomenological shift to studying discursive constructs through empirical measurement of a presentational field. Since there is not much evidence that the field of discursive constructs is likely to exhaust itself, the longevity of constructivism research seems assured. Finally, as this chapter was being completed, an entire issue of the *Western Journal of Speech Communication* was devoted to the topic "Communication and Consciousness" ("Communication," 1986).

This attenuated overview of hermeneutics and phenomenology points to the value of this research in setting an actor-centered agenda for substantive focus in communication, as well as offering a rich method for construct definition and refinement. As the hermeneutician would undoubtedly notice, the communication researcher, no less than the actual communicant, is constantly engaged by a multitextual phenomenon. We are immersed in intrapersonal, interpersonal, organizational, and systemic communication during much of our public and private lives. Fortunately, neither the researcher nor the practitioner is able to attend to all levels of interpretative "density" at the same time. From what my colleagues in the sciences tell me, however, we are only beginning to raise the questions of level and priority of influence. It may be among these prior issues that hermeneutics and phenomenology offer their greatest value.

SEMIOTICS AND STRUCTURALISM

Semiotics and structuralism are close enough together conceptually that they dwell constantly upon their own differences. Nonetheless, I will stress certain commonalities of theme and emphasize works that offer an introduction to this nomenclature. Semiotics presents us with one further difficulty in that some of its more sophisticated forms claim to be a sort of science. I will not evaluate this claim but merely bring the matter to the attention of those better able to consider it.

The various strands of semiotics may be traced to two very different conceptual sources. First, there is the very important work of American pragmatic philosopher Charles Sanders Peirce. Peirce's theory of signs was part of a phenomenology of perception and meaning that bears little in common with a second source of contemporary understanding, the linear information-transmission model of communication filtered through the somewhat unlikely cultural lens of French linguistics. This may be why the study of semiotics ranges from the highly impressionistic critiques of Barthes (1968) to elaborate mathematical models of codes and transformations. Given such extravagant diversity, we are fortunate in having available several useful introductory works.

The philosophical origins of semiotics are overviewed by Lyne (1980). Specifically centered on the seminal influence of Peirce, Lyne's essay introduces the contemporary reader to the first systematic interpretation of signs and their attendant functions, explaining how Peirce's pragmatic philosophical assumptions inform a developing logic of signs.

Among the most accessible overviews of contemporary semiotics is Leach's *Culture and Communication* (1976). Although purportedly written for an advanced undergraduate reader, this work is neither simplistic nor removed from scholarly concerns. What is most applicable to its aim is a careful didacticism of treatment. Basic terms are defined. We are told how sign and symbol relationships are created and discovered in a rich diversity of contexts. Most important, we are instructed as to how semiotics might actually be employed as a methodology in communication research. Communication is conceptualized as a kind of meaning-event constituted by signs and their interpretations. The perspective will frustrate some mainstream research assumptions, but Leach is careful to offer a detailed list of his classic sources (e.g., Malinowski, Levi-Straus, Jakobson).

The French tradition in semiotics requires a range of introduction entirely its own. I recommend Guiraud's *Semiology* (1975) and Barthes's *Elements of Semiology* (1968). Guiraud and Barthes examine virtually identical conceptual territory: signs, signifiers and systems, codes and their variations, denotation and connotation, and programs for related research. Both presume that semiology is a science of communication carefully delimited from outside frames of reference.

The study of semiotics takes on a more interesting range of implications when viewed alongside some recent developments in social anthropology. Chief among these is the work of Geertz and Douglas, who share with the semioticians the belief that communication is dependent upon an internally consistent framework of connectives within a common culture. Unlike the semioticians, these scholars are concerned with connections among symbols rather than signs. They believe that the commonality of a logic of connections must stop once we come to the limits of the cultural community. Because of these beliefs, they admit the possibility of time, change, and even transformation in symbol systems. Geertz (1983) presents a provocative attempt to get at the limits of discourse in systems of understanding that are, like much of our own discipline, undergoing "revision." Douglas comes closer to the semiology mold, largely because of her implicit denial of an actional dimension in the various "logics" she continues to uncover (Douglas, 1954, 1960, 1982). Put another way, she sometimes has a tendency to treat symbols as if they were signs.

The literature on semiotics and social anthropology is much larger than what is described here. But a few interim conclusions may still be appropriate. At first glance, this appears to be an area with important but untapped implications for social science research. Although the assumptions that guide semiotics seem diametrically opposed to those of, say, social cognition, there are still exciting prospective developments in relational network research and message variables generally, to say nothing of that rapidly expanding gray area in media studies where content analysis meets "critical research." Having said this much, however, I suspect there are reasons why more has not been done. The vocabularies of semiotics and anthropology are imposing, and there is a tendency of both schools of thought to treat their research object as a matrix of relationships whose rigor is completely internalized. Although there is no semiotic "law" against experimental research, the univocal lawlike quality of its logic seems outside the probabilistic presumptions of social science experimentation.

Social anthropology is in a somewhat different situation, and could offer a powerful corrective to the tendency toward psychological reductionism in interpersonal communication. Yet, the cultural variable is a rare commodity in communication research (Katriel & Philipsen, 1981, is a refreshing counterexample). To the semiotic and anthropological traditions, the *message* is a loose linguistic metaphor for the larger system of sociocultural relationships. For many social scientists of communication, however, the larger system of relationships is a loose relational metaphor for whatever the *message* is. This conceptual inversion is not to deny that some intersystemic discussion might one day prove useful.

MARXISM AND SOCIAL THEORY

A great deal of contemporary ferment and friction between "humanists" and "scientists" can be found within Marxism and social theory. We have noted the tendency of social science to bracket or suspend "outside" conditions and circumstances in both the definition and the model explanations of its object, presumably, *communication*. One reason for the confounding ambiguity of social theory to social science (in addition to its taxing Germanic jargon) is its tendency to remove the brackets from social science research—to let all "outside" factors in—at the same time as it purports to be a science. The source of this ambiguity may be traced back to the seminal text for much of social theory: the work of Marx himself.

In a difficult but powerful analysis of Marxism, Gouldner (1980) suggests that there is a fundamental ambivalence in Marxism between necessity as determinism (i.e., the material conditions that are purportedly causal for all "meaning" and action) and necessity as imperative (i.e., the climactic rhetorical sense that we *must* act). This ambivalence informs everything from the role of consciousness formation in revolutionary action to the status of cultural products in the social order. Moreover, the ambivalence is covered over by compelling but slippery concepts such as, "the totality," the "superstructure," even *ideology*. As a result of this initial problem, there is what may be called a scientific Marxism as well as a romantic revolutionary Marxism. The scientific Marxism is preoccupied with the formation of those conditions that might bring about a "revolutionary situation." The romantic revolutionary Marxism, believing that thought, desire, and will are all formative ingredients in the transformation of society, is considerably less stable. It is uncomfortable with science generally, given to utopian exhortations ("revolution for the hell of it") and, predictably, prolonged pessimism and melancholia. Each style of thought has some basis in the original texts of Marx, and each has its contemporary adherents.

The most conspicuous example of utopian, romantic Marxism and social theory is the core scholarship behind the Frankfurt school. This is where the most trenchant and consuming criticism of "positivistic" social science may be found. Horkeimer, Adorno, Bloch, Benjamin, and Marcuse were primarily social critics, with a strikingly similar religious heritage. As I argued elsewhere (Farrell & Aune, 1979), the critical posture of the Frankfurt school was so sweeping in its compass as virtually to preclude any practical discourse. In a work that pursues a similar theme, *The Tragedy of the Enlightenment*, Connerton (1980) argues that the Frankfurt school drove its own critical reason into a double bind, rendering itself politically impotent in the process. I would stop short of the self-destructive motive Connerton appears to discover within the intellectual legacy of Frankfurt, but his is a challenging interpretation.

There are, in the midst of the critical negation of romantic Marxism, some intriguing contributions to the study of communication. The unlikely blend of Freud, Marx, and a primitive language pragmatics led to fascinating and pioneering work on communication in the family (which Frankfurt could be said to have founded as an area of research), the distortions of propaganda and "administrative" communication generally, and perhaps most pivotal, the classic *The Authoritarian Personality* (Adorno, Frenkel-Brunswick, Levinson, & Sanford, 1950). The models of communication generated by Frankfurt theory are simplistic, and even such contemporary theorists as Schiller (1969) employ a mimetic view of media domination that reduces all communication to the status of a dependent variable "product." For all these difficulties, there is a sense in which the very development of a communication science owes something to this odd assortment of alienated intellectuals. The analogy that comes to mind is the paradoxical origins of contemporary sociology in Spencer and Comte.

There is also a scientific Marxism and social theory. Here it is difficult *not* to think of Habermas, whose seminal contributions to philosophy, ethics, criticism, history, art, linguistics, and communication defy conventional disciplinary boundaries. Since the 1950s, when he was Adorno's research assistant, Habermas has been at work on a vast philosophical project designed to reinvigorate the criticism of society while maintaining a defensible foundation for the social and natural sciences. Not all of Habermas's work, of course, is of equal relevance to the social science of communication. The early studies, *Knowledge and Human Interests* (1971) and *Theory and Practice* (1974), are absorbed with conventional philosophical questions of epistemology and meaning that are rooted in the touchstones of German thought. The works are nonetheless important because of their implications for social science research methods and programs, as well as for the much-discussed "linguistic turn" in critical theory. In revitalizing the most "modernist" heritage of the Frankfurt school, Habermas sought to reinterpret Marxism from a communicative perspective. By reintroducing certain Kantian postulates presupposed by the very practice of dialogic reflection (an optimal communication practice) Habermas was able to allow for an aspect of "reason" and critique that is not historically determined and that, therefore, cannot be cancelled out by the cumulative weight of events alone. For Habermas, then, the project of Modernity is not over, and the prospect for reason is always available. There is, in other words, no contradiction between the interests we have in our inquiry and the validation of what inquiry reveals through the mediation of others. The validation is fundamentally communicative.

Habermas's theory of communication incorporates insights from analytic philosophy, argumentation, speech act theory, and systems analysis, together with a healthy dose of Western pragmatism. What results is a vision of ordinary discourse that is language-centered, audience dependent, grounded in reflective reason, and admitting to a developmental logic of communicative and (later) moral competence. Each of these aspects of the theory has received considerable scholarly attention. Beyond the challenging content of the Habermas conceptualizations, there have already been important implications in the collaborative aims, methods, and topical agenda of social science research. But understandably, there has been no systematic empirical research program to incorporate all relevant aspects of the theory itself. Since a full bibliography on Habermas would exhaust these pages, I can best recommend McCarthy's *The Critical Theory of Jurgen Habermas* (1978) as a systematic introduction. Habermas poses almost an inventional agenda for social scientists interested in the construct-formation phase of theory development in communication. We may sense some range of variation by mentioning two other social theory writers who take demonstrably different paths.

Wilden's *System and Structure: Essays in Communication and Exchange* (1977) defies any category system I could imagine. Best to consider this difficult work a kind of amalgam of repressed connections among social-psychological philosophies and research paradigms. Communication is modeled upon the idea of exchange, and an information-based concept of exchange at that. But Wilden (one of the founders of the

British Marxist tradition) is well aware of the political ramifications of terminologies, so each is a kind of experiment in the politics of social science as well. A Lacanian analysis yields (if that is the proper term) the phallocentrism in most post-Freudian therapeutic literature, structuralism gives us an analogue to law in late Capitalism, and so forth. Wilden's work provides a virtual inventory of fascinating reflections on the consequences of social science models *as* communication behavior.

An indication of how far the British Marxist tradition has come from its eclectic beginnings can be found in Giddens, *A Contemporary Critique of Historical Materialism* (1981). This important work is less interested in the tour de force variations of radical social theory than in the implications of communication media for Marx's original formulations. The result is something unique: a theory of structuration that is *not* tied to a deterministic developmental process. Acquisition and concentration of power are not, in Giddens's view, entirely the consequence of controlled *means of production*. In late capitalism, power has come to equal the long-distance control of information, and its capacities for surveillance and discipline of those who might deviate from norms of conduct. Giddens thus can argue that both the stakes and the rules of intersystemic conflict have changed, even as entirely different developmental types of systems coexist within a parallel span of time. It is, as he puts it, a nonevolutionary view of history. One does not have to endorse the same critical theory agenda as Giddens to appreciate the implications for both social analysis and empirical research that follow from his perspective. The program of Giddens, and social theory generally, presents the kind of challenge that is implicit in the best contributions from the philosophy of communication. Social science research in communication, as our editors (Chapter 3 in this volume) note, is no more about language or words alone than it is about numbers. Rather words and numbers are only tools for capturing invariant features of a much more elusive phenomenon: relationships of meaning among persons.

NONRATIONAL PHILOSOPHY, OR DECONSTRUCTION

The very presumption that we can make true and reliable statements about such features of social life has been called into question by a fourth general category of speculative thought, nonrational philosophy, or deconstruction. Since I make no attempt to capture all the nuances of this amorphous area of research, I will discuss it cautiously and generally, using its lessons as a basis for some tentative conclusions about our overall task.

When we speak of the movement away from rationalism in the theory and criticism of texts, we are reflecting the influence of Foucault and

Derrida. Several useful interpretive works help introduce the lay reader to these imposing French philosophers, including Megill's *Prophets of Extremity* (1985) and Said's *The World, the Text, and the Critic* (1983); for an exposition and critique of Derrida alone, see also Rorty (1982). All these works concede the radical challenge deconstruction poses to conventional, speaker-centered approaches to meaning and communication.

Although there are major and controversial differences between the two writers, what binds Derrida and Foucault together is their rejection of what might be called the "logocentric" preoccupation of Western thought generally, encapsulated by the primacy of a singular, knowing subject in the classic philosophic texts (e.g., Plato, Aristotle, Descartes, Kant, Hegel). If philosophy is "dead," if it has not satisfied its all-consuming quest for a truth-in-itself that may be known to the unified self, one possible reason is that the quest was terribly wrongheaded from the beginning. The very idea of a stable subject-object relationship to truth is without foundation. For Derrida particularly, this stable logocentrism is typified in the primacy he believes to have been accorded speech throughout the history of ideas. With speech, we assume a speaker who means what he says, a listener to whom the meaning is apparent, and so forth. Note that these very conditions of communicative truth resemble the program of Habermas. But, the net cast by nonrational philosophy catches a much larger range of nemeses than social theory and analytic philosophy. The point is to remove the subject from discourse, to replace the primacy of speech with the phenomenon of writing or the "text," and to replace the quest for truth with the interpretation (or "misreading") of meaning. When Rorty (1982) observes that literary criticism is the new philosophy, this is what he means (or at least it is one of the things his text means, to borrow a locution). Overall, the process of systematic misreading is designed to place what the author intends the text to do in opposition to what the text itself tends to assert in a kind of defiance of the author's purported ownership of meaning. This is what its practitioners refer to as deconstruction.

At this point, the agendas of Derrida and Foucault take off in sharply different directions. Foucault, being the more overtly political of the two, is interested in the way rules of discourse formation define and exclude membership in various forms of affiliation. Definitions of reason and sanity, guilt and responsibility, discipline and authority, gender and autonomy all offer unexamined margins of power and domination. Again, it is not that the language is controlled by some sinister subject so much as the language itself controls its use. For Foucault, then, deconstruction is a concerted attempt to see what has been left out of the picture. For Derrida, despite his protestations, the practice is more traditionally academic. By reinventing the meanings of our classic texts, he would hope to restore something of the fluidity and richness in the prospects for meaning in language.

To theorists in communication, I suspect that the work of deconstruction is more interesting to read about than to actually read. Foucault (1972, 1973, 1977) and Derrida (1972, 1974, 1981) have had something of the same influence upon the humanities that Kuhn and Popper had on the progressive vision of science. These are the sort of contentious thinkers who distrust orderly formations of any kind, who enjoy watching the pieces tumble and the people scatter. Why, then, should the serious student of communication science care about their cognitive vandalism? Primarily because they have exploited a core myth about the way communication occurs and have taken their exploits to a disturbingly extreme implication.

CONCLUSION

Communication among persons seems to have much more to do with the invention of meaning than with the discovery of truth. Add to this the truism that, as communicating agents, we are never able to exert total control over what our symbols, signals, utterances, message units, and information *mean*. Nonetheless, as theorists, we claim to be able to make not only meaningful, but also *true* statements about the phenomenon of communication generally, as well as the principles best able to explain its character. Viewed from the perspective of Foucault and Derrida, then, the whole process of scientific experimentation has a great deal more in common with deconstruction than might be supposed. I say this not so much to debunk either enterprise as to place them both in perspective.

Communication science progresses to the extent that it can generate hypotheses that might be invalidated. Whether we are dealing in the realms of decision theory, mass communication, deception, interpersonal cognition, network analysis, or their numerous specialized offshoots, we search for a kind of coherence that is not insulated from the world of choice and chance, but rather can be overturned—at any moment—by their insinuation. This is a fragile truth at best. It is both enriched and challenged by the equally different approaches to communicative meaning offered by contemporary schools of thought in the humanities. Each perspective I have examined has its own category system for the overall practice of communication. Drawing upon such category systems, the studies of argument, rules approaches, myth, ritual, text, and metaphor each offer an opportunity for conceptual invention, as well as a potential angle of vision on what we ourselves *do* in communication. There would be no contradiction in thinking as a hermeneutician, a semioticist, a social theorist, or even a deconstructionist, and thinking as a communication scientist. There would, of course, be extraordinary tension. But only through such extraordinary tension do the extraordinary possibilities for communication science persist.

REFERENCES

Adorno, T. W., Frenkel-Brunswick, E., Levinson, D. J. & Sanford, R. N. (1950). *The authoritarian personality.* New York: Science Editions.
Apel, K.-O. (1972). The a'priori of communication and the foundation of the humanities. *Man and World, 5.*
Barthes, R. (1968). *Elements of semiology.* New York: Hill and Wang.
Burleson, B. K., & Kline, S. L. (1979). Habermas' theory of communication: A critical explication. *Quarterly Journal of Speech, 65, 4.*
Campbell, P. N. (1975). The *personae* of scientific discourse. *Quarterly Journal of Speech, 61.*
Cohen, G.A. (1972). Karl Marx and the withering away of social science. *Philosophy and Public Affairs,* (Winter).
Communication and consciousness. (1986). *Western Journal of Speech Communication, 50*(1).
Connerton, P. (1980). *The tragedy of enlightenment: An essay on the Frankfurt School.* Cambridge: Cambridge University Press.
Derrida, J. (1972). *Positions.* Paris: Minuit.
Derrida, J. (1974). *De la grammatologie.* Paris: Minuit.
Derrida, J. (1981). *Dissemination* (Barbara Johnson, Trans.). Chicago: University of Chicago Press.
Douglas, M. (1954). The Lele of the Kasai. *African worlds* (D. Forde, Ed.). London: Oxford University Press.
Douglas, M. (1960). Blood-debts among the Lele. *Journal of the Royal Anthropological Institute, 90*(1).
Douglas, M. (1982). *Essays in the sociology of perception* (Douglas, Ed.). London: Routledge & Kegan Paul.
Edie, J. (1976). *Speaking and meaning.* Bloomington: Indiana University Press.
Farrell, T. B., & Aune, J. A. (1979). Critical theory and communication: A selective literature review. *Quarterly Journal of Speech, 65,*(1).
Foucault, M. (1972). *The archaeology of knowledge and the discourse on language* (A.M. Sheridan Smith, Trans.) New York: Harper & Row.
Foucault, M. (1973). *The order of things: An archaeology of the human sciences.* New York: Vintage Books.
Foucault, M. (1977). *Language, counter-memory, practice: Selected essays and interviews* (D. Bouchard & S. Simon, Trans.). Ithaca, NY: Cornell University Press.
Gadamer, H.-G. (1975). *Truth and method.* New York: The Seabury Press.
Gadamer, H.-G. (1976). *Hegel's dialectic: Five hermeneutical studies.* New Haven, CT: Yale University Press.
Geertz, C. (1983). *Local knowledge: Further essays in interpretive anthropology.* New York: Basic Books.
Giddens, A. (1981). *A contemporary critique of historical materialism: Vol. 1. Power, property and the state,* Berkeley: University of California Press.
Gouldner, A. W. (1973). "Romanticism and classicism: Deep structures in social science." *Diogenes, 82.*

Gouldner, A. W. (1980). *The two Marxisms: Contradictions and anomalies in the development of theory.* New York: Oxford University Press.

Guiraud, P. (1975). *Semiology.* London: Routledge & Kegan Paul.

Habermas, J. (1971). *Knowledge and human interests.* Boston: Beacon.

Habermas, J. (1974). *Theory and practice.* Boston: Beacon.

Hyde, M. J. (1980). "The experience of anxiety: A phenomenological investigation." *Quarterly Journal of Speech, 66,(2).*

Hyde, M. J. (1982). *Communication philosophy and the technological age.* Tuscaloosa: University of Alabama Press.

Hyde, M. J., & Smith, C. (1979). "Hermeneutics and rhetoric: A seen but unobserved relationship." *Quarterly Journal of Speech, 65,(2).*

Katriel, T., & Philipsen, G. (1981). "What we need is communication": "Communication" as a cultural category in some American speech. *Communication Monographs, 48*(4).

Kuhn, T. (1977). *The essential tension: Selected studies in scientific tradition and change.* Chicago: University of Chicago Press.

Lyne, J. R. (1980). Rhetoric and semiotic in C.S. Peirce. *Quarterly Journal of Speech, 66*(2).

Leach, E. (1976). *Culture and communication: The logic by which symbols are connected.* Cambridge: Cambridge University Press.

McCarthy, T. A. (1978). *The critical theory of Jurgen Habermas.* Cambridge: MIT Press.

Megill, A. (1985). *Prophets of extremity: Nietzsche, Heidegger, Foucault, Derrida.* Berkeley: University of California Press.

Nagel, T. (1986). *The view from nowhere.* New York: Oxford University Press.

Ricoeur, P. (1974). *The conflict of interpretations.* Evanston, IL: Northwestern University Press.

Ricoeur, P. (1976). *Interpretation theory: Discourse and the surplus of meaning.* Fort Worth: Texas Christian University Press.

Ricoeur, P. (1977). *The rule of metaphor: Multi-disciplinary studies of the creation of meaning in language.* Toronto: University of Toronto Press.

Ricoeur, P. (1984). *Time and narrative, Vol. 1.* Chicago: University of Chicago Press.

Ricoeur, P. (1985). *Time and Narrative, Vol. 2.* Chicago: University of Chicago Press.

Rorty, R. (1982). *Consequences of pragmatism.* Minneapolis: University of Minnesota Press.

Said, Edward W. (1983). *The world, the text, and the critic.* Cambridge: Harvard University Press.

Schiller, H. I. (1969). *Mass communication and American empire.* New York: Augustus M. Kelley.

Schrag, C. (1975). *Communicative praxis and the space of subjectivity.* Bloomington: Indiana University Press.

Schutz, A. (1964). *Collected papers II: Studies in social theory.* The Hague: Martinus Nijhoff.

Sloan, T. O. (1971). The interpreter's house revisited. *Quarterly Journal of Speech, 57*(1).

Stewart, J. (1981). Hermeneutic phenomenology and communication research. *Quarterly Journal of Speech, 67*(1).

Weimer, W. B. (1977). Science as a rhetorical transaction. *Philosophy and Rhetoric, 10.*

Weimer, W. B. (1983). Why all knowing is rhetorical. *Journal of the American Forensic Association, 20.*

Wilden, A. (1972). *System and structure: Essays in communication and exchange.* London: Tavistock.

PART II
LEVELS OF ANALYSIS

5 Levels of Analysis: An Introduction

STEVEN H. CHAFFEE
Stanford University

CHARLES R. BERGER
Northwestern University

WE have discussed (especially in Chapter 3) four levels at which communication can be conceptualized and studied empirically. These are analyzed in the four chapters this part of the book comprises. This is not to suggest that these four are the only possibilities. Many distinctions of much finer grade could be—and often are—made in differentiating theoretical approaches to communication research.

But that has not often been the problem as we see it. This volume is dedicated to the proposition that *at least* four levels need to be kept in mind. That has only rarely been the case. Most researchers focus their thinking on, say, the interpersonal level and differentiate it from adjacent levels such as that of the individual actor or the social network. Others, working perhaps at the level of the local community, are aware of alternative possibilities—the nation, or the family or local institutions within the community. But community-level researchers are as a rule unlikely to bear in mind interpersonal processes, or vice versa. More crucial even, specialists in these different levels rarely consult with one another; frequently they are housed in different departments at many universities and present their research to separate academic bodies.

By selecting the four-level model as our organizing scheme for this book, we are consciously attempting to change this state of affairs. It is our hope that through theoretical integration of concepts and issues across these different levels, which have in effect been separate academic subcultures, we can move the field of communication toward a more fundamental integration of research and, more broadly, knowledge. Although we have chosen the tradition of communication *science* for concentration here—that is our area of expertise, as it is for almost every contributor to this volume—we would commend this multilevel way of thinking about communication to those who approach it from different intellectual traditions (see Farrell, Chapter 4). Philosophical and humanistic disciplines can also, we believe, be enriched by maintaining a perspective that keeps the many levels of human communication activity in mind.

In this section, each level is examined in detail within a single chapter. In the later sections of the book, various topics of communication study will be examined at each level. The reader can envision the organization of these sections in terms of a two-dimensional matrix. The four levels chapters of this part constitute the four rows of this matrix. The 16 topical chapters of Parts III and IV will then form 16 columns, so that the total book has a 4-by-16 or 64-cell format, so to speak. To date, not all of these conceptual cells have produced a significant body of scientific research; it is another general purpose of this book to identify some relatively empty spots in our field.

To lay the groundwork of four levels of communication analysis we have invited authors who are widely noted for their research contributions at the level we have assigned to them, but whose work has pointedly *not been limited to that level.* For example, Hewes and Planalp (Chapter 6) make a strong case for analyzing the individual in communication science. They show persuasively how a cognitive approach to explaining communicative conduct is superior to trait or transactional approaches. But the authors of the three following chapters, each of which deals with a supraindividual level, have also tested individual-level theories, and Hewes and Planalp are in their turn well known for work on interpersonal communication. Our macro-level authors, McLeod and Blumler (Chapter 9), have done notable work on such sub-macroscopic entities as parent-child communication structures within the family, and personal and social gratifications people receive from use of mass media.

Given this catholicity of vision, we might expect the authors of these four levels chapters to relate their discussions to one another's levels more than they have. But in doing justice to a particular level an author naturally becomes something of an advocate for that type of analysis. The reader should not suppose, simply because these chapters carry a flavor of advocacy, that these leading communication scientists would be incapable of working at other levels. They have all done so, extensively in some cases. These chapters should be taken as position papers prepared for the sake of stimulating scientific dialogue; they are not expositions of narrow personal positions.

A few further points need to be made about these levels. One is the distinction between what we might call the *level of discourse* and the *level of analysis.* Questions, hypotheses, statements, inferences, and conclusions about human communication take place in the form of discourse. Knowledge is in that sense highly semantic in nature. On the other hand, scientific research procedures such as data collection, coding, aggregation, and statistical operations take place in the form of empirical analysis. Although this book consists almost wholly of words, the overwhelming majority of scientific studies to which it refers have at their core data analyses such as tables of numerical entries that represent amounts and frequencies, coefficients of association, or tests of the statistical significance of differences. This dual nature of communication science, or more exactly its dual existence in the forms of discourse and analysis, is not inherently problematic. Indeed it is a strength to the extent that these two kinds of intellectual activity coincide. But that is not as easily done as said. We often find research at one level of analysis interpreted at a different level of discourse.

An example of mixing levels can be found in public opinion polling. A research agency may gather a large number of individual opinions and analyze them statistically; they are then presented in discursive form as if they represent the opinion of a macrosocial entity (the "public"). As Price and Roberts (Chapter 25) stress, there is much more than this to the communication processes involved in public opinion. Similar problems associated with aggregating individuals into social units are discussed by Cappella (Chapter 7), Bochner and Eisenberg (Chapter 18), Fitzpatrick (Chapter 19), and Gudykunst (Chapter 27).

Functional analysis of communication, which is dealt with extensively in Part III of this book, is particularly vulnerable to confusions between the level of discourse and the level of analysis, and even more to problems of inferring dysfunctions at one level but overlooking positive functions at another. That kind of concern lies properly in those later chapters; but it is important to bear in mind in reading the next four chapters that these levels represent choices for both analysis and discourse, and that the relationship between the two needs to be kept in mind.

We present these four levels, then, as a menu of alternatives. They are not rival schools of thought, but complementary approaches that can serve to strengthen one another in the pursuit of understanding communication. Theoretical development of our field has been hindered by the tendency of scholars to "choose up sides," specializing in just one level and rejecting others without fully considering what they have to offer.

This does not mean that we think everyone should try to do everything at every level. Eclecticism carries no particular virtue, and specialization is a well-proven method of producing high-quality work. But communication scientists should keep themselves aware of the general perspectives, and potential strengths, of many different levels of analysis and discourse.

6 The Individual's Place in Communication Science

DEAN E. HEWES
University of Illinois, Urbana-Champaign

SALLY PLANALP
University of Illinois, Urbana-Champaign

THE individual is the locus of social action. At least that impression is conveyed by a host of theorists including cognitive psychologists (Carroll & Payne, 1976; Pylyshyn, 1984; Vaina & Hintikka, 1984), much of the tradition of rhetoric (as in Bitzer, 1968), social exchange theorists (Blau, 1964; Homans, 1974; Thibaut & Kelley, 1959), constructivists (Kelly, 1955; Mancuso & Adams-Webber, 1982; O'Keefe & Delia, 1982; but see O'Keefe, Delia, & O'Keefe, 1980), social cognition researchers (Fiske & Taylor, 1984; Sorrentino & Higgins, 1986) and many students of human communication (Greene, 1984; Roloff & Berger, 1982; Seibold & Spitzberg, 1982; Sillars, 1985).

Although all these theorists recognize the importance of the social contexts of individual choice (especially Bitzer, 1968; Blau, 1964; Kelley & Thibaut, 1978), an increasing number of voices arising from widely diverse perspectives have challenged the extent to which the individual holds a favored position in their theorizing. These voices highlight the essentially social nature of communication, concluding that interacting aggregates (dyads, relationships, groups, organizations, societies) may be more appropriate units of analysis and that communication must be essentially conventionalized to be functional (see Fisher & Hawes, 1971; Grossberg, 1982; O'Keefe et al., 1980; Poole, Seibold, & McPhee, 1986; Rogers & Farace, 1975). At stake in this contest of viewpoints is the place of the individual in the study of human communication.

Appropriate to our title, we discuss this issue, attempting to shed some light on the relationship between the process of communication and the individual's place in that process. Of course, how one conceives of communication determines how one studies and theorizes about it (Delia, 1977)—but only in part. The advantages to be gained from a conceptual framework have triggered an almost endless supply of definitional arguments, metaphors, and meta-theoretical stances advanced to reveal the "correct" framework for investigating communication (see Berger & Bradac, 1982; Cronen, Pearce, & Harris, 1982; Cushman & Whiting, 1972; Delia, 1977; W. Fisher, 1984, 1985; Planalp & Hewes, 1982; see

Cappella, Chapter 7 in this volume). This is precisely what should be happening. Conceptual diversity is a precondition for selecting a viable, productive basis for any sort of theory (Feyerabend, 1975); however, it is not the *only* precondition. The properties of the phenomenon itself limit the set of frameworks that do it justice (Papincau, 1979; Suppe, 1974; but see Feyerabend, 1975).[1] Our purpose in this chapter is to examine two fundamental properties of the human communication process and to use those properties to locate the place of the individual in this process. Our position is threefold: The place of the individual in communication has been vastly oversimplified in current theory and research; certain approaches to the study of the individual's place in the process of communication are more productive than others; and once the place of the individual in communication theory is understood, movement toward the study of the interactive character of communication will be greatly facilitated.

TWO FUNDAMENTAL PROPERTIES
OF COMMUNICATION

Identifying fundamental properties of communication is always a dangerous task. There numerous lists of such from which to choose, and they seldom overlap (see Bruner, 1978; Dance & Larson, 1976; Poole, Folger, & Hewes, 1987). Moreover, for our selection to be fruitful, we must show that these basic properties are generated, in whole or in part, by some mechanism that resides in the individual. Only thus can we specify the importance of individual-level analysis for a science of communication. To begin, then, let us turn to the properties.

Impact

Perhaps no other property of communication is so commonly linked to its definition than impact (Hewes, 1986). If person A's behavior affects person B's subsequent behavior or cognitive/emotive state, then communication has taken place; if not, then it has not (Cappella, Chapter 7; Fisher, 1970; Hewes, Planalp, & Streibel, 1980; Steinfatt & Miller, 1974; Stevens, 1950). Such specific communication phenomena as "responsiveness" (Davis, 1982) and "control" (Gottman, 1979) all evidence this property of communication. In fact, the importance of impact to communication is what moves it out of the sterile realm of Chomskian competence (Chomsky, 1975) into the intriguingly messy world of performance.

The problem, of course, is that the production of potentially meaningful behavior by no means guarantees impact. Impact can range from none to complete control. As a consequence, *an adequate account of human communication must identify the mechanism, or mechanisms, that generate the degree of impact that a person's behavior has on another's behavior or cognitive/emotive state.* Failure to expose such mechanisms leaves communication theorists with no specifiable boundaries for their discipline; it offers no basis for explaining degrees of impact; it offers no aid to pedagogy for increasing or decreasing the effects of communication (as in Hewes, 1979a). On the positive side, when such mechanisms are specified—as they are in Cappella and Folger's (1980) explanation of the impact of messages on behavior change—a richer, more productive theory emerges, one that demonstrates clearly the importance of a more complex understanding of the place of the individual in a science of communication.

Intersubjectivity

Intersubjectivity is both a central product of and a central contributor to human communication (Gurwitsch, 1974; Poole et al., 1986; Schutz, 1967; Schutz & Luckmann, 1973). Intersubjectivity is established through knowledge shared by participants in social interaction based on common experience and communication (Gurwitsch, 1974). Simultaneously, intersubjectivity is necessary for communication (Schutz, 1967; Shutz & Luckmann, 1973). Without it, social actors can no longer presume that they share perspectives on the understanding of events. Without this presumption communication is halting or ineffective (Schutz & Luckmann, 1973).

When shared knowledge exists, social actors can engage in constructing a common "world" of interconnected beliefs and inferences (Smith, 1985). Thus intersubjectivity provides the grounding for specific communication phenomena such as coordination (Cronen et al., 1982), coorientation (Laing, Phillipson, & Lee, 1966; Pavitt & Cappella, 1979; see Price & Roberts, Chapter 25), misunderstanding (Richards, 1965), emotional empathy (Denzin, 1984), and identity negotiation (McCall & Simmons, 1978), to name but a few.

Intersubjectivity exists by degrees (Poole et al., 1987). Consequently, *an adequate account of human communication must identify the mechanism, or mechanisms, that generate degrees of intersubjectivity.* Failure to bring to light such mechanisms leaves communication theorists with no way to explain misunderstanding and its effects on relational definition (Planalp, 1985), conflict (Brehmer & Hammond, 1977), the success of deception (Zuckerman, DePaulo, & Rosenthal, 1981) and the lack of coordination. On the other hand, an understanding of such mechanisms greatly facilitates intervention in and correction of misunderstanding—as illustrated, for example, by Brehmer and Hammond's applications of their social judgement theory to real conflicts deriving from misunderstanding (Brehmer & Hammond, 1977; Hammond, Stewart, Adelman, & Wascoe, 1975). Their theory not only identifies sources of misunderstanding, it also explains why misunderstanding persists even when one or both parties have attempted to correct the sources of that misunderstanding. Theories such as Brehmer and Hammond's enrich our understanding of the function of the individual in understanding interactive manifestations of communication.

Impact and intersubjectivity are properties against which any explanation of human communication can be judged adequate. To the extent that an approach has heuristic value in identifying the mechanisms that explain why and under what circumstances varying degrees of these two properties will emerge, it is a productive way to view human communication.

THREE APPROACHES TO
COMMUNICATION SCIENCE

Approaches to the study of human communication abound. To limit our discussion to only three is to do injustice to some. Yet it is a necessary injustice. We have chosen three approaches that have had a recent, dominant impact on communication research. Roughly speaking *trait* approaches to communication place the locus of action in the predispositions of individuals to initiate action or to react to behavior. *Transindividual* approaches describe regularities in communication as emergent, conventionalized, products of social aggregates (dyads, relationships, groups, organizations, culture, etc.). *Cognitive/interpretive* approaches emphasize the importance of the individual's complex cognitive abilities to interpret and produce communication. Trait, transindividual, and cognitive/interpretive approaches are widely represented in the literature and encompass many other approaches. For example, communication apprehension (McCroskey, 1982) and constructivism (Delia, O'Keefe, & O'Keefe, 1982) are both trait approaches though they differ markedly in other ways. Similarly relational communication research (see Berger, 1985, pp. 452-455; Fisher, 1978, Chapter 7) shares certain central assumptions with discourse analysis (see Stubbs, 1983), thus both belong among transindividual approaches. Interpretive theory (see Rabinow & Sullivan, 1979) has points of overlap with cognitive research (see Planalp & Hewes, 1982) that manifest themselves in cognitive/interpretive approaches (see D'Andrade, 1981; Winograd, 1980).

We have chosen these three approaches not only for their current popularity and scope. They also offer a range of perspectives on the centrality of the individual in communication theory (trait approaches having most, to transindividual, least) and the complexity of the individual's contribution to communication (cognitive/interpretive, most, to transindividual, least). Thus they represent a useful set of contrasts to locate the place of the individual in a science of communication.

Trait Approaches

Trait approaches to human communication place the individual as central and offer a very simplified version of the capacities the individual brings to bear in social interaction. These characteristics of the trait approach arise from the very definition of a trait—a stable predisposition to behavior (Mischel, 1968). Thus human beings are conceived of primarily as bundles of predispositions, and these predispositions are relatively stable across time and across specified contexts. These dispositions are, for the most part, taken as givens. The behaviors they explain, however, may be quite varied including a host of *actions,* such as avoiding communication (Hewes & Haight, 1979) or higher-order behaviors, such as adaptation to others (Delia et al., 1982; Snyder & Ickes, 1985).

While the trait approach has been used widely in predicting social behavior (Blass, 1977; but see Hewes & Haight, 1979; Mischel, 1973; Parks, 1980), it has certain inherent limitations. Most central of these is that the mechanisms that generate the prediction of traits are missing. As Quine (1974) put it, "I once expressed my view of predispositions by saying that a disposition is a promissory note for an eventual description in mechanical terms" (p. 14). Precisely the same argument applies to dispositions to behave or adapt (Hirschberg, 1978; Wiggins, 1974). To say that leaves in northern climates have a predisposition to fall from trees in autumn is not a very satisfying explanation. To say that a person avoids communication because they have a disposition to do so is equally unrewarding. The same could be said of all trait explanations (Alston, 1975). This limitation becomes especially important when taken in conjunction with our two central properties of communication.

Consider, first, degrees of impact. Generally speaking the trait approach can and has been used with some success to predict either the sender's powers of impact or the receiver's responsiveness to a message. In the former case, studies of charisma or leadership ability often take this tack (Kenny & Zaccaro, 1983). In the latter case, this is done in the study of persuadability with the use of simple action-prediction traits such as self-esteem (McGuire, 1968) or dogmatism (Vacchiano, 1977). More consistent and stronger results are usually obtained by the use of such traits as cognitive differentiation (O'Keefe & Delia, 1982), self-monitoring (Snyder, 1979) or self-awareness (Roloff, 1980) to predict adaptation of behavior. A problem arises, however, when one reaches for an explanation. For example, high self-monitors should be more persuadable, at least in their public statement, because (1) they attend to the exigencies of the situation more than do low self-monitors who look inward to their attitudes and beliefs, *or* (2) they have greater amounts and quality of social information than low self-monitors and thus can better assess the socially correct response to the situation, *or* (3) they are generally more skillful than low self-monitors at identity management and use those skills to adapt better to the attitudinal atmosphere of a given situation (Snyder, 1979). Each of these explanations is directly derivable from the work on self-monitoring in some stage of its history, none is refutable given the evidence available, and each posits implicitly the existence of some generative mechanism that stands behind the trait and provides the "real" explanation. This is true in almost all trait research. One need only read Hale and Delia (1976) to spot the gap between the complexity of their picture of social actors and the simplified picture induced by the use of the cognitive differentiation trait. Moreover, other personality researchers, when faced with the complexity of the humans they have tried to describe, have been forced to abandon strictly trait approaches (see Greene & Sparks, 1983; McCroskey, 1982).

We face much the same problem when trait approaches are applied to the property of degrees of intersubjectivity, although here additional problems arise. Intersubjectivity implies that two or more actors share an understanding of some events. Since trait approaches emphasize individual differences, two kinds of traits could predict degrees of intersubjectivity—those traits related to the understanding of some event *outside* the person possessing them and those traits *within* the individual that tend to create misunderstanding.[2] Thus in the former case researchers might study intersubjectivity with such trait variables as locus of control (Lefcourt, 1976) authoritarianism (Cherry & Byrne, 1977), or racism (Brigham, 1971) because these traits center on the individual's beliefs about the world, either one's ability to control reinforcement or one's orientation to the treatment of others. People similar in one of these traits might be supposed to share an understanding of an event evocative of their beliefs. Unfortunately, holding such beliefs in common does not guarantee that they will be deemed relevant by either or both parties in reacting to a specific event. Such beliefs are often so diffuse and potentially contradictory in implementation (see Brigham, 1971, on racial attitudes) that it is hard to see how they could lead to strong predictions concerning the degree of intersubjectivity. An additional set of mechanisms concerned with interpretation and implementation of beliefs need to be added to predict whether the beliefs were called into play with regard to a specific event. The traits themselves are not enough.

In the latter case, where traits lead to misunderstanding, similar problems arise. As an example, one might predict that a personal trait of competitiveness would dispose a person to believe that others are also competitive even when this is not the case (Kelley & Stahelski, 1970). Thus the uncritical projection of self-traits onto others, as well as traits involving a lack of perceptiveness, could be used to predict degrees of misunderstanding or lack of intersubjectivity. Nevertheless, at the very best, the knowledge that these predispositions exist by itself can never tell us when they will prove to be detrimental to intersubjectivity. Lack of skill is not damaging unless the context calls for that skill; projecting oneself onto others does not necessarily lead to errors in judgment; some others really are like ourselves. And even if these traits were predictive, the explanation for degrees of intersubjectivity would be just as barren as that for degrees of impact. Predispositions do not explain much. Whenever trait theorists have been pressed to explain why a trait works, they have been forced to look for the mechanisms *behind* that trait, mechanisms outside the realm of predispositions that almost always involve processes of interpretation and production of behavior or adaptation (Cantor & Kihlstrom, 1985; Greene & Sparks, 1983). Trait approaches, when successful, *do* warn us that something about individuals is the locus of causality for social action (Briggs, 1985), but by oversimplifying explanations of individuals' capabilities they do not take us far enough. They tell us *that* individuals are important in the study of human communication but not *how* or *why.*

Transindividual Approaches

These approaches to human communication draw attention away from the individual as the locus of social action, refocusing it instead on social aggregates such as relationships, groups, organization, and society as the ultimate sources of explanations of interaction. The general strategy characterizing these approaches is to obviate the individual's place in communication science by placing a heavy emphasis on the function of context.

The notion of context is central to all explanations of communication (Bochner & Krueger, 1979). For instance, trait approaches accept context either implicitly or explicitly. Implicitly it stands behind the central trait assumption of cross-situational consistency. Traits bring coherence to a set of behaviors because certain behaviors in certain contexts are relevant to—are symptoms of—the trait (Hewes & Haight, 1979; Mischel, 1968). Further, a number of trait theorists have incorporated contextual factors into their theories (see McCroskey, 1982; Spielberger, 1966) or as part of the natural extension of trait theories (Endler, 1982; Greene & Sparks, 1983; Mischel, 1978).

Context also plays a central role in transindividual approaches. It does so in one of two ways. In *behavioral contingency* versions of transindividual approaches, research centers on sequential patterns of interaction between individuals or among group members and assumes that there are no processes unique to the individuals who produce and apprehend messages (but see Cappella & Greene, 1982). Thus, for instance, Fisher and Hawes (1971; Hawes, 1972) warn of the poverty of psychological (individual-level) analysis of communication and charge researchers to adopt an "interact system model." This model makes the "interact"— the juxtaposition of two communicative acts—the basic unit of analysis for communication research. Either member of the interact can serve as the context for the understanding of the other, although there seems to be a strong preference for seeing the first member as the context for the second (Hawes, 1972). Moreover, the whole approach leads to a trans-individual orientation. As Rogers and Farace (1975) note,

> A distinctive aspect of relational analysis is that it necessitates at least a dyadic level of analysis . . . [B]oth actors must participate in the defini-tion of the relationship. Thus the smallest unit of relational analysis is a paired exchange of two messages [the interact]. (p. 226)

This same preoccupation with behavioral contingency at the transindi-vidual level of analysis is characteristic of systems theory (see Fisher, 1980) and phasic (see Ellis & Fisher, 1975; Hawes & Foley, 1976; Poole, 1981) studies of small group communication. It also appears implicitly in every attempt using sequential analytic techniques such as Markov chains (Hewes, 1980); semi-Markov models (Hewes et al., 1980) and time-series regression (Cappella, 1980) to demonstrate com-munication impact (adaptation, mutual influence) on some dyadic or group outcome (Hewes, 1986; see Cappella, Chapter 7).

Context is also crucial to the second of the transindividual ap-proaches—*conventionalized versions*. Knowledge of contexts, and the communicative forms and interpretations appropriate to them, is seen as shared by members of some linguistic community. Consequently, indi-viduals are viewed as culturally interchangeable entities (Schutz & Luck-mann, 1973) with shared knowledge of communication resources and appropriate settings who contribute to the creation of some intersubjec-tive project (a conversation, an interpretation of a particular event) that can be understood by all members of that linguistic community (see Coulthard, 1977; Doelger, 1985; Frentz & Farrell, 1976; Jackson & Jacobs, 1980; Labov, 1972; Sacks, Schegloff, & Jefferson, 1978; Searle, 1969; Stubbs, 1983). Thus conventionalized versions, like behavioral contingency versions, transcend the individual by making simplifying assumptions about the individual's contribution to communication. Since each individual's contribution to a communicative exchange is highly conventionalized, the possibilities of unique contributions or joint mis-understanding are disregarded.[3]

On the one hand, each of these two versions of transindividual ap-proaches—behavioral contingency and conventionalized versions—cor-rectly emphasizes the truly social nature of communication. In that sense, they take us further toward dealing with the issues of impact and intersubjectivity than do trait approaches. On the other hand, because both versions make highly simplifying assumptions about the individual's place in communication, they do not address these issues adequately. Consider first the problem of explaining degrees of impact.

In order to explain the degrees of impact that a message might have on some other's subsequent behavior or cognitive/emotive state, a mechanism or mechanisms that can produce varying degrees of impact must be identified. Unfortunately, both versions of the transindividual approach fail to provide such mechanisms. For example, behavioral contingency versions focus primarily on impact as a descriptive property of communication (see Fisher, Glover, & Ellis, 1977; Hewes, 1979a). Concepts such as order and structure as well as the actual magnitudes of contingent probabilities are all used to *describe* the degree of impact of one message on another (Hewes, 1980). Only rarely are the mechanisms that produce degrees of impact taken as objects of study (for instance, Saine & Bock, 1973; Saine, Schulman, & Emerson, 1974). When serious efforts are made to explore these mechanisms in some detail, they typically reveal the need to incorporate individual-level analysis. To illustrate, even the simplest explanations of behavioral contingencies, those of operant conditioning, seem to require an understanding of individuals' goals (Ringen, 1976; Skinner, 1974) and their awareness of the conditioning process (Dulany, 1961); more empirically adequate analyses include the responding individual's interpretation of the other's initiating behavior (Cappella & Greene, 1982; Patterson, 1982), the goals of the respondent, and the anticipated reactions of the initiator or observers to the respondent's behavior (Street & Giles, 1982). Thus it can be shown empirically that factors that form part of the mechanisms to explain behavioral contingencies derive from the individual.

Conventionalized versions also suffer problems in explaining *degrees* of impact. Because they are based on the recurrence of conventionalized patterns of behavior in socially sanctioned contexts, conventionalized versions of transindividual approaches do a very good job of describing high impact. Adjacency pairs (Jackson & Jacobs, 1980), turn-taking (Sacks et al., 1978), playing the "dozens" (Labov, 1972) all give a strong sense of the prescribed order of discourse. When that order fails or is only partially played out, however, conventionalized approaches face difficulties. In these cases of low impact, one can only say that some cognitive or emotive state that is a prior condition for the conventionalized pattern failed (Graham, 1985). There is no guarantee that this failure will manifest itself in subsequent discourse, and there is nothing within these explanations to explain why the failure occurred or the timing of the failure. To explain less than perfect impact requires that one look to each individual's interpretations of the discourse, the context, and the goals and understandings of the other (Hewes, 1979b). An explanation of degrees of impact requires that individuals be deconventionalized.

Explanations of degrees of intersubjectivity fare no better for the transindividual approaches. Behavioral consistency approaches either fail to address this issue altogether or do so by treating the coders used in this work as "cultural informants" (Bakeman & Gottman, 1986, p. 28) and category schemes as sets of conventionalized acts (see Hawes, 1972; Poole & Folger, 1981). In short, when issues of intersubjectivity are addressed at all, they are handled by making behavioral contingency versions into conventionalized versions. The question then becomes, How well do conventionalized versions explain *degrees* of intersubjectivity?

The answer is that they do not do it very well. Conventionalized versions *are* very useful in explaining intersubjectivity itself almost by definition. If individuals are culturally interchangeable entities with shared knowledge of events and communication resources for talking about those events, then intersubjectivity is attainable almost by definition.[4] It either exists by virtue of the stock of common experiences and a common symbol system or it is achieved eventually by means of those same resources (see Morris & Hopper, 1980; Poole et al., 1986).

Here, as in explanations of degrees of impact, conventionalized versions find themselves in theoretical hot water. By virtue of oversimplifying individuals' potential contributions to communication, conventionalized versions lack the ability to explain less-than-perfect intersubjectivity. This can be illustrated in one of the strongest theoretical efforts to cope with the problem of intersubjectivity, Poole and Doelger's (1986) theory of developmental processes in group decision making.

Poole and Doelger, drawing on Poole's (1983) contingency theory of decision development, attempt to describe factors that disrupt the smooth flow of discussion in task-oriented small groups. They recognize that many disruptions emerge because group members do not share a common understanding of the nature of the task or of the process to be followed to achieve it. Thus they consider intersubjectivity to be both essential for effective decision making and potentially problematic. The adequacy of their attempts to identify sources of low intersubjectivity, however, are hampered by their commitment to a transindividual perspective. For example, Poole and Doelger (p. 59) note that "high difficulty 'objective' tasks will result in (a) more different individual [task] representations, (b) more disagreements over collective representations, and (c) less clarity and completeness of representations than will low difficulty tasks." Other factors, such as the existence of shared procedural norms or a clear definition of the problem should result in more collective task representation (more intersubjective understanding about the task). Note that every factor (e.g., high difficulty) is cast at the transindividual level; yet, these transindividual variables do not in themselves explain why misunderstanding or unvoiced disagreement (differing individual task representations) occur. In one sense the factors are almost tautological: They all suggest that lack of intersubjectivity exists because of lack of intersubjectivity. Lack of consensus about procedure leads to lack of consensus about task representations—which include procedures (Poole & Doelger, 1986, p. 51). In another sense, however, these factors point to the need for individual-level analysis. Perhaps some tasks are "difficult" because they are complex enough or ambiguous enough to tax individuals' capacities to comprehend them. Perhaps the existence of procedural norms reduces the cognitive demands on individual decision makers, letting them focus on the management of conversation (Hewes, 1986). While these may not be the real reasons behind Poole and Doelger's (1986) propositions, they do illuminate the problem faced by theorists concerned with transindividual units of analysis who try to explain degrees of intersubjectivity.

Transindividual approaches to communication offer a constant reminder that communication is a *social* enterprise. That insight, largely ignored by trait approaches, must be central to any theory of communication. Nevertheless, the advances made by transindividual approaches are made at the expense of oversimplifying the place of the individual in communication theory. As we have demonstrated, these oversimplifications make it difficult to identify the mechanisms that explain degrees of impact and intersubjectivity.

Cognitive/Interpretive Approaches

A third alternative approach to the study of communication is what we call the cognitive/interpretive approach. This approach emphasizes the internal, psychological processes involved in interpreting and producing messages and other social behavior (see Hewes & Planalp, 1982; Planalp & Hewes, 1982, for more details). Like trait approaches, the cognitive approach is able to account for individual differences but does so by appeal to differences in cognitive structures that lead to different interpretations of messages and behaviors or different plans of action. Like transindividual approaches, the cognitive approach also deals with observable behavior but never in isolation from ongoing interpretive and production processes. Perhaps the greatest strength of this approach is that it can account for subjective reactions to "objective" messages and behaviors.

It does so by explaining how information in messages is acquired, retained, altered, and acted upon by appeal to a cognitive system that follows general principles yet at the same time makes use of capacities and knowledge structures that may differ substantially from one person to the next. For example, one might explain how two listeners could come away with somewhat different interpretations of a text depending on how much they knew about the topic, what was on their minds at the time, how much time they had to think about it, whether it conjured up memories of similar texts, and the uses to which they intended to put the information, to name just a few factors. At the same time, texts also impose constraints that make some interpretations more reasonable than others. For example, interpretations must be grounded in socially shared word meanings, must be based on inferences that are consistent with common knowledge of the world, and cannot be guided by entirely idiosyncratic concerns and goals. In short, messages serve as general frameworks from which interpretations are constructed through the operation of cognitive processes.

The cognitive system consists of two basic, interrelated components—cognitive processes and knowledge structures (Planalp & Hewes, 1982; Hewes & Planalp, 1982). Briefly, cognitive processes are operations performed on incoming information such as focusing on particular aspects, drawing inferences from it, storing it in memory, retrieving it when needed, selecting plans of action based on it, and implementing those plans. Knowledge structures are organized repositories of information about the world, including the social world, that inform experience and action. Both components must be considered together because there is virtually constant interplay between them (Anderson, 1978). Existing knowledge structures guide the focus of attention to novel events, are the basis of inference, serve as frameworks for storing and retrieving memories, and provide a basis for formulating and implementing action plans (Berger, in press). Similarly, cognitive processes are the means by which knowledge is acquired, updated, and integrated.

The heuristic value of studying communication by appeal to cognitive processes and knowledge structures has been demonstrated in almost every domain of inquiry. Consider, for instance, recent work in the areas of message interpretation (van Dijk & Kintsch, 1983; Hewes, Graham, Doelger, & Pavitt, 1985), message production (Berger & Kellermann, 1983; Greene, 1984; O'Keefe & Delia, 1982), nonverbal communication (Woodall & Folger, 1985), relational communication (Planalp, 1985), small group communication (Kellermann & Jarboe, 1986; Leff & Hewes, 1981), organizational communication (Jablin, 1982), and mass communication (Reeves & Garramone, 1983), to name a few. Clearly the emphasis of the cognitive approach is on processing information but it is also compatible with concerns for motivation and emotion. In fact, sophisticated models of cognition have stimulated renewed interest and important breakthroughs in the study of goal-oriented behavior (Wilensky, 1983b) and emotion (Isen, 1984; Izard, Kagan, & Zajonc, 1984; Mandler, 1984).

As we have noted elsewhere (Planalp & Hewes, 1982), cognition is not a source of basic goals but a means of determining how they might be pursued intelligently. For example, hunger is hardly cognitive, but finding ways of satisfying hunger requires knowledge of the world and the use of incoming information to determine the most effective means of getting food from that world. Nevertheless, human beings seldom pursue distinct goals single-mindedly (Schutz, 1967) but instead gather and retain information almost as an end in itself to be used for any number of other purposes when needed. This seems to be especially true in the social world (Berger & Calabrese, 1975). When particular goals are salient, however, they exert strong influence over which knowledge structures are accessed and how information is processed (Cohen & Ebbesen, 1979; Nisbett & Ross, 1980).

It is also very difficult to separate cognition from emotion at almost any level. Debates over whether cognition or emotion is primary (Lazarus, 1984; Zajonc, 1984) illustrate the difficulties of untangling the two. At the most basic level, preference judgments (presumably emotional; Zajonc, 1980) are based on recognition of stimuli as familiar (presumably cognitive; Mandler & Shebo, 1983). More sophisticated emotional responses are certainly based on more sophisticated construals of emotion-producing situations (Berscheid, 1983; Roseman, 1984). The expression of emotion also depends on assessments of the appropriateness of certain emotions in certain situations, as captured in the notion of "display rules" (Ekman, 1982, p. 17-19). Finally, the fact that we can talk about our feelings and empathize with others based on verbal expressions of their feelings indicates at minimum that there is cognitive recoding of felt emotions into language and vice versa.

Cognitive/interpretive approaches contain a much more complex view of the individual than do either trait or transindividual approaches. Is all this complexity necessary? We believe it is and endeavor to illustrate that below. For the moment though, suffice to say that both trait and transindividual approaches fell err to problems precisely because they oversimplify individuals. Traits are promissory notes on explanation because the generative mechanism that produced trait-related behavior or adaptation is missing from trait theories. Transindividual theories cannot cope effectively with degrees of intersubjectivity because they do not encompass individual differences in the resources that make intersubjectivity possible. In what follows, we show that the complexity of the cognitive approach is necessary to overcome these theoretical deficiencies.

THE HEURISTIC VALUE OF
A COGNITIVE/INTERPRETIVE APPROACH:
TWO APPLICATIONS

To illustrate more fully how studying cognition improves our understanding of the degree of impact and intersubjectivity produced by messages, we turn to two areas of research that are basic to communication—discourse processing and social metacognition. Discourse-processing research deals with the cognitive processes and knowledge structures involved in interpreting and producing texts. Research in social metacognition deals with one person's cognitions about the *other* person's cognitions. Both areas of research are important to communication because together they explain how speakers adapt their messages to the interpretive processes of listeners and how listeners adapt their interpretations to speakers' production processes. By understanding cognition, both researchers and ordinary social actors are able to assess the degree of impact their messages are likely to have and to design messages to produce the intended impact. If intersubjectivity is the goal, knowledge of interpretive and production processes makes it possible to assess whether the other person shares in one's knowledge and how messages might be used to foster intersubjectivity.

Discourse Processing

Of the many different approaches to the study of connected discourse (van Dijk, 1985), discourse processing focuses on speakers'/writers' and listeners'/readers' psychological processes and so is grounded most strongly in the individual level of analysis. While messages themselves are also important, the emphasis is on understanding how they are produced and comprehended. Winograd (1977, p. 64) states this position most strongly in claiming that "the text is a concrete trace of the processes, and its structure needs to be understood in terms of the processing structure." It is not, however, necessary to believe that the text is completely determined by psychological processes and hence reducible to them to grant that texts are produced and comprehended through psychological processes and hence are better understood when those processes are considered.

The following discussion of discourse-processing literature, though not exhaustive, illustrates how the same knowledge structures and cognitive processes that guide information processing in general also guide processing of information from messages. To emphasize the parallels, we follow the same organization pattern used earlier to describe the cognitive system. Research focusing on knowledge structures and processing functions is reviewed, links between knowledge and processing are noted, and work that bridges discourse processing, goals, and emotions is examined.

Knowledge structures. One of the most substantial contributions that computer simulations have made to our understanding of communication is to make explicit the vast amount of organized world knowledge that is necessary to comprehend even the simplest texts (Planalp, 1986, for review). Experimental research has further illustrated that comprehension is founded on knowledge structures such as scripts (Bower, Black, & Turner, 1979; Haberlandt & Bingham, 1982), frames (Charniak, 1982), story grammars (Brewer, 1985), and schemas (Planalp, 1985). Variations in the type and amount of knowledge that is available have also been found to produce dramatic differences in interpretation. For example, texts have been cleverly designed to demonstrate that comprehension is next to impossible without the appropriate prior knowledge and that certain ambiguous texts may be interpreted quite differently depending on what knowledge is cued in the title (Bransford, 1979, chap. 5; Dooling & Lachman, 1971; Kozminsky, 1977). Other work has shown substantial differences in both the amount and kind of information gleaned from texts depending on readers' expertise (Fiske, Kinder, & Larter, 1983; Spilich, Vesonder, Chiesi, & Voss, 1979), and differences in experts' and novices' abilities to gather additional information by asking questions (Miyake & Norman, 1979).

It is not difficult to extrapolate these findings to concerns for the impact of messages and strategies for optimizing it. The type and degree of impact depends, at least in part, on the listener's knowledge. It is not just that complex and sophisticated messages will be wasted on naive listeners/readers compared to experts; precise differences in comprehension processes can also be isolated and used to design messages more effectively. For example, Fiske et al. (1983) found that politically naive people who read texts about an unknown Third World country based their inferences very strongly on prior knowledge of Third World countries, whereas experts were more likely to draw inferences that were consistent with the text but inconsistent with their prior knowledge of Third World countries. To correct for this bias, messages targeted to naive readers might be designed to emphasize how the new information is different from what they might expect. Work on baseball expertise (Spilich et al., 1979; Chiesi, Spilich, & Voss, 1979) also indicates that naive readers are less able than experts to remember events, especially sequences of events that they cannot link to goals, and to anticipate their consequences. Messages for naive readers might have more impact if links between actions and goals were stated explicitly.

Similarly, it is important to understand the role of knowledge structures in comprehension in order to achieve intersubjectivity. In this case, intersubjectivity is a direct extension of impact because intersubjectivity is achieved when a speaker can control the impact a message has on the listener's knowledge in order to bring it into alignment with his or her own knowledge. It also becomes clear that some degree of intersubjectivity is necessary for effective communication. If knowledge is shared, listeners' comprehension is guided by the same knowledge that guides speakers' production so that their conceptions of what was said are similar. If they have either substantially different knowledge (as with experts talking to novices) or access to different knowledge, the two conceptions may differ dramatically and misunderstanding may result unless messages can be designed to compensate for the differences in knowledge.

Cognitive processes. The impact of a message also depends on the degree to which it is the focus of attention, how it is stored and retrieved from memory, how it is integrated with other messages and prior knowledge, what inferences are drawn from it, how it is chosen from among possible alternatives and how it is implemented. Most of these cognitive processes have been investigated in some depth in the discourse processing literature, and a great deal is known about how they function and how they interact with knowledge structures.

The process that has been studied the least in the context of connected discourse is *focusing,* although studies of attentional processes in word and sentence comprehension go back decades (Treisman, 1964). Different messages or different aspects of the same message are more likely to be focused upon than others, and the degree of focus partially determines its impact (Reichman, 1985). Focus alone, however, does not guarantee impact but simply admits information for further processing. For this reason, most investigations of focus of attention either rely on indirect measures such as reading time (Swann & Read, 1981), segmentation, and memory (Cohen & Ebbesen, 1979) or use crude, all-or-nothing measures of focus such as channel switching among video- or audiotapes (Berscheid & Graziano, 1979; White & Carlston, 1983). These latter two studies also show that focus is guided by prior knowledge; Swann and Read found greater focus on consistent information, whereas White and Carlston observed a shift in focus when prior knowledge was first confirmed then later disconfirmed.

The processes that have been studied most thoroughly in the context of connected discourse are *integration* and *inference.* Integration refers to the process of making connections among parts of a text or between a text and prior knowledge. Included among studies of integration are studies of on-line integration during reading (Carpenter & Just, 1977; Clark & Haviland, 1977) many studies of conversational coherence that admit a significant mental component (e.g., Ellis, 1983; Hobbs, 1982; Planalp, Graham, & Paulson, 1985; Tracy, 1985), and studies of information updating (van Dijk & Kintsch, 1983, p. 342). Inference refers to the process of supplying information that goes beyond what is explicitly stated in the text in order to bridge gaps (Clark, 1975), understand important events (Goetz, 1979), or respond appropriately (Kemper, Estill, Otalvaro, & Schadler, 1985). Reiser and Black (1982) state that "accounting for inference is the key to modeling language understanding, since a major proportion of the information communicated in a discourse is left implicit" (p. 229).

Memory for discourse has also received considerable research effort, although the processes of *storage* and *retrieval* have not always been separated. From a cognitive perspective, the issue of *how well* texts are remembered (Hjelmquist & Gidlund, 1985; Stafford & Daly, 1984) is a special case of the issue of *how* texts are remembered. That is, if we understand how memory traces are constructed and accessed when needed, we have a deeper understanding of the circumstances under which those traces do or do not replicate the original event. One consistent finding is that knowledge structures exert considerable influence on memory traces both at the time of storage and retrieval (Anderson & Pichert, 1978; Borland & Flammer, 1985) and serve as a basis for reconstructive memory of the original event even if separated in time and context from it (Spiro, 1980).

In fact, the influence of prior knowledge on all three processes just discussed—integration, inference, and memory—has been demonstrated time and again in research on story grammars. Story grammars are knowledge structures for conventional story forms that guide how information from stories is integrated into a coherent whole (Pollard-Gott, McCloskey, & Todres, 1979), how inferences are made (Stein & Glenn, 1979), and how information about the story is stored and retrieved from memory (Mandler, 1978; Thorndyke, 1977). Controversy still reigns over the area because it is not clear whether people have knowledge structures for stories (Mandler & Goodman, 1982), knowledge structures for the human plans and action often depicted in stories (Wilensky, 1983a), or both (Brewer, 1985). In any case, knowledge in some form guides integration, inference, and memory. Virtually identical evidence for the influence of scripts on the processing of texts about everyday events gives additional corroboration (Bower et al., 1979).

The last two processes, *selection* and *implementation* have received surprisingly little attention considering that they represent all of discourse production. Greene (1984) reviewed the literature on message selection and implementation and described the several levels at which it operates. Cognitive models have been used to account for idea generation (van Dijk & Kintsch, 1983, pp. 294-301), story telling (Haslett, 1986), selection of persuasive messages (Sillars, 1980), deception leakage (Greene, O'Hair, Cody, & Yen, 1985), and verbal and action slips (Motley, Baars, & Camden, 1983; Norman, 1981). It is also evident from these studies that selection and implementation cannot be separated from knowledge. For example, Haslett (1986) demonstrated that storytelling is guided by story grammars and Norman (1981) found one type of action slip to be caused by faulty activation of schemas.

A message's degree of impact obviously depends on the cognitive processes of focusing, integration and inference, storage and retrieval, and selection and implementation. Messages will have impact to the degree that the listener's attention is focused on them, the appropriate connections are made, conclusions are drawn that go beyond the text, the material is stored in memory for later use, retrieved when needed, and used to select and implement the listener's own messages later. Similarly, speakers and listeners are able to achieve intersubjectivity to the extent that they focus on the same information, integrate it in the same way, draw the same inferences, store and retrieve it similarly, and select and implement their subsequent messages in light of their common knowledge.

Ties to goals and emotions. Intuition tells us that goals and emotions influence how speakers produce messages and how listeners comprehend them, but literature on discourse processing goes one step further to explicate those influences by appeal to their effects on knowledge and processing. Goals and knowledge interact in discourse processing in at least two major ways. First, knowledge of goals and how they are achieved or thwarted is critical for interpreting most texts about people since characters in narratives (Wilensky, 1983a), soap operas (Owens, Bower, & Black, 1979), and newspaper stories (Schank & Abelson, 1977) tend to do things for reasons that readers need to understand. Second, speakers draw on knowledge of how to achieve goals in formulating their own messages and listeners use that same knowledge to infer speakers' goals from what they say (Bruce, 1983).

These and other studies have also demonstrated how goals influence processing either directly or indirectly through the knowledge structures they call up. For instance, Owens et al. (1979) found that beliefs about the motives of characters in stories affected how quickly the stories were comprehended, what inferences were drawn, and how the stories were remembered. If we concur with Wilensky and colleagues' arguments that story grammars consist of knowledge of plans rather than knowledge of conventional text structures (Black & Wilensky, 1979; Wilensky, 1983a), all the studies discussed earlier that link story grammars to integration, inference, memory, and production can be seen instead as linking goals, knowledge, and cognitive processes. Finally, two studies have demonstrated how goals influence the degree to which prior knowledge guides cognitive processes. Spiro (1980) found that when people were told they would be asked for their reactions to stories, memory for the stories was influenced by their implicit theories; but when they were told that they would be asked to recall the stories, it was not. Similarly, Cohen and Ebbesen (1979) found that people who were asked to watch a videotape in order to form an impression of the person in it were more influenced by their implicit personality theories (person schemas) than people who were instructed to watch the tape in order to remember the details of the task depicted in it.

Ties between emotions and discourse processing come in two basic forms that parallel the ties between goals and discourse processing. First, texts are often about emotions, either the emotions of characters in stories or the emotions of either the producer or interpreter of the text, so that information about emotions must be processed from and into discourse as is information about any other topic (Davitz, 1969; Dyer, 1983). Second, emotions influence the cognitive processes involved in message production and interpretation directly. For example, Martins (1982) found that affectively loaded material in stories was processed more deeply and hence was recalled better and was more likely to be placed in summaries of the stories than was other material that was more affectively bland. Forgas, Bower, and Krantz (1984) found that mood produced strong effects on judgments and recall of social interaction. In addition, a number of the effects of positive and negative mood on cognitive processes reviewed in Isen (1984) are easily extended to communicative situations. Positive moods tend to make positive material more accessible in memory, to make judgments more positive, and to make people more friendly, open, and giving. Such effects may also lead to more pleasant topics of discussion, more pleasant feelings toward the partner, and more positive interactions in general. The effects of negative mood are found consistently *not* to be the reverse of the effects of positive mood, perhaps because people try to repair bad moods by self-consciously focusing on positive thoughts and being on good behavior. As a result, the effects of negative moods on communicative behavior as mediated through cognitive processes are probably less predictable.

To summarize, the literature on discourse processing reveals a complex cognitive system that guides the interpretation and production of messages. Structures of world knowledge play a major role, as do the processes of focusing, integration and inference, storage and retrieval, selection and implementation. Important links among cognition, goals and emotions were also noted in the discourse literature. Throughout this section, it was also argued that knowledge of how cognition guides message interpretation and production will help communication scholars understand when and how messages have impact and lead to intersubjectivity.

In the next section we extend the analysis to a second domain of application—social metacognition. We examine literature indicating that people are aware of the cognitive processes of others and adapt their messages to optimize impact and intersubjectivity in light of that knowledge. In this sense, ordinary social actors are intuitive scientists (Heider, 1958; Kelly, 1955) who recognize that knowledge and cognitive processes guide how their interaction partners interpret and produce messages.

Social Metacognition

Metacognition refers to people's cognition about their *own* cognition (Wellman, 1985: 1), so *social metacognition* may be used more specifically to refer to a person's cognition about *another* person's cognition. It includes knowledge of the other person's knowledge, awareness of where the other's attention is directed, memory for the other person's memory, and so on. Work on perspective-taking, especially in children (e.g., Clark & Delia, 1977), certainly falls under the rubric of social metacognition but will not be reviewed here, in part because it has been reviewed extensively elsewhere (Flavell, 1974) and in part because we chose to focus on studies that target specific components of the cognitive system. By analyzing social metacognition according to the components of knowledge, cognitive processes and links among cognition, goals, and emotion, we are able to determine the extent to which social actors consider specific aspects of their interaction partners' cognitive systems instead of making more global judgments of their current thoughts, attitudes, and personal characteristics.

Just as cognition in general deals with both input and output processes and discourse processing includes both message interpretation and production, social metacognition is necessary for both speakers and listeners. Effective listeners interpret messages by considering what the speaker must have had in mind, and effective speakers produce messages by considering how their messages are likely to be interpreted. Thus whenever possible we consider each component of social metacognition from both speaker and listener roles.

Knowledge structures. As was discussed in the section on knowledge in discourse processing, research attention has been devoted to how differences in the amount of knowledge people have about a particular topic (i.e., expertise) affect how they interpret messages on that topic. By extension, it was argued that speakers could optimize the impact of their messages by taking those differences into account. Indeed, there is evidence that they do just that. Speakers adapt their messages to the level of knowledge they expect their listeners to have; and if they are wrong, communication suffers (Harris, Begg, & Upfold, 1980). Further, Higgins, McCann, and Fondacaro (1982) found that speakers were more likely to "stick to the facts" (i.e., emphasize description over interpretation) when they believed their listeners had different information than when they believed they shared the same information.

There is also evidence that listeners consider speakers' knowledge in interpreting messages. In two separate studies, Hewes et al. (1985; Doelger, Hewes, & Graham, 1986) found that listeners noted discrepancies between what they knew and what they presumed the speaker to know based on the message (what they call "background cues") and used those discrepancies to reinterpret the message. Thus the impact the message has depends on the listener's assessment of the speaker's knowledge.

Finally, there is a direct connection between knowledge of the other's knowledge and intersubjectivity. Effective communication requires not only that people share knowledge (intersubjectivity) but also that they know they share knowledge, as can be demonstrated at a number of levels. For instance, most discourse is based on culturally shared knowledge found in scripts, schemas, frames, and plans, as discussed earlier. If persons mistakenly believe that their interaction partners share knowledge when they do not, or do not share it when they do, communication leads to serious misunderstanding (Hewes, 1979b). At another level, Clark (1985) argues that the effective use of indirect requests, implicature, definite reference, and nouns depends on the two interaction partners building up common ground over the course of a conversation and each being aware of that common ground. At still another level, Wegner, Giuliano, and Hertel (1985) discuss how relational partners know what the other knows, either because they share the same knowledge or because one person knows *that* the partner knows something but not *what* the partner knows. Such mutual knowledge makes intimacy and coordination possible but can also be the source of such relational problems as boredom, excessive dependence, and (if overestimated) misunderstandings.

Cognitive processes. Effective communication also depends on interactors being cognizant of each others' cognitive processes, including what information is the *focus* of the other's attention. For example, public speakers are admonished to use attention-getting devices in their introductions to make sure audience members focus on the speech. In conversation, people are presumed to be focused on what is currently being said so that if they want to change the topic, they should cue listeners to the change in focus (Planalp & Tracy, 1980). Listeners, too, take speakers' foci of attention into account in interpreting their messages. For example, deictic expressions such as "this" and "that" draw the listener's attention to something by locating it with reference to the speaker (DeVilliers & DeVilliers, 1978, p. 123) and sometimes require that the listener recognizes his or her *this* as the speaker's *that*. A good deal of the time, however, both speaker and listener will have a common focus and assume it in their messages. Clark (1985, p. 200) offers a memorable example. I point to ten men jogging, one of whom is naked, and say, "That man is my neighbor." We both know to which man I am referring.

Examples of social metacognition dealing with *integration* processes also abound. Conversational coherence requires that speakers give listeners cues that are sufficient to make the connections they intend (Planalp et al., 1985). To use a very basic example, stating "He is my best friend" after a discussion about two men would be ambiguous and thus difficult to integrate but after a discussion of a man and a woman would pose no problem. Similarly, listeners integrate information from messages under the assumption that speakers intend for them to see a connection. Grice (1975) gives several examples, including the presumed connection between "Smith doesn't seem to have a girlfriend these days" and "He has been paying a lot of visits to New York lately" (p. 51). Clark and Haviland (1977) also explicate how speakers and listeners coordinate integration through the given-new contract. Speakers indicate through paralinguistic emphasis or cleft sentences which part of a message is given (already known to the listener) and which is new, thus enabling listeners to integrate efficiently new information with prior knowledge. Listeners rely on speakers to designate given and new information accurately, and comprehension suffers when cues are not used correctly.

Speakers and listeners are also aware of how *inferences* are made. Because speakers can count on listeners to make inferences, they need not (and in fact should not in the interests of efficiency) state information they know listeners will supply (Harris & Monaco, 1978; Hopper, 1981). Knowledge of listeners' likely inferences can also be used to mislead, as in the following commercial: "During the coldcatching season, have him gargle twice a day with full-strength Gargoil. Watch his diet, see he gets plenty of sleep and there's a good chance he'll have fewer colds or milder colds this year" (Harris, 1977). Listeners, too, anticipate what inferences speakers intend them to make and on occasion may use inference to malign speaker's intentions (e.g., *A:* "I like your new haircut"; *B:* "So you didn't like the old one").

Adaptation to the other person's *storage* and *retrieval* processes also seems to take place. For example, skillful speakers recognize that their listeners can remember only a few main points (Miller, 1956), remember personally meaningful material and jokes better than blander statements (Keenan, MacWhinney, & Mayhew, 1977), and are more likely to remember vivid than pallid information (Nisbett & Ross, 1980, chap. 3). Listeners also recognize that speakers' messages may be influenced by information that is easily retrieved, producing an availability bias that listeners can correct for in interpreting the message (Hewes et al., 1985; Doelger et al., 1986). Yet there are also times when listeners fail to correct for others' retrieval processes, such as Ross, Amabile, and Steinmetz's (1977) finding that question askers were judged more knowledgeable than question answerers without recognizing that any relevant information can be retrieved to formulate a question but specific, targeted information must be retrieved to answer it. Shared memories also develop through talking over common experiences and may make retrieval of specific events more efficient and thorough (Wegner et al., 1985).

Finally, interaction partners may be aware of constraints on each others' *selection* and *implementation* processes. For example, leading questions can be used to restrict the answerer's response selections to no-win choices (e.g., "Have you stopped beating your wife, yes or no?") or answers that provide biased information (Snyder & Swann, 1978). Conversely, listeners seem to be aware of sources of implementation errors when they interpret too much or too little control, response latencies, speech errors, speech hesitations, and other behaviors as cues to deception (Zuckerman et al., 1981).

The importance of interaction partners' awareness of each other's cognitive processes should be obvious by now. Speakers are better able to assess and optimize the impact of a message if they know what listeners are focusing on, how they are likely to integrate information and draw inferences from it, what they are likely to remember, and how they will select and implement their responses. But the impact also depends on what the listeners think speakers are focusing on, what inferences they are inviting, and so on. Social metacognition is also integral to intersubjectivity in the sense that shared knowledge results from awareness of each others' cognitive processes and attempts to bring them into alignment. Without social metacognition, we might have intersubjectivity but we might not know that we do and hence could not take advantage of it in coordinating activity or correct misunderstandings if they occurred.

Ties to goals and emotions. Extending our analysis of social metacognition to other concerns at the individual level of analysis, we now consider whether people are aware of how goals and emotions are linked to cognition. Again, it seems that they are. Hewes et al. (1985; Doelger et al., 1986) found that listeners reinterpret messages when they believe they are biased by either self-serving or altruistic goals. Wilensky (1983b) also argues at length for the importance of assessing the other's goals and how they are likely to be pursued for both understanding the other and planning one's own behavior. At the very least we must know whether our goals are shared or in conflict.

Similarly, we seem to be aware of how other people's cognitions affect their emotions (and vice versa) and adapt our own messages accordingly. For example, Thoits (1984) indicates that an effective strategy for helping others is to help them reinterpret the situation as less threatening or hopeless or to relabel the cause of distress as simple tiredness or physical illness. The strategy of "looking on the brighter side" also suggests some awareness that negative affect promotes memory for negative events and that asking the other to remember positive events might help to reverse the process.

Throughout this discussion of cognitive/interpretive approaches, we have emphasized the importance of such cognitive processes as focusing, integration, inference, storage, retrieval, selection, and implementation and their interrelationships with knowledge of self, context, and other (social metacognition). This elaborate view of individuals is the cornerstone on which communication theory must be based. It is certainly possible to examine conventionalized sequences or trait-behavior linkages. They are informative in their own right. But as we begin to explain these regularities and why they sometimes fail, cognitive/interpretive approaches become essential.

EXTENSIONS:
COGNITION AND COMMUNICATION PROCESSES

To this point we have demonstrated that knowledge of individual cognitive process is essential to the ability to explain both degrees of communication impact and intersubjectivity. Moreover, we have attempted to justify the use of a richer, more complex picture of the individual than that offered by either trait or transindividual approaches to the study of human communication. Not only are individuals complex but that complexity must be a part of the explanation of a host of communicative phenomena.

In this last section we address, albeit speculatively, the place of a cognitive/interpretive approach in explanations of communication process (Berlo, 1960; Mortensen, 1972). Communication processes are the links between the mental life of one individual and the conjoint lives of two or more individuals. Although our explanations of both impact and intersubjectivity are part of this linking process, cognitive/interpretive approaches are all too often identified with intraindividual, not social, action (Nisbett & Ross, 1980; Taylor, 1981), with the interpretation or production of social stimuli but not with the interaction between individuals (Sampson, 1981). As a step toward overcoming these stereotypes of cognitive/interpretive explanations, we offer the following three-level typology of those explanations as applied to communication processes.

Explanations of the Seemingly Social

Ofttimes cognitive interpretive explanations can serve a positive function by offering the kind of nonsocial explanation they are stereotyped as providing. They give us a natural foil for transindividual explanations that confuse the existence of a temporal pattern of communication with need for some transindividual mechanism to explain it. For instance, observing some attitude change taking place in both parties in a dyadic discussion would *appear* to warrant an explanation based on mutual influence. Nevertheless, there are alternative cognitive explanations that would account for the observed changes without reference to the ongoing communication (see Hewes, 1986, p. 280; Poole & Hunter,

1980; Tesser, 1978). In other words, a number of cognitive mechanisms exist that can produce self-generating temporal change without reference to transindividual explanations. For the sake of simplicity these cognitive mechanisms should serve as viable alternatives to transindividual explanations. Consider some examples.

Mutual gaze is often considered a sign of interactants' joint availability and permeability to one another (Knapp, 1983; Rubin, 1970). Mutual gaze is seen as something special relationally, something that separates it from simple eye gaze (Argyle & Dean, 1965), something that makes it a transindividual variable. Recent research, however, does not support this view. Mutual gaze now seems to be the accidental result of each individual's goal to focus attention on the other person thereby reducing uncertainty (Rutter, Pennington, Dewey, & Swain, 1984; Strongman & Champness, 1968). Or consider Hewes's (1986) explanation of communication influence in decision making. Phasic patterns in group communication are often taken as signs of the operation of some transindividual mechanism, some General Systems principle (Fisher, 1980), mutual influence (Hewes et al., 1980), or structuration (Poole, 1983; Poole & Doelger, 1986). Each of these transindividual perspectives can be contrasted with a cognitive one. Hewes's (1986) socioegocentric model generates an explanation of the seemingly influential nature of communication on decision making. His model is based on the operation of (1) two competing individual goals, (2) limitations of each individual's capacities to juggle both goals at the same time, (3) each individual's cognitive processes, and (4) one purely structural (noninfluence-carrying) communication process that *as a set* explain the evidence that has heretofore justified only a transindividual perspective. Thus in these two cases, explanations of mutual gaze and communicative influence on group decision making, the cognitive/interpretive approach makes it possible to identify nonsocial mechanisms that explain seemingly social processes. This is a useful tactic. To be true to our claims as communication theorists, we should always contrast our assertions about the social nature of phenomena with alternative explanations, usually cognitive/interpretive explanations, that reduce the seemingly social to the individual. Thus are the viability and the parsimony of our claims put to the test.

Explanations of the Etiology of Conventions

As we noted previously, the cognitive/interpretive approach encompasses both idiosyncratic and conventionalized knowledge about context, roles, and communication resources. But cognitive/interpretive approaches can do much more. They also offer the potential to explain the emergence of conventions used to structure interaction across time (see Planalp & Tracy, 1980). That is, inherent *shared* limitations in cognitive processes, or the interface between cognitive processes and knowledge, can explain the evolution of conventionalized patterns of communication. A few examples should suffice to make this point.

Clark and Haviland (1977) identified a social rule—the "given-new contract"—in which a speaker must provide "given" information first so that the listener can compute an antecedent for "new" information. Computing a unique antecedent permits the speaker to store new information appropriately, to resolve ambiguities in interpretation, and to draw correct inferences. Similarly, Planalp and Tracy's (1980) explanation of norms of topic change or topic extension (Tracy, 1985) identifies the goal of comprehensibility and a cognitive process of information integration as the sources of the etiology of social rules. Social rules such as turn-taking and the structure and effectiveness of indirect acts (questions, requests, polite forms) may also have evolved to their present form, in part, from shared cognitive limitations. Regardless, cognitive/ interpretive mechanisms offer a promising hunting ground for the antecedents of social rule development. These social rules, in turn, provide ways of understanding the process of communication.

Explanations of the Interactively Social

Communication processes are not limited to the production of conventionalized forms (Poole et al., 1986). Both the structure and the interpretation of discourse evolve over time. The very intricacy of this process has led some to refer to it as emergent and, therefore, not predictable, although explainable ex post facto (Ellis, 1980; O'Keefe et al., 1980). To us this seems a bit like surrendering before the battle has been fought. Emergence need not be magical! Just because conversation is a heavy mixture of cognition, emotion, social metacognition, cognitive process, and social rules does not put it beyond the reach of the scientific enterprise.

ELIZA, Weizenbaum's (1967, 1976) interactive program simulating an initial psychiatric interview, creates a remarkable illusion of having understood and responded appropriately to a human interactant even though it has limited world knowledge and no social metacognitive abilities (Weizenbaum, 1976, p. 189-191). In fact many human interactants, even knowing that ELIZA is a computer program, respond to it as if it were another human being. If ELIZA can accomplish so much without the full capacities of the human actor, and do so in a completely predictable manner, what might we accomplish by taking those capacities into account?

Hints are already available. For example Graham (1985) has presented a preliminary analysis of simultaneous talk that predicts when turn-taking rules will be followed (see Sacks et al., 1974), when they will be violated, and what form that violation will take—all this from the operation of two sets of rules and the cognitive limitations of the interactants. Thus Graham has begun to explore the why, when, and how of violations of social norms in ongoing conversations. Similarly, recent investigations of second-guessing (Doelger et al., 1986; Hewes et al., 1985; Hewes & Planalp, 1982) also demonstrate the possibility of extending cognitive work to the study of communication processes. These extensions begin with the results of social metacognition (hypotheses about the true nature of the source's message) and begin to explore interactants' use of those hypotheses to engage in social strategies with one or more other interactants in order to test those hypotheses. This work even examines the proactive structuring of social networks to facilitate second-guessing when the need for it arises. Here the effort does not simply end with an interpretation of a message as the output of some cognitive process. Instead, that interpetation is seen as triggering social interaction which itself must cycle again through second-guessing.

And cognitive/interpretive work on the interactively social has not stopped there. Van Dijk and Kintsch's (1983) situational model offers great promise for the effective application of sophisticated cognitive/ interpretive theorizing to the study of the process of communication. Schank (1984), Hintikka (1984), Gunther (1984), and many others are already exploring this rich field of application (Lehnert, 1978; Reichman, 1985; Vaina & Hintikka, 1984). No, emergence need not be magical. But to study it we need a strong understanding of the complexity of individuals. An understanding of the individual's knowledge, cognitive capacities and emotion is the necessary point of departure for building adequate theories of communication. That is the place of the individual in a science of communication.

NOTES

1. We are arguing here that while *interpretations* of phenomena may be partially theory governed, the original data need not be. Certainly theories guide perception but they do not rule it (Planalp & Hewes, 1982; Suppe, 1974, pp. 192-199).

2. Degrees of intersubjectivity could be predicted from the *similarity* of beliefs (trait) *that two* or more individuals hold about some object, event, or person outside themselves. Degrees of intersubjectivity might also be predicted by the degree to which *one* individual possesses some trait that makes him or her less open to others or less skillful in perceiving others' orientations toward some object, event, or person.

3. We are arguing here that while conventionalized theories have an ex post facto mechanism for identifying *that* a misunderstanding has occurred (A didn't follow rule X therefore A did not know X was applicable or was not competent to perform X), the mechanisms that would explain *why* and *when* a misunderstanding will take place are missing from these conventionalized theories.

4. While it is true that Schutz (1967; Schutz & Luckman, 1973) gives a great deal of attention to the effects of lack of "mediacy" of experience (direct experience) as a barrier to strong intersubjectivity, his solution to the problem of intersubjectivity rests strongly on his presumption of a common symbol system and shared experience, even if not "mediate."

REFERENCES

Alston, W. P. (1975). Traits, consistency, and conceptual alternatives for personality theory. *Journal for the Theory of Social Behavior, 5,* 17-47.
Anderson, J. R. (1978). Arguments concerning representations for mental imagery. *Psychological Review, 85,* 249-277.
Anderson, R. C., & Pichert, J. W. (1978). Recall of previously unrecallable information following a shift in perspective. *Journal of Verbal Learning and Verbal Behavior, 17,* 1-12.
Argyle, M., & Dean, J. (1965). Eye contact, distance, and affiliation. *Sociometry, 28,* 289-304.
Bakeman, R., & Gottman, J. M. (1986). *Observing interaction.* London: Cambridge University Press.
Berger, C. R. (1985). Social power and interpersonal communication. In M. L. Knapp & G. R. Miller (Eds.), *Handbook of interpersonal communication.* Newbury Park, CA: Sage
Berger, C. R. (in press). Planning, affect and social action generation. In L. Donohew, H. Sypher, & E. T. Higgins (Eds.), *Communication, social cognition and affect.* Hillsdale, NJ: Lawrence Erlbaum.
Berger, C. R., & Bradac, J. J. (1982). *Language and social knowledge.* London: Edward Arnold.
Berger, C. R. & Calabrese, R. (1975). Some explorations in initial interaction and beyond: Toward a developmental theory of interpersonal communication. *Human Communication Research, 1,* 99-112.
Berger, C. R., & Kellermann, K. A. (1983). To ask or not to ask: Is that a question? In R. N. Bostrom (Ed.), *Communication yearbook 7.* Newbury Park, CA: Sage.
Berlo, D. K. (1960). *The process of communication.* New York: Holt, Rinehart & Winston.
Berscheid, E. (1983). Emotion. In H. H. Kelley, E. Berscheid, A. Christensen, J. H. Harvey, T. L. Huston, G. Levinger, E. McClintock, L. A. Peplau, & D. R. Peterson (Eds.), *Close relationships.* New York: Freeman.
Berscheid, E., & Graziano, W. (1979). The initiation of social relationships and interpersonal attraction. In R. L. Burgess & T. L. Huston (Eds.), *Social exchange in developing relationships.* New York: Academic Press.
Bitzer, L. (1968). The rhetorical situation. *Philosophy and Rhetoric, 1,* 1-14.
Black, J. B., & Wilensky, R. (1979). An evaluation of story grammars. *Cognitive Science, 3,* 213-230.
Blass, T. (Ed.). (1977). *Personality variables in social behavior.* Hillsdale, NJ: Lawrence Erlbaum.
Blau, P. M. (1964). *Exchange and power in social life.* New York: John Wiley.
Bochner, A. P., & Krueger, D. L. (1979). Interpersonal communication theory and research: An overview of inscrutable epistemologies and muddled concepts. In D. Nimmo (Ed.), *Communication yearbook 3.* New Brunswick, NJ: Transaction.
Borland, R., & Flammer, A. (1985). Encoding and retrieval processes in memory for prose. *Discourse Processes, 8,* 305-317.

Bower, G. H., Black, J. B., & Turner, T. (1979). Scripts in memory for text. *Cognitive Psychology, 11*, 177-220.

Bransford, J. D. (1979). *Human cognition: Learning, understanding and remembering.* Belmont, CA: Wadsworth.

Brehmer, B., & Hammond, K. R. (1977). Cognitive factors in interpersonal conflict. In D. Druckman (Ed.), *Negotiations: Social-psychological perspectives.* Newbury Park, CA: Sage.

Brewer, W. F. (1985). The story schema: Universal and culture-specific properties. In D. R. Olson, N. Torrance, & A. Hildyard (Eds.), *Literacy, language, and learning.* New York: Cambridge University Press.

Briggs, S. R. (1985). A trait account of social shyness. P. Shaver (Ed.). *Review of personality and social psychology* (Vol. 6). Newbury Park, CA: Sage.

Brigham, J. C. (1971). Racial stereotypes, attitudes, and evaluations of and behavioral intentions toward negroes and whites. *Sociometry, 36*, 360-380.

Bruce, B. (1983). Plans and discourse. *Text, 3*, 253-259.

Bruner, J. S. (1978). From communication to language: A psychological perspective. In I. Markova (Ed.), *The social context of language.* New York: John Wiley.

Cantor, N., & Kihlstrom, J. F. (1985). Social intelligence: The cognitive basis of personality. In P. Shaver (Ed.), *Review of personality and social psychology* (Vol. 6). Newbury Park, CA: Sage.

Cappella, J. (1980). Structural equation modeling: An introduction. In P. Monge & J. Cappella (Eds.), *Multivariate techniques in communication research.* New York: Academic Press.

Cappella, J. N., & Folger, J. P. (1980). An information processing explanation of attitude-behavior inconsistency. In D. P. Cushman & R. McPhee (Eds.), *Message-attitude-behavior relationship.* New York: Academic Press.

Cappella, J. N., & Greene, J. O. (1982). A discrepancy-arousal explanation of mutual influence in expressive behavior for adult and infant-infant interaction. *Communication Monographs, 49*, 89-114.

Carpenter, P. A., & Just, M. A. (1977). Integrative processes in comprehension. In D. LaBerge & J. Samuels (Eds.), *Perception and comprehension.* Hillsdale, NJ: Lawrence Erlbaum.

Carroll, J. S., & Payne, J. W. (Eds.), (1976). *Cognition and social behavior.* Hillsdale, NJ: Lawrence Erlbaum.

Charniak, E. (1982). Context recognition in language comprehension. In W. G. Lehnert & M. H. Ringle (Eds.), *Strategies for natural language processing.* Hillsdale, NJ: Lawrence Erlbaum.

Cherry, F. & Byrne D. (1977). Authoritarianism. In T. Blass (Ed.), *Personality variables in social behavior.* Hillsdale, NJ: Lawrence Erlbaum.

Chiesi, H. L., Spilich, G. J., & Voss, J. F. (1979). Acquisition of domain-related information in relation to high and low domain knowledge. *Journal of Verbal Learning and Verbal Behavior, 18*, 257-273.

Chomsky, N. (1975). *Reflections on language.* New York: Pantheon Books.

Clark, H. H. (1975). Bridging. In R. Schank & B. Nash-Webber (Eds.), *Theoretical issues in natural language processing.* Cambridge: MIT Press.

Clark, H. H. (1985). Language use and language users. In G. Lindsey & E. Aronson (Eds.), *The handbook of social psychology* (Vol. 2). New York: Random House.

Clark, H. H., & Haviland, S. W. (1977). Comprehension and the given-new contact. In R. O. Freedle (Ed.), *Discourse production and comprehension* (Vol. 1). Norwood, NJ: Ablex.

Clark, R. A., & Delia, J. G. (1977). Cognitive complexity, social perspective-taking, and functional persuasive skills in second- to ninth-grade children. *Human Communication Research, 3*, 128-134.

Cohen, C. E., & Ebbesen, E. B. (1979). Observational goals and schema activation: A theoretical framework for behavior perception. *Journal of Experimental Social Psychology, 15,* 305-329.

Coulthard, M. (1977). *An introduction to discourse analysis.* Hong Kong: Longman Group, Ltd.

Cronen, V. E., Pearce, W. B., & Harris, L. M. (1982). The coordinated management of meaning: A theory of communication. In F.E.X. Dance (Ed.), *Human communication theory.* New York: Harper & Row.

Cushman, D., & Whiting, G. (1972). An approach to communication theory: Toward consensus on rules. *Journal of Communication, 22,* 217-238.

Dance, F.E.X., & Larson, C. E. (1976). *The functions of human communication: A theoretical approach.* New York: Holt, Rinehart & Winston.

D'Andrade, R. G. (1981). The cultural part of cognition. *Cognitive Science, 5,* 179-195.

Davis, D. (1982). Determinants of responsiveness in dyadic interaction. In W. Ickes & E. S. Knowles (Eds.), *Personality, roles & social behavior.* New York: Springer-Verlag.

Davitz, J. R. (1969). *The language of emotion.* New York: Academic Press.

Delia, J. G. (1977). Constructivism and the study of human communication. *Quarterly Journal of Speech, 63,* 66-83.

Delia, J. G., O'Keefe, B. J., O'Keefe, D. J. (1982). The constructivist approach to communication. In F.E.X. Dance (Ed.), *Human communication theory.* New York: Harper & Row.

Denzin, N. K. (1984). *On understanding emotion.* San Francisco: Jossey-Bass.

DeVilliers, J. G., & DeVilliers, P. A. (1978). *Language acquisition.* Cambridge, MA: Harvard University Press.

Doelger, J. A. (1985). *A descriptive analysis of complaints in conversation.* Paper presented to the Speech and Language Sciences Division of the Speech Communication Association Convention, Denver, CO.

Doelger, J. A., Hewes, D. E. & Graham, M. L. (1986). Knowing when to "second-guess": The mindful analysis of messages. *Human Communication Research, 12,* 301-338.

Dooling, D. J., & Lachman, R. (1971). Effects of comprehension on retention of prose. *Journal of Experimental Psychology, 88,* 216-222.

Dulany, D. E. (1961). Hypotheses and habits in verbal "operant conditioning." *Journal of Abnormal and Social Psychology, 63,* 251-263.

Dyer, M. G. (1983). The role of affect in narratives. *Cognitive Science, 1,* 211-242.

Ekman, P. (Ed.). (1982). *Emotion in the human face.* Cambridge: Cambridge University Press.

Ellis, D. G. (1980). Ellis on Hewes. *Quarterly Journal of Speech, 66,* 437-439.

Ellis, D. G. (1983). Language, coherence, and textuality. In R. T. Craig & K. Tracy (Eds.), *Conversational coherence: Form, structure, and strategy.* Newbury Park, CA: Sage.

Ellis, D., & Fisher, B. (1975). Phases of conflict in small group development: A Markov analysis. *Human Communication Research, 1,* 195-212.

Endler, N. S. (1982). Interactionism comes of age. In M. P. Zanna, E. T. Higgins, & C. P. Herman (Eds.), *Consistency in social behavior* (Vol. 2). Hillsdale, NJ: Lawrence Erlbaum.

Feyerabend, P. (1975). *Against method.* London: Versa.

Fisher, B. A. (1970). Decision emergence: Phases in group decision-making. *Speech Monographs, 37,* 53-66.

Fisher, B. A. (1978). *Perspectives on human communication.* New York: Macmillan.

Fisher, B. A. (1980). *Small-group decision-making* (2nd ed.). New York: McGraw-Hill.

Fisher, B. A., Glover, T. W., & Ellis, D. G. (1977). The nature of complex communication systems. *Communication Monographs, 44,* 231-240.

Fisher, B. A., & Hawes, L. C. (1971). An interact system model: Generating a grounded theory of small groups. *Quarterly Journal of Speech, 57,* 444-453.

Fisher, W. R. (1984). Narration as a human communication paradigm: The case of public moral argument. *Communication Monographs, 51,* 1-22.

Fisher, W. R. (1985). The narrative paradigm: An elaboration. *Communication Monographs, 52,* 347-367.

Fiske, S. T., Kinder, D. R., & Larter, W. M. (1983). The novice and the expert: Knowledge-based strategies in political cognition. *Journal of Experimental Social Psychology, 19,* 381-400.

Fiske, S. T., & Taylor, S. E. (1984). *Social cognition.* Reading, MA: Addison-Wesley.

Flavell, J. H. (1974). The development of inferences about others. In T. Mischel (Ed.), *Understanding other persons.* Oxford: Basil Blackwell.

Forgas, J. P., Bower, G. H., & Krantz, S. E. (1984). The influence of mood on perceptions of social interactions. *Journal of Experimental Social Psychology, 20,* 497-513.

Frentz, T. S., & Farrell, T. B. (1976). Language action: A paradigm for communication. *Quarterly Journal of Speech, 62,* 333-349.

Goetz, E. T. (1979). Infering from text: Some factors influencing which inferences will be made. *Discourse Processes, 2,* 179-195.

Gottman, J. M. (1979). *Marital interaction: Experimental investigations.* New York: Academic Press.

Graham, M. L. (1985). *An integrative framework for explaining simultaneous talk.* Paper presented to the Speech and Language Sciences Division of the Speech Communication Association Convention, Denver, CO.

Greene, J. O. (1984). A cognitive approach to human communication: An action assembly theory. *Communication Monographs, 51,* 289-306.

Greene, J. O., O'Hare, H. D., Cody, M. J., & Yen, C. (1985). Planning and control of behavior during deception. *Human Communication Research, 11,* 335-364.

Greene, J. O. & Sparks G. G. (1983). Explication and test of a cognitive model of communication apprehension: A new look at an old construct. *Human Communication Research, 9,* 349-366.

Grice, H. P. (1975). Logic and conversation. In P. Cole & J. L. Morgan (Eds.), *Studies in syntax* (Vol. 3). New York: Seminar Press.

Grossberg, L. (1982). Does communication theory need intersubjectivity? Toward an immanent philosophy of interpersonal relationships. In M. Burgoon (Ed.), *Communication yearbook 6.* Newbury Park, CA: Sage.

Gunther, A. (1984). Some ways of representing dialogues. In L. Vaina & J. Hintikka (Eds.), *Cognitive constraints on communication.* Boston: D. Reidel.

Gurwitsch, A. (1974). *Phenomenology and the theory of science.* Evanston, IL: Northwestern University Press.

Haberlandt, K., & Bingham, G. (1982). The role of scripts in the comprehension and retention of texts. *Text, 2,* 29-46.

Hale, C., & Delia, J. G. (1976). Cognitive complexity and social perspective-taking. *Communication Monographs, 43,* 195-203.

Hammond, K. R., Stewart, T. R., Adelman, L., & Wascoe, N. (1975). *Report to the Denver City Council and Mayor regarding the choice of handgun ammunition for the Denver Police Department* (Program of Research on Human Judgment and Social Interaction Report No. 179). Boulder: University of Colorado, Institute of Behavioral Science.

Harris, G., Begg, I., & Upfold, D. (1980). On the role of the speaker's expectations in interpersonal communication. *Journal of Verbal Learning and Verbal Behavior, 19*, 597-607.

Harris, R. H. (1977). Comprehension of pragmatic implications in advertising. *Journal of Applied Psychology, 62*, 603-608.

Harris, R. J., & Monaco, G. E. (1978). Psychology of pragmatic implication: Information processing between the lines. *Journal of Experimental Psychology: General, 107*, 1-22.

Haslett, B. (1986). A developmental analysis of children's narratives. In D. G. Ellis & W. A. Donahue (Eds.), *Contemporary issues in language and discourse processes.* Hillsdale, NJ: Lawrence Erlbaum.

Hawes, L. (1972). Development and application of an interview coding system. *Central States Speech Journal, 23*, 92-99.

Hawes, L., & Foley, J. (1976). Group decisioning: Testing a finite stochastic model. In G. Miller (Ed.), *Explorations in interpersonal communication.* Newbury Park, CA: Sage.

Heider, F. (1958). *The psychology of interpersonal relations.* New York: John Wiley.

Hewes, D. E. (1979a). The sequential analysis of social interaction. *Quarterly Journal of Speech, 65*, 56-73.

Hewes, D. E. (1979b). *Discourse can't "behave": Structure, structure, where is the structure?* Paper presented to the Speech Communication Seminar on Research on Interactive Discourse, San Antonio, TX.

Hewes, D. E. (1980). Stochastic modeling of communication processes. In P. R. Monge & J. N. Cappella (Eds.), *Multivariate techniques in human communication research.* New York: Academic Press.

Hewes, D. E. (1986). A socio-egocentric model of group decision-making. In R. Y. Hirokawa & M. S. Poole (Eds.), *Communication and group decision-making.* Newbury Park, CA: Sage.

Hewes, D. E., Graham, M. L., Doelger, J., & Pavitt, C. (1985). "Second-guessing": Message interpretation in social networks. *Human Communication Research, 11*, 299-334.

Hewes, D. E., & Haight, L. (1979). The cross-situational consistency of communicative behaviors: A preliminary investigation. *Communication Research, 6*, 243-270.

Hewes, D. E., & Planalp, S. (1982). There is nothing as useful as a good theory . . . : The influence of social knowledge on interpersonal communication. In M. E. Roloff & C. R. Berger (Eds.), *Social cognition and communication.* Newbury Park, CA: Sage.

Hewes, D. E., Planalp, S., & Streibel, M. J. (1980). Analyzing social interaction: Some excruciating models and exhilarating results. In D. Nimmo (Ed.), *Communication yearbook 4.* New Brunswick, NJ: Transaction.

Higgins, E. T., McCann, C. D., & Fondacaro, R. (1982). The "communication game": Goal-directed encoding and cognitive consequences. *Social Cognition, 1*, 21-37.

Hintikka, J. (1984). Rules, utilities, and strategies in dialogical games. In L. Vaina & J. Hintikka (Eds.), *Cognitive constraints on communication.* Boston: D. Reidel.

Hirschberg, N. (1978). A correct treatment of traits. In H. London (Ed.), *Personality: A new look at metatheories.* New York: John Wiley.

Hjelmquist, E., & Gidlund, A. (1985). Free recall of conversations. *Text, 5*, 169-185.

Hobbs, J. R. (1982). Towards an understanding of coherence in discourse. In W. D. Lehnert & M. H. Ringle (Eds.). *Strategies for natural language processing.* Hillsdale, NJ: Lawrence Erlbaum.

Homans, G. C. (1974). *Social behavior: Its elementary forms* (2nd ed.). New York: Harcourt Brace Jovanovich.

Hopper, R. (1981). The taken-for-granted. *Human Communication Research, 7,* 195-211.

Isen, A. M. (1984). Toward understanding the role of affect in cognition. In R. S. Wyer, Jr., & T. K. Srull (Eds.), *Handbook of social cognition* (Vol. 3). Hillsdale, NJ: Lawrence Erlbaum.

Izard, C. E., Kagan, J., Zajonc, R. C. (Eds.). (1984). *Emotions, cognition, and behavior.* Cambridge: Cambridge University Press.

Jablin, F. M. (1982). Organizational communication: An assimilation approach. In M. E. Roloff & C. R. Berger (Eds.), *Social cognition and communication.* Newbury Park, CA: Sage.

Jackson, S., & Jacobs, S. (1980). Structure of conversational argument: Pragmatic bases for the enthymeme. *Quarterly Journal of Speech, 66,* 251-265.

Keenan, J. M., MacWhinney, B., & Mayhew, D. (1977). Pragmatics in memory: A study of natural conversation. *Journal of Verbal Learning and Verbal Behavior, 16,* 549-560.

Kellermann, K., & Jarboe, S. (1986). *Conservatism in judgment: Is the risky shift-ee really risky, really?* Paper presented to the Information Systems Division of the International Communication Association Convention, Chicago, IL.

Kelley, H. H., & Stahelski, A. J. (1970). Social interaction basis of cooperators' and competitors' beliefs about others. *Journal of Personality and Social Psychology, 16,* 66-91.

Kelley, H. H., & Thibaut, J. W. (1978). *Interpersonal relations.* New York: John Wiley.

Kelly, G. A. (1955). *A theory of personality.* New York: Norton.

Kemper, S., Estill, R., Otalvaro, N., & Schadler, M. (1985). Questions of facts and questions of inferences. In A. C. Graesser & J. B. Black (Eds.), *The psychology of questions.* Hillsdale, NJ: Lawrence Erlbaum.

Kenny, A., & Zaccaro, S. J. (1983). An estimate of variance due to traits in leadership. *Journal of Applied Psychology, 26,* 7-21.

Knapp, M. L. (1983). Dyadic relationship development. In J. M. Wiemann & R. P. Harrison (Eds.), *Nonverbal interaction.* Newbury Park, CA: Sage.

Kozminsky, E. (1977). Altering comprehension: The effect of biasing titles on text comprehension. *Memory and Cognition, 5,* 482-490.

Labov, W. (1972). Rules for ritual insults. In D. Sudnow (Ed.), *Studies in social interaction.* New York: Free Press.

Laing, R. D., Phillipson, H., & Lee, C. (1966). *Interpersonal perception.* New York: Harper & Row.

Lazarus, R. S. (1984). On the primacy of cognition. *American Psychologist, 39,* 124-129.

Lefcourt, H. M. (1976). *Locus of control.* Hillsdale, NJ: Lawrence Erlbaum.

Leff, M. C., & Hewes, D. E. (1981). Topical invention and group communication: Towards a sociology of inference. In G. Ziegelmueller & J. Rhodes (Eds.), *Dimensions of argument.* Annandale, VA: Speech Communication Association.

Lehnert, W. G. (1978). *The process of question answering.* Hillsdale, NJ: Lawrence Erlbaum.

Mancuso, J. C., & Adams-Weber, J. C. (Eds.), (1982). *The construing person.* New York: Praeger.

Mandler, G. (1984). *Mind and body.* New York: Norton.

Mandler, G., & Shebo, B. J. (1983). Knowing and liking. *Motivation and Emotion, 7,* 125-144.

Mandler, J. M. (1978). A code in the node: The use of a story schema in retrieval. *Discourse Processes, 1,* 14-35.

Mandler, J. M., & Goodman, M. S. (1982). On the psychological validity of story structure. *Journal of Verbal Learning and Verbal Behavior, 21,* 507-523.

Martins, D. (1982). Influence of affect on comprehension of a text. *Text, 2,* 141-154.
McCall, G. J., & Simmons, J. L. (1978). *Identities and interactions* (2nd ed.). New York: Free Press.
McCroskey, J. C. (1982). Oral communication apprehension: A reconceptualization. In M. Burgoon (Ed.), *Communication yearbook 6.* Newbury Park, CA: Sage.
McGuire, W. J. (1968). Personality and susceptibility to social influence. In E. F. Borgatta and W. W. Lambert (Eds.), *Handbook of personality theory and research.* Chicago: Rand McNally.
Miller, G. A. (1956). The magical number seven plus or minus two: Some limits on capacity for processing information. *Psychological Review, 63,* 81-96.
Mischel, W. (1968). *Personality and assessment.* New York: John Wiley.
Mischel, W. (1973). Toward a cognitive social learning reconceptualization of personality. *Psychological Review, 80,* 252-283.
Mischel, W. (1978). Personality research: A look at the future. In H. London (Ed.), *Personality.* New York: John Wiley.
Miyake, N., & Norman, D. A. (1979). To ask a question, one must know enough to know what is not known. *Journal of Verbal Learning and Verbal Behavior, 18,* 357-364.
Morris, G. H., & Hopper, R. (1980). Remediation and legislation in everyday talk: How communicators achieve consensus. *Quarterly Journal of Speech, 66,* 266-274.
Mortensen, C. D. (1972). *Communication.* New York: McGraw-Hill.
Motley, M. T., Baars, B. J. & Camden, C. T. (1983). Experimental verbal slip studies: A review and an editing model of language encoding. *Communication Monographs, 50,* 79-101.
Nisbett, R., & Ross, L. (1980). *Human inference.* Englewood Cliffs, NJ: Prentice-Hall.
Norman, D. A. (1981). Categorization of action slips. *Psychological Review, 88,* 1-15.
O'Keefe, B. J., & Delia, J. G. (1982). Impression formation processes and message production. In M. E. Roloff & C. R. Berger (Eds.), *Social cognition and communication.* Newbury Park, CA: Sage.
O'Keefe, B. J., Delia, J. G., & O'Keefe, D. J. (1980). Interaction analysis and the analysis of interactional organization. In N. K. Denzin (Ed.), *Studies in symbolic interaction* (Vol. 3). Greenwich, CT: JAI Press.
Owens, J., Bower, G. H., & Black, J. B. (1979). The "soap opera" effect in story recall. *Memory and Cognition, 7,* 185-191.
Papineau, D. (1979). *Theory and meaning.* Oxford: Clarendon Press.
Parks, M. R. (1980). A test of the cross-situational consistency of communication apprehension. *Communication Monographs, 47,* 220-232.
Patterson, M. L. (1982). A sequential functional model of nonverbal exchange. *Psychological Review, 89,* 231-249.
Pavitt, C., & Cappella, J. (1979). Coorientational accuracy in interpersonal and small group discussions: A literature review, model, and simulation. In D. Nimmo (Ed.) *Communication yearbook 3.* New Brunswick, NJ: Transaction.
Planalp, S. (1985). Relational schemata: A test of alternative forms of relational knowledge as guides to communication. *Human Communication Research, 12,* 3-29.
Planalp, S. (1986). Scripts, story grammars, and causal schemas. In D. G. Ellis & W. A. Donohue (Eds.), *Contemporary issues in language and discourse processes.* Hillsdale, NJ: Lawrence Erlbaum.
Planalp, S., Graham, M., & Paulson, L. (1985). *Cohesive devices in conversation.* Paper presented to the Language and Speech Sciences Division of the Speech Communication Association Convention, Denver, CO.
Planalp, S., & Hewes, D. E. (1982). A cognitive approach to communication theory: *Cogito ergo dico?* In M. Burgoon (Ed.), *Communication yearbook 5.* New Brunswick, NJ: Transaction.

Planalp, S. & Tracy, K. (1980). Not to change the topic but . . . : A cognitive approach to the management of conversation. In D. Nimmo (Ed.), *Communication yearbook 4.* New Brunswick, NJ: Transaction.

Pollard-Gott, L., McCloskey, M., & Todres, A. K. (1979). Subjective story structure. *Discourse Processes, 2,* 251-281.

Poole, M. S. (1981). Decision development in small groups I: A comparison of two models. *Communication Monographs, 48,* 1-24.

Poole, M. S. (1983). Decision development in small groups III: A multiple sequence model of group decision-making. *Communication Monographs, 50,* 321-341.

Poole, M. S., & Doelger, J. A. (1986). Developmental processes in group decision-making. In R. Y. Hirokawa & M. S. Poole (Eds.), *Communication and group decision-making.* Newbury Park, CA: Sage.

Poole, M. S., & Folger, J. P. (1981). A method for establishing the representational validity of interaction coding schemes: Do we see what they see? *Human Communication Research, 8,* 26-42.

Poole, M. S., Folger, J. P., & Hewes, D. E. (1986). Analyzing interpersonal interaction. In M. Roloff & G. R. Miller (Eds.), *Interpersonal processes: New directions in communication research.* Newbury Park, CA: Sage.

Poole, M. S., & Hunter, J. E. (1980). Behavior and hierarchies of attitudes: A deterministic model. In P. Cushman & R. McPhee (Eds.), *The message-attitude-behavior relationship.* New York: Academic Press.

Poole, M. S., Seibold, D. R., & McPhee, R. D. (1986). A structurational approach to theory-building in group decision-making research. In R. Y. Hirokawa & M. S. Poole (Eds.), *Communication and group decision-making.* Newbury Park, CA: Sage.

Pylyshyn, Z. W. (1984). *Computation and cognition.* Cambridge: MIT Press.

Quine, W. V. (1974). *The roots of reference.* LaSalle, IL: Open Court.

Rabinow, P., & Sullivan, W. M. (Eds.), (1979). *Interpretive social science: A reader.* Berkeley: University of California Press.

Reeves, B., & Garramone, G. M. (1983). Television's influence on children's encoding of personal information. *Human Communication Research, 10,* 257-268.

Reichman, R. (1985). *Getting computers to talk like you and me.* Cambridge: MIT Press.

Reiser, B. J., & Black, J. B. (1982). Processing and structural models of comprehension. *Text, 2,* 225-252.

Richards, I. A. (1965). *The philosophy of rhetoric.* New York: Oxford University Press.

Ringen, J. D. (1976). Explanation, teleology, and operant behaviorism: Purposive behavior. *Philosophy of Science, 43,* 223-253.

Rogers, L. E., & Farace, R. V. (1975). An analysis of relational communication in dyads: New measurement procedures. *Human Communication Research, 1,* 222-239.

Roloff, M. E. (1980). Self-awareness and the persuasion process: Do we really *know* what we are doing? In M. E. Roloff & G. R. Miller (Eds.), *Persuasion: New directions in theory and research.* Newbury Park, CA: Sage.

Roloff, M. E., & Berger, C. R. (Eds.). (1982). *Social cognition and communication.* Newbury Park, CA: Sage.

Roseman, I. J. (1984). Cognitive determinants of emotion: A structural theory. In P. Shaver (Ed.), *Review of personality and social psychology* (Vol. 5). Newbury Park, CA: Sage.

Ross, L., Amabile, T. M., & Steinmetz, J. L. (1977). Social roles, social control and biases in social perception processes. *Journal of Personality and Social Psychology, 35,* 485-494.

Rubin, Z. (1970). The measurement of romantic love. *Journal of Personality and Social Psychology, 16,* 265-272.

Rutter, D.R., Pennington, D. C., Dewey, M. E., & Swain, J. (1984). Eye contact as a chance product of individual looking: Implications for the intimacy model of Argyle and Dean. *Journal of Nonverbal Behavior, 8,* 250-258.

Sacks, H., Schegloff, E., & Jefferson, G. (1978). A simplest systematics for the organization of turn-taking for conversation. In J. Schenkein (Ed.), *Studies in the organization of conversational interaction.* New York: Academic Press.

Saine, T., & Bock, D. (1973). The effects of reward criteria on the structure of interaction in problem solving groups. *Southern Speech Communication Journal, 39,* 55-62.

Saine, T. J., Schulman, L. S., & Emerson, L. C. (1974). The effects of group size on the structure of interaction in problem-solving groups. *Southern Speech Communication Journal, 40,* 333-345.

Sampson, E. E. (1981). Cognitive psychology as ideology. *American Psychologist, 36,* 730-743.

Schank, R. (1984). Looking for a process model of dialogue: Speculations from the perspective of artificial intelligence. In L. Vaina & J. Hintikka (Eds.), *Cognitive constraints on communication.* Boston: D. Reidel.

Schank, R. C., & Abelson, R. P. (1977). *Scripts, plans, goals and understanding.* Hillsdale, NJ: Lawrence Erlbaum.

Schutz, A. (1967). *The phenomenology of the social world* (G. Walsh and F. Lehnert, Trans.). Evanston, IL: Northwestern University Press.

Schutz, A. & Luckmann, T. (1973). *The structures of the life-world* (R. M. Zaner and H. T. Engelhardt, Jr., Trans.). Evanston, IL: Northwestern University Press.

Searle, J. R. (1969). *Speech acts.* Cambridge: Cambridge Univ. Press.

Seibold, D. R., & Spitzberg, B. H. (1982). Attribution theory and research: Review and implications for communication. In B. Dervin & M. Voigt (Eds.), *Progress in communication sciences* (Vol. 3). Norwood, NJ: Ablex.

Sillars, A. L. (1985). Interpersonal perception in relationships. In W. Ickes. (Ed.), *Compatible and incompatible relationships.* New York: Springer-Verlag.

Sillars, A. L. (1980). The stranger and the spouse as target persons for compliance-gaining strategies: A subjective expected utility model. *Human Communication Research, 6,* 265-279.

Skinner, B. F. (1974). *About behaviorism.* New York: Alfred Knopf.

Smith, F. (1985). A metaphor for literacy: Creating worlds or shunting information? In D. R. Olson, N. Torrance, & A. Hildyard (Eds.), *Literacy, language and learning.* New York: Cambridge University Press.

Snyder, M. (1979). Self-monitoring processes. In L. Berkowitz (Ed.), *Advances in experimental social psychology* (Vol. 12). New York: Academic.

Snyder, M., & Ickes, W. (1985). Personality and social behavior. In G. Lindzey & E. Aronson (Eds.), *Handbook of social psychology* (Vol. 2) (3rd ed.). New York: Random House.

Snyder, M., & Swann, W. B., Jr. (1978). Hypothesis-testing processes in social interaction. *Journal of Personality and Social Psychology, 36,* 1202-1212.

Sorrentino, R. M., & Higgins, E. T. (Eds.). (1986). *Handbook of motivation and cognition.* New York: Guilford Press.

Spielberger, C. D. (1966). *Anxiety and behavior.* New York: Academic Press.

Spilich, G. J., Vesonder, G. T., Chiesi, H. L., & Voss, J. F. (1979). Text processing of domain-related information for individuals with high and low domain knowledge. *Journal of Verbal Learning and Verbal Behavior, 18,* 275-290.

Spiro, R. (1980). Accommodative reconstruction in prose recall. *Journal of Verbal Learning and Verbal Behavior, 19,* 84-95.

Stafford, L., & Daly, J. A. (1984). Conversational memory: The effects of recall mode and memory expectancies on remembrances of natural conversations. *Human Communication Research, 10,* 379-402.

Stein, N. L., & Glenn, C. G. (1979). An analysis of story comprehension in elementary school children. In R. Freedle (Ed.), *New directions in discourse processing* (Vol. 2). Norwood, NJ: Ablex.

Steinfatt, T., & Miller, G. R. (1974). Communication in game theoretic models of conflict. In G. Miller & H. Simons (Eds.), *Perspectives on communication in social conflict.* Englewood Cliffs, NJ: Prentice-Hall.

Stevens, S. (1950). Definition of communication. *Journal of the Acoustical Society of America, 22,* 689-690.

Street, R. L., & Giles, H. (1982). Speech accommodation theory: A social cognitive approach to language and speech behavior. In M. E. Roloff & C. R. Berger (Eds.), *Social cognition and communication.* Newbury Park, CA: Sage.

Strongman, K. T., & Champness, B. G. (1968). Dominance hierarchics and conflict in eye contact. *Acta Psychologica, 28,* 376-386.

Stubbs, M. (1983). *Discourse analysis: The sociolinguistic analysis of natural language.* Chicago: University of Chicago Press.

Suppe, F. (Ed.), (1974). *The structure of scientific theories.* Urbana: Univ. of Illinois Press.

Swann, W. B., Jr., & Read, S. (1981). Self-verification processes: How we sustain our self-conceptions. *Journal of Experimental Social Psychology, 17,* 351-372.

Taylor, S. E. (1981). The interface of cognitive and social psychology. In J. H. Harvey (Ed.), *Cognition, social behavior, and the environment.* Hillsdale, NJ: Lawrence Erlbaum.

Tesser, A. (1978). Self-generated attitude change. In L. Berkowitz (Ed.), *Advances in experimental social psychology* (Vol. 11). New York: Academic Press.

Thibaut, J., & Kelley, H. H. (1959). *The social psychology of groups.* New York: John Wiley.

Thoits, P. A. (1984). Coping, social support, and psychological outcomes. In P. Shaver (Ed.), *Review of personality and social psychology* (Vol. 5.). Newbury Park, CA: Sage.

Thorndyke, P. W. (1977). Cognitive structures in comprehension and memory of narrative discourse. *Cognitive Psychology, 9,* 77-110.

Tracy, K. (1985). Regulating conversational coherence: A cognitively grounded rules approach. In R. L. Street, Jr., & J. N. Cappella (Eds.), *Sequence and pattern in communicative behavior.* Baltimore: Edward Arnold.

Treisman, A. M. (1964). Verbal cues, language and meaning in selective attention. *American Journal of Psychology, 77,* 206-219.

Vacchiano, R. B. (1977). Dogmatism. In T. Blass (Ed.), *Personality variables in social behavior.* Hillsdale, NJ: Lawrence Erlbaum.

Vaina, L., & Hintikka, J. (Eds.), (1984). *Cognitive constraints on communication.* Boston: D. Reidel.

Van Dijk, T. A. (1985). Introduction: Discourse analysis as a new cross-discipline. In T. A. Van Dijk (Ed.), *Handbook of discourse analysis* (Vol. 1). New York: Academic Press.

Van Dijk, T. A., & Kintsch, W. (1983). *Strategies of discourse comprehension.* New York: Academic Press.

Wegner, D. M., Giuliano, T., & Hertel, P. T. (1985). Cognitive interdependence in close relationships. In W. Ickes (Ed.), *Compatible and incompatible relationships.* New York: Springer-Verlag.

Weizenbaum, J. (1967). Contextual understanding by computers. *Communications of the ACM, 10,* 474-480.

Weizenbaum, J. (1976). *Computer power and human reason.* New York: W. H. Freeman.

Wellman, H. (1985). The origins of metacognition. In D. L. Forrest-Pressley, G. E. MacKinnon, & T. G. Waller (Eds.), *Metacognition, cognition and human performance* (Vol. 1). New York: Academic Press.

White, J. D., & Carlston, D. E. (1983). Consequences of schemata for attention, impressions, and recall in complex social interactions. *Journal of Personality and Social Psychology, 45,* 538-549.

Wiggins, J. S. (1974). *In defense of traits.* Invited address at the Ninth Annual Symposium on Recent Developments in the Use of the MMPI, Los Angeles.

Wilensky, R. (1983a). Story grammars versus story points. *Behavioral and Brain Sciences, 6,* 579-623.

Wilensky, R. (1983b). *Planning and understanding.* Reading, MA: Addison-Wesley.

Winograd, T. (1977). A framework for understanding discourse. In M. A. Just & P. Carpenter (Eds.), *Cognitive processes in comprehension.* New York: John Wiley.

Winograd, T. (1980). What does it mean to understand language? *Cognitive Science, 4,* 209-241.

Woodall, W. G., & Folger, J. P. (1985). Nonverbal cue context and episodic memory: On the availability and endurance of nonverbal behaviors as retrieval cues. *Communication Monographs, 52,* 319-333.

Zajonc, R. B. (1980). Feeling and thinking: Preferences need no inferences. *American Psychologist, 35,* 151-175.

Zajonc, R. B. (1984). On the primacy of affect. *American Psychologist, 39,* 117-123.

Zuckerman, M., DePaulo, B. M., & Rosenthal, R. (1981). Verbal and nonverbal communication of deception. In L. Berkowitz (Ed.), *Advances in experimental social psychology* (Vol. 14). New York: Academic Press.

7   Interpersonal Communication: Definitions and Fundamental Questions

JOSEPH N. CAPPELLA
University of Wisconsin—Madison

I F the history of science teaches us anything, it is that observation and description are the heart of scientific inquiry. Theories come and go; paradigms come and go; philosophies of science come and go. But observations and the descriptions in which they participate when precise, accurate, and informative, remain to be absorbed by new theories, new paradigms, and new philosophies of science, Norwood Russell Hanson and his school notwithstanding (Hanson, 1958). Scientific knowledge requires that we observe what we speculate about and that we speculate about the implications of what we observe. Knowledge is separable from scientific knowledge at the boundary of observation.

So should it be with our approach to the study of the human behaviors of communication among persons. Our knowledge of these behaviors and their regularities, if any, will increase as our bases of observation and description increase. Coherence, regularity, and understanding are, of course, not guaranteed by mere observation; but the absence of informed, precise, and accurate observation, whether qualitative or quantitative, guarantees that our knowledge will be, in the worst sense of the cliché, "mere speculation." In the human sciences, where the questions posed affect in significant ways the lives, psyches, and the relationships of people, knowledge seekers must be intimates of the empirical world. The nature of their particular intimacies, whether qualitative or quantitative, are less important than the discoveries the methods yield.

The present chapter will not be a compendium of discoveries from the human science of interpersonal communication. Indeed, such an effort would be a brief one at best or a long but excuse-laden one at worst. Neither will I attempt to trace carefully past traditions of research nor recent trends; I will not exercise the reader with lengthy descriptions of esoteric theory. That is the important task of other reviews in this and other volumes (Knapp & Miller, 1985). Rather, this chapter will raise classes of questions that any theory of interpersonal and interactive behavior must answer. These questions will arise as a natural consequence of definitional issues and their resolution. Within each of these classes of questions, exemplary studies will be discussed, methodological concerns raised, and future research proposed.

DEFINING INTERPERSONAL COMMUNICATION

Selected Previous Definitions

Attempts to define whole domains of inquiry are usually doomed to be inaccurate or incomplete. No sooner has the pen been lifted from paper but an uncooperative researcher will have published a new line of inquiry that seems not to fit the newly penned definition. Actually, the most accurate and least explicit definition of interpersonal communication as a field of study would be what researchers do and what they allow other researchers to publish under the title of interpersonal communication. On this view, a definition of interpersonal communication will always be incapable of capturing the history and dynamic current affairs that characterize an active and lively scholarly community bridging several disciplines.

Definitions of domains of inquiry have a very different function. They sensitize communities by taking account of trends and, indeed, making trends. Definitions will bring certain elements into the foreground, force other elements to the background, and bring new elements forward. In this way, a definition of a field of inquiry is more like an economic indicator than it is like the economy itself.

Economic indicators are only useful when compared to earlier indicators of economic state. So it is with definitions of interpersonal communication. One must have the baseline definitions before one can reasonably interpret the new indicators. Unfortunately, there are as many definitions of interpersonal communication as there are basic textbooks of interpersonal communication (which have been fruitful and multiplied!). Fortunately, only a few of these have had a significant impact on the conduct of research in interpersonal communication in the last decade. They include the definitions put forward by Berger and Bradac (1982), Bochner (1984), Hinde (1979), and Miller and Steinberg (1975).

These definitions offer several features significant to the characterization of interpersonal communication. These include (1) the assumption that interpersonal communication involves the transfer of idiosyncratic, personalized, and psychological information rather than generalized, role-related, or sociological and cultural information, (2) an emphasis on reciprocal feelings and bonds, (3) a tendency to define interpersonal *relationships* but not interpersonal communication, and (4) a tendency to avoid the explicit inclusion of interaction and, when it is described at all, to describe the interleaving of actions.

The most important feature is the first one and is adopted in some form by all four sets of authors. Miller and Steinberg (1975, p. 22) set forward the distinction in their influential textbook in this way:

> When predictions about interpersonal communication outcomes are based primarily on a cultural or sociological level of analysis, the communicators are engaged in noninterpersonal communication; when predictions are based primarily on a psychological level of analysis, the communicators are engaged in interpersonal communication.

This distinction is pursued throughout their textbook to distinguish interpersonal relationships and strategies from noninterpersonal ones. Bochner (1984, p. 550) also adopts the distinction: "For a bond to be interpersonal, the parties must have particularized knowledge of each other." Berger and Bradac (1982, p. 12) follow the trend when they note that "interpersonal communication is a relatively unique form of communication the appearance of which depends upon the relative knowledge levels of participants." When knowledge is psychological, communication is interpersonal. Hinde (1979, p. 38) too notes the distinction separating formal from personal relationships on the basis of individual versus group knowledge.

These authors are representative of a rich tradition that recognizes in some way the distinction between personal and impersonal relationships (Bochner, 1984). None of these authors denies that communication takes place in noninterpersonal settings or that the study of formal, role-defined, or impersonal relationships is necessary. Rather, I believe that they are undoing historical injustice. Studies of intimate relationships had not been well represented in the empirical literature in communication. By defining interpersonal communication in terms of personalistic information exchange, studies of interpersonal communication are redirected toward the study of personal relationships and away from the study of impersonal relationships. This redirection has been a benefit to the field in that a significant neglect has been redressed.

On the negative side, interpersonal communication should not be so narrowly defined. The significant relationships that occur in such role-defined settings as those involving doctors and patients or teachers and students should not be defined as nonentities. In these settings people participate in communication as fully, albeit differently, as they do in more personal settings. Role-specific interactions should be as much a part of the domain of interpersonal inquiry as are more personalized interactions. Our studies as well as our definitions must recognize differences between types of relationships where that is appropriate, but these differences should not lead to the exclusion of significant contexts of interaction because of the particular swing of a historical moment.

The second characteristic of these definitions is an emphasis on reciprocal feelings as characteristic of established interpersonal bonds. This feature is central only to Bochner's (1984) description of interpersonal communication. Presumably, established interpersonal relationships are marked by reciprocity of both positive and negative behaviors. What is significant about Bochner's claim is not that there is no evidence for it; indeed, both Bochner's (1984) review and other reviews (Cappella, 1985b; Street & Giles, 1982) point out the positive effects of reciprocity and the effects of positive identification and cohesion on reciprocity. Nevertheless, most interpersonal relationships are marked by periods of increased separation and claims for autonomy, even in the context of increased convergence and similarity that reciprocity implies (Altman, Vinsel, & Brown, 1981). The conflict between approach and avoidance, union and autonomy, dependence and interdependence that even common experience defines as the way people approach their relationships dictates that our definitions of interpersonal communication remain open to the complementarity, divergence, and compensatory reactions that will occur in all relationships, including those in which the interpersonal bond has been cemented.

The third, and perhaps the most disturbing, characteristic is the pervasive tendency to offer careful definitions of interpersonal relationships but to avoid defining interpersonal communication. For Berger and Bradac (1982) interpersonal communication is simply information exchange at the psychological level. Miller and Steinberg (1975, p. 29) take the odd view that "interpersonal communication occurs when one person bases predictions about another person's responses on psychological data." Bochner's (1984) chief concern is with bonding, so communication is seen as a means to that end. Nevertheless, communication is concerned with selective and specific response, the chief consequence of which is influence; interpersonal communication is never explicitly defined. Hinde (1979) takes the opposite tack arguing that we know that relationships exist by virtue of the interactions they produce. When past interactions affect future interactions so that the interactional history is carried over into the present, then a relationship exists.

What is peculiar about these treatments is that interpersonal communication takes a subsidiary role to interpersonal relations. Certainly interpersonal relations deserve definition, but not to the exclusion of a serious consideration of interpersonal communication. If definitions serve a sensitizing function for the research enterprise and if our definitions give short shrift to features specific to interpersonal communication, then our own lack of self-reflexiveness will limit the scope of research.

The final point about previous definitions concerns a certain imprecision in defining interaction. Hinde (1979, p. 15) suggests that interactions are mutual and that they consist of interchanges in which "A shows
behavior X to . . . B, or A shows X to B and B responds with Y." Miller
and Steinberg (1975, p. 40) refer to the transactional character of interactions that imply that "we have an impact on other people and they have
an impact on us." The problem with these superficially accurate definitions of interaction is that they do not clearly separate the interleaving of
actions from interactions. Interleaved actions are the alternating actions
by persons A and B in which A's actions are not produced by any influence
of B's action but are simply baseline actions run off by A regardless
of the actions by B; similarly for B. Interactions require characteristics
something like those hinted at by Miller and Steinberg (1975). A and B
must have an impact on one another over and above the normal or baseline sequence that A and B would enact separately. Whether A and B do
have an influence on one another separates the interleaving of actions,
which is hardly of interest to interpersonal communication researchers,
from interaction.

Defining Interpersonal Communication Anew

The selected review of definitions of interpersonal communication
above suggests that a new definition (1) be broad enough so as not to
exclude a priori a set of interpersonal relationships, (2) avoid a bias
toward interactions that are reciprocal, (3) have interpersonal communication rather than interpersonal relations as its focus, and (4) clearly
define interchange so that it is interactional.

The definition of mutual influence promoted here is one I have
described elsewhere (Cappella, 1985b). Let X_I be the Ith behavior type
for person A and let Y_J be the Jth behavior type for person B. I and J are
simply convenient indices used to mark the set of behaviors $\{X\}$ and the
set $\{Y\}$ which are the behaviors for A and B, respectively, manifested
in face-to-face interactions: interruptions, topical shifts, disclosures,
requests, and the like. A and B are said to be interaction when the following conditions are met:

$$P [X_I(t + k) \mid Y_J(k)] > O \text{ with } k > O \qquad [1]$$
$$P [X_I(t + k) \mid Y_J(k)] < \text{ or } > P [X_I(t)] \qquad [2]$$
$$\text{similarly for B with X and Y reversed} \qquad [3]$$

Note that t + k refers to time, at time unit t + k; and the mark "|" should
be read as "given that." In ordinary words these conditions state that (1)
the probability of A enacting a certain behavior at a certain time given
that B enacted either the same or a different behavior at some earlier
time is not zero (equation 1); however, (2) this probability must be sig-

nificantly greater or less than A's own baseline probability of acting or ignoring B's prior action (equation 2); and (3) interaction requires that the same conditions hold for B (equation 3).

The definition of interaction proposed in statements (1) to (3) is somewhat more general than first glance might suggest. The relationship between A's subsequent and B's prior behavior has been represented as discrete time at lag k. This was done for simplicity and convenience. Continuous time at any lag could have also been employed. Similarly, A's subsequent action is made to depend on a single action by B at a single prior time. In principle, A's subsequent action could be made to depend upon two, three, or more prior behaviors, although such complexities would be cumbersome to represent.

Conceptually, the set of behaviors {X} and {Y} are limited only to the observable behaviors enacted by persons A and B. Excluded from this set are such psychological variables as personality, affective reaction, perceived intensity, and satisfaction, and such situational factors as role and social normative constraints. Included in this set are not only the set of more objective behaviors such as loudness, speech rate, and postural state but also the more inferential behaviors such as intimacy of question, hostility of language choice, and dominance. The broadness of the behavioral categories allows the definition to include comfortably such processes as mutual influence (Cappella, 1981), turn-taking (Duncan & Fiske, 1977), conversational pragmatics (Levinson, 1983; McLaughlin, 1984), negotiation (Putnam & Jones, 1982), and group phasic structure (Poole, 1981, 1983), among others.

Some implications. Statements (1) through (3) represent an exercise in "definitional minimalism." The definition makes few controversial commitments about the nature of interpersonal communication and does so intentionally. The one commitment it does make is to the interactional character of interpersonal communication, emphasizing that for interpersonal communication to occur each person must affect the other's observable behavior patterns relative to their typical or baseline patterns. Surely this is a necessary condition for face-to-face communication and it is a condition that has been passed over lightly in recent conceptualizations of the interpersonal communication process.

One of the noncommitments made by my definition is the intentional avoidance of discussion of the quality of the information exchanged, personal or impersonal. The definition includes any encounter in which enacted behaviors meet the criteria for interaction. Role-determined encounters (e.g., doctor-patient interactions) are not relegated to the null condition of "noninterpersonal" communication. Rather, all encounters that are interactions are interpersonal, although they may differ significantly on the types of information exchanged, the intimacy and trust felt, and so on.

The definition does not take a stand on whether interactions will tend to be reciprocal or compensatory. Both are possible in interpersonal encounters, whether the relationships are well adjusted or filled with animosity. Our definitions not only should avoid bias toward positive behaviors only (Bochner, 1984) but also should avoid a bias toward a single type of interaction pattern.

Finally, the definition does not take a stand on the question of intentionality of behavior, whether the behaviors are symbols or signs, or on the capacities of the individuals participating in the interaction. Omission of these questions does not signify their lack of importance or their lack of relevance. Rather, it signals a belief that high-quality observation and description of the minimal observable patterns of interaction takes precedence over questions that are primarily philosophical. These philosophical questions must be raised but they must not be debated and answered in the context of ignorance about the very processes that the debate concerns. I believe that the minimal definition of the necessary conditions for interpersonal communication advanced above represents a reasonable strategy at this stage of knowledge: Be inclusive rather than narrow, emphasize what can be readily observed given current observation technologies, avoid controversial assumptions that cannot be resolved, and set down the minimal necessary conditions for the phenomenon.

Some possible objections. A variety of objections can be raised to the definition proffered above. The first is that although the necessary conditions for interpersonal communication may have been identified, interpersonal relations have been left undefined. Of course, the intention is to counter the trend toward defining interpersonal relations and to define only interpersonal communication. However, the relationship between the two deserves comment and follows the discussion of Hinde (1979). Interpersonal relations are not congruent with the set of interactions in which a particular pair of persons engages. Certainly interpersonal communication is the means through which particular relationships are created. In turn, some representation of the relationship is stored as knowledge by each party and that representation and the expectations which it generates can affect subsequent interactions (see Hewes & Planalp, Chapter 6 in this volume). One cannot simply observe a particular interaction and hope to obtain a snapshot of the relationship. Rather, one must observe a sequence of interactions to observe the effects of prior interactions, as translated through the relational knowledge, on subsequent interactions. If the mental representation of a relationship were a veridical translation of the interaction that gave rise to it, then the relationship would be nothing more than the accumulation of interactions. However, memory is anything but a passive receptacle for experience being actively involved in reconstruction, selective retention and learning, and in the integration of information from multiple sources (Anderson, 1985; Kintsch, 1977; Tulving, 1983). The translation from interaction to relational knowledge cannot be veridical.

A second objection might hold that the definition of statements (1) through (3) concerns interaction but not communication, so that a definition of interpersonal interaction but not interpersonal communication has been offered. Several responses can be made to this objection. On the view of certain theorists (Ashby, 1963), communication and interaction as defined above are congruent. For Ashby, two systems are said to be in communication when the output of one system is the input for the other and affects the output of that system. That is precisely the definition of statements (1) through (3). One rejoinder to the equation of interaction with communication is that communication is intentional, symbolic, goal directed, and so on. My response is a redundant one: Even if these features are required, it is premature for us to make our definitions so narrow and it is unproductive for us to debate issues that are unresolvable on empirical grounds. Our studies should not be restricted to a preselected class of phenomena when the criteria for their selection and for their observation is so tenuous.

A second rejoinder to the equation of interaction and communication is that a variety of God's creatures from insects to chimpanzees to prelinguistic infants exhibit patterns of interaction whereas only adult humans converse. When pushed to distinguish conversation from interaction, opponents might claim that conversations are about something (ideas, concepts, principles, etc.) whereas interactions are not, and that conversations involve understanding and interpretation whereas interactions do not necessarily. As to the first point, interactions are always about something in the same way that conversations are. For example, the interaction patterns of bees studied by von Frisch (1962) are about the location of food sources; interactions among male chimpanzees are often about dominance (Smith, 1977). The major difference between conversations and interactions on this point is that at least some of the time conversationalists can tell us what their conversations are about, whereas nonhumans and prelinguistic humans cannot make such identifications. This point verifies the self-reflective character of the participants more than it clarifies the distinction between interaction and conversation. Anyway, linguistic humans are not so mentally agile when it comes to identifying the relational agendas hidden in their conversations (see Giles & Wiemann, Chapter 12).

As to the second point, understanding and interpretation will distinguish conversation from interaction only in some theory of understanding that clearly differentiates understanding as a human mental capacity distinct from the mental capacities of nonhuman and prelinguistic human organisms to perceive, categorize, and respond. The usual differentiation is that human understanding is more like problem solving than it is like simple mental associations or complex mental dictionaries (Bransford & McCarrell, 1974). Such complex problem solving is presumed to be beyond the mental abilities of nonhuman organisms. However, such wisdom has been seriously challenged (Griffin, 1984) with the observation of what can only be described as problem solving in a wide variety of animal, bird, and insect species. The bottom line is that the distinction between conversation and interaction while clearly one of degree is certainly not one of kind.

A third major objection to the definition of interaction put forward in statements (1) through (3) does not concern its relationship to interpersonal communication but rather its incompleteness. O'Keefe, Delia, and O'Keefe (1980) have argued that left-to-right, or sequential, definitions of interactions are incomplete in significant ways because they fail to account for the hierarchical or embedded nature of many remark sequences. A simple case in point is as follows:

    A1: A Black Russian with little ice please.
    B1: Are you 21?
    A2: I thought the law goes into effect January 1!
    B2: December 1.
    A3: No, I'm 20.
    B3: Sorry, I can't help you.

The distinguishing character of this example is that the remark B3 is the answer to A1 but is separated from it with four intervening remarks, two question-answer pairs; the three question-answer pairs are embedded hierarchically within one another. They are not organized as a left-to-right sequence. The conclusion that one might reach is that sequential definitions like those of statements (1) to (3) cannot account for examples A1 to B3. In fact, this is exactly the same issue that Chomsky (1957) raised in reaction to the left-to-right sequential grammars of information theory and learning theory. Despite the success of Chomsky's arguments and the hierarchically organized grammars that he introduced, several theorists have shown that in principle sequential grammars can account for these cases (Kaufer, 1979). Further, the most useful grammars for simulating human understanding have been modifications of sequential grammars rather than Chomsky's hierarchical models. Sequential models of interaction cannot easily handle hierarchical embedding of actions, as shown in the example above, but they are not incapable of doing so in principle.

Other problems with the definition in (1) through (3) such as establishing a baseline measure, the place of explanation in this highly descriptive definition, and mutual versus individual influence will be deferred to later sections. We next turn to classification of questions that are suggested by the definition and that will organize interpersonal communication research within and between levels of communication inquiry.

FOUR CLASSES OF QUESTIONS ABOUT INTERPERSONAL COMMUNICATION

The definition of interpersonal communication advanced here suggests four categories of questions that may be asked by researchers. For convenience these categories will be labeled zero-, first-, second-, and third-order questions. Zero-order questions concern the set of behaviors {X} and {Y}, their types and structures. First-order questions involve the baseline probabilities, their production and their perception by receivers. Second-order questions, unique to the interpersonal level, concern interaction patterns themselves. Third-order questions step beyond the definitional boundaries of interpersonal communication to include relationship factors. This final category focuses upon the two-way linkage between relationship factors and interaction patterns, and interaction patterns and relational outcomes.

Relationships to Other Levels

These sets of questions make clear, at least in outline, the relationship between the interpersonal level and the other levels of communication inquiry. First-order questions are especially relevant to the intraindividual level because they pose questions about encoding and decoding of verbal and nonverbal behaviors. Certain third-order questions are the same questions about culture and society and their institutions that one must raise in asking if society is different from the sum of the individuals in that society. One may ask the same question of relational types and outcomes. Is an interpersonal relationship an entity uniquely different from its parts? Is a relationship reducible to the interactions that gave rise to it or do the interactions, like those in the society at large, create an interpersonal institution that exists for its members as a reality greater than any of them?

The only class of questions that is unique to the interpersonal level is the second-order. These questions deal centrally with the defining characteristic of interpersonal communication, namely, interaction. This is not to claim that the other classes of questions are irrelevant to interpersonal communication. I hope my remarks and the derivation of these classes of questions all speak to the opposite claim. Rather, the study of interpersonal communication must proceed through all classes of questions simultaneously in bootstrap fashion. In the process, questions relevant to the intraindividual and organizational and social levels will necessarily be posed and answered.

In the subsequent sections each of the four classes of questions are taken up in turn. Critical distinctions are made, exemplary research is discussed, methodological issues raised, and future research proposed.

ZERO-ORDER QUESTIONS

Time and space will not permit comprehensive overviews of literature and issues relevant to zero-order questions. With respect to serious and comprehensive reviews of the structure and function of interpersonal behaviors, four recent summaries of literature will assist the reader interested in a broader coverage of issues related to coding reliability and validity (Folger, Hewes, & Poole, 1984), to functional groupings of behaviors (Cappella & Street, 1985), and to the role of nonverbal (Burgoon, 1985) and verbal behaviors (Jacobs, 1985) in interpersonal communication.

Critical Distinctions and Critical Research

The definition of interpersonal communication advocated earlier brings into prominence two important zero-order topics: the classes of behavior to be observed and the time units in which the observations will occur. Certainly by proposing a definition that invokes behavioral contingencies and their time order as central concepts one cannot avoid a serious consideration of time and behavior classifications.

Time. Any researcher who chooses to make and record observations of interpersonal communication will necessarily make choices about the time units of the observations. For example, in choosing to study influence attempts (Jackson & Jacobs, 1983) one implicitly assumes that an event occurs every so often that is identifiable as an influence attempt. The observer marks time by the occurrence of these events and not by ticks of the clock. The most fundamental distinction that can be made with respect to time is between real or clock time and event time. The former is marked by the occurrence and duration of behaviors as they occur relative to an arbitrarily started clock. The latter is marked by the occurrence of defined events and their temporal order regardless of the elapsed real time between events or elapsed time from the beginning to the end of an event (Cappella & Street, 1985; Folger et al., 1984).

Significant programs of research have been carried out under the assumption that time is marked by the clock. Research by Jaffe and Feldstein (1970) employed an objectively defined conception of time to study and represent talk and silence sequences in informal conversations.

Their 300-millisecond time unit has been shown to be a valid unit for studying talk and silence sequences (Cappella & Streibel, 1979) and close to the minimum perceptual unit (250 milliseconds) in the recognition of conversational pauses (Walker & Trimboli, 1982). The important issue with respect to clock time is the elapsed time between observations relative to the shortest duration of real cycles or real state changes. When the observation time is much shorter than the minimum duration of real cycles or real state changes, then the behavior under observation appears to be much more stable than it actually is. This would be due to numerous observations of "no change" (see for example, Hayes, Meltzer, & Wolf, 1970). When the observation time is longer than the minimum duration of real cycles or real state changes, then some observations of real change will have been missed. Arundale (1977) has given a careful treatment to these issues.

Objective time involves little or no inference on the part of the observer as to the time at which observations will be made. Of course, this does not make the choice of a sampling time arbitrary. Rather, validation of a minimum sampling unit in clock time is made against criteria that are theoretical or predictive. For example, Warner, Waggener, and Kronauer (1983) studied rhythms of pausing in dialogues as a function of respiratory rhythms. Their fundamental time unit needed only to be one-half the duration of the shortest respiratory period in normal social conversation. Street (1983) found that one-minute durations of speech rate predicted adaptation between children and an experimenter as a function of age but that half-minute units did not. In Warner's research, theoretical predictions dictated the smallest clock-time sampling unit while in Street's research actual prediction dictated the choice of minimum sampling unit. With longer time spans of study (e.g., the formation of a committed relationship) the same criteria for choice of a sampling unit hold. Sampling units in objective time may be somewhat ad hoc but they must be validated either predictively or theoretically.

The second type of time samples are event samples. These can be illustrated with the ways that the event called a conversational turn has been defined. Several research programs have defined the conversational turn, with some identifications being highly automatic (Jaffe & Feldstein, 1970) others being more inferential (Duncan & Fiske, 1977; Matarazzo & Wiens, 1972). The issue of whether an event occurs or not depends upon the definition of the category and not upon any ambiguity over the nature of time. The consequence of this conclusion is that problems with event time are not the same as problems with clock time. Clock time raises questions about the validity of the sampling unit. Event time creates problems in sampling only to the extent that the events themselves are ambiguous or difficult to observe.

A third conception of time can be called phenomenological time. In this case, time is defined from the point of view of the participants to or observers of the interaction. In phenomenological time, real time is shrunk, expanded, and, in general, restructured according to the perspective of participants or observers. For example, Dittman (1962, 1972; Dittman & Llewellyn, 1969) and Boomer (1963, 1965, 1978) have concluded that the phonemic clause is an important encoding unit because pauses, hesitations, and body movements tend to occur between phonemic units. Other researchers have argued on the basis of alternating periods of hesitancy and fluency in speech that the encoding unit is larger than the phonemic clause (Beattie, 1978; Butterworth, 1975; Butterworth & Goldman-Eisler, 1979). Newtson and his colleagues (Newtson, 1976; Newtson, Enquist, & Bois, 1977) found that observers of social interactions chunked social sequences more finely and more grossly as a function of their need to attend to them and their goals in each situation. Each of these lines of inquiry offers information about how interpersonal communication might be organized perceptually and cognitively for actors, participants, and observers.

What is especially important about studies of phenomenological time is the relationship between the structure of the interaction as viewed by the interactants or observers and the interaction as conceived by clock or event time. For example, much research has emphasized the significance of the turn and the topic as natural units in the organization and evolution of the interaction. However, if the organization of the interaction on the basis of the turn does not agree with the organization of the interaction as seen by observers or by participants, then one must question the centrality of topic or turn as an organizing factor in interpersonal communication. Recent work has tried to assess the fit between observers' chunking of the interaction and that based on topical groupings (Palmer & Badzinski, 1986).

Behavior. The set of behaviors that could be observed in an interpersonal encounter is potentially enormous, in principle infinite. Even with multiple levels of subcategories, no simple category system such as verbal, vocal, and kinesic could hope to provide an informative and comprehensive observation system. Future research applications cannot anticipate all the observations that will be needed or will be technologically possible.

Rather than simply summarize previous work, it will be more useful to discuss category systems themselves. Three ways of conceptualizing interpersonal behaviors will be discussed: (1) categorizing on the basis of the degree of inference required of the observer, (2) grouping on the basis of function, and (3) mapping of unique behaviors onto particular meanings.

Behaviors can be distinguished on the basis of the degree of inference required of observers as they attribute meaning to the act. At one end of the continuum of inference are objective behaviors. Some behaviors are objective because the observer attributes no additional meaning to the behavior, simply taking the behavior "as is." Jaffe and Feldstein's (1970) work with vocalizations and pauses comes close to this pole of the continuum. In such research, the observer makes choices in the observational process, but these choices are not allied with the interpretation of the behavior. At the other pole of the continuum are behaviors presumed to have a particular interpersonal function or meaning. For example, the equilibrium theory of Argyle and Dean (1965) is a theory about affiliation and the behavioral reactions to demonstrated affiliative behaviors. In particular, behaviors such as eye gaze, distance, and self-disclosure are presumed to have an affiliative function.

Middle points on the continuum fall to behaviors such as Duncan and Fiske's (1977) definition of the turn. Although this behavior appears to be quite objective, its definition requires an assessment of the speaker's intent which, itself, is a kind of implicit meaning analysis. Many other behaviors appear to fall toward the objective end of the continuum but when examined closely require considerable inference. This is particularly true when the behavior is context sensitive or content determined. Jacobs (1985) offers a good example with the category of "requests." Remarks as diverse as "Would you mind if we go home?," "Tomorrow's an early day for me," and "Don't start drinking another beer!" can all be interpreted as requests to leave an evening's affair. To do so requires an inference and belief structure on the part of the observer that is very complex and is often implicit. On the other hand, an objective definition of requests may miss the richer cases that depend upon prior knowledge and context of occurrence.

Categorizing behaviors in terms of an inferential continuum has an important sensitizing function. By noting that some behaviors are treated as objective, one recognizes that the behavior has been given no interpretation or meaning. In such a case, radical operationism reigns with one behavior having no relationship to any other since no behavior participates in any larger conceptual grouping. Such a radical science of interpersonal communication would have no parsimony. At the other extreme, interpreted behaviors are often built on assumptions about the behavior's function or meaning that are never themselves tested. A careful science must not only conduct precise observations but must recognize the assumptions upon which those observations are made and evaluate them empirically. If a personality researcher put together a set of items that were claimed to assess achievement motive, scientific standards would require that the items be shown to be both reliable and valid. No less should be required of behavioral observations. Put simply, behaviors that have interpretations supplied by the observers must be validated. The methods of validation, themselves under some dispute, will be discussed in the section on methodology. However, no observer, no matter how insightful, should be allowed the unilateral authority to ascribe complex and subtle meanings to behaviors.

A second approach to categorizing behaviors concerns their grouping. If the myriad verbal, vocal, and kinesic behaviors that operate in interpersonal communication are all independent of one another, then the researcher is faced with the rather foreboding prospect that the study of each behavior must be taken up anew without guidance from work on other behaviors. At the same time researchers are recognizing that one cannot study behaviors one at a time (Burgoon, 1985; Cappella, 1981; Eidinger & Patterson, 1983) because the absence of reaction in one behavioral domain may be compensated by a strong reaction in another behavioral domain.

One of the most obvious reasons that behavioral groupings are used is efficiency and parsimony. Because there is such a huge variety of visual, aural, and tactile stimuli in interpersonal communication, research must seek commonalities across behaviors. One strategy to increase parsimony is to understand how behaviors group together. A second reason for grouping comes from the analogy to test construction. When constructing psychological tests, researchers try to develop parallel items for the concept being measured. If the concept has dimensions or there are several concepts that are a part of the test, then methods are employed to determine how individual test items group together as indicators of the underlying constructs. One would not begin by analyzing every item as if it were distinct from every other. The same should be true with multiple behaviors.

A third reason may be found in the implicit assumption that interpersonal behaviors are related to interpersonal judgments. This literature (reviewed by Cappella, 1985b) finds that people's judgments about others fall into a small number of categories: association (positivity-negativity), control (dominance-submission), and sometimes a formality-informality and an activity dimension. These judgments must arise from people's behaviors so that the variety of behavior may function to produce only a small number of types of judgments. Thus behaviors may be grouped through their pattern of association to important interpersonal judgments. Unless we understand how they group, we will not understand how they inform interpersonal perceptions.

Three strategies for grouping behaviors can be used. The first is a direct analogy to the patterns of empirical covariation in test construction. Behaviors that group should be behaviors that correlate. A better procedure than correlation among summary measures would be temporal covariation among behaviors. By using patterns of temporal covariation, we would learn whether behaviors increase and decrease together over time and whether behaviors are temporally independent. Preliminary work in our own laboratories has shown that such behaviors as face-directed gaze and object-focused gestures covary temporally with the speaking and listening roles. Although not surprising, these results confirm the importance of separating behaviors enacted while listening from those enacted while speaking (Rime, in press).

Two other strategies advocated for grouping behaviors are related to basic approaches to establishing the meaning of any sign: meaning as perception and meaning as intention. The latter approach has been advocated by Patterson (1982b, 1983; Eidinger & Patterson, 1983) and the former has been advocated by Cappella (1985b; Cappella & Street, 1985). The approaches are not competitors but rather are complementary. They argue that verbal, vocal, and kinesic behaviors are associated with certain motivational, personality, and intentional states of senders and also that they produce certain perceptions, interpretations, or judgments in receivers. Those behaviors that are linked to the same motivational or intentional state are presumably functionally equivalent to one another in encoding. Eidinger and Patterson (1983) conducted a very thorough review of the literature on nonverbal behaviors related to various types of control motivations. On the decoding side, those behaviors that produce the same perceptual judgment may be viewed as functionally equivalent. Shrout and Fiske (1982) showed that five behaviors used by interaction partners accounted for substantial portions of the variance in observers' judgments of persons' sociability. These two pairs of researchers employed different methods and different assumptions about the source of meaning but both were concerned with how behaviors can be judged to be equivalent.

A final type of behavioral grouping has received little or no attention. By focusing upon behaviors separately or upon behavioral equivalence, we ignore the possibility that certain behavioral combinations may produce unique meanings not readily deducible from the behaviors separately. A classic study by Ellsworth and Carlsmith (1968) makes the point clearly. High face-directed gaze is usually interpreted more positively than high gaze aversion, at least in neutral social contexts. When high gaze and high gaze aversion are coupled with positive comments on another's performance, the usual reactions obtain. When high and low gaze are coupled with comments critical of performance, the usual results are reversed with the high gaze-criticism combination producing more negative reactions than the high gaze aversion-criticism combination. Very few studies of this type exist. They are significant because they help us understand how behaviors function in context and understand the relative power of behaviors that are in competition.

The third classification of behaviors focuses upon the attempt to map specific behaviors onto specific meanings. Most verbal and nonverbal behaviors do not have a one-to-one relationship to a particular meaning. For example, eye gaze can function as a sign of positive affect, as a sign of dominance or threat, as an indicator of attentiveness, or as a means to monitor interesting, threatening, or novel stimuli. The particular function depends upon the situation and the context (Cappella, 1983). A significant line of work in the nonverbal area has sought to establish unique meanings for particular kinesic or vocal manifestations. Perhaps the most well-known studies of this type concern facial displays of emotion (Ekman, 1972; Ekman, Friesen, & Ellsworth, 1972). The most important findings here are that certain configurations of facial musculature are the result of internal emotional experiences and that these facial configurations are recognized as particular emotions by a wide variety of cultures.

A one-to-one relationship between a sign and its meaning makes available a powerful and unequivocal indicator of psychological state (even granting cultural display rules and various motivations for deceit). Although only a little research on specialized behavioral configurations and their meanings has been done to date, that is changing. Work by Scherer (1984) and others is trying to specify the relationship between a variety of vocal parameters as indicators of emotional state and interpersonal judgments. The results are promising so far. Research in this area is painstaking, requiring powerful tools and extremely fine analysis of microscopic differences between behavioral states. Future research cannot continue to treat behaviors in gross categories. For example, all smiles are not identical in structure and function. But forming valid distinctions between the structural differences, let alone the functional differences, will require considerable effort in the research community. The payoff, if it comes, will be substantial gains in knowledge and benchmark information concerning behavioral signs and their meanings.

Critical Methodological Issues

The previous section carefully avoided dealing with the variety of ways of coding verbal, vocal, and kinesic behavior and instead focused upon issues concerning behavioral observation. In an attempt to summarize the section, two words would be prominent: meaning and validity. The development of theoretically and pragmatically useful observational systems for interpersonal communication research will depend upon careful and precise observation. Objective observations devoid of interpretation will be neither parsimonious nor theoretically useful. The methods for establishing accurate observations and for validating interpretative frameworks for behavior are unique to the interpersonal communication level and so will be treated briefly here (see also Folger et al., 1984).

Reliability. Two types of reliability are crucial to accurate observations in interpersonal communication studies: unitizing and categorizing. These types of reliability are also unique to interpersonal communication research. Unitizing reliability tries to assure that actions seen by one observer are also seen by another observer. Unitizing reliability does not assess whether two or more observers identify an action as the same type or not, only that they agree that an action has taken place. This type of reliability is clearly a necessary condition for later judgments. Unitizing reliability cannot be established by simply comparing the number of observation units identified by two or more coders since it would be possible for them to agree perfectly in number overall and to never agree on the location of any particular action. Rather, unitizing reliability requires that observers compare their identified units time point by time point (Folger et al., 1984; Krippendorff, 1980).

Unfortunately, the vast majority of interaction research never checks for unitizing reliability. This failure creates a modest crisis in observational accuracy. With relatively complex observational systems such as those of Rogers and Farace (1975) or Stiles (1978) the absence of unitizing reliability makes it impossible to know that observers are consistently identifying the same units for subsequent categorization. Unitizing reliability is therefore the sine qua non of observational studies.

Unitizing reliability only insures that observers consistently identify that actions of some sort have occurred at specified instants. Categorizing reliability goes one step further in assessing whether the observers consistently place the action in the same category or not. Unfortunately, categorizing reliability is often assessed globally rather than on an act-by-act basis. Global categorizing reliability can be very misleading. Suppose that two observers observe 20 instances of actions to be sorted into one of four categories, say A, B, C, and D. It is easy to show an example in which the two observers agree perfectly on the total *number* of A's, B's, C's and D's so that their global reliability is perfect but disagree on every instance of coding when compared act by act. This is a strong counterexample against the use of global reliability. Unfortunately, reports of global reliability are much more common in the literature than are reports of act-by-act reliability.

Another unfortunate tendency in the research literature is the reporting of uncorrected agreement statistics, even when calculated on an act-by-act basis. Percentage agreement might seem like a reasonable method to report reliability. However, when the true distribution of categories is not equally probable but strongly unequal, then the probability for two or more coders to agree at high levels by chance alone is itself high. Agreement statistics must be corrected for chance agreements before they can be meaningfully reported.

In sum, reliability, so important in all scientific research, has special requirements in interpersonal communication studies. Reliability must be established for the units of observation and then the categories. The categorizing reliability must also be established on an act-by-act basis and corrected for chance agreements. Krippendorff (1980) gives an excellent treatment of reliability pertinent to interpersonal communication and applicable to all levels of measurement.

The potential effects of unreliability are more severe in interpersonal communication studies than in other domains. Hewes (1985) has shown that the contingent probabilities, which are central to interaction studies, can be badly distorted from their true values in the face of unreliability across a set of categories. Put simply, the distortion of the contingent probability is due to the summative effects of the unreliabilities in the behaviors that enter the contingent probability. The solution of course is accurate and reliable observation that is properly assessed.

Validity. The question of validity arises whenever an observer assigns an interpretation to a behavior. In interpersonal communication research a particular controversy has arisen between Folger and Poole (1982) and Rogers and Millar (1982) over acceptable procedures for assigning meaning to behaviors. Folger and Poole have argued that because observational schemes, like that of Rogers and Farace (1975), assume that certain actions have been given implicit meanings of dominance and submission by researchers, then these implicit meanings must be checked. The primary method of checking is representational validity, in which the researcher's assigned meanings are compared to the meanings assigned by ordinary users of the behaviors. Rogers and Millar counter that the requirements of representational validity require of subjects knowledge that is too subtle (Nisbett & Wilson, 1977) and that successful use of the scheme in prediction is sufficient validation of the meanings assigned by the researchers.

The validation issue is a significant one because it is at the very heart of the necessity and the proper method for validation of behavioral observations. First let us consider the necessity argument. The issue revolves around whether construct validity is a necessary type of validity for behaviors. Consider an analogy. A researcher discovers a set of self-report questions that are excellent predictors of audience adaptation in message selection. The researcher calls the items "flexibility." Now the labeling of the items is either arbitrary or the items do indeed get at some aspect of individual flexibility. If other workers are to be able to use the concept of flexibility in other hypotheses and theories, and not merely be tied to the items of the flexibility test, then independent evidence of the construct's labeling must be obtained. The ability to take a concept from one research domain to another requires that the concept have a valid link to its operations and not simply be an arbitrarily assigned name. Similarly, the validation of interpretations of behaviors must be completed if the concept represented by the interpretation is to be transferable to other domains of theory and research. Predictive validity is very weak evidence of the validity of a construct because in this test the operational measure predicts the outcome regardless of the name attached to the operation.

Folger and Poole (1982) argue for a particular type of construct validity—representational. This form of validation is based upon what Harré and Secord (1973) have called the "open souls" doctrine. In the particular case of validating observational schemes the doctrine would have researchers directly ask language users how they would interpret examples of observational categories. Whether people are sufficiently aware of their interpretations of a wide variety of behaviors in a wide variety of circumstances is a matter of some dispute (Nisbett & Wilson, 1977) and considerable research (Ericsson & Simon, 1984). The question is not whether people have interpretations of social acts such as remarks and certain tones of voice; they certainly do. The question is whether their interpretations in the context of direct inquisition would be the same as their interpretations as participants who either produce or receive such remarks. The "open souls" approach to validation presumes that the interpretation of disinterested observers is equivalent to the reactions produced by a participant who is involved, threatened, aroused, bored, and so on.

The resolution of this controversy is to consider the question of validity of interpretive observation systems as central to the study of first-order questions. However, the methods of validation should be various. The assumption that people are "open souls" to be explored with the crude instrumentation of direct inquisition is dubious. Rather, these highly direct methods should be complemented by techniques that seek the same information in less direct fashion. But direct predictive validity alone is not sufficient; it can only indicate that the operations employed share variance with one another and cannot indicate the appropriateness of the interpretation applied to the behavior.

Summary and Future Directions

This section on zero-order questions has dealt primarily with issues in the measurement of verbal, vocal, and kinesic behavior in interpersonal communication. No attempt was made to review the observational systems that might be employed in studying interpersonal communication. The reader interested in such an overview should consult Scherer and Ekman (1982), Burgoon (1985), Jacobs (1985), and other chapters in this volume. This section has emphasized several particular issues for current and future observational work: accuracy, meaning, parsimony, and assumption checking.

Despite the difficulties, studies of interactional behaviors cannot continue simply to proliferate observational systems. The time for consolidation and integration is upon us, before interactional research is drowned by the mass of data and data-gathering techniques.

FIRST-ORDER QUESTIONS

First-order questions are concerned with factors affecting the encoding of behaviors and the decoding of behaviors within interpersonal communication settings. This literature is voluminous and can barely be touched in this chapter. Recent reviews of the various aspects of the literature are available in several of the chapters in Knapp and Miller (1985) and in the present volume.

Critical Distinctions and Critical Research

The definition of interpersonal communication put forward in statements (1) through (3) raise two important types of first-order questions. The first is a production or encoding question: What are the psychological and social (but not interactive) factors that account for variation in the baseline probability of acting? This question is important because the baseline probability is the criterion against which mutual influence must be judged. Knowing whether and how the baseline changes with situational and psychological changes determines whether baselines need to be adjusted with changing circumstances. The second subclass is a decoding question that arises from the implicit assumption that the probability of response depends upon the other's actual behavior rather than the responder's perception of that behavior. If perceptions are veridical, then the definition of statements (1) through (3) can stand; otherwise, the definition must be modified to include perceived responses.

First-order questions are actually asked at the intrapersonal level of communication inquiry. They have obvious relevance to the interpersonal level for the reasons just cited, but contribute more to the theoretical knowledge of the level below. Interestingly, more researchers conduct what they would identify as interpersonal research on first-order questions than any other type. As we proceed I will clarify why this identification has been made.

Encoding factors. The categories of factors that can affect behavioral output in interaction can be grouped as follows: environmental or situational factors, and psychological or intraindividual factors. The former set refers to factors that exist outside the person: situational factors, role relationships, and social normative constraints. The latter set refers to conditions existing within the person. This set can be further broken down into relatively stable individual characteristics such as personality factors, habits, and dispositions, and relatively transient individual characteristics such as affective states, cognitive states, and physiological states. Affective states include both global affect such as positive and negative feeling (the evaluative component of attitude) and particular affect such as the emotions of anger, fear, sadness, and so on. Cognitive states include attributions, beliefs, goals, intentions, expectations, and perceptions (in turn including interpretations and understandings). Physiological states include both autonomic arousal and cognitive activation.

These categories provide a relatively complete system for pigeonholing encoding studies. Of course, the categories do have somewhat permeable boundaries. For example, much of the recent research in personality has argued that predictions from personality to behavior must include significant interactions with situational factors (Endler & Magnusson, 1976; Hewes & Haight, 1979; Parks, 1980). Similarly, attitudes are usually assumed to have both affective and cognitive components (Fishbein & Ajzen, 1975) so that attitude falls into more than one category. Confusion could also arise with relatively enduring cognitive states such as cognitive complexity (O'Keefe & Sypher, 1981), which have the characteristics of personality traits. Studies of this sort could find a place in either category.

The purpose of this category system is not to develop a completely well-defined method for organizing first-order questions but rather to be a vehicle that brings certain issues into focus. The first issue concerns when first-order encoding questions are relevant to the interpersonal level and when they are relevant to the intrapersonal level. As implied in earlier discussions, first-order questions that deal with psychological factors are always relevant to the intrapersonal level of inquiry. The particular conditions under which the study is done determine whether the first-order question is significant to interpersonal communication work. Any situational, affective, cognitive, personality, or physiological factor that gives rise to behavior *in an interactive context* makes that factor relevant to interpersonal communication research.

The above claim is best seen by counterexample. Attributions that we make for another's actions may or may not have a subsequent effect on our interactions with that other. If the other is a spouse, then attributions of personal untrustworthiness have a high likelihood of affecting subsequent interactional behaviors. If the other person is a political candidate, rather than a spouse, subsequent interactions are unlikely. The attributional processes are likely to be similar but the former example is relevant to the interpersonal communication level while the latter is relevant to the intrapersonal and probably social levels of analysis. The point of this modest distinction is to argue that the vast bulk of research labeled interpersonal research is just as relevant to the intrapersonal level as the interpersonal level and that to make a first-order question an interpersonal one requires that the link to interactional behaviors be made clear.

A second issue arises from empirical versus phenomenological approaches to the effects of environmental factors on behavioral output. Few would have any difficulty accepting the link between psychological states and individual behavioral action. However, the link between external environment and an individual's behavioral response may be mediated by the individual's perception of the situation (McHugh, 1968). In this case, the perceived situation would predict behavioral outcomes (Forgas, 1979). The important issue here is not which approach—empiricist or phenomenological—is correct, but rather the checking that is necessary when research operates out of one perspective or the other. On the empiricist side, the finding that a set of situations produces differential behavioral outcomes is insufficient information. One must carry out careful manipulation checks of the situations to ascertain what features lead them to be treated differently by the subjects. These manipulation checks are actually nothing more than situational perceptions.

On the phenomenological side, a finding that subjects' perceptions of situations produce differential behavioral outcomes is insufficient information. One must also attempt to discover how the perceptions of the situations, which are presumably different from the situations themselves, came about. In short, empiricist and phenomenological approaches, when carefully done methodologically and when pursued theoretically, dovetail in the information that they should provide. One need not make an exclusive choice between them.

A third reason for providing a category system for first-order encoding questions is to provide a means of illustrating significant lines of research while being somewhat comprehensive. The role of situation in interpersonal communication research has recently been surveyed by Cody and McLaughlin (1985). Within this arena, one of the most lively lines of inquiry has concerned the relationship between situational factors and compliance-gaining and compliance-resisting actions (Miller, Boster, Roloff, & Siebold, 1977; Fitzpatrick & Winke, 1979; McLaughlin, Cody, & Robey, 1980; Dillard & Burgoon, 1985).

The role of personality and other stable personal factors in behavioral output has been recently reviewed by Giles and Street (1985). The personality factor that has probably received the most research attention in the interpersonal communication literature is communication apprehension (McCroskey, 1977), variously labeled predisposition to verbal behavior (Mortensen & Arnston, 1974), reticence (Phillips, 1968), and social anxiety (Leary, 1983). Surprisingly little of the research on this trait has examined its relationship to overt verbal and nonverbal behavior. Burgoon and Koper (1984) did conduct such a study, and Dillard and Spitzberg (1984) reported a meta-analysis of the relationship between social anxiety and behavioral outcomes.

The relationship between affect and behavior was recently reviewed by Bowers, Metts, and Duncanson (1985). Although the relationship between specific emotions and behavioral outcomes has been limited to the study of facial affect (Ekman, 1982) and vocal characteristics (Scherer, 1984), that between general affect and behavioral outcome has been extensively studied (Harper, Wiens, & Matarazzo, 1978).

The relationship between physiological state and behavior was reviewed by Cappella (1983), although the number of studies on this hypothesis are limited. Finally, to my knowledge no reviews are available on the influence of cognitive factors on behavior (but see Hewes & Planalp, 1982; Planalp & Hewes, 1982; also Hewes & Planalp, Chapter 6). This may be due to the diversity of variables that could be lumped under the cognitive heading. Significant research has been conducted relating cognitive complexity to actions (O'Keefe & Sypher, 1981) in interpersonal communication settings.

The final issue made painfully prominent by the category scheme of this section is the limitation to linear effects from the factor to behavioral output. In fact, many of the separate categories of predictors will interact in predicting behavioral outcome. Patterson (1982a) has made this point with respect to the simple relationship between affect and behavioral outcome. He argues that a cognitive factor, such as goals or intentions, can in some circumstances override an affective factor. For example, Ickes, Patterson, Rajecki, and Tanford (1982) found that subjects who expected to interact with a cold partner smiled as much as those expecting to interact with a warm partner (in comparison to the control) because those expecting an unpleasant interaction tried to minimize the possibility of hostility from the other person. A study of this sort illustrates the kind of complex interactions that can arise among situational, cognitive, personality, and affective factors as predictors of behavioral outcomes.

The interaction of multiple factors affecting behavioral baseline will probably require a meta-analysis (Hunter, Schmidt, & Jackson, 1982). Experiments that manipulate many separate factors simultaneously are difficult to carry out and produce ecological validity problems. The relative variance accounted for by situational, affective, cognitive, and physiological predictors is crucial for understanding stability and variability in baseline behavioral activity. Meta-analytical techniques may be the only way of ascertaining the relative predictive value of these classes of effects on interpersonal behaviors.

Decoding factors. In specifying the relationship between behavior and output factors, the set of categories from the previous section changes only slightly. Dropped from the set of outcomes are the relatively stable intraindividual factors such as personality, age, sex, and socioeconomic status, as well as environmental factors such as situation. Verbal and non-verbal behaviors clearly cannot, by definition, alter factors that change very slowly or not at all. The transient categories of affective, cognitive, and physiological states remains. These groups of outcome factors include attitude and belief changes as a result of message effects and per-ceptions of the message sender in terms of power, dominance, affection, competence, and so on. Also included under the cognitive subcategory of perceptions are understandings and interpretations of incoming mes-sages. No references to reviews of the literature linking verbal, vocal, and kinesic behavior to these psychological states will be made here because the reviews cited earlier are comprehensive enough to include the reversed causal ordering from behaviors to outcomes.

The multifunctionality of most verbal and nonverbal behavior (Pat-terson, 1982b; Hewes, 1979) argues against assuming the single-cause/single-effect pattern in research on the effects of behavior on psycho-logical output. Thus high amounts of gaze behavior may lead to judg-ments of positive regard or to judgments of dominance, or both, depending on the social situation. As with encoding questions, interac-tions between outcomes may produce complex results.

The fundamental question that arises in the decoding area is the ques-tion of whether the probability of response depends upon perceived behavior or actual behavior. This is the empiricist-phenomenological issue raised in the previous section. There is little doubt that perceptions of behavior will in some situations differ from the behaviors on which they are based. This claim does not accept the superiority of the phe-nomenological position. As before, the crucial issue is not *that* percep-tions differ from behaviors but *how* they differ from behaviors. Simply replacing behavior with the perception of behavior will not answer this question. Rather, one must assume that individuals can describe why their perceptions differ from their observations. This is a dubious assumption. A second strategy would map empirically the relationship between a range of behavior and the perception of that behavior and from this relationship specify the operational filter that must be operat-ing between behavior and its perception. The significance of the phe-nomenological argument is being granted, but the method of obtaining the data necessary to evaluate the relationship between behavior and per-ception is empirical. The comprehensive data necessary to carry out such analyses have only begun to be gathered.

The nature of such data involves both summary measures of behav-ioral activity and summary measures of various perceptual judgments. The problem with such studies is that they must involve coding large numbers of different behaviors because we have such limited knowledge about which behaviors will be good predictors of perceptual judgments. In the domain of kinesic and vocal behaviors work by Shrout and Fiske (1982) and Burgoon, Buller, Hale, and deTurck (1984) has tried to predict judgments of affiliativeness and intimacy, immediacy, emotionality, and dominance. In the area of verbal and vocal behaviors recent work by Mulac, Lundell, and Bradac (in press) and Bradac and Mulac (1984) has tried to account for aspects of the powerfulness of speech on the basis of an extensive set of verbal behaviors. All of this work is promising in providing a solid empirical basis to the behavior-perception relationship. The work also contributes to our knowledge about functional groupings of behavior and begins to link interpersonal behavior to interpersonal perceptions—an important step in reintroducing interpersonal communication to the study of interpersonal relationships.

Although much more research in the behavior-perception tradition needs to be done using summary measures of behavior and perception, more dynamic studies ought to be considered as well. For example, if temporal perceptions of interactants were available from judges, then those dynamic perceptions could be the output series predicted by the person's own behaviors. In this way, a more dynamic and complete picture of how perceptions arise from behaviors could be obtained.

The domain of first-order questions is necessarily extremely broad in its compass; however, certain types of questions that may seem to fit within this domain are in fact omitted. Research that does not directly consider the signs and symbols of interpersonal communication is not directly relevant to the class of first-order questions. Examples would include hypotheses about A's personality and B's perception of that personality, the relationship between situational factors and cognitive attributions, cognitive reactions and affective responses, and so on. These are omitted because when these questions are ends in themselves, our knowledge about the behaviors and patterns of interpersonal interaction is not directly advanced. Of course, researchers sometimes begin with these questions in order to investigate message effects later. Research on the gender-linked language effect (Mulac & Lundell, 1982) began with attributional differences between male-generated and female-generated written speech samples. This work quickly moved to the specific verbal factors that produced these attributions. The important lesson of Mulac's research and the theme of this section is that message outcomes and message effects in interactional contexts make intraindividual processes relevant to interpersonal communication.

Critical Methodological Issues

The domain of first-order questions is too broad to make useful methodological comments. However, a few issues can be discussed within the context of message results and message effects, which is the focus of the class of first-order questions.

Unfortunately, much of the research that is classifiable as first-order interpersonal communication research is done with self-report measures of behavior. Certainly, self-report measures are an efficient first step in evaluating hypotheses for their potential utility. Even this pragmatic goal is often not in the best interests of research on first-order questions. First, since many of the output and input measures for first-order research must be self-report measures because they are reports of psychological states (e.g., personality or perceptions of dominance), then the covariation between this group of self-reports and self-report measures of behavior raises the problem of artifactual covariation due to the common methods factor. The covariance of such can be minimized by placing temporal or conceptual distance between the behavioral self-report and the psychological self-report measures. But even with such care a second problem arises. When people report behaviors they can be reporting their cultural expectations of what behaviors can or should be enacted in the situations and they are limited to reporting only those behaviors accessible to memory and to introspection.

When the relationship between messages and various outputs is the object of study, a significant problem in message selection and statistical analysis can arise. This has come to be known as the message-as-fixed-effects problem (Bradac, 1983; Clark, 1973; Hewes, 1983; Jackson & Jacobs, 1983). This problem has several different, but related, features. The first is that to avoid the possibility that a given effect is due to a particular message choice, the effect should be demonstrated with multiple versions of the message. This replication can be achieved as a direct replication with no significant feature of the message altered or as a sampling of messages from a specified population (e.g., of student-delivered speeches) or levels of a specified dimension (e.g., language intensity). A second part of the fixed effects problem is statistical and concerns whether the message manipulation should be considered a random or fixed effects variable. The reader is directed to the original articles for a discussion of this matter, but the decision clearly hinges on whether messages are samples from a specifiable population or fixed representatives of a level of some manipulated variable.

Summary and Future Directions

The class of first-order questions is extremely broad, covering questions that are primarily operative at the intraindividual level of inquiry. They become relevant to the interpersonal level when message effects and message outcomes in turn affect interpersonal interactions. Otherwise, the research on first-order questions is best considered intraper-sonal inquiry carried out in the interpersonal context.

Baseline probabilities of acting are certainly influenced by a wide variety of factors from situational to physiological. Comprehensive knowledge of the effects of these classes of effects will require, I believe, meta-analytic studies that quantitatively summarize results and have the ability to assess relative variance explained as well as interactive effects. Research concerning message effects on interpersonal judgments is only beginning and our knowledge in this domain is very limited. However, some research has been conducted and the process of mapping from behavior to perception has started. Success in this domain of research will have effects on zero-order questions related to the functional group-ing of behaviors and to those linking the study of interpersonal interac-tion to the study of interpersonal relations.

Finally the era has passed in which studies measuring "amount of communication" were considered observational studies. Researchers now measure many behavioral categories under the assumption of mere data exploration and the assumption that strong individual differences in behavior necessitate multiple behavioral observations on each person. Researchers do need to investigate wider ranges of behavior to under-stand the limits of the effects of these behaviors and limitations in their production, but these are refinements in research programs that have moved toward serious and comprehensive observational work.

SECOND-ORDER QUESTIONS

Second-order questions are central to the study of interpersonal com-munication as conceptualized in this chapter. These questions concern the pattern of interaction between persons directly. If interpersonal com-munication is anything, it is directly and deeply related to the way that one person's messages cause those of another to be different from what they would be otherwise. Thus this section is of critical importance in understanding the conceptual and methodological issues facing a sci-ence of communication at the interpersonal level.

Critical Distinctions and Critical Studies

The definition of interpersonal communication as behavioral influ-ence suggests two distinct subclasses of processes. The first concerns individual and mutual adaptation and assumes, in the former case, that a particular person adjusts their behavior to that of the other over and above baseline probability and, in the latter case, that each person adjusts to the other. The crucial feature in this first subclass is tracking "who is adapting to whom"; at issue is the type and extent of adaptation that persons make to one another behaviorally. The second subclass, not officially recognized as a part of the definition of statements (1) through (3), drops any consideration of an individual's or pair's adaptation and focuses upon the pattern of association between adjacent or lagged messages regardless of the source of the messages. At issue is not adaptation by a person but a pattern among message units. Let us label these two subclasses adaptation studies (individual and mutual) and message pattern studies.

Several up-to-date reviews of these two subclasses of second-order questions are available. Adaptation studies have been overviewed by Cappella (1981, 1985b), Giles and Powesland (1975), Patterson (1976, 1982a), and Street and Giles (1983); message pattern studies have received excellent treatments at the hands of Levinson (1983) and McLaughlin (1984). The remainder of this section discusses certain of the larger conceptual issues facing research in these two subclasses.

Message pattern studies. The definition of interpersonal communication advocated in this chapter is clearly oriented toward adaptation studies. Modifying the definition for message pattern studies involves substituting for X_I and Y_I a representation of the set of enactable behaviors Z_M so that the contingent probability becomes $P[Z_M (t + k) \mid Z_N (t)]$ where N and M may or may not be the same. Note that the individual actors have been suppressed and only the contingency between behaviors remains. As before, the baseline probability $P [Z_M (t + k)]$ must be known before the significance of the contingent probability can be assessed.

Within the class of message pattern studies are two subtlely, but significantly, different approaches to message-message sequences. The first focuses primarily, but not exclusively, on dyadic behavior so that message sequences are easily linked to the persons enacting the messages. This work is exemplified by the work of Cody and McLaughlin (1985). The second focuses primarily, but not exclusively, upon group behavior (of groups larger than two) so that the sources of the messages are difficult to identify. This work is exemplified by the research of Fisher and Drecksel (1983), Ellis and Fisher (1975), and Hawes and Foley (1973). Let us take up these two types in turn.

One of the most informative and intelligent summaries of the dyadic message pattern research is that of McLaughlin (1984). She organizes the available research into several categories employing functional groupings. The functional groupings include coherence, regulation, sequencing, preventatives, and repairs. The coherence function concerns the ways that interactants try to make antecedent and subsequent remarks make sense together, in much the same ways—although not by employing the same strategies—that writers do in making sentences cohere into paragraphs and paragraphs into essays. The study of conversational coherence then, depends significantly on the nature of comprehension. Thus research finds that remarks that extend other remarks at least locally (see McLaughlin, 1984, p. 55) are more coherent than nonextensions, that topical shifts to which the information is immediate are more coherent than distant ones (Planalp & Tracy, 1980; Reichman, 1978), and that extensions of the thesis are more coherent than extensions of the event under discussion (Tracy, 1982).

The regulation function concerns the way speakers and listeners control the allocation of their roles in conversation (Duncan & Fiske, 1977; Sacks, Schegloff, & Jefferson, 1974), create and react to moments of awkward silence (McLaughlin & Cody, 1982), and negotiate overlapping speech. The sequencing function as discussed by McLaughlin (1984) concerns the regularized pairings of remarks, often called adjacency pairs, which arise from the classification of various speech act types. The request-response pair is a typical adjacency pair that has received a great deal of attention in terms of the nature of indirect requests (Nofsinger, 1976), presequences that cue that a request is coming, insertion sequences that indicate that some precondition for the speech act has not been met, and so on (Jackson & Jacobs, 1983).

Preventatives are attempts to minimize or avoid threats to face during an interaction episode. These are usually carried out by actors in anticipation of their own threats to face and so are not of interest to studies of message pattern across actors. Repairs are attempts to fix some breakdown in the conversation, in the remarks made in the conversation, or in some event outside the conversation as made by the speaker or listener. When repairs are responses to some accusation by the other person, then the research is relevant to message pattern studies. Work by McLaughlin, Cody, and Rosenstein (1983) has found that when reproaches are more aggravating, more aggravating responses are obtained; when reproaches are mitigating, more mitigating responses are obtained. Thus the pattern is one of reciprocity at the level of the message.

Much of the research reviewed by McLaughlin (1984), labeled here as message pattern research, offers fascinating and informative insights into the organization and sequencing of messages in interpersonal encounters. This research often adopts qualitative methods of study rather than quantitative methods. This methodological choice has been made partly for philosophical reasons (Garfinkel, 1977; Harré & Secord, 1973; Schutz, 1977) and partly because the focus has been on the content of the acts rather than their linguistic structure or their quantity. Qualitative techniques may be more appropriate when the meaning of the remark is directly at issue since interpretations can be imposed directly by those closest to the data. The dangers of unchecked interpretation—that is, interpretations whose intersubjectivity has not been assessed—will be discussed below. However, the work of McLaughlin and Cody (McLaughlin, Cody, & O'Hair, 1983; McLaughlin, Cody, & Rosenstein, 1983) shows that one can blend quantitative and qualitative methods so that each profits from the strengths of the other.

The dyadic message pattern studies can be seen as more relevant to work in language pragmatics than work in interpersonal communication. Pragmatically oriented linguists (Brown & Yule, 1983; Levinson, 1983) have exhibited a deep interest in the research on conversational structure. Interpersonal communication is, after all is said and done, concerned with the way communication is linked to the relationships between persons, not to the structures of conversations that various linguistic communities can have. This is not to imply that this first class of message pattern studies is necessarily irrelevant to interpersonal communication; it is not. However, a change in the use of this research may be necessary. For example, the study of relational control could proceed from a study of the number and types of reproaches and responses that each member of the pair employs. Similarly, the explicitness of coherence devices in conversation may decrease as relationships are more well established, implying that the type of coherence necessary could be an indicator of relationship stage. The general point is that in order for message pattern findings to be relevant for interpersonal communication research, treatment of message sequences alone must be abandoned and attention must be turned to the originators and recipients of messages.

The second group of message pattern studies is represented by the work of Fisher, Hawes, and Ellis, in which various types of groups from interview dyads through task and consciousness-raising groups to quarantined military pairs are observed for patterns of dominant, submissive, and neutral remark pairs. Message pairs are the fundamental unit of analysis in this work, and sequences between adjacent message pairs are observed and codified using variations of the Ericson and Rogers (1973) coding system. The results reported in this line of work make no mention of who the initiator or who the receiver of the remark is. Rather, the focus is solely upon the types of *remark* sequences. The following comments focus upon the implicit assumptions that are being made when the originator and recipient of the message are so ignored as to become unretrievable.

One can argue that in the group context keeping track of individuals as well as what they say is practically prohibitive. Indeed, there are problems in doing so (but see Hewes, 1979) but one must weigh these burdens against the possible information loss and the radical assumptions about group communication that one must make. With regard to information loss, consider a two-person interaction in which only positive and negative remarks are being observed. In the first part of the interaction suppose that A responds negatively to B's positive comments and B's response to A's positive comments is also positive. This yields high values for the contingent probabilities $p(-|+)$ and $p(+|+)$, which ignore the source of the activity. If in the second half of the interaction B is negative to A's positive comments and A's response to B's positive comments is also positive, then once again $p(-|+)$ and $p(+|+)$ have high values. However, the patterns between A and B and, very possibly, their interpersonal relationship have changed between the first and second periods. Thus the study that ignores the source and receiver of the messages runs the risk of missing significant relational changes. This is an unacceptable risk for a study of interpersonal communication, although it may not be unacceptable for a study of interaction structure.

In group contexts if one assumes that the source of a message is irrelevant to the overall pattern of interaction, then one is implicitly assuming that message sequences contribute equally to the group's climate of communication. Sources of the interaction are assumed to be irrelevant. Thus if hostile remarks beget hostile remarks in subgroups involving persons A, B, and C in the first part of the interaction and the same patterns obtain but for persons C, D, and F in the second part of the interaction, then conclusions that ignore the message source and destination must assume that the "climate of hostile retaliation" was constant for the group even though the actions were perpetrated by different subgroups. There is no question that information has been lost in these observational procedures. Whether the loss is critical depends crucially on whether the assumption that communicative exchanges contribute equally to group climate is valid in the context of the particular research question.

In some situations this assumption may be valid. For example, as the group size increases, individuals may be less able to recognize which comments are directed at themselves and which at the group as a whole. In such a scenario, exchanges within subgroups may be less important than group-level interchanges. However, with small groups, and certainly with groups of two, persons will tend to see and hear remarks and gestures as directed at them as individuals so that keeping track of source and destination becomes more important. Although the assumption about group climate may ultimately prove to be a viable one, it seems unwise to make such a powerful assumption without putting it to the test. The assumption to be tested is not whether the group interaction structure differs from the interaction structure of specified subgroups; evidence on that assumption is likely to show that they do (Hewes, Planalp, & Streibel, 1980). The assumption to test is whether participants' and observers' perceptions of the group climate differ when interaction patterns in subgroups differ significantly from group patterns as compared to when the subgroups and the group as a whole do not differ.

In the absence of such a test, the group climate assumption must be left as an interesting and powerful, but untested and dubious, hypothesis.

Adaptation studies. In contrast to the group-level message pattern studies reviewed above, adaptation studies keep track of the individuals sending and receiving the messages. These studies have been overviewed elsewhere (Cappella, 1981, 1985b) under the descriptors "mutual influence," "convergence," "interspeaker influence," and so on. Despite minor differences in these labels, they all refer to the set of processes in which behavior by one person influences the behavior emitted by another over baseline levels. Most adaptation studies are concerned with the extent and direction of adaptation of person A to person B; that is, adaptation is individual adaptation rather than adaptation of the dyad or group.

The chief areas of research on adaptation in adult interactions include the regulation of speaking turns (Duncan & Fiske, 1977), involvement (Davis, 1982), dominance (Rogers, Courtright, & Millar, 1980), speech variables (Cappella & Planalp, 1981; Jaffe & Feldstein, 1970), such kinesic behaviors as eye gaze (Kaplan, Firestone, Klein, & Sodikoff, 1983), gesture, orientation and posture, distance (Aiello, 1972, 1973), self-disclosure (Davis, 1976, 1977), language choice, dialect and accent (Giles & Powesland, 1975), intimate questions (Anderson, 1976), negotiation (Putnam, 1985; Putnam & Jones, 1982), and accounts and repairs (Cody & McLaughlin, 1985). Research on individual adaptation in interactions involving children and adults includes speech variables (Street, 1983), forms of turn-taking (Stern, Jaffe, Beebe, & Bennett, 1975), movement (Beebe, Stern, & Jaffe, 1979), involvement (Thomas & Martin, 1976), and gaze (Blehar, Lieberman, & Ainsworth, 1977).

Although the research literature on adaptation is too complex and too voluminous to summarize here, general trends within this literature can be stated. First, individuals are relatively consistent in the behaviors they exhibit within a conversational situation (Cappella, 1984) and this consistency is greater than the degree of adaptation to the other person. Second, adaptation occurs in a wide variety of behaviors from verbal to motor and from intentional to unconscious, thus indicating its pervasiveness in the behavioral program. Third, for many behaviors adaptation toward and adaptation away from the other's behavior is observed often with clear trends in one or the other direction. For example, all reviews of the distance literature find that people compensate or move away from others in some fashion (e.g., verbally or with gaze aversion) when distances are too close. However, certain social conditions produce deviations from this general trend (Hale & Burgoon, 1984). Fourth, situational, personal, and relational factors can affect the type of adaptation, moving it from "adaptation toward" to "adaptation away" under the proper configuration of conditions. Finally, adaptation occurs not only with a wide variety of behaviors but also occurs across the developmental spectrum, being observed early in the social life of infants.

These general conclusions suggest that adaptation is ingrained deeply in the interaction patterns of the human organism. Furthermore, we must be willing to entertain the notion that these adaptations exist and help guide the interactions of less advanced species as well (Griffin, 1984; Smith, 1977). Given these findings, one cannot help but be impressed by the centrality of behavioral adaptation to the human, and perhaps animal, experience. It is only fitting that such a process be at the heart of our definition of and research into what we refer to nobly as interpersonal relations. What remains to be seen is whether adaptation, mutual or individual, predicts important relational outcomes. That is the concern of a subsequent section on third-order questions.

Critical Methodological Issues

Methodological issues in the study of message sequences whether from an adaptation or from a message pattern point of view are extremely important. For the more quantitative adaptation studies, the reason is that the sequential character of the observations introduces problems in data handling that are not well known to social scientists. The problems are primarily ones of temporal dependence in observations and the probability that members of a dyad do not yield behavioral observations that are independent of one another. For the more qualitative studies, problems arise with the confidence that one can have with observations derived from the insights of a single well-schooled observer thoroughly immersed in his or her data. These concerns with qualitative and with quantitative methods will be taken up in turn.

Qualitative methods. Most of the qualitative procedures employed in the study of social interaction are strongly empirical in orientation. Certainly the techniques of inquiry advocated by Garfinkel (1977) and Harré and Secord (1973), while critical of quantitative methods, do nevertheless accept empiricist inquiry. A science of human communication can readily accept these methods as applied to interpersonal communication except for two features. Highly inferential observations create reliability problems. The example of types of requests given earlier is representative. When requests are categorized on the basis of content rather than structure, obtaining reliable observations is very difficult. Since much of the excellent research on message patterns requires content-based observational decisions rather than structural decisions and since the reliability of these content decisions is often unchecked, then the reproducibility of the findings will be questioned; however, researchers should not forego content-based observational systems. Given their significance and their complexity, they require reliability assessments even more than do other observational systems.

In most qualitative message pattern studies no attempt is made to show that observed message sequences exceed the chance baseline probability. Without a baseline probability, one cannot judge whether the observed sequence differs from a chance sequence. In many cases, the observed sequence is so obviously not due to chance alone that a test, for example, request-denial sequences against chance baselines would be ludicrous. However, when researchers turn their attention to subtler effects, as have Kendon (1970) in postural shifts and Goodwin (1981) with eye gaze and turn regulation, then the necessity of having baseline information against which to compare observed patterns is very important. The errors promulgated by the research of Condon and Ogston (1967) and Condon and Sander (1974) in movement synchrony (see McDowall, 1978) must not be allowed to undermine the excellent work that has already come out of the qualitative studies of message patterns.

Quantitative methods. Although the definition of adaptation implies strongly that adaptation is a temporal phenomenon requiring sequential observations, some research has employed more static designs to provide at least minimal information on how people adjust to confederates and to one another. The relatively static designs create one set of statistical problems and the relatively dynamic designs another set. The issues raised here are unique to the study of interpersonal communication. Let us consider these in turn.

One of the most common procedures used to estimate the effects of a given behavior upon the behavioral response employs a confederate who is coached to adopt different levels of behavior with different subject groups. The mean response of subjects to each behavioral level indicates whether adaptation toward or away or some other more complex adaptation has occurred. Such designs create several difficulties. First, only a limited number and limited range of behaviors can be manipulated because of limitations in the confederate's ability to control what are often low awareness behaviors. Second, the usual high variability in the amount (duration or percentage) or rate of behavior across subjects requires that the effects be large or that the power be high. The first of these requirements is unlikely and the second is unfeasible with observational studies. The best alternative is to obtain a baseline of behavior for all subjects and to use difference scores or a covariance model to minimize the within-cell variance.

The major objection that can be raised to confederate studies of course is that they lack ecological validity as the confederates must enact a highly scripted routine. However, with intact dyads or groups the mean level of behavior for individuals is not necessarily independent for persons within the same group. This violation of the independence assumption can have disastrous consequences for significance testing should the

researcher simply go forward treating the individual responses as independent (Kraemer & Jacklin, 1979). The alternatives are several and
none of them is completely satisfactory. One could operate at the group
rather than the individual level of analysis. This solution reduces what is
probably, for reasons of economy, already low power. If one is willing
to forego power considerations, group responses must be created from
individual responses and this step involves a certain amount of capriciousness. A second solution requires the foresight to employ designs
such as those advocated by Kraemer and Jacklin (1979) in order to separate individual effects with little loss of power. This design has recently
been updated to the multivariate case (Mendoza & Graziano, 1982). A
third, and often neglected solution, is to employ various forms of nested
and split-plot designs as appropriate (Miller-Tutzauer, 1984), testing for
effects due to group or dyad, and moving to the individual level when
these group effects are not significant. None of these solutions is optimal, but certainly any one of them is superior to simply eliminating half
of the data in dyadic cases and more in group cases.

Neither the confederate nor intact group designs for studying adaptation separates person from dyadic effects. The problem is that adaptation should be assessed for individuals within dyads if possible and must
be assessed relative to a baseline level for the particular person. Neither
of the above designs gets at individual adjustment. In addition, how is it
possible to get a baseline behavior for person A that is relevant to the
interactional context but is not a part of a particular interaction, say with
person B. Any baseline for A obtained from an interaction with another
will be tainted by the influences of that particular other and, hence, will
not be a baseline for A but will be a baseline for A with B. Of course, A
cannot interact without some B being present. The solution to this problem conceptually is simply to have person A interact with several different others and take as a baseline the probability of A's acting averaged
across partners.

Kenny and his associates (Kenny & LaVoie, 1984; Warner, Kenny, &
Stoto, 1979) have not only suggested designs of this sort but have worked
the complex statistical analyses necessary to obtain and test measures
of dyadic adjustment for individuals across dyadic partners and dyadic
adjustment unique to particular dyads. In the "social relations model,"
as it is called, measures of sending and receiving are also readily available for baseline information. The social relations model holds considerable promise for investigating, without the artificiality of confederate
designs, natural interactions, and obtaining measures of general and
unique adaptation. The design does require some additional data gathering but the potential payoff appears to be worth the effort (Fitzpatrick &
Dindia, 1986; Montgomery, 1984). Despite its power, the social rela-

tions model does not and cannot provide direct information on sequential patterning that is the heart of the definition of interpersonal communication advocated here.

Standard methods of data analysis cannot be directly transferred to sequential data in part because of the temporal covariation that usually exists in sequential observations. This lack of independence creates biases in significance tests that, under certain conditions, will not be minimized even in the large sample case (Hibbs, 1974).

The fundamental form of the data that faces the researcher studying adaptation processes is two series of observations, one for each of the persons in a dyadic interaction, one observation per time-sampling unit. Unlike some time series data, social interaction does not suggest which of the two series is the input series and which the output series. In many applications in economics and politics, clear causal priority exists beforehand and this information can be used in modeling the size and direction of effects.

For most interpersonal interactions causal priority is very much at issue with the direction, amount, and kind of behavioral influence from A to B and vice versa. Gottman (1979) in fact defined control in his married couples in terms of which partner had the greater statistical influence on the other. When an input and output series can be clearly and unequivocally defined, data handling is simpler. On more substantive grounds, a research question may indicate that asymmetric influence between partners should result from or predict certain other relational factors. Recent developments in econometrics (Geweke, 1978) and elsewhere (Gottman & Ringland, 1981) have provided techniques that may be useful in determining which of two series—and hence which of two people in interaction—is the more controlling influence.

Usually, questions about adaptation are not interested merely in causal priority but are also interested in the direction and magnitude of the adaptation, as well as the time between behavioral manifestation and its effect (lag time). The methods most commonly employed to answer these questions are time series (McCleary & Hay, 1980), time series regression (Cappella, 1980), lag sequential techniques (Sackett, 1978, 1979), and Markov techniques (Hewes, 1975, 1980) although other less common procedures are also used. Time series and time series regression techniques are primarily suited to such continuous measures of behavior as speech rate (Cappella & Planalp, 1981; Street, 1982) while lag sequential and Markov techniques are designed to handle categorical data such as talk-silence sequences (Jaffe & Feldstein, 1970), relational control (Ellis, 1979; Ellis & Fisher, 1975), and negotiation (Putnam & Jones, 1982).

Summary and Future Directions

Much of the work on message patterns and adaptation is complementary. Unfortunately, this efficient division of labor has not been as advantageous to researchers as it might have been, since representatives from each group have tended to ignore one another's work. Part of the reason for this mutual ignorance is the unfortunate confound between methodology and the content of variables being studied. Most of the studies of interactional content have been primarily qualitative whereas studies of vocal and kinesic factors have primarily employed quantitative methodologies. A second reason is that many of the qualitatively oriented researchers have roots in or biases toward the more sociological traditions (Cicourel, 1974; Garfinkel, 1977; Schutz, 1977) while the quantitative types have looked to psychological work for their theories and research traditions. A third reason is that some of the content-based research has been aimed at the study of the structure of conversation while some of the vocal and kinesic work has been conducted in service of interpersonal communication concerns. Thus for some researchers the ultimate goals have been different.

This separation of lines of inquiry need not, and indeed should not, continue. If adaptation in interpersonal communication is to be understood in all of its behavioral manifestations, then research must be directed at the content of interactions as much as the vocal and kinesic features. If conversational structure is to be understood in all of its behavioral manifestations, then research must be concerned with the subtle vocal and kinesic processes as much as the more obvious aspects of verbal content. Since research in both approaches is strongly empiricist, workers have a rich observational data base from which to generalize using their own unique methodological biases. McLaughlin and Cody and their colleagues (McLaughlin, Cody, & O'Hair, 1983; McLaughlin, Cody, & Rosenstein, 1983) have given us excellent examples of research richly cross-fertilized by work conducted in both domains.

THIRD-ORDER QUESTIONS

This fourth group of questions takes the next logical step in the study of interpersonal communication, asking about the association between relationship states (and relationship outcomes) and communication patterns, whether conceived as adaptive patterns or message patterns. This category links the behavioral patterns that define interpersonal communication to intraindividual perceptions and cognitions and the socially defined relationships that exist above and below the interpersonal level.

Critical Distinctions and Critical Research

A variety of distinctions must be made before the types of third-order questions can be completely specified. These distinctions include (1) the difference between individual patterns and group patterns of interaction, (2) the distinction between relational factors as antecedents and relational factors as consequents of interaction patterns, and (3) the distinction between individual and social measures of relationship.

The distinction between individual and group patterns of interaction was made in the earlier section on second-order questions. Basically, one type of interactive pattern involves the adaptation of person A's behavior to that of the partner and the partner's to person A's. These two measures can be different and characterize the individuals separately. A second type of interactive pattern characterizes the group as a whole by either combining the individuals' patterns in a unique way or by ignoring the individuals and summarizing only the message patterns. For example, if one is observing positively and negatively toned behavior in marital dyads, one can characterize the degree of reciprocity for husband and wife separately; or one can combine the husband's and wife's reciprocity into an index of dyadic reciprocity; or one can ignore the husband and wife, summarizing the tendency for positive to beget positive behavior and negative to beget negative behavior. In sum, the researcher can study individual or group interaction patterns. The group patterns can be obtained by combining individuals or by observing message patterns alone.

The second distinction involves the obvious potential for mutual causal influence between relationship factors and interaction patterns. Anyone who has seriously considered both interpersonal communication and interpersonal relationships (e.g., Hinde, 1979) assumes that each has the potential to affect the other. In the research context, one would expect that the type of implicit or explicit relationship between persons, even in interviewing situations (Street, 1986), should be taken into account in predicting the types of interactive behavior. Similarly, the skills approach and the systems approach to marital functioning both assume that the pattern of interaction between partners can predict not only satisfaction and longevity, but also the ideological character of the relationship.

The third distinction tries to clarify subtle differences between group and individual measures of relationship states. This distinction parallels that for interaction patterns. Some measures of relationship state are directed at group or social levels in the sense that these levels are meant to characterize the relationship as a whole. One type of these social measures of relationship state is created through some combination procedure, involving measures taken from the individuals involved. For example, relational satisfaction may be treated as the average satisfaction obtained from the partners. In these cases the social measure is created by an ad hoc procedure that combines the individual measures. A second type of social measure of relationship state applies to all those in the situation at the same time and is not dependent on individual assessments. Such measures can include the longevity of the relationship, the relative social status of the persons as defined by the society (e.g., in doctor-patient settings), the sexual status of the relationship (homosexual, heterosexual), and so on. Such descriptors of the relationship avoid the disagreements inherent in individual measures but, of course, are limited in that phenomenological variables such as satisfaction are not in their purview. A third subtype of relational state measures are the individual measures of perception of the relationship or perceived relational outcome that are treated as individual measures and not combined in any way.

These distinctions are offered here because the important hypotheses in third-order questions involve causal direction between interpersonal communication and interpersonal relationship factors and the match between levels of predictor and predicted variables.

Matching levels. Studies that seek to establish associations between relationship factors and interaction patterns must match the level of variables used, either group to group or individual to individual. The reasons for this matching requirement are both statistical and theoretical. Let us consider the statistical reasons first. Suppose one were correlating a group-level variable, disagreement (measured as the sum of differences between partner's attitudes on issues sensitive to the relationship), with an individual-level variable, positive or negative response to the other's positive or negative action. The disagreement measure is the same for both persons but the interpersonal communication measure is different for each individual. If one simply treats the disagreement score as the same for both persons, then an artifactual correlation has been introduced so that the disagreement measures are not independent across the subjects within pairs in the sample. Neither can one simply drop one of the individual measures randomly. Which one shall it be? Which person's reaction is less important to the association with disagreement? Since disagreement as measured here is clearly a social-level variable, the only solution is to develop a combination of the individual patterns, which together constitute a social-level pattern of interaction. The same considerations hold in general.

The issue is not only a statistical one; it is a theoretical one. Sociologists, such as Berger and Luckman (1967), have been asking how, on the one hand, societal-level phenomena can develop from the interactions among people and, on the other hand, how interactions among people can be determined by society. This question of the relationship between social institutions and individual behavior is a fundamental issue in sociological theory. To the extent that relationships exist as more than the sum of the perceptions of the persons within a relationship, then the classical question of sociological theory is also a central question of the study of interpersonal relationships and interpersonal communication.

Berger and Luckman (1967) take up exactly these issues in their book on social reality. They give a simple and straightforward answer to the question of how social reality can constrain the actions of the individuals within a society. It is that society and its institutions exist as a part of reality for people born into that society. If the social reality dictates a pattern of action, reason Berger and Luckman, then acting in accord with its dictates is no more unusual than acting in accord with the dictates of physical reality.

In answering the question of how society's institutions, norms, and conventions come to be in the first place, Berger and Luckman offer a more complex explanation. Assuming that persons engage in habitual actions and that for reasons of predictability and efficiency others mimic these actions, then a pattern of interaction and, more important, an expected pattern of action develops. This pattern hardens and thickens over time as the reasons for it are eventually lost in history. The pattern is followed simply because it is. For third parties who come to this microcosmic society, the pattern exists outside of them and, hence, has a reality greater than would be attributed simply to a pattern of expectations.

When applied to interpersonal situations, Berger and Luckman's explanations have points of similarity and difference. When people define themselves as having this or that type of relationship, then the reality of that definition and the mutual expectations that the definition engenders, even when implicit, can constrain their patterns of interaction. The dissimilarity derives from the difference between a relationship and a social institution. Eventually the originators of social institutions are lost to history, leaving only the institution with its norms and conventions. This is true only for some interpersonal relationships (e.g., well-defined role relationships); for other interpersonal relationships, such as those within families and mating pairs, persons within the relationship have defined it and its boundaries. In turn, they can redefine those relationships. In this case, the institution which is the interpersonal relationship does not outlive its originators.

Both definitions of relationships and definitions of social institutions can be questioned by individuals, but individuals acting alone cannot change institutions any more than a single individual can change a socially defined relationship by acting unilaterally. The difference, however, is not one of quality but one of quantity. Social relationships, like social institutions, have a reality greater than that of their makers.

The study of the association between individual patterns of social interaction and socially defined relationships is the same conceptual question that sociological theorists raise about the origin and development of social institutions. This mixing of levels, individual and social, is not a theoretical error by any means. Rather, it is a complex processual question requiring much more careful data and theory than the mere statistical correlation of individual with group-level variables.

The research literature. What can be readily studied then are relationship factors and interaction patterns at the same level of abstraction, group or individual. The research on these topics cannot be comprehensively reviewed here but articles by Cappella (1985b), Street (1986), and Fitzpatrick and Badzinski (1985; and see Fitzpatrick, Chapter 19) offer more complete treatments of the interaction and the relationship literatures.

Two major problems arise in attempting to categorize the research literature for third-order questions. First, the major categorization dimension in addition to level of abstraction (group or individual) is causal direction. Specifically, does the research attempt to predict *to* or to predict *from* interaction pattern? Some of the very best research in this area is done with established dyads, such as married couples. In many of these cases, it is not possible to unravel whether the causal priority is from relationship type to interaction pattern or vice versa (Williamson & Fitzpatrick, 1985) or whether the direction is from satisfaction to reciprocity or vice versa (Pike & Sillars, 1985). The authors of the research are careful to make no casual claims either, but our inability to make no statements stronger than correlational ones is very limiting.

Where causal priority can be untangled, the situation is usually one involving little relational history. For example, Thakerar, Giles, and Cheshire (1982) studied the effects of status differences on patterns of actual and perceived speech rate accommodation while Genesee and Bourhis (1982) studied the effects of code switching in bilingual settings on perceptions of the other person. The former case examined the effect of a relational state on interaction pattern while the latter considered the effects of manipulated code-switching patterns on relational perceptions. Both are laboratory studies with valuable results for the general set of human role relationships but are much less relevant to the study of more intimate and established relationships.

The point is that causal information is not merely of academic interest in the study of interpersonal communication but of paramount pragmatic interest. Just as static information hinders and limits our knowledge of interaction patterns, so too the static knowledge that we obtain from people in established relationships limits what we can know and what we can advise for these important relationships. This lack of knowledge makes it impossible to guess whether interventions into beliefs about the relationship would be more effective than interventions in patterns of interaction in inducing changes in the relational climate.

The second major problem with the research literature relevant to third-order questions is that there is very little of it. Few researchers have made the significant commitments of time and energy necessary to complete studies that require natural or created dyads and careful observation of an extensive set of behaviors. The recent work by Gottman (1979), by Courtright, Millar, and Rogers-Millar (1979) and Millar, Rogers-Millar, and Courtright (1979), and by Noller (1984) coupled with the research cited above by Williamson and Fitzpatrick (1985) and Pike and Sillars (1985) represent some of the few exceptions to this rule. The challenge to researchers is to begin serious and programmatic research in this area, which is so much at the heart of interpersonal communication.

Critical Methodological Issues

Since the research literature on third-order questions is so sparse, few significant methodological matters have been raised. Some general comments relevant to the basic issues treated under this category can be made, however. These issues concern interaction pattern, level of abstraction, and causal priority.

Third-order questions concern the association between relationship factors and *patterns* of interaction, not distributional characteristics such as the amount, rate, or duration of some behavior. Such distributional characteristics may be of interest for a variety of reasons, but interpersonal communication is fundamentally concerned with behavioral contingency rather than mere amounts.

The previous section argued that third-order questions must use variables that are matched in their level of abstraction. When one of the relationship variables is a group-level variable that is created as a sum, average, or whatever, arbitrariness becomes an issue. Since simple techniques such as summing are completely ad hoc and ignore the potential variation between partners, researchers should work at the individual level whenever data and the research question permit. However, working at the individual level of analysis requires attention to the lack of independence that persons within dyad or within group create. The previous section on second-order questions discussed this problem. By working at the individual level the researcher can avoid charges of arbitrariness and charges that natural variation has been ignored. In addition, when individual level findings (for example, from husbands to wives and from wives to husbands) show little difference, then one can move back to the group level without arbitrarily ignoring natural variation in the data.

When the research question or other considerations require working at the group level, even though the operational definitions provide individual level data, then some precautions against ignoring within-group variation are in order. Fitzpatrick (1984) has used an interesting technique of separating relational types into those where the partners agree on the relationship definition and those in which the partners disagree about the definition. This technique can be easily generalized to other individual measures of relational states. The advantage of this technique is that the natural variation existing between partners is not simply ignored but is included as a characteristic to be explained.

Untangling the causal influences from relational factors to communication patterns and back again is not a significant methodological problem for relationships without a history. Indeed, some experimental work has been done on both parts of these causal paths. However, with established relationships no simple methodological tricks or statistical manipulations are available to unconfound the intertwined factors of relationship and interaction. To my knowledge, serious attacks on this question have not been made. When they are, they will no doubt require long-run temporal data that begin at the early stages of a relationship and follow both relational state descriptors and interaction patterns over relatively long periods of time. The only other alternatives for untangling causal priority are to follow the same classes of variables over time, waiting for significant changes in the relationship or the interaction pattern as a result of outside disturbances and observing whether or not the interruptions transfer some effect to the other series. These quasi-experiments (Cook & Campbell, 1979) come as close to experimental manipulations as is possible with established relationships.

Summary and Future Directions

In the domain of third-order questions both practical and theoretical questions exist in juxtaposition. Fundamental theoretical questions arise about the nature of relationships as social entities or individual entities, about the direction of causal influence between relationship factors and interaction patterns, and about the linkage between socially defined relationships and individual interactions. At the same time, these questions are not merely the speculations of academics unconnected to the world of real human relations. In fact, third-order questions represent the tie not only between the study of interpersonal communication and the study of interpersonal relations but also between research and policy. Interpersonal communication cannot be a closed research enterprise no matter how fascinating the temporal covariation between behavior X and behavior Y. That covariation must matter at some point to the experiences of the persons who enact the behaviors.

CONCLUSIONS

The goals of this chapter have been related to the definition of interpersonal communication put forward at the outset. That definition has adopted what I have called a minimalist approach. Whatever changes subsequent research and subsequent chroniclers in the field make in the definition, the centrality of mutual adaptation will not be lost. The fundamental claim is simply that if interpersonal communication has any essential feature, it is that persons influence one another's behavior over and above that attributed to normal baselines of action. The remainder of the chapter has explored a variety of implications that this definition highlights primarily by focusing upon four classes of research and theoretical questions that a science of interpersonal communication must answer. These questions are not offered as a laundry list of previous and future research but rather as fundamental issues that the research community must address.

The classes of zero-order through third-order questions have brought into focus (1) issues on observation, meaning, validity, and reliability, (2) issues related to the production of baseline behaviors and the differences between behavior as stimulus and the perception of behavior, (3) the centrality of mutual adaptation and message patterns to the social functioning of the human organism, and (4) the association between interaction patterns and relational states in their causal relationship and in their definition as individual or social phenomena.

Issues that have been a part of classical theoretical controversies in the social and behavioral sciences have arisen naturally through the definition of statements (1) through (3). The study of interpersonal communication is not, simply because it is a relatively new field of inquiry, divorced from these controversies. Meaning, validity, and accuracy are as central to the observational studies of interpersonal behaviors as they are to philosophers and methodologists. Even those social theorists who have emphasized the importance of understanding a phenomenon to the exclusion of its quantification are immediately pressed into the study of intersubjective understanding lest they find themselves occupying the skeptic's ground defending an incommunicable subjective understanding. Disagreement between the phenomenologist who claims that perception of the environment dictates response and the behaviorist who claims that the environment dictates response also occurs within the boundaries of interpersonal communication studies. In discussing this issue under the category of first-order questions, I have tried to show that each side stops its inquiry at precisely the point where its own assumptions should be tested. Informative research will not stop where it should move forward toward the test of its own operating assumptions. Finally, the debate over social and individual conceptions of relational states has occupied social theorists from the beginning of sociological theory. The analogy between social institutions and social relationships is a strong one. The issues of how society produces individual behavior and how individual behavior produces society are the same questions, in macrocosm, that need to be asked about interpersonal relationships and interpersonal communication.

One might be concerned that the approach that has been taken here is too analytical, giving precedence to the parts rather than the whole system. This is a fair criticism that requires the caveat that analysis is only one-half of the dialectical process, which has synthesis as its opposite pole. A comprehensive science of interpersonal communication requires proceeding on all four fronts simultaneously, keeping clearly in one's mind the fundamental questions that guide research and theory.

Students of interpersonal communication who have emphasized qualitative forms of data acquisition and have emphasized *verstehen* over prediction may argue that they have received too few pages in this chapter. I am certainly open to that objection. However, those who claim to be developing a science of interpersonal communication have certain, minimal requirements of the knowledge that they are willing to admit. The basic requirement is that the research methods produce intersubjectively verifiable conclusions. This requirement does not imply what methods are required for intersubjectivity since I, for one, am willing to admit a variety of methods. But intersubjectivity cannot be an afterthought or merely a philosophical issue appended to discussions in order to avoid the alienation of pure subjectivism. Intersubjectivity meets the spirit of the basic scientific drive for public knowledge, while the methods for insuring intersubjectivity are negotiable.

Finally, one can object to this chapter on the grounds that it is barren with respect to the theories that operate within interpersonal communication. To that charge I am guilty but not without defense. This chapter opened with the claim that although theories come and go, observations—and, it appears, fundamental issues—remain for subsequent theorists to use in their puzzle solving. Thus I have elected to avoid discussions of theory because they, too, shall pass away. But theories are not reviewed here for another reason. Theories are explanations of phenomena that occur at some level. Pains have been taken to describe the phenomena of interpersonal communication but, I believe, the explanations for these phenomena operate at levels above and below the interpersonal in the hierarchy of communication processes. Thus to explain individual production and individual response patterns requires explanations that are actually intraindividual in their focus (e.g., Burgoon, 1978; Cappella & Greene, 1982; Hale & Burgoon, 1984; Patterson, 1982a; Street & Giles, 1983), fitting more comfortably on the level below. To explain message patterns and social-level phenomena requires explanations that are primarily sociological and societal in their focus (Berger & Luckman, 1967; Brown & Levinson, 1978; Roloff,

1981; Searle, 1969). For these reasons one must look above and below the level of inquiry for explanations of the phenomena that one has described. In this way the levels of communication inquiry are tightly interwoven: Not only are individuals parts of dyads and groups and groups part of larger social units but our understanding of how groups and dyads function in interpersonal communication depends upon explanations available only at other levels of inquiry.

REFERENCES

Aiello, J. R. (1972). A test of equilibrium theory: Visual interaction in relation to orientation, distance, and sex of the interactants. *Psychonomic Science, 27,* 335-336.

Aiello, J. R. (1973). Male and female behavior as a function of distance and duration of an interviewer's directed gaze: Equilibrium theory revisited. (Doctoral dissertation, Michigan State University). *Dissertation Abstracts International, 33,* 4482B-4483B.

Altman, I., Vinsel, A., & Brown, B. B. (1981). Dialectical conceptions in social psychology: An application to social penetration and privacy regulation. In L. Berkowitz (Ed.), *Advances in experimental social psychology* (Vol. 14, pp. 107-160). New York: Academic Press.

Anderson, D. R. (1976). Eye contact, topic intimacy, and equilibrium theory. *Journal of Social Psychology, 100,* 313-314.

Anderson, J. R. (1985). *Cognitive psychology and its implications* (2nd ed.). New York: W. H. Freemen.

Argyle, M., & Dean, J. (1965). Eye contact, distance and affiliation. *Sociometry, 28,* 289-304.

Arundale, R. B. (1977). Sampling across time for communication research: A simulation. In P. M. Hirsch, P. V. Miller, & F. G. Klein (Eds.), *Strategies for communication research* (pp. 257-285). Newbury Park, CA: Sage.

Ashby, W. R. (1963). *An introduction to cybernetics.* New York: Science Editions.

Beattie, G. W. (1978). Floor apportionment and gaze in conversational dyads. *British Journal of Social and Clinical Psychology, 17,* 7-15.

Beebe, B., Stern, D., & Jaffe, J. (1979). The kinesic rhythm of mother-infant interactions. In A. W. Siegman & S. Feldstein (Eds.), *Of speech and time* (pp. 23-34). Hillsdale, NJ: Lawrence Erlbaum.

Berger, C. R., & Bradac, J. J. (1982). *Language and social knowledge.* London: Edward Arnold.

Berger, P. L., & Luckman, T. (1967). *The social construction of reality.* Garden City, NJ: Doubleday.

Blehar, C. M., Lieberman, A. F., & Ainsworth, M.D.S. (1977). Early face-to-face interaction and its relation to later infant-mother attachment. *Child Development, 48,* 182-194.

Bochner, A. P. (1984). The functions of human communication in interpersonal bonding. In C. C. Arnold & J. W. Bowers (Eds.), *Handbook of rhetorical and communication theory* (pp. 544-621). Boston: Allyn & Bacon.

Boomer, D. S. (1963). Speech disturbance and body movement in interviews. *Journal of Nervous and Mental Disease, 136,* 263-266.

Boomer, D. S. (1965). Hesitation in grammatical encoding. *Language and Speech, 8,* 148-158.

Boomer, D. S. (1978). The phonemic clause: Speech unit in human communication. In A. W. Siegman & S. Feldstein (Eds.), *Nonverbal behavior and communication* (pp. 245-262). Hillsdale, NJ: Lawrence Erlbaum.

Bourhis, R. Y. (1985). The sequential nature of language choice in cross-cultural communication. In R. L. Street & J. N. Cappella (Eds.), *Sequence and pattern in communicative behavior* (pp. 120-141). London: Edward Arnold.

Bowers, J. W., Metts, S. M., & Duncanson, W. T. (1985). Emotion and interpersonal communication. In M. L. Knapp & G. R. Miller (Eds.), *Handbook of interpersonal communication* (pp. 500-550). Newbury Park, CA: Sage.

Bradac, J. J. (1983). On generalizing cabbages, messages, kings and several other things: The virtues of multiplicity. *Human Communication Research, 9,* 181-187.

Bradac, J. J., & Mulac, A. (1984). A molecular view of powerful and powerless speech styles: Attributional consequences of specific language features and communicator intentions. *Communication Monographs, 51,* 307-319.

Bransford, J. D., & McCarrell, N. S. (1974). A sketch of a cognitive approach to comprehension. In W. B. Weimar & D. S. Palermo (Eds.), *Cognition and the symbolic processes* (pp. 189-229). Hillsdale, NJ: Lawrence Erlbaum.

Brown, G., & Yule, G. (1983). *Discourse analysis.* Cambridge: Cambridge University Press.

Burgoon, J. K. (1978). A communication model of personal space violations: Explication and initial test. *Human Communication Research, 4,* 129-142.

Burgoon, J. K. (1985). Nonverbal signals. In M. L. Knapp & G. R. Miller (Eds.), *Handbook of interpersonal communication* (pp. 344-390). Newbury Park, CA: Sage.

Burgoon, J. K., Buller, D. B., Hale, J. L., & DeTurck, M. (1984). Relational messages associated with nonverbal behaviors. *Human Communication Research, 10,* 351-378.

Burgoon, J. K., & Koper, R. J. (1984). Nonverbal and relational communication associated with reticence. *Human Communication Research, 10,* 601-627.

Butterworth, B. (1975). Hesitation and semantic planning in speech. *Journal of Psycholinguistic Research, 4,* 75-87.

Butterworth, B., & Goldman-Eisler, F. (1979). Recent studies on cognitive rhythm. In A. W. Siegman & S. Feldstein (Eds.), *Of speech and time* (pp. 211-224). Hillsdale, NJ: Lawrence Erlbaum.

Cappella, J. N. (1980). Structural equation modeling: An introduction. In P. R. Moge & J. N. Cappella (Eds.), *Multivariate techniques in human communication research* (pp. 57-109). New York: Academic Press.

Cappella, J. N. (1981). Mutual influence in expressive behavior: Adult-adult and infant-adult dyadic interaction. *Psychological Bulletin, 89,* 101-132.

Cappella, J. N. (1983). Conversational involvement: Approaching and avoiding others. In J. M. Wiemann & R. P. Harrison (Eds.), *Nonverbal interaction* (pp. 113-152). Newbury Park, CA: Sage.

Cappella, J. N. (1984). The relevance of the microstructure of interaction to relationship change. *Journal of Social and Personal Relationships, 1,* 239-264.

Cappella, J. N. (1985a). Controlling the floor in conversation. In A. W. Siegman & S. Feldstein (Eds.), *Multichannel integration of nonverbal behavior* (pp. 69-103). Hillsdale, NJ: Lawrence Erlbaum.

Cappella, J. N. (1985b). The management of conversations. In M. L. Knapp & G. R. Miller (Eds.), *Handbook of interpersonal communication* (pp. 393-438). Newbury Park, CA: Sage.

Cappella, J. N., & Greene, J. O. (1982). A discrepancy-arousal explanation of mutual influence in expressive behavior for adult-adult and infant-adult interaction. *Communication Monographs, 49,* 89-114.

Cappella, J. N., & Planalp, S. (1981). Talk and silence sequences in informal conversations. III: Interspeaker influence. *Human Communication Research, 7,* 117-132.

Cappella, J. N., & Street, R. L. (1985). Introduction: A functional approach to the structure of communicative behaviour. In R. L. Street & J. N. Cappella (Eds.), *Sequence and pattern in communicative behaviour* (pp. 1-29). London: Edward Arnold.

Cappella, J. N., & Streibel, M. S. (1979). Computer analysis of talk-silence sequences: The FIASSCO system. *Behavioral Research Methods and Instrumentation, 11*, 384-392.

Chomsky, N. (1957). *Syntactic structures*. The Hague: Mouton.

Cicourel, A. (1974). *Cognitive sociology: Language and meaning in social interaction*. New York: Free Press.

Clark, H. H. (1973). The language-as-fixed-effect fallacy: A critique of language statistics in psychological research. *Journal of Verbal Learning and Verbal Behavior, 12*, 335-359.

Cody, M., & McLaughlin, M. L. (1985). Models for the sequential construction of accounting episodes: Situational and interactional constraints on message selection and evaluation. In R. L. Street & J. N. Cappella (Eds.), *Sequence and pattern in communicative behaviour* (pp. 50-69). London: Edward Arnold.

Condon, W. S., & Ogston, W. D. (1967). A segmentation of behavior. *Journal of Psychiatric Research, 5*, 221-235.

Condon, W. S., & Sander, L. W. (1974). Synchrony demonstrated between movement of the neonate and adult speech. *Child Development, 45*, 456-452.

Cook, T. D., & Campbell, D. T. (Eds.) (1979). *Quasi-experimentation: Design and analysis issues for field settings*. Chicago: Rand-McNally.

Courtright, J., Millar, F. E., & Rogers-Millar, L. E. (1979). Domineeringness and dominance: Replication and expansion. *Communication Monographs, 46*, 179-192.

Davis, D. (1982). Determinants of responsiveness in dyadic interaction. In W. Ickes & E. S. Knowles (Eds.), *Personality, roles, and social behavior* (pp. 85-139). New York: Springer-Verlag.

Davis, J. D. (1976). Self-disclosure in an acquaintance exercise: Responsibility for level of intimacy. *Journal of Personality and Social Psychology, 33*, 787-792.

Davis, J. D. (1977). Effects of communication about interpersonal process on the evolution of self-disclosure in dyads. *Journal of Personality and Social Psychology, 35*, 31-37.

Dillard, J. P., & Burgoon, M. (1985). Situational influences on the selection of compliance-gaining messages. Two tests of the predictive utility of the Cody-McLaughlin typology. *Communication Monographs, 52*, 289-304.

Dillard, J. P., & Spitzberg, B. H. (1984). Global impressions of social skills: Behavioral predictors. In R. N. Bostrom (Ed.), *Communication yearbook 8* (pp. 446-463). Newbury Park, CA: Sage.

Dittmann, A. T. (1962). The relationship between body movements and moods in interviews. *Journal of Consulting Psychology, 26*, 480.

Dittmann, A. T. (1972). The body movement speech rhythm relationship as a cue to speech encoding. In A. W. Siegman & B. Pope (Eds.), *Studies in dyadic communication* (pp. 135-152). New York: Pergamon.

Dittmann, A. T., & Llewellyn, L. G. (1967). The phonemic clause as a unit of speech encoding. *Journal of Personality and Social Psychology, 6*, 341-349.

Duncan, S., & Fiske, D. W. (1977). *Face-to-face interaction*. Hillsdale, NJ: Lawrence Erlbaum.

Eidinger, J. A., & Patterson, M. L. (1983). Nonverbal involvement and social control. *Psychological Bulletin, 93*, 30-56.

Ekman, P. (1972). Universals and cultural differences in facial expressions of emotion. In J. Cole (Ed.), *Nebraska symposium on motivation* (Vol. 19, pp. 207-283). Lincoln: University of Nebraska Press.

Ekman, P. (1982). Methods for measuring facial action. In K. Scherer & P. Ekman (Eds.), *Handbook of methods in nonverbal behavior research* (pp. 45-135). Cambridge: Cambridge University Press.

Ekman, P., Friesen, W. V., & Ellsworth, P. (1972). *Emotion in the human face.* New York: Pergamon.

Ellis, D. E. (1979). Relational control in two group systems. *Communication Monographs, 46,* 153-166.

Ellis, D. G., & Fisher, B. A. (1975). Phases of conflict in small group development: A Markov analysis. *Human Communication Research, 1,* 195-212.

Ellsworth, P. P. & Carlsmith, J. M. (1968). The effects of eye contact and verbal content on affective response to dyadic interaction. *Journal of Personality and Social Psychology, 10,* 15-20.

Endler, N. S., & Magnusson, D. (Eds.) (1976). *Interactional psychology and personality.* New York: John Wiley.

Ericson, P. M., & Rogers, L. E. (1973). New procedures for analyzing relational communication. *Family Process, 12,* 245-267.

Ericsson, K. A., & Simon, H. A. (1984). *Protocol analysis: Verbal reports as data explanation.* Cambridge: MIT Press.

Fishbein, M., & Ajzen, I. (1975). *Belief, attitude, intention, and behavior.* Reading, MA: Addison-Wesley.

Fisher, B. A., & Drecksel, G. L. (1983). A cyclical model of developing relationships. *Communication Monographs, 50,* 66-78.

Fitzpatrick, M. A. (1984). A typological approach to marital interaction: Recent theory and research. In L. Berkowitz (Ed.), *Advances in experimental social psychology* (Vol. 18, pp. 1-47). New York: Academic Press.

Fitzpatrick, M. A., & Badzinski, D. M. (1985). All in the family: Interpersonal communication in kin relationships. In M. L. Knapp & G. R. Miller (Eds.), *Handbook of interpersonal communication* (pp. 687-736). Newbury Park, CA: Sage.

Fitzpatrick, M. A., & Dindia, K. (1986). *Couples and other strangers: Conversational involvement in spouse-stranger interactions.* Paper presented at the International Communication Association Conference, Chicago, IL.

Fitzpatrick, M. A., & Winke, J. (1979). You always hurt the one you love: Strategies and tactics in interpersonal conflict. *Communication Quarterly, 27,* 1-11.

Folger, J. P., Hewes, D. E., & Poole, M. S. (1984). Coding social interaction. In B. Dervin & M. Voight (Eds.), *Progress in the communication sciences* (pp. 115-161). Norwood, NJ: Ablex.

Folger, J. P., & Poole, M. S. (1982). Relational coding schemes: The question of validity. In M. Burgoon (Ed.), *Communication yearbook 5* (pp. 235-248). New Brunswick, NJ: Transaction.

Forgas, J. P. (1979). *Social episodes: The study of interaction routines.* London: Academic Press.

Garfinkel, H. (1977). What is ethnomethodology? In F. R. Dallmayr & T. A. McCarthy (Eds.), *Understanding and social inquiry* (pp. 240-266). Notre Dame, IN: University of Notre Dame Press.

Genesee, R., & Bourhis, R. Y. (1982). The social psychological significance of code-switching in cross-cultural communication. *Journal of Language and Social Psychology, 1,* 1-27.

Geweke, J. (1978). Testing the exogeneity specification in the complete dynamic simultaneous equation model. *Journal of Econometrics, 7,* 163-185.

Giles, H., & Powesland, P. F. (1975). *Speech style and social evaluation.* London: Academic Press.

Giles, H., & Street, R. L. (1985). Communicator characteristics and behavior. In M. L. Knapp & G. R. Miller (Eds.), *Handbook of interpersonal communication* (pp. 205-262). Newbury Park, CA: Sage.

Goodwin, C. (1981). *Conversational organization: Interaction between speakers and hearers.* New York: Academic Press.

Gottman, J. M. (1979). *Marital interaction.* New York: Academic Press.

Gottman, J. M., & Ringland, J. T. (1981). The analysis of dominance and bidirectionality in social development. *Child Development, 52,* 393-412.

Griffin, D. R. (1984). *Animal thinking.* Cambridge, MA: Harvard University Press.

Hale, J. L. & Burgoon, J. K. (1984). Models of reactions to changes in nonverbal immediacy. *Journal of Nonverbal Behavior, 8,* 287-314.

Hanson, N. R. (1958). *Patterns of discovery.* Cambridge: Cambridge University Press.

Harper, R. G., Wiens, A. N., & Matarazzo, J. D. (1978). *Nonverbal communication: The state of the art.* New York: John Wiley.

Harré, H. & Secord, P. F. (1973). *The explanation of social behavior.* Totowa, NJ: Littlefield Adams.

Hawes, L. C., & Foley, J. M. (1973). A Markov analysis of interview communication. *Speech Monographs, 40,* 208-219.

Hayes, D. P., Meltzer, L., & Wolf, G. (1970). Substantive conclusions are dependent on techniques of measurement. *Behavioral Science, 15,* 265-269.

Hewes, D. E. (1975). Finite stochastic modeling of communication processes. *Human Communication Research, 1,* 271-283.

Hewes, D. E. (1979). The sequential analysis of social interaction. *Quarterly Journal of Speech, 65,* 56-73.

Hewes, D. E. (1980). Stochastic modeling of communication processes. In P. R. Monge & J. N. Cappella (Eds.), *Multivariate techniques in human communication research* (pp. 393-427). New York: Academic Press.

Hewes, D. E. (1983). Confessions of a methodological puritan: A response to Jackson and Jacobs. *Human Communication Research, 9,* 187-191.

Hewes, D. E. (1985). Systematic biases in coded social interaction data. *Human Communication Research, 11,* 554-574.

Hewes, D. E. & Haight, L. (1979). The cross-situational consistency of communication behaviors. *Communication Research, 6,* 243-270.

Hewes, D. E. & Planalp, S. (1982). There is nothing as useful as a good theory . . . : The influence of social knowledge on interpersonal communication. In M. E. Roloff & C. E. Berger (Eds.), *Social cognition and communication* (pp. 107-150). Newbury Park, CA: Sage.

Hewes, D. E., Planalp, S., & Streibel, M. S. (1980). Analyzing social interaction: Some excruciating models and exhilirating results. In D. Nimmo (Ed.), *Communication yearbook 4* (pp. 123-144). New Brunswick, NJ: Transaction.

Hibbs, D. A. (1974). Problems of statistical estimation and causal inference in time series regression models. In H. L. Costner (Ed.), *Sociological methodology 1974* (pp. 252-308). San Francisco: Jossey-Bass.

Hinde, R. A. (1979). *Towards understanding relationships.* London: Academic Press.

Hunter, J. E., Schmidt, F. L., & Jackson, G. B. (1982). *Meta-analysis.* Newbury Park, CA: Sage.

Ickes, W. J., Patterson, M. L., Rajecki, D. W., & Tanford, S. (1982). Behavioral and cognitive consequences of reciprocal versus compensatory responses to pre-interaction expectancies. *Social Cognition, 1,* 160-190.

Jackson, S., & Jacobs, S. (1983). Generalizing about messages: Suggestions for design and analysis of experiments. *Human Communication Research, 9,* 169-181.

Jacobs, S. (1985). Language. In M. L. Knapp & G. R. Miller (Eds.), *Handbook of interpersonal communication* (pp. 313-343). Newbury Park, CA: Sage.

Jacobs, S., & Jackson, S. (1983). Strategy and structure in conversational influence attempts. *Communication Monographs, 50,* 285-304.

Jaffe, J., & Feldstein, S. (1970). *Rhythms of dialogue.* New York: Academic Press.

Kaplan, K. J., Firestone, I. J., Klein, K. W., & Sodikoff, C. (1983). Distancing in dyads: A comparison of four models. *Social Psychology Quarterly, 46,* 108-115.

Kaufer, D. (1979). *An investigation of the formal theory of grammatical competence and two empirical interpretations of that theory.* Doctoral dissertation, University of Wisconsin—Madison.

Kendon, A. (1970). Movement coordination in social interaction: Some examples described. *Acta Psychologica, 35,* 101-125.

Kenny, D. A., & LaVoie, L. (1984). The social relations model. In L. Berkowitz (Ed.), *Advances in experimental social psychology* (pp. 141-182). New York: Academic Press.

Kinstch, W. (1977). *Memory and cognition* (2nd ed.). New York: John Wiley.

Knapp, M. L., & Miller, G. R. (Eds.). (1985). *Handbook of interpersonal communication.* Newbury Park, CA: Sage.

Kraemer, H. C., & Jacklin, C. N. (1979). Statistical analysis of dyadic social behavior. *Psychological Bulletin, 86,* 217-224.

Krippendorff, K. (1980). *Content analysis.* Newbury Park, CA: Sage.

Leary, M. R. (1983). *Understanding social anxiety.* Newbury Park, CA: Sage.

Levinson, S.C. (1983). *Pragmatics.* Cambridge: Cambridge University Press.

Matarazzo, J. D., & Wiens, A. N. (1972). *The interview: Research on its anatomy and structure.* Chicago: Aldine-Atherton.

McCall, G. J. & Simmons, J. L. (1978). *Identities and interactions* (2nd ed.). New York: Free Press.

McCleary, R., & Hay, R. A. (1980). *Applied time series analysis for the social sciences.* Newbury Park, CA: Sage.

McCroskey, J. C. (1977). Oral communication apprehension: A summary of recent theory and research. *Human Communication Research, 4,* 78-98.

McDowall, J. J. (1978). Interactional synchrony: A reappraisal. *Journal of Personality and Social Psychology, 36,* 963-975.

McHugh, P. (1968). *Defining the situation: The organization of meaning in social interaction.* Indianapolis, IN: Bobbs-Merrill.

McLaughlin, M. L. (1984). *Conversation: How talk is organized.* Newbury Park, CA: Sage.

McLaughlin, M. L., & Cody, M. J. (1982). Awkward silences: Antecedants and consequences of the conversational lapse. *Human Communication Research, 8,* 299-316.

McLaughlin, M. L., Cody, M. J., & O'Hair, H. D. (1983). The management of failure events: Some contextual determinants of accounting behavior. *Human Communication Research, 9,* 208-224.

McLaughlin, M. L., Cody, M. J., & Robey, C. S. (1980). Situational influences on the selection of strategies to resist compliance-gaining attempts. *Human Communication Research, 7,* 14-36.

McLaughlin, M. L., Cody, M. J., & Rosenstein, N. E. (1983). Account sequences in conversations between strangers. *Communication Monographs, 50,* 102-125.

Mendoza, J. L., & Graziano, W. G. (1982). The statistical analysis of dyadic social behavior: A multivariate approach. *Psychological Bulletin, 92,* 532-540.

Millar, F. E., Rogers-Millar, L. E., & Courtright, J. A. (1979). Relational control and dyadic understanding: An exploratory predictive regression model. In D. Nimmo (Ed.), *Communication yearbook 3* (pp. 213-224). New Brunswick, NJ: Transaction.

Miller, G. R., Boster, F., Roloff, M. E., & Seibold, D. (1977). Compliance-gaining message strategies: A typology and some findings concerning effects of situational differences. *Communication Monographs, 44,* 37-51.

Miller, G. R., & Steinberg, M. (1975). *Between people*. Chicago: Science Research Associates.

Miller-Tutzauer, C. (1984). *On designs long forgotten: Statistical techniques for handling mutual influence in social interaction*. Paper presented to the Speech Communication Association Conference, Chicago.

Montgomery, B. M. (1984). Individual differences and relational interdependencies in social interaction. *Human Communication Research, 11,* 33-60.

Morley, D. D. (1984). Corrections to lag sequential results in communication research: An introduction. *Human Communication Research, 11,* 121-123.

Mortensen, C. D., & Arnston, P. H. (1974). The effects of predispositions toward verbal behavior on interaction patterns in dyads. *Quarterly Journal of Speech, 61,* 421-430.

Mulac, A., & Lundell, T. L. (1982). An empirical test of the gender-linked language effect in a public speaking setting. *Language and Speech, 25,* 243-256.

Mulac, A., Lundell, T. L., & Bradac, J. J. (in press). Male-female language differences and attributional consequences in a public speaking situation: Toward an explanation of the gender-linked language effect. *Communication Monographs*.

Newtson, D. (1976). Foundations of attribution: The perception of ongoing behavior. In J. H. Harvey, W. J. Ickes, & R. F. Kidd (Eds.), *New directions in attribution research* (Vol. 1, pp. 223-247). Hillsdale, NJ: Lawrence Erlbaum.

Newtson, D., Enquist, G., & Bois, J. (1977). The objective basis of behavior units. *Journal of Personality and Social Psychology, 12,* 847-862.

Nisbett, R. E., & Wilson, T. (1977). Telling more than we can know: Verbal reports on mental processes. *Psychological Review, 84,* 231-259.

Nofsinger, N. E. (1976). Answering questions indirectly. *Human Communication Research, 2,* 171-181.

Noller, P. (1984). *Nonverbal communication and marital interaction*. Oxford: Pergamon Press.

O'Keefe, B., Delia, J., & O'Keefe, D. (1980). Interaction analysis and the analysis of interactional organization. In N. K. Denzin (Ed.), *Studies in symbolic interactionism* (Vol. 3, pp. 25-57). Greenwich, CT: JAI Press.

O'Keefe, D. J., & Sypher, H. E. (1981). Cognitive complexity measures and the relationship of cognitive complexity to communication. *Human Communication Research, 7,* 72-92.

Palmer, M. T., & Badzinski, D. (1986). *Topics as natural discourse processing units*. Paper presented at the International Communication Association Conference, Chicago.

Parks, M. R. (1980). A test of the cross-situational consistency of communication apprehension. *Communication Monographs, 47,* 220-232.

Patterson, M. L. (1976). An arousal model of interpersonal intimacy. *Psychological Review, 83,* 235-245.

Patterson, M. L. (1982a). A sequential functional model of nonverbal exchange. *Psychological Review, 89,* 231-249.

Patterson, M. L. (1982b). Personality and nonverbal involvement: A functional analysis. In W. Ickes & E. S. Knowles (Eds.), *Personality, roles, and social behavior* (pp. 141-164). New York: Springer-Verlag.

Patterson, M. L. (1983). *Nonverbal behavior: A functional perspective*. New York: Springer-Verlag.

Phillips, G. M. (1968). Reticence: Pathology of normal speakers. *Speech Monographs, 35,* 39-49.

Pike, G. R., & Sillars, A. L. (1985). Reciprocity and marital communication. *Journal of Social and Personal Relationships, 2,* 303-324.

Planalp, S., & Hewes, D. E. (1982). A cognitive approach to communication theory: *Cogito ergo dico?* In M. Burgoon (Ed.), *Communication yearbook 5* (pp. 49-77). New Brunswick, NJ: Transaction.

Planalp, S., & Tracy, K. (1980). Not to change the topic but . . . : A cognitive approach to the management of conversation. In D. Nimmo (Ed.), *Communication yearbook 4* (pp. 237-258). New Brunswick, NJ: Transaction.

Poole, M. S. (1981). Decision development in small groups I: A comparison of two models. *Communication Monographs, 48,* 1-24.

Poole, M. S. (1983). Decision development in small groups II: A study of multiple sequences in decision-making. *Communication Monographs, 50,* 206-232.

Putnam, L. L. (1985). Bargaining as task and process: Multiple functions of interaction sequences. In R. L. Street & J. N. Cappella (Eds.), *Sequence and pattern in communicative behaviour* (pp. 225-242). London: Edward Arnold.

Putnam, L. L., & Jones, T. S. (1982). Reciprocity in negotiations: An analysis of bargaining interaction. *Communication Monographs, 49,* 171-191.

Reichman, R. (1978). Conversational coherency. *Cognitive Science, 2,* 283-327.

Rime, B. (in press). Nonverbal communication or nonverbal behavior? Towards a cognitivo-motor theory of nonverbal behavior. In S. Moscovici & W. Doise (Eds.), *Current issues in European social psychology* (Vol. 1). Cambridge: Cambridge University Press.

Rogers, L. E., Courtright, J. A., & Millar, F. E. (1980). Message control intensity: Rationale and preliminary findings. *Communication Monographs, 47,* 201-219.

Rogers, L. E., & Farace, R. V. (1975). Analysis of relational communication in dyads: New measurement procedures. *Human Communication Research, 1,* 222-239.

Rogers, L. E., & Millar, F. (1982). The question of validity: A pragmatic response. In M. Burgoon (Ed.), *Communication yearbook 5* (pp. 249-257). New Brunswick, NJ: Transaction.

Roloff, M. E. (1981). *Interpersonal communication: The social exchange approach.* Newbury Park, CA: Sage.

Sackett, G. P. (1978). Measurement in observational research. In G. P. Sackett (Ed.), *Observing behavior* (Vol. 2, pp. 25-44). Baltimore: University Park Press.

Sackett, G. P. (1979). The lag sequential analysis of contingency and cyclicity in behavioral interaction research. In J. P. Osofsky (Ed.), *Handbook of infant development* (pp. 623-649). New York: John Wiley.

Sacks, H., Schegloff, E. A., & Jefferson, G. (1974). A simplest systematics for the organization of turn-taking for conversation. *Language, 50,* 696-735.

Scherer, K. (1984). The state of the art in vocal communication: A partial view. In A. Wolfgang (Ed.), *Nonverbal behavior* (pp. 41-73). Lewiston, NY: C.J. Hogrefe.

Scherer, K., & Ekman, P. (Eds.). (1982). *Handbook of methods in nonverbal behavior research.* Cambridge: Cambridge University Press.

Schutz, A. (1977). Concept and theory formation in the social sciences. In F. R. Dallmayr & T. A. McCarthy (Eds.), *Understanding and social inquiry* (pp. 225-239). Notre Dame, IN: University of Notre Dame Press.

Searle, J. R. (1969). *Speech acts: An essay in the philosophy of language.* Cambridge: Cambridge University Press.

Shrout, P. E., & Fiske, D. W. (1982). Nonverbal behavior and social evaluation. *Journal of Personality, 49,* 115-128.

Smith, W. J. (1977). *The behavior of communicating.* Cambridge, MA: Harvard University Press.

Stern, D. N., Jaffe, J., Beebe, B., & Bennett, S. L. (1975). Vocalizing in unison and in alteration: Two modes of communication within the mother-infant dyad. *Annals of the New York Academy of Sciences, 263,* 89-100.

Stiles, W. B. (1978). *Manual for the taxonomy of verbal response modes.* Chapel Hill, NC: Institute for Research in Social Science.

Street, R. L. (1982). Evaluation of noncontent speech accommodation. *Language and Communication, 2,* 13-31.

Street, R. L. (1983). Noncontent speech convergence in adult-child interactions. In R. N. Bostrom (Ed.), *Communication yearbook 7* (pp. 369-395). Newbury Park, CA: Sage.

Street, R. L. (1986). Interaction processes and outcomes in interviews. In. M. L. McLaughlin (Ed.), *Communication yearbook 9* (pp. 215-250). Newbury Park, CA: Sage.

Street, R. L., & Giles, H. (1982). Speech accommodation theory: A social cognitive approach to language and speech behavior. In M. Roloff & C. Berger (Eds.), *Social cognition and communication* (pp. 193-226). Newbury Park, CA: Sage.

Thakerar, J. N., Giles, H., & Cheshire, J. (1982). Psychological and linguistic parameters of speech accommodation theory. In C. Fraser & K. R. Scherer (Eds.), *Advances in the social psychology of language* (pp. 205-255). Cambridge: Cambridge University Press.

Thomas, E.A.C., & Martin, J. A. (1976). An analysis of parent-infant interaction. *Psychological Review, 83,* 141-156.

Tracy, K. (1982). On getting the point: Distinguishing "issues" from "events"—an aspect of conversational coherence. In M. Burgoon (Ed.), *Communication yearbook 5* (pp. 279-302). New Brunswick, NJ: Transaction.

Tulving, E. (1983). *Elements of episodic memory.* Oxford: Clarendon Press.

von Frisch, K. (1967). *The dance and orientation of bees* (C. E. Chadwick, Trans.). Cambridge, MA: Harvard University Press.

Walker, M. B., & Trimboli, C. (1982). Smooth transitions in conversational interactions. *Journal of Social Psychology, 117,* 305-306.

Warner, R., Kenny, D. A., & Stoto, M. (1979). A new round-robin analysis of variance for social interaction data. *Journal of Personality and Social Psychology, 37,* 1742-1757.

Warner, R. M., Waggener, T. B., & Kronauer, R. E. (1983). Synchronized cycles in ventilation and vocal activity during spontaneous conversational speech. *Journal of Applied Physiology, 54,* 1324-1334.

Williamson, R. N., & Fitzpatrick, M. A. (1985). Two approaches to marital interaction: Relational control patterns in marital types. *Communication Monographs, 52,* 236-252.

8 The Network Level of Analysis

PETER R. MONGE
University of Southern California

WHILE the field of social network analysis has existed for little
more than half a century, it is a research area that has experienced tremendous growth. This explosion in interest has
occurred across a wide variety of social science disciplines including
anthropology, management science, organizational psychology, political science, social psychology, sociology, and human communication.
Given the diversity of social scientists who are interested in network
analysis, it is not surprising that some of this research does not have
much to do with human communication. What is surprising is that a
great amount of it does.

To synthesize and integrate this rapidly expanding knowledge base,
a large number of extensive and comprehensive reviews of network
research have been written over the past twenty-five years (e.g., Alba,
1982; Burt, 1980; Eisenberg et al., 1985; Farace & Mabee, 1980; Fombrun, 1982; Lincoln, 1982; McPhee, 1985; Mitchell, 1974; Monge,
Edwards, & Kirste, 1978; Monge & Eisenberg, 1987; Porter & Roberts,
1976; Rogers & Kincaid, 1981; Shaw, 1964; Tichy, 1981; Tichy & Fombrun, 1979; Tichy, Tushman, & Fombrun, 1979; Whetten, 1981). It is
not the purpose of this chapter to replicate these extensive compendia
either in depth or in comprehensiveness. Rather, as one of the overview
chapters of this handbook, the purpose is to articulate how the network
level enriches our understanding of communication and other social
processes, both by itself and in consort with variables from other levels.

This chapter is organized into five sections. The first provides an overview of the major network methods and techniques. The second, third,
and fourth sections focus on representative network analysis at three
sublevels: personal, organizational, and interorganizational/societal.
The final section briefly discusses the relation of network analysis to the
other levels of communication that are covered in this handbook.

An Overview of Communication Network
Methods and Techniques

Human communication is a multifaceted process. At one level of analysis, humans possess a variety of communication attributes, in addition to a large number of other human traits. Attributes are traditionally conceptualized as properties or characteristics of the individual. For example, psychological theory treats attitudes, values, and beliefs as attributes of individuals. Communication theory has also conceptualized many of its variables as attributes. For example, communicator style (Norton, 1978), credibility (Berlo, Lemert, & Mertz, 1969-1970), and competence (Monge, Bachman, Dillard, & Eisenberg, 1982) are viewed as attributes of communicators. Similarly, the amount and kind of evidence, the nature of appeals, and the intensity of language have been studied as attributes of messages. Delia (1977) labels this tradition of research a "variables approach."

Important as individual attributes are in explaining human life, a number of social theorists (Blau, 1982; Burt, 1980; Merton, 1975) have argued that they provide at best only a partial account of human behavior, and at worst a misleading and inaccurate account. These theorists have argued that there are group and social phenomena that cannot be explained by the attributes of the individuals that make up the social unit. Durkheim (1964), for example, postulated a set of "social facts" that are not a part of individual consciousness but serve to constrain individual behavior. Marx identified collective group situations—that is, social classes—as determinative of individual behavior. These theorists share the perspective that "there is a level of organization within societies which cannot be adequately understood by simply observing individual behavior" (Berkowitz, 1982, p. 11).

An example of the problem of the proper level of analysis is provided by the recent debate over alternative conceptualizations of the notion of organizational climates (Glick, 1985). The basic idea of organizational climate is that there are relatively enduring characteristics of organizations that describe the working environment (James & Jones, 1976). By analogy to attributes of meteorological climate (temperature, rainfall, humidity), organizational climate theory postulates a series of characteristics such as formality, openness, and quality.

Given general consensus on this definition, the problem became one of gathering and interpreting appropriate data. Originally, people were asked to report their individual perceptions of climate. These perceptions were then aggregated to some larger unit of analysis—the work group, division, or entire organization—to represent the organizational climate. It should be clear that this procedure aggregates individual attributes and perceptions and uses them to represent the entire unit. Guion

(1973) and James and Jones (1976) have argued, however, that this procedure failed to provide a valid account of the larger unit of analysis; it does not represent relations or higher order collective attributes. As a result, new procedures have been developed that provide data at the level of analysis to which inferences are to be made. For example, Joyce and Slocum (1984) utilized a clustering technique to identify emergent clusters of people that shared similar views of the organizational climate irrespective of the formal work group to which they belonged. Other researchers have asked organization members to discuss the various dimensions of organizational climate and arrive at a consensual position called "collective" climate. A third procedure utilizes a coorientation perspective (McLeod & Chaffee, 1973). It invites respondents to provide their views of the climate as well as their perceptions or predictions of how relevant others in their group or unit view it. Perceptual agreement and accuracy are then used to define groups that share the same climate.

These procedures do not invalidate the original perceptions of individuals; in fact, what is now called psychological climate represents the views of each individual toward the climate in the organization. Organizational climate, however, is now taken to refer to higher-level perceptions of the organization. This means that researchers now have four alternative procedures that lead to four distinct concepts. They may (1) ask people to report their individual perceptions to obtain psychological climates, (2) aggregate these individual perceptual reports by work group or across other levels to obtain organizational climate, (3) ask respondents to report how they think others in the organization view the climate, or (4) try to induce respondents to arrive at a consensual view of the organization's climate. Glick (1985) argues that all four types of climate analysis—psychological, aggregate, coorientation, and consensual—provide conceptually distinct and important information.

At the network level of analysis, communication processes involve relationships rather than attributes (Monge & Miller, 1985). A relationship is not the property of an individual; it is a characteristic that is defined in reference to two or more people taken together. A communication network, then, is a structure that is built on the basis of communication relationships.

Though the network is one of this handbook's four levels of analysis, Burt (1980) notes that networks themselves contain and should be analyzed from several levels. These levels are the personal (sometimes called ego) networks, group networks, organizational networks and interorganizational networks. (Burt combines the last two categories into one, the systems level.)

Personal or ego networks are the communication linkages that people maintain with other individuals (Burt, 1980). These contacts may be extensive or limited, and in any given network are likely to vary considerably from individual to individual.

Group networks describe the patterns and structure of people who communicate more with each other than they do with the rest of the people in the larger network (Alba, 1982). Groups emerge by being densely connected regions of the network. Determining the degree of density and also the extent to which the group is connected to other groups and individuals in the network are important analytic objectives.

Organizational networks represent the structural differentiation of organizations. This is accomplished by network articulation that assigns individuals to network roles (Farace, Monge, & Russell, 1977). Typically, these roles include group member, a linking person (a "liaison" or "bridge"), and a "star" or "isolate." This level of analysis examines the entire internal organizational system and identifies its component parts.

Interorganizational networks are the configurations of communication relations between organizations (Lincoln, 1982). Structural differentiation is accomplished at this level by articulation of a set of organizations rather than a collection of individuals. In one sense, this can be viewed as a simple redefinition of the system, in which individuals are replaced with organizations. This is certainly true if data are collected from all organizations that make up the interorganizational network. However, it is also possible to take a more limited perspective. Since they examine individuals within their organizational boundaries, organizational networks are "internal analyses." Equally interesting, however, is the question of how the organization is linked to other organizations. This is a different question than how a set of organizations is linked together, which is the typical focus of analysis at the interorganizational level. One can think of an organization's external linkages as that organization's external or "personal" network.

These levels are helpful in organizing the objectives of network analysis. It is important to recognize, however, that they are no more than useful heuristics. Occasionally, research problems arise that do not easily fall into one or the other category. The discussion in the previous paragraph of an organization's external network is an example of a research issue that requires some flexibility in applying the levels framework.

Communication Relations in Networks

The general notion of a network is one that is familiar to virtually everyone since we have all had extensive experience with physical networks such as streets and highways, telephone lines, power lines, and water pipes. Despite this familiarity with networks in general, communication networks are difficult to identify. The difficulty stems from the fact that communication networks are typically constituted of abstract human behavior over time rather than physical material such as concrete, wires, and pipes.

Communication networks, then, are the regular patterns of person-to-person contacts that can be identified as people exchange information in a human social system (Farace et al., 1977). By observing the communicative behavior of people over time we can infer who is informationally connected to whom, and thus we infer a communication network.

All communication networks are constructed out of two elements: a set of communicators and one or more relations among the communicators. The relations define the nature of the connections among the communicators. Many forms of relations can be used to study societal networks. For example, a kinship relation could be "is the parent of," "is the sister of," or "is married to." An authority relation could be of the form "reports to" or "supervises"; a resource relation might be "shares workers with" (Monge & Miller, 1985). Communication networks are constructed out of communication relations, which describe the nature of information flow among people. Typical communication relations are "shares information with," "talks to," "receives reports from," and "discusses new ideas with."

Relations possess several important conceptual properties that define the nature of the network. The first of these is the *number of people* involved in the relation. A relationship that is defined for pairs of people is dyadic. If three people are involved, the relationship is triadic. For example, the relationship "reports to" is dyadic since it pairs subordinates with their supervisors. Likewise, "a ménage à trois" is triadic since it is defined by the domestic linkages among three people. Higher-order relations are possible, but are very rare in network research. The number of people involved in the relation should not be confused with the number of people that constitute the network. Dyadic, triadic, and higher order relations can all be defined in networks that contain any number of people.

A second property is the *strength* or *intensity* of the relation. Strength refers to the quantity or amount of the relationship between the pairs or triples of people in the network. Historically, most relations have been conceptualized as "present" or "absent," which is a categorical or binary level of measurement (Alba, 1982). More recently, relations have been conceived of as varying in, for example, the "amount of interaction" between pairs of people (Richards, 1985). Amount may also be viewed as the frequency or duration of communication over some period of time (Monge & Contractor, in press).

A third property of relations is *symmetry*. This property describes the directionality of flow in the relation. If the relationship is defined equally in both directions, the relation is symmetric. For example, the relation "communicates with" is symmetrical since both people are viewed as sending and receiving information. If the relationship implies a one-way directional flow, it is asymmetric. One asymmetric relation that has received considerable attention by the Securities and Exchange Commission is "gives insider information"; it is an asymmetric relation since one person is the giver and the other is the receiver.

Finally, relations may be characterized by the property of *transitivity*. In a transitive relation, if one person is related to a second and the second person is related to a third, then the first is also related to the third via the same relation. The relation between the first and third persons is implied by the relation of the first to the second and the second to the third. For example, if person A is a coworker of person B, and B is a coworker of person C, then A must also be a coworker of C. In an intransitive relation, however, the A to C implication does not hold. For example, A "communicates with" B and B "communicates with" C says nothing about whether A "communicates with" C; it can be an intransitive relation.

In addition to the four conceptual properties of relations there are two measurement properties: *reciprocity* and *multiplexity*. Reciprocity refers to the degree to which the two people who are related each report the same relation. Reciprocity, then, pertains to the agreement among respondents about the existence or strength of their relations with each other. For example, if two respondents report communicating with each other very frequently, their reciprocity would be high. Likewise, if both report that they very seldom communicated with each other, their reciprocity would also be high. But if one person reports that the two communicate very frequently and the other reports that they seldom communicate, the dyad would have low reciprocity.

Multiplexity refers to the fact that more than one relation may be defined for any given set of people. Traditionally, communication network analysis has focused on uniplex relations. Recent work on structural equivalence (Burt, 1978) emphasizes the importance of examining multiple relations.

Communication networks are often presented in graphic form. Typically, people are represented as points (or nodes or vertices) and the relations as lines or "linkages" (also called "arcs" or "edges"). Each of the properties of relations discussed above can be represented in the graph. For example, an asymmetrical relation corresponds to a line with an arrowhead that points in the direction of the flow.

Network Articulation

Network articulation is the process of identifying the component parts of a network (Farace et al., 1977). These components represent the five major network roles that people can fulfill: (1) a membership role, in the groups or clusters that constitute the networks; (2) a connecting role, which links the clusters together; (3) a star role, where a large number of linkages are centered; (4) an isolate role, where relatively few linkages are located; and (5) a boundary-spanning role, which links the network to its environment (Katz & Kahn, 1978; Tichy & Fombrun, 1979).

The process of network articulation assigns each person a network role. The person is typically given a label that corresponds to the role category. Thus people who belong to groups are called group members. Those who connect groups together are called "bridges" if they are a member of one of the groups and "liaisons" if they connect groups to which they do not belong. People upon whom many linkages are centered are called "stars," while those who have few linkages are "isolates." Finally, those who connect a network to its environment are called boundary spanners (Adams, 1976, 1980). Individuals often play different roles in different networks. For example, a person may be an internal star or isolate in the task communication network but a boundary spanner in the innovation communication network.

Network Metrics

Network articulation is sometimes the principal focus of network analysis. More typically, however, analysis centers on quantifying characteristics of the network. Tichy (1981) provides a list of network metrics that have been developed to represent different characteristics. Most of these metrics have alternative computational forms for describing both individual- and organizational-level networks. The best known typology uses size, reachability, density (or connectedness), and centrality.

Network size is the simplest metric. At the individual level it refers simply to the number of people to whom a person is linked. At the network level, it indicates the total number of linkages in the network.

The reachability and density metrics are built upon the notion of a "path," a connected sequence of linkages by which it is possible to move from one point to another in the network. The length of a path is equal to the number of linkages in the path. As Alba (1982) points out, "the concept of a path leads easily to notions of *reachability* and *connectedness*. One point is reachable from another if there is a path from the second to the first, and a part of a graph is connected if each of its points is reachable from every other" (p. 52).

Reachability can be defined from the perspective of the individual or of the entire network. For personal networks, reachability is the number of linkages it takes to connect one individual to another in the network. At the organizational level, reachability is the average number of links separating individuals. If the average link distance among people were 2 or 3, the network would be very high in reachability; if it were 10 to 15, reachability would be very low.

Density, or connectedness, indicates the degree to which people have a large number of communication linkages to others in the network. It is the ratio of actual to potential contacts. For a personal network, it describes the proportion of the total number of people to whom a person in the network is connected by means of a path of a specified length. For an entire network, it is the proportion of linkages that exist relative to the total number of linkages that would exist if everyone were linked directly to everyone else.

As Freeman's (1979) review demonstrates, centrality has been frequently used in network research. Typically, every member in a network is assigned a centrality value on the basis of one of two criteria. The first criterion is the extent to which a person is near all the other people in the network. This version of centrality is computed by averaging each individual's distance from every other individual. The second criterion is based on Freeman's (1977) idea of "betweenness." As Alba (1982) says, "an individual is central to the extent that he or she lies on the shortest path between others and thus has the potential for control over their communication" (p. 59).

All these metrics are useful for describing characteristics of communication networks at all levels of analysis, including personal, organizational, and interorganizational networks. Network metrics create quantitative variables like those characteristic of attribute data; consequently, they can be used with other variables to analyze relationships between communication networks and other social processes.

Theoretical Perspectives on Communication Networks

Rogers and Kincaid (1981) assert that the communication network is an emerging paradigm for the study of human communication. Jablin (1980) says it is one of the two major perspectives for studying organizational communication.

Monge and Eisenberg (1987) describe the three major theoretical perspectives on communication networks: relational, positional, and cultural. Although these three perspectives are not fully developed theories, they differ considerably in their theoretical orientations and assumptions.

Historically, the relational school has been the dominant paradigm in communication network analysis. It focuses on the direct and indirect connections among members of the network. This leads to an emphasis on identifying network roles through network articulation and the computation of network metrics, such as centrality and density. The relational school of thought is also identified with emergent rather than designated or formal networks (compare Monge & Eisenberg, 1987, with Dansereau & Markham, 1987).

The positional school was based upon the early sociological role theories of Parsons (1951), Homans (1950), Merton (1957), and Katz and Kahn (1978). These theorists viewed a communication network as the pattern of relations among the set of positions and roles in society and its institutions. These roles specified obligatory communication relations for people who occupy various positions. Positions and roles determined who should say what to whom, and the consequent communication networks.

More recently, the positional perspective has been based on the principle of structural equivalence, which identifies social or communication structure on the basis of similarities in patterns of relations (Burt, 1978; Lorraine & White, 1971). People are considered to be structurally equivalent when they have patterns of relations similar to other people in the network who occupy their same status. For example, two managers at the same level in an organization would be viewed as structurally equivalent if they communicate to the same executives, managers, and subordinates even if they do not talk to each other.

It is important to understand the differences and similarities in rationales between the two methods. Alba (1982) summarizes them as follows:

> The relational approach focuses essentially on the pathways in networks; the positional approach on patterns of similarity in relational configurations. The former lends itself to analyses in which the social processes occurring in a network are conceptualized in terms of "communication," using that term in the broadest possible sense, and the latter to a delineation of hierarchical structure. Neither approaches excludes the other, and neither is reducible to the other. Indeed, they ultimately complement each other. (p. 63)

The third theoretical perspective, the cultural, has only recently begun to influence research on communication networks. This perspective focuses on symbols and meanings that are used to transmit message content through the communication networks. The significance of these symbols, however, is not their role in transmitting specific messages. Rather, their primary importance lies in their capacity to create language communities and cultures (Ortner, 1984). This stems from the fact that communication is the mechanism by which we make sense out of our social world by continually transmitting messages that require us to make and affirm collective social interpretations of reality (Riley, 1983). From this view, communication and communication networks are essential in the creation of the fundamental human social structures we call cultures (McPhee, 1985). Monge and Eisenberg (1987) suggest that one important way to operationalize this perspective is to study semantic networks in order to identify organizational subcultures.

A Process View of Structure

The traditional idea of structure is a simple one. Researchers think of networks as relatively stable and unchanging patterns that exist over time. While this view is certainly valid, it is equally true that networks are constantly changing.

One reason for the traditional view of structure is that we tend to think of it in relation to parts of an object. We think of the structure of an organization as the arrangements of its people or departments and divisions. But a process also has a structure, which is the usual *sequence of activities* that constitute the process. Hence a manufacturing process contains a specific set of steps to convert raw materials into finished products. That sequence is the structure of the process. The process is the conduct of the various activities; the structure of the process is the arrangement of the activities. Structure is the form and is most easily recognizable in contrast with other possible arrangements and forms—that is, in contrast to other structures. In short, structure can be conceptualized as either the arrangement of parts or the arrangement of activities.

But structures also change, often quite rapidly. Structures can be changed by adding or deleting component parts or relations, or by rearranging the parts. The same is true for the structure of activities. Hence, by organizing or reorganizing, as Monge and Eisenberg (1987) illustrate, and by structuring and restructuring, it is possible to mean that components have been added or deleted, relations have been altered, or the existing components and/or relations have been rearranged. There is a process of reorganizing that itself has a structure.

PERSONAL COMMUNICATION NETWORKS

All but the most isolated of us live in a world in which communication links us with a fairly large number of people. From the point of view of the individual, these connections are personal networks (Laumann, 1973). They consist of the set of direct and indirect contacts that people maintain at any point in time (Burt, 1980). Personal networks link people to their set of contacts across the full range of human experience, including family members and occupational, political, social, religious, and recreational partners.

Personal networks expand as communication relationships are established with new people; they contract as existing relationships diminish or are terminated. Some of the connections in personal networks are very close and intense, as is the case with many family ties. Others, such as many business and social acquaintances, are less close and intense. Some personal connections exist for a long time, as is the case with many family ties and life-long friends and business associates. Others are more recent and transient, as friends may be added and dropped throughout life.

People employ their personal networks to accomplish a variety of things. As will be shown in this section, personal networks affect the educational and occupational aspirations of children, influence development of romantic relationships, influence the jobs people find, and impact on organizational socialization and career development.

Family Ties

At the outset of this chapter the distinction was made between analysis of individual-level attributes and analysis of network relations. By far the majority of research to date has been limited to one level or the other. As Ridley and Avery (1979) observe, very little research has been conducted that explores the relationship between the two levels. Recently, however, investigators have begun to address this issue in an attempt to understand how these two types of data are related (Burgess & Huston, 1979).

One of the most interesting areas is the relationship between interpersonal relationships and network involvement. This research is based on the premise that interpersonal relations are not initiated, maintained, and terminated in a social vacuum; rather, they are significantly influenced by the context of the social and communication networks in which both persons are involved.

Pursuing this premise, Parks, Stan, and Eggert (1983) studied the relation between romantic involvement and social network involvement. Participants in the study were undergraduate students who were involved in premarital romantic relationships. They were asked to report on their relations with their romantic partner and on their involvement in both their own and their partner's family and social networks. Network involvement included perceived support from people in both networks, level of communication with network members, and attraction to members of both networks. Parks et al. hypothesized that involvement in and social support from the members of the family and social networks of both partners would be positively related to their romantic involvement. The data strongly supported the hypotheses.

Subsequent research has extended this finding in two important ways. Parks and Adelman (1983) showed that involvement in communication networks significantly predicted the stability of the romantic relationship. Specifically, they were able to predict correctly 90% of the couples that were still together at the end of three months and 83% of those who had dissolved the relationship. The results showed that the study participants

> experienced less uncertainty about their romantic partners and were less likely to break up when they communicated more often with their partner's family and friends, received greater support for their romantic rela-

tionship from family and friends, communicated more often with their partners, and perceived greater similarity to their partners. (p. 55)

The second extension focused on same-sex friendships rather than romantic relations. As in the research on romantic partners, Eggert and Parks (1987) found that involvement in communication networks was a significant predictor of same-sex friendship involvement. However, they also found that the pattern of network involvement was considerably different for the two types of interpersonal relationships:

Support from the adolescents' own network linked equally or stronger with friendship development than did support from the partner's network. The antithesis occurred in dating relationships; support from the partner's network had stronger links with relational development, than did support from the adolescents' own network. Taken together, these findings suggest an egocentric network connection in best friendships versus a more sociocentric network connection in dating relationships. (p. 17)

A number of scholars have criticized interpersonal research for ignoring the social context in which interpersonal relations exist (Burgess & Huston, 1979; LaGaipa, 1981; Parks et al., 1983). The same criticism can be leveled against network researchers: They have generally ignored interpersonal processes among members of the networks they study. The emerging line of research described above is attempting to resolve this problem by developing theories, hypotheses, and research designs to integrate these two levels of analysis.

Obtaining a Job

A modest amount of research has focused on the question of how people obtain jobs. While there are many aspects to this question, part of the answer lies in communication networks.

In a provocative and frequently cited article, Granovetter (1973) articulated a set of hypotheses relating to a concept he called the "strength of weak ties." His argument centers around the difference between weak and strong ties and the implications of this distinction for various human activities. Strong ties are frequent and enduring linkages to close friends, relatives, and associates. By contrast, weak ties are relatively infrequent communication linkages that connect people to distant acquaintances and casual friends.

A network made up of strong ties will be densely connected; many of the possible linkages will actually exist. A network of weak ties will be sparsely connected; only a few of the possible connections will exist. Granovetter reasoned that people in densely connected networks are likely to have access to and share the same information. Since the network is dense, what one person knows all of the others are likely to know also. But weak ties can serve as bridges to people outside a person's primary group. The weak ties then provide access to people who are likely to have new information that is not shared by a person's own group. As Granovetter (1982) says,

> It follows that individuals with few weak ties will be deprived of information from distant parts of the social system and will be confined to the provincial news and views of their close friends. This will not only insulate them from the latest ideas and fashions, but also may put them in a disadvantaged position in the labor market where advancement can depend . . . on knowing about appropriate job openings at just the right time. (p. 106)

Granovetter's (1974) research showed that people were nearly twice as likely to hear about new jobs through weak ties than strong ties. With some qualifications, this finding has generally been supported by Ericksen and Yancey (1980) and Lin, Ensell, and Vaughn (1981). Summarizing these research efforts, Granovetter (1982) states, "The results of these studies are very encouraging but not conclusive" (pp. 129-130).

Societal Networks: "It's a Small World"

In the late 1950s de Sola Pool and Kochen (1978-1979) began to examine the number of acquaintances of people in different social classifications. They reasoned that different occupations, social classes, and age and sex groups had differential access to other people who possessed information, power, or other important resources. Their data supported this generalization, as did the work of Gurevitch (1961).

During the next two decades an ingenious series of studies by Milgram (1967, 1969) and his associates (Korte & Milgram, 1970; Travers & Milgram, 1969) and White (1970, 1973) was conducted that explored this area and became known as the "small world studies" (Milgram, 1967). This name stems from the expression people use when they meet a stranger who is acquainted with a friend: "It's a small world."

The basic research design consisted of selecting a sample of people in a specific geographical location (e.g., Los Angeles) and a set of "target" others who resided in a different location (e.g., New York). The "starters" were provided with the name of the target and instructions that specified that they were to try to deliver the packet to the target person according to the specified rules. Usually, this meant that they were to give it to someone they knew personally, who in turn was to hand it to someone they knew personally, until the final person delivered it directly to the target person. Variations on this design included providing the target's occupation, address, and so on. Participants provided the researchers with their names and locations. Thus a set of contact chains was generated that could be traced and analyzed with network techniques.

Milgram (1967) discovered that it took an average of 7.3 links to connect sources with unknown targets who were on opposite ends of the continental United States. An interesting replication of this research revealed that almost as many links were required to link sources and targets at a large midwestern university (Shotland, 1976). Shotland interpreted this as indicating that large universities contain virtually as much social distance as the country as a whole.

Subsequent research by Travers and Milgram (1969) revealed that contact chains for sources who tried to reach their targets through occupational and professional associates were smaller (an average of 4.6 links) than for sources who tried to reach their targets through residential contacts (6.1 links). Korte and Milgram (1970) also found significant differences in the contact networks for targets in white and black communities, even when the racial identity of the targets was unknown to the sources. These differences include a larger number of completed chains and a higher probability of success in exclusively white chains than white-black chains or exclusively black chains, and a higher level of contact overlap in white than in black contact networks.

While interesting, Korte and Milgram's work does not explain these results. Further, until these results are extensively replicated, caution should be exercised in accepting the differences as anything more than a product of the times and social structure of the late 1960s. Nonetheless, this line of research demonstrates that the communication networks in which we all participate link us more closely than might otherwise have been thought. Furthermore, there are significant structural factors in society that significantly determine the nature and extent of these networks. Despite the enormous number of people in the world, contemporary human society is indeed a small world, at least in terms of network connections.

While the small world approach is an interesting line of network research, it is not without its faults. As Farace et al. (1977) point out,

> each person in the chain passes the message on to one person, an approach which reduces the likelihood of measurement of contact redundancy. Similarly, because only one route taken by a message is documented, it is not suited to general descriptions of communication load [in the networks]. (p. 211)

Further, they state,

> A major drawback to this approach is its high degree of artificiality. It is based on an introduced message and a relatively unreal task—forwarding

the message, via persons who are personally known, to an unfamiliar target. Therefore, it is unlikely to reflect the actual communication patterns that would occur in day-to-day activities. (p. 212)

Finally, the Milgram method completely ignores the content of the message and/or the purposes of the linkers. Yet as White (1970, 1973) indicated, when people search through their contact networks to accomplish particular tasks, they use them very differently than when they passively transmit a letter to a known other. Several researchers have examined a number of contact networks for specific objectives such as getting a job (Granovetter, 1974) and searching for an abortionist (Howell, 1969).

ORGANIZATIONAL NETWORKS

The study of communication networks in organizations is traditionally separated into two areas: formal networks and emergent networks. Typically, formal networks are those designated by someone with authority to prescribe who should communicate with whom. By contrast, emergent networks (also sometimes called informal networks) evolve from day-to-day interactions among people, irrespective of whether someone has specified that they communicate. The literature on formal networks is thoroughly reviewed by Dansereau and Markham (1987) and Stork and Tushman (1987); emergent networks are described in detail by Monge and Eisenberg (1987), who review factors that influence the emergence of communication networks and consequences for the people in them.

Boundary spanning is an area that incorporates both formal and informal networks but is not covered by the recent reviews. The literature on boundary spanning is reviewed here as illustrative of the issues involved in organizational networks and their relationships to the larger world.

Organizational Boundaries

Communication network research in organizations has assumed that it is possible to identify the boundaries of the organization. By identifying an organization's boundaries the researcher identifies the people who should be included in the analysis. On the surface this may seem like a simple task, but closer inspection suggests otherwise. Weick (1976, 1979), for example, developed the concept of "partial inclusion" to describe the fact that the behavior of people in organizations is only a part of their total behavior. Often, their activity outside the organization has significant bearing on their behavior inside it.

The image this conveys is one of people embedded in extensive communication networks both within and outside an organization. As we move more toward this view, organizational boundaries become more diffuse and difficult to identify. As Lincoln (1982) suggests, eventually we might be led to view organizational boundaries as epiphenomena: "A real appreciation for the social structural features of organizations may require that we look past these (formal structures and boundaries) to the ways organizations represent clusters of particular kinds of ties embedded in more inclusive social arrangements" (p. 26).

The significance of the ability to identify boundaries relates to how internal linkages differ from external linkages.

> If boundaries are hard, objective facts, then links across them might be thought to have a very different quality from links within them. But if boundaries are vague, permeable and shifting, perhaps there is no reason to treat organizational relations separately. An interorganizational tie (or organization-environment tie) might simply be seen as another network link which just happens to span the boundaries of what some observers view as separate organizations. (Lincoln, 1982, p. 27)

Despite these ambiguities, organizations must identify their boundaries and distinguish their environments from what they consider to be themselves. The flow of information through internal networks is essential to organizational functioning; but organizations must also establish linkages with relevant parts of their environment. Without the ability to gather and distribute information with the environment, most organizations would languish in isolation. Boundary spanning is the process by which organizations accomplish this task.

Boundary Spanning

Adams (1976) and Katz and Kahn (1978) define boundary spanning as the process by which members of an organization communicate with the environment. There are five major boundary-spanning activities: "(1) transacting the acquisition of organizational inputs and the disposition of outputs, (2) filtering inputs and outputs, (3) searching for and collecting information, (4) representing the organization to its external environments, and (5) protecting the organization and buffering it from external threat and pressure" (Adams, 1980, p. 328).

Adams (1976, 1980) describes boundary spanning as a networking process. The boundary spanner must develop two distinctive networks, one internal and one external. The boundary spanner then serves as liaison between the two networks. This process is much like "gatekeeping." In the two-step flow model of diffusion (Katz, 1957), gatekeepers have access to information not generally available to other members of their primary group. Gatekeepers select and transmit information that they believe their less well-informed associates should have (Rogers, 1983). Similarly, a media gatekeeper is one who determines what content is made available to the public. The primary distinction between the two concepts is the emphasis on the role of communication networks. For Adams, the primary function of the boundary spanner is the development and maintenance of the internal and external networks.

The role of the boundary spanner is complex. People who work in these positions must be sensitive to social cues and flexible in adapting their behavior to various circumstances. Self-monitoring was developed by Snyder (1974) to indicate the extent to which people can accurately perceive and adapt to a variety of social situations. It operates in a variety of interpersonal contexts. Caldwell and O'Reilly (1982) showed that high self-monitors are perceived to be more effective boundary spanners than low self-monitors.

Tushman and Scanlan (1981) carefully examined the role of boundary spanners within organizations. They identified three types of highly connected organizational individuals, only one of which they called boundary spanning: (1) internal stars, who were highly connected employees, though their connections were primarily with others in their own organizational unit; (2) external stars, who were well connected, but primarily with people who were external to the organization; and (3) boundary spanners, who were well connected both internally and externally. Their research showed that only boundary spanners—that is, only people who were both internally and externally connected—were identified by others in the organization as valuable sources of new ideas.

Tushman and Scanlan (1981) discuss the role of boundary spanner in the context of information environments. Information environments are idiosyncratic language/coding schemes and local conceptual frameworks. They develop because of the specialization required to accomplish divergent organizational tasks. The boundary spanner is a person who works in two or more information environments, at least one of which is inside the organization and another of which is in the external environment. A principal task of the boundary spanner is to translate knowledge from one environment to another. This includes several separate functions: (1) a searching function to scan the environment for information, (2) an evaluating function to assess its value to the organization, and (3) a translating function to convert the information from one environment into the best equivalent in the other environment.

In addition to dealing with information in the environment, a person who fulfills a boundary-spanning role must cope with the internal organizational structure. Leifer and Huber (1977) were interested in the relation between the perceived informational uncertainty in the environment and the flexibility of the organizational structure. Their basic argument is that higher informational uncertainty requires an organization to develop more flexible internal structures to deal with the uncertainty. Conversely, if environmental information is fairly predictable, organizations can develop fixed and rigid structures to process the information. Leifer and Huber found that flexibility of structure and frequency of boundary-spanning activity are highly related. They also found that the relationship between flexibility of structure and perceived environmental uncertainty was contingent on the level of boundary-spanning activity, specifically for those people who are high boundary spanners.

Jemison (1984) examined the importance of boundary-spanning roles in executive level strategic decision making. He derived a tripartite classification of boundary-spanning roles: (1) information acquisition and control, which determines what information is selected from the environment and who receives it within the organization; (2) domain determination and interface, which determines the nature of the organization's clients and who maintains contact with them; and (3) physical input control, which regulates kind, quality, and rate of acquisition of environmental inputs. He found that the role of domain determination and interface exercised the greatest influence over executive strategic decision making, though this is somewhat dependent upon the technology of the organization. Jemison reports that boundary-spanning activities accounted for nearly 60% of the variance in the strategic decision making.

All this suggests that people are rather extensively involved in communication networks outside their organizations. Some networks in which they are involved are personal and completely unrelated to their work inside the organization. Other networks are quite informal, and yet have considerable impact on work performance and organizational functioning. Finally some people are involved in external networks because boundary spanning is part of their job.

INTERORGANIZATIONAL AND SOCIETAL NETWORKS

With rare exceptions such as boundary spanning, communication researchers have restricted their investigations to intraorganizational communication networks. Despite this fact, there is a 25-year tradition of interorganizational research, dating back to the pioneering articles of Levine and White (1961) and Litwak and Hylton (1962; see also, Guetzkow, 1965). Though much of the early research focused on the exchange of goods and material resources, more recent work has given attention to communication and information linkages (Eisenberg et al., 1985). This section discusses issues regarding interorganizational communication networks.

Mohr (1982) describes the flurry of writing and research that characterized the field during the 1960s and early 1970s. He also noted, however, a decline of interest in the late 1970s; and by the time of his book's publication he declared the field all but dead. Ironically, during the 1980s several major theoretical and empirical papers have been published on interorganizational relations (Adams, 1980; Aldrich & Whetten, 1981; Boje & Whetten, 1981; Gottfredson & White, 1981; Leblebici & Salancik, 1982; Mariolis & Jones, 1982; Pennings, 1980; Provan, 1983; Rice & Richards, 1985; Whetten, 1981).

Interorganizational Linkages

Though much of the early research focused on the exchange of goods and material resources, (Mitchell, 1973; Warren, 1967) more recent work has been concerned with communication and information linkages. Eisenberg et al. (1985) developed a two-dimensional taxonomy of interorganizational linkages that distinguishes linkage type from linkage level. Like Zeitz (1980), they define two types of linkages on the basis of their transactional content: (1) material and (2) symbolic or informational. They also describe three levels at which information and material may be exchanged: institutional, representative, and personal. According to Eisenberg et al.,

> An *institutional* linkage occurs when information or materials are exchanged between organizations without the involvement of specific organizational roles or personalities (e.g., routine data transfers between banks). A *representative* linkage occurs when a role occupant who officially represents an organization within the system has contact with a representative of another organization (e.g., an interagency committee to formulate joint policies). The emphasis here is on the official nature of the transaction and the representative capacities of the individuals. Finally, a *personal* linkage occurs when an individual from one organization exchanges information or materials with an individual in another organization, but in a nonrepresentative or private capacity (i.e., via friendship or "old school" ties). (p. 237)

There are two opposing schools of thought about why organizations establish interorganizational relations and the role of communication in that process. The first centers on the principle of coordination and cooperation; the second rests on the idea of competition and control.

Van de Ven and Walker (1981) summarize a developmental view of the coordination perspective:

> The growth of an interorganizational relation is viewed as a dynamic cyclical process. A need for resources stimulates communications with organizations that have complementary domains since they are likely to have needed resources. These communications have the purpose of developing consensus and norms of equity on the terms of a relationship to transact resources. Resources are exchanged incrementally in order to allow participants to gradually develop trust, observe equity, work out misunderstanding, and commit themselves to become increasingly dependent upon each other. (p. 253)

Several writers have emphasized the role of competition and control in establishment of interorganizational networks. Levine and White (1961) and Aiken and Hage (1968) were among the first to argue that organizations compete for scarce resources; they establish interorganizational linkages only when they cannot achieve their goals with their own resources. They further assert, as does Marrett (1971), that fear of the loss of organizational autonomy and power leads organizations to avoid establishing interorganizational linkages. Aldrich and Whetten (1981), Alinsky (1971), and Kidder (1981) all emphasize that competing goals often lead organizations into conflict. When this happens, they typically give priority to their own rather than collective goals, even if they must resort to coercion and force. It is not necessary to adopt only one of these perspectives. Zeitz (1980) believes that both processes operate in interorganizational relations, often simultaneously: "The mutual dependence which serves as a basis for exchange provides fertile ground both for acts of cooperation and acts of conflict and opposition" (p. 82).

A number of researchers have attempted to identify the factors that lead to linkage formation. Aiken and Hage (1968) determined that organizations are more likely to link to others when they have active internal communication networks and are decentralized, informal, and complex. Galaskiewicz (1979) found that large organizations that control disposable funds and depend upon the local community for cash flow are more centralized in interorganizational community networks than their smaller, less affluent counterparts. Levine and White's (1961) research demonstrated the importance of two factors: dependence on local resources and domain consensus, which is the overlap of goals, procedures, and client populations.

Although it may not be immediately apparent, the research tradition just described is based on a proletariate perspective. It attempts to explain what typical workers in public agencies and private-sector firms do to forge linkages with other organizations to accomplish collective goals. A related line of thinking and research has centered on the corporate and social elite.

Interorganizational Linkages of the Corporate Elite

Most capitalist societies are significantly influenced by the interests of private businesses. In turn these enterprises are dominated by the interests of the few thousand large corporations that control most of the corporate wealth in the world. The executives who control these corporations make up the corporate elite.

One of the ways in which elites exercise control is by membership on a corporation's board of directors. Useem (1980) estimates that "membership in the corporate elite probably numbers at most two or three hundred thousands" (p. 42) in the United States. Yet this group exercises an inordinate amount of influence, not only within the corporate world, but throughout the larger society as well (Berg & Zald, 1978; Domhoff, 1970; Pfeffer & Salancik, 1978).

But corporate elites rarely hold membership on only one board of directors. To obtain and share the information they need to exercise control, they hold overlapping memberships on multiple boards. These "interlocking directorates" provide regular and consistent patterns of interorganizational contact among the corporate elite (Fennema & Schijf, 1978-1979; Pennings, 1980).

Useem (1980, pp. 54-55) reports that

> these interlocking directorships are sufficiently dispersed and extensive to bring the managers and directors (and, among their ranks, an unknown but large percentage of the principal owners) of virtually *all* major companies into direct or indirect contact. Studies of the 797 largest firms in 1969, for instance, revealed that the interlocking directorates united in a single network more than 90% of these firms' more than 8,600 directors; moreover, the network is sufficiently cross-cutting that removal of the most interlocked nodes does not greatly alter its inclusiveness (Mariolis, 1975; Levine & Roy, 1975).

Research on interlocking directorates suggests that they are formed as part of deliberate corporate strategies to improve performance of the firm. Allen (1974), Galaskiewicz (1979), Pfeffer (1972), and others find this to be the case in sales, purchasing, credit, and public reputation.

These findings suggest that major segments of capitalist societies are controlled by densely connected networks of elite power and influence. This reaches beyond the bounds of business. Many of the corporate elite are also part of the social and political elite. For example, leading business associations to which many of the elite belong exercise enormous influence on both local and national political decisions. They are also frequently involved in civic, artistic, and other high-status activities.

Many scholars have been interested in the origins of the elite, that is, in the question of how elites achieve that status (Alba & Moore, 1978; Domhoff, 1970; Mills, 1956; Moore & Alba, 1982). A number of factors have been identified that center on exclusivity. These include exclusive kinship within the elite, personal or family wealth, and exclusive education. As Useem (1980) says, "Business, associational, educational, and kinship networks comprise mutually reinforcing strands of cohesion" (p. 58).

Alba and Moore (1978) studied networks of 941 elites from the American Leadership Study. It included people in 10 major institutional sectors including public and private organizations covering all major areas of corporate and political life. The major focus was on identifying the "social circle" of the elite. A social circle is a network metric similar to the concept of clique. The difference between the two is that members are "integrated" into a circle on the basis of short chains of interaction, whereas members are integrated into cliques on the basis of face-to-face contacts.

In the Alba and Moore study 65 members were isolates, but the remaining 876 were connected so that it was possible to find a path between any pair of individuals! The study found 442 overlapping cliques that were aggregated into a social circle composed of a dense clique at the center of the circle with numerous linkages to other groups. The central circle contained individuals covering the economic and political spectrum. Alba and Moore (1978) conclude

> We believe that our analysis of this elite network provides important evidence of the integration of political elites in the United States. The existence of a central circle facilitates communication and interaction both within a large, diverse leadership group and between the members of that circle and more specialized elite groups. (p. 184)

Professional Networks: Invisible Colleges

In a classic study Crane (1972) described those professions where the primary contacts are among similar professionals who are geographically dispersed. She called these long-distance networks "invisible colleges"; the world of academics provides a prime example. Though professors have to maintain personal networks with colleagues at their home universities, successful professors also maintain extensive contacts with professors at other universities around the world. The network is maintained by reading each others' published works and by correspondence, telephone, and professional meetings.

Burt (1982) analyzed journal publication patterns in sociological methodology, and found a strong influence attributable to the invisible college. He surveyed the publication preferences for experts in the field and for others associated with them in relation to their actual publication patterns. He says, "the expressed interests of the elite experts in journals as outlets for significant work in sociological methodology could be viewed as reflections of journal norms systematically maintained by the network of interpersonal influences among the experts" (p. 253).

In many ways, Crane (1972) reports, the invisible college is more important to the long-term success of a professor than is a local network. An invisible college is a primary mechanism for keeping abreast of important new research, for learning about events in the profession, for effectively placing one's graduates, and for attracting new students and faculty.

Networks of Social Support

Few people in modern society live isolated lives. Our daily activities tend to be deeply intertwined with the daily lives and activities of many others. In contrast to earlier eras when emphasis was placed on independence, contemporary life requires interdependence. Research by de Sola Pool and Kochen (1978-1979) indicates that some people maintain acquaintance networks with as many as 2,000 to 3,000 other people. They report that white collar workers contacted an average of 540 persons and blue collar workers an average of 140 persons in a 100-day period.

Despite the large number of others to which most people are connected, Pattison and Pattison (1981) indicate that the typical person depends on approximately 25 family members, close friends, neighbors, and coworkers for social support. Albrecht and Adelman (1984) define social support as "a network or configuration of personal ties where affect and/or instrumental aid is exchanged" (p. 4).

Obtaining and maintaining social support is an essential aspect of human life. It is equally important for everyday activities and special instances of personal crisis and life stress. In the former case it affects how people view and feel about themselves, their behavior, and their relations with others. In the latter, it provides help to deal with difficult human experiences such as illness, death, divorce, job burnout, and other major life transitions.

Albrecht, Adelman, and Associates (in press) organize the main research findings about social support around the major properties of networks: size, heterogeneity, reciprocity, changes over time, multiplexity, and density. They compare the networks for healthy individuals with networks of those classified as disturbed. "Normals" have larger networks, they report,

> have been found to communicate with their contacts frequently, and have a balanced reciprocity of affective caring and instrumental assistance. In contrast, disturbed populations such as schizophrenics have smaller networks (8-12 persons) of shorter relational duration, with low reciprocity and low affect.

They also report that "individuals who have low density, heterogeneous network structures are likely to fare better than those who do not" (Albrecht et al., in press).

Social support networks can be viewed as the personal networks that people maintain to enhance their well-being and to cope with difficult life events. However, they can also be viewed as societal networks. People in helping professions, such as health, religion, education, social work, and law, participate in social support networks to maintain the structure of society and the well-being of its members. From either perspective, this is an important area of future research for communication scholars.

FUTURE RESEARCH

This chapter began with an overview of essential concepts and theories of network analysis, and then described representative research at three network levels: personal, organizational, and interorganizational or societal. This final section discusses the relationship of network analysis to communication behaviors at other levels of analysis. Figure 8.1 summarizes the possible relations. One axis is labeled "levels of network analysis." These are personal networks, group and organizational networks, and interorganizational and societal networks. The other axis is labeled "levels of communication study": the intrapersonal, interpersonal, network, and societal levels discussed throughout this handbook. Each cell shows a possible combination of network analysis and communication variables that could fruitfully be studied. Little research has been done in this area, so much of what is said in this final section must be considered conjectural.

The intrapersonal level. Little is known about the relation between individual-level cognitive and communicative processes and communication networks. A pioneering study by Walker (1985) investigated the hypothesis that individuals' positions in an organizational network would predict their cognitions about their firm's products and processes. Network position accounted for nearly a quarter of the variance in cognition. Walker suggested that people who are located in similar places in the network structure have similar experiences and hence develop similar ways of thinking about products and processes. This study points to questions of the relation between intrapersonal communication variables and networks. For example, Do different cognitive styles lead to different role relations in a network, such as stars, liaisons, and boundary spanners? Is cognitive complexity a good predictor of network involvement or participation? How is information-processing capacity related to the development of personal networks?

The interpersonal level. The studies by Parks and colleagues (Parks & Adelman, 1983; Parks et al., 1983) and by Milardo (1982) are among the first to examine the development of interpersonal relations in the context of communication networks. Level of connectedness in each other's networks was a significant predictor of the development and stability of a relationship. Milardo (1982) demonstrated that as couples become more deeply involved with one another, they tend to withdraw from por-

	Intrapersonal	Interpersonal	Network and Organizational	Societal
Personal	Communication liaison or isolate roles and cognitive style	Personal kinship networks and the development of romantic relations	Size of personal networks and organizational communication effectiveness	Size of personal support networks and societal anomic
Group and Organizational	Group network density and individual cognitive complexity and attitudes	Level of network centrality and supervisor/subordinate communication relations	Degree of boundary spanning and richness of information about organizational environments	Level of group isolation and societal information gap
Interorganizational and Societal	Interorganizational information flow and individual communicator competence	Density of network of social support agencies and stability of marital communication	Inter-organizational network density and organizational performance	Density of elite social circles and spiral of silence or agenda setting

(left axis label) **Levels of Network Analysis**

Figure 8.1. The relation between levels of network analysis and levels of other communication variables. Each cell entry contains a representative example of potential research between any two levels of analysis.

tions of their individual networks and forge joint networks. Similarly, the social support literature looks at the effect of networks of supportive people on individual and relational adjustment to difficult life events.

These studies point to other interesting questions that center on the relationship between networks and interpersonal relations. How can our theories of interpersonal relations be broadened to include the contextual dimensions of networks? For example, Parks and Adelman (1983) introduced network sources of uncertainty in their test of Berger and Calabrese's (1975) uncertainty reduction theory of the development of interpersonal relations. Albrecht and Adelman (1984) undertook a similar task for social support networks. Having demonstrated the empirical importance of network sources of uncertainty, these ideas should now be formally incorporated in an elaboration of the original theory. Other areas of empirical research are also interesting. How does network participation affect supervisor-subordinate relations? How do the kinship networks of romantic partners from different ethnic, cultural, or religious backgrounds adjust to the development of the romantic relationship?

The organizational level. Most research on communication networks in organizations has focused on one level of analysis. As indicated earlier, most researchers look for antecedents and outcomes of network involvement. Rarely have they investigated how network participation at one level of analysis is related to networks at other levels. For example, are people with a small personal social network outside of work (the individual level) more likely to be isolates in their work networks (the organizational level)? Are boundary spanners more likely to be densely connected within the organization than people who fulfill other communication roles?

The societal level. Many forms of social groupings exist. Computer devotees create bulletin boards to exchange information about computers (and many other things). Churches, singles groups, parents groups, and professional associations form social support networks to help people through difficult life transitions. Organizations develop interorganizational linkages to exchange information and resources. Government organizations develop information networks to help individuals obtain the resources that are available to them, especially for medical and legal needs. How are all these societal networks related to individual, interpersonal, and organizational communication variables? For example, are people who are communication apprehensive less able to use government information networks?

Finally, two caveats seem appropriate. First, it is one thing to suggest interesting and provocative cross-level hypotheses and questions, but quite another to conduct the research. Special problems with cross-level research need to be taken into account. These include the choice of units and levels of analysis (Haney, 1980), aggregation and disaggregation (Firebaugh, 1978; Hanan, 1971), and problems in cross-level influences (Glick, 1980; Roberts, Hulin, & Rousseau, 1978). Second, as Reardon and Rogers (1986) argue, historical accident has led to the development of a false intellectual dichotomy between two traditional areas of inquiry, interpersonal communication and mass communication. It does not take much imagination to extend their argument to the position that all boundaries between communication specialities are contrived, including the levels approach used to organize this book. Whatever the outcome of that debate, one of the most useful benefits of the organization of the handbook is that it should lead us to examine the usefulness of the levels approach itself.

REFERENCES

Adams, J. S. (1976). The structure and dynamics of behavior in organizational boundary roles. In M. D. Dunnette (Ed.), *Handbook of industrial and organizational psychology* (pp. 1175-1199). Chicago: Rand McNally.

Adams, J. S. (1980). Interorganization processes and organization boundary activities. In L. Cummings & B. Staw (Eds.), *Research in organizational behavior* (Vol. 2, pp. 321-355). Greenwich, CT: JAI Press.

Aiken, M. & Hage, J. (1968). Organizational interdependence and interorganizational structure. *American Sociological Review, 33,* 912-930.

Alba, R. D. (1982). Taking stock of network analysis: A decade's results. In S. Bacharach (Ed.), *Research in the sociology of organizations* (Vol. 1, pp. 39-74). Greenwich, CT: JAI Press.

Alba, R. D., & Moore, G. (1978). Elite social circles. *Sociological Methods and Research, 7,* 167-188.

Albrecht, T. L., & Adelman, M. B. (1984). Social support and life stress: New directions for communication research. *Human Communication Research, 11,* 3-32.

Albrecht, T. L., & Adelman, M. B., & Associates (in press). *Communicating social support.* Newbury Park, CA: Sage.

Aldrich, H., & Whetten, D. (1981). Organization-sets, action-sets, and networks: Making the most of simplicity. In P. Nystrom & W. Starbuck (Eds.), *Handbook of organizational design* (Vol. 4). New York: Oxford University Press.

Alinsky, D. (1971). *Rules for radicals: A practical primer for realistic radicals.* New York: Random House.

Allen, M. P. (1974). The structure of interorganizational elite cooptation: Interlocking corporate directorates. *American Sociological Review, 39,* 393-406.

Allen, T. (1977). *Managing the flow of technology.* Cambridge: MIT Press.

Berg, I., & Zald, M. N. (1978). Business and society. *Annual Review of Sociology, 4,* 115-143.

Berger, C. R., & Calabrese, R. J. (1975). Some explorations in initial interaction and beyond: Toward a developmental theory of interpersonal communication. *Human Communication Research, 1,* 99-112.

Berkowitz, S. D. (1982). *An introduction to structural analysis: The network approach to social research.* Toronto: Butterworths.

Berlo, D. K., Lemert, J. B., & Mertz, R. J. (1969-1970). Dimensions for evaluating the acceptability of message sources. *Public Opinion Quarterly, 33,* 563-576.

Blau, P. M. (1982). Introduction: Diverse views of social structure and their common denominator. In P. M. Blau & R. K. Merton (Eds.), *Continuities in structural inquiry* (pp. 1-23). Newbury Park, CA: Sage.

Boje, D., & Whetten, D. (1981). Strategies and constraints affecting centrality and attributions of influence in interorganizational networks. *Administrative Science Quarterly, 26,* 378-395.

Burgess, R., & Huston, T. (Eds.). (1979). *Social exchange in developing relationships.* New York: Academic Press.

Burt, R. S. (1978). Cohesion versus structural equivalence as a basis for network subgroups. *Sociological Methods and Research, 7,* 189-212.

Burt, R. S. (1980). Models of network structure. *Annual Review of Sociology, 6,* 79-141.

Burt, R. S. (1982). *Toward a theory of action.* New York: Academic Press.

Caldwell, D. F., & O'Reilly III, C. A. (1982). Boundary spanning and individual performance: The impact of self-monitoring. *Journal of Applied Psychology, 67,* 124-127.

Crane, D. (1972). *Invisible colleges: Diffusion of knowledge in scientific communities.* Chicago, IL: University of Chicago Press.

Dansereau, F., & Markham, S. (1987). Formal networks: Interpersonal. In F. Jablin, L. Putnam, K. Roberts, & L. Porter (Eds.), *Handbook of organizational communication.* Newbury Park, CA: Sage.

Delia, J. G. (1977). Constructivism and the study of human communication. *Quarterly Journal of Speech, 63,* 66-83.

de Sola Pool, I., & Kochen, M. (1978-1979). Contacts and influence. *Social Networks, 1,* 5-51.

Domhoff, G. W. (1970). *The higher circles: The governing class in America.* New York: Random House.

Durkheim, E. (1964). *The rules of sociological method.* London: Free Press.

Eggert, L. L., & Parks, M. R. (1987). Communication network involvement in adolescents' friendships and romantic relationships. In M. McLaughlin (Ed.), *Communication yearbook 10.* Newbury Park, CA: Sage.

Eisenberg, E. M., Farace, R. V., Monge, P. R., Bettinghaus, E. P., Kurchner-Hawkins, R., Miller, K., & Rothman, L. (1985). Communication linkages in interorganizational systems. In B. Dervin & M. Voigt (Eds.), *Progress in communication sciences* (Vol. 6, pp. 210-261). Norwood, NJ: Ablex.

Ericksen, E., & Yancey, W. (1980). *Class, sector and income determination.* Unpublished manuscript, Department of Sociology, Temple University.

Farace, R. V., & Mabee, T. (1980). Communication network analysis methods. In P.R. Monge & J.N. Cappella (Eds.), *Multivariate techniques in human communication research* (pp. 365-391). New York: Academic Press.

Farace, R. V., Monge, P. R., & Russell, H. M. (1977). *Communicating and organizing.* Reading, MA: Addison-Wesley.

Fennema, M., & Schijf, H. (1978-1979). Analyzing interlocking directorates: Theory and methods. *Social Networks, 1,* 297-332.

Firebaugh, G. (1978). A rule for inferring individual-level relationships from aggregate data. *American Sociological Review, 43,* 557-572.

Fombrun, C. J. (1982). Strategies for network research in organizations. *Academy of Management Review, 7,* 280-291.

Freeman, L. C. (1977). A set of measures of centrality based on betweenness. *Sociometry, 40,* 35-41.

Freeman, L. C. (1979). Centrality in social networks: Conceptual clarification. *Social Networks, 1,* 215-239.

Galaskiewicz, J. (1979). *Exchange networks and community politics.* Newbury Park, CA: Sage.

Glick, W. H. (1980). Problems in cross-level inferences. In K. H. Roberts & L. Burstein (Eds.), *New directions for methodology of social and behavioral science: Issues in aggregation* (No. 6, pp. 17-30). San Francisco: Jossey-Bass.

Glick, W. H. (1985). Conceptualizing and measuring organizational and psychological climate: Pitfalls in multilevel research. *Academy of Management Review, 10,* 601-616.

Gottfredson, L. S., & White, P. E. (1981). Interorganizational agreements. In P. C. Nystrom & W. H. Starbuck (Eds.), *Handbook of organizational design* (Vol. 1, pp. 471-486). New York: Oxford University Press.

Granovetter, M. (1973). The strength of weak ties. *American Journal of Sociology, 78,* 1360-1380.

Granovetter, M. (1974). *Getting a job.* Cambridge, MA: Harvard University Press.

Granovetter, M. (1982). The strength of weak ties: A network theory revisited. In P. V. Marsden & N. Lin (Eds.), *Social structure and network analysis* (pp. 105-130). Newbury Park, CA: Sage.

Guetzkow, H. (1965). Communications in organizations. In J. G. March (Ed.), *Handbook of organizations* (pp. 354-413). Chicago, IL: Rand McNally.

Guion, R. M. (1973). A note on organizational climate. *Organizational Behavior and Human Performance, 9,* 120-125.

Gurevitch, M. (1961). *The social structure of acquaintanceship networks.* Doctoral dissertation, Massachusetts Institute of Technology, Cambridge.

Haney, W. (1980). Units and levels of analysis in large-scale evaluation. In K. H. Roberts & L. Burstein (Eds.), *New Directions for methodology of social and behavioral science: Issues in aggregation* (No. 6, pp. 1-16). San Francisco: Jossey-Bass.

Hannan, M. T. (1971). *Aggregation and disaggregation in sociology.* Lexington, MA: Lexington Books.

Homans, G. C. (1950). *The human group.* New York: Harcourt, Brace & World.

Howell, N. (1969). *The search for an abortionist.* Chicago, IL: University of Chicago Press.

Jablin, F. M. (1979). Superior-subordinate communication: The state of the art. *Psychological Bulletin, 86,* 1201-1222.

Jablin, F. M. (1980). Organizational communication theory and research: An overview of communication climate and network research. In D. Nimmo (Ed.), *Communication yearbook 4* (pp. 327-347). New Brunswick, NJ: Transaction.

James, L. R., & Jones, A. P. (1976). Organizational structure: A review of structural dimensions and their conceptual relationships with individual attitudes and behavior. *Organizational Behavior and Human Performance, 16,* 74-113.

Jemison, D. B. (1984). The importance of boundary spanning roles in strategic decision-making. *Journal of Management Studies, 21,* 131-152.

Joyce, W. F., & Slocum, J. W., Jr. (1984). Collective climate: Agreement as a basis for defining aggregate climates in organizations. *Academy of Management Journal, 27,* 721-742.

Katz, E. (1957). The two-step flow of communication: An up-to-date report on an hypothesis. *Public Opinion Quarterly, 21,* 67-78.

Katz, D., & Kahn, R. (1978). *The social psychology of organizations* (2nd ed.). New York: John Wiley.

Kidder, T. (1981). *The soul of a new machine.* Boston: Little, Brown.

Korte, C. & Milgram, S. (1970). Acquaintanceship networks between racial groups: Application of the small world method. *Journal of Personality and Social Psychology, 15,* 101-108.

LaGaipa, J. J. (1981). A systems approach to personal relationships. In S. Duck & R. Gilmour (Eds.), *Personal relationships 1: Studying personal relationships* (pp. 67-89). New York: Academic Press.

Laumann, E. O. (1973). New directions in the study of community elites. *American Sociological Review, 38,* 212-230.

Leblebici, H., & Salancik, G. R. (1982). Stability in interorganizational exchanges: Rulemaking processes of the Chicago board of trade. *Administrative Science Quarterly, 27,* 227-242.

Leifer, R., & Huber, G. P. (1977). Relations among perceived environmental uncertainty, organizational structure, and boundary spanning behavior. *Administrative Science Quarterly, 22,* 235-247.

Levine, J. H., & Roy, W. S. (1975). *A study of interlocking directorates: Vital concepts of organization.* Unpublished manuscript, Department of Sociology, Dartmouth College.

Levine, S., & White, P. (1961). Exchange as a conceptual framework for the study of interorganizational relationships. *Administrative Science Quarterly, 5,* 583-601.

Lin, N., Ensel, W. M., & Vaughn, J. C. (1981). Social resources and strength of ties:

Structural factors in occupational status attainment. *American Sociological Review, 46*, 393-405.

Lincoln, J. R. (1982). Intra- (and inter-) organizational networks. In S. Bacharach (Ed.), *Research in the sociology of organizations* (Vol. 1, pp. 1-38). Greenwich, CT: JAI Press.

Litwak, E., and Hylton, L. F. (1962). Interorganizational analysis: A hypothesis on coordinating agencies. *Administrative Science Quarterly, 6*, 395-420.

Lorraine, F. P., & White, H. C. (1971). Structural equivalence of individuals in social networks. *Journal of Mathematical Sociology, 1*, 49-80.

McLeod, J., & Chaffee, S. (1973). Interpersonal approaches to communication research. *American Behavioral Scientist, 16*, 469-499.

McPhee, R. D. (1985). Formal structure and organizational communication. In R. D. McPhee, & P. K. Tompkins (Eds.), *Organizational communication: Traditional themes and new directions* (pp. 149-177). Newbury Park, CA: Sage.

Mariolis, P. (1975). Interlocking directorates and control of corporations: The theory of bank control. *Social Science Quarterly, 56*, 425-439.

Mariolis, P., & Jones, M. H. (1982). Centrality in corporate interlock networks: Reliability and stability. *Administrative Science Quarterly, 27*, 571-587.

Marrett, C. (1971). On the specification of interorganizational dimensions. *Sociology and Social Research, 56*, 83-99.

Merton, R. K. (1957). The role set: Problems in sociological theory. *British Journal of Sociology, 8*, 106-120.

Merton, R. K. (1975). Structural analysis in sociology. In P. M. Blau (Ed.), *Approaches to the study of social structure* (pp. 1-17). New York: Free Press.

Milardo, R. M. (1982). Friendship networks in developing relationships: Converging and diverging social environments. *Social Psychology Quarterly, 45*, 162-172.

Milgram, S. (1967). The small world problem. *Psychology Today, 1*, 61-67.

Milgram, S. (1969). Interdisciplinary thinking and the small world problem. In M. Sherif & C. Sherif (Eds.), *Interdisciplinary relationships in the social sciences.* Chicago, IL: Aldine.

Mills, C. W. (1956). *The power elite.* New York: Oxford University Press.

Mitchell, J. C. (1973). Networks, norms and institutions. In J. Boissevain & J. C. Mitchell (Eds.), *Network analysis.* (pp. 15-35). The Hague: Mouton.

Mitchell, J. C. (1974). Social networks. *Annual Review of Anthropology, 3*, 279-299.

Mohr, L. B. (1982). *Explaining organizational behavior.* San Francisco: Jossey-Bass.

Monge, P. R., Bachman, S. G., Dillard, J. P., & Eisenberg, E. M. (1982). Communicator competence in the workplace: Model testing and scale development. In M. Burgoon (Ed.), *Communication yearbook 5* (pp. 505-527). New Brunswick, NJ: Transaction Books.

Monge, P. R., & Contractor, N. (in press). Measurement techniques for the study of communication networks. In C. Tardy (Ed.), *Instrumentation in communication research.* Norwood, NJ: Ablex.

Monge, P. R., Edwards, J., & Kirste, K. (1978). The determinants of communication and communication structure in large organizations: A review of research. In B. Ruben (Ed.), *Communication yearbook 2* (pp. 311-331). New Brunswick, NJ: Transaction Books.

Monge, P. R., & Eisenberg, E. M. (1987). Emergent networks. In F. Jablin, L. Putnam, K. Roberts, & L. Porter (Eds.), *Handbook of organizational communication.* Newbury Park, CA: Sage.

Monge, P. R., & Miller, G. R. (1985). Communication networks. In A. Kuper & J. Kuper (Eds.), *The social science encyclopedia* (pp. 130-131). London: Routledge & Kegan Paul.

Moore, G., & Alba, R. D. (1982). Class and prestige origins in the American elite. In P. V. Marsden & N. Lin (Eds.), *Social structure and network analysis* (pp. 39-60). Newbury Park, CA: Sage.

Norton, R. W. (1978). Foundation of a communicator style construct. *Human Communication Research, 4,* 99-112.

Ortner, S. (1984). Theory in anthropology since the sixties. *Journal for the Comparative Study of Society and History,* 126-166.

Parks, M. R., & Adelman, M. B. (1983). Communication networks and the development of romantic relationships: An expansion of uncertainty reduction theory. *Human Communication Research, 10,* 55-79.

Parks, M. R., Stan, C. M., & Eggert, L. L. (1983). Romantic involvement and social network involvement. *Social Psychology Quarterly, 46,* 116-131.

Parsons, T. (1951). *The social system.* New York: Free Press.

Pattison, E. M., & Pattison, M. L. (1981). Analysis of schizophrenic psychosocial networks. *Schizophrenia Bulletin, 7,* 135-143.

Pennings, J. M. (1980). *Interlocking directorates.* San Francisco: Jossey-Bass.

Pfeffer, J. (1972). Size and composition of corporate boards of directors: The organization and its environment. *Administrative Science Quarterly, 17,* 218-228.

Pfeffer, J., & Salancik, G. (1978). *The external control of organizations.* New York: Harper & Row.

Porter, L. W., & Roberts, K. H. (1976). Communication in organizations. In M. Dunnette (Ed.), *Handbook of industrial and organizational psychology* (pp. 1553-1589). Chicago, IL: Rand McNally.

Provan, K. G. (1983). The federation as an interorganizational linkage network. *Academy of Management Review, 8,* 79-89.

Reardon, K., & Rogers, E. M. (1986). *Interpersonal and mass communication: A false dichotomy.* Paper presented at the annual convention of the Speech Communication Association, Chicago.

Rice, R. R., & Richards, W. D., Jr. (1985). An overview of network analysis methods and programs. In B. Dervin & M. Voigt (Eds.), *Progress in communication sciences* (Vol. 7, pp. 105-165). Norwood, NJ: Ablex.

Richards, W., Jr. (1985). Data, models, and assumptions in network analysis. In R. McPhee & P. Tompkins (Eds.), *Organizational communication: Traditional themes and new directions* (pp. 109-128). Newbury Park, CA: Sage.

Ridley, C., & Avery, A. (1979). Social network influence on the dyadic relationship. In R. Burgess & T. Huston (Eds.), *Social exchange in developing relationships* (pp. 223-246). New York: Academic Press.

Riley, P. (1983). A structurationalist account of organizational culture. *Administrative Science Quarterly, 28,* 414-437.

Roberts, K. H., Hulin, C. L., & Rousseau, D. M. (1978). *Developing an interdisciplinary science of organizations.* San Francisco, CA: Jossey-Bass.

Rogers, E. M. (1983). *Diffusion of innovations* (3rd ed.). New York: Free Press.

Rogers, E. M., & Kincaid, D. L. (1981). *Communication networks: Toward a new paradigm for research.* New York: Free Press.

Shaw, M. E. (1964). Communication networks. In L. Berkowitz (Ed.), *Advances in experimental social psychology* (pp. 111-147). New York: Academic Press.

Shotland, R. L. (1975). *University communication networks: The small world method.* New York: John Wiley.

Snyder, M. (1974). The self-monitoring of expressive behavior. *Journal of Personality and Social Psychology, 30,* 526-537.

Stork, D., & Tushman, M. (1987). Formal networks: Organizational and extraorganizational. In F. Jablin, L. Putnam, K. H. Roberts & L. Porter (Eds.), *Handbook of organizational communication.* Newbury Park, CA: Sage.

Tichy, N. M. (1981). Networks in organizations. In P. Nystrom & W. Starbuck (Eds.), *Handbook of organizational design* (Vol. 2, pp. 225-249). New York: Oxford University Press.

Tichy, N., & Fombrun, C. (1979). Network analysis in organizational settings. *Human Relations, 32,* 923-965.

Tichy, N., Tuchman, M., & Fombrun, C. (1979). Social network analysis for organizations. *Academy of Management Review, 4,* 507-519.

Travers, J., & Milgram, S. (1969). An experimental study of the small world problem. *Sociometry, 32,* 425-443.

Tuchman, M. L., & Scanlan, T. J. (1981). Boundary spanning individuals: Their role in information transfer and their antecedents. *Academy of Management Journal, 24,* 289-305.

Useem, M. (1980). Corporations and the corporate elite. *Annual Review of Sociology, 6,* 41-77.

Van de Ven, A. H., & Walker, G. (1981). *The dynamics of interorganizational coordination* (Discussion Paper 110, Center for the Study of Organizational Innovations). University of Pennsylvania, The Wharton School.

Walker, G. (1985). Network position and cognition in a computer software firm. *Administrative Science Quarterly, 30,* 103-130.

Warren, R. (1967). The interorganizational field as a focus for investigation. *Administrative Science Quarterly, 12,* 396-419.

Weick, K. E. (1976). Educational organizations as loosely coupled systems. *Administrative Science Quarterly, 21,* 1-19.

Weick, K. E. (1979). *The social psychology of organizing* (2nd ed.). Reading, MA: Addison-Wesley.

Whetten, D. (1981). Interorganizational relations: A review of the field. *Journal of Higher Education, 52,* 1-28.

White, H. (1970). Search parameters for the small world problem. *Social Forces, 49,* 259-264.

White, H. (1973). Everyday life in stochastic networks. *Sociological Inquiry, 43,* 43-49.

Zeitz, G. (1980). Interorganizational dialectics. *Administrative Science Quarterly, 25,* 72-88.

9 The Macrosocial Level of Communication Science

JACK M. McLEOD
University of Wisconsin—Madison

JAY G. BLUMLER
University of Leeds and University of Maryland

T HE contours of communication study have been transformed in the past two decades by a considerable growth of macro-level inquiry. Most affected have been approaches to mass communication, with increasing attention to the ideological role of the media; the relationship of media organizations to society; the production process; the roles and values of media professionals; the global flow of information; and the societal impact of new communication technologies. Developments in semiotics and sociolinguistics have highlighted complex relationships between cultural forms and social identity, constraining "texts" and negotiating "readers", and socially based convention of encoding and decoding. Resurgent critical theory and cultural studies operate almost entirely at this level. Macrosocial issues dominated a 1983 symposium on "Ferment in the Field" (Gerbner, 1983) and the 1985 Convention of the International Communication Association's "Cross-Paradigm Dialogues." New journals provide outlets for writing on communication systems, institutions, and processes (e.g., *Critical Studies in Mass Communication, Media, Culture and Society, European Journal of Communication*).

Has this anything to do with "communication science"? "Scientific" is probably not what first comes to mind when academics are given the term "macroscopic communication theory and research." But is the macrosocial beyond the reach of scientific discipline, or is this simply due to intellectual predilections? Our position is the following:

(1) Scientific criteria are, in principle, as applicable to macrosocial theory and research as to any other level of communication inquiry.

AUTHORS' NOTE: We are grateful to Connie M. Hoxie, graduate student in the School of Journalism and Mass Communication, University of Wisconsin—Madison, for aid in the preparation of this chapter.

(2) The time is ripe to apply such criteria, although realization of the scientific potential of macro-level scholarship will require release from certain dominant, imprisoning intellectual frameworks.
(3) In explaining how communication systems and social systems are organized, scientific inquiry is often comparative, over both time and space.

The scientific credentials of macrosocial theory and research are, however, less securely established than for any other level of analysis considered in this volume. For three reasons it has attracted an unscientific image, deterring investigators of scientific bent.

First, macroscopic considerations enter most visibly into our field's exercises of grand polemic, where the merits and deficiencies of opposed paradigms are contested. Field polemics concerns differing political values about communication: consensus, pluralism, objectivity, impartiality, participatory democracy, equality, compromise, etc. It pivots on convictions about the reality of communication orders: hegemony, liberal democracy, media imperialism, etc. It is about what is presumed to be self-evident—so that the scientist's painstaking collection and sifting of evidence is not required.

Polemical exchange brings influential assumptions to the surface. It helps to clarify issues of study direction and priorities. It affirms the importance of communication systems. But it also deters scholars who see such discourse as beyond their professional competence. The uncomfortable relationship between values and science plays a part. Because devotees of the macrosocietal are perceived to ignore the distinction between normative and scholarly considerations, the macroscopic level has been discounted as a place for testable theory.

Second, macrosocial thought is associated with holistic approaches— "total" explanation. If everything is connectable with everything else, there can never be closure; inquiry can never stop because it leads inexorably on to everything else. Such a perspective does not match the conditions of scientific research, which progresses through bounded inquiries; at any point issues may have to be temporarily closed and partial explanations sought.

Third, the "universalism" of prominent macrosocial standpoints seems to exclude a scientifically organized effort. The assumption that the media hold some fixed and unvarying relationship to the worlds of politics and economics abolishes those sources of difference and variation that are the meat and drink of social science. Universalism is also at odds with the impression emerging from cross-national research that national media systems differ more than might have been expected. There may be a lot of variation to play with in macro-level communication systems and processes.

Despite these aversive images and a certain historic neglect, there are signs that the time is ripe for scientific advance at the macrosocial level.

Among behaviorally oriented communication researchers, dissatisfaction with the narrowness and repetitiveness of their data gathering has bred a self-questioning spirit. Among critical scholars, a realization is growing that solid evidence is needed if their work is to have impact. They are also discovering that audience reactions are not automatic outcomes of media content, which in turn is not a straightforward product of media control structures (Fejes, 1984).

Another encouraging sign is scientifically motivated comparative communication research projects by different kinds of scholars committed to collaboration. These include studies of the European election campaigns of 1979 and 1984 (Blumler, 1983; Siune, McQuail, & Blumler, 1984); portrayal of families and women on television (Linné & Hartmann, 1986; Thoveron, 1986); mass media agenda setting in the United States and the United Kingdom (Gurevitch, Blumler, & Weaver, 1986); creation of "advanced wired cities" in different societies (Dutton, Blumler, & Kraemer, 1986); new communication technology policies in Western societies (McQuail & Siune, 1986); comparative broadcasting finance (Blumler, Brynin, & Nossiter, 1986); constituency-level communication in legislative election campaigns (Goldenberg & Traugott, 1984); cross-cultural television fiction (Liebes & Katz, 1986); and television news portrayals of social conflict (Adoni, Cohen, & Mane, 1984).

There are still many critical and behavioral communication scholars who relate to each other as if at war, with no middle ground and no basis for cooperation or mutual learning. Some critical theorists dismiss any work that has no connection with ideology; the behaviorally trained investigator may demand hard and replicable data. The answer to both must come from the quality of evidence produced by scientific macrosocial research.

NOTIONS OF LEVELS AND SYSTEMS

Previous attempts to organize the communication research field have concentrated on "what" scholars do and "how" they do it. The categories thus reflect combinations of the phenomena studied (interpersonal versus mass communication), goals sought (basic versus applied), intellectual tradition (social science versus humanism), methods used (experiments versus surveys versus content analysis), nature of the data (quantitative versus qualitative), and the part of a communication model examined (communicator versus message versus audience). These distinctions tend to force neophyte scholars into choices they might not have to make. They separate much that could be integrated, but also combine much that needs separation.

Theory building requires concepts that are defined and measured at the same level of abstraction as the phenomena being explained. The history of communication research is replete with examples of mixing "sociological" and "psychological" variables to maximize prediction. This results in confusion over causal processes and little understanding. Another tendency is "system-jumping"—using a concept defined at one level of analysis as an explanation at another. This is illogical and leads to faulty policy recommendations. For example, it was once thought that if communication raised need-achievement motivation in individuals, an achieving society would result (McClelland, 1961). There is also reverse system-jumping. If we improved diffusion of information (Rogers & Shoemaker, 1971) or made media more available (Lerner, 1957), the individual subsistence farmer would supposedly benefit.

Levels of analysis do not in themselves constitute theories, although they may shape theories. They belong in the realm of meta-theory. What determines the level of analysis of any theoretical and/or empirical work is the unit being observed (e.g., synapse, individual, society) and the degree of abstraction used to analyze that unit. Communication at the physiological level uses variables describing cellular, brain, or nervous system functioning. Intrapersonal variables describe cognitive processing, personality style, and the like. Interpersonal communication theory adds variables reflecting relationships between individuals. Social systems are analyzed in terms of the properties, relations, and processes of organized collections of individuals, including institutions, laws, and norms. This institutional quality makes the study of macrosocial communication frustrating and yet all the more rewarding.

Theoretical statements are often made about the role of communication in societies, but the evidence for testing hypotheses from those statements is based on data about individuals. For example, it is frequently asserted that the increasing dominance of television over print has lowered the quality of election campaigns. Properties of campaigns cannot logically be inferred solely from effects on individuals, but the supporting evidence consists of associations between high individual use of television news relative to print and various negative individual political outcomes: low information (Becker & Whitney, 1980; Patterson & McClure, 1976); low trust and political efficacy (Robinson, 1975, 1976); and emphasis on candidate images in making voting decisions (McLeod, Glynn, & McDonald, 1983). These findings are certainly germane to the theoretical statement, but there is much more to the complexities of media and electoral politics than cognitive effects on individual voters.

These are examples of what Lazarsfeld (1959) labeled *analytical* variables. Nations can be compared on the basis of variables with individual counterparts (e.g., hours spent watching television) or without them (e.g., standard deviations of television time). The latter type of dispersion variable is the key indicator for one important mass communication issue, the widening or narrowing "knowledge gap" (Donohue,

Tichenor, & Olien, 1975; Ettema & Kline, 1977; McLeod, Bybee, & Durall, 1979).

Lazarsfeld (1959) specified two other types of variables more clearly appropriate to social systems and more independent of individuals. *Structural* variables describe relations between individuals (e.g., sociometric choice in a small group) or between subunits in a larger social system (e.g., strength of communication links between community organizations). *Global* variables deal with a collective situation irrespective of its relation to individual members (e.g., "richness" in number of sources of information; type of media ownership and control). Macrosocial system research mostly confines itself to analytical variables formed by aggregating individual data. This reflects imbalance and lack of attention to structural and global variables.

The idea of levels of analysis for communication theory presupposes the concept of "system," a bounded set of interrelationships between units. Systems are most usefully viewed not as static but as dynamic organizations in constant change. Systems differentiate; units within the system specialize and develop interdependence with other units. Relationships within the system can be analyzed, as can those between the system and other systems. A given unit can belong to one subsystem under some conditions and to other subsystems under other conditions.

The analysis of a system reflects the theoretical and methodological strategies of the researcher. Systems can be described in terms of their parts, their processes, their antecedents, or their consequences. Systems can be viewed either as closed, where over time all causal influences are present, or open, where new variables exert influence at different times. Change can be seen as either emanating within the system (internally) or entering from outside (externally). These options lead to very different kinds of theoretical systems.

Communication can be seen as a process necessary for both control and change in any social system. Communication may also be thought of as a social system, as in the term "media system." This has been defined in varied ways. Some refer to a particular media organization (e.g., *New York Times*, BBC). Others think of media system as a set of organizations within a medium (e.g., U.S. commercial television) or across media (e.g., the news media). Still others include media organizational roles, information sources, and audience members.

Regardless of the boundaries of the media system, its systematic character can serve at least three functions. First, it provides structured role expectations regardless of who fills those roles. The *structural* dimension is not confined to formal positions; it may include, for example, relationships with news sources. We can also speak of audience roles as part of a larger media system. Second, systems provide continuity over time, reflecting the influence of the past on present ways of doing things.

This *historical* dimension was evident in research on the first European parliamentary election, where policies for television were largely drawn from the election broadcasting traditions of each individual country (Blumler, 1983).

Media systems exhibit a third function, what might be termed the *power* dimension, in constraining those hoping to achieve their goals within them. While the goals of media organizations may be shared by journalists and others within them (and even by news sources and others outside), the individual actors are also pursuing their own goals. The journalists' goals may reflect a struggle for vertical mobility or may derive from professional commitments potentially in conflict with organizational goals.

All three functions represent dimensions scholars can aim to account for at the macrosocial level. This has implications for the kinds of data needed in order to understand systems functioning.

Mass media systems are inter-related and interdependent. The boundaries of the system are defined according to the requirements of the research problem. As long as we have observable properties, we can close the system temporarily for scholarly examination. These boundaries may be "media-centric" (closing to a given media organization) or more broadly delineated (focusing, for example, on a communication system comprising news sources, media personnel, and the audience).

Media systems differ from other types of social systems in that they make contact with an extraordinary variety of external systems—political, economic, and cultural. This reflects the broad responsibilities that media systems assume as mediators between societal institutions. The interdependence with other systems and the mediating role are among the reasons why, contrary to some political-economic media theorists, we maintain that media systems are not entirely derivable from their social structure or culture. That is, knowing the economic and political system of a nation does not permit easy prediction as to what its media system will be like. Media arrangements are admittedly partially dependent on both social structure and culture, but important characteristics of them are *sui generis,* meriting study in their own right.

Media systems also depend upon economic, political, and other social systems. Regardless of the form of financial support, media systems must operate within economic constraints. Political arrangements not only provide the legal framework for operation of the media system but also represent common, complementary, and antagonistic interests.

It follows from the *sui generis* qualities of media systems that scholars should identify distinctive features of media systems, specifying dimensions to facilitate comparisons between nations or communities. A distinctive cultural feature of media organizations is their independence from other systems and efforts to preserve it. Patterns of shifting dependence and resulting struggles to preserve autonomy invite research.

In general, the search for conflict is a valuable strategy for examination of media systems. Burns (1977) traced much conflict in the BBC to adherence to three different role orientations: a commitment to traditional cultural "standards" as goals for public broadcasting; adherence to the craft of making "good television"; and a pragmatic emphasis on management goals and audience ratings. Blumler, Gurevitch, and Nossiter (1986) found the contrasting perspectives of the news and the current affairs departments of the BBC to be systematically related to conflicting views over how the organization should cover British election campaigns.

Finally, macrosocial communication analysis can often be advanced by constructing a model of the main elements and relationships of interest. McQuail and Windahl (1981) point out that models have an "*organizing function* by ordering and relating systems to each other and by providing us with images of wholes that we might not otherwise perceive." They also highlight key relationships for theory building, clarify hypotheses by expressing them diagrammatically, and indicate links to other subsystems. Blumler and Thoveron (1983) modeled the elements of an election broadcasting system for comparative research in nine European Economic Community (EEC) countries during the first European parliamentary elections. Their scheme included actor roles (politicians, mediators, and audience electors); forms of media and contents; direction of dominant message flows; filters standing between senders and receivers, which might or might not let messages pass; and links to national party and media systems.

THE NEED FOR MACRO-LEVEL
COMMUNICATION SCHOLARSHIP

In the 1970s communication research in the United States was widely criticized as lopsided. Virtually defining the field in terms of effects on individuals, it had ignored a host of larger controversies from which the real world of mass communication cannot be isolated (Blumler, 1978). Is the modern communication system a plural set of media outlets, serving the differential needs of a pluralist society, or a set of conformist institutions conveying the ingredients of a socially conservative consensus? How are the functions of social control and social change intertwined? What determines the power relations between media and other institutional sectors in the social system? These issues remind us that communication science without a macro component would be impoverished and seriously incomplete. There are three fundamental reasons why macro-level communication scholarship is essential. These have to do with our need for understanding, for policy, and for analyzing media systems in their own terms.

The first reason, a strategy for greater understanding, is *to extend the range of settings in which hypotheses of communication science at other levels can be tested; to stretch the external validity of propositions of other levels; and to identify the circumstances in which such propositions apply.*

Most empirical observation of communication phenomena has been confined to a single national or local media system. Consequently, although many propositions about functions of the mass media are couched in universal terms, the evidence in support of them is almost always culture specific. In politics, for example, it may be true that the mass media set voters' issue agendas (McCombs & Shaw, 1972), erode trust in leaders and the legitimacy of institutions (Robinson, 1975), foster spectator orientations (Patterson, 1980), tell people what is safe to talk about (Noelle-Neumann, 1983), and depict the urban world as a violent and unsafe place (Gerbner, Gross, Morgan, & Signorielli, 1980). But it would really be quite staggering, given the world's many different cultural, stratification, political, and media systems, if these inferences from a few Western societies were to apply around the globe.

Universality of communication influences would be plausible only if media systems were (a) transnationally similar and (b) autonomous from influences stemming from the sociopolitical environment. As to the former, it may be (as Golding, 1977, and Golding & Elliott, 1979, allege) that journalists throughout the West approach their jobs under the influence of highly similar self-images, news values, and legitimating creeds—and that their approach has been transferred to underdeveloped societies as well. But this is an empirical question; the evidence for it is thin, and there is much contrary evidence. For example, research into European election communication produced a "revelation of the complexity of campaign communication processes and of the intrusion into them of culturally unique features at many points" (Blumler, 1983). The other condition—universal media autonomy—flies in the face of all we know about the impact of the varying pressures that are imposed on journalists in different political systems.

Replication, then, is an essential antidote to unwarranted generalization from findings in one system. Replication strategies should not be pursued indiscriminately, but in sites with theoretical justifications in the form of reasons for supposing that in varying circumstances communication might work differently (see Gudykunst, Chapter 27 in this volume).

One can replicate across societies. For example, does agenda setting work in countries other than the United States, where it was originally tested? Agenda setting might be a peculiarly American phenomenon.

Political controversy in the United States tends to revolve around sharply focused issues, which shift from year to year. American media are organized to facilitate agenda setting (e.g., the 22-minute television news program, hierarchically ordering items from top to bottom). Does the spiral of silence operate in countries other than the one, West Germany, from which that concept emerged? Predicated on a supposed fear of isolation from voicing unpopular views, it could be culturally defined. This might explain recent nonreplication in the United States (Glynn & McLeod, 1985).

Replication can also be attempted across communities within a country. For example, how does legislative incumbency translate into media coverage across constituencies with differing candidate-status patterns? One might replicate individual-level research to generate macro-level propositions. For example, if there is more evidence of agenda setting among lower-status individuals with weaker ties to the organized political system, that might tell us something about communication features of the society (McLeod, Becker, & Byrnes, 1974). In uses and gratifications research, cognitive needs might not tie as closely to knowledge gain in systems that do not cherish and reward cognitive motivation. Different national audience responses to an international television program might tell us something about cultural distinctiveness. Thus replication is a genuinely macrosocial exercise, to be undertaken on the assumption that system features should make a difference to the empirical association.

In sum, replications of hypotheses of communication science in different settings are important in their own right, for gaining knowledge about other aspects of society, for telling us how communication operates at other levels, and for forcing reconceptualizations of theories. Replicated macrosocial research should help to transcend naive universalism. Theories should be generally applicable and "able to cross national boundaries" (Glynn & McLeod, 1984), but good theory should include propositions about how phenomena will differ in varying conditions.

A second reason for undertaking macrosocietal research is that *most policy issues involving the organization of communication arise at that level.* Media institutions, for example, are not mere conduits of information flows without consequence in their own right. They may help to realize or thwart a whole range of potentially valid purposes: fair access, opportunities for opinion leadership, equality of informational power, representation of social groupings, avoidance of manipulation, fulfillment of audience needs, or promotion of an informed democracy. Only evidence on media relationships to other institutions can clarify what is happening and what might need to be put right.

This is not to proclaim a scientific authority over values but to accept the assumption on which, according to Chaffee and Berger (Chapter 3), a science of human communication rests; namely, that "behavior can be both understood and improved through systematic study." Some policy recommendations can be addressed to individuals (e.g., parents might be urged to control their children's TV viewing habits or to talk to them about what they have seen), but even these appeals have to be initiated by macro-level institutions. Almost all communication policy issues focus on the organization, practices, and consequences of media for related social institutions.

For example, proposed communication roles in the development of Third World societies are based on analyses of media organization in the societies concerned, and of national media systems in the international market or vis-à-vis domestic power centers (Katz & Wedell, 1978). To clarify for the British government alternative ways of financing the BBC, Blumler, Brynin, and Nossiter (1986) examined the scheduling and programming consequences of different funding arrangements in seven countries. These ranged from full advertising through mixed sources to purely public grants. Similarly, on the basis of comparative newsroom observation in Britain and the United States, Blumler, Gurevitch, and Nossiter (1986) evaluated advantages for service to viewers and the needs of democracy of several different ways of combining bulletin-type campaign reporting with more extended political analysis.

A third reason for macro-level research stems from the essence of communication as a relationship spanning individuals or systems. Media institutions are intermediate agencies, standing between would-be sources of communication and would-be consumers. Thus *social system linkages are at the very heart of media systems and need to be traced for their architecture, dynamics, and effects.* This is not to suggest that the mass media serve merely as hyphens, connecting various spheres. There is far more interaction, interpenetration, and influence between media systems and cultural, political, and economic systems than such a passive metaphor could capture.

Media institutions are indispensable to realization of the objectives of institutions in other spheres. For example, in the political system, the transmission of initiatives from leaders to led and of expectations the other way round is largely performed by the media system. Conflicts and potential accommodations between crucial subgroups (management/ labor, conservatives/liberals, Wasps/ethnics, heterosexuals/homosexuals, etc.) are frequently aired and tried out via media. Advertising in commercial media facilitates market transactions of modern economies by structuring consumer choice. Communication sources therefore develop strategies of manipulation, ingratiation, and control to enhance their chances in the media. Media personnel tailor their offerings to suppositions about what viewers, listeners, and readers will find interesting, significant, exciting, relevant, plausible, and comprehensible, which are ultimately rooted in societal cultures.

A strong impression of the system character of communication arrangements emerged from research on the role of television in the European parliamentary elections to voters in nine EEC countries in 1979 (Blumler, 1983). For example: (a) Although the election was unprecedented, policies for presenting it to viewers were brought closely into line with each country's existing model of domestic general election organization. (b) The range of campaign communicators was quite narrow, implying that their participation was system legitimated, unlike that of others whose involvement would have been resented by established figures. (c) In the issues they addressed, different types of communicators (e.g., politicians and journalists) were more like their national counterparts than like their international peers. System features, in other words, had helped to align their contributions toward each other. (d) Both journalists and politicians were influenced by their impressions of how audience members might react to European election talk. They entered "into 'mental' relations with the audience, styling their messages according to images they [had] formed of its likely receptivity to their wares."

HISTORICAL REASONS FOR
MACROSOCIAL RESEARCH NEGLECT

Given the strong reasons for macro-level scholarship, it is curious that empirically based communication research until rather recently had neglected the study of mass communication phenomena in social system terms. It is useful to think of four broad historical eras in the development of mass communication as a research field: early awareness of societal consequences of communication prior to the twentieth century; attempts to develop research dating from the early parts of this century; efforts to construct mass communication as a field starting in the early 1950s; and the reconstruction of the field beginning around 1970 (compare Delia, Chapter 2).

Nineteenth-Century Theories

We could begin with Plato and Aristotle, whose conceptions of communication had much to do with what we now call problems of social control. For our purposes, however, it is better to start with the analyses of society that emerged in Western Europe in the late nineteenth century largely in response to the industrial revolution. Many of these analyses included conjecture about the role of the press, so they have obvious relevance to macrosocietal communication scholarship. In an attempt to demonstrate early European concern with communication, Lang (1979) cites particularly Tarde (1890) on the role of the press in the formation of public opinion. The contribution of these early works to macrosocial communication theory is limited by their lack of specificity. The press was only one among many social institutions characterizing the "modern" world. Further, analyses were cast in terms of "ideal types" based on dichotomies representing preindustrial societies at one extreme and industrial societies at the other. These included Maine's (1885) status-contract, Toennies' (1887) gemeinschaft-gesellschaft, and Durkheim's (1893) mechanical-organic solidarity. Each end of the spectrum was packed with a compound of characteristics, often without any clear empirical referent. More recent scholars have had difficulty generating continuous variables from these analyses.

While the "modern" end of these dichotomies included both high levels of both social disorganization and problems and the rise of press power, these were not seen as inescapably linked, the press as necessarily contributing to social problems. Rather, nineteenth-century theorists considered as problematic the question of whether social institutions in the industrial world could compensate for the loss of the close personal ties and stable norms of earlier times. Social theorists of the twentieth century vary on this question. Cooley (1909), Dewey (1927), Park (1938), and Wirth (1948) acknowledged the potential dangers of press influence but realized its limited power, and each saw the newspaper as potentially playing a compensatory and integrative role in society.

More negative views were embodied in mass society models, in which the media increased alienation and provided a substitute reality for isolated, passive, and gullible audiences (Arendt, 1951; Fromm, 1941; Kornhauser, 1959; Mills, 1956; Ortega y Gasset, 1932). It is important to note, however, that "mass society" was not a label applied by those theorists themselves; rather it was a construction by Kornhauser (1959) and by Bramson (1961) that loosely classified a collection of writers who, though they shared some assumptions, represented a wide range of ideological viewpoints. The legacy of the nineteenth-century theorists did not automatically imply powerful and negative media effects, nor did later scholars unanimously assume such effects.

Setting the Research Agenda

Although content analyses of newspapers began almost a century ago (Speed, 1893) and readership studies of audiences go back at least to 1902 (Scott, 1921; Scott, Clothier, & Spriegel, 1949), such traces are too scattered to discern their overall tie to macrosocietal concerns. More instructive are attempts to set a research agenda starting with Max Weber (1910) and his prospectus for a sociology of the press in Germany. Lang (1979) notes that Weber's proposal had a solid empirical basis, a feature that is counter to current stereotypes of European traditions. Weber dealt with audience effects along with more macroscopic questions such as capitalistic organization of the press and the origins of national press systems.

Empirical analysis also played an important role in the Institute of Social Research in Germany. From its beginnings at Frankfurt in the early 1920s through the amplification of critical theory, the institute attempted to reconcile theory and facts, not replace one with the other. One of the institute's major activities under director Carl Grunberg was documentation of workers' movements. What distinguished the institute from dominant American and German scholarship was its interdisciplinary and critical strategy. The role and structure of communication was but one aspect in the macro analyses offered. The Institute acquired financial independence in order to support intellectual independence, and fostered "pure research" to counter the trend in universities toward "practical training" (Jay, 1973). Yet founding members Max Horkheimer and Friedrich Pollock, along with later joiners such as Erich Fromm and Theodor W. Adorno, wholeheartedly believed in the applicability of their work. Jay describes the tension for the left-wing intellectual of "maintaining a critical distance from the movement on whose victory he counts." The research agenda was not a list of topics but an approach: In exploration of social phenomena, theory development was placed before fact gathering; in politics, theory before praxis.

If popular stereotypes of American communication research were valid, we would expect research in the United States from the earliest days to be descriptive, individualistic, and lacking in social concern. Yet the agenda offered by one of the founders of journalism education, Willard G. Bleyer (1924), reveals a distinctly reformist outlook. He called for the analysis of accuracy and completeness, for the influence of editorials in bringing about reforms, for the assessment of press effects on the ideas and ideals of the readers, and for the analysis of the influence of publicity and propaganda in newspapers. Bleyer's recommendation for study of the effects of competition on news policy resembles what Weber had proposed a decade earlier. Although Bleyer's academic background was in the humanities, he had considerable influence in aligning the teaching of journalism with the social sciences and in providing a rationale for doing so (Bleyer, 1931). For Bleyer, journalism education was justified primarily because of media influences on society, and he pushed well beyond reform to "constructive journalism" (1916, 1934).

A better-known communication research agenda was that of Paul Lazarsfeld (1948). He identified 16 types of mass media effects by crossing four sources of influence acting on four types of objects. For our purposes here, it is worth noting that at least one of these sources is of macrosocial significance—the socioeconomic control structure of the media; and at least two of the objects being influenced have social system relevance—the social group and the institutional structure of society. Overall, roughly half of the potential effects in Lazarsfeld's 16-cell matrix were not individualistic but macrosocial in conception. Although Lazarsfeld himself tended to study only a limited portion of his effects matrix using largely survey research methods, his vision of communication research included a much greater variety. Earlier he had seen a vitalizing role for critical theory, a clearly macrosocial perspective using mainly nonempirical methods (Lazarsfeld, 1941), and had collaborated with Adorno.

Even these few examples of research agenda setting prior to 1950 indicate macro conceptions of the role of the mass media on both sides of the Atlantic Ocean. Yet microindividual work flourished while macrosocial research was neglected. The decline of European macrosocietal work is the result of its being uprooted by Hitler and World War II. But on the American side it was self-inflicted. Journalism educators assumed a powerful role for the media and taught reporting and editing on the premise that good technique would lead somehow to positive social effects, bad technique to negative influence of the media. Communication research in scattered social science fields saw communication as a relatively minor and limited aspect of larger social questions. These assumptions, though working from different directions, discouraged testing of macro communication hypotheses, which were formulated as answers and expressed in normative terms—not as research questions.

Emergence as a Field

The start of communication as an autonomous academic discipline is hard to date, but a good case can be made for the 1954 publication of Wilbur Schramm's *The Process and Effects of Mass Communication*. It was only in the 1950s that independent research centers and doctoral programs began using the labels "communication" or "mass communication." Schramm (1954) stitched together more than three dozen papers on communication by social scientists from many disciplines. Roughly half of the chapters were conceptualized in macrosocietal terms, a proportion retained in a revised edition 17 years later (Schramm & Roberts, 1971). If his editorial selections were evenhanded with respect to level of analysis, Schramm's (1954) selection of information theory and representational learning theory as models for "how communication works" could scarcely stimulate macrosocial research. These models, though, reflected quite well what was happening in the 1950s in social science generally and in the larger political scene.

It is difficult to capture the heady optimism of social science in the postwar years when communication was becoming an academic field.

Social scientists could find funding not only through applied research contracts but also for basic research grants advancing themselves and their disciplines. They became more prominent in academic circles as student enrollments grew, although their legitimacy was viewed with suspicion by "hard" scientists. Anxious to use new and improved techniques of data gathering and analysis to advance their claims of being "objective and scientific," they conspicuously avoided "arm-chair theorizing" and the older techniques of observation and analysis. Those activities are often central to macrosocial theory and research.

Optimism permeated many aspects of American science and technology in the postwar era. Enthusiasts believed the same technology that helped to win the war could be used to solve economic and social problems throughout the world. Social science could help clarify these problems, and communication was a likely vehicle to transmit technology and knowledge to the "underdeveloped" peoples of the world. The neutrality of social science knowledge was tacitly assumed. Researchers, by making results available to all, would allow the best ideas to triumph. These views of social science seem naive today, but it was not until the political upheavals of the late 1960s that the neutrality and control of knowledge were strongly challenged. This social scientific elan had a formative and persistent influence on American communication research and its neglect of macrosocial research.

Communication researchers arrived late at the table of social science celebration. Those from other social sciences could use their affiliations to pursue their research objectives; few identified themselves with communication and many went on to study other topics. The new self-designated communication scholars of the 1950s and 1960s sought legitimacy and research guidance wherever they could. Social psychology seemed an excellent field to emulate. It too was a latecomer to social science; and after the contributions of social psychologists to research projects in World War II, it was enjoying marked growth and prominence at the time Schramm was constructing the field. Various aspects of communication were among the major variables social psychologists examined, and their bilevel theorizing had considerable appeal.

If emulation of social psychology was a good choice generally, it was not a productive one for macrosocietal communication research. Experimental studies of attitude change in World War II (Hovland, Lumsdaine, & Sheffield, 1949) had been a major part of Schramm's (1954) *Process and Effects* reader. Attitude change became the dominant idea of social psychology with the entrance of cognitive balance theories (Festinger, 1957; Heider, 1958; Newcomb, 1953; Rosenberg, 1960). Of these homeostatic theories even the most "social" simply analyzed the relationship between a person's perceptions of others' opinions and the actual opinions expressed by others (Newcomb, 1953). More generally in social psychology, "social" tended to be defined as the group created in the laboratory or the small primary group; attention was drawn away from variables of larger social systems.

It is instructive to note what did not appear in early formulations of the communication field. Although Schramm (1954) chose four selections concerning "communicating to another culture," none dealt with the then-prominent hypothesis of Whorf (1938) that a person's experience of the world is shaped by that person's language. Psycholinguistics, which might have bridged mass and interpersonal communication, did not "take off" until the early 1960s. Sociolinguistics, the study of the interactions of language structure and speech performance with social structure, became salient enough later in the decade to become a chapter (Grimshaw, 1973) in the *Handbook of Communication* (Pool, Frey, Schramm, Maccoby, & Parker, 1973). But at the beginning of the field, mass communication and the study of language were peculiarly compartmentalized. More generally, the separation of mass communication from other forms of communication behavior was fostered by the division of academic departments into journalism, with its professional and social science roots, and speech communication, with origins in the humanities.

The Columbia University research program of Lazarsfeld and his colleagues had tremendous impact on the field. Macrosocial research was particularly influenced by two voting studies (Lazarsfeld, Berelson, & Gaudet, 1948; Berelson, Lazarsfeld, & McPhee, 1954) and personal influence research (Katz & Lazarsfeld, 1955). These studies gained a strong hold on the field (Gitlin, 1978, refers to them as the "dominant paradigm") despite the fact that they represented small, homogeneous communities in a pretelevision era. Each contained proper cautionary notes about its limitations and the need for replication, but even today we find social science texts that treat their conclusions as enduring specimens of knowledge.

Our understanding of voting behavior and interpersonal processes was greatly enhanced, but the early studies focused on the individual voter or consumer. Individualistic concepts such as selective exposure and reinforcement, or at most interpersonal models such as the "two-step flow," predominated in data analysis and interpretation. There were no community variables, and no concern for structural constraints; demographic differences were viewed as individual "predispositions." The Decatur study of personal influence ignored considerations of power and conflict at the community or society level. A homeostatic model of small group functions—drawn from social psychology—served as the intellectual background to the empirical analysis. The researchers looked for consensus formation within groups, not conflict between groups. There was an absence of structure. Katz and Lazarsfeld (1955) implied that inter-personal communication flowed on all topics, equally across all sectors and status levels of the community. Except in public affairs, opinion leaders were seen as status equals to their followers. The lack of gener-ality of opinion leadership across various spheres of influence supported an egalitarian view of society. Given this study's widespread acceptance at the time, it is not surprising that community conflict did not break through as an important topic for communication research until the 1970s (Tichenor, Donohue, & Olien, 1980).

In the years following the Columbia studies, analysts invoked a sharp contrast between the knowledge of media effects gained from the voting and personal influence studies and previous images of powerful, direct, and universal media effects on isolated and gullible audience members. The latter views of powerful effects were supposed to have been widely accepted until Lazarsfeld and others came along to dispel the notion. The theory of powerful effects was variously ridiculed as "hypodermic" (Katz, 1960), "bullet" (Schramm & Roberts, 1971), and "magic bul-let" (Lowery & DeFleur, 1983); at the societal level it was associated with mass society theory. Theories of powerful effects appear to have been a straw man set up for rhetorical and pedagogical purposes, but the assertion of near universal pre-World War II acceptance of powerful effects has endured. It is true that propaganda analysts following Lass-well (1927) inferred strong audience impact from the examination of content alone, that influential writers like Walter Lippmann (1922) por-trayed a gullible public, and that there was considerable public and offi-cial concern about the effects of propaganda from World War I through World War II. In the 1940s many American high school students were exposed to the Lee and Lee (1939) analysis of propaganda techniques ("card stacking," "glittering generalities") in the hope that they could combat propaganda when they encountered it. It is also true, however, that the Payne Fund studies of the early 1930s (Charters, 1933; Peterson & Thurstone, 1933) had showed varied but certainly not powerful effects of movies on children. The universality of effects was challenged by data showing differential effects depending on various aspects of background and personality. Hovland et al. (1949) showed that experimental effects of propaganda were unlikely to be direct and universal. In any event, mass society theories were only one among many macrosocial perspec-tives of the pre-1950 era. The equating of macrosocial theory with a naive view of powerful media effects did little to stimulate further theo-rizing and research at that level.

Klapper (1960) and Berelson (1959) went even further toward con-veying an impression that media effects are minor and embedded in a host of necessary conditions. This was partly an outcome of the Colum-bia group's focus on persuasion in the alteration of attitudes and behavior. Had information been the focus, a stronger assessment might have been made. Berelson went on to try to assemble and catalog the findings of mass communication along with everything else he believed to be known about human behavior (Berelson & Steiner, 1964). The effort seemed naive even then, but it was assumed that knowledge of human behavior was invariant over time and place.

Although there was a decline in research activity on social effects of media during the 1950s and early 1960s, we should not imply that the Klapper doctrine of limited effects was universally accepted. McQuail (1984) mentions four researchers who realized that effects could be important without the media being necessary and sufficient (Blumler, 1964; Halloran, 1964; Key, 1961; Lang & Lang, 1959). A decade later their views of stronger and more diversified effects became much less the minority view in the field.

The search for legitimacy took many directions for researchers entering the communication field in the 1950s and 1960s. Lacking specific theoretical guidance, some turned to concepts and hypotheses borrowed from diverse fields while others tried to articulate highly abstract models that would capture communication processes and effects at all levels. Many of the borrowed concepts turned out to have little payoff for communication theory, and there tended to be a time lag between the appearance of a concept in its original field and its appearance in communication research. Models of the communication process—those using source-receiver terminology for example—proved to be overly general, lacking in their generation of theoretical propositions and failing to convey any sensitive understanding of human communication behavior.

Many researchers tried to find solace in methodological innovation in lieu of guiding theory. Over the years, various statistical and methodological techniques were seized upon: Factor analysis, the semantic differential, and Q-methodology were followed by present-day path analysis, Galilean coordinate systems, and Lisrel. These require large data sets, which individual-level measures provide in greatest abundance. To the extent that survey research and experimentation were particularly attractive research techniques in the United States, macrosocial analyses were neglected by communication research for many years.

Recent Developments

During the late 1960s and early 1970s, communication research began to show signs of both growth and maturity. In the United States an increasing number of college students studying communication supported a dramatic increase in teachers of communication and in the volume of their research. With more scholars looking for new topics and doing research on a wider range of effects using more sensitive analytic techniques, it is not surprising that an image of much stronger media impact emerged with evidence to back it up. The growing evidence of media effects eventually attracted the attention of other social science disciplines, particularly political science, where traditional wisdom was being challenged. It became apparent, for example, that political party affiliation was declining in level and in its ability to predict voting behavior. It was suspected that television might be replacing the party as a source of influence (Nie, Verba, & Petrocik, 1976). A growing number of American political scientists focused on the role of mass media in elections (Graber, 1980; Patterson, 1980; Patterson & McClure, 1976; Ranney, 1983; Robinson, 1977; Robinson & Sheehan, 1983).

Outside the United States communication was becoming, from the early 1960s onward, an increasingly respectable sphere of study, in which from the outset societal perspectives were natural, central and legitimate—even obligatory. Many forces encouraged scholars in Europe, Latin America, and Asia to look at communication in macroscopic terms.

One was a reaction against the perceived overpreoccupation of American research with individual-level audience phenomena. Halloran (1974) argued for an extension of the field's boundaries in two directions. One was toward "the factors that govern or influence what the media make available" for consumption, which are a selection of what could be provided and not just a matter of chance. Researchers should be asking questions about the "development of media institutions," their "organization and structure," their patterns of "control, resources and technology," as well as studying the "professional values and day-to-day operations of those working in the media" (p. 5). Nor should this be individualized; it was *not* a matter of studying the *personal* decisions of a gatekeeper (see White, 1950). The other step was to explore the social environment surrounding mass media functioning. In Halloran's (1974) words,

> What is made available by the media, and consequently what helps to shape attitudes and values, will be influenced by a whole series of economic, legal, political, professional and technological considerations. [So,] to understand the part played by the media in our society, we must study the whole communication process [in] these appropriate contexts. (p. 6)

A second major source of influence was the rise of television as a mass medium while communication researchers were looking for objects of study. Television's problematic relations to state authority and to the marketplace were best addressed through macrosocial policy concepts. There was also a gradual loss of faith among supporters of the political left that the forces of history were basically on their side. The obstacles to progressive political change were far more powerful and the props to prevailing social orders far more enduring than expected. Among these, the roles of communication organization, professional assumptions, and patterned messages deserved special consideration.

Fourth, there was the liberation of a host of colonies from their imperial masters and their entry as ostensibly sovereign and independent actors into what eventually proved to be a highly structured, hierarchical, and uncongenial international arena of political, economic, and communication power. Studies of cultural dependency, constraints on communication roles in national development, and imbalances in news flows followed.

Probably the controversiality of communication arrangements in many non-American societies is a fifth factor of some significance. Media organizations need not be commercial enterprises, their contents need not be shielded from political influence, nor their public obligations lightly enforced. In many countries, diverse models of media organization exist side by side, their rival merits regularly compared and debated. Consider, for example, the Scandinavian preoccupation with communication as a force that may serve or hamper culturally supported egalitarian commitments (Thunberg, Nowak, Rosengren, & Bengt, 1982), the German preoccupation with relations between media elites and political elites, and the British fascination with the interplay of media systems and social class systems.

Conditions may be ripe for a reconstruction of the field reclaiming much of the earlier macrosocial legacy of communication. The last decade of communication research in the United States has broken away from the postwar mold of short-term attitudinal effects on individuals. Longitudinal designs have made possible the assessment of longer-term effects, and informational and other cognitive effect criteria have been studied that are more suitable to macrosocial concerns. Effects on populations (e.g., the increased homogenization of outlook among audience members) rather than on individuals are conducive to answering macro-level questions. Although the study of differential effects has a long history, the systematic study of structural variation in effects is of relatively recent origin.

There appears also to be a lessening of the compartmentalization of research that separated the audience from other parts of the communication process. This is particularly evident in the recent return to the macro-level study of mass media organizations (e.g., Bagdikian, 1983; Blumler, 1969; Blumler & Gurevitch, 1986; Burns, 1977; Epstein, 1973; Fishman, 1980; Gans, 1979; Tuchman, 1978; Tunstall, 1971).

Contact with humanistic perspectives has also enriched the study of communication messages (see Farrell, Chapter 4). Whereas for many years Berelson's (1952) emphasis on the *manifest* content of messages and its attendant focus on intercoder reliability held sway, the perspectives of semiotics and more subtle and latent, if less reliable, meanings of messages have begun to balance the content analyses of communication messages. A given message may produce varying readings by the audience and these alternative readings may be organized according to cultural and social structural location (Hall, 1977; Liebes & Katz, 1986; Morley, 1980).

SCIENTIFIC EXPLANATION
AND SOCIAL SYSTEM ANALYSIS

At a minimum, science requires acceptable measurement in the controlled observation or manipulation of key concepts. Second, there should be a high ratio of relationships between these explicated concepts and unverifiable assertions about undefined concepts. Third, there should be some form of control over contaminating or confounding influences, and serious consideration should be given to alternative explanations. Fourth, there is a need for at least one formal comparison of a given group or system with an explicit or implicit control group. Thus in both its abstract theoretical statements and in the gathering of evidence, theory should be falsifiable. Finally, the set of theoretical statements must be sufficiently abstract to separate research from sheer description. The level of abstraction of theory at the social system level will, of necessity, vary greatly. But unless it has some generality across time and place, it can hardly be called scientific.

In setting out this rough list of minimal conditions for scientific research conducive to the development of knowledge, we must be careful to clarify what is not required. No particular method is essential nor is any approach inherently superior to any other. In fact, the accumulation of knowledge at the social system level is more likely to result from a combination of methodological strategies. Although we should avoid assuming that all theoretical explanations are equally valid, reality is so profoundly complex that no single theoretical approach can provide more than a partial explanation.

We find many of the arguments raised by Manicas and Secord (1983) to be appropriate to the issues of theoretical development at the macrosocial level. They adopt the "realist critique" in the "new philosophy of science" (Bhaskar, 1975, 1982; Harré, 1972) in asserting that theories are "constitutive of the known world, but that they are not *of* the world." That is, theories do not and cannot capture the reality of the entire world, and theories and their constituent concepts are not "out there" in some kind of natural state. They are built by the theorist. Events of the world are complex composites, a temporary concatenation of many causal forces acting at various levels; hence, these events are not fully capturable by any given theory nor should they be. Their prediction may be made on an actuarial basis. One might proceed in the prediction process by plugging variables from many theories at different levels of abstraction into a grand stepwise regression. However strong a prediction might be produced in this manner, it does not constitute an explanation providing a "sense of understanding" and it is not the stuff of science.

One need not buy all the particulars of the realist position to benefit from its implications for communication research. Theories are attempts at partial explanations of communication behavior that are examined by developing temporarily closed systems that are in contrast to the "real world," which is an open system. Theories are thus limited in several respects. Their temporary nature constrains application to the particular set of variables and conditions so enclosed. Theories are also limited in their conceptualization to a given level of abstraction; one seeks to establish their validity at the given level and not by seeking superiority over explanations framed at other levels.

The goal of science, according to this argument, is more to achieve a sense of understanding within level and with temporary closure rather than to predict behavior in all levels and conditions. Understanding is most likely when we look at human behavior consistently within a given level of analysis.

The Manicas and Secord position has many implications for communication research. If there are no "natural" variables out there waiting to be discovered and measured in near perfect form, then measurement must be preceded by painstaking explication of conceptual definitions with dimensions and multiple indicators. Measurement tries to reflect these conceptual definitions, but the measurement of their indicators is apt to be highly imperfect.

Forms of Explanation

Theory can be defined as an organized explanation of a pattern of observed or to-be-observed events or behaviors. In the macrosocial case, this would be an assertion of "why" a given pattern of relationships occurs. It is often claimed there is a lack of theory in communication, but in the broadest sense there is almost too much theory because so many explanations of social phenomena have been offered. The average person no less than the scholar is apt to make assertions about why things are as they are. What seems lacking is not the availability of explanations but rather their organization in a manner such that they might be compared and evaluated.

Prescientific Forms

Many explanations emerge in everyday life, informally and piece-meal. Detailed moment-by-moment accounts of events may be important data for developing or testing hypotheses, but *sheer description* offered in the guise of explanation is scientifically deficient; it lacks parsimony. Without some organizing concepts and a comparative aspect, description has no generality across time and space. The "how" it happened is there, but the "why" is missing.

Another common explanation from everyday life is the substitution of a label for the description of a phenomenon. *Categorization* is a pseudo-explanation, though it makes more concrete that which we may have been only partially aware of previously. Television weatherpersons, for example, have "explained" extended bitter American winters as resulting from the "Siberian Express" and the "Alberta Clipper." Explanation requires at least two independently observed variables, that which is being explained and the antecedent or other variable used to explain it. Categorization involves only one variable in subsuming specific events under a general label. It can be an important research activity but should not be mistaken for explanation.

The assertion of *communality*—that large numbers of people share the same behavior or situation—is often given as an explanation of individual behavior. For example, physicians sometimes assure a patient that many others are suffering from the same affliction. Even if the process of diffusion from the aggregate to the person were specified, it would answer a question different from the patient's query of how to deal with the illness. One communication example of communality, the prevalence of a particular genre of television program, does not in itself explain how the genre originated nor why it developed, persisted, or declined.

Another kind of nonscientific explanation involves the *presumption of causality* from inadequate evidence. The media critic who asserts that "If kids spend five hours a day with TV, it must have effects" is offering an inference with an element of plausibility. But when the critic goes on to assume that particular effects can be inferred from the content, that audience analysis is unnecessary, and that extended exposure is sufficient to produce such effects, then a very shaky explanation is being offered.

Contiguity is a form of explanation whereby a variable is thought to be caused by another variable solely because they covary in time or space. This reasoning may err in attributing connection or causal direction. For example, television could be seen as the cause of a drop in U.S. voter turnout because television has increasingly been chosen as the dominant election news medium since taking the lead over newspapers in the mid

1960s while voter turnout declined from 1964 to 1980. Without further evidence that television reliance and voter turnout are functionally connected, though, this reasoning may constitute a historical fallacy. A different logical problem, an ecological fallacy, is illustrated by a U.S. study showing that states with the highest levels of pornographic material purchased were also those with the highest incidence of rape. Without individual data showing that pornography is more likely to be read by rapists than by others, we can only see this as a provocative finding without a strong claim to valid explanation.

Acceptable But Incomplete Explanations

Scholars use forms of explanation that are in various ways more elaborate than those of the general public. *Prediction,* the successful estimation of the value of a variable given the value of another variable, has been advanced as a crucial element in a scientific approach. In its purest form, prediction is represented by a regression equation or other mathematical function. Although many communication researchers espouse the view that successful prediction is necessary to call a theoretical perspective scientific, far fewer would argue for prediction as a sufficient condition as well.

The pure positivist position—that sheer prediction represents an adequate explanation—is best illustrated for macrosocial communication research in the Project Revere studies of information diffused from leaflets, conducted between 1951 and 1953 under the direction of Stuart Dodd (DeFleur, 1956; described more fully in Lowery & DeFleur, 1983). The data consisted of plotted coordinates for eight communities, each point representing the ratio of leaflets per capita distributed in a given city and the percentage of respondents who learned the message. Because the eight data coordinates nearly matched predictions based on a classical formula, the mathematical function was reported as if it constituted a scientific explanation. The "who" and "when" were learned, but not the "why."

Another approach to macrosocial explanation is the *location* of various communicator and audience groups in terms of their demographic characteristics. Demographic analyses of media audiences have a long history, but again there is a question of whether knowing the location of the audience tells us *why* any given category uses a given type of content. A demographer might consider the question irrelevant and assert that because only nominal definitions (e.g., education is "years of schooling completed") are used, there is no ambiguity of surplus meaning involved. Others would counter that the "why" is crucial and that even such an apparently straightforward variable becomes complex if we wish to understand the relationship of education to audience behavior.

We would have to go well beyond mere years of schooling to examine a host of other manifestations—including the subject matter studied and type of school—and to control for many other variables that might be related to education.

Quite often in macrosocial analyses we are dealing with an institutional pattern that has endured for some time and originated long before the contemporary situation being analyzed. In such cases, an analysis of the *historical* origins of the enduring pattern becomes an attractive approach to explanation. Many social scientists treat contemporary social phenomena as if they had no history. History has long been a vital but most often separate part of communication research. It is possible to treat the origins and development of media institutions historically in combination with other perspectives, say that of diffusion (DeFleur & Ball-Rokeach, 1982); but we should be cautious about assuming that a historical account of the origins of a pattern represents a complete explanation of the contemporary pattern. The origins of a pattern may not account for its persistence, for example. Stinchcombe (1968) illustrates an approach whereby a functional model is used to explain persistence.

Functional analysis seeks an explanation for the persistence of a pattern in the favorable consequences from previous enactment of the pattern, specifically, success in reducing tension for the system generally or for those controlling the system. Tensions are viewed as arising outside the social system to disturb some homeostatic mechanism or principle. The pattern is one of synthesis in response to tension; its persistence in the future is thus determined by its success at adaptation. Variations of this functional model dominated the field of sociology and macrosocietal analyses for 20 years following World War II. (The Columbia University researchers discussed earlier were clearly influenced by it.) Functionalism was attacked from all sides, the criticisms taking a toll sufficient to induce its severe decline since the late 1960s. It has had something of a rebirth in recent years (reflected in a defense by Alexander, 1981) including reapplication to mass communication.

The attacks on functionalism, and more generally on functional explanations, center on a conservative bias inherent in seeking patterns that repeat and stabilize the system. The focus on stability and control may prevent adequate attention to how the system changes. Rapid change may simply be beyond the ability of functional explanation. There is a question of what is chosen as the homeostatic principle; if quiescence is the criterion, there is a conservative bias, but could not patterns that induce change be the alternative criterion used? Another problem with functional explanations is that tension is seen as emanating only from outside the system, thus ignoring tensions that come from contradictions within the system. Unless the theorist is alert to the possibilities that a given pattern could be partially or totally dysfunctional or irrelevant, it could be falsely inferred that all patterns are functional and indispensable. Finally, there is a danger that individual motives and goals will be substituted for societal constructs as homeostatic principles, thus reducing societies to the level of individual functioning.

Reductive explanations that invoke the characteristics and behavior of individuals to explain patterns of social systems have their roots in the approaches of social psychology discussed earlier. Certainly no social system explanation should be discrepant or inconsistent with knowledge of behavior at other levels. The question is really the dominance of the cognitive properties of individuals in explaining social systems and the degree to which such properties are seen as autonomous. In terms of dominance of reductive explanations, it is very different to assert that social systems are *nothing but* collections of individuals from including assumptions about individuals in a larger set of social system assumptions. Individual properties can be seen as somehow emerging and acting independently of social systems, but they also can be seen as being shaped by social systems. Realistic assumptions about individual behavior are necessary to social system theory, but total recourse to reduction is the coward's way out of hard intellectual problems.

Normative explanations are rather different from others in that they deal not with attempts to stipulate how social systems *do* operate but rather with specification of how they *should* or *could* work according to some preexisting set of criteria. This sometimes entails a set of ideal types found nowhere in perfect form but proposed in order to provide the strongest possible contrast between types. "Ideal" is used here as reflecting the pure case of what a pattern or system might be like if uncontaminated by other constraints—not "ideal" in the sense of being the "best" alternative. In many cases, we have a strong sense of which type is preferred by the author, but other types may be regarded with varying levels of rejection. The classic "four theories of the press" (Siebert, Peterson, & Schramm, 1956) is one such normative theory. The problem with it and other ideal types is that the unwary reader may mistake the types as representations of how press or other systems actually work. Ideal types may serve as standards against which observations of performance may be measured but they do not in themselves serve as valid forms of explanation.

We could add more forms of explanation that are used to explain various social system patterns. As is the case for those discussed above, none is likely to approach complete explanation. It is difficult to argue that any set of explanatory forms could be ordered meaningfully from best to worst. Certain explanations may be better than others for attacking certain types of research problems, but even a reasonably satisfying explanation would seem to require combinations of explanatory forms and approaches rather than relying on a single "best" perspective.

Dimensions of Choice
in Theory Construction

The communication scholar attempting to construct theory at the macrosocial level will encounter a set of seemingly different but less-than-well-articulated theoretical perspectives from which to choose. They are better seen as sketchy orientations than as logically constructed systems. To make sense of these perspectives and to have a meaningful basis of choice, we can identify certain dimensions on which the various perspectives can be located.

The first is the focus on *stability* versus *change*. It is difficult for any theoretical perspective to explain both of these adequately. Explaining how social control is maintained may require a different type of theorizing than does the analysis of system change. Perspectives that concentrate on the stability of systems also tend to use *equilibrium* or homeostatic models, often borrowed from biology, to represent the adjustive qualities of the social system. They see threats of potential change in the form of tensions from sources *external* to the system. At the *change* end of the stability-change continuum, theorists focus on *conflict* models, where the impetus to change is generated from strains or contradictions between *internal* forces in the system.

The perspective most clearly representing the stability/equilibrium-external source of change ends of the continua is functionalism (Breed, 1955; Lasswell, 1948; Lazarsfeld & Merton, 1948; Merton, 1957; Wright, 1960, 1974). But even here the pattern is not uniform. Lasswell's well-known "Structure and Function of Communication in Society" (1948) was a prototypic functional analysis, but Lasswell was a proponent of strong media effects throughout his long career—a position contrary to the "limited effects" view attributed to functionalism. Tichenor and his colleagues use functional language to some extent but deal with conflict and change in their community studies (Donohue, Tichenor, & Olien, 1975; Tichenor, Donohue, & Olien, 1970; Tichenor, Donohue, & Olien, 1980).

Critical theory in its various forms (e.g., Adorno & Horkheimer, 1972; Hall, 1977, 1982; Murdock & Golding, 1977; Schiller, 1969; Smythe, 1977) most clearly falls into the change/conflict-internal source of change ends of the continua. The basic economic and political arrangements are the ultimate sources of power and conflict, the exact role of the media being played out differently in the several varieties of this perspective. Social control is a central theme but its outcome is certainly not maintenance of harmony. Change originates within the system, except in analyses of media imperialism in developing nations where the sources of change are external Western capitalist nations (Boyd-Barrett, 1982; Golding, 1977); the system in this case is really the international economic sphere.

Other perspectives tend to take less clear positions on stability and change. Demographic analyses, especially the example of Lazarsfeld, Berelson, and Gaudet (1948), imply a stabilizing tendency of demographic factors; little attention has been given to the possibility that demographic relationships to communication might change over time. Modern versions of mass society theory diverge somewhat with respect to control and change. Gerbner focuses on the role of mass media in maintaining social control (Gerbner et al., 1980) but also considers change when stressing the importance of a shift to television as the dominant medium (Gerbner, 1967). Noelle-Neumann (1983) describes cyclical change and conflict in her spiral of silence theory but also conceives of public opinion as a form of social control. Various perspectives of diffusion (Katz & Lazarsfeld, 1955; Rogers, 1962; Savage, 1981) clearly concentrate on change in the form of information and influence but the source of change is external (Western nations and their technology) except for those formulations stressing information from audience demand (Rogers, 1976).

Power of communication and mass media. Another set of dimensions involves the power of communication and the mass media generally to affect social systems. Critical theorists and the mass society revivalists (Gerbner, 1967; Noelle-Neumann, 1983) stipulate strong effects of mass communication. The early versions of diffusion theory also envisioned strong media effects, but later estimates have portrayed their relative ineffectiveness especially when pitted against interpersonal communication (Katz & Lazarsfeld, 1955). Relatively weak effects largely in the direction of strengthening social control are dominant in both functional and demographic analyses, with the exception of Lasswell (1948) in the former case.

McQuail (1984) has adapted a fourfold table from Rosengren (1981) to illustrate theoretical differences in the influence relationships of mass media (more generally culture) and social structure. Mass media and social structure can each influence or not influence the other, thus generating four potential patterns: interdependence (mutual influence); idealism (media system influencing social structure but not the reverse); materialism (social structure influencing the media system but not the reverse); and autonomy (both operating with relative independence).

A possible weakness of this fourfold typology is the failure to identify any theoretical perspective clearly falling into the interdependence cell. Perhaps some functional analyses do this, although the direction of influence is often unclear. More explicit examples might be derived from models of political communication positing "a close interaction between political advocates and media professionals, in the course of which the two sides may virtually be said to constitute a subtly composite unity" (Blumler & Gurevitch, 1981, p. 469; see also Nimmo, 1978). This implies a two-way flow of influence, ultimately traceable to the fact that each side needs the other if it is to pursue its own goals effectively:

> Politicians need access to the communication channels that are controlled by the mass media, including the hopefully credible contexts of audience reception they offer. Consequently, they must adapt their messages to the demands of formats and genres devised inside such organizations and to their associated speech styles, story models and audience images. . . . Likewise, journalists cannot perform their task of political scrutiny without access to politicians for information, news, interviews, action and comment. (Blumler & Gurevitch, 1981, p. 477)

The resulting paths of reciprocal influence may be multiple, with politicians having to adapt their behaviors more in certain respects and journalists in others. Thus seeing the dominant direction of influence as varying according to circumstances could be a useful model. DeFleur and Ball-Rokeach (1982) imply such varying media-audience relationships in their dependency theory of media effects.

Idealism, the power of media systems to influence social change, is clearly stated in diffusion theory (Rogers, 1962), the media determinism of Innis (1950), McLuhan (1964), and Altheide (1985), in cultivation theory (Gerbner et al., 1980), and various formulations of cultural imperialism (Boyd-Barrett, 1982; Schiller, 1969).

Materialism, the power of social structure to dominate media systems, is found most clearly in the political economy branch of critical theory (Murdock & Golding, 1977; Smythe, 1977) and with somewhat lesser clarity in the Frankfurt school (Adorno & Horkheimer, 1972), hegemonic (Althusser, 1971), and social-cultural (Hall, 1982) approaches within critical theory that give somewhat greater degrees of autonomy to the superstructural features of ideology and communication. Demographic analyses of communicators and audiences argue, at least implicitly, for social location strongly influencing communication effects. In the Columbia voting studies, for example, selective exposure was determined by the person's demographic characteristics (Lazarsfeld et al., 1948).

The fourth of McQuail's patterns, autonomy, is also difficult to match with existing perspectives. It would be naive to suggest that media systems are totally independent from economic and political forces, but it may be useful nonetheless to conceptualize the elements of partial autonomy of media systems manifested in journalistic processes that are not simply outgrowths of political and economic systems.

Other dimensions of choice. Other choices in the construction of macrosocial theory divide within rather than between existing theoretical perspectives. It matters a great deal, for example, whether we set out to construct a model of society into which the mass media and language systems are fitted or, alternatively, we start with the media system or with language-speech systems as our central focus. What is set as the foreground focus is apt to be highly differentiated conceptually and what lies in the background is apt to appear in simplified form or, at worst, be taken as a given. No theorist can put everything in the foreground, although perhaps groups of researchers might try to do so. Critical theory alone among existing perspectives makes a clear choice that one must begin with a theory of society from which to analyze the media and other institutions (Bennett, 1979; Murdock & Golding, 1978). Because other macrosocial perspectives have their historic roots in social sciences other than communication, by implication they represent theories of society from which propositions about communication might be taken. There are signs, however, that with the growth and specialization of the field, communication theory might be shifting toward the development of media-centric and language-centric theories. Detailed analyses of journalistic organizations and studies of divergent audience readings of specific media content may signal the beginnings of more formal approaches to theory construction.

Another choice in the construction of macrosocial theory is the type of social unit singled out for investigation. As long as they are conceptualized as social relationships, the source of the explanation and what is being explained could be variables appropriate to total societies, communities, organizations, or primary groups. In a classic example, Shils and Janowitz (1948) explained the ability of German army units (organization) to withstand hardship by the leadership and interpersonal cohesion of the small fighting unit (primary group)—not by the holding power of the fascist symbols of the larger system (society). Macrosocial work has become much more productive with respect to both societies and organizations in recent years, while communities have occasionally been the site but seldom the theoretical focus of research. A notable exception is the Tichenor et al. research program.

Theories vary in the extent to which they focus on prediction or understanding. This is reflected particularly in the conceptualization of variables, research design, and analysis of data. Prediction pushes one toward simpler but reliable measures, more empirical research strategies, and the measurement of short-term effects. The goal of understanding leads the researcher to more complex concepts and relationships, more varied research strategies, and longer-term and more varied (if less easily accessible) effects.

The conception of communication itself opens another set of dimensions. We can see communication as requiring just a bit of fixing to make it perfect or we can see it as full of noise and fraught with difficulties. Another choice is between communication as transmission or as ritual

(Carey, 1977). The early work on diffusion conceived of communication as transmission from experts to users; more recently the images of mutual exchange have become more common. Finally, theories differ over how much they focus on the process of communication versus its result.

Components of Theory: Some Problems and Comments

Our definition of theory as "an organized explanation of a pattern of observed or to-be-observed events or behaviors" requires a more complete discussion. We have given examples of explanations that are unsatisfactory from a scientific point of view and others that are more satisfactory but incomplete. We have tried to illustrate some dimensions of choice for theory construction but have said little about the component parts of theory—the ingredients necessary to build theory.

For our purposes here, we specify six components of theory along with examples of common problems and suggestions for possible remedies: *postulates,* the first premises, strategies, or biases of the perspective; *conceptual framework,* the collection of defined variables used to characterize what is being explained and the explanatory terms; *theoretical linkages,* the assumptions that logically lead to causal or other forms of relationship between concepts, and the theoretical statements thus developed; *measurement,* the procedures for observing and classifying the research concepts; *research design* for testing hypotheses linking the observed variables; and *inferences* to be drawn from the evidence.

Postulates

Theoretical statements about communication processes and effects often come to us lacking in specification of their ancestry and where they fit into other issues. It is useful to state insofar as possible the values and world view each assertion represents and whatever context would help to understand it.

Unstated value premises. Sometimes public policy discussion and resultant funding for research forces "natural" concepts on the macro investigator along with their unspecified value premises: for example, political participation or knowledge of agricultural practices are good; aggressive behavior or perceptions of a "scary world" are bad. Sometimes investigators finding evidence of communication impact on the fortunes of a given institution presume its worth in some scale of values that is not explicated, such as the recent growth of American political science literature deploring the tendency for television to take over the communication functions previously performed by a stronger party system (Patterson, 1980; Polsby, 1980).

There is now fairly widespread agreement that a value-free science is impossible. Nowhere is this more apparent than at the macrosocial level in communication. Rather than pretend values do not exist, we can make clear our values insofar as we are aware of them. Public policy and funding possibilities bring other values into play. The question is whether the researcher's own set of values is sufficiently compatible with those of the funding source to justify participation. The leeway to explore other consequences and discuss the limitations of the unstated assumptions is also a factor. Some negative consequences occur at some level in any generally positive communication effect, and vice versa.

Naive humanitarianism. Certain lines of comparative research reflect an unstated postulate, namely, that identifying the psychic unity of mankind will somehow contribute to the common good of the world. From this first premise research has been overtly designed to identify "basic communalities" in public opinion structures (Cantril, 1965; Gallup, 1976-1977), to verify the common foundations of cognitive perception (Osgood, Suci, & Tannenbaum, 1957) and to "broaden knowledge of the common bases of behavior" when people use communication for problem solving (Edelstein, 1985).

Although establishment of regularities across systems is a legitimate scientific aspiration, to treat this as the essential "point of view of the comparativist" (Edelstein, 1985) is to demolish the macrosocial as a level of inquiry in its own right. It flouts the indispensable macro-level assumption that different forms of sociopolitical and communication organization will differentially constrain behavior.

Conceptual Framework

The need to provide clear and unambiguous definitions of all research concepts constituting a theoretical perspective is a particularly difficult task at the macrosocial level. The level of complexity of multiperson units combined with a host of measurement difficulties presents a formidable obstacle to explication and seems to have discouraged many authors. In much of the writing at this level, it is easy to get the impression that muddy prose and vague concepts are necessary.

Global typologizing. Some varieties of macrosocietal conceptualization amount to little more than an overall classification of phenomena into categories, overlooking a host of potentially significant features. Press system classification is notoriously prone to this tendency (Siebert et al., 1956). It can also be seen in recent work dividing the world's mass media systems into just three types: Western, Communist, and underdeveloped. Although drawing gross distinctions between broad types of systems may be clarifying for certain purposes, it is unlikely to be particularly fruitful for theory construction. It implies that complex systems are reducible to some master characteristic or single dimension. Ideal-type conceptualization may also impute a greater difference between systems than is really the case (e.g., that the Communist press system of the Soviet Union is totally controlled, while that of the U.S. press is totally free).

The division of media systems into a few gross types ignores theoretically important variance within categories. Within Western societies, there can be large differences in the autonomy/subordination of media institutions to state and party control. In Communist systems, there can be big differences in the authorized projection of social problems and conflicts. In authoritarian systems, large differences can be noted in independent reporting efforts. In underdeveloped societies, the practice of development journalism may be more or less advanced and more or less critical of ruling authorities and their policies.

Ignoring complexity. Whether for purposes of keeping theoretical discussion simple or of meeting the requirements of funding agencies, macro-level researchers are prone to use simple labels (e.g., objectivity, news values, development, knowledge, participation) for complex concepts without adequately defining and differentiating them. Because certain terms appear so frequently in the professional and public discourse, they may take on the quality of being "natural," as if they were really "out there." The simple label may mask the fact that a variety of different behaviors and activities have been combined. Careful examination and explication of "natural" concepts may lead to the conclusion that a given label is simply too vague to serve as a research concept. At the least, clear explication is called for, first identifying and then defining whatever dimensions might be subsumed under the more general concept.

Theoretical Linkages

Assertions about the relationships, causal or other, between defined concepts constitute theoretical statements. Underlying these assertions are potentially testable assumptions about human behavior and institutions that logically lead to the theoretical statements. Our understanding of theoretical perspectives would be enhanced greatly if theorists were to state these assumptions and to work through the logic of their conclusions. Unfortunately, this is seldom the case and much of the confusion and misunderstanding in macrosocial work results from this failure.

False universality. There is a tendency in macrosocial analyses to treat theoretical statements as if they were universally applicable over time and across and within societies. Propositions specifying the conditions under which the statement will hold (contingent conditions) or under which they will hold in greater or lesser strength (contributory conditions) are unusual but perhaps more common today than in the past. It is often the fate of those who do build such complexities into their work to find it papered over with universality by those citing it in reviews of the research area. For example, the finding that agenda setting is largely confined to the less politically active sectors of the public (McLeod et al., 1974) has been translated into a less differentiated positive finding by later reviewers. Similarly, the impact of class divisions on both media output and audience reaction, well documented in Britain, has at times been unthinkingly exported as if findings from a particular society applied equally to all societies.

Monocausal theories. Theories are sometimes stated as if there were but a single cause. This is most common in substructural varieties of critical theory (Garnham, 1979; Smythe, 1977) where, despite taking account of various political and social forces, the place of the media system in the economic system is treated as ultimately decisive. There is a tendency to gravitate toward a power constraints model of social system influences on mass media performance. Such a model posits certain functions that media are supposed to serve (by virtue of authoritative norms or communicators' claims) and then shows how dependence on external power centers blocks and limits their realization. For example, liberal press theory promises a robust and wide open exchange of ideas; but the subservience of newspapers and television to the market, or to cultural assumptions, argues otherwise.

We have only very fragmentary evidence as to the potentially diverse social system-based influences on media performance and other communication outcomes. To insist too firmly on only one line of influence is to close off other patterns that can be uncovered. Instead, one can adopt a research strategy of anticipating other lines of influence that could operate or perhaps interact with economic arrangements.

Single consequences. On the effects side, there is an equivalent weakness to the monocausality problem. There is a tendency to postulate only one set of consequences, usually either positive or negative, for a given linkage. In critical theory, for example, the possibility that a liberal media system may include tendencies that undermine ideological props of the status quo as well as projecting them has not been seriously entertained until recently. From another perspective, Alexander's (1981) otherwise highly sophisticated functionalist account of the contribution to a society's normative integration made by differentiated media systems (not formally tied to other power centers) deals only with the integrative tendencies and not the potentially disintegrative ones. Other examples may be found in American writings that postulate a host of depoliticizing effects of modern journalism, including the delegitimating impact of television news (Robinson, 1977), the narcotizing dysfunction of news reports (Lazarsfeld & Merton, 1948), and a denigration of political leaders and institutions with consequential heightening of voter skepticism and dampening of participatory impulses and readiness to vote (Ranney, 1983).

It is likely that any communication or other influence strong enough to merit study will produce not a single consequence but many. These are not unlikely to have both positive and negative implications for any set of evaluative criteria. Research designs should anticipate multiple and potentially opposite outcomes. Consequences may be delayed or sequentially arranged (e.g., media exposure leads to interpersonal discussion, which then has social consequences; McLeod et al., 1979). Longitudinal multiwave designs with measures of potentially mediating processes are appropriate to expanded perspectives on consequences.

Dichotomous assumptions. Intellectual arguments often utilize overstatement for the sake of clarity. The hypodermic effects model, for example, may have been a convenient straw man set up as a contrast to an overdrawn limited effects position. Unfortunately, this writing strategy makes all too easy the false inference that media must have either strong direct effects or none at all. Other false dichotomies are apparent: Influence must come from the media or from people but not both; the audience must be either active or passive but not varying by time and situation.

Although useful as illustrative devices, dichotomies may be mistaken for discontinuous discrete positions. The continuous dimension underlying them may be lost on those to whom the dichotomy is presented. In theoretical reasoning blanket assumptions are dangerous. It is better to assume that under certain conditions the effects will be stronger, interpersonal sources will be more important, the audience more active in certain ways. These assumptions can then serve not as articles of faith, but as themselves constituting propositions testable in later research.

Measurement

In a broad sense, measurement is the statement of how the research concepts are to be observed. Beyond the usual problems of measurement common to all levels of communication research, macrosocial investigation faces a number of *characteristic* problems of measurement not common to other levels. Evaluation of measurement quality is no less crucial here. We are quite often measuring complex multidimensional constructs with multiple indicators. These require special care.

Availability of appropriate evidence. We seek explanations beyond the individual but much of our measurement is simply an aggregation of information from or about individuals. The data gathered from individuals are summed to come to macrosocial conclusions. As McLeod and Reeves (1980) point out,

For example, if some members of the audience are found to become more informed by using media content, it is sometimes assumed that such information gain must be functional for the society. But societal consequences cannot be inferred solely from estimates of the number of changes. The social location (e.g., social class) of those gaining information must be considered in assessing system consequences. The same problem applies to the term "public opinion," which is often used as a grand reification of individually measured opinions having little connection to their mode of organization in the community or society. (p. 18)

It is not that measures aggregated from individuals should be entirely eschewed but (a) their use as "stand-ins" for macro-level traits should be considered and used if they are defensible, and (b) they should be supplemented wherever possible with more genuinely macro-level variables. Unfortunately, the global social system variables are not always ready to hand in official reports and statistics in forms that would closely match an investigator's conceptual needs. The construction of appropriate global variables is apt to require a painstaking search through masses of variegated documentary material, including statutes, charters and financial records (Blumler & Gurevitch, 1975). Because of the need to compare across national systems, organizations, etc., researchers must ascertain what data are available for the various systems and try to find different ways of bringing them together within common analysis frames. This will involve a struggle to standardize conceptual definitions across systems and requires ingenuity in constructing composite indices out of multiple and diverse criteria.

Confounding of variables. Unlike cognitive-level survey research where sample sizes may be in hundreds and key variables in dozens, in macro-level work one is likely to have more significant variables than cases. Further, social system variables are likely to be "block billed" (Rosenberg, 1968) in that several variables may be highly correlated.

Where cross-system surveys with large sample sizes are available, the most common tendency is to simply ignore the fact that the N is really the number of systems and to proceed using the number of respondents in each system as the N for statistical purposes. Other approaches are possible. To cope with this problem, even the relatively large-scale nine-nation European election communication research (Blumler, 1983) was obliged to undertake a series of bounded analyses, each concentrating on a few key variables.

Measurement equivalence. The cross-system reliability of main indicators may be at issue. Convenience dictates the use of uniform instruments, yet what Przeworski and Teune (1970) term "system interference" may diminish the real equivalence of common measures. For example, what counts as political participation (which one might wish to correlate with media use) in one society (say, voting in the United States) could be far less relevant to another (say, in the Soviet Union, where attendance at party meetings might be more apposite). In recommending more cross-national analysis of media system influence on audience uses and gratifications, Blumler, Gurevitch, and Katz (1985) also caution against

> quick and dirty comparative research, whereby measures of audience gratifications, designed for one national setting, are dropped into a survey in another country, just to see what turns up. There is no reason a researcher in Taiwan, say, should seek respondents' reactions to gratification statements reflecting Israelis' pride in their statehood. (p. 268)

Research Design and Hypothesis Testing

Strategies for gathering evidence and testing hypotheses require special care in macrosocial research. Within-nation variance might be between subcultures, between communities with differing levels of media access, or between media organizations where ownership, management styles, and the like might vary. Societies with differing media systems but relatively comparable economic and political systems might be particularly apt for between-nation comparisons.

Unmitigated inductionism. Much cross-system research is based on administration of common instruments without cross-system theory. As Blumler and Gurevitch (1975) put it, work of this kind "is inimical to progressive continuity. It trades in no pre-defined problems, the resolution of which would open up yet other issues for scrutiny. It lights no torch that can be handed on from one investigator to the next." This is not to condemn every recourse to induction or to argue that all macrosocial research should spring from theoretical propositions tested by data. Exploratory comparisons can be highly appropriate in still relatively undeveloped fields. When adopted, however, the fruits of induction should be explicitly used for theory building.

Making Inferences from Evidence

The goal of a research design is to produce evidence that provides clear answers to research questions. It is then the obligation of the researcher to make sense out of the evidence assembled, to place it in a larger context, and to suggest new directions for research.

Ungrounded inferences. A high proportion of macrosocial work either states inferences that run well beyond the evidence or draws so few inferences that one wonders why all the effort was expended to do the research.

Much polemical writing falls into the first category, where the conclusions are strong but the evidence is weak or not apparent. At the other extreme are descriptive studies of media systems bound to a single time and place. The apparent contradiction of single case studies being by definition noncomparable and hence restricted in inference power becomes noncontradictory if the observer conceptualizes dimensions on which the single case might be compared to others. Implicit comparisons in time and place are possible and these are superior to the endless detail of sheer description.

ADVANCING MACROSOCIAL INQUIRY: PROSPECTS AND EXAMPLES

The prospects for making significant scientific advances in macrosocial communication theory and research appear relatively propitious. As major issues centering on communication systems' relations to social systems have moved up the field's agenda, it is no longer acceptable for their treatment to remain rooted in realms of polemic, untested assertion and personal critique. Attention is increasingly likely to be directed to complex and dynamic macro-level processes by the need to understand the impact of new communication and information technologies, which are provoking policy responses from government and adaptations from established media industries. The growing internationalization of communication studies may also play a part, giving serious scholars more opportunities as well as incentives to fashion cross-national inquiries.

The aim of this section is to suggest lines of inquiry that would open the door further to macrosocial communication research possibilities. But first it may be useful to map the essential features of this level as we have defined it.

Systems as Foci
of Comparative Research

The macrosocial level of communication research is concerned with the analysis of communication-relevant systems. They may be communication systems *per se* or social systems examined for their communication implications. The appropriate strategy for macrosocial system analysis is comparative, based on the presumption that different system parameters (i.e., different manners in which systems are structured) will differentially encourage or constrain communication roles and behaviors belonging to, organized by, or exposed to them. Creative macrosocial theorizing, however, will follow the exhortation of Przeworski and Teune (1970) to substitute "variables for proper names of systems," explicitly postulating, applying, and revising potentially formative dimensions of cross-system variation. It will also explicate expected relationships between and influences of such sources of variation.

The macrosocial systems that could be studied in this way come in many shapes and sizes. Just using four social unit forms (society, community, organization, and primary group), two types of comparisons (between and within such units), and at least two major types of communication content (news or public affairs and entertainment) yields a $4 \times 2 \times 2$, or 16-cell, matrix of macroscopic research focus possibilities. Even this does not exhaust all the possibilities. Depending on one's analytical purpose, it is permissible, for example, to work with notions of "media systems" (incorporating several organizations within a medium or across media) or of more specialized types of "communication systems." A common example of the latter is the political communication system, narrower versions of which might include, say, an election communication system or even an election broadcasting system.

The potential system locales of scientific macrosocial inquiry are therefore legion. There can be cross-national analyses, say, of media organizations (as in Blumler & Gurevitch's, 1986, observation study of BBC and NBC journalists' agenda-setting roles), media messages (as in Hallin & Mancini's, 1984, content analysis of Italian and American TV news coverage of a trip to Europe by President Reagan), audience roles (as in Blumler, Cayrol, & Thoveron's, 1978, study of the election communication gratifications sought by Belgian, British, and French voters), and audience responses and effects (as in an in-progress attempt by Adoni and Cohen to chart the acceptance by adolescents of media versions of social conflicts in Britain, Germany, Israel, South Africa, and the United States). There can be similar forms of cross-community research—as in Tichenor et al.'s (1980) investigation of the influence of community conflict levels on press reporting and local inhabitants' issue awareness, or in Clarke and Evans' (1983) study of the impact on journalists' roles, press coverage, and citizen knowledge of congressional campaigns varying in vigor and type of race. Of course community media systems could also be compared cross-nationally, or even with their own *national* media equivalents. Primary groups could also be a focus of comparison within communities, societies, or even cross-nationally (e.g., a comparison of the uses of television by families varying in structure or culture). Other culturally defined communities can also be deployed in meaningful system comparisons, as in the Liebes and Katz (1986) research into the interpretations of the TV series *Dallas* given by members of different ethnic subgroups within and across societies.

Possible Lines of Further Research

Extending Existing Theory

We suspect that virtually all the major social theories of communication absorbing scholarly energies at present could benefit from macro-social research scrutiny. Gains would flow, not only from the enlargement of settings in which such theories would be tested, but also from the pressure to *elaborate* them by defining those system circumstances in which their leading propositions could take modified forms. This is because such theories often hinge on concepts that have been implicitly accepted as virtually axiomatic but that when considered might vary across systems. Three examples may be mentioned.

One is the theory of mass media agenda setting. Most empirical work in this tradition has tested the hypothesis that increased media emphasis on certain issues results in increased public concern over those same issues (Weaver, Wilhoit, & Semetko, 1986). There has been little systematic study, however, of the underlying premise of a discretionary power for journalists to define the public agenda by filtering and shaping reality. Such an issue is best explored through a comparative analysis, predicated on the assumption that the contributions of the media to the formation of political agendas will be shaped by the political structures and cultures of the societies in which they operate. Consequently, Gurevitch et al. (1986) have recently proposed a set of system factors that might explain variability in media discretionary power across polities: (a) The valuation of politics and politicians in the political culture; (b) the prevalence of "sacerdotal" or "pragmatic" orientations to politics and politicians in the professional culture of journalists; (c) the level of professionalization reached in the organization of political persuasion and campaign marketing; and (d) the intensity of competition among news media for audience patronage.

Second, theories that propose that the mass media (particularly television) have become a prime source of socially constructed reality for audience members are another case in point. In the cultivation theory of Gerbner et al. (1980), these rest on the assumption that TV portrayals of social reality depart appreciably from other depictions and records of social reality. A comparative approach would introduce the elaborating proposition that the reality distortion (or divergence) in media content varies across systems due to (a) normative constraints in the surrounding cultural environment, (b) social and political controls over the major mass media, or (c) differences of mass media organization. To exemplify, stereotypical media portrayals of the elderly might be more prevalent in cultures valuing modernity, innovation, and youth (a); the organization and activity of the women's movement might have an effect on the range of female role models presented in media fare (b); and the output of more commercially competitive media might be impregnated with more episodes and reports of extreme and atypical violence (c). Corresponding hypotheses of differential cultivation effects on heavy media consumers could follow as well.

Third, there is the often cited, yet in a sense neglected, dependency theory of media effects (Ball-Rokeach & DeFleur, 1976). This was explicitly propounded as a macrosocietal model, encouraging "treatment of both the media and its audience as integral parts of a larger social system" in contrast to "conceptualizations that focus on the stimulus-response probabilities of individuals acting in a situational field." Curiously, since its propagation, the concept of dependency has been heavily "psychologized," repeatedly taking the form of measures of individual behaviors and beliefs. Yet there is promising scope for macro-level research in the original, more system-oriented formulation. Ball-Rokeach and DeFleur proposed that as societies grow more complex and the quality of communication technology improves, the mass media assume a larger number of unique information functions, on which their audiences become more dependent; second, that in societies with developed media systems, audience dependency on media information resources increases as the level of structural conflict and the pace of social change increase; and third, that with heightened dependency, a number of cognitive, affective, and behavioral media effects are more likely. It should not be beyond a research team's capability to devise operational indicators for cross-system analysis of societal complexity and conflict levels, postulating and testing associated implications in the "more dependent" cases.

Systematizing Media Studies

Most research on mass media organization, ownership, controls, occupations, content, and audiences has been pursued within strictly national compartments. Partial exceptions are the study of journalists, television news, and election campaign communication (Blumler, 1983; Blumler & Gurevitch, 1986; Golding & Elliott, 1979; Köcher, 1986; Weaver et al., 1986). There are a number of other growth points, however, from which such work could be extended.

As an example, there are a variety of media occupational roles, which, in different organizations, may reflect different linkages to societal institutions and produce different styles of performance with different consequences. Cross-national surveys of holders of other occupations, such as media executives, producers, and directors of drama and entertainment programs, could examine these variables in broader models of the communication systems to which they belong.

Second, the uses and gratifications approach could lead to macro-level theorizing and research. If people's political and social roles affect their expectations for communication, then societies with different social and political structures should generate different audience roles. A three-nation analysis of viewers' attitudes to election campaign messages in Belgium, Britain, and France (Blumler et al., 1978) found that voters' campaign communication responded to several system influences. Comparative analysis of media gratifications might address the relative explanatory power of media factors (how content offerings are structured by the dominant mass media in different societies) as against cultural factors (how national traditions favor certain ways of using media materials) in shaping audience expectations.

Third, mass media finance offers another focus for macrosocietal research. Many national broadcasting systems, which were traditionally organized as public service institutions and financed from noncommercial sources, are under pressure to accept advertisements or to compete for audiences against new channels funded entirely by advertising. Two opposed hypotheses, open to comparative study, have shaped much of the debate provoked by these developments. One ascribes to competitive advertising an overriding power to transform the goals and motivations of broadcasting executives and producers; the other would expect the thrust of such financial incentives to be checked and controlled by the traditional organizational structures into which they will have been inserted.

Relationships of Social Systems to Communication Systems

First, we wonder whether the central theses of critical theory—for example, that mass communication chiefly reinforces hegemonic ideologies, "selling" the institutional status quo—could not be translated into more differentiated terms, opening them up to cross-system examination. Classical Marxism insisted on grounding "scientific" analysis in the historical development of contradictions between the forces and relations of production, including close attention to the concrete conditions prevalent in a given society at a particular time. Guided by sensitivity to such societal specificities and differences, it should be possible (even exciting) to derive from within a Marxist framework a set of dimensions along which modern capitalist societies might vary, with corresponding implications for differences of communication role. Cross-system theorizing of this kind might take account of such factors as these: (a) the stage of development reached in the occupational and class structure; (b) relations between class divisions and other bases of social and political organization and cleavage; (c) manifestations of "class consciousness" in party organization, trade union organization and their literatures, as well as in popular culture more widely; (d) relations of the national society to the international economic order; and (e) relations of the media system to the commercial and public spheres. Working, for example, with Hall's (1982) stress on the politics of signification and his designation of media content as the site of an active "class struggle in language," one could try to specify the societal conditions that might affect the balance of communicated representations. Or, depending on the severity of the underlying structural contradictions making for societal crises, varying responses of communication agencies might be postulated. Hypotheses of a differential reception of media messages by different audience sectors could also be generated, following the empirical concerns of Morley (1980) and Fejes (1984).

Second, the determinants and mechanisms of mass media access might profitably be explored through macro-level research. Its importance is due to the fact that much of the power of the press stems, not from its ability to initiate ideas but from its "need to be selective in choosing what to escalate and what to leave languishing" (Tichenor et al., 1980, p. 19). In all media systems there is a hierarchy of "accredited witnesses," whose views get aired. The voices that tend to be favored might vary significantly according to such factors as (a) the organization of political systems, which tend to have embedded within them certain leading political roles that translate more or less automatically into roles of spokespersonship and rights to media attention (e.g., Fishman, 1982); (b) the fabric of large pressure groups, representing significant interests and causes, including their articulation to or independence from party systems; (c) journalists' orientations to the spectrum of social institutions, depending on the degree of respect to which they are regarded as entitled by the dominant value system; (d) the social and educational backgrounds of media personnel in a position to influence selection decisions; (e) the structure of media ownership (Bagdikian, 1983); and (f) the relationship between owners and regulators of information system technology (Mosco, 1982).

A closely related third approach might focus on the "mediation" of statements and events presented to publics through mass communication channels. Kelly and Siune (1983) present intriguing evidence of much cross-national variance in television news during the European parliamentary elections of 1979. For American television news, Hallin (1985) reports big shifts over two decades in sound-bite lengths. Such measures could be examined in relation to the degree to which the media system is amenable to access for politicians' messages on their own terms.

Fourth, "cultural" influences on mass media organization, functions, content, and audience roles and responses could be examined macrosocietally in a number of interesting directions. There are cultural differences across both nations and subgroups that could impinge on communication in a variety of ways:

Constraining how communicators address publics. Cayrol (1983) found that journalists' opinions on how television should present the first European parliamentary elections varied according to opinion in their countries toward European integration. Holding their own attitudes to European unification constant, a more extensive coverage with a more "European" slant was recommended more often by journalists in societies shown to be more "pro-European" by opinion poll evidence.

Impinging on content. Soap operas, a common genre, might in different cultures pivot on different sorts of conflicts, present different sorts of plot resolutions or highlight different sorts of values at stake. Another focus could be political rhetoric, with different idioms to be expected in cultures varying in the strength of their support for populist values.

Guiding the performance by the mass media of their function of the "reinforcement of social norms" (Lazarsfeld & Merton, 1948). In principle, it should follow that if canons of public morality are variable across cultures, then media activity to enforce them should vary correspondingly as well. American political culture, taking a low view of politicians' integrity, may foster journalistic enforcement of social norms against the dangers of official corruption. Such pressures seem less prevalent in Britain, where a cultural counterpart might be found in assumptions about a social order that is presumed virtually to be natural. This could help explain why so many critical theory analysts of British media content find that it upholds what they term a societal consensus in one policy sphere after another (Cohen & Young, 1973).

Shaping audience responses. Liebes and Katz (1986) illustrate the scope available for subcultural research on the reception of internationally diffused media materials. Analyzing discussions of an episode of *Dallas* by focus groups of different ethnic origins in Israel and the United States, they found much evidence of differential perceptions and responses.

Social and Communication Change

A dynamic outlook is in strikingly short supply in macrosocial communication research. Yet communication systems are not rooted in indissoluble cement. We need to build a catalog of different types of mechanisms through which social or communication change interactions may be processed.

Two active topics in this area should attract those strategies of dimensionalizing and modeling of communication system variables that have been recommended throughout this chapter. One is the role of communication in development. The truism is widely accepted that communication forces in isolation cannot significantly mobilize energies for development and that their operation will be molded by forces in the surrounding social context.

A second topic is the impact of new communication technologies. Case studies of the introduction of "wired cities" in different societies have yielded several dimensions that might facilitate the comparative analysis of other such developments (Dutton et al., 1986). For example, the scale and speed of adoption, the role of central planning, and the integration and blend of new media and institutions with what already exists could be affected by a number of mediating and differentiating factors.

Finally, we are struck by the infrequent utilization of time series data to track significant communication system developments, relating them to trends in other spheres, such as the economy, political organization, and public opinion. For some purposes, appropriate data do exist and need to be drawn on more often and imaginatively to test theoretical propositions. There may also be a case for a consortium of media research schools and agencies to identify a set of additional indices of communication organization, content, and audience behavior, which would be useful to compile on a periodic basis.

COMPARISONS NOT ODIOUS

A common theme of this chapter is the necessity in macrosocial communication research for creative, self-conscious, and explicit comparative analysis in several senses. This is not just a matter of making comparisons but of setting things up right for arriving at valid and illuminating comparisons. Thus we have emphasized, first, the need for a comparative awareness of the diverse theoretical perspectives that are available for addressing macrosocial phenomena, choosing that which is best adapted to one's study problem—or even those opposed perspectives that could be systematically tested against each other in the course of research. There is, second, the need to find and set out one's postulates, concepts, and dimensions clearly, so that one knows *why* one is comparing social systems. Third, there is the careful choice of system sites, between which comparisons might be fruitful, looking not just for places where instruments can be fielded but for ones across which substantial variance on the key dimensions can be expected. Fourth, there is all that is involved in devising the measures by means of which effective comparisons can be made.

Much communication research has not been purposively and systematically comparative in these senses. Yet one can only understand a

316 LEVELS OF ANALYSIS

given system by comparing it with others, just as one can only clarify the generalizability of a favored theory by testing it in multiple systemic circumstances. In that dual sense, then, comparative analysis is a prescription for those communication scholars who wish better and more amply to "know themselves."

REFERENCES

Adoni, H., Cohen, A. A., & Mane, S. (1984). Social reality and television news: Perceptual dimensions of social conflicts in selected life areas. *Journal of Broadcasting, 28,* 33-49.

Adorno, T., & Horkheimer, M. (1972). The cultural industry: Enlightenment as mass deception. In *The dialectics of enlightenment.* New York: Herder & Herder.

Alexander, J. C. (1981). The mass news media in systemic, historical and comparative perspective. In E. Katz & T. Szecsko (Eds.), *Mass media and social change.* Newbury Park, CA: Sage.

Altheide, D. L. (1985). *Media power.* Newbury Park, CA: Sage.

Althusser, L. (1971). Ideology and ideological state apparatuses. In *Lenin and philosophy and other essays.* London: New Left Books.

Arendt, H. (1951). *The origins of totalitarianism.* New York: Harcourt Brace Jovanovich.

Bagdikian, B. H. (1983). *The media monopoly.* Boston: Beacon Press.

Ball-Rokeach, S. J., & DeFleur, M. L. (1976). A dependency model of mass media effects. *Communication Research, 3,* 3-21.

Becker, L. B., & Whitney, D. C. (1980). Effects of media dependencies on audience assessment of government. *Communication Research, 7,* 95-120.

Bennett, T. (1979). *Formalism and marxism.* London: Methuen.

Berelson, B. (1952). *Content analysis as a tool of communication research.* New York: Free Press.

Berelson, B. (1959). The state of communication research. *Public Opinion Quarterly, 23,* 1-6.

Berelson, B., Lazarsfeld, P. F., & McPhee, W. N. (1954). *Voting: A study of opinion formation in a presidential campaign.* Chicago: University of Chicago Press.

Berelson, B., & Steiner, G. (1964). *Human behavior: An inventory of scientific findings.* New York: Harcourt Brace Jovanovich.

Bhaskar, R. (1975). *A realist theory of science.* Leeds, England: Leeds Books.

Bhaskar, R. (1982). Emergence, explanation and emancipation. In P. F. Secord (Ed.), *Explaining social behavior: Consciousness, behavior and social structure.* Newbury Park, CA: Sage.

Bleyer, W. G. (1916). *Types of news writing.* Boston: Houghton Mifflin.

Bleyer, W. G. (1924). Research problems and newspaper analysis. *Journalism Quarterly, 1*(March), 17-22.

Bleyer, W. G. (1931). What schools of journalism are trying to do. *Journalism Quarterly, 8*(March), 35-44.

Bleyer, W. G. (1934). Freedom of the press and the New Deal. *Journalism Quarterly, 11*(March), 22-35.

Blumler, J. G. (1964). British television: The outlines of a research strategy. *British Journal of Sociology, 15,* 223-233.

Blumler, J. G. (1969). Producers' attitudes towards the television coverage of an election. In P. Halmos (Ed.), *The sociology of mass communicators* (Sociological Review Monographs 13: 85-115).

Blumler, J. G. (1978). Purposes of mass communication research: A transatlantic perspective. *Journalism Quarterly, 55,* 219-230.

Blumler, J. G. (Ed.). (1983). *Communicating to voters: Television in the first European parliamentary elections.* Newbury Park, CA: Sage.

Blumler, J. G., Brynin, M., & Nossiter, T. J. (1986). Broadcasting finance and programme quality: An international review. *European Journal of Communication, 1,* 343-364.

Blumler, J. G., Cayrol, R., & Thoveron, G. (1978). *La television: Fait-elle l'election?* Paris: Presses de La Fondation Nationale des Sciences Politiques.

Blumler, J. G., & Gurevitch, M. (1975). Towards a comparative framework for political communication research. In S. H. Chaffee (Ed.), *Political communication.* Newbury Park, CA: Sage.

Blumler, J. G., & Gurevitch, M. (1981). Politicians and the press: An essay in role relationships. In D. D. Nimmo & K. R. Sanders (Eds.), *Handbook of political communication.* Newbury Park, CA: Sage.

Blumler, J. G., & Gurevitch, M. (1986). *The election agenda-setting roles of television journalists: Campaign observation at the BBC and NBC.* Paper presented at the International Communication Association Convention.

Blumler, J. G., Gurevitch, M., & Katz, E. (1985). Reaching out: A future for gratifications research. In K. E. Rosengren, L. A. Wenner, & P. Palmgreen (Eds.), *Media gratifications research: Current perspectives.* Newbury Park, CA: Sage.

Blumler, J. G., Gurevitch, M., & Nossiter, T. J. (1986). Setting the television news agenda: Campaign observation at the BBC. In I. Crewe & M. Harrop (Eds.), *Political communications: The general election campaign of 1983.* Cambridge: Cambridge University Press.

Blumler, J. G., & Thoveron, G. (1983). Analyzing a unique election: Themes and concepts. In Blumler (Ed.), *Communicating to voters: Television in the first European parliamentary elections.* Newbury Park, CA: Sage.

Boyd-Barrett, J. O. (1982). Cultural dependency and the mass media. In M. Gurevitch, T. Bennett, J. Curran, & J. Woollacott (Eds.), *Culture, society and the media.* London: Methuen.

Bramson, L. (1961). *The political context of sociology.* Princeton: Princeton University Press.

Breed, W. (1955). Social control in the newsroom. *Social Forces, 33,* 326-335.

Burns, T. (1977). *The BBC: Public institution and private world.* London: Macmillan.

Cantril, H. (1965). *The pattern of human concerns.* New Brunswick, NJ: Rutgers University Press.

Carey, J. W. (1977). Mass communication research and cultural studies: An American view. In J. Curran, M. Gurevitch, & J. Woollacott (Eds.), *Mass communication and society.* London: Edward Arnold.

Cayrol, R. (1983). Broadcasters and the election campaign: Attitudes to European and professional orientations. In J. G. Blumler (Ed.), *Communicating to voters: Television in the first European parliamentary elections.* Newbury Park, CA: Sage.

Charters, W. W. (1933). *Motion pictures and youth: A summary.* New York: Macmillan.

Clarke, P., & Evans, S. (1983). *Covering campaigns: Journalism in congressional elections.* Stanford: Stanford University Press.

Cohen, S., & Young, J. (1973). *The manufacture of news: Deviance, social problems and the mass media.* London: Constable.

Cooley, C. H. (1909). *Social organization: A study of the larger mind.* New York: Scribner's.

DeFleur, M. L. (1956). A mass communication model of stimulus response relationships: An experiment in message diffusion. *Sociometry, 19*(March), 21-22.

DeFleur, M. L., & Ball-Rokeach, S. J. (1982). *Theories of mass communication* (4th ed.). New York: Longman.

Dewey, J. (1927). *The public and its problems.* New York: Holt, Rinehart & Winston.

Donohue, G. A., Tichenor, P. J., & Olien, C. N. (1975). Mass media and the knowledge gap: A hypothesis reconsidered. *Communication Research, 2,* 3-23.

Durkheim, E. (1893). *De la division du travail social.* Paris: Alcan.

Dutton, W. H., Blumler, J. G., & Kraemer, K. L. (1986). *Wired cities: Shaping the future of communications.* White Plains, NY: Knowledge Industry Publications.

Edelstein, A. S. (1985). *Paradigm dialogue on comparative communication research: Epistemological and methodological issues.* Paper presented at the International Communication Association.

Epstein, E. J. (1973). *News from nowhere.* New York: Vintage.

Ettema, J. S., & Kline, F. G. (1977). Deficits, differences and ceilings: Contingent conditions for understanding the knowledge gap. *Communication Research, 4,* 179-202.

Fejes, F. (1984). Critical mass communications research and media effects: The problem of the disappearing audience. *Media, Culture and Society, 6,* 219-232.

Festinger, L. (1957). *A theory of cognitive dissonance.* Evanston, IL: Row, Peterson.

Fishman, M. (1980). *Manufacturing the news.* Austin: University of Texas Press.

Fishman, M. (1982). News and nonevents: Making the visible invisible. In J. S. Ettema & D. C. Whitney (Eds.), *Individuals in mass media organizations: Creativity and constraint.* Newbury Park, CA: Sage.

Fromm, E. (1941). *Escape from freedom.* New York: Holt, Rinehart & Winston.

Gallup, G. (1976-1977). Human needs and satisfactions: A global survey. *Public Opinion Quarterly, 40,* 459-467.

Gans, H. (1979). *Deciding what's news.* New York: Vintage.

Garnham, N. (1979). Contribution to a political economy of mass communication. *Media, Culture and Society, 1,* 123-146.

Gerbner, G. (1967). Mass media and human communication theory. In F.E.X. Dance (Ed.), *Human communication theory.* New York: Holt, Rinehart & Winston.

Gerbner, G. (Ed.). (1983). Ferment in the field [Special Issue]. *Journal of Communication, 33*(Summer).

Gerbner, G., Gross, L., Morgan, M., & Signorielli, N. (1980). The "mainstreaming" of America: Violence profile no. 11. *Journal of Communication, 30*(Summer), 10-29.

Gitlin, T. (1978). Media sociology: The dominant paradigm. *Theory and Society, 6,* 205-253.

Glynn, C., & McLeod, J. M. (1984). Public opinion du jour: Its impact on communication and voting behavior. *Public Opinion Quarterly, 48,* 731-740.

Glynn, C., & McLeod, J. M. (1985). Implications of the spiral of silence theory for communication and public opinion research. In D. D. Nimmo & K. R. Sanders (Eds.), *Political communication yearbook 1.* Carbondale: Southern Illinois University Press.

Goldenberg, E. N., & Traugott, M. W. (1984). *Campaigning for congress.* Washington, DC: Congressional Quarterly Press.

Golding, P. (1977). Media professionalism in the Third World: The transfer of an ideology. In J. Curran, M. Gurevitch, & J. Woollacott (Eds.), *Mass communication and society.* London: Edward Arnold.

Golding, P., & Elliott, P. (1979). *Making the news.* London: Longman.

Graber, D. A. (1980). *Mass media and American politics.* Washington, DC: Congressional Quarterly Press.

Grimshaw, A. D. (1973). Sociolinguistics. In I. de Sola Pool, F. W. Frey, W.L. Schramm, N. Maccoby, & E. B. Parker (Eds.), *Handbook of communication.* Chicago: Rand McNally.

Gurevitch, M., Blumler, J. G., & Weaver, D. (1986). *The formation of campaign agendas in the U.S. and Britain: A conceptual introduction.* Paper presented at the International Communication Association Convention.

Hall, S. (1977). Culture, the media and the "ideological effect." In J. Curran, M. Gurevitch, & J. Woollacott (Eds.), *Mass communication and society.* London: Edward Arnold.

Hall, S. (1982). The rediscovery of ideology: Return of the repressed in media studies. In M. Gurevitch, T. Bennett, J. Curran, & J. Woollacott (Eds.), *Culture, society and the media.* New York: Methuen.

Hallin, D. C. (1985). The rise of the ten second bite: Changing conventions in television coverage of the presidency, 1965-1985. Paper presented at the Southern Political Science Association Convention.

Hallin, D. C., & Mancini, P. (1984). Speaking of the president: Political structure and representational form in U.S. and Italian television news. *Theory and Society, 13,* 829-850.

Halloran, J. D. (1964). *The effects of mass communication, with special reference to television* (Working Paper No. 1). Leicester: Leicester University Press.

Halloran, J. D. (1974). *Mass media and society: The challenge of research.* Leicester: Leicester University Press.

Harré, R. (1972). *Philosophies of science.* Oxford: Oxford University Press.

Heider, F. (1958). *The psychology of interpersonal relations.* New York: John Wiley.

Hovland, C. I., Lumsdaine, A. A., & Sheffield, F. D. (1949). *Experiments on mass communication.* Princeton: Princeton University Press.

Innis, H. (1950). *Empire and communication.* Oxford: Clarendon Press.

Jay, M. (1973). *The dialectical imagination: A history of the Frankfurt school and the Institute of Social Research 1923-1950.* Boston: Little, Brown.

Katz, E. (1960). Communication research and the image of society: A convergence of two traditions. *American Journal of Sociology, 64,* 435-440.

Katz, E. & Lazarsfeld, P. F. (1955). *Personal influence.* New York: Free Press.

Katz, E., & Wedell, G. (1978). *Broadcasting and the Third World.* London: Macmillan.

Kelly, M., & Siune, K. (1983). Television campaign structures. In J. G. Blumler (Ed.), *Communicating to voters: Television in the first European parliamentary elections.* Newbury Park, CA: Sage.

Key, V. O. (1961). *Public opinion and American democracy.* New York: Knopf.

Klapper, J. (1960). *The effects of mass communication.* New York: Free Press.

Köcher, R. (1986). Bloodhounds or missionaries: Role definitions of German and British journalists. *European Journal of Communication, 1,* 43-64.

Kornhauser, W. (1959). *The politics of mass society.* New York: Free Press.

Lang, K. (1979). The critical functions of empirical communication research: Observations on German-American influences. *Media, Culture and Society, 1,* 83-96.

Lang, K., & Lang, G. E., (1959). The mass media and voting. In E. J. Burdick & A. J. Brodbeck (Eds.), *American voting behavior.* New York: Free Press.

Lasswell, H. D. (1927). *Propaganda technique in the World War.* New York: Knopf.

Lasswell, H. D. (1948). The structure and function of communication in society. In L. Bryson (Ed.), *The communication of ideas.* New York: Institute for Religious and Social Studies.

Lazarsfeld, P. F. (1941). Remarks on administrative and critical research. In *Studies in Philosophy and Social Science.* Pittsburgh: University of Pittsburgh Press.

Lazarsfeld, P. F. (1948). Communication research and the social psychologist. In *Current trends in social psychology.* Pittsburgh: University of Pittsburgh Press.

Lazarsfeld, P. F. (1959). Evidence and inference in social research. In D. Lerner (Ed.), *Evidence and inference.* New York: Free Press.

Lazarsfeld, P. F., Berelson, B., & Gaudet, H. (1948). *The people's choice.* New York: Columbia University Press.

Lazarsfeld, P. F., & Merton, R. K. (1948). Mass communication, popular taste and organized social action. In L. Bryson (Ed.), *The communication of ideas.* New York: Institute for Religious and Social Studies.

Lee, A. M., & Lee, E. B. (1939). *The fine art of propaganda: A study of Father Coughlin's speeches.* New York: Harcourt Brace Jovanovich.

Lerner, D. (1957). Communication systems and social systems. *Behavioral Science, 2,* 266-275.

Liebes, T., & Katz, E. (1986). Patterns of involvement in television fiction: A comparative analysis. *European Journal of Communication, 1,* 151-171.

Linné, O., & Hartmann, P. (1986). Family differences on television. *European Journal of Communication, 1,* 407-420.

Lippmann, W. (1922). *Public opinion.* New York: Macmillan.

Lowery, S., & DeFleur, M. L. (1983). *Milestones in mass communication research: Media effects.* New York: Longman.

Maine, H.J.S. (1885). *Popular government.* London: Murray.

Manicas, P. T., & Secord, P. F. (1983). Implications for psychology of the new philosophy of science. *American Psychologist, 38,* 399-413.

McClelland, D. C. (1961). *The achieving society.* Princeton: Van Nostrand.

McCombs, M. E., & Shaw, D. L. (1972). The agenda-setting function of the media. *Public Opinion Quarterly, 36,* 176-187.

McLeod, J. M., Becker, L., & Byrnes, J. (1974). Another look at the agenda setting function of the press. *Communication Research, 1,* 131-166.

McLeod, J. M., Bybee, C. R., & Durall, J. A. (1979). Equivalence of informed political participation: The 1976 presidential debates as a source of influence. *Communication Research, 6,* 463-487.

McLeod, J. M., Glynn, C. J., & McDonald, D. G. (1983). Issues and images: The influence of media reliance in voting decisions. *Communication Research, 10,* 37-58.

McLeod, J. M., & Reeves, B. (1980). On the nature of mass media effects. In S. B. Withey & R. P. Abeles (Eds.), *Television and social behavior: Beyond violence and children.* Hillsdale, NJ: Lawrence Erlbaum.

McLuhan, M. (1964). *Understanding media.* London: Routledge & Kegan Paul.

McQuail, D. (1984). *Mass communication theory: An introduction.* Newbury Park, CA: Sage.

McQuail, D., & Siune, K. (1986). *New media politics: Comparative perspectives in Western Europe.* London: Sage.

McQuail, D., & Windahl, S. (1981). *Communication models for the study of mass communications.* London: Longman.

Merton, R. K. (1957). *Social theory and social structure* (rev. ed.). New York: Free Press.

Mills, C. W. (1956). *The power elite.* New York: Oxford University Press.

Morley, D. (1980). *The "nationwide" audience* (Television Monograph No. 11). London: British Film Institute.

Mosco, V. (1982). *Pushbutton fantasies: Critical perspectives on videotex and information technology.* Norwood, NJ: Ablex.

Murdock, G., & Golding, P. (1977). Capitalism, communication and class relations. In J. Curran, M. Gurevitch, & J. Woollacott (Eds.), *Mass communication and society.* London: Edward Arnold.

Murdock, G., & Golding, P. (1978). Theories of communication and theories of society. *Communication Research, 5,* 339-356.

Newcomb, T. M. (1953). An approach to the study of communicative acts. *Psychological Review, 60,* 393-404.

Nie, N. H., Verba, S., & Petrocik, J. R. (1976). *The changing American voter.* Cambridge, MA: Harvard University Press.

Nimmo, D. D. (1978). *Political communication and public opinion in America.* Santa Monica, CA: Goodyear.

Noelle-Neumann, E. (1983). *The spiral of silence: Our social skin.* Chicago: University of Chicago Press.

Ortega y Gasset, J. (1932). *The revolt of the masses.* New York: Norton. (Original work published 1930)

Osgood, C. E., Suci, G. J., & Tannenbaum, P. H. (1957). *The measurement of meaning.* Urbana: University of Illinois Press.

Park, R. E. (1938). Reflections on communication and culture. *American Journal of Sociology, 44,* 187-205.

Patterson, T. E. (1980). *The mass media election: How Americans choose their president.* New York: Praeger.

Patterson, T. E., & McClure, R. D. (1976). *The unseeing eye: The myth of television power in national elections.* New York: Putnam.

Peterson, R. C., & Thurstone, L. L. (1933). *Motion pictures and the social attitudes of children.* New York: Macmillan.

Polsby, N. W. (1980). The news media as an alternative to party in the presidential selection process. In R. A. Goldwin (Ed.), *Political parties in the eighties.* Washington, DC: American Enterprise Institute.

Pool, I. de S., Frey, F. W., Schramm, W. L., Maccoby, N. & Parker, E. B. (Eds.). (1973). *Handbook of communication.* Chicago: Rand McNally.

Przeworski, A., & Teune, H. (1970). *The logic of comparative social inquiry.* New York: John Wiley.

Ranney, A. (1983). *Channels of power: The impact of television on American politics.* New York: Basic Books.

Robinson, M. J. (1975). American political legitimacy in one era of electronic journalism: Reflections on the evening news. In D. Cater & R. Adler (Eds.), *Television as a social force: New approaches to TV criticism.* New York: Praeger.

Robinson, M. J. (1976). Public affairs television and the growth of political malaise: The case of "The Selling of the Pentagon." *American Political Science Review, 70,* 409-432.

Robinson, M. J. (1977). Television and American politics: 1956-1976. *Public Interest, 48,* 3-39.

Robinson, M. J., & Sheehan, M. A. (1983). *Over the wire and on TV: CBS and UPI in campaign '80.* New York: Russell Sage Foundation.

Rogers, E. M. (1962). *The diffusion of innovations.* New York: Free Press.

Rogers, E. M. (1976). Communication and development: The passing of a dominant paradigm. *Communication Research, 3,* 213-240.

Rogers, E. M., & Shoemaker, F. F. (1971). *Communication of innovations: A cross-cultural approach.* New York: Free Press.

Rosenberg, M. J. (1960). An analysis of affective-cognitive consistency. In C. I. Hovland & M. J. Rosenberg (Eds.), *Attitude organization and change.* New Haven: Yale University Press.

Rosenberg, M. (1968). *The logic of survey analysis.* New York: Basic Books.

Rosengren, K. E. (1981). Mass media and social change: Some current approaches. In E. Katz & T. Szecsko (Eds.), *Mass media and social change.* Newbury Park, CA: Sage.

Savage, R. L. (1981). The diffusion of information. In D. D. Nimmo & K. R. Sanders (Eds.), *Handbook of political communication.* Newbury Park, CA: Sage.

Schiller, H. (1969). *Mass communication and American empire.* New York: Augustus M. Kelly.

Schramm, W. L. (1954). *The process and effects of mass communication.* Urbana: University of Illinois Press.

Schramm, W. L., & Roberts, D. F. (1971). *The process and effects of mass communication* (rev. ed.). Urbana: University of Illinois Press.

Scott, W. D. (1921). *The psychology of advertising in theory and practice.* Boston: Small, Maynard.

Scott, W. D., Clothier, R. C., & Spriegel, W. R. (1949). *Personnel management: Principles, practices and point of view.* New York: McGraw-Hill.

Shils, E. A., & Janowitz, M. (1948). Cohesion and disintegration in the Wehrmacht in World War II. *Public Opinion Quarterly, 12,* 280-315.

Siebert, F. S., Peterson, T., & Schramm, W. L. (1956). *Four theories of the press.* Urbana: University of Illinois Press.

Siune, K., McQuail, D., & Blumler, J. G. (1984). Broadcasting European elections. *Electoral Studies, 3,* 256-263.

Smythe, D. W. (1977). Communications: Blindspot of Western Marxism. *Canadian Journal of Political and Social Theory, 1,* 120-127.

Speed, J. G. (1893). Do newspapers now give the news? *The Forum, 15,* 705-711.

Stinchcombe, A. L. (1968). *Constructing social theories.* New York: Harcourt Brace Jovanovich.

Tarde, G. (1890). *Les Lois de l'imitation: Etude Sociologique.* Paris: Felix Alcan.

Thoveron, G. (1986). European televised women. *European Journal of Communication, 1,* 289-300.

Thunberg, A., Nowak, K., Rosengren, K. E., & Bengt, S. (1982). *Communication and equality: A Swedish perspective.* Stockholm: Almquist & Wiksell.

Tichenor, P. J., Donohue, G. A., & Olien, C. N. (1970). Mass media and differential growth in knowledge. *Public Opinion Quarterly, 34,* 158-170.

Tichenor, P. J., Donohue, G. A., & Olien, C. N. (1980). *Community conflict and the press.* Newbury Park, CA: Sage.

Toennies, F. (1887). *Gemeinschaft und gesellschaft.* Leipzig: Fues's Verlag.

Tuchman, G. (1978). *Making news: A study in the construction of reality.* New York: Free Press.

Tunstall, J. (1971). *Journalists at work.* London: Constable.

Weaver, D. H., Wilhoit, G. C., & Semetko, H. (1986). *The role of the press in the formation of campaign agendas in Britain and the United States.* Paper presented at the International Communication Association Convention.

Weber, M. (1910). *Zeitungwesen.* Report to the first meeting of the German Sociological Society, Deutsche Gesellschaft fur Soziologie, 39-62.

White, D. M. (1950). The "gate keeper": A case study in the selection of news. *Journalism Quarterly, 27,* 383-390.

Whorf, B. L. (1938). Some verbal categories of Hopi. *Language, 14,* 275-286.

Wirth, L. (1948). Consensus and mass communication. *American Sociological Review, 13*(February), 1-15.

Wright, C. R. (1960). Functional analysis and mass communication. *Public Opinion Quarterly, 24,* 605-620.

Wright, C. R. (1974). Functional analysis and mass communication revisited. In J. G. Blumler & E. Katz (Eds.), *The uses of mass communications.* Newbury Park, CA: Sage.

PART III
FUNCTIONS

10 Functions of Communication: An Introduction

STEVEN H. CHAFFEE
Stanford University

CHARLES R. BERGER
Northwestern University

HUMANS are purposeful beings, and they use communication for many of their purposes. The concept of "functions" reminds us of this central fact. The functions that communication can serve exist in endless variety—as endless as human purposes themselves—so we cannot hope to be comprehensive here. We must be selective, and in the context of our four-level scheme (see Part II) we should be analytical as well.

The following six chapters examine some very broad functions for which people rely on communication heavily. In the first, McQuail (Chapter 11) provides an overview of this kind of analysis. It develops a matrix of its own, using levels and then types of functions at each level, and lists numerous examples of functions within each cell.

The remaining five chapters deal with themes that have stimulated a great deal of research. The first two examine the basic tools of communication: language (Giles & Wiemann, Chapter 12) and nonverbal signals (Knapp, Cody, & Reardon, Chapter 13). In both cases, though, functions for which people use these tools are stressed. Giles and Wiemann are particularly concerned, for example, about the role language plays in reflecting and creating social power. Knapp, Cody, and Reardon focus on the role played by nonverbal signals in the deployment and detection of deceptive communication. O'Keefe and Reid-Nash (Chapter 14) examine the long-standing tradition of research on socialization, both to and via communication, across levels of analysis.

The final two chapters in this section address some very broad social functions that have been subjects of extensive scientific study. Miller (Chapter 15) looks at the basic human task of persuasion and the gaining of compliance. Roloff (Chapter 16) takes on the topic of conflict at each level of analysis, showing both the functional and dysfunctional aspects of human conflict. Neither persuasion nor conflict management would be conceivable without the capacity to communicate. At the same time, neither is easily accomplished. Communication skills and techniques have a long way to go in achieving such purposes as compliance-gaining or social harmony.

The term "function" often arouses criticism in academic circles—a concern that is evident in McQuail's chapter, where he describes himself as a nonfunctionalist. The assumptions of functional analysis have been attacked in sociology as conservative, unscientific, tautological, and generally to be eschewed. We do not mean to conjure up that debate, interesting as it might be, by use of the title "Functions" here. Rather, we simply wish to group these chapters by calling attention to a loose linking premise. We—in common with other students of communication, scientific and otherwise—have no difficulty in assuming that communication is mostly a purposeful activity.

11 Functions of Communication: A Nonfunctionalist Overview

DENIS McQUAIL
University of Amsterdam

I T is quite common in many of the disparate and often unrelated areas of work that belong to communication science to find references to communication as being "functional" or to particular "functions" assigned to communication. Yet it is difficult to discover any systematic functional framework for theory and research that is widely accepted or that spans the several levels of communication analysis treated in this book.

At an early stage in the development of the study of communication, Lasswell (1948) did try to sketch such a framework. He named three general functions of all communication: "surveillance of the environment" (monitoring, intelligence gathering for security and adaptation), "correlation of parts" (for integration), and "transmission of the cultural heritage" (for social continuity). This scheme was picked up mainly as a guide to organizing propositions about mass communication, especially its effects (Wright, 1960, 1974).

Although functional terminology is quite liberally used in other branches of communication, a functionalist theory seems only to have been influential as a guide to research regarding mass media. It has particularly given rise to the "uses and gratifications" approach to the study of media audiences, which aims to identify, describe, and quantify people's motives for attending to mass communication (Blumler & Katz, 1974; Palmgreen, Rosengren, & Wenner, 1985).

An exception to the absence of a systematic functionalist consideration outside mass media is the work of Dance and Larson (1976). They organized their theoretical discussion of human communication around three basic functions that differ somewhat from Lasswell's: "linking" (of individuals to the environment), "mentation" (development of higher mental processes), and "regulatory" (regulation of human conduct). Despite this kind of theoretical work and the research into media audience motivations, no framework exists for comparing the many phenomena that have at one time or another been regarded as communication functions. Suggestions like those of Lasswell and Dance seem somewhat arbitrary or idiosyncratic, derived from no clear antecedent logic or body of evidence. For this reason, a new starting point has been adopted here and will be outlined below.

The subtitle of this chapter requires some explanation. The approach offered here is "nonfunctionalist" mainly in that it does not rest on any particular variety of functionalist theory. It is at best agnostic about the status of functionalism in the context of the controversy that has raged for some years within sociology. I am even inclined to the view expressed by Giddens (1979), that functionalism is too discredited to be of further use as a theory. Nevertheless it is useful to follow Max Weber and retain the concept of *function* for "provisional orientation and practical illustration." It can be especially helpful in this way here, given the continued currency of the term in communication study.

Reasons for rejection of *functionalism* are not strictly relevant to this presentation, but the central problem is worth some attention. In virtually all serious functionalist theory, the essential element is a relation of *necessity* between one phenomenon and another, or between act and action. Thus functionalist explanations are ultimately *causal* explanations; to say that something is a function of something else is to say that one thing causes another or that something is necessarily dependent on another. Propositions of this kind can rarely be demonstrated in social life, so that functionalism always carries a good deal of excess baggage. To say, for instance, that a given conversation between persons A and B has a "linking function" may entail the following: that person A *needs* to be linked to B; that A is *dependent* on B; and that linking will be an *effect,* whether intended or not, of the conversation. It would be difficult even in such a simple case to demonstrate any of these propositions— even if they were all true. One can qualify a functional formulation to eliminate unwanted corollaries, but that would be a tedious business.

The approach here is also nonfunctionalist because it gives a meaning to the term "function" that was expressly rejected by Merton (1957), the theorist who probably did most to promote functional analysis of mass communication: the meaning of task, or purpose. Merton argued that function should only be used to refer to effects or consequences, whether consciously intended or not, and whether beneficial or not for the human system concerned. He was, in doing so, being true to a causal, deterministic model that he hoped to rescue from its confused state.

A particular weakness of a truly functionalist analysis of communication is the implicit supposition that all communication has a manifest or latent utility. By confining attention in this discussion to purposeful (problem-solving) communication behavior, some attempt has been made to evade this doubtful and unnecessary proposition. Much communication is either *purposeless* or an end in itself—for intrinsic satisfaction and without ulterior motive or expected consequences. This applies to interpersonal contact and self-expression as well as to reception of communication by way of arts and mass media (McQuail, 1984). For the most part, such communication cannot be validly or usefully analyzed in those functional terms that have been chosen for the present discussion.

The present approach is not without its own difficulties, despite its attempt to be pragmatic and to escape from a debate that has grown sterile. To a sociologist, the approach may seem to fall into the trap of subjectivism and individualism; a behavioral psychologist is equally unlikely to be happy with an approach that seems unduly voluntaristic and mentalistic. The defense offered is simply that no effort will be made to choose between, let alone elaborate on, any particular theory in which the terms collected here might be deployed. The aim is simply to inventory certain recurrent features of human communication, to promote comparison across levels of analysis according to a consistent usage of the term "function."

FUNCTION AS PURPOSE

The choice made here is to take the point of view of the actor and assign meaning to actions from this perspective. A function, then, is a purposeful communication activity as it might seem to the acting unit or agent, such as a person, group, or organization. The fact that a given action might occur without conscious motivation or awareness of any goal is not strictly relevant to the construction of a typology of communication actions. Nor does it matter if the meaning assigned could equally be expressed as a goal or an effect. In an empirical investigation it clearly does matter. But in complex human behavior "consequences" and "purposes" are often interchangeable, and consequences can occur without any clearly identifiable purpose or cause.

To treat function as purpose is not only to choose the perspective of a communicating agent. It is also to choose a moment in time in a process, at the end of which lies an outcome—whether or not intended or even expected, whether satisfactory to the initiator or not. Before this moment there is assumed to exist a condition that may account for the communication act, which can be labeled a "problem." (Here, "problem" does not imply a negative aspect, but includes the wider notion of choice or decision.) For purposes of classifying different types of communication acts, it is enough to assume an *association in time* between problem and *act,* without necessarily assuming any *causal* connection between problem and *action.* We are seeking to establish patterns, regularities, or "rules of the game" rather than to pursue causal-sequential analysis or to establish necessary connections between circumstances and actions. Our view of function is essentially a meaning or reference that links a perceived problem with a particular kind of communication act, as differentiated by content, form, or direction.

The main elements needed to define the nature of communication functions in the sense of tasks or purposes are (1) an acting unit, or agent, (2) a communicative action; and (3) a set of labels indicating the meaning of a category of acts. The first of these is relatively easy to arrive at; it is largely given by the levels of analysis that structure this volume. Communicating agents can be individuals, or any group, organization, or other collective body that acts either internally in relation to its own members or externally in relation to other individuals or collective bodies or to its own environment.

Communication acts are behaviors that involve producing, sending, receiving, storing, processing, or seeking information or messages. Messages, for this purpose, are symbolic constructs that have a meaningful reference to sender, receiver, or environment. The criterion of meaningfulness requires that the message or information be understandable to the actors involved. Thus it should convey information (i.e., serve to reduce uncertainty) and senders should be able to assume that information will be received more or less as intended. Receivers in turn should have some confidence that what they take as meaning corresponds to what was intended.

Little need be said here of the varied nature of messages. There are numerous symbolic codes, languages, and forms of expression that may well be associated with a particular communication function; some may even be necessary for some communication purposes. For the most part, however, languages (whether verbal, kinetic, pictorial, or whatever) and channels (social, physical, or other) are sufficiently versatile to serve many different kinds of functions. Associations between forms of message, channel used, and meaning carried are usually culturally or situationally determined and are highly variable. It would make little sense to approach the question of communication functions by this route.

A CONCEPTUAL FRAMEWORK

There is not, as we have noted, any universal framework through which to arrive at a set of functionally descriptive labels. But lists of functions and communication needs do exist, and by collecting them from different studies it would be possible to extract the recurrent themes. A second approach would be to identify theories that posit functions for communication. Both these possibilities have their drawbacks, though. There are too many extant lists of functions, conceptualized at too many different levels. There are also numerous theories, too diverse to integrate. In a review of theories of psychological motivations for attending to mass media, for example, McGuire (1974) was able to derive 16 kinds of motives or functions from an even larger number of theoretical perspectives. To achieve even this measure of economy he had to limit rather strictly the scope of his work. He noted that many thousands of words could "fall under the motivational rubric," and that a brief consideration of any small area of social behavior would reveal a large number of motives associated with communication acts; according to our definition here, each of these might be considered a function.

One way to construct a schema of communication functions is to begin with the dimensions used by McGuire to generate his theoretical categories of motivation, even though they were only intended for discussion of one kind of communication act—receiving mass media. In themselves these dimensions indicate key functional categories, and in combination they can generate even more.

McGuire first distinguishes *cognitive* from *affective* behaviors. The former stresses instrumentality and rationality; the latter, emotional satisfactions, feelings, and values. The cognitive kinds of behavior can be readily paralleled at more complex levels of social organization—for instance, in the formal decision-making processes of organizations and societies. The "affective" category does not strictly apply to units other than human individuals, but there is a loose parallel in the cultural, evaluative, and symbolizing aspects of wider social communication, with a potential for integration and social solidarity. The second distinction McGuire draws is between an orientation to *stability* or *growth*, thus to preservation or to change; this is more easily recognized at all levels of social organization. The third dimension, *active* versus *passive*, is equally universal since any unit act of communication can be considered as either action or reaction. The fourth—internal versus external orientation of action—is also clearly relevant to classifying the purpose of a wide range of communicative acts.

Certain other dimensions have to be considered to take account of the wider scope of the present discussion. The most important addition, which can be called *connection versus disconnection,* is peculiarly important for communication, which can be a means of establishing either similarity or difference, contact or avoidance, cooperation or conflict. To a degree this dimension corresponds with the "linking" function of Dance and Larson (1976). The location of communication acts in time raises the possibility of distinguishing between communication oriented to the past (e.g., storage of information), the present, or the future. The spatial aspect of communication also indicates a significant difference between lateral and vertical communication in any hierarchical situation. The variable of symmetry in communication relationships has consequences for the direction and amount of flow of communication, as well as its content. We might also make use of a dimension of communication introduced by Innis (1950) in which orientation to time (i.e., toward continuity) is posed as an alternative to spatial orientation (i.e., toward the extent of influence or reach of information at a given time).

We should differentiate not only between motives for communication but also among types of acts—producing, sending, receiving, and so forth. These terms are a good deal more complex than they look. "Receiving," for example, includes attention giving, registering, decoding, and interpretation. Each process can be elaborated to disclose a sequence of stages or subprocesses. This underlines the magnitude of any attempt to inventory functions by taking account of the main dimensions, the types of communication, and the levels of analysis. The interrelation of these three alone would produce a large matrix that would require still further subdivision. There is consequently a need to begin at a yet higher level of generality. The aim should be to establish broad categories of communication function, which would have equal potential for reference to each level of analysis and which capture the important components of the dimensions discussed.

To arrive at such a scheme we can employ the problem-solving formulation (see above) to deploy the elements that have been described. We are thus concerned with situations in which acting units (agents of communication) exist in an environment of other units, objects, or events and use communication to find solutions to problems they experience. Problems are either generated in the environment or are self-generated, involving a wish to act on the environment. This formulation presupposes that communication is a dynamic process, having a direction and thus a source and destination (which are not the same as cause and effect). According to our view of function we are concerned mainly with the question of why persons engage in communication acts. This focuses us on the relation between problem as experienced, defined, or chosen by the acting unit, and the communication solution adopted. The functional label is in a sense a description of this relationship.

The main categories for the typology of communication functions can be arrived at by using these materials in one further step. In the most elementary case there are limited possibilities for locating the source of any problem and the destination or orientation of any communication solution. Problems can originate either within the communicating unit or in its environment. Similarly, solutions are directed either toward the environment, or inward—toward the unit itself. (The meaning of "direction" here has to do with the location of the point to which a message is directed or the point on which the communication act should have some effect.) If these two basic alternatives are cross-tabulated, as in Figure

11.1, they can identify the main kinds of communication function, in the sense of task or purpose.

The tentative labels for the four cells are not directly given by the logic of the dichotomy. They are somewhat subjective descriptions of different categories of communication purpose, informed by the literature as discussed briefly above. Type I, concerning internally originated problems and internally oriented solutions, typically has to do with such matters as consciousness, identity, and consistency. "Identity" might even be a better term than "Being" here, but it has too little connotation of growth and change. These ideas are carried by the label "Being," echoing Maslow's (1968) discussion of a hierarchy of human needs extending from the physiological upward to needs for growth and self-actualization of an aesthetic, moral, and intellectual kind. A difficulty in going further with this exploration of the nature of these basic categories is that any explanation (and the descriptive labels used) must vary according to the *level* at which the scheme is applied. The labels given in Figure 11.1 lean to a certain extent toward the individual or interpersonal level. The bias cannot be easily removed, so the following discussion should be regarded as illustrating the meaning of these basic categories at the various levels. Type I functions, at whatever level, are likely to involve acts of communication that have to do more with producing, storing, and processing information than with sending, exchanging, seeking, or receiving it.

Type II, labeled "Adaptation," concerns the response to changes, challenges, or pressures from the environment that threaten to disturb normal functioning or survival. The emphasis in this cell is on stability rather than growth, on the passive more than the active, and on more "cognitive" than "affective" kinds of communication. The concepts of balance, consistency, and homeostasis are relevant in this context, as is the notion of communication as link to the environment (Davison, 1959).

		Problem originates:	
		Within unit (internally)	In environment (externally)
Communication solution is directed:	Internally	Type I (Being)	Type II (Adaptation)
	Externally	Type IV (Control)	Type III (Affiliation)

Figure 11.1. Basic typology of communication functions.

Type III ("External-external") has to do with interactive relations between units or (just possibly) between unit and environment. A term from social psychology meaning a drive toward liking and attachment seems appropriate. Equal weight, however, may in practice need to be given to the reverse tendency—toward disconnection or dissociation, in which communication can play an equally important part.

Finally Type IV, labeled "Control," refers to any actively chosen purposes of changing or manipulating the environment (including other units within it). The label "Control" is somewhat strong, but alternatives—such as "guidance" or "regulation"—are either too weak or too specific in their meaning. The emphasis is on initiatives taken by the acting unit in its own interest. The kinds of communication act most often involved have to do with producing, sending, exchanging, and seeking information. Depending on the context and level, though, they could be affective as well as cognitive.

In the sections that follow these four types are examined at each of five levels and a provisional inventory of communication functions for each level is proposed.

INTRAPERSONAL COMMUNICATION

Intrapersonal communication refers primarily to thinking and information-processing activities that are not externally observable although the person concerned may be aware of them (Roloff & Berger, 1982). At this level of analysis we are concerned mainly with the seeking out, reception, interpretation, and further processing of messages or signals from an environment of objects, events, and other people. The category of Being functions is most salient at this level and is often the key to other functions.

This approach assumes a tendency by the individual to acquire and maintain a consistent self-image, a set of values, a maximum of self-satisfaction, and a frame of reference to make consistent sense of incoming information. Communication not only allows a person to collect and process materials for these ends, it permits self-monitoring through listening to one's own utterances. Much communication of this type is nonutilitarian—it is not calculated to achieve specific ends—but rather consummatory—an end in itself (Carey, 1975). It has to do with the formation and expression of an identity and a consciousness of the self.

External communication feeds into this process, since individuals use messages received to build the self and also to compare themselves with real or fictional others. They also reflect on their past experience, if necessary reshaping their perception of it to maximize a favorable self-concept. The subcategories of functions relating to Being include

- maintaining consistent and positive self-image,
- self-reinforcing of values,
- self-monitoring, and
- developing self and consciousness of self

In respect of Adaptation, the thrust of most theory is to emphasize a need to maintain a cognitive balance with the environment. This assumes the individual seeks to avoid the sense of discomfort arising from a discrepancy between the self-image and images held by others or what the environment seems to require. The processes involved are more passive or reactive than active, and the aim is self-preservation rather than growth (in contrast to Being functions). At this level, the logic of the notion of adaptation is that attention is paid to external matters for internal purposes. The emphasis is thus on seeking, receiving, and processing messages rather than on producing and sending.

The most relevant body of theory is that of balance and dissonance, which posits that perceived discrepancies stimulate acts of information seeking (Festinger, 1957; Newcomb, 1953). Another relevant body of theory is that concerned with attribution, which according to McGuire (1974) "depicts a person as an implicit theorist attributing causes and motives to occurrences in experience and responding to any occurrences, not so much in terms of its appearance as in terms of causal interpretations that one makes of it" (on attribution theory see also Heider, 1958; Jones & Davis, 1965; Kelley, 1967). The sources of messages relevant to adaptation can be varied, ranging from personal encounters to mass communicated accounts of remote events.

While formally, according to the terms of Figure 11.1, adaptation relates to externally originated problems, some causes may lie within the self, as when aging or sickness alter a person's relation to an environment. Many of the situations prompting a search for internally oriented communication solutions have to do with socially instituted role requirements that are liable to change. Thus processes of finding and adopting appropriate models, frames and scripts for behavior (Schank & Abelson, 1977) comprise an important set of communication functions in themselves. In the literature on attitude formation and change, reference is made to an ego-defensive motive (Katz, 1960) that leads a person to adopt self-supportive attitudes in a threatening environment. This may be considered a separate internal communication function related to adaptation. Communication functions relevant to intrapersonal adaptation, then, include

- attending to or monitoring the environment;
- interpreting the environment;
- reducing cognitive dissonance;

- reducting uncertainty;
- acquiring or constructing appropriate models, scripts, schemas;
- presenting self to accord with external expectations or circumstances; and
- ego-defensive attitude formation.

There is little to be said about Affiliation that is not better dealt with at the interpersonal level. Intrapersonal Affiliation functions are basically the same as those for Adaptation, although they differ according to the dimensions discussed earlier, being more concerned with keeping contact and avoiding isolation. They are more active than passive, more affective than cognitive, and more concerned with growth than with stability. One kind of communication process described in the literature on attitude formation (e.g., Kelman, 1960) is *identification;* this refers to the wish to adopt ideas, appearance, or other attributes of valued others in order to feel or to demonstrate a close relationship and attachment. There are several ways in which communication can help in this process. In summary, additional functions at this level include

- identification with valued others,
- expressing social proximity or distance, and
- comparison with others.

A consideration of Control functions at the intrapersonal level does not generate important new items. However, our framework emphasizes the intention of acting on the environment for personally chosen ends, so it would be appropriate to emphasize also the production of communication, the development of communication skills, and the expression of the result. Although from one point of view control is the reverse of adaptation, many of the communication devices described by Goffman (1974) under such names as "facework" and "framing" are equally suited to manipulation of as adaption to an environment. We can summarize by adding the item

- manipulation of impression formation.

INTERPERSONAL COMMUNICATION

The change of level is signaled by the fact that we now consider persons as exchanging messages with other persons, thus as engaged in formulating and sending messages as well as receiving and processing them. At issue is purposeful interaction with others in social relationships in which communication plays an indispensable part. The sphere of interpersonal communication still accounts for a major part of communication behavior for the average person, a fact reflected by the very large body of relevant literature (e.g., Berger & Bradac, 1982; Miller, 1976; Roloff & Berger, 1982). Obviously this activity overlaps with communication at other levels (groups, organizations, society, etc.), and it is convenient to consider an additional criterion relating to the *topic* of communication as well as to the number of participants. Thus interpersonal communication is that which, in a variety of settings, deals primarily with informal matters of personal interest to participants. As to the number of participants, most interpersonal communication probably occurs in dyadic settings (Wilmot, 1975), but a certain proportion occurs in group situations of indeterminate extent. Where, as in the case of couples, a very clear dyadic formation is involved, communication may lead to the emergence of the dyad (couple) as a new acting unit in communication, with its own needs and purposes of communication. This process may be seen in functional terms, according to our scheme, as

- formation and growth of the dyad as a joint identity.

In other situations of interpersonal communication, the acting unit remains the individual and there is little reason to add to what has been said above with respect to Being functions.

With respect to Adaptation there is more to be said of interpersonal relationships, since communication forms part of a continuous process of exchange and monitoring between persons. The relevant communication acts and purposes are stimulated by the other person in the process of maintaining or deepening a relationship. In this context, the process is characteristically reactive, cognitive, and concerned with stability and connection. It is oriented to the present, is usually lateral rather than vertical, and primarily involves exchange. Terms that describe these communication functions are

- monitoring,
- feedback, and
- coorientation.

Affiliation functions are most central at the interpersonal level, where the actors are primarily concerned with establishing contact or marking differences; communication is relevant to both. It should be noted that interpersonal relations can be between persons in a close environment or persons widely separated physically (and even socially). The wider the separation, the more important is communication. For instance, a relationship can exist with a public hero or a movie star, a personality known only by way of mass media. In closer, more equal relationships, communication is important, but there are other kinds of commonality to cement the relationship, such as social similarity and location.

Identification and internalization (see above) are accomplished through selection and interpretation of communication in the spheres of values, consciousness, ideas, and behavior. A wide range of communication acts can be involved in Affiliation functions, but predominant are the production, expression, and exchange of messages. There are also many communicative ways in which attraction or deference can be expressed in speech, body language, and writing. Devices have been identified in conversational analysis for opening contacts or signaling attraction and agreement. We can summarize the main functions as

- establishing contact,
- expressing deference or attachment,
- offering symbolic gratification or reward to another,
- establishing vicarious contact with valued other (identification),
- establishing social distance through symbols, and
- breaking contact.

A part of what has been said is also relevant to Control—that is, to communication strategies enabling one person to dominate, influence, or direct another in a relationship. These include favorable presentation of self, offering symbolic rewards or punishments, establishing and controlling areas of communicative competence, claiming attention, monopolizing time in interaction, controlling the agenda for any discussion, and setting the terms on which exchanges take place. This kind of communication function is always active, more or less planned, and usually related to extension and growth.

The motive and means can be either cognitive or affective; the orientation is always external and in the interest of the self. An example in the cognitive sphere would be the employment of "expert" knowledge or argument to establish oneself as an influential person or opinion leader on a subject. An example in the affective sphere would be nonverbal behavior, such as physical contact, to establish higher status or to show affection. Much research on conversational patterns identifies devices people use to control the flow of talk for relational advantage. In some hierarchical contexts, such as parent- or teacher-child relationships, communicative control by command, threat, or rebuke is quite overt. Most informal interaction is more competitive, though, and communicative devices carry the burden of attempts to gain (or resist) control. We should add to our list the following sub-functions:

- gaining compliance by symbolic reward or punishment,
- exerting influence through expert knowledge,

- establishing higher status by initiating contact,
- attracting attention,
- setting interpersonal agendas, and
- monopolizing time in interaction.

SOCIAL GROUP COMMUNICATION

Groups are sets of persons with close, long-term ties of association and communication; almost all aspects of social group life can be expressed in terms of communicative functions (Cartwright & Zander, 1968; Homans, 1951). Since groups have a stable consciousness and identity, the notion of Being needs is particularly relevant. Many communicative devices are likely to be involved most fundamentally in marking the boundaries of the group. A precondition and sign of group membership is frequent interaction among members—much more frequent within than across group boundaries. Through this process, common norms and a sense of group identity are developed. Group members often identify themselves as belonging, via distinct expressive forms such as speech, appearance, or style of behavior. Often group subcultures develop, with further consequences for identity and consciousness.

Groups vary in the importance attached to communication for sustaining them. Those that are formally institutionalized (e.g., families) or based on necessary and recurrent cooperation (e.g., work groups) are less reliant on communication for their continuity than are informal and voluntary groups. The main communication functions in this sphere are

- expressing group identity,
- marking boundaries by symbols,
- forming common norms and values, and
- developing and continuing group consciousness.

Adaptation functions in relation to the environment are in general less salient for most groups than they are for individuals or more complex organizational units, partly because most groups do not have exclusive boundaries. Their members have multiple memberships; their environments do not usually exert pressures to adapt in ways that require consistent or organized response; and many groups are "inwardly" oriented, without very pressing survival needs. There are exceptions, but the general categories of adaptive communication function are still similar to those for individuals or organizations (see below).

Affiliation aspects of group life are also not unique although they are important and have much to do with communication activities and norms. Thus the "solidarity" function is very salient in groups, and much communication within the group is directed at achieving this end. This is predominantly affective and informal, concerned with stability rather than growth, with internal connectedness and with disconnection at the boundary. We can at least list the following items as communication functions:

- expressing solidarity, and
- maintaining communicative contact for belonging.

Most groups do not, as suggested, seek or have to act on their environment or to Control other groups, although some such relationships can be found in informal social life. The aspect of Control is thus most relevant *within* groups, generally by way of an unofficial hierarchy of leaders and followers. The lines of this hierarchy can be marked by the frequency, direction, and the initiation of communication of all kinds. Communication is also used to discipline directly, to publicize group norms, and to signal any deviance. At this level, we can make a first entry for "diversionary" activities in the form of games, parties, or amusements that help to release tension and offer rewards for participation and conformity, in general serving solidarity. The following is a summary of communication Control functions at this level:

- gaining, marketing, or maintaining status;
- developing, disseminating, and enforcing group norms;
- publicizing deviance from norms;
- giving symbolic rewards or punishments; and
- contact, tension release, and diversion through amusement.

FORMAL ORGANIZATIONS AND SOCIAL NETWORKS

The discussion must here cover such a wide range of situations that it takes on an increasingly general and approximate character. Between group and society there are many kinds of organizational and institutional networks, which have little in common except a general measure of formality of their communication arrangements. That is, they have rules about who should communicate with whom through which channels and for what purpose (Goldhaber, 1979; Porter & Roberts, 1977; Rogers & Rogers, 1976). It follows that functions of communication in the sense of tasks and purposes should be more explicit and recognizable in formal organizations, although many do remain implicit and hidden.

To deal with the diversity of organizational life, theorists often attempt to classify organizations into functional categories. Etzioni

(1961) divided them globally into three types—coercive, calculative, or normative—according to the nature of power and compliance between higher- and lower-level participants. The coercive organization, such as the army unit or prison, makes open use of force or the threat of it; the calculative organization, such as the business firm and most work organizations, relies on material reward and self-interest as bases for control; the normative organization, such as a church or a political party, depends on voluntary attachment and internalization of values. These are important bases of variation for the character of communicative relations and the balance of functions. Wider social institutions that also give rise to communication networks may be loosely classified in the same way as organizations. For instance, legal and taxation bureaucracies would belong to the coercive category, institutions of consumption and entertainment are calculative, and political and educational institutions normative.

Functions related to Being, identity, and expression are most important for normative organizations, where a widespread consciousness of belonging is a precondition of membership and of the organization's very existence. Communication, often through rituals of various kinds (e.g., church services, elections, rallies), serves to diffuse and reinforce a sense of identity. This function is not entirely absent in coercive organizations, but there its character is quite different. The use of badges, uniforms, and rituals has a more punitive character, exemplifying communication as a substitute for violence. It is difficult to separate Being from Control functions where the latter is inwardly directed. Even business firms often seek to acquire and express an identity or image and may encourage an esprit de corps around a corporate philosophy. Given the reservations noted about diversity of units and the difficulty of separating functions, the main Being functions at the organizational level seem to be

- formation of organizational identity and its expression through symbols; and
- value formation, internal diffusion, and external expression.

As far as Adaptation is concerned, most organizations have elaborate arrangements for collecting intelligence about the environment in which they operate, for processing this information, and for making decisions in response. These communication functions may be clearly represented by such activities as opinion polling, market research, and data processing. These activities are most obvious in calculative organizations, which are sensitive to an economic or political climate. Coercive organizations are relatively insulated from their environments and self-sufficient on a day-to-day basis. Those with a normative character are likely to be inner directed and to respond only slowly to external change or pressure. They may avoid or try to reduce communication inputs that threaten fundamental values, as in the case of secularization of religious belief systems. A summary listing of organizational control functions includes

- monitoring and surveillance of environment;
- information seeking, gathering, and processing;
- feedback and exchange; and
- internal articulation of tasks and roles.

Solidarity and differentiation of members by task or status are related to Affiliation as well as to Being (as discussed above). In formal organizations there are informal networks—mainly horizontal, between status equals—that lead to attachment patterns of members. These often provide chains and networks that function as alternatives to official channels, carrying gossip and rumor. External affiliation (one organization with another) is most evident in the case of normative organizations, where Being needs are also paramount. Thus political and religious groups are likely to signal their attachment to, or differences from, other groups, in order both to cement their identity and boundaries and to form coalitions. In summary, affiliative functions of organizations include

- maintaining formal networks and encouraging informal ones;
- marking and maintaining boundaries of organization;
- promote solidarity, attachment, and integration; and
- providing social events for bonding and sense of belonging.

The Control group of functions is vital to all organizations, especially in their internal aspects. As noted, coercive organizations use threats of violence or symbolic punishment, such as public degradation, to produce long-term submission. More pronounced in normative organizations is the reverse tendency—to give symbolic rewards for conformity to valued behavior. External control is expressed mainly through attempts to recruit new members and to mobilize support. Most normative organizations have as a central purpose the extension of their boundaries by acquiring and activating nominal adherents. For this reason, the organization enters into elaborate communication activities. The calculative organization typically makes the most extensive use of communication for internal control and the integration of activities. The importance of communication for control of the environment varies from one kind of calculative organization to another, but production and retail companies use extensive advertising and public relations methods to regulate and act on their environment. Such tactics have been adopted by other kinds of organizations that might seem to have more direct means of control at their disposal, such as government bureaucracies. Organizational advancement (or preservation) seem to exert a strong pressure to communicate to the world outside, influencing clients, public opinion, and competitors. Relevant functional items include

- symbolic punishment and reward;
- attention gaining and retaining;
- marking hierarchy;
- giving commands;
- expert guidance;
- informal network management;
- propaganda, recruitment, and image making; and
- mobilization of members and other support.

SOCIETYWIDE COMMUNICATION

Since societies are usually acting units only in the context of international economic and political relations, much of societal communication has already been accounted for by considering organizations and institutions and the innumerable informal contacts and networks of social life. Yet there are also many occasions when communication activities can be interpreted as serving purposes for the whole society or ends that might seem intrinsic to the continued existence of a given society in a world community (Deutsch, 1963). Mostly we have to refer to nation states whose Being and identity requirements are served by, for instance, symbols of power, unity, and continuity. Obvious examples are political ceremonies, rituals directed either internally toward members or externally toward other states. Cultural activities and artifacts also have this dual orientation.

The whole national society or state is not the only arena where social life is played out or most directly experienced. Often, our contact with society is at the level of region, city, or local community. The extent to which major social institutions of politics, justice, culture, and so on are organized at the level of community or region rather than nation varies a good deal according to circumstances of history, geography, and economic development. Nearly everywhere the communication system and its functions will vary accordingly, so that the greater the localization of social life, the more the significance of, for instance, local mass media compared to national media or local interpersonal communication networks compared to wider ties. Most advanced societies have developed communication systems at each level. The following outline of functions is written mainly with a view to the national level; but in the case of each main functional type, a parallel version could be worked out for the local or regional community. In most cases, the translation can be achieved by substituting "local" for "national" and "community" for "society" in the list of summarized functions.

Insofar as functions have a problem-solving basis, the relevant problems are those of maintaining unity and patriotism and of transmitting national values, political traditions, and a cultural heritage over time and space. The means of such transmission are varied, but mass media are of increasing importance in large, heterogeneous modern societies. Almost everywhere the media retain a national character more than either a local or an international character. Where the media are weak or lack a societal cultural identity, as is often the case at the community level, this is construed as a problem. Being needs for societies can be summed as follows:

- reproducing and expressing national identity,
- disseminating national values and consciousness,
- diffusion and continuity of culture and language,
- storing and recording a national past or traditions, and
- cultural and artistic production.

The Adaptation function is largely carried out for societies at the level of institutions, by way of political and economic instruments that monitor and respond to changes in the world environment and interact in a global economic and political system. Internally, a permanent process of change is at work, responding to internally and externally generated pressures. Essential processes include correlating internal change to avoid or resolve conflict or discontinuity and making sense (from the members' perspective) of change so as to minimize individual (ultimately aggregate) disjunction from the environment. A summary list includes

- monitoring external environment for changes (warning);
- monitoring internal changes, pressures, and conflicts;
- political and economic exchanges;
- conflict avoidance, reduction, and resolution;
- self-criticism by society; and
- change and diffusion of innovations.

Affiliation functions are interwoven with others, but communication offers numerous possibilities for developing internal solidarity and consciousness of identity. It offers a basis for connection either by the common reception of the same messages from society or through active interchanges. We can specify the following:

- connecting members of society by common networks and content,
- promoting solidarity or attachment by way of national rituals,
- marking boundaries of society and culture, and
- forming alliances and coalitions.

As at the organizational level, much of the burden of Control and direction within and between societies falls on communication. Initially this takes place within established institutional networks; it is often amplified and supplemented through mass communication. One control function has to do with the identification of leaders and the legitimation of sources of power and status. This calls for continuous reaffirmation, explicit or implicit, often by way of mass media. Power relations are made visible so that force is less likely to be required to keep order. Another control function is the relay of instructions, regulations, and rules to citizens. A third is the task of publicizing and disseminating values and norms through symbolic rewards and punishment, again often by mass communication. Fourth, there is a mobilizing, activating, and motivating function related to specific ends such as consumption, work, health, and military service. Finally, there is a set of activities and processes that have to do with release of tension and amusement. These are now largely the province of mass communication, but have been equally evident in festivals, holidays, fairs, and games.

Externally, control functions take on a somewhat different form, the most important concerning international political relations. Here communication is subordinate to real power, but it is not insignificant in projecting favorable images, influencing foreign opinion, and in bargaining in the public arena. International propaganda activities for national ends can usually be discerned, often in somewhat concealed forms within culture and information. Societal control functions of a communicative kind can be summarized as

- identifying status and legitimating power;
- relaying instructions, regulations, and information;
- disseminating values and norms;
- mobilizing and activating;
- establishing consensus and shaping climates of opinion;
- diversion, tension release, and entertainment;
- projecting national images;
- training in valued skills; and
- attention gaining and agenda controlling.

THE INTERRELATION
OF COMMUNICATION FUNCTIONS

This description of societywide functions, like those that have preceded it, has been written in a formal and rather abstract way, trying to stay true to the conceptual framework presented in Figure 11.1. In particular, care has been taken to observe the guidelines of treating a function as a purposeful (or potentially so) act of a communicating agent (a person, group, organization, or society). In other words, communication has been looked at from one particular perspective—that of an individual or collective unit. This has been done for consistency and economy of presentation, but we should not forget that the more complex the unit (e.g., a community or society), the harder it is to locate a single perspective and the more subordinate units are also interacting and communicating functionally. Thus the higher-level functions actually depend on functions of lower-level component units, and the functionality for senders (the communication agents) depends on the willingness and even purposiveness of receivers.

At each level above that of the single person, there is a complementarity of perspective on communicative acts according to whether one is sending or receiving, and the perceived function will vary accordingly. Since the chosen usage of the term function is essentially *subjective* in character (in that function depends on the purpose seen by the actor), it follows that the functional meaning of a communication act or event may well differ according to the perspective adopted. For instance, the same political news item on television might be seen as neutral monitoring of the political environment by the news organization, as propaganda or mobilization by the political organization to which the report refers, and as a form of entertainment by some audience members. Within an organization, an informal friendly approach by a manager to a subordinate might be open to interpretation at face value by the recipient as a means to resolve personal tension for the manager and, from the organizational point of view, as part of the wider control mechanism. Much communication will be viewed by participants in complementary and mutually consistent ways, depending on the clarity or ambiguity of the communication acts concerned.

To illustrate further, we may refer to findings of research on mass media uses and gratifications. Mass communication may be viewed as purposeful according to some perceived societal needs (interrelation, surveillance, control, etc.), but rests on a foundation of innumerable individual free acts of choice to attend to mass media. Research over several decades (Blumler & Katz, 1974; Klapper, 1960; Palmgreen et al., 1985) has demonstrated that individuals in media publics also behave in patterned and regular ways and frequently give a functional meaning to their reception behavior in terms that reflect and help to sustain the higher-level purposes. For instance, a large part of media choice and use can be classified, according to the self-reports of the individuals involved, as serving a range of functions, of which the following are among the most common: acquiring useful or orienting information, developing values and opinions, gaining self-insight and a sense of identity, gaining and maintaining desirable social contact, increasing an empathy with others, helping in the performance of social roles, finding emotional fulfillment and release, and reducing insecurity. These individual motives for receiving communication correspond to and underpin the main societal and community purposes for *communicating,* as outlined above. While this kind of research seems to have been more common in relation to mass media than for other communication channels and contexts, there is reason to suppose similar patterns of motivation for attending to communication can also be uncovered in other communication contexts (Katz, Gurevitch, & Haas, 1973). It may even be the case that in other contexts (e.g., family, neighborhood, organization) motives are more salient and conscious than in the case of mass communication, which encourages minimally motivated behavior.

CONCLUSION

This presentation began with a warning about the functional approach. Yet there are evident uses for the approach that merit detailed discussion. It is difficult to strike an adequate balance between the risks and the potential rewards. The main risk, aside from fundamental problems with the complete functionalist theory mentioned at the outset, lies in the "reification" of whatever communication phenomena we locate under different functional labels. By calling something a particular kind of function we appear to identify and categorize it in a secure and unique way. It thus acquires much more certainty and durability than the evidence usually justifies. We risk placing unlike phenomena together and ignoring possible alternative meanings of the same communication event. Communication phenomena are especially complex, ambiguous, and susceptible to alternative interpretations. If, however, we continually keep in mind that our own labeling is merely a provisional way of ordering phenomena on the basis of limited information, we may help make sense of diverse and confusing observations. We can use a category framework of the kind described here for recording, comparing, and interrelating observations, and can modify or extend the framework as needed for the particular case or situation under study.

Application of functional analysis is "prescientific" in that there is no agreement on a single functional paradigm spanning the different levels of human communication or even for a single level. Locating observations under functionally descriptive labels is not in itself a scientific result but rather a means to further analysis and understanding of what is going on. Further, there are no firmly established strategies or methods for functional analysis of communication. Even where one deploys a clearly derived and theoretically supported scheme of the kind suggested by McGuire (1974), there are no firm rules for categorizing cases and data. Much depends on the judgment of the investigator.

Evidence for making allocations in functional terms comes mainly from three sources: studies of the effects of communication (always hard to establish); subjective accounts of participants (never fully reliable); and observation of communication behavior as it happens (ambiguous). Each of these has its own limitations and difficulties, which are inherent in the methods that have to be used. There is a fourth possibility: gaining supplementary evidence from an analysis of the content of the message. It is tempting to construct a functional picture on the basis of content analysis alone, but the temptation should be avoided since it greatly adds to the danger that the functional analysis will be no more than a subjective and "pseudoscientific" account by one author. All four methods have something to recommend them and normally more than one is used at a time. However one collects evidence, it is essential for research to have a clear theoretical starting point and to develop a clear, economical, and logical set of functional categories. The absence of any generally agreed-upon single version of either is not necessarily an obstacle to research, and there remains some scope for moving closer to both. Finally, much communication is not functional in the sense outlined here, but is an end in itself or without purpose. For that reason, the scheme presented here is by no means applicable to all communication.

REFERENCES

Berger, C. R., & Bradac, J. J. (1982). *Language and social knowledge*. London: Edward Arnold.
Blumler, J. G., & Katz, E. (Eds.). (1974). *The uses of mass communications*. Newbury Park, CA: Sage.
Carey, J. W. (1975). A cultural approach to communication. *Communication, 2*, 1-2.
Cartwright, D., & Zander, A. (Eds.). (1968). *Group dynamics* (2nd ed.). London: Tavistock.
Dance, F.E.X., & Larson, C. E. (1976). *The functions of human communication*. New York: Holt, Rinehart & Winston.
Davison, W. P. (1959). On the effects of communication. *Public Opinion Quarterly, 24*, 343-360.

Deutsch, K. W. (1963). *The nerves of government*. New York: Free Press.
Etzioni, A. (1961). *Complex organizations*. New York: Free Press.
Festinger, L. (1957). *A theory of cognitive dissonance*. New York: Row Peterson.
Giddens, A. (1979). *Central problems in social theory*. London: Macmillan.
Goffman, I. (1974). *Frame analysis: An essay in the organization of experience*. Cambridge, MA: Harvard University Press.
Goldhaber, G. (1979). *Organizational communication*. Dubuque, IA: W.C. Brown.
Homans, G. (1951). *The human group*. London: Routledge & Kegan Paul.
Heider, F. (1958). *The psychology of interpersonal relations*. New York: John Wiley.
Innis, H. (1950). *Empire and communication*. Oxford: Clarendon Press.
Jones, E. E., & Davis, K. E. (1965). From acts to dispositions: The attribution process in human perception. In L. Berkowitz (Ed.), *Advances in experimental social psychology*. New York: Academic Press.
Katz, D. (1960). The functional approach to the study of attitudes. *Public Opinion Quarterly, 24,* 163-204.
Katz, E., Gurevitch, M., & Haas, H. (1973). On the use of mass media for important things. *American Sociological Review, 38,* 164-181.
Kelman, H. (1961). Processes of opinion change. *Public Opinion Quarterly, 25,* 57-78.
Kelley, H. H. (1967). Attribution theory in social psychology. In D. Levine (Ed.), *The Nebraska symposium on motivation*. Lincoln: University of Nebraska Press.
Klapper, J. T. (1960). *The effects of mass communication*. New York: Free Press.
Lasswell, H. (1948). The structure and function of communication in society. In L. Bryson (Ed.), *The communication of ideas*. New York: Harper & Row.
Maslow, A. (1968). *Toward a psychology of being*. New York: Van Nostrand.
McGuire, W. J. (1974). Psychological motives and communication gratification. In J. G. Blumler & E. Katz (Eds.), *The uses of mass communications* (pp. 167-196). Newbury Park, CA: Sage.
McQuail, D. (1984). With the benefit of hindsight: reflections on uses and gratifications research. *Critical Studies in Mass Communication, 1*(2), 177-193.
Merton, R. K. (1957). *Social theory and social structure*. New York: Free Press.
Miller, G. R. (Ed.). (1976). *Explorations in interpersonal communication*. Newbury Park, CA: Sage.
Newcomb, T. (1953). An approach to the study of communicative acts. *Psychological Review, 60,* 393-404.
Palmgreen, P., Rosengren, K. E., & Wenner, L. A. (Eds.). (1985). *Media gratification research: Current perspectives*. Newbury Park, CA: Sage.
Porter, L. W., & Roberts, K. H. (Eds.). (1977). *Communication in organizations*. Harmondsworth: Penguin.
Rogers, E. M., & Rogers, R. A. (1976). *Communication in organizations*. New York: Free Press.
Roloff, M., & Berger, C. R. (Eds.). (1982). *Social cognition and communication*. Newbury Park, CA: Sage.
Schank, R., & Abelson, R. (1977). *Scripts, plans, goals and understandings*. Hillsdale, NJ: Lawrence Erlbaum.
Wilmot, W. W. (1975). *Dyadic communication*. Reading, MA: Addison-Wesley.
Wright, C. R. (1960). Functional analysis and mass communication. *Public Opinion Quarterly, 24,* 605-620.
Wright, C. R. (1974). Functional analysis and mass communication revisited. In J. G. Blumler & E. Katz (Eds.), *The uses of mass communications* (pp. 197-212). Newbury Park, CA: Sage.

12 Language, Social Comparison, and Power

HOWARD GILES
University of Bristol

JOHN M. WIEMANN
University of California, Santa Barbara

WITHIN the title of this chapter are concepts that have been afforded considerable social significance by others in the past. We are of course referring here to "language" and "power" explicitly, and to "communication" implicitly. For instance, in tying the concept of communication to power and language, it has been argued (Blakar, 1985) that

> communication constitutes a basic precondition of all social intercourse. No social system, organization or society can be established or maintained, or changed, without communication . . . If using our imaginations, we try and conceive of man or woman as completely lacking communicative powers, we immediately realise the absurdity of this autistic being—unable to participate and unqualified for membership in any social organization . . . It is via language that reality is grasped and conceptualized as well as inherited from generation to generation. (p. 11)

At the same time, Hawley (1963) has said,

> It should be obvious that power in the social sphere, as with energy in the physical world, is ubiquitous . . . every social act is an exercise of power, every social relationship is a power equation, and every social group or system is an organization of power. (p. 422)

That potential power in relationships has been the focus of much research. For example, Russell (1938) attempted to "prove that the fundamental concept in social science is Power in the sense in which energy is the fundamental concept in physics" (p. 10). Research at the interpersonal and group levels, for example, has demonstrated that power (also termed control, status, etc.) is a central feature of a variety of social relationships. Early work with task groups showed that control-oriented components of communication were influential in decision making and productivity (Bales, 1950; Borgotta, 1964; Borgotta, Cottrell, & Mann,

1958; Carter, 1954). Their work was extended into the interpersonal realm (see Becker & Krug, 1964; Foa & Foa, 1972; Leary, 1957; Lorr & McNair, 1965), where it emerged as the factor accounting for the largest proportion of explained variance in interpersonal behavior (e.g., Bochner, Kaminski, & Fitzpatrick, 1977). It has also been shown to be part of people's phenomenological experience of relationships (Wiemann & Krueger, 1980). Hence, by discussing the interrelationships among language, communication, and power we are dealing with some of the central components of human social life (see Berger, 1985).

We begin by considering some of the ways that the social sciences have studied language in its social context over the last 20 years. Language can oftentimes *reflect, build upon, and determine* the nature of individuals' social perceptions, their interpersonal and intergroup relations, as well as the society in which they are a participating force. Not every single sociolinguistically oriented study can be encapsulated by our tripartite mold; after all, language behaviors obviously exist for functions other than social power and control (see Patterson, 1983; Street & Cappella, 1985). Nevertheless, the above conceptual net captures a large proportion of the extant literature. We will, however, point to some of the cumulative weaknesses of these "sociolinguistic" approaches and then propose an emergent conceptual framework that remedies their deficiencies.

While our inclinations are *inter*disciplinary, the advances we will suggest and the assumptions underlying them are distinctly *social psychological,* given our own baseline territories. Yet we make no apologies for this approach even though it has been conspicuous by its absence until quite recently (see, for example, Giles, Robinson, & Smith, 1980; Giles & St. Clair, 1985; Robinson, 1983). Finally, the study of language in all its social contexts is a vast empirical and theoretical exercise crossing many academic boundaries. It is beyond the scope of this chapter to do justice to all its intrigues and intricacies. Hence, our contribution is only a biased selection of the data, language variables, ideas, and methods.

PREVIOUS APPROACHES
TO LANGUAGE, POWER, AND SOCIETY

In the late 1950s and early 1960s, the study of language focused on explaining why it was that persons could produce an endless stream of novel sentences, many of which had never been uttered by anyone else before, and yet were readily understood by others. The answer at that time (Chomsky, 1957, 1965) was that there are a limited number of, albeit complex, grammatical rules from which an infinite number of sentences can be transformed (Koerner, 1983). This work stimulated research in the study of child language development and brought new life to the field of (cognitive) psycholinguistics. Nevertheless, the impact of this approach, which we will term "language *without* social context" (see Figure 12.1), seemed to draw most researchers away from considering language as a social instrument used for communicative purposes. Over the last two decades, however, three approaches to language have emerged that do not take social context as a given and are more communicative in origin.

The "Language *Reflects* Context" Paradigm

The first of these, which appeared arguably in part as a reaction to the earlier *a*social perspective, asserts that language use is prescribed and proscribed largely by the situation in which it is spoken, including the characteristics of the speakers involved (e.g., Fishman, 1966; Gumperz, 1964; Gumperz & Hymes, 1972; Hymes, 1967; Labov, 1966). This "language *reflects* context" paradigm (Figure 12.1) is built on the now well-established foundation that we all have speech *repertoires* from which we can select to meet the normative demands of situations. Most space will be devoted to research emanating from this approach, as it is the cornerstone of sociolinguistic inquiry even today.

One of the most influential concepts in the sociolinguistic literature is "diglossia," which relates to the use of two languages or dialects in bilingual or bidialectal societies, each serving different functions with different status connotations (see Fishman, 1967; Hawkins, 1983). This phenomenon is an excellent example of this approach to language, power, and society. The so-called low (L) variety of language or dialect is most often confined to such areas as the home, everyday activities, and friendship, while the high (H) variety is often acquired later in the socialization process and is reserved for use in more formal and public arenas (Herman, 1961). Fishman (1972) proposed five general social domains in his own research: the family, neighborhood, religion, education, and employment. He notes that for bilingual Mexican Americans in the United States, Spanish might be used in the context of the family, neighborhood or religion, but English would be used at work or in the classroom. An important feature of this analysis is that, given the two varieties fulfilling separate functions in the various domains cited, their linguistic structures will represent this functional disparity and not be equivalent. In many multilingual societies a simple dichotomy into H and L varieties is grossly insufficient (Platt, 1977). For this reason, he invoked the notion of *polyglossia,* illustrating it by the case of the ethnic Chinese in Malaysia who have a speech repertoire that includes six varieties for use in particular subdomains.

LANGUAGE
WITHOUT
CONTEXT

                   LANGUAGE REFLECTS CONTEXT

                            LANGUAGE BUILDS UPON CONTEXT

                                      LANGUAGE DETERMINES CONTEXT

1960 ———————————————————————▶1995

Figure 12.1. Approaches to the study of language, power, and society.

The above conceptual framework for speech diversity in multilingual societies has been elaborated for examining similar processes in monolingual communities. To this end, a variety of taxonomies have emerged over the years that attempt to specify how objective characteristics of social situations (e.g., the age of the person addressed) affect particular speech patterns, and even the minutiae of vowel and consonant variants (see for example, Ervin-Tripp, 1969; Giles & Powesland, 1975; Hymes, 1967). While Labov's (1966) study showing that speakers' phonological variants become more prestigious sounding as the context changes from informal chat to formal reading (see Romaine, 1982; Trudgill, 1974) is a classic case in point, Joos's (1962) illustration is immediately compelling. He provides five variants on a request for the time, moving down from more formal ("frozen") to informal ("intimate"), for example:

(1) I should be glad to be informed of the correct time.
. . .
(5) Time?

The taxonomists' approaches have differentially weighted various situational determinants of language. Thus Brown and Fraser (1979) suggest that "purpose is the motor which sets the chassis of setting and participants going" (p. 34; Argyle, Furnham, & Graham, 1981), while Giles and Powesland (1975) argue that the characteristics of the person spoken to are fundamental features of the situation determining speech style and nonverbal behaviors (Bell, 1984). Giles and associates have developed "speech accommodation theory" that examines, in propositional terms, the motivations underlying and the consequences arising from various shifts in language, including moving toward, away from, complementing, and even competing with the person addressed (Giles, Mulac, Bradac, & Johnson, in press; Street & Giles, 1982; Thakerar, Giles, & Cheshire, 1982). We now outline very briefly some of the ways that language can reflect intraindividual, interindividual, intergroup, and institutional characteristics.

The Language of Intrapersonal Dynamics

That communicators' language behaviors can be a function of the personality and physical characteristics of the participants involved seems intuitively to be a reasonable proposition. Indeed there is an enormous literature in the field of development mapping the changes that occur on a wide variety of grammatical, phonological, discourse, and nonverbal levels during childhood, revealing not only the shifts toward the linguistic maturity of adulthood (e.g., Robinson, 1984; Wells & Robinson, 1982) but also the unique phases that emerge during this period (Snow & Ferguson, 1977). While middle age is extremely underresearched, adolescence (Romaine, 1984) and old age (Giles & Ryan, 1986) are increasing in empirical and theoretical importance. Relatedly, Laver and Trudgill (1979) have discussed the ways in which physique and height can determine various vocal qualities (e.g., a tall well-built man may for reasonable physiological reasons have a deeper and louder voice than his less endowed peers), and Scherer (1979) has reviewed studies showing that such stable and transitory qualities of individuals as extraversion and depression can be indicated linguistically. Furthermore, Cappella (1981) has reviewed studies showing how individuals' levels of physiological arousal can mediate their nonverbal behavioral patterns. A recent review of the literature concerning the influence of individual differences dimensions (e.g., self-monitoring, cognitive complexity) on verbal, vocal, and nonverbal indices of behavior failed to produce clearcut main effects for these intraindividual parameters (Giles & Street, 1985). Such factors did have effects but usually only in *interaction* with other sociodemographic and contextual variables. For instance, highly anxious individuals displayed a linguistic profile of distress (e.g., speech disfluencies) only when talking about or being in an emotionally arousing situation (Scherer, 1979).

The Language of Interpersonal Relations

The type of relationship apparent between interlocutors has shown more definitive main effects for language behaviors (Fielding & Fraser, 1978). Berger (1979) has, from a cognitive perspective, characterized initial encounters between people as involving the reduction of uncertainty and has outlined the language behaviors used strategically to this end. For instance, mutual interrogation followed by self-disclosures allows participants to not only make their partner more predictable but engenders more certainty about responding "appropriately" themselves. Complementarily, Brown and Fraser (1979) point to the importance of the affective nature of interpersonal encounters and apparent role relationships. Asymmetrical status and power roles are found cross-culturally in address terms (Brown & Gilman, 1960; Ervin-Tripp, 1972) and in nonverbal distancing patterns by differential use of interpersonal space (Hall, 1966), backward lean, and differential gaze patterns (Henley, 1977). Among the many contexts where status and/or power differences abound and have pragmatic significance are in the doctor's consulting room (Pendleton & Hasler, 1983; Street & Wiemann, in press) and in the courtroom (O'Barr, 1982).

Knapp (1983), following Altman and Taylor (1973), has discussed eight dimensions of language and communicative behavior that differentiate short- from long-term encounters (e.g., breadth and depth of disclosures, smoothness). Moreover, he argues that relationships develop toward greater intimacy through five stages of initiating, experimenting, intensifying, integrating, and bonding, each of which has discernible language correlates (Knapp, 1984). For instance, "intensifying" is associated with increasing taken-for-granteds (Hopper, 1981), increasing use of private codes and neologisms (Hopper, Knapp, & Scott, 1981) and more direct expressions of commitment. Knapp argues in his "staircase" model that the dissolution of relationships is concomitant with a decrease in intimacy. Hence, he posits, again with language correlates, five phases that typify relationship tumble down to actual termination.

Duck (1982) has criticized the notion that relationship decline is simply the *reverse* of its development, claiming that there are distinct and unique features associated with dissolution. Baxter (1984), in a similar vein, argues that the process of relationship breakdown can take many different paths. She provides a trajectory model elucidating these various ends. Furthermore, Baxter (1985) discusses the language behaviors associated with unilateral and bilateral disengagement in terms of two orthogonal dimensions, namely, directness and other-orientedness (see also Berger & Bradac, 1982; Miller & Parks, 1982). Thus the quadrant of high directness and other-orientedness would be marked communicationally by explicit "state-of-the-relationship talk" and "negotiated farewells." Baxter also discusses the individual and relational attributes that would increase the likelihood of linguistic directness (e.g., androgeny, prior closeness).

Marital relationships have been the target of much research with communication factors being highly associated with relational dissatisfaction or distress (see Noller & Fitzpatrick, in press; Spanier, 1976) and divorce (Kitson, Babri, & Roach, 1985). This literature shows marital nonadjustment to be manifest in negative vocal, verbal, and non-verbal channel inconsistencies, lowered information exchange, fewer self-disclosures, and the like (Gottman, 1979; Lederer & Jackson, 1967; Noller, 1982). Moreover, there often appears to be asymmetry in distressed couples such that wives respond even to small affective changes in their spouses whereas husbands do not react to even significant emotional changes in their wives. Gottman (1982), exploring sequentially the nature of conflict situations in distressed and adjusted couples, suggests that a communication feature of adjusted couples is their ability to deescalate, linguistically, potential negative affect when it emerges (see also Krueger, 1982). Finally, Fitzpatrick (1984) has been able to discriminate polythetically and empirically three couple types (traditionals, independents, and separates, as well as various "mixed" types) based on their subjective appraisals of their own interdependence, relational ideology, and communicative expressiveness. Moreover, she has been able to present a linguistic profile of these types (Fitzpatrick, Fallis, & Vance, 1982; Fitzpatrick, Vance, & Witteman, 1984; see Fitzpatrick, Chapter 19 in this volume).

The Language of Intergroup Relations

Intergroup communication is a growing area of research spanning many different types of between-category encounters (Gudykunst, 1986; see Gudykunst, Chapter 27), much of which has been concerned with male and female linguistic and communication differences. While early research suggested that females are prone to use less powerful language (grammatically and nonverbally) than their male counterparts (Barron, 1971; Lakoff, 1973; Zimmerman & West, 1975), over the years, few consistent differences have been established between the sexes (Kramarae, 1981; Thorne, Kramarae, & Henley, 1984). Indeed those that have emerged tend, in Western societies, to be a matter of degree rather than kind (Smith, 1985) and are extremely sensitive to situational issues (Brouwer, 1982; Giles & Street, 1985). At the same time, convincing evidence is emerging (see Mulac & Lundell, 1986) across a wide array of ages and written and spoken contexts, suggesting distinctive gender-linked differences in language usage. The findings indicate that what constitutes so-called male and female language styles differs markedly across socioverbal contexts, and that the cues people use to attribute, say, written prose, to a man or woman writer also vary considerably depending on the domain. The "gender-linked language effect" is not evident in mixed-sex dyads, however, where members of each sex accommodate linguistically (see Street & Giles, 1982) to their stereotypes of the other sex's behavior (Mulac, Wiemann, Yoerks, & Gibson,

1983). Brown and Levinson (1979) argue that whatever differences are ultimately and convincingly associated with any particular social category are not so much due to membership in the group itself as to the nature of the power relationships prevailing between specific groups at the time; change the power structure and the language will follow in due course (see Berger, 1985; Bourhis, 1984; Leet-Pettigrini, 1980).

Other areas of intergroup concern include the relations between socioeconomic classes and between ethnic groups, which often cannot be separated empirically (see Sebastian & Ryan, 1985). In the former domain, while many linguistic and communication differences have been identified most of which can be considered in "deficit" terms— that is, working-class individuals are less expressive nonverbally, use less diverse vocabulary and more ungrammaticalities, etc. (Edwards, 1979; Robinson, 1978)—controversy still rages concerning their origins and evaluative and communicative consequences (Edwards, 1983). Claims have been made that these findings are elicited from middle-class respondents in extremely formal, abstract, stressful, and biased contexts (Stipeck & Nelson, 1980) and that in any case the language of working-class people is no less rule-based, logical, or rich than middle-class language. It has been argued that working-class language should be considered "different" rather than substandard (Labov, 1972; Robinson, 1978; Trudgill, 1975), a position often relevant in minority, ethnic situations (Baugh, 1983; Kochman, 1982). Different or substandard, these linguistic differences function as class or group "markers" that provide the opportunity for easy ingroup/outgroup distinctions (both desired and undesired) for sustaining and expressing valued group identity (Edwards & Giles, 1984; Milroy, 1980; Ryan, 1979).

Common processes may underlie any situation where individuals define themselves in terms of their group memberships, be they religious, generational, occupational, disciplinary, gender, or ethnic. In this vein, Tajfel and Turner (1979) consider the extremes of two types of interaction:

> At one extreme is the interaction . . . which is fully determined by . . . inter-personal relationships and individual characteristics and not at all affected by various social groups . . . to which [interactants] belong. The other extreme consists of interactions . . . which are fully determined by [interactants'] memberships [in] various social groups . . . and are not at all affected by the inter-individual personal relationships. (p. 34)

These two extremes define either end of a bipolar continuum labeled interindividual and intergroup encounters, respectively. The more that members of a group conceive of an encounter toward the intergroup pole, the more behavioral uniformity they will display toward outgroup members and the more they will treat them in an undifferentiated manner rather than as individuals (Tajfel & Turner, 1979).

Tajfel and his coworkers have developed a theory for understanding behavior at the intergroup end of the continuum (Tajfel, 1982; Turner & Giles, 1981). While we are no longer convinced that interindividual and intergroup encounters are poles of a single continuum (these terms more likely describe poles of orthogonal continua), ramifications of intergroup work in the *ethnolinguistic* sphere have been important for understanding interethnic relations (e.g., Giles & Johnson, 1981, in press-a). In essence, "ethnolinguistic identity theory" (Beebe & Giles, 1984; Giles & Johnson, in press) suggests that when individuals identify with a social group, they desire to derive satisfaction from their membership in it. The realization of the affect associated with ingroup identity comes through making intergroup comparisons between the position of one's own group and that of other groups on such valued dimensions as power, resources, capabilities, and the like.

Much of the theory and empirical research deriving from it is concerned with understanding the conditions necessary and the language strategies used for achieving a positive ingroup identity, given that speech style and nonverbal aspects of language can be important dimensions of ethnic identity (Edwards, 1985; Giles, 1977; Giles & Saint-Jacques, 1979), nationalist movements (Weinstein, 1979), and multicultural policies (Bourhis, 1984; Edwards, 1984). Hence, in line with Tajfel and Turner's (1979) thinking, when a member of an ethnic group defines an encounter *subjectively* as an intergroup one, he or she will wish to assume a positive social identity. One important strategy for achieving this goal might involve linguistic differentiation from those who are (usually) outgroup members (Giles & Johnson, 1986; Taylor & Royer, 1980; see Gudykunst, Chapter 27).

The process of "psycholinguistic distinctiveness" (Giles, Bourhis, & Taylor, 1977) could be manifest by code-switching to one's ingroup language, emphasizing the ingroup dialect by either broadening one's accent or adopting ingroup slang and discourse structures, and so on (Giles, 1979). In short, linguistic *divergence* accrues (Bourhis, Giles, Leyens, & Tajfel, 1979; Lambert, 1979) according to a format that depends on a variety of intergroup variables. Included among these are the legitimacy and stability of the perceived status relations existing between the two groups (Turner & Brown, 1978) and the speakers' cognitive representations of the degree to which structural factors favor the group or not (Bourhis, 1985; Bourhis & Sachdev, 1984; Giles & John son, in press). Of additional importance is the extent to which speakers identify with other meaningful (nonethnic) social categories (e.g., occupation, trade union membership) having positive group identities in which individuals themselves have high within-group status (Giles & Johnson, 1981). But even in *intra*group encounters, the ethnic tongue or code can fulfill a basic, supportive function in the absence of material resources (Milroy, 1982).

Thus far discussion has emphasized the influence of intergroup perceptions of situation on encoding speech variables; however, *decoding* processes may also be affected (see Bourhis, Giles, & Lambert, 1975; Doise, Sinclair, & Bourhis, 1976; Genesee & Bourhis, 1982). For example, perceiving a situation in intergroup terms or an individual as a category member may be expected to have repercussions on the attributions made about that situation or individual (Hewstone & Jaspars, 1984; Jaspars & Hewstone, 1982).

The intergroup perspective has also been established in the second-language learning domain where ethnic minorities are learning the dominant group's tongue (Beebe & Giles, 1984; Giles & Byrne, 1982). Although other social psychological models have paid lip service to the dynamics of ethnic group relations (Gardner, 1985), the intergroup model suggests that learners' cognitive representations of the intergroup structure can have a fundamental influence on the level of proficiency they attain, or at least to which they perform. This position also has implications beyond *individual* learners. It claims that under certain conditions, if sufficient members of the subordinate ethnic group acquire levels of proficiency that threaten the perceived ethnolinguistic superiority of the dominant collectivity, the latter will redefine its own valued language (perhaps by lexical, phonological, and semantic innovations, grammatical and intonational restructurings, and discourse and nonverbal modifications) in order to maintain the linguistic differential in their favor (see Ullrich, 1971).

Finally, spoken language is not simply a reflection of one's social category membership but can indicate individuals' conceptions of and feelings toward such membership (Giles, Scherer, & Taylor, 1979). For instance, vocal and nonverbal cues allow us not only to categorize a person as a female but also can reflect her gender identity (Smith, 1980) and political ideology (Giles, Smith, Ford, Candor, & Thakerar, 1980). Similarly, Taylor, Meynard, and Rheault (1977) found among French Canadian students in Montreal that attitudes toward Quebec nationalism had an inverse relationship to their English proficiency levels. Lack of acquiring good linguistic skills in the language of a sociopolitically powerful outgroup need not have to do with cognitive deficiencies as much as with *social* factors; it is a rational, group-based tactic in search of a positive social identity and social power (see also Flores & Hopper, 1975; Mercer, Mercer, & Mears, 1979).

Language and the Media

There is little direct research available on how the media's language might reflect the values of society or the interests of those who are involved in and or fund these institutions (Beardsmore, 1984; Vesterguard & Schroder, 1985); yet there is much of relevance here that will be discussed under our final social approach to language and society. There is a growing literature in multilingual societies on issues of institutional support for ethnic minorities to gauge how much vitality they have in terms of proliferating their group values through use of the native tongue in radio, newspapers, magazines, television, and the like (Breton, 1971; Clyne, 1982). Relatedly, black and Hispanic participation in network television is roughly equivalent to their proportion of the population (see Greenberg, 1982). However, Anderson, Fine, and Anderson (1983) note that black English vernacular in *Roots II* was restricted to lower-class and old blacks and, in any case, the vocal characteristics of it were stereotypical and did not correspond with real life usage.

Greenberg (1972) has shown that viewers with least direct contact with blacks are most likely to use TV as their main resource regarding how blacks use language. Moreover, Baptista-Fernandez and Greenberg (1980) claim that much of the depiction of Hispanics in the media occurs in a very limited number of programs where other Hispanics are the focus of attention and oftentimes involved in socially undesirable behaviors. As Greenberg (1982) points out, while American white relationships on TV involve family language characterized by affective support, information seeking and giving, TV depictions of black families involve far more verbal conflict (see O'Keefe & Reid-Nash, Chapter 14).

It is widely held that much of our literature and media are linguistically sexist (Cheshire, 1984; Cooper, 1984; McConnell-Ginet, Borker, & Furman, 1980). Kramarae (1982) has pointed this out extensively with respect to proverbs, advice to women on their use of language, and in the role of women as broadcasters. In general it is a depressing state of affairs to see even in the 1980s that women and girls (in magazines, advertisements, fiction, TV drama) are not typically afforded linguistic participation as equals with men and boys, and even when they are, their linguistic roles and verbal content frequently are stereotypical (Howitt, 1982). Giles (1980) found that 83% of the voices or final persuasive-appeal voice-overs were male in British TV commercials. Indeed, use of mechanical voices or computer simulations today (e.g., in cars, vending machines) still follow largely the old sexist lines; that is, female voices are in general associated with lower status or socioemotional roles.

The psychological costs of these linguistic and nonverbal depictions have not been greatly studied (Hyde, 1984; Martyna, 1980; McKay, 1980) but evidence suggests, despite the fact that even children bring to the media an already established interpretive sexist frame (Durkin, 1984), that continued absorption can have predictable consequences on sex role conceptions throughout adolescence (Morgan, 1982). Gerbner, Gross, Morgan, and Signorielli's (1980a) work on "cultivation effects" (see however, Hirsch, 1981; Wober & Gunter, 1982) as well as Tversky and Kahneman's (1980) availability heuristic support this observation.

Older men and women are even less well-depicted than their younger counterparts (Petersen, 1973). Over-65-year-olds are underrepresented, and the language of the elderly is "silence" (Davis & Kubey, 1982). Again, exceptions can be found, especially in daytime soap operas; but in the main, the elderly are depicted in language terms as fulfilling their age role stereotype. Thus they are heard to be silly, ineffectual, and incompetent (Gerbner & Signorielli, 1979).

In sum, Western societies (at least) can be considered, albeit with many attendant provisos, to embrace elements of racism, sexism, and ageism in the media. The language forms endemic to them perpetuate related prejudices.

The Reflection of Power

Language not only reflects objective indices of context but is also a barometer of how individuals define the situation as they see it and their own identity at that time (Forgas, 1983; Smith, Giles, & Hewstone, 1982). The role of *power* in the "language reflects context" paradigm exists because it is "the establishment" that dictates what is normatively appropriate language behavior in formal, public situations. For instance, in bilingual, or even bidialectal situations, where ethnic majority and minority peoples coexist, second language learning is dramatically *unidirectional;* that is, it is very uncommon for the dominant group to acquire the linguistic habits of the subordinate collectivity (see however, the "migrant ruler" situation, Giles, 1978). Indeed it is no accident that cross-culturally what is "standard," "correct," and "cultivated" language behavior is that of the aristocracy, the upper or ruling classes and their institutions (Trudgill, 1975); that is, the language of the most powerful—politically and economically (Drake, 1980; St. Clair, 1982). This is not to envisage a static state of affairs—far from it. First, while the voluminous, cross-national literature on "language attitudes" shows that listeners evaluate speakers on audiotape who use the prestige language forms highly on competence dimensions (see Giles & Edwards, 1983; Giles, Hewstone, Ryan, & Johnson, in press; Ryan & Giles, 1982), speakers' evaluations and communicative expectations are also sensitive to changes in the social structure. Second, while unidirectionality holds sway, in some situations there are limits to which subordinate groups may encroach linguistically on the relevant dominant outgroups before various social sanctions are applied against them (e.g., use of obscenities by females; see Burgoon & Miller, 1985; Kramarae, 1981).

The "Language *Builds* on Context" Paradigm

That language derives much of its meaning from the context in which it is spoken is an assumption reflected in the "language *builds on* context" paradigm (see Figure 12.1). This view suggests that interactants share an array of assumptions; in fact, we must, otherwise communication would never take place (see Hewes & Planalp, Chapter 6). The more shared assumptions we have between us, the greater "intersubjectivity" there will be (e.g., Rommetveit, 1979). Interestingly, Knapp's (1983) model of relationship development explores the way romantic partners "intensify" their intimacy by developing the use of so-called taken-for-granteds (Hopper, 1981). Conversely, Ragan and Hopper (1984) note that in novels usually the last encounter depicted between lovers involves a "suspension of the let-it-pass rule," the so-called consensus on dissensus. That is, one or other of the characters peppers his or her conversations with "what do you mean?" or similar statements. This indicates a *sudden lack* of intersubjectivity between them, thereby legitimizing (perhaps strategically) an exit from the relationship by the perpetrator (see Baxter, 1985).

Of course, in everyday conversations much is "let past" without its meaning being made clear either because of its lack of significance to the listener or the listener's belief that "all will be revealed in due course." Interactants at times count on the fact that they will not be taken to task on each point, thus facilitating purposeful (intentional) misunderstandings, deceptions, and other similar less-than-truthful episodes. The fact that both parties can be seen as cooperating in these little deceptions should be of interest to communication researchers but to date has attracted little attention. Furthermore, what is envisaged as "shared" is a perennial difficulty in communication, particularly in intergroup encounters (Dube-Simard, 1983; Gumperz, 1982; Hewstone & Giles, 1986; Milroy, 1984; Platt & Weber, 1984).

Much of language builds on shared presuppositions and shared knowledge about our social contexts; so much of our language has a level of meaning beyond that of the referents of the words themselves, namely, that which reveals something about the intentions of the speaker, the so-called illocutionary force. The more the shared presuppositions of relative power in a relationship—say, between mother and child, doctor and patient, employer and employee, and the like—the more illocutionary force can be used to good effect. Take an example provided by Ervin-Tripp (1980) of a mother wanting her child to put on his new pair of shoes. She does not give him a forthright command, but nevertheless, provides it implicitly:

Mother: Where are those nice new shoes I bought for you yesterday, Johnny?

Child: In the closet [said with a grin].

Mother: Don't you get clever with me; you get those shoes right now, young man, before I . . .

The powerful can thus use language to influence others when the surface structure of their words appears *polite* and where commands are unnecessary (see Brown & Levinson, 1978).

Obviously, although attempts at compliance-gaining by the powerful can be linguistically meted out subtly and prosocially, when the target is considered a protagonist or a personal/group threat the language of the appeal can be noxious and verbally aggressive, as in case of the "circumvention" and "punishment appeal" strategies of "deceit" and "warning," respectively (see Miller, 1983; Wiseman & Schenck-Hamlin, 1981).

The "Language *Determines* Context" Paradigm

The third, more social and communicative approach to language is built upon a sociology of knowledge perspective and deals far more squarely with the relationship between language and power. This we term the "language *determines* context" paradigm (see Figure 12.1). It has been argued, in fact, that any utterance *is* the context for the utterances that follow (Bavelas, 1983; Grice, 1975; Nofsinger, 1976; Schegloff & Sacks, 1973; Sluzki, Beavin, Tarnopolsky, & Vernon, 1967). Thus a speaker can attempt to influence his or her interlocutor by strategic linguistic choices that effectively manipulate the context. The more powerful speakers are, the greater the conversational and relational control they can exert (Wiemann, 1985). Control of the semantic environment has been shown to be important at all levels of analysis, from people's perception of the world around them (Whorf, 1941) through the mental health of families (Watzlawick, Beavin, & Jackson, 1967) to the agendasetting role played by the media (McCombs & Shaw, 1972).

There are very few *inherent social* laws (Kelvin, 1972); hence, each culture decides on norms of appropriacy and deviance and uses language to help construct its social reality (Berger & Luckmann, 1966). Numerous studies suggest that our language forms (e.g., color terms, terms for types of physical phenomena, such as different kinds of taste, snow, etc.) can influence greatly the types of perceptions and sociophysical discriminations we make (see Fishman, 1980). But the relationship between language and cognition is more intricate and more active than just this perceptual socialization by what is culturally provided for us linguistically. By our very mouths we can influence our own cognitions. The language forms we use to describe a specific event to a *particular* other will distinctly affect our memory of the original event in such a manner as to be consonant with the nature of our linguistic expressions (Higgins & McCann, 1984; Higgins & Rholes, 1978). For instance, asking students to relate the ins and outs of a recent and novel social event to either a peer or an elderly person might induce the storytellers to overaccommodate their messages to the latter (Ryan, Giles, Bartolucci, & Henwood, 1986). This might be achieved by means of simplified grammar and slow speech rate to the elderly, owing to unfavorable stereotypes young people hold of the competence of the aged (Rubin & Brown, 1975).

There are other levels beyond the referential, propositional content of words and phrases, and the present approach focuses on the *evaluative* meaning behind expressions and statements. Eiser (1980) reported that forcing students to write essays using adjectives that were potentially biased either for or against the values inherent in the specified topic (e.g., on capital punishment: starry-eyed, oversentimental vs. callous, sadistic) had a rather predictable effect not only on the tenor of their products but on their own subsequently expressed attitudes on this social issue. Similarly, there are *few* terms available in the English language for categorizing different phases of, or feelings toward, the intimate relationships in which we participate (Bradac, 1983). This contributes to our experience of many relations as full of uncertainty (Baxter & Wilmont, 1984; Berger & Calabrese, 1975; Gudykunst, 1985; Meill & Duck, 1982; Parks & Adelman, 1983).

This third approach to language, power, and society suggests that we can rarely be evaluatively neutral; our descriptions are frequently a reflection of our social attitudes. Perhaps more important, however, is the finding that the language we use to describe events and people influences the framework of our understanding of these phenomena. In this vein, Giles and Hewstone (1982) presented a model with language acting as an independent variable determining context. They proposed various propositions outlining when and how speech will influence the initial definition and later redefinitions of the situation, who will usually be responsible for initiating such actions, and under what conditions speech will be *the* salient cue to contextual definition and redefinition (see Bradac, 1982).

Power enters the picture squarely here as it is the powerful—whether they be news reporters, politicians, authority figures, or the like—who can determine subtly our perception of events by the language they adopt.

For example, Husband (1977) found that news reports concerning black immigrants to Britain were more often than not associated with adjectives suggesting unfavorable evaluations, namely, "control," "conflict," "swamping," "violence," and so on. Such associative language then is bound to affect our views because of the evaluative overtones of the words and expressions used (see also Kress, 1983; Potter, Stringer, & Wetherell, 1984). Language forms used by the news media can also distract us from the emotional connotations of what is really happening in our physical and social environment; for example, press releases reporting the Vietnam War referred to massive air raids as "routine limited duration protective reactions" (Tromel-plotz, 1981, p. 75). Ross (1984) has undertaken a compelling examination of the writing of the U.S. Defense Department and State Department with respect to preparedness for nuclear war. He argues that use of jargon, nominal style and depersonalizations gives the impression of "everything being under control." For example, the use of an abbreviation such as "6559 MT" hardly conveys the true horror of "6,559,000,000 tons of dynamite"!

Conversely, Blakar (1975) has pointed to the *conserving* nature of language. His example is the Norwegian word for Member of Parliament, which originally included the suffix "-man." The Norwegians changed the evaluative connotations to neutralize the sexist form by switching to an androgynous suffix, "-representative." However, in a very short period of time, the new term had acquired its former associative characteristics as witnessed by a newspaper article that referred to the Parliament-representatives *and their wives;* now the supposed neutral individual has a wife! Interestingly enough, the socially influential can use language to *avoid* restricting the definition of a given situation, thereby maintaining control of its ambiguity until a strategic, "safer" point in the conversation or relationship arises (Scotton, 1979).

In sum then, a current trend in the area of language and society seems to be that powerful groups use language as *one,* albeit very important, way of establishing, maintaining, and legitimizing the status quo.

LIMITATIONS OF PREVIOUS APPROACHES

The above are three clearly visible lines of inquiry that encapsulate much work in language and society. Other vantage points are, however, apparent. For instance, Furnham (1986) shows that frequently we choose the situation that best fits the message we wish to convey, thereby exerting manifestly more control over our environments. For instance, people tend to opt for the written mode rather than verbal face-to-face encounters for delivering personally critical views or bad news. Notwithstanding, there are at least four cumulative "weaknesses" in the aforementioned approaches.

FUNCTIONS

First, the three *social* perspectives, while overlapping implicitly in the work of just a few scholars (e.g., Bruner, 1975; Gumperz, 1982; Rommetveit, 1979), are treated as autonomous approaches. There is now a need to integrate them into a coherent view of language, communication, and society.

Second, we can detect the influence of the social cognition perspective on workers in communication science and social psychology of language (e.g., Greene & Cody, 1985; Kraut & Higgins, 1984; Roloff & Berger, 1982). A caricature of this social cognitive animal is the lone individual, imbued with various biases unbeknownst to itself, processing as best it can the social information thrown at it. However, and notwithstanding its situational potency, this perspective is off the mark and does a disservice to our complex and negative transactions with social reality. To the contrary, Kellerman & Berger (1984) rightly remind us that oftentimes individuals actively *seek out* the information they require for processing. These authors have examined how people can procure information from others while masking their intent nonobviously. Hewes and associates (Hewes, Graham, Doelger, & Pavitt, 1985; Hewes & Planalp, 1982) on the decoding side demonstrate that individuals are active by "second-guessing" when and how people debug and defuse some of the biases inherent in others' messages to them.

All in all, the picture then is of us as speaker-hearers (see McGregor, 1986) subtly trying to "pull the wool over the ears" of others by backing up and down the rocky continuum from transmitting veridical truth to telling deliberate lies (Bradac, Friedman, & Giles, 1986; DePaulo, Stone, & Lassiter, 1985; Ekman, 1985; see Knapp, Cody, & Reardon, Chapter 13) with uncomfortable stops in between, issuing nonstraightforward but not-dishonest "disqualifications" to avoid various difficulties (Bavelas, 1983)—this, too, in the face of trying to decide among the truths, biases, evasions, and lies of those talking *to* us. Hence, any rules (e.g., Cushman & Whiting, 1973; Grice, 1975; Harré & Secord, 1972; Shimanoff, 1980) or "communication games" (Higgins, Fondacaro, & McCann, 1981) approaches to interpersonal communication per se are of limited theoretical value. Taking the games approach, nowhere in the encoder *or* in the overly dichotomized recipient sides of this information-exchange slanted model have we an appreciation of such disguised emission and detection. The solution is not *just* to infuse these models with *added* "disguise" propositions. We need now more radical theoretical conceptions that attempt to articulate the negotiative, relational, and transactional nature of language, and represent adequately the emerging picture of the "skeptical" and "crafty" communicator in all of us.

Third, there is a skewed dichotomy in our previous *social* approaches between the powerful and the powerless. The view that emerges is that of the powerful as the determiners of rules, meanings, and contexts while the powerless are rule, meaning, and context *followers*. Although researchers working on relational communication have attended to the negotiation of control at that level (see Wiemann, 1985), little work has dealt with the communication of those who have had control forced on them. There now seems to us to be the need for a theory that also focuses upon the linguistic "victims" of power, similar to a social psychological perspective on social change (Tajfel, 1974, 1978; Tajfel & Turner, 1979). It is usually *subordinate* power groups in society that innovate and question the status quo by linguistic and nonlinguistic means (Giles, 1978, 1979).

Furthermore, while the third social approach discussed above is currently in vogue, one begins to feel wary of reading anything or listening to anyone without thinking how they are manipulating communication to their own devices . . . power elites lurking everywhere with their linguistic weapons drawn! We find it difficult to conceive of linguistic Machiavellians behind every nook and cranny. For instance, Fishman (1980) has shown in a case study of three egalitarian, married couples that the wives evidence "powerless" language (see Bradac & Mulac, 1984; Lind & O'Barr, 1979; Scotton, 1985) to the extent that they use $2\frac{1}{2}$ times as many tag questions and five times the number of hedges as their husbands. However, closer examination of these linguistic products showed that they did not simply occur randomly throughout conversations, as might be predicted from a traditional language and power perspective. They were used (and in the same way, albeit less often, by husbands) when they were attempting to obtain their spouses' complete attention and detailed judgment. Rather than being a reflection of a low power position within the family, women used these devices actively and creatively to achieve their communicational goals and solve interpersonal problems.

Fourth, there has been an overly *referential* emphasis on the functions of language. Perhaps this is understandable given that the impetus for the more social approaches was a reaction against the "language without context" paradigm, but this has been detrimental to understanding the *symbolic* function of language for our social identities (Giles & Johnson, 1981; Gumperz, 1982; Milroy, 1982). That is, not only the context of the talk, but the mere act of talking or not has symbolic value (see Wiemann, Chen, & Giles, 1986).

TOWARD AN INTEGRATIVE VIEW OF LANGUAGE IN COMMUNICATION

We need a theory that can (1) integrate the symbolic and referential functions of language for our individual, relational, and multiple group identities; (2) focus upon the creative role of majority and minority collectivities in society while recognizing the dynamic nature of language change and evolution (Aitchison, 1981; Peng, 1976); and (3) feature the interface between the ways that language reflects, builds upon, and determines social reality, as well as highlight the dynamic, skeptical, crafty communicative qualities we all share.

Some Theoretical Priorities for Interpersonal Communication

Interpersonal communication is a plethora of quite discrete topics and research domains, yet we hope to have shown from the foregoing that these intermingle in fascinating, intricate ways. An important integrative mechanism is the mediating role of *social power*. We have observed this at the institutional level in terms of news and media language, with its emotional, political, and evaluative predispositions and potentially ultimately discriminatory impact. It clearly emerged at the intergroup level, through reactions to what is "standard, correct and proper" to speak and acquire. At the interindividual level, it operates in terms of communicative competence (Spitzberg & Cupach, 1984; Wiemann, 1977; Wiemann & Bradac, in press-a, in press-b; Wiemann & Kelly, 1981), self-presentation, relational definition (Millar & Rogers, 1976; Sluzki & Beavin, 1965; Wiemann, 1985), as well as in the latter phases of relationship disengagement. Finally, it emerges intraindividually by influencing our thought processes as a by-product of the language in which we are socialized and the nature of the speech we accommodate to others present (and sometimes absent).

Another complexity emerges from the fact that the institutional, intergroup, interindividual, and intrapsychic levels are not mutually exclusive conceptually. For instance, it is clear that spouses' language patterns cannot only *reflect* the status of heterosexual relationships, but can equally likely, and simultaneously, *determine* them as well (Bradac, 1983); the same bidirectionality is also apparent with respect to language and institutional life (O'Barr, 1983). Even more compelling are taken-for-granteds that not only *build upon* relationships but can also *reflect* the development of them, as well as contribute to the determination of their ultimate downfall. In actual fact then, the present conceptual systems are extremely susceptible to yet another set of intricate interrelationships. How then can we achieve some valued theoretical parsimony in the face of these interlocking spirals? Our preliminary proposals are founded in the processes of

↔ "self"-concept/social identity ↔ social comparison ↔ "self"-esteem ↔ social influence needs ↔ language behaviors ↔ social cognitions ↔ "self"-presentation ↔

A brief consideration of this model makes clear that each aspect influences and is influenced by all the others, either directly or indirectly. Space does not permit, nor does the present state of theory justify, a detailed exposition of all linkages depicted. For ease of exposition, let us enter the cycle above at the "self"-esteem construct, although it could be entered at any point. One's estimate of self-worth must, to a certain extent, come from one's own private observations, attributions, and projected consequences of one's own actions, cognitions, and feelings. These are subjective yardsticks that are largely constructed idiosyncratically—termed henceforth "intra-individual comparisons"—and are a feature of a self-reflexive model of the human being (Farr, 1980). Yet, given we exist in a world where our reality is socially constructed (Berger & Luckmann, 1966), from a symbolic interactionist perspective our conceptions of our own value come from appraising how *others* see us (Mead, 1934). Hence in Festinger's (1954) terms, we make "social comparisons" (Suls & Miller, 1977), particularly in contexts where norms are subjectively ill-defined or unavailable (see McKirnan & Hamayan, 1984) to establish our own self-esteem. Tajfel (1974) extended this essentially interpersonal comparison process to the intergroup level for application when individuals wish to assess the affect associated with their *social identity.*

In a similar vein, Giles and Fitzpatrick (1984) argued for the need in relational situations to make *couple comparisons.* Recall the notion that the development, as well as the dissolution, of relationships is fraught with stressful uncertainties (Berger & Bradac, 1982; Berger & Calabrese, 1975). We may use couple comparisons then, and those carefully chosen as interindividual ones for their appropriateness (Festinger, 1954), as useful templates for judging our own relationship status (see Milardo, 1982). In other words, we have not only self-concepts or self-identities, but relational and group ones as well. In this context, it might be worthwhile reformulating Tajfel and Turner's (1979) bipolar interindividual continuum to constitute an orthogonal, tridimensional space wherein self, relational, and group situations could be construed each along a high to low continuum. Of course, the factors that determine the relative perceived saliency of individual, relational, or group identities at a given time constitute an important area of further inquiry (see Ward, 1984), as do the type and nature of the social comparisons that ensue.

This chapter has also made clear that our identification can be created and established by another form of social comparison not explicitly acknowledged by Festinger, namely, "media/institutional" comparisons. After all, we gain access to what we should or could be like, how we might talk, and why the world is as it is from TV, newspapers, novels, and the like (e.g., Ragan & Hopper, 1984). Zillman and Bryant (1982) make this argument with respect to viewing of pornography and the internal construction via this media-social comparison of what is standard nonverbal sexual fare for the consumer of it (see also Malamuth & Donner-stein, 1982). Media comparisons, of course, not only feed our relational identities (Fallis, Fitzpatrick, & Friedstadt, 1985) but also our indi-vidual and group esteems (see O'Keefe & Reid-Nash, Chapter 14).

Tedeschi (1972, 1974) has argued that the acquisition and mainte-nance of social power and influence is a fundamental social motivation. He sees this desire as mediating our self-presentations, most of which are manifest linguistically (see Tedeschi, Lindskold, & Rosenfeld, 1985). Hence, we strategically and tactically wish to establish and create posi-tive impressions along the dimensions desired in socially influential oth-ers. Having managed such a construction allows us considerable social power over others and our environment. Obviously, on other occasions we do not have the luxury of asserting ourselves because we have to pro-tect or defend our spoiled identities and save face (Arkin, 1981; Goff-man, 1959). Tedeschi provocatively suggests that feelings of positive esteem are not autonomous but are barometers of how much social influ-ence we are enjoying and the extent of the interpersonal power we hold.

An important aspect of self-presentation theory is that we do not sit idle and passively accept social comparisons from others. By communi-cation (Baumeister, 1982) we attempt to manage others' impressions of us, thereby being active in formulating our own individual, group, and relational esteem and, hence, identities (see Cushman & Cahn, 1985). Thus impression management research needs to be modestly extended to acknowledge explicitly the role of group relational presentations.

Although there is some appreciation of it in the literature (e.g., Cline, 1983; Wiemann & Bradac, in press-a; Wiemann & Kelly, 1981), empiri-cal work has not attended much to the possibility and theoretical conse-quences of the *relationship* itself being a unit of analysis. When we are talking in couples, very often we do not treat others in terms of their indi-vidual contributions but rather construe their conversations as "couple talk" (Giles & Fitzpatrick, 1984). Indeed, when talking to a group we may leave with the oft-quoted "feeling of the meeting" rather than recall in detail individual contributions to it. Earlier we discussed notions of speech divergence, and these can be now considered exemplars of indi-viduals' *group presentations*. Illustrations of the relational presentation include "couple-disclosures" (we did . . . ; our feelings are . . .), expressed egalitarian ideals, manifest affection by various nonverbal signals, and the like. As Oakes and Turner (1980) showed, the opportu-nity to achieve a positive group identity by discriminating from a rele-vant outgroup may bolster one's sense of *individual* self-worth; so too might a positive relational presentation achieve similar benefits.

Although the role of communication science or sociolinguistics has not been appreciated by social psychologists working in the self-presentation arena, it is apparent that our language attitudes (Ryan & Giles, 1982) mediate our self-presentations (Coupland, 1984, 1985; Giles et al., in press). In other words, the crafty, skeptical communicator can use the social knowledge that deep pitch, fast speech rate, standard dialect, and dynamic style are associated with perceived competence in order to construct his or her self-presentations. The process of group presentation is also mediated by sociolinguistic expectations regarding ingroup rhetoric, jargon, slang, and nonverbal style.

Of course, the crafty, skeptical decoder is sometimes attuned to the range of language presentations that can be second-guessed. Bearing in mind the fact that we are self-reflective speaker-hearers, we can monitor and adjust the nature of our self-presentations so as to maximize our impact or reduce any ineffectualities (Weary & Arkin, 1981). Needless to say, and as stressed strongly by Giles and Street (1985), our actual language behaviors are determined by a multitude of social cognitions besides those of self-presentation in order to meet the demands of the situation. One's beliefs about the value of talk (be it small talk [see Knapp, 1984], group discussion, etc.) could be crucial determinants of the energy invested in conversation, thereby affecting the nature of language behaviors emitted (Wiemann et al., 1986).

This conceptualization allows us then to knit together the three social processes outlined at the beginning of this chapter while recognizing the craftiness and skepticism associated with linguistic skills and communicative competence. Language reflects social reality, builds upon it, and determines it so as to maintain or defend, create or legitimize the social power and influence we desire in order to organize and make sense of social reality (Coleman, 1985). Our perspective holds out social comparison and self-presentation theories as key processes at the intraindividual, relational, intergroup, and institutional levels of analysis. It opens a panoply of questions concerning how language operates in more detail to facilitate our social influence pursuits, and does so in a more integrative manner than hitherto.

Obviously, no one conceptualization can encapsulate the depth and diversity of language and social relationships. Nonetheless, we must be aware that traditional academic boundaries are fading, merging, and redefining themselves very quickly. We should be wary of compartmentalizing each other from other divisions of communication science that are integral, if not fundamental, to our concerns. Take for example the media. When processed by individuals, this field provides many of the topics and themes and supplies much of the meat and content of interpersonal encounters (McLeod, Fitzpatrick, Glynn, & Fallis, 1982). Such experiences, of course, in turn affect our attention to and processing and evaluation of the media. Relatedly, a significant influence in the relatively high rate of TV-watching by the elderly and the comfort many of them derive from it might well be the dissatisfying, even demeaning interpersonal communication they often have with those younger than themselves (Ryan et al., 1986).

Language and power are central to understanding human social life. In our lifetimes the physical components of power have been developed beyond our wildest nightmares, with communication technology progressing beyond our wildest dreams. Is it not about time society spent appreciably more resources developing the *social* components of language, communication, and power? It has been argued that human infants are inherently disposed toward communication (Bruner, 1975; Trevarthen, 1974). Biologically wired to communicate we may be, socially sophisticated enough to know *naturally* how to control this linguistic power we are not!

REFERENCES

Aitchison, J. (1981). *Language change: Progress or decay?* Bumpay, Suffolk: Fontana.

Altman, I., & Taylor, D. A. (1973). *Social penetration: The development of interpersonal relationships.* New York: Holt, Rinehart & Winston.

Anderson, C., Fine, M. G., & Anderson, F. L. (1983). Black talk on television: A constructivist approach to viewers' perceptions of BEV in Roots II. *Journal of Multilingual and Multicultural Development, 4,* 181-196.

Argyle, M., Furnham, A., & Graham, J. A. (1981). *Social situations.* Cambridge: Cambridge University Press.

Arkin, R. M. (1981). Self-presentation styles. In J. T. Tedeschi (Ed.), *Impression management theory and social psychological research* (pp. 311-333). New York: Academic Press.

Bales, R. (1950). *Interaction process analysis.* Reading, MA: Addison-Wesley.

Baptista-Fernandez, P., & Greenberg, B. (1980). The context, characteristics and communication behaviors of blacks on television. In B. Greenberg (Ed.), *Life on television* (pp. 13-21). Norwood, NJ: Ablex.

Barron, N. (1971). Sex-typed language: The production of grammatical cases. *Acta Sociologica, 14,* 24-72.

Baugh, J. (1983). *Black street speech.* Austin: University of Texas Press.

Baumeister, R. F. (1982). A self-presentation view of social phenomena. *Psychological Bulletin, 91,* 3-26.

Bavelas, J. (1983). Situations that lead to disqualification. *Human Communication Research, 9,* 130-145.

Baxter, L. A. (1984). Trajectories of relationship disengagement. *Journal of Social & Personal Relations, 1,* 29-48.

Baxter, L. A. (1985). Accomplishing relationship disengagement. In S. Duck & D. Perlmann (Eds.), *Understanding personal relationships* (pp. 243-265). Newbury Park, CA: Sage.

Baxter, L. A., & Wilmot, W. M. (1984). Secret tests: Social strategies for acquiring information about the state of the relationship. *Human Communication Research, 11,* 171-202.

Beardsmore, H. B. (Ed.). (1984). Language and television. *International Journal of the Sociology of Language, 48.*

Becker, W., & Krug, R. (1964). A circumplex model of social behavior in children. *Child Development, 35,* 371-396.

Beebe, L., & Giles, H. (1984). Speech-accommodation theories: A discussion in terms of second-language acquisition. *International Journal of the Sociology of Language, 46,* 5-32.

Bell, A. (1984). Language style as audience design. *Language in Society, 13,* 145-204.

Berger, C. R. (1979). Beyond initial interaction: Uncertainty, understanding and the development of interpersonal relationships. In H. Giles & R. N. St. Clair (Eds.), *Language and social psychology* (pp. 122-144). Baltimore: University Park Press.

Berger, C. R. (1985). Social power and interpersonal communication. In M. L. Knapp & G. R. Miller (Eds.), *Handbook of interpersonal communication* (pp. 439-499). Newbury Park, CA: Sage.

Berger, C. R., & Bradac, J. J. (1982). *Language and social knowledge.* London: Edward Arnold.

Berger, C. R., & Calabrese, R. J. (1975). Some explorations in initial interaction and beyond: Toward a developmental theory of interpersonal communication. *Human Communication Research, 1,* 99-112.

Berger, P., & Luckmann, T. (1966). *The social construction of reality: A treatise in the sociology of knowledge.* Garden City, NY: Doubleday.

Blakar, R. M. (1975). How sex roles are represented, reflected and conserved in the Norwegian language. *Acta Sociologica, 14,* 515-534.

Blakar, R. M. (1985). Towards a theory of communication in terms of preconditions: A conceptual framework and some empirical explorations. In H. Giles & R. N. St. Clair (Eds.), *Recent advances in language, communication and social psychology* (pp. 10-40). Hillsdale, NJ: Lawrence Erlbaum.

Bochner, A., Kaminski, E., & Fitzpatrick, M. A. (1977). The conceptual domain of interpersonal communication behavior: A factor analytic study. *Human Communication Research, 3,* 291-302.

Borgotta, E. (1964). The structure of personality characteristics. *Behavioral Science, 9,* 8-17.

Borgotta, E., Cottrell, L., & Mann, J. (1958). The spectrum of individual interaction characteristics: An interdimensional analysis. *Psychological Reports, 4,* 279-319.

Bourhis, R. Y. (1984). Cross-cultural communication in Montreal: Two field studies since Bill 101. *International Journal of the Sociology of Language, 46,* 33-47.

Bourhis, R. Y. (1985). The sequential nature of language choice in cross-cultural communication. In R. L. Street, Jr., & J. N. Cappella (Eds.), *Sequence and pattern in communicative behavior* (pp. 120-141). London: Edward Arnold.

Bourhis, R. Y., Giles, H., & Lambert, W. E. (1975). Social consequences of accommodating one's style of speech: A cross-national investigation. *International Journal of Language, 6,* 55-72.

Bourhis, R. Y., Giles, H., Leyens, J.-P., & Tajfel, H. (1979). Psycholinguistic distinctiveness: Language divergence in Belgium. In H. Giles & R. St. Clair (Eds.), *Language and social psychology* (pp. 158-185). Oxford: Blackwell.

Bourhis, R. Y., & Sachdev, I. (1984). Vitality perceptions and language attitudes. *Journal of Language and Social Psychology, 3,* 97-126.

Bradac, J. J. (1982). A rose by another name: Attitudinal consequences of lexical variation. In E. B. Ryan & H. Giles (Eds.), *Attitudes towards language variation: Social and applied contexts* (pp. 99-115). London: Edward Arnold.

Bradac, J. J. (1983). The language of lovers, flovers, and friends: Communicating in personal and social relationships. *Journal of Language and Social Psychology, 2,* 141-162.

Bradac, J. J., Friedman, E., & Giles, H. (1986). A social cognitive approach to propositional communication: Speakers lie to hearers. In G. McGregor (Ed.), *Speaking for hearers* (pp. 127-151). Oxford: Pergamon.

Bradac, J. J., & Mulac, A. (1984). Attributional consequences of powerful and power-less speech styles in a crisis-intervention context. *Journal of Language and Social Psychology, 3,* 1-19.

Breton, R. (1971). Institutional completeness of ethnic communities and personal relations of immigrants. In B. R. Blishen, F. E. Jones, K. D. Naegels, & J. Porter (Eds.), *Canadian society: Sociological perspectives* (pp. 51-68). Toronto: Macmillan.

Brouwer, D. (1982). The influence of the addressee's sex on politeness in language use. *Linguistics, 20,* 697-711.

Brown, P., & Fraser, C. (1979). Speech as a marker of situation. In K. R. Scherer & H. Giles (Eds.), *Social markers in speech* (pp. 33-108). Cambridge: Cambridge University Press.

Brown, P., & Levinson, S. (1978). Universals in language usage: Politeness phenomena. In E. N. Goody (Ed.), *Questions and politeness* (pp. 56-310). Cambridge: Cambridge University Press.

Brown, P., & Levinson, S. (1979). Social structure, groups and interaction. In K. R. Scherer & H. Giles (Eds.), *Social markers in speech* (pp. 291-342). Cambridge: Cambridge University Press.

Brown, R., & Gilman, A. (1960). The pronouns of power and solidarity. In T. Sebeok (Ed.), *Style in language* (pp. 253-276). New York: Free Press.

Bruner, J. S. (1975). From communication to language—a psychological perspective. *Cognition, 3,* 253-286.

Burgoon, M., & Miller, G. R. (1985). An expectancy interpretation of language and persuasion. In H. Giles & R. N. St. Clair (Eds.), *Recent advances in communication, language and social psychology* (pp. 199-229). Hillsdale, NJ: Lawrence Erlbaum.

Cappella, J. N. (1981). Mutual influence in expressive behavior: Adult and infant-adult dyadic interaction. *Psychological Bulletin, 89,* 101-132.

Carter, L. (1954). Evaluating the performance of individuals as members of small groups. *Personnel Psychology, 7,* 477-484.

Cheshire, J. (1984). The relationship between language and sex in English. In P. Trudgill (Ed.), *Applied sociolinguistics* (pp. 33-50). London: Academic Press.

Chomsky, N. (1957). *Syntactic structures.* The Hague: Mouton.

Chomsky, N. (1965). *Aspects of the theory of syntax.* Cambridge: MIT Press.

Cline, R. (1983). The acquaintance process as relational communication. In R. N. Bostrom (Ed.), *Communication yearbook 7* (pp. 396-413). Newbury Park, CA: Sage.

Clyne, M. G. (1982). *Multilingual Australia.* Melbourne: River Seine.

Coleman, L. (1985). Language and the evolution of identity and self-concept. In F. Kessel (Ed.), *The development of language and language researchers: Essays in tribute to Roger Brown.* Hillsdale, NJ: Lawrence Erlbaum.

Cooper, R. L. (1984). The avoidance of androcentric generics. *International Journal of the Sociology of Language, 50,* 5-20.

Coupland, N. (1984). Accommodation at work: Some phonological data and their implications. *International Journal of the Sociology of Language, 46,* 49-70.

Coupland, N. (1985). "Hark, hark the lark": Social motivations for phonological style shifting. *Language and Communication, 5,* 153-171.

Cushman, D., & Cahn, D. (1985). *Communication in interpersonal relationships.* Albany: State University of New York Press.

Cushman, D., & Whiting, G. A. (1973). An approach to communicaton: Toward consensus on rules. *Journal of Communication, 22,* 217-283.

Davis, R. H., & Kubey, R. W. (1982). Growing older on television and with television. In D. Pearl, L. Bouthilet, & J. Lazar (Eds.), *Television and behavior* (pp. 201-208). Rockville, MD: National Institute of Mental Health.

DePaulo, B., Stone, J. I., & Lassiter, G. D. (1985). Telling ingratiation lies: Effects of target sex and target attractiveness on verbal and nonverbal deceptive success. *Journal of Personality and Social Psychololgy, 48*, 1191-1208.

Doise, W., Sinclair, A., & Bourhis, R. Y. (1976). Evaluation of accent convergence and divergence in cooperative and competitive intergroup situations. *British Journal of Social and Clinical Psychology, 15*, 247-252.

Drake, G. (1980). The social role of slang. In H. Giles, W. P. Robinson, & P. M. Smith (Eds.), *Language: Social psychological perspectives* (pp. 63-70). Oxford: Pergamon.

Dryden, C., & Giles, H. (in press). Language, social identity and health. In H. Beloff & A. Coleman (Eds.), *Psychology Survey 6*. Leicester: British Psychological Society.

Dube-Simard, L. (1983). Genesis of social categorization, threat to identity, and perceptions of social injustice: Their role in intergroup communication breakdown. *Journal of Language and Social Psychology, 2*, 183-206.

Duck, S. (1982). A topography of relationship disengagement and dissolution. In S. Duck (Ed.), *Personal relationships 4: Dissolving relationships* (pp. 141-162). London: Academic Press.

Durkin, K. (1984). Children's accounts of sex-role stereotypes. *Communication Research, 11*, 341-362.

Edwards, J. R. (1979). *Language and disadvantage*. London: Edward Arnold.

Edwards, J. R. (1983). Review of J. Honey, *The language trap. Journal of Language and Social Psychology, 2*, 67-76.

Edwards, J. R. (Ed.). (1984). *Linguistic minorities, policies and pluralism*. London: Academic Press.

Edwards, J. R. (1985). *Language, society and identity*. Oxford: Blackwell.

Edwards, J. R., & Giles, H. (1984). Applications of the social psychology of language: Sociolinguistics and education. In P. Trudgill (Ed.), *Applied sociolinguistics* (pp. 119-158). London: Academic Press.

Eiser, J. R. (1980). *Cognitive social psychology*. London: McGraw-Hill.

Ekman, P. (1985). *Telling lies: Clues to deceit in the marketplace, politics and marriage*. New York: Norton.

Ervin-Tripp, S. M. (1969). Sociolinguistics. *Advances in Experimental Social Psychology, 4*, 91-165.

Ervin-Tripp, S. M. (1972). On sociolinguistic rules: Alternation and co-occurrence. In J. Gumperz & D. Hymes (Eds.), *Directions in sociolinguistics* (pp. 213-250). New York: Holt, Rinehart & Winston.

Ervin-Tripp, S. M. (1980). Speech acts, social meaning and social learning. In H. Giles, W. P. Robinson, & P. M. Smith (Eds.), *Language: Social psychological perspectives* (pp. 389-396). Oxford: Pergamon.

Fallis, S. F., Fitzpatrick, M. A., & Friestad, M. S. (1985). Spouses' discussions of television portrayals of close relationships. *Communication Research, 12*, 59-81.

Farr, R. (1980). Homo loquiens in social psychological perspective. In H. Giles, W. P. Robinson, & P. M. Smith (Eds.), *Language: Social psychological perspectives* (pp. 409-413). Oxford: Pergamon.

Fielding, G., & Fraser, C. (1978). Language and interpersonal relations. In I. Markova (Ed.), *The social context of language* (pp. 217-232). London: John Wiley.

Festinger, L. (1954). A theory of social comparison processes. *Human Relations, 7*, 117-140.

Fishman, J. A. (1966). *Language loyalty in the United States*. The Hague: Mouton.

Fishman, J. A. (1967). Bilingualism with and without diglossia: Diglossia with and without bilingualism. *Journal of Social Issues, 23*, 29-38.

Fishman, J. A. (1972). The relationship between micro- and macro-sociolinguistics in the study of who speaks what language to whom and when. In J. B. Pride & J. Holmes (Eds.), *Sociolinguistics* (pp. 15-32). Harmondsworth: Penguin.

Fishman, P. (1980). Conversational insecurity. In H. Giles, W. P. Robinson, & P. M. Smith (Eds.), *Language: Social psychological perspectives* (pp. 127-132). Oxford: Pergamon.

Fitzpatrick, M. A. (1984). A typological approach to marital interaction: Recent theory and research. In L. Berkowitz (Ed.), *Advances in experimental social psychology* (Vol. 18, pp. 1-47). New York: Academic Press.

Fitzpatrick, M. A., Fallis, S., & Vance, L. (1982). Multifunctional coding of conflict resolution strategies in marital dyads. *Family Relations, 31,* 61-70.

Fitzpatrick, M. A., Vance, L., & Witteman, H. (1984). Interpersonal communication in the casual interaction of marital partners. *Journal of Language and Social Psychology, 3,* 81-96.

Flores, N., & Hopper, R. (1975). Mexican Americans' evaluations of spoken Spanish and English. *Communication Monographs, 42,* 91-98.

Foa, U., & Foa, E. (1972). Resource exchange: Toward a structural theory of interpersonal communication. In A. Siegman & B. Pope (Eds.), *Studies in dyadic communication* (pp. 291-323). New York: Pergamon.

Forgas, J. (1983). Language, goals, and situation. *Journal of Language and Social Psychology, 2,* 267-293.

Furnham, A. (1986). Assertiveness through different media. *Journal of Language and Social Psychology, 5,* 1-11.

Gardner, R. C. (1985). *Social psychology and second language learning.* London: Edward Arnold.

Genesee, F., & Bourhis, R. Y. (1982). The social psychological significance of code-switching in cross-cultural communication. *Journal of Language and Social Psychology, 1,* 1-28.

Gerbner, G., Gross, L., Morgan, M., & Signorielli, N. (1980a). Some additional comments on the cultivation analysis. *Public Opinion Quarterly, 44,* 408-410.

Gerbner, G., Gross, L., Morgan, M., & Signorielli, N. (1980b). Aging with television: Images on television drama and conceptions of social reality. *Journal of Communication, 30*(1), 37-47.

Giles, H. (Ed.). (1977). *Language, ethnicity and intergroup relations.* London: Academic Press.

Giles, H. (1978). Linguistic differentiation between social groups. In H. Tajfel (Ed.), *Differentiation between social groups* (pp. 361-393). London: Academic Press.

Giles, H. (1979). Ethnicity markers in speech. In K. R. Scherer & H. Giles (Eds.), *Social markers in speech* (pp. 251-290). Cambridge: Cambridge University Press.

Giles, H. (1980). Accommodation theory: Some new directions. *York Papers in Linguistics, 9,* 105-136.

Giles, H., Bourhis, R. Y., & Taylor, D. M. (1977). Towards a theory of language in ethnic group relations. In H. Giles (Ed.), *Language, ethnicity and intergroup relations* (pp. 307-348). London: Academic Press.

Giles, H., & Byrne, J. L. (1982). An intergroup model of second language acquisition. *Journal of Multilingual and Multicultural Development, 3,* 17-40.

Giles, H., & Edwards, J. R. (Eds.). (1983). Language attitudes in multilingual settings. *Journal of Multilingual and Multicultural Development, 4* (2-3).

Giles, H., & Fitzpatrick, M. A. (1984). Personal, group and couple identities: Towards a relational context for the study of language attitudes and linguistic forms. In D. Schiffrin (Ed.), *Meaning, form and use in context: Linguistic applications* (pp. 253-277). Washington, DC: Georgetown University Press.

Giles, H., & Hewstone, M. (1982). Cognitive structures, speech and social situations: Two integrative models. *Language Sciences, 4,* 188-219.

Giles, H., Hewstone, M., Ryan, E. B., & Johnson, P. (in press). Research in language attitudes. In U. Ammons, N. Dittmar, & K. J. Mattheier (Eds.), *Sociolinguistics: Handbook of the science of language.* Berlin: de Gruyter.

Giles, H., & Johnson, P. (1981). The role of language in ethnic group relations. In J. C. Turner & H. Giles (Eds.), *Intergroup behavior* (pp. 199-243). Oxford: Blackwell.

Giles, H., & Johnson, P. (1986). Perceived threat, ethnic commitment, and inter-ethnic language behavior. In Y. Y. Kim (Ed.), *Current studies in interethnic communication* (pp. 91-116). Newbury Park, CA: Sage.

Giles, H., & Johnson, P. (in press). New directions in language maintenance: A social psychological approach. *International Journal of the Sociology of Language.*

Giles, H., Mulac, A., Bradac, J. J., & Johnson, P. (1987). Speech accommodation theory: The first decade and beyond. In M. L. McLaughlin (Ed.), *Communication yearbook 10* (pp. 13-48). Newbury Park, CA: Sage.

Giles, H., & Powesland, P. F. (1975). *Speech style and social evaluation.* London: Academic Press.

Giles, H., Robinson, W. P., & Smith, P. M. (Eds.). (1980). *Language: Social psychological perspectives.* Oxford: Pergamon.

Giles, H., & Ryan, E. B. (Eds.). (1986). Language, communication and the elderly. *Language and Communication, 6* (1-2).

Giles, H., & St. Clair, R. N. (Eds.). (1985). *Recent advances in language, communication and social psychology.* Hillsdale, NJ: Lawrence Erlbaum.

Giles, H., & Saint-Jacques, B. (Eds.). (1979). *Language and ethnic relations.* Oxford: Pergamon.

Giles, H., Scherer, K. R., & Taylor, D. M. (1979). Speech markers in social interaction. In K. R. Scherer & H. Giles (Eds.), *Social markers in speech* (pp. 343-381). Cambridge: Cambridge University Press.

Giles, H., Smith, P. M., Ford, B., Condor, S., & Thakerar, J. N. (1980). Speech style and the fluctuating salience of sex. *Language Sciences, 2,* 260-282.

Giles, H., & Street, R. L., Jr. (1985). Communicator characteristics and behavior. In M. L. Knapp & G. R. Miller (Eds.), *Handbook of interpersonal communication* (pp. 205-262). Newbury Park, CA: Sage.

Giles, H., Taylor, D. M., & Bourhis, R. Y. (1973). Towards a theory of interpersonal accommodation through language: Some Canadian data. *Language in Society, 2,* 177-192.

Goffman, E. (1959). *The presentation of self in everyday life.* Garden City, NY: Doubleday.

Gottman, J. (1979). *Marital interaction.* New York: Academic Press.

Gottman, J. (1982). Emotional responsiveness in marital conversations. *Journal of Communication, 32,* 108-120.

Greenberg, B. (1972). Children's reactions to TV blacks. *Journalism Quarterly, 49,* 5-14.

Greenberg, B. (1982). Television and role socialization: An overview. In D. Pearl, L. Bouthilet, & J. Lazar (Eds.), *Television and behavior* (pp. 179-200). Rockville, MD: National Institute of Mental Health.

Greene, J. O., & Cody, M. J. (Eds.). (1985). Cognitive processes and speech production. *Journal of Language and Social Psychology, 4* (3-4).

Grice, P. (1975). Logic and conversation. In P. Cole & J. L. Morgan (Eds.), *Syntax and semantics* (Vol. 3, pp. 43-58). New York: Academic Press.

Gudykunst, W. B. (1985). A model of uncertainty reduction in intercultural encounters. *Journal of Language and Social Psychology, 4,* 79-98.

Gudykunst, W. B. (Ed.). (1986). *Intergroup communication.* London: Edward Arnold.

Gumperz, J. (1964). Linguistic and social interaction in two communities. *American Anthropologist, 66* (Suppl. 6, Pt. 2), 137-153.

Gumperz, J. (Ed.). (1982). *Language and social identity.* Cambridge: Cambridge University Press.

Gumperz, J., & Hymes, D. (Eds.). (1972). *Directions in sociolinguistics.* New York: Holt, Rinehart, & Winston.

Hall, E., (1966). *The hidden dimension.* Garden City, NY: Doubleday.

Harré, R., & Secord, P. (1972). *The explanation of social behavior.* Oxford: Blackwell.

Hawkins, P. (1983). Diglossia revisited. *Language Sciences, 5,* 1-20.

Hawley, A. H. (1963). Community power and urban renewal. *American Journal of Sociology, 68,* 422-431.

Henley, N. M. (1977). *Body politics: Power, sex and nonverbal behavior.* Englewood Cliffs, NJ: Prentice-Hall.

Herman, S. (1961). Explorations in the social psychology of language choice. *Human Relations, 14,* 149-164.

Hewes, D., Graham, M. L., Doelger, J., & Pavitt, C. (1985). Second guessing: Message interpretation in social networks. *Human Communication Research, 11,* 299-334.

Hewes, D., & Planalp, S. (1982). There is nothing as useful as a good theory . . . : The influence of social knowledge on interpersonal communication. In M. E. Roloff & C. R. Berger (Eds.), *Social cognition and communication.* (pp. 107-150). Newbury Park, CA: Sage.

Hewstone, M., & Giles, H. (1986). Social groups and social stereotypes in intergroup communication: Review and model of intergroup communication breakdown. In W. B. Gudykunst (Ed.), *Intergroup communication* (pp. 10-26). London: Edward Arnold.

Hewstone, M., & Jaspars, J. (1984). Social dimensions of attribution. In H. Tajfel (Ed.), *The social dimension* (Vol. 2, pp. 379-404). Cambridge: Cambridge University Press.

Higgins, E. T., Fondacaro, R., & McCann, C. D. (1981). Rules and roles: The "communication game" and speaker-listener processes. In W. P. Dickson (Ed.), *Children's oral communication skills* (pp. 289-312). New York: Academic Press.

Higgins, E. T., & McCann, C. D. (1984). Social encoding and subsequent attitudes, impressions, and memory: "Context-driven" and motivational aspects of processing. *Journal of Personality and Social Psychology, 47,* 26-39.

Higgins, E. T., & Rholes, W. S. (1978). "Saying is believing": Effects of message modification on memory and liking for the person described. *Journal of Experimental Social Psychology, 14,* 363-378.

Hirsch, P. (1981). On not learning from one's own mistakes. *Communication Research, 8,* 3-38.

Hopper, R. (1981). The taken-for-granted. *Human Communication Research, 7,* 195-211.

Hopper, R., Knapp, M., & Scott, L. (1981). Couples' personal idioms: Exploring intimate talk. *Journal of Communication, 31*(1), 23-33.

Howitt, D. (1982). *Mass media and social problems.* Oxford: Pergamon.

Husband, C. (1977). News media, language and race relations: A case study in identity maintenance. In H. Giles (Ed.), *Language, ethnicity and intergroup relations* (pp. 211-240). London: Academic Press.

Hyde, S. (1984). Children's understanding of sexist language. *Development Psychology, 20,* 697-706.

Hymes, D. (1967). Models of the interaction of language and social setting. *Journal of Social Issues, 23,* 8-28.

Jaspars, J.M.F., & Hewstone, M. (1982). Cross-cultural interacton, social attribution and intergroup relations. In S. Bochner (Ed.), *Cultures in contact: Studies in cross-cultural interaction* (pp. 127-156). Oxford: Pergamon.

Joos, M. (1962). The five clocks. *International Journal of American Linguistics, 28,* Part 5.

Kellermann, K., & Berger, C. R. (1984). Affect and the acquisition of social information: Sit back, relax, and tell me about yourself. In R. Bostrom (Ed.), *Communication yearbook 8* (pp. 412-445). Newbury Park, CA: Sage.

Kelvin, P. (1972). *The bases of social behavior.* London: Methuen.

Kitson, G. C., Babri, K. B., & Roach, M. J. (1985). Who divorces and why: A review. *Journal of Family Issues, 6,* 255-294.

Knapp, M. L. (1983). Dyadic relationship development. In J. M. Wiemann & R. P. Harrison (Eds.), *Nonverbal interaction* (pp. 179-208). Newbury Park, CA: Sage.

Knapp, M. L. (1984). *Interpersonal communication and human relationships* (pp. 29-56). Boston: Allyn & Bacon.

Kochman, T. (1982). *Black and white styles in conflict.* Chicago: Chicago University Press.

Koerner, K. (1983). The Chomskyan "revolution" and its historography: A few critical remarks. *Language and Communication, 3,* 147-170.

Kramarae, C. (1981). *Women and men speaking.* Rowley, MA: Newbury House.

Kramarae, C. (1982). Gender: How she speaks. In E. B. Ryan & H. Giles (Eds.), *Attitudes towards language variation: Social and applied contexts* (pp. 84-98). London: Edward Arnold.

Kraut, R. E., & Higgins, E. T. (1984). Communication and social cognition. In R. S. Wyer & T. K. Srull (Eds.), *Handbook of social cognition* (Vol. 3, pp. 87-129). Hillsdale, NJ: Lawrence Erlbaum.

Kress, G. (1983). Linguistic processes and the mediation of "reality": The problems of newspaper language. *International Journal of the Sociology of Language, 40,* 43-57.

Krueger, D. L. (1982). Marital decision-making: A language-action analysis. *Quarterly Journal of Speech, 68,* 273-287.

Labov, W. (1966). *The social stratification of English in New York City.* Washington, DC: Center for Applied Linguistics.

Labov, W. (1972). The logic of nonstandard English. In P. P. Giglioli (Ed.), *Language and social context* (pp. 179-216). Harmondsworth: Penguin.

Lakoff, R. (1973). Language and women's place. *Language in Society, 2,* 45-80.

Lambert, W. E. (1979). Language as a factor in intergroup relations. In H. Giles & R. St. Clair (Eds.), *Language and social psychology* (pp. 186-192). Oxford: Blackwell.

Laver, J., & Trudgill, P. (1979). Phonetic and linguistic markers in speech. In K. R. Scherer & H. Giles (Eds.), *Social markers in speech* (pp. 1-32). Cambridge: Cambridge University Press.

Leary, T. (1957). *Interpersonal diagnosis of personality.* New York: Ronald.

Lederer, W. J., & Jackson, D. D. (1967). *The mirages of marriage.* New York: Norton.

Leet-Pelligrini, H. (1980). Conversational dominance as function of gender and expertise. In H. Giles, W. P. Robinson, & P. M. Smith (Eds.), *Language: Social psychological perspectives* (pp. 97-104). Oxford: Pergamon.

Lind, E. A., & O'Barr, W. M. (1979). The social significance of speech in the courtroom. In H. Giles & R. N. St. Clair (Eds.), *Language and social psychology* (pp. 66-87). Baltimore: University Park Press.

Lorr, M., & McNair, D. (1965). Expansion of the interpersonal behavior circle. *Journal of Personality and Social Psychology, 2,* 823-830.

MacKay, D. (1980). Language, thought and social attitudes. In H. Giles, W. P. Robinson, & P. M. Smith (Eds.), *Language: Social psychological perspectives* (pp. 89-96). Oxford: Pergamon.

Malamuth, N. M., & Donnerstein, E. (1982). The effects of aggressive-pornographic mass media stimuli. In L. Berkowitz (Ed.), *Advances in experimental social psychology* (Vol. 15, pp. 103-136). New York: Academic Press.

Martyna, W. (1980). The psychology of the generic masculine. In S. McConnell-Ginet, R. Borker, & N. Furman (Eds.), *Women and language in literature and society* (pp. 69-78). New York: Plenum.

McCombs, M., & Shaw, D. (1972). The agenda-setting function of the press. *Public Opinion Quarterly, 36,* 176-187.

McConnell-Ginet, S., Borker, R., & Furman, N. (Eds.). (1980). *Women and language in literature and society.* New York: Plenum.

McGregor, G. (Ed.). (1986). *Language for hearers.* Oxford: Pergamon.

McKirnan, D. J., & Hamayan, E. V. (1984). Speech norms and attitudes towards outgroup members: A test of a model in a bicultural context. *Journal of Language and Social Psychology, 3,* 21-38.

McLeod, J. M., Fitzpatrick, M. A., Glynn, C. J., & Fallis, S. F. (1982). Television and social relations: Family influences and consequences for interpersonal behavior. In D. Pearl, L. Bouthilet, & J. Lazar (Eds.), *Television and behavior* (pp. 69-78). Rockville, MD: National Institute of Mental Health.

Mead, G. H. (1934). *Mind, self and society.* Chicago: Chicago University Press.

Mercer, N., Mercer, E., & Mears, R. (1979). Linguistic and cultural affiliation. In H. Giles & B. Saint-Jacques (Eds.), *Language and ethnic relations* (pp. 15-26). Oxford: Pergamon.

Meill, D., & Duck, S. (1982). *Charting the development of personal relationships.* Paper presented at the International Conference on Personal Relations, Madison, Wisconsin.

Milardo, R. M. (1982). Friendship networks in developing relationships: Converging and diverging social environment. *Social Psychology Quarterly, 45,* 162-172.

Millar, F., & Rogers, L. E. (1976). A relational approach to interpersonal communication. In G. Miller (Ed.), *Explorations in interpersonal communication* (pp. 87-103). Newbury Park, CA: Sage.

Miller, G. R. (1983). On various ways of skinning symbolic cats: Recent research on persuasive message strategies. *Journal of Language and Social Psychology, 2,* 123-140.

Miller, G. R., & Parks, M. (1982). Communication in dissolving relationships. In S. Duck (Ed.), *Personal relations 4: Dissolving personal relationships* (pp. 127-154). London: Academic Press.

Milroy, L. (1980). *Language and social networks.* Oxford: Blackwell.

Milroy, L. (1982). Language and group identity. *Journal of Multilingual and Multicultural Development, 3,* 207-216.

Milroy, L. (1984). Comprehension and context: Successful communication and communication breakdown. In P. Trudgill (Ed.), *Applied sociolinguistics* (pp. 7-32). London: Academic Press.

Morgan, M. (1982). Television and adolescents' sex role stereotypes: A longitudinal study. *Journal of Personality and Social Psychology, 43,* 947-955.

Mulac, A., & Lundell, T. (1986). Linguistic contributions to the gender-linked language effect. *Journal of Language and Social Psychology, 5,* 81-101.

Mulac, A., Wiemann, J. M., Yoerks, S., & Gibson, T. (1983, July). *Male/female language differences and their effects in like-sex and mixed-sex dyads: A test of interpersonal accommodation and the gender-linked language effect.* Paper delivered at the 2nd International Conference on Social Psychology and Language, Bristol.

Nofsinger, R. (1976). On answering questions indirectly: Some rules in the grammar of doing conversation. *Human Communication Research, 2,* 172-181.

Noller, P. (1982). Channel consistency and inconsistency in the communications of married couples. *Journal of Personality and Social Psychology, 43,* 732-741.

Noller, P., & Fitzpatrick, M. A. (Eds.). (in press). *Marital communication.* Clevedon: Multilingual Matters.

Oakes, P. J., & Turner, J. C. (1980). Social categorization and intergroup behavior: Does minimal intergroup discrimination make social identity more positive? *European Journal of Social Psychology, 10,* 295-301.

O'Barr, W. M. (1982). *Linguistic evidence: Language, power and strategy in the courtroom.* New York: Academic Press.

O'Barr, W. M. (1983). The study of language in institutional contexts. *Journal of Language and Social Psychology, 2,* 241-252.

Parks, M. R., & Adelman, M. B. (1983). Communication networks and the development of romantic relationships. *Human Communication Research, 10,* 55-80.

Patterson, M. (1983). *Nonverbal behavior: A functional perspective.* New York: Springer-Verlag.

Peng, F. (1976). A new explanation of language change: The sociolinguistic approach. *Forum Linguisticum, 1,* 67-94.

Pendelton, D., & Hasler, J. (Eds.). (1983). *Doctor-patient communication.* London: Academic Press.

Petersen, M. (1973). The visibility and image of old people on television. *Journalism Quarterly, 50,* 569-573.

Platt, J. (1977). Review of H. Giles & P. F. Powesland, *Speech style and social evaluation. Lingua, 28,* 98-100.

Platt, J., & Weber, H. (1984). Speech convergence miscarried: An investigation into inappropriate accommodation strategies. *International Journal of the Sociology of Language, 46,* 131-146.

Potter, N., Stringer, P., & Wetherell, M. (1984). *Texts and social context.* London: Routledge & Kegan Paul.

Ragan, S. L., & Hopper, R. (1984). Ways to leave your lover: A communicational analysis of literature. *Communication Quarterly, 32,* 310-317.

Robinson, W. P. (1978). *Language management in education: The Australian context.* Sydney: Allen & Unwin.

Robinson, W. P. (Ed.). (1983). Plenary papers at the 2nd (Bristol) International Conference on Social Psychology and Language. *Journal of Language and Social Psychology, 2* (2-4).

Robinson, W. P. (Ed.). (1984). *Communication in development.* London: Academic Press.

Roloff, M., & Berger, C. R. (Eds.). (1982). *Social cognition and communication.* Newbury Park, CA: Sage.

Romaine, S. (Ed.). (1982). *Sociolinguistic variation in speech communities.* London: Edward Arnold.

Romaine, S. (1984). *The language of children and adolescents.* Oxford: Blackwell.

Rommetveit, R. (1979). On the architecture of intersubjectivity. In R. Rommetveit & R. M. Blakar (Eds.), *Studies of language, thought, and communication* (pp. 93-107). London: Academic.

Ross, H. H. (1984). Speaking the unspeakable: The language of civil defense research. In J. Learing & L. Keyes (Eds.), *The counterfeit ark: Crisis relocation for nuclear war* (pp. 24-48). Cambridge, MA: Ballinger.

Rubin, K. H., & Brown, I. D. R. (1975). A life-span look at person perception and its relationship to communicative interaction. *Journal of Gerontology, 30,* 461-468.

Russell, B. (1938). *Power: A new analysis.* London: Allen & Unwin.

Ryan, E. B. (1979). Why do low-prestige language varieties persist? In H. Giles & R. St. Clair (Eds.), *Language and social psychology* (pp. 145-175). Oxford: Blackwell.

Ryan, E. B., & Giles, H. (Eds.). (1982). *Attitudes towards language variation: Social and applied contexts.* London: Edward Arnold.

Ryan, E. B., Giles, H., Bartolucci, G., & Henwood, K. (1986). Psycholinguistic and social psychological components of communication by and with the elderly. *Language and Communication, 6,* 1-22.

Schegloff, E., & Sacks, H. (1973). Opening up closings. *Semiotica, 8,* 289-327.

Scherer, K. R. (1979). Personality markers in speech. In K. R. Scherer & H. Giles (Eds.), *Social markers in speech* (pp. 147-210). Cambridge: Cambridge University Press.

Scotton, C. M. (1979). Code switching as a "safe choice" in choosing a lingua franca. In W. C. McCormack & S. Wurm (Eds.), *Language and society: Anthropological issues* (pp. 71-83). The Hague: Mouton.

Scotton, C. M. (1985). What the heck, sir: Style shifting and lexical coloring as features of powerful language. In R. L. Street, Jr., & J. N. Cappella (Eds.), *Sequence and pattern in communicative behavior* (pp. 103-119). London: Edward Arnold.

Sebastian, R. J., & Ryan, E. B. (1985). Speech cues and social evaluation: Markers of ethnicity, social class and age. In H. Giles & R. N. St. Clair (Eds.), *Recent advances in language, communication and social psychology* (pp. 112-143). Hillsdale, NJ: Lawrence Erlbaum.

Shimanoff, S. B. (1980). *Communication rules: Theory and research.* Newbury Park, CA: Sage.

Sluzki, C., & Beavin, J. (1965). Simetria y complementaridad: Una definicion operacional y una tipologia de parejas. *Acta Psiquiatrica y Psicologica de America Latina, 11,* 321-330.

Sluzki, C., Beavin, J., Tarnopolsky, A., & Veron, E. (1967). Transactional disqualification: Research on the double bind. *Archives of General Psychiatry, 16,* 494-504.

Smith, P. M. (1980). Judging masculine and feminine social identities from content-controlled speech. In H. Giles, W. P. Robinson, & P. M. Smith (Eds.), *Language: Social psychological perspectives* (pp. 121-126). Oxford: Pergamon.

Smith, P. M. (1985). *Language, the sexes, and society.* Oxford: Blackwell.

Smith, P. M., Giles, H., & Hewstone, M. (1982). New horizons in the study of speech and social situations. In B. Bain (Ed.), *The sociogenesis of language and human conduct* (pp. 297-310). New York: Plenum.

Snow, C., & Ferguson, C. A. (Eds.) (1977). *Talking to children.* Cambridge: Cambridge University Press.

Spanier, G. B. (1976). Measuring dyadic adjustment: New scales for assessing the quality of marriage and other dyads. *Journal of Marriage and the Family, 38,* 15-28.

Spitzberg, B., & Cupach, W. R. (1984). *Interpersonal communication competence.* Newbury Park, CA: Sage.

St. Clair, R. N. (1982). From social history to language attitudes. In E. B. Ryan & H. Giles (Eds.), *Attitudes toward language variation: Social and applied contexts* (pp. 167-174). London: Edward Arnold.

Stipeck, D., & Nelson, K. (1980). Communication efficiency of middle- and lower-SES dyads. *Human Communication Research, 6,* 168-177.

Street, R. L., Jr., & Cappella, J. N. (Eds.). (1985). *Sequence and pattern in communicative behavior.* London: Edward Arnold.

Street, R. L., Jr., & Giles, H. (1982). Speech accommodation theory: A social cognitive approach to language and speech behavior. In M. Roloff & C. R. Berger (Eds.), *Social cognition and communication* (pp. 193-226). Newbury Park, CA: Sage.

Street, R. L., Jr., & Wiemann, J. M. (in press). Patient satisfaction with physician interpersonal involvement, expressiveness, and dominance. In M. L. McLaughlin (Ed.), *Communication yearbook 10* (pp. 591-612). Newbury Park, CA: Sage.

Suls, J. M., & Miller, R. L. (1977). *Social comparison processes.* New York: John Wiley.

Tajfel, H. (1974). Social identity and intergroup behavior. *Social Science Information*, *13*, 65-93.
Tajfel, H. (Ed.). (1978). *Differentiation between social groups*. London: Academic Press.
Tajfel, H. (Ed.). (1982). *Social identity and intergroup relations*. Cambridge: Cambridge University Press.
Tajfel, H., & Turner, J. C. (1979). An integrative theory of intergroup conflict. In W. G. Austin & S. Worchel (Eds.), *The social psychology of intergroup relations* (pp. 33-47). Belmont, CA: Brooks/Cole.
Taylor, D. M., Meynard, R., & Rheault, E. (1977). Threat to identity and second language learning. In H. Giles (Ed.), *Language, ethnicity and intergroup relations* (pp. 99-118). London: Academic Press.
Taylor, D. M., & Royer, E. (1980). Group processes affecting anticipated language choice in intergroup relations. In H. Giles, W. P. Robinson, & P. M. Smith (Eds.), *Language: Social psychological perspectives* (pp. 185-192). Oxford: Pergamon.
Tedeschi, J. T. (1972). *Social influence processes*. Chicago: Aldine.
Tedeschi, J. T. (Ed.). (1974). *Perspectives on social power*. Chicago: Aldine.
Tedeschi, J. T., Lindskold, S., & Rosenfeld, P. (1985). *Introduction to social psychology* (pp. 65-96). New York: West.
Thakerar, J. N., Giles, H., & Cheshire, J. (1982). Psychological and linguistic parameters of speech accommodation theory. In C. Fraser & K. R. Scherer (Eds.), *Advances in the social psychology of language* (pp. 205-255). Cambridge: Cambridge University Press.
Thorne, B., Kramarae, C., & Henley, N. (Eds.). (1984). *Language, gender and society*. Rowley, MA: Newbury House.
Trevanthen, C. (1974, May 2). Communication with a 2-month-old. *New Society*, p. 230.
Tromel-plotz, S. (1981). Review article: The languages of oppression. *Journal of Pragmatics*, *5*, 67-80.
Trudgill, P. (1974). *Sociolinguistics*. Harmondsworth: Penguin.
Trudgill, P. (1975). *Accent, dialect and the school*. London: Edward Arnold.
Turner, J. C., & Brown, R. J. (1978). Social status, cognitive alternatives and intergroup relations. In H. Tajfel (Ed.), *Differentiation between social groups* (pp. 201-234). London: Academic Press.
Turner, J. C., & Giles, H. (Eds.). (1981). *Intergroup behavior*. Chicago: Chicago University Press.
Tversky, A., & Kahneman, D. (1980). Causal schemas in judgements about uncertainty. In M. Fishbein (Ed.), *Progress in social psychology* (Vol. 1, pp. 49-72). Hillsdale, NJ: Lawrence Erlbaum.
Ullrich, H. E. (1971). Linguistic aspects of antiquity: A dialect study. *Anthropological Linguistics*, *13*, 106-113.
Vestergaard, R., & Schroder, K. (1985). *The language of advertising*. Oxford: Blackwell.
Watzlawick, P., Beavin, J. H., & Jackson, D. (1967). *Pragmatics of human communication*. New York: Norton.
Ward, R. A. (1984). The marginality and salience of being old: When is age relevant? *Gerontologist*, *24*, 227-232.
Weary, G., & Arkin, R. M. (1981). Attributional self-presentation. In J. H. Harvey, M. J. Ickes, & R. Kidd (Eds.), *New directions in attribution theory and research* (Vol. 3, pp. 225-247). Hillsdale, NJ: Lawrence Erlbaum.
Weinstein, B. (1979). Language strategists: Redefining political frontiers on the basis of linguistic choices. *World Politics*, *31*, 345-364.

Wells, G., & Robinson, W. P. (1982). The role of adult speech in language develop-
    ment. In C. Fraser & K. R. Scherer (Eds.), *Advances in the social psychology of
    language* (pp. 11-76). Cambridge: Cambridge University Press.
Whorf, B. (1941). The relationship of habitual thought and behavior to language. In
    L. Sapir (Ed.), *Language, culture and personality: Essays in memory of Edward
    Sapir* (pp. 75-93). Menasha, WI: Sapir Memorial Publication Fund.
Wiemann, J. M. (1977). Explication and test of a model of communicative competence.
    Human Communication Research, 3, 195-213.
Wiemann, J. M. (1985). Interpersonal control and regulation in conversation. In R. L.
    Street, Jr., & J. N. Cappella (Eds.), *Sequence and pattern in communicative behav-
    ior* (pp. 85-102). London: Edward Arnold.
Wiemann, J. M., & Bradac, J. J. (in press-a). Metatheoretical issues in the study of
    communicative competence: Structural and functional approaches. *Progress in
    Communication Science, 9.*
Wiemann, J. M., & Bradac, J. J. (in press-b). *Communicative competence: A theoreti-
    cal analysis.* London: Edward Arnold.
Wiemann, J. M., Chen, V., & Giles, H. (1986, November). *Beliefs about talk and
    silence in a cultural context.* Paper presented at the annual meeting of the Speech
    Communication Association, Chicago.
Wiemann, J. M., & Kelly, C. W. (1981). Pragmatics of interpersonal competence. In
    C. Wilder-Mott & J. H. Weakland (Eds.), *Rigor and imagination: Essays from the
    legacy of Gregory Bateson* (pp. 283-297). New York: Praeger.
Wiemann, J. M., & Krueger, D. (1980). The language of relationships: I. Description.
    In H. Giles, W. P. Robinson, & P. M. Smith (Eds.), *Language: Social psychological
    perspectives* (pp. 55-61). Oxford: Pergamon.
Wiseman, R. L., & Schenck-Hamlin, W. (1981). A multidimensional scaling valida-
    tion of an inductively-derived set of compliance-gaining strategies. *Communication
    Monographs, 48*, 251-270.
Wober, M., & Gunter, B. (1982). Television and personal threat: Fact or artifact? A
    British survey. *British Journal of Social Psychology, 21*, 43-51.
Zillmann, D., & Bryant, J. (1982). Pornography, sexual callousness and the trivializa-
    tion of rape. *Journal of Communication, 32*, 10-21.
Zimmerman, D., & West, C. (1975). Sex roles, interruptions and silences in conversa-
    tion. In B. Thorne & N. Henley (Eds.), *Language and sex: Dominance and differ-
    ence* (pp. 105-129). Rowley, MA: Newbury House.

13 Nonverbal Signals

MARK L. KNAPP
University of Texas, Austin

MICHAEL J. CODY
KATHLEEN KELLEY REARDON
University of Southern California

THE theory and research associated with nonverbal signals, primarily that amassed since 1950, has been summarized and analyzed from several different perspectives. There are syntheses of nonverbal studies dealing with sex differences (Hall, 1984, 1985; Mayo & Henley, 1981), methodology (Scherer & Ekman, 1982) and nonverbal signals manifested in specific contexts—for example, pedagogy (Smith, 1979, 1984) and psychotherapy (Davis, 1984). By far the two most common approaches view that literature as informative about some particular body region or regions and as informative about how various body parts work together to signal certain communicative goals or help to achieve desired interaction outcomes. Knapp (1978) and Harper, Wiens, and Matarazzo (1978) represent the body region approach, reviewing studies associated with eye behavior, facial expressions, vocal cues, body postures, gestures, and appearance. Extensions of the human body such as the role of space, environmental stimuli, and clothing are also included. Burgoon (1980, 1985), Burgoon and Saine (1978), and Heslin and Patterson (1982) represent the outcome approach, bringing together research from various body regions and body extensions to show how multisignal clusters and sequences work together in communicating the nature of one's relationship to another, influencing others, regulating the flow of interaction, expressing affect, achieving accuracy and understanding, and so on.

Throughout this seeming analytic diversity, however, lies the virtually uniform application of the findings from nonverbal theory and research to dyadic or interpersonal communication contexts. Viewing nonverbal signals in the context of two person conversations has provided many useful insights, but it also has some liabilities. First, the prevalence of the interpersonal perspective sometimes causes us to apply inappropriately the findings from noninterpersonal (noninteractive) studies to interpersonal situations. Second, the prevalence of the interpersonal perspective tends to inhibit scholarship and thinking focused on other levels of nonverbal activity and the interdependent relationships among levels. Third, the lack of information concerning the nature of nonverbal processes at different levels leaves a gap in our ability to identify appropriate paths to competent performances at a given level. In short, a continued reliance on nonverbal signals as an exclusively interpersonal phenomenon may distort our understanding of some extant work, inhibit the pursuit of valuable future work on other levels of communicative activity, and restrict our ability to explain the processes and rules associated with competent behavior at different levels of functioning.

Therefore, in this chapter we offer a more expansive vision of the study of nonverbal signals by examining the nature of nonverbal studies at multiple levels, and showing how a multilevel perspective can be used to view the body of literature concerned with nonverbal signals associated with the act of lying.

NONVERBAL STUDIES
AND MULTILEVEL PERSPECTIVES

As noted earlier, any behavior representative of a particular body region (facial expressions, eye gaze, etc.) or multiple nonverbal signals enacted toward the accomplishment of a particular goal (lying, expressing emotion, persuading, etc.) may be examined on different levels of functioning. Examples from each of these approaches are used to illustrate and help define the following levels.

Individual Level

Studies at the individual level focus on the behavioral performance and/or interpretive processes of a single person. The focus of study concerns an individual's reaction to some controlled stimulus—human or otherwise. Individual performance or individual interpretive processes are the focus. A great many studies of nonverbal behavior fall into this category. Four approaches are common.

First, there are studies that seek to describe the enactment and structure of a particular behavior (facial, proxemic, self-touch, etc.) devoid of any possible influence of an unconstrained interaction partner. (See Ekman, 1982, for examples in the study of facial expressions.) Another approach, often using the behaviors obtained by the preceding method, tries to identify interpretations given to various nonverbal stimuli presented to the subject. In both of the preceding approaches (enactment and interpretation) various personal (sex, age) and/or personality (self-esteem, Machiavellianism) characteristics of the individual are manipulated. (See Rosenthal, 1979, for examples.)

The third focus at the individual level seeks to identify cognitive and emotional processes underlying the performance of various nonverbal behaviors. Questions that typify this approach include the following: To what extent is pausing behavior a manifestation of impaired cognitive processes (Goldman-Eisler, 1968)? To what extent are different thought processes represented by different directions of eye gaze? (See Bakan, 1971, for examples.) To what extent is a particular nonverbal behavior consciously enacted (Ekman & Friesen, 1969b)? To what extent are the muscles used in various facial expressions of emotion responsible for the experienced feeling of emotion? (See various positions in Buck, 1980; Ellsworth & Tourangeau, 1981; Hager & Ekman, 1981; Izard, 1981; Kraut, 1982; Laird, 1984; Tomkins, 1981; Tourangeau & Ellsworth, 1979; Zuckerman, Klorman, Larrance, & Spiegel, 1981.) Finally, some nonverbal researchers are concerned with the synchrony of an individual's behavior, that is, the extent to which speed and body movements are in synchrony or whether two types of body movement are in sync (Kendon, 1972).

Interpersonal Level

Analyses of nonverbal behavior at this level are focused on the *product* of the interacting pair. As at the individual level, the performance and interpretation of behavior is of interest; but now the focus is on how patterns of behavior exhibited by the pair are negotiated and mutually influenced. Both interactants are performer and interpreter, contributing to a jointly produced product. Perhaps the studies most representative of this approach in the nonverbal area are those dealing with mutual influence, interactional synchrony, and some of the studies of speaking-turn exchange.

Cappella (1981, 1985; see Chapter 7 in this volume) has reviewed the mutual influence studies that originated with Argyle and Dean's (1965) intimacy equilibrium model. The major focus of these studies is on compensation and reciprocity of behavior. With strangers, for example, increases in proximity to close distances will most likely elicit compensatory reactions on the part of the other interactant (e.g., increased distance, decreased eye gaze, less direct body orientation, and decreased response duration). Although there are factors that serve to offset the general trend, eye gaze usually elicits reciprocal acts except in negatively charged interactions, when the reverse effect obtains. Generally, people reciprocate or match behavior when it is perceived to be congruent with their expectations or involvement preferences and to compensate or offset their partners' behavior when it violates their expectations and preferences.

Those who study the extent to which body movements of each interactant are synchronized have found some evidence of simultaneous changes in the direction of movement, particularly during periods of rapport and attention (Condon, 1976; Kendon, 1970; LaFrance, 1979) even though the extent and timing of this synchronization is still not entirely clear.

The study of how people exchange speaking turns must by definition actively consider interactive processes. For example, a speaker's head direction toward the auditor increases the likelihood that the auditor will attempt to take the speaking turn; the number of turn-yielding cues seems to have a similar effect. (See Duncan & Fiske, 1977; Duncan, Brunner, & Fiske, 1979.) Rosenfeld (1978) provides a summary of other studies that have integrated such speaker-listener perspectives as the nature and placement of listener responses, first mentioned by Dittmann (1972).

Group/Organization Level

At this level the characteristics of the individual communicators and the mutuality of behavior of previous levels are coupled with a group identification for analysis (see Giles & Wiemann, Chapter 12; Gudy-kunst, Chapter 27). At the individual level, various group characteristics (age, sex, race) distinguish communicators from all others. Thus a woman may exhibit a different pattern of eye gaze than a man as an individual difference, but at the group level this person is communicating as a representative of the group "women" as well as an individual woman. Such messages may be communicated within or outside the group/organization of the communicator. Studies at this level may examine message sending and receiving of a particular group representative or multiple sources identified with the same group/organization. When multiple communicators are involved, the access to and responsibility for specific nonverbal signals changes dramatically. Determining exactly what stimuli provided the basis for responses and for whom becomes a much more complex problem at this level. Nonverbal signals at this level may be a particular behavior displayed by a single person, behavior exhibited by many persons, or a symbol representing the group but not associated with any particular person's behavior. The following are illustrative of nonverbal studies at this level.

In some groups and organizations the way persons are expected to express emotions facially and vocally may be linked to the image of the group/organization and the members' roles (Rafaeli & Sutton, 1986). Sutton and Denison (1986) found three different expectations for the communication of emotion by surgical nurses. They were expected to be unemotional (or "professional") in the operating room, to be warm and concerned with patients, and encouraged to display their "true feelings" (such as rage and disgust) when interacting informally with other nurses. Expectations associated with other occupations require different on the job nonverbal displays. Salesclerks, flight attendants, receptionists, waiters, waitresses, and servants are generally expected to be friendly, courteous, and happy; judges are supposed to behave impartially; funeral directors in a somber manner; bouncers and bill collectors in a threatening or assertive way; and professional phone interviewers are expected to have an unbiased vocal tone. Like Hochschild (1983) we assume nonverbal encoding and decoding abilities are highly relevant to fulfilling one's occupational role successfully.

Some other approaches to the study of nonverbal behavior at the group level include the effects of temperature and humidity on the development of group riots (Baron & Ransberger, 1978; Carlsmith & Anderson, 1979); the role of architectural design on patterns of interaction in an organization (Baum & Valins, 1979; Festinger, Schacter, & Bach, 1950; Sommer & Ross, 1958); patterns of interaction associated with where members of a group sit (Adams, 1969; Porter & Geis, 1981; Strodtbeck & Hook, 1961); and the effects of high density and crowding on group behavior (Draper, 1973; Schmidt & Keating, 1979; Stockdale, 1978).

Society Level

This level incorporates the features of the previous levels, but now the distinguishing characteristic is that multiple groups are involved. Usually, studies of this type involve one or more people displaying a signal or signals to multiple groups to elicit their reaction. However, it may also involve an action that we, as a culture, produce, to which a specific other or others will respond. And, like the interpersonal and group levels, this level also involves a mutuality of response, even though the process takes longer and changes are more difficult to identify. Nonverbal signals at this level may also be put before the public by a third party— someone who takes a transaction originally performed at the interpersonal or group level and reconstitutes its level by reporting it to the public for consumption and evaluation.

Nonverbal signals displayed by people on television are normally classified at this level. In some cases it may be the attractiveness of a political candidate or the candidate's smile or frown that comes under scrutiny in the context of the candidate's persuasiveness (Bryski & Frye, 1979-1980; Tiemens, 1978). Apparently, the television news commentator who introduces a story about a political candidate also displays subtle signals that indicate positive or negative orientations (Friedman, Mertz, & Dimatteo, 1980). Such cultural symbols as a salute to the flag or other pervasive societal actions such as marching in Nazi Germany (Bosmajian, 1968) are included in the analyses at this level. At least two approaches have been taken in studies of cultural differences and similarities in nonverbal behavior. Milgrim (1970) studied the ways New York City residents coped with the high density environment, and methods of successful coping in residential sections of China and Tokyo have also been reported (Aiello & Thompson, 1980). Attempts have also been made to determine cross-cultural similarities associated with a particular behavior (e.g., interruptions, greeting, facial expressions) that would then allow researchers to identify the rules imposed by each society to account for the differences. Perhaps the most ambitious effort in this area has been the work of Ekman and his colleagues (Ekman, Friesen, & Ellsworth, 1982).

Processes Studied at All Levels

Even though they may manifest themselves in different ways at different levels, studies of nonverbal communication at all levels are minimally concerned with perception, meaning, information processing, time or timing, and the signals themselves. A few examples will suffice.

Perceptual gatekeeping may manifest itself at the individual level as a cognitive process involving repression; perceptual gatekeeping at the societal level may focus on media managers and the actions of public relations experts. Meaning at the individual level involves the associations of a single person; at the interpersonal level meanings for each individual are overlaid with relational meanings. There is an increasing number of realities as one goes from the individual to the societal level. One area of information processing that has received considerable attention at the individual level concerns the role of the right and left hemispheres of the brain in processing nonverbal signals; but at the group level, information processing may involve a pattern of hostile expressions transmitted from one family member to another. The timing of nonverbal feedback at the interpersonal level is usually immediate, but as the level increases in scope, delays in timing occur. Time may also be an important contextual feature for each level; for instance, at what point in relationship time are the relevant nonverbal signals enacted and interpreted, or at what point in the cultural history of a particular society are various artifacts representative? Even the signals themselves are likely to exhibit differences at different levels. Surely some signals enacted by people without an interaction partner will alter as copresence obtains; increased intimacy is likely to bring forth more idiosyncratic signals at all levels; and we might expect that as a signal is intended for more people, it will become more stereotypical, ritualized, and repeated.

Interlevel Analysis

Communication events may function at multiple levels. Thus analyses of the same data may be performed using different level perspectives. Furthermore, changes at one level are likely to mark changes at other levels as well. In short, the interplay between levels is an important factor in the theoretical underpinning of any analysis by level. Miller (1978) has shown a remarkable interdependency and organization among several biological and social systems: cells, organs, organisms, groups, organizations, societies, and supranational systems. Our schema is limited to four levels. The following are but two examples of studies that have attempted to bridge levels in nonverbal analyses.

Cline (1985) bridges the interpersonal and societal levels as she frames a political interview between Walter Cronkite and former U.S. President Gerald Ford, broadcast on national TV from the Republican National Convention, not as a political message for society but as a therapeutic, interpersonal interview—with Cronkite as the therapist. This, Cline argues, explains Ford's otherwise enigmatic responses that involved unexpectedly high levels of openness and self-exploration atypical of televised interviews at a national political convention. Cline's moment-by-moment analysis of the interview shows how Cronkite created a therapeutic climate by verbal and nonverbal behavior. Utterance rate, posture, eye gaze, and facial expressions of the interviewer seemed to take precedence, for Ford, over the fact that it was a nationally televised event.

Chesebro (1984) bridges the individual and societal levels by showing how they mutually affect one another, analyzing media on the one hand and neurophysiological processes on the other to illustrate the ways in which mental patterns and world views are part and parcel of both levels. Chesebro integrates meaning, information processing, and perception to show how the selective perception of the media creates a selective perception of reality; how habitual mental patterns lead to particular world-views. Whole societies share frames of reference for deciding which acts should and should not be brought into consciousness—just as individuals and families do.

ILLUSTRATIVE CASE:
LEVELS OF LYING

The subject of lying (and the broader concept of deception) have long been of philosophical interest, but in the 1970s and 1980s the confluence of a variety of issues and events brought an avalanche of attention to the subject. Watergate, government pronouncements about the Vietnam war, requirements for properly informing the subjects of social science research, requests that employees submit to polygraph tests as a requirement for employment, management of the confidentiality of clients and journalists' informants, fair handling of undercover police operations such as ABSCAM, and more personal issues—such as the extent to which an "open marriage" works and whether it is proper to lie to a dying relative—all focused attention on and demanded greater understanding of lying. For communication scholars, questions surrounding lying and deception are central to understanding and explaining the nature of effective communication (achieving one's desired response or responses). For instance, when is the exclusion of information in message construction simply part of an effective strategy and when is it considered a lie? Nonverbal scholars actively pursued the nature of lying behavior; believing that liars are not capable of controlling all their behaviors at once, it was thought that while they focus on verbal control, nonverbal signals "leak" our and reveal their deceptiveness.

Individual Level

Most empirical efforts to understand the role of nonverbal signals in lying behavior address individual behavior, even though the investigators often discuss their findings as applicable to interactive contexts. Some studies of individual nonverbal behavior may have utility for understanding interpersonal transactions and some may not. Studies of individual behavior are so classified because (1) the focus of analysis concerns an individual's cognitive or physiological processes linked to deceptive actions; (2) the focus of analysis concerns one or more characteristics (personal or personality) of an individual liar; or (3) the focus of analysis concerns a particular signal or behavioral cluster manifested by an individual communicator. The research designs and theory applicable to this level do not provide for two people who can freely affect one another's behavior. This holds for decoding (lie detection behavior) as well as encoding behavior. Liar and lie detection behavior are analyzed separately.

The typical research design, not involving a polygraph, follows these steps:

(1) Research subjects are asked by the experimenter to lie about a stimulus presented to them—for example, sweet or sour drinks (Feldman, Jenkins, & Popoola, 1979; Feldman & White, 1980), pleasant or unpleasant pictures (Ekman & Friesen, 1974); or about something they already believe—for example, an opinion about the likability of a person (DePaulo & Rosenthal, 1979) or a personally salient issue (Knapp, Hart, & Dennis, 1974). These same subjects (or others) are asked to tell the truth. In a few studies, lies and truths have emerged from choices made by the subjects rather than at the direction of the E. In these designs, Ss are put in a situation where they actually cheat on a task or are implicated in cheating because their partner, a confederate of the experimenter, cheated or persuaded them to cheat.

(2) Subjects are then videotaped as they lie or tell the truth to a camera or to an interviewer unfamiliar to the subjects. The interviewer's behavior is controlled, usually limited to asking prescribed questions. The behaviors recorded on this one occasion are the only ones studied.
(3) Selected individual behaviors of liars and truth tellers are then quantified and compared. Liar and truth-teller videotapes or audiotapes can then be used as a stimulus tape for lie detection studies.

Note, however, that studies using this basic paradigm differ in that some studies have liars lie while describing (or responding to) a slide show (hence no "interviewer" sits directly in front of the liar or truth teller); some studies have liars lie directly into a video camera or an audio recorder; other studies have liars lie during an ongoing interview; and other studies create situations where the subject does not know the study is about deceit, is implicated in an unethical act, and is accused of committing an offense. These distinctions are important, since procedures that do not obligate the liar to attend to an interviewer's presence may enable him or her to effect better control over some behaviors (see below).

Three questions are of fundamental interest at the individual level of analysis: (1) What cognitive and physiological processes account for why and how nonverbal behaviors differ between liars and truth tellers? (2) How do individuals behave nonverbally when confronted with the lie task (or, more precisely, what kinds of cues consistently differentiate lie and truth responses)? (3) Can lying be identified accurately by observers of unknown liars?

Processes Underlying Lying

No single individual variable is directly associated with deceit (Zuckerman, DePaulo, & Rosenthal, 1981). Instead, several processes or psychological variables experienced by communicators differentiate liars from truth tellers. Traditional literature on deception has chiefly explored three within individual processes: intent, arousal, and control. The first of these is fundamental, since it has to do with defining precisely what is meant by lying.

Intent and awareness. In both social science research (Ekman, 1985; Knapp & Comadena, 1979; Zuckerman et al., 1981) and philosophy (Bok, 1978; Chisholm & Freehan, 1977) lying is normally designated a consciously intentional behavior—what Goffman (1959) called "barefaced lies," those "for which there can be unquestionable evidence that the teller knew he lied and willfully did so" (p. 61). Zuckerman et al. (1981) and others uniformly point out that nonverbal scholars operationalize the act of deception as one in which the actor intends to foster in another person a belief or understanding the actor knows to be false.

Such conceptualizations are central to the belief that there are nonverbal signals associated with lying. Liars who know they are lying are believed to be most likely to exhibit states of emotion, arousal, or faulty message presentation that observers use as clues to detecting lying. For some lies, intent may be at a high level of awareness. Hample (1980) argues that two out of three lies he obtained from responses to an open-ended questionnaire reflected selfish intent, but the reasons for lying outlined by Camden, Motley, and Wilson (1984) seem to cover a wide spectrum and virtually mirror the reasons we tell the truth, namely, to acquire, maintain, and protect physical, social, and psychological resources.

Turner, Edgley, and Olmstead (1975) found that reasons for constructing fabrications during conversations (to conceal things or to distort facts) included face concerns, relationship concerns, exploitation motives (i.e., power or influence), reduction of tension, and to gain situational control. Lindskold and Walters (1983) reported that respondents had clear-cut ideals about the "permissibility" of lies based on the liar's perceived intentions. Lies were considered more permissible if (1) lies saved others from shame or hurt, (2) lies protected people from punishment or disapproval for a minor failing that hurts no one; (3) lies were told to public officials, so long as no harm followed; and (4) lies were told to protect some gain the liar had previously acquired, but to which the liar was not actually entitled. The least permissible lies were ones where liars could cause others to do something to bring about a benefit for the liar, but which cost the actors, and lies that hurt others for the liar's personal gain.

Intent is obviously more complex than we have treated it thus far, and the focus on consciously intentional behavior may represent a more specialized type of lying than has heretofore been acknowledged. The study of self-deception raises some thorny issues about consciousness that, in turn, affect assumptions we make about arousal and leakage signals. Goleman (1985), for example, maintains that much of our behavior is enacted at a low level of awareness; that one side of the brain may know something the other does not; that much is blocked from our consciousness; and that habitual lies can become truths for the liar. Gur and Sackeim (1979) say we can hold two contradictory beliefs simultaneously and one may not be subject to awareness. Thus the working premise that a liar knows the truth and deliberately tries to modify it may actually represent a variety of gradations, depending on how much truth is known. Similarly, display rules for making affects and verbalizations may be performed at different levels of awareness. A consciously intentional lie may become conscious and less intentional over time, or the intent may only be revealed to the liar after he or she overtly reveals it through a slip of the tongue or some subconsciously revealing behavior.

Arousal and emotions. Lying behavior is also commonly assumed to have an emotional component to it as well. The stronger the emotion (e.g., fear of being caught, guilt, shame, etc.), the reasoning goes, the greater the likelihood of displaying specific arousal behaviors that can be used in detection. A corollary assumption, emanating from the psychophysiological research on lie detection, presumes liars will exhibit behavioral indicators of an aroused state—even if a specific emotion is not indicated via facial or body channels. Zuckerman et al. (1981), and others, distinguish between arousal and emotion. Arousal, they suggest, is a more generalized state that evokes "difficult to control" responses such as pupil dilation, heart rate, and changes in voice pitch. In this framework emotions are more particularized. They may be positive (as in duping delight) or negative (as in anger). Not all nonverbal research makes such distinctions, however, because the nature of the relationship between general arousal and specific emotions is not clear.

Buck (1984) points out that lies may also be nonemotional or simply stressful, even though research and theory thus far has emphasized emotional responses to lying. Nonemotional lies are normally associated with inconsequential matters but may also typify some of the studies of college students who are asked to role play or lie about their attitudes on presumably ego-involving issues—studies that are guided by theoretical assumptions that liars will experience emotional responses. The manifestation of stress, rather than a particular emotion, may be associated with the liar's experienced conflict about the act of dissimulation itself. These distinctions regarding liars' experienced states are directly linked to our understanding of how well liars control the manifestation of their state. The key assumption in detecting deception is that liars will have trouble controlling all the manifestations of emotional states; but if emotions are nonexistent or mildly experienced, detection ability may decrease sharply. Sometimes truth tellers may also be aroused, but preliminary evidence suggests that even under such conditions there are still reliable differences in the behavior of truth tellers and liars (deTurck & Miller, 1985).

Control and motivation. The third internal process thought to be of importance to lying behavior, and which permeates theory and research in this area, is the motivation and ability to control one's own behavior (Ekman & Friesen, 1969a). Behavioral control has been viewed from several different perspectives. How motivated is the liar to control his or her behavior? Ekman (1985, p. 91), summarizing his work, says that even though highly motivated deceivers may do well at masking information, their aroused state may reveal detectable clues; and that the least detectable condition would probably be a liar who had an intermediate level of motivation. Is preparation and/or training useful in a liar's attempt to control his or her behavior? Studies to date show that given time to rehearse or prepare, a liar may be able to do a better job of controlling some behaviors (not all) than if he or she must lie spontaneously (Greene, O'Hair, Cody, & Yen, 1985; O'Hair, Cody, & McLaughlin, 1981; Miller, deTurck, & Kalbfleisch, 1983). And, if a person is able to take advantage of relaxation or biofeedback training, he or she may be able to exercise considerable control over the physiological measures of polygraph tests (Corcoran, Lewis, & Garver, 1978).

Are some behaviors easier to control than others? Generally, the argument is made that verbalizations (i.e., selection of words) and facial expressions are much more under liars' control than their tone of voice, speech errors, blinking, and nervous mannerisms commonly called adaptors. Still, verbal slips and the inability to keep a story "straight" as well as facial asymmetry or micromomentary facial expressions commonly escape control and provide deception clues. Signal control, then, appears to be related to the complexity of the lie as well as to motivation and rehearsal.

Signals Indicative of Deception

From the inception of deception research, the identification of behaviors that would distinguish liars from truth tellers has been a major goal. Kraut (1980), for example, tried to identify behaviors that consistently characterized liars in a variety of studies and concluded from his review of research that deceivers (compared with truth tellers) exhibit more blinking, longer response latency, more grooming adaptors, and more errors/hesitations in their speech. Others, however, argue that *"there is no sign of deceit itself*—no gesture, facial expression, or muscle twitch that in and of itself means that a person is lying" (Ekman, 1985, p. 90). Similarly, Buck (1984) summarizes, "All in all, it appears that there are no cues which are consistently revealing of deception across all deceivers and deception situations" (p. 239). The same behavior, as Kraut (1978) found, can be perceived very differently as the level of suspicion is varied. Observers who suspected lying were even more suspicious of a self-serving answer when it was preceded by a long pause, but trusting observers became even more trusting of a self-damaging answer if it was preceded by the same length pause. In one case, the pause was interpreted as time needed to create a lie; in the other, it was perceived as time needed to decide how to phrase an answer in the least damaging way. Thus it may be unrealistic to expect to find behaviors that transcend all types of deception in all situations; instead, it may be more profitable to examine signals associated with the processes believed to be associated with some types of lying.

Signals associated with each of the processes noted above can be grouped together, and we can take a stab at predicting which types of cues are likely to be leaked. Two approaches have been used in the study of how different processes are related to cue leakage. First, some studies have conducted a meta-analysis of all studies on deception in order to identify the set of nonverbal indicators that are significantly and consistently leaked by liars (DePaulo, Stone, & Lassiter,1985; Zuckerman et al., 1981; Zuckerman & Driver, 1985). After consistent sources of leakage are identified, theorists attempt to group the detectable signals in terms of the underlying processes (e.g., control) based on theory and logic. On the other hand, a growing body of studies have attempted to manipulate purposefully the psychological features of the laboratory events in which deception takes place so that different types of lies are constructed (ones that are more motivating, ones where controllability is increased or decreased, etc.). The logic underlying these latter studies is that if relatively few cues are leaked consistently across deception contexts, then it is at least possible to increase leakage for some types of lies by placing liars in a particular lying context where one of the underlying processes has been maximized (or minimized). The first approach identifies fewer cues as related to deception, but ones that are generalizable; the second approach tries to see if greater overall leakage can be obtained by manipulating underlying process, but results are less generalizable. Nonetheless, we will first discuss how each process is linked theoretically to particular signals and whether the cues are consistently related to deception. Then we will focus our attention on the several studies that manipulated types of lies.

Engaging in deceit may induce a state of general arousal. Since members of a society may be encouraged to believe that lying is morally wrong and should be punished, communicators experience a state of heightened arousal when engaged in deceit. Heightened arousal is reflected in changes in the autonomic response system and provides the impetus for reliable detection via psychophysiological means (Waid & Orne, 1981). Nonverbal behaviors indicative of arousal include increased pupil dilations (Nunnally, Knott, Duchnowski, & Parker, 1967; Scott, Wells, Wood, & Morgan, 1967), increased eyeblinks (Meyer, 1953), higher pitch (Scherer, 1981), and speech errors and hesitations (Kasal & Mahl, 1965; Siegman, 1979). Meta-analytic work indicates that signals indicative of arousal are in fact consistently linked to deception: Liars are more likely than truth tellers to have increased pupil dilation, to have a higher pitched voice, to blink frequently, to have more speech errors and to have more speech hesitations. Lying is arousing.

In terms of a second process, control, one can expect that few cues associated with the face would be leaked. In fact, it is likely that liars could be so well prepared that they indeed sound prepared (DePaulo et al., 1985; Zuckerman et al., 1981). Also, it is possible that liars could be so well rehearsed that they are "primed" with the answer, producing short response latencies and short messages (Greene et al., 1985; O'Hair et al., 1981). Meta-analytic work demonstrates that few cues related to the face are in fact leaked by liars; moreover, cues reflecting less involvement with the message or topic, greater nonimmediacy, and reduced commitment are associated with deception (dePaulo et al., 1985). Note, however, that the most general statement concerning the process of control deals with "channel discrepancies." The more control a liar attempts to achieve over one channel, the more leakage results in another channel since communicators cannot control all behaviors at once. Thus if liars are telling ingratiating lies, for example, they might know that they should put on a happy face and smile but they might leak body cues or leak deception in the tone of their verbal expressions. On the other hand, if liars communicate messages over an intercom system and do not believe that their faces are being monitored, they might leak facial cues (Krauss, 1981). Generally speaking, then, liars attempt to control the part of the body they believe to be monitored and leak in the least monitored channel. Yet, nearly all studies conducted in deception to date have involved either face-to-face communication contexts or instances where the communicators knew that cameras were present. Thus liars have typically effected control over facial displays and word selections (as opposed to body-related cues and tone of voice).

Liars may experience some type of emotional response when deceiving others, and the particular type of leakage to be observed will depend on the type of emotion experienced. If anxiety is induced, it is possible that at least three classes of behaviors will be evidenced (DePaulo et al., 1985; Knapp et al., 1974): nervous responses (fidgeting, stuttering, stammering, and adaptors), disaffiliative behaviors (longer silences, longer response latencies, decreased eye contact, and reduced participation in conversations), and image protection (nodding, agreeing, yielding turn, etc.—generally any tactic that would draw attention away from oneself). Guilt responses, however, might be more directly related to distancing oneself from the conversational event (and from the lie itself), thus resulting in more negative statements, lower levels of immediacy, increased interpersonal distancing, and more hedges. Liars experiencing duping delight, however, might display greater vocal confidence, more pleasant facial displays, and perhaps increased extraversion cues when enjoying the act of deceiving their partners successfully. However, the typical study on deception has often manipulated at least some type of negative affect (either guilt or anxiety), and several cues involved with negative affects have been leaked consistently by liars: increasing adapting behaviors, more frequent speech errors, more speech hesitations, more frequent use of negative statements, less immediacy, more hedging or leveling terms, and more irrelevant statements (DePaulo et al., 1985; DePaulo, Rosenthal, Rosenkrantz, & Green, 1982; Zuckerman et al., 1981).

Finally, although not discussed above as a distinct underlying process, some scholars have argued that cognitive difficulty is one variable that differentiates liars from truth tellers since lying is often a more difficult task than truth telling. High cognitive burden or experienced uncertainty in message construction may increase speech hesitations and pupil dilation. Goldman-Eisler (1968) found that hesitations are related to cognitive load; Kahneman (1973) found that pupils are dilated when speakers concentrate on difficult problems. Since liars who experience uncertainty may not be able to think of as many concrete details as truth tellers, liars are more likely to make irrelevant statements, be vague, lack details (Cody, Marston, & Foster, 1984; Kraut, 1978), and use more generalizing terms (Knapp, Hart, & Dennis, 1974). Cognitively difficult messages may take longer to prepare and may contain more speech errors (Cody et al., 1984; DePaulo et al., 1985; Zuckerman et al., 1981). Further, as lies become increasingly difficult to encode, liars may speak more briefly than truth tellers and use fewer words. Liars may evidence fewer speech-centered body movements, since communicators tend to restrict such gestures as illustrators when concentrating (Ekman & Friesen, 1972; Greene et al., 1985). Meta-analytic work indicates that several of these variables are leaked consistently by liars: irrelevant statements, leveling terms, pupil dilation, speech errors, decreased speech length, and speech hesitations.

If each of these nonverbal signals is indicative of each of the particular processes, then it would be possible to predict specific lie behaviors with some accuracy if one could assess the operation of underlying processes. The behaviors manifested by a liar who tells a lie where controllability is high but arousal, anxiety, and difficulty are low are considerably different than the behaviors manifested by a liar who tells a lie where controllability is difficult to achieve and where arousal, anxiety, and difficulty are high. Further, manipulating the context in which lies are told so that the importance of these processes varies ought to have an impact on which behaviors are leaked. Three "lie types" have been explored to date:

Motivated lies. Some studies induce liars to lie convincingly by promising them payment of some type of reward for a quality performance. In Exline, Thibaut, Hickey, and Gumpert (1970) successful lying (denying wrongdoing) meant that the liars would not be reported to the Dean's Office. In other studies, the only incentive to lie convincingly was some extra credit given for class participation. It goes without saying that there are many variations of high and low motivation that have not been explored, but the studies that have manipulated motivation find that highly motivated liars blink less, engage in less head nodding, fewer adaptors, fewer postural shifts, and higher pitch than their less motivated counterparts (Zuckerman et al., 1981; Zuckerman & Driver, 1985). Highly motivated liars may effect greater control over the verbal message (i.e., word selections) and actually increase cue leakage in nonverbal channels (DePaulo, Lanier, & Davis, 1983; DePaulo et al., 1985). In terms of the processes noted above, high motivation increases arousal and the desire not to be detected, and increases the cognitive burden of the deception by prompting liars to concentrate more on communication.

Prepared Lies. Some studies allow liars time to prepare and rehearse the lie while other studies trap liars into telling lies when the liar does not know that the particular line of questioning is going to surface (i.e., "spontaneous" lies). There is some evidence that when liars are prepared and rehearsed they exhibit shorter response latencies, engage in less postural shifting, fewer gestures, and provide very brief messages that lack spontaneity compared to behavior elicited from unprepared liars (Zuckerman et al., 1981; see also Greene et al., 1985). Spontaneous lies, however, require liars to create messages and transmit them off the top of their heads; thus, spontaneous lies contain more pauses and nonfluencies and lack specific detail (Cody et al., 1984; Kraut, 1978).

In terms of the processes described above, preparation time functions to increase one's ability to effect control and may, to some degree, reduce cognitive difficulty of encoding the fabrication by reducing the speaker's feelings of uncertainty. In a recent meta-analytic review, Zuckerman and Driver (1985) found that planned deception was associated with more pupil dilation, somewhat more smiling, fewer gestures, more postural shifts, shorter response latencies, somewhat shorter answers, and faster speech rates than unplanned deception. Many of these results indicate, first, that prepared liars are primed (they tell briefer lies and talk earlier and more briefly), and second, that prepared liars may experience greater anxiety or arousal by focusing attention or awareness on their role as liars.

Narrative lies. Following from Hocking, Bauchner, Kaminski, and Miller (1979), a small number of studies have explored lies involving the fabrication of factual information, such as grade point averages, vacation areas visited, and false places of employment (Cody et al., 1984; Cody & O'Hair, 1983; Greene et al., 1985; O'Hair, Cody, & Behnke, 1985; O'Hair et al., 1981). Narrative lies are ones in which the liar has a relatively large number of choices about details he or she can transmit about a particular topic—as when liars are asked to describe a typical day at a place of employment where they never actually worked. Some lies may be relatively easy to tell because they are short "yes" or "no" responses. Such lie responses contain few speech errors or pauses.

However, a liar who has to lie for a full minute or to list activities that occurred during a fictitious event will probably not be able to create as many specific details or speak for as long as a truth teller. Also, liars may leak the fact that they are uncertain by employing more generalizing terms, such as "the usual stuff," or "stuff like that," "you know," and the like (Cody et al., 1984; Knapp et al., 1974). Of the processes discussed above, longer narrative lies increase the speaker's level of uncertainty and cognitive difficulty.

Future research is needed to determine (1) whether the four processes discussed above operate to affect leakage and whether the indicators we have listed reflect each of these processes and, (2) whether manipulating underlying processes does in fact increase predictability of cue leakage. Nonetheless, we are left with the conclusions that few cues consistently differentiate liars and truth tellers across all deception contexts and that we must study more carefully the contexts within which lies are communicated.

The behavioral signals manifested by *detectors* of deception have not been given much research attention. Most research designs do not allow deception detectors to manifest self-generated and developing strategies by identifying liars. The behavior used by detectors in making their judgments (e.g., that suspicious detectors may be more likely to rely on the voice than the face for clues) and the extent to which judges know what they are looking for as clues to deception (generally they seem to) have been of interest, but lie-catching behavior per se is relatively unexplored.

The perceptual orientation used by detectors who are told specifically to look for lying behavior has been the primary area of interest. Many studies in nonverbal communication, person perception, and cognitive psychology (e.g., Atkinson & Allen, 1983; Cantor, Mischel, & Schwartz, 1982; Cohen & Ebesen, 1979; Jeffrey & Mischel, 1979) indicate that instructions given to observers or raters have a pronounced impact on how much effort observers expend as well as the cues to which they attend. One may expect, then, that when observers are asked to view tapes of speakers or interviewees simply to "gain an impression," observers may elect to attend to a wide range of behavio.. in order to form an impression of the actor's competence or likability (an "additive model" relying on top-down processing). By contrast, when observers are led to believe that the actors are engaged in deliberate behaviors, observers may "segment" ongoing streams of behavior into finer gradations and focus attention on more specific cues (a "significant clue" model relying on "bottom-up" processing).

When instructed to determine whether an actor is lying, observers may attempt to seek out what they believe are significant cues and attend to different types of cues depending upon their availability in different observational conditions (face-only, body-only, etc.). Riggio and Friedman (1983) gave observers specific instructions to detect lying behavior and found that they seemed to seek out specific cues—invalid ones dealing with the face and valid ones in the body and verbal messages. Kraut (1978) also found detectors relied on body cues and verbal message cues. Zuckerman, Kernis, Driver, and Koestner (1984) reported that observers segmented ongoing streams of behavior (i.e., videotaped performances) into finer gradations when they were suspicious of deceit, and Toris and DePaulo (1984) found that suspicious observers (ones who thought that the interviewee would possibly lie) were not more accurate in detecting deception, were less confident of judgments, and rated all interviewees as more deceptive. Being suspicious does not seem to increase the observers' ability to detect deception.

Individual differences. Ekman (1985) maintains that there are four types of leakage signals (slips of the tongue, emotional tirades, emblematic slips, and microexpressions) that are not as dependent on knowledge of individual liar communication style for interpretation as are other signals. But a number of efforts have been made to investigate individual differences—even though, curiously, many of these studies have focused on accuracy rather than stylistic features. Individuals high in self-monitoring and Machiavellianism would be expected to show greater skill in lying, but the results are mixed. High self-monitors (when compared with lows) do seem to be more effective liars when they have time to prepare their lie (Miller et al., 1983). One of the reasons for this may be the high self-monitor's desire to have as much information as possible about the target and situation when preparing a lie (Elliott, 1979). People who score high on a measure of Machiavellianism do not necessarily do a better job of lying than their less manipulative counterparts (Knapp et al., 1974; O'Hair et al., 1981). But when there is strong motivation to succeed coupled with a highly stressful situation, highly Machiavellian liars may lie very effectively (Exline et al., 1970; Geis & Moon, 1981).

Other studies of individual differences offer some isolated findings. Introverts and children do not seem to do a very good job of lying because there is so much leakage of affect. Test anxious students exhibited negativity in lying behavior (Mehrabian, 1971). Kraut (1980) maintained that more socialized people have higher skin conductance responses and are therefore more likely than less socialized people to give off signals that would allow them to be classified as deceptive (when they were). Differences between males and females have been the object of some study, but it is difficult to make many generalizations at this time. Females tend to be more accurate than males in judging emotions, but this does not necessarily translate into increased deception accuracy since females often politely disattend to leaky channels (DePaulo & Jordan, 1982; Rosenthal & DePaulo, 1979a, 1979b). One study dealing with ingratiating lies found females more easily detected than males when lying (DePaulo et al., 1985).

From his studies Ekman (1985) identifies effective or skilled liars as people who know their own ability; who have confidence and little apprehension about being caught; who do not differ from less skilled liars on a variety of personality tests; who have a history of successful experiences with lying; and whose deceptive skills are known by those who know them well. Riggio and Friedman (1983) found that individuals who score high on dominance, exhibition, and emotional sending ability were more successful at deception.

What about individual differences among human lie detectors? As with previous areas, the study of individual differences in lie detectors has been of less interest to researchers than have studies of the liars themselves. Kraut and Poe (1980) reported that individual differences did not play much of a role in determining whom to search as smugglers; whether they were professional customs inspectors, laypeople, or successful inspectors, all used the same criteria for screening: young, lower socioeconomic class, hesitations before answering, avoidance of eye gaze, and so on. Buck (1984) indicates that one of the most important individual difference behaviors that is central to lie detector behavior concerns differences in perception: "There may well be individual differences in attention patterns that strongly influence the kinds of information that one extracts from a given situation, including information relevant to deception" (p. 241). One factor related to attention patterns is the familiarity of the detector with the deceiver. When sufficiently motivated to look for deception, familiarity appears to increase accuracy (Brandt, Miller, & Hocking, 1982). A questionnaire study using a small number of high school and college students suggests another individual difference that may be related to deception perception, religious commitment. The stronger the religious commitment and formal religious background, the greater the likelihood that a person will report more instances of lying in everyday life (Maier & Lavrakas, 1976).

Interpersonal Level

At his level of analysis, we would expect to find several differences from the studies of individual behavior. Now the focus for study is the interacting pair. Achieving control over the process is much more difficult, and the object of study has become infinitely more complex. Interpersonal communication requires a consideration of the cognitive/emotional processes, overt behavior, and perceptual processes of two involved interactants. Individual actions combine to form jointly produced patterns (see Cappella, Chapter 7). Obviously, some of the results from studies at the individual level may have application at the interpersonal level, but at present there has not been enough representative research at the interpersonal level to know exactly what can be generalized from the individual level. At least three issues take on a special importance at this level—issues that will ultimately help us define interpersonal lies and lying behavior: mutual influence, multiple exposure, and familiarity.

Mutual influence. If we conceptualize lying behavior as a transaction, then the behaviors of liar and lie detector (or target) can be considered as they influence one another. The melding of various combinations of cognitive/emotional states, signals and individual differences produces something that affects and is affected by each individual. Two studies show how a liar's behavior can be influenced by his or her interaction partner. Fugita, Hogrebe, and Wexley (1980) had liars lie to a purported "expert" in lie detection or a person who purportedly had no expertise in this area. When the liars lied to the expert, they maintained more eye gaze and glanced more frequently at the interviewer than when lying to the "novice." Pennebaker and Chew (1985) had an interviewer sit one meter in front of people told to lie and stared right at their chin. Not surprisingly, such monitoring resulted in a decrease in facial behaviors by monitored liars (fewer changes in eye movement and facial expressiveness).

Exactly how we collaborate in covering a liar's deceit, or what happens when we use different information or accusation strategies (probing, leading questions, setting traps, etc.) in response to different liar tactics, is something we know very little about even though most scholars acknowledge that mutual influence is descriptive of the process. Obviously, the complex nature of mutual influence is difficult to capture and may require methods that differ from those used at the individual level. Qualitative case studies of con men (Hankiss, 1980) and liars may help to identify some of the ways we mutually collaborate in lies of various types. Or, mutual influence in deception could be conceptualized and studied in a way similar to the investigations of how people mutually influence one another during the communication of another outcome which is strongly associated with nonverbal manifestations, intimacy (Cappella, 1981; Patterson, 1983). From this perspective, researchers might try to find out what situations, expectations, and manifest behaviors will evoke a reciprocity of lies, and what kind of compensatory behaviors are likely to occur with different types of lies and in different situations. In general, what lying and detection strategies tend to co-occur?

Multiple exposure. Some lies are told in a brief, single, one-time utterance, but interpersonal lies are more likely to be of an ongoing nature. It may be the development and/or repetition of a lie during the course of a single encounter, or the process may develop over the course of several encounters. Hample (1980) indicates that many lies are told repeatedly and "field-tested" for costs and benefits. Exactly how this field-testing takes place, how the nature of a lie (and the attendant behavior) changes over time, and how the target's behavior is affected by multiple exposure are questions we need to answer in order to better understand the nature of nonverbal signalling and lying.

Familiarity. Generally it is assumed that the more we have been exposed to another person's normal truth-telling behavior, the more accurate we are when exposed to a person's verbal and nonverbal signals reflecting a state of arousal, a specific emotion, or verbalizations that seem inconsistent with previous behavior (Ekman, 1985). Studies that have provided up to six video exposures to an unknown person's behavior prior to judging the person for truth-telling or lying (Brandt et al., 1982) and studies that have used married couples (Comadena, 1982) have generally confirmed that having a baseline for typical behavior increases accuracy in lie detection. We do not know much about how relationship conditions alter perceptual skills since we may not look for deception cues among intimates or may wish to be deceived by them (McCornack & Parks, 1986).

And although research thus far has focused on the lie detector's familiarity with the liar, interpersonal studies also need to determine how the liar may use this familiarity as part of his or her deception strategy. Further, the issue of familiarity requires the comparison of behavior not between groups of liars and truth-tellers but of the same people over time.

Group/Organization Level

At this level of analysis, the number of players in the game of deception increases; now the focus of analysis is lying behavior that permeates and influences an entire group. The same elements examined at the individual level and interpersonal level (the actors, the motivations for lying, the nature of the message or messages, the situations, the process of detection, and the consequences) still need to be examined; but they are likely to manifest themselves differently at this level, although the exact nature of the differences and similarities is yet to be identified. One difference may help to explain why few nonverbal scholars have explored lies at this level. The communicators at this level may not always have access to auditory and visual signals, so more reliance is placed on verbal indices. Nevertheless, as noted in the examples of deception research in this area, nonverbal signals are sometimes available and may be critical in encoding and decoding lying at the group level.

Even though lies may be made by individuals, the lie at this level is either made on behalf of a group or because of one's group membership. Lies at this level may occur within the group or organization itself or may be externally directed (i.e., to another group or individual). Detection, in turn, may be an individual or group effort. There are relatively few in-depth investigations of lying behavior per se (not to mention nonverbal studies) at the group/organization level, even though two related themes—openness and secrecy—provide some important foundation work for future investigations in this area. The predominant mode of study thus far is analytical or critical, as contrasted with the experimental method that predominates in explorations at the individual level.

Lies may be embedded in the functioning of groups that vary considerably in their formality and organization. Two studies, for example, examined communication patterns used by subordinated groups with the members of the dominant group. Stanbeck and Pearce (1981) identified three forms of deceptive communications, all of which may make use of nonverbal displays: "passing," when a member of the subordinate group acts as if he or she was a member of the dominant group; "shucking," when a member of the subordinate group acts like what he or she knows the dominant group expects even though it is just facade; and "dissembling," when a member of the subordinate group acts like he or she knows what the dominant group members expect but does not consider the behavior to be relevant to his or her group status. Logue (1981) writes of a similar situation when he discusses concealment and deception as responses of black slaves. Slaves, says Logue, learned to deceive their white owners by using familiar words in ways that were confusing or infused with new and private meanings that only slaves could understand. Deception was also a part of singing: "As long as the *sound* of the singing created a mood acceptable to whites or the language was perceived by owners as meaningless, blacks could communicate thoughts and concerns unmentionable publicly in other forms" (Logue, 1981, p. 44).

Other examples of analyses at the group level include Greenberg's (1982) account of the disinformation campaign used by the Allied military forces against the Nazis prior to the 1944 invasion of Normandy. Bok (1983) observes that military secrecy (and, by implication, deception) can indeed confound one's foes but also one's supporters—as the Pentagon Papers revealed about the U.S. involvement in Vietnam. Other examples of secrecy and deception at the group/organization level are found in Bok's (1983) discussion of secret societies, investigative journalism, and academic social science. The journalist and the scientist may both argue that lying and secrecy are necessary in order for them to expose the truth about various social ills that would otherwise go undiscovered. Scientists lie to experimenters as well as subjects in double-blind experiments. And even though scientists in academia routinely profess to subscribe to openness and sharing of information, deception among this group does take place. Watson (1968), for example, writes in

The Double Helix that he and his collaborator, Francis Crick, tried to keep their competitors ignorant of the progress they were making while trying to discover the structure of DNA, using publication deadlines and waiting periods to protect and reveal as they saw fit. Not much has been written about family lies, but Bochner (1984) suggests that lying and deception (along with openness) may be important in the development and maintenance of bonded, long-term relationships and healthy functioning families.

The formal business organization is another source of lies at the group level. Instead of emphasizing the nature of verbal or nonverbal signals, though, the information available focuses on the motivation for lying and topics and conditions likely to spawn deception. Steele (1975), in noting what assumptions permeate corporations and lead to low information disclosure, may also have pinpointed factors that lead to a climate of group deception. One assumption, which Steele calls "the satellite theory of communication," says that it is better to communicate something indirectly than to do so directly, taking pride in "what we don't have to say." The assumptions associated with the "great lie" approach suggest: "My responsibilities require that I either withhold information from, or lie to those below me in the system for the good of both them and the world" (p. 25). Steele goes on to list various risks involved in disclosing information in some organizations—risks that may also act as triggers for deception. As Perry and Barney (1981) note, when workers perceive management has imposed unrealistic standards for performance it is not unreasonable to expect they will lie about their performance. Or, in the case of whistle-blowing and leaks, the organization may be perceived as unresponsive to internal criticism, favoring the suppression of undesirable truths (Stewart, 1980). Thus leakage in this context at the group level is still an indicator of deception that, despite all efforts at containment, slips out. The difference is that at this level it is not nonverbal behavior within an individual but the verbal behavior of an individual (or group) who are members of the organization.

Steele (1975) also makes an important distinction between private and public audiences as the receivers of information put out by the corporation. Good images and rosy pictures are more likely to be reserved for public audiences. But, as Steele observes, the same process can occur between groups within the same company. For example, the marketing department may see a meeting with the manufacturing department as within the public arena and provide a carefully crafted message about forecasts, manpower needs, and so on that does not accurately represent what is believed to be the truth. The manufacturing group then operates on the basis of what amounts to an internal press release and ends up putting unreasonable demands on the marketing department.

Societal Level

When an individual or group communicates with the public at large and it is perceived as a lie, we have a representative instance for analysis at the societal level. As at other levels, some lies may be well prepared and intentional; others may be undertaken with considerably less awareness. Sometimes interactions that originally occur at other levels are reported to the public at large and thereby achieve dimensions analyzable at the societal level. For example, when Neville Chamberlain, Britain's prime minister, reported to Parliament (and the world) in 1938 that Hitler was a man who could be relied on, that Hitler had given his word that he wanted peace, and that Chamberlain believed Hitler "means what he says," a case of interpersonal lying assumed societal implications and was subject to public evaluation. Whenever the public is asked to make a judgment about the truth or falsity of a message (even though it was not originally communicated to the public) it assumes characteristics of mass consumption and societal effects (see Ettema & Whitney, Chapter 24).

Normally the process at this level involves a deceptive message or messages communicated to the public and either public opinion, an agency, or an individual (purportedly representing the public) acting as lie detector. Sometimes the public plays the role of choosing between two accounts of the truth, one from the supposed liar and one from the lie detector. The National Council of Teachers of English annually gives an award to someone or some agency in public life—usually associated with government—that best exemplifies the vagueness, imprecision, and ambiguity associated with "doublespeak." The words "liar" and "deceiver" are avoided, but the implication is clear that the doublespeak committee is a watchdog for instances of deception directed at the society at large.

It is not surprising that verbal statements are the targets for analysis, given the potential problems in getting the public to believe the intentionality of many nonverbal signals. Public standards for evaluating lies are always in the process of change so the "climate of the times" becomes an important measure of potential or actual effects. Norms associated with lying at all communication levels (in government, in marriage, or when lying to a dying relative) constantly affect one another and make up the climate of the times. One common norm about lying in this culture has been the tendency to reserve the various forms of the term "lie" for only the most extreme and provocative circumstances. Instead we prefer to say that the person made an "outright fabrication," that the person showed a "reckless disregard for the truth," that the statement was a "malicious misrepresentation," and the like. Our own lies are similarly designated (i.e., we make a "misstatement" rather than lie; Safire, 1980).

The reasons given for lying at this level are not unlike those at other levels: to mobilize the public toward some goal (as with the facts about the Vietnam war), to sell (as with advertising), or to keep from knowing (as with Watergate). Nor are the tactics especially different; withholding information, over- and understatement, refusal to provide information, deliberate misinformation, and inaccurate information used to mislead.

The research methods at this level are varied. Standard and repeatable messages in the form of advertisements, presidential speeches, or news reports can be manipulated in controlled experiments, while analytical or critical approaches are more suitable for multiact, multiperson and multimedia deception campaigns. Lying itself is not manipulated as it is at the individual level. Instead, only those circumstances in which messages have been made and lying either is admitted or is suspected from contrary evidence/testimony are studied. The studies of lying on the societal level have primarily concerned advertising and politics, although other public deceptions do gain notoriety and analysis (e.g., the hoax perpetrated by author Clifford Irving about Howard Hughes's biography; Phelan, 1982).

Advertising. By definition, the mass media represent ways of communicating with large segments of society. Large numbers of people are exposed and potentially far-reaching effects are possible. Misleading messages about a product or service are of interest for their direct effects as well as for the possibility that they will provide a role model for acceptable behavior.

The study of deceptive advertising has emphasized strategy, detection, and effects. Studies of strategy question the extent to which "puffery" is actually lying and whether the Federal Trade Commission (FTC) should make this decision for the American public (Glassman & Pieper, 1980; Oliver, 1979; Rotfeld & Rotzoll, 1980). The issue of what actually constitutes a lie becomes even more ambiguous (for the FTC or the public) when words are omitted and pictures are used to imply a particular message (Crock, 1978; Shimp & Preston, 1981). Obviously, this phenomenon, which makes the lie detector's job even more difficult, may be of particular interest to nonverbal scholars. The ads in question are made available to many people, but not everyone views them with the same tolerance or understanding. Thus the question of who is being deceived is a critical issue and one Armstrong, Gural, and Russ (1980) argue has not yet been adequately answered; although Barry (1980) has devised a seven-step plan for detecting deception in children's advertising. Glassman and Pieper (1980) address the issue of effects when they report some evidence suggesting that deceptive ads may not be as influential as many believe. Barbour and Gardner's work (1982) adds that at least in the area of pricing, attempts to provide nondeceptive guidelines may indeed be perceived as even more deceptive.

Politics. Bok (1978) makes the following statement about the American public's changing view of lying by their political leaders:

> In 1960, many Americans were genuinely astonished to learn that President Eisenhower had lied when asked about the U-2 incident, in which an American spy plane and pilot had been forced down in the Soviet Union. But only fifteen years later, battered by revelations about Vietnam and Watergate, 69 percent of the respondents to a national poll (Cambridge Survey Research, 1975, 1976) agreed that "over the last ten years, this country's leaders have consistently lied to the people." (p. xviii)

There are times when political leaders are asked to make statements to the American people via television, which allows the viewers to examine nonverbal signals that may suggest deception; but much of the emphasis in this area concerning signals and/or strategies of deception focuses on verbal behavior or written documents. Ekman (1985), in a discussion of the Watergate testimony by government officials, pointed out that inconsistencies within one's verbal report or discrepancies between the verbal report and other "known" facts are important clues to deceit. The public liar, then, has to anticipate when a lie will be necessary, invent a line that will fit the changing circumstances, and remember the line once it has been made public. Alker (1976), using Bolinger's (1973) ideas on how deception is revealed linguistically, studied presidential press conferences where statements were made that could later be compared with contrary factual information. The various linguistic forms in this study did not distinguish the deceptive statements in press conferences from truthful ones. But Carpenter (1981) used an analysis of the presidential debates of 1976 to develop the hypothesis (which was later confirmed in an analysis of a suspect's testimony in a police interrogation) that lexical diversity would increase as one became more cautious in responding. The problem, of course, is that caution may be associated with some lies and liars, but it is also a common practice among truth-tellers. Axelrod and Zimmerman (1981) examined over 30 years of *Pravda* and *Izvestia* for information regarding how reliably these Russian information sources would attempt various types of direct deception—that is, strategic lies unfilled threats, and diplomatic fictions. According to the researchers, on occasions when the stakes were high enough so the potential gain from deception would outweigh the loss of newspaper credibility, the central Soviet press would be used to tell lies.

Rank (1980, 1984) has researched detection of deception in political rhetoric using the common warnings against undocumented charges or claims, indirectness, and so on, even though the association of these clues with deception per se is not clearly established. Bok (1978) also seeks standards for evaluating the need for secrecy and lying in government and politics. Her evaluation of the consequences of such behavior emphasizes the ethical perspective:

> Political lies, so often assumed to be trivial by those who tell them, rarely are. They cannot be trivial when they affect so many people and when they are so peculiarly likely to be imitated, used to retaliate, and spread from the few to the many. When political representatives or entire governments arrogate to themselves the right to lie, they take power from the public that would not have been given up voluntarily. (p. 175)

CONCLUSION

Several observations seem evident from the foregoing review. The study of nonverbal behavior has been largely limited to the study of individual liars. As the level of analysis incorporates more people into the deceptive act, more attention seems to be given to verbal manifestations of lying. Given our increasing knowledge of various types of lies, liars, and lying situations, it seems increasingly futile to seek nonverbal or verbal clues that will, in all instances, provide clues to deception. Probably the most accurate detection strategy at all levels will be to identify signals associated with control, arousal, intent, and the like and interpret them within the framework of some key situational variables. As the responsibility for the lie can be diffused to others, as lies may be at the group and society levels, we will no doubt need to revise our views of control and arousal developed at the individual level. The review also makes it clear that we have emphasized the behavior of the liar and spent far less effort examining the behavior of lie detectors, the strategies used and the signals manifested at every level and the interactive effects of such behavior. Detector behavior has primarily been confined to measures of accuracy in identifying lying behavior.

REFERENCES

Adams, R. S. (1969). Location as a feature of instructional interaction. *Merrill-Palmer Quarterly, 15,* 318-319.

Aiello, J. R., & Thompson, D. W. (1980). Personal space, crowding and spatial behavior in a cultural context. In I. Altman, A. Rappoport, & J. R. Wohlwill (Eds.), *Human behavior and environment* (Vol. 4). New York: Plenum.

Alker, H. A. (1976). *Mystification and deception in presidential press conferences.* Paper presented at the meeting of the American Psychological Association, Washington, DC.

Argyle, M., & Dean, J. (1965). Eye contact, distance and affiliation. *Sociometry, 28,* 289-304.

Armstrong, G. M., Gural, M. N., & Russ, F. A. (1980). Defining and measuring deception in advertising: a review and evaluation. In J. H. Leigh & C. R. Martin (Eds.), *Current issues and research in advertising 1980* (pp. 17-39). Ann Arbor: Division of Research, Graduate School of Business Administration, University of Michigan.

Atkinson, M. L., & Allen, V. L. (1983). Perceived structure of nonverbal behavior. *Journal of Personality and Social Psychology, 45,* 458-463.

Axelrod, R., & Zimmerman, W. (1981). The Soviet press on Soviet foreign policy: A usually reliable source. *British Journal of Political Science, 11,* 183-200.

Bakan, P. (1971). The eyes have it. *Psychology Today, 4,* 64-67.

Barbour, F. L., & Gardner, D. M. (1982). Deceptive advertising: A practical approach to measurement. *Journal of Advertising, 11,* 21-30.

Baron, R. A., & Ransberger, V. M. (1978). Ambient temperature and the occurrence of collective violence. The "long hot summer" revisited. *Journal of Personality and Social Psychology, 36,* 351-360.

Barry, T. E. (1980). A framework for ascertaining deception in children's advertising. *Journal of Advertising, 9,* 11-18.

Baum, A., & Valins, S. (1979). Architectural mediaton of residential density and control: Crowding and regulation of social contact. In L. Berkowitz (Ed.), *Advances in experimental social psychology* (Vol. 12). New York: Academic Press.

Bochner, A. P. (1984). The functions of human communication in interpersonal bonding. In C. C. Arnold & J. W. Bowers (Eds.), *Handbook of rhetorical and communication theory* (pp. 544-621). Boston: Allyn & Bacon.

Bok, S. (1978). *Lying: Moral choice in public and private life.* New York: Pantheon Books.

Bok, S. (1983). *Secrets.* New York: Pantheon Books.

Bolinger, D. (1973). Truth is a linguistic question. *Language, 49,* 539-550.

Bosmajian, H. A. (1971). The persuasiveness of Nazi marching and der kampf um die strasse. In H. A. Bosmajian (Ed.), *The rhetoric of nonverbal communication,* Glenview, IL: Scott, Foresman.

Brandt, D. R., Miller, G. R., & Hocking, J. E. (1982). Familiarity and lie detection: A replication and extension. *Western Journal of Speech Communication, 46,* 276-290.

Brandt, D. R., Miller, G. R., & Hocking, J. E. (1980). The truth-deception attribution: Effects of familiarity on the ability of observers to detect deception. *Human Communication Research, 6,* 99-110.

Bryski, B. G., & Frye, J. K. (1979-1980). Nonverbal communication in presidential debates. *Australian Scan, 7-8,* 25-31.

Buck, R. (1980). Nonverbal behavior and the theory of emotion: The facial feedback hypothesis. *Journal of Personality and Social Psychology, 38,* 811-824.

Buck, R. (1984). *The communication of emotion.* New York: Guilford Press.

Burgoon, J. K. (1980). Nonverbal communication in the 1970s: An overview. In D. Nimmo (Ed.), *Communication yearbook 4* (pp. 179-197). New Brunswick, NJ: Transaction.

Burgoon, J. K. (1985). Nonverbal Signals. In M. L. Knapp & G. R. Miller (Eds.), *Handbook of interpersonal communication* (pp. 344-390). Newbury Park, CA: Sage.

Burgoon, J. K., & Saine, T. (1978). *The unspoken dialogue: An introduction to nonverbal communication.* Boston: Houghton Mifflin.

Camden, C., Motley, M., & Wilson, A. (1984). White lies and interpersonal communication. A taxonomy and preliminary investigation of social motivation. *Western Journal of Speech Communication, 48,* 309-325.

Cantor, N., Mischel, W. R., & Schwartz, J. C. (1982). Social knowledge: Structure, content, use and abuse. In A. H. Hastorf & A. M. Isen (Eds.), *Cognitive social psychology* (pp. 33-72). New York: Elsevier/North Holland.

Cappella, J. N. (1981). Mutual influence in expressive behavior: Adult-adult and infant-adult interaction. *Psychological Bulletin, 89,* 101-132.

Cappella, J. N. (1985). The management of conversations. In M. L. Knapp & G. R. Miller (Eds.), *Handbook of interpersonal communication* (pp. 393-438). Newbury Park, CA: Sage.

Carlsmith, J. M., & Anderson, C. A. (1979). Ambient temperature and the occurrence of collective violence: A new analysis. *Journal of Personality and Social Psychology, 37,* 337-344.

Carpenter, R. H. (1981). Stylistic analysis for law enforcement purposes: A case study of a language variable as an index of a suspect's caution in phrasing answers. *Communication Quarterly, 29,* 32-39.

Chesebro, J. W. (1984). The media reality: Epistemological functions of media in cultural systems. *Critical studies in mass communication, 1,* 111-130.

Chisholm, R., & Freehan, T. (1977). The intent to deceive. *Journal of Philosophy, 74,* 143-159.

Cline, R. J. (1985). The Cronkite-Ford interview at the 1980 republican national convention: A therapeutic analogue. *Central State Speech Journal, 36,* 92-104.

Cody, M. J., Marston, P. J., & Foster, M. (1984). Deception: Paralinguistic and verbal leakage. In R. Bostrom (Ed.), *Communication yearbook 8* (pp. 466-490). Newbury Park, CA: Sage.

Cody, M. J., & O'Hair, H. D. (1983). Nonverbal communication and deception: Differences in deception cues due to gender and communicator dominance. *Communication Monographs, 50,* 175-192.

Cohen, C. S., & Ebbesen, E. B. (1979). Observational goals and schema education: A theoretical framework for behavior perception, *Journal of Experimental Social Psychology, 15,* 305-329.

Comadena, M. E. (1982). Accuracy in detecting deception: Intimate and friendship relationships. In M. Burgoon (Ed.), *Communication yearbook 6* (pp. 446-472). Newbury Park, CA: Sage.

Condon, W. S. (1976). An analysis of behavior organization. *Sign Language Studies, 13,* 285-318.

Corcoran, J.F.T., Lewis, M. D., & Garver, R. B. (1978). Biofeedback—conditioned galvanic skin response and hypnotic suppression of arousal: A pilot study of their relation to deception. *Journal of Forensic Sciences, 23,* 155-162.

Crock, S. (1978, August 11). FTC is seeking ways to decide if pictures in advertising convey false impressions. *Wall Street Journal,* p. 2.

Davis, M. (1984). Nonverbal behavior and psychotherapy process research. In A. Wolfgang (Ed.), *Nonverbal behavior: Perspectives, applications, intercultural insights* (pp. 203-228). Toronto: Hogrefe.

DePaulo, B. M., & Jordan, A. (1982). Age changes in deceiving and detecting deceit. In R. S. Feldman (Ed.), *Development of nonverbal behavior in children* (pp. 151-180). New York: Springer-Verlag.

DePaulo, B. M., Lanier, K., & Davis, T. (1983). Detecting deceit of the motivated liar. *Journal of Personality and Social Psychology, 45,* 1096-1103.

DePaulo, B. M., & Rosenthal, R. (1979). Telling lies. *Journal of Personality and Social Psychology, 37,* 1713-1722.

DePaulo, B. M., Rosenthal, R., Rosenkrantz, J., & Green, C. R. (1982). Actual and perceived cues to deception: A closer look at speech. *Basic and Applied Social Psychology, 3,* 291-312.

DePaulo, B. M., Stone, J. I., & Lassiter, G. D. (1985). Telling ingratiating lies: Effects of target sex and target attractiveness or verbal and nonverbal deception success. *Journal of Personality and Social Psychology, 48,* 1191-1203.

deTurck, M. A., & Miller, G. R. (1985). Deception and arousal: Isolating the behavioral correlates of deception. *Human Communication Research, 12,* 181-201.

Dittmann, A. T. (1972). Developmental factors in conversational behavior. *Journal of Communication, 22,* 404-423.

Draper, P. (1973). Crowding among hunter-gatherers: The !Kung bushmen. *Science, 182,* 301-303.

Duncan, S., Brunner, L. J., & Fiske, D. W. (1979). Strategy signals in face-to-face interaction. *Journal of Personality and Social Psychology, 37,* 301-313.

Duncan, S., & Fiske, D. W. (1977). *Face-to-face interaction: Research, methods, and theory.* Hillsdale, NJ: Lawrence Erlbaum.

Ekman, P. (Ed.). (1982). *Emotion in the human face* (2nd ed.). New York: Cambridge University Press.

Ekman, P. (1985). *Telling lies.* New York: Norton.

Ekman, P., & Friesen, W. V. (1969a). Nonverbal leakage and clues to deception. *Psychiatry, 32,* 88-105.

Ekman, P., & Friesen, W. V. (1969b). The repertoire of nonverbal behavior: Categories, origins, usage and coding. *Semiotica, 1,* 49-98.

Ekman, P., & Friesen, W. V. (1972). Hand movements. *Journal of Communication, 22,* 353-374.

Ekman, P., & Friesen, W. V. (1974). Detecting deception from the body or face. *Journal of Personality and Social Psychology, 29,* 288-298.

Ekman, P., Friesen, W. V., & Ellsworth, P. (1982). What are the similarities and differences in facial behavior across cultures? In P. Ekman (Ed.), *Emotion in the human face* (2nd ed.). New York: Cambridge University Press.

Elliott, G. C. (1979). Some effects of deception and level of self-monitoring on planning and reacting to a self-presentation. *Journal of Personality and Social Psychology, 37,* 1282-1292.

Ellsworth, P. C., & Tourangeau, R. (1981). On our failure to disconfirm what nobody ever said. *Journal of Personality and Social Psychology, 40,* 363-369.

Exline, R. V., Thibaut, H., Hickey, C. B., & Gumpert, P. (1970). Visual interaction in relation to Machiavellianism and an unethical act. In R. Christie & F. L. Geis (Eds.), *Studies in Machiavellianism* (pp. 53-75). New York: Academic Press.

Feldman, R. S., Jenkins, L., & Popoola, O. (1979). Detection of deception in adults and children via facial expressions. *Child Development, 50,* 250-255.

Feldman, R. S., & White, J. B. (1980). Detecting deception in children. *Journal of Communication, 30,* 121-128.

Festinger, L., Schachter, S., & Back, K. (1950). *Social pressures in informal groups: A study of human factors in housing.* New York: Harper & Row.

Friedman, H. S., Mertz, T. I., & Dimatteo, M. R. (1980). Perceived bias in the facial expressions of television news broadcasters. *Journal of Communication, 30,* 103-111.

Fugita, S. S., Hogrebe, M. A., & Wexley, K. N. (1980). Perceptions of deception: Perceived expertise and detecting deception, successfulness of deception and nonverbal cues. *Personality and Social Psychology Bulletin, 6,* 637-643.

Geis, F. L., & Moon, T. H. (1981). Machiavellianism and deception. *Journal of Personality and Social Psychology, 41,* 766-775.

Glassman, M., & Pieper, W. I. (1980). Processing advertising information: Deception, salience, and inferential formation. *Journal of Advertising, 9,* 3-10.

Goffman, E. (1959). *The presentation of self in everyday life.* Garden City, NY: Doubleday.

Goldman-Eisler, F. (1968). *Psycholinguistics: Experiments in spontaneous speech.* New York: Academic Press.

Goleman, D. (1985). *Vital lies, simple truths: The psychology of self-deception.* New York: Simon & Schuster.

Greenberg, I. (1982). The role of deception in decision theory. *Journal of Conflict Resolution, 26,* 139-156.

Greenwald, A. G., & Leavitt, C. (1984). Audience involvement in advertising: Four levels. *Journal of Consumer Research, 11,* 581-592.

Greene, J. O., O'Hair, H. D., Cody, M. J., & Yen, C. (1985). Planning and control of behavior during deception. *Human Communication Research, 11,* 335-364.

Gur, R. C., & Sackheim, H. A. (1979). Self deception: A concept in search of phenomenon. *Journal of Personality and Social Psychology, 37,* 147-169.

Hager, J. C., & Ekman, P. (1981). Methodological problems in Tourangeau and Ellsworth's study of facial expression and experience of emotion. *Journal of Personality and Social Psychology, 40,* 358-362.

Hall, J. A. (1984). *Nonverbal sex differences.* Baltimore: John Hopkins University Press.

Hall, J. A. (1985). Male and female nonverbal behavior. In A. W. Siegman & S. Feldstein (Eds.), *Multichannel integration of nonverbal behavior* (pp. 195-226). Hillsdale, NJ: Lawrence Erlbaum.

Hample, D. (1980). Purposes and effects of lying. *Southern Speech Communication Journal, 46,* 33-47.

Hankiss, A. (1980). Games con men play: The semiosis of deceptive interaction. *Journal of Communication, 30,* 104-112.

Harper, R. G., Wiens, A. N., & Matarazzo, J. D. (1978). *Nonverbal communication: The state of the art.* New York: John Wiley.

Heslin, R., & Patterson, M. L. (1982). *Nonverbal behavior and social psychology.* New York: Plenum.

Hochschild, A. R. (1983). *The managed heart.* Berkeley: University of California Press.

Hocking, J. E., Bauchner, J., Kaminiski, E., & Miller, G. R. (1979). Detecting deceptive communication from verbal, visual and paralinguistic cues, *Human Communication Research, 6,* 33-46.

Izard, C. E. (1981). Differential emotions theory and the facial feedback hypothesis of emotion activation: Comments on Tourangeau and Ellsworth's "The role of facial response in the experience of emotion." *Journal of Personality and Social Psychology, 40,* 350-354.

Jeffrey, K. M., & Mischel, W. (1979). Effects of purpose on the organization and recall of information in person perception. *Journal of Personality, 47,* 397-419.

Kahneman, D. (1973). *Attention and effort.* Englewood Cliffs, NJ: Prentice-Hall.

Kasal, S. V., & Mahl, G. F. (1965). The relationship of disturbances and hesitations in spontaneous speech to anxiety. *Journal of Personality and Social Psychology, 1,* 425-433.

Kendon, A. (1970). Movement coordination in social interactions: Some examples described. *Acta Psychologica, 32,* 100-125.

Kendon, A. (1972). Some relationships between body motion and speech: An analysis of an example. In A. W. Siegman & B. Pope (Eds.), *Studies in dyadic communication.* Elmsford, NY: Pergamon Press.

Knapp, M. L. (1978). *Nonverbal communication in human interaction* (2nd ed.). New York: Holt, Rinehart & Winston.

Knapp, M. L., & Comadena, M. E. (1979). Telling it like it isn't: A review of theory and research on deceptive communications. *Human Communication Research, 5,* 270-285.

Knapp, M. L., Hart, R. P., & Dennis, H. S. (1974). An exploration of deception as a communication construct. *Human Communication Research, 1,* 15-29.

Krauss, R. M. (1981). Impression formation, impression management, and nonverbal behaviors. In E. T. Higgins, C. P. Herman, & M. P. Zanna (Eds.), *Social cognition: The Ontario symposium* (Vol. 1, pp. 323-341). Hillsdale, NJ: Lawrence Erlbaum.

Kraut, R. E. (1978). Verbal and nonverbal cues in the perception of lying. *Journal of Personality and Social Psychology, 36,* 380-391.

Kraut, R. E. (1980). Humans as lie detectors: Some second thoughts. *Journal of Communication, 30,* 209-216.

Kraut, R. E. (1982). Social pressure, facial feedback, and emotion. *Journal of Personality and Social Psychology, 42,* 853-863.

Kraut, R. E., & Poe, D. (1980). On the line: The deception judgement of customs inspectors and laymen. *Journal of Personality and Social Psychology, 39,* 784-798.

LaFrance, M. (1979). Nonverbal synchrony and rapport: Analysis by the cross-lag panel technique. *Social Psychology Quarterly, 42,* 66-70.

Laird, J. D. (1984). The real role of facial response in the experience of emotion: A reply to Tourangeau and Ellsworth, and others. *Journal of Personality and Social Psychology, 47,* 909-917.

Lindskold, S., & Walters, P. S. (1983). Categories for acceptability of lies. *Journal of Social Psychology, 120,* 129-136.

Logue, C. M. (1981). Transcending coercion: The communicative strategies of black slaves on antebellum plantations. *Quarterly Journal of Speech, 67,* 31-46.

Maier, R. A., & Lavrakas, P. J. (1976). Lying behavior and evaluation of lies. *Perceptual and Motor Skills, 42,* 575-581.

Mayo, C., & Henley, N. M. (1981). Deception detection and relationship development: The other side of trust. In M. L. McLaughlin (Ed.), *Communication yearbook 9* (pp. 377-389). Newbury Park, CA: Sage.

McCornack, S. A., & Parks, M. R. (1986). Deception detection and relationship development: The other side of trust. In M. L. McLaughlin (Ed.) *Communication yearbook 9* (pp. 377-389). Newbury Park, CA: Sage.

Mehrabian, A. (1971). Nonverbal betrayal of feeling. *Journal of Experimental Research in Personality, 5,* 64-73.

Meyer, D. R. (1953). On the interaction of simultaneous responses. *Psychological Bulletin, 50,* 204-220.

Miller, G. R., deTurck, M. A., & Kalbfleisch, P. J. (1983). Self-monitoring, rehearsal, and deceptive communication. *Human Communication Research, 10,* 97-117.

Miller, J. G. (1978). *Living systems.* New York: McGraw-Hill.

Milgrim, S. (1970). The experiences of living in cities. *Science, 167,* 1461-1468.

Nunnally, J. C., Knott, P. D., Duchnowski, A., & Parker, R. (1967). Pupillary response as a general measure of activation. *Perception and Psychophysics, 2,* 149-155.

O'Hair, D., Cody, M. J., & Behnke, R. R. (1985). Communication apprehension and vocal stress as indices of deception. *Western Journal of Speech Communication, 49,* 286-300.

O'Hair, H. D. Cody, M. J., & McLaughlin, M. L. (1981). Prepared lies, spontaneous lies, Machiavellianism, and nonverbal communication. *Human Communication Research, 7,* 325-339.

Oliver, R. L. (1979). An interpretation of the attitudinal and behavioral effects of puffery. *Journal of Consumer Affairs, 13,* 8-27.

Patterson, M. L. (1983). *Nonverbal behavior: A functional perspective.* New York: Springer-Verlag.

Pennebaker, J. W., & Chew, C. H. (1985). Behavioral inhibition and electrodermal activity during deception. *Journal of Personality and Social Psychology, 49,* 1427-1433.

Perry, T. L., & Barney, J. B. (1981). Performance lies are hazardous to organizational health. *Organizational Dynamics, 10*, 24-36.

Phelan, J. (1982). *Scandals, scamps and scoundrels.* New York: Random House.

Porter, N., & Geis, F. (1981). Women and nonverbal leadership cues: When seeing is not believing. In C. Mayo & N. M. Henley (Eds.), *Gender and nonverbal behavior.* New York: Springer-Verlag.

Rafaeli, A., & Sutton, R. I. (1986). *The expression of emotion as part of the work role.* Unpublished manuscript, Department of Industrial Engineering and Engineering Management, Stanford University.

Rank, H. (1980). Analyzing political rhetoric. *English Journal, 69*, 38-43.

Rank, H. (1984). *The pep talk.* Park Forest, IL: Counter-Propaganda Press.

Riggio, R. E., & Friedman, H. S. (1983). Individual differences and cues to deception. *Journal of Personality and Social Psychology, 45*, 899-915.

Rosenfeld, H. M. (1978). Conversational control functions of nonverbal behavior. In A. W. Siegman & S. Feldstein (Eds.), *Nonverbal behavior and communication,* Hillsdale, NJ: Lawrence Erlbaum.

Rosenthal, R. (Ed.). (1979). *Skill in nonverbal communication: Individual differences.* Cambridge, MA: Oelgeschlager, Gunn & Hain.

Rosenthal, R., & DePaulo, B. M. (1979a). Sex differences in accommodation in nonverbal communication. In R. Rosenthal (Ed.), *Skill in nonverbal communication* (pp. 68-103). Cambridge, MA: Oelgeschlager, Gunn & Hain.

Rosenthal, R., & DePaulo, B. M. (1979b). Sex differences in eavesdropping on nonverbal cues. *Journal of Personality and Social Psychology, 37*, 273-285.

Rosenthal, R., Hall, J. A., Di Matteo, M. R., Rogers, P. L., & Archer, D. (1979). *Sensitivity to nonverbal communication: The PONS test.* Baltimore: Johns Hopkins University Press.

Rotfeld, H. J., & Rotzoll, K. B. (1980). Is advertising puffery believed? *Journal of Advertising, 9*, 16-20.

Safire, W. (1980, October 5). Gross distortions. *New York Times Magazine,* pp. 10-12.

Scherer, K. R. (1981). Speech and emotional states. In J. Darby (Ed.), *The evaluation of speech in psychiatry and medicine* (pp. 189-220). New York: Grune & Stratton.

Scherer, K., & Ekman, P. (Eds.). (1981). *Handbook of methods in nonverbal behavior research.* New York: Cambridge University Press.

Schmidt, D. E., & Keating, J. P. (1979). Human crowding and personal control: An integration of the research. *Psychological Bulletin, 86*, 680-700.

Scott, T. R., Wells, W. H., Wood, D. Z., & Morgan, D. I. (1967). Pupillary response and sexual interest reexamined. *Journal of Clinical Psychology, 23*, 433-438.

Shimp, T. A., & Preston, I. L. (1981). Deceptive and non-deceptive consequences of evaluative advertising. *Journal of Marketing, 45*, 22-31.

Siegman, A. W. (1979). The tell tale voice. In A. W. Siegman & S. Feldstein (Eds.), *Nonverbal behavior and communication* (pp.183-243). Hillsdale, NJ: Lawrence Erlbaum.

Smith, H. A. (1984). State of the art of nonverbal behavior in teaching. In A. Wolfgang (Ed.), *Nonverbal behavior: Perspectives, applications, intercultural insights* (pp. 171-202). Toronto: Hogrefe.

Smith, H. A. (1979). Nonverbal communication in teaching. *Review of Educational Research, 49*, 631-672.

Sommer, R., & Ross, H. (1958). Social interaction in a geriatric ward. *International Journal of Social Psychiatry, 4*, 128-133.

Stanbeck, M. H., & Pearce, W. B. (1981). Talking to "the man": Some communication strategies used by members of "subordinate" social groups. *Quarterly Journal of Speech, 67*, 21-30.

Steele, F. (1975). *The open organization.* Reading, MA: Addison-Wesley.

Stewart, L. P. (1980). "Whistle blowing": Implications for organizational communication. *Journal of Communication, 30,* 90-101.

Stockdale, J. E. (1978). Crowding: Determinants and effects. In L. Berkowitz (Ed.), *Advances in Experimental Social Psychology* (Vol. 11). New York: Academic Press.

Strodtbeck, F., & Hook, L. (1961). The social dimensions of a twelve man jury table. *Sociometry, 24,* 297-415.

Sutton, R. I., & Denison, D. R. (1986). *Surgical nurses: Issues in the design of a loosely-bound team.* Unpublished manuscript, Department of Industrial Engineering and Engineering Management, Stanford University.

Tiemens, R. K. (1978). Television's portrayal of the 1976 presidential debates: An analysis of visual content. *Communication Monographs, 45,* 362-370.

Tomkins, S. S. (1981). The role of facial response in the expression of emotion: A reply to Tourangeau and Ellsworth. *Journal of Personality and Social Psychology, 40,* 355-357.

Toris, C., & DePaulo, B. M. (1984). Effects of actual deception and suspiciousness of deception on interpersonal perceptions. *Journal of Personality and Social Psychology, 47,* 1063-1073.

Tourangeau, R., & Ellsworth, P. C. (1979). The role of facial response in the experience of emotion. *Journal of Personality and Social Psychology, 37,* 1519-1531.

Turner, R. E., Edgley, C., & Olmstead, C. (1975). Information control in conversations: Honesty is not always the best policy. *Kansas Journal of Sociology, 11,* 69-89.

Waid, W. M., & Orne, M. T. (1981). Cognitive, social and personality processes as the psychological detection of deception. In L. Berkowitz (Ed.), *Advances in experimental social psychology* (Vol. 14, pp. 61-106). New York: Academic Press.

Watson, J. D. (1968). *The double helix.* New York: Atheneum.

Zuckerman, M., DePaulo, B. M., & Rosenthal, R. (1981). Verbal and nonverbal communication of deception. In L. Berkowitz (Ed.), *Advances in experimental social psychology* (Vol. 14, pp. 2-59). New York: Academic Press.

Zuckerman, M., & Driver, R. E. (1985). Telling lies: Verbal and nonverbal correlates of deception. In A. W. Siegman & S. Feldstein, (Eds.), *Multichannel integrations of nonverbal behavior* (pp. 129-147). Hillsdale, NJ: Lawrence Erlbaum.

Zuckerman, M., Kernis, M. R., Driver, R., & Koestner, R. (1984). Effects of actual deception and expected deception. *Journal of Personality and Social Psychology, 46,* 1173-1182.

Zuckerman, M., Klorman, R., Larrance, D. T., & Spiegel, N. H. (1981). Facial, autonomic, and subjective components of emotion: The facial feedback hypothesis versus the externalizer-internalizer distinction. *Journal of Personality and Social Psychology, 41,* 929-944.

14 Socializing Functions

GARRETT J. O'KEEFE
Colorado State University

KATHALEEN REID-NASH
Lee College

A N often recurring research focus in communication science has been the socializing functions of communication. The core concern is the development of children within a society, and the maintenance of the social order through that process. Child raising is assumed to be a critical task within any social structure, and the means and modes of communication applied to that process have significant impact. The role of parents is of course regarded as paramount in the process (see Hartup, 1979), but schools, peers (see Damon, 1983), and mass media—particularly television (National Institute of Mental Health [NIMH], 1982; Surgeon General, 1972)—are noteworthy factors as well.

However, concern with socialization is by no means limited to child raising. As adults move through their lifetimes and confront change in their families, educational statuses, work situations, and the like, they need to adapt or be "resocialized" to form new behaviors and roles (Brim, 1968; Dion, 1985; Mortimer & Simmons, 1978; Riley, Foner, Hess, & Toby, 1969). This evolution continues into elder adulthood (Chappel & Orbach, 1986; Riley et al., 1969). The continuing socialization process over the life span is similarly dependent upon effective uses of appropriate communication sources, channels, and modes.

Nor is interest in the topic limited to consideration of communication as an independent or intervening variable in the socialization process. Attention is also given to the ways in which individuals are socialized into communicative behaviors, including language capability as well as interpersonal and mass communication usage habits and skills (Diez, 1984; Hymes, 1972; McLeod & O'Keefe, 1972). Although socialization has been primarily investigated through research at the intrapersonal level, many productive explorations have been pertinent to communication and socialization at the interpersonal, organizational, and societal levels.

We will begin with some general perspectives on the concept of socialization and its current evolution, particularly as tied to communication research. Certain conceptual and methodological issues will be noted.

We will then explore research on socialization and communication at each of the four levels of analysis. Specification of problems inherent in the research will then be provided, with suggestions for their resolution.

PERSPECTIVES ON SOCIALIZATION

While difficult to define in the narrow sense, socialization entails "the process by which individuals acquire the knowledge, skills, and dispositions that make them more or less able members of society" (Brim, 1966, p. 3). It thus involves social learning on the part of an individual in the acquisition of the "personal and group loyalties, the knowledge, skills, feelings, and desires that are appropriate for a person of his age, sex, and particular social status, especially as these have relevance to adult role performance" (Clausen, 1968, p. 7).

Socialization integrates the individual into the social structure, as distinct from what Damon (1983) calls individuation, or the development of one's sense of self or personality. Socialization has been primarily considered from either the viewpoint of the society or the viewpoint of the individual. Macroscopically, the research question is how the culture is transmitted to individuals to assure its maintenance and functioning. Social structural variables of major interest include population ecology, economics and resource allocation, politics or power structures, and institutionalized value systems (Inkeles, 1968). How socialization is perceived also depends on one's view of society. A more traditional "consensus" perspective assumes greater normative agreement and harmony, with little deviance. A "conflict" perspective poses numerous competing norms and value systems within a given society, with more tension and competition (McCron, 1976).

A useful distinction is made in the anthropological literature between *socialization* and *enculturation* (Whiting, 1968). Enculturation involves the transmission of information, norms, and values about the society, its components, and processes, but with no direct utilitarian relevance to one's activities in that society. Socialization, on the other hand, refers directly to the transmission of information, norms, values, and skills pertinent to one's performance (or survival) in the social setting. Thus everything "socially relevant" that one receives communication about is not necessarily socialization; rather, it encompasses only those things that add to one's competence in a given social position or role.

Socialization is also distinguished from persuasion and education. Socialization may involve "persuasive" or "educational" processes, but its results yield relatively more enduring change in matters of consequence to the individual or the social structure. The difference is a matter of degree, not unlike that between the constructs of "attitude" and "value."

Socialization as an Active Pursuit

While the macroscopic view tends to regard those being socialized as quite passive, the trend at the individual level of analysis has been toward perceiving socializees as being far more active in pursuing learning experiences, interpreting and processing them, and exerting greater control over their outcomes (see Johnsson-Smaragdi, 1983; Zigler & Seitz, 1978). The emergence of cognitive development and information processing as the dominant paradigm in individual-level socialization has contributed much to this view (see Baldwin, 1969; Youniss, 1980; Zigler & Child, 1973).

There are many situations, particularly among adolescents and adults, in which the individual has a strong desire to assume a new role or pattern of behavior and takes an active role in (1) anticipating the need to learn requisite cognitions, attitudes, and behaviors; (2) seeking out individuals, information, or experiences that facilitate learning; (3) engaging in activities that bring about the desired change; and (4) "reality testing" to evaluate progress toward the desired goals. In this "proactive" socialization mode, communication behavior by the socializee is a critical variable (see Berlyne, 1960). Anticipatory socialization (Merton, 1967) is particularly salient here; it involves taking on values of a role or group one wants to partake in, facilitating the later actual socialization process.

Even with young children, as White (1959) has suggested, learning or gaining competence in a new role or behavior can be rewarding in its own right, and may be sought for that very reason. Dorr (1980) stresses the active participation of small children in their television viewing behaviors.

Rosengren (1983, 1986) notes that despite the emergence of this "active" view, the bulk of socialization research still empirically treats the socializee as passive (as an "object," not a "subject"), and that research usually assumes a consensual rather conflicting social structure. He advocates comparison of socialization outcomes where (1) the recipient is passive and the societal situation conflictful, (2) an active recipient is in a consensual society, and (3) an active socializee confronts a conflicting society. Rosengren points to the ubiquitous mass media as agents of socialization, at times interacting with parents and schools and at other times supplanting them.

In terms of interpersonal communication, socialization has come to be considered more of an interactive, reciprocal process, and less a matter of an agent transmitting information to a recipient. Rather, socialization involves a continuing interaction between individuals and those who attempt to influence them, "an interaction that undergoes many phases and changes" (Clausen, 1968, p. 6). Wentworth (1980) similarly emphasizes the interactive aspects of socialization, and recommends greater attention to the social contexts through which "the ability to reproduce society is transferred from member to novice" (p. 79). Organizational socialization or assimilation has become more concerned with the impact of new recruits upon organizational functioning (Jablin, 1985; Jablin & Krone, Chapter 23 in this volume).

Socialization Processes Over
the Life Cycle

Among adults in particular, motivation to "be socialized" or, more simply, to change and adapt, may explain the kinds of strategies used and the success of the socializing experience. Because adults have previously been through socializing situations, they are likely to be more aware of and practiced at it.

There is ample evidence that adaptation does not end at the termination of adolescence but rather continues throughout the life cycle. As Brim (1968) has noted, the lives of new waves of 18-year-olds entering the mainstream year by year do not necessarily follow those of their predecessors. Nor can we assume that adults currently entering their sixties follow the life styles of those who did so a few years ago. During the middle years adults are met with such resocializing experiences as marriage, child raising, divorce, and changes in career and community settings.

While the basic processes remain similar for adult and child socialization experiences, some distinctions with particular import for communication need to be taken into account. One concerns the relative consistency of "basic" personality—largely shaped in childhood—over the adult years (Mortimer & Simmons, 1978). Childhood socialization experiences have arguably greater potential for impact in that they are likelier to "bend the twig" that grows into the tree. Moreover, the content of such experiences includes such essential components as the regulation of biological drives and development of self-image (Brim, 1966). Adult socializing experiences are far less apt to result in such influential consequences, centering more upon relatively specific roles and norms (Berger & Luckman, 1967). Adults can also exert much more resistance to socialization norms with which they disagree. Thus we are less concerned with the media as agents of adult socialization.

The context of adult socialization differs as well in that the child or adolescent is quite clearly related to the role of student or learner, while the adult is usually less constrained to "perform" in a learner role and has greater choice in choosing nonconforming options (Dion, 1985; Mortimer & Simmons, 1978). Moreover, communication between agent and influencee in the adult setting is likelier to be marked by open interaction and exchange, and be less directed "at" the socializee.

Finally, adults are more likely to enter voluntarily into situations in which socialization to new roles or norms is required (Brim, 1968). Such self-initiated change can result in greater satisfaction with a successful transition on the part of the individual. Such change would also seem likely to involve more active use and manipulation of communication channels by the socializee, as opposed to the case in which socialization demands imposed by other agents may be transmitted by communications to which the individual is expected to react.

SOCIALIZATION AND COMMUNICATION IN CONTEXT

The fields of socialization and communication both deal with processes that are difficult to define empirically. Both easily fall prey to reliance upon linear cause-effect models. Lasswell's (1948) outline of communication "Who says what in which channel to whom with what effect?" can be paraphrased to describe socialization as "Who learns what from whom under what circumstances with what effects?" (Greenstein, 1965). But both fields have come to recognize that interactive components are important and that the recipients may play active roles in what takes place (see Rosengren, Wenner, & Palmgreen, 1985). Finally, both tend to emphasize research efforts that are limited to particular content areas, sometimes at the expense of the cross-content integration necessary for theory development.

Investigations of the relationship between communication and socialization require a choice of whether communication is to be regarded as an independent, dependent, or intervening variable. The bulk of existing thinking and work has dealt with communication as an independent variable or "agent" of socialization. Studies of the impact of television alone on children likely account for the majority of such investigations (see NIMH, 1982). Scarcer have been socialization-based studies utilizing communication as the dependent variable—for example, emphasizing how individuals are socialized into various communicative orientations and behaviors (see McLeod, Fitzpatrick, Glynn, & Fallis, 1982). Communication may also be considered as an intervening variable, as in investigations of how variation in the modality or means of communication emanating from the same socializing agent may make a difference in outcomes (see Chaffee, 1977).

CONCEPTUAL AND METHODOLOGICAL
CONSIDERATIONS

In any of the above cases, if communication behavior is to be the focus of inquiry a general paradigm guiding the research requirements should involve (1) explicit, empirical conceptualizations of the patterns of communication behavior being addressed; (2) a similar explication of the factors antecedent to (or predictors of) the communication behaviors; and (3) causal delineation of the effects and consequences of the communication behaviors both in and of themselves and as functions of their interactions with antecedent variables.

This approach rests upon the assumption that investigations of communication and socialization toward both theoretical and policy-related ends will be most productive if they entail more than either only basic descriptions of communication behavior and its predictors, or possible outcomes of such behaviors in terms of direct effects. Rather, at a minimum such research should include an interactive process approach containing all such components.

Some Basic Requirements

As noted by McLeod and O'Keefe (1972) socialization-based models in general require stringent conceptual and methodological frameworks. In terms of data, for a full analysis five kinds of variables need to be addressed simultaneously: (1) age or life cycle position of the person being influenced; (2) the agent or source of influence; (3) the type of learning processes involved in the socialization process (e.g., modeling versus social-interactive); (4) the social structural constraints impinging upon the learning process (e.g., education levels, community type); and (5) the dependent variable or the type of behavior that is the focus of the socialization process.

Socialization thus involves interaction among agent, situation, and recipient; understanding of the relationships among all three is highly dependent upon adequate specification of the type of learning mechanism involved (McLeod & Brown, 1976). The agent-situation-recipient relationship for learning by modeling, for example, can place heavier emphasis on the observational abilities and activities of the socializee or on the environment in which the act takes place. The agent, or role model, may be relatively passive or even unaware of being involved in a learning process. But reinforcement models of learning necessarily depend upon the agent's active participation in the reward or punishment of given behaviors on the part of the socializee. In a social-interactive perspective (e.g., Wentworth, 1980), greater emphasis is placed upon the situation of source and receiver. Neither individual needs to make a conscious effort at socialization processes per se. More important may be the way in which the learning stimuli are displayed during the interaction, and the characteristics of the interaction—for example, the role relationships between the interactants or the kinds of communicative behaviors being performed.

Cross-Level Considerations

The bulk of the theory and research pertinent to socialization has been confined to the intrapersonal level of inquiry dealing with the development of the individual. However, socialization also applies to the interpersonal, organizational, and macrosocietal levels in several ways. As Chaffee and Berger note in Chapter 3, agents of socialization can include the self (through active learning), interpersonal relationships with others (family and peer communication), organizations such as schools and churches, and such macrosocietal entities as mass media content.

Moreover, individuals can be viewed as being socialized into interpersonal, organizational, and societal roles. Children are expected to develop skill and competence in interpersonal discussion (Delia & O'Keefe, 1979), and adults are expected to do likewise in marital relations (see Fitzpatrick, Chapter 19). At the organizational level, adolescents typically need to learn to cope with the formats and rules of peer group relationships (Coleman, 1980). The study of the socialization of individuals into occupational roles is a long-standing research tradition (Moore, 1969), and the functioning of the political system depends upon adequate stimuli to involve the young in it (Greenstein, 1965). Socialization processes also serve functions for groups, social systems, and other collectivities.

INTRAPERSONAL SOCIALIZATION

Studies of the intrapersonal socializing functions of communication with respect to role development have focused upon (1) politics (2) gender roles, (3) age roles, (4) ethnic/racial roles, and (5) consumer roles. Two other content areas more akin to personality/behavioral trait development have also been closely scrutinized in terms of communication's impact on them: antisocial behavior (particularly aggression) and prosocial behavior (primarily altruism). Most recently, interest has also developed in the socialization of children with respect to their emotional capacities. To the above we can add yet another criterion content area— communication itself.

Political Socialization

Clearly the most conceptually and methodologically complete topical work relating communication to socialization has been in the arena of political socialization, dealing with the processes by which individuals gain politically relevant cognitions, attitudes, and behaviors. As Chaffee (1977) has indicated, there is a potpourri of possible models through which causal linkages among mass media, interpersonal communication, and individual political orientations can be viewed. Likely the most productive are those regarding communication as either an independent variable in its own right or as a factor contingent upon such varying conditions as level of political interest.

Moreover, research has been broached not only at the intrapersonal but at all four levels of analysis. At the intrapersonal level, for example, exposure to news media—particularly newspapers—has been found predictive of political knowledge (Atkin & Gantz, 1978; Chaffee, Ward, & Tipton, 1970) as well as sense of political efficacy (Chaffee, 1977) and presidential campaign involvement (Chaffee et al., 1970).

In one of the very few instances of application of an interpersonal level model to socialization, Chaffee, McLeod, and Wackman (1973) measured parent-child pairs as units of analysis in terms of the extent to which socio-oriented and concept-oriented communication styles were emphasized. Children engaged in "pluralistic" communicatory relationships with their parents—in which high conceptual skills were emphasized and social constraints minimized—were found to score highest in political awareness, participation, and media use. Contrarywise, youths engaged in "protective" parental relationships (i.e., low concept and high socio-orientation) scored lowest on those political attributes.

Organizational-level formal education has long been recognized as a critical ingredient in political socialization (see Hess & Torney, 1967), and rather extensive system-level analyses of the process have served as guiding models (Almond & Verba, 1963; Easton & Hess, 1962). As Atkin (1981) has suggested, however, there are significant gaps in the research in terms of linkages between the levels of analysis, as well as in the range of dependent variables examined.

Gender, Age, and Ethnic/Racial
Role Socialization

Linkages between communication and such more "personal" areas of socialization as integration into appropriate gender, age, and ethnic/racial roles have received less attention in the literature. With respect to mass media influences on such socialization, content analysis remains the most prevalent form of inquiry into all areas, with clear findings that the media—particularly television—tend to offer inaccurate and often stereotypical views of all three types of roles (Barcus, 1983; Greenberg, 1982).

However, the more meaningful question of the impact of such content upon audiences, especially children, remains largely unanswered. While heavier viewing of television by children appears to be associated with more sex role stereotyping on their part (Beuf, 1974), the medium can also be used to downplay or even reverse stereotypes (Miller & Reeves, 1976). As Williams, LaRose, and Frost (1981) suggest, the quantity of stereotypical behavior shown on television may not be as important as the qualities of the characters in terms of their more personal and emotional qualities. Role models tend not to be stereotypes but more "real" characters with identifiable and admirable human attributes. Given the significant changes in sex roles over the past two decades and the wide variety of social, economic, and cultural factors coming into play (see Spence, Deaux, & Helmreich, 1985), it is curious that more dynamic, causally based empirical research has not delved into the communication-related aspects of these changes.

Age role stereotyping on television has been most obvious in portrayals of elderly persons, but its impact remains unexamined (Davis & Kubey, 1982; Kubey, 1980). A more important issue in this content area would appear to be uses of media by aged persons in facilitating their own socialization to retirement, health changes, and the like (Rubin, 1982). The long-term socializing impact of television on cultural minority group members and perceptions of them remains a largely open issue as well (Greenberg & Atkin, 1982).

Consumer Socialization

Somewhat more headway has been gained in examining ways in which communication interacts with various kinds of consumer orientations, and the bulk of that research has concerned the impact of television advertising on children. Findings indicate that children learn information about products from television and form positive attitudes of those products based on what they view (Atkin, 1980; Ward, Wackman, & Wartella, 1977). However, the same research suggests that such contingent conditions as family and peer group relations can ameliorate such mediated influences. The extent of the impact of advertising on long-term development of children's cognitions, attitudes, and behaviors with respect to their roles as consumers remains uncertain.

Antisocial Behavior

Numerous reviews (e.g., Comstock, Chaffee, Katzman, McCombs, & Roberts, 1978; Huesmann, 1982) have attempted to summarize and interpret the voluminous and often contradictory array of studies dealing with the impact of portrayals of violence on television on aggressive dispositions and behaviors among young viewers. The research reviewed leaves little doubt that viewership of violence generally correlates with aggressive behavior.

In the context of socialization as the term is used here, concern is more with the influence of television and other forms of communication on children's aggressive or antisocial orientations as enduring traits, and the evidence on that issue has been particularly difficult to assess. Panel studies have produced some evidence that increased aggressive behavior may persist given a continuing diet of televised violence over time (Lefkowitz, Eron, Walder, & Heusmann, 1977; Singer & Singer, 1980). However, evidence is less clear on the direction of causal linkages given such repeated exposure (Cook, Kendzierski, & Thomas, 1983; Milavsky, Kessler, Stipp, & Rubens, 1982).

Despite the popular emphasis on television as a source of stimulation for both aggressive and altruistic behaviors, the bulk of the research evidence points to family and peers as clearly the more influential socializers (Bandura, 1977; Krebs & Miller, 1985). With respect to communication variables per se, Krebs and Miller note the sometimes significant effects of the "preaching" of appropriate behaviors to children by adults.

Prosocial Behavior

In a major review of research on the influence of television on such prosocial behaviors as altruism, generosity, friendliness, rule adherence, and fear reduction, Rushton (1980, 1982) concluded that the medium can modify viewers' behaviors in a prosocial direction. The evidence for short-term change is quite conclusive based upon both laboratory experiments and field studies. However, the question again remains of the duration of such effects in naturalistic long-range socializing situations.

Socialization to Emotions

Recent work on the psychology of emotions has led to concern with what aspects of emotions are influenced by social relations and how it is that emotions become integrated within social structure and norms (Lewis & Saarni, 1985). The aspect of emotional expression is of particular interest to communication researchers, and offers a promising new front for inquiry into socialization per se. This component "consists of the observable and potentially communicative changes in facial, vocal, and kinesis behavior that occur with changes in emotional state" (Lewis & Saarni, 1985, p. 3). Socialization and biology are blended here as independent factors that lead to emotional development.

Emotional socialization processes are heavily based upon what has shaped an individual's interactions with other members of society. Camras (1985) suggests, for example, that "the child may learn what emotions are appropriate in particular situations and what are the socially acceptable means of displaying these emotions" (p. 141) through interpersonal relationships. Dorr (1985) notes that traditional socialization processes

> include direct explication by others, reinforcements and punishments administered by others, observation of others, self-reinforcement and children's use of their various and sundry experiences with emotion to generate meaning, principles, conceptual systems, and/or rules. (p. 56)

Face-to-face interaction is not necessarily the only context in which socialization can occur:

> In particular, the less common emotions . . . and [those] less directly related to the child's current developmental, social, and cultural status are likely to be socialized in contexts other than those of face-to-face interaction directly involving the child. (Dorr, 1985, p. 81)

Dorr has distinguished four categories of contexts in which emotional socialization can take place: (1) personal, ongoing experience with emotion; (2) observation of live, ongoing experience with emotion; (3) observation of a framed, ongoing experience with emotion (e.g., via mass media); and (4) remembrance or recall of previous emotional experiences.

Socialization to Communication

The development of language and speech in infancy is the most universal socializing experience, and the literature on development of language is far too rich and complex to be reviewed here. The work is typically tied more to the cognitive development of children; reviews may be found in Jenkins (1969), Damon (1983), and Feagans, Garvey, and Golinkoff, with Greenberg (1984).

Investigation of the means by which individuals are socialized into various forms of communication orientations and behaviors is of critical import to an understanding of both communication and socialization processes. But, as McLeod et al. (1982) point out, the area is vastly underresearched. Descriptive studies of variations in media behavior by such variables as age, education and income abound (Comstock et al., 1978), and use of television viewing motivations as descriptors has become more prevalent (Frank & Greenberg, 1980). But even the use of such variables in elaborate multivariate designs does little to explain the development of media habits over time.

Some of the more promising approaches to date in this area include the use of the above-noted family communication pattern dimensions to predict television usage patterns (Lull, 1980; McLeod & Brown, 1976). For example, socio-oriented families watched more television than did the concept-oriented and tended to use it more for social-interactive purposes. This type of research has the added advantage of separating communication variables into independent and dependent modes within the same conceptual framework: Interpersonal communication is used to predict television use.

In a test of the more interactive aspects of socialization, Wilson (1984) found that influences in parent-adolescent dyads during a political campaign were bidirectional: Parents who talked with their children about the campaign were likely to show issue opinion changes in the direction of their offsprings' opinions, and (as was more expected) children changed opinions in the direction of their parents. Moreover, the direction of influence was predicted in part by the extent of newspaper usage on the part of the parties involved. Whichever parent-adolescent partner read more appeared to have an upper hand in the process.

Taking a somewhat different approach, Chaffee and Tims (1982) propose a developmental sequence of media usage among adolescents (from radio to television to newspapers to magazines) and use multivariate analyses to identify education and parental media use variables as antecedent to such development. Tims (1984) found socialization to newspaper exposure—but not television news exposure—among adolescents to be dependent in part upon parental behaviors. Similarly, in an elaborate longitudinal study of Swedish adolescents, Johnsson-Smaragdi (1983) presents quite convincing evidence of adolescent modeling of parental television viewing, but with no reverse effect of children on parents. Moreover, television viewing appeared to enhance rather than constrict adolescent interaction with family and peers. In a multivariate examination of the development of grade schoolers' reading skills, Roberts, Bachen, Hornby, and Hernandez-Ramos (1984) found linkages between attitudinal and behavioral orientations toward television and reading ability.

INTERPERSONAL RELATIONS AND SOCIALIZATION

The socialization of individuals into dealing with interpersonal units—and indeed the social evolution of those units—has been indirectly addressed from a number of perspectives. The symbolic interactionist view of Mead (1934) held that shared meaning develops in the course of interpersonal communication through shared significant symbols. Such symbols, with the spoken word the most notable example, evoke similar responses in both parties. Sharing of symbols is enhanced by each communicative partner's mentally assuming the role of the other, and with both mutually adjusting to the total interactive situation.

The more recent perspective of the social psychology of interpersonal attraction once again emphasizes the communicative outcomes of role taking, shared knowledge, and self-disclosure, as well as mutual responsibilities and norms for maintaining and regulating the relationship (Berscheid, 1985). Empirical data on the nature and pattern of communicative acts facilitating such outcomes are lacking, although traditional studies on affiliation and friendship formation have indicated that the exchange of personal information is a primary determinant (Newcomb, 1961). The process of self-disclosure in interpersonal dyads is a compelling topic in its own right in terms of socialization. While variation in self-disclosing communication on the part of individuals may be in part accounted for by personality trait characteristics, situational factors appear more significant, with disclosure by a communication partner a highly salient one (Chelune & Associates, 1979).

Other clues come from studies of socialization into marriage (see Hill & Aldous, 1969, for an extensive discussion), where the taking of more formalized roles may either enhance or constrain interpersonal communication. Again, however, the modes of communication through which adults are socialized into marital roles remain less well specified. (See Fitzpatrick, Chapter 19, for further discussion.)

Berger (1979) makes the case that too much emphasis has been placed on attraction and liking as the criterion variables in relationship development. He suggests that more attention be paid to how dyads develop knowledge and understanding of one another, and suggests that key determinants of such are such antecedent factors as incentives for mutual understanding and perceived likelihood of future interaction. Active (e.g., verbal interrogation), passive (e.g., social comparison), and interactive (e.g., self-disclosure) strategies toward increased understanding are discussed as well.

Duck (1976) stresses the need for examining the information-based communication processes in constructing more comprehensive models of the development of acquaintanceships and friendships. Interactive models based upon coorientation (McLeod & Chaffee, 1973), which also take a cognitively oriented approach, may have utility in investigating the development of relationships. Coorientation models take into account the degree of (1) actual agreement between partners on an issue, (2) accuracy of perceptions of each other's position on the issue, and (3) perceived agreement from the point of view of each partner on the issue. Tracing such relational attributes over time can be instructive in delineating the strengthening or decline of relationships, at least with respect to particular salient issues, including those involving parents and children (O'Keefe, 1973; Price & Roberts, Chapter 25).

ORGANIZATIONS, NETWORKS, AND SOCIALIZATION

Investigations of the social assimilation process have generally taken the form of either more interactive studies of how individuals come together into groups (see Newcomb, 1961) or of how groups exert conforming influences upon new members (see Festinger, 1951; Moscovici, 1985). In either case communication is regarded as implicitly taking place and serving such functions as information sharing, exerting social pressure, negotiation, and the like. Clearly, group members do become socialized to group norms, and in turn have an impact on changes in those norms. However, studies of the process have largely been concerned with initial structural considerations (e.g., physical proximity) or with end result consequences (e.g., opinion sharing and consensus). The substantial literature on group interaction (see Blumberg, Hare, Kent, & Davies, 1983) deals with communication processes at some length, but much less from the point of view of socialization than those of task performance, conflict resolution, networking, leadership, and negotiation.

The stages of development of groups have been explored as well, with some attention paid to the communicative patterns inherent in each stage. In a sense, such development can be regarded as the "socialization" of the group as a unit to the situation or task at hand. Numerous models of the stages have been offered, depending upon the type and functions of the group (see Hare, 1976; Lacoursiere, 1980). Most follow in many respects a functional view of group development formulated by Parsons (1961) that includes the following phases, which may vary in order of occurrence: (1) latent pattern maintenance, or the commitment by members toward normative group behaviors; (2) adaptation, including the adaption of group resources toward goal attainment; (3) integration, referring to the integrating of subsystems of the group to allow effective functioning; and (4) goal attainment, or the achieving of goals that provide group equilibrium. Bales and Strodtbeck (1951) identified communication patterns over the course of group meetings as consisting of an initial information-gathering stage, followed by information evaluation and opinion giving, and closing with socioemotional support as the task is completed.

Assimilation Into Organizations

Studies of socialization to work (see Moore, 1969)—a more formal assimilation process—have evolved into more general emphasis on socialization to organizations overall. Recent work in this area has decidedly emphasized more communication-oriented variables. Organizational socialization is the "process by which a person learns the values and norms and required behaviors that permit him to participate as a member of the organization" (Van Maanen 1976, p. 67). The initial impact of the socialization process is greatest as the individual first affiliates with the organization; however, as with most adult socialization experiences the process likely continues as changes occur in both organization and the individual.

Jablin (1982; Jablin & Krone, Chapter 23) provides a more interactive communication perspective to organizational socialization by viewing it in terms of both how the organization influences the individual and how in turn the individual may modify the organization. He defines organizational assimilation as "the process by which organizational members become a part of, or are absorbed into, the culture of an organization" (Jablin, 1982, p. 256).

Jablin indicates that interpersonal communication, particularly between superiors and subordinates, is a highly important component of the assimilation process. He suggests two important outcomes of the organization assimilation process: (1) employee perceptions of the communication climates of an organization, and (2) the extent to which workers participate in an organization's communication networks.

SOCIAL SYSTEMS, LANGUAGE, AND SOCIALIZATION

As Clausen (1968) has noted, "Human society is dependent upon a measure of consensus among its members—consensus about goals to be sought and the means of attaining them" (p. 3). He adds that such consensus emerges through communication, and that it rests upon shared symbols and norms that are acquired in the process of socialization. The very development of social systems is inherently tied to the nature and extent of operative communication systems and networks (see Pool, 1973). For example, the formation of communities or organizations has been tied to an increasing proportion of social contact and communication flow within the structure (Deutsch, 1956).

Societal-level inquiry into the socializing role of communication has involved a wide array of theorizing. Whorf (1952) postulated that language development is the foundation for other essential attributes of a given society or culture, including common modes of human thought processes. McLuhan (1964) argued that the type of mass medium predominant in a society shapes its prevalent cognitive style, with "linear" thinking most characteristic of print-based societies and a more "simultaneous" style typical in oral and/or video-centered ones. Ellul (1965) positioned propaganda as a key communicative ingredient in cultural development. Propaganda indeed may be an overlooked element in socialization, particularly if we take Clausen's view that socialization and social control are the complementary bases for social order and unity.

Mass communications systems may also be examined for their possible impacts on the "cultivation" of individuals to various characteristics of a society emphasized in its media (Gerbner & Gross, 1976). Television has been hypothesized to lead to widespread misperceptions of the "social realities" of a given social environment (Hawkins & Pingree, 1982).

Social Structure and Language

A somewhat controversial view of the impact of social structure on language, and vice versa, is that of Bernstein (1970), who postulates that greater diversity within social systems results in greater variation in speech behavior. He specifically distinguishes between restricted codes of speech, which he argues are more typical of lower-class English-speaking families, and elaborated codes, more likely found in middle-class families. In brief, restricted speech codes involve more concrete statements of fact or authority, with less in the way of abstraction or reasoning offered. Elaborated codes on the other hand contain more complex sentence structures with greater emphasis on attribution and abstract thinking (see Giles & Wiemann, Chapter 12).

Bernstein's work is of particular interest because it has implications for at least three levels of analysis. At the systems level it is inferred that the codes serve a social control function, allowing the middle class greater linguistic as well as social flexibility and mobility. The interpersonal level serves as the locus for interactive transmission of the code from parent to child. Finally, the code becomes fixed intrapersonally into the speech personality of the individual, with social class a discriminating variable. However, Bernstein is not without his critics, and while the empirical evidence is strongly suggestive it is far from conclusive. Labov (1979) offers evidence that lower-class language among American blacks is in fact highly complex and "elaborated," but it appears less so because of the cultural biases of middle-class educators and scholars. Previously Labov (1968) had presented interesting evidence of anticipatory socialization on the part of lower-class but upwardly mobile persons in the early adoption of middle-class phonetics.

Cultures and Languages in Contact

Grimshaw (1973) notes with irony that the greatest opportunity to examine cultures and languages coming into contact with one another and the impact of that on social behavior and structure occurred with the massive immigrations to the United States in the early decades of this century. Yet virtually no scientific studies of these were carried out due to a lack of interest in that topic by sociologists and linguists. Most attention was given to social and political assimilation processes, to which language differences were seen at best as a hindrance.

More recently there has been considerably more interest in the result of contact between languages as a consequence of immigration, commercial or political interaction, or conquest. Fishman (1972) has made a cogent case for immigration policies that promote bilingual language development for immigrants while maintaining their parent language in the interest of linguistic and cultural diversity. There is an obvious tension in this perspective in that overly zealous loyalty to one's own language on the part of newcomers could be detrimental to assimilation; immigrant groups with insulative religious ties may be more successful in maintaining their language, but less so at socializing into the new culture. Yum (1982) considers the diversity of communication channels—as opposed to sheer quantity of communication—used by the immigrant to be an important impetus to ease of assimilation. She also found that among Korean immigrants in Hawaii, length of tenure was a significant predictor of diversity, suggesting a reciprocal process of changes in degrees of socialization and communication patterns over time (see Giles & Wiemann, Chapter 12; Gudykunst, Chapter 27).

Gardner (1979) places second-language acquisition at the center of social psychology. He regards it as a situation in which the student is faced with "not simply learning new information which is part of his own culture but rather of acquiring symbolic elements of a different ethnolinguistic community" (p. 193). Thus elements of another culture are imposed into one's own life space, and "the student's harmony with his own cultural identity and his willingness or ability to identify with other cultural communities become important considerations in the process of second language acquisition." Apart from intelligence and language aptitude, Gardner identifies motivation to orient to new language and culture as a prime determinant of the success of second-language acquisition, along with situational anxiety, or anxiety reactions aroused in specific situations in which secondary language use would be appropriate (see Giles & Wiemann, Chapter 12).

Need for cultural identity may be critical in language maintenance as well. In their research on the maintenance of Spanish by southwestern U.S. Hispanics, Christian and Christian (1966) emphasize the embeddedness of Hispanic culture in the language and the need to maintain that cultural reality as distinct from the mainstream Anglo culture.

Grimshaw (1973) points to increasing interest in the development and functions of pidgin and creole languages, which typically emerge in situations involving contact between highly dissimilar languages and cultures when one culture is subservient to the other (e.g., in colonization). He suggests more attention to variations in those languages that may accompany changes in the social, political, and economic structure of the cultures (e.g., decolonization).

PROBLEMS IN THE CURRENT APPROACHES

There are several problems common to the surveyed research above. These indicate that a more conceptually unified approach to studying the socializing functions of communication could be highly productive. Here are some key problems:

(1) The preponderance of work has been carried out at the intrapersonal level of analysis, especially the work that is empirically based. Scholarship on the interpersonal, organizational and systems levels of analysis, while innovative, is also more speculative.

(2) Most studies at the intrapersonal level concern influences of mass media—and television in particular. The potential impacts of interpersonal or informal organizational interaction on intrapersonal socialization are given little consideration from a communication perspective.

(3) Most researchers, while noting the active role of the recipient in socialization, in practice treat individuals as reactors to the process. Little methodological consideration is given to their active involvement in it.

(4) With respect to mass media per se, the dominant methodology used has been macrosocietal analyses of media content relevant to each area. While it is necessary to establish that content does indeed exist that has potential for socializing influence, all too often the research is not developed beyond that point.

(5) Much of the research relies upon highly general measures of gross exposure to media content (e.g., "time spent with TV") while more sensitive measures of specific forms of motivations for using media are underutilized.

(6) A socialization perspective entails rather sophisticated multivariate designs incorporating indicators of life cycle position, source of influence, type of learning process, and structural variables. Seldom are more than two or at most three of these factors considered in any one study.

(7) Longitudinal, or even short-term panel, designs have been used in only a limited number of instances. Apart from their utility in examining causal relationships, such designs are necessary to determine whether the effects being found are simply short-run ones or are more enduring.

(8) The dependent variable or criterion for socialization is often limited to a single indicator.

(9) Research conceptualization and design are generally tied to the content area as opposed to attempting to seek out commonalities across all socialization-relevant research. (For example, seldom does political socialization research attempt to borrow or share underlying concepts or measures with consumer socialization research.)

COMPETENCE

In this section one particular perspective on socialization is offered as a framework under which the socializing functions of communication might be more productively examined. This perspective incorporates the concept of *competence* as a key ingredient. White (1959, 1960) defines competence in its broader biological sense as "an organism's capacity to interact effectively with its environment" (1959, p. 298). In the case of man, White identifies competence as primarily being learned over time (as opposed to being innate) and postulates that individuals have an intrinsic motivation to gain competence. Labeled "effectance motivation," it is viewed as propelling humans toward more self-perceived competent states and as providing a sense of self-reward when such states are reached. In sum, White views individuals as being motivated to "do well" at what they undertake and a belief that a task has been well done is gratifying in its own right.

Clausen (1968) ties competence more closely to formal socialization processes in defining it as "capability for effective performance for self and society" (p. 6). Smith (1968) finds this the key question of socialization research: "What do we know, and what do we need to know, about the conditions under which people come to function as competent members of society?" (p. 272). He also notes an important appeal of the concept as being its "rootedness in the view of the organism as an *active* (rather than merely *re*active) participant in *inter*action with the environment, and [its] close linkage to motivational processes" (p. 273). Moreover, competence bridges the traditionally divergent role theory and symbolic interaction perspectives on socialization. It may be viewed as either the outcome of a succession of interactive socializing experiences, or as a criterion for effective role performance (Inkeles, 1968; Smith, 1968).

A more varied concept of competence is also gaining some currency in the interpersonal communication literature (see Bostrom, 1984). As McCroskey (1984) notes, the term has been applied to encompass a number of attributes in diverse situations relating basically to forms of competence in effective communication. We need to emphasize that our use of the term is more narrowly restricted to its definition in the socialization literature as a criterion variable. To date, it has not been developed as a linkage between communication and socialization.

Advantages of a Competence Viewpoint

The concept of competence has value in communication-based socialization research. It assumes not only an interactive process of socialization that has utility for communication theory, but it necessitates a view of the socializee as an active participant. Competence, at least in White's view, requires a motivational component, which is also critical for communication as interaction. It also allows for a perspective on communication being an independent, intervening, or dependent variable in socialization processes. That is, communication may serve as the agent in the development of competence; or as a facilitating factor; or competence in communication may be an outcome of a socializing process.

While intuitively appearing to be an individual-level concept, in a more general sense competence may be applicable to interpersonal, macrosocietal, and network levels of analysis as well. Socialization allows an individual to develop the competence necessary to cope successfully with a particular role or situation. Interpersonal interaction variables may well facilitate that development; indeed interpersonal relationships may be categorized as to their levels of competence in effective functioning (e.g., the degree of competence between marriage partners for successful child raising). Similarly, groups and networks may be evaluated in terms of their competence on a number of dimensions in effectively meeting goals. The effective functioning of a society may be evaluated in terms of the degree of competence with which the criteria set for established roles are met (e.g., the extent of active citizen participation in voting that allows for a competent functioning of the political system).

Focus on a concept of competence can assist in formulating more cohesive communication-based models and theories of socialization. It can serve at least as an organizing rubric for criterion variables that need to be considered in investigating the socializing functions of communication.

In a similar vein, the concept can help tie together the disparate content areas assumed under the general theme of communication and socialization (e.g., political socialization, consumer socialization, and sex role socialization) by attempting to provide both a common perspective and a common set of criterion variables.

Possible Directions

We assume it is particularly useful from a communication perspective to regard socialization as being in effect a gaining of competence in ability to perform appropriately in many different social roles and situations. Our own recent work has utilized a more limited construct of competence (see O'Keefe 1985; O'Keefe & Reid-Nash, 1982), as a device for evaluating the influences of public information campaigns on social learning.

The specific variables include a collection of dependent variables often identified in communication effects and persuasion studies (see McGuire, 1985; Percy & Rossiter, 1980). With respect to a particular topic, situation, or role, individuals vary in competence on the basis of their (1) *awareness* of information necessary to their appropriate performance, (2) holding of positive *attitudes* concerning their own abilities to act successfully as well as the inherent value of the such actions, (3) sense of *capability* in being able to perform adequately, (4) *motivation* to engage in the actions, and (5) actual *engagement* in the actions. To these a sixth is added at this point: the extent to which an individual can effectively *evaluate* the outcomes of the above in order to assess his or her performance.

Competence is distinct from persuasion process models in that it deals with levels of effect in a nonlinear way. It assumes that individuals can, for example, be behaviorally competent while not necessarily being attitudinally or informationally competent with respect to a given topic, situation, or role. Our research on the effects of a public information campaign advocating greater citizen involvement in crime prevention found that the campaign had greater attitudinal effects on some persons while not necessarily having informational effects, while for other individuals it stimulated behavioral changes without concurrent attitudinal change (O'Keefe, 1985).

CONCLUSION

Investigations of the socializing functions of communication continue to be vital to the development of communication science. Socialization and communication have much in common as processes as well. While most inquiry into the relationship between them has focused on the intrapersonal level, there is ample room for productive research at the interpersonal, organizational, and macrosocietal levels.

Research on communication and socialization at the intrapersonal level has traditionally emphasized political socialization; gender, age, and ethnic role socialization; consumer socialization; and the development of antisocial and prosocial personality and behavioral traits. More recently attention has turned to socialization of emotional traits and, more important, to mass and interpersonal communication processes.

Interpersonal research involving socialization has evolved from early symbolic interaction perspectives to concern with such issues as interpersonal attraction, and recent work places more emphasis on information sharing and understanding. At the organizational level, the impact of communication network patterns on newcomers is an emerging area. Systems-level inquiry has been closely tied to the relationships between social structure and language, as well as on the consequences of intercultural contact for language and communication.

REFERENCES

Almond, G., & Verba, S. (1963). *The civic culture*. Princeton, NJ: Princeton University Press.

Atkin, C. (1980). Television advertising and socialization to consumer roles. In NIMH, *Television and behavior: Ten years of scientific progress and implications for the eighties: Vol. 2. Technical reviews*. Rockville, MD: NIMH.

Atkin, C. (1981). Communication and political socialization. In D. Nimmo & K. Sanders (Eds.), *Handbook of political communication*. Newbury Park, CA: Sage.

Atkin, C., & Gantz, W. (1978). Television news and the child audience. *Public Opinion Quarterly, 42*, 183-198.

Atkin, C., Greenberg, B., & McDermott, S. (1983). Television and race role socialization. *Journalism Quarterly, 60*, 407-414.

Baldwin, A. (1969). A cognitive theory of socialization. In D. Goslin (Ed.), *Handbook of socialization theory and research*. Chicago: Rand McNally.

Bales, R., & Strodtbeck, F. (1951). Phases in group problem solving. *Journal of Abnormal and Social Psychology, 46*, 485-495.

Bandura, A. (1977). *Social learning theory*. Englewood Cliffs, NJ: Prentice-Hall.

Barcus, F. (1983). *Images of life on children's television*. New York: Praeger.

Berger, C. (1979). Beyond initial interaction: Uncertainty, understanding, and the development of interpersonal relationships. In H. Giles & R. St. Clair (Eds.), *Language and social psychology*. Baltimore: University Park Press.

Berger, P., & Luckman, T. (1967). *The social construction of reality*. Garden City, NY: Doubleday.

Berlyne, D. (1960). *Conflict, arousal and curiosity*. New York: McGraw-Hill.

Bernstein, B. (1970). "A sociolinguistic approach to socialization: With some reference to educability." In F. Williams (Ed.), *Language and poverty: Perspectives on a theme*. Chicago: Markham.

Berscheid, E. (1985). "Interpersonal Attraction." In G. Lindzey & E. Aronson (Eds.), *Handbook of social psychology* (Vol. 2). New York: Random House.

Beuf, A. (1974). Doctor, lawyer, household drudge. *Journal of Communication, 24*, 142-145.

Blumberg, H., Hare, A., Kent, V., & Davies, M. (1983). *Small groups and social interaction*. New York: John Wiley.

Bostrom, R. (1984). *Competence in communication*. Newbury Park, CA: Sage.

Brim, O. (1966). Socialization through the life cycle. In O. Brim & S. Wheeler (Eds.), *Socialization after childhood.* New York: John Wiley.

Brim, O. (1968). Adult socialization. In J. Clausen (Ed.), *Socialization and society.* Boston: Little, Brown.

Camras, L. (1985). "Socialization of affect communication." In M. Lewis & C. Saarni (Eds.), *The socialization of emotions.* New York: Plenum Press.

Chaffee, S. (1977). Mass communication in political socialization. In S. Renshon (Ed.), *Handbook of political socialization.* New York: Free Press.

Chaffee, S., McLeod, J., & Wackman, D. (1973). Family communication patterns and adolescent political participation. In J. Dennis (Ed.), *Socialization to politics: A reader.* New York: John Wiley.

Chaffee, S., & Tims, A. (1982). News media use in adolescence: Implications for political cognitions. In M. Burgoon (Ed.), *Communication yearbook 6.* Newbury Park, CA: Sage.

Chaffee, S., Ward, S., & Tipton, L. (1970). Mass communication and political socialization. *Journalism Quarterly, 47,* 647-659.

Chelune, G., & Associates. (1979). *Self-disclosure: Origins, patterns, and implications of openness in interpersonal relationships.* San Francisco: Jossey-Bass.

Christian, J., & Christian, C., Jr. (1966). Spanish language and culture in the Southwest. In J. Fishman (Ed.), *Language loyalty in the United States.* The Hague: Mouton.

Clausen, J. (1968). Introduction. In J. Clausen (Ed.), *Socialization and society.* Boston: Little, Brown.

Coleman, J. (1980). Friendship and the peer group in adolescence. In J. Adelson (Ed.), *Handbook of adolescent psychology.* New York: John Wiley.

Comstock, G., Chaffee, S., Katzman, N., McCombs, M., & Roberts, D. (1978). *Television and human behavior.* New York: Columbia University Press.

Cook, T., Kendzierski, D., & Thomas, S. (1983). The implicit assumptions of television research: An analysis of the 1982 NIMH report on television and behavior. *Public Opinion Quarterly, 47,* 161-201.

Damon, W. (1983). *Social and personality development.* New York: Norton.

Davis, R., & Kubey, R. (1982). Growing old on television and with television. In NIMH, *Television and behavior: Ten years of scientific progress and implications for the eighties: Vol. 2. Technical reviews.* Rockville, MD: NIMH.

Delia, J., & O'Keefe, B. (1979). Constructivism: The development of communication in children. In E. Wartella (Ed.), *Children communicating: Media and development of thought, speech and understanding.* Newbury Park, CA: Sage.

Deutsch, K. (1956). Shifts in the balance of communication flows. *Public Opinion Quarterly, 20,* 143-160.

Diez, M. (1984). Communication competence: An interactive approach. In R. Bostrom (Ed.), *Communication yearbook 8.* Newbury Park, CA: Sage.

Dion, K. (1985). Socialization in adulthood. In G. Lindzey & E. Aronson (Eds.), *Handbook of social psychology.* (Vol. 2). New York: Random House.

Dorr, A. (1985). Contexts for experience with emotion, with special attention to television. In M. Lewis & C. Saarni (Eds.), *The socialization of emotions.* New York: Plenum.

Duck, S. (1976). Interpersonal communication in developing acquaintance. In G. Miller (Ed.), *Explorations in interpersonal communication.* Newbury Park, CA: Sage.

Easton, D., & Hess, R. (1962). The child's political world. *Midwest Journal of Political Science, 16,* 229-246.

Ellul, J. (1965). *Propaganda.* New York: Knopf.

Feagans, L., Garvey, C., & Golinkoff, R., with Greenberg, M., Harding, C., & Bohannon, J. (1984). *The origins and growth of communication.* Norwood, NJ: Ablex.

Festinger, L. (1951). Informal social communication. *Psychological Review, 57,* 271-282.

Fishman, J. (1972). *Language in sociocultural change.* Stanford: Stanford University Press.

Frank, R., & Greenberg, M. (1980). *The public's use of television.* Newbury Park, CA: Sage.

Gardner, R. (1979). Social psychological aspects of second language acquisition. In H. Giles & R. St. Clair (Eds.), *Language and social psychology.* Baltimore: University Park Press.

Gerbner, G., & Gross, L. (1976). Living with television: The violence profile. *Journal of Communication, 26,* 173-199.

Greenberg, B. (1982). Television and role socialization: An overview. In NIMH, *Television and behavior: Ten years of scientific progress and implications for the eighties: Vol. 2. Technical reviews.* Rockville, MD: NIMH.

Greenberg, B., & Atkin, C. (1982). Learning about minorities from television: A research agenda. In G. Berry & C. Mitchell-Kernan (Eds.), *Television and the socialization of the minority child.* New York: Academic Press.

Greenstein, F. (1965). *Children and politics.* New Haven, CT: Yale University Press.

Grimshaw, A. (1973). Sociolinguistics. In I. Pool & F. Frey (Eds.), *Handbook of communication.* Chicago: Rand McNally.

Hagestad, G., & Neugarten, B. (1985). Aging and the life course. In H. Binstock & E. Shanas (Eds.), *Handbook of aging and the social sciences* (2nd ed.). New York: Van Nostrand.

Hare, A. (1976). *Handbook of small group research.* New York: Free Press.

Hartup, W. (1979). The social worlds of childhood. *American Psychologist, 34,* 944-950.

Hawkins, R., & Pingree, S. (1982). Using television to construct social reality. *Journal of Broadcasting, 25,* 347-364.

Hess, R., & Torney, J. (1967). *The development of political attitudes in children.* Chicago: AVC.

Hill, R., & Aldous, J. (1969). Socialization for marriage and parenthood. In D. Goslin (Ed.), *Handbook of socialization theory and research.* Chicago: Rand McNally.

Huesmann, R. (1982). Television violence and aggressive behavior. In NIMH, *Television and behavior: Ten years of scientific progress and implications for the eighties: Vol. 2. Technical reviews.* Rockville, MD: NIMH.

Hymes, D. (1972). On communicative competence. In J. Pride & J. Holmes (Eds.), *Sociolinguistics.* London: Penguin.

Inkeles, A. (1968). Society, social structure and child socialization. In J. Clausen (Ed.), *Socialization and society.* Boston: Little, Brown.

Inkeles, A. (1969). Social structure and socialization. In D. Goslin (Ed.), *Handbook of socialization theory and research.* Chicago: Rand McNally.

Jablin, F. (1982). Organizational communication: An assimilation approach. In M. Roloff & C. Berger (Eds.), *Social cognition and communication.* Newbury Park, CA: Sage.

Jablin, F. (1984). Assimilating new members into organizations. In R. N. Bostrom (Ed.), *Communication yearbook 8.* Newbury Park, CA: Sage.

Jablin, F. (1985). Task/work relationships: A life-span perspective. In M. Knapp & G. Miller (Eds.), *Handbook of interpersonal communication.* Newbury Park, CA: Sage.

Jenkins, J. (1969). The acquisition of language. In D. Goslin (Ed.), *Handbook of socialization theory and research.* Chicago: Rand McNally.

Johnsson-Smaragdi, U. (1983). *TV use and social interaction in adolescence: A longitudinal study.* Stockholm: Almquist & Wiksell.

Krebs, D., & Miller, D. (1985). "Altruism and aggression." In G. Lindzey & E. Aronson (Eds.), *Handbook of social psychology* (Vol. 2). New York: Random House.

Kubey, R. (1980). Television and aging: Past, present and future. *Gerontologist, 20,* 16-35.

Labov, W. (1968). Reflections of social processes in linguistic structures. In J. Fishman (Ed.), *Readings in the sociology of language.* The Hague: Mouton.

Labov, W. (1979). The logic of nonstandard English. In V. Lee (Ed.), *Language development.* New York: John Wiley.

Lacoursiere, R. (1980). *The life cycle of groups.* New York: Human Sciences.

Lasswell, H. (1948). The structure and function of communication in society. In L. Bryson (Ed.), *The communication of ideas.* New York: Harper & Row.

Lefkowitz, M., Eron, L., Walder, L., & Huesmann, R. (1977). *Growing up to be violent: A longitudinal Study of the Development of Aggression.* New York: Pergamon.

Lewis, M., & Michalson, L. (1983). *Children's emotions and moods: Developmental theory and measurement.* New York: Plenum.

Lewis, M., & Saarni, C. (1985). "Culture and emotions." In M. Lewis & C. Saarni (Eds.), *The socialization of emotions.* New York: Plenum.

Lull, J. (1980). Family communication patterns and the social uses of television. *Communication Research, 7,* 319-334.

McCron, R. (1976). Changing perspectives in the study of mass media and socialization. In J. Halloran (Ed.), *Mass media and socialization.* Leeds: Kavanagh & Sons.

McGuire, W. (1985). The nature of attitudes and attitude change. In G. Lindzey & E. Aronson (Eds.), *Handbook of social psychology* (Vol. 2). Reading, MA: Addison-Wesley.

McLeod, J., & Brown, J. (1976). The family environment and adolescent television use. In J. Brown (ed.), *Children and television.* London: Collier Macmillan.

McLeod, J., & Chaffee, S. (1973). Interpersonal approaches to communication research. *American Behavioral Scientist, 16,* 469-499.

McLeod, J., Fitzpatrick, M., Glynn, C., & Fallis, S. (1982). Television and social relations: Family influences and consequences for interpersonal behavior. In NIMH, *Television and behavior: Ten years of scientific progress and implications for the eighties: Vol. 2. Technical reviews.* Rockville, MD: NIMH.

McLeod, J., & O'Keefe, G. (1972). The socialization perspective and communication behavior. In P. Tichenor & F. Kline (Eds.), *Current perspectives in mass communication research.* Newbury Park, CA: Sage.

McLuhan, M. (1964). *Understanding media.* New York: McGraw-Hill.

Mead, G. (1934). *Mind, self, and society.* Chicago: University of Chicago Press.

Merton, R. (1967). *Social theory and social structure.* New York: Free Press.

Milavsky, R., Kessler, R., Stipp, H., & Rubens, W. (1982). *Television and aggression: A panel study.* New York: Academic Press.

Miller, M., & Reeves, B. (1976). Dramatic TV content and children's sex-role stereotypes. *Journal of Broadcasting, 20,* 35-50.

Moore, W. (1969). Occupational socialization. In D. Goslin (Ed.), *Handbook of socialization theory and research.* Chicago: Rand McNally.

Mortimer, J., & Simmons, R. (1978). Adult socialization. In R. Turner, J. Coleman, & R. Fox (Eds.), *Annual review of sociology.* Palo Alto, CA: Annual Reviews.

Moscovici, S. (1985). Social influence and conformity. In G. Lindzey & E. Aronson (Eds.), *Handbook of social psychology* (Vol. 2). New York: Random House.

National Institute of Mental Health. (1982). *Television and behavior: Ten years of scientific progress and implications for the eighties.* Rockville, MD: NIMH.

Newcomb, T. (1961). *The acquaintance process.* New York: Holt, Rinehart & Winston.

O'Keefe, G. (1973). Coorientation variables in family study. *American Behavioral Scientist, 16,* 513-535.

O'Keefe, G. (1985). Taking a bite out of crime: The impact of a public information campaign. *Communication Research, 12,* 147-178.

O'Keefe, G., & Reid-Nash, K. (1982). *Fear arousal in a media information campaign: Some preliminary findings.* Paper presented to Annual Convention of the Midwest Association for Public Opinion Research, Chicago.

Parsons, T. (1961). An outline of the social system. In T. Parsons, E. Shils, K. Naegele, & J. Pitts (Eds.), *Theories of society.* New York: Free Press.

Percy, L., & Rossiter, J. (1980). *Advertising strategy: A communication theory approach.* New York: Praeger.

Pool, I. (1973). Communication systems. In I. Pool & F. Frey (Eds.), *Handbook of communication.* Chicago: Rand McNally.

Porter, L., Lawler, E., & Hackman, J. (1975). *Behavior in organizations.* New York: McGraw-Hill.

Riley, M., Foner, A., Hess, B., & Toby, M. (1969). Socialization for the middle and later years. In D. Goslin (Ed.), *Handbook of socialization theory and research.* Chicago: Rand McNally.

Roberts, D. (1985). Effects of mass communication. In G. Lindzey & E. Aronson (Eds.), *Handbook of Social Psychology* (Vol. 2). New York: Random House.

Roberts, D., Bachen, C., Hornby, M., & Hernandez-Ramos, P. (1984). Reading and television: Predictors of reading achievement at different age levels. *Communication Research, 11,* 9-49.

Rosengren, K. (1983). Communication research: One paradigm, or four? *Journal of Communication, 33,* 185-207.

Rosengren, K. (1986). Media linkages between culture and other societal systems. In M. McLaughlin (Ed.), *Communication yearbook 9.* Newbury Park, CA: Sage.

Rosengren, E., Wenner, L., & Palmgreen, P. (1985). *Media gratification research: Current perspectives.* Newbury Park, CA: Sage.

Rubin, A. (1982). Directions in television and aging research. *Journal of Broadcasting, 26,* 537-551.

Rushton, J. (1980). *Altruism, socialization and society.* Englewood Cliffs, NJ: Prentice-Hall.

Rushton, J. (1982). Television and prosocial behavior. In NIMH, *Television and behavior: Ten years of scientific progress and implications for the eighties: Vol. 2. Technical reviews.* Rockville, MD: NIMH.

Singer, J., & Singer, D. (1980). *Television, imagination and aggression: A study of preschoolers' play.* Hillsdale, NJ: Lawrence Erlbaum.

Smith, M. (1968). Competence and socialization. In J. Clausen (Ed.), *Socialization and society.* Boston: Little, Brown.

Spence, J., Deaux, K., & Helmreich, R. (1985). Sex roles in contemporary American society. In G. Lindzey & E. Aronson, *Handbook of social psychology* (Vol. 2). New York: Random House.

Surgeon General's Scientific Advisory Committee on Television and Social Behavior. (1972). *Television and social behavior.* Washington, DC: Government Printing Office.

Tims, A. (1984). *Socialization to the news media during adolescence.* Paper presented to Annual Convention of Speech Communication Association, Chicago.

Van Maanen, J. (1976). Breaking in: Socialization to work. In R. Dubin (Ed.), *Handbook of work, organization and society.* Chicago: Rand McNally.

Ward, S., Wackman, D., & Wartella, E. (1977). *How children learn to buy: The development of consumer information processing skills.* Newbury Park, CA: Sage.

Wentworth, W. (1980). *Context and understanding: An inquiry into socialization theory.* New York: Elsevier.

White, R. (1959). Motivation reconsidered: The concept of competence. *Psychological Review, 66,* 297-333.

White, R. (1960). Competence and the psychosexual states of development. In M. Jones (Ed.), *Nebraska Symposium on Motivation 1960.* Lincoln: University of Nebraska Press.

Whiting, J. (1968). Socialization: Anthropological aspects. In *International encyclopedia of the social sciences* (Vol. 14). New York: Collier-Macmillan.

Whorf, B. (1952). *Collected papers in metalinguistics.* Washington, DC: Foreign Service Institute.

Williams, F., LaRose, R., & Frost, F. (1981). *Children, television and sex-role stereotyping.* New York: Praeger.

Wilson, D. (1984). *Political opinion change in parent-adolescent dyads.* Paper presented at the Annual Convention of the Association for Education in Journalism and Mass Communication, Gainesville, FL.

Youniss, J. (1980). *Parents and peers in social development* Chicago: University of Chicago Press.

Yum, J. (1982). Communication diversity and information acquisition among Korean immigrants in Hawaii. *Human Communication Research, 8,* 154-169.

Zigler, E., & Child, I. (1973). *Socialization and personality development.* Reading, WA: Addison-Wesley.

Zigler, E., & Seitz, V. (1978). Changing trends in socialization theory and research. *American Behavioral Scientist, 21,* 721-746.

15   Persuasion

GERALD R. MILLER
Michigan State University

TWO generalizations strike me as appropriate starting points for this chapter. First, with the possible exception of language, more has undoubtedly been written and said about persuasion than any other single process, problem, or issue relating to human communication. In the past 22 years, three editions of the *Handbook of Social Psychology* have appeared. The two-volume maiden edition of this classic reference work (Lindzey, 1954) contains chapters by Bert Green on attitude measurement and by Carl Hovland on the effects of the mass media. In addition, several of the other chapters traffic heavily in material germane to persuasion. The ambitious, five-volume second edition (Lindzey & Aronson, 1969) offers a chapter on attitudes and attitude change (which lists 42 pages of relevant references), by William McGuire; attitude measurement, by William Scott; effects of the mass media, by Walter Weiss; and numerous other chapters touching on issues relevant to persuasion. The most recent two-volume edition (Lindzey & Aronson, 1985) contains an updated chapter on attitudes and attitude change by McGuire (also listing 42 pages of references, albeit a number of different ones from the earlier chapter), and chapters by Serge Moscovici on social influence and conformity, Donald Roberts and Nathan Maccoby on effects of mass communication, and Robyn Dawes and Tom Smith on attitude and opinion measurement. Once again, material of interest to students of persuasion surfaces in many of the other chapters.

Nor is evidence of the pervasive interest in persuasion limited to the three editions of this handbook. The influential early series of Yale volumes, edited by Carl Hovland and his associates, deals almost exclusively with persuasive communication. The *Handbook of Rhetorical and Communication Theory* (Arnold & Bowers, 1984), authored entirely by people whose disciplinary roots lie in speech communication and communication, provides chapters on changing attitudes and gaining compliance, by Michael Burgoon, Judee Burgoon, and myself; maintaining public values, by Roderick Hart; and the rhetoric of social movements, by Herbert Simons, Elizabeth Mechling, and Howard Schreier. Finally, to avoid further belaboring of a perhaps already belabored point, a frequency count of the topics dealt with in articles appearing in the major journals of speech communication, communication, social psychology, journalism, and other related areas would likely reveal that persuasion is represented as amply as any other topic—though I cannot say for certain, since I have not undertaken this arduous task.

The continuing interest in matters of persuasion stems partially from the fact that symbolic inducement and symbolic control have traditionally been conceived of as issues of central import to the communication scholar. From Aristotle's (1954) classical conception of rhetoric as the art of discovering persuasive proofs, to Berlo's (1960, p. 12) assertion that "we communicate to influence—to affect with intent," to Miller and Steinberg's (1975, p. 12) contention that "the basic function of all communication is to control the environment so as to realize certain physical, economic, or social rewards from it" runs an unsevered thread linking human symbolizing and message-making with human influence and control. To be sure, some critics have charged that this concern with influence and control has often been blown out of scholarly and ethical proportion, but even the most trenchant skeptics are willing to grant that persuasion is *an* important function of human communication, even if it is not *the* sole or predominant function.

Aside from its scholarly justification, however, persuasion stimulates perennial interest because of its potential social significance. Those who occupy positions of power in society have an abiding concern with ways that communication can be used to cement their privileged positions. It is certainly no accident that most communication research funded by government agencies and private corporations centers on improving the persuasive effectiveness of messages emanating from these powerful collectivities—whether the issue is selling agricultural innovations to underdeveloped societies, selling beer to perpetually thirsty consumers, or selling political candidates to a fickle electorate; the name of the communicative game is persuasion. Conversely, the "have nots" of society look to persuasive communication as one tool for promulgating social change, for unseating the present power structure, or, at the very least, for reducing the starkly apparent economic and social inequities between those who wield political and economic power and those who do not. Indeed, one need not even look to weighty matters of business and state to discover the deeply rooted social significance of persuasion: Almost every individual ponders how she or he can communicate so as to be lauded more, liked more, and loved more. Thus even if there were no compelling scholarly reasons for studying persuasion, its social centrality would ensure its continued investigation.

The preceding discussion of persuasion's social import provides a convenient transition for my second generalization: Despite the vast number of pages written and the countless studies undertaken about persuasion, many students of communication find it impossible to shake the uneasy feeling that we have precious little reliable, socially relevant knowledge about it. Laments regarding our collective ignorance about persuasion are commonplace, and more than one communication researcher has been heard to characterize persuasion research as a scholarly dead end. In short, while students of persuasion have labored long and diligently, the fruits of their labors continue to be viewed with skepticism.

Precise evaluation of this claim regarding collective ignorance about the process and outcomes of persuasion is, of course, impossible. It is one thing to say that not all that *ideally* should be known is known, quite another to assert that nothing (or "almost nothing," or "not enough") has been discovered. The systematic empirical study of persuasion is a relatively recent scholarly innovation, its roots extending less than 50 years deep into the intellectual topsoil. Moreover, much early research centered on verifying knowledge claims generally thought to be part of the conventional wisdom and commonsense; consider, for instance, the frequently replicated finding that high-credible sources are more persuasive than their low-credible counterparts. Unexciting as such findings may be, adherence to an empiricist epistemology dictated that the work must be done. Nor are all present findings this mundane: To mention but two examples, work on inducing resistance to persuasion (e.g., McGuire, 1961, 1962, 1964; McGuire & Papageorgis, 1961) and counterattitudinal advocacy (Festinger & Carlsmith, 1959; Miller, 1973) has yielded interesting, intuitively nonobvious results. Thus there are grounds for offering a more charitable assessment of current progress in persuasion research than the most severe critics have been prone to offer.

Notwithstanding this fact, however, it seems fair to say that the search for scientific knowledge about persuasion has been slowed by several dominant research attitudes and practices. The first of these is an ideological aversion against studying—or at least, an ideological reluctance to study—a number of variables that doubtless exert a powerful impact in many persuasive transactions. Simons's (1974) charge that the field subscribes to a "drawing room" conception of persuasion has much to recommend it. As a consequence, considerable energy has been expended in examining the persuasive effects of such dimensions of credibility as *competence* and *trustworthiness*. By contrast, the role of *means control,* or the extent to which the persuader controls rewards and punishments of import to the persuasive target (Kelman, 1961), has been largely ignored, even though any informed layperson knows it is a variable that explains much of the variance in numerous persuasive transactions. Similarly, hardly any attention has been directed at the role of physical attractiveness in the persuasive process; indeed, until Berscheid, Walster, and their colleagues (e.g., Berscheid, 1981; Berscheid & Walster, 1974) placed them in front of the investigative mirror in the late 60s, "looks" had been largely overlooked by social and behavioral researchers, even though it is all but universally agreed that beauty, skin deep though it may be, provides a persuasive edge in daily social commerce. There are undoubtedly multiple reasons for these omissions, and others like them, but certainly one relevant deterrent is the implicit (and occasionally explicit) value judgment that persuasive life should not go on this way, that people should not be able to wield social influence because of carrots, sticks, and beguiling features.

A second reason for the perceived lack of progress in persuasion research stems from the tendency of researchers to study persuasion almost solely from the vantage point of mass media and public communication—that is, a one-to-many context. While some branching out to other contexts, such as the interpersonal arena, has occurred in recent years, an observation Michael Burgoon and I made in 1978 is still relevant:

> Most persuasion research [relies] on a one-to-many situational context. In the traditional persuasion study, a relatively large aggregate of receiver/persuadees—a classroom of students, the members of a PTA, and so forth—is exposed to a message attributed to an individual or an institutional source. With few exceptions [a] linear, unidirectional view of the "transaction" is enforced by the fact that the message is not even presented live. Instead the persuadees read it, or see and/or hear it on video or audiotape, a procedure that prevents any meaningful reciprocal influence by the audience. After message exposure, the persuadees respond to some measure of persuasive effect, usually a paper-and-pencil assessment of attitude change. Thus, the entire enterprise closely resembles a public speaking or mass media setting, though even here the fit is far from perfect, since there is little opportunity for the kinds of audience social facilitation effects one would expect in real-life communicative settings. (Miller & Burgoon, 1978, p. 33)

Since only a small percentage of communicative exchanges takes place in this one-to-many context, why have researchers mined it so extensively? One possible explanation has already been mentioned: the fact that much persuasion research has been supported and sponsored by parties who are primarily interested in exerting influence in this context. Furthermore, though the import of persuasive encounters in face-to-face, more interpersonal settings is easily endorsed, the process is not so easily studied in such environs, particularly if the investigator places a premium on the kinds of control procedures that permit relatively unambiguous isolation of relevant variables. To seat 50 undergraduate students in a classroom and measure the persuasive impact of a written or spoken message is one thing, to "shadow" each student individually, as persuasive messages are exchanged in dormitory rooms, cafeterias, bars, and faculty offices—to mention but a few possible settings for such exchanges—is quite another, both pragmatically and ethically.

A third limitation of prior research lies in its almost exclusive reliance on a single persuasive message. Despite the obvious fact that most of us are bombarded every day with a barrage of persuasive messages, employing widely varying strategies and tactics, about particular issues, ideas, or individuals, persuasion researchers have continued the quest for knowledge and understanding by examining the immediate, and often transient impact of one message. Although this approach usually leaves them with the comforting thought that they have a reasonable grasp of what, if anything, is making a difference, it is a dismally inadequate representation of how persuasion functions in daily social life. This is not to deny the occasional powerful impact of a single persuasive communication, but rather to emphasize that, as a rule, people's attitudes and behaviors are shaped by exposure to multiple competing messages.

In addition to issues of accessibility and research control, it should be candidly admitted that the allure of single-message studies is linked to the prevailing system of professional rewards. Promotions and tenure are directly related to the frequency of publication, rather than the contribution of a particular endeavor. In the language of the claim I am making, faculty colleagues, deans, and provosts are more persuaded by a series of persuasive messages, each representing a separate publication, than by one scholarly tour de force. Small wonder, then, that many researchers have clung to the simple, rewarding old ways of conducting persuasion research and have largely resisted exploring alternatives they themselves have endorsed.

Although far from a comprehensive inventory of problems plaguing current persuasion research (see, e.g., Miller & Burgoon, 1978; Miller, Burgoon, & Burgoon, 1984), the three limitations mentioned above, along with my opening remarks about the pervasiveness of persuasion research, serve to define my central aims in this chapter. Since the voluminous persuasion literature defies exhaustive synthesis in a chapter of modest length, I shall not attempt this task, even though the term "handbook" is often associated with it. Instead, I will sample selectively from work relevant to the intrapersonal and interpersonal levels of communication, and will conclude with a brief postscript concerning the macrosocietal level. Furthermore, given the limitations of most prior persuasion research, I will undertake this journey critically, seeking to underline gaps in the present literature and to suggest promising avenues for future research. Hopefully, the end product, while certainly not illuminating all the nooks and crannies, will cast a few rays of light on areas of persuasion research presently clouded by theoretical, empirical, and procedural shadows—though whether my remarks improve or impair vision is for the reader to decide.

A WORKING DEFINITION OF "PERSUASION"

The definition of "persuasion" that guides my discussion closely parallels a definition of "being persuaded" formulated six years earlier (Miller, 1980b, p. 15):

The term "persuasion" refers to situations where attempts are made to modify behavior by symbolic transactions (messages) that are sometimes, but not always, linked with coercive force (indirectly coercive) and that appeal to the reason and emotions of the intended persuadee(s).

Several implications of this definition merit attention. First, persuasion is conceived to be a process that is both *social* and *symbolic*. To say that persuasion is social is to underscore the requirement that persuasive transactions involve a minimum of two human transactants. To be sure, numerous intrapersonal processes powerfully affect persuasive message exchanges, some of the more important of which will be considered in the next section of this chapter. Moreover, an assortment of ordinary language terms refer to persuasion as an intrapersonal process—for example, "talking oneself into something" and "self-persuasion." But despite these facts, the primary focus of the student of persuasion concerns symbolic exchanges between two or more persons that aim at modifying their behaviors in some way.

To say that persuasion is symbolic underscores the primacy of *communication;* it stresses that primary interest is directed at the verbal and nonverbal code systems employed by the transactants. Granted, the persuasive power of the word is often buttressed by coercive means at the disposal of the persuader; as the definition duly recognizes, persuasion is frequently *indirectly coercive*. But when bombing runs on Tripoli replace words to Qaddafi *threatening* bombing runs if Libya does not abandon its terrorist activities (to use but one currently relevant example) indirectly coercive persuasion is replaced by directly coercive acts of warfare. In terms of my earlier renunciation of the "drawing room" conception of persuasion, then, the definition grants that persuasive effectiveness often requires more than words, while at the same time emphasizing the centrality of words and their accompanying nonverbal behaviors to the persuasive process.

Persuasion seeks to *modify behavior* in one of three ways: by changing existing responses, by reinforcing existing responses, or by shaping new responses (Miller, 1980b). Traditionally, persuasion has been conceived of primarily in terms of the first objective; examples of suasory discourse usually stress such things as persuading smokers to quit smoking, persuading farmers using traditional methods to adopt modern farming practices (as in the voluminous literature on diffusion of innovations; see, e.g., Rogers, 1962, 1983; Rogers & Shoemaker, 1971), or persuading property owners opposed to a millage increase to vote for it. As important and challenging as this objective may be, it is only part of the vital social role played by persuasion. Throughout the formative years of development—and for that matter, throughout the entire life cycle—socialization and learning rely heavily on persuasive messages that seek to shape stable response patterns where no stable patterns previously existed. And even when these patterns have been established, most of them are constantly challenged by competing messages from other persuasive communicators. Thus to ensure that these learned predispositions persist, response-reinforcing persuasive messages are essential. For the most part, the literature has referred to this latter objective as *inducing resistance to persuasion* (McGuire, 1961, 1962, 1964; McGuire & Papageorgis, 1961). Though the distinction may have some pragmatic value, I prefer to conceive of such *immunizing* messages (McGuire, 1969) as persuasive transactions.

Finally, to say that persuasive messages appeal to the reason and emotions of intended persuadees partially sustains a venerable practice that dates back at least as far as the Aristotelian distinction between *logos* (logical proof) and *pathos* (emotional proof). Some writers have pushed the distinction further, arguing that *conviction* is a process relying on symbolic appeals to reason while *persuasion* derives its effectiveness from symbolic appeals to emotion. The wisdom of this strict dichotomy has been questioned (Rowell, 1932a, 1932b; Woolbert, 1917), and the arguments against it strike me as convincing. Attempts to distinguish crisply between logical and emotional appeals have been problematic (Becker, 1963) for almost all ordinary language conveys emotional overtones. Thus as I have suggested elsewhere, "it seems more useful to conceive of persuasive discourse as an amalgam of logic and emotion, while at the same time granting that particular messages may differ in the relative amount of each element" (Miller, 1980b, p. 15).

INTRAPERSONAL FACTORS

Earlier I expressed my preference for conceptualizing the persuasive process as a social transaction involving the linkage of two or more communicators via messages aimed at achieving particular attitudinal and behavioral outcomes. Notwithstanding my bias, the vast majority of scientific excursions into the realm of persuasion have numbered intrapersonal factors as traveling companions. Such factors are viewed as essential explanatory mechanisms for understanding both the responses of intended persuadees cast in the traditional role of message recipients—as in the case of those most venerable of persuasive concepts, *attitude* and *attitude change*, or in the more recent concern with *cognitive responses* to persuasive messages (Petty & Cacioppo, 1986a, 1986b; Petty, Ostrom, & Brock, 1981a)—and the responses of intended persuadees cast in the more novel role of persuasive communicators—as in the case of the lengthy debate over the antecedent mediators of persuasive effects resulting from engaging in *counterattitudinal advocacy* (Miller, 1973). An examination of these intrapersonal issues should serve the dual purpose of placing them in historical and scientific perspective and of identifying persistent problems and ambiguities associated with them. Obviously, however, my remarks concerning these issues should be interpreted as relating to the other levels of analysis covered later in this chapter, not as sovereign attempts to provide answers to crucial questions regarding the persuasive process.

Attitude and Attitude Change

In 1935, Gordon Allport confidently proclaimed *attitude* to be the most important concept in developing a viable discipline of social psychology. DeFleur and Westie (1963, p. 17) cautiously assert, "Perhaps no other concept from the behavioral sciences has been used so widely by theorists and researchers as the term *attitude*." Nowhere is the investigational hegemony of the attitude construct more apparent than in the persuasion literature; save for a handful of exceptions, attitude change has consistently remained the standard for assessing the relative impact of persuasive messages.

Several obvious considerations account for this continuing widespread allegiance. Intuitively, modeling persuasion as a process in which symbolic stimuli (persuasive messages) trigger internal evaluative predispositions (attitudes) that subsequently motivate desired overt behaviors (compliance with persuasive objectives) makes sense. After all, the argument goes, how can people be expected to behave in prescribed ways if they are not favorably inclined toward the prescriptions? Thus conventional wisdom has long held that "education" (translated "attitude change") must precede demands for action or behavioral change, particularly in a democratic society: Neither the white citizens of the American South nor the Afrikaners of South Africa can be expected to integrate their societies until they have acquired favorable attitudes toward integration. Nor can children be relied upon to comply with persuasive demands because of the lure of tokens or M&Ms; instead, they must first be convinced that the demanded actions and behaviors are "good for them." In short, though people are sometimes guilty of failing to practice their persuasive preachments—What parent has not on occasion abandoned rational reasons in favor of the carrot or the stick?—favorable attitudes are typically pictured as logical precursors of compliant behaviors.

Moreover, the prevailing conception of attitudes as internal mediators of behavior fits nicely with the consensual view of theory construction in the social and behavioral sciences. Spence's (1944) insightful comment that theories in the behavioral sciences primarily consist of the postulation of intervening variables to account for observed regularities in and deviations from observable stimulus-response linkages is as accurate today as it was in 1944: The phrase "theories of attitude change" remains practically synonymous with the phrase "theories of persuasion," and the mechanisms invoked to explain the process of attitude formation and change—*cognitive inconsistency, learning, attributional processes, counterarguing,* and the like—share common status as scientific shorthand labels for private events assumed to be occurring, if at all, *within* persuasive communicators. Though there has been no shortage of tinkering with various mechanisms—and, hence, various theories—the fundamental metatheoretical logic has escaped largely unscathed, so much so that heretics such as Skinner (1953, 1971), who have challenged the prevailing preoccupation with real or imagined mental events, have been saddled with the potentially pejorative label *atheoretic.*

Finally, as noted earlier in this chapter, attitude change has continued its reign as the dominant signpost of persuasive effects because of methodological and procedural convenience. In their typical operational form as paper-and-pencil scale-marking behaviors, attitudes can be quickly and conveniently measured. Compare, for example, the relatively minor logistical problems resulting from asking male respondents to report verbally how they feel about conferring greater social, economic, and political equality to women with the horrendous difficulties involved in "tailing" these same males and observing how they actually treat women they encounter in social, economic, and political arenas. Furthermore, the equal-appearing interval scales common to most persuasion studies lend themselves to mathematical operations that are impossible with nominal or ordinal behavioral measures of persuasive impact; in common parlance, they permit "more complex" data analyses. In a field perennially self-conscious about its scientific status and where such status is often equated with methodological and statistical sophistication, the capability to perform complex mathematical operations is a prized possession. And lest the preceding prognosis seems unduly cynical, it should also be stressed that the unraveling of some theoretical puzzles requires persuasion researchers to probe complex relationships represented by higher-order interactions; probes that can only be successfully completed with intervally scaled data.

While the three considerations discussed above have contributed heavily to the centrality of the attitude and attitude change constructs in persuasion research, chinks in the protective armor surrounding these intrapersonal factors have resulted in difficult theoretical and method-ological problems. To some extent, the notion that the persuasive pro-cess is best modeled by conceiving of attitudes as precursors of behavior stems from the widely shared bias toward viewing communicative trans-actions as highly mindful, cognitive events—a bias called into question by communication scholars (e.g., Berger & Douglas, 1982; Miller, 1977). Such a mindful bias implies that individuals possess neatly orga-nized cognitive and affective maps of their overall attitude structures and that these maps constitute a master plan for guiding and directing responses to persuasive messages.

A less mindful view holds that most people do not devote a great deal of cognitive contemplation to how they feel about various matters; as a result, they may often have no clear picture or even be largely ignorant of their attitudes regarding a particular object, act, or situation. In the absence of a sharply defined attitudinal stance, individuals are likely to examine their behaviors as the best available evidence for inferring their attitudes, at least under certain conditions (Bem, 1965, 1968, 1972). In terms of Zetterberg's (1965) scheme for classifying propositions, the posited relationship between attitudes and behaviors thus can be more usefully conceived of as *reversible* rather than *irreversible:* To illustrate using Bem's familiar example, people may reason, "I must like brown bread, because I'm always eating it" (behavior implying attitudes) instead of, or in addition to, "I like brown bread, so I should eat some for breakfast" (attitudes implying behavior).

Not only does Bem's self-perception theory reverse the prevailing temporal linkage between attitudes and behaviors, certain assumptions of cognitive consistency theories, particularly cognitive dissonance theory (Festinger, 1957) as applied to forced compliance situations (Festinger & Carlsmith, 1959), foster the conclusion that behaviors fre-quently play a powerful role in shaping subsequent attitudes. Results of numerous studies (see, e.g., Brehm & Cohen, 1962; Miller, 1973; Miller & Burgoon, 1973; Wicklund & Brehm, 1976) clearly demon-strate that when individuals are induced to engage in belief-discrepant behaviors, including advocating attitudinally discrepant positions, they subsequently report more favorable attitudes toward the initially belief-discrepant activity or position. Thus to return to a previous example, even if persons report initially unfavorable attitudes toward integration, their participation in integrated activities or their presentation of mes-sages supporting integration may culminate in more favorable attitudes toward integration, an outcome that refutes the conventional wisdom regarding the necessity of changing attitudes before successful behav-ioral changes can be instituted. These issues will be examined more fully in the later section dealing with counterattitudinal advocacy.

Both the theoretical indispensibility and the procedural superiority of the attitude and attitude change constructs are called into question by one of the most persistent problems facing persuasion researchers: the misleadingly labeled *attitudes versus behavior problem* (see e.g., Cushman & McPhee, 1980; Liska, 1975). Stated in ordinary language, the problem arises from the fact that how people say they feel about something often fails to correspond with their other behaviors, a commonly recognized social phenomenon that accounts for the popularity of such adages as "Actions speak louder than words" and "Talk's cheap!" Stated in the more technical argot of persuasion researchers, the problem can be phrased as follows: Verbal indicators of attitude, such as the paper-and-pencil scale-marking behaviors obtained in most persuasion studies, typically correlate minimally with other attitudinally consistent behaviors.

The misleading label attached to the problem stems from the fact that researchers have fallen prey to a reification fallacy. Since some type of scale designed to elicit verbal responses (e.g., Gillham & Woelfel, 1977; Guttman, 1944; Likert, 1932; Osgood, Suci, & Tannenbaum, 1957; Thurstone & Chave, 1929) has been used in all but a handful of attitude and attitude change studies, these measures have come to be regarded, in some mysterious way, *as the attitude itself,* whereas other types of attitudinally related responses have been labeled *behaviors.* Actually, of course, given the prevailing view of attitudes as intervening variables, no behavioral index, including indices based on verbal reports, provides a direct measure of attitude or attitude change: All statements about these two constructs are, of necessity, inferential. Thus the problem facing persuasion researchers centers on the low correlation between verbal attitudinal responses and other types of attitudinally related behaviors. Yet even this conclusion rests on scanty evidence, since few studies have compared the relationship between two or more operational indicants of attitude (see DeFleur & Westie, 1958; Festinger, 1964, for examples of studies undertaking such comparisons).

When labeled accurately, the existence of this problem is less disturbing and surprising than many writers have pictured it. Campbell (1963) emphasizes that the response threshold for verbal behavior is typically low; stated differently, verbal manifestations of attitude usually involve relatively low effort and potential cost. By contrast, giving money, spending time circulating petitions, risking incarceration, and being executed, to mention but a few other potential indicants of attitude, are usually more effortful and costly; in Campbell's terms, the response threshold is higher for such behaviors. If laypersons are not surprised that many persons who profess support of the Democratic Party, the American Civil Liberties Union, and the National Organization for Women resist contributing time or money to these organizations' causes, students of persuasion should scarcely be perplexed by this fact.

Moreover, in numerous daily communicative transactions, verbal conformity with a particular position is itself sufficient to satisfy would-be persuaders. When attempting to win an argument, a simple verbal assent such as "That's right!" or "I agree!" often signals success, and the assertion "78% of those surveyed agree with the President's arms control policy" serves as ample evidence that an address from the Oval Office was on target. In a society increasingly dominated by symbols, it is both theoretically and socially valuable to understand how persuasive messages can be used to shape and alter verbal responses.

Such considerations aside, however, the fact remains that optimally useful theories of persuasion should permit reasonably accurate prediction of other message effects besides verbal responses; though communication researchers have a valid interest in "talk," other persuasive outcomes also demand attention. At least two broad strategies offer promise in pursuing this objective. First, attempts can be made to refine and extend the mediational calculus used to determine probable persuasive outcomes. The work of Fishbein and his colleagues (Ajzen & Fishbein, 1969, 1970; Fishbein, 1963, 1965, 1966, 1967a, 1967b; Fishbein & Ajzen, 1972, 1974; Fishbein & Raven, 1962) represents a case in point. Second, widespread acceptance of the scientific superiority of the *latent process* (DeFleur & Westie, 1963) or *readiness to respond* (Miller et al., 1984) view regarding attitude and attitude change—that is, the conceptualization of attitude as an intervening variable—can be challenged more aggressively (Miller, 1980a) or at least supplemented and extended by work that conceptualizes attitude as *behavioral consistency* or *response probability* (DeFleur & Westie, 1963; Green, 1954; Miller et al., 1984). At very least, persuasion researchers should relax their slavish commitment to scale-marking behavior and conduct more studies using other behavioral measures of persuasive effect. If nothing else, such an extension would permit more confident assessment of the consistency, or convergent validity, of various behavioral indicants of attitude and attitude change. Lip service has long been paid to this latter strategy, but since talk is also reasonably cheap in the research arena, it remains to be seen whether these verbal protestations will begin to be more widely accompanied by other attitudinally consistent behaviors.

Cognitive Responses

As the preceding section illustrates, students of persuasion have always evinced a lively interest in cognitive responses; indeed, so venerable a treatise as Aristotle's (1954) *Rhetoric* discusses numerous concepts grounded in the cognitive and affective states of persuasive communicators. The term is used here in a more restricted sense to refer to several lines of recent theorizing and inquiry that view cognitive responses, generally, as "all the thoughts that pass through a person's mind while he or she anticipates a communication, listens to a communication, or reflects on a communication" (Petty, Ostrom, & Brock, 1981b, p. 7). More particularly, a cognitive response is conceptualized as "a unit of information pertaining to an object or issue that is the result of cognitive processing" (Cacioppo, Harkins, & Petty, 1981, p. 37). Advocates of a cognitive responses approach argue that "an understanding of the thoughts produced in the persuasion context is essential if the process of attitude change is to be understood fully" (Petty et al., 1981b, p. 15).

In terms of an earlier observation in this chapter, the preceding definitions and contentions underscore the fact that a concern with cognitive responses emphasizes the mindful nature of persuasion, at least if satisfactory understanding of its processes and outcomes is to be achieved. This is not to say that attitude and behavior change never occur somewhat mindlessly; indeed, one of the most extensively studied cognitive response models of persuasion, Petty and Cacioppo's (1968a, 1986a, 1986b) elaboration likelihood model, posits two routes to persuasion: a central, or mindful route, characterized by cognitive processing and evaluation of message content; and a peripheral, or mindless route, characterized by affective responses to extra-message cues such as source or context. Though the theoretical posture differs, the major conclusion closely resembles one drawn much earlier by Kelman (1961) in his discussion of social influence processes: Persuasive effects accruing from the peripheral route are relatively ephemeral and highly dependent upon the maintenance of external contingencies of reinforcement; effects resulting from the central route are relatively enduring and less dependent upon continuing external reinforcement—in a sense, these effects are seen as having greater motive force, or functional autonomy.

Space does not permit a detailed assessment of the research fruits yielded by this reaffirmation of the scientific hegemony of intrapersonal cognitive processes; for that matter, the harvest is far from complete, and any such blanket evaluation would be premature. That the approach has generated interesting research (e.g., Petty & Cacioppo, 1986a, 1986b) and is beginning to generate scholarly controversy (e.g., Stiff, 1986) are certainly points in its favor. Moreover, the general assumptions of the cognitive responses approach provide an interesting, and potentially useful way of reconceptualizing the findings of numerous persuasion studies conducted from varying theoretical perspectives (e.g., Burgoon & Miller, 1985; Petty et al., 1981a). Finally, whether an asset or a liability, the renewed concern with cognitive responses squares nicely with the prevailing and persisting value judgment that theories of persuasion *ought to be* grounded in rationality and reflection rather than the emotional caprices of message recipients or the coercive weapons of message sources.

Despite the potential utility of the cognitive responses construct, two notes of caution should be sounded. First, even the most enthusiastic proponents of the approach grant that the information processing that does occur is often biased (e.g., Petty & Cacioppo, 1986b); only when potential persuadees are relatively uncommitted about a matter is the cognitive calculus likely to proceed according to classical principles of rational thought. Biased processing results largely from the salience of previously acquired information, but the salience of such information is frequently triggered by peripheral cues associated with message sources or contexts. Given this fact, such peripheral cues assume added theoretical importance, so much so that it may be possible to explain many important persuasive outcomes without invoking inferences to mediating cognitive processes.

Second, no one seriously questions that in many persuasive transactions, effectiveness hinges largely on peripheral source and context cues. While these circumstances are of theoretical import, my aim here is to stress their social significance. Optimally useful theories of persuasion must eventually achieve the objective of ecological validity; that is, they must provide empirical insights into the workings of persuasion as it is *actually practiced* in daily communicative commerce. In this era of 30-second commercials and political plugs that seem to rely heavily on the peripheral route for their effectiveness, healthy skepticism about the eventual heuristic worth of complex information-processing models emphasizing cognitive responses is warranted; indeed, cynics might assert that the necessary message content requirements for invoking such models are limited to academic debates and to media sources serving a distinct minority of the population. To take this position is not to dismiss totally the value of the cognitive responses construct but rather to suggest that it may fall considerably short of the status of a useful universal mechanism for dealing with persuasive effects.

Counterattitudinal Advocacy

Counterattitudinal advocacy itself is not an intrapersonal factor, but rather a full-blown persuasive paradigm. When used with persuasive intent, counterattitudinal advocacy involves a situation where *"an individual is induced, by some means, to encode and/or to present a persuasive message that demonstrably conflicts with his initial attitudes. . . .* Central to this persuasive paradigm is the assumption that the individual will, in a sense, *persuade himself,* rather than *being persuaded* by another"* (Miller, 1973). Since this paradigm assigns the central symbolizing role to the intended persuadee, Burgoon and I (Miller & Burgoon, 1973) chose to characterize it as an *active participation* paradigm in contrast to the more traditional *passive reception* paradigm where persuadees are the targets of messages emanating from persuasive sources.

When seeking explanations for the persuasive efficacy of counterattitudinal advocacy, however, intrapersonal factors have typically been of central import. Because the earliest research employing the paradigm was closely wedded to cognitive dissonance theory, it is hardly surprising that dissonance theory interpretations have assumed a prominent place in the literature. Festinger (1957; Festinger & Carlsmith, 1959) contends that counterattitudinal advocacy derives its persuasive impact from the dissonant cognitions (1) I believe X, and (2) I am publicly advocating non-X), an explanation subsequently labeled the "early" dissonance view. Later dissonance theorizing (e.g., Aronson, 1968; Carlsmith, 1968) departs from Festinger's position by shifting the locus of the dissonant cognitions:

> In the experiments on counterattitudinal advocacy . . . I would suggest that it is incorrect to say that dissonance existed between the cognitions "I believe the task is dull" and "I told someone that the task was interesting" [the manipulation used by Festinger and Carlsmith, 1959]. . . . What is dissonant is the cognition "I am a decent, truthful human being" and the cognition "I have misled a person; I have conned him into believing something which just isn't true; he thinks that I really believe it and I cannot set him straight because I probably won't see him again." (Aronson, 1968, p. 24)

In a nutshell, then, the "early" dissonance interpretation stresses the illogical link between cognitions per se while the "later" explanation centers on the moral dilemma engendered by lying to potentially vulnerable message recipients.

Regardless of disagreement concerning the locus of cognitive dissonance, all dissonance theorizing stresses the central role of *justification* in mediating the persuasive impact of counterattitudinal advocacy. If the advocate can identify other cognitions to justify her or his belief-discrepant message behavior, the likelihood of self-persuasion (i.e., attitudinal or behavioral change consistent with the initially belief-discrepant position) is sharply diminished. In other words, certain features of the situation, such as substantial monetary reward or minimal perceived choice, permit the advocate to reduce cognitive dissonance while remaining persuasively unaffected: Magnitude of justification is thus inversely related to self-persuasion following counterattitudinal advocacy. Furthermore, there is consensus that justification is best conceptualized as an intervening variable rooted in the perceptions of counterattitudinal advocates themselves; indeed, the research has suffered persistent criticism because researchers have usually manipulated justifying features of the situation with little or no concern for the meaning assigned to these features by research participants cast in the role of counterattitudinal advocates (e.g., Aronson, 1966; Miller, 1973; Rosenberg, 1965, 1966).

Further complicating the situation is the fact that another theoretical posture reverses the hypothesized relationship between justification and self-persuasion: Conflict or incentive theorists (Elms & Janis, 1965; Janis, 1968; Janis & Gilmore, 1965) posit a direct relationship between the two variables. Stated in everyday language, these theorists contend that self-persuasion is furthered by rewarding people handsomely for lying, a contention that squares nicely with commonsense reasoning. A number of studies exist to support both the dissonance and the conflict interpretations of the influence of justification on self-persuasion; fully a decade of research on counterattitudinal advocacy is dominated by disputes arising from the real or ostensibly competing claims of the two positions.

In addition to the center-stage debate regarding intrapersonal factors waged by dissonance and conflict theorists, a plethora of alternative theoretical postures have been championed, including self-perception (Bem, 1965, 1968, 1972), functional analysis (Baron, 1968; Kelman et al., 1969), and role enactment (Berger, 1972; Bodaken, 1976) interpretations. By and large, champions of these alternative theoretical postures have reinterpreted the existing body of counterattitudinal advocacy research, substituting different mediational concepts to explain observed outcomes, with an occasional added study reported to further reinforce their particular theoretical preference. In one or two instances (e.g., Bem & McConnell, 1970) it has been claimed that a critical study has established the primacy of a particular interpretation over alternative interpretations predicting the same outcomes, but a dispassionate reading indicates that such studies typically fall short of this objective.

Since the early 70s, interest in counterattitudinal advocacy research has waned, although occasional attempts have been made to resolve the confusion wrought by a welter of conflicting theoretical interpretations and diverse research findings (e.g., Gerard, Conolley, & Wilhelmy, 1974; Wicklund & Brehm, 1976). While the precise reasons for this demise in interest cannot be documented, it has probably resulted at least partially from the confusing morass of intervening constructs invoked to explain counterattitudinal advocacy processes and outcomes. To the extent that this is true, it is also unfortunate, for most students of persuasion agree counterattitudinal advocacy is a paradigm capable of yielding interesting, socially significant persuasive findings. As a consequence, it is certainly worthy of continued empirical pursuit, even if the exact intrapersonal factors contributing to its effectiveness remain elusive.

INTERPERSONAL FACTORS

The most cursory perusal of current communication literature reveals a gaping void between the theoretically and socially self-evident importance of persuasion in interpersonal relationships, on the one hand, and the scholarly preoccupations of persuasion researchers, on the other. Whether interpersonal communication is viewed from a situational or developmental perspective (Miller, 1978; Miller & Sunnafrank, 1982), no one would question that persuasion is an integral thread in its relational fabric. But despite this fact, mainstream persuasion research has remained largely divorced from the interpersonal arena. To be sure, certain concepts central to the study of interpersonal relationships—for instance, *interpersonal attraction* (Berscheid, 1985; Berscheid & Walster, 1978) and *interpersonal influence* (Goffman, 1959, 1969; Seibold, Cantril, & Meyers, 1985)—smack of persuasive overtones, as do particular problem areas investigated largely in interpersonal settings—such as, bargaining and negotiation (Bachrach & Lawler, 1981; Donohue, 1981; Donohue, Diez, & Hamilton, 1984; Druckman, 1977; Morley & Stephenson, 1977; Pruitt, 1981; Rubin & Brown, 1975). Nevertheless, that body of literature commonly designated by the descriptive label "persuasion" has only recently begun to reflect much interest in interpersonal factors.

Several reasons can be posited for this discrepancy. As the fledgling discipline of communication has developed, there have been few efforts to overlay some conceptual master plan upon it. Instead, problem areas have been carved out operationally; thus, " 'persuasion research' has typically been defined as the paradigms employed, the problems investigated, and the outcomes assessed by those who call themselves persuasion researchers" (Miller & Burgoon, 1978). While such operational definitions are probably next to inevitable during a discipline's formative stages, and while they may in fact have much to recommend them, they are pitched at a level of abstraction that overlooks (or perhaps more aptly "underlooks") higher-order concepts and generalizations. The consequences of this shortcoming are certain to include considerable redundancy and wasted effort, as well as a degree of conceptual sterility.

The critical reader might understandably opine that the preceding reason suffers from an element of question begging, for to observe that the persuasion literature fails to emphasize interpersonal factors because persuasion researchers have neglected to study them falls considerably short of a convincing explanation. In defense of my logic, the primary intent of the preceding paragraph is to underscore the somewhat myopic view of persuasion research that has dominated the field and to signal the existence of a substantial body of persuasion research that has not been labeled as such. Nevertheless, some speculation as to *why* interpersonal factors have traditionally been short changed should prove informative. Since the two reasons that strike me as most relevant have been discussed earlier, they can be dealt with relatively briefly.

First, the social circumstances that initially fostered lively interest in the scientific study of persuasion were largely grounded in issues involving mass audiences. While certainly evincing concern for theoretical development, the seminal work of Hovland and his colleagues arose largely because of practical interests concerning mass wartime persuasion: In a nutshell, how could the vast persuasive resources of the United States government best be used to speed the defeat of the Axis enemy? Coupled with this concern for enhancing the persuasive effectiveness of the mass media was a note of foreboding, voiced by numerous social critics and students of communication, regarding the potential schizophrenic effects of media persuasion campaigns: Just as the media provided the potential for marshaling public support and action in pursuit of desirable social aims, they were also deemed capable of enslaving the populace in the sort of lockstep conformity and compliance envisioned by such popular pundits as Huxley and Orwell. Indeed, most of the early voting research (e.g., Lazarsfeld, Berelson, & Gaudet, 1948) sought to determine the extent to which this disturbing specter of media influence intruded in the political process (this was sometimes referred to as the *hypodermic needle model* of media effects). It is worth noting, however, that this research provided one of the earliest acknowledgements of the potentially important role of interpersonal factors in the persuasive process, the two-step flow hypothesis (Katz, 1957; Katz & Lazarsfeld, 1955), which posited the flow of media messages to opinion leaders who make persuasive use of the information in face-to-face settings. Notwithstanding such exceptions, however, persuasion research has been inextricably linked with large audience concerns; so much so that, as I have argued elsewhere (Miller & Burgoon, 1978), the late 1960s zeitgeist that fostered a heightened interest in the study of interpersonal communication also provoked a pejorative image of "persuasion" as synonymous with "mass manipulation practiced by the reigning power structure."

Returning to a recurring theme of this chapter, the second reason why interpersonal factors have traditionally failed to achieve an important status in persuasion research lies in the procedural difficulties involved in studying them. The procedural characteristics of the prototypical persuasion study have been described earlier; suffice to reiterate that most findings are the product of a research design involving single messages

transmitted to relatively large, impassive audiences. To devise procedures for investigating persuasive transactions in interpersonal relationships remains a methodological horse of a different color; indeed, as I
will shortly discuss more fully, attempts to achieve this objective have
largely relied on role-playing responses to hypothetical interpersonal
scenarios, an approach that raises thorny questions regarding ecological
validity.

Given the complexity of the preceding problems, my goal in this
section is, again, modest. Specifically, I shall examine several considerations that strike me as particularly relevant to achieving greater understanding of the role of interpersonal factors in the persuasive process,
using as points of departure concepts and issues of perennial interest to
persuasion researchers. Although interpersonal factors will be stressed,
the assumption remains that the various levels of analysis cannot be
understood *en vacuo;* interpersonal transactions are profoundly influenced by both the intrapersonal and macrosocietal levels.

Persuasive Means and Ends:
The Case of Credibility

That certain perceived characteristics of sources exert a marked
impact on the effectiveness of persuasive messages is one of the most
well-documented and widely accepted generalizations of persuasion
research. Aristotle (1954) lumps three such source characteristics under
the label *ethos,* or ethical proof: Roughly translated, ethical proof refers
to the good sense, goodwill, and good morals of the speaker. In one of
the first studies to use the term *source credibility,* Hovland and Weiss
(1951) found that communicators who were perceived as *competent* (good
sense) and *trustworthy* (good morals) were more successful persuaders
than communicators perceived less positively on these two attributes.
Approaching the issue somewhat differently, Kelman (1961) identifies
three sources of power for *influence agents,* his label for persuasive
sources: *means control,* which, as noted earlier, refers to the source's
capability to control rewards and punishments; *attractiveness,* which
refers to the extent that receivers see the source as someone with whom
they would like to form a satisfying role relationship; and *credibility,*
which refers to the expertise of the source—in other words, the good
sense dimension identified by Aristotle and the competence dimension
studied by Hovland and Weiss. Kelman posits a crucial difference
between the first two sources of power as opposed to the third: Attitudinal or behavioral change resulting from *compliance* (means control) and
identification (attractiveness) is less autonomous and can be maintained
only by continued *surveillance* in the case of means control, or *salience*
in the case of attractiveness; change resulting from *internalization* (credi-

bility) is more autonomous and will be maintained under conditions of *issue relevance* regardless of whether or not the source is physically or psychologically present.

Beginning in the mid-1960s, considerable attention was devoted to factor analytic studies designed to isolate empirically the dimensions of credibility (e.g., Berlo, Lemert, & Mertz, 1969; McCroskey, 1966). Though the factors differ somewhat from study to study, the two dimensions of competence and trustworthiness emerge consistently. In addition to these recurring factors, such dimensions as dynamism (an energy or assertiveness characteristic) and sociability (a friendliness characteristic) have also surfaced in particular studies.

The scientific value of this factor analytic sound and fury remains an open question. The initial impetus for the work was based on the defensible justification that the dimensions of credibility conjured by persuasion theorists and researchers should be empirically tested using actual target audiences; one frequently encountered the caveat that the credibility construct's dimensionality should be based on observational data rather than armchair speculation. Nevertheless, it does not appear that our understanding of the relationships between credibility and other variables has advanced much. Speaking of the impact of the Berlo et al. (1969) study, Cronkhite and Liska (1980, p. 101) assert trenchantly, "In the succeeding 15 years little was done with the credibility construct other than to analyze similar sets of semantic differential scales used by a variety of subject populations to rate a variety of sources." Even if this indictment is viewed as too uncharitable, it seems apparent that persuasion researchers have been overly enamored with conducting factor analyses of the credibility construct, with the result being that much of the recent scholarly dialogue about credibility consists of procedural and statistical nit-picking about the relative merits of this or that study or analytic approach.

Another problem with most credibility research lies in the almost exclusive reliance on a monadic approach to assessing credibility (Mertz, 1966; Miller, 1972). A monadic approach operationalizes credibility unidirectionally, treating it as an audience member's evaluation of a persuasive communicator. Mertz argues for the superior conceptual logic of a dyadic approach, summarizing its major assumptions as follows:

In contrast to the singular focus of monadic approaches to the variable, one can conceptualize credibility by stressing the *source-receiver relationship* which is implied by credibility judgments. This conceptualization asserts a source's influence potential to be a joint function of (1) receiver evaluations of the message source, and (2) receiver self-evaluations. Under this approach, a source's acceptability as a source of information and opinion in a given message situation is determined by a series of self-source comparisons on specific judgmental dimensions [e.g., one's own perceived level of knowledge about the particular issue (self-compe-tence) versus the communicator's perceived level of knowledge about the particular issue (source-competence)]. To the extent that the receiver rates the source as *higher than self* on these dimensions—whatever his absolute rating—he will tend to accept the proffered influence. On the other hand, when the receiver judges the message source *lower than self* on these dimensions, he will reject the source's influence attempts. Thus, a source's credibility and subsequent influence potential are seen to depend, not on his absolute rating, but on his evaluative standing relative to receiver self-evaluation. (1966, pp. 12-13)

In essence, Mertz argues that it is impossible to interpret the meaning of a source's credibility ratings apart from additional information about the raters themselves. Suppose, for example, that on a set of competence scales ranging from one (minimally competent) to seven (maximally competent), a receiver reports an average rating of three for the source. On an absolute basis, this rating suggests perceptions of modest credi-bility. Further suppose, however, that the receiver rates his or her own competence as one. Since the source is perceived as more competent than the receiver, the potential for persuasion exists. By contrast a receiver may assign an average rating of six to a source and yet be highly resistant to persuasion because of a self-competence rating of seven. The superiority of such dyadic comparative measures strikes me as self-evident, but though Mertz presented his case 20 years ago, I am unaware of any subsequent studies of credibility using his dyadic measurement approach.

While surely germane to persuasion in interpersonal settings, the pre-ceding comments about prior work on credibility are equally relevant to all three levels of analysis covered in this chapter. Two additional issues are particularly important to my analysis of interpersonal factors. First, as I have stressed elsewhere, "With few exceptions . . . credibility has been treated as an antecedent, independent variable which influences subsequent persuasive outcomes, rather than a *persuasive outcome* wor-thy of study in its own right" (Miller & Burgoon, 1978, p. 34). Stated in the language of this section's title, credibility has usually been viewed as a functional *means* to some persuasive end, not as an important persua-sive *end* in itself.

Given the dominant approach to persuasion research outlined earlier, this bias is hardly surprising. In most large audience settings, primary persuasive concern centers on such matters as selling some product or gaining support for some political candidate or policy. To the extent that achievement of these primary persuasive goals is enhanced or hindered by the persuader's credibility, understanding of this variable's instrumen-tal contribution to an overall equation of persuasive effectiveness has been deemed paramount. Sensible as such a position may seem, its limitations have lately become apparent at even the macrosocietal level: One need not be a particularly astute social observer to discern that contemporary political campaigns are increasingly geared toward selling favorable *images* of candidates themselves instead of rallying support for specific policies and priorities of the competing parties.

This concern with credibility as a persuasive end is even more apparent in many interpersonal relationships. To recognize this fact is not to deny that being perceived positively is instrumentally important in interpersonal relationships: Highly credible interpersonal communicators are no doubt accorded more social deference, are afforded a wider, more attractive range of choices for establishing social relationships, and, in general, are more apt to "get their way" than their less credible counterparts. Nevertheless, in most interpersonal relationships, "people devote the preponderance of their persuasive energies to *selling themselves,* and to a lesser extent, other persons" (Miller & Burgoon, 1978, p. 33) for no other apparent end than being liked and accepted.

When viewed in this light, the necessity of understanding as much as possible about *credibility formation*—that is, the process by which communicators use symbolic inducements to persuade others to perceive them more positively—becomes theoretically and socially apparent. This problem has been pursued on several fronts, including work on how specific verbal and nonverbal message elements affect credibility assessments (e.g., Baker, 1965; Giles & Powesland, 1975; Giles & Street, 1985; Jones, 1964; Miller & Hewgill, 1964; Sereno & Hawkins, 1967; Sharp & McClung, 1966); research dealing with the relationship of the more global construct, *communicator style,* to judgments of credibility (Giles & Street, 1985; Norton, 1983; Norton & Warnick, 1976); and studies of how information and topic sequencing influence perceived credibility (e.g., Berger, Gardner, Clatterbuck, & Schulman, 1976; Berger, Gardner, Parks, Schulman, & Miller, 1976). Though these investigations have yielded valuable insights about credibility formation, many questions about the process remain unanswered. Moreover, few of the studies conducted to date have examined credibility formation as it occurs in actual interpersonal transactions but have relied instead on large audience settings or, at best, role-playing responses to hypothetical interpersonal scenarios.

Just as communicators in interpersonal relationships are likely to evince a keen interest in credibility enhancement for its own sake, they are also apt to manifest considerable concern for the personal consequences of their persuasive strategies. Stated differently, persuasive communicators placed in mass and public settings often are motivated largely, or even solely, by a desire to achieve their immediate persuasive objectives; parties to interpersonal persuasive transactions usually share a common interest in the *relational implications* of their message exchanges. Consider, for instance, the use of falsehood and deceit to achieve an immediate behavioral aim such as selling some product, delivering a vote for some candidate, or "winning" some argument about relational priorities for spending time or money. Miller, Mongeau, and Sleight (1986) observe that in most impersonal, large audience settings, concern for being caught in a lie is limited to the potential negative effects of deception detection on these immediate goals—for example, "If this buyer realizes I am lying about the mileage on this car, he will not buy it." By contrast, "personal [interpersonal] relationships are characterized by the partners' concern for relational outcomes. To be trapped in a lie not only thwarts the immediate objective of the deceit, it also casts a pall over the relationship itself" (Miller et al., 1986, p. 508)—for example, "If my spouse realizes I am lying about my whereabouts last night, she will not only know that I was not inputting data at the computer center, she will also regard me as a less trustworthy and less attractive partner."

Stated in a nutshell, my argument about the conceptualization and investigation of credibility in interpersonal relationships goes as follows: *When contrasted with impersonal, large audience settings, interpersonal settings are characterized first, by a greater concern for development and maintenance of credibility for its own sake; second, by a more pronounced interest in the influence of persuasive message choices on subsequent perceptions of credibility.* Among the research implications of this expanded interest in credibility as a legitimate persuasive end in itself is heightened concern with the persuasive impact of the markedly differing gamut of symbolic strategies potentially available to persuasive communicators. I will turn next to this issue.

Catching Flies with Honey and Vinegar:
Compliance-Gaining Message Strategies

In 1967, two sociologists, Marwell and Schmitt, generated a list of 16 compliance-gaining message strategies (Table 15.1). Of the 16 strategies, 15 can be readily translated into specific symbolic inducements, while the single exception, *liking,* consists of a variety of verbal and nonverbal behaviors that seek to set the affective stage for a subsequent persuasive appeal. The persuasive force of particular strategies hinges on several different motivational considerations:

Certain strategies seek to heighten the salience of particular persuadee self-attitudes—e.g., the *moral appeal* strategy relies on the assumption that people wish to perceive themselves as honest and upright, while the *altruism* strategy assumes people like to be seen as cooperative, helpful, and concerned with the welfare of others. Other strategies depend primarily on conjuring a positive image of the compliance-seeker—e.g., the persuasive force of *liking* depends on painting a pleasant, friendly picture of the compliance-seeker, while the success of the *expertise* strategies hinges on the perception that the compliance-seeker is knowledgeable about the "way things are." Still another group of strategies aims at triggering an appropriate dispositional state in the persuadee—e.g., both *threat* and *promise* function this way, with the former seeking to stimulate fear or anxiety and the latter anticipation or appetite. Finally, some of the strategies combine more than one of these intervening outcomes—*pregiving* both contributes to a positive image of the compliance-seeker as a generous person and sets the stage for subsequent appeals to persuadee self-attitudes regarding fairness and reciprocity. In the last analysis, of course, the persuasive proof of the pudding is in the behavior, for regardless of the precise mediating mechanism, the compliance-seeker is hopeful the specific strategy or strategies employed will induce the message target to behave as desired. (Miller, Boster, Roloff, & Seibold, 1987)

Using the 16 strategies generated by Marwell and Schmitt (1967), Miller, Boster, Roloff, and Seibold (1977) conducted the first communication study dealing with compliance-gaining message strategies. Respondents in this study were asked to rate the likelihood they would use each of the 16 strategies in one of four hypothetical scenarios involving face-to-face persuasive communication. Though Miller et al. sought to manipulate the degree of interpersonalness by varying the descriptions of the participants' relational history (i.e., relative strangers versus close romantic partners) all four scenarios met situational criteria (Miller, 1978) for defining interpersonal communication. From its outset, then, persuasion research on compliance-gaining message strategies has departed from the investigational norm by relying heavily on interpersonal settings. Seibold et al. (1985, p. 560) assert that "this research fuses traditional persuasion concerns and newer interpersonal foci," while Wheeless, Barraclough, and Stewart (1983) argue that it has made the study of persuasion in interpersonal situations more viable than in the early and middle 1970s.

Since the initial Miller et al. undertaking in 1977, communication researchers have generated more than 50 published studies and conference papers that probe various issues associated with compliance-gaining message strategies (for reviews see, e.g., Miller, 1983; Miller et al., 1987; Seibold et al., 1985; Wheeless et al., 1983). Readers may experience a slight attack of scientific déjà vu upon discovering that, as in the case of communicator credibility, persistent attention has been directed at identifying response-derived strategy dimensions, or strategy typologies (e.g., Burgoon, Dillard, Doran, & Miller, 1982; Hunter & Boster, 1987; Wiseman & Schenck-Hamlin, 1981). Unfortunately, these studies have produced a wide variety of factor solutions, as well as inter-

TABLE 15.1
Marwell & Schmitt's Typology Using an Example
Involving Relational Dissolution

(1) Promise	(If you comply, I will reward you.) You offer to release community property if your relational partner will agree to dissolution.
(2) Threat	(If you do not comply, I will punish you.) You threaten to take all community property if your relational partner will not agree to dissolution.
(3) Positive Expertise	(If you comply, you will be rewarded because of "the nature of things.") You tell your relational partner that it will be a lot easier on both of you if he or she agrees to the dissolution.
(4) Negative Expertise	(If you do not comply, you will be punished because of "the nature of things.") You tell your relational partner that if he or she does not agree to the dissolution, it will be an extremely difficult emotional experience for both of you.
(5) Pregiving	(Actor rewards target before requesting compliance.) You finance a vacation for your relational partner to visit friends before telling him or her you wish to dissolve the relationship.
(6) Aversive Stimulation	(Actor continuously punishes target making cessation contingent on compliance.) You refuse to communicate with your relational partner until he or she agrees to discuss the possibility of dissolution.
(7) Debt	(You owe me compliance because of past favors.) You point out to your relational partner that you have sacrificed to put him or her through college and that he or she owes it to you to let you live your life as you desire.
(8) Liking	(Actor is friendly and helpful to get target in "good frame of mind" so that he or she will comply with the request.)
(9) Moral Appeal	(A moral person would comply.) You tell your relational partner that a moral person would let someone out of a relationship in which he or she no longer wished to participate.
(10) Positive Self-Feeling	(You will feel better about yourself if you comply.) You tell your relational partner that he or she will feel better about him- or herself if he or she lets you go.
(11) Negative Self-Feeling	(You will feel worse about yourself if you do not comply.) You tell your relational partner that denying you your freedom will make him or her feel like a terrible person.
(12) Positive Altercasting	(A person with "good" qualities would comply.) You tell your relational partner that because he or she is a mature, intelligent person, he or she will want you to do what is best for you.

(continued)

TABLE 15.1 Continued

(13) Negative Altercasting	(Only a person with "bad" qualities would not comply.) You tell your relational partner that only someone who is cruel and childish would keep another in a relationship which the other desired to leave.
(14) Altruism	(I need your compliance very badly, so do it for me.) You tell your relational partner that he or she must free you from the relationship to preserve your sanity.
(15) Positive Esteem	(People you value will think better of you if you comply.) You tell your relational partner his or her friends and relatives will think highly of him or her for letting you go.
(16) Negative Esteem	(People you value will think worse of you if you do not comply.) You tell your relational partner his or her friends and relatives will be ashamed of him or her if he or she tries to prevent you from leaving.

SOURCE: From Miller & Parks (1982, pp. 146-147).

pretations of these solutions, thus presenting a confused picture for interested researchers.

Given the lack of parsimony inherent in Marwell and Schmitt's (1967) original 16-strategy list, as well as the subsequent confusion faced when naive respondents attempt to "make sense" of the list, more economical typologies of compliance-gaining message strategies are mandated. One approach to this problem has been to devise typologies rooted in a mixture of existing theory, research, and speculation. Berger (1985, pp. 484-491) describes a Strategy Attribute Schema that holds promise for developing more comprehensive generalizations about strategy selection. Miller and Parks (1982) suggest a four-category typology based on the two dimensions of reward-oriented versus punishment-oriented strategies and communicator-onus versus communicatee-onus strategies. As Figure 15.1 reveals, all of Marwell and Schmitt's 16 strategies can be grouped in the four types of strategies generated by the two dimensions of Miller and Parks.

The scheme suggested by Miller and Parks seems relevant to another issue that has captured the attention of several researchers, namely, the appropriate level of abstraction for labeling a message element a strategy. Given the sensible definitional premise that a strategy may subsume multiple message tactics, it can be argued persuasively that the message elements labeled "strategies" by prior researchers might more usefully be conceived of as "tactics." Berger (1985, p. 485) notes that "there may be numerous tactical variations for a given strategy" and goes on to

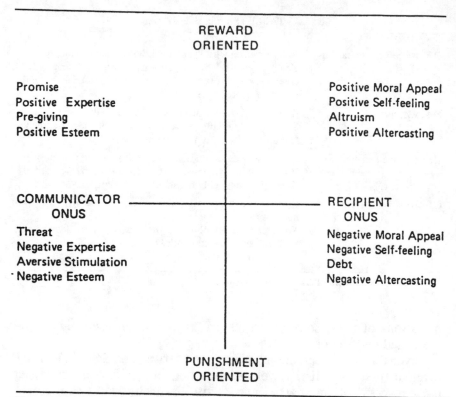

Figure 15.1. Four-category typology of compliance-gaining message strategies. From Miller & Parks (1982); the Marwell and Schmitt strategies have been slightly modified by eliminating the *liking* strategy and by substituting *positive moral appeal* for the original *moral appeal* strategy.

say that "any number of verbal messages could be sent to depict threat, and a large number of nonverbal variations could also be used to instantiate the strategy."

Applying this reasoning to Figure 15.1 results in the conclusion that there are four general compliance-gaining message strategies available to persuasive communicators: *reward-oriented/communicator-onus* strategies, *reward-oriented/communicatee-onus* strategies, *punishment-oriented/communicator-onus* strategies, and *punishment-oriented/communicatee-onus* strategies. Stated differently, a persuader may elect to stress either the positive outcomes accruing from compliance (reward-oriented) or the negative consequences of noncompliance (punishment-oriented). Having made this choice, the persuader may then opt to manipulate the rewards or punishments directly (communicator-onus) or to try to stimulate in the intended persuadee positively or negatively self-reinforcing contingencies (communicatee-onus). For each of these four broad strategic choices, there are numerous tactical message options; for example, as Figure 15.1 reveals, this reconceptualization changes the status of Marwell and Schmitt's list from "strategies" to "tactics."

More abstract, economical typologies of compliance-gaining message strategies can also help to alleviate the possibility of an *overly mindful* (Berger & Douglas, 1982) conception of the process of generating persuasive messages. Implicit in the term "strategy" is some level of conscious awareness or deliberate choice, but as was emphasized earlier, it is likely that many persuasive exchanges are relatively short on cognitive activity, thus calling into question the relevance of such phrases as "choosing strategies" or "selecting strategies." Indeed, as I have suggested elsewhere (Miller, 1982; see also Boster & Stiff, 1984), it seems plausible that many persuasive communicators acquire relatively narrow strategy repertoires by learning and conditioning, and continue to use these repertoires regardless of persuasive circumstances. If this is the case, it is highly improbable that, in the heat of persuasive battle, communicators are capable of cognitively juggling a voluminous list of strategies and arriving at reasoned judgments concerning the relative merits of each one. In fact, there is considerable evidence that naive research participants, and even coders who have received some training, err frequently when attempting to apply the Marwell and Schmitt strategies to persuasive transactions. By contrast, when using the four-category typology of Miller and Parks (1982), Senter and Miller (1983) found that following a 15-minute explanation research participants could sort message elements into the appropriate category with almost perfect reliability and could write with few errors symbolic inducements that fit the defining criteria of the four strategy types.

To harken yet again to a well-worn refrain, however, the most thorny problem facing those seeking understanding of how compliance-gaining message strategies function in interpersonal surroundings is an observational one. Two choices exist: The researcher may ask respondents *to report the strategies they would use* in various face-to-face settings, or the researcher may *observe the strategies actually used* in such settings. While the former approach is much simpler and has been used far more extensively, it is rife with inferential difficulties, whether respondents are supplied with prepared "checklists" of strategies (e.g., Marwell & Schmitt, 1967; Miller et al., 1977; Williams & Boster, 1981; Wiseman & Schenck-Hamlin, 1981) or are asked to compose their own strategies from scratch (Clark, 1979). Though Burleson et al. (1986) argue for the superiority of the latter self-report procedure, Seibold et al. (1986) nicely capture the difficulty inherent in both self-report procedures:

Neither method [procedure] permits study of situated message *use* or, by extension, compliance-gaining effectiveness. At issue here is the distinction between message "use" and message "choices." The encompassing construct is message use, for it presumes choices. . . . The subconstruct is message choice, and it may or may not correspond to message use. . . . We must remember, then, that findings yielded from *both* selection and construction methods inherently say little about message use, for both methods yield artificially induced rated or written responses to hypothetical situations involving single goals, time constraints, artificial environments, and proximally distant social stimuli. . . . In neither case do these message *choice* results inherently say anything about situated message use in the "real world." (pp. 5-6)

More generally and emphatically, then, the message is clear: *If persuasion researchers want to understand how compliance-gaining message strategies function in interpersonal settings—or, for that matter, how any symbolic inducement functions in any communicative setting— they must come to grips with the necessity of observing actual message exchanges.* Although this dictum is fundamental and easily comprehended, I have repeatedly stressed that it is often endorsed but seldom followed (for exceptions, see, Boster & Lofthouse, 1986; Boster & Stiff, 1984). Moreover, it is most difficult to follow in the interpersonal arena. Laying aside difficulties and excuses, the fact still remains that theoretical and empirical advances hinge on the ability of researchers to devise ways of observing actual communicative practices in interpersonal settings. This blunt judgment marks a good point for writing finis to the discussion of interpersonal factors.

MACROSOCIETAL FACTORS: A CHAPTER POSTSCRIPT

The macrosocietal importance attached to persuasion has been underscored several times throughout this chapter and elsewhere in this volume (see Price & Roberts, Chapter 25; Rogers & Storey, Chapter 26). Consistent with the Western democratic value of government empowered and legitimized by ballots not bullets, persuasive campaigns are generally viewed as one of the linchpins of the political process. The vast appetite for consumer goods so essential to the continued well-being of the economy is at the same time fueled and sated by a glut of media advertising. Simply stated, persuasive messages emanating from large audience settings are given tremendous credit for shaping, reinforcing, and changing public attitudes and behaviors. Nor are the hypothesized effects of media messages limited to the area of intentional influence, though this intentional area is of primary concern in this chapter. In addition, such messages are thought to provide generalized role models for large segments of society and to paint pictures of the society that are viewed as gospel, even when they depart radically from "objective reality." A recent volume (Bryant & Zillmann, 1986) devotes 16 chapters to possible effects of media messages, including such diverse areas as television addiction (Smith, 1986), social learning of aggression (Tan, 1986), and prosocial effects of television (Johnston & Ettema, 1986).

Given limited remaining page space, wide breadth of issues and problems, and numerous reviews and syntheses of the macrosocietal aspects of persuasion (e.g., Pearl, Bouthilet, & Lazar, 1982; Roberts & Maccoby, 1985; Wartella, Whitney, & Windahl, 1983; Weiss, 1969; Whitney, Wartella, & Windahl, 1982; Wilhoit & deBock, 1980, 1981), I will content myself with two brief judgmental comments in this postscript. First, it strikes me that the tendency to focus research on problem areas of applied significance—violence, pornography, treatment of minorities, alcohol and drug usage, and the like—often slows the search for theoretical explanations of macrosocietal persuasive processes and outcomes. The grounds for this assertion rest in a failure to pitch research efforts at the proper level of abstraction, to seek generalizations about the impact of this or that kind of media message content on recipient attitudes and behaviors rather than striving to develop and test overarching theoretical propositions and empirical generalizations about the effect of media messages *in general* on target audiences. Though the analogy is far from perfect, the results often seem akin to those that would have been produced by learning theorists had they chosen to direct research at topics such as how to learn to dress, how to learn to cross the street, how to learn to consume food, and so on, instead of seeking more general laws, or principles, of learning. Though some macrosocietal persuasion research dealing with currently "hot" problem areas is all but inevitable, it should be buttressed by work focusing on more general theoretical and empirical concerns.

Finally, as I have argued elsewhere (Miller, 1986, 1987), it appears that investigators have only begun to scratch the surface of the interconnectedness between the macrosocietal level, on the one hand, and the intrapersonal and interpersonal levels, on the other. More specifically, extensive exposure to media persuasive messages is likely to predispose persons "*to view other people as undifferentiated role occupants—simplistic cultural and sociological caricatures—rather than individuals*" (Miller, 1986, p. 136). To the extent that media messages exert such posited effects on basic mechanisms of person perception and cognitive processing, they profoundly influence persuasive transactions at all levels of analysis examined in this chapter. Only time and additional research will provide an answer to this final conjecture.

REFERENCES

Ajzen, I., & Fishbein, M. A. (1969). The prediction of behavioral intentions in a choice situation. *Journal of Experimental Social Psychology, 5,* 400-416.

Ajzen, I., & Fishbein, M. A. (1970). The prediction of behavior from attitudinal and normative variables. *Journal of Experimental Social Psychology, 6,* 466-487.

Allport, G. E. (1935). Attitudes. In C. Murchison (Ed.), *Handbook of social psychology* (Vol. 2, pp. 798-844). Worcester, MA: Clark University Press.

Aristotle, (1954). *Rhetoric.* (W. R. Roberts, Trans.). New York: Random House.

Arnold, C. C., & Bowers, J. W. (Eds.). (1984). *Handbook of rhetorical and communication theory.* Newton, MA: Allyn & Bacon.

Aronson, E. (1966). The psychology of insufficient justification: An analysis of some conflicting data. In S. Feldman (Ed.), *Cognitive consistency: Motivational antecedents and behavioral consequents* (pp. 109-133). New York: Academic Press.

Aronson, E. (1968). Dissonance theory: Progress and problems. In R. P. Abelson, E. Aronson, W. J. McGuire, T. M. Newcomb, M. J. Rosenberg, & P. H. Tannenbaum (Eds.), *Theories of cognitive consistency: A sourcebook* (pp. 5-27). Chicago: Rand McNally.

Bachrach, S. B., & Lawler, E. J. (1981). *Bargaining: Power, tactics, and outcomes.* San Francisco: Jossey-Bass.

Baker, E. E. (1965). The immediate effects of perceived speaker disorganization on speaker credibility and audience attitude change in persuasive speaking. *Western Speech, 29,* 148-161.

Baron, R. M. (1968). Attitude change through discrepant action: A functional analysis. In A. G. Greenwald, T. C. Brock, & T. M. Ostrom (Eds.), *Psychological foundations of attitudes* (pp. 297-326). New York: Academic Press.

Becker, S. L. (1963). Research on emotional and logical proofs. *Southern Speech Journal, 28,* 198-207.

Bem, D. J. (1965). An experimental analysis of self-persuasion. *Journal of Experimental Social Psychology, 1,* 199-218.

Bem, D. J. (1968). Attitudes as self-descriptions: Another look at the attitude-behavior link. In A. G. Greenwald, T. C. Brock, & T. M. Ostrom (Eds.), *Psychological foundations of attitudes* (pp. 197-215). New York: Academic Press.

Bem, D. J. (1972). Self-perception theory. In L. Berkowitz (Ed.), *Advances in experimental social psychology* (Vol. 6, pp. 2-63). New York: Academic Press.

Bem, D. J., & McConnell, H. K. (1970). Testing the self-perception explanation of dissonance phenomena: On the salience of premanipulation attitudes. *Journal of Personality and Social Psychology, 14,* 23-31.

Berger, C. R. (1972). Toward a role enactment theory of persuasion. *Speech Monographs, 39,* 260-276.

Berger, C. R. (1985). Social power and interpersonal communication. In M. L. Knapp & G. R. Miller (Eds.), *Handbook of interpersonal communication* (pp. 439-499). Newbury Park, CA: Sage.

Berger, C. R., & Douglas, W. (1982). Thought and talk: "Excuse me, but have I been talking to myself?" In F.E.X. Dance (Ed.), *Human communication theory: Comparative essays* (pp. 42-60). New York: Harper & Row.

Berger, C. R., Gardner, R. R., Clatterbuck, G. W., & Schulman, L. S. (1976). Perceptions of information sequencing in relationship development. *Human Communication Research, 3,* 29-46.

Berger, C. R., Gardner, R. R., Parks, M. R., Schulman, L., & Miller, G. R. (1976). Interpersonal epistemology and interpersonal communication. In G. R. Miller

(Ed.), *Explorations in interpersonal communication* (pp. 149-171). Newbury Park, CA: Sage.

Berlo, D.K. (1960). *The process of communication.* New York: Holt, Rinehart & Winston.

Berlo, D. K., Lemert, J. B., & Mertz, R. J. (1969). Dimensions for evaluating the acceptability of message sources. *Public Opinion Quarterly, 33,* 563-576.

Berscheid, E. (1981). An overview of the psychological effects of physical attractiveness and some comments upon the psychological effects of knowledge of the effects of physical attractiveness. In G. W. Lucker, K. Ribbens, & J. A. McNamara (Eds.), *Psychological aspects of facial form* (Monograph No. 11, Craniofacial Growth Series). Ann Arbor, MI: Center for Human Growth and Development.

Berscheid, E. (1985). Interpersonal attraction. In G. Lindzey & E. Aronson (Eds.), *Handbook of social psychology* (3rd ed., Vol. 2, pp. 413-484). New York: Random House.

Berscheid, E., & Walster, E. (1974). Physical attractiveness. In L. Berkowitz (Ed.), *Advances in experimental social psychology* (Vol. 7, pp. 157-215). New York: Academic Press.

Berscheid, E., & Walster, E. (1978). *Interpersonal attraction* (2nd ed.). Reading, MA: Addison-Wesley.

Bodaken, E. M. (1976). An empirical test of a role enactment model of persuasion. *Human Communication Research, 2,* 330-337.

Boster, F. J., & Lofthouse, L. J. (1986). *Situational and individual difference determinants of the persistence and content of compliance gaining behavior: A test of the generalizability of some compliance gaining message choice findings.* Paper presented at the annual meeting of the Speech Communication Association, Chicago.

Boster, F. J., & Stiff, J. B. (1984). Compliance-gaining message selection behavior. *Human Communication Research, 10,* 539-556.

Brehm, J. W., & Cohen, A. R. (1962). *Explorations in cognitive dissonance.* New York: John Wiley.

Bryant, J., & Zillmann, D. (Eds.). (1986). *Perspectives on media effects.* Hillsdale, NJ: Lawrence Erlbaum.

Burgoon, M., Dillard, J. P., Doran, N. E., & Miller, M. D. (1982). Cultural and situational influences on the process of persuasive strategy selection. *International Journal of Intercultural Relations, 6,* 85-100.

Burgoon, M., & Miller, G. R. (1985). An expectancy interpretation of language and persuasion. In H. Giles & R. N. St. Clair (Eds.), *Recent advances in language, communication, and social psychology* (pp. 199-229). London: Lawrence Erlbaum.

Burleson, B. R., Wilson, S. R., Waltman, M. S., Goering, E. M., Ely, I. K., & Whaley, B. B. (1986). *Item desirability effects in compliance-gaining research: Seven empirical studies showing why the checklist methodology produces garbage.* Paper presented at the annual meeting of the Speech Communication Association, Chicago.

Cacioppo, J. T., Harkins, S. G., & Petty, R. E. (1981). The nature of attitudes and cognitive responses and their relationships to behavior. In R. E. Petty, T. M. Ostrom, & T. C. Brock (Eds.), *Cognitive responses in persuasion* (pp. 31-54). Hillsdale, NJ: Lawrence Erlbaum.

Campbell, D. T. (1963). Social attitudes and other acquired behavioral dispositions. In S. Koch (Ed.), *Psychology: A study of a science* (Vol. 6, pp. 94-172). New York: McGraw-Hill.

Carlsmith, J. M. (1968). Varieties of counterattitudinal behavior. In R. P. Abelson, E. Aronson, W. J. McGuire, T. M. Newcomb, M. J. Rosenberg, & P. H. Tannenbaum (Eds.), *Theories of cognitive consistency: A sourcebook* (pp. 803-809). Chicago: Rand McNally.

Clark, R.A. (1979). The impact of self-interest and desire for liking on selection of persuasive strategies. *Communication Monographs, 46,* 257-273.

Cronkhite, G., & Liska, J. R. (1980). The judgment of communicant acceptability. In M. E. Roloff & G. R. Miller (Eds.), *Persuasion: New directions in theory and research* (pp. 101-139). Newbury Park, CA: Sage.

Cushman, D. P., & McPhee, R. D. (Eds.). (1980). *Message-attitude-behavior relationship: Theory, methodology, and application.* New York: Academic Press.

DeFleur, M. L., & Westie, F. R. (1958). Verbal attitudes and overt acts: An experiment on the salience of attitudes. *American Sociological Review, 23,* 667-673.

DeFleur, M. L., & Westie, F. R. (1963). Attitude as a scientific concept. *Social Forces, 42,* 17-31.

Donohue, W. A. (1981). Development of a model of rule use in negotiation interaction. *Communication Monographs, 48,* 106-120.

Donohue, W. A., Diez, M. E., & Hamilton, M. (1984). Coding naturalistic negotiation interaction. *Human Communication Research, 10,* 403-425.

Druckman, D. (1977). *Negotiations: Social-psychological perspectives.* Newbury Park, CA: Sage.

Elms, A. C., & Janis, I. L. (1965). Counter norm attitudes induced by consonant versus dissonant conditions of role playing. *Journal of Experimental Research in Personality, 1,* 50-60.

Festinger, L. (1957). *A theory of cognitive dissonance.* Stanford: Stanford University Press.

Festinger, L. (1964). Behavioral support for opinion change. *Public Opinion Quarterly, 28,* 404-417.

Festinger, L., & Carlsmith, J. M. (1959). Cognitive consequences of forced compliance. *Journal of Abnormal and Social Psychology, 58,* 203-210.

Fishbein, M. A. (1963). An investigation of the relationship between beliefs about an object and the attitude toward that object. *Human Relations, 16,* 233-239.

Fishbein, M. A. (1965). A consideration of beliefs, attitudes, and their relationship. In I. D. Steiner & M. Fishbein (Eds.), *Current studies in social psychology* (pp. 107-120). New York: Holt, Rinehart & Winston.

Fishbein, M. A. (1966). The relationships between beliefs, attitudes, and behavior. In S. Feldman (Ed.), *Cognitive consistency: Motivational antecedents and behavioral consequents* (pp. 199-223). New York: Academic Press.

Fishbein, M. A. (1967a). A behavior theory approach to the relations between beliefs about an object and the attitude toward the object. In M. A. Fishbein (Ed.), *Readings in attitude theory and measurement* (pp. 389-400). New York: John Wiley.

Fishbein, M. A. (1967b). Attitude and the prediction of behavior. In M. A. Fishbein (Ed.), *Readings in attitude theory and measurement* (pp. 477-492). New York: John Wiley.

Fishbein, M. A., & Ajzen, I. (1972). Attitudes and opinions. In P. H. Mussen & M. R. Rosenzweig (Eds.), *Annual review of psychology* (Vol. 6, pp. 487-544). Palo Alto, CA: Annual Reviews.

Fishbein, M. A., & Ajzen, I. (1974). Attitudes toward objects as predictors of single and multiple behavioral criteria. *Psychological Review, 81,* 59-74.

Fishbein, M. A., & Raven, B. H. (1962). The AB scales: An operational definition of belief and attitude. *Human Relations, 15,* 35-44.

Gerard, H. B., Conolley, E. S., & Wilhelmy, R. A. (1974). Compliance, justification, and cognitive change. In L. Berkowitz (Ed.), *Advances in experimental social psychology* (Vol. 7, pp. 217-247). New York: Academic Press.

Giles, H., & Powesland, P. F. (1975). *Speech style and social evaluation.* New York: Academic Press.

Giles, H., & Street, R. L., Jr. (1985). Communicator characteristics and behavior. In M. L. Knapp & G. R. Miller (Eds.), *Handbook of interpersonal communication* (pp. 205-261). Newbury Park, CA: Sage.

Gillham, J. C., & Woelfel, J. (1977). The Galileo system of measurement: Preliminary evidence for precision, stability, and equivalence to traditional measures. *Human Communication Research, 3,* 222-234.

Goffman, E. (1959). *The presentation of self in everyday life.* Garden City, NY: Doubleday.

Goffman, E. (1969). *Strategic interaction.* Philadelphia: University of Pennsylvania Press.

Green, B. F. (1954). Attitude measurement. In G. Lindzey (Ed.), *Handbook of social psychology* (pp. 335-369). Cambridge, MA: Addison-Wesley.

Guttman, L. (1944). A basis for scaling qualitative data. *American Sociological Review, 9,* 139-150.

Hovland, C. I., & Weiss, W. (1951). The influence of source credibility on communication effectiveness. *Public Opinion Quarterly, 15,* 635-650.

Hunter, J. E., & Boster, F. J. (1987). An empathy model of compliance-gaining message selection. *Communication Monographs, 54,* 63-84.

Janis, I. L. (1968). Attitude change via role playing. In R. P. Abelson, E. Aronson, W. J. McGuire, T. M. Newcomb, M. J. Rosenberg, & P. H. Tannenbaum (Eds.), *Theories of cognitive consistency: A sourcebook* (pp. 810-818). Chicago: Rand McNally.

Janis, I. L., & Gilmore, J. B. (1965). The influence of incentive conditions on the success of role playing in modifying attitudes. *Journal of Personality and Social Psychology, 1,* 17-27.

Johnston, J., & Ettema, J. (1986). Using television to best advantage: Research for prosocial television. In J. Bryant & D. Zillmann (Eds.), *Perspectives on media effects* (pp. 143-164). Hillsdale, NJ: Lawrence Erlbaum.

Jones, E. E. (1964). *Ingratiation.* New York: Appleton-Century-Crofts.

Katz, E. (1957). The two-step flow of communication: An up-to-date report on an hypothesis: *Public Opinion Quarterly, 21,* 61-78.

Katz, E., & Lazarsfeld, P. F. (1955). *Personal influence.* New York: Free Press.

Kelman, H. C. (1961). Processes of opinion change. *Public Opinion Quarterly, 25,* 57-78.

Kelman, H. C., Baron, R. M., Sheposh, J. P., Lubalin, J. S., Dabbs, J. M., & Johnson, E. (1969). *Studies in attitude-discrepant behavior.* Unpublished manuscript, Department of Psychology, Harvard University.

Lazarsfeld, P. F., Berelson, B., & Gaudet, H. (1948). *The people's choice.* New York: Columbia University Press.

Likert, R. (1932). A technique for the measurement of attitudes. *Archives of Psychology,* Whole No. 140.

Lindzey, G. (Ed.). (1954). *Handbook of social psychology.* Reading, MA: Addison-Wesley.

Lindzey, G., & Aronson, E. (Eds.). (1969). *Handbook of social psychology* (2nd ed.). Reading, MA: Addison-Wesley.

Lindzey, G., & Aronson, E. (Eds.). (1985). *Handbook of social psychology* (3rd ed.). New York: Random House.

Liska, A. E. (Ed.). (1975). *The consistency controversy: Readings on the impact of attitude on behavior.* New York: Schenkman.

Marwell, G., & Schmitt, D. R. (1967). Dimensions of compliance-gaining behavior: An empirical analysis. *Sociometry, 30,* 350-364.

McCroskey, J. C. (1966). Scales for the measurement of ethos. *Speech Monographs, 33,* 65-72.

McGuire, W. J. (1961). Resistance to persuasion conferred by active and passive prior refutation of the same and alternative counterarguments. *Journal of Abnormal and Social Psychology, 63,* 326-332.

McGuire, W. J. (1962). Persistence of the resistance to persuasion induced by various types of prior belief defenses. *Journal of Abnormal and Social Psychology, 64,* 241-248.

McGuire, W. J. (1964). Inducing resistance to persuasion: Some contemporary approaches. In L. Berkowitz (Ed.), *Advances in experimental social psychology* (Vol. 1, pp. 191-229). New York: Academic Press.

McGuire, W. J. (1969). The nature of attitudes and attitude change. In G. Lindzey & E. Aronson (Eds.), *Handbook of social psychology* (2nd ed., Vol. 3, pp. 136-314). Reading, MA: Addison-Wesley.

McGuire, W. J., & Papageorgis, D. (1961). The relative efficacy of various types of prior belief-defense in producing immunity against persuasion. *Journal of Abnormal and Social Psychology, 62,* 327-337.

Mertz, R. J. (1966). *Acceptance of persuasive influence as related to three dimensions of source evaluation.* Unpublished doctoral dissertation, Department of Communication, Michigan State University.

Miller, G., Boster, F., Roloff, M., & Seibold, D. (1977). Compliance-gaining message strategies: A typology and some findings concerning effects of situational differences. *Communication Monographs, 44,* 37-50.

Miller, G. R. (1972). Speech: An approach to human communication. In R. W. Budd & B. D. Ruben (Eds.), *Approaches to human communication* (pp. 383-400). New York: Spartan Books.

Miller, G. R. (1973). Counterattitudinal advocacy: A current appraisal. In C. D. Mortensen & K. K. Sereno (Eds.), *Advances in communication research* (pp. 105-152). New York: Harper & Row.

Miller, G. R. (1977). On the pervasiveness and marvelous complexity of human communication: A note of skepticism. *Journal of the Annual Fresno Conference in Communication, 4,* 1-18.

Miller, G. R. (1978). The current status of theory and research in interpersonal communication. *Human Communication Research, 4,* 164-178.

Miller, G. R. (1980a) Afterword. In D. P. Cushman & R. P. McPhee (Eds.), *Message-attitude-behavior relationship: Theory, methodology, and application* (pp. 319-327). New York: Academic Press.

Miller, G. R. (1980b). On being persuaded: Some basic distinctions. In M. E. Roloff & G. R. Miller (Eds.), *Persuasion: New directions in theory and research* (pp. 11-28). Newbury Park, CA: Sage.

Miller, G. R. (1982). *Effects of persuasive message strategy selection on family members' attitudes toward the family.* Unpublished manuscript, Department of Communication, Michigan State University.

Miller, G. R. (1983). On various ways of skinning symbolic cats: Recent research on persuasive message strategies. *Journal of Language and Social Psychology, 2,* 123-140.

Miller, G. R. (1986). A neglected connection: Mass media exposure and interpersonal communicative competence. In G. Gumpert & R. Cathcart (Eds.), *Inter/media: Interpersonal communication in a media world* (3rd ed., pp. 132-139). New York: Oxford University Press.

Miller, G. R. (1987). Media messages and information processing in interpersonal communication: "Generally speaking . . . ." *Information and Behavior.*

Miller, G. R., Boster, F. J., Roloff, M. E., & Seibold, D. R. (1987). MBRS rekindled: Some thoughts on compliance gaining in interpersonal settings. In M. E. Roloff &

G. R. Miller (Eds.), *Interpersonal processes: New directions in communication research.* Newbury Park, CA: Sage.

Miller, G. R., & Burgoon, M. (1973). *New techniques of persuasion.* New York: Harper & Row.

Miller, G. R., & Burgoon, M. (1978). Persuasion research: Review and commentary. In B. D. Ruben (Ed.), *Communication yearbook 2* (pp. 29-47). New Brunswick, NJ: Transaction Books.

Miller, G. R., Burgoon, M., & Burgoon, J. K. (1984). The functions of human communication in changing attitudes and gaining compliance. In C. C. Arnold & J. W. Bowers (Eds.), *Handbook of rhetorical and communication theory* (pp. 400-474). Newton, MA: Allyn & Bacon.

Miller, G. R., & Hewgill, M. A. (1964). The effect of variations in nonfluency on audience ratings of source credibility. *Quarterly Journal of Speech, 50,* 36-44.

Miller, G. R., Mongeau, P. A., & Sleight, C. (1986). Fudging with friends and lying to lovers: Deceptive communication in interpersonal relationships. *Journal of Social and Personal Relationships, 3,* 495-512.

Miller, G. R., & Parks, M. R. (1982). Communication in dissolving relationships. In S. Duck (Ed.), *Personal relationships 4: Dissolving relationships* (pp. 127-154). New York: Academic Press.

Miller, G. R., & Steinberg, M. (1975). *Between people: A new analysis of interpersonal communication.* Chicago: Science Research Associates.

Miller, G. R., & Sunnafrank, M. J. (1982). All is for one but one is not for all: A conceptual perspective of interpersonal communication. In F.E.X. Dance (Ed.), *Human communication theory: Comparative essays* (pp. 220-242). New York: Harper & Row.

Morley, I., & Stephenson, G. (1977). *The social psychology of bargaining.* London: Allen & Unwin.

Norton, R. (1983). *Communicator style.* Newbury Park, CA: Sage.

Norton, R., & Warnick, B. (1976). Assertiveness as a communication construct. *Human Communication Research, 3,* 62-66.

Osgood, C. E., Suci, G. J., & Tannenbaum, P. H. (1957). *The measurement of meaning.* Urbana: University of Illinois Press.

Pearl, D., Bouthilet, L., & Lazar, J. (Eds.). (1982). *Television and behavior: Ten years of scientific progress and implications for the eighties* (Vol. 2). Rockville, MD: Department of Health and Human Services.

Petty, R. E., & Cacioppo, J. T. (1986a). *Communication and persuasion: Central and peripheral routes to attitude change.* New York: Springer-Verlag.

Petty, R. E., & Cacioppo, J. T. (1986b). The elaboration likelihood model of persuasion. In L. Berkowitz (Ed.), *Advances in experimental social psychology* (Vol. 19, pp. 123-205). New York: Academic Press.

Petty, R. E., Ostrom, T. M., & Brock, T. C. (Eds.). (1981a). *Cognitive responses in persuasion.* Hillsdale, NJ: Lawrence Erlbaum.

Petty, R. E., Ostrom, T. M., & Brock, T. C. (1981b). Historical foundations of the cognitive response approach to attitudes and persuasion. In R. E. Petty, T. M. Ostrom, & T. C. Brock (Eds.), *Cognitive responses in persuasion* (pp. 1-29). Hillsdale, NJ: Lawrence Erlbaum.

Pruitt, D. G. (1981). *Negotiation behavior.* New York: Academic Press.

Roberts, D. F., & Maccoby, N. (1985). Effects of mass communication. In G. Lindzey & E. Aronson (Eds.), *Handbook of social psychology* (3rd ed., Vol. 2, pp. 539-598). New York: Random House.

Rogers, E. M. (1962). *Diffusion of innovations.* New York: Free Press.

Rogers, E. M. (1983). *Diffusion of innovations* (3rd ed.). New York: Free Press.

Rogers, E. M., & Shoemaker, F. F. (1971). *Communication of innovations: A cross-cultural approach* (2nd ed.). New York: Free Press.

Rosenberg, M. J. (1965). When dissonance fails: On eliminating evaluation apprehension from attitudinal measurement. *Journal of Personality and Social Psychology, 1,* 28-42.

Rosenberg, M. J. (1966). Some limits of dissonance: Toward a differentiated view of counter-attitudinal performance. In S. Feldman (Ed.), *Cognitive consistency: Motivational antecedents and behavioral consequents* (pp. 135-170). New York: Academic Press.

Rowell, E. Z. (1932a). Prolegomena to argumentation (Part I). *Quarterly Journal of Speech, 18,* 1-13.

Rowell, E. Z. (1932b). Prolegomena to argumentation (Part II). *Quarterly Journal of Speech, 18,* 224-248.

Rubin, J. Z., & Brown, B. R. (1975). *The social psychology of bargaining and negotiation.* New York: Academic Press.

Seibold, D. R., Baya, N. K., Berteotti, C. R., Burgener, S. C., McCornack, S. A., McQuillan, L. P., & Rivers, R. (1986). *Gar'bage or gar baj'-It's all where you place the accent.* Paper presented at the annual meeting of the Speech Communication Association, Chicago.

Seibold, D. R., Cantrill, J. G., & Meyers, R. A. (1985). Communication and interpersonal influence. In M. L. Knapp & G. R. Miller (Eds.), *Handbook of interpersonal communication* (pp. 551-611). Newbury Park, CA: Sage.

Senter, M. M., & Miller, G. R. (1983). *Catching flies with honey and with vinegar: Persuasive message strategy choice in relational dissolution.* Unpublished manuscript, Department of Communication, Michigan State University.

Sereno, K. K., & Hawkins, G. J. (1967). The effects of variations in speakers' nonfluency upon audience ratings of attitude toward the speech topic and speakers' credibility. *Speech Monographs, 34,* 58-64.

Sharp, H., Jr., & McClung, T. (1966). Effects of organization on the speaker's ethos. *Speech Monographs, 33,* 182-183.

Simons, H.W. (1974). The carrot and stick as handmaidens of persuasion in conflict situations. In G. R. Miller & H. W. Simons (Eds.), *Perspectives on communication in social conflict* (pp. 172-205). Englewood Cliffs, NJ: Prentice-Hall.

Skinner, B. F. (1953). *Science and human behavior.* New York: Macmillan.

Skinner, B. F. (1971). *Beyond freedom and dignity.* New York: Knopf.

Smith, R. (1986). Television addiction. In J. Bryant & D. Zillmann (Eds.), *Perspectives on media effects* (pp. 109-128). Hillsdale, NJ: Lawrence Erlbaum.

Spence, K. W. (1944). The nature of theory construction in contemporary psychology. *Psychological Review, 51,* 47-68.

Stiff, J. B. (1986). Cognitive processing of persuasive message cues: A meta-analytic review of the effects of supporting information on attitudes. *Communication Monographs, 53,* 75-89.

Tan, A. S. (1986). Social learning of aggression from television. In J. Bryant & D. Zillmann (Eds.), *Perspectives on media effects* (pp. 41-55). Hillsdale, NJ: Lawrence Erlbaum.

Thurstone, L. L., & Chave, E. J. (1929). *The measurement of attitudes.* Chicago: University of Chicago Press.

Wartella, E., Whitney, D. C., & Windahl, S. (Eds.). (1983). *Mass communication review yearbook* (Vol. 4). Newbury Park, CA: Sage.

Weiss, W. (1969). Effects of the mass media of communication. In G. Lindzey & E. Aronson (Eds.), *Handbook of social psychology* (2nd ed., Vol. 5, pp. 77-195). Reading, MA: Addison-Wesley.

Wheeless, L. R., Barraclough, R., & Stewart, R. (1983). Compliance-gaining and power in persuasion. In R. Bostrom (Ed.), *Communication yearbook 7* (pp. 105-145). Newbury Park, CA: Sage.

Whitney, D. C., Wartella, E., & Windahl, S. (Eds.). (1982). *Mass communication review yearbook* (Vol. 3). Newbury Park, CA: Sage.

Wicklund, R. A., & Brehm, J. W. (1976). *Perspectives on cognitive dissonance.* Hillsdale, NJ: Lawrence Erlbaum.

Wilhoit, G. C., & deBock, H. (Eds.). (1980). *Mass communication review yearbook* (Vol. 1). Newbury Park, CA: Sage.

Wilhoit, G. C., & deBock, H. (Eds.). (1981). *Mass communication review yearbook* (Vol. 2). Newbury Park, CA: Sage.

Williams, D. L., & Boster, F. J. (1981). *The effect of beneficial situational characteristics, negativism, and dogmatism on compliance-gaining message selection.* Paper presented at the annual meeting of the International Communication Association, Minneapolis.

Wiseman, R. L., & Schenck-Hamlin, W. (1981). A multidimensional scaling validation of an inductively-derived set of compliance-gaining strategies. *Communication Monographs, 48,* 251-270.

Woolbert, C. H. (1917). Conviction and persuasion: Some considerations of theory. *Quarterly Journal of Public Speaking, 3,* 249-264.

Zetterberg, H. L. (1965). *On theory and verification in sociology* (3rd ed.). New York: Bedminster Press.

16 Communication and Conflict

MICHAEL E. ROLOFF
Northwestern University

> All men have in them an instinct for conflict
> At least all healthy men.
> —Hilaire Belloc, *The Silence of the Sun*

The opening quotation provides two important insights into human conflict. First, given an inherent tendency toward conflict, it should be both pervasive and inevitable. Conflict is part of much human experience. Individuals wrestle with diverse, complex, and often inconsistent stimuli in order to acquire some understanding of their environment and themselves. Couples with different backgrounds attempt to intertwine their respective interests and behaviors so that a satisfying relationship results. Groups of organizational members possessing different levels of authority and task information attempt to reach consensus about the "best" means of increasing productivity. And, collectivities or their representatives press their particular views of societal institutions in order to redress prior injustices and preclude future ones. Indeed, Fisher and Ury (1981) have argued that conflict tendencies are increasing at such a rate that conflict has become a "growth industry."

Second, conflict is not abnormal and, if handled properly, may actually improve the human condition. The individual who perceives inconsistency in self or others may have a veridical perception and consequently, discover an explanatory principle that will increase his or her understanding. Relational partners who confront their differences can modify their relationship so that greater joint benefits and mutual affection result. Given a knowledge gap between organizational members at different levels of the authority structure, conflict could afford the opportu-

AUTHOR'S NOTE: As with any project of this size, one incurs many debts. Thanks to Charles Berger for allowing me the extra time to pursue the vast amount of information needed; Robert Bell, James Ettema, Peter Miller, and Charles Berger for serving as "sounding boards" and occasional archivists; my former students who patiently understood why their projects were on hold until this was completed; my wife Karen who put up with clatter of word processing late into the night; and to my young daughters, Erika, Katrina, and Carlissa, who make conflict so easy to observe.

nity for greater feedback, adaptation, and innovation. And, to the extent that societal institutions are modified so that all collectivities are treated justly, societal cohesiveness should increase.

While conflict may have a number of benefits, people often associate it with war, strikes, and violence (Hocker & Wilmot, 1985). Given such a negative image, it is not surprising to find readers viewing theoretical pieces on the positive functions of conflict with a skeptical eye. Part of this doubt probably results from coercive attempts to resolve conflict rather than from conflict itself. A variety of other methods might be used to end a conflict, including communication. Since most conflict theorists view the establishment of lines of communication as a necessary condition for effective conflict resolution (e.g., Deutsch, 1973), it is proper that scholarship focused on communication and conflict be reviewed in this volume. This chapter will focus on the relationship between communication and conflict at various levels. The first section will define the two terms and each of the subsequent four sections will review relevant theory and research conducted at each of the four levels described in this handbook: intrapersonal, interpersonal, organizational, and mass communication.

DEFINITIONS

An examination of the literature indicates no shortage of definitions of either conflict (Fink, 1968) or communication (Dance & Larson, 1976). Given the diversity of the material relevant to this discussion, general definitions provide greater range of coverage and hence, are more suitable for our purpose. According to Deutsch (1973, p. 10) "conflict exists whenever *incompatible* activities occur. . . . An action that is incompatible with another action prevents, obstructs, interferes, injures, or in some way makes the latter less likely or less effective." While clearly focused on the incompatibility of activities, it leaves flexibility with regard to the unit (e.g., individual, relationship, organization, or societal group) or activities (e.g., cognition, exchange, task orientation, or societal participation) to be studied. Communication constitutes the production, transmission, and interpretation of symbols. This definition also provides sufficient flexibility with regard to units and activities.

With these two definitions in mind, we argue that communication and conflict are interdependent. Both processes can have important influences on the other. Communication can cause conflict, be symptomatic of conflict, and may be an effective mode of conflict resolution (Hocker & Wilmot, 1985). The degree of conflict can affect the types of symbols produced (e.g., Raush, Barry, Hertel, & Swain, 1974), patterns of observed communications (e.g., Putnam & Jones, 1982), and the interpretation of communication cues (e.g., Wilson & Nisbett, 1978). While the empirical evidence for mutual influence suggests causal ambiguity, it demonstrates the relevance of research related to both processes. The remainder of this chapter will amplify that relationship.

INTRAPERSONAL CONFLICT AND COMMUNICATION

Intrapersonal communication is the production, transmission, and interpretation of symbols *within an individual*. It constitutes the inner experience of people as they attempt to make sense of or discern a pattern in stimuli related to self and others. This definition assumes that intrapersonal communication is driven by and directed toward the creation of understanding or in other words, uncertainty reduction. Individuals develop implicit theories about some stimuli they encounter in order to better predict their occurrence and consequently, control them (Hewes & Planalp, 1982; Wegner & Vallacher, 1977). Since the construction of these explanations is carried out through thought processes, the communication stimuli at the intrapersonal level are thoughts. While this form of communication is internal, persons may construct explanations about their behavior, relational partners, work environments, or events that are reported via the mass media. Therefore, intrapersonal communication can be affected by and can affect factors at other communication levels. Intrapersonal conflict occurs when there is incompatibility or inconsistency among an individual's cognitive elements. This implies that a new cognitive element is at variance with a prior explanation or expectation. Thus intrapersonal conflict reflects a challenge to a person's basis for prediction and control resulting in greater uncertainty. This section will examine research related to the frequency and resolution of intrapersonal conflict.

Frequency of Intrapersonal Conflict

Inner turmoil is unavoidable (Deutsch, 1973). While a variety of sources contribute to internal dissension, an important one stems from inconsistency between cognition and behavior. Research indicates low correlations between behavior and expressed attitudes (Wicker, 1969; Zanna & Olson, 1982) and personality traits (Mischel, 1968). This implies that individuals' conceptions of their behavior could be at variance with self-related cognitions, and that observers who are aware of actors' self-images may be equally dismayed at their incongruent behavior.

While this research seems to support Deutsch's conclusion, there are limiting factors. First, individuals may not closely monitor all of their behavior and, hence, are unaware of any inconsistencies. This may be especially likely when behavior is habitual (Langer, 1978) or when it occurs at a micro level (Argyle, 1975). Second, behavior tends to be consistent with *relevant* attitudes (Snyder, 1982), self-schemata (Markus, 1977), and personality traits (Mischel & Peak, 1982). If so, then an individual and, perhaps, observer may only be aware of how a given action is related to a particular internal standard but not to others with which it might be inconsistent. Thus many behaviors may be interpreted as consistent and generate minimal intrapersonal conflict. Nevertheless, if an individual is made aware of behavioral incongruity, challenges to his or her cognitive structure should occur and internal communication aimed at discovering the reasons for the inconsistency should ensue (Wong & Weiner, 1981).

Methods of Reducing Intrapersonal Conflict

When an inconsistency is perceived, it is generally assumed that tension arises. For example, Festinger (1957) argued that cognitive dissonance occurs when two related cognitive elements do not fit together well and that dissonance produces a drive to reduce inconsistency. While Festinger was not explicit as to why inconsistency should be drive producing, Pepitone (1968) observed that individuals need to maintain a system for understanding phenomena. Inconsistency threatens the validity of the framework and uncertainty results. When inconsistency is perceived, subsequent internal communication could be aimed at reducing uncertainty but not necessarily the inconsistency. Kelmen and Baron (1968) noted that instead of actually restoring consistency through changes in the cognitive system or behavior, individuals can maintain inconsistency but reduce the tensions associated with it. If a person has a well-formed attitude or self-schemata, the most effective method of reducing uncertainty may be to "explain away" the inconsistency. To modify the cognitive structure may imply a new and potentially risky course of thinking and acting.

In order to reduce uncertainty, a "plausible" account for the discrepancy must be provided. One set of "plausible" accounts stem from environmental causes for the inconsistent action. Attribution research indicates that actors, as opposed to observers of the actors, tend to account for their actions through situational factors (see Ross, 1977). Therefore, when made aware of an inconsistency, an actor can define it as irrelevant to the self-image since external factors produced the incongruency and the cognitive structure need not be changed. Consistent with this reasoning, dissonance research indicates that minimal attitudinal or behavioral changes occur unless actors believe that they chose the inconsistent behavior (see Petty & Cocioppo, 1981), foresaw negative consequences (see Wicklund & Brehm, 1976), and/or perceive that observers of the action will not accept an explanation for the inconsistency (see Petty & Cocioppo, 1981). For the person with a relatively undefined cognitive structure, perceiving a behavior as inconsistent with some standard may not stimulate much uncertainty and may even constitute the basis for predicting future behavior (Bem, 1972).

While much of the aforementioned research has been concerned with how self-generated inconsistency is resolved, other studies have focused on how inconsistencies in perceptions of others are resolved. While the search for plausible explanations should be similar to that of actors it is constrained somewhat by the tendency of observers to attribute internal rather than external causes for behavior. Observers may rely upon three mechanisms for handling inconsistent impressions (Wegner & Vallacher, 1977). One method is termed *univalence* and involves the total acceptance of an explanation consistent with a new perception or total rejection of the new perception in favor of the old one. A second method is *aggregation* and involves accepting the old image and new information as valid, with no attempt to explain the inconsistency. *Integration* occurs when the perceiver accepts both the initial impression and the inconsistent perception as valid but develops an explanation for their existence.

Although univalence and integration should result in reductions in uncertainty, aggregation leaves the inconsistency unaccounted for and uncertainty may remain high. Aggregation may only occur when the perceiver does not anticipate having to act upon his or her impressions of another and therefore the consequences of uncertainty are low. Not having to communicate about a set of contradictory traits reduces the amount of effort put into integrating them into a coherent pattern (Davis & Wicklund, 1972). Choosing univalence or integration could depend upon the extent of discrepancy between new information and a prior impression. If information is not highly inconsistent with a schema, it may be assimilated or distorted in such a fashion that it appears consistent or may be attributed to temporary situational causes and forgotten (Crocker, Fiske, & Taylor, 1984). If the information is in gross conflict with the cognitive structure, a "plausible" explanation may be more difficult to construct and cognitive structure will change.

Thus intrapersonal conflict is a source of uncertainty. It threatens the validity of a person's basis for predicting and controlling events. People are not likely to be aware of all of their behaviors or the implications of those actions for a wide range of cognitions. When intrapersonal conflict is perceived, the individual seeks an explanation for the disconfirmation. If a "plausible" explanation is found, the cognitive structure may not change much. If not, some alteration takes place.

INTERPERSONAL CONFLICT AND COMMUNICATION

Interpersonal communication constitutes the production, transmission, and interpretation of symbols by *relational partners*. This definition implies that each communicator has acknowledged the other's existence and, to some degree, will be responsive to the other's behavior. Our conceptualization also assumes that current behavior is affected by prior relational history or by anticipated relational outcomes (Hinde, 1979). Within this framework, interpersonal communication functions as a means of resource exchange and as a method by which partners coordinate their actions so as to produce the relational rewards vital to relationship growth and maintenance (Roloff, 1981b).

Interpersonal conflict involves the existence of incompatible actions between relational partners, thus decreasing their mutual rewards. This section will be subdivided into three major areas: frequency of interpersonal conflict, intrapersonal conflict and communication in relationships, and relational conflict and communication.

Frequency of Interpersonal Conflict

Conflict within close relationships has been hypothesized to be frequent and intense (e.g., Coser, 1956), and Sprey (1969, p. 703) has gone so far as to suggest that "family harmony must be considered a problematic rather than normal state of affairs." Close interdependency, frequent scrutiny of motives, and attempts to negotiate relational rules have all been posited as factors that lead to greater conflict in intimate relationships (Altman & Taylor, 1973). Several studies support this conjecture (Argyle & Furnham, 1983; Birchler, Weiss, & Vincent, 1975; Braiker & Kelley, 1979; Swensen, Eskew, & Kohlhepp, 1981; Vincent, Weiss, & Birchler, 1975).

Intrapersonal Conflict and Communication in Relationships

Intrapersonal conflict, communication, and uncertainty are important aspects of interpersonal relationships. Relational partners try to reduce uncertainty about themselves (Cushman & Craig, 1976; McCall & Simmons, 1978) and others (Berger & Bradac, 1982) through communication. Uncertainty makes the coordination of relational behavior difficult. One method of reducing uncertainty is the construction of relational roles that specify expectations and duties for a given occupant. While a role may add a measure of predictability for relational partners, it may also lead to internal dissension and later increases in uncertainty. We will examine three role-related conflicts: self-focused, partner-focused, and relational-focused.

Self-focused role conflict. At least three of these conflicts can be identified. In some cases, a self-role incongruity may occur (Sarbin & Allen, 1968). This problem develops when relational partners are expected to enact roles that are inconsistent with their self-concepts. For example, an independent person may have difficulty with role constraints imposed by marriage. These conflicts may be resolved when the role occupant changes the self in the direction of the role or avoids inconsistent roles (Backman & Secord, 1968). Second, interrole conflict occurs when a single individual occupies several incompatible roles (Sarbin & Allen, 1968). For example, work schedules, excessive time commitments, and job-related fatigue make the fulfillment of family roles difficult (Plack, Staines, & Lang, 1980). Finally, role incompetency may stimulate intrapersonal conflict because role enactment is below standards of performance. If the role has been incorporated into one's self-image and if one cannot rationalize the poor role performance, conflict may be intense (e.g., McCall & Simmons, 1978).

Partner-focused role conflict. Since relational roles provide a basis for predicting the partner's behavior, deviations from those expectations should stimulate uncertainty. Intrapersonal conflict occurs when the relational partner's role performance is of lower quality or different from those expected by the perceiver. Murstein (1971) found that couples who made "good courtship progress" evidenced greater perceived role fit, and Nye and McLaughlin (1976) reported that 36% of the variance in wives' and 9% of husbands' marital satisfaction was accounted for by the quality of their partner's role performance. However, these inadequate role performances might be attributed to external factors and thus attenuating role conflict (Hall & Taylor, 1976).

Relational-focused role conflict. Individuals not only have expectations about how roles should be enacted but also possess notions of how effort put forth within those roles should be associated with the distribution of relational resources. Walster, Walster, and Berscheid (1978) argue that relational partners evaluate their outcomes according to an equity principle that assumes equal relative gains for each relational partner. If unequal gains are perceived, both the beneficiary and victim of the inequity will feel distressed. These feelings may be resolved by thinking about justifications for the inequity or distorting relative contributions and gains. Both dating couples and newlyweds are less distressed if they reported being treated equitably rather than over- or underbenefited (Hatfield, Utne, & Traupmann, 1979). Also, equitably treated dating part ners were more certain their relationship would be intact one year and five years later than those under- or overbenefited.

If inner role conflicts are not adequately handled, the relationship may be in jeopardy. Indeed, Bahr, Chappel, and Leigh (1983) discovered that the quality of own and partner's role enactment combined with the degree of role consensus accounted for 44% of wives' and 35% of husbands' variance in marital satisfaction.

Relational Communication and Conflict

Conflict within a relational partner may be resolved through internal communication; hence, it may never be apparent to the other partner. Occasionally, however, internal conflicts come to the attention of both partners and may "explode forth." When mutual perception of incompatibility occurs, relational conflict has arisen. Our analysis of this conflict type will focus upon the mutual perception of incompatibility and resulting overt communication behaviors.

Mutual perception of incompatibility. Relational conflict may stem from disagreement over three aspects of a behavioral enactment. The *degree* to which the partners agree that a given action is incompatible is the first aspect. One partner may accuse the other of making his or her own role enactment more difficult. For example, working wives experience greater conflict between work and home roles when their husbands have traditional sex role orientations (Beutell & Greenhaus, 1983) or if their husbands are career-oriented and there are children in the family (Beutell & Greenhaus, 1982). Or, this conflict may arise from a self-centered bias in which spouses assume that they contribute more to a joint task (including marital activity) than their partners are willing to acknowledge (Ross & Sicoly, 1979; Thompson & Kelley, 1981).

This basic conflict may escalate to a second level at which the partners disagree over the *causes* of a behavior enactment. When people encounter negative behavior emitted toward them (especially if directed from an intimate), they will likely try to understand why it occurred. Differing explanations will produce attributional conflict (Horai, 1977; Orvis, Kelley, & Butler, 1976). This conflict may stem from the tendency of actors to explain their behavior (and especially behavior having negative consequences) by citing external causes or temporary internal states while observers (and especially victims of the behavior) attribute internal traits or dispositions (Kelley, 1979; Orvis et al., 1976; Passer, Kelley, & Michela, 1978). Such conflicts may be irresolvable (Orvis et al., 1976). Among partners who are dissatisfied with their relationship, these conflicts occur with greater frequency (Holtzworth-Munroe & Jacobson, 1985; Jacobson, McDonald, Follette, & Berley, 1985).

The final area of disagreement may stem from the *perceived implica-tions* of an act for continuation of the relationship. Not all conflicts over behavioral enactments are judged to be equally significant for the future of the relationship. At least two factors determine when salience will increase. First, the greater the number of unresolved relational conflicts, the greater the likelihood that a current disagreement will be perceived as important (Birchler & Webb, 1977; Filley, 1975; Jacobson, Follette, & McDonald, 1982). Second, certain rules may constitute critical rela-tional bonds, the single violation of which may be sufficient to threaten the relationship. For example, Argyle and Henderson (1984) found that the violation of such friendship rules as keeping confidences, volun-teering to help in time of need, and avoiding public criticism were very frequent causes of the breakup of friendships. Conflicts are less severe and easier to resolve when focused upon the occurrence of a behavioral enactment than when they escalate to the attributional or relational sig-nificance level (Kelley, 1979). High levels of conflict may divert atten-tion away from the development of solutions and toward blaming and retribution. Those processes may cause the accused to engage in face-saving behavior, thus escalating conflict further.

Overt communication behaviors. Since overt communications may have a direct bearing upon conflict resolution and may themselves become a cause of conflict (see Braiker & Kelley, 1979), we will next focus upon communication preferences, patterns, and interpretations.

(1) Communication Preferences. When in conflict, individuals often demonstrate preferences for certain communication styles. Research in this area has focused on three factors that influence such preferences: socialization, gender, and attributions.

A person's background can have a strong influence on how they deal with conflict. Specifically, one's family and peers may serve as role models for how conflicts should be resolved (Bandura, 1973). For example, abused children are more likely to become abusive adults (Carroll, 1977; Rosenbaum & O'Leary, 1981; Ulbrich & Huber, 1981). Relationships have been found between family (Roloff & Greenberg, 1980; Steinmetz, 1977) and peer (Roloff & Greenberg, 1980) conflict behavior and preferences for both pro- and antisocial modes of conflict resolution.

There are gender differences in preferences for modes of conflict reso-lution. Females in dating relationships are perceived to be more emo-tional in conflict interactions than males (Kelley et al., 1978; Sullaway & Christensen, 1983), and males reciprocate their female partner's con-ciliatory attempts while females respond to such attempts with greater rejection and less support (Lochman & Allen, 1979; Raush et al., 1974).

A social exchange approach may explain these gender differences (Scanzoni, 1979). Historically, wives have been at a bargaining disadvantage relative to their husbands because of lowered access to crucial resources. However, as women have attained greater access to such resources as jobs and education, their perceptions of gender roles have become more egalitarian. Modern gender role wives show greater preferences to enter the work force, view their jobs as of equal or greater importance than their husbands', are more likely to bargain individualistically rather than collectivistically (e.g., "do this because it is best for me" rather than "do this because it is best for the family"), and are more successful at bargaining with their husbands than are their traditional counterparts. Wives (and especially gender role moderns) may be confrontative in dealing with their husbands whereas husbands may avoid conflicts (postpone) or refute their wives' reasons as a way of trying to maintain their relative advantage (see Fitzpatrick, Chapter 19 in this volume).

These differences may also be explained by differential reactions to stress. Marriage is a more stressful state of affairs for wives than husbands (Pearlin, 1974; Shafer & Keith, 1980). Women are prone to externalize their emotions, while men tend to internalize theirs (Buck, Miller, & Caul, 1974; Buck, Savin, Miller, & Caul, 1972). Consequently, wives are more likely to express frustrations resulting from conflict than are their husbands.

Attributional conflict also occurs in heterosexual relationships. Both genders may assume that each responds to conflict and stress in a similar manner; thus, a confrontative female may be perceived by a controlled male as unstable, whereas the controlled male may be perceived as uncaring or uninvolved in the relationship. But, these attributions may be incorrect. Notarius and Johnson (1982) found that wives were significantly more negative than husbands in an interaction, but husbands showed greater physiological reactions to their wives' negative speech than the wives manifested in response to the husbands'. Thus the wives appeared more upset but *physiologically* the husbands were more aroused (Notarius & Johnson, 1982).

A final factor that may influence communication preferences are attributions of responsibility for conflict. People are more likely to reciprocate physical aggression if it is perceived as intentional rather than accidental or normative (Dyck & Rule, 1978; Epstein & Taylor, 1967; Greenwell & Dengerink, 1973; Nickel, 1974). Beyond aggression, blaming oneself for a conflict is negatively correlated with the use of conflict avoidance and coercive strategies and positively correlated with self-disclosure and problem-solving behavior (Sillars, 1980b). When the other is perceived to be at fault, communicators either try to avoid the conflict or, conversely, become more confrontative (Sillars, 1980a, 1980b). Thus a person's preference for modes of conflict resolution may be based upon socialization, gender, or attributions. However, since most of this research has neglected the *interactive* nature of conflict, the next section will examine communication patterns that occur within these interactions.

(2) Communication Patterns. Message exchange research has focused on differences between happily and unhappily married couples. Within this context are two general theoretical perspectives: social learning, and the structural model. The social learning approach posits that when marital partners are in conflict, they could change each other's behavior through positive reinforcements or coercive actions (e.g., Patterson & Reid, 1970). Because coercive behaviors usually result in temporary compliance, aversive messages are reinforced. However, such short-term solutions as coercion carry with them long-term liabilities. Coerced persons may reciprocate negative behaviors, decrease positive exchanges, or avoid coercive partners altogether (Birchler et al., 1975).

Within conflict interactions, distressed marrieds enact more negative and fewer positive social reinforcers than nondistressed couples (Billings, 1979; Birchler et al., 1975; Koren, Carlton, & Shaw, 1980; Vincent et al., 1975). However, Gottman et al. (1976) found that when couples coded their *own statements* as intended to be positive or negative, distressed and nondistressed couples did not differ. In addition, while Margolin and Wampold (1981) reported that nondistressed couples enacted more positive problem-solving behaviors than their distressed counterparts, distressed and nondistressed couples did not differ in the frequency of verbal or nonverbal negative messages.

Gottman's (1979) structural model of marital interaction posits that conflict interactions between distressed marrieds tend to be more structured and patterned than between nondistressed marrieds; thus, nondistressed couples have greater capability to alter the course of their interactions. Apparently, distressed couples do repeat particular stimulus-response sequences further into a conversation than do nondistressed couples (Ting-Toomey, 1983).

The structural model makes three predictions about communication patterns. First, like social learning theory's hypothesis, nondistressed couples are expected to be more positive and less negative toward one another. Gottman's (1979) research indicates that distressed couples encode greater frequencies of negative and neutral nonverbal cues than nondistressed couples, providing support for this prediction.

Second, the model predicts that distressed marrieds will be more likely to reciprocate negative behavior than nondistressed couples but the two types of dyads will not differ in their reciprocation of positive communication. This hypothesis has been supported for negative nonverbal cues (Gottman, 1979; Margolin & Wampold, 1981) but contrary to the prediction, distressed couples are more likely to reciprocate positive affect in the early stages of an interaction but less so in later ones (Gottman, 1979).

Finally, the structural model predicts that the communication of one of the members of a distressed dyad can be predicted by his or her partner's behavior to a greater extent than the partner's can be predicted from that person's. Gottman (1979) reported that only in high conflict interactions, wives in distressed marriages are more reactive to their husband's emotional changes than the husbands are to the wives' and that no gender differences were observed in nondistressed marriages.

Perhaps the greatest limitation of Gottman's approach stems from its reliance upon lag sequential analysis for measures of reciprocity and structure. Recently, Sillars and Weisberg (in press) have argued that reliance upon methods that assume rigid, lagged responses may obscure some of the confusion, chaos, and subtle shifts that characterize conflictive interactions. Furthermore, the particular patterns observed through statistical measures may not fit the phenomenological experience of communicators (see Roloff & Campion, 1985).

(3) Communication Interpretation. Little research has focused on how relational partners interpret the symbols in their interactions. Gottman et al. (1976) addressed this issue and found that misinterpretation of the intent behind communication may characterize those in distressed marriages. Moreover, distressed couples tend to attribute their spouse's negative communication in a conflict to internal factors and the positive to external factors whereas the reverse is true of nondistressed couples (Jacobson et al., 1985). Thus misinterpretation or second-guessing of intent may impede conflict resolution. We will focus on two potential causes of misunderstanding in conflict.

First, misinterpretation may result from faulty decoding skills. In distressed marriages, husbands are less able to interpret their wives' nonverbal cues while their wives can successfully decode their husbands' (Gottman & Porterfield, 1981; Noller, 1980). However, this result could stem from either the male's lack of ability (Gottman & Porterfield, 1981) or from his lack of motivation (Noller, 1981).

A second source of misinterpretation may result from faulty encoding skills. Distressed husbands are poor encoders of nonverbal affect (Noller, 1980; Sabatelli, Buck, & Dreyer, 1982) and distressed wives are more likely to communicate inconsistent affect across communication channels (Noller, 1982). Further, if partners use modes of conflict resolution that do not amplify upon their positions or rationales, understanding may be lower (Roloff, 1976). Threats (Carnevale, Pruitt, & Selheimer, 1981; Kimmel, Pruitt, Maganeu, Konar-Golband, & Carnevale, 1980), domineering behavior (Courtright, Millar, & Rogers-Millar, 1979), and conflict avoidance (Knudson, Sommers, & Golding, 1980) reduce understanding between conflicting parties while problem-solving behaviors increase it (Kimmel et al., 1980). However, good decoding skills (Rosenthal & DePaulo, 1979) and understanding (Sillars et al., 1984) are negatively correlated with relational satisfaction. Knowing does not always lead to happiness.

Conflict is a frequent part of everyday relational life. Role conflicts may prompt internal dissension, and conflicting behavioral enactments may escalate into disputes over causes and significance for relational futures. While some communication behaviors may facilitate effective conflict resolution, others may inhibit it.

ORGANIZATIONAL COMMUNICATION AND CONFLICT

Organizational communication constitutes the production, transmission, and interpretation of symbols by *organizational members*. Organizational members are persons who see themselves as part of or representatives of a body of formally interconnected and interdependent individuals. The primary function of organizational communication is to coordinate the actions of the membership so that organizational goals are met, or, as noted by Cushman and Craig (1976), to create consensus about production. This broad function can be subdivided into the three subprocesses of discovery, implementation, and maintenance of efficient task-oriented behaviors (Farace, Monge, & Russell, 1977).

Organizational conflict occurs when members engage in activities that are incompatible with those of colleagues within their network, members of other collectivities, or unaffiliated individuals who utilize the services or products of the organization. These disputes may be focused on the value of organizational objectives, methods of achieving those goals, the degree to which standards are being realized, and/or the fair distribution of rewards associated with goal achievement. Organizational communication and conflict will be discussed in five parts: frequency of organizational conflict, intrapersonal conflict and communication in organizations, interpersonal conflict and communication in organizations, intergroup conflict and communication in organizations, and extraorganizational conflict and communication.

Frequency of Organizational Conflict

Conflict is an inherent part of organizational life (e.g., Brett, 1984; Pondy, 1967; Thomas, 1976). Middle managers report spending over 25% of their time in conflicts with superiors, peers, and subordinates, and across ranks managers report about 20% of their time involves trying to regulate such disputes (Thomas & Schmidt, 1976). Furthermore, responsibility for dealing with conflicts may be associated with formal managerial role requirements (Tornow & Pinto, 1976).

The inevitability of organizational conflict stems from a variety of sources. First, the large size of organizations makes supervision of activities difficult (Downs, 1967). Consequently, out of maliciousness or lack of information, organizational members behave in ways contrary to organizational objectives. Second, the structure of an organization may stimulate conflict. Given the pervasiveness of division of labor, separate but interdependent sections of an organization may compete for control of resources and areas of responsibility (Downs, 1967) and the authority structure may pit those with authority against those who lack it (Kipnis, 1972). Third, organizational conflict may result from processes necessary for coordinating actions. Individuals' goals may be sacrificed for those of the larger organization. This loss of individuality may alienate persons from the larger organization (Argyris, 1957). Fourth, conflict may result from organizational change and adaptation. Conflict may be associated with internal adjustment to changing technology and factors in the organizational environment (Katz & Kahn, 1966). Finally, conflict may occur because of turmoil external to the organization. Dissension in society may be infused into organizations (Brown & Brown, 1983).

While these factors may not be a complete list, they suggest that conflict may be a permanent part of organizations. Indeed, Cyret and March (1963) speculated that organizations are never able to resolve conflict completely but instead engage in "quasi-resolution of conflict."

Intrapersonal Conflict and Communication in Organizations

Despite the efforts of organizations to establish a clear, stable, and predictable internal environment, uncertainty and intrapersonal conflict are frequent occurrences. We will examine two types: role conflict and policy decision making.

Role conflict. In order to coordinate the activities of large numbers of interdependent members, organizations have constructed organizational roles (Kahn, Wolfe, Quinn, Snoek, & Rosenthal, 1964). These roles are often the focus of formal and informal socialization processes for new members (Van Maanen & Schein, 1979). However, despite these efforts, members may find that role expectations do not conform to reality, resulting in intrapersonal conflict (Jablin, 1982; Louis, 1980; see Jablin & Krone, Chapter 23).

Katz and Kahn (1966) identified several types of organizational role conflicts including intersender, intrasender, interrole, person-role, and role overload. In their classic work, Kahn et al. (1964) found that 40 to 50% of workers surveyed reported experiencing role conflicts. Since this work, two meta-analyses of this literature indicate that role conflict is negatively related to organizational involvement, commitment, general job satisfaction, and may predict the propensity to quit (Fisher & Gitelson, 1983; Jackson & Schuler, 1985).

While role conflict may have dire consequences, in most cases it may not be difficult to resolve. Van De Vliert (1981) found that in 76% of the cases of role conflict, only one of the roles was legitimately sanctioned, had negative sanctions attached to its performance, or both. Consequently, the most frequent method of coping was choosing one particular role over another.

Policy decision making. Organizational members may encounter intrapersonal conflict as a result of decisions made on the job. The costs of seeking adequate information about the decision (Downs, 1967), quasirational decision making (Hammond & Brehmer, 1973), and "groupthink" (Janis, 1972; Longley & Pruitt, 1980) all make these choices problematic.

After encountering negative feedback about a decision, one might expect that it might simply be revoked; however, decision makers may continue to invest resources in failed policies and decisions (Bazerman, Beekun, & Schoorman, 1982; Rubin & Brockner, 1975; Staw, 1976). Such entrapment is equally likely for individuals and group decision makers (Bazerman, Guiliano, & Appleman, 1984). Entrapment may result from three factors (Staw, 1981). First, a decision maker may feel that his or her credibility will be harmed if a decision fails or is revoked (Bazerman et al., 1982; Bazerman et al., 1984; Rubin, Brockner, Small-Weil, & Nathanson, 1980; Staw, 1976). Second, entrapment may occur because of leadership role models who were successful through perseverence in the "face of adversity" (Brockner, Rubin, & Lang, 1981; Nathanson et al., 1982). Finally, continued investment is more likely when the decision maker believes that success will result with continued resources (Staw & Fox, 1977). Thus organizational decision makers may persevere in the belief that a bad decision was wise.

Interpersonal Conflict and Communication
in Organizations

Interpersonal relationships are important factors in organizational behavior and vice versa. Work schedules can create conflict in family relationships (Shamir, 1983) and family responsibilities (e.g., young children) are related to organizational problems such as absences, tardiness, inattention, and inefficiency (Crouter, 1984). However, superior-subordinate relationships on the job are also of critical importance to organizations (Jablin, 1979).

Interpersonal conflict appears frequently in these job relationships. In comparison to a variety of other types of relationships (e.g., parent, friends), people report that their relations with a work supervisor are less satisfactory and more conflictive (Argyle & Furnham, 1983). The dynamics of these conflicts can harm the quality of the work relationship and reduce satisfaction with the organization (Burke, 1970; Howat & London, 1980; Infante & Gorden, 1985; Richmond, Wagner, & McCroskey, 1983). Our analysis will focus on mutual perceptions of incompatibility and the overt communication behaviors enacted within these disputes.

Mutual perception of incompatibility. The perceptions of superiors and subordinates may marginally be related to one another. For example, Howat and London (1980) reported a modest correlation (.35) between superior and subordinate estimates of how frequently they were in conflict with each other. Baird (1977) found weak correlations (.13 to .21) between superior's and subordinate's estimates of the subordinate's performance. Smircich and Chesser (1981) reported no relationship between superiors' ratings of subordinates' performance and subordinates' estimates of how superiors would rate them. Since organizations typically base part of a member's salary on performance, these findings imply that this process is rife with disagreement.

When conflict occurs in performance appraisal, attributional conflict can result as superiors and subordinates generate explanations for poor performance (Green & Mitchell, 1979). Superiors are more likely to attribute a subordinate's poor performance to internal rather than external causes, and this propensity increases when the subordinate has had a bad performance record and the consequences of the poor performance are severe (Mitchell & Wood, 1980). Conflict may escalate when subordinates attribute their poor performance to situational factors (Gioia & Sims, 1985). Such disputes may have serious consequences for a subordinate if motivational problems are recorded in the subordinate's permanent record (Riccillo & Trenholm, 1983).

Overt communication behaviors. At some point, the conflicting perceptions may emerge and the superior and subordinate may communicate about them. We will focus on their selection, transmission, and interpretation of such symbols.

(1) Selection Processes. Bacharach and Lawler's (1980) theory of power in organizations distinguishes between two types of organiza-

tional power: authority and influence. Authority is the structural component of power and is grounded within the office held by the individual, whereas influence is an informal type of power emerging from an individual's personality or expertise.

Given their analysis, superiors should be better able to bring to bear formal sanctions than their subordinates who may have to rely primarily upon influence. Superiors rely upon control strategies to a greater extent than subordinates while subordinates select more problem-solving approaches (Kipnis, Schmidt, & Wilkinson, 1980; Putnam & Wilson, 1982). However, superiors who have a great deal of confidence and experience avoid the use of authority-based power (Conrad, 1983; Goodstadt & Kipnis, 1970; Instone, Major, & Bunker, 1983; Kipnis & Cosentino, 1969; Kipnis & Lane, 1962) and instead rely upon their personal influence (Goodstadt & Hjelle, 1973; Goodstadt & Kipnis, 1970). If a supervisor perceives the cause of a subordinate's poor performance to be internally based, punitive responses are more likely (Green & Liden, 1980; Mitchell & Wood, 1980; Riccillo & Trenholm, 1983).

(2) Communication Transmission. While research focused on superior-subordinate conflict interactions has employed limited communication situations, there is evidence of mutual influence in their behaviors. Subordinates may enact different conflict communication depending upon the particular approach chosen by the superior. An authority who attempts to intimidate rather than reward disagreeing subordinates may find them forming into retaliatory coalitions (Freedman, 1981; Lawler, 1975). Subordinates who communicate accounts of external causes for their poor performance are less likely to receive punitive communication from their superiors than are subordinates who provide no information or are hostile (Gioia & Sims, 1986; Goodstadt & Hjelle, 1973; Goodstadt & Kipnis, 1970; Wood & Mitchell, 1981).

(3) Interpretation of Communication. Superior-subordinate conflicts may also suffer from misunderstanding. In some cases, misunderstanding results from conflict avoidance. A subordinate may fear that conflict could lead to reprisal by the superior and may be unduly compliant, positive (Musser, 1982), or may even avoid proposing new ideas (Miller, 1982). The same tendency can be found among superiors. Consequently, superiors' true evaluations may not be discerned by subordinates during performance evaluation (Fisher, 1979).

Competitive tactics may also inhibit understanding. An attack upon a person's self-concept in a problem-solving discussion results in greater misunderstanding and rejection than if accepting statements are made (Tjosvold, Johnson, & Lerner, 1981). On the other hand, a cooperative approach to controversy in which the individuals have a frank and open but not rejecting discussion enhances understanding (Tjosvold, 1982; Tjosvold & Deemer, 1980).

Intergroup Conflict and Communication in Organizations

Intergroup conflict occurs when the collective interests of a particular group are incompatible with those of another. While this form of conflict implies each member of a group is in conflict with those of another, quite often the actual dispute is carried out between representatives (e.g., departmental heads, or labor-management negotiators). We will focus on two types of intergroup conflicts in organizations: interdepartmental and labor-management.

Interdepartmental conflict. Organizations frequently cluster individuals into specialized work groups. Each group may concentrate its efforts on the completion of a different subgoal. Despite the separation of these groups, they are still interdependent. They compete for resources, but their efforts must coalesce. Often this interdependence leads to conflict (Thomas, Walton, & Dutton, 1972). When interdepartmental conflict occurs, the opposing parties may adopt a tough, distributive bargaining stance or a more problem-solving, integrative one (Dutton & Walton, 1966). Departments employing a distributive rather than integrative approach limit their interdepartmental communication to representatives, appeal their conflicts to superiors, resort to formal rules when making interdepartmental decisions, see greater interdepartmental differences, and engage in more negative stereotyping and story telling (Walton, Dutton & Fitch, 1966). In addition, when group representatives feel strong commitments to their constituency, their tough, distributive bargaining produces agreements that are not in the best interest of the larger system in which they reside (Vidmar, 1971; Vidmar & McGrath, 1970).

Persons with higher authority in the organization may be compelled to mediate the dispute (Sheppard, 1983). While the presence of a mediator may increase the quality of agreements ending intergroup disputes, it may also lower mutual trust between group representatives and lower satisfaction with the negotiations (Vidmar, 1971). Although no research has focused on the effectiveness of different styles of authority intervention, scholars have argued for both inquisitorial (Sheppard, 1983) and adversarial methods (Notz, Starke, & Atwell, 1983).

Labor-management disputes. Two forms of conflict have been identified in collective bargaining: intragroup and interrepresentative. Intragroup conflict occurs within labor and management constituencies (Walton & McKersie, 1965). Because these groups are heterogeneous, there may be little consensus about goals or strategies (e.g., Rabbie &

Huygen, 1974). Consequently, certain group members must mediate among those who are more radical and those who advocate softer positions (Colosi, 1983). The primary strategy is to soften hard-line expectations (McKersie, Perry, & Walton, 1965). This may be facilitated when groups perceive the consequences of a work stoppage to be grave (Peterson & Tracy, 1977).

If hard-liners prevail, accountability pressures induce representatives to use tough bargaining (Klimoski, 1972; Roloff & Campion, in press; Slusher, 1978; Tjosvold, 1977a, 1977b; Wall, 1981) and deadlocks are more likely (Roloff & Campion, in press). Under some conditions, hard-liners can be effectively used by the representative. Bargainers make significant concessions when encountering a representative who bargains softly but has a radical constituency (Wall, 1977). However, the effectiveness of this strategy is limited to situations where offers are within the acceptable bargaining range of the opponent (Friedland, 1983).

Interrepresentative conflict occurs between the leaders of the two opposing groups. This form of bargaining places representatives in a quandry as to the best strategy to use (Tedeschi & Rosenfeld, 1980). A tough bargaining strategy might achieve significant benefits for the constituency (e.g., Donohue, 1981) but also run the increased risk of deadlocks (Bateman, 1980; Putnam & Jones, 1982; Tjosvold & Huston, 1978). Softer strategies avoid an impasse but yield smaller outcomes and, potentially, contract rejection (Odewahn & Krislov, 1973).

To resolve this dilemma negotiators may start by being tough (high offers and strong rhetoric) but later switch to problem-solving behaviors (information exchange, creation of alternative settlements). Such an approach may enhance one's perceived sincerity and legitimacy before starting the search for a mutually beneficial agreement (Pruitt, 1981). Successful collective bargaining appears to progress through distributive bargaining phases to problem-solving ones (Morley & Stephensen, 1977).

The presence of a third party may facilitate concession making without loss of face or pressure from constituencies (Rubin, 1980). Representatives can retreat from hard-line positions while giving the appearance that they are cooperating rather than giving in to the opposition.

Extraorganizational Communication
and Conflict

Organizations may be in conflict with other organizations over the exchange of goods and services, and organizations that provide support services for one another may be in conflict (Adams, 1976; Rosenberg & Stern, 1971; Stern, 1971; Stern, Sternthal, & Craig, 1973). It is in the interest of organizational members or boundary spanners to press for the goals of their employer, but their frequent contact with other organizations and groups may convince them that outside agents have legitimate interests as well. Boundary spanners do experience greater amounts of role conflict (Fisher & Gitelson, 1983). If their ambivalence is perceived by other group members, then increased pressure may be brought to bear on them (Wall & Adams, 1974), resulting in their adoption of tougher bargaining strategies (Carnevale, Pruitt, & Britton, 1979; Clopton, 1984; Gruder, 1971; Gruder & Rosen, 1971) and deadlocks (Gruder & Rosen, 1971; Tjosvold, 1977b). Fortunately, if boundary role occupants can establish a long-term, cooperative arrangement with a client (Ben-Yoav & Pruitt, 1984; Roering, Slusher, & Schooler, 1975) or if they perceive a mutual threat from a competitor (Hunger & Stern, 1976), they may be able resist accountability pressure and achieve agreements that are mutually rewarding.

Conflict may be encountered in various aspects of the work place. Roles may conflict and seemingly wise decisions may fail. One may find significant disagreement with a direct supervisor, and one's work group or status group may be in conflict with others. Beyond internal squabbling, one may also have to contend with other organizations whose interests conflict with those of one's own.

MASS COMMUNICATION AND CONFLICT

Mass communication constitutes the production, transmission, and interpretation of symbols by members of mass media organizations, unaffiliated individuals who appear in media accounts, consumers of media messages, and/or representatives of groups concerned about media performance. The primary function of mass communication is to provide an account of what is and/or should be entertaining, informative, important, or in some way useful to a particular audience. As the media reflect, highlight, and promote issues within their messages, they help create consensus about cultural institutions and problems (Cushman & Craig, 1976). Conflict at the mass level involves the existence of incompatible activities among media actors, representatives, audiences, and/ or institutional groups. As such, conflict may be evidenced within media content, the reactions of audiences while decoding the content, the message creation process, and pressure brought to bear by those representing various media audiences.

The discussion of mass communication and conflict will be divided into five parts: frequency of conflict in mass media content, intrapersonal conflict and the mass media, interpersonal conflict and the mass media, organizational conflict in the mass media, and mass communication and conflict at the cultural level.

Frequency of Conflict in Mass Media Content

The mass media communicate diverse images of events, people, objects, and the relationships among them. Conflict is a common theme running through mass media entertainment and news content.

Conflict in entertainment content. Conflict is frequently portrayed in such entertainment content as tv drama (Comstock, Chaffee, Katzman, McCombs, & Roberts, 1978; Greenberg, 1969), fictionalized magazine stories (Clark & Blankenburg, 1972), and books (Haskins, 1969). Conflict's special appeal to the tv drama producers is its swift and sudden action within the time constraints and competition with other sources of entertainment (Baldwin & Lewis, 1972; Cantor, 1972; Greenberg, 1969). In addition, industry competition makes conflict an available theme from which to draw story ideas (Comstock, 1980). Finally, the portrayal of conflict creates suspense (Greenberg, 1969; Zillmann, 1980), humor (Stocking, Sapolsky, & Zillmann, 1978), and enjoyment (Diener & Woody, 1981).

Conflict in news content. Given conflict is a pervasive phenomenon in society, it is not surprising that it is frequently described in newspapers (Clark & Blankenburg, 1972; Cony, 1953), news magazines (Gans, 1979), and tv news stories (Clark & Blankenburg, 1972; Gans, 1979). The reason for this focus arises from factors within both the media and their audiences. Members of news media prefer stories containing conflict and especially those affecting large groups of people (Atwood, 1970; Ward, 1967). Stories containing conflict have increased chances for publication or broadcast (Gans, 1979). Furthermore, consumers of the news share this interest in stories of wide-reaching conflict (Atwood, 1970).

Intrapersonal Conflict and the Mass Media

In some cases, the mass media purposefully challenge the attitudes and behaviors of their audience (e.g., editorials, information campaigns, investigative reporting). Even entertainment content may advance certain causes by highlighting and ridiculing audience stereotypes. Given professional productions and potentially large audiences, the mass media have powerful potential for inducing intrapersonal conflict and, by advocating positions, for creating immense change (see Rogers & Storey, Chapter 26).

However, there are five obstacles that make the realization of that potential difficult. First, the audience may be composed of individuals who already agree with the message and hence will experience no increase in intrapersonal conflict (e.g., Ball-Rokeach, Grube, & Rokeach, 1981; Hur & Robinson, 1978).

Second, media messages may be interpreted and distorted by cognitive structures so that messages are not conflictive. The notion that people interpret media messages within existing cognitive structures can be found in research related to sex roles (Drabman et al., 1981; Durkin, 1984; Eisenstock, 1984; Goff, Goff, & Lehrer, 1980; Koblinsky, Cruse, & Sugawara, 1978), racial attitudes (Atkin, Greenberg, & McDermott, 1983; Brigham & Giesbrecht, 1976; Chapko & Lewis, 1975; Surlin, 1974; Surlin & Bowden, 1976; Tate & Surlin, 1976; Vidmar & McGrath, 1974; Wilhoit & deBock, 1976), and political preferences (Donohue, 1973-1974; Sigelman & Sigelman, 1984).

Third, individuals may only expose themselves to counterattitudinal messages when confident that they can refute them (Frey, 1986). Persons counterargue against media messages thought to be biased (Stevenson & Greene, 1980) or contradictory to their beliefs (Tan, 1975).

Fourth, audiences will feel less conflict from and be less influenced by those portrayals they define as unrealistic. For example, the perceived reality of black tv characters is positively related to self-reported learning about blacks from tv (Atkin et al., 1983) and perceived reality of tv violence is positively related to measures of viewer aggressiveness (Atkin, 1983; Feshbach, 1972; McLeod, Atkin, & Chaffee, 1972a, 1972b).

Finally, individuals may receive inputs from several nonmediated sources including some that support an individual's cognitive structure and attack the credibility of tv portrayals (e.g., Greenberg & Reeves, 1976; Messaris & Kerr, 1984). Only if these additional sources are weak (Gross & Morgan, 1985; Robertson & Rossiter, 1977; Rothschild, 1979) or are supportive of media portrayals (Buerkel-Rothfuss, Greenberg, Atkin, & Neuendorf, 1982; Corder-Bolz, 1980) should media challenges be effective.

To be successful, media persuaders must be able to get a message before an audience, have it accurately interpreted, overcome counterarguing, and make it appear realistic and superior to alternative sources of information. This is rarely achievable through a single mediated message and may not always occur as a result of larger campaigns (see Rogers & Storey, Chapter 26).

Interpersonal Conflict and the Mass Media

Interpersonal and mass communication are intertwined. Media usage frequently occurs in interpersonal settings (Bower, 1973; Lyle & Hoffman, 1972), facts garnered from the media are used in interpersonal arguments (Greenberg, 1975), and media presentations include models of how people relate to one another (Barbatsis, Wong, & Herek, 1983).

This interface will be examined in two areas: the media as stimulants of interpersonal conflict, and the role of the media in interpersonal conflict resolution.

The media as stimulants of interpersonal conflict. There are three ways in which the media may cause interpersonal conflict. First, while the reported frequency of conflicts between parents and adolescents and between spouses over the amount of media use is not large (Gantz, 1985; Lyle & Hoffman, 1972), it can be an irritant. For example, when children watch cartoons and fathers watch the news, they become sufficiently engrossed that they are unresponsive to interpersonal communication directed at them (Stoneman & Brody, 1983). Moreover, Gantz (1985) found that 47% of spouses felt that their partners were occasionally more interested in the TV than what they had to say.

Second, adolescents report that they disagree with their parents over preferences for a variety of media (Lyle & Hoffman, 1972) and conflicts over tv program preferences occur frequently between siblings (Lyle & Hoffman, 1972). When these conflicts occur, parental preferences appear to dominate over those of children (Lull, 1978, 1982; Wand, 1968) and older siblings are more successful at getting their way than younger ones (Lull, 1978; Lyle & Hoffman, 1972; Zahn & Baran, 1984). Conflict over media preferences occur infrequently between spouses (Gantz, 1985) and when they do they are resolved noncoercively (Gantz, 1985; Raush et al., 1974).

The final conflict occurs because media portrayals are at variance with the relational experiences of users. For example, family interactions in prime time are largely of an affiliative rather than conflictive nature (Greenberg et al., 1980) and even soap operas show high degrees of self-disclosure as people try to resolve their problems (Fine, 1981). Since viewing family programs is positively correlated with believing that families are affiliative and compliant (Buerkel-Rothfuss et al., 1982), and among male viewers viewing soap operas is positively correlated with believing in the effectiveness of talk for solving problems (Alexander, 1985), consuming these portrayals might create dissatisfaction with one's relationships (see, Glennon & Butsch, 1982). While this speculation is not confirmed for children's feelings about their parents (Miller & Beck, 1976), Fallis, Fitzpatrick, and Friedstad (1985) found that among couples whose marital life deviated most from idealized TV portrayals there was a positive relationship between TV viewing and communication about TV portrayals and marital issues. Such media-stimulated communication might become heated as the partners broke with their typical pattern of avoidance (Fitzpatrick, 1977; Fitzpatrick & Best, 1979; Sillars, Pike, Jones, & Redmon, 1983) and used media portrayals to demonstrate their partners' inadequacies.

Finally, TV advertisements may increase requests for products by children, which if denied lead to interpersonal conflict with a parent (Atkin, 1975a, 1975b). These conflicts can prompt anger (Sheikh & Moleski, 1977), rejection (Goldberg & Gorn, 1978) and even aggression (Sheikh & Moleski, 1977) from the child; and if the product is attractively advertised, neither parental reasoning nor coercion may reduce the child's desire for it (Prasad, Rao, & Sheikh, 1978).

The role of the media in interpersonal conflict resolution. The media may influence conflict resolution in three ways. First, by watching TV programs relational partners may be able to disengage and "cool off" from an argument (Gantz, 1985; Lull, 1978; Rosenblatt & Cunningham, 1976). Second, relational partners may use the media as a punishment for transgressions. When children enjoy watching TV, denial of that privilege may be used by parents as negative reinforcement (Lull, 1980; Lyle & Hoffman, 1972).

Finally, media messages may provide models of how conflicts can be resolved (Roloff, 1981a). Probably the best known research bearing upon this issue is focused upon the impact of televised violence on viewer aggression. Cook, Kendzierski, and Thomas (1983) reviewed recent work in that area and concluded that TV models who employ violence to resolve conflict probably have a small, causal impact upon similar use among viewers. However, by focusing almost exclusively on violence, researchers have ignored other methods of conflict resolution portrayed on TV. For example, Dominick, Richman, and Wurtzele (1979) reported that a larger proportion of problems on action/adventure, situation comedy, and general dramas were resolved through assertiveness (standing up for one's rights in a noninjurious fashion) or through receiving help than by physical or verbal aggression. Television characters are typically perceived by adolescent viewers to employ prosocial discussion (e.g., self-disclosure) and verbal aggression as conflict resolution modes (Roloff & Greenberg, 1979a). Further, the perceived use of both pro- and antisocial modes of conflict resolution are correlated with the reported use of the same modes (Roloff & Greenberg, 1979b).

A second limitation results from excluding other causal agents such as family, peers, and direct experience (Bandura, 1973). By focusing primarily upon TV, an exaggerated picture of its importance may result. A few studies that have examined other causal agents have found that measures of TV are *slightly* better predictors than interpersonal models (McLeod et al., 1972a, 1972b; Lefkowitz, Eron, Walder, & Huesmann, 1977; Meyer, 1973; Singer, Singer, & Rapaczynski, 1984) while others suggest that interpersonal sources are *much* better predictors than TV viewing (Dominick & Greenberg, 1972; Roloff & Greenberg, 1980; Milavsky, Kessler, Stipp, & Rubens, 1982). Given differences in measurement and in methods of conducting multiple regressions, firm conclusions are difficult to reach. But it seems clear that TV violence is not the only causal agent and was of minor importance compared to factors such as peer and parental aggression.

Organizational Conflict in the Mass Media

Media messages are created by individuals who work within organizations. Consequently, they may experience conflicts common to other organizations. We will focus on four: role conflict, superior-subordinate conflict, intergroup conflict, and extraorganizational conflict.

Role conflict. Media professionals occupy roles possessing certain responsibilities, and the nature of these responsibilities may not be viewed similarly by all organizational members with whom they come into contact (Burgoon, Burgoon, & Atkin, 1982). Nor may they be consistent with the standards of the role occupant. We will focus on three types of role conflict.

The first type occurs when the personal views of a role occupant are in conflict with organizational policy. For example, Breed (1955) argued that newspapers often have an implicit policy that guides the acceptability of certain interpretations of people and events in the news. Journalists often find this policy to differ from their personal values (Burgoon et al., 1982). Conflict is especially likely in newspapers with politically conservative editors and policies (Flegel & Chaffee, 1971; Tunstall, 1971). The severity of this conflict is abated somewhat by organizational socialization (Breed, 1955), self-selection by journalists into newspapers and specialities with congruent policies (Sigelman, 1973; Tunstall, 1971), and voluntary severance from the job (Gans, 1979).

Second, when reporters investigate stories, information that contradicts their beliefs may be uncovered. Generally, reporters will provide accurate accounts even if facts contradict their personal views (Starck & Soloski, 1977) and may even overcompensate by presenting more belief-discrepant information (Kerrick, Anderson, & Swales, 1964). Professionally imposed standards of objectivity may reduce inner turmoil since they represent "plausible" externally based explanations for inconsistent behaviors.

The final role conflict stems from divergence between professional standards and the quality of role performance. Many media producers and writers believe they are far more creative and talented than is evidenced in their TV work and some even avoid watching their own material (Cantor, 1971, 1974).

Superior-subordinate conflict. Media organizations are structured into a vertical hierarchy. Editors and producers play supervisory roles and are themselves accountable to others. A variety of factors may put those in authority at odds with those at lower levels. Individuals at higher levels of media organizations are politically more conservative (Bogart, 1974; Gans, 1979) and more concerned about the organization (Bogart, 1974) and financial matters (Bagdikian, 1974). In addition, role occupants at different levels of the hierarchy disagree about how their respective jobs should be performed (Burgoon et al., 1982; Joseph, 1982). Those at lower levels may be concerned primarily with professional and personal quality rather than revenue matters (Flegel & Chaffee, 1971).

Despite these differences, the severity of superior-subordinate conflicts may be reduced. Open conflict can be costly to both the subordinate (Burgoon et al., 1982) and the superior (Diamond, 1974). Consequently, both groups may prefer to deal with conflict covertly or indirectly (Argyris, 1974). Reporters may tone down phrases, prepare adequate documentation (Gans, 1979), or engage in more devious activity such as turning in stories just before its deadline, bypassing an editor, or redefining a story into the area of a sympathetic editor (Sigal, 1973). For their part, editors may only make minor revisions, seek compromise language (Gans, 1979), and may defer to a reporter having greater story knowledge (Warner, 1971) or a proven track record (Gans, 1979; Sigal, 1973; Warner, 1971).

Intergroup conflict. Media organizations are composed of groups that are differentiated based upon authority (e.g., union-management) and function (e.g., interdepartmental). Intergroup conflict can occur along both dimensions. For example, newspaper editors are significantly more hostile toward the Newspaper Guild than are journalists, and among nonunion journalists some fear editor retaliation (including firing, bad assignments) if they help form a union (Fedler & Taylor, 1981).

Furthermore, different staffs or departments in a news organization may be in conflict over stories, broadcast time or line space, and prominence within the news format (Bagdikian, 1974; Sigal, 1973). Such internal competition may result in secrecy and distrust among colleagues (Argyris, 1974), and obstruction in the use of facilities (Gans, 1979). Potentially, this conflict may affect the kind of news that is reported as different news divisions highlight the dramatic and downplay the ordinary aspects of their stories in order achieve prime location in a news presentation (Gans, 1979).

Beyond staff disputes, groups focused on the business side of the organization may be in conflict with those concerned primarily with the process of creating media messages (Bogart, 1974). Media content may antagonize advertisers, making the jobs of those in sales more difficult; or advertisers may not wish to buy time around shows favored by production people unless they attract the right audience (Brown, 1971).

Often individuals involved with the business side have some experience in production areas and vice versa (Bogart, 1974). Therefore, they are sympathetic to each groups' problems. In addition, in large and successful media operations, those who are most concerned with revenue generation have little day to day knowledge and involvement in story content and placement (Bowers, 1967; Gans, 1979). Consequently, little conflict can take place prior to publication or broadcast.

Extraorganizational conflict. Media organizations do not operate in a vacuum. Their environment includes a variety of organizations with which they are interdependent. Occasionally, disputes emerge.

The media sometimes find themselves in conflict with support groups. The networks may be in conflict with production companies over creative control (Cantor, 1979, 1980) or with local affiliates about perceived political and geographical bias (Brown, 1971; Gans, 1979), and news organizations and advertisers may not always agree over their press coverage (Brooks, 1970; Sethi, 1977). While these conflicts do occur, most producers realize that real power over creative control resides with the networks (Cantor, 1980); local affiliates are not able to exert much influence over network news (Gans, 1979); and media officials exercise discretion with regard to advertisers' sensibilities (Gans, 1979).

However, a variety of organizations have sought to pressure the media (and especially TV) into improving the portrayals of the groups they represent or reflecting their client group's values in programming. These groups have pressured advertisers, boycotted media output, bought media stock, urged government action, and at times engaged in open confrontation (Cantor, 1980). While successfully raising the consciousness of producers (Cantor, 1980; Comstock, 1980), programmers (Lewis, 1969-1970), advertisers (Bogart, 1980a), and stimulating government action with regard to children's advertising (Comstock, 1980), Cantor (1980) has noted that overall, the content of TV entertainment has remained remarkably the same.

Finally, an important function of the media is to serve as a "watchdog" on governmental activity (Siebert, Peterson, & Schramm, 1956). Consequently, the press may "dig" for information while government officials may try to control their discoveries (Sigal, 1973). When damaging information is found, officials may bring strong pressure to bear on the media (Gans, 1979; Sigal, 1973). However, both reporters and officials "use" each other in a variety of ways (Fico, 1984; Sigal, 1973) and are similar in their news orientations (Dyer & Nayman, 1977; Hilton, 1966). Reporters identify more with legislators than they do with their own editors or news directors (Dyer & Nayman, 1977). Thus the two groups have a basis for cooperation and reporters may play a role in the creation of legislation (Cook et al., 1983; Dyer & Nayman, 1977).

Mass Communication and Conflict at the Cultural Level

The media provide information that most people cannot discern through observation of their immediate environment and, hence, may make individuals aware of trends in the larger culture. Within that context, the media could operate as a conflict suppressor by downplaying societal problems or an instigator by highlighting them. This section will examine both points of view.

The media as suppressors of cultural conflict. Because the media are themselves powerful societal institutions and have frequent contacts with other such institutions, they are assumed to have a vested interest in perpetuating the political and social order. In addition, because they seek to establish profitable markets, their entertainment content skirts controversial issues; and journalistic standards of objectivity preclude taking a strong stance on social problems. Furthermore, their tendency to focus on violent crime may increase the dependency of citizenry on authority figures. The net result is support for and dependence on the system (see Gerbner & Gross, 1976).

Support for this position can be summarized in the following six generalizations:

(1) *Because newspaper stories* (Davis, 1952; Graber, 1979; Jones, 1976; Sheley & Askins, 1981) *and TV entertainment* (Dominick, 1973; Estep & Macdonald, 1983) *exaggerate the rate of violent crimes and risks of victimization* (Gerbner, Gross, Jackson-Beeck, Jeffries-Fox, Signorielli, 1978), *exposure to TV and newspapers is positively correlated with judgments about the prevalence of crime* (Davis, 1952; Graber, 1980; Gerbner et al., 1977; Gerbner et al., 1978; Gerbner, Gross, Signorielli, Morgan, & Jackson-Beeck, 1979; Jaehnig, Weaver, & Fico, 1981) *and TV exposure is positively correlated with fear of being victimized* (Gerbner, Gross, Morgan, & Signorielli, 1980), *especially among groups portrayed on TV as victims* (Morgan, 1983).

(2) *Because TV entertainment portrays women in stereotypical roles* (see Busby, 1975, 1985), *exposure to TV is positively related to sexism, particularly among females* (Gross & Morgan, 1985; McGhee & Frueh, 1980; Morgan, 1982; Zuckerman, Singer, & Singer, 1980).

(3) *Because TV entertainment portrays limited interracial contact and conflict* (Baptista-Fernandez & Greenberg, 1980; Weigel, Loomis, & Soja, 1980), *exposure to TV portrayals of minorities is negatively related to concern about racial problems* (Volgy & Schwarz, 1982).

(4) *Because TV entertainment portrays professionals such as police* (Dominick, 1973; Estep & Macdonald, 1983; Haney & Manzolati, 1978) *and*

medical doctors (Gerbner, Morgan, & Signorielli, 1982; Turow & Coe, 1985) *as generally successful in performing their jobs, exposure to programs portraying these characters is positively related to belief in their effectiveness* (Dominick, 1974; Gunter & Wober, 1983; Haney & Manzolati, 1978; Slater & Elliott, 1982; Volgy & Schwarz, 1982).

(5) *Because the news media negatively frame social advocacy groups* (e.g., Glasgow University Media Group, 1976; Hartmann, 1975-1976) *and especially militant ones* (Pride & Clarke, 1973; Shoemaker, 1984), *exposure to this coverage results in negative judgments about their legitimacy, viability, stability, and favorability* (Shoemaker, 1982).

(6) *Because TV entertainment skirts controversial issues* (Gerbner et al., 1982) *and news organizations try to balance coverage of disputes* (e.g., Hallin, 1984), *exposure to TV is positively related to holding conventional attitudes* (Weigel & Jessor, 1973), *moderate political beliefs* (Gerbner, Gross, Morgan, & Signorielli, 1984), *and may result in converging political, social, and economic beliefs among normally divergent groups* (Gerbner et al., 1982).

While these summary statements imply a strong case against the media, cautions should be noted. For example, not all research has found that tv exposure measures are positively related to fear of crime (Hughes, 1980; Piepe, Crouch, & Emerson, 1977; Pingree, 1983; Slater & Elliott, 1982; Wober, 1978; Wober & Gunter, 1982), sexism (Perloff, 1977; Repetti, 1984), or belief in the adequacy of the healthcare system (Culbertson & Stemple, 1985). Further, tv exposure does not appear to be associated with crime-related beliefs in the same way across subgroups (Doob & Macdonald, 1979; Gerbner et al., 1980). Moreover, the primary use of correlational data makes the direction of causality ambiguous. And finally, the magnitude of the effects across these areas is small both on an absolute basis (Hirsch, 1980) and compared to other potential predictors (Doob & Macdonald, 1979; Hirsch, 1980; Roberts, 1981).

The mass media as instigators of cultural conflict. The media might also play a pivotal role in causing cultural conflict. This perspective focuses on three ways in which they instigate controversy.

First, it is alleged that overly critical press coverage purportedly stems from a generally liberal bent among working journalists, the watchdog function of the press, and the necessity of presenting interesting, dramatic news. Consequently, the press attempts to denigrate authority and conservative figures and policies.

Lefever (1974, 1975) concluded that during the Vietnam era, CBS news content included large numbers of statements critical of the war and South Vietnam while including themes mildly supportive of North Vietnam. However, the methodology of this study has been questioned

(Frank, 1975). Other studies suggest that network coverage included largely neutral statements with roughly equal numbers of positive and negative ones (Pride & Wamsley, 1972; Russo, 1971) and, as the war progressed, criticism of both supporters and critics of the war (Hallin, 1984). Further, content analyses of network coverage of the ecology movement (Pride & Richards, 1975), student movement (Pride & Richards, 1974), and race relations (Pride & Clarke, 1973) indicate that the direction of press coverage of government varies with topic, type of government unit, and, even when critical, typically includes positive statements.

But perhaps the most important factor in press coverage is that it directs criticism at particular officials or policies rather than the system as a whole. Content analyses of press coverage of the Vietnam war (Hallin, 1984) and Watergate scandal (Miller, Goldenberg, & Erbring, 1979) indicate that press criticism was not directed at the democratic system of government and, in fact, supported it.

Robinson (1976) has argued that as a result of critical press coverage, a political malaise has developed such that political efficacy is negatively related to reliance on TV news (Robinson, 1976) or total TV viewing (Berman & Stookey, 1980; Gerbner et al., 1978). Further, exposure to newspaper criticism of government is positively related to political cynicism (Miller et al., 1978). However, exposure to TV news (Rubin, 1978; O'Keefe, 1980) and newspapers (Becker & Whitney, 1980; Miller et al., 1979) has been positively correlated with support for government, especially among those most reliant on those news sources (Miller & Reese, 1982). Belief in governmental institutions may be sufficiently strong that scandals such as Watergate may only impact upon the credibility of the principal parties, not the political system as a whole (McLeod, Brown, Becker, & Ziemke, 1977; Sniderman, Neuman, Citrin, McCloskey, & Shanks, 1975).

A second form of cultural conflict may result from press coverage of social advocacy groups. Because conflict and especially militant confrontation is newsworthy (Snyder & Kelly, 1977; Bogart, 1980b), advocacy groups may adopt confrontational strategies as a means of drawing media attention (Rada, 1977). Hence the potential for media coverage may encourage militancy that, if covered, may then influence public opinion and government action.

The question of whether such coverage of demonstrations and protests actually serves the purpose of the social advocates is unclear. Press coverage of antiwar demonstrations during the Vietnam era appeared to have short-term *counterproductive* impacts on public opinion and no influence on governmental decision making about the war (Berkowitz, 1973). By contrast passage of civil rights legislation was immediately preceded by increased coverage of civil rights demonstrations by the *New York Times* (Burstein, 1979), and the extent of Vietnam protests covered by the *New York Times* was positively related to antiwar votes in the U.S. Senate prior to 1970 but negatively correlated after that point (Burstein & Freudenburg, 1978).

The mixed effects of such coverage could result from several factors. In some cases, the press are aware they are being manipulated and include overt disclaimers about the demonstration (Levy, 1981). In addition, the press may rely upon officials rather than (or in addition to) the demonstrators for information about the groups' cause (Paletz, Fozzard, & Ayanian, 1982). Further, time pressure for stories may result in minimal discussion of the underlying causes for the protest (Murdock, 1973), and conservative editorial biases may reduce the significance attached to such protests (Madden, 1971; Mann, 1974). Finally, while media coverage of a conflict may be an effective method of stimulating awareness in the early stages of a dispute, it may not be an effective forum for the development of solutions (Burstein & Freudenburg, 1978); and its continued coverage may actually stimulate increasingly negative attitudes toward participants (e.g., Robinson, 1974).

The final instigative role of the media stems from their alleged part in stimulating dissatisfaction among the citizenry. By covering conflict, turmoil, scandals, and generally "bad" news, confidence in society as a whole may be shaken. Indeed, TV exposure has been positively correlated with feelings that the lot of the average person is getting worse (Gerbner et al., 1978), interpersonal mistrust (Gerbner et al., 1977, 1978, 1979, 1980; Hawkins & Pingree, 1980, 1981; Pingree & Hawkins, 1981), and negative evaluations of one's own life (Morgan, 1984). Further, exposure to bad news can instill suspiciousness and competitiveness toward others (Blackman et al., 1977). While such alienation is not universally correlated with media exposure (e.g., McLeod, Ward, & Tancill, 1965-1966) and may be of less importance than other factors (e.g., Hirsch, 1980), the media may stimulate some reduction in societal cohesiveness.

Thus there is a measure of evidence for the role of the media as *both* suppressors and instigators of cultural conflict. While the magnitude of their effect is not large and their influence may diminish with direct involvement of their audience with a conflict (Hartmann & Husband, 1973; Adoni, Cohen, & Mane, 1984), the media may play both roles. They may highlight societal problems that at times have negative impacts upon cultural cohesiveness but this process is done within a framework that prevents radical conflict and change in the political or social system.

CONCLUSION

While this review is perhaps tiring, it is not exhaustive. Within each of the pools of research, there are eddies of activity of which the general nature of this report precluded discussion. However, there are general patterns. First, it is clear that conflict is pervasive. Across communication levels people may experience conflicts in their internal thoughts, relationships, work environments, and media use. Second, within each level of conflict there are factors that serve to protect individuals from extreme turmoil. Schemata may distort incoming information so that it is not inconsistent or direct attention toward "plausible" explanations for it. Satisfied relational partners may generally overlook conflicts or engage in behaviors that decrease the likelihood of their escalation. Organizational members may come to accept the predominant values of their work environment, utilize indirect methods of power, and try to establish long-term cooperative relations with other organizations. And while the media may occasionally prompt conflict, they do not promote radical change.

Conflict suppression or avoidance provides necessary stability for individual and coordinated action, but it may also have negative effects. Given that open controversy is a normal (Folger & Poole, 1984) and beneficial (Tjosvold & Johnson, 1977, 1978) part of decision making, its suppression could lead to misunderstanding, lack of innovativeness, resentment, and long-term conflict escalation (see, Tjosvold & Johnson, 1978; Tjosvold, 1982). Unfortunately, minimal research has focused across communication levels in this seemingly necessary balance between conflict avoidance and confrontation.

From an epistemological view, our analysis of levels highlights several needs. While a pattern of research could be traced across levels, that pattern was imposed by this reviewer and not necessarily the researchers. Scholars studying similar phenomena across or within levels are not always aware of each other's research. This segmentation is lamentable. Research has not investigated potential contextual differences in similar conflict processes. For example, we found role conflicts in relationships, organizations, and the mass media, yet research does not tell us whether their occurrence, intensity, and frequency varies across them. Nor can we tell whether conflicts in one domain influence those in another.

While specialization and research costs make such inquiry difficult, it provides a more systematic study of communication and conflict that more accurately reflects the way they occur in the "real world." After all, it is possible to wake up to family conflict in the morning, read about scandal and crime in the morning newspaper, experience disputes at work during the day, come home to relational turmoil, watch societal controversies during the evening news, see violent conflict in TV entertainment, and think about them much of the time!

REFERENCES

Adams, J. S. (1976). The structure and dynamics of behavior in organizational boundary roles. In M. Dunnette (Ed.), *Handbook of industrial and organizational psychology* (pp. 1175-1199). Chicago: Rand McNally.

Adoni, H., Cohen, A. A., & Mane, S. (1984). Social reality and television news: Perceptual dimensions of social conflict in selected life areas. *Journal of Broadcasting, 28,* 33-49.

Alexander, A. (1985). Adolescents' soap opera viewing and relational perceptions. *Journal of Broadcasting and Electronic Media, 29,* 295-308.

Altman, I., & Taylor, D. A. (1973). *Social penetration: The development of interpersonal relationships.* New York: Holt, Rinehart & Winston.

Argyle, M. (1975). *Bodily communication.* New York: International Universities Press.

Argyle, M., & Furnham, A. (1983). Sources of satisfaction and conflict in long-term relationships. *Journal of Marriage and the Family, 45,* 481-493.

Argyle, M., & Henderson, M. (1984). The rules of friendship. *Journal of Social and Personal Relationships, 1,* 211-237.

Argyris, C. (1957). *Personality and organization: The conflict between the system and the individual.* New York: Harper & Brothers.

Argyris, C. (1974). *Behind the front page.* San Francisco: Jossey-Bass.

Atkin, C. (1975a). Effects of television advertising on children—Survey of preadolescent's responses to television commercials (Report #6). Washington, DC: Office of Child Development.

Atkin, C. (1975b). The effects of television advertising on children: Survey of children's and mother's responses to television commercials (Report #8). Washington, DC: Office of Child Development.

Atkin, C. (1983). Effects of realistic tv violence vs. fictional violence on aggression. *Journalism Quarterly, 60,* 615-621.

Atkin, C., Greenberg, B. S., & McDermott, S. (1983). Television and race role socialization. *Journalism Quarterly, 60,* 407-414.

Atwood, L. E. (1970). How newsmen and readers perceive each others' story preferences. *Journalism Quarterly, 47,* 296-302.

Backman, C. W., & Secord, P. F. (1968). The self and role selection. In C. Gordon & K. J. Gergen (Eds.), *The self in social interaction: Vol. 1. Classic and contemporary perspectives* (pp. 289-296). New York: John Wiley.

Bacharach, S. B., & Lawler, E. J. (1980). *Power and politics in organizations.* San Francisco: Jossey-Bass.

Bagdikian, B. H. (1974). Professional personnel and organizational structure in the mass media. In W. P. Davison & F.T.C. Yu (Eds.), *Mass communication research: Major issues and future directions* (pp. 122-142). New York: Praeger.

Bahr, S. J., Chappell, C. B., & Leigh, G. K. (1983). Age at marriage, role enactment, role consensus, and marital satisfaction. *Journal of Marriage and the Family, 45,* 795-803.

Baird, L. S. (1977). Self and superior rating of performance: As related to self-esteem and satisfaction with supervision. *Academy of Management Journal, 20,* 291-300.

Baldwin, T. F., & Lewis, C. (1972). Violence in television: The industry looks at itself.

In G. A. Comstock & E. A. Rubinstein (Eds.), *Television and social behavior Vol. 1: Media content and control* (pp. 290-373). Washington, DC: Government Printing Office.

Ball-Rokeach, S. J., Grube, J. W., & Rokeach, M. J. (1981). "Roots: The Next Generation"—Who watched and with what effect? *Public Opinion Quarterly, 45,* 56-68.

Bandura, A. (1973). *Aggression: A social learning analysis.* Englewood Cliffs, NJ: Prentice-Hall.

Baptista-Fernandez, P., & Greenberg, B. S. (1980). The context, characteristics and communication behaviors of blacks on television. In B. S. Greenberg (Ed.), *Life on television: Content analyses of U.S. TV drama* (pp. 13-21). Norwood, NJ: Ablex.

Barbatsis, G. S., Wong, M. R., & Herek, G. M. (1983). A struggle for dominance: Relational communication patterns in television drama. *Communication Quarterly, 31,* 148-155.

Bateman, T. S. (1980). Contingent concession strategies in dyadic bargaining. *Organizational Behavior and Human Performance, 26,* 212-221.

Bazerman, M. H., Beekun, R. I., & Schoorman, F. D. (1982). Performance evaluation in a dynamic context: A laboratory study of the impact of a prior commitment to the ratee. *Journal of Applied Psychology, 67,* 873-876.

Bazerman, M. H., Giuliano, T., & Appelman, A. (1984). Escalation of commitment in individual and group decision making. *Organizational Behavior and Human Performance, 33,* 141-152.

Becker, L. B., & Whitney, D. C. (1980). Effects of media dependencies: Audience assessment of government. *Communication Research, 7,* 95-120.

Bem, D. J. (1972). Self-perception theory. In L. Berkowitz (Ed.), *Advances in experimental social psychology* (Vol. 6, pp. 1-62). New York: Academic Press.

Ben-Yoav, O., & Pruitt, D. G. (1984). Accountability to constituents: A two edged sword. *Organizational Behavior and Human Performance, 34,* 283-295.

Berger, C. R., & Bradac, J. (1982). *Language and social knowledge: Uncertainty in interpersonal relations.* London: Edward Arnold.

Berkowitz, W. R. (1973). The impact of anti-Vietnam demonstrations upon national public opinion and military indicators. *Social Science Research, 2,* 1-14.

Berman, D. R., & Stookey, J. A. (1980). Adolescents, television, and support for government. *Public Opinion Quarterly, 47,* 330-340.

Beutell, N. J., & Greenhaus, J. H. (1982). Interrole conflict among married women: The influence of husband and wife characteristics on conflict and coping behavior. *Journal of Vocational Behavior, 21,* 99-110.

Beutell, N. J., & Greenhaus, J. H. (1983). Integration of home and nonhome roles: Women's conflict and coping behavior. *Journal of Applied Psychology, 68,* 43-48.

Billings, A. (1979). Conflict resolution in distressed and nondistressed married couples. *Journal of Consulting and Clinical Psychology, 47,* 368-376.

Birchler, G. R., & Webb, L. J. (1977). Discriminating interaction behaviors in happy and unhappy marriages. *Journal of Consulting and Clinical Psychology, 45,* 494-495.

Birchler, G. R., Weiss, R. L., & Vincent, J. P. (1975). Multimethod analysis of social reinforcement exchange between maritally distressed and nondistressed spouse and stranger dyads. *Journal of Personality and Social Psychology, 31,* 349-360.

Blackman, J. A., Hornstein, H. A., Divine, C., O'Neill, M., Steil, J., & Tucker, L. (1977). Newscasts and the social actuary. *Public Opinion Quarterly, 41,* 295-313.

Bogart, L. (1974). The management of the mass media. In W. P. Davison & F.T.C. Yu (Eds.), *Mass communication research: Major issues and future directions* (pp. 143-170). New York: Praeger.

Bogart, L. (1980a). After the Surgeon General's Report: Another look backward. In S. B. Withey & R. P. Abeles (Eds.), *Television and social behavior: Beyond violence and children* (pp. 103-134). Hillsdale, NJ: Lawrence Erlbaum.

Bogart, L. (1980b). Television news as entertainment. In P. H. Tannenbaum (Ed.), *The entertainment functions of television* (pp. 209-250). Hillsdale, NJ: Lawrence Erlbaum.

Bower, R. T. (1973). *Television and the public.* New York: Holt, Rinehart & Winston.

Bowers, D. R. (1967). A report on activity by publishers in directing newsroom decision. *Journalism Quarterly, 44,* 43-52.

Braiker, H. B., & Kelley, H. H. (1979). Conflict in the development of close relationships. In R. L. Burgess & T. L. Huston (Eds.), *Social exchange in developing relationships* (pp. 135-168). New York: Academic Press.

Breed, W. (1955). Social control in the newsroom: A Functional analysis. *Social Forces, 33,* 326-335.

Brett, J. M. (1984). Managing organizational conflict. *Professional Psychology: Research and Practice, 15,* 664-678.

Brigham, J. C., & Giesbrecht, L. W. (1976). "All in the Family": Racial attitudes. *Journal of Communication, 26,* 69-74.

Brockner, J., Rubin, J. Z., & Lang, E. (1981). Face-saving and entrapment. *Journal of Experimental Social Psychology, 17,* 68-79.

Brooks, J. M. (1970). *A sociological study of commercial broadcast organizatons.* Unpublished dissertation, Ohio State University.

Brown, L. D., & Brown, J. C. (1983). Organizational microcosms and ideological negotiation. In M. H. Bazerman & R. J. Lewicki (Eds.), *Negotiating in organizations* (pp. 227-248). Newbury Park, CA: Sage.

Brown, L. L. (1971). *Television: The business and the box.* New York: Harcourt Brace Jovanovich.

Buck, R., Miller, R. E., & Caul, W. F. (1974). Sex, personality, and physiological variables in the communication of affect via facial expression. *Journal of Personality and Social Psychology, 30,* 587-596.

Buck, R., Savin, V. J., Miller, R. E., & Caul, W. F. (1972). Communication of affect through facial expression in humans. *Journal of Personality and Social Psychology, 23,* 362-371.

Buerkel-Rothfuss, N. L., Greenberg, B. S., Atkin, C. K., & Neuendorf, K. (1982). Learning about the family from television. *Journal of Communication, 32,* 191-201.

Burgoon, J. K., Burgoon, M., & Atkin, C. K. (1982). *What is news? Who decides? And how?* Michigan State University: American society of newspaper editors.

Burke, R. J. (1970). Methods of resolving superior-subordinate conflict: The constructive use of subordinate differences and disagreements. *Organizational Behavior and Human Performance, 5,* 393-411.

Burstein, P. (1979). Public opinion, demonstrations, and the passage of antidiscrimination legislation. *Public Opinion Quarterly, 43,* 157-172.

Burstein, P., & Freudenburg, W. (1978). Changing public policy: The impact of public opinion, antiwar demonstrations, and war costs on senate voting on Vietnam war motions. *American Journal of Sociology, 84,* 99-122.

Busby, L. J. (1975). Sex-role research on the mass media. *Journal of Communication, 25,* 107-131.

Busby, L. J. (1985). The mass media and sex-role socialization. In J. R. Dominick & J. E. Fletcher (Eds.), *Broadcasting research methods* (pp. 267-295). Boston: Allyn & Bacon.

Cantor, M. G. (1971). *The Hollywood producer: His work and his audience.* New York: Basic Books.

Cantor, M. G. (1972). The role of the producer in choosing children's television content. In G. A. Comstock & E. A. Rubinstein (Eds.), *Television and social behavior: Vol. 1. Media content and control* (pp. 259-289). Washington, DC: Government Printing Office.

Cantor, M. G. (1974). Producing television for children. In G. Tuchman (Ed.), *The tv establishment: Programming for power and profit* (pp. 103-118). Englewood Cliffs, NJ: Prentice-Hall.

Cantor, M. G. (1979). The politics of popular drama. *Communication Research, 6,* 387-406.

Cantor, M. G. (1980). *Prime-time television: Content and control.* Newbury Park, CA: Sage.

Carnevale, P.J.D., Pruitt, D. G., & Britton, S. D. (1979). Looking tough: The negotiator under constituent surveillance. *Personality and Social Psychology Bulletin, 5,* 118-121.

Carnevale, P.J.D., Pruitt, D. G., & Seilheimer, J. (1981). Looking and competing: Accountability and visual access in integrative bargaining. *Journal of Personality and Social Psychology, 40,* 111-120.

Carroll, J. C. (1977). The intergenerational transmission of family violence: The long-term effects of aggressive behavior. *Aggressive Behavior, 3,* 289-299.

Chapko, M. K., & Lewis, M. H. (1975). Authoritarianism and *All in the Family. The Journal of Psychology, 90,* 245-248.

Clark, D. G., & Blankenburg, W. B. (1972). Trends in violent content in selected mass media. In G. A. Comstock & E. A. Rubinstein (Eds.), *Television and social behavior: Vol. 1. Media content and control* (pp. 188-243). Washington, DC: Government Printing Office.

Clopton, S. W. (1984). Seller and buying firm factors affecting industrial buyers' negotiation behavior and outcomes. *Journal of Marketing Research, 21,* 39-53.

Colosi, T. (1983). Negotiation in the public and private sectors: A core model. *American Behavioral Scientist, 27,* 229-253.

Comstock, G. (1980). *Television in America.* Newbury Park, CA: Sage.

Comstock, G., Chaffee, S., Katzman, N., McCombs, M., & Roberts, D. (1978). *Television and human behavior.* New York: Columbia University Press.

Conrad, C. (1983). Power and performance as correlates of supervisors' choice of modes of managing conflict: A preliminary investigation. *Western Journal of Speech Communication, 47,* 218-228.

Cony, E. R. (1953). Conflict-cooperation content of five American dailies. *Journalism Quarterly, 30,* 15-22.

Cook, F. L., Tyler, T. R., Goetz, E. G., Gordon, M. T., Protess, D., Leff, D. R., & Molotch, H. L. (1983). Media and agenda setting: Effects on the public, interest groups leaders, policy makers, and policy. *Public Opinion Quarterly, 47,* 16-35.

Cook, T. D., Kendzierski, D. A., & Thomas, S. V. (1983). The implicit assumptions of television research: An analysis of the 1982 NIMH report on *Television and Behavior. Public Opinion Quarterly, 47,* 161-201.

Corder-Bolz, C. R., (1980). Mediation: The role of significant others. *Journal of Communication, 30,* 106-118.

Coser, L. (1956). *The functions of social conflict.* New York: Free Press.

Courtright, J. A., Millar, F. E., & Rogers-Millar, L. E. (1979). Domineeringness and dominance: Replication and expansion. *Communication Monographs, 46,* 180-192.

Crocker, J., Fiske, S. T., & Taylor, S. E. (1984). Schematic bases of belief change. In R. Eiser (Ed.), *Attitudinal judgment* (pp. 198-226). New York: Springer-Verlag.

Crouter, A. (1984). Spillover from family to work: The neglected side of the work-family interface. *Human Relations, 37,* 425-442.

Culbertson, H. M., & Stempel, G.H., III (1985). "Media malaise:" Explaining personal optimism and societal pessimism about health care. *Journal of Communication, 35,* 180-190.

Cushman, D. P., & Craig, R. T. (1976). Communication systems: Interpersonal implications. In G. R. Miller (Ed.), *Explorations in Interpersonal Communication* (pp. 37-58). Newbury Park, CA: Sage.

Cyret, R. M., & March, J. G. (1963). *A behavioral theory of the firm.* Englewood Cliffs, NJ: Prentice-Hall.

Dance, E., & Larson, C. (1976). *The functions of human communication: A theoretical approach.* New York: Holt, Rinehart & Winston.

Davis, D., & Wicklund, R. A. (1972). An objective self-awareness analysis of communication sets. In S. Duval & R. A. Wicklund (Eds.), *A theory of objective self-awareness* (pp. 180-184). New York: Academic Press.

Davis, F. J., (1952). Crime news in Colorado newspapers. *American Journal of Sociology, 57,* 325-330.

Deutsch, M. (1973). *The resolution of conflict: Constructive and destructive processes.* New Haven, CT: Yale University Press.

Diamond, E. (1974). "Reporter power" takes root. In M. Emery & T. C. Smythe (Eds.). *Readings in mass communication* (2nd ed., pp. 67-73). Dubuque, IA: Wm C. Brown.

Diener, E., & Woody, L. W. (1981). Television violence, conflict, realism, and action: A study in viewer liking. *Communication Research, 8,* 281-306.

Dominick, J. R. (1973). Crime and law enforcement on prime-time television. *Public Opinion Quarterly, 37,* 241-250.

Dominick, J. R. (1974). Children's viewing of crime shows and attitudes on law enforcement. *Journalism Quarterly, 51,* 5-12.

Dominick, J. R., & Greenberg, B. S. (1972). Attitudes toward violence: The interaction of television exposure, family attitudes, and social class. In G. A. Comstock & E. A. Rubinstein (Eds.), *Television and social behavior: Vol. 3. Television and adolescent aggressiveness* (pp. 314-335). Washington, DC: Government Printing Office.

Dominick, J. R., Richman, S., & Wurtzel, A. (1979). Problem-solving in tv shows popular with children: Assertion vs. aggression. *Journalism Quarterly, 56,* 455-463.

Donohue, T. R. (1973-1974). Impact of viewer predispositions on political tv commercials. *Journal of Broadcasting, 18,* 3-15.

Donohue, W. A. (1981). Development of a model of rule use in negotiation interaction. *Communication Monographs, 48,* 106-120.

Doob, A. N., & MacDonald, G. E. (1979). Television viewing and fear of victimization: Is the relationship causal? *Journal of Personality and Social Psychology, 37,* 170-179.

Downs, A. (1967). *Inside bureaucracy.* Boston: Little, Brown.

Drabman, R. S., Robertson, S. J., Patterson, J. N., Jarvie, G. J., Hammer, D., & Cordua, G. (1981). Children's perception of media-portrayed sex roles. *Sex Roles, 7,* 379-389.

Durkin, K. (1984). Children's accounts of sex-role stereotypes in television. *Communication Research, 11,* 341-362.

Dutton, J. M., & Walton, R. E. (1966). Interdepartmental conflict and cooperation: Two contrasting studies. *Human Organization, 25,* 207-220.

Dyck, R. J., & Rule, B. G. (1978). Effect on retaliation of causal attributions concerning attack. *Journal of Personality and Social Psychology, 36,* 521-529.

Dyer, C. S., & Nayman, O. G. (1977). Under the capitol dome: Relationships between legislators and reporters. *Journalism Quarterly, 54,* 443-453.

Einsiedel, E. F., Salomone, K. L., & Schneider, F. P. (1984). Crime: Effects of media exposure and personal experience on issue salience. *Journalism Quarterly, 61,* 131-136.

Eisenstock, B. (1984). Sex-role differences in children's identification with counterstereotypical televised portrayals. *Sex Roles, 10,* 417-430.

Epstein, S., & Taylor, S. P. (1967). Instigation to aggression as a function of degree of defeat and perceived aggressive intent of the opponent. *Journal of Personality, 35,* 265-289.

Estep, R., & MacDonald, P. T. (1983). How prime time crime evolved on TV, 1976-1981. *Journalism Quarterly, 60,* 293-300.

Fallis, S. F., Fitzpatrick, M. A., & Friestad, M. S. (1985). Spouses' discussion of television portrayals of close relationships. *Communication Research, 12,* 59-81.

Farace, R. V., Monge, P. R., & Russell, H. M. (1977). *Communicating and organizing.* Reading, MA: Addison-Wesley.

Fedler, F., & Taylor, P. (1981). Reporters and the Newspaper Guild: Membership attitudes and salaries. *Journalism Quarterly, 58,* 83-88.

Feshbach, S. (1972). Reality and fantasy in filmed violence. In J. P. Murray, E. A. Rubinstein, & G. A. Comstock (Eds.), *Television and social behavior Vol. 2: Television* and *social learning* (pp. 318-345). Washington, DC: Government Printing Office.

Festinger, L. (1957). *A theory of cognitive dissonance.* Stanford: Stanford University Press.

Fico, F. (1984). How lawmakers use reporters: Differences in specialization and goal. *Journalism Quarterly, 61,* 793-800.

Filley, A. C. (1975). *Interpersonal conflict resolution.* Glenview, IL: Scott, Foresman.

Fine, M. G. (1981). Soap opera conversations: The talk that binds. *Journal of Communication, 31,* 97-107.

Fink, C. F. (1968). Some conceptual difficulties in the theory of social conflict. *Journal of Conflict Resolution, 12,* 412-460.

Fischer, C. D. (1979). Transmission of positive and negative feedback to subordinates: A laboratory investigation. *Journal of Applied Psychology, 64,* 533-540.

Fisher, C. D., & Gitelson, R. (1983). A meta-analysis of the correlates of role conflict and ambiguity. *Journal of Applied Psychology, 68,* 320-333.

Fisher, R., & Ury, W. (1981). *Getting to yes: Negotiating agreement without giving in.* Boston: Houghton Mifflin.

Fitzpatrick, M. A. (1977). A typological approach to communication in relationships. In B. Ruben (Ed.), *Communication yearbook 1* (pp. 263-278). New Brunswick, NJ: Transaction.

Fitzpatrick, M. A., & Best, P. (1979). Dyadic adjustment in relational types: Consensus, cohesion, affectional expression, and satisfaction in enduring relationships. *Communication Monographs, 46,* 168-178.

Flegel, R. C., & Chaffee, S. H. (1971). Influences of editors, readers, and personal opinions on reporters. *Journalism Quarterly, 48,* 645-651.

Folger, J. P., & Poole, M. S. (1984). *Working through conflict: A communication perspective.* Glenview, IL: Scott, Foresman Company,

Frank, R. S. (1975). The IAS case against CBS. *Journal of Communication, 25,* 186-189.

Freedman, S. C. (1981). Threats, promises, and coalitions: A study of compliance and retaliation in a simulated organizational setting. *Journal of Applied Social Psychology, 11,* 114-136.

Frey, D. (1986). Recent research on selective exposure to information. In L. Berkowitz (Ed.), *Advances in experimental social psychology* (Vol. 19, pp. 41-80). New York: Academic Press.

Friedland, N. (1983). Weakness as strength: The use and misuse of a "my hands are tied" ploy in bargaining. *Journal of Applied Social Psychology, 13,* 422-426.

Gans, H. J. (1979). *Deciding what's news: A study of CBS Evening News, NBC Nightly News, Newsweek and Time.* New York: Random House.

Gantz, W. (1985). Exploring the role of television in married life. *Journal of Broadcasting and Electronic Media, 29,* 65-78.

Gerbner, G., & Gross, L. P. (1976). Living with television: The violence profile. *Journal of Communication, 26,* 172-199.

Gerbner, G., Gross, L. P., Eleey, M. F., Jackson-Beeck, M., Jeffries-Fox, S., & Signorielli, N. (1977). Tv violence profile no. 8: The highlights. *Journal of Communication, 27,* 171-180.

Gerbner, G., Gross, L. P., Jackson-Beeck, M., Jeffries-Fox, S., & Signorielli, N. (1978). Cultural indicators: Violence profile no. 9. *Journal of Communication, 28,* 176-207.

Gerbner, G., Gross, L. P., Morgan, M., & Signorielli, N. (1980). The "mainstreaming" of America: Violence profile no. 11. *Journal of Communication, 30,* 10-29.

Gerbner, G., Gross, L. P., Morgan, M., & Signorielli, N. (1982). Charting the mainstream: Television's contributions to political orientations. *Journal of Communication, 32,* 100-127.

Gerbner, G., Gross, L. P., Morgan, M., & Signorielli, N. (1984). Political correlates of television viewing. *Public Opinion Quarterly, 48,* 283-300.

Gerbner, G., Gross, L. P., Signorielli, N., Morgan, M., & Jackson-Beeck, M. (1979). The demonstration of power: Violence profile no. 10. *Journal of Communication, 29,* 177-196.

Gerbner, G., Morgan, M., & Signorielli, N. (1982). Programming health portrayals: What viewers see, say, and do. In D. Pearl, L. Bouthilet, & J. Lazar (Eds.), *Television and behavior: Ten years of scientific progress and implications for the eighties* (pp. 291-307). Rockville, MD: National Institute of Mental Health.

Gioia, D. A., & Sims, H. P., Jr. (1985). Self-serving bias and actor-observer differences in organizations: An empirical analysis. *Journal of Applied Social Psychology, 15,* 547-563.

Gioia, D. A., & Sims, H. P., Jr. (1986). Cognition-behavior connections: Attribution and verbal behavior in leader-subordinate interactions. *Organizational Behavior and Human Decision Processes, 37,* 197-229.

Glasgow University Media Group. (1976). *Bad news* (Vol. 1). London: Routledge & Kegan Paul.

Glennon, L. M., & Butsch, R. (1982). The family as portrayed on television 1946-1978. In D. Pearl, L. Bouthilet, & J. Lazar (Eds.), *Television and behavior: Ten years of scientific progress and implications for the eighties* (pp. 264-271). Rockville, MD: National Institute of Mental Health.

Goff, D. H., Goff, L. D., & Lehrer, S. K. (1980). Sex-role portrayals of selected female television characters. *Journal of Broadcasting, 24,* 467-478.

Goldberg, M. E., & Gorn, G. J. (1978). Some unintended consequences of tv advertising on children. *Journal of Consumer Research, 5,* 22-29.

Goodstadt, B., & Hjelle, L. A. (1973). Power to the powerless: Locus of control and the use of power. *Journal of Personality and Social Psychology, 27,* 190-196.

Goodstadt, B., & Kipnis, D. (1970). Situational influences on the use of power. *Journal of Applied Psychology, 54,* 201-207.

Gottman, J. M. (1979). *Marital interaction: Experimental investigations.* New York: Academic Press.

Gottman, J. M., & Porterfield, A. L. (1981). Communicative competence in the nonverbal behavior of married couples. *Journal of Marriage and the Family, 43,* 817-824.

Gottman, J. M., Notarius, C., Markman, H., Bank, S., Yoppi, B., & Rubin, M. E. (1976). Behavior exchange theory and marital decision making. *Journal of Personality and Social Psychology, 34,* 14-23.

Graber, D. A. (1979). Is crime news excessive? *Journal of Communication, 29,* 81-92.

Green, S. G., & Liden, R. C. (1980). Contextual and attributional influences on control decisions. *Journal of Applied Psychology, 65,* 453-458.

Green, S. G., & Mitchell, T. R. (1979). Attributional processes of leaders in leader-member interactions. *Organizational Behavior and Human Performance, 23,* 429-458.

Greenberg, B. S. (1969). The content and context of violence in the mass media. In R. K. Baker & S. J. Ball (Eds.), *Mass media and violence* (Vol. 11, pp. 423-452). Washington, DC: Government Printing Office.

Greenberg, B. S., Hines, M., Buerkel-Rothfuss, N., & Atkin, C. K. (1980). Family role structures and interactions on commercial television. In B. S. Greenberg (Ed.), *Life on television: Content analyses of U.S. TV drama* (pp. 149-172). Norwood, NJ: Ablex.

Greenberg, B. S., & Reeves, B. (1976). Children and the perceived reality of television. *Journal of Social Issues, 32,* 86-97.

Greenberg, S. R. (1975). Conversations as units of analysis in the study of personal influence. *Journalism Quarterly, 52,* 128-131.

Greenwell, J., & Dengerink, H. A. (1973). The role of perceived versus actual attack in human physical aggression. *Journal of Personality and Social Psychology, 26,* 66-71.

Gross, L., & Morgan, M. (1985). Television and enculturation. In J. R. Dominick & J. E. Fletcher (Eds.), *Broadcasting research methods* (pp. 221-234). Boston: Allyn & Bacon.

Gruder, C. L. (1971). Relationships with opponent and partner in mixed-motive bargaining. *Journal of Conflict Resolution, 15,* 403-416.

Gruder, C. L., & Rosen, N. A. (1971). Effects of intragroup relations on intergroup bargaining. *International Journal of Group Tensions, 1,* 301-317.

Gunter, B., & Wober, M. (1983). Television viewing and public trust. *British Journal of Social Psychology, 22,* 174-176.

Hall, J. A., & Taylor, S. E. (1976). When love is blind: Maintaining idealized images of one's spouse. *Human Relations, 29,* 751-761.

Hallin, D. C. (1984). The media, the war in Vietnam, and political support: A critique of the thesis of an oppositional media. *Journal of Politics, 46,* 2-24.

Hammond, K. R., & Brehmer, B. (1973). Quasi-rationality and distrust: Implications for internation conflict. In L. Rappoport & D. A. Summers (Eds.), *Human judgment and social interaction* (pp. 338-390). New York: Holt, Rinehart & Winston.

Haney, C., & Manzolati, J. (1978). Television criminology: Network illusions of criminal justice realities. In E. Aronson (Ed.), *Readings about the social animal* (pp. 120-130). New York: W. H. Freeman.

Hartmann, P. (1975-1976). Industrial relations in the news media. *Industrial Relations Journal, 6,* 4-18.

Hartmann, P., & Husband, C. (1973). The mass media and racial conflict. In S. Cohen & J. Young (Eds.), *The manufacture of news: A reader* (pp. 270-283). Newbury Park, CA: Sage.

Haskins, J. B. (1969). The effects of violence in the printed media. In R. K. Baker & S. J. Ball (Eds.), *Mass media and violence Vol. 11* (pp. 493-502). Washington, DC: Government Printing Office.

Hatfield, E., Utne, M. K., & Traupmann, J. (1979). Equity theory and intimate rela-
    tionships. In R. L. Burgess & T. L. Huston (Eds.), *Social exchange in developing
    relationships* (pp. 99-134). New York: Academic Press.
Hawkins, R. P., & Pingree, S. P. (1980). Some processes in the cultivation effect. *Com-
    munication Research, 7*, 193-226.
Hawkins, R. P., & Pingree, S. P. (1981). Uniform messages and habitual viewing:
    Unnecessary assumptions in social reality effects. *Human Communication
    Research, 7*, 291-301.
Hewes, D. E., & Planalp, S. (1982). There is nothing as useful as a good theory . . . :
    The influence of social knowledge on interpersonal communication. In M. E. Roloff
    & C. R. Berger (Eds.), *Social cognition and communication* (pp. 107-150). New-
    bury Park, CA: Sage.
Hilton, C. (1966). *Reporting the legislature: A study of newsmen and their sources.*
    Unpublished master's thesis, University of Washington.
Hinde, R. A. (1979). *Toward understanding relationships.* New York: Academic
    Press.
Hirsch, P. M. (1980). The "scary world" of the nonviewer and other anomalies: A
    reanalysis of Gerbner et al.'s findings on cultivation analysis. Part 1. *Communica-
    tion Research, 7*, 403-456.
Hocker, J. L., & Wilmot, W. W. (1985). *Interpersonal conflict* (2nd ed.). Dubuque,
    IA: Wm. C. Brown.
Holtzworth-Munroe, A., & Jacobson, N. S. (1985). Causal attributions of married
    couples: When do they search for causes? What do they conclude when they do?
    Journal of Personality and Social Psychology, 48, 1398-1412.
Horai, J. (1977). Attributional conflict. *Journal of Social Issues, 33*, 88-100.
Howat, G., & London, M. (1980). Attributions of conflict management strategies in
    supervisor-subordinate dyads. *Journal of Applied Psychology, 65*, 172-175.
Hughes, M. (1980). The fruits of cultivation analysis: A reexamination of some effects
    of television viewing. *Public Opinion Quarterly, 44*, 287-302.
Hunger, J. D., & Stern, L. W. (1976). An assessment of the functionality of the super-
    ordinate goal in reducing conflict. *Academy of Management Journal, 19*, 591-605.
Hur, K. K., & Robinson, J. R. (1978). The social impact of "Roots." *Journalism Quar-
    terly, 55*, 19-24.
Infante, D. A., & Gordon, W. I. (1985). Superiors' argumentativeness and verbal
    aggressiveness as predictors of subordinates' satisfaction. *Human Communication
    Research, 12*, 117-125.
Instone, D., Major, B., & Bunker, B. B. (1983). Gender, self-confidence, and social
    influence strategies: An organizational simulation. *Journal of Personality and
    Social Psychology, 44*, 322-333.
Jablin, F. M. (1979). Superior-subordinate communication: The state of the art. *Psy-
    chological Bulletin, 86*, 1201-1222.
Jablin, F. M. (1982). Organizational communication: An assimilation approach. In
    M. E. Roloff & C. R. Berger (Eds.), *Social cognition and communication* (pp. 255-
    326). Newbury Park, CA: Sage.
Jackson, S. E., & Schuler, R. S. (1985). A meta-analysis and conceptual critique of
    research on role ambiguity and role conflict in work settings. *Organizational Behav-
    ior and Human Decision Processes, 36*, 16-78.
Jacobson, N. S., Follette, W. C., & McDonald, D. W. (1982). Reactivity to positive
    and negative behavior in distressed and nondistressed married couples. *Journal of
    Consulting and Clinical Psychology, 50*, 706-714.
Jacobson, N. S., McDonald, D. W., Follette, W. C., & Berley, R. A. (1985). Attribu-
    tional processes in distressed and nondistressed married couples. *Cognitive Therapy
    and Research, 9*, 35-50.

Jaehnig, B., Weaver, D. H., & Fico, F. (1981). Reporting crime and fearing crime in three communities. *Journal of Communication, 31,* 88-96.

Janis, I. L. (1972). *Victims of groupthink.* Boston: Houghton-Mifflin.

Jones, E. T. (1976). The press as metropolitan monitor. *Public Opinion Quarterly, 40,* 239-244.

Joseph, T. (1982). Reporters' and editors' preferences toward reporter decision making. *Journalism Quarterly, 59,* 219-222.

Kahn, R. L., Wolfe, D. M., Quinn, R. P., Snoek, J. D., & Rosenthal, R. A. (1964). *Occupational stress: Studies in role conflict and ambiguity.* New York: John Wiley.

Katz, D., & Kahn, R. L. (1966). *The social psychology of organizations.* New York: John Wiley.

Kelman, H. C., & Baron, R. M. (1968). Determinants of modes of inconsistency dilemmas: A functional analysis. In R. P. Abelson, E. Aronson, W. J. McGuire, T. M. Newcomb, M. J. Rosenberg, & P. H. Tannenbaum (Eds.), *Theories of cognitive consistency: A sourcebook* (pp. 670-683). Chicago: Rand McNally.

Kelley, H. H. (1979). *Personal relationships: Their structures and processes.* Hillsdale, NJ: Lawrence Erlbaum.

Kelley, H. H., Cunningham, J. D., Grisham, J. A., Lefebvre, L. M., Sink, C. R., & Yablon, G. (1978). Sex differences in comments made during conflict within close heterosexual pairs. *Sex Roles, 4,* 473-492.

Kerrick, J. S., Anderson, T. E., & Swales, L. B. (1964). Balance and the writer's atttitude in news stories and editorials. *Journalism Quarterly, 41,* 207-215.

Kimmel, M. J., Pruitt, D. G., Magenau, J. M., Konar-Goldband, E., & Carnevale, P.J.D. (1980). Effects of trust, aspiration and gender on negotiation tactics. *Journal of Personality and Social Psychology, 38,* 9-22.

Kipnis, D. (1972). Does power corrupt? *Journal of Personality and Social Psychology, 24,* 33-41.

Kipnis, D., & Cosentino, J. (1969). Use of leadership powers in industry. *Journal of Applied Psychology, 53,* 460-466.

Kipnis, D., & Lane, W. P. (1962). Self-confidence and leadership. *Journal of Applied Psychology, 46,* 291-295.

Kipnis, D., Schmidt, S. M., & Wilkinson, I. (1980). Intraorganizational influence tactics: Explorations in getting one's way. *Journal of Applied Psychology, 65,* 440-452.

Klimoski, R. J. (1972). The effects of intragroup forces on intergroup conflict resolution. *Organizational Behavior and Human Performance, 8,* 363-383.

Knudson, R. M., Sommers, A. A., & Golding, S. L. (1980). Interpersonal perception and mode of resolution in marital conflict. *Journal of Personality and Social Psychology, 38,* 751-763.

Koblinsky, S. G., Cruse, D. F., & Sugawara, A. I. (1978). Sex role stereotypes and children's memory for story content. *Child Development, 49,* 452-458.

Koren, P., Carlton, K., & Shaw, D. (1980). Marital conflict: Relations among behaviors, outcomes, and distress. *Journal of Consulting and Clinical Psychology, 48,* 460-468.

Langer, E. (1978). Rethinking the role of thought in social interaction. In J. H. Harvey, W. J. Ickes, & R. F. Kidd (Eds.), *New directions in attribution research* (Vol. 1, pp. 35-58). Hillsdale, NJ: Lawrence Erlbaum.

Lawler, E. J. (1975). An experimental study of factors affecting the mobilization of revolutionary coalitions. *Sociometry, 38,* 163-179.

Lefever, E. W. (1974). *Tv and national defense: An analysis of CBS news 1972-1973.* Boston: Institute for American Strategy.

Lefever, E. W. (1975). CBS and national defense, 1972-73. *Journal of Communication, 25,* 181-185.

Lefkowitz, M. M., Eron, L. D., Walder, L. O., & Huesmann, L. R. (1977). *Growing up to be violent: A longitudinal study of the development of aggression.* New York: Pergamon.

Levy, M. R. (1981). Disdaining the news. *Journal of Communication, 31,* 24-31.

Lewis, J. D. (1969-1970). Programmer's choice: Eight factors in program decision-making. *Journal of Broadcasting, 14,* 71-82.

Lochman, J. E., & Allen, G. (1979). Elicited effects of approval and disapproval: An examination of parameters having implications for counseling couples in conflict. *Journal of Consulting and Clinical Psychology, 47,* 634-636.

Longley, J., & Pruitt, D. G. (1980). Groupthink: A critique of Janis's theory. In L. Wheeler (Ed.), *Review of personality and social psychology Vol. 1* (pp. 74-93). Newbury Park, CA: Sage.

Louis, M. R. (1980). Surprise and sense making: What newcomers experience in entering unfamiliar organizational settings. *Administrative Science Quarterly, 25,* 226-251.

Lull, J. (1978). Choosing television programs by family vote. *Communication Quarterly, 26,* 53-57.

Lull, J. (1980). Family communication patterns and the social uses of television. *Communication Research, 7,* 319-334.

Lull, J. (1982). How families select television programs: A mass-observational study. *Journal of Broadcasting, 26,* 801-811.

Lyle, J., & Hoffman, H. R. (1972). Explorations in patterns of television viewing by preschool-age children. In E. A. Rubinstein, G. A. Comstock, & J. P. Murray (Eds.), *Television and social behavior: Vol. 4. Television in day-to-day life* (pp. 257-273). Washington, DC: Government Printing Office.

Madden, T. J. (1971). Editor authoritarianism and its effect on news display. *Journalism Quarterly, 48,* 660-666.

Mann, L. (1974). Counting the crowd: Effects of editorial policy on estimates. *Journalism Quarterly, 51,* 278-285.

Margolin, G., & Wampold, B. E. (1981). Sequential analysis of conflict and accord in distressed and nondistressed marital partners. *Journal of Consulting and Clinical Psychology, 49,* 554-567.

Markus, H. (1977). Self-schemata and processing information about the self. *Journal of Personality and Social Psychology, 35,* 63-78.

McCall, G. J., & Simmons, J. L. (1978). *Identities and interactions: An examination of human associations in everyday life* (rev. ed.). New York: Free Press.

McGhee, P. E., & Frueh, T. (1980). Television viewing and the learning of sex-role stereotypes. *Sex Role, 6,* 179-188.

McKersie, R. B., Perry, C. R., & Walton, R. E. (1965). Intraorganizational bargaining in labor negotiations. *Journal of Conflict Resolution, 9,* 463-481.

McLeod, J. M., Atkin, C. K., & Chaffee, S. H. (1972a). Adolescents, parents, and television use: Adolescent self-report measures from Maryland and Wisconsin samples. In G. A. Comstock & E. A. Rubinstein (Eds.), *Television and social behavior: Vol. 3. Television and adolescent aggressiveness* (pp. 173-238). Washington, DC: Government Printing Office.

McLeod, J. M., Atkin, C. K., & Chaffee, S. H. (1972b). Adolescents, parents, and television use: Self-report and other-report measures from the Wisconsin sample. In G. A. Comstock & E. A. Rubinstein (Eds.), *Television and social behavior: Vol. 3. Television and adolescent aggressiveness* (pp. 239-313). Washington, DC: Government Printing Office.

McLeod, J. M., Brown, J. D., Becker, L. B., & Ziemke, D. A. (1977). Decline and fall at the White House: A longitudinal analysis of communication effects. *Communication Research, 4,* 3-22.

McLeod, J. M., Ward, S., & Tancill, K. (1965-1966). Alienation and uses of the mass media. *Public Opinion Quarterly, 29,* 583-594.

Messaris, P., & Kerr, D. (1984). TV-related mother-child interaction and children's perceptions of TV characters. *Journalism Quarterly, 61,* 662-666.

Meyer, T. P. (1973). Children's perceptions of favorite television characters as behavioral models. *Educational Broadcasting Review, 7,* 25-33.

Miller, A. H., Goldenberg, E. N., & Erbring, L. (1979). Type-set politics: Impact of newspapers on public confidence. *American Political Science Review, 73,* 67-84.

Miller, M. D. (1982). Friendship, power and the language of compliance-gaining. *Journal of Language and Social Psychology, 1,* 111-121.

Miller, M. M., & Reese, S. D. (1982). Media dependency as interaction: Effects of exposure and reliance on political activity and efficacy. *Communication Research, 9,* 227-248.

Miller, W. C., & Beck, T. (1976). How do TV parents compare to real parents? *Journalism Quarterly, 53,* 324-328.

Milavsky, J. R., Kessler, R. C., Stipp, H. H., & Rubens, W. S. (1982). *Television and aggression: A panel study.* New York: Academic Press.

Mischel, W. (1968). *Personality and assessment.* New York: John Wiley.

Mischel, W., & Peake, P. K. (1982). Beyond deja vu in the search for cross-situational consistency. *Psychological Review, 89,* 730-755.

Mitchell, T. R., & Wood, R. E. (1980). Supervisor's responses to subordinate poor performance: A test of an attributional model. *Organizational Behavior and Human Performance, 25,* 123-138.

Morgan, M. (1982). Television and adolescents' sex role stereotypes: A longitudinal study. *Journal of Personality and Social Psychology, 43,* 947-955.

Morgan, M. (1983). Symbolic victimization and real world fear. *Human Communication Research, 9,* 146-157.

Morgan, M. (1984). Heavy television viewing and perceived quality of life. *Journalism Quarterly, 61,* 499-504.

Morley, I., & Stephenson, G. (1977). *The social psychology of bargaining.* London: Allen & Unwin.

Murdock, G. (1973). Political deviance: The press presentation of a militant mass demonstration. In S. Cohen & J. Young (Eds.), *The manufacture of news* (pp. 156-175). Newbury Park, CA: Sage.

Murstein, B. I. (1971). A theory of marital choice and its applicability to marital adjustment. In B. I. Murstein (Ed.), *Theories of attraction and love* (pp. 100-151). New York: Springer.

Musser, S. J. (1982). A model for predicting the choice of conflict management strategies by subordinates in high-stakes conflict. *Organizational Behavior and Human Performance, 29,* 257-269.

Nathanson, S., Brockner, J., Brenner, D., Samuelson, C., Countryman, M., Lloyd, M., Rubin, J. Z. (1982). Toward the reduction of entrapment. *Journal of Applied Social Psychology, 12,* 193-208.

Nickel, T. W. (1974). The attribution of intention as a critical factor in the relation between frustration and aggression. *Journal of Personality, 42,* 482-492.

Noller, P. (1980). Misunderstandings in marital communication: A study of couples' nonverbal communication. *Journal of Personality and Social Psychology, 39,* 1135-1148.

Noller, P. (1981). Gender and marital adjustment level differences in decoding messages from spouses and strangers. *Journal of Personality and Social Psychology, 41,* 272-278.

Noller, P. (1982). Channel consistency and inconsistency in the communications of married couples. *Journal of Personality and Social Psychology, 43,* 732-741.

Notarius, C. I., & Johnson, J. S. (1982). Emotional expression in husbands and wives. *Journal of Marriage and the Family, 44,* 483-489.

Notz, W. W., Starke, F. A., & Atwell, J. (1983). The manager as arbitrator: Conflicts over scarce resources. In M. H. Bazerman & R. J. Lewicki (Eds.), *Negotiating in organizations* (pp. 143-164). Newbury Park, CA: Sage.

Nye, F. I., & McLaughlin, S. (1976). Role competence and marital satisfaction. In F. I. Nye (Ed.), *Role structure and the analysis of the family* (pp. 191-205). Newbury Park, CA: Sage.

Odewahn, C. A., & Krislov, J. (1973). Contract rejections: Testing the explanatory hypotheses. *Industrial Relations, 12,* 289-296.

O'Keefe, G. (1980). Political malaise and reliance on media. *Journalism Quarterly, 57,* 122-128.

Orvis, B. R., Kelley, H. H., & Butler, D. (1976). Attributional conflict in young couples. In J. H. Harvey, W. J. Ickes, & R. F. Kidd (Eds.), *New directions in attribution research* (Vol. 1, pp. 353-386). Hillsdale, NJ: Lawrence Erlbaum.

Paletz, D. L., Fozzard, P. A., & Ayanian, J. Z. (1982). The I.R.A., the Red Brigades, and the F.A.L.N. in the *New York Times. Journal of Communication, 32,* 162-171.

Passer, M. W., Kelley, H. H., & Michela, J. L. (1978). Multidimensional scaling of the causes for negative interpersonal behavior. *Journal of Personality and Social Psychology, 36,* 951-962.

Patterson, G. R., & Reid, J. B. (1970). Reciprocity and coercion: Two facets of social systems. In C. Neuringer & J. L. Michael (Eds.), *Behavior modification in clinical psychology* (pp. 133-177). New York: Appleton-Century-Crofts.

Pepitone, A. (1968). The problem of motivation in consistency models. In R. P. Abelson, E. Aronson, W. J. McGuire, T. M. Newcomb, M. J. Rosenberg, & P. H. Tannenbaum, (Eds.), *Theories of cognitive consistency: A sourcebook* (pp. 319-326). Chicago: Rand McNally.

Pearlin, L. T. (1974). Sex roles and depression. In N. Datan & L. Ginsberg (Eds.), *Proceedings of fourth life span, developmental psychology conference: Normative life crises* (pp. 183-198). New York: Academic Press.

Perloff, R. M. (1977). Some antecedents of children's sex-role stereotypes. *Psychological Reports, 40,* 463-466.

Peterson, R. B., & Tracy, L. (1977). Testing a behavioral theory model of labor negotiations. *Industrial Relations, 16,* 35-50.

Petty, R. E., & Cacioppo, J. T. (1981). *Attitudes and persuasion: Classic and contemporary approaches.* Dubuque, IA: Wm. C. Brown.

Piepe, A., Crouch, J., & Emerson, M. (1977). Violence and television. *New Society, 41,* 536-538.

Pingree, S. (1983). Children's cognitive processes in constructing social reality. *Journalism Quarterly, 60,* 415-422.

Pingree, S., & Hawkins, R. (1981). U.S. programs on Australian television: The cultivation effect. *Journal of Communication, 31,* 97-105.

Pleck, J. H., Staines, G. L., & Lang, L. (1980). Conflicts between work and family life. *Monthly Labor Review, 103,* 29-32.

Pondy, L. R. (1967). Organizational conflict: Concepts and models. *Administrative Science Quarterly, 12,* 296-320.

Prasad, V. K., Rao, T. R., & Sheikh, A. A. (1978). Mother vs. commercial. *Journal of Communication, 28,* 91-96.

Pride, R. A., & Clarke, D. H. (1973). Race relations in television news: A content analysis of the networks. *Journalism Quarterly, 50,* 319-328.

Pride, R. A., & Richards, B. (1974). Denigration of authority? Television news coverage of the student movement. *Journal of Politics, 36,* 637-660.

Pride, R. A., & Richards, B. (1975). The denigration of political authority in television news: The ecology issue. *Western Political Quarterly, 28,* 635-645.

Pride, R. A., & Wamsley, G. L. (1972). Symbol analysis of network coverage of Laos incursion. *Journalism Quarterly, 49,* 635-640.

Pruitt, D. G. (1981). *Negotiation behavior.* New York: Academic Press.

Putnam, L. L., & Jones, T. S. (1982). Reciprocity in negotiations: An analysis of bargaining interaction. *Communication Monographs, 49,* 171-191.

Putnam, L. L., & Wilson, C. E. (1982). Communicative strategies in organizational conflicts: Reliability and validity of a measurement scale. In M. Burgoon (Ed.), *Communication yearbook 6* (pp. 629-652). Newbury Park, CA: Sage.

Rabbie, J. M., & Huygen, K. (1974). Internal disagreements and their effects on attitudes toward in- and outgroup. *International Journal of Group Tensions, 4,* 222-245.

Rada, S. E. (1977). Manipulating the media: A case study of a Chicano strike in Texas. *Journalism Quarterly, 54,* 109-113.

Raush, H. L., Barry, W. A., Hertel, R. K., & Swain, M. A. (1974). *Communication, conflict and marriage.* San Francisco: Jossey-Bass.

Repetti, R. I. (1984). Determinants of children's sex stereotyping: Parental sex-role traits and television viewing. *Personality and Social Psychology Bulletin, 10,* 457-468.

Riccillo, S. C., & Trenholm, S. (1983). Predicting managers' choice of influence mode: The effects of interpersonal trust and worker attributions on managerial tactics in a simulated organizational setting. *Western Journal of Speech Communication, 47,* 323-339.

Richmond, V. P., Wagner, J. P., & McCroskey, J. C. (1983). The impact of style, use of power, and conflict management style on organizational outcomes. *Communication Quarterly, 31,* 27-36.

Roberts, C. (1981). Children's and parent's television viewing and perceptions of violence. *Journalism Quarterly, 55,* 556-564.

Robertson, T. S., & Rossiter, J. R. (1977). Children's responsiveness to commercials. *Journal of Communication, 27,* 101-106.

Robinson, M. J. (1974). The impact of the televised Watergate hearings. *Journal of Communication, 24,* 17-30.

Robinson, M. J. (1976). Public affairs television and the growth of political malaise: The case of "The Selling of the Pentagon." *The American Political Science Review, 70,* 409-432.

Roering, K. J., Slusher, E. A., & Schooler, R. D. (1975). Commitment to future interaction in marketing transactions. *Journal of Applied Psychology, 60,* 386-388.

Roloff, M. E. (1976). Communication strategies, relationships, and relational changes. In G. R. Miller (Ed.), *Explorations in interpersonal communication* (pp. 173-196). Newbury Park, CA: Sage.

Roloff, M. E. (1981a). Interpersonal and mass communication: An interdisciplinary link. In G. C. Wilhoit & H. deBock (Eds.), *Mass communication review yearbook* (Vol. 2, pp. 428-444). Newbury Park, CA: Sage.

Roloff, M. E. (1981b). *Interpersonal communication: The social exchange approach.* Newbury Park, CA: Sage.

Roloff, M. E., & Campion, D. E. (1985). Conversational profit seeking: Interaction as social exchange. In R. L. Street & J. N. Cappella (Eds.), *Sequence and pattern in communicative behavior* (pp. 161-189). London: Edward Arnold.

Roloff, M. E., & Campion, D. E. (in press). On alleviating the debilitating effects of accountability on bargaining: Authority and self-monitoring. *Communication Monographs.*

Roloff, M. E., & Greenberg, B. S. (1979a). Resolving conflict: Methods used by tv characters and teenage viewers. *Journal of Broadcasting, 23,* 285-300.

Roloff, M. E., & Greenberg, B. S. (1979b). Sex differences in choice of modes of conflict resolution in real-life and television. *Communication Quarterly, 27,* 3-12.

Roloff, M. E., & Greenberg, B. S. (1980). Tv, peer, and parent models for pro- and anti-social conflict behaviors. *Human Communication Research, 6,* 340-351.

Rosenbaum, A., & O'Leary, D. (1981). Marital violence: Characteristics of abusive couples. *Journal of Consulting and Clinical Psychology, 49,* 63-71.

Rosenberg, L. J., & Stern, L. W. (1971). Conflict management in the distribution channel. *Journal of Marketing Research, 8,* 437-442.

Rosenblatt, P. C., & Cunningham, M. R. (1976). Television watching and family tensions. *Journal of Marriage and the Family, 38,* 105-111.

Rosenthal, R., & DePaulo, B. M. (1979). Sex differences in accommodation in nonverbal communication. In R. Rosenthal (Ed.), *Skill in nonverbal communication: Individual differences* (pp. 68-103). Cambridge: Oelgeschlager, Gunn & Hain.

Ross, L. (1977). The intuitive psychologist and his shortcomings: Distortions in the attribution process. In L. Berkowitz (Ed.), *Advances in experimental social psychology* (Vol. 10, pp. 173-220). New York: Academic Press.

Ross, M., & Sicoly, F. (1979). Egocentric biases in availability and attribution. *Journal of Personality and Social Psychology, 37,* 322-336.

Rothschild, N. (1979). *Group as a mediating factor in the cultivation process among young children.* Unpublished master's thesis. University of Pennsylvania.

Rubin, A. M. (1978). Child and adolescent television use and political socialization. *Journalism Quarterly, 55,* 125-129.

Rubin, J. Z. (1980). Experimental research on third-party intervention in conflict: Toward some generalizations. *Psychological Bulletin, 87,* 379-391.

Rubin, J. Z., & Brockner, J. (1975). Factors affecting entrapment in waiting situations: The Rosencrantz and Guildenstern effect. *Journal of Personality and Social Psychology, 31,* 1054-1063.

Rubin, J. Z., Brockner, J., Small-Weil, S., & Nathanson, S. (1980). Factors affecting entry into psychological traps. *Journal of Conflict Resolution, 24,* 405-426.

Russo, F. D. (1971). A study of bias in TV coverage of the Vietnam war: 1969 and 1970. *Public Opinion Quarterly, 35,* 539-543.

Sabatelli, R. M., Buck, R., & Dreyer, A. (1982). Nonverbal communication accuracy in married couples: Relationship with marital complaint. *Journal of Personality and Social Psychology, 43,* 1088-1097.

Sarbin, T. R., & Allen, V. L. (1968). Role theory. In G. Lindzey & E. Aronson (Eds.), *The handbook of social psychology* (2nd ed., Vol. 1, pp. 488-567). Reading, MA: Addison-Wesley.

Scanzoni, J. (1979). *Sex roles, women's work, and marital conflict.* Lexington, MA: Lexington Books.

Schafer, R. B., & Keith, P. M. (1980). Equity and depression among married couples. *Social Psychology Quarterly, 43,* 430-435.

Sethi, S. P. (1977). The schism between business and American news media. *Journalism Quarterly, 54,* 240-247.

Shamir, B. (1983). Some antecedents of work-nonwork conflict. *Journal of Vocational Behavior, 23,* 98-111.

Sheikh, A. A., & Moleski, L. M. (1977). Conflict in the family over commercials. *Journal of Communication, 27,* 152-157.

Sheley, J. F., & Ashkins, C. D., (1981). Crime, crime news, and crime views. *Public Opinion Quarterly, 45,* 492-506.

Sheppard, B. H. (1983). Managers as inquisitors: Some lessons from the law. In M. H. Bazerman & R. J. Lewicki (Eds.), *Negotiating in organizations* (pp. 193-213). Newbury Park, CA: Sage.

Shoemaker, P. J. (1982). The perceived legitimacy of deviant political groups: Two experiments on media effects. *Communication Research, 9,* 249-286.

Shoemaker, P. J. (1984). Media treatment of deviant political groups. *Journalism Quarterly, 61,* 66-75.

Siebert, F. S., Peterson, T. B., & Schramm, W. (1956). *Four theories of the press.* Urbana: University of Illinois Press.

Sigal, L. V. (1973). *Reporters and officials: The organization and politics of newsmaking.* Lexington, MA: D.C. Heath.

Sigelman, L. (1973). Reporting the news: An organizational analysis. *American Journal of Sociology, 79,* 132-151.

Sigelman, L., & Sigelman, C. K. (1984). Judgments of the Carter-Reagan debate: The eyes of the beholders. *Public Opinion Quarterly, 48,* 624-628.

Sillars, A. L. (1980a). Attributions and communication in roommate conflicts. *Communication Monographs, 47,* 180-200.

Sillars, A. L. (1980b). The sequential and attributional structure of conflict interactions as a function of attributions concerning the locus of responsibility and stability of conflicts. In D. Nimmo (Ed.), *Communication yearbook 4* (pp. 217-235). New Brunswick, NJ: Transaction.

Sillars, A. L., Pike, G. R., Jones, T. S., & Murphy, M. A. (1984). Communication and understanding in marriage. *Human Communication Research, 10,* 317-350.

Sillars, A. L., Pike, G. R., Jones, T. S., & Redmon, K. (1983). Communication and conflict in marriage. In R. Bostrom (Ed.), *Communication yearbook 7* (pp. 414-429). Newbury Park, CA: Sage.

Sillars, A. L., & Weisberg, J. (in press). Conflict as a social skill. In M. E. Roloff & G. R. Miller (Eds.), *Interpersonal processes: New directions in communication research.* Newbury Park, CA: Sage.

Singer, J. L., Singer, D. G., & Rapaczynski, W. S. (1984). Family patterns and television viewing as predictors of children's beliefs and aggression. *Journal of Communication, 34,* 73-89.

Slater, D., & Elliott, W. R. (1982). Television's influence on social reality. *Quarterly Journal of Speech, 68,* 69-79.

Slusher, E. A. (1978). Counterpart strategy, prior relations, and constituent pressure in a bargaining simulation. *Behavioral Science, 23,* 470-477.

Smircich, L., & Chesser, R. J. (1981). Superiors' and subordinates' perceptions of performance: Beyond disagreement. *Academy of Management Journal, 24,* 198-205.

Sniderman, P. M., Neuman, W. R., Citrin, J., McClosky, H., & Shanks, J. M. (1975). Stability of support for the political system: The initial impact of Watergate. *American Politics Quarterly, 3,* 437-457.

Snyder, D., & Kelly, W. R. (1977). Conflict intensity, media sensitivity and the validity of newspaper data. *American Sociological Review, 42,* 105-123.

Snyder, M. (1982). When believing means doing: Creating links between attitudes and behavior. In M. P. Zanna, E. T. Higgins, & C. P. Herman (Eds.), *Consistency in social behavior: The Ontario symposium Vol. 2* (pp. 105-130). Hillsdale, NJ: Lawrence Erlbaum.

Sprey, J. (1969). The family as a system in conflict. *Journal of Marriage and the Family, 31,* 699-706.

Starck, K., & Soloski, J. (1977). Effect of reporter predisposition in covering controversial story. *Journalism Quarterly, 54,* 120-125.

Staw, B. M. (1976). Knee-deep in the big muddy: A study of escalation commitment to a chosen course of action. *Organizational Behavior and Human Performance, 16,* 27-44.

Staw, B. M. (1981). The escalation of commitment to a course of action. *Academy of Management Review, 6,* 577-587.

Staw, B. M., & Fox, F. V. (1977). Escalation: The determinants of commitment to a chosen course of action. *Human Relations, 30,* 431-450.

Steinmetz, S. K. (1977). *The cycle of violence: Assertive, aggressive, and abusive family interaction.* New York: Praeger.

Stern, L. W. (1971). Potential conflict management mechanisms in distribution channels: An interorganizational analysis. In D. N. Thompson (Ed.), *Contractual marketing systems* (pp. 111-145). Boston: Heath-Lexington Books.

Stern, L. W., Sternthal, B., & Craig, C. S. (1973). Managing conflict in distribution channels: A laboratory study. *Journal of Marketing Research, 10,* 169-179.

Stevenson, R. L., & Greene, M. T. (1980). A reconsideration of bias in the news. *Journalism Quarterly, 57,* 115-121.

Stocking, S. H., Sapolsky, B., & Zillmann, D. (1977). Sex discrimination in prime time humor. *Journal of Broadcasting, 21,* 447-457.

Stoneman, Z., & Brody, G. H. (1983). Family interactions during three programs. *Journal of Family Issues, 4,* 349-365.

Sullaway, M., & Christensen, A. (1983). Assessment of dysfunctional interaction patterns in couples. *Journal of Marriage and the Family, 45,* 653-660.

Surlin, S. H. (1974). Bigotry on air and in life: The Archie Bunker case. *Public Telecommunications Review, 2,* 34-41.

Surlin, S. H., & Bowden, E. (1976). *The psychological effect of television characters: The case of Archie Bunker and authoritarian viewers.* Paper presented at the annual meeting of the Association for Education in Journalism in College Park, Maryland.

Swensen, C. H., Eskew, R. W., & Kohlhepp, K. A. (1981). Stage of family life cycle, ego development, and the marriage relationship. *Journal of Marriage and the Family, 43,* 841-853.

Tan, A. S. (1975). Exposure to discrepant information and effect of three coping modes. *Journalism Quarterly, 52,* 678-684.

Tate, E. D., & Surlin, S. H. (1976). Agreement with opinionated TV characters across cultures. *Journalism Quarterly, 53,* 199-203.

Tedeschi, J. T., & Rosenfeld, P. (1980). Communication in bargaining and negotiation. In M. E. Roloff & G. R. Miller (Eds.), *Persuasion: New directions in theory and research* (pp. 225-248). Newbury Park, CA: Sage.

Thomas, K. (1976). Conflict and conflict management. In M. D. Dunnette (Ed.), *Handbook of industrial and organizational psychology* (pp. 889-935). Chicago: Rand McNally.

Thomas, K. W., & Schmidt, W. H. (1976). A survey of managerial interest with respect to conflict. *Academy of Management Journal, 19,* 315-318.

Thomas, K. W., Walton, R. E., & Dutton, J. M. (1972). Determinants of interdepartmental conflict. In M. Tuite, R. E. Walton, & M. Radnor (Eds.), *Intraorganizational decision making* (pp. 45-69). Chicago: Aldine.

Thompson, S. C., & Kelley, H. H. (1981). Judgments of responsibility for activities in close relationships. *Journal of Personality and Social Psychology, 41,* 469-477.

Ting-Toomey, S. (1983). An analysis of verbal communication patterns in high and low marital adjustment groups. *Human Communication Research, 9,* 306-319.

Tjosvold, D. (1977a). Commitment to justice in conflict between unequal status persons. *Journal of Applied Social Psychology, 2,* 149-162.

Tjosvold, D. (1977b). The effects of the constituent's affirmation and the opposing negotiator's self-presentation in bargaining between unequal status groups. *Organizational Behavior and Human Performance, 18,* 146-157.

Tjosvold, D. (1982). Effects of approach to controversy on superiors' incorporation of subordinates' information in decision making. *Journal of Applied Psychology, 67,* 189-193.

Tjosvold, D., & Deemer, D. K. (1980). Effects of controversy within a cooperative or competitive context on organizational decision making. *Journal of Applied Psychology, 65,* 590-595.

Tjosvold, D., & Huston, T. L. (1978). Social face and resistance to compromise in bargaining. *The Journal of Social Psychology, 104,* 57-68.

Tjosvold, D., & Johnson, D. W. (1977). The effects of controversy on cognitive perspective-taking. *Journal of Educational Psychology, 69,* 679-685.

Tjosvold, D., & Johnson, D. W. (1978). Controversy within a cooperative or competitive context and cognitive perspective-taking. *Contemporary Educational Psychology, 3,* 376-386.

Tjosvold, D., Johnson, D. W., & Lerner, J. (1981). Effects of affirmation and acceptance on incorporation of opposing information in problem-solving. *Journal of Social Psychology, 114,* 103-110.

Tornow, W. W., & Pinto, P. R. (1976). The development of a managerial job taxonomy: A system for describing, classifying, and evaluating executive positions. *Journal of Applied Psychology, 61,* 410-418.

Tunstall, J. (1971). *Journalists at Work. Specialist correspondents: Their news organizations, news sources, and competitor-colleagues.* London: Constable.

Turow, J., & Coe, L. (1985). Curing television's ills: the portrayal of health care. *Journal of Communication, 35,* 36-51.

Ulbrich, P., & Huber, J. (1981). Observing parental violence: Distribution and effects. *Journal of Marriage and the Family, 43,* 623-631.

Van De Vliert, E. (1981). A three-step theory of role conflict resolution. *Journal of Social Psychology, 113,* 77-83.

Van Maanen, J., & Schein, E. H. (1979). Toward a theory of organizational socialization. In B. M. Staw (Ed.), *Research in organizational behavior* (pp. 209-264), Greenwich, CT: JAI Press.

Vidmar, N. (1971). Effects of representational roles and mediators on negotiation effectiveness. *Journal of Personality and Social Psychology, 17,* 48-58.

Vidmar, N., & McGrath, J. E. (1970). Forces affecting success in negotiation groups. *Behavioral Science, 15,* 154-163.

Vidmar, N., & Rokeach, M. (1974). Archie Bunker's bigotry: A study in selective perception and exposure. *Journal of Communication, 24,* 36-47.

Vincent, J. P., Weiss, R. L., & Birchler, G. R. (1975). A behavioral analysis of problem solving in distressed and nondistressed married and stranger dyads. *Behavioral Therapy, 6,* 475-487.

Volgy, T. J., & Schwarz, J. E. (1982). Tv entertainment programming and sociopolitical attitudes. *Journalism Quarterly, 59,* 150-155.

Wall, J. A., Jr. (1977). Intergroup bargaining: Effects of opposing constituent stances, opposing representative's bargaining, and representative's locus of control. *Journal of Conflict Resolution, 21,* 459-474.

Wall, J. A., Jr. (1981). An investigation of reciprocity and reinforcement theories of bargaining behavior. *Organizational Behavior and Human Performance, 27,* 367-385.

Wall, J. A., Jr., & Adams, J. S. (1974). Some variables affecting a constituent's evaluations of and behavior toward a boundary role occupant. *Organizational Behavior and Human Performance, 11,* 390-408.

Walster, E., Walster, G. W., & Berscheid, E. (1978). *Equity: Theory and research.* Boston: Allyn & Bacon.

Walton, R. E., Dutton, J. M., & Fitch, H. G. (1966). A study of conflict in the process, structure, and attitudes of lateral relationships. In A. H. Rubenstein & C. J. Haberstroh (Eds.), *Some theories of organizations* (pp. 444-465). Homewood, IL: Richard D. Irwin.

Walton, R. E., & McKersie, R. B. (1965). *A behavioral theory of labor negotiations: An analysis of a social interaction system.* New York: McGraw-Hill.

Wand, B. (1968). Television viewing and family choice differences. *Public Opinion Quarterly, 32,* 84-94.

Ward, W. (1967). *News values, news situations and news selections.* Unpublished doctoral dissertation, University of Iowa.

Warner, M. (1971). Organizational context and control of policy in the television newsroom: A participant observation study. *British Journal of Sociology, 22,* 283-294.

Wegner, D. M., & Vallacher, R. R. (1977). *Implicit psychology: An introduction to social cognition.* New York: Oxford University Press.

Weigel, R. H., & Jessor, R. (1973). Television and adolescent conventionality: An exploratory study. *Public Opinion Quarterly, 37,* 76-89.

Weigel, R. H., Loomis, J. W., & Soja, M. J. (1980). Race relations on prime time television. *Journal of Personality and Social Psychology 39,* 884-893.

Wicker, A. W. (1969). Attitudes vs. actions: The relationship of verbal and overt behavioral responses to attitude objects. *Journal of Social Issues, 25,* 41-78.

Wicklund, R. A., & Brehm, J. W. (1976). *Perspectives on cognitive dissonance.* Hillsdale, NJ: Lawrence Erlbaum.

Wilhoit, G. C., & deBock, H. (1976). "All in the Family" in Holland. *Journal of Communication, 26,* 75-85.

Wilson, T. D., & Nisbett, R. E. (1978). The accuracy of verbal reports about the effects of stimuli on evaluations and behavior. *Social Psychology, 41,* 118-131.

Wober, J. M. (1978). Televised violence and paranoid perception: The view from Great Britain. *Public Opinion Quarterly, 42,* 315-321.

Wober, M., & Gunter, B. (1982). Television and personal threat: fact or artifact? A British survey. *British Journal of Social Psychology, 21,* 239-247.

Wong, P., & Weiner, B. (1981). When people ask "why" questions, and the heuristics of attributional search. *Journal of Personality and Social Psychology, 40,* 650-663.

Wood, R. E., & Mitchell, T. R. (1981). Manager behavior in a social context: The impact of impression management on attributions and disciplinary actions. *Organizational Behavior and Human Performance, 28,* 356-378.

Zahn, S. B., & Baran, S. J. (1984). It's all in the family: Siblings and program choice conflict. *Journalism Quarterly, 61,* 847-852.

Zanna, M. P., & Olson, J. M. (1982). Individual differences in attitudinal relations. In M. P. Zanna, E. T. Higgins, & C. P. Herman (Eds.), *Consistency in social behavior: The Ontario symposium* (Vol. 2, pp. 75-104). Hillsdale, NJ: Lawrence Erlbaum.

Zillmann, D. (1980). Anatomy of suspense. In P. H. Tannenbaum (Ed.), *The entertainment functions of television* (pp. 133-164). Hillsdale, NJ: Lawrence Erlbaum.

Zuckerman, D. M., Singer, D. G., & Singer, J. I. (1980). Children's television viewing, racial and sex-role attitudes. *Journal of Applied Social Psychology, 10,* 281-294.

PART IV
CONTEXTS

17 Contexts of Communication: An Introduction

STEVEN H. CHAFFEE
Stanford University

CHARLES R. BERGER
Northwestern University

I N Part III we have seen the diverse functions communication can serve. We now turn to another, related perspective for viewing communication science. In this final major part of the handbook we present 10 chapters in which scholars who study communication in distinct social and institutional settings outline these subfields as they are seen from within. We asked them to consider all four levels of discourse and analysis (see Chapter 5), but communication science has not been pursued with equal vigor at every level in every context. Still, these authors have found at least some research or theory to comment upon at each level within their respective areas of concentration.

These chapters diverge widely in the intellectual perspectives they represent. In communication, as in any science, there are various schools of thought, and the same general setting can evoke quite different approaches. The home provides a good example of the intellectual diversity of communication scientists. Chapters 18 through 20 address separate concerns that exist side by side in the home.

Bochner and Eisenberg (Chapter 18) examine the problem of the family, Fitzpatrick (Chapter 19) looks at marital relations, and Wartella and Reeves (Chapter 20) consider children. Not only are these different topics, they are addressed from unique theoretical perspectives. Bochner and Eisenberg examine the role played by paradoxical communication and other communication patterns in the production of psychopathology in family members. Theirs is a systems perspective. Fitzpatrick offers a variety of theoretical perspectives from which to view marital processes and outcomes. Wartella and Reeves draw much of their perspective from the literatures of language and cognitive development. Consumer behavior, Ward's focus in Chapter 21, is also a home-centered concern (as is O'Keefe & Reid-Nash's in Chapter 14 on socialization). But these too follow from viewpoints and assumptions that give each a distinctive flavor. Both consumer behavior and socialization are concepts that flow from system-oriented perspectives rather than the viewpoint of the family or the child.

The work setting is the common context of Chapters 22 through 24, but again they are quite diverse. Pettegrew and Logan (Chapter 22) are concerned with the topic of health care, which might be thought of as home-related too; but most of the research has instead concerned professional-patient communication in institutional settings. Jablin and Krone (Chapter 23) are concerned with the work organization more generically, and specifically with the problem of assimilation into it. While their interests are related to Monge's (Chapter 8) analysis of the network/organizational level, there is little substantive overlap between the two chapters.

The study of professional mass communicators, addressed by Ettema and Whitney with Wackman (Chapter 24), shares the work context with the two prior chapters and yet is oriented as well to the community and nation. That is, while mass communicators work in an immediate organizational context, their audiences—both local and national—establish contexts that determine how they communicate and how we evaluate their product.

More macroscopic are the topics of the final three chapters of Part IV. Price and Roberts (Chapter 25) deal with public opinion, which involves many processes linking various levels of analysis, but which still finds its ultimate force in the context of political processes of a community or nation-state. Campaigns, examined by Rogers and Storey (Chapter 26), are generally conducted within community or larger contexts. Much of the best campaign research, as they demonstrate, has been done in international settings, notably in developing countries of the Third World.

Finally, Gudykunst (Chapter 27) examines variation between nations in the ways communication activities are conducted. But even when viewed in comparative and international contexts, communication involves processes at every level from the individual or interpersonal relationship on up. Even though we have ordered these 10 chapters from the relatively micro- to macroscopic in terms of context, our four-level scheme (see Part II) is maintained within each. The result is an interweaving of topic and level that constitutes a distinct "communication perspective" for our science.

Viewing communication science from a contextual point of view runs the risk of encouraging theoretical and empirical fragmentation. When researchers study what are ostensibly different contexts, the theoretical languages they use refer to similar theoretical constructs with different words. Since communication can take place in literally thousands of different contexts, there is the possibility for confusion and overlap in theory and research efforts.

These potentially negative consequences are ameliorated to some degree by the levels of analysis scheme that undergirds this book. The chapters in this section can be ordered in a coherent way, even though they deal with a wide variety of contexts and intellectual perspectives. This suggests the integrative potential of the levels of analysis approach. Nevertheless, we need continued efforts to see commonalities across contexts so that *general theories* of human communication can be developed.

18 Family Process: System Perspectives

ARTHUR P. BOCHNER
University of South Florida

ERIC M. EISENBERG
University of Southern California

T HIS chapter reviews the literature on family process associated with system perspectives on family interaction. The term "family process" typically is used to emphasize the nonlinear and nonindividualistic qualities of families and to highlight the pragmatic goals to which family process research is directed. Inquiry on family process focuses on two scientific objectives: (1) to predict and control family-based disorders, and (2) to interpret and understand the meanings of family experience. As a communication science, family process has both empiricist and hermeneutic objectives (Bochner, 1985).

Why should students of communication concern themselves with the literature on family process? The primary reason is that several of our foundational communication concepts originated in or were greatly advanced by the early research programs associated with family process, for example, the nuances of metacommunication and paradox (Haley, 1976; Wilder-Mott, 1981). A second reason is that the family of origin is generally considered to be the earliest and most powerful source of influence on one's personality (Winch, 1977) as well as a primary locus of support and/or rejection throughout life (McCubbin, Cauble, & Patterson, 1982). Furthermore, it is generally assumed, whether rightly or wrongly, that the interpersonal difficulties associated with family life have much to do with communication. Third, the study of the family *as a whole* offers an opportunity to transcend the narrow and confining domination of dyadic models of interpersonal communication and thus bring conceptions of interpersonal communication into greater congruence with the interactional complexity of the system under observation (Ricci & Selvini-Palazzoli, 1984). Finally, the family process literature is highly pragmatic. The focus is on how to enrich or to cure families, and the achievement of these pragmatic goals is largely dependent on the validity of certain pragmatic premises about change.

We have narrowed the scope of this review to the literature on family process for three reasons. First, space limitations do not permit an exhaustive review of the entire literature relevant to family communication. Second, two other chapters in this volume are charged with the responsibility for reviewing research relevant to the question of how particular subsystems of the family operate—specifically, marital communication and child development (see Fitzpatrick, Chapter 19 in this volume; Wartella & Reeves, Chapter 20). Thus we will be dealing only incidentally with these topics (see Fitzpatrick & Badzinski, 1985, for a more comprehensive review). Third, we believe the family process perspective provides a coherent framework from which we can provide a useful synthesis of existing research.

SYSTEMIC FOUNDATIONS

Systemic descriptions of families were introduced in the 1950s, elaborated in the 1960s, and fortified in the 1970s (Guerin, 1976; Hoffman, 1983). The corpus of communication theory on which these descriptions are based is usually credited to the Bateson project on human communication (Bateson, 1972; Bateson, Jackson, Haley, & Weakland, 1956; Haley, 1976a; Weakland, 1981). However, there were a number of researchers and clinicians located in different parts of the United States who were investigating or treating families as systems at about the same time, in particular Bowen (1966), Wynne (Wynne, Rycoff, Day, & Hirsch, 1958) and Whitaker (1958). The Bateson project was not, as it is sometimes assumed, clinically inspired, but rather had as its objective the development of a general theory of human communication. In addition to Bateson, the original research team consisted of Haley and Weakland.

The Bateson research project was founded on certain basic premises about logical types and contexts of learning extrapolated from Whitehead and Russell's *Principia Mathematica* (1910). Since the funding for this project was based on the promise of extending communication theory to the mysteries of schizophrenic speech, Bateson and his colleagues attempted to apply general notions about classification and paradox to patterns of schizophrenic transaction. Having been impressed by the potential applicability of cybernetics to living systems, they hypothesized that the bizarre responses of schizophrenic children may actually be adaptive to their learning context.

In 1954 Jackson, a supervising psychiatrist at the same V.A. hospital, joined the Bateson project as a psychiatric consultant. Jackson (1957) had observed instances in which families seemed to *require* symptomatic behavior; that is, if the symptomatic person improved, someone else in the family would get sick. Thus he found the adaptability hypothesis compatible with his own notion of "family homeostasis," the idea that families seek to maintain equilibrium at any cost, even if the only way to maintain it is through symptomatic behavior. Haley later generalized this principle, calling it "the first law of human relationships." Haley's law states that "when one person indicates a change in relation to another, the other will act upon the first so as to diminish and modify the change" (Haley, 1963, p. 189).

The first generation of theorizing about family systems was dominated by these loosely applied cybernetic notions, which Hoffman (1981) has called "the homeostatic paradigm." Although the concepts associated with the homeostatic paradigm were never rigorously developed or formally explicated during this period (see Ariel, Carel, & Tyano, 1984), the scope and purposes of this paradigm are not difficult to identify. First, homeostasis is a metaphorical (or theoretical) way of describing the functioning of a system. Second, research conducted in the 1950s at the National Institute of Mental Health in Bethesda (Redl & Wineman, 1965) and at MRI in Palo Alto (Bateson, Jackson, Haley, & Weakland, 1956) had repeatedly observed that when patients were released from the hospital and returned to their families, they were highly likely to relapse, or some other member of the family was likely to get sick. This resistance to change apparently was accomplished by processes of self-regulation that could usefully be described as "homeostatic mechanisms." Third, the homeostatic paradigm represented an epistemological turn away from thinking of "forces" or "causes" and toward thinking of "relationships" and "contexts;" away from emphasizing what goes on "under the skin" or "inside the head" and toward a focus on the communicative behavior that takes place between people; away from linear models and toward recursive or circular descriptions. Selvini-Palazzoli and her colleagues (Selvini-Palazzoli, Boscolo, Cecchin, & Pratta, 1978, pp. 5-6) have summarized aptly this epistemological shift:

> The acceptance of these hypotheses requires an epistemological change, in the original sense of the Greek verb *epistamai,* which means to put oneself "over" or "higher" in order to better observe something. To do this, we must abandon the causal-mechanistic view of phenomena, which has dominated the sciences until recent times, and adopt a systemic orientation. With this new orientation . . . the members of the family [are seen] as elements in a circuit of interaction. None of the members of the circuit have unidirectional power over the whole, although the behavior of any one of the members of the family inevitably influences the behavior of the others. At the same time it is epistemologically incorrect to consider the behavior of one individual the *cause* of the behavior of the others. This is because every member influences the others, but is in turn influenced by them. The individual acts upon the system, but is at the same time influenced by the communications he receives from it. . . . Saying that the behavior of one individual is the *cause* of the behavior of other individuals is an epistemological error. The error derives from the arbitrary punctuation which isolates such behavior from the pragmatic context of preceding behaviors that can be traced back to infinity. Even a

behavior which, in various ways, reduces its apparent victim to impotence is not a "behavior-power," but rather a "behavior-response." And yet, whoever thinks of himself as being in the superior position believes himself the one with power, just as the one in the "inferior" position thinks of himself as the one without it. We, however, know these convictions to be wrong: the power belongs neither to the one nor the other. *The power is only in the rules of the game which cannot be changed by the people involved in it.*

Additionally, the homeostatic paradigm incorporated the entire arsenal of Batesonian communication concepts: (1) the idea that communication involves multiple levels of messages that coexist on at least two simultaneous levels, the analogic and the digital; (2) context as a field of meanings; (3) the notion of punctuating sequences of interaction; (4) the importance of defining the relationship and the various tacit modes of communication that are used to define it; (5) the concepts of symptomatic and therapeutic paradoxes; (6) symmetrical and complementary forms of relationship; (7) metacommunication, framing and reframing, and strategic modes of altering contexts (Bateson, 1972; Haley, 1963; Stanton, 1981; Watzlawick, Beavin, & Jackson, 1967; Watzlawick, Weakland, & Fisch, 1974; Wilder-Mott & Weakland, 1981).

The homeostatic paradigm has recently encountered some severe criticism, and for several good reasons. First of all, family systems not only remain the same, they also change, sometimes suddenly. Homeostasis cannot explain such changes, particularly when viewed as the maintenance of a family's current stability (Dell, 1982; Speer, 1970). Speer (1970) astutely pointed out the irony involved in basing a field committed to helping families change on a paradigm about how they do not change. Second, to speak of homeostatic mechanisms as restoring the family to its status quo, or functioning to diminish change, is to imply rather strongly a linear causal effect connecting the mechanism, such as family rules (Ford, 1983; Jackson, 1957, 1965; Sorrells & Ford, 1969), to particular outcomes, such as resistance to change. This is precisely the kind of causal thinking that system theories intended to correct. Third, the homeostatic paradigm's central premise of resistance to change inappropriately differentiates the family from its environment, making it seem as if the family resists changes proposed by the environment (Dell, 1982). It would be more appropriately systemic to view the family system or environment as one wider context in which "there is no such thing as resistance; there is only misunderstanding of reality or refusal to accept reality" (Dell, 1982, p. 31).

Dell (1982) has proposed an evolutionary paradigm of family systems specifically targeted at correcting these deficiencies. Charging that homeostasis is "an epistemological error," "an erroneous scientific idea," and "a flawed concept," Dell argues that the concept of *coherence* should replace homeostasis. According to Dell, "the coherence of interactional situations needs no explanation other than that the coherence is a natural, spontaneous phenomenon that arises when living organisms spend time together (1982, p. 36). Although he may have overstated the case, the epistemological basis of Dell's arguments is well founded. It is still too early to tell, though, how much impact the coherence notion will have on the next generation of family system theories.

Midrange Perspectives

In this section, we describe three intermediate models of family process. These midrange perspectives fall between the more general paradigms reviewed in the previous section and the applied techniques generally associated with family therapy. Sluzki (1983) refers to these models as "translations" of the systems perspective. The three models we shall examine are (1) the interactional, (2) the structural, and (3) the constructivist (see Sluzki, 1983).

The interactional view. Of the three perspectives we shall review, this is the one most closely identified with communication theory. The interactional view emphasizes directly observable messages, that is, statements and/or actions of family members. This focus on messages draws attention to several important features of interaction. First, it is assumed that "there is no such thing as a simple message" (Weakland, 1976, p. 117) because communicators are sending and receiving several messages simultaneously. Some messages are used to qualify or modify the meaning of other messages. Thus no single message can be adequately understood without considering the messages that qualify or frame its meanings. Second, the analytical distinction between the report and command level of messages (Ruesch & Bateson, 1951) indicates that every message is a double message insofar as it is both stimulus and response; that is, it serves both informative and directive functions. It is this later function, the directive influence of a message, that is central to the interactional view. As Weakland states it, "Small signals may easily have large effects (and thus) the potential importance of communicative influence on behavior is great, and should never be neglected" (1976, p. 117). Third, there is no beginning or end to an ongoing sequence of interaction. Which message is seen as stimulus and which as response is an arbitrary choice, as is the decision to call communicators "sources" and "receivers." Nevertheless, participants normally punctuate their sequences of interaction according to a simple linear model of cause and effect. These causal punctuations are viewed as a major source of the difficulties experienced by troubled families. Fourth, interactional sequences tend to be self-perpetuating and repetitive. The structure of the family is defined in terms of its repetitive interactional sequences. Family members typically behave in whatever way is necessary to keep the sequence going (Haley, 1976; Sluzki, 1983). These highly predictable sequences of interaction are sometimes referred to as "family rules" (Ford, 1983; Jackson, 1965; Sorrells & Ford, 1969) since the family is acting "as if" it were following a particular rule. Fifth, no matter how unusual a particular person's behavior may seem, it is sensible within its own particular communicative context. The critical questions for the observer are these: (1) What function does the behavior serve in the family context? and (2) How does the behavior fit with the interactional sequences of the family (Weakland, 1976)?

The structural view. The social organization of the family is the pivotal concern in the structural view. It is assumed that the codes regulating human relationships, the so-called structuring forces, are manifested in the operational patterns of the system (Aponte & VanDeusen, 1981). Minuchin (1974) has written the clearest description of the structural view. He defines family structure as "the invisible set of functional demands that organizes the ways in which family members interact" (Minuchin, 1974, p. 71). These functional demands constitute the family's systems of constraint. The first system of constraint involves universal rules of family organization, for example, parents will have more influence than children. The second system of constraint is the mutual expectations of family members built up over years of living together, often through a process of implicit negotiation.

Minuchin (1974) suggests that families are normally differentiated into subsystems that carry out family functions. There are three principal subsystems:

(1) *The spouse subsystem* includes only the husband and wife and has as its goal the achievement of complementarity and mutual support. Spouses normally feel the tensions created by each one's dialectical need for both independence and dependence. Each must find a way "to give in without feeling he has given up" (Minuchin, 1974, p. 56). The problems of the spouse subsystem are complicated by the demands placed upon the spouses by other subsystems. It is essential, argues Minuchin, that the spouses create "a haven in which they can give each other emotional support" (1974, p. 57), but this can only be achieved by establishing a clear boundary that sets them off and protects them from the intrusions of other subsystems.

(2) *The parenting subsystem* involves the nurturing and disciplining responsibilities associated with relations between parents and children. These responsibilities are often experienced by parents as oppositions, since disciplining requires controlling and/or restricting (authority-based outcomes) while nurturing requires emotional support and/or greater freedom for the children (intimacy-based outcomes). It is not difficult to see why parenting is a process that "no one goes through . . . unscathed" (Minuchin, 1974, p. 58).

(3) *The sibling subsystem* refers to the relations among children in the same family. For children, it is the primary context of learning how to relate to peers, particularly how to cooperate and how to compete. The connection between sibling relations and extrafamilial peer relations is also important. If there is a radical difference between the transactional patterns operating in the family and the patterns that normally operate in peer relations outside the family, the children may encounter difficulties in establishing friendships and adapting to the world outside the family (see, e.g., Henry, 1973, pp. 99-187).

The structural view calls attention to several operational dimensions of family structure. First, there are *boundaries* that differentiate and separate individuals and subsystems in the family. Clarity of the *boundaries* is viewed as the most important quality of family structure. Clarity means not only that all of the family members know the boundaries but also that the boundaries are appropriate to the functional demands confronting the family. There are two general forms of inappropriateness: *disengagement* and *enmeshment*. Disengagement refers to cases in which the boundaries are inappropriately rigid, making it difficult to achieve communication across the subsystems and thus endangering the protective functions of the family. Enmeshment refers to cases in which the boundaries are inappropriately diffuse resulting in an overinvolved and overprotective structure that inhibits privacy (Hoffman, 1975).

Second, there are the *coalitions* that develop in families aligning individuals in joint action against others (Aponte, 1976; Haley, 1976b; Hoffman, 1977). When these coalitions develop into alliances that cut across generational boundaries—alliances that are kept hidden from the third person and may be denied at the metacommunicative level—they are called "perverse triangles" (Haley, 1976b).

Third, the boundaries and coalitions essentially define who is in and who is out, as well as who is for and who is against. Thus *power* is a fundamental dimension of family process (Aponte & Vanduesen, 1981). Unlike the individualistic conceptions of power that dominate the social science literature, however, power is defined in terms of the family's structure, its hierarchy, and transactional operations. If a family's set of operations is changed, its power structure is changed too.

The constructivist view. The constructivist view is both a theory of knowledge and a meta-theory of family process. The constructivists renounce "metaphysical realism" and thereby break away from the representational theory of knowledge that emphasizes correspondence between knowledge and objective reality (von Glasersfeld, 1984). Instead of correspondence to reality, they emphasize "a search for *fitting* ways of behaving and thinking" based on a view of knowledge "as something that an organism builds up in the attempt to order the as such amorphous flow of experience by establishing repeatable experiences and relatively reliable relations between them" (von Glasersfeld, 1984,

p. 39). Constructivism thus emphasizes the world views—constructs, belief structures, paradigms—that individuals use to organize and/or operate on their experience (Von Foerster, 1984; Watzlawick, 1984).

Most of the literature on family process takes for granted the constructivist view of the relationship between knowledge and reality. For instance, Sluzki (1983) looks upon the family as the place where each of us develops a blueprint of the world, our sense of "the way things are." This ordering of experience, called "reality constructing," is often viewed as the central feature of family experience (Berger & Kellner, 1964; Berger & Luckmann, 1967; Hess & Handel, 1959; Laing, 1969). Ordinarily, an individual's sense of belonging to a particular family is tied to the reality-organizing structures shared by family members. These structures constitute a "family ideology," a set of belief-oriented constructs that are recursively tied to the family's interaction patterns. *The interaction patterns evolve from the family's ideology and reinforce it.* The circuit connecting family ideology and interaction patterns is thus a self-perpetuating one that is difficult to break. This premise is particularly important to family practitioners (see, e.g., Haley, 1976; Minuchin, 1974; Stanton, 1981). Most of the structural and strategic forms of family therapy are oriented toward altering the family's reality premises—that is, its ideology—by changing its interaction patterns.

FAMILY PROCESS, PSYCHOPATHOLOGY, AND SOCIAL DEVIANCE

The inspiration behind the family process movement was the premise that efforts to understand and treat various forms of psychopathology, such as schizophrenia, had failed to take into account the interactional context within which psychopathology develops and is maintained. If family experience results in a "blueprint of the way things are," then disturbances in thinking (about the way things are) may result from the learning context of the family rather than from what is inside the individual (i.e., the individual's psychic or genetic endowment). The implication of this premise is that psychopathology is an interpersonal rather than an intrapsychic disorder. An individual's strange behavior can then be seen as a symptom of a disturbed family context rather than a disturbed individual. This paradigmatic shift from an individual/deterministic/cause-and-effect conception to a contextual/processual/a-causal one is consonant with the systems perspective out of which it emerged (Bateson, 1966, 1970, 1972, 1978; Helmerson, 1983; Hoffman, 1981; Sluzki & Ransom, 1976).

The issue of what causes schizophrenia (and other forms of psychopathology) is the unifying concern that ties together family interaction research and family therapy. The more research evidence the field can accumulate in support of an interactional etiology, the more confidence it can have in a family-oriented method of treatment. The credibility of family therapy is at least partially dependent on how strong a case it can build for the interactional etiology hypothesis.

Our review of the literature relating family processes to psychopathology and/or social deviance has two objectives. First, we shall briefly describe the communication or interactional constructs that have played a central role in this body of empirical research. Then, we shall summarize the current status of this line of research. Helmerson (1983) has published a recent review of this literature that we find difficult to improve on. Hence we shall highlight some of his observations. Readers who are interested in a more comprehensive review of this literature should consult the reviews by Mishler and Waxler (1965), Riskin and Faunce (1972), Jacob (1975), Goldstein and Rodnick (1975), Doane (1978), and Liem (1980).

The Bateson research team (Bateson et al., 1956) published the first paper that attempted to describe formally what was going on in the family of the schizophrenic. Their *double-bind* theory presented a broad outline of a communication theory about the origins of schizophrenia. They defined schizophrenia as the acquisition of mental habits that inevitably lead to crazy-sounding talk. These mental habits are acquired from repeated experiences of interaction in which the discontinuity between logical types is breached, specifically when a vulnerable individual receives "a primary negative injunction, a secondary injunction conflicting with the first at a more abstract level and enforced by punishments or signals which threaten survival, and a third negative injunction prohibiting the victim from escaping the field" (Haley, 1976, p. 69). Although the Bateson group suggested that this pattern could involve other members of the family, their examples emphasized dyadic interactions between victimizing mothers and victimized children. Their paper was interpreted as describing an interpersonal situation in which the victim is "damned if he does and damned if he doesn't," but a careful reading shows clearly that a double-binding context is one in which the victim cannot choose one without choosing the other. His bind is that "if he obeys, he is disobeying, and if he disobeys, he is obeying"(Haley, 1976, p. 71).

Double bind never amounted to much as a rigorous description of interpersonal sequences or as a testable theory of how schizophrenia evolves. Although empirical researchers made numerous attempts to test the theory by counting double binds (Abeles, 1976), it is obvious, at least in retrospect, that the theory was not designed to be tested in this way. A decade after the publication of the original paper, Bateson referred to the double-bind theory as "slippery—so slippery that perhaps no set of empirical facts could contradict it" (Bateson, 1966, p. 415). The double bind, then, was not so much a scientific theory as a language of interpersonal relations reflecting a new epistemology.

Building upon Haley's observation that in families with a schizophrenic patient each family member is reluctant to admit either that his behavior is controlled by the other members of the family or that he himself regulates their behavior, Selvini-Palazzoli and her colleagues (1978) have described the interaction between spouses in such families as a "game without end." Accordingly, the schizophrenic transaction involves spouses whose positions in the relationship are identical and symmetrical. Each wants to control the definition of the relationship and tries to do so; and each one constantly runs the risk of being defeated by the other. Since each of the parties becomes painfully vulnerable to the other, the only way out is to avoid committing to any definition of the relationship at all: *"Each must disqualify his own definition of the relationship before the other has a chance to do it"* (Selvini-Palazzoli et al., 1978, pp. 24-25). The transactional moves that characterize the "schizophrenic game" include such maneuvers as partial or total disqualification of the message, topic discontinuity, non sequitur, and a "deadly and subtle" form of disqualification called *autodisconfirmation* in which "*it is the very author of the message who qualifies himself as nonexistent,* expressing in some way, 'I'm not really here, I don't exist in the relationship with you'" (Selvini-Palazzoli et al., 1978, p. 25). The crux of the schizophrenic game is the reluctance of the players to assume a definable position in the relationship, making it impossible to determine who has the advantage, that is, who is the winner and who is the loser. It is a game without escape and without closure.

One of the earliest programmatic attempts to better understand and explain the interactional problems and styles of families with a child labeled schizophrenic was Wynne et al. (1958). Wynne had studied with Talcott Parsons at Harvard (Wynne, 1983) and the Parsonian influence aroused his interest in examining the connection between the family's organization as a whole and stages of schizophrenic processes. Wynne's research team audiotaped therapy sessions; watched each other conduct therapy from behind one-way mirrors; and thoroughly discussed what they saw and heard, formulating and criticizing hypotheses about family processes. In one of their first published reports from this research program, Wynne et al. (1958) described the manner in which these families deal with conflicts between the need for identity and the need for relation generally experienced by all families. These families were unable to achieve "genuine complementarity." They were fearful of openly affirming their member's individual identities, believing that expressions of independence run the risk of demolishing the family's togetherness. The solution to the identity/relatedness dilemma chosen by these families is *pseudomutuality,* an intense and persistent effort to sustain the perception that each member's behavior and expectations are complementary to those of other family members. Symptomatic individuals find it particularly difficult to engage in experiences inside or outside the family that would result in differentiating themselves from other family members.

Shortly after publication of the pseudomutuality paper, Wynne and others began to focus specifically on the stylistic qualities of family communication (Singer & Wynne, 1965; Wynne & Singer, 1963). They assumed that in order to share meanings, it is necessary for members of the family to share a focus of attention. Thus the communicational disorders observed in the families of certain schizophrenics were construed as "transactional thought disorders," characterized by the inability to focus attention with other family members (Wynne & Singer, 1963). Wynne and Singer's research program on transactional thought disorders concentrated on the communication deviances of these presumably disturbed families. Communication deviance was broadly construed as a measure of the difficulties members of these families had in constructing "a consistent visual image or a consistent construct from the speaker's words" (Singer, Wynne, & Toohey, 1978, p. 500). The measurement of communication deviance (CD) used in their studies included 32 categories of CD that were significantly different in the disturbed families than in the control families (Singer & Wynne, 1965, 1966; Singer et al., 1978; Wynne, Singer, Bartko, & Toohey, 1977).

Blakar, a Norwegian social scientist, heads up a research program on psychopathology based on assumptions about communication that are similar to those of Wynne's group. Finding previous conceptions of communication to be loosely defined, too implicit, and excessively vague, Blakar tried to develop a research framework and methodology based on "essential aspects of communication" that distinguish communication from related processes and activities. Blakar based his definition of communication on Rommetveit's communication theory (1973, 1980), which suggests that "the most essential characteristic of communication is that something is being made known to somebody" (Blakar, 1980). Blakar was convinced by the research conducted in the 1960s that families containing members with certain psychopathological symptoms are less efficient communicators than their "normal" counterparts (see Haley, 1972). They have more difficulty communicating their preferences and they take longer to complete tasks. Blakar argued that in order to explain why communication is so inefficient in these families, it is necessary to concentrate on the *qualitative* dimensions of communication, particularly the conditions that make it possible for one person to make something known to another person. Favoring a social-cognitive conception of successful communication, Blakar grounded his research program on the assumption that "the most basic precondition for successful communication . . . to take place at all, is that the participants have established *'a shared social reality'*, a common here-and-now within which the exchange of messages can take place" (Blakar, 1980, p. 222).

Blakar devised an ingenious methodology that operationalized his basic premise about the preconditions for successful communication. Participants (couples and/or other family members) were put into a communication situation in which they did not share the same "reality" (premises) about their present situation and they did not know that they were not sharing the same "reality." Thus one of the essential preconditions for successful communication was not satisfied. The participants believed they were in the "same" situation, but they were not. Helmerson (1983, p. 40), who has reviewed these studies more closely than the present authors, concluded that Blakar's "experimental task was found to discriminate parents of schizophrenics from parents of normal offspring in the same elegant manner that Wynne and Singer's design had demonstrated the relationship between communication deviance in parents and severity of disorder in their offspring."

In this section, we have identified five communicational characteristics of families with a member labeled schizophrenic: (1) double binds, (2) autodisconfirmation, (3) pseudomutuality, (4) communication deviance, and (5) failure to share a common here-and-now. Obviously, these are not the only dimensions of communication worthy of attention in studies of "disturbed" families. We have chosen to emphasize these over others because they have survived the test of time. In considering these qualities as significant dimensions of communication associated with the presence of schizophrenia, readers should be apprised of two important limitations of this review. First, we have concentrated only on describing the communication processes of families with a member labeled schizophrenic, though the trend in recent years has been to apply family process notions to other forms of family-based "social deviance," particularly drug addiction (see Stanton, 1978, 1979) and psychosomatic illness (Liebman, Minuchin, Baker, & Rosman, 1976; Minuchin et al., 1975; Minuchin, Rosman, & Baker, 1978). Second, we have focused only on communication and/or essential prerequisites to communication. There is an enormous literature pertaining to structural correlates of psychopathology (symbiotic enmeshment, dominance structures, coalition and perverse triangles, breaching of boundaries, role strains, etc.) that has not been included in this review.

Etiology of psychopathology. As we have seen, the communication style of families with an identified schizophrenic is characteristically different from control or "normal" families. These families show considerably more communication deviance, find it more difficult to share a focus of attention, are more inefficient at problem solving, and lack awareness of each other's reality-orienting premises. As impressive as these results may seem, they do not speak directly to the issue of causation. The correlations that have been reported show a strong association between communication style and psychopathology, but do not rule out the rival hypothesis that deviance in communication style and social/ cognitive ability develops *"along with"* or as a *response to* psychopathology (Helmerson, 1983, p. 42). As Reiss (1976) has accurately pointed out, in order to demonstrate a causal link between family variables and schizophrenia "the causal role of the variable must be linked with schizophrenia as opposed to other conditions and states, . . . [have] an impact on the individual before the onset of schizophrenia, and . . . not [be] confounded with a covarying or concomitant variable that is the 'true' etiological variable" (Reiss, 1976, p. 181).

Studies that have attempted to assess the causal impact of family variables have been of three types. The first type examines what happens when schizophrenic children interact for a time with normal parents. These studies are methodologically flawed and rarely done (Helmerson, 1983). Reported studies have yielded inconsistent results. Waxler (1974) found that schizophrenic children rarely disrupt the performance of normal parents, but often improve their own performances after such interactions. However, Liem (1974, 1976) reported that such experiences result in poorer performances both for normal and schizophrenic parents.

The two other sets of studies involve cross-sectional and longitudinal assessments of "high-risk families." These studies are grouped together here because the cross-sectional research consists mainly of preliminary analyses of data gathered in the first stage of longitudinal studies conducted at UCLA (Goldstein & Rodnick, 1975) and the University of Rochester (Doane, West, Goldstein, Rodnick, & Jones, 1981; Doane et al., 1982; Wynne, 1980). In the UCLA studies, risk is defined in terms of child attributes associated with a "preschizophrenic" syndrome. Although the UCLA cross-sectional studies suggest that the chances of "becoming schizophrenic" are greater for preschizophrenic children whose parents show higher levels of deviant communication, the reactive hypothesis cannot be ruled out because there is no way of determining precisely when children become schizophrenic or what the developmental pattern involves (Helmerson, 1983). The higher levels of parental communication deviance may be simply a reaction to the preschizophrenic syndrome, which may or may not contribute significantly to the child's later diagnosis as schizophrenic.

The Rochester cross-sectional studies define risk according to the psychiatric condition of parents. The criterion was whether the hospitalized parent was schizophrenic or nonschizophrenic. Several of these studies have reported relatively strong associations between high parental CD scores and ego-impaired male children (Doane, 1977; Ritzler, Singer, Cole, & Fisher, 1977). Assuming ego impairment is part of the schizophrenic syndrome, it is reasonable to conclude that high parental CD increases the risk for male children.

The main flaw of all cross-sectional research is that there is no way to determine whether or not individuals classified as high risk become schizophrenic. This methodological obstacle is overcome in the five-year longitudinal report on the UCLA families, which Helmerson refers to as "a milestone in family interaction research" (Helmerson, 1983, p. 45). The results reported by Doane and her associates (1981) are impressive indeed. They found that 9 of the 11 young adults who ended up classified as "extended schizophrenia spectrum" had parents who had high CD scores five years earlier, while 19 of the 26 children who ended up after five years with nothing worse than "normal and mild and marked character neuroses" had parents whose earlier CD scores were low. This is the first study to provide convincing evidence of the presence of parental communication dysfunctions *before* the diagnosis of schizophrenia. While it is not yet clear precisely how communication deviance contributes to schizophrenia, these longitudinal results may support a causal link.

Helmerson (1983) made several observations about this line of family process research that are worth underscoring as we close this section. First, we have not discussed studies of family structure that incorporate such interactional measures as total talk time, interruptions, who follows whom, and content analysis. Such measures have been shown to have little discriminative power (Doane, 1978; Jacob, 1975) and to require inferential judgments that are not clearly justifiable (e.g., connecting talking time with dominance). Second, the results that have accrued from efforts to relate structure to outcome are disappointing. The reviews published by Jacob (1975) and Goldstein and Rodnick (1975) came to the same conclusion as Helmerson (1983). These studies are limited by "methodological flaws," "questionable operationalizations," and "unresolved epistemological issues" (Helmerson, 1983, p. 98). Third, the number of studies focusing on schizophrenia has declined, while studies of drug addiction, alcoholism, and psychosomatic illness have increased. We also expect an increase in studies of how families are affected by illnesses such as cancer and/or heart disease. Finally, it has become a ritual to comment on the ambiguity of definitions of communication and to point out how frequently linear methodologies are applied inappropriately as operationalizations of mutual causal or recursive relationships. While there have been some notable improvements in the conceptualization and operationalization of communication (e.g., Wynne and Blakar), the cleavage between a constructivist epistemology and the predominantly linear methodologies utilized in research is far too large.

Intensive studies. Up to this point we have concentrated on nomothetic studies of family interaction conducted in the empiricist tradition (Bochner, 1986). While we have been impressed with the progress of research on family-based psychopathology, we are not yet convinced that this research can be generalized to "real" families. Nomothetic research seeks to establish general laws that would make it possible to predict and control psychopathology. Thus it restricts observation to a relatively small range of structured interaction experiences that may be unrepresentative of the way families interact in their own homes. The only way to overcome this deficiency is to prolong the time period in which families are observed and attempt to observe them unobtrusively. The preferred method is intensive field research. We were disappointed to find that Helmerson's (1983) review of family interaction and psychopathology completely ignored intensive case studies of family interaction (see e.g., Bott, 1971; Handel, 1967; Henry, 1973; Hess & Handel, 1959; Kantor & Lehr, 1975). These studies are more thickly textured than other studies and they add important insights about the dynamics of family interaction. We will end our discussion of psychopathology by highlighting a few of the observations made by Henry (1973) in his landmark study *Pathways to Madness.* Readers interested in a review of some of the other idiographic studies should consult Bochner (1976).

Henry (1973) studied five families, four of which had an institutionalized child and a fifth in which the mother had experienced repeated psychotic episodes. He spent between five and eight days with each family. One of the families provided a room for him; in three others he arrived in time for breakfast and left when the family retired for the night. Twenty years after its first printing, Henry's study still towers over other attempts to draw conclusions about psychological illness from direct observation of families in their natural habitat. While many observers have looked upon the mundane activities of daily life as trivial, Henry (1973) was able to show that a "relentless examination of the commonplace" can produce profound insights that could not possibly be seen in the researcher's laboratory or the psychologist's clinic.

Looking over his experiences with all of the families, Henry (1973) reached several conclusions about family-based psychopathology. First, *family interaction is highly complex.* So many things are happening at the same time that it is difficult to make sense of all of it. Even in the "sickest" families, there are always signs of health. Given the complexity of family life, it is doubtful that psychopathology could ever be ascribed to a single cause. Second, *there is more cruelty and less compassion in "miserable" families.* Cruelty is a function of vulnerability for without vulnerability cruelty would be impossible. Disturbed families tend to exploit their most vulnerable members. Somehow these families have failed to understand the importance of compassion. In Henry's opinion, the "judicious application of compassion" is essential (Henry, 1973, p. 449). Third, in disturbed families *at least one person is viewed as an "enemy" and treated as one.* Usually, the adversary (or scapegoat) is one of the children. Interestingly enough, the children who are not treated this way are usually better off. Fourth, *family members do not know how to restrain their reactions when it is necessary to do so.* They fight when they ought to submit; they have learned the subtle art of entrapment and know how to appear innocent when they are guilty of triggering another's emotional impulses, what Henry calls "turning the other person on" (Henry, 1973, p. 449). Fifth, *there is distortion in the means of satisfaction.* For instance, spouses substitute the affection received from a child for what is absent from their own relationship. Sixth, they *take life too seriously.* There is very little joy and not much humor in these families. They seem to have "a compulsion to murder pleasure" (Henry, 1973, p. 452). Finally, *these families exhibit considerable "pathogenic leveling,"* a form of "concordant misperception" in which "the sick are treated as if well, the young are treated as if they were older and vice versa, strangers are treated like old friends, and so on" (Henry, 1973, p. 453).

NORMAL AND HEALTHY FAMILIES

The primary goal of research relating family processes to psychopathology and/or social deviance is to gain an understanding of these processes sufficient to prevent and/or cure family disorders. Of course, the definition of what is socially or psychologically "deviant" depends largely on what is considered "normal." It would be comforting to be able to present an interactional baseline of "normality" against which interaction in "disturbed" families could be compared. No such baseline exists. The rule of thumb applied in most family interaction research either is to classify families as normal if none of the family members presents a symptom or if the family is not engaged in therapy. The research we have reviewed strongly suggests that these methods of classifying families as normal are unacceptable. First, we know of only one study that has been able to cross-validate the clinical classification of normal and abnormal families by listening or viewing tapes of their interaction (Blakar, 1980), and this study focused only on dyadic interaction. The evidence of an interactional difference between the "normal" family and the family containing a symptomatic individual that could serve as a baseline for cross-validation is "no more than indicative" (Haley, 1973, p. 36). Second, much of the activity in the psychotic families seems within "normal limits" (Henry, 1973). The main difference is that "they seem to go to extremes and do too many things that are upsetting" (Henry, 1973, p. xx). However, there is always some allevi-ating health in these families. Third, by defining normality as the absence of abnormality, one runs the risk of confusing conventionality with nor-mality, and implying that there is something particularly "good" or "right" about how such families function. Jackson (1967, p. 161) sug-gested almost twenty years ago that the concept of a normal family is a myth:

> As a student of the family for many years, I think it is safer to say there is no such thing as a normal family any more than there is a normal indi-vidual. There are parents who appear to live in extreme harmony together but who have nervous children, and parents who get along miserably but whose children appear to be functioning well. When one hears the expression, "Gee, they're a normal family," the speaker is usually refer-ring to some facet of family living and not to the total family interaction, which is unknown to the casual observer. Such statements are usually made by persons who value conformity and see this family as one that lives up to all of the ideals of the ladies magazines, including the cardinal principle of "togetherness." Truly, such behavior has little to do with mental health. There are cultures and families within our own culture, in which the family structure is very different from what is commonly con-sidered normal. Yet the individuals therein are creative and productive. (p. 161)

Jackson's (1967) observations remain just as true today. For example, Fisher, Giblin, and Hoopes (1982) recently conducted a study in which 208 nonclinical families were asked to rank order the importance of 34 aspects of family process in terms of their importance to family func-tioning. These families strongly endorsed the value of family unity and togetherness, however, such results clash with judgments of therapists who generally view adaptability as more critical to the functioning of families than cohesion (Fisher & Sprenkle, 1978).

How can we arrive at a conception of normality that avoids the trap-pings of ideology and convention? It is probably too much to hope for or expect a conception of normality that would be culture-free and devoid of ideology. But after 30 years of investigating family process, we should be able to offer some propositions about normal family function-ing that resist the temptation to attribute all of the difficulties in family life to communication and too often result in such banal generalities as "communication must be clear, direct, and honest" or "each member of the family must be dealt with equitably." One of the main obstacles to reaching this goal is the term "normal." Unless we are to be satis-fied with a purely statistical concept of normality, the variety of families that fall under the heading "normal" simply is too large. We agree with Skynner's (1961) suggestion that "adequate families" should be clearly distinguished from "optimal families." Although the term "normal" family applies to both, we are interested principally in optimal family functioning.

The family life cycle. There is a vast literature on family development that describes how families evolve over time. Families progress through a sequence of predictable stages that define transitions in the course of the family's history (Hill, 1964). The pivotal concerns are usually the arrival or departure of family members (Wynne, 1984), such as birth of the first child or last adolescent leaving home. As many as 24 different stages have been identified (Rodgers, 1960). In terms of family functioning, the most important aspect of development is the fact that the stages in the family life cycle march inexorably forward regardless of whether the family members are psychologically or interpersonally prepared for them. The most difficult stages to accommodate are those that directly alter the family structure in unexpected ways, such as illness, separation or death.

Dialectical tensions. There are two oppositions that cut across the developmental stages of the family life cycle. The first is the tension between differentiation and integration, which was discussed earlier in terms of individuality and mutuality and is sometimes referred to as independence/dependence or identity/stability (Askham, 1976). All of the relationships in the family are subject to conflicts associated with these opposing forces. The well-functioning family somehow finds a way for its members to achieve satisfactory separateness without damaging the family's sense of wholeness. The second opposition involves the tension between change and stability. The family life cycle imposes changes on the family structure; in other words, the family cannot *not* change. Yet most families resist structural changes, as Haley (1963) implies by his first law of human relationships. Change is usually experienced as uncertainty. The healthy family copes with this stress by finding a way to hold onto its sense of security in the face of the threat posed by uncertainty.

Problem-solving skills. The evolutionary and dialectical qualities of family life make it obvious that all families experience stress. One of the main differences between healthy and unhealthy families is how they deal with stressful impasses. Riskin's (1976) intensive study of "nonlabeled families" suggests that healthy families are able to find solutions to their problems that do not escalate the severity of the problem; the solution does not become the problem (Riskin, 1976; Weakland, Fisch, Watzlawick, & Bodin, 1974). As Bodin (1981, p. 274) expresses it, "problems [may] persist but they do not paralyze." This nonescalating quality of optimal functioning has been emphasized by Gottman as a mark of healthy marital communication as well (Gottman, 1982). How do optimally functioning families manage to defuse these potentially explosive conflicts? The clinical reports we have examined identify the following features as characteristic of optimal functioning: (1) Members of optimally functioning families rarely take an oppositional attitude toward each other (Skynner, 1981); they are not looking to blame each other or to find a scapegoat for their problems. Unlike their more troubled counterparts, they are trusting rather than paranoid. Henry (1973) expresses their attitude brilliantly when he suggests that the "secret to sanity is to exaggerate the goodness of the world." (2) Optimally functioning families enjoy themselves. Their interaction has a spontaneous quality to it. They are humorous and witty (Skynner, 1981). (3) Optimally functioning families are not preoccupied with themselves. They do not overanalyze their problems looking for hidden motivations and unconscious intentions (Aponte & VanDeusen, 1981). They do not take family life too seriously. (4) Optimally functioning families usually maintain conventional boundaries. There is an unyielding parental coalition (Skynner, 1981) and little confusion in the family about what the hierarchy should be (Aponte & VanDeusen, 1981).

SUMMARY

This review has attempted to overcome the scattered and disconnected nature of family communication research by concentrating on a restricted but coherent body of theory and research on family interaction. Our focus has been the system perspectives on family process. These perspectives emphasize the functioning of the family as a whole unit governed by mechanisms of self-regulation that maintain its equilibrium. The homeostatic paradigm on which many system perspectives are based transformed the study of the family from an individualistic to a relational subject, giving priority to recursive descriptions over linear models. The homeostatic paradigm has proved limited in its scope; it cannot explain how families change. An evolutionary model that seems better suited to the epistemological commitments of cybernetics has recently been developed as a counterpoint to the homeostatic paradigm.

The system perspectives have been translated into several schools of thought that operationalize the premises of cybernetics. The interactional view focuses on the dimensions of messages and the self-perpetuating and repetitive sequences of interactional patterns in the family. The structural view emphasizes the organizational features of the family, particularly the ways in which boundaries and hierarchies constrain family experience. The constructivist view represents the epistemological commitments of these loosely applied cybernetic conceptions. Constructivists reject the representational theory of knowledge and stress instead the individual's participation in the construction of what is "real."

The research literature associated with family process has addressed the question of how family interaction is associated with psychopathology and/or social deviance. Five interactional patterns and/or dimensions of communication have been strongly associated with the presence of a family member diagnosed as schizophrenic: (1) double-bind sequences, (2) autodisconfirmation, (3) pseudomutuality, (4) communication deviance, and (5) failure in the capacity to share a common here-and-now. There is increasing evidence that parental communication deviance is not only associated with psychopathology of the family but may cause it. This evidence, however, is not yet conclusive. Future research utilizing longitudinal designs will undoubtedly help to clarify whether the association is causal.

Intensive case studies of family interaction have shown the importance of observing the commonplaces of daily interactions in the homes of families. The intensive studies are more thickly textured than the clinic and laboratory studies. They provide insights that are not nearly as intuitively obvious as quantitative studies tend to be. The way family members handle vulnerability seems to be a discriminating factor, showing up in both qualitative and quantitative studies. The judicious application of compassion may be the most important skill to master in the struggle to prevent or alleviate suffering in families (Henry, 1973).

The intensive and clinical studies of families suggest that the difference between "them" and "us" is not that great. There are signs of health in the sickest families and signs of sickness in healthy families. Definitions of what constitutes a normal family usually emphasize conventional values and fail to distinguish between adequate and optimal functioning. The stages of family development and the oppositional struggles pitting individuality against mutuality and change against stability virtually guarantee that no family will be completely free of stress. Optimally functioning families are capable of coping with the problems of family development without creating solutions that exacerbate their problems. They are more affiliative than oppositional; more lighthearted than serious; and more spontaneous than introspective. We do not yet know how to facilitate optimal functioning.

REFERENCES

Abeles, G. (1976). Researching the unresearchable: Experimentation on the double-bind. In C. Sluzki & D. Ransom (Eds.), *Double bind: The foundation of the communicational approach to the family* (pp. 113-149). New York: Grune & Stratton.

Aponte, H. (1976). Underorganization in the poor family. In P. Guerin (Ed.), *Family therapy: Theory and practice* (pp. 432-448). New York: Gardner.

Aponte, H., & VanDeusen, J. (1981). Structural family therapy. In A. Gurman & D. Kniskern (Eds.), *The handbook of family therapy* (pp. 310-360). New York: Brunner/Mazel.

Ariel, S., Carel, C., & Tyano, S. (1984). A formal explication of the concept of family homeostasis. *Journal of Marital and Family Therapy, 10,* 337-349.

Askham, J. (1976). Identity and stability within the marriage relationship. *Journal of Marriage and the Family, 38,* 535-547.

Bateson, G. (1966). Slippery theories. *International Journal of Psychiatry, 2,* 415-417.

Bateson, G. (1970). A systems approach. *International Journal of Psychiatry, 9,* 242-244.

Bateson, G. (1972). *Steps to an ecology of mind.* New York: Ballantine.

Bateson, G. (1978). The birth of a matrix or double bind and epistemology. In M. Berger (Ed.), *Beyond the double bind.* New York: Brunner/Mazel.

Bateson, G., Jackson, D., Haley, J., & Weakland, J. (1956). Toward a theory of schizophrenia. *Behavioral Science, 1,* 251-264.

Berger, P., & Kellner, H. (1964). Marriage and the construction of reality: An exercise in microsociology of knowledge. *Diogenes, 46,* 1-24.

Berger, P., & Luckmann, T. (1967). *The social construction of reality.* Garden City, NY: Anchor Books.

Blakar, R. (1973). An experimental method for inquiring into communication. *European Journal of Social Psychology, 3,* 415-425.

Blakar, R. (1980). Psychopathology and familial communication. In M. Brenner (Ed.), *The structure of action* (pp. 211-263). New York: St. Martins.

Bochner, A. (1976). Conceptual frontiers in the study of communication in families: An introduction to the literature. *Human Communication Research, 2,* 381-397.

Bochner, A. (1985). Perspectives on inquiry: Representation, conversation, and reflection. In M. Knapp & G. Miller (Eds.), *Handbook of interpersonal communication* (pp. 27-58). Newbury Park, CA: Sage.

Bodin, A. (1981). The interactional view: Family therapy approaches of the mental research institute. In A. Gurman & D. Kniskern (Eds.), *The handbook of family therapy* (pp. 267-309). New York: Brunner/Mazel.

Bott, E. (1971). *Family and social network: Roles, norms, and external relationships in ordinary urban families.* New York: Free Press.

Bowen, M. (1966). The use of family theory in clinical practice. *Comprehensive Psychiatry, 7,* 345-374.

Dell, P. (1982). Beyond homeostasis: Toward a concept of coherence. *Family Process, 21,* 21-41.

Doane, J. (1977). *Parental communication deviance as a predictor of child competence in families with a schizophrenic and nonschizophrenic parent.* Unpublished doctoral dissertation, University of Rochester.

Doane, J. (1978). Family interaction and communication deviance in disturbed and normal families: A review of research. *Family Process, 17,* 357-376.

Doane, J., Jones, J., Fisher, L., Ritzler, B., Singer, M., & Wynne, L. (1982). Parental communication deviance as a predictor of competence in children at risk for adult psychiatric disorder. *Family Process, 21,* 211-223.

Doane, J., West, K., Goldstein, M., Rodnick, E., & Jones, J. (1981). Parental communication deviance and affective style: Predictors of subsequent schizophrenia spectrum disorders in vulnerable adolescents. *Archives of General Psychiatry, 38,* 679-685.

Fisher, B., Giblin, P., & Hoopes, M. (1982). Healthy family functioning: What therapists say and what families want. *Journal of Marital and Family Therapy, 8,* 273-284.

Fisher, B., & Sprenkle, D. (1978). Therapist's perceptions of healthy family functioning. *International Journal of Family Counseling, 6,* 1-10.

Fitzpatrick, M., & Badzinski, D. (1985). All in the family: Interpersonal communication in kin relationships. In M. Knapp & G. Miller (Eds.), *Handbook of interpersonal communication* (pp. 687-736). Newbury Park, CA: Sage.

Ford, F. (1983). Rules: The invisible family. *Family Process, 22,* 135-145.

Goldstein, M., & Rodnick, E. (1975). The family's contribution to the etiology of schizophrenia: Current status. *Schizophrenia Bulletin, 14.*

Gottman, J. (1982). Emotional responsiveness in marital conversations. *Journal of Communication, 32,* 108-120.

Guerin, P. (1976). Family therapy: The first twenty-five years. In P. Guerin (Ed.), *Family therapy: Theory and practice* (pp. 2-22). New York: Gardner.

Haley, J. (1963). *Strategies of psychotherapy.* New York: Grune & Stratton.

Haley, J. (1972). Critical overview of present status of family interaction research. In J. Framo (Ed.), *Family Interaction: A dialogue between family researchers and family therapists* (pp. 13-40). New York: Springer.

Haley, J. (1976a). Development of a theory: A history of a research project. In C. Sluzki & D. Ransom (Eds.), *Double bind: The foundation of the communicational approach to the family* (pp. 59-104). New York: Grune & Stratton.

Haley, J. (1976b). *Problem-solving psychotherapy.* San Francisco: Jossey-Bass.

Handel, G. (1967). *The psychological interior of the family.* Chicago: Aldine.

Helmerson, P. (1983). Family interaction and communication in psychopathology. *European Monographs in Social Psychology, 34,* 1-142.

Henry, J. (1973). *Pathways to Madness.* New York: Vintage.

Hess, R., & Handel, G. (1959). *Family worlds: A psychological approach to family life.* Chicago: University of Chicago Press.

Hill, R. (1964). Methodological issues in family development research. *Family Process, 3,* 186-206.

Hoffman, L. (1971). Deviation amplifying processes in natural groups. In J. Haley (Ed.), *Changing families: A family therapy reader* (pp. 285-311). New York: Grune & Stratton.

Hoffman, L. (1975). "Enmeshment" and the too richly cross-joined family. *Family Process, 14,* 457-468.

Hoffman, L. (1977). Breaking the homeostatic cycle. In P. Guerin (Ed.), *Family therapy: Theory and practice* (pp. 501-519). New York: Gardner.

Hoffman, L. (1981). *Foundations of family therapy.* New York: Basic Books.

Jackson, D. (1957). The question of family homeostasis. *Psychiatric Quarterly Supplement, 31,* 79-90.

Jackson, D. (1965). The study of the family. *Family Process, 4,* 1-20.

Jackson, D. (1967). Differences between normal and abnormal families—communication within the family: A panel discussion. In N. Ackerman, F. Beatman, & S. Sherman (Eds.), *Expanding theory and practice in family.* New York: Family Service Association of America.

Jacob, T. (1975). Family interaction in disturbed and normal families: A methodological and substantive review. *Psychological Bulletin, 82,* 33-65.

Kantor, D., & Lehr, W. (1975). *Inside the family.* San Francisco: Jossey-Bass.

Laing, R. (1969). *The politics of the family and other essays.* New York: Random House.

Lewis, J., Beavers, W., Gossett, J., & Phillips, V. (1976). *No single thread: Psychological health in family systems.* New York: Brunner/Mazel.

Liebman, R., Minuchin, S., Baker, L., & Rosman, B. (1976). The role of the family in the treatment of chronic asthma. In P. Guerin (Ed.), *Family therapy: Theory and practice* (pp. 309-324). New York: Gardner.

Liem, J. (1974). Effects of verbal communications of parents and children: A comparison of normal and schizophrenic families. *Journal of Consulting and Clinical Psychology, 42,* 438-450.

Liem, J. (1976). Intrafamily communication and schizophrenic thought disorder: An etiologic or responsive relationship? *Clinical Psychologist, 29,* 28-30.

Liem, J. (1980). Family studies of schizophrenia: An update commentary. *Schizophrenia Bulletin, 6,* 429-455.

McCubbin, H., Cauble, A., & Patterson, J. (1982). *Family stress, coping, and social support.* Springfield, IL: Charles C Thomas.

Minuchin, S. (1974). *Families and Family Therapy.* Cambridge, MA: Harvard University Press.

Minuchin, S., Baker, L., Rosman, B., Liebman, R., Hilman, L., & Todd, T. (1975). A conceptual model of psychosomatic illness in children. *Archives of General Psychiatry, 32,* 1031-1038.

Minuchin, S., Rosman, B., & Baker, L. (1978). *Psychosomatic families: Anorexia nervosa in context.* Cambridge, MA: Harvard University Press.

Mishler, E., & Waxler, N. (1965). Family interaction processes and schizophrenia: A review of current theories. *Merrill-Palmer Quarterly of Behavior and Development, 11,* 269-315.

Mishler, E., & Waxler, N. (1968). *Interaction in families: Experimental study of family process and schizophrenia.* New York: John Wiley.

Redl, F., & Wineman, D. (1965). *Controls from within: Techniques for the treatment of the aggressive child.* New York: Macmillan.

Reiss, D. (1976). The family and schizophrenia. *American Journal of Psychiatry, 133,* 181-1985.

Ricci, C., & Selvini-Palazzoli, M. (1984). Interactional complexity and communication. *Family Process, 23,* 169-176.

Riskin, J. (1976). Non-labelled family interaction: Preliminary report on a prospective study. *Family Process, 15,* 433-439.

Riskin, J., & Faunce, E. (1972). An evaluative review of family interaction research. *Family Process, 11,* 365-455.

Ritzler, B., Singer, M., Cole, R., & Fisher, L. (1977, April). *Parental communication deviance and competence of children at risk for schizophrenia.* Paper presented at Eastern Psychological Association Convention.

Rodgers, R. (1960). *Proposed modifications of Duvall's family life cycle stages.* Paper presented at the American Sociological Association Meeting, New York.

Ruesch, J. and Bateson, G. (1951). *Communication: The social matrix of psychiatry.* New York: Norton.

Selvini-Palazzoli, M., Boscolo, L., Cecchin, G., & Prata, G. (1978). *Paradox and counterparadox: A new model in the therapy of the family in schizophrenic transaction.* New York: Jason Aronson.

Singer, M., & Wynne, L. (1965). Thought disorder and family relations of schizophrenics: IV. Results and implications. *Archives of General Psychiatry, 12,* 201-212.

Singer, M., Wynne, L., & Toohey, M. (1978). Communication disorders and the families of schizophrenics. In L. Wynne, R. Cromwell, & S. Matthysse (Eds.), *The nature of schizophrenia: New approaches in research and treatment* (pp. 499-511). New York: John Wiley.

Skynner, A. (1981). An open systems, group-analytic approach to family therapy. In A. Gurman & D. Kniskern (Eds.), *The handbook of family therapy* (pp. 39-84). New York: Brunner/Mazel.

Sluzki, C. (1983). Process, structure and world views: Toward an integrated view of systemic models in family therapy. *Family Process, 22,* 469-476.

Sluzki, C., & Ransom, D. (1976). *Double bind: The foundation of the communicational approach to the family.* New York: Grune & Stratton.

Sorrells, J. & Ford, J. (1969). Toward an integrated theory of families and family therapy. *Psychotherapy: Theory, Research, Practice, 6,* 150-160.

Speer, D. (1970). Family stress: Morphostasis and morphogenesis, or is homeostasis enough? *Family Process, 9,* 259-278.

Stabenau, J., Tupin, J., Werner, M., & Pollin, W. (1965). A comparative study of families of schizophrenics, delinquents, and normals. *Psychiatry, 28,* 45-59.

Stanton, M. (1978). Family treatment of drug problems: A review. In R. Dupont, A. Goldstein, & J. O'Donnell (Eds.), *National Institute of Drug Abuse Publication* (pp. 133-150).

Stanton, M. (1979). Drugs and the family. *Marriage and Family Review, 2,* 1-10.

Stanton, M. (1981). Strategic approaches to family therapy. In A. Gurman & D. Kniskern (Eds.), *Handbook of family therapy* (pp. 361-402). New York: Brunner/Mazel.

Von Foerster, H. (1984). On constructing a reality. In P. Watzlawick (Ed.), *The Invented Reality* (pp. 41-61). New York: Norton.

von Glasersfeld, E. (1984). An Introduction to radical constructivism. In P. Watzlawick (Ed.), *The invented reality* (pp. 17-40). New York: Norton.

Watzlawick, P. (1984). Components of ideological "realities." In P. Watzlawick (Ed.), *The invented reality* (pp. 206-247). New York: Norton.

Watzlawick, P., Beavin, J. & Jackson, D. (1967). *Pragmatics of human communication.* New York: Norton.

Watzlawick, P., Weakland, J., & Fisch, R. (1974). *Change: Principles of problem formation and problem resolution.* New York: Norton.

Weakland, J. (1976). Communication theory and clinical change. In P. Guerin (Ed.), *Family therapy: Theory and practice* (pp. 111-128). New York: Gardner.

Weakland, J. (1981). One thing leads to another. In C. Wilder-Mott & J. Weakland (Eds.), *Rigor and imagination: Essays from the legacy of Gregory Bateson.* New York: Praeger.

Weakland, J., Fisch, R., Watzlawick, P., & Bodin, A. (1974). Brief therapy: Focused problem resolution. *Family Process, 13,* 141-168.

Westley, W., & Epstein, N. (1976). *The silent majority.* San Francisco: Jossey-Bass.

Whitaker, C. (Ed.). (1958). *Psychotherapy of chronic schizophrenic patients.* Boston: Little, Brown.

Whitaker, C., & Keith, D. (1981). Symbolic-experiential family therapy. In A. Gurman & D. Kniskern (Eds.), *The handbook of family therapy* (pp. 187-225). New York: Brunner/Mazel.

Whitehead, A., & Russell, B. (1910). *Principia mathematica.* Cambridge: Cambridge University Press.

Wilder,-Mott, C. (1981). Rigor and imagination. In C. Wilder-Mott & J. Weakland (Eds.), *Rigor and imagination: Essays from the legacy of Gregory Bateson* (pp. 5-42). New York: Praeger.

Wilder-Mott, C., & Weakland, J. (1981). *Rigor and imagination: Essays from the legacy of Gregory Bateson.* New York: Praeger.

Winch, R. (1977). *Familial organization.* New York: Free Press.

Wynne, L. (1980, March 11-13). *University of Rochester child and family study: Summary progress report.* Paper presented at High Risk Plenary Conference, San Juan, Puerto Rico.

Wynne, L. (1983). Family research and family therapy: A reunion. *Journal of Marital and Family Therapy, 9,* 113-117.

Wynne, L. (1984). The epigenesis of relational systems: A model for understanding family development. *Family Process, 23,* 297-318.

Wynne, L., Ryckoff, I., Day, J., & Hirsch, S. (1958). Pseudo-mutuality in the family relations of schizophrenics. *Psychiatry, 21,* 205-220.

Wynne, L., & Singer, M. (1963). Thought disorder and family relations of schizophrenics: I. A research strategy. *Archives of General Psychiatry, 9,* 191-198.

Wynne, L., Singer, M., Bartko, J., & Toohey, M. (1977). Schizophrenics and their families: Recent research on parental communication. In J. Tanner (Ed.), *Developments in psychiatric research.* London: Hodder & Stoughton.

19 Marital Interaction

MARY ANNE FITZPATRICK
University of Wisconsin—Madison

T HE majority of adults in contemporary western society marry. Between 90 and 95% of all Americans marry at least once and most divorced persons remarry within five years (Bane, 1976). The high divorce rate does not suggest wide dissatisfaction with the institution of marriage per se but rather with a particular spouse. In addition to the prevalence of marriage as a relational form, analyzing the communication that occurs between spouses illuminates important dynamics of marriage and, at the same time, reveals vital principles of interpersonal communication. No attempt to understand human behavior can be wholly successful without an understanding of the close relationships that form the theme and foundation of the human condition (Kelley et al., 1983). And, communication plays an integral part in the stability, maintenance, and change that occurs in close relationships.

Some argue that specific theoretical work on marriage or other forms of close relationships is unnecessary (Berkowitz, 1985). These scholars assert that in order to understand relational processes, the analyst needs only to calibrate the scope conditions of current theories of basic social and psychological processes. This argument overlooks two salient aspects of marital processes. First, marital interaction processes often operate at the extreme levels of variables. Second, there are a number of unique properties of close relationships such as marriage that do not exist in other social entities (Weick, 1978).

A theorist may consider male-female relations, for example, as an instance of intergroup relations and analyze male-female relations in much the same way as cross-race, -class, or -ethnic group relations (Tajfel, 1981). The analogy drawn between race, class, ethnicity, and sex breaks down, however, in two fundamental ways. First, genetic assimi-

AUTHOR'S NOTE: Preparation of this chapter was supported in part by Grant No. MH 40813-01 from the National Institute of Mental Health and Grant No. UW 871251 from the Wisconsin Alumni Research Foundation to the author. I would like to thank Charles R. Berger, Northwestern University, Patricia Noller, University of Queensland, Diane Badzinski and Isabelle Bauman, University of Wisconsin, for their insightful comments on earlier versions of this manuscript. For their conscientious work compiling the bibliography, special praise should be given to Ann Sapa, Yolanda Hicks, and Vicki Tolbert.

lation through intergroup mating between races, ethnic groups, and social classes is possible: We can envision a society blind to these distinctions. Genetic assimilation of male and female is impossible, however, because both sexes are needed for reproduction. No society will ever be "sex blind" (Rossi, 1985). Second, unlike members of other ingroup-outgroup categories, individual males and females are drawn to one another and form relationships that most societies legitimate through informal norms and formal laws.

Unlike most reviews of marital communication, this chapter considers marital interaction at various levels of analysis. An examination of basic knowledge across the levels of analysis most often represented in the disciplines of social science is essential in explaining all forms of human relationships, with marriage being no exception. Research reviews discussing advances in the area may decrease the numerous prejudices that exist against the scientific study of relationships (Hinde, 1979). In the area of personal relationships, there is a great struggle between what is known and what is believed. Many writers rush to explain "facts" before they are clearly shown to exist. More than any other phenomenon in current society, there is a mutual interpretative interplay between the scientific study of relationships and those whose activities constitute its subject matter. This double hermeneutic influences the study of marriage, as well as the marriages ongoing in society at a given time (Giddens, 1984).

Marriage is a relationship in which males and females are exposed to strong influences of diverse types over extended periods of time. These influences can be categorized as individual biological and psychological processes, marital interaction, social networks, and social contexts. The "levels of analysis" framework implied in these sets of influences on marriage is a necessary analytic device that, nevertheless, needs to be read with caution. Marriage can be affected by a large number of causal conditions, emerging from inside and outside the marriage. Since causation can occur on various levels simultaneously, difficulty obtains in assessing relative contributions of any given effect (Kelley, 1979). This framework also suggests that the review be limited to marital relationships between males and females; although, some investigators have noted the similarities between intimate relationships among heterosexuals and homosexuals (Peplau, Cochran, Rook, & Padesky, 1978; Peplau & Gordon, 1983).

This chapter reflects the state of the field, with particular emphasis on work completed in the last decade, and is limited to theories and research concerned with marriage. Work on relationships in general is omitted. This chapter has four parts. First, we begin with an overview of the major dependent variable in the study of marriage: marital success.

This section discusses the major ways that marital success has been defined and examined and makes suggestions for improving the measurement process. The second section of the chapter surveys the major meta-theoretical models used to study marital processes. The influence of each of these models can be clearly traced throughout the literature on marriage. The underlying assumptions of the social exchange perspective, for example, have dominated both microsocietal and macrosocietal explanations of marital processes. The third and fourth sections cover microsocietal and macrosocietal perspectives on marriage, respectively.

MARITAL SUCCESS

For the chatelains and knights in medieval France, the success of a marriage was judged by the degree to which the joining of a given male and female strengthened family position and reinforced local class lines (Duby, 1983). In the latter part of the twentieth century, marital success is evaluated along different lines. Generally, marital success is measured with one of three major dependent variables: marital stability, adequacy of function, and marital quality.

Research in the decades of the 1940s, 1950s and 1960s focused on marital quality or satisfaction rather than marital stability or dissolution. Underlying this choice of research focus were values supporting the concept that stable but alienated marriages were of limited theoretical or pragmatic interest: Marital stability was uninteresting if the marriage was not a happy one. The additional unstated assumption, still widely held in the literature, is that highly satisfactory marriages are ipso facto permanent marriages (Nye, 1979). The increasing emphasis on the study of divorce, desertion, and remarriage, largely as a response to pragmatic social concerns, still ignores the stable but unhappy marriage.

Marital Stability

Marital stability is defined as whether or not a given marriage is intact. A stable marriage is one that is terminated only by the natural death of one spouse. The measurement is straightforward, requiring categorization as married, divorced, or separated (see, however, Bohannon, 1970, for his discussion of the six stations of divorce). But there are no standardized measures that tap steps or stages in the process of dissolution, although moves in this direction are being made (Booth, Johnson, & Edwards, 1983; Weiss & Cerreto, 1980). Early theoretical work located three major determinants of marital stability: positive affect toward the spouse, constraints against dissolution, and unattractive alternatives to marriage (Levinger, 1974; Nye, White, & Frideres, 1973). Of these three variables, positive affect has been given the most attention more recently. Currently, marital stability appears to be primarily related to the degree of happiness or contentment experienced by couples, both with particular aspects of the relationship and with the overall quality of the relationship (Lewis & Spanier, 1979; Spanier & Lewis, 1980). Effort has turned to explicating the causes of marital happiness in the hopes of better predicting the ultimate exogenous variable of longevity; however, a major social institution such as marriage hinges on the relatively unstable foundation of the satisfaction experienced by its members. Many cultural critics identify the centrality of affect in modern marriages as *the problem* with current American society (Shorter, 1975). Institutions that rise and fall on the emotions of participants are inherently unstable.

If marriage is a "nomos-building" institution, divorce may be taken as a sign of social anomie or disintegration. Stack (1980) found that a 1% increase in divorce is related to a .54% increase in suicide. Causally linking these two variables is called into question, however, by the work of Ryan (1981), who found no relationship between either marital status or marital happiness and feelings of alienation and isolation. Marital instability research has been criticized because it is atheoretical and most samples are not representative (Levinger & Moles, 1976). Furthermore, few longitudinal studies have been reported.

Marital Functioning

Marital functioning is the accomplishment of major marital or family goals. These goals may include the appropriate or nonpathogenic socialization of children (Waxler & Mischler, 1970) or the stabilization of the adult personality (Parsons & Bales, 1955). Successful marital functioning may involve the development of interaction competencies (Farber, 1964). Embedded in the concept of functioning is a consideration of the "normalcy" of a marriage. There are at least three discriminable uses of the term normal in this area (see Bochner & Eisenberg, Chapter 18 in this volume). The first is the *clinically ideal,* including what the theorist considers reasonable standards of mental and physical health. Within this view, the psychological problems of a child are taken as prima facie evidence of marital dysfunction (Haley, 1962). The second is the *generalized model of conduct* often indicated by statistical averages. With the 700% increase in the divorce rate in America in this century, divorce and remarriage are developing statistically identifiable patterns of regularity and becoming "institutionalized" (Price-Bonham & Balswick, 1980). In the clinical and research literature, there are references to the "healthy" divorce (Goldsmith, 1982) as well as the development of scales of divorce adjustment. The third sense of normal is what is perceived as *morally right* by members of the family. The male, middle-class, white bias in the research demands a consideration of family processes from the point of view of various ethnic and racial groups (Staples & Mirande, 1980).

Marital Quality

In the last half of the twentieth century, the quality of life for many Americans is more likely to be determined by the quality of the marital relationship than by the traditional measures of income and so forth (Campbell, 1981). Consequently, *marital quality* is the most frequently studied dependent variable in the literature. Serious debate surrounds the use of the various concepts in this area (Burr, 1973; Hicks & Platt, 1970). Some theorists focus only on marital satisfaction (e.g., Burr, 1973) yet others maintain that a marriage is much more than subjective feelings about the relationship (e.g., Spanier, 1976). Marital quality and such related concepts as satisfaction, happiness, adjustment, lack of distress, or integration refer to a number of subjectively experienced dimensions and evaluations of the marital relationship. Marital quality questionnaires include scales measuring amount of conflict, degree of agreement, shared activities, self-ratings of happiness, perceived permanence of the marriage, and so forth. Although debate continues about the definition of this construct, the intercorrelations among the instruments used to measure these various concepts are very high.

Not only have questionnaires been completed by individual husbands and wives, but also ratings of a couple's happiness have been made by other family members (Kolb & Strauss, 1974); by interviewers (Birchler, Weiss, & Vincent, 1975; Haynes, Chavez, & Samuel, 1984); and by the fact that a couple has applied for marital therapy. Margolin (1978) examined the intercorrelations of two self-report measures of marital satisfaction, two observer-rated measures, and two measures requiring spouses to monitor each others behavior. Only three significant correlations obtained among the possible 15 and these were between the two self-report measures; the two observational measures; and one self-report and one spouse-monitoring measure, which were both from the same person. Multitrait, multimethod studies (Campbell & Fiske, 1959) will help to untangle these confusing skeins of evidence. The appearance of these studies in the literature is encouraging (e.g., Boals, Peterson, Farmer, Mann, & Robinson, 1982). Conceptual work is also needed, however, to explain why divergence and convergence in ratings of marital satisfaction occur not only between husbands and wives but between insiders' and outsiders' perspectives. Despite the advances in measurement technology (Filsinger, 1983), the major marital quality measures are self-report questionnaires.

Most questionnaires contain many subscales relating to various dimensions of marital quality as well as overall, summary statements of the individual's evaluation of the marriage. The two most frequently used instruments are the Locke-Wallace (1959) and the Spanier (Spanier & Felsinger, 1983) scales. The latter is a revised version of the former. Aside from the general problems with self-report measures, problems peculiar to the marital area arise. One is the negative skewness of distributions of overall evaluations of marriages. About 95% of the respondents in Terman's (1938) study reported their marriages as significantly happier than average and very few people in national surveys report themselves or their marriages as unhappy overall. This skewness may attenuate correlations, although skewness actually makes correlations unstable.

A second set of problems has been explicated by Norton (1983) as a justification for his marital quality measure. Previous investigators have summed across evaluations of a marriage in different domains (e.g., attitudinal agreement, sexual expression); thus the measures obscure what they should clarify. Spanier and Thompson (1982) present convincing evidence that the dyadic adjustment scale (DAS) is a valid and reliable multidimensional marital assessment scale. Considering each of the four components of the dyadic adjustment construct (i.e., cohesion, satisfaction, consensus, and affectional expression) separately allows the analyst to examine how the variables individually and in combination relate to evaluations of marital quality. In one investigation, Pittman, Price-Bonham, and McKenry (1983) developed a causal model of the DAS factor of cohesion.

A third set of problems concerns appropriate units of analysis. To make the leap from the individual level to the interpersonal level requires either linking observational data or a procedure for combining individual data into dyadic (structural) measures. Although devising structural measures is a problem in many areas of marriage and family study, the problem is particularly acute in the study of marital quality. A lack of consensus on marital quality between husbands and wives can represent inaccuracy of perception, different criteria for evaluating the quality of the marriage, differential sensitivity to response sets, and so forth. Although it is possible that disagreement stems from the difference between one valid and one invalid report, it is more likely that both reports represent important statements about the quality of the marriage (White & Brinkerhoff, 1978).

The typical way *individual* assessments of a marriage are aggregated to assign *couples* to a happy or unhappy category unnecessarily loses a good deal of information. Paradigmatic research in this area proceeds by having each husband and wife independently complete scales of some aspect of marital quality. The husbands and wives who score above a certain average are assigned to the happily married group while those husbands and wives who score below a certain score are assigned to the unhappily married group. At times, couple scores are added and divided by 2, a procedure that has little to recommend it other than simplicity. These methods may confound *agreement* between a husband and wife on their level of marital quality with the actual level of marital quality. Couples in the happily married group are those who evaluate their marriage as qualitatively high on the dimensions of interest and who may agree on those evaluations. Equivalent total scores on a marital quality index may emerge from each partner seeing different aspects of the marriage as positive. These couples are contrasted with those who score lower and who may either agree or disagree with the spouse on these dimensions. Rather than obscuring agreement and marital quality, agreement on the level of marital quality may be the important variable to study. Generally, agreement between husbands and wives on marital quality is rarely high. Locke (1951) found a husband-wife marital happiness correlation of .36 and the correlation on the Snyder Marital Satisfaction Inventory for husbands and wives is .37 (Snyder, Wills, & Kesler, 1981). Significantly higher correlations may suggest spousal collusion. Procedurally and ethically, spouses should not be left alone without a researcher present to complete questionnaires about their marriage (Locke, 1951). In general, these findings are so robust that there are two marriages in any given relationship: his marriage and her marriage (Bernard, 1972).

Some resolve the problem of two marriages by sampling both members of the dyad and then reporting the scores for husbands and wives separately. Although this procedure puts an end to "wives family sociology" (Safilios-Rothschild, 1969), it does not answer the question of estimating the dyadic level of analysis. Others resolve the problem by suggesting various weighting and averaging schemes for husband and wife data (White & Brinkerhoff, 1978) or use the husband data to respecify models of the wife's behavior as a function of both partners subjective outcomes (Fried & Udry, 1980). An interesting methodological suggestion is that of Thompson and Williams (1982), who argue that Lisrel measurement models (Jöreskog & Sörbom, 1978) can be used to estimate the measurement error and variable structure underlying husband and wife data in order to compare couple models to individual husband and wife models.

Despite these proposed methodological solutions, many argue that the only approach to resolving this problem is a theoretical one. The measurement of structure requires explicit specification of the rules that link individuals to dyads: aggregation rules. Methodological techniques may provide vacuous "solutions" to theoretical problems.

Summary and recommendations. First, in the area of marital success as well as with other outcomes of marriage, theorists need to consider whether they are concerned with dyadic or individual-level properties.

Bernard (1972) maintains that there are no truly shared experiences in marriage. This view contrasts with Berger and Kellner's (1975) that marriage involves the development of a shared definition of reality ("his," "hers," and "theirs"). Measurement models can be developed to test the individual versus shared nature of the marital experience. Second, the use of dependent variables that are both methodologically and conceptually related to one another cries out for a meta-analysis. It would be helpful, for example, to take the information presented in one of the classic reviews of marital quality and assess the degree to which a meta-analysis of the same literature would yield the same substantive conclusions. Third, divorce should not be the primary focus of attention. Attempts should be made to study stable relationships, regardless of their quality (Bell, Daly, & Gonzalez, 1986; Dindia & Baxter, 1986). Fourth, the procedures for questionnaire administration and development need to be standardized. Questionnaires must be filled out privately and placed in sealed envelopes (Bradburn & Sudman, 1979). When working with diverse populations, the reading difficulty of these questionnaires needs to be examined. For example, the Relational Dimensions Instrument (Fitzpatrick & Best, 1979) frequently used to categorize nonuniversity samples of married couples, has a seventh-grade reading difficulty level. One study (Dentch, O'Farrell, & Cutter, 1980) found that of the nine self-report marital assessment measures, all had reading difficulties substantially higher than the seventh-grade level. Since daily newspapers are written on the sixth-grade level, marital quality instruments should probably not exceed this level.

Finally, marital quality is part of an intricate causal chain and increasing attention needs to be paid to its status as an independent variable, capable of predicting a number of other concepts. Not only *being married* but the quality of that marriage needs to be considered in studies that relate marriage to health, economic, structural factors, and so forth. In the wake of the feminist movement, it is easy for the scholarly community to criticize earlier definitions of marital success that specified the successful marriage as one in which the wife was subordinate to the husband (Hicks & Platt, 1970). While it is always easier to see the ideological blind spots of previous generations, it is much more difficult to detect current biases.

THEORETICAL PERSPECTIVES ON MARRIAGE

Six major meta-theoretical perspectives have dominated the study of marriage during the past 25 years. These perspectives differ from one another in that each has different philosophical and historical beginnings as well as different assumptions about the nature of humankind and society. Analyzing marriage from each one of these perspectives provides a number of unique insights (Hage, 1972).

(1) The *structural-functional* position identifies the structural elements or subsystems of a given social system and specifies their functional significance in the maintenance of the system. The very nature of group interaction creates a need for role specialization. Instrumental and expressive activities are viewed as the specialized responsibilities of males and females, respectively. This allocation arises out of the biological acts of childbearing and nursing (Parsons & Bales, 1955). This approach has been applied to the family (Bell & Vogel, 1960) and in the clinical literature on marital processes (Minuchin, 1974). Since males and females do not demonstrate a strict instrumental/expressive task dichotomy (Crano & Aronoff, 1978) this position no longer adds much to our understanding of marriage.

(2) The *interactionist* position assumes that people respond to their environment in terms of the meaning that the environment has for them rather than its physical properties. People create and negotiate roles in the course of their social interaction rather than merely play out culturally determined scripts (Burr, Leigh, Day, & Constantine, 1979). According to this perspective, husbands and wives make their own roles in marriage within some very loosely determined guidelines (Peplau, 1983; Udry, 1974). Although their theoretical statements were not well formulated, Waller (1938) and Bolton (1961) are early interactionists because of their concern for process and the stages of redefinition of the situation. An interactionist theory of the middle range is Burr's theory of marital satisfaction (Burr et al., 1979). This theory has four central propositions. First, perceived quality of the role enactment in a relationship and satisfaction experienced in the relationship are positively related. Second, the more important a role expectation is to a person, the greater the effect that the quality of role enactment has on that person. Third, the greater the relative deprivation of one's situation as a whole, the less one's satisfaction with the situation. Fourth, the amount of consensus on relevant role expectations in a relationship and satisfaction are positively related.

(3) The *conflict* position maintains that marriage is a social process in which members must face the perpetual problem of coming to terms with each other's conflicting, though not necessarily opposing, interests (Sprey, 1979). Within this perspective, marital harmony is seen as an abnormal state of affairs. Sprey (1985) argues that the figures on family violence are astounding: In more than 90% of American families, spouses do not physically attack one another! Scanzoni and Fox's model (1980) is another conflict interpretation of marriage, focused specifically on the conflict latent in the gender differences (see Roloff, Chapter 16). A variant of the conflict perspective is intergroup relations (Tajfel, 1981). This theory postulates both an external (societal-level) and an

internal (psychological) representation of reality. The social world is partitioned into groups. Individuals internally represent relevant social categories and these representations come to shape beliefs about and evaluations of social categories. Giles and his associates (Giles, Robinson, & Smith, 1980; Ryan & Giles, 1982; Scherer & Giles, 1979) have shown how an intergroup relations perspective informs the study of language variations and evaluations of outgroup members (see Giles & Wiemann, Chapter 12). Giles and Fitzpatrick (1985) showed that marital relationships can be viewed within this perspective.

(4) The *exchange* perspective maintains that humans avoid costly behavior and seek rewarding statuses, relationships, interactions, and feeling states in order to maximize their outcomes. The exchange theory of marital satisfaction contains three third-order propositions. First, the greater the social and personal resources available for marital role functioning, the higher the marital quality. Second, the greater the spouses' satisfaction with their life style, the greater the marital quality. Third, the greater the rewards from spousal interaction, the greater the marital quality (Lewis & Spanier, 1979). Objections to exchange views of marital quality have been elaborated by Bochner (1983).

(5) *Systems theories* posit that a marriage is a system that operates through transactional patterns. Repeated transactions establish patterns of how, when, and to whom to relate. Raush, Barry, Hertel, and Swain (1974) have applied information theory measures—a subtype of system theory—to study change and constancy in newlywed dyads through the birth of the first child. Boss (1977, 1980) has studied the process of boundary maintenance in families with a father missing in action. Overall, however, very little research has been done on the marital system per se. Systems theory concepts are often used to compare the interaction patterns of normal versus troubled families. Raush, Grief, and Nugent (1979) concluded that despite the appeal of the systems theories and the related interactional viewpoint (Watzlawick, Weakland, & Fisch, 1974), the differences that emerge in the most careful studies seem trivial in contrast to the dramatic pathology afflicting some of the families (see Bochner, 1985; Bochner & Eisenberg, Chapter 18).

(6) *Developmental perspectives* focus on the repeated pattern of organization, disorganization, and change that families follow. Such positions try to account for the continuities and discontinuities in family life. There have been attempts to incorporate family developmental theories into individual developmental models (Hill & Mattessich, 1977; Hooper & Hooper, 1979). Within current family development work, there are two major schools of thought: the *life-course* perspective and the *life-cycle* perspective.

(a) A *life-course perspective* (Elder, 1979) probes the impact of historical events on human behavior, especially as applied to family living, by examining an individual's age-structured pathways across settings from birth to death. The chronological age of an individual, cohort member-ship, and the duration of stay in various stages are the major variables examined. In this perspective, marriage is viewed as the joining of two life histories (Liker & Elder, 1983). Elder and Rockwell (1976) exam-ined the temporal variations and outcomes of marriage patterns for women of a certain cohort. In a study of the Great Depression cohort, Liker and Elder (1983) found that under economic pressure, men who had been irritable and moody types before being faced with hard times became increasingly unstable and maritally distressed.

(b) A *life-cycle perspective* assumes that important transitions bring about changes in the internal dynamics of a family (Duvall, 1977; Rodgers, 1973). Duvall's (1977) classic work marks stages according to the pres-ence of children, their ages, parents' participation in the work force, and death. One theory representative of this line of thought deals with mari-tal satisfaction of parents (Rollins & Galligan, 1978). Marital satisfac-tion is best represented by a U-shaped curve with the dip in satisfaction occurring soon after the birth of the first child; the curve only begins to climb when the last child leaves home, although satisfaction never reaches its early marriage high (Rollins & Cannon, 1974; Rollins & Feldman, 1970; Spanier, Lewis, & Cole, 1975). The U-shaped curve may represent only positive interaction; a linear decline occurs across age for negative sentiments toward the spouse (Gilford & Bengtson, 1979).

These cross-sectional designs confound cohort differences with selec-tive survival rates and contain other methodological difficulties (Klein, Jorgensen, & Miller, 1978). Cohort effects are particularly problematic because, with few exceptions, most families and family members expe-rience transitions at about the same ages (Norton, 1980). Spanier, Sauer, and Larzelere (1979) compared three possible stratification schemes for studying family development: stage of the family life cycle, marriage cohort, and birth cohort. These researchers, using a variety of statistical techniques and a large random sample, found no method to be superior for either analytic use or predictive capability (see also Nock, 1979).

Both Nock (1981) and Menaghan (1983) found that family transitions produced few negative effects on life and relational satisfactions. Nev-ertheless, since there are no clear differences in the role demands for family members at different stages of family life cycles, theoreticians are loath to disregard life-cycle concepts. Some theoreticians clearly demand a focus on stages (e.g., Aldous, 1978) when a couple or family have established a new stability. Regrettably, many theoretical approaches to the life cycle ignore the gender of the individual (Rossi, 1985). Others are expressly interested in studying the transition period.

The transition out of marriage through the natural death of one spouse has been studied primarily from an epidemiological framework. Of particular interest has been the question, Is the life expectancy of one spouse affected by the death of the other? Conjugal bereavement ranks high on most stress indices. In a review of the previous 17 years of research, Jacobs and Ostfeld (1977) concluded that there is a pattern of excess mortality in the bereaved, especially males. The duration of risk appears to vary by age (the younger being at greater risk) and is no more than two years. These authors argue that the mortality of bereavement results from an organismic response to loss; however, alternative explanations for these data abound. The "loss effect," as it is termed, received strong support in a number of reviews of the literature (e.g., Kastenbaum & Costa, 1977; Rowland, 1977). In a systematic review of the evidence for this effect, however, Stroebe and his colleagues (Stroebe, Stroebe, Gergen, & Gergen, 1981) argue persuasively that the evidence is weaker than usually suggested. Their analysis revealed shortcomings in nearly every study.

Summary and recommendations. A meta-theoretical perspective likely to gain ascendancy is that of structuration theory (Giddens, 1976, 1984). This approach attempts to place equal emphasis on both structure and process and sees each in a dialectical relationship with the other. This perspective is particularly appropriate to an examination of personal relationships and marriage because of its concern for understanding the historical forces at work on the phenomena of interest. The intergroup relations approach extended to marriage also holds promise.

MICROSOCIETAL LEVEL

The concepts appropriate to this level of analysis include the biological, psychological, and primary group processes related to communication in marriage.

Biological Processes

The persistent differences between men and women and the variations in the extent to which such differences are found throughout the life course are a function not only of social and historical processes (Shorter, 1982) but also the underlying biological processes of sexual differentiation and maturation (Rossi, 1985). How does the analyst estimate whether biological variability produces differences in social behavior? Four criteria can be applied (Parsons, 1982; Rossi, 1985): (1) The pattern involves consistent correlations between social behavior and a physiological sex attribute; (2) the pattern is found in infants and young children before major socialization influences take hold or the pattern emerges with the onset of puberty when body morphology and hormonal secretion change rapidly; (3) the pattern is stable across cultures; (4) the pattern is found across species, particularly the higher primates most genetically like humans. Only two of these patterns need be observed before biological factors are involved. To what degree are biological factors involved in marriage?

Marriage appears to fit the third criterion since all societies contain provisions for some relationship between adults of the opposite sexes that may be designated by the term "marriage" (Reiss, 1976). Marriage clearly does *not* fit pattern four. Marriage appears to be pivotal in the evolution of our species. In most theories dealing with evolution, the ability of human adult males and females to bond, share, and work together in the raising of their offspring *differentiates* them from other higher-order primates. The division of labor between the sexes, paternal investment patterns, as well as prolonged periods of juvenile dependency are viewed as the crucial characteristics of human societies (Lancaster, 1985).

The sex ratio appears to change the organization of relationships between males and females in a society (Guttentag & Secord, 1983). When women are in undersupply, they find themselves more likely to be in the traditional roles of wife and mother and the division of labor is strong. When women are in oversupply, the society places less value on marriage and family and more value on sexual libertarianism and feminist ideology. Thus the relative numbers of males and females available for marriage may exert an influence on the nature and type of personal relationships in a society (Guttentag & Secord, 1983). In addition, the improvement in the quality of gynecological care for women, the increase in the use and efficiency of birth control devices, safe abortions, and so forth formed the physical platform for equality between the sexes (Shorter, 1982).

Current preferences in mate choices have changed. No longer is good heredity or good housekeeping at the top of a preference list for a potential mate (Buss & Barnes, 1986). Preferences in mate choices for males and females have consequences for assortative mating and sexual selection. Preferred mate characteristics can be consensually ordered, with kind or understanding, exciting personality, intelligent, physically attractive, and healthy highly valued. These characteristics may serve as cues to marital survival and satisfaction or, alternately, these characteristics may be cues to reproductive investment (Buss & Barnes, 1986). Consensually valued characteristics probably enter into the equity and exchange processes in the marital marketplace. Relative to women, men prefer mates who are physically attractive, although women more than men prefer mates who are college-educated and show good earning potential. Both socialization and evolutionary biological explanations can be offered for these replicated sex differences. Since women's reproductive fertility and value are tied to health and age, physical attractiveness serves as a proximate cue. Reproductive fitness extends beyond fertility. The economic advantages provided by males also help offspring.

The purpose of this section is to suggest that gender differentiation is not merely a creation of patriarchy, socialization, or capitalist production (Rossi, 1985). Gender differentiation is grounded in a sex dimorphism that serves the fundamental purpose of reproducing the species. Following the logic of the four patterns discussed at the beginning of this section, sexual dimorphism with biological contributions can be claimed in sensory sensitivity (e.g., Haviland & Malatesta, 1981), general activity level and aggression (e.g., Gove, 1985), cognitive skills such as spatial visualization and to a lesser extent verbal skills (e.g., Maccoby & Jacklin, 1974), and parenting behavior (Peterson, 1980; Rossi, 1977). All of these have implications for marital communication patterns.

Summary and recommendations. Ignoring the fact that the essential basis for marriage is the joining of a male and a female leads to a number of theoretical blind spots. Few of our theories seek an integration of biological and social factors. As more knowledge becomes available concerning the neurological, hormonal, and physiological differences between males and females, theories of marriage and the family may suffer if they fail to include these factors. This is not to argue for a simple-minded theory of biological determinism. It is a call for the incorporation of biological factors in theories of marital and family development when warranted.

Science is a socially embedded activity. Each step in the scientific method is profoundly affected by the values, opinions, biases, beliefs and even political interests of scientists. Each new truth is partial, incomplete, and culture bound. At the beginning of the century women's brains were "proven" to be smaller than those of men. Such scientific work both reinforced and grew out of the climate of social Darwinism rampant at the time (Gould, 1981). Realizing these facts, many feminists fear any theory arguing for a biological component in human behavior. The fear of the use to which scientific evidence may be put should not necessarily constrain the construction and testing of scientific theories of human behavior.

Psychological Processes

Males and females are assumed to be both cognitive and social creatures. Husbands and wives are cognitive in that they represent external reality internally, often in a languagelike form. This internal representation can be manipulated (transformed, and so forth) in a variety of ways. And this internal representation guides behavior. To argue that husbands and wives are cognitive creatures does not ignore affect or emotions. Emotions or feelings are one form of internal representation, as are propositions or images.

Individual Differences

The individual perspective on marriage has persisted throughout this century. Initially, the set of sociodemographic factors (e.g., social class, religion) that led to marital happiness was sought. This enterprise was supplanted by the investigation of the psychological traits that influence the development of happy marriages.

Aspects of the relationship between psychological processes and marriage that are usually studied include (1) psychological variables in mate selection, (2) the relationship between such variables and marital satisfaction, (3) mate selection and perceptual patterns between spouses, and (4) the relationship between interspousal perceptions of personality or role behavior and marital satisfaction. Both the actual and the perceptual patterns support the similarity concept in mate selection; yet this similarity does not necessarily lead to marital satisfaction. Congruence of role enactments and role expectations appears to be more strongly related to marital adjustment.

This section will not catalogue the personality characteristics related to marital satisfaction (e.g., Baucom & Aiken, 1984). Most of the variance in marital satisfaction is explained not by the individual characteristics of one spouse but by some interpersonal factor (Gottman, 1979). More variance is explained, for example, by a *matching* of each spouse's ability to tolerate conflict than any one spouse's level of consideration for others. Personality traits predict marital happiness because these traits actually tap differences in interactional styles between husbands and wives (Fitzpatrick & Badzinski, 1985).

Gender, which is usually studied under the rubric of husband and wife differences, has received much attention. Psychological differences between males and females in general may influence the direction of the marriage. One fundamental difference between males and females may be the relative value each places on close relationships (Pollack & Gilligan, 1983). Women place more emphasis on morality, intimacy, attachments, and caring across the life cycle. Men, who value notions of justice and equality more than connection and nurturance between people, tend to withdraw from relationships, while women strive to sustain connections (Gilligan, 1982). The position that males and females may differ fundamentally in their emphasis on justice versus connection is not without controversy (Kerber et al., 1986; Walker, 1984). The concern for maintaining connections may explain why females appear to monitor relationships more closely and are aware of interpersonal problems sooner than are males (Rubin, Peplau, & Hill, 1981). The work of maintaining relationships and the consequent decreases in self-esteem when relationships disintegrate may be the women's burden (Fitzpatrick & Indvik, 1982).

Summary and recommendations. Little will be learned from the study of husband-wife differences until researchers anchor their studies in theoretical models. A major mediating factor between one's biological sex and an individual's communicative behavior with the spouse is one's psychological gender. Some concern should be manifested for the psychological commitment each spouse has to traditional male and female roles.

Cognitive Models

The self-concept has not been abandoned by cognitive theories (Berger, 1987). Rather, the personality variables relevant to the explanation of individual behavior have been reconstructed in terms of flexible mental structures and processes rather than the stable and consistent behavioral dispositions envisaged by conventional psychometric approaches. Included under the discussion of cognitive models are implicit theories of communication in relationships, social exchange models of marriage, equity theory, attribution theory, and marital schemata.

Individuals have implicit theories of relationships (Planalp, 1984; Rands & Levinger, 1979) that guide their information processing, and they can hold dysfunctional beliefs about relationships (Eidelson & Epstein, 1982). The strong correlations between marital satisfaction and self-reports of communication behavior may constitute evidence for strongly held beliefs in our culture about the role of communication in marriage (Fitzpatrick & Badzinski, 1985). The happily married believe that they have remarkably good communication with their spouses. "Good" communication includes openness (Chelune, 1979), self-disclosure of thoughts and feelings (Levinger & Senn, 1967), perceived accuracy of nonverbal communication (Navran, 1967), and a fair number of successful communicative exchanges (Bienvenu, 1970).

Social exchange models of relationship maintenance argue that we "buy" the best relationship we can get—the most rewarding, the least costly, and the best value relative to other relationships (Foa & Foa, 1975; Homans, 1961; Roloff, 1981; Thibaut & Kelley, 1959). Within these models, relationships progress through sequences. At the end of a sequence, participants evaluate their rewards and costs and decide whether or not to remain in the relationship. In close relationships, individuals also weigh the investments they have made in the past in the relationship (Kelley et al., 1983). In incremental exchange theory, rewards and costs are expected to change with each occurrence and partners are aware of these changes (Levinger & Huesmann, 1980). Although some theorists believe that romantic relationships and marriage should be nonexchange relationships (e.g., Milardo & Murstein, 1979), this belief says little about behavior. According to Altman and Taylor's (1973) social penetration theory, the gradual exchange of personal information increases in both breadth and depth of topics as relationships develop. Reward-cost ratios affect trajectories of relationships. The assumption that relationship progress is linear and unidirectional with increasing openness between people has been questioned (Altman, Vinsel, & Brown, 1981). Relationships are dialectical; they continually cycle through superficial and deeper contact with repeated ebbs and flows of self-disclosure. The issue may not be whether people use exchange principles in their intimate relationships but whether the rules of exchange are the same in all relational types (Clark, 1981). Exchange relationships demand repayment, and in similar currency.

Equity theory (Walster, Walster, & Berscheid, 1978), although somewhat similar to social exchange notions, deals with individuals' evaluations of the fairness of exchanges. Satisfaction with relationships occurs when individuals perceive that what they got out of a relationship (i.e., rewards minus costs) is proportional to their inputs. In inequitable relationships, the inputs and outcomes are not proportional between partners. Underbenefitted spouses are distressed because they tend to feel angry at the unfairness of their relationship exchanges and overbenefited spouses tend to feel guilty and hence dissatisfied. The prediction that overbenefited spouses will be distressed contrasts with social exchange models, which assume that the major principle in relationships is to maximize one's rewards while minimizing one's costs. The overbenefited appear to have accomplished this objective, yet it leaves them with marital distress and guilt. Couples in inequitable marriages may be more depressed than couples in equitable marriages (Schafer & Keith, 1980). The state of inequity induces attempts to restore the balance, and this is especially true among the underbenefitted.

Conceptually, these theories overemphasize one type of reward allocation. People may use several different allocation norms rather than only considering the *equitable* distribution of rewards (Leventhal, 1976). Some use *equity* norms, which suggest that relative contributions should be rewarded; others use *equality* norms, which suggest equal distribution according to the needs of the individual. Of course, justice may not be the only standard applied in human relationships. Simple preferences may hold sway. Methodological difficulties also abound in the measurement of equity (Schumm & Kirn, 1982). When couples are treated in these designs, repeated measures or Kraemer and Jacklin's (1979) solution should be considered. More important than measurement problems are the conceptual problems. We need to know more about the judgment heuristics used by couples in interpersonal exchanges. When and how are equity, equality, justice, and fairness standards applied?

Attribution theories consider how spouses arrive at estimates of the causes of their one behavior as well as the causes of the actions of their partners. Kelley's 1979 book, which linked the development and maintenance of relationships to the kinds and types of attributions individuals make about themselves, the partner, and the relationship, stimulated a number of interesting studies of the functions of attributions in marriage (e.g., Bernal & Golann, 1980; Doherty, 1981; Newman, 1981). Sillars (1980) demonstrated that the assignment of dispositional causes to a roommate's negative behavior lead to conflict avoidance strategies and eventual termination of the relationship. Couples may search for explanations and justifications as a way of maintaining or qualifying the relationships. However, attribution-as-communication may be a double-edged sword: A husband might become angry when he attributes his distress to his wife's neglect (Harvey, Weber, Yarkin, & Stewart, 1982; Newman, 1981). There is a distinct tendency for couples to overattribute responsibility for relational conflicts to the negative personality characteristics of the spouse (Orvis, Kelley, & Butler, 1976). Unfortunately, attribution theories present static models of cognition. Such perspectives argue that individuals assign causes to the behaviors of themselves and of others but do not suggest why or even how such processes operate.

A theoretical explanation for the regularities in marital interaction observed in different types of couples has been proposed by the present author (Fitzpatrick, 1984, 1985). Specifically, individuals are hypothesized to have knowledge structures or *marital schemata* that represent the external world of marriage and provide guidelines about how to interpret incoming data. Marital schemata operate to specify the nature and organization of information relevant to the partner and the marriage and to plan and direct activity relevant to the schemata (Neisser, 1967). This hypothesis emerges from a program of research on marriage conducted over the past 10 years (Fitzpatrick, 1984). When individuals are asked to respond to the Relational Dimensions Instrument (Fitzpatrick, 1977)—a series of questions on major dimensions of marriage—three definitions emerge: traditional, independent, or separate. Traditionals hold conventional orientations about marital and family values, are very interdependent in their marriages, and willingly engage in conflicts with their spouses over serious issues. Independents are very liberal in their orientations toward family life, are moderately interdependent in their marriages, and are habituated to conflict with their spouses. Separates are ambivalent about their family values, not very interdependent in their marriages, and avoid all types of marital conflict.

Although the Relational Dimensions Instrument does not contain all of the major dimensions of marital interaction and does not isolate the *content* of an individual's marital schema, the instrument can tap sub-groups of individuals who hold different marital schemata. There are four advantages to treating the basic orientations toward marriage uncovered in previous research as marital schemata. First, this view allows the researcher to make a number of specific, theoretically derived predictions concerning message processing. Schemata direct attentional focus for they make classes of messages from the spouse salient (Hastie, 1981; Taylor & Fiske, 1978). Second, this theoretical stance leads to predictions about what spouses store in memory from interactions with one another. Schema-inconsistent information may lead to relational crises and redefinitions. Since the dimensions contain more information than the level of marital satisfaction of a couple, the marital schema yields more information concerning inputs to—and not only outcomes of—marital interaction. Such a perspective may explain why different interaction patterns lead to specific levels of marital satisfaction.

Third, proof of the existence and operation of marital schemata may advance our understanding of general social cognitive processes because this work has the potential to show how schemata operate in domains where affect is highly salient. Fourth, adopting a social cognitive perspective offers a way to understand how couples assign meaning to their own messages. Many programs of research (Fitzpatrick, 1984; Gottman, 1979; Markman, 1984; Weiss, 1984) have coded the ongoing interaction of spouses and demonstrated the patterned nature of that interaction. How the participant evaluates the messages of the spouse is rarely studied with these models (Markman, 1984).

Recent research (Fallis, Fitzpatrick, & Friestad, 1985; Giles & Fitzpatrick, 1985) has shown promise in demonstrating that the three relational definitions are marital schemata. Giles and Fitzpatrick (1984) found that individuals have stable views of marriage that correspond to the marital typology (Fitzpatrick, 1984). Furthermore, these views contained clear specifications of the types of messages exchanged in various couple types. In a different investigation with married couples, Fallis et al. (1984) found that television viewing of various relationship forms affected both amount and kind of marital communication. They argued that individuals' marital definitions represent schemata that control whether television content is seen as relevant and consistent (Hastie, 1981). The arguments for gender schemata (Bem, 1984) and for role schemata (Kinder, Peters, Abelson, & Fiske, 1980) suggest that individuals may process messages from the spouse and about the marriage in terms of the traditional, independent, and separate schemata.

Summary and recommendations. It is surprising that very little research has been conducted on the social cognitive processes underlying marital communication. Forgas (1981) considers the communicative aspect to be the very essence of social cognition. According to Markus and Zajonc (1985), "social cognitions are both the sources and the products of a social process in which communication is the main vehicle" (p. 213). Indeed, these authors suggest that the major new method in studying social cognition will be dialogue, supplementing the paradigm of reaction time and recognition memory. Along with the move to study "hot cognitions," the discussion of the cognitive processes involved in marital communication is long overdue.

To study marital schemata, the analyst must have a clear notion of the *content* of a particular structure. Markus (1977; Markus & Smith, 1981) has had success with the self-schemata because of the long history of individual-level personality measurement. The marital typology contains enough information to be relevant in the development of experiments to test for process. Furthermore, seeing the types as representing schemata of marriage offers an explanation for the different interaction processes and outcomes that define the types. In addition to the schema concept, the study of cognitive processes underlying communication between married partners represents a fruitful new direction. In considering models of human relationships, the analyst makes certain assumptions about the nature of human rationality (Abelson & Levi, 1985), and these assumptions should be checked. Only a cognitive perspective helps to sort out the errors and the biases from the heuristics used by couples in their message exchanges. Systematic errors imply systematic processes (see Hewes & Planalp, Chapter 6).

Affect Models

Few would argue with the commonsense notion that emotion in close relationships is an important area of study. Many would be surprised to find, however, that relatively little attention has been paid until recently to this topic (For overviews, see Bowers, Metts, & Duncanson, 1985; Bradbury & Fincham, 1986). Liking has been tied into the concept of attitude since the beginning (Berscheid, 1982) and consequently manifested a cognitive tone. Personal relationships are being reconceptualized as emotional states and the study of emotional communication in marriage is burgeoning (Gaelick, Bodenhausen, & Wyer, 1985). From a variety of different sources comes the general conclusion that distressed couples are more predictable, interact less often, are less positive, more negative and more likely to reciprocate negative behaviors. These differences are most pronounced when couples are in situations where they need to settle conflicts or resolve differences (see Fitzpatrick & Badzinski, 1985, for a review).

The major treatment of love in marriage (Hatfield & Walster, 1978) argues that love exists on a continuum from passionate to companionate love. Passionate love is intense, romanticized, and sexual while companionate love is steadier, realistic, and based on shared interests and values. A similar distinction has been made between liking and loving (Rubin, 1973). The first large scale study of sexual love was conducted by Davis (1929). This survey examined the sex lives of 10,000 married and unmarried women. Other work quickly followed (Dickinson & Beam, 1932; Hamilton, 1929). Despite what might be considered the quaintness of the questions (e.g., the fear of the bride during the first intercourse) and the necessity for the writers to argue in prefaces that they were scientists of human behavior and not playing to the prurient interests of the readers, these works have much to recommend them besides their historical curiosity. Each tried to sort out the role of sexuality in human relationships and its contribution to the level of personal happiness experienced by married couples.

Reiss (1981) argues that two broad ideologies are implicated in any social situation involving sexuality. The first is the traditional-romantic ideology and the second is the modern-naturalistic ideology. These ideologies found in dating couples are very similar to those of married couples (Fitzpatrick, 1984). For some couples, sexuality is an important expression of long-term love and commitment between partners while for others it is a form of personal expression and/or even physical exercise. Studies on the ideology of relationships reinforce the importance of examining the meaning of sexual events in the lives of married couples. When the concept of meaning is introduced, the study of sexuality in marriage is supplanted by a concern for the study of human communication. Couples' ability to discuss their needs and desires predicts their adjustment in the marriage.

In Western society, the marriage bond brings with it a concept of sexual exclusivity, although the behavior of individuals often markedly deviates from the practices they preach. A continuing research focus has been the nature of extramarital sex (EMS). Most research investigations have taken one of the following forms: (1) surveys examining incidence rates and correlates of EMS; (2) empirical studies that attempt to account for EMS by testing a variety of predictor variables and test the hypotheses by comparing EMS and non-EMS samples; (3) studies that have viewed extramarital sexual permissiveness as the significant attitudinal precursor of EMS. A major problem in this area is definitional. In many surveys only intercourse is used to define EMS. A broader range of sexual behaviors may need to be specified. Since 1970, survey data indicate that the population parameters of extramarital coitus appear to be approaching 50% for married men and women. Both characteristics of the marriage and personal readiness characteristics and not social background factors predict EMS. Premarital sexual permissiveness also appears to be strongly related to EMS (Thompson, 1983).

One typical research paradigm used to study marital affect is to compare dimensions of affective interaction between spouses to those of strangers. In these repeated measures designs, couples interact both with the spouse and with another opposite-sex stranger. This research shows that males are more expressive with their wives than with other women and females more instrumental with their husbands (Heiss, 1962; Leik, 1963); and married people are far more negative to one another and less polite than they are to strangers (Birchler et al., 1975; Ryder, 1968; Winter, Ferreira, & Bowers, 1973). These *spouse-stranger* designs continue to appear in the literature and have been used to study self-disclosure (Morton, 1978) and familiarity (Premo & Stiles, 1984). Fitzpatrick and Dindia (1986) have criticized this design on methodological grounds and used the more appropriate round-robin block design (Kenny & LaVoie, 1984).

The major communication variable studied under the rubric of affect is self-disclosure (Dindia, 1985). Although early research viewed self-disclosure as a personality trait, more recent research treats self-disclosure as the process of social exchange. The shift in focus not only indicates a concern for the context in which communication takes place but also a belief that consideration of self-disclosure illuminates processes of relational development more generally (Altman & Taylor, 1973; Fitzpatrick, 1987). Self-disclosure is rewarding because it signals to the listener the speaker's willingness to trust and share. Central to the notion of self-disclosure as the process of social exchange is the notion of reciprocity. Two different definitions of reciprocity, equivalent and covariant, have been used in the self-disclosure area (Hill & Stull, 1982). Equivalent exchange asks if the rewards provided to the husband by the wife are equal in value to the rewards provided by the wife to the husband. Equivalence on some dimensions may not always be rewarding (Chelune, 1979). Covariant exchange suggests that changes in the husband's rewards covary with changes in the wife's rewards (n.b., equivalence always implies covariance but covariance does not always imply equivalence).

Self-report studies show a positive correlation between the self-disclosures of husbands and wives (Burke, Weir, & Harrison, 1976; Hendrick, 1981). There is also a high positive correlation between self-disclosure and marital satisfaction, but a high disclosure of negative feelings is negatively correlated with marital satisfaction (Chelune, Waring, Vosk, Sultan, & Ogden, 1984; Levinger & Senn, 1967). Using an equity theory approach, imbalances or discrepancies in affective self-disclosure between married partners were related to dissatisfaction with the marriage (Davidson, Balswick, & Halverson, 1983). The outcomes for disclosing negative emotions may depend less on the unpleasantness of the emotion expressed than on the degree to which the expressed emotion honors or threatens the face needs of the communicator (Shimanoff, 1986). Badovski (1986) found significant differences by couple type (Fitzpatrick, 1984) in both public and private situations regarding preferences for avoidant, cooperative, and aggressive face work. Fitzpatrick (1977) found significant differences by couple type in willingness to disclose both to marital partners and to people in general. Differences in the breadth, depth, and amount of self-disclosure in one-career versus two-career couples have also been uncovered, with dual career couples more able to disclose to one another (Rosenfeld & Welsh, 1985).

Summary and recommendations. Consideration of the basic emotional processes underlying marital communication is an important new direction. There has been too much focus on the study of self-disclosure and not enough on the variety of other verbal and nonverbal message systems that couples can use to communicate affect to one another. Furthermore, self-disclosure needs to be studied within a theoretical framework other than social exchange. How spouses communicate their emotional responses to one another and to the relationship appears to be one valuable conceptual framework to be explored.

Conversational Models

Despite the "logocentric" focus of our theories of communication and relationships (Bradac, 1983), relatively few analyses of language patterns in marriage have been undertaken. This is unfortunate because marriage may be viewed as a private culture and culture is both displayed and transmitted by the language patterns of group members. Conversations between couples or "that familiar predominant kind of talk in which two or more participants freely alternate in speaking" (Levinson, 1983, p. 284) are infrequently examined. Topic shifts in marital dialogues (Crow, 1983) and decision making in the dual career couple (Krueger, 1982) are two examples of research exploring conversational processes in marriage. Individuals can describe their marriages metaphorically (Stephens, 1986). Individuals who described their marriage in paradoxical terms were significantly less adjusted and interdependent than were those who used other metaphoric descriptions.

Language mediates the world of interpersonal relationships through the codes used by couples in their conversations with each other. A code reflects a shared grammatical and semantic structure between spouses. A syntactic code indicated by more linguistic elaboration, modification, structural complexity, and less contextual presupposition mark the discourse of the independent couple (Ellis & Hamilton, 1986; Fitzpatrick, Lindass, & Bauman, 1986). Traditionals use a pragmatic code that implies the presuppositions of meaning based on relatively clear role prescriptions and conventional patterns of behavior; that is, the comments of traditionals do more work in fewer words because of the shared and clear nature of their roles.

A major issue in studies of marital conversation is the degree to which such discourse is strategic. Under what conditions do couples interact mindlessly (Berger & Roloff, 1982) and under what conditions do these husbands and wives plan their exchanges to achieve certain goals? Further distinctions can be made between prospective planning prior to an interaction and emergent monitoring during an encounter. Anticipated or experienced difficulty is associated with awareness of communication activity (Baxter & Philpott, 1985). Compliance-gaining (Witteman & Fitzpatrick, 1986), generating liking for oneself with an interaction partner (Bell, 1986), and strategies for maintaining one's marriage (Dindia & Baxter, 1986) are examples of strategic message choice studies.

A number of regularities in likelihood of compliance-gaining message use are seen across programs of research (Berger, 1985; Cody & McLaughlin, 1985). For example when couples were placed in situations to gain compliance from one another, the types and kinds of strategies used were significantly more restricted than those strategies generally found in compliance-gaining studies (Dillard & Fitzpatrick, 1985; Witteman & Fitzpatrick, 1986). The majority of couples attempted to gain compliance from their spouses by simply requesting it. These findings suggest that even when individuals attempt to be strategic, they may have rather limited communication repertoires.

Summary and recommendations. There is a great need for theoretical work and descriptive research on language use among intimates (Berger & Bradac, 1982). Much can be learned about language processes in general by studying how language functions in established relationships. An obvious point of departure would be to study the gender-linked language effect. Do intimates use the gender-specific language patterns found in formal speaking situations (Mulac, Lundell, & Bradac, 1986)?

Social Competence

The issue of communication competence in marriage is a consistent theme in the literature. Montgomery (1981), for example, defines "quality communication" and suggests the existence of a set of skills that can be learned to ensure a better relationship. Central to the study of social competence are nonverbal communication skills. Nonverbal communication better estimates the state of the relationship between spouses because it ties closely into the emotional nature of the marriage and because it is less amenable to "faking." Harmonious marital relationships are marked by closer physical distances, direct body orientation, and more immediate and relaxed posture (Beier & Sternberg, 1977).

Newlywed couples are better able to read the nonverbal messages of their spouse than are dating couples. The wife's skill seems to be particularly important (Sabatelli, Buck, & Dreyer, 1982). Wives who were good encoders (easy for judges to read) had husbands with few marital complaints and were relatively satisfied themselves. Wives who were especially skilled at decoding their husband's poorly sent nonverbal messages were also in happier marriages. Contrary to this finding are those of Gottman and Porterfield (1981), who reported that the husband's ability to read his wife's nonverbal communication is more predictive of the degree of marital happiness than the wife's ability to read the husband's.

Noller's (1984) research has shown that in distressed marriages, husbands seem to suffer a communication skills deficit. Husbands in unhappy marriages appear unable to receive the messages of their spouses correctly and have problems in sending clear messages, especially positive ones. In comparing spouses and strangers, however, what appears to be a communication skills deficit is actually a performance deficit. Husbands and wives in distressed marriages do less well in reading the marital communication of their spouses than they do in reading the communication of strangers.

Many therapeutic and intervention programs operate on the assumption that individuals need to be taught communication skills to improve the relationship. The research indicating that husbands and wives may have the skills but not use them in marital communication exchanges suggests very different intervention techniques. Furthermore, a common type of program—the marital enrichment program—although established to help couples learn to communicate, actually teaches very little. Witteman and Fitzpatrick (in press) have recently examined these programs and compared them unfavorably to therapeutic interventions. Behavior changes in marital communication appear to be facilitated by some type of skills training and not merely discussing effective communication as is typically done in church-sponsored marital enrichment sessions (Ford, Bashford, & Dewitt, 1984).

Summary and recommendations. More careful theoretical work needs to be done in the area of social competence in marriage. The efforts to date have involved cataloging the typical communication skills of the happily and the unhappily married. Skills focus on particular abilities while competence involves a general evaluation of the quality of a person's overall performance in the relationship. A competence framework (McFall, 1982) argues that not only motor deficits but cognitive and physiological deficits and strengths need to be integrated to offer a complete model of marital competence.

Interaction

The assessment of marital interaction entails conceptual and methodological considerations distinct from the consideration of the individual. With a focus on the dyad as a unit, the priority becomes an examination and understanding of relationship variables. The key question at this level of analysis is, How is the intricate system connecting two intimate partners described, analyzed, and explained (Margolin, 1983)? Early research viewed the family as a small, face-to-face primary group and tried to apply the theories of small group functioning in a direct way to marital processes. However the family is organizationally handicapped (Hill, 1965) and has unique decision processes (Aldous, Condon, Hill, Straus, & Tallman, 1971). On a number of relevant dimensions, the family differs markedly from task-oriented small groups (Hess, 1981).

In this section, we examine three major approaches to marital interaction: coorientational models of marital communication, typological models of marital interaction, and interaction models.

Coorientational Models

Coorientational models (Laing, Phillipson, & Lee, 1966; McLeod & Chaffee, 1972) measure the outcomes of the communication process: agreement, accuracy, and understanding. Agreement is the congruence of direct perspectives. Accuracy refers to predicting the spouse's unique attitudes and perceptions. Understanding involves the congruence of perspectives with meta-perspectives (my perception of your perspective versus your perspective). Sillars and Scott (1983) review a good deal of research on the question of the accuracy of interpersonal perception in close relationships and suggest a number of conditions under which accuracy in perception may falter. Fitzpatrick and Indvik (1979) found that coorientational accuracy differed depending on the ideological values and level of interdependence in a marriage. Knudson, Sommers, and Golding (1980) measured the interpersonal perceptions of couples as they watched a videotape of one of their own conflicts. Couples who resolved the issue by engaging the conflict at hand were contrasted to those who avoided discussing the issue. Engaging the issue at hand was related to increases in spouse's access to one another's interpersonal perceptions whereas avoidance was associated with decreases in shared perceptions.

Summary and recommendations. Methodological difficulties abound in the measurement of coorientational accuracy (Gage & Cronbach, 1955). Couples who have high levels of agreement may guess one another's position via projection or the imputation of a similar response to the partner. Both projective and stereotypic accuracy may be important in their own right (Fitzpatrick & Indvik, 1979). Many communication situations occur, even between intimates, that require only stereotypic information. Couples do not necessarily have to use all the information at their disposal about one another in all their exchanges.

Typological models

The search for ways to categorize couples has been an extremely active one (Filsinger, McAvoy, & Lewis, 1982). Based on the assumption that different types of couples can be expected to communicate differently, typological approaches assume that within any heterogeneous sample of couples it is possible to find a few, discrete patterns of relationships. These patterns will be exhibited in both the self-reports of couples and, at least under certain conditions, in their interaction with one another. Some researchers assume that the best way to categorize couples or families is through their interaction patterns, especially particular patterns of control in conversations with the spouse (Ericson & Rogers, 1973; Sluzki & Beavin, 1965). Based on observations of couples as they communicate with one another, two types of couples can be discriminated: symmetrical and complementary. Symmetrical couples, or those whose predominant pattern of communication involves the exchange of similar control moves, have higher levels of role discrepancy. When these couples are defined by a high number of competitive attempts to be in control, however, they have lower levels of marital satisfaction (Rogers, 1972).

Complementary couples, or those whose predominant pattern of communication with the spouse is opposite in control maneuvering, have different levels of marital satisfaction and role discrepancy depending on which spouse is in the controlling position. Husband-dominant couples report higher levels of satisfaction and less role discrepancy than do wife-dominant couples (Millar & Rogers, 1976; Courtright, Millar, & Rogers-Millar, 1979). These findings on complementary couples are consonant with the general research in the area of power and marital satisfaction (Gray-Little & Burke, 1983). One explanation for these findings is the *husband-incapacity role hypothesis:* When the husband retreats from the marriage and refuses to fulfill his marital role, a vacuum is created; the wife fills the vacuum but with deleterious consequences for the marriage.

Other typological approaches assume that it is better to construct a series of dimensions related to interaction and base the categorization of marriages on those dimensions (Fitzpatrick, 1984). The most extensive empirical typology of marital relationships is the work of myself and my colleagues (Fitzpatrick & Badzinski, 1985). The marital types isolated in this program of research differ both in self-reports about a variety of relational issues and also in their patterns of communication during casual and conflictual interactions. The typology has been shown capable of predicting interaction differences between couples in a number of laboratories other than my own, both in the United States (e.g., Badovski, 1986; Ellis & Hamilton, 1986; Sillars, Pike, Redmon, & Jones, 1983) and abroad (Noller & Hiscock, 1986). Other investigators working independently have also found in samples of both engaged (Huston, Surra, Fitzgerald, & Cate, 1981) and divorcing couples (Kressel, Jaffee, Tuchman, Watson, & Deutsch, 1980) types of marriages remarkably similar to those of the typology.

Summary and recommendations. Although two types of couples—symmetrical and complementary—have been isolated in studies of control, another type called the parallel couple is logically possible. The parallel couple is capable of switching control strategies depending on the context. More research across different topics and for longer interaction time periods may uncover parallel couples. Typologies offer one way to conceptualize the dyadic level of analysis. To be effective, the types must be tied into a network of constructs and shown to be more than an artifactual clustering of items or groups. Dindia and Fitzpatrick (1985) have compared the major approaches to categorizing marriage and show how well each does in fulfilling the fundamental goals of science.

Interaction Models

The study of interaction processes, defined as the sequential analysis of verbal and nonverbal messages involving chains of interpersonal exchanges, represents a revolution in thinking and research about interpersonal relationships (Gottman, 1982; Penman, 1980). Haley (1962) argued that such a perspective required a new language that included interactional constructs. Others have said that new research technologies were also necessary (Gottman, 1982; Lamb, Suomi, & Stephenson, 1979). Theoretical arguments in the interactional framework (Watzlawick, Beavin, & Jackson, 1967) and in the family literature (Kantor & Lehr, 1975; Lederer & Jackson, 1968) are replete with statements about the primacy of interaction sequences. Many studies stop short of analyzing the patterning in the communication between spouses over time; however, there are a growing number of exceptions to this rule (Fitzpatrick, 1984; Gottman, 1979; Hahlweg & Jacobson, 1984; Margolin & Wampold, 1981; Raush et al., 1974; Rogers-Millar & Millar, 1979; Schaap, 1982; Sillars, Pike, Jones, & Murphy, 1984; Ting-Toomey, 1983).

Coding of most marital interaction is done on six dimensions: dominance, affect, communication clarity, information exchanges, conflict (overt tension), and support/validation. Markman and Notarius (in press) give examples of research in each of these categories. Bavelas, Rogers, and Millar (1985) have done a comparative analysis of some of the major coding schemes in this area. Many of these coding schemes use the same behaviors to signify different constructs, thus some validation work is clearly needed. The verbal and nonverbal content of an interaction per se can be examined as well as characteristics of such verbal and nonverbal codes as quality, intensity (activity, tension, tempo), and diversity.

Williamson and Fitzpatrick (1985) have studied the intensity of the control moves of husbands and wives defined into one of the Fitzpatrick

(1984) marital typology clusters. Courtright, Millar, and Rogers (1980) offer a different way to study message intensity in marital interaction. Diversity has not been the object of much sequential analysis, unless it is defined as the different communication strategies spouses use in discussing different topics (Fitzpatrick, 1984). In one study, Gottman (1979) examined flexibility (similar to diversity) by looking at the size of the Z-scores in lag sequential analysis. This approach was criticized, however, by Allison and Liker (1982). The issue of diversity in interaction needs further consideration because diversity in interactional style may be the key ingredient in communication competence.

Seven major theories or models have been proposed as explanations of interaction in marriage. These models are summarized as follows:

(1) *Behavior Exchange Model of Marital Interaction.* The quality of the exchanges, such as the ratio of positive to negative exchanges, determines the degree of marital distress. Further, the reactivity hypothesis argues that recent events are particularly salient to distressed spouses, whereas for nondistressed spouses subjective satisfaction is relatively independent of such events (Jacobson, Follette, & McDonald, 1982). Recently, the cognitions that couples hold about the relationship, the spouse and the nature of the rewards and costs have been seen as important (Jacobson, 1984).

(2) *Behavioral Competency Model.* This model isolates the coping skills and external stresses relevant for all couples as they progress through normal developmental changes (Markman, 1984). The basic thesis of this model is that interactional deficits precede the development of marital distress. Excellent support in longitudinal investigations exists for this model (Kelly, Huston, & Cate, 1985).

(3) *Social Learning Model.* This emphasizes social reinforcement through quid pro quo. Behaviors displayed by partners are lawfully related; that is, each spouse's behavior is controlled by discriminative and reinforcing stimuli provided by the other partner. The role of nonverbal communication in contextualizing and modifying conversations between intimates is also stressed (Weiss, 1981).

(4) *Relational Control Model.* Communication involves both content and relational-level information. Each turn in an interaction offers a definition of how the speaker sees his or her relationship to the other interactant. The conversational partner may accept, reject, or ignore this relational bid (Rogers & Farace, 1975).

(5) *Structural Model of Marital Interaction (SMMI).* Marital interaction is patterned: Structure is a constraint determined by the reduction in uncertainty in temporal patterns of communication between partners (Gottman, 1979). This model offers four hypotheses that are well supported by the research conducted by Gottman and his associates (Gottman, 1979).

(6) *Interdependence Model.* Marriage involves interdependence among a number of shared organized behavioral sequences. When a spouse is

interrupted in the completion of an organized behavioral sequence and alternate routes to complete the sequence are blocked, emotion occurs. Positive affect occurs if the interruption is seen as benign or controllable, leads to the accomplishment of a goal sooner than expected, or removes something previously disruptive (Berscheid, 1983; Fitzpatrick, in press; Mandler, 1984).

(7) *Physiological Theory of Marital Interaction.* Basic biological differences exist in response baseline return for physiological arousal for males and females. Hence, husbands are more easily aroused during tense interactions with their wives and are slower to return to baseline levels. Communication functions in this model to relieve the stress of the situation for husbands. Patterning occurs at the physiological level for husbands and wives (Levinson & Gottman, 1983). The unhappily married show a high degree of physiological response to one another's comments. This ANS arousal can be dangerous (Mandler, 1984) and may be related to the typical stress diseases that males suffer.

Summary and recommendations. The first three models of marital interaction are exchange models that have recently been modified to include cognitive factors. Three major trends in the research on couples have resulted in the inclusion of cognitive variables in these models (Jacobson, 1984). First, distressed couples have significantly higher reactivity to negative behavior from spouses than do their nondistressed counterparts. Second, nondistressed couples respond positively and *noncontingently* to their spouses. Third, distressed couples are notoriously unreliable as observers of events in their own relationships. Together, these points suggest the operation of different cognitive states or processes in distressed and nondistressed marriages. Much more descriptive research is needed on the characteristic facets of interaction and their structure in marital communication. More research on the language code is needed. Concerns for representational validity or the matching of the researcher, couple, and community perspectives on linguistic choices would be useful (Folger, Hewes, & Poole, 1983).

MACROSOCIETAL LEVEL

The concepts to be considered at the macrosocietal level are those defined as properties of social systems. These include social networks, communities, and organizations; aggregates within society, such as social class, gender and age grades, ethnicity and race; and societies.

Social Networks

Classic models of family stress and coping (Burr, 1973; Hill, 1949) pose this question: Which families, under what conditions, involving what resources and coping behaviors, are better able to handle family crises (McCubbin et al., 1980)? The family crises that have been studied include normative transitions (e.g., the birth of a child) as well as non-normative transitions (e.g., war, illness). Family crises are often studied in the context of the whole family and not the marital dyad per se.

The major variable that determines how families cope with stress is the degree of social support available to families. Although social support has a number of different definitions (see House, 1981 for a comprehensive discussion), a reasonable one is offered by Cobb (1976): Social support is information exchanged at the interpersonal level that leads individuals to believe they are cared for and loved, esteemed and valued, and part of a network of individuals who are mutually obligated and understanding of one another. In the study of marriage and social networks, Elizabeth Bott's book (Bott, 1971) on the topic stands at the forefront of work completed since World War II. Bott's hypothesis is that the connectedness of husbands' and wives' separate social networks is positively associated with marital role segregation. Despite the elegance of this hypothesis, the empirical support for it is mixed (Gordon & Downing, 1978; Lee, 1979). Although the structure of spouses' networks does have an effect on marital integration, the effect may be compensatory rather than the mediating effect that Bott suspected.

The social contexts or networks in which close relationships find themselves exert a reciprocal and interactive effect on the development of relationships (Milardo, 1983, 1985). Social networks of pair members have been conceptualized in two ways. First, the network of significant others has been considered (e.g., Parks, Stan, & Eggert, 1982). Numerous problems surround this conceptualization, according to Milardo (1983): the lack of reliability and validity of measures, pressure on respondents to present socially desirable responses, and the omission of what Granovetter (1973) called weak ties. Also ignored are the potentially important negative ties (Rook, 1984). The buffering hypothesis (stressful life events are buffered by positive supports from significant others and thus are less likely to lead to psychiatric symptoms) ignores the opposite side of the social interaction coin. Negative interaction may make life worse. The emphasis on the number of social contacts rather than the quality of those contacts may be misplaced.

Second, interactive networks are defined as those with whom one engages in face-to-face interaction. The two key issues, according to Milardo (1983), are whether the reported interactions are immediate or retrospective and whether the researcher or the respondent is responsible for aggregation of data. Retrospective accounts have been attacked for their lack of reliability and validity (Bernard & Killworth, 1977; Killworth & Bernard, 1979). A number of newer techniques have circumvented the problems of these accounts: self-reports of social events completed daily (Wheeler & Nezlek, 1977), or completed as soon as possible after a ten-minute interaction (Milardo, 1982); time-sampling procedures aided by telephones (Huston, 1982); structured diaries completed daily (Peterson, 1979); the use of paging devices (Larson, Csikszentmihalyi, & Graef, 1982). Given the differential metrics that respondents may use in generating estimates of frequency and so forth, the researcher should be responsible for aggregating data.

As partners become more involved with one another they tend to withdraw from social networks (Johnson & Milardo, 1984). The withdrawal of the couple causes social anxiety and attempts by network members to interfere in the relationship. The degree of interference by the network appears to be curvilinear across the cycle of the relationship. In a theoretical elaboration of his earlier work, Milardo (in press) links a variety of structural network characteristics, such as size, density, and interconnectedness, to internal relational processes.

Summary and recommendations. Work on marital networks, particularly studies that will link developmental changes in marriage to network factors, is needed. The interesting aspect of the network studies that have been done to date is that they often begin their investigations because of a distaste for individual-level explanations of social behavior that ignore the context in which interaction occurs. These same researchers, however, appear perfectly comfortable in linking the individual to a social system variable such as a network. The dyadic level of analysis is again ignored in these theories and research.

Aggregates Within Society

As we have seen, developmental theories deal in a variety of ways with the concept of age. There are, however, two other social aggregates that are often the focus of theoretical and empirical attention: social class and gender.

Social Class

Propinquity defines the field of eligibles. The usual outcome of propinquity is that individuals tend to marry others from similar social categories (Adams, 1979). The study of social class differences in marriage is concerned with the study of differences between, rather than within, groups. A differentiation between the Marxist concept of class and the Weberian concept of status must be made (Otto, 1979). The Marxist concept of class differentiates groups according to their production and acquisition of goods. The Weberian concept of status classifies groups according to their consumption of goods as represented by their life styles.

Numerous studies have tried to estimate how social class affects marital behavior. Rare are works that investigate *why* social class affects marital processes. Three classes of theories have attempted to answer the causal question (see Gecas, 1979, for a related discussion of social class and parental behaviors). The first class represents the *ideational theories,* which maintain that marital processes differ across social classes because of different values, beliefs, and/or ideologies that individuals within various social strata hold. Such theories suggest that marital practices are more likely to change in segments of society that have closest access to, and are more receptive to, agencies or agents of change such as educational institutions, public media, and experts. The work of Komarovsky (1964) and Rubin (1976) fits into this category.

The second group of theories comprises the *structural theories,* which stress the mediating function between social class and marital processes of family structure and such process variables as size, division of labor, and patterns of authority. Bernstein (1973) argues that codes are the sediment of social class. The conditions of life associated with social class affect the development of two distinct codes: the restricted and the elaborated. These two codes are realized in two different types of social relations characteristic of groups. The restricted code creates a sense of social solidarity while the elaborated code does not presume to understand the intent of the other. For couples in a given social class, the roles they adopt lead to the differential use of language forms.

The *psychological states theories* constitute the third group. These theories state that the major emphasis in our society is on achievement in the world of work. Success or the lack of it in the occupational sphere has psychological consequences for the individual. Lower social class status has negative consequences for psychological adjustment, interpersonal competence, and sense of esteem. These theories have generally been abandoned (Otto, 1979).

Summary and recommendations. A problem arises with these theories when occupation is treated unidimensionally rather than as a system involving a complex set of factors ranging from the organizational setting within a particular cultural milieu to the timing of various jobs. Job and career trajectories and pressures, geographical mobility, and time demands all affect marital and family processes (see Jablin & Krone, Chapter 23). The facets of work cannot be subsumed under social class (Kanter, 1977).

Gender

A fierce debate rages around the terms utilized in this area. Sherif (1982) argues, for example, the term "sex role" has become a boxcar carrying an assortment of sociological and psychological data along with an explosive mix of untested assumptions and myths. More important, this term is often used as an *explanation,* thus deflecting deeper, more careful consideration of the issues (Deaux, 1984). I will use the term "sex" to refer to biological characteristics while I reserve the term "gender" to suggest nonbiological characteristics or a social category. There was a virtual explosion of research on gender roles throughout the 1970s (Scanzoni & Fox, 1980). Gender roles have been studied in terms of social stratification, the division of labor by sex, and gender belief systems.

Social stratification. At the macrosociological level, gender roles are structured such that men represent the dominant and women the subordinate group. Systems of sex stratification typically foster women's economic and psychological dependence on marriage. Women's social status and their access to resources are dependent on relationships with men. The general status of women in society is associated with increases in the amount of violence directed against them in a domestic context. Although feminists argue that as the status of women increases the amount of violence that they experience will decrease, Yllo (1983) presents contrary findings. At both low and high levels of female status, women experience a greater amount of domestic violence. In states where women have high status not only are these women more likely to be the victims of violence, they are also more likely than lower status women to be the perpetrators of violence against their husbands. Kalmuss and Straus (1982) suggest that economically dependent women tolerate abuse from their husbands since they may have no alternative to marriage.

Despite the fact that systems of sex stratification promote marriage as the only viable alternative for women, marriage appears to represent a better support system for males than for females. Comparisons of married males to married females show that males are advantaged in terms of their levels of morbidity, mental health, and depression. The differences are reversed when unmarried and married women are compared. Gove (1978) argues that these differences can be directly attributed to the gender roles that women are forced to assume in Western society. Gove (1978) challenges the Dohrenwends' position (Dohrenwend & Dohrenwend, 1978) that the personality disorders shown by men are the functional equivalents of the mental distress or disorganization shown by females. While the absolute level of psychological distress has increased in the population as a whole, sex differences in distress have actually decreased. This trend has been replicated by researchers in Canada, Sweden, and the United States and with a variety of different research designs (Hagnell, 1981; Kessler & McRae, 1981, 1983; Murphy, 1984; Srole & Fischer, 1980). Changes in both male and female employment patterns account for these differences, with more females working and a higher rate of unemployment existing for males (McLanahan & Glass, 1986).

The literature on life satisfaction of males and females is inconsistent. Some studies show no differences while others find that men are consistently more satisfied (Campbell, 1981; Gurin, Veroff, & Feld, 1960). Although general life satisfaction data are ambiguous, the effects of having had children on husbands and wives and on their marriages are clear. Data from five national surveys indicate that parenthood has negative consequences for the psychological well-being of adults (e.g., Campbell, Converse, & Rogers, 1976; Glenn & McLanahan, 1981). Parents report less global happiness, less satisfaction with their lives, and more psychological distress than adults who have never had children. Between 1957 and 1976, there were extremely strong shifts downward in the reported satisfaction of husbands and wives in their parental roles (McLanahan & Adams, 1985). These effects are quite pervasive and end to hold up across various sex and racial groups (Glenn & McLanahan, 1982).

Division of labor by sex. Men do exchange-value work in the society, which gains rewards and status in the public sphere. Women do use-value work in which goods and services are produced for immediate consumption in the private sphere. The differentiation of labor by gender is deeply ingrained in domestic and occupational roles. Research in the past 10 years has documented these differences and explored their consequences (Miller & Garrison, 1982). In general, such investigations show continuing gender inequity in household and occupational roles. There appears to be occupational, organizational, and industrial sex segregation at work (Staines & Libby, 1986). The sexes meet as people who do different types of work, come from different organizational niches, have different levels of power and prestige, and do not tend to meet in equal numbers. Such arrangements make gender highly salient, and the problems of tokenism are a live issue (Kanter, 1977). Despite these difficulties, the aggregate mental health of women increases as they enter the labor force; yet their husbands suffer from lower self-esteem and depression. The negative effects for husbands do not seem to occur because of their domestic task work overloads (Kessler & McCrae, 1982). The outcomes of labor force participation and a variety of other division of labor by sex schemes are based on the degree to which the behaviors are consistent with sex role preferences (Atkinson & Huston, 1984; Ross, Mirowsky, & Huber, 1983).

Relatively less attention has been paid to the mechanisms maintaining the sexual division of labor. In this area the theorists can see clearly how the barriers encountered at one level create constraints in other realms. For example, the occupations of husbands and wives affect their fertility decisions (Ericksen, Yancey, & Ericksen, 1979). Another mechanism suggested by feminists is the feminization of love and the accompanying emphasis on the independence of men. The social organization of love strengthens the power of men over women in the work place not only by encouraging women to devote themselves to home and family but also by supporting the belief that money and the dreams of achievement are not very important to women (Cancian, 1985).

Staines and Libby (1986) review the three major adult roles of spouse, parent, and worker. Work and family roles tend to complement one another in the case of men yet compete in the case of women (Near, Rice, & Hunt, 1980). The only aspect of a spousal role studied in great detail, if indeed it can be considered part of a spousal role, is housework. The distribution of the amount and type of housework is a continuing focus of attention (Atkinson & Huston, 1984). The relationship between family life and work has been viewed as segmented and independent, as compensating for each other's deficiencies in fulfilling the needs of an individual, or as "spilling over" or generalizing the attitudes or behaviors of one domain to the other. Although none of these approaches has received decisive empirical support, the spillover model captures the interdependency of work and family roles (Cooper & Marshall, 1978; Gutek, Nakamura, & Nieva, 1981).

How work spills over into family life has been examined. The effect of a wife's labor force participation on her children and her marriage constitutes one major topic of investigation (Locksley, 1980; Rallings & Nye, 1979). Another major theme has been the effects of husbands' job-related mobility or separation on their wives and families (Boss, 1977). Despite repeated calls for such research on how family life effects work (Bailyn, 1977), few investigations have focused on the effect of marital and family processes on work outcomes. The research points to the effects of wife support and help in a husband's professional attainment (e.g., Kanter, 1977), career decisions (e.g., Jones & Butler, 1980), and health (e.g., Matteson & Ivancevich, 1979).

Perhaps the most frequently discussed occupational and family interface is the dual career couple. Careers are occupations requiring specialized training and a regular sequence of related jobs in a hierarchy of prestige. The focus on dual career couples represents a narcissistic preoccupation on the part of the writers. About 79% of the articles on this topic are authored or coauthored by women. If coauthored, the other writer generally has the same last name (Aldous, 1982). Dual career couples are a numerical rarity in our society. While prevalence is not the only reason to spend a good deal of energy on a research topic in the social sciences, all other things being equal, the common is to be preferred to the rare.

Gender belief systems. Norms that refer to the evaluations of and reactions to the sexual stratification system and the sexual division of labor are gender belief systems. Within these belief systems there are attitudes and behaviors toward roles, representations of males and females, and gender stereotypes. The traditional or complementary marital roles support differentiated and complementary family roles—wives are responsible for child rearing and husbands for employment. Independent or modern couples support egalitarianism between husbands and wives and an equal sharing of home and work tasks. Problematically, the behavior of husbands and wives may differ from their expressed preferences, and husbands and wives may disagree with one another over these issues (Fitzpatrick, 1984).

In Western society, marriage has undergone a series of transformations from an *institutional* to a *companionate* system (with traditional roles) to the current *parallel* system. In the parallel system, the shared ideology of husbands and wives supports egalitarianism, as does their behavior. The transformation to a parallel marital system is far from complete because the transition from complementary to parallel marital roles involves conflict between ideology and behavior. Thomson, Czajka, and Williams (1984), for example, have shown that various combinations of agreement and disagreement on gender role behaviors affect how spouses calculate the status benefits, stress, and opportunity costs that having children holds for the marriage.

A gender-based model of marital decision making (Scanzoni & Fox, 1980) argues that marriage is best conceived as a study of interdependent persons whose potentially conflicting interests or preferences require joint decision making. Thus gender orientations of husbands and wives should predict a range of decision making, bargaining, and conflict characteristics. Research lends strong support for their model (Fitzpatrick, 1984). Traditional couples, who support conventional male and female roles, use radically different patterns of persuasion, bargaining, and conflict resolution than do independent couples, who have more egalitarian gender role preferences.

The representations of males and females in a variety of media and popular culture outlets has long been a concern. These outlets are said both to represent larger cultural ideals and to reinforce existing attitudes and values (Hawkins & Pingree, 1982). The more important social effects to study may be the unintended effects (Giddens, 1984). The study of the effects of television and other mass media sources on belief systems, values, stereotypes, and social behavior are one such side effect of television (Siegel, 1982). Gender role presentations on television represent traditional orientations to male and female role enactments (Greenberg, 1980). Fallis et al. (1985) argue that two different marital interaction patterns can be discerned on prime time television: traditional (complementary) and independent (parallel). In both sets, the given marital organizational pattern is presented as rewarding and satisfying to both partners.

Two other trends in the representation of gender in the media deserve mention. Violent content in the media may lead to a habituation to sex and violence in interpersonal relationships (Huesmann, 1982; Zillmann, 1982). For example, husbands exposed to soft-core erotica tend to devalue the sexual and physical attractiveness of their own partners (Kendrick, Gutierres, & Goldberg, 1986). A wife's desire for more open communication and disclosure by her husband is supported by the mass media. There is more social pressure on men to express their feelings than for women to enjoy sex.

Summary and recommendations. In the study of gender and society, the researcher is faced with the question of the degree to which his or her theory of communication revolves around one dominant ideological perspective. In its strongest form, ideology may not control the answers that researchers find but may more insidiously control the types of questions asked. Feminists have argued that marital research prior to the 1970s involved the legitimation of vested male interests. The rise in the number of studies on gender shows some attention to documenting male and female roles in society. Rather than focusing on dual career families, researchers should develop typologies blocking out the various patterns that occupational and family roles can take.

Gender role preferences may be shifting but the changes in both attitudes and behaviors occur with glacially slow movements and in certain social strata before others. It is not always attitudes toward these gender roles that change first, followed by behavior; often the behavior changes before the attitudes (Miller & Garrison, 1982). The move from the companionate to the parallel marriage may take as much time as the previous move from the institutional marriage to the companionate marriage.

Societies. The process by which marriages are constructed varies widely across societies. The nature of the family structure relates to mate selection. The closer the society is to the nuclear family model, the more likely that the criterion for the selection of a marital partner is romantic love (Van den Berghe, 1978). Across all societies, marriage bestows kinship. Any definition of kinship (marriage) must include some reference to the social relationship, its behavioral content, and the regulatory power of norms expressed in terms of rights and duties (Verdon, 1981).

The social context as represented in the historical, political and economic environment in which a given marriage takes place influences the relationship between married partners, the strength and intensity of the regulatory power of norms, as well as what constitutes the rights and duties of husbands and wives. In colonial America, for example, intimacy between husbands and wives involved the sharing of physical and not psychological space (Gadlin, 1977). Popular marriage in former centuries was affectionless, formed and held together by considerations of lineage and property (Shorter, 1975). Families' living arrangements produced this distance by limiting the possibility of spontaneous face-to-face interaction. The emotional isolation of husbands and wives was accomplished through the strict demarcation of work assignments and sex roles.

Nostalgia for a tradition that never existed can prejudice our understanding of the contemporary family. Changes in household composition, in the demography of kinship, and in the relationship between the family and other institutions have contributed to the greater emotional significance that marriage holds (Laslett, 1978). Until about 50 years ago, for example, one partner died about the time the last child left home. Today one may be married about 48 years with 20 to 25 years in the empty nest phase.

Summary and recommendations. Both cross-cultural and cross-historical studies of marriage and family help scientists uncover the sometimes covert assumptions of their own theoretical work as well as to see the limitations of their models. In our society, marriage occupies a privileged status among the significant validation relationships for adults (Berger & Kellner, 1975). More than any other historical period, marriage has increased significance for the development of personal identity and emotional gratification. The argument that marriage has become more significant to individual identity is not a sentimental view, focused only on positive interaction. Marriage is one of the few relationships in society where the expression of strong feelings is still legitimate; hence the possibility exists of strong positive and negative interaction.

CONCLUSION

Three major themes may be said to cut across the research on marital communication at all levels of analysis throughout this century. The first is the commitment to the strengthening and protection of the American family. In the public debate surrounding whether there should be a national policy of the family, no public voice even questioned the assumption that the family in its present form should be saved. Feminists and Marxists of various orientations hold perspectives that argue that marital relationships are the ultimate destructive forms of human freedom and creativity (Cooper, 1970). Yet these voices are rarely given serious hearing in the public arena.

The second theme is that changes in the society have a far greater impact on the study of marital processes than do basic research agendas. The pragmatic concerns of funding agencies revolve around devising answers to public policy questions. Because of the increasing divorce rate, research on divorce and its outcomes has gone up dramatically, to the detriment of basic theoretical work on processes that undergird relationships.

The third theme in this chapter is the centrality of communication across the levels of analysis of marriage. The discovery of similar patterns of thought within different intellectual disciplines, each with its own data and disparate viewpoints, suggests the existence of more general paradigms or orientations toward viewing phenomena. Communication is the general paradigm that connects these disparate levels of analysis of marriage. The centrality of communication in modern marriage, whether in working through the structural difficulties inherent in gender or in expressing affect toward the spouse, is the link across the levels of analysis and the key to understanding marriage in this era.

REFERENCES

Abelson, R. P., & Levi, A. (1985). Decision making and decision theory. In G. Lindzey & E. Aronson (Eds.), *The handbook of social psychology* (3rd ed., Vol. 1, pp. 231-310). New York: Random House.

Adams, B. N. (1979). Mate selection in the United States: A theoretical summarization. In W.R. Burr, R. Hill, F.I. Nye, & I.L. Reiss (Eds.), *Contemporary theories about the family* (Vol. 1, pp. 259-267). New York: Free Press.

Aldous, J. (1978). *Family careers: Developmental change in families*. New York: John Wiley.

Aldous, J. (1982). *Two paychecks: Life in dual-earner families*. Newbury Park, CA: Sage.

Aldous, J., Condon, T., Hill, R., Straus, M., & Tallman, I. (1971). *Family problem solving*. Hinsdale, IL: Dryden Press.

Allison, P. D., & Liker, J. K. (1982). Analyzing sequential categorical data on dyadic interation: A comment on Gottman. *Psychological Bulletin, 91*, 393-403.

Altman, I., & Taylor, D. A. (1973). *Social penetration: The development of interpersonal relationships*. New York: Holt, Rinehart & Winston.

Altman, I., Vinsel, A., & Brown, B. B. (1981). Dialectic conceptions in social psychology: An application to social penetration and privacy regulation. In L. Berkowitz (Ed.), *Advances in experimental social psychology* (pp. 107-160). New York: Academic Press.

Atkinson, J., & Huston, T. L. (1984). Sex role orientation and division of labor early in marriage. *Journal of Personality and Social Psychology, 46*, 330-345.

Badovski, S. L. (1986). A study for preference of face-work: The role of marital satisfaction and couple type. Master's thesis, Illinois State University.

Bailyn, L. (1977). Involvement and accommodation in technical careers: An inquiry into the relation to work at mid-career. J. Van Maaner (Ed.), *Organizational careers: Some new perspectives* (pp. 109-132). New York: John Wiley.

Bane, M. J. (1976). *Here to stay: American families in the twentieth century*. New York: Basic Books.

Baucom, D. H., & Aiken, P. A. (1984). Sex role identity, marital satisfaction, and response to behavioral marital therapy. *Journal of Consulting and Clinical Psychology, 52*, 438-444.

Bavelas, J. B., Rogers, L. E., & Millar, F. E. (1985). Interpersonal conflict. In T. A. Van Dijk (Ed.), *Handbook of discourse analysis* (Vol. 4, pp. 9-26). London: Academic Press.

Baxter, L., & Philpott, J. (1985). *Conditions conducive to awareness of communication activity*. Paper presented at the Western Speech Communication Association Convention in Fresno, CA.

Beier, E. G., & Sternberg, D. P. (1977). Subtle cues between newlyweds. *Journal of Communication, 27*, 92-103.

Bell, N. W., & Vogel, E. F. (1960). Toward a framework for functional analysis of family behavior. In N. W. Bell, & E. F. Vogel (Eds.), *A modern introduction to the family* (pp. 33-48). New York: Free Press.

Bell, R. (1986). *Affinity seeking among married couples.* Paper presented at the Speech Communication Association Convention in Denver.

Bell, R., Daly, J., & Gonzalez, C. (1986). *Affinity-maintenance in marriage.* Paper presented at the International Communication Association Convention, Chicago.

Bem, S. L. (1984). Androgeny and gender schema theory: A conceptual and empirical integration. In T. B. Sanderegger (Ed.), *Psychology and gender: Nebraska symposium on motivation* (pp. 179-226). Lincoln: University of Nebraska Press.

Berger, C. R. (1987). Self-conception, social information processing and communicative behavior. In J. McCroskey & J. Daly (Eds.), *Personality and interpersonal communication* (pp. 275-304). Newbury Park, CA: Sage.

Berger, C. R., & Bradac, J. J. (1982). *Language and social knowledge: Uncertainty in interpersonal relations.* London: Edward Arnold.

Berger, C. R., & Roloff, M. E. (1982). Thinking about friends and lovers: Social cognition and relational trajectories. In M. E. Roloff & C. R. Berger (Eds.), *Social cognition and communication* (pp. 151-192). Newbury Park, CA: Sage.

Berger, P., & Kellner, H. (1975). Marriage and the construction of reality. In D. Brisset & C. Edgley (Eds.), *Life as a theater: A dramaturgical handbook* (pp. 219-233). Chicago: Aldine.

Berkowitz, L. (1985). Conversations with Professors Leonard Berkowitz and Harold Kelley: Is there a need for a field of personal relationships? In Milardo (Ed.), *International society for the study of personal relationships news.* Orono: University of Maine.

Bernal, G., & Golann, S. (1980). Couple interaction: A study of the punctuation process. *International Journal of Family Therapy, 2,* 47-56.

Bernard, H. R., & Killworth, P. D. (1977). Informant accuracy in social network data II. *Human Communication Research, 4,* 3-18.

Bernard, J. (1972). *The future of marriage.* New York: World Publications.

Bernstein, B. (1973). *Class, codes and control: Vol. 2. Applied studies toward a sociology of language.* London: Routledge & Kegan Paul.

Berscheid, E. (1983). Emotion in close relationships. In H. Kelley, E. Berscheid, A. Christensen, J. J. Harvey, T. L. Huston, G. Levinger, E. McClintock, L. A. Peplau, & D. R. Peterson (Eds.), *Close relationships* (pp. 110-168). New York: W.H. Freeman.

Berscheid, E. (1982). Attraction and emotion in interpersonal relationships. In M. S. Clark & S. J. Fiske (Eds.), *Affect and cognition* (pp. 57-92). Hillsdale, NJ: Lawrence Erlbaum.

Bienvenu, M. J. (1970). Measurement of marital communication. *Family Coordinator, 19,* 26-31.

Birchler, G. R., Weiss, R. L., & Vincent, J. P. (1975). Multimethod analysis of social reinforcement exchange between maritally distressed and nondistressed spouse and stranger dyads. *Journal of Personality and Social Psychology, 31,* 349-360.

Boals, G. F., Peterson, D. R., Farmer, L., Mann, D. F., & Robinson, D. L. (1982). The reliability, validity, and utility of three data modes in assessing marital relationships. *Journal of Personality Assessment, 46,* 85-95.

Bochner, A. P. (1983). The functions of human communication in interpersonal bonding. In C. C. Arnold & J. W. Bowers (Eds.), *Handbook of rhetorical and communication theory* (pp. 544-621). Boston: Allyn & Bacon.

Bochner, A. (1985). Perspectives on inquiry: Representation, conversation & reflection. In M. L. Knapp & G. R. Miller (Eds.), *Handbook of interpersonal communication* (pp. 27-58). Newbury Park, CA: Sage.

Bohannon, P. (1970). The six stations of divorce. In P. Bohannon (Ed.), *Divorce and after* (pp. 29-55). Garden City, NY: Doubleday.

Bolton, C. D. (1961). Mate selection as the development of a relationship. *Marriage and Family Living, 22,* 234-240.

Booth, A., Johnson, D., & Edwards, J. N. (1983). Measuring marital instability. *Journal of Marriage and the Family, 45,* 387-394.

Boss, P. G. (1977). A clarification of the concept of psychological father presence in families experiencing ambiguity of boundary. *Journal of Marriage and the Family, 39,* 141-151.

Boss, P. G. (1980). The relationship of psychological father absence, wife's personal qualities and wife/family dysfunction in families of missing fathers. *Journal of Marriage and the Family Process, 45,* 541-549.

Bott, E. (1971). *Family and social network* (2nd ed.). New York: Free Press.

Bowers, J. W., Metts, S. M., & Duncanson, W. T. (1985). Emotion and interpersonal communication. In M. L. Knapp & G. R. Miller (Eds.), *Handbook of interpersonal communication* (pp. 500-550). Newbury Park, CA: Sage.

Bradac, J. J. (1983). The language of lovers, flovers and friends: Communicating in social and personal relationships. *Journal of Language and Social Psychology, 2,* 141-162.

Bradburn, N., & Sudman, J. (1979). *Improving interview method and questionnaire design.* San Francisco: Jossey-Bass.

Bradbury, T. N., & Fincham, F. D. (1986). Assessment of affect. In K. O'Leary (Ed.), *Assessment of marital discord.* Hillsdale, NJ: Lawrence Erlbaum.

Burke, R. J., Weir, T., & Harrison, D. (1976). Disclosure of problems and tensions experienced by marital partners. *Psychological Reports, 38,* 531-542.

Burr, W. R. (1973). *Theory construction and the sociology of the family.* New York: Harcourt Brace Jovanovich.

Burr, W. R., Leigh, G. K., Day, R. D., & Constantine, J. (1979). Symbolic interaction and the family. In W. R. Burr, R. Hill, F. I. Nye, & I. L. Reiss (Eds.), *Contemporary theories about the family* (Vol. 2, pp. 42-111). New York: Free Press.

Buss, D. M., & Barnes, M. (1986). Preferences in human mate selection. *Journal of Personality and Social Psychology, 50,* 559-570.

Campbell, A. (1981). *The sense of well being in America: Patterns and trends.* New York: McGraw-Hill.

Campbell, A., Converse, P. E., & Rodgers, W. L. (1976). *The quality of American life: Perceptions, evaluations, and satisfactions.* New York: Russell Sage Foundation.

Campbell, D. T., & Fiske, D. W. (1959). Convergent and discriminate validation by the multitrait-multimethod matrix. *Psychological Bulletin, 56,* 81-105.

Cancian, F. M. (1985). Gender politics: Love and power in the private and public spheres. In A. S. Rossi (Ed.), *Gender and the life course* (pp. 253-264). Hawthorne: Aldine.

Chelune, G. J. (1979). Measuring openness in interpersonal communication. In G. J. Chelune (Ed.), *Self-disclosure* (pp. 1-27). San Francisco: Jossey-Bass.

Chelune, G. J., Waring, E. M., Vosk, B. N., Sultan, F. E., & Ogden, J. K. (1984). Self-disclosure and its relationship to marital intimacy. *Journal of Clinical Psychology, 40,* 216-219.

Clark, M. S. (1981). Noncomparability of benefits given and received: A cue to the existence of friendship. *Social Psychology Quarterly, 44,* 375-381.

Cobb, S. (1976). Social support as a moderator of life stress. *Psychosomatic Medicine, 38,* 300-314.

Cody, M. S., & McLaughlin, M. L. (1985). The situation as a construct in interpersonal communication research. In M. L. Knapp & G. R. Miller (Eds.), *Handbook of interpersonal communication* (pp. 263-312). Newbury Park, CA: Sage.

Cooper, C. L., & Marshall, J. (1978). Sources of managerial and white collar stress. In C. L. Cooper & R. Payne (Eds.), *Stress at work* (pp. 81-105). New York: John Wiley.

Cooper, L. (1970). *The death of a family.* New York: Pantheon Books.

Courtright, J. A., Millar, F. E., & Rogers-Millar, L. E. (1979). Domineeringness and dominance: Replication and extension. *Communication Monographs, 46,* 179-192.

Courtright, J. A., Millar, F. E., & Rogers, L. E. (1980). Message control intensity as a predictor of transactional redundancy. In D. Nimmo (Ed.), *Communication yearbook 4* (pp. 199-216). New Brunswick, NJ: Transaction.

Crano, W. D., & Aronoff, J. A. (1978). A cross-cultural study of expressive and instrumental role complementarity in the family. *American Sociological Review, 43,* 463-471.

Crow, B. K. (1983). Topic shifts in couple's conversations. In R. T. Craig & K. Tracy (Eds.), *Conversational coherence: Form, structure, and strategy* (pp. 136-156). Newbury Park, CA: Sage.

Davidson, B., Balswick, J., & Halverson, C. (1983). Affective self-disclosure and marital adjustment: A test of equity theory. *Journal of Marriage and the Family, 45,* 93-102.

Davis, K. (1929). *Factors in the sex life of twenty-two hundred women.* New York: Harper & Row.

Deaux, K. (1984). From individual differences to social categories: Analysis of a decade's research on gender. *American Psychologist, 39,* 105-116.

Dentch, G., O'Farrell, T., & Cutter, H. (1980). Readability of marital assessment measures used by behavioral marriage therapists. *Journal of Consulting and Clinical Psychology, 48,* 790-792.

Dickinson, R. L., & Beam, L. (1932). *A thousand marriages: A medical study of sex adjustment.* Baltimore: Willams and Wilkins.

Dillard, J. P., & Fitzpatrick, M. A. (1985). Compliance-gaining in marital interaction. *Personality and Social Psychology Bulletin, 11,* 419-433.

Dindia, K. (1985). Affiliation and resource exchange: A functional approach to self-disclosure. In R. L. Street, Jr., & J. N. Cappella (Eds.), *Sequence and pattern in communication behavior* (pp. 142-160). London: Edward Arnold.

Dindia, K., & Baxter, L. (1986). *Strategies used by marital partners to maintain and to repair their relationship.* Paper presented at the International Communication Association Convention, Chicago.

Dindia, K., & Fitzpatrick, M. A. (1985). Marital communications: Three approaches compared. In S. Duck & D. Perlman (Eds.), *Sage series in personal relations* (Vol. 1, pp. 137-157). Newbury Park, CA: Sage.

Doherty, W. J. (1981). Cognitive processes in intimate conflict: I. Extending attribution theory. *American Journal of Family Therapy, 9,* 1-13.

Dohrenwend, B. S. & Dohrenwend, B. P. (1978). Some issues in research on stressful life events. *Journal of Nervous and Mental Distress, 166,* 7-15.

Duby, G. (1983). *The knight, the lady, and the priest: The making of a modern marriage in medieval France.* New York: Pantheon Books.

Duvall, E. M. (1977). *Marriage and family development.* Philadelphia: Lippincott.

Eidelson, R. J., & Epstein, N. (1982). Cognition and relationship maladjustment: Development of a measure of dysfunctional relationship beliefs. *Journal of Consulting and Clinical Psychology, 50,* 715-720.

Elder, G. (1979). Family history and the life course. In T. Hareven (Ed.), *Transitions: The family and the life course in historical perspective* (pp. 17-64). New York: Academic Press.

Elder, G. H., & Rockwell, R. C. (1976). Marital timing in women's life patterns. *Journal of Family History, 1,* 34-53.

Ellis, D. & Hamilton, M. (1986). Syntactic and pragmatic code in interpersonal communication. *Communication Monographs, 52,* 264-278.

Ericksen, J. A., Yancey, W. L., & Ericksen, E. P. (1979). The division of family roles. *Journal of Marriage and the Family, 41,* 301-313.

Ericson, P. M. & Rogers, L. E. (1973). New procedures for analyzing relational communication. *Family Process, 12,* 245-257.

Fallis, S. I., Fitzpatrick, M. A., & Friestad, M. (1985). Spouses' discussion of television portrayals of close relationships. *Communication Research, 12,* 59-82.

Farber, B. (1964). *Family organization and interaction.* San Francisco: Chandler.

Filsinger, E. E. (1983). A machine-aided marital observation technique: The dyadic interaction scoring code. *Journal of Marriage and the Family, 45,* 623-632.

Filsinger, E. E., McAvoy, P., & Lewis, R. A. (1982). An empirical typology of dyadic formation. *Family Process, 21,* 321-335.

Fitzpatrick, M. A. (1977). A typological approach to communication interrelationships. In B. Rubin (Ed.), *Communication yearbook 1* (pp. 263-275). Rutgers: Transaction.

Fitzpatrick, M. A. (1984). A typological approach to marital interaction: Recent theory and research. In L. Berkowitz (Ed.), *Advances in Experimental Social Psychology* (Vol. 18, pp. 1-47). Orlando, FL: Academic Press.

Fitzpatrick, M. A. (1985). *The effect of marital schemata in marital communication.* National Institute of Mental Health Grant.

Fitzpatrick, M. A. (1987). Marriage and verbal intimacy. In V. J. Derlega & J. Berg (Eds.), *Self-disclosure: Theory, research, and therapy* (pp. 131-154). New York: Plenum.

Fitzpatrick, M. A., & Badzinski, D. (1985). All in the family: Communication in kin relationships. In M. L. Knapp & G. R. Miller (Eds.), *Handbook of interpersonal communication* (pp. 687-736). Newbury Park, CA: Sage.

Fitzpatrick, M. A., & Best, P. (1979). Dyadic adjustment in traditional, independent, and separate relationships: A validation study. *Communication Monographs, 46,* 167-178.

Fitzpatrick, M. A., & Dindia, K. (1986). Couples and other strangers: Talktime in spouse-stranger interaction. *Communication Research, 13,* 625-652.

Fitzpatrick, M. A., & Indvik, J. (1979). *What you see may not be what you have: Communicative accuracy in marital types.* Paper presented at the Speech Communication Association Convention, San Antonio.

Fitzpatrick, M. A., & Indvik, J. (1982). The instrumental and expressive domains of marital communication. *Human Communication Research, 8,* 195-213.

Fitzpatrick, M. A., Lindass, M. L., & Bauman, I. (1986). *Language codes in couple types.* Unpublished manuscript, University of Wisconsin—Madison, Center for Communication Research.

Foa, U. G., & Foa, E. B. (1975). *Resource theory of social exchange.* Morristown, NJ: General Learning Press.

Folger, J. P., Hewes, D., & Poole, M. S. (1983). Coding social interaction. In B. Dervin & M. Voight (Eds.), *Progress in communication science* (pp. 45-80). Norwood, NJ: Ablex.

Ford, J. D., Bashford, M. B., & Dewitt, K. N. (1984). Three approaches to marital enrichment: Toward optimal matching of participants and interventions. *Journal of Sex and Marital Therapy, 10,* 41-48.

Forgas, J. P. (1981). *Social cognition: Perceptives on everyday understanding.* London: Academic Press.

Fried, F. S., & Udry, J. (1980). Normative pressures on fertility planning. *Population and Environment: Behavioral and Social Issues, 3,* 199-209.

Gadlin, H. (1977). Private lives and public order: A critical view of the history of intimate relations in the United States. In G. Levinger & H. L. Raush (Eds.), *Close relationships: Perspectives on the meaning of intimacy* (pp. 33-72). Amherst: University of Massachusetts Press.

Gaelick, L., Bodenhausen, G. V., & Wyer, R. S. (1985). Emotional communication in close relationships. *Journal of Personality and Social Psychology, 49,* 1246-1265.

Gage, N. L., & Cronbach, L. J. (1955). Conceptual and methodological problems in interpersonal perception. *Psychological Review, 62,* 411-422.

Gecas, V. (1979). The influence of social class on socialization. In W. R. Burr, R. Hill, F. I. Nye, & I. L. Reiss (Eds.), *Contemporary theories about the family* (Vol. 1, pp. 365-404). New York: Free Press.

Giddens, A. (1976). *New rules of sociological method: A positive critique of interpretive sociologies.* London: Hutchinson.

Giddens, A. (1984). *The constitution of society: Outline of the theory of structuration.* Cambridge: Polity Press.

Giles, H., & Fitzpatrick, M. A. (1985). Personal, couple and group identities: Towards a relational context for language attitudes and linguistic forms. In D. Schiffrin (Ed.), *Meaning, form and use in context: Linguistic application* (pp. 253-277) Washington, DC: Georgetown University Press.

Giles, H., Robinson, W. P., & Smith, P. M. (Eds.). (1980). *Language: Social psychological perspectives.* New York: Pergamon.

Gilford, R., & Bengtson, V. (1979). Measuring marital satisfaction in three generations: Positive and negative dimensions. *Journal of Marriage and the Family, 41,* 387-398.

Gilligan, C. (1982). *In a different voice: Psychological theory and women's development.* Cambridge: Harvard University Press.

Glenn, N. D., & McLanahan, S. (1981). The effects of offspring on the psychological well-being of older adults. *Journal of Marriage and the Family, 43,* 409-421.

Glenn, N. D., & McLanahan, S. (1982). Children and marital happiness: A further specification of the relationship. *Journal of Marriage and the Family, 44,* 63-72.

Goldsmith, J. (1982). The postdivorce family system. In F. Walsh (Ed.), *Normal family processes* (pp. 297-330). New York: Guilford.

Gordon, M., & Downing, H. (1978). A multivariate test of the Bott hypothesis in an urban Irish setting. *Journal of Marriage and the Family, 40,* 585-593.

Gottman, J. M. (1979). *Marital interaction: Experimental investigations.* New York: Academic Press.

Gottman, J. M. (1982). Temporal form: Toward a new language for describing relationships. *Journal of Marriage and the Family, 44,* 943-962.

Gottman, J. M., & Porterfield, A. L. (1981). Communicative competence in the nonverbal behavior of married couples. *Journal of Marriage and the Family, 43,* 817-824.

Gould, S. J. (1981). *The mismeasure of man.* New York: Norton.

Gove, W. R. (1978). Sex differences in mental illness among adult men and women: An evaluation of four questions raised regarding the evidence on the higher rates of women. *Social Science and Medicine, 12,* 187-198.

Gove, W. R. (1985). The effect of age and gender on deviant behavior: A biosocial perspective. In A. S. Rossi (Ed.), *Gender and the life course* (pp. 15-144). Hawthorne: Aldine.

Granovetter, M. S. (1973). The strength of weak ties. *American Journal of Sociology, 78,* 1360-1380.

Gray-Little, B. & Burks, N. (1983). Power and satisfaction in marriage: A review and critique. *Psychological Bulletin, 93,* 513-538.

Greenberg, B. (1980). *Life on television: A content analysis of U.S. TV drama.* Norwood, NJ: Ablex.

Gurin, G., Veroff, J., & Feld, S. (1960). *Americans view their mental health.* New York: Basic Books.

Gutek, B. A., Nakamura, C. Y., & Nieva, V. F. (1981). The interdependence of work and family roles. *Journal of Occupational Behavior, 2,* 1-16.

Guttentag, M., & Secord, P. F. (1983). *Too many women? The sex ratio question.* Newbury Park, CA: Sage.

Hage, J. (1972). *Techniques and problems of theory construction in sociology.* New York: John Wiley.

Hagnell, O. (1981). The Lundby Study on psychiatric morbidity. In S. A. Mednick, A. E. Baert, & B. P. Bachman (Eds.), *Prospective longitudinal research* (pp. 12-54). Oxford: Oxford University Press.

Hahlweg, K., & Jacobson, N. S. (1984). *Marital interaction: Analysis and modification.* New York: Guilford.

Haley, J. (1962). Family experiments: A new type of experimentation. *Family Process, 1,* 265-293.

Hamilton, G. (1929). *A research in marriage.* New York: A&C Boni.

Harvey, J. H., Weber, A. L., Yarkin, K. L., & Stewart, B. E. (1982). An attributional approach to relationship breakdown and dissolution. In S. Duck & R. Gilmour (Eds.), *Personal relationships* (Vol. 4, pp. 107-126). New York: Academic Press.

Hastie, R. (1981). Schematic principles in human memory. In E. T. Higgins, C. P. Herman, & M. P. Zanna (Ed.), *Social cognition: The Ontario symposium, 1* (pp. 155-177). Hillsdale, NJ: Lawrence Erlbaum.

Hatfield, E., & Walster, G. W. (1978). *A new look at love.* Reading, MA: Addison-Wesley.

Haviland, J., & Malatesta, C. (1981). The development of sex differences in nonverbal signals: Fallacies, facts, and fantasies. In C. Mayo & N. Henley (Eds.), *Gender and Nonverbal Behavior* (pp. 182-208). New York: Springer-Verlag.

Hawkins, R., & Pingree, S. (1982). Television's influence on social reality. In D. Pearl, L. Bouthilet, & J. Lazar (Eds.), *Television and behavior: Ten years of scientific progress and implications for the eighties* (pp. 224-247). Washington, DC: Government Printing Office.

Haynes, S. N., Chavez, R. E., & Samuel, V. (1984). Assessment of marital communication and distress. *Behavioral Assessment, 6,* 315-321.

Heiss, J. (1962). Degree of intimacy in male-female interaction. *Sociometry, 25,* 197-208.

Hendrick, I. S. (1981). Self-disclosure and marital satisfaction. *Journal of Personality and Social Psychology, 40,* 1150-1159.

Hess, R. D. (1981). Approaches to the measurement and interpretation of parent-child interaction. In R. W. Henderson (Ed.), *Parent-child interaction: Theory, research, and prospects* (pp. 207-234). New York: Academic Press.

Hicks, M. W., & Platt, M. (1970). Marital happiness and stability: A review of the research in the sixties. *Journal of Marriage and the Family, 32,* 553-574.

Hill, C., & Stull, D. (1982). Disclosure reciprocity: Conceptual and measurement issues. *Social Psychology Quarterly, 45,* 233-244.

Hill, R. (1949). *Families under stress.* New York: Harper & Row.

Hill, R. (1965). Decision-making and the family life cycle. In E. Shanas & G. Streibl (Eds.), *Social structure and the family: Generational relations* (pp. 113-139). Englewood Cliffs, NJ: Prentice-Hall.

Hill, R., & Mattessich, P. (1977). *Reconstruction of family development theories: A progress report.* Paper prepared for the Theory Development and Methodology Workshop, National Council on Family Relations Annual Meeting, San Diego, CA.

Hinde, R. A. (1979). *Towards understanding relationships.* New York: Academic Press.

Homans, G. (1961). *Social behavior: Its elementary forms.* New York: Harcourt Brace Jovanovich.

Hooper, J. O., & Hooper, F. H. (1979). *Family and individual developmental theories: Conceptual analysis and speculations.* Paper prepared for the theory and method construction workshop of the annual meeting of the National Council on Family Relations, Boston, MA.

House, J. S. (1981). *Work stress and social support.* Reading, MA: Addison-Wesley.

Huesmann, R. L. (1982). Television violence and aggressive behavior. In D. Pearl, L. Bouthilet, & J. Lazar (Eds.), *Television and behavior: Ten years of scientific progress and implications for the eighties* (pp. 126-137). Washington, DC: Government Printing Office.

Huston, T. L. (1982). *The typography of marriage: A longitudinal study of changes in husband-wife relationships over the first year.* Paper presented at the International Conference on Personal Relationships, Madison, Wisconsin.

Huston, T. L., Surra, C. A., Fitzgerald, N. M., & Cate, R. M. (1981). From courtship to marriage: Mate selection as an interpersonal process. In S. Duck & R. Gilmour (Eds.), *Personal relationships: Vol. 2. Developing personal relationships* (pp. 53-90). New York: Academic Press.

Jacobs, S., & Ostfeld, A. (1977). An epidemiological review of the mortality of bereavement. *Psychosomatic Medicine, 39,* 344-357.

Jacobson, N. S. (1984). A component analysis of behavioral marital therapy: The relative effectiveness of behavior exchange and communication/problem-solving training. *Journal of Consulting and Clinical Psychology, 52,* 295-305.

Jacobson, N. S., Follette, W. L., & McDonald, D. W. (1982). Reactivity to positive and negative behavior in distressed and nondistressed married couples. *Journal of Consulting and Clinical Psychology, 50,* 706-714.

Johnson, M. P., & Milardo, R. M. (1984). Network interference in pair relationships: A social psychological recasting of Slater's theory of social regression. *Journal of Marriage and the Family, 46,* 893-899.

Jones, A. P., & Butler, M. C. (1980). A role transition approach to the stresses of organizationally induced family role disruption. *Journal of Marriage and the Family, 42,* 367-376.

Jöreskog, K. G., & Sörbom, D. (1978). *LISREL IV-A general computer program for estimation of a linear structural system by maximum likelihood methods* [Computer Program].

Kalmuss, D. S., & Straus, M. A. (1982). Wife's marital dependency and wife abuse. *Journal of Marriage and the Family, 44,* 277-86.

Kanter, R. M. (1977). *Men and women of the corporation.* New York: Basic Books.

Kantor, D., & Lehr, W. (1975). *Inside the family.* New York: Harper & Row.

Kastenbaum, R., & Costa, P. T. (1977). Psychological perspectives on death. *Annual Review of Psychology, 28,* 225-249.

Kelley, H. H. (1979). *Personal relationships: Their structures and processes.* Hillsdale, NJ: Lawrence Erlbaum.

Kelley, H., Bersheid, E., Christensen, A., Harvey, J. H., Huston, T. L., Levinger, G., McClintock, E., Peplau, L. A., & Peterson, D. R. (1983). *Close relationships.* New York: W.H. Freeman.

Kelly, C., Huston, T. L., & Cate, R. M. (1985). Premarital relationship corrolates of the erosion of satisfaction in marriage. *Journal of Social and Personal Relations, 2,* 167-178.

Kendrick, D. T., Gutierres, S. E., & Goldberg, L. (1986). *Influence of popular erotica on judgments of strangers and mates.* Unpublished manuscript, Arizona State University.

Kenny, D. A., & LaVoie, L. (1984). The social relations model. In L. Berkowitz (Ed.), *Advances in experimental social psychology* (Vol. 18, pp. 48-101). New York: Academic Press.

Kerber, L. K., Greeno, C. G., Maccoby, E. E., Luria, Z., Stack, C. B., & Gilligan, C. (1986). On "In a different voice": An interdisciplinary forum. *Signs: Journal of Women in Culture & Society, 11,* 304-333.

Kessler, R. C., & McRae, J., Jr. (1981). Trends in sex and psychological distress. *American Sociological Review, 47,* 216-227.

Kessler, R. C., & McRae, J., Jr. (1982). The effect of wives' employment on the mental health of married men and women. *American Sociological Review, 47,* 216-227.

Kessler, R. C., & McRae, J., Jr. (1983). Trends in the relationships between sex and attempted suicide. *Journal of Health and Social Behavior, 24,* 98-110.

Killworth, P. D., & Bernard, H. R. (1979). Informant accuracy in social network data III: A comparison of triadic structure in behavioral and cognitive data. *Social Networks, 2,* 19-46.

Kinder, D. R., Peters, M. D., Abelson, R. P., & Fiske, S. T. (1980). Presidential prototypes. *Political Behavior, 2,* 315-337.

Klein, D. M., Jorgensen, S. R., & Miller, B. C. (1978). Research methods and developmental reciprocity in families. In R. M. Lerner & G. B. Spanier (Eds.), *Child influences on marital and family interaction: A life-span perspective* (pp. 107-135). New York: Academic Press.

Knudson, R. M., Sommers, A. A., & Golding, S. L. (1980). Interpersonal perception and mode of resolution in marital conflict. *Journal of Personality and Social Psychology, 38,* 751-763.

Kolb, T. M., & Strauss, M. (1974). Marital power and marital happiness in relation to problem-solving ability. *Journal of Marriage and the Family, 36,* 752-766.

Komarovsky, M. (1964). *Blue collar marriage.* New York: Random House.

Kraemer, H. C. & Jacklin, C. N. (1979). Statistical analysis of dyadic social behavior. *Psychological Bulletin, 86,* 217-224.

Kressel, K., Jaffee, N., Tuckman, B., Watson, C., & Deutsch, M. (1980). A typology of divorcing couples: Implications for mediation and the divorce process. *Family Process, 19,* 101-116.

Krueger, D. L. (1982). Marital decision making: A language-action analysis. *Quarterly Journal of Speech, 68,* 273-287.

Laing, R. D., Phillipson, H., & Lee, A. R. (1966). *Interpersonal perception: A theory and method of research.* New York: Springer.

Lamb, M. E., Suomi, S. J., & Stephenson, G. R. (1979). *Social interaction analysis: Methodological issues.* Madison: University of Wisconsin Press.

Lancaster, J. B. (1985). Evolutionary perspectives on sex differences in the higher primates. In A. S. Rossi (Ed.), *Gender and the life course* (pp. 3-27). Hawthorne: Aldine.

Larson, R., Csikszentmihalyi, M., & Graef, R. (1982). Time alone in daily experience: Loneliness or renewal? In L. A. Peplau & D. Perlman (Eds.), *Loneliness: A sourcebook of current theory, research and therapy* (pp. 125-143). New York: John Wiley.

Laslett, B. (1978). Family membership, past and present. *Social Problems, 25,* 476-490.

Lederer, W. J., & Jackson, D. D. (1986). *The mirages of marriage.* New York: Norton.

Lee, F. R. (1979). Effects of social networks on the family. In W. R. Burr, R. Hill. F. I. Nye, & I. L. Reiss (Eds.), *Contemporary theories about the family* (pp. 27-56). New York: Free Press.

Lee, G. R. (1980). Kinship in the seventies: A decade review of research and theory. *Journal of Marriage and the Family, 42,* 923-934.

Leik, R. K. (1963). Instrumentality and emotionality in family interaction. *Sociometry, 26,* 131-145.

Leventhal, G. S. (1976). The distribution of rewards and resources in groups and organizations. In L. Berkowitz & E. Walster (Eds.), *Advances in experimental social psychology* (Vol. 9, pp. 51-85). New York: Academic Press.

Levinger, G. (1974). A three-level approach to attraction: Toward our understanding of pair relatedness. In T. L. Huston (Ed.), *Foundations of interpersonal attraction* (pp. 100-120). New York: Academic Press.

Levinger, G., & Huesmann, L. R. (1980). An "incremental exchange" perspective on the pair relationship: Interpersonal reward and level of involvement. In K. K. Gergen, M. S. Greenberg, & R. H. Willis (Eds.), *Social exchange: Advances in theory and research* (pp. 11-41). New York: Plenum.

Levinger, G., & Moles, O. (1976). *Divorce and separation: Context, causes, and consequences.* New York: Basic Books.

Levinger, G., & Senn, D. J. (1967). Disclosure of feelings in marriage. *Merrill-Palmer Quarterly of Behavioral Development, 13,* 237-249.

Levinson, D. J. (1980). Toward a conception of the life course. In N. Smelser & E. Erikson (Eds.), *Themes of work and love in adulthood* (pp. 265-290). Cambridge: Harvard University Press.

Levinson, R. W., & Gottman, J. M. (1983). Marital interaction: Physiological linkage and affective exchange. *Journal of Personality and Social Psychology, 45,* 587-597.

Levinson, S. C. (1983). *Pragmatics.* New York: Cambridge University Press.

Lewis, R. A., & Spanier, G. (1979). Theorizing about the quality and the stability of marriage. In W. R. Burr, R. Hill, F. I. Nye, & I. L. Reiss (Eds.), *Contemporary theories about the family* (Vol. 1, pp. 268-294). New York: Free Press.

Liker, J. K., & Elder, G. H. (1983). Economic hardship and marital relations in the 1930s. *American Sociological Review, 3,* 343-359.

Locke, H. J. (1951). *Predicting adjustment in marriage: A comparison of a divorced and happily married group.* New York: Henry Holt.

Locke, H. J., & Wallace, K. M. (1959). Short marital-adjustment tests: Their reliability and validity. *Marriage and Family Living, 21,* 251-255.

Locksley, A. (1980). On the effects of wives' employment on marital adjustment and companionship. *Journal of Marriage and the Family, 43,* 337-346.

Maccoby, E., & Jacklin, C. (1974). *The psychology of sex differences.* Stanford: Stanford University Press.

Mandler, G. (1984). *Mind and body: The psychology of emotion and stress.* New York: Norton.

Margolin, G. (1978). A multilevel approach to the assessment of communication positiveness in distressed marital couples. *International Journal of Family Counseling, 6,* 81-89.

Margolin, G. (1983). Behavioral marital therapy: Is there a place for passion, play and other non-negotiable dimensions? *The Behavioral Therapist, 6,* 65-68.

Margolin, G., & Wampold, B. E. (1981). Sequential analysis of conflict and accord in distressed and nondistressed marital partners. *Journal of Consulting and Clinical Psychology, 49,* 554-567.

Markman, H. J. (1984). The longitudinal study of couples' interactions: Implications for understanding and predicting the development of marital distress. In K. Hahlweg & N. S. Jacobsen (Eds.), *Marital interaction: Analysis and modification* (pp. 253-284). New York: Guilford.

Markman, H. J., & Notarius, C. I. (in press). Coding marital and family interaction: Current status. In T. Jacob (Ed.), *Family interaction and psychopathology: Theories, methods, and findings.* New York: Plenum.

Markus, H. (1977). Self schemata and processing information about the self. *Journal of Personality and Social Psychology, 35,* 63-78.

Markus, H., & Smith, J. (1981). The influence of self-schemata on the perception of others. In N. Cantor & J. Kihlstrom (Eds.), *Personality, cognition, and social interaction* (pp. 233-262). Hillsdale, NJ: Lawrence Erlbaum.

Markus, H. & Zajonc, R. B. (1985). The cognitive perspective in social psychology. In G. Lindzey & E. Aronson (Eds.), *The handbook of social psychology* (3rd ed., Vol. 1, pp. 137-230). New York: Random House.

Matteson, M. T., & Ivancevich, J. M. (1979). Organizational stressors and heart disease: A research model. *Academy of Management Review, 4,* 347-357.

McCubbin, H. I., Joy, C. B., Cauble, A. E., Comeau, J. K., Patterson, J. M., & Needle, R. H. (1980). Family stress and coping: A decade review. *Journal of Marriage and the Family, 42,* 855-871.

McFall, R. M. (1982). A review and reformation of the concept of social skills. *Behavioral Assessment, 4,* 1-33.

McLanahan, S., & Adams, J. (1985). *Parental dissatisfaction.* Unpublished manuscript, University of Wisconsin—Madison, Center for Demography and Ecology.

McLanahan, S. S., & Glass, J. S. (1986). *A note on the trend in sex differences in psychological distress.* Unpublished manuscript, University of Wisconsin—Madison, Center for Demography and Ecology.

McLeod, J. M., & Chaffee, S. H. (1972). The construction of social reality. In J. T. Tedeschi (Ed.), *The social influence processes* (pp. 50-99). Chicago: Aldine.

Menaghan, E. (1983). Marital stress and family transitions: A panel analysis. *Journal of Marriage and the Family, 45,* 371-386.

Milardo, R. M. (1982). Friendship networks in developing relationships: Converging and diverging social environments. *Social Psychology Quarterly, 45,* 162-172.

Milardo, R. M. (1983). Social networks and pair relationships: A review of substantive and measurement issues. *Sociology and Social Research, 68,* 1-18.

Milardo, R. M. (1985). Personal choice and social constraint in close relationships: Applications of network analysis. In V. J. Derlega & B. A. Winstead (Eds.), *Friendship and social interaction* (pp. 11-36). New York: Springer-Verlag.

Milardo, R. M., & Murstein, B. I. (1979). The implications of exchange orientation on the dyadic functioning of heterosexual cohabitation. In M. Cook & G. Wilson (Eds.), *Love and attraction* (pp. 161-206). Oxford: Pergamon.

Millar, F. E., & Rogers, E. (1976). A relational approach to interpersonal communication. In G. R. Miller (Ed.), *Explorations in interpersonal communication* (pp. 87-104). Newbury Park, CA: Sage.

Miller, J., & Garrison, H. H. (1982). Sex roles: The division of labor at home and in the workplace. *Annual Review of Sociology, 8,* 237-62.

Minuchin, P. (1974). *Families and family therapy.* Cambridge, MA: Harvard University Press.

Montgomery, B. M. (1981). The form and function of quality communication in marriage. *Family Relations, 30,* 21-30.

Morton, T. L. (1978). Intimacy and reciprocity of exchange: A comparison of spouses and strangers. *Journal of Personality and Social Psychology, 37,* 72-81.

Mulac, A., Lundell, T. L., & Bradac, J. J. (1986). Male/female language differences and attributional consequences in a public speaking situation: Toward an explanation of the gender-linked language effect. *Communication Monographs, 53,* 115-129.

Murphy, J. (1984). Stability of prevalence depression and anxiety disorders. *Archives of General Psychiatry, 41,* 990-997.

Navran, L. (1967). Communication and adjustment in marriage. *Family Process, 6,* 173-184.

Near, J. P., Rice, R. W., & Hunt, R. G. (1980). The relationship between work and nonwork domains: A review of empirical research. *Academy of Management Review, 5,* 415-29.

Neisser, U. (1967). *Cognitive psychology.* New York: Appleton.

Newman, H. (1981). Communication within ongoing intimate relationships: An attributional perspective. *Personality and Social Psychology Bulletin, 7,* 59-70.

Nock, S. (1981). Family life-cycle transitions: Longitudinal effects on family members. *Journal of Marriage and the Family, 43,* 703-714.

Nock, S. L. (1979). The family life cycle: Empirical or conceptual tool? *Journal of Marriage and the Family, 41,* 15-26.

Noller, P. (1984). *Nonverbal communication and marital interaction.* New York: Pergamon.

Noller, P, & Hiscock, H. (1986). *Fitzpatrick's marital typology: An Australian replication.* Paper presented at the International Conference on Personal Relationships, Herzlya, Israel.

Norton, A. J. (1980). The influence of divorce on traditional life-cycle measures. *Journal of Marriage and the Family, 42,* 63-69.

Norton, R. (1983). Measuring marital quality: A critical look at the dependent variable. *Journal of Marriage and the Family, 45,* 141-151.

Nye, F. I. (1979). Choice, exchange, and the family. In W. R. Burr, R. Hill, F. I. Nye, & I. L. Reiss (Eds.), *Contemporary theories about the family* (Vol. 2, pp. 1-41). New York: Free Press.

Nye, F. I., White, L., & Frideres, J. (1973). Role competence and marital dissolution. *International Journal of Sociology of the Family, 3,* 324-345.

Olson, D. H., McCubbin, H. I., & Associates. (1983). *Families: What makes them work.* Newbury Park, CA: Sage.

Orvis, B. R., Kelley, H. H., & Butler, D. (1976). Attributional conflict in young couples. In J. H. Harvey, W. J. Ickes, & R. E. Kidd (Eds.), *New directions in attribution research* (Vol. 1, pp. 353-386). Hillsdale, NJ: Lawrence Erlbaum.

Otto, L. B. (1979). Antecedents and consequences of marital timing. In W. R. Burr, R. Hill, F. I. Nye, & I. L. Reiss (Eds.), *Contemporary theories about the family* (Vol. 1, pp. 101-126). New York: Free Press.

Parks, M. R., Stan, C. M., & Eggert, L. L. (1982). *Romantic involvement and social network involvement.* Paper presented at the International Conference on Personal Relationships, Madison, WI.

Parsons, J. E. (1982). Biology, experience, and sex dimorphic behaviors. In W. R. Gove & G. R. Carpenter (Eds.), *The fundamental connection between nature and nurture* (pp. 137-170). Lexington: Lexington Books.

Parsons, T., & Bales, R. F. (1955). *Family socialization and interaction process.* New York: Free Press.

Penman, R. (1980). *Communication processes and relationships.* New York: Academic Press.

Peplau, L. A. (1983). Roles and gender. In H. Kelley, E. Berscheid, A. Christensen, J. J. Harvey, T. L. Huston, G. Levinger, E. McClintock, L. A. Peplau, & D. R. Peterson (Eds.), *Close relationships* (pp. 220-264). New York: W.H. Freeman.

Peplau, L. A., Cochran, S. D., Rook, K., & Padesky, C. (1978). Loving women: Attachment and autonomy in lesbian relationships. *Journal of Social Issues, 34,* 7-27.

Peplau, L. A., & Gordon, S. L. (1983). The intimate relationships of lesbians and gay men. In E. R. Allgeier & N. B. McCormick (Eds.), *The changing boundaries: Gender roles and sexual behavior* (pp. 41-71). Palo Alto, CA: Mayfield.

Peterson, A. C. (1980). Biopsychosocial processes in the development of sex-related differences. In J. E. Parsons (Ed.), *The psychology of sex differences and sex roles* (pp. 31-56). Washington, DC: Hemisphere.

Peterson, D. R. (1979). Assessing interpersonal relationships by means of interaction records. *Behavioral Assessment, 1,* 221-236.

Pittman, J. F., Price-Bonham, S., & McKenry, P. (1983). Marital cohesion: A path model. *Journal of Marriage and the Family, 45,* 521-531.

Planalp, S. (1984). *Relational schemata: An interpretive approach to relationships.* Unpublished doctoral dissertation, University of Wisconsin—Madison.

Pollack, S., & Gilligan, C. (1983). Images of violence in thematic apperception test stories. *Journal of Personality and Social Psychology, 42,* 159-167.

Premo, B. E., & Stiles, W. B. (1984). Familiarity in verbal interactions of married couples versus strangers. *Journal of Social and Clinical Psychology, 1,* 209-230.

Price-Bonham, S., & Balswick, J. O. (1980). The noninstitutions: divorce, desertion, and remarriage. *Journal of Marriage and the Family, 42,* 959-972.

Rallings, E. M., & Nye, F. I. (1979). Wife-mother employment, family, and society. In W. Burr, R. Hill, F. I. Nye, & I. L. Reiss (Eds.), *Contemporary theories about the family* (Vol. 1, pp. 203-226). New York: Free Press.

Rands, M., & Levinger, G. (1979). Implicit theories of relationship: An intergenerational study. *Journal of Personality and Social Psychology, 37,* 645-661.

Raush, H. L., Barry, W. A., Hertel, R. K., & Swain, M. A. (1974). *Communication, conflict, and marriage.* San Francisco: Jossey-Bass.

Raush, H. L., Grief, A. C., & Nugent, J. (1979). Communication in couples and families. In W. R. Burr, R. Hill, F. I. Nye, & I. L. Reiss (Eds.), *Contemporary theories about the family* (Vol. 1, pp. 468-492). New York: Free Press.

Reiss, I. L. (1981). Some observations on ideology and sexuality in America. *Journal of Marriage and the Family, 43,* 271-283.

Reiss, I. L. (1976). *Family systems in America* (2nd ed.). New York: Holt-Dryden.

Rodgers, R. H. (1973). *Family interaction and transaction: The developmental approach.* Englewood Cliffs, NJ: Prentice-Hall.

Rogers, L. E. (1972). *Dyadic systems and transactional communication in a family context.* Unpublished doctoral dissertation, Michigan State University.

Rogers, L. E., & Farace, R. V. (1975). Relational communication analysis: New measurement procedures. *Human Communication Research, 1,* 222-239.

Rogers-Millar, L. E., & Millar, F. E. (1979). Domineeringness and dominance: A transactional view. *Human Communication Research, 5,* 238-246.

Rollins, B. C., & Cannon, K. L. (1974). Marital satisfaction over the family cycle: A reevaluation. *Journal of Marriage and the Family, 36,* 271-282.

Rollins, B. C., & Feldman, H. (1970). Marital satisfaction over the family life cycle. *Journal of Marriage and the Family, 32,* 20-28.

Rollins, B. C., & Galligan, R. (1978). The developing child and marital satisfaction of parents. In R. M. Lerner & G. B. Spanier (Eds.), *Child influences on marital and family interaction: A life-span perspective* (pp. 71-106). New York: Academic Press.

Roloff, M. E. (1981). *Interpersonal communication: The social exchange approach.* Newbury Park, CA: Sage.

Rook, K. S. (1984). The negative side of social interaction: Impact on psychological well-being. *Journal of Personality and Social Psychology, 46,* 1097-1108.

Rosenfeld, L. B., & Welsh, S. M. (1985). Differences in self-disclosure in dual-career and single-career marriages. *Communication Monographs, 52,* 253-263.

Ross, C. E., Mirowsky, J., & Huber, J. (1983). Dividing work, sharing work, and in-between: Marriage patterns and depression. *American Sociological Review, 48,* 809-823.

Rossi, A. (1977). A biosocial perspective on parenting. *Daedalus, 106,* 1-31.

Rossi, A. (1985). Gender and parenthood. In A. Rossi (Ed.), *Gender and the life course* (pp. 161-192). New York: Aldine.

Rowland, K. F. (1977). Environmental events predicting death for the elderly. *Psychological Bulletin, 84,* 349-372.

Rubin, L. (1976). *Worlds of pain: Life in the working class family.* New York: Basic Books.

Rubin, Z. (1973). *Liking and loving, invitation to social psychology.* New York: Holt, Rinehart & Winston.

Rubin, Z., Peplau, L. A., & Hill, C. T. (1981). Loving and leaving: Sex differences in romantic attachments. *Sex roles, 7,* 821-835.

Ryan, E. B., & Giles, H. (Eds.). (1982). *Attitudes towards language variation: Social and applied contexts.* London: Edward Arnold.

Ryan, J. (1981). Marital status, happiness and anomia. *Journal of Marriage and the Family, 43,* 643-649.

Ryder, R. G. (1968). Husband-wife dyads versus married strangers. *Family Process, 7,* 233-238.

Sabatelli, R. M., Buck, R., & Dreyer, A. (1982). Nonverbal communication accuracy in married couples: Relationships with marital complaints. *Journal of Personality and Social Psychology, 43,* 1088-1097.

Safilios-Rothschild, C. (1969). Family sociology or wives' family sociology? A cross-cultural examination of decision-making. *Journal of Marriage and the Family, 31,* 290-301.

Scanzoni, J., & Fox, G. L. (1980). Sex roles, family and society: The seventies and beyond. *Journal of Marriage and the Family, 42,* 743-756.

Schaap, C. (1982). *Communication and adjustment.* Lisse, Netherlands: Swets & Zeitlinger, B.V.

Schafer, R. B., & Keith, P. M. (1980). Equity and depression among married couples *Social Psychology Quarterly, 43,* 430-435.

Scherer, K. R., & Giles, H. (Eds.). (1979). *Social markers in speech.* Cambridge: Cambridge University Press.

Schumm, W. R., & Kirn, J. E. (1982). Evaluating equity in the marital relationship: An alternative approach. *Psychological Reports, 51,* 759-762.

Sherif, C. W. (1982). Needed concepts in the study of gender identity. *Psychology of Women Quarterly, 6,* 375-398.

Shimanoff, S. (1986). *Types of emotional disclosures and request compliance between spouses.* Paper presented at the International Communication Association Convention in Chicago.

Shorter, E. (1975). *The making of the modern family.* New York: Basic Books.

Shorter, E. (1982). *A history of women's bodies.* New York: Basic Books.

Siegel, A. E. (1982). Social beliefs and social behavior: Introductory comments. In D. Pearl, L. Bouthilet, & J. Lazar (Eds.), *Television & behavior: Ten years of scientific progress and implications for the eighties* (pp. 175-178). Washington, DC: Government Printing Office.

Sillars, A. (1980). *Communication and attributions in interpersonal conflict.* Unpublished doctoral dissertation, University of Wisconsin—Madison.

Sillars, A. L., & Scott, M. D. (1983). Interpersonal perception between intimates: An integrative review. *Human Communication Research, 10,* 153-176.

Sillars, A., Pike, G. R., Redmon, K., & Jones, T. S. (1983). Communication and conflict in marriage: One style is not satisfying to all. In R. Bostrom (Ed.), *Communication yearbook 7* (pp. 414-431). Newbury Park, CA: Sage.

Sillars, A. L., Pike, G. R., Jones, T. S., & Murphy, M. A. (1984). Communication and understanding in marriage. *Human Communication Research, 10,* 317-350.

Sluzki, C. E., & Beavin, J. (1965). Simetra y complementaridad: Una definicion operacional y una tipologia de parejas. *Acta Psiquiatrica y Psicologica de America Latina, 11,* 321-330.

Snyder, D. K., Wills, R. M., & Kesler, T. W. (1981). Empirical validation of the marital satisfaction inventory: An actuarial approach. *Journal of Consulting and Clinical Psychology, 49,* 262-268.

Spanier, G. B. (1976). Measuring dyadic adjustment: New scales for assessing the quality of marriage and similar dyads. *Journal of Marriage and the Family, 38,* 15-28.

Spanier, G. B., & Filsinger, E. E. (1983). The dyadic adjustment scale. In E. E. Filsinger (Ed.), *Marriage and family assessment* (pp. 155-168). Newbury Park, CA: Sage.

Spanier, G. B., & Lewis, R. A. (1980). Marital quality: A review of the seventies. *Journal of Marriage and the Family, 42,* 825-839.

Spanier, G. B., Lewis, R. A., & Cole, C. L. (1975). Marital adjustment over the family life cycle: The issue of curvilinearity. *Journal of Marriage and the Family, 37,* 263-275.

Spanier, G. B., Sauer, W., & Larzelere, R. (1979). An empirical evaluation of the family life cycle. *Journal of Marriage and the Family, 41,* 27-38.

Spanier, G. B., & Thompson, L. (1982). A confirmatory analysis of the dyadic adjustment scale. *Journal of Marriage and the Family, 44,* 731-738.

Sprey, J. (1979). Conflict theory and the study of marriage and the family. In W. R. Burr, R. Hill, F. I. Nye & I. L. Reiss (Eds.), *Contemporary theories about the family* (Vol. 2, pp. 130-159). New York: Free Press.

Sprey, J. (1985). Editorial comments. *Journal of Marriage and the Family, 47,* 3.

Srole, L., & Fischer, A. K. (1980). The midtown Manhattan longitudinal study vs. "the mental paradise lost" doctrine: A controversy joined. *Archives of General Psychiatry, 37,* 209-221.

Stack, S. (1980). The effects of marital dissolution on suicide. *Journal of Marriage and the Family, 42,* 83-91.

Staines, G. L., & Libby, P. L. (1986). Men and women in role relationships. In R. D. Ashmore & F. K. Del Boca (Eds.), *The social psychology of female-male relations: A critical analysis of central concepts* (pp. 211-258). New York: Academic Press.

Staples, R., & Mirande, A. (1980). Racial and cultural variations among American families: A decennial review of the literature on minority families. *Journal of Marriage and the Family, 42,* 887-903.

Stephens, T. (1986). *On linguistic and social forms.* Unpublished manuscript Renslauer University.

Stroebe, M. S., Stroebe, W., Gergen, K. J., & Gergen, M. (1981). The broken heart: Reality or myth? *Omega, 12,* 87-106.

Tajfel, H. (1981). *Human groups and social categories: Studies in social psychology.* Cambridge: Cambridge University Press.

Taylor, S. E., & Fiske, S. T. (1978). Salience, attention and attribution: Top of the head phenomena. In L. Berkowitz (Ed.), *Advances in experimental social psychology* (Vol. 11, pp. 249-288). New York: Academic Press.

Terman, L. M. (1938). *Psychological factors in marital happiness.* New York: McGraw-Hill.

Thibaut, J. W., & Kelley, H. H. (1959). *The social psychology of groups.* New York: John Wiley.

Thompson, A. P. (1983). Extramarital sex: A review of the research literature. *Journal of Sex Research, 19,* 1-22.

Thompson, E., & Williams, R. (1982). Beyond wives' family sociology: A method for analyzing couple data. *Journal of Marriage and the Family, 44,* 999-1008.

Thomson, E., Czajka, J. L., & Williams, R. (1984). *Marital roles and the demand for children.* Paper presented at the annual meetings of the American Sociological Association, San Antonio, TX.

Ting-Toomey, S. (1983). An analysis of verbal communication patterns in high and low marital adjustment groups. *Human Communication Research, 9,* 306-319.

Udry, R. J. (1974). *The social context of marriage.* Philadelphia: Lippincott Company.
Van den Berghe, P. L. (1978). *Human family systems: An evolutionary view.* New York: Elsevier.
Verdon, M. (1981). Kinship, marriage, and the family: An operational approach. *American Journal of Sociology, 86,* 796-818.
Walker, L. J. (1984). Sex differences in the development of moral reasoning: A critical review. *Child Development, 55,* 677-691.
Waller, W. (1938). *The family: A dynamic interpretation.* New York: Dryden.
Walster, E., Berscheid, E., & Walster, G. W. (1976). New directions in equity research. In L. Berkowitz & E. Walster (Eds.), *Advances in experimental social psychology* (Vol. 9, pp. 1-42). New York: Academic Press.
Walster, E. H., Walster, G. H., & Berscheid, E. (1978). *Equity: Theory and research.* Boston: Allyn & Bacon.
Watzlawick, P., Beavin, J. H., & Jackson, D. D. (1967). *Pragmatics of human communication.* New York: Norton.
Watzlawick, P., Weakland, J., & Fisch, R. (1974). *Change: Principles of problem formation and problem resolution.* New York: Norton.
Waxler, N. E., & Mischler, E. G. (1970). Sequential patterning in family interaction: A methodological note. *Family Process, 9,* 211-220.
Weick, K. E. (1978). *The social psychology of organizing.* Reading, MA: Addison-Wesley.
Weiss, R. L. (1981). The new kid on the block: Behavioral systems approach. In E. E. Filsinger & R. A. Lewis (Eds.), *Assessing marriage: New behavioral approaches* (pp. 22-37). Newbury Park, CA: Sage.
Weiss, R. L. (1984). Cognitive and behavioral measures of marital interaction. In K. Hahlweg & N. S. Jacobson (Eds.), *Marital interaction: Analysis and modification* (pp. 232-252). New York: Guilford.
Weiss, R. L., & Cerreto, M. C. (1980). The marital status inventory: Development of a measure of dissolution potential. *American Journal of Family Therapy, 8,* 80-85.
Wheeler, L., & Nezlek, J. (1977). Sex differences in social participation. *Journal of Personality and Social Psychology, 45,* 943-953.
White, L. K., & Brinkerhoff, D. B. (1978). Measuring dyadic properties: An exploratory analysis. *International Journal of Sociology of the Family, 8,* 219-229.
Williamson, R. N., & Fitzpatrick, M. A. (1985). Two approaches to marital interaction: Relational control patterns in marital types. *Communication Monographs, 52,* 236-252.
Winter, W. D., Ferreira, A. J., & Bowers, N. (1973). Decision-making in married and unrelated couples. *Family Process, 12,* 83-94.
Witteman, H., & Fitzpatrick, M. A. (1986). Compliance-gaining in marital interaction: Power bases, power processes, and outcomes. *Communication Monographs, 53,* 130-143.
Witteman, H., & Fitzpatrick, M. A. (in press). A social scientific evaluation of marital enrichment programs. *Journal of Social and Clinical Psychology.*
Yllo, K. (1983). Sexual equality and violence against wives in American states. *Journal of Comparative Family Studies, 14,* 67-86.
Zillmann, D. (1982). Television viewing and arousal. In D. Pearl, L. Bouthilet, & J. Lazar (Eds.), *Television and behavior: Ten years of scientific progress and implications for the eighties* (pp. 53-67). Washington, DC: Government Printing Office.

20 Communication and Children

ELLEN WARTELLA
University of Illinois, Urbana-Champaign

BYRON REEVES
Stanford University

T HIS chapter (like this entire volume) attempts to bring together research that has typically been reviewed separately. Theoretically, this means combining studies about communicating individuals with those about communication in dyads, groups, and society. Topically, this means combining the traditional areas of interpersonal and mass communication as well as areas that are often considered outside communication studies. Organizationally, this probably means putting too much in too small a space. Nevertheless, we have opted for liberal boundaries in this review. The potential error is that some research programs are ignored. This may be acceptable, however, given the large number of reviews available on children (e.g., Mussen, 1983). A benefit may be a broad view of intellectual similarities often masked by the organization of departments, associations, and journals.

The fear that everything is relevant pertains to no other chapter more than this one. To be sure, we focus on children to the exclusion of adults and older adolescents. But topics and levels of analysis in all other chapters are relevant. Children process information; talk with family, siblings, and friends; participate in organizations (schools and social groups); interact with media; have opinions; are socialized to politics; and so on. So we must limit the scope of our review without (we hope) jeopardizing the major goal of the volume—to join research in areas that could share theory but rarely even share citations.

We will attempt to show that several apparently disparate areas are in fact similar. Examples have been chosen to highlight similarities across literatures. Three major themes emerge across disciplines: (1) Children's experience and knowledge are shown to be important determinants—in addition to the limitations imposed by cognitive skills—of how children understand themselves and the world; (2) there is increased emphasis on processing concepts such as attention and memory, beyond qualities of developmental stages such as egocentrism; and (3) interactions between social context and mental abilities are emphasized. These changes have reduced dependence on Piagetian theories of cognitive development and they have highlighted (sometimes due to methodological advances) competencies in processing and sense making at early ages.

We review three broad areas: (1) learning to communicate (acquisition of language for individual children), (2) communicating with others (social aspects of communication and communicative competence), and (3) mediated communication (interactions with media). These areas involve efforts from different disciplines (linguistics, psychology, sociology, anthropology) and questions at different levels of analysis.

LEARNING TO COMMUNICATE:
LANGUAGE ACQUISITION

Language is not an abstract construction of the learned or of dictionary makers, but is something arising out of the work, needs, ties, joys and affections of long generations of humanity and has its bases broad and low and close to the ground. (Walt Whitman)

This quote from "Slang in America" embodies some of the basic tenets of language development. Language acquisition is a social enterprise; much of children's language is tied to interactions with objects and people, and language develops over time both for the individual and for successive generations. The next two sections consider how children learn to use language and how they learn to communicate with others. This separation highlights differences between language development and communicative development. The section titled "Learning to Communicate" considers the acquisition of language, how children acquire grammar and word meanings, and the general relationship between cognitive and language development. Language involves more than the construction of messages, however; it also involves conversation. The next section will focus on the social aspects of language use.

A distinction between language acquisition and communicative competence is arbitrary, but there are some good arguments for the separation. Bierwisch (1980) lists three reasons for separate consideration: (1) Some uses of language are not communicative (e.g., the babbling of babies), (2) there are instances of communication that are clearly nonlinguistic (e.g., nonverbal gestures and paralinguistic cues), and (3) the rules of linguistic versus pragmatic verbal communication may be different (nongrammatical speech is communicative). Moreover, consideration of communicative development, unlike language development, *must* include the cultural and social conventions that provide information and through which children learn to communicate in a social context (Shatz, 1983). Although it is clear that communicative experiences can facilitate language acquisition (see Hoff-Ginsberg & Shatz, 1982), the two are not easily equated. So questions about language development are not reducible to principles of communicative development or vice versa.

Developmental psychologists also provide reasons for a separate treatment of linguistic and communicative development. For instance, there is evidence of children who have language difficulties but who *can* communicate (Shatz, 1983). Second, there have been no adequate accounts of language development based on prior communicative achievements (Shatz, 1982). Third, both Karmiloff-Smith (1981) and Bowerman (1982) have demonstrated that some language development (e.g., the organization of grammar at different stages of development) may proceed from children's internal notion of orderliness and not from communicative pressures. The study of language development, then, is the study of how children learn to *talk*. Although infants can be observed attempting to communicate (crying, tugging on mother's clothes, etc.), it is the rapid language growth between 10 months and 5 years that is usually considered under the topic of language development.

What are the origins of language? According to Sinclair (1982), interest in language development goes back to the earliest writings in which people reflected on the nature of being human. Herodotus in 400 B.C. recorded a psycholinguistic experiment in language development (Sinclair, 1982). Charles Darwin (1974) studied language development by keeping a diary of a child's speech from infancy to age 3. (Since then, but probably not because of Darwin, the diary method has been a mainstay in studies of child language.) Three questions have concerned scholars of language development: (1) How do children acquire syntax or the rules for forming words and combining them into phrases and sentences? (2) How do children learn the meaning of words (semantics)? and (3) What is the relationship of general cognitive development to language development?

The study of syntax (acquisition of grammatical rules) has been heavily influenced by Chomsky's (1957) theory of transformational generative grammar. Chomsky maintains that underlying abstract rules account for linguistic structure, that rules are "autonomous and independent of meaning" (Chomsky, 1957, p. 17), and that the rules are innately programmed in humans through a language-specific acquisition device. Chomsky's ideas about the acquisition of grammar have generated considerable empirical research about how children learn grammar in the first few years of life.

The basic measure of linguistic advancement has been the mean length of utterance (MLU) in morphemes (Maratsos, 1983). An utterance like *girl's ball* is 3 MLU since *girl* is one morpheme, *'s* is another morpheme, and *ball* is a third morpheme. Roger Brown (1973) identified five major MLU stages of language acquisition (1.75, 2.25, 2.75, 3.50, and 4.0) during the first 3 years of life. These stages describe the growth of children's abilities to string words into utterances during early language development. Studies of word strings have afforded tests of Chomsky's notions of language development. Brown (1973) summarized the major developments in grammar that are correlated with the five MLU stages and that describe language between birth and 3 years. For instance, the use of possessive inflection ("John's dog") appears in Stage II, auxiliary verbs ("can," "do") and the use of conjunctions ("I want eggs and some cereal") appear in Stage V (MLU of 4.0 morphemes). After Stage V there is no stability in the development of syntactical complexity. That does not mean, however, that children's grammar stops developing. Even between 5 and 14 years of age grammar continues to change as children master relational terms and begin to use passive verbs, and quantifiers, adjectives, adverbs, and mood voice (Rice & Kemper, 1984).

Considerable research has been devoted to studying the syntax of Stage I speech, the earliest grammatical development of language. A review by Maratsos (1983) concluded that

> the most important result of the study of early speech is the now common agreement that semantic-cognitive categories, such as actionality, actorhood, location, recurrence, possession and nomination play central roles in the child's grammatical analyses, that is, the child analyzes aspects of the situational meanings of words to account for how they may be ordered with respect to each other. (p. 712)

Phrases such as *David ball* (possessor, possessed object) or *Mommy walk* (agent-action) or *big ball* (attribute-modified object) are all indicative of a young child's interest in the permanence and recurrence of objects. Contrary to Chomsky's claim that situational meaning is irrelevant to children's early language, recent research suggests that grammar is not independent of the semantic and pragmatic aspects of language. Children's earliest language use is now thought to involve the rudimentary ordering of words, and includes semantic analysis of word meaning as well as pragmatic and sequential analyses of how words and phrases are put together. Moreover, according to Maratsos (1983), early speech shows little uniformity among children. While only a small set of structural meanings and combinations can account for Stage I speech, as Braine (1963) suggested, they are not uniform across children. Individuals differ in the acquisition and use of grammatical structures, a finding counter to Chomsky's idea of innate programming of grammar for all humans.

General theories of syntax acquisition are no longer nativist. Chomsky's major impact was to remind us that children are not unbiased observers and processors. This highlighted the human predisposition for language. It is important to realize that Chomsky's theory competed with behaviorist accounts of language acquisition prominent in the 1950s. The behaviorists argued that language, like other aspects of learning, was the result of imitation and reinforcement. Chomsky helped to pinpoint the inadequacy of these theories of language acquisition by suggesting empirical tests that refuted behaviorism. As Chomsky claimed, the language environment of very young children is inadequate to support the behaviorists' claim that language is acquired through imitation.

Bloom, Hood, and Lightbown (1974) demonstrated that some children do not imitate language at all. Moreover, child caretakers often provide inadequate feedback to young children and often their comments are "degenerate, full of errors and provide little feedback about correctness of utterances" (Maratsos, 1983, p. 768). But Chomsky's notions of language development are inadequate as well. A major influence of the empirical studies prompted by Chomsky's theory was to point out, contrary to the theory, the importance of semantic and pragmatic analyses of language acquisition. Language development involves more than learning grammar and, as the research on children's early speech indicates, semantic and pragmatic aspects of language influence the development of grammar.

Semantics, the study of word meanings, has received considerable attention in the last 15 years. Unlike the work on syntax, studies of children's early word acquisition have been heavily influenced by Piaget. He maintained that general cognitive development influenced language development, and that the emergence of language in children is dependent on the ability to represent words mentally (Piaget & Inhelder, 1969). Piaget expected cognitive precursors to language use. American scholars in the early 1970s siezed the Piagetian position on language acquisition as an alternative to Chomsky, and used Piaget's ideas to guide studies of cognition and language acquisition.

Good evidence about the influence of cognitive development on language comes from studies of children's acquisition of early word meanings. These studies, mostly descriptive research about children's first words, have identified a small set of words that are consistent across children and cultures and that tend to be predominantly object related (Bloom, 1970, 1973; Brown, 1973). For instance, young children's first 50 to 200 words are dominated by objects ("dog," "cat," "chair"), situations ("pick up," "put"), and states ("want," "make," "go"; Clark, 1983). Nelson (1978) has demonstrated that when children begin to talk during the second year of life their first sentences are also object centered. Typically, they are about objects ("that ball"), actions and objects ("hit ball"), or the recurrence of objects ("more juice"). Interpreted within a Piagetian framework, object word use by toddlers is thought to correspond to the development of object permanence, the major cognitive developmental attainment of toddlers. Thus a young child's prior cognitive development is thought to influence use of object words.

Other evidence for the conceptual underpinnings of language use comes from studies about children's acquisition of color terms (e.g., red, blue). These words tend to be mastered as a set, suggesting that it is conceptual relatedness that influences linguistic acquisition (Bartlett, 1978). Children's nonlinguistic understanding of spatial relationships (in front of, behind, in, on, under) also influences the acquisition of location terms (Clark, 1977; Johnston & Slobin, 1979). Other studies about word acquisition have examined words in a particular domain (e.g., dimensional terms, "big," "small," "high," "low," and "wide"; Donaldson & Wales, 1970). Results consistently show that the order of acquisition for word meanings is from simple to more complex concepts (e.g., "big" and "small" precede "high" and "deep"; Donaldson & Wales, 1970).

In all these studies, children's early word use is used to *infer* prior cognitive developmental accomplishments. More recent studies have examined whether cognitive development precedes language development. Studies of statistical relationships between cognitive task performance and linguistic performance (e.g., Bates, 1979; Miller, Chapman, Branston, & Reichle, 1980) find that cognitive knowledge does not always precede word use. There is no consistent relationship between measures of cognitive performance and language performance across a variety of measures of cognitive skills and language use (Elliott, 1979).

Other evidence that contradicts Piaget comes from training studies of children's language performance. Rice (1980), for example, examined the relationship between children's categorical knowledge and understanding of color terms. Knowledge of color terms was measured prior to training in these terms. Although Rice found that prior categorical knowledge helped children learn color terms more easily, it was not a prerequisite for learning color words. Two children she studied mastered color terms easily without prior categorical knowledge.

There is little evidence that *specific* cognitive structures precede linguistic performance, although early descriptive studies of word use suggest that cognitive understanding influences the growth of early word meanings. The best tests related to this conclusion are the training studies because they require the investigator to specify precisely the cognitive skill expected to influence language performance. Here too, the evidence for a strong cognitive Piagetian position is weak. Although child language scholars do not subscribe to a strong cognitive position any longer, many do not want to discard Piaget completely. Karmiloff-Smith (1979) argues that Piaget has called attention to the active nature of children's mental abilities and that his theory does offer an interpretation of why early word acquisition is object based. However, as Rice and Kemper (1984) note, Piaget's account of language development has two major flaws: (1) The role of specific mental processes such as memory and attentional systems in language acquisition are not explained, and (2) social interaction and children's social knowledge are underestimated as influences on language development. The flaws found in the nativist position of Chomsky and the cognitive position of Piaget have led to a middleground position. Rice and Kemper's (1984)

> major conclusion is that there is no one, general pervasive relationship between children's nonlinguistic and linguistic knowledge. Instead, there is a network of tenuous links between localized areas of cognitive and linguistic knowledge. Furthermore, the direction of influence varies from one link to another; cognitive development may influence language acquisition, yet language may affect cognition. The types of links shift with the child's ontogenetic development. It depends on (1) the nature of the cognitive competencies involved; (2) the nature of the linguistic competencies involved; (3) the level of mental development involved; and (4) the nature of the tasks and evidence. (p. 113)

COMMUNICATING WITH OTHERS: COMMUNICATIVE COMPETENCE

Language development does not account for all of children's communicative accomplishments. In addition to learning how to construct linguistic messages (the topic of the last section), children learn how to use language and nonverbal skills to communicate with others in a variety of situations. Communicative competence is an umbrella term for studies of how children communicate with others. As Shatz (1983) notes, the ability to communicate is influenced by cognitive, linguistic, and social knowledge, and the term "communicative competence" encompasses the pragmatic aspects of how communication is accomplished. According to Saville-Troike (1982)

> communicative competence involves knowing not only the language code, but also what to say to whom, and how to say it appropriately in any given situation. It deals with the social and cultural knowledge speakers are presumed to have to enable them to use and interpret linguistic forms. (p. 22)

This section will review the relationships between development of language skills, communicative competence, growth of referential communicative skills, impact of care givers on development of communicative ability, and influence of world knowledge on communicative competence.

First, what is the relationship between language and communicative competence? Until recently, this question was framed in Piagetian terms, usually as a question about the influence of egocentrism on communicative ability. Piaget (1926) argued that children's communicative performance before age 7 or 8 was egocentric, that is, not adapted to the listener. With the publication of Flavell's (1963) exposition of Piaget's theory, substantial research on egocentric speech began. Contradictory findings quickly accumulated. Many of the early studies supporting Piaget's position involved anecdotal descriptions of unadapted speech. In addition, referential communication tasks that involve self versus other encoding techniques were used to test for aggregate differences in group performance rather than individual differences in the production of messages (e.g., Flavell, Botkin, Fry, Wright, & Jarvis, 1968). Correlational studies compared performance on measures of egocentrism and listener-adapted tasks. Typically, the correlations were low (about .30 according to Dickson, 1982). More important, observational studies of children's conversations by Maratsos (1973) and Shatz and Gelman (1973) were able to provide evidence that, contrary to Piaget, children as young as 3 or 4 *could* spontaneously adapt their speech to the age of the listener. In 1975, Glucksburg, Krauss, & Higgins had concluded that egocentrism was too broad a concept. By 1979, Asher argued that "communication effectiveness involves a number of separate skills whose relevance to performance varies as a function of the nature of the listener and the nature of the task" (p. 194). And in 1981 Shantz concluded that role-taking played only a minor role in referential communication.

Dickson (1982), after reviewing 100 studies of referential communication, did conclude, however, that there was some evidence that children's abilities to give directions (referential tasks) improved as children grew older. The more important question is how age *interacts* with other variables in communicative performance tasks. Dickson suggested that age should be tightly controlled in correlations with communicative performance or as a covariate in analyses using performance measures as a dependent variable.

What other factors affect referential communicative performance? Although a few studies report sex differences in referential communicative performance, Dickson (1982) argues that there are fewer sex differences across studies than would be expected by chance. There are, however, consistent social class differences in referential communicative tasks; middle-class, well-educated children and college students have a different style of encoding compared to lower-class peers. Middle-class youths use more part-descriptive and holistic descriptions compared to lower-class children, who use more inferential descriptions

(Dickson, 1974; Heider, 1971; Johnston & Singleton, 1977). There are no similar social class differences in communication accuracy studies (Dickson, 1982).

Clearly research on communicative competence has moved away from strict Piagetian ideas about the role of cognitive abilities in communicative performance. Research attention is focused on development of conversational skills in young children, the growth of knowledge about people and events that influence conversational output, and environmental influences on development of communicative skills. In these areas, the influence of Dell Hymes (1974), Vygotsky (1962), and Mead (1930) is clear. These theorists have presented strong arguments for the importance of social environment.

Evidence is accumulating that learning of conversational skills begins at birth. For instance, observational investigations of parent-infant interactions show that children, even before they can talk, are treated as communicative partners by parents. Bateson (1975) observed alternating patterns in infant-mother interaction (indicative of early proto-conversations) with a 2- to 4-month old infant. Turn-taking in conversations has also been observed in the patterned interactions of 9- to 18-month old children (Bates, 1976). The classic study in this area (Bloom, Rocissano, & Hood, 1976) examined children's utterances preceding adult speech. They found 18-month-old children at the two-word stage (MLU Stage I) who demonstrated turn-taking to adult utterances and who responded more frequently to questions than nonquestions in the conversations. The children's speech was not, however, contingent on the topic of the preceding adult utterance.

Kaye and Charney (1980) showed that mothers attempted to maintain conversations with 2-year-olds beyond two turns by using turnabouts. This occurs when the mother makes another request of the child to respond again after the child's initial response and then the mother expands on that response. Even children as young as two can respond to the nonspecific request of "What?" (Wilcox & Webster, 1980), and by age 3 children can respond to nonspecific requests and produce requests for more clarification or more information (Revelle, Karabenick, & Wellman, 1981). By age 4, children are accomplished at tailoring specific requests to clarify initial questions (Revelle et al., 1981). Children's use of communicative strategies to maintain conversations also increases between 3 and 5 years of age. These strategies include initiating and maintaining conversational topics, pursuing a line of discussion, and using politeness to achieve goals (see Haslett, 1984).

Thus evidence is accumulating that during the first few years (from birth to age 2) children acquire important social understanding about communication. They learn pragmatics of conversations (such as turn-taking and question asking) and they acquire important information about people and events. Piaget's notion of nonsocially directed egocentric talk is no longer a viable account of conversations, even for 2-year-olds. This does not mean, however, that very young children are competent communicators by adult standards. There is certainly development of communicative skills into the grade school years and beyond. Children's syntactic, semantic, and pragmatic knowledge about communication continues to expand in school. For instance, preschoolers show little understanding of words supporting logical inference such as *even* and *only* (Johnson & Maratsos, 1977). They also lack an understanding of sarcasm and of language that requires subtle interpretation (Shatz, 1983). Younger elementary school children have less well-organized knowledge, which impedes performance on communicative tasks (Pratt, Scribner, & Cole, 1977). Moreover, children's ability to think about what they are saying (meta-communicative skills) improves as children grow older (Flavell, 1977). Delia and O'Keefe (1979) have demonstrated that children in middle childhood (ages 5 to 12) can adapt messages to a listener's needs. This is a function of the complexity of children's interpersonal constructs (as indicated by differentiated and abstract constructs) for describing other people and communicative strategies.

In addition to conversational skills, preschool children develop an important understanding of people, events, and social relationships, all of which influence linguistic and conversational abilities. For instance, young children (ages 3 to 4) shift their communicative style when addressing younger as opposed to older children (Shatz & Gelman, 1973). Children can also vary directives according to the age, familiarity, or dominance of the listener (Ervin-Tripp, 1977). Shields (1978) and Bretherton, McNew, & Beeghly-Smith (1981) have demonstrated that children's language by age 2 shows an implicit understanding of "mind" and knowledge that people have perceptions, intentions, feelings, and experiences. These inferences are based on observations of nursery school children's interchanges with peers during school play. All of these studies indicate that even very young children have knowledge about people.

During the preschool years, children also acquire social knowledge about events and settings. Nelson (1978) demonstrated that preschool children have at least a general understanding of temporally organized event sequences or "scripts." She asked children aged 3 to 8 "to tell what happens when . . . " and found that even 3-year-olds were able to recite a reasonable sequence of events for such events as eating and shopping.

All of these findings suggest that "children's communicative skills develop as a function of growing knowledge in a variety of cognitive, social and linguistic domains, and as the child becomes better able to organize and utilize knowledge" (Shatz, 1983, p. 878). Researchers need to demonstrate, however, that conclusions about children's communicative ability are based on reasonable inferences about children's performance in real-world communicative tasks that the child clearly understands.

COMMUNICATING WITH THE MEDIA

This section considers how children communicate with media. In some ways, the preposition "with" is disconcerting. Popular images of children's use of media are of a "passive" viewer. On the other hand, much of the past 15 years of research on how children make sense of television demonstrates that viewing *actively* engages children. Moreover, the types of media and specific program choices within each medium are indicative and expressive aspects of a child's personality and life style. In this section we will consider children's use of mass media, their ability to process and make sense of messages, and social learning that results from media use. Children's active choice of media as well as their active processing of media content will be highlighted. However, we will also suggest that structural characteristics of messages and the family environment influence children's responses and the range of media children are involved with at different ages.

The medium children first use is television. Most reviews conclude that between 2 and 4 years of age children become regular users of television (e.g., Roberts & Bachen, 1982); however, some studies suggest that for some children television use begins much earlier, even during infancy. For instance, Hollenbeck and Slaby (1979) found evidence of babies as young as 6 to 12 months visually and verbally responding to television for an average of 1 to 2 hours a day. Lemish (1986) reported that babies 1 and 2 years old regularly watched *Sesame Street* at full attention for as long as 30-40 minutes at a time. There was also considerable complexity in infants' interactions with *Sesame Street*.

Although babies do see television, use increases most dramatically during the preschool years, dipping slightly when school begins (age 5 to 6) and then rising again up to early adolescence and finally decreasing during teenage years. Most estimates of the average time children spend with television are based on Nielsen data. Estimates for 1985 indicate the television set is on 7 hours a day in the average American household. But this average clearly overestimates the amount of time children spend *watching* television. Moreover, there is growing evidence of variation in television use across different family types. Medrich, Roizin, and Buckley (1981) reported that more than 35% of a sample of California families were classified as "constant television households" because they reported having the television set turned on most of the afternoon, during dinner, and most of the evening. These families were structurally different from the non-constant television households, showing a higher incidence of single parents, less parental education, and lower family income.

There are other sources of variation in media use among children. Perhaps the best recent evidence is from studies conducted by the Newspaper Advertising Bureau in the late 1970s on how children and families use newspapers and other mass media. In a national sample of 817 households with children ages 6 to 17, there were striking differences in children's use of media depending on age and family type. For instance, just as children's use of television increases during grade school so too does use of newspapers. One-third of 6- to 8-year-olds reported "ever" reading a newspaper, compared to 61% of 9- to 11-year-olds, three-quarters of the 12- to 14-year-olds, and more than four-fifths of the 15- to 17-year-olds. Moreover, the same children who read newspapers regularly are most likely to read books and magazines. Of 6- to 8-year-olds who read newspapers 21% reported reading other material "every day," and among 15- to 17-year-olds 44% of those who read newspapers report reading other materials "every day."

The type and amount of reading is strongly related to family background. Children whose parents regularly read a newspaper are more likely to be readers themselves. For example, 57% of 13- to 14-year-olds whose parents both read a newspaper are regular readers of one, compared to 21% of children whose parents are not regular newspaper readers. Children from poorer, nonwhite, rural, and single-parent homes are also less likely to be readers of newspapers as well as other magazines and books. For instance, as many as one-half of the children in lower status families rarely, if ever, see their mother or father reading a book.

Other media—often forgotten by researchers—are receiving increased attention. They include movies, radio, records, and tapes. The Newspaper Advertising Bureau (1980) study found that although only one-third of 6- to 8-year-olds reported listening to the radio "yesterday" or playing records "yesterday," the proportion increased substantially among teenagers. Nine in ten 15- to 17-year-olds reported listening to the radio and 60% reported playing records. Similarly, children's movie attendance increases substantially from age 6 through the teen years (22% of 6- to 8-year-olds attended movies weekly compared to 48% of 15- to 17-year-olds). Among teenagers it is the children from affluent families who attend most frequently—twice or more per month. In a recent review of research on children's audio use (records, tapes, and radio), Christenson, De Benedittis, and Lindlof (1985) argued that audio media play an important role in children's lives. This is true even for grade school children. For example, in a 1984 study, 42% of fourth- and fifth-graders claimed they listened to the radio "most every day," and 68% had a record player in their room. In the Newspaper Advertising Bureau study (1980) about one-third of children aged 6 to 11 reported "a lot" of free time devoted to records and tapes. Clearly audio use is an important and often forgotten element in children's media environments.

One additional element is children's use of new media, particularly new technologies such as computers, video games, and videocassettes. These new technologies are quickly diffusing. For instance, between 1981 and 1984 the number of computers available in American schools rose from 33,000 to 631,000 (Chen & Paisley, 1985). How these technologies alter children's media use patterns is currently under investigation. As Chen and Paisley's most recent review suggests, microcomputers in particular are quickly being adopted by the well-educated and information-rich homes where children are already immersed in media. How these new media technologies alter other media use, or affect social learning and cognitive processes, are current subjects of research.

Children's Processing of Media

Before reviewing literature about processing and content effects of media, it is important to note the differences between research on language and communicative competence and research on children and media. One of the important goals of this review is to suggest the usefulness of combining these areas; however, it is more difficult to fit this last category in with the previous two than it is to demonstrate similarities between language development and communicative abilities. Similarities, although seldom acknowledged in the media literature, do exist. First, recent research has begun to examine the relationship between language on television and development of language more generally. Second, there has been a shift away from Piagetian studies of media and cognitive development. Current research examines processing concepts, such as attention and memory, and processing efficiencies, such as the use of scripts to understand television narrative and to categorize people and objects. There is also a realization that younger children understand more about television than was previously thought and that competencies related to understanding are as much based on experience and knowledge as on the limitations of developmental stages. Finally, there is new interest in the social context of television viewing as a supplement to studies of *intrapersonal* processing.

Theory in the media literature is usually different from previously reviewed research about language and competence. Theory that guides media research about children is largely *borrowed* from developmental, social, and cognitive psychology. Consequently, theories that explain children's development with respect to diverse stimuli are matched with a few particular, although pervasive, activities—namely, processing media. This has at times put considerable distance between the theories

and the activities they explain. And this distance has an important implication for research. It has often meant that theory is a provocative starting point for considering research questions rather than a formal system
of explanation and prediction. Unfortunately, this also means that many
different theories are indistinguishable. Historically, shifts from social
learning to developmental explanations have been noted (Wartella &
Reeves, 1985), but it has always been true that children respond differently to media as they grow older. Consequently, many early reviews of
this literature are still appropriate because they acknowledged considerable age differences (e.g., Roberts, 1973). Even the classic studies of
media proposed and supported hypotheses about age differences (Charters, 1933; Schramm, Lyle, & Parker, 1961). The *mechanisms* deemed
responsible for the differences—experiences versus cognitive abilities
versus social interactions—have changed, but perhaps with fewer implications for this literature than we imagine, especially considering that
public concern and governmental policy have been the driving forces
behind research agendas.

This section reviews current research on media and children in two
broad categories: message processing and effects of message content.
Most conceptions of research about children and media center on effects
of content—violence, advertising, news, sexual themes, or educational
material. The topics most often associated with the area are effects of
prime time violence or of Saturday morning sugared cereal commercials.
Although popular descriptions of research still reflect a bias toward message content, the research does not. Clearly more citations are generated about children's *processing* of media than for all studies of content
effects. Considerations of media processing are about issues such as
message structure, mental representation of symbols, processing of narratives, attention, comprehension, and understanding. It is important to
note that the theory behind these efforts does not focus on message
content. Many different categories of content are used interchangeably
(e.g., entertainment, violence, advertisements, and children's television
programs such as *Sesame Street*); the results are expected to generalize
across genre and content, but are specific to a single medium, usually
television.

One of the most prominent research areas about processing of television looks at message structure and the relation of structure to attention,
comprehension, and understanding. There has been a corresponding
emphasis on effects of message structure with adults (often based on the
same theories and methods), owing in large part to a recognition that it is
the forms of television that are unique, not the content. The forms of
television include visual features (spatial frequency, picture complexity,
animation), camera movement (pans and zooms), editing techniques
(cuts and pacing), and features of the audio and language (loudness,

sound/silence, sentence complexity). An emphasis on form has high-lighted different dependent variables, notably attention and comprehension. Also, the research has recognized that these criteria not only vary between children but also *within* a child *over time.*

One of the most studied concepts has been attention, usually defined as the time when children's eyes are focused on the television screen as opposed to other distractions (e.g., toys, mother). Children's attention to television changes in relation to identifiable message attributes. Attention does not fluctuate randomly over the course of viewing. However, a second major result is that attention comes and goes in regular cycles, at least in part independent of program attributes. This means that program features can cause attention to commence (or terminate) but that once initiated, it is increasingly likely that attention will be maintained. Anderson and Lorch (1983) labeled this "attentional inertia."

Children's attention to television varies in relation to program features and characteristics of children. Using children's programs such as *Sesame Street* and *Mister Rogers' Neighborhood,* Anderson and colleagues (Alwitt, Anderson, Lorch, & Levin, 1980; Anderson, 1983) have shown that attention is initiated and maintained by features such as movement, certain voices (women and other children), changes of scene, applause, laughing, and sound effects. Krull and Husson (1979) reported similar findings with features such as set and scene complexity and the visual presence of speakers.

The viewer characteristic most studied is age. Time devoted to the screen changes from the sporadic glances of 6-month-old infants (Hollenbeck & Slaby, 1979) to the majority (55%) of a viewing session for 5-year-olds. The greatest increases occur between ages 2 and 3 (Anderson, 1983). Older children look at the screen longer, once attracted, and they look more frequently (Anderson & Levin, 1976; Anderson, Alwitt, Lorch, & Levin, 1979). A year-long study of home observations of viewing in 16 families confirmed these results, although the observations suggested that full attention to television occurs at even an earlier age (Lemish, 1986). Children in the 18- to 24-month range watched *Sesame Street* at nearly full attention for as long as 30-40 minutes.

Various "codes" of American television have been analyzed with respect to children's attention. Huston and Wright (1983) distinguish between forms that are perceptually salient and those that are reflective. Perceptually salient forms elicit children's attention. They usually involve a quick change or a visual or auditory surprise (Huston & Wright, 1983). Reflective forms encourage repetition and elaboration of content and usually appear as dialogue, singing, and moderate action levels. Huston and Wright argue that perceptually salient codes are markers, signaling children that a certain type of content will follow

(Huston & Wright, 1983). In contrast, reflective codes maintain (rather than elicit) attention and aid in rehearsal, reflection, and comprehension (Rice, Huston, & Wright, 1982). Interpretation of these codes changes with age as children become more adept at decoding television codes that help them allocate attention to program characteristics that increase comprehension.

The attention research seems primarily motivated by an interest in determining what children comprehend and remember from television. The two families of theory guiding this research appear quite different, but likely form two complementary parts of a larger synthesis. One view holds that children *react* to television cues reflexively and that understanding proceeds rotely once attention has been initiated with a visual or auditory surprise. Attention is merely a necessary condition for learning, not a guide (Bandura, 1977). Singer and Singer (1983), for example, claim that television features elicit an orienting response in children and that many programs (e.g., *Sesame Street*) continually exploit this response by designing formats that favor constant change. They further claim that constant orienting is detrimental to learning and understanding. Other studies are also concerned with reactions to television and acknowledge that television is responsible for constant orientation, but they find that performance is not jeopardized; the orientations may directly facilitate learning of material that immediately follows visual surprises (Zillmann, 1982; Zillmann & Bryant, 1981). Anderson also finds that such orientations facilitate learning from television, but because children *actively* select content that is comprehensible (Anderson & Lorch, 1983). This reverses the causal interpretation, suggesting that a desire to *comprehend* guides attention. Anderson's work, as well as research by Huston and Wright, Krull, and others, constitutes a second family of theories concerned more with how children make sense of television than with how television elicits reactions.

In addition to the relationship of attention to comprehension, other recent studies have continued to look at two other features of comprehension: retention and inference making. Age changes in retention are quite apparent. Second-graders can remember significantly less information central to a television plot than can fifth- or eighth-graders (Collins, Wellman, Keniston, & Westby, 1978). Further, retention is not affected by a relationship between scenes. Younger children remember as much information when scenes are jumbled as when they are presented in a logical order.

Inferences refer to the information children assign to television that goes beyond what is available on the screen. By testing children's recognition memory for explicit information versus information that is merely suggested, Collins and associates find that children improve with age in their ability to make inferences about essential program features, although they correctly answer a greater proportion of explicit than implicit questions (Collins et al., 1978). Younger children (second-graders) are less likely to make an inference than older six-graders, even though they are aware of the explicit information from which an inference could be made (Collins et al., 1978). Older children are also more likely to attempt implicit links between different scenes, indicating advancement to more abstract logical abilities as suggested by Piaget. Similar to the language literature, however, it could be that these advancements are attributable to increased *experience* and *familiarity* with television plots.

Retention of information in television stories has also been examined by Collins (1983). Age changes similar to those for inferences are apparent. Younger children can remember significantly less information central to a television plot than can fifth- and eighth-graders (Collins et al., 1978).

Another significant research program has suggested that features of television represent a unique "symbol system" that serves as the basis for learning and comprehension (Salomon, 1979). Similar to McLuhan's claim, Salomon suggests that even if the medium is not *the* message, it is certainly influential. Symbols themselves can have meaning; and when combined with novel content, they can yield different meanings. Symbol systems require different amounts of mental energy to process and represent internally. The types of symbols present in a particular medium (e.g., words rather than pictures) cultivate a style of information processing dependent primarily on the effort required to produce internal representations of content. The most obvious example is that pictures (from television or film) are easier to represent than written words because words require translation into a visual code before the information is stored for later use.

Salomon has used the concept of "amount of invested mental effort" (AIME) to study children's comprehension of media information. For example, greater amounts of AIME (for a viewer or reader) result in greater comprehension (Salomon, 1981). The amount of AIME can be dependent on children's expectations about a medium or particular content. Comprehension is increased when children *expect* that television messages will be difficult to process (Salomon & Leigh, 1984), when viewing departs from expectations, or when children are instructed to learn (Salomon, 1983). Further, there may be medium-specific expectations that influence AIME. Television may signal that little effort is required whereas reading suggests from the outset that processing will be difficult.

In a recent review of "metacognition," Desmond (1985) discussed other organizing concepts that help children make sense of television by guiding their thinking. Many studies of children's processing of television employ versions of the concept of schemata. "Schemata" generally refers to hypothetical cognitive structures that represent associations among units of information (Cohen, 1981). Research on media and children has used this concept and another similar concept—scripts, special types of schema useful for representing social action as a sequence of events (Reeves, Chaffee, & Tims, 1982). Children's processing of television narratives has particularly benefited from conceptualizing stories as scripts. Collins and Wellman (1982) showed that the information children retain from television is most likely to conform to stereotyped actions and events, cued by isolated and familiar occurrences. Also, when asked to predict actions most likely to happen next, children base predictions on a generalized notion of common event sequences on television. Both of these results were more likely for younger than older children (second-graders as opposed to fifth- and eighth-graders). Older children were more able to respond on the basis of unique cues in a story rather than depend on stereotyped scripts.

Similar to research with adults, research on children's use of schemata in processing television predicts the type of information children retain. Meadowcroft and Reeves (1985) measured children's level of schema development (high or low) and experimentally manipulated exposure to a story that was either structured according to a schema or randomly sequenced. The development of story schema (highly correlated with age among the sample of 5- to 8-year-olds) was related to reduced processing effort (as measured by a secondary task reaction time method) and to increased memory for central story content. Other similar treatments of schema concepts include comprehension schema (Anderson, Lorch, Field, & Sanders, 1981), guided memory for television plots (Huston & Wright, 1983), stereotypes used in person perception (Reeves & Garramone, 1983), use of schema to remember story narratives (Baker & Stein, 1981), and the use of television schemas to construct stories about hypothetical events (Watkins, Cojuc, Mills, Kwiatek, & Tan, 1982).

An area of recent media research similar (at least topically) to the language literature examines speech on television. Attempts have been made to describe television language and to examine its impact on the development of vocabulary, written communication, and school achievement. Even though a great deal of attention is placed on visual (as opposed to linguistic) symbols on television, children attend to television in toto (Rice & Wartella, 1981). For the child viewer, content and form are intertwined and are not consciously processed as separate features. Although not a unique code for television, language varies considerably in television presentations. Rice (1984) has identified three different "packages" of language in children's programs: (1) programs with little language but salient visual forms (e.g., *Road Runner* cartoon series); (2) those with moderate levels of dialogue and references to new words (e.g.,

Mister Rogers' Neighborhood); and (3) programs with few surprising production techniques but considerable dialogue and other features such as grammatically incomplete sentences or references to people or events that are not immediately present (e.g., *Gilligan's Island*).

Rice has suggested that language interacts with other codes on television (particularly visual features) to influence attention and comprehension. And television producers' use of language may even parallel the adjustments that adults make when speaking, to maximize children's comprehension. Similar to the visual code, children must make sense of language on television by applying appropriate knowledge that is necessary for interpretation. However, unlike the medium-specific visual code, which must be learned from direct experience with television, generic codes like language are part of the child's other communicative experiences. Consequently, the development of knowledge about television language is more likely dependent on learning *outside* of the television context. As language develops, children can better interpret television's language and television can aid in subsequent language learning.

The exact manner in which television influences language development (as well as parallel concerns about reading and general school achievement) has been discussed since the first major studies of television's introduction (Himmelweit, Oppenheim, & Vince, 1958; Schramm, Lyle, & Parker, 1961). Unfortunately, as Hornik (1981) notes, few studies have gone beyond bivariate correlational analyses of television exposure and language development or school achievement. However, one experimental study demonstrates that 3- to 5-year-old children can learn novel words by viewing television (Rice & Woodsmall, 1986). More important, most of the available literature does not rely heavily on theories of language development but rather on more simple notions of media effects. One recent program of research has attempted to remedy earlier problems, although few relationships have emerged to date (Roberts, Bachen, Hornby, & Hernandez-Ramos, 1984). When appropriate controls are considered in the relationship between amount of viewing time and reading ability, there are no significant correlations at a single time point or lagged across several years.

One of the deficits noted about the language research was that studies were guided mostly by ideas about cognitive development to the exclusion of important social and contextual factors that could influence communicative abilities. In past media research, there have been suggestions that the interpersonal context of viewing, usually the presence of parents or adults, is an important aid to learning from television (e.g., Ball & Bogatz, 1970). A recent laboratory study (Collins, 1981) has demonstrated a mechanism at least partially responsible for increased comprehension: Adult coviewers are able to focus children's attention on implicit relationships between scenes in a sequence or on scenes central to a story.

Observational techniques have been particularly useful for showing that television is often understood through interpersonal interactions with siblings and parents. Messaris and Kerr (1983) noted, however, that global measures of parental viewing are often not useful in predicting children's viewing. Rather, it is in specific, even microscopic, instances of viewing that context matters. A recent study by Lemish and Rice (1984) demonstrated language effects of specific interventions by parents. These results are also applicable to television and language; however, the important component of interpersonal contact *during* viewing stresses social context. They observed babies between 6 months and 2 and one-half years old. Four categories of children's verbalizations while watching television were observed, the last two of which involve interaction with parents: (1) designating objects, characters, and animals on the screen by pointing or identifying names; (2) actual use of language to describe content; (3) questions to mothers and fathers (and their responses) about the content; and (4) repetition of television dialogue or of parents' comments about the content. Of special interest were situations where television content was used by parents to initiate and elaborate other verbal interactions. Lemish and Rice (1984) refer to television as a "pictorial story book," where children learn to talk, label, repeat, and elaborate action on the screen.

Other studies of preschool and elementary school children also demonstrate the importance of parental interaction during viewing. Messaris and Sarett (1981) noted that parents frequently talk to children about interpretations of television. Reid (1979) has observed child-parent discussions about television advertising and found considerable instruction about the purposes of advertising and how to evaluate advertising claims critically. While this study observed only nine children (although extensively), the results were consistent with many other areas of research; children understand television better (and at an earlier age) than descriptions derived from interviews outside the viewing situation suggest.

Children do not talk with parents only, of course. Alexander, Ryan, & Munoz (1984) observed sibling pairs in their homes and found that ongoing interactions while watching television were important for younger children's learning. Although talk related specifically to the screen represented less than 40% of sibling discussions, there were instructive exchanges. Older brothers and sisters helped identify characters and events. Children also discussed how things are produced on television, predicted what would happen, and discussed what was real and not. An important conclusion from these processing studies is that knowledge about television is not just a result of general cognitive development; it is also a function of growth in real-world knowledge, viewing experience, and social context.

Effects of Specific Content

The processing studies are clearly interested in how children make sense of the media environment and, therefore, they are similar to research on language and competency. The studies about effects of specific content, however, ask more about what changes than about how and why. With notable exceptions, studies in these areas suggest a more passive relationship between children and media, as media, by their sheer presence, alter children's behavior and ideas about the world. These efforts, while still the major identifying tags for the field, are consequently somewhat less related to other studies in this review. This is perhaps most true for the areas tied directly to specific content (violence and advertising) and somewhat less true for content effects in the areas of social reality and social roles.

The violence area has been most visible recently because of continued industry and scientific controversy over how to interpret the significance of findings about the relationship between viewing and aggression (ABC Social Research Unit, 1983; Cook, Kendziersky, & Thomas, 1983; Freedman, 1984; Milavsky, Kessler, Stipp, & Rubens, 1982; Walsh, 1983). While there are significant new citations available about media violence (e.g., Milavsky et al., 1982), many of the studies are procedurally similar to past efforts, even if they can boast of more substantial designs. Several current reviews are available, but most concentrate more on tallying votes about whether effects exist than on attempts to explain how and why the effects occur (e.g., Huesmann, 1982; Singer & Singer, 1983). Also, the reviews have moved the age range of interest slightly higher, from a predominant concern with children to an interest that often begins with early adolescence.

There have, however, been continued attempts to theorize about this specific effect. Some relate new and previous results to the processing of other media content. The theoretical area most similar to past work is social learning theory, the focus of two recent reviews about the learning of aggression from television (Pearl, 1982; Tan, 1986). Even though this perspective, which still depends mostly on the work of Bandura, guided some of the first studies about violence (many of them more than 20 years ago), Tan argues that it is still the most comprehensive explanation available. He says that it explains not only modeling of televised violence but also why the relationship between viewing and aggression, although positive and causal, is in most cases small. It is interesting to note that current thinking about the processing of media in general has reverted (or come full circle?) to propositions consistent with this theory. Notably, this includes emphasis on experience rather than limited cognitive abilities as a determinant of how children make sense of media.

Two traditional explanations for violence effects are mostly absent from current research (within the last 5 years) although for different reasons. Studies that propose catharsis explanations are gone, most likely because the theory was wrong (Huesmann, 1982). Also, studies that propose an intervening process of arousal are less frequent in the violence literature, although there are several discussions of arousal in effects of pornography on adults (Malamuth & Billings, 1986), and of the use of television for excitement and the transfer of excitation after viewing (Zillman, 1982). While all of these efforts concentrate on autonomic arousal, there have been some efforts to study cortical arousal with children in response to negative (and usually violent) television programs. Davidson (1984) has shown, for example, hemisphere asymmetry in the brain for processing of emotional television content such that negative material produces greater cortical arousal in the right hemisphere. This may be linked to automatic reactions that could promote aggressive responses (Reeves & Lange, 1986).

There are also important retrospective examinations of the violence literature that benefit from current work in cognitive psychology and information processing. These theories are not as specific about developmental patterns (other than the suggestion that processing somehow works better for older children) but they do begin to acknowledge the importance of the experiences and memories activated by messages. In a recent review, Berkowitz and Rogers (1986) explicitly replace past explanations of media effects based on principles of conditioning with concepts of mental association, principally priming. According to theories of priming, when a thought is activated, related thoughts are brought into awareness based on "associative pathways." This increases the probability that related thoughts will come to mind again, thus priming their occurrence. The authors argue that a priming explanation is particularly relevant to effects of violence that are not lasting but occur for relatively brief periods. Violent television primes aggressive thoughts, but the associations decay if they are not periodically reinforced.

The other traditional content area of interest, advertising, has experienced a parallel decline in the number of studies devoted to it. This is perhaps attributable (as with the violence research) to a decline in regulatory interest (Wartella & Reeves, 1985). Nevertheless, there are a few studies that both continue past directions and bring this area more in line with other research emphasizing processing. Most studies have extended and confirmed the intentional influence of advertising, almost exclusively television commercials, on children's brand awareness, product information and preference, requests for purchase, and amount of consumption (Atkin, 1982). Fewer have examined other side effects such as parent-child conflict over purchases, aggressive behavior associated with product disappointment, learning about social roles from commercials, or learning about life-style orientations. Few studies have gone beyond confirming associations between exposure and various cognitive, affective, and behavioral outcomes. Some consistencies with other areas, however, can be seen. The previously reviewed research by Reid (1979), for example, exemplifies a trend toward earlier recognition of processing skills related to advertising.

A final research area that deals with specific content of media is the study of social reality—occupations, gender roles, person perception, and perceptions of realism. The most prominent of these areas, studies of social reality conducted by Gerbner and colleagues, suggest that it is television's content rather than its forms that is unique. This research argues that the extent to which television distorts social reality (particularly in the presentation of violence but also with other content) leads viewers to have distorted beliefs about the real world that favor the lessons of television (Gerbner, Gross, Signorielli, Morgan, & Jackson-Beeck, 1979). The applicability of the results to child audiences, however, has perhaps been overstated. A majority of the 48 publications about social reality reviewed by Hawkins and Pingree (1982) use adult samples, and those that sample school children usually begin with sixth or seventh grade. Nevertheless, there are studies with elementary aged children as young as 7 and 8. These studies have found positive but small relationships between the amount of viewing and prevalence of violence and interpersonal mistrust (Gerbner et al., 1979; Hawkins & Pingree, 1982). As Hawkins and Pingree note in their review, there is little explanation offered for how these effects occur. And the intervening mechanisms that have been proposed—for example, mainstreaming and resonance—seem applicable more to established life experiences relevant to adult viewers.

There are other similar areas of research that in spite of theoretical similarity are rarely reviewed with studies of social reality. One area is social roles—those of family, gender, race, occupations, and age (Greenberg, 1982). Much of the research, however, is directed at describing content; and those studies that do examine effects are often limited to documenting associations between viewing and perceptions of roles (e.g., Abel, Fontes, Greenberg, & Atkin, 1980—occupational roles; Buerkel-Rothfuss, Greenberg, & Atkin, 1981—family roles; Greenberg & Atkin, 1978—race roles; Korzenny & Neuendorf, 1980—age roles; and Miller & Reeves, 1976—gender roles).

In another similar area, children's perception of television characters, there are similar associational studies that show that amount of viewing is correlated with the attributes that children use to describe others and the variation in how the attributes are applied (Reeves & Garramone, 1982). Another study attempted to explain the processing mechanisms related to television's influence on children's descriptions of other people (Reeves & Garramone, 1983). Similar to the suggestions of Berkowitz and Rogers (1986), elementary school children were either "primed" with representative examples of television people or were shown no television. They were then asked to describe a new person in their school. Those who had watched television were more likely than the control group to use attributes associated with television (humor and physical attractiveness) to describe the new person.

CONCLUSION

How do we summarize these disparate areas of research on children and communication? As suggested in the beginning, several tightly drawn and distinct research areas about children's communicative activities characterize this literature. Research has proceeded at different levels of analysis, with separate agendas for research and with relatively little interaction between areas. Consequently, studies of children's language development, for example, have only recently been applied (albeit by analogy) to studies of how children make sense of television (e.g., Lemish & Rice, 1984).

More important, little theoretical or research attention has been devoted to issues of how one level of analysis imposes constraints on other levels. For instance, how might language development influence or constrain children's learning from television? How might children's media behavior constrain interpersonal communicative activity? Indeed, is there any reason to expect *in all cases* that levels must be related? Certainly scholars have not organized studies to answer these questions. By and large *different* researchers, embedded in different research traditions, have been conducting studies of children communicating at separate levels of analysis. Moreover, the preoccupations of research traditions are manifested in different theoretical movements and different methodological commitments. Research methods, although seldom acknowledged as determinants of research results, have had an important role in shaping literatures. For example, descriptive studies of young children's word use characterize the early 1970s research on the development of children's word meaning, whereas experimental methods tend to be employed to study children's abilities to comprehend television narratives.

Beginning in the 1960s, researchers at *each* level were influenced by grand-scale theories of child development, most notably those of Piaget. This was true regardless of whether there was significant interaction between the areas. At each level, research was preoccupied with the question of how overall *cognitive* development and cognitive abilities influenced communicative behavior. To this extent, Piaget's theory influenced research at all levels of analysis. This gave rise to a variety of studies of age differences in communicative activities and a concentration on questions about the cognitive basis of communication.

Although the specific research questions and studies prompted by Piaget's theory differ at each level of analysis, there are similarities in the direction of research at each level that have followed from this common core. First, theoretical developments are moving away from grand descriptions of how children's cognitive abilities influence their communicative ability. More attention is now given to the *specific* cognitive skills that interact with specific communicative skills such as the development of word meaning, grammar, knowledge of people, conversational ability, or interpretation of television narrative. Across these three research domains, therefore, there is movement toward specifying the mental activities involved in communicating. This places less reliance on global theories of cognitive development and more on accounts of how certain communicative acts are performed.

Second, there are more mechanisms invoked to account for communicative development. Rather than viewing communicative outcomes as a result of underlying cognitive abilities, communicative development is seen as the result of cognitive-environmental interaction. Additionally, there is attention to how communicative abilities are influenced by the physical development of children, although we have not highlighted this literature.

Third, these changes have resulted in greater attention to methodologies that better uncover children's true communicative abilities. This has led to use of multiple methods to assess children's communicative performance with the result that we now believe children have greater competence at younger ages than past methods suggested.

In spite of similarities in conclusions about different areas of research on children and communication, it is difficult to end this review with an enthusiastic prescription that future research consider each area *within* a particular study. There are benefits in reviewing areas together to determine common problems in theory and methods, but it is not necessary that each effort to study children and communication simultaneously consider language, competence, peers, family, and media—or each of these at all levels of analysis. Overall, this could lessen the chances of answering questions about the specific processes associated with various communicative activities. Dependence on the word "children" as an organizing term for reviews, however, remains viable primarily because it is a human interest in the *people* at this stage of life that motivates scientific inquiry.

REFERENCES

ABC Social Research Unit. (1983). *A research perspective on television and violence.* New York: American Broadcasting Companies, Inc.

Abel, J., Fontes, B., Greenberg, B., & Atkin, C. (1980). *The impact of television on children's occupational role learning.* Unpublished report, Michigan State University, East Lansing.

Alexander, A., Ryan, M. S., & Munoz, P. (1984). Creating the learning context: Investigations on the interaction of siblings during television viewing. *Critical Studies in Mass Communication, 1,* 345-364.

Alwitt, L. F., Anderson, D. R., Lorch, E. P., & Levin, S. R. (1980). Preschool children's visual attention to attributes of television. *Human Communication Research, 7,* 52-67.

Anderson, J. A. (1983). Television literacy and the critical viewer. In J. Bryant & D. R. Anderson (Eds.), *Children's understanding of television: Research on attention and comprehension.* New York: Academic Press.

Anderson, D. R., Alwitt, L. F., Lorch, E. P., & Levin, S. R. (1979). Watching children watch television. In G. Hale & M. Lewis (Eds.), *Attention and cognitive development.* New York: Plenum.

Anderson, D., & Levin, S. R. (1976). Young children's attention to "Sesame Street." *Child Development, 47,* 806-811.

Anderson, D., & Lorch, E. P. (1983). Looking at television: Action or reaction. In J. Bryant & D. Anderson (Eds.), *Children's understanding of television.* New York: Academic Press.

Anderson, D., Lorch, E. P., Field, D. E., & Sanders, J. (1981). The effects of TV program comprehensibility on preschool children's visual attention to television. *Child Development, 52,* 151-157.

Anglin, J. M. (1977). *Word, object, and conceptual development.* New York: Norton.

Asher, S. R. (1979). Referential communication. In G. J. Whitehurst & B. J. Zimmerman (Eds.), *The functions of language and cognition.* New York: Academic Press.

Atkin, C. K. (1982). Television advertising and socialization to consumer roles. In D. Pearl, L. Bouthilet, & J. Lazar (Eds.), *Television and behavior: Ten years of scientific progress and implications for the eighties.* Washington, DC: Government Printing Office.

Baker, L., & Stein, N. L. (1981). The development of prose comprehension skills. In C. Shantz & B. Hayes (Eds.), *Children's prose comprehension: Research and practice.* Newark, NJ: International Reading Association.

Ball, S. J., & Bogatz, G. A. (1970). *The first year of "Sesame Street": An evaluation.* Princeton, NJ: Educational Testing Service.

Bandura, A. (1977). *Social learning theory.* Englewood Cliffs, NJ: Prentice-Hall.

Bartlett, E. J. (1978). The acquisition of the meaning of color terms: A study of lexical development. In R.N. Campbell & P.T. Smith (Eds.), *Proceedings of the NATO Conference on the psychology of language.* New York: Plenum.

Bates, E. (1976). *Language and context: The acquisition of pragmatics.* New York: Academic Press.

Bates, E. (1979). *The emergence of symbols: Cognition and communication in infancy.* New York: Academic Press.

Bateson, M. C. (1975). Mother-infant exchanges: The epigenesis of conversational interaction. In D. Aaronson & R. W. Rieber (Eds.), *Developmental psycholinguistics and communication disorders* (Annals of the New York Academy of Sciences, Vol. 263). New York: New York Academy of Sciences.

Berkowitz, L., & Rogers, K. H. (1986). A priming effects analysis of media influ-
ences. In J. Bryant & D. Zillmann (Eds.), *Perspectives on media effects.* New York:
Lawrence Erlbaum.
Bierwisch, M. (1980). Semantic structure and illocutionary force. In J. R. Searle,
F. Kieter, & M. Bierwisch (Eds.), *Speech act theory and pragmatics.* Dordrecht,
The Netherlands: D. Reidel.
Bloom, L. (1970). *Language development: Form and function in emerging grammars.*
Cambridge: MIT Press.
Bloom, L. (1973). *One word at a time.* The Hague, Mouton.
Bloom, L., Hood, L., & Lightbown, P. (1974). Imitation in language development: If,
when, and why? *Cognitive Psychology, 6,* 380-420.
Bloom, L., Rocissano, L., & Hood, L. (1976). Adult-child discourse: Developmental
interaction between information processing and linguistic knowledge. *Cognitive
Psychology, 8,* 521-552.
Bowerman, M. (1978). Systematizing semantic knowledge: Changes over time in the
child's organization of word meaning. *Child Development, 49,* 977-987.
Bowerman, M. (1982). Reorganizational processes in language development. In E.
Wanner & L. R. Gleitman (Eds.), *Language acquisition: The state of the art.* Cam-
bridge: Cambridge University Press.
Braine, M.D.S. (1963). The ontogeny of English phrase structure: The first phase.
Language, 39, 3-13.
Bretherton, I., McNew, S., & Beeghly-Smith, M. (1981). Early person knowledge as
expressed in gestural and verbal communication: When do infants acquire a "theory
of mind"? In M. E. Lamb & L. R. Sherrod (Eds.), *Infant social cognition.* Hills-
dale, NJ: Lawrence Erlbaum.
Brown, R. (1973). *A first language: The early stages.* Cambridge: Harvard University
Press.
Buerkel-Rothfuss, N., Greenberg, B., & Atkin, C. (1981). *Children's family role learn-
ing from television.* Unpublished report, Michigan State University, East Lansing.
Charters, W. W. (1933). *Motion pictures and youth: A summary.* New York: Macmillan.
Chen, M., & Paisley, W. (Eds.). (1985) *Children and microcomputers: Research new-
est medium.*
Chomsky, N. (1957). *Syntactic structures.* The Hague: Mouton.
Chomsky, N. (1965). *Aspects of the theory of syntax.* Cambridge: MIT Press.
Christenson, P. G., De Benedittis, P., & Lindlof, T. R. (1985). Children's use of audio
media. *Communication Research, 12,* 327-343.
Clark, E. V. (1973a). Non-linguistic strategies and the acquisition of word meanings.
Cognition, 2, 161-182.
Clark, E. V. (1973b). What's in a word? On the child's acquisition of semantics in his
first language. In T. E. Moore (Ed.), *Cognitive development and the acquisition of
language.* New York: Academic Press.
Clark, E. V. (1977). Strategies and the mapping problem in first language acquisition.
In J. Macnamara (Ed.), *Language learning and thought.* New York: Academic
Press.
Clark, E. V. (1983). Meanings and concepts. In P. H. Mussen (Ed.), *Handbook of child
psychology* (4th ed., vol. 3). New York: John Wiley.
Cohen, C. E. (1981). Goals and schemata in person perception: Making sense from the
stream of behavior. In N. Cantor & J. F. Kihlstrom (Eds.), *Personality, cognition,
and social interaction.* Hillsdale, NJ: Lawrence Erlbaum.
Collins, W.A. (1981). Recent advantages in research on cognitive processing and tele-
vision viewing. *Journal of Broadcasting, 25,* 327-334.
Collins, W. A. (1983). Interpretation and inference in children's television viewing.
In J. Bryant & D. R. Anderson (Eds.), *Children's understanding of television:
Research on attention and comprehension.* New York: Academic Press.

Collins, W. A., & Wellman, H. (1982). Social scripts and developmental changes in representations of televised narratives. *Communication Research, 9,* 380-399.

Collins, W. A., Wellman, H., Keniston, A., & Westby, S. (1978). Age-related aspects of comprehension and inference from a televised dramatic narrative, *Child Development, 49,* 389-399.

Cook, T. D., Kendzierski, D. A., & Thomas, S. V. (1983). The implicit assumptions of television research: An analysis of the 1982 NIMH report on television and behavior. *Public Opinion Quarterly, 47,* 161-201.

Davidson, R. J. (1984). Hemispheric asymmetry and emotion. In K. R. Scherer & P. Ekman (Eds.), *Approaches to emotion.* New York: Lawrence Erlbaum.

Darwin, C. (1974). A biographical sketch of an infant. In H. Gruber, *Darwin on man.* London: Wildwood House. (Original work published 1887)

Delia, J., & O'Keefe, B. (1979). Constructivism: The development of communication in children. In E. Wartella (Ed.), *Children communicating.* Newbury Park, CA: Sage.

Desmond, R. J. (1985). Metacognition: Thinking about thoughts in children's comprehension of television. *Critical Studies in Communication, 2,* 338-351.

Dickson, W. P. (1974). The development of interpersonal referential communication skills in young children using an interactional game device. *Dissertation Abstracts International, 35,* 3511A. (University Microfilms No. 74-27, 008.)

Dickson, W. P. (1982). Two decades of referential communication research: A review and meta-analysis. In C. J. Brainerd & M. Pressley (Eds.), *Verbal processing in children: Progress in cognitive developmental research.* New York: Springer-Verlag.

Donaldson, M., & Wales, R. J. (1970). On the acquisition of some relational terms. In J. R. Hayes (Ed.), *Cognition and the development of language.* New York: John Wiley.

Elliott, N. (1979). Language and cognition in the developing child. In E. Wartella (Ed.), *Children communicating.* Newbury Park, CA: Sage.

Ervin-Tripp, S. (1977). Speech acts and social learning. In K. Basso & H. Selby (Eds.), *Meaning in anthropology.* Albuquerque: University of New Mexico Press.

Flavell, J. H. (1963). *The developmental psychology of Jean Piaget.* New York: Van Nostrand.

Flavell, J. H., Botkin, P. T., Fry, C. L., Jr., Wright, J. W., & Jarvis, P. E. (1968). *The development of role-taking and communication skills in children.* New York: John Wiley.

Flavell, J. H. (1977). *Cognitive development.* Englewood Cliffs, NJ: Prentice-Hall.

Freedman, J. L. (1984). Effect of television violence on aggressiveness. *Psychological Bulletin, 96,* 227-246.

Gerbner, G., Gross, L., Signorielli, N., Morgan, M., & Jackson-Beeck, M. (1979). The demonstration of power: Violence profile no. 10. *Journal of Communication, 29,* 177-195.

Glucksberg, S., Krauss, R. M., & Higgins, E. T. (1975). The development of referential communication skills. In F. D. Horowitz (Ed.), *Review of child development research* (Vol. 4). Chicago: University of Chicago Press.

Greenberg, B. (1982). Television and role socialization: An Overview. In D. Pearl, L. Bouthilet, & J. Lazar (Eds.), *Television and behavior: Ten years of scientific progress and implications for the eighties.* Washington, DC: Government Printing Office.

Greenberg, B., & Atkin, C. (1978). *Learning about minorities from television.* Paper presented at the UCLA Center for Afro-American Studies Conference, Los Angeles.

Haslett, B. (1984). Communication development in children. In R. Bostrom (Ed.), *Communication yearbook 8.* Newbury Park, CA: Sage.

Hawkins, R., & Pingree, S. (1982). Television's influence on constructions of social reality. In D. Pearl, L. Bouthilet, & J. Lazar (Eds.), *Television and behavior: Ten years of scientific research and implications for the eighties.* Washington, DC: Government Printing Office.

Heider, E. R. (1971). Style and accuracy of verbal communication within and between social classes. *Journal of Personality and Social Psychology, 18,* 37-47.

Himmelweit, H. T., Oppenheim, A. N., & Vince, P. (1958). *Television and the child.* London: Oxford University Press.

Hoff-Ginsberg, E., & Shatz, M. (1982). Linguistic input and the child's acquisition of language. *Psychological Bulletin, 92,* 3-26.

Hollenbeck, J., & Slaby, R. G. (1979). Infant visual responses to television. *Child Development, 50,* 41-45.

Hornik, R. C. (1981). Out-of-school television and schooling: Hypotheses and methods. *Review of Educational Research, 51,* 199-214.

Huesmann, L. (1982). Violence and aggression. In D. Pearl, L. Bouthilet, & J. Lazar (Eds.), *Television and behavior: Ten years of scientific progress and implications for the eighties.* Washington, DC: Government Printing Office.

Huston, A. C., & Wright, J. C. (1983). Children's processing of television: The informative functions of formal features. In J. Bryant & D. R. Anderson (Eds.), *Children's understanding of television.* New York: Academic Press.

Hymes, D. (1974). *Foundations in sociolinguistics: An ethnographic approach.* Philadelphia: University of Pennsylvania Press.

Johnson, C. N., & Maratsos, M. P. (1977). Early comprehension of mental verbs: Think and know. *Child Development, 48,* 1743-1747.

Johnston, R. P., & Singleton, C. H. (1977). Social class and communication style: The ability of middle and working class five year olds to encode and decode abstract stimuli. *British Journal of Psychology, 68,* 237-244.

Johnston, J. R., & Slobin, D. (1979). The development of locative expressions in English, Italian, Serbo-Croatian and Turkish. *Journal of Child Language, 6,* 529-545.

Kaye, K., & Charney, R. (1980). How mothers maintain "dialogue" with two-year-olds. In D. Olson (Ed.), *The social foundations of language and thought.* New York: Norton.

Karmiloff-Smith, A. (1979). *A functional approach to child language.* Cambridge: Cambridge University Press.

Karmiloff-Smith, A. (1981). The grammatical marking of thematic structure in the development of language production. In W. Deutsch (Ed.), *The child's construction of language.* London: Academic Press.

Korzenny, F., & Neuendorf, K. (1980). Television viewing and self-concept of the elderly. *Journal of Communication, 30,* 71-80.

Krull, R., & Husson, W. (1979). Children's attention: The case of TV viewing. In E. Wartella (Ed.), *Children communicating.* Newbury Park, CA: Sage.

Lemish, D. (1986). The pampered "Sesame Street" viewer. In T. Lindlof (Ed.), *Natural audiences.* Norwood, NJ: Ablex.

Lemish, D., & Rice, M. (1984). *Toddlers, television, and talk: Observation in the home.* Paper presented at the International Communication Association Convention, San Francisco.

Leonard, L. B., & Kaplan, L. (1976). A note on imitation and lexical acquisition. *Journal of Child Language, 3,* 449-455.

Malamuth, N. M., & Billings, V. (1986). The functions and effects of pornography: Sexual communication versus the feminist models in light of research findings. In J. Bryant & D. Zillmann (Eds.), *Perspectives on media effects.* New York: Lawrence Erlbaum.

Maratsos, M. P. (1973). Nonegocentric communication abilities in preschool children. *Child Development, 44,* 697-700.

Maratsos, M. P. (1983). Some current issues in the study of the acquisition of grammar. In P. H. Mussen (Ed.), *Handbook of child psychology* (4th ed., Vol. 3). New York: John Wiley.

Mead, G. H. (1934). *Mind, self, and society.* Chicago: University of Chicago Press.

Meadowcroft, J., & Reeves, B. (1985). *Children's attention to television: The influence of story schema development on allocation of mental effort and memory.* Paper presented to the Speech Communication Association, Denver.

Medrich, E. A., Roizin, J. A., & Buckley, S. (1981). *The serious business of growing up: A study of children's lives outside of school.* Berkeley: University of California Press.

Messaris, P., & Kerr, D. (1983). Mother's comments about TV: Relation to family communication patterns. *Communication Research, 11,* 175-194.

Messaris, P., & Sarett, C. (1981). On the consequences of television-related parent-child interaction. *Human Communication Research, 7,* 226-244.

Milavsky, J. R., Kessler, R. C., Stipp, H. H., & Rubens, W. S. (1982). *Television and aggression: A panel study.* New York: Academic Press.

Miller, J. F., Chapman, R. S., Branston, M. B., & Reichle, J. (1980). Language comprehension in sensorimotor states V and VI. *Journal of Speech and Hearing Research, 23,* 284-311.

Miller, M. M., & Reeves, B. (1976). Dramatic TV content and children's sex-role stereotypes. *Journal of Broadcasting, 20,* 35-50.

Mussen, P. H. (1983). *Carmichael's manual of child psychology.* (Vols. 1-4). New York: John Wiley.

Nelson, K. (1978). Early speech in its communicative context. In F. Minific & L. Lloyd (Eds.), *Communicative and cognitive abilities: Early behavioral assessment.* Baltimore: University Park Press.

Pearl, D., Bouthilet, L., & Lazar, J. (Eds.). (1982). *Television and behavior: Ten years of scientific progress and implications for the eighties.* Washington, DC: Government Printing Office.

Piaget, J. (1926). *The language and thought of the child.* New York: Harcourt Brace Jovanovich.

Piaget, J., & Inhelder, B. (1969). *The psychology of the child.* New York: Basic Books.

Piatelli-Palmarini, M. (1980). *Language and learning: The debate between Jean Piaget and Noam Chomsky.* Cambridge, MA: Harvard University Press.

Pratt, M. W., Scribner, S., & Cole, M. (1977). Children as Teachers: Developmental studies of instructional communication. *Child Development, 48,* 1475-1481.

Reeves, B., Chaffee, S., & Tims, A. (1982). Social cognition and mass communication. In M. Roloff & C. Berger (Eds.), *Social cognition and communication.* Newbury Park, CA: Sage.

Reeves, B., & Garramone, G. (1982). Children's person perception: Generalization from television to real people. *Human Communication Research, 8,* 317-326.

Reeves, B., & Garramone, G. (1983). Television's influence on children's encoding of person information. *Human Communication Research, 10,* 119-136.

Reeves, B., & Lang, A. (1986). *Emotional television scenes and hemispheric specialization.* Paper presented to the International Communication Association, Chicago.

Reid, L. (1979). The impact of family group interaction on children's understanding of television advertising. *Journal of Advertising, 8,* 13-19.

Revelle, G. L., Karabenick, J. D., & Wellman, H. M. (1981, April). *Comprehension monitoring in preschool children.* Paper presented at the meeting of the Society for Research in Child Development, Boston.

Rice, M. L. (1980). *Cognition to language: Categories, word meanings and training.* Baltimore: University Park Press.

Rice, M. L. (1984). The words of children's television. *Journal of Broadcasting, 28,* 365-372.

Rice, M. L., Huston, A. C., & Wright, J. C. (1982). The forms and codes of television: Effects on children's attention, comprehension, and social behavior. In D. Pearl, L. Bouthilet, & J. Lazar (Eds.), *Television and behavior: Ten years of scientific progress and implications for the eighties.* Washington, DC: Government Printing Office.

Rice, M. L., & Kemper, S. (1984). *Child language acquisition.* Baltimore: University Park Press.

Rice, M. L., & Wartella, E. (1981). Television as a medium of communication: Implications for how to regard the child viewer. *Journal of Broadcasting, 25,* 365-372.

Rice, M. L., & Woodsmall, L. (1986). *Lessons from television: Children's word learning when viewing.* Unpublished manuscript: University of Kansas.

Roberts, D. (1973). Children and communication. In I. D. Pool, F. W. Frey, W. Schramm, N. Maccoby, & E. Parker (Eds.), *Handbook of communication.* Chicago: Rand McNally.

Roberts, D., & Bachen, C. (1982). Mass communication effects. In D. C. Whitney & E. Wartella (Eds.), Mass communication review yearbook (pp. 29-78). Newbury Park, CA: Sage.

Roberts, D., Bachen, C., Hornby, M., & Hernandez-Ramos, P. (1984). Reading and television: Predictors of reading achievement at different age levels. *Communication Research, 11,* 9-49.

Salomon, G. (1979). *Interaction of media, cognition and learning.* San Francisco: Jossey-Bass.

Salomon, G. (1981). Introducing AIME: The assessment of children's mental involvement with television. In H. Gardner & H. Kelly (Eds.), *Children and the worlds of television.* San Francisco: Jossey-Bass.

Salomon, G. (1983). Television watching and mental effort: A social psychological view. In J. Bryant & D. R. Anderson (Eds.), *Children's understanding of television: Research on attention and comprehension.* New York: Academic Press.

Salomon, G., & Leigh, J. C. (1984). Predispositions about learning from print and television. *Journal of Communication, 34,* 119-135.

Saville-Troike, M. (1982). *The ethnography of communication: An introduction.* Baltimore: University Park Press.

Schramm, W., Lyle, J., & Parker, E. B. (1961). *Television in the lives of our children.* Stanford: Stanford University Press.

Shantz, C. U. (1981). The role-taking of children's referential communication. In W. P. Dickson (Ed.), *Children's oral communication skills.* New York: Academic Press.

Shatz, M. (1982). On mechanisms of language acquisition: Can features of the communicative environment account for development? In E. Wanner & L. R. Gleitman (Eds.), *Language acquisition: The state of the art.* Cambridge: Cambridge University Press.

Shatz, M. (1983). Communication. In P.H. Mussen (Ed.), *Handbook of child psychology* (4th ed., Vol. 3). New York: John Wiley.

Shatz, M., & Gelman, R. (1973). The development of communication skills: Modification in the speech of young children as a function of listener (Monographs of the Society for Research in Child Development 38, 5, Serial No. 152).

Shields, M. M. (1978). The child as psychologist: Construing the social world. In A. Lock (Ed.), *Action, gesture and symbol: The emergence of language.* London: Academic Press.

Sinclair, A. (1982). Some recent trends in the study of language development. *International Journal of Behavioral Development, 5*, 413-431.

Singer, J. L., & Singer, D. G. (1983). Psychologists look at television: Cognitive, developmental, personality, and social policy implications. *American Psychologist, 38*, 826-834.

Slobin, D. I. (1973). Cognitive prerequisites for the acquisition of grammar. In C. A. Ferguson & D. I. Slobin (Eds.), *Studies of child language development.* New York: Holt, Rinehart & Winston.

Tan, A. S. (1986). Social learning of aggression from television. In J. Bryant & D. Zillmann (Eds.), *Perspectives on media effects.* New York: Lawrence Erlbaum.

Templin, M. C. (1957). Certain language skills in children: Their development and interrelationships. (University of Minnesota Institute of Child Welfare Monograph 26).

Vygotsky, L. (1962). *Thought and language.* Cambridge: MIT Press.

Walsh, J. (1983). Wide world of reports. *Science, 220*, 804-805.

Wartella, E., & Reeves, B. (1985). Historical trends in research on children and media: 1900 to 1960. *Journal of Communication, 35*, 118-133.

Watkins, B., Cojuc, J., Mills, S., Kwiatek, K. K., & Tan, C. Z. (1982). *Children write about TV and real life: The relationship of prime-time televiewing to children's schematic representations.* Paper presented to the International Communication Association.

Wilcox, M. J., & Webster, E. J. (1980). Early discourse behavior: An analysis of children's responses to listener feedback. *Child Development, 51*, 1120-1125.

Zillmann, D. (1982). Television viewing and arousal. In D. Pearl, L. Bouthilet, & J. Lazar (Eds.), *Television and behavior: Ten years of scientific progress and implication for the eighties.* Washington, DC: Government Printing Office.

Zillmann, D., & Bryant, J. (1981). Uses and effects of humor in educational television. In J. Baggaley (Ed.), *Proceedings of the third international conference on experimental research in televised instruction.* St. John's: Memorial University of Newfoundland.

21 Consumer Behavior

SCOTT WARD
University of Pennsylvania

CONSUMER behavior focuses on transactions between sellers, or "marketers," and consumers, or "buyers." Most consumer behavior researchers are interested in economic transactions resulting in consumption of goods and services. Many, however, define their interests more broadly, to include the marketing of ideas or positions, where "consumption" refers to accepting advocated positions and adopting new behaviors. For example, anti-smoking advertising campaigns urge smokers to accept ideas and quit smoking. In a broad sense, then, studies of propaganda, voting behavior, and any phenomena involving advocacy are studies of consumer behavior.

As a field, consumer behavior is most often aligned with marketing departments in business schools. Consequently, most research is concerned with efforts of business organizations to market goods and services. In business, marketers are concerned with assessing demand for goods and services, analyzing competitive and environmental factors, and then recommending and implementing decisions regarding product design, pricing, promotion and distribution. The composite of these decisions is the marketing program for a product or service. For example, a stereo component manufacturer might decide to produce only very high-quality products, to price them accordingly, to package them in particular ways, and distribute them through stereo specialty stores rather than through discounters. This manufacturer would accordingly advertise in high-quality publications aimed at serious stereo enthusiasts rather than through mass circulation media.

Communication issues are an integral part of such marketing decisions. For example, products themselves communicate value in terms of their appearance. Brand names also connote value: consider Heinekin versus Budweiser, Jordache versus Levi-Strauss, Mercedes versus Chevrolet. Distribution choices also communicate things about products: we expect higher-quality stereos, more technical advice, and service responsiveness from a stereo specialty store as opposed to a discount outlet. Advertising and promotion are the primary controllable means marketers have to communicate with customers. This is particularly true for marketers of goods and services bought by individual consumers since markets are large and other means of communicating are not feasible. For marketers of goods and services bought by other organizations, however, interpersonal communication (i.e., salespeople) is the norm. Markets are generally more concentrated, and information must be tailored to specific needs of a buying company.

Not all communications about a company or its products are under the control of the marketer (see Figure 21.1). "Control" means the marketer's ability to dictate aspects of a product that may communicate value to consumers. For example, decisions about a product's quality may affect consumer perceptions and evaluations, and advertising media and copy decisions are also product-related communications under the control of the marketer. Obviously, marketers only control the stimulus, that is, the product and advertising for the product; consumer reactions to the stimulus are uncontrolled. Consumers in a marketer's target audience may not be exposed to the advertising, or they may be exposed but respond very differently than the advertiser intended. Other events are also beyond the marketer's control, such as unfavorable publicity resulting from a product recall or negative interpersonal communication about a product.

Other aspects of interpersonal communication are also relevant to the study of consumer behavior. Marketers exert some control over interpersonal communication through the sales force. However, this control is far from complete. We have all heard some salespeople negatively evaluate their products. Marketers have no control over interaction between buyers and potential buyers of products. Studies show that interaction between early adopters of a new product and later adopters has a strong effect on the rate of sales (Robertson, 1971). Interpersonal communication in social organizations, such as families and businesses, has powerful effects on consumption. In some cases, marketers attempt to influence interpersonal communication about the product. Consider, for example, the influence of children on parents' purchases of soft drinks, candy, and breakfast cereals. Although self-regulatory advertising codes regarding children prohibit direct appeals to get children to influence their parents to buy, intrafamily purchase requests do frequently occur.

COMPARING CONSUMER BEHAVIOR AND COMMUNICATION SCIENCE

Consumer and communication researchers have much in common. As suggested above, much consumer behavior research focuses on mass and interpersonal communication phenomena per se. Only the context varies; communication messages are advertisements or other forms of marketer-controlled communication, and the researcher of consumer behavior is interested in interpersonal communication usually in terms

	Personal	Impersonal
Marketer Controlled	• salespeople • company seminars • 800-number information lines • trade shows	• media advertising • point-of-purchase displays • packaging • sales promotions
Not Controlled by the Marketer	• word of mouth from friends, family, and acquaintances • professional advice • personal consumption experiences	• editorial and news material

Figure 21.1. Categories of information sources.

of proscribed roles of buyers and sellers or of family members communicating about behaviors that ultimately involve consumption. But the basic notions are quite similar. In mass communication research, the questions of "who says what to whom through what channel with what effects" sound equally relevant to consumer behavior researchers. In interpersonal communication, the basic concepts of roles, norms, language, signs, and codes are also useful to understand contexts of interest to consumer behavior researchers.

The field of consumer behavior grew as behavioral sciences gained acceptance among academics and marketing practitioners in the last three decades (see Delia, Chapter 2 in this volume). Perhaps the earliest consumer behavior studies were called "motivation research," referring to individual depth interviews in which consumers were asked about their product perceptions and buying behavior. This early research tradition was based on Freudian psychoanalytic techniques and gained widespread acceptance among marketers in the 1950s as a way of determining "hidden motives" underlying buying patterns (Dichter, 1964; Newman, 1957).

The field was stimulated by the applied needs of marketers. As survey research techniques developed and computers made large-scale data processing possible, consumer behavior studies reflected the need for quantitative information for specific decisions. For example, early studies assessed consumer attitudes toward brands and measured recall of advertising campaigns.

In universities, the academic study of consumer behavior developed as researchers borrowed theories and concepts from "parent" behavioral sciences—notably, psychology and sociology. For example, early studies examined cultural and subcultural variations in consumption. The concept of attitude was utilized in studies seeking to predict consumer behavior, and the concept of "opinion leadership" was borrowed from sociology to explain the role of interpersonal influence in the sales of new products (Ward & Robertson, 1973).

As the field developed, emphasis shifted to theory development and advances in measurement. For example, in the late 1970s several models of consumer behavior were proffered to portray functional relationships among variables associated with purchase behavior. Currently much effort in the field is devoted to developing mathematical expressions of relationships. For example, multivariate techniques such as conjoint analysis and Lisrel represent significant advances over earlier methodologies for examining multivariate interactions.

In many ways, the development of consumer behavior parallels the development of research and theory in mass communication. Both communication sciences and consumer behavior research seek general theories, and the fields have experienced similar phases (e.g., borrowing concepts from parent disciplines, developing general models, and making advances in measurement). Since consumer behavior research focuses on advocacy and transaction, at least some of the field may be viewed as a subset of more general communication research. This chapter will survey some areas of particular overlap.

COMMUNICATION IN CONSUMER BEHAVIOR RESEARCH

For consumer researchers, communication is most often a variable in studies of other phenomena. As Figure 21.2 suggests, communication is

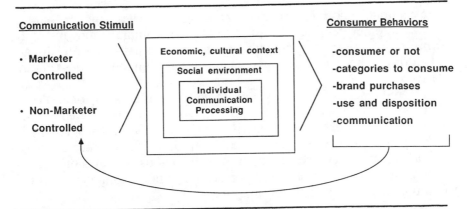

Figure 21.2. Communication in consumer behavior research.

treated as a stimulus, or independent variable; as a process, or mediating variable; and sometimes as a dependent variable. As an independent variable, studies most often focus on different types of mass media or interpersonal messages, that is, source and message variables in advertising or personal selling and advertising campaign decisions, such as scheduling and repetition of advertisements. Communication as an independent variable has also been viewed as a second-order consequence of mass communication exposure as, for example, in studies of the "two-step flow" of mass communication.

Interests in communication as an independent variable are also reflected in evaluation studies—atheoretical descriptive research, such as copy tests, that are used by marketers to develop and select from among alternative advertising executions and to evaluate effects of advertising after it has been presented. However, some investigators have studied communication stimuli with more conceptual and theoretical interests. For example, Wartella (1979) used Watt and Krull's (1974) operationalization of information theory constructs to examine the effects on children of advertising that varies in audiovisual complexity.

In recent years, a great deal of attention has been given to communication as a mediating variable. This is reflected in information-processing research in consumer behavior. This area has borrowed heavily from concepts in psychology, particularly memory processes and perception. Communication is studied as a mediating variable in research on consumer life styles. If individuals interact with their social and cultural environments, as Figure 21.2 suggests, symbolic communication influences an individual's desire to position him- or herself in those larger contexts. Much consumption is symbolic, intending to communicate something to others, such as status, life style, interests.

Finally, consumer behavior researchers are interested in communication as a dependent variable. In some cases, marketing campaigns advocate communication; for example, anti-drug abuse campaigns encourage talking to other people. Also of interest are communications resulting from consumption—in particular, expressions of satisfaction and dissatisfaction to other consumers, which become stimuli themselves (Figure 21.2).

The remainder of this chapter examines consumer behavior as a context for communication research. It will focus on three areas: (1) the communication effects perspective, especially advertising; (2) the information-processing perspective, a new area of consumer behavior research that includes selection, evaluation, and use of consumer information; and (3) the transactional perspective, emphasizing interpersonal communication related to consumption.

THE COMMUNICATION EFFECTS PERSPECTIVE

For many marketers, the most important means of reaching consumers is mass media advertising. Probably the "oldest" area of consumer behavior research focuses on effects of individual advertisements and whole advertising campaigns. Perhaps the earliest "model" of advertising effectiveness was the "direct effects" model (Bauer, 1963; Bauer & Bauer, 1960; see also Delia, Chapter 2; McLeod & Blumler, Chapter 9; Rogers & Storey, Chapter 26). The idea of powerful mass media potential reflects early thinking in microeconomics. In the classical economic sense, consumers are assumed to be rational and to act on the basis of "perfect" information about consumption alternatives. While such ideas might have served early economic theories, they did a disservice to emerging theories of communication. Consumers were assumed to attend to all advertising, and to obtain all available information about products, to make optimal buying decisions. The relative newness of mass media probably also fostered the idea that they are very powerful forces.

From a marketer's perspective, however, advertising did not appear so powerful. As a cost, advertising was justified by its ability to generate sales revenues. But marketers realized that many variables affect sales, in addition to advertising. The question became how to conceptualize advertising so that effects on sales could be predicted. A management consultant, Russell Colley, suggested that advertisers evaluate advertising in terms of short-term "communication effects" rather than in terms of ultimate behavioral effects (sales results).

Colley (1961) defined communication results in terms of a hierarchy—from awareness, to interest, to formation of favorable attitudes, and finally to action. These cognitive and behavioral states can be assessed through field research and, Colley argued, be used to evaluate the effectiveness of an advertising campaign. Of course, many issues surrounding the hierarchy are apparent: There need not be any progression of individual consumers through the hierarchy; some individuals may become aware of a brand through advertising, but fail to become interested in acquiring additional information, and so forth. In fact, taking the hierarchical notion too seriously could result in making a significant marketing error: creating an advertisement that is sure to get attention (measured by awareness and recall) but that fails to do anything more. Advertisements that feature very attractive people or funny scenes are cases in point. For example, despite a very humorous and memorable series of advertisements for Alka-Seltzer, sales continued to decline slowly as other brands of antacids eroded its market share. The issue seems to be, what could be expected of advertising for such an old, well-known brand? When a product has been on the market for many years, most consumers are aware of it, so advertising is not needed to increase awareness or to get consumers to try it. By this point in the product's history, Alka-Seltzer's market was quite stable. About all that could reasonably be expected of advertising for Alka-Seltzer would be to keep current users from switching to new competitors; the humorous ads did not seem to achieve this objective.

Nonetheless, the notion of a hierarchy of communications effects became the basis for early research on advertising effectiveness, and advertising campaigns were planned to achieve levels of awareness, to create, maintain or change attitudes, and so forth. Later, McGuire (1978) examined dynamics of the hierarchy. He proposed a "compensation principle": high levels of response in one part of the hierarchy may actually be related to lower levels in other parts of the hierarchy. This suggests that cognitive processing of some parts of a message may divert attention and effort from other parts of a message. Some empirical data support this notion.

In an article in *Harvard Business Review* Cox (1960) analyzed advertising strategies using concepts from early communication research, particularly findings from the Yale attitude change research program of Hovland, Lumsdaine, and Sheffield (1949). For example, Cox related the concept of "sleeper effect" to mass media advertising, suggesting that advertisements might have different effects immediately after exposure, compared to later, due to different rates of memory decay for source versus content.

While Cox's article did much to stimulate thinking about communication concepts, for a variety of reasons one cannot simply translate these results to the consumer context. First, the issue of external validity is particularly important in evaluating the applicability of research results from laboratory experiments to the consumer behavior context. In the case of advertising communication, the stimuli are short commercials, which are often viewed casually and repeatedly by subjects who are not very involved in the subject matter.

Such early attempts to apply communication concepts sparked consumer research examining effects on intraindividual states. For example, an important managerial problem is scheduling advertising campaigns. How often should particular advertisements be used? For how long? Advertising scheduling decisions depend critically upon consumer memory processes: How long do consumers remember advertising, and how do these response functions change over time?

Consumer researchers have approached this problem in field experiments by varying the conditions of exposure to advertising, and measuring recall or recognition over time. For example, Strong (1972) found greater advertising recognition when consumers were exposed to weekly intervals of magazine advertising than to either monthly or daily intervals. Zielske (1959) examined effects on recall and its decay, comparing weekly versus monthly ads. These studies are suggestive of how mass communication processes have been studied in the consumer behavior context. The studies are driven by applied questions of marketers, utilize concepts from "parent" disciplines, and focus on communication effects rather than on receiver variables.

In recent years, it is fair to say that consumer behavior researchers have shown less interest in communication effects research, probably for some of the same reasons that such research lost favor among mass communications researchers. The principal problem is the necessity of hypothetical constructs, to infer cognitive processes from input-output research designs. Additionally, so many variables affect responses to advertising—scheduling, repetition, message factors, audience experiences—that researchers have turned from viewing communication as a series of effects, to conceptualizing it as a process involving both senders and receivers. This is the domain of information processing.

THE INFORMATION-PROCESSING PERSPECTIVE

Consumer researchers have studied patterns of information people acquire and use in making purchase decisions. This treats information in the broadest information-theory sense, as uncertainty reduction. The focus is on "external" sources of information as distinct from information gained from personal experience with a product. The absolute amount of information search appears rather low, even for costly product purchases. For example, only about half of consumers visit more than one outlet or consider more than one brand for expensive products such as automobiles and appliances (Newman & Staelin, 1972).

The amount of time and effort consumers devote to searching for information is related to a number of factors. First, external search is inversely related to both the breadth of experience (the number of brands purchased in a product category) and the depth of experience (the number of purchase decisions previously made; Hughes, Tinic, & Neast, 1969). Simply stated, as consumers gain experience in purchasing particular products, they do not need to rely on external sources of information. Amount of search is affected by the degree of satisfaction consumers feel with brands within a product category; the greater the satisfaction, the less need to search for information. Consumers exert more time and effort to gather information if they have not made purchases in a product category for a long time. Finally, product categories characterized by frequent changes in prices, technologies, and styles arouse greater information search. Products in the home electronics market are an example (Robertson, Ward, & Zielinski, 1984).

Perceived risk. Information search has also been related to the degrees of social and economic risk consumers perceive in a purchase situation (Cox, 1967). When uncertainty concerning purchase alternatives and purchase consequences is high, and when the importance of the purchase is also high, perceived risk is greatest. Many consumer researchers have explored two types of risk: social risk, relating to perceptions of how other people may view a consumer who purchases a particular product; and economic risk, relating to product performance at a given price.

Information overload. Consumer researchers have examined costs of information search, including what has come to be called "information overload." Reflecting the classical economics view discussed earlier, one might believe that more information is better when it comes to product evaluation and decisions. For example, consumer activists have called for more information on product labels, more information at the point of sale, and so forth. This assumes a kind of consumer rationality, perhaps even a linear relationship between amount of information available and information search. Some further argue that consumers would make more "rational" and satisfying product choices if more information were available. Research does not necessarily support this idealistic view.

One study found that, as the amount of information increases up to a point the amount of search also increases, but then search decreases with still more information (Jacoby, Speller, & Kohn, 1974). This study examined the relationship between amount of information and the quality of consumer decisions, measured by comparing products chosen with the consumer's "ideal" for various products. The authors concluded that "subjects felt better with more information, but actually made poor purchase decisions" (p. 63).

Other studies of consumer uses of product information have focused on issues such as unit pricing, nutritional information, and truth-in-lending disclosures. This detailed product information is not used much by consumers, but there is considerable variance depending on how the information is displayed, and on individual differences: In general, consumers who are more affluent or highly educated engage in more information search for relatively expensive, durable goods (e.g., automobiles, microwave ovens) than do less educated and less affluent consumers. Role perceptions also affect information search. One study found a relationship between women's perceptions of their family role and the amount of information search for food products. In terms of life-style descriptors, "liberated" women as well as "traditionalists" (those who prepare meals as their parents did) show less information search than family-centered "mother" types.

"Micro" Aspects of Consumer Information Processing

Early studies in consumer behavior focused on cognitive processes—most often attitude formation and change in input-output research—that inferred the presence of attitudes and assessed the magnitude of changes as a function of some combination of independent variables. The field shifted to more process-oriented research in response to calls to study communication and consumption phenomena more directly.

The shift from attitude research to information-processing research was led by three streams of inquiry. To examine consumer information processing related to consumer decisions directly, Bettman (1979) had consumers verbalize their thoughts while shopping for various items ("thought protocols"). To assess consumer responses to advertising communication, Wright (1974) utilized concepts of cognitive responses, such as counterarguing and connections that occur while people are exposed to advertising. To approach issues regarding advertising scheduling, Krugman (1965) developed the concept of "low involvement" to characterize the nature of consumer interaction with advertising for some types of products.

Thought protocols. Research emanating from Bettman's early work on thought protocols has resulted in much more elaborate understanding of how consumers select, comprehend, store, and retrieve information from communications (Bettman, 1979). Consumer information processing focuses on initial aspects of earlier "hierarchy of effects" models. The difference is that the information-processing view more clearly portrays the relationships between the stages and takes into account the critical role of memory processes. Additionally, information-processing notions in consumer behavior research are not so concerned with relating cognitive states to purchase behavior. Instead the focus is on specific cognitive processes.

The essential notions of consumer information-processing research are shown in Figure 21.3. If a consumer is a member of an audience for

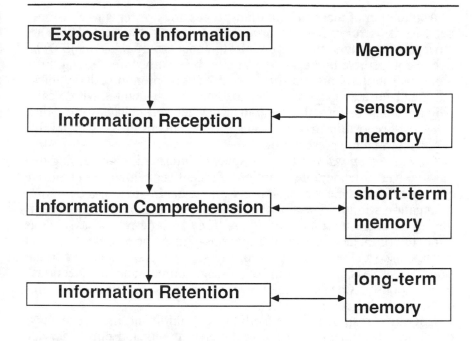

Source: Robertson, Ward, & Zielinski (1984).

Figure 21.3. Model of information processing.

an advertising vehicle, such as a publication or a television program, exposure to advertising information is possible. Whether information is actually received is another question. Information reception is seen as a state of cognitive readiness and attention. Some degree of arousal is a necessary but not sufficient condition for further processing. Very high levels of arousal (as under conditions of extreme stress) may narrow the focus of attention to only a few aspects of incoming information and bias internal search for additional information in memory to only the most readily available information.

Research on the next step, comprehension, focuses on how incoming information is integrated with existing information in memory. Short-term memory is viewed as the center of active information processing while long-term memory may be accessed to interpret incoming information. Long-term memory is conceived in terms of basic memory research—memory nodes, scripts, and schemas. Memory control processes are also understood in terms of memory research concepts: rehearsal, coding, transfer, placement, and the like.

Application of these information-processing concepts to consumer behavior is useful in devising product positioning strategies. These are attributes marketers may communicate about a particular brand, relative to competitive brands. For example, beers are stored in long-term memory in terms of product forms, such as light, premium, dark, and so on. One beer attempted to reorganize memory structures with a campaign stressing that it is the "beer to have when you're having more than one." IBM repositioned one of its PCs to a small business computer that is good for making presentations.

Cognitive responses. Another aspect of information processing that has received considerable attention in recent years are the "cognitive responses" consumers experience while attending to marketing communication stimuli. These responses refer to actual cognitive events during exposure to communications. They include responses such as "counterarguments" (internal refutations of message claims), "support arguments" (feelings of support for message claims), "source derogation" (negative characterization of message source), and "connections" (associations between the audience member's personal life and elements of the marketing communication).

Cognitive responses may facilitate or inhibit the impact of mass communication messages such as advertisements and public service announcements; moreover, these variables reflect specific processes occurring during exposure. Two experiments illustrate their usefulness.

Ray, Ward, & Reed (1976) were interested in improving pre-test methods for anti-drug abuse public service announcements (PSAs). Advertising agencies use a variety of pre-test methods to determine the likely effects of specific advertisements or campaigns. The simplest and least expensive methods include laboratory measures of recall, comprehension, and affect in which consumers respond to advertisements via paper-and-pencil tests after viewing ads under controlled conditions. More costly are "test markets," or field experiments. Test markets involve running alternative advertising in several markets that are matched on various criteria (e.g., city size, location, sales). The dependent measure under these more natural conditions is most often sales. In other words, test markets are simply input-output research designs in a field setting.

In the case of PSAs, budget considerations usually preclude expensive pretesting methods such as field experiments; at best it would be difficult to specify just what "sales" should be measured. The objectives for anti-drug abuse PSAs are indirect and cognitive response measures are more appropriate to them. The impact of these PSAs depends on whether the audience member counterargues, for example.

In a series of experiments, Ray et al. exposed groups of junior and senior high school students, and a group of parents, to three different PSAs. Different groups of subjects saw different commercials, which were inserted in programming materials and surrounded by other advertising messages. Following exposure, subjects completed a questionnaire designed to measure cognitive responses. Additionally, a measure of "drug abuse as a social problem" was included to assess more general effects of the messages, and interest in receiving a booklet or more information was also measured. The senior high sample, which was closest to the PSAs target audience, differed from both the parent and the junior high students. The seniors did not respond differently to the different ads, as the other two samples did; they made the fewest connections, and they reported the most counterarguments. These specific findings could never have been gleaned from traditional test-market methods.

Other variables also affect cognitive responses. Wright (1974) examined responses of consumers who were exposed to identical messages transmitted via print and broadcast media. He also manipulated the level of involvement with the content of the message by telling half of the subjects that they would be asked to evaluate the product in the advertisement, while the other half received no such information. Respondents were instructed to list all thoughts relevant to the product or the message that occurred to them during exposure. Wright found no differences in recall, but respondents exposed to print media generated far more counterarguments, source derogation, and support arguments than did consumers exposed to the broadcast media. Moreover, the number of counterarguments generated by those exposed to the broadcast message did not vary with level of involvement, but in the print message condition highly involved consumers generated far more counterarguments than did those with little involvement.

Low involvement. The "low involvement" model was initially posed by Herbert Krugman (1965). Much debate concerns whether involvement is essentially a cognitive variable or an interaction between an individual's cognitive state and the salience of the product category. In any case, we have seen how the concept of involvement mediates effects of advertising. Figure 21.4 outlines the basic distinctions, based on variations in involvement and information.

Under conditions of high involvement and differences between brands, the classic cognitive learning model is most appropriate; involved consumers form beliefs, make evaluations (or form attitudes), and then purchase. Under high involvement conditions, but where few differences are perceived between brands, consumers may simply purchase and then later form beliefs and evaluations based on their postpurchase experience. They may make attributions to the purchased product or reduce dissonance by justifying their purchase. For example, while buying an

	High Involvement	Low Involvement

Significant Differences Between Brands	MODEL
	    Beliefs
	    Evaluation
	    Behavior
	
	THEORY
	    Cognitive Learning
	
	DECISION PROCESS
	    Complex Decision
	    Making or Brand
	    Loyalty
		MODEL
		    Beliefs
		    Behavior
		    Evaluation
		
		THEORY
		    Low Involvement
		    Decision Making
		
		DECISION PROCESS
		    Variety Seeking

Few Differences Between Brands	MODEL
	    Behavior
	    Beliefs
	    Evaluation
	
	THEORY
	    Dissonance or
	    Attribution Theory
	
	DECISION PROCESS
	
	    Dissonance
	    Reduction or
	    Attribution
		MODEL
		    Beliefs
		    Behavior
		
		THEORY
		    Low Involvement
		    Decision Making
		
		DECISION PROCESS
		
		    Inertia

SOURCE: From Henry Assael, *Consumer behavior and marketing action* (Boston: Kent Publishing Co., 1981), p. 80. © 1981 by Wadsworth, Inc. Reprinted by permission of PWS-Kent Publishing Co., a division of Wadsworth, Inc.

Figure 21.4. A classification of four types of consumer behavior.

automobile or purchasing a carpet may be highly involving to most consumers, in some cases there is little prepurchase deliberation (besides shopping for price differences). Few consumers may be willing to undertake the considerable effort in learning how to evaluate fully such complex products. In these cases, mass communications may play only a limited role, making consumers aware of a few differences between brands. Marketers may try to establish the idea that there really are many differences in order to influence cognitive learning processes. For example, long-distance telephone service providers other than AT&T attempt to convince consumers that all long distance services are essentially alike but that savings can be realized by choosing one of them. AT&T counters with messages designed to influence consumers that there are many differences between competing services and that the decisions require careful attention to many factors besides price.

Under low involvement conditions, consumers may believe that there are big differences between brands, but still not devote a great deal of deliberation to purchase decisions. In such cases, variety seeking may occur within a range of brands that are all seen as "acceptable" by consumers; advertising can influence purchase probabilities by altering a few beliefs about brands. Much advertising for detergents, cold remedies, and cereals provides examples, as a brand introduces a new ingredient, for example.

Finally, under low involvement conditions if consumers perceive few differences between brands, little if any evaluation may go on. The advertiser's task is to break the inertia in purchasing habits for these relatively simple, routinely purchased products (e.g., soft drinks, beer, cigarettes). It may be said that consumers do not feel much or care much in such product categories, and enormous amounts of advertising may be required to stimulate any cognitions, much less change in sales.

Summary. The "one way" communication effects model was replaced in information processing research by a two-way notion, suggesting that consumers have prior experiences and cognitions that mediate the impact of advertising. These cognitive structures are the critical battleground for marketers, as they attempt to create, maintain, or alter perceptions, attitudes, affect, and other cognitions about products and ideas.

If the two-way model was useful in orienting marketers to consider cognitive variables, it had a seductive effect in establishing the hierarchy of effects as a model for advertising generation and measurement. The hierarchy portrays consumers as moving from rudimentary cognitions (recognition, recall) through affective states (liking and preference) to purchase intention and, ultimately, purchase. The hierarchical notion may indeed be appropriate for a variety of marketing situations—for example, if a marketer is introducing a new, complex product. But it still assumes an underlying rationality, which may not be appropriate for all marketing situations and may not reflect the most useful conceptualization of communication.

More recent concepts such as thought protocols, cognitive responses and involvement have helped to change thinking about mass communication effects on consumers. Perhaps the most important change has been to refocus consumer behavior research from input-output designs of advertising effects to research that seeks to examine the actual processes that occur when consumers are exposed to mass communication.

INTERPERSONAL LEVEL OF ANALYSIS

Consumer behavior researchers have examined several dimensions of interpersonal communication, including the diffusion of innovations, opinion leadership, impact of reference groups on consumption, and communication in families and business organizations. In this section, we examine conceptualizations and research dealing with communication in business organizations and families, and focus on interpersonal communication in dyadic, salesperson-buyer interaction.

This interpersonal research has paralleled the transition from intrapersonal input-output designs to communication processes. For example, studies of salesperson-buyer interaction supplanted earlier research that sought to find personality characteristics of successful salespeople (Stevens, 1958). Also, early studies of organizational buying behavior simply tried to construct flow charts of communications linking various individuals in a company, without any sense of the nature of the communication network portrayed (see O'Shaughnessy, 1977; Steckel & O'Shaughnessy, 1983). More recent research focuses on concepts of decision-making units and decision-making processes that explore the role of communications in the dynamics of decisions in organizational settings (seminal early studies include Webster & Wind, 1972; Wilson, 1975).

Family Communication and Consumer Behavior

Early studies of consumption behavior in the family context focused on roles marriage partners play in planning and implementing consumption and the degrees of power and autonomy of husbands and wives. A late 1950s study found husbands generally more dominant across purchase decisions, although wives had more power in lower socioeconomic strata (Sharp & Mott, 1956).

More recent research has focused on the nature of decision making at different points in the purchase decision process. For example, Davis and Rigaux (1974) classified married couples' purchases in terms of whether they were syncratic (joint decision making), autonomic (specialized decision making), or husband- or wife-dominant. They examined the influence of husband and wife across three decision stages: problem recognition, search for information, and final decision. There was a trend toward specialization (autonomic decision making) among couples seeking to gather information about housing, vacations, and the like. Other studies have found that newly married couples are likely to engage in syncratic decision making for a wide range of products, but specialization takes place as the marriage becomes established.

Communication concepts are particularly relevant in studies of conflict resolution in family decision making. Families may disagree over the goals of consumption ("Will the purchase satisfy our needs?"); over the product or brand being considered; and/or over the purchase process ("Should we buy it now or later? What should we look for?"). Families may adopt normative (i.e., relatively standardized) mechanisms to avoid conflict, and instrumental (i.e., relatively specific to the problem) mechanisms to solve conflicts.

Among normative mechanisms, families might take steps to avoid probable sources of conflict by deferring to impersonal constraints ("It's not in the budget") or by establishing an arbitrary rule ("We'll never get a video game, and that's that"). Alternatively, families may establish rights, duties, and responsibilities, such as assigning particular consumption tasks to each family member. Families may also establish equality of treatment of family members and set up a routine so that everyone is satisfied eventually (e.g., one child can pick the fast food restaurant this time, but the other gets to pick it next time).

When conflicts do arise, instrumental mechanisms may be used to deal with them. Families might increase facilities for family satisfaction (as when parents buy a second toy for a sibling to resolve ownership issues), establish priorities, or grant new autonomy to some family member (see Davis, 1976; Roloff, Chapter 16).

Another view of family decision making is offered by Davis (1976). He describes strategies for when family members agree or disagree about goals and suggests how these strategies may be implemented. For example, when family members disagree about goals, persuasion strategies include impugning the disagreeing family member's competence or motives ("the irresponsible critic"), appealing to special competence ("feminine intuition"), attempting to coopt other family members while shopping together, and outright coercion. Family members may also pool resources in coalitions to persuade another family member. Bargaining strategies involve trade-offs among conflicting family members—for example, making agreement on a purchase conditional on control over the next purchase ("OK, buy the VCR, but next year we get a car"), or justifying an unsanctioned purchase activity by appealing to impulse or to forgetfulness ("I'll get it next time.").

These streams of conceptualizations and research in the area of family decision making assume communication, but the hypothesized interactions are rarely examined directly or tied into more general theory. The focus is most often on husband-wife interaction; children are rarely included in family buying behavior conceptualizations, and purchasing units other than married couples are rarely studied. Finally, while some research has documented changing buying habits and changes in role structures and role relationships over the life cycle of families, little attention has been paid in traditional studies of family consumer behavior to learning processes.

Consumer socialization. In recent years, communication researchers have sought to remedy these shortcomings by focusing on processes of "consumer socialization." The ways in which children acquire knowledge, skills, and attitudes relevant to functioning in the marketplace have been examined among pre-teenage children (Ward, Wackman, & Wartella, 1979) and among children and adolescents (see O'Keefe & Reid-Nash, Chapter 14).

The work of Moschis (1985) and Moschis and Moore (1979) is particularly instructive since they have creatively used a conceptualization of family interaction emanating from the field of communication research: McLeod & Chaffee's (1972) family communication patterns (FCP) typology. Building on Newcomb's (1953) A-B-X coorientation model, McLeod and Chaffee found two relatively uncorrelated dimensions of communication structure within families: socio-oriented, which emphasizes social relationships and harmony within the home; and concept-oriented, which stresses A-X relationships and encourages children to form their own ideas about the world. The resulting four-fold typology of "laissez-faire," "protective," "pluralistic" and "consensual" family communication environments is well known.

Studies have related FCP to children's media use, interest in public affairs, and other phenomena, but Moschis and Moore (1979) and their colleagues have utilized the typology to understand family consumer behavior and such related phenomena as consumer socialization, brand preferences, retail store patronage, and adolescent career decisions. Moschis (1985) poses a series of hypotheses for direct and indirect parental influences on offsprings' developing patterns of consumer behavior. Based on his research, he notes that outcomes such as brand and store preferences, motivations for consumption, and skills in evaluating information in advertising depend not only on the family communication environment but also on product characteristics.

Moschis also hypothesized several different communication processes that operate in the "transmission of consumer behaviors from parent to child." He distinguishes among purposive consumer training, observation of parental consumer behaviors, and positive reinforcement, as mechanisms that underlie children's consumer learning from parents. In earlier research, Ward et al. (1977) found in a study of 5- to 12-year-olds that relatively direct communication between parents and children was related to developing consumer skills among younger children, while observational learning (modeling parental behaviors) was more likely to be related to consumer learning variables among older children.

Summary. Early studies of consumer decision making in families focused exclusively on roles and role relationships. The emphasis was on relative degrees of power held by husbands and wives, and the exercise of that power in making purchase decisions. Later research, exemplified by Davis, focused on various types of husband-wife relationships and their implications for decision making across purchase decision stages. Other conceptualizations have focused on conflict resolution within families.

These studies rarely focus on communication. Moreover, there is little concern with learning beyond documenting changes as families move through the life cycle from early marriage through later adult years. Moschis and his colleagues have shifted the focus from husband-wife and role relationships to actual family consumer behavior, including that of offspring, and from decision making to consumer learning.

THE ORGANIZATIONAL LEVEL

The term "consumer" most often connotes an individual searching for product information, attending to advertising, deliberating about purchases, and negotiating the transaction. However, a significant stream of consumer behavior research focuses on industrial consumers, referring to individuals in companies and other types of for-profit and nonprofit organizations that are involved in purchasing decisions. In these cases, the consumer is a company president, purchasing agent, engineer, secretary, or other employee who has a direct or indirect influence on goods and services procured by the organization. The marketer in such cases is another organization, which offers the goods and services. For example, IBM sells office products, such as typewriters and word processors, as well as large, mainframe computers. Its renowned sales force is a team of people trained to interact with individuals with various organizational job responsibilities to cultivate a sale.

In contrast to consumer goods and services, marketing to organizations is characterized by multiple individuals involved in the purchase decision, long purchase decisions, and a greater role for personal selling as opposed to mass media advertising. Since organization purchases are often costly, customized, and complex, personal selling is required as opposed to the more simple, less costly decisions for everyday consumer goods. Consequently, research has focused on "sales-buyer interaction" to refer to communication between the industrial salesperson and members of the decision-making unit within a buying organization.

Sales-Buyer Interaction

Just as the interest of consumer marketers is ultimately in sales results, industrial marketers are most interested in what kinds of salespeople and techniques are most likely to result in the greatest sales volume with the least associated costs. As noted in the introduction to this section, initial consumer behavior research in this area reflected earlier eras of behavioral research in that studies attempted to isolate the most important "personality" variables associated with successful selling. Other research attempted to isolate presentation rules and scenarios salespeople could use to ensure success (Corey, 1976). Most of these investigators assumed a one-way flow of influence, not unlike the one-way model of mass communication effects discussed earlier.

An example of such early research is the "sales grid" of Blake and Mouton (1970). This is a framework for salesperson selection and training, based on two dimensions: concern for the customer and concern for the sale. Individuals with high concern for the customer but low concern for the sale were thought to be effective by leveraging their personal relationship with the buyer. On the other hand, individuals high in concern for the sale but low in concern for the customer were thought to be effective through their hard-driving approach. Such grids may provide useful characterizations, but they tell us nothing about dyadic interaction. For example, should a sales force manager assign a hard-driving salesperson to work on an account in which his or her main contact would be an analytical person? That is, do opposites attract, or do birds of a feather flock together?

Studies of dyadic communication have moved us beyond posing questions from folklore. The earliest studies examined the importance of similarities between salespeople and buyers. Research in other contexts has consistently demonstrated that similarity is related to liking, perhaps because individuals who are similar have a greater pool of things to discuss. Interaction with similar others may prove easier and more rewarding than the often awkward interactions between highly dissimilar people. Studies in marketing contexts confirm the similarity-liking relationship: Positive relationships are found between customer-salesperson similarity and sales success. Many dimensions of similarity appear to be involved, including physical characteristics and backgrounds. In one study, similarity was found to be more important than expertise in achieving sales (Brock, 1965). A salesperson in a hardware store was trained to use one of two approaches whenever his customer was interested in buying paint: he portrayed himself either as an expert or simply as having painting problems and needs similar to the customer's. The latter approach yielded greater sales.

Conceptualizations and research in this area finally focused on interaction per se with the work of Weitz (1978, 1981). Building on leadership research in social psychology, Weitz posed a "contingency framework" for sales effectiveness across different kinds of selling situations. For Weitz, sales effectiveness is contingent on four major factors: (1) the behavior of the salesperson in customer interactions, (2) the salesperson's resources, (3) the customer's buying task, and (4) the customer-salesperson relationship. Weitz (1978) expanded on this framework with his ISTEA sales process model. ISTEA is an acronym for the five elements of his model: impression formation, strategy formulation, transmission, evaluation, and adjustment. Weitz stresses the concepts of empathy and adaptability—the abilities to monitor the customer's leanings, feelings, and reactions and to adapt to them on a moment-by-moment basis in sales interactions. The model and its elements are suggestive of coorientation models in communication and psychology.

Weitz found that variations in abilities during the two initial stages—impression formulation and strategy formulation—account for 20% of the variance in field sales performance. This corroborates earlier findings that more effective salespeople understand more of the feedback from customers, especially nonverbal cues, and are better able to summarize customer feedback and respond appropriately.

CONCLUSION

This chapter has focused on the relationship between the fields of consumer behavior and communication research. In particular, the interest has been in describing areas of consumer behavior research as a context for concepts and applications from communication research. Particular attention has been given to changes in conceptualizations and research approaches in consumer behavior research. In many respects, changes in the two fields paralleled each other, perhaps mirroring changes in other behavioral sciences as well. Considerable cross-fertilization between the two fields of study has occurred.

This chapter has not addressed issues regarding the role of consumer and communication research at the macro level of societal functioning. There are no studies in economics that attempt to support or refute the proposition that advertising is "justified" in a country's or a society's economy. Moreover, discussions of the role of marketing activities in creating or satisfying wants or needs quickly degenerate into a competition among personal values and a semantic argument.

For instance, some argue that communication regulates consumption, thereby maintaining economic stability, while others argue that such communication only benefits large companies. This argument would seem to deny the emergence of "niche" products, which are developed in many markets and rely more on precise satisfaction of needs in a narrowly defined market segment than on mass advertising. For example, Hewlett-Packard sells a very narrow range of relatively expensive and feature-rich hand-held calculators that are expressly designed for scientists and engineers. The company spends very little compared to its competitors on marketing communication, yet the Hewlett-Packard product is a viable one because it satisfies the particular needs of a specific subsegment.

Consumer behavior research can also be questioned regarding the uses to which it is put. Some would argue that it is ultimately used by marketers to create and exploit consumer needs. The counterargument debates the definition of "wants" and "needs," and questions the motives of critics who impose their values on others. Moreover, the alleged ability of marketing communication to "create needs" ignores the fact that 8 out of 10 new products fail (in the sense that they do not reach sales objectives), which suggests that consumer behavior research is not yet yielding information that fully characterizes consumer needs in a valid and reliable way, or that marketers have simply not utilized and implemented that information in an effective way. Another alternative, of course, is that consumers are not easily "misled" into purchasing things they do not "really need." The question of what "real needs" are forces one to consider the role of personal values. Many find needs for status, belonging, and prestige are illegitimate and believe that consumption should only satisfy the essential material requisites of life. That others satisfy status needs by purchasing a Mercedes-Benz or Perrier water may offend some, but to impose the values of some on others is questionable.

The field of consumer behavior research has proven to be a fertile one for communication researchers. There seems to be no single area of consumer behavior research that could not benefit from applications of communication research. The breadth and depth of both fields hold considerable promise for each other. It would seem that the communication researcher need only choose the most interesting domain.

REFERENCES

Assael, H. (1981). *Consumer behavior and marketing action.* Boston: Kent Publishing.

Bauer, R. (1963). The initiative of the audience. *Journal of Advertising Research, 3*(2), 2-7.

Bauer, R., & Bauer, A. (1960). America, mass society, and mass media. *Journal of Social Issues, 16,* 3.

Bettman, J. (1979). *An information processing theory of consumer choice.* Reading, MA: Addison-Wesley.

Blake, R., & Mouton, J. (1970). *The grid for sales excellence: Benchmarks for effective salesmanship.* New York: McGraw-Hill.

Brock, T. (1965). Communicator-recipient similarity and decision change. *Journal of Personality and Social Psychology,* 650-654.

Colley, R. H. (1961). *Defining advertising goals for measured advertising results.* New York: Association of National Advertisers.

Corey, E. (1976). *Industrial marketing: Cases and concepts* (2nd ed.). Englewood Cliffs, NJ: Prentice-Hall.

Cox, D. (1960). Clues for advertising strategists. *Harvard Business Review.*

Cox, D. (1967). *Risk taking and information handling in consumer behavior.* Boston: Harvard Business School.

Davis, H. (1976). Decision-making within the household. *Journal of Consumer Research, 2,* 241-260.

Davis, H., & Rigaux, B. (1974). Perception of marital roles in decision processes. *Journal of Consumer Research, 1,* 51-63.

Dichter, E. (1964). *Handbook of consumer motivations.* New York: McGraw-Hill.

Hovland, C., Lumsdaine, A., & Sheffield, F. (1949). *Experiments on mass communication.* Princeton: Princeton University Press.

Hughes, G., Tinic, S., & Neast, P. (1969). Analyzing consumer information processing. In *Marketing involvement in society and the economy* (pp. 235-240). Chicago: American Marketing Association.

Jacoby, J., Speller, D., & Kohn, C. (1974). Brand choice behavior as a function of information load. *Journal of Marketing Research, 11,* 63-69.

Krugman, H. (1965). The impact of television advertising: learning without involvement. *Public Opinion Quarterly, 29,* 349-356.

McGuire, W. (1978). An information processing model of advertising effectiveness. In H. Davis & A. Silk (Eds.), *Behavior and management sciences in marketing* (pp. 156-180). New York: John Wiley.

McLeod, J., & Chaffee, S. (1972). The construction of social reality. In J. Tedeschi (Ed.), *The social influence processes* (pp. 50-99). Chicago: Aldine.

Moschis, G. (1985). The role of family communication in consumer socialization of children and adolescents. *Journal of Consumer Research, 11,* 898-913.

Moschis, G., & Moore, R. (1979). Decision making among the young: a socialization perspective. *Journal of Consumer Research, 6,* 101-112.

Newcomb, T. M. (1953). An approach to the study of communicative acts. *Psychological Review, 60,* 393-404.

Newman, J. (1957). *Motivation research and marketing behavior.* Boston: Harvard University Press.

Newman, J., & Staelin, R. (1972). Pre-purchase information seeking for new cars and major household appliances. *Journal of Marketing Research, 9,* 249-257.

O'Shaughnessy, J. (1977). Aspects of industrial buying behavior relevant to supplier account strategies. *Industrial Marketing Management, 6*(1), 15-22.

Ray, M., Ward, S., & Reed, J. (1976). Protesting of anti-drug abuse education and information campaigns. In R. Ostman (Ed.), *Communication research and drug education* (pp. 193-221). Newbury Park, CA: Sage.

Robertson, T. (1971). *Innovative behavior and communication.* New York: Holt, Rinehart & Winston.

Robertson, T., Ward, S., & Zielinski, J. (1984). *Consumer behavior.* Glenview, IL: Scott, Foresman.

Sharp, H., & Mott, P. (1956). Consumer decisions in the metropolitan family. *Journal of Marketing, 23,* pp. 239-243.

Steckel, J., & O'Shaughnessy, J. (1983). *Measuring power in the organizational buying center.* Paper presented at Columbia University Business School.

Stevens, S. (1958). The application of social findings to selling and the salesman. In *Aspects of modern management* (Report No. 15, pp. 85-94). New York: American Management Association.

Strong, E. C. (1972). *The effects of repetition on advertising: A field study.* Unpublished doctoral dissertation, Stanford University.

Ward, S., & Robertson, T. (1973). *Consumer behavior: Theoretical sources.* Englewood Cliffs, NJ: Prentice-Hall.

Ward, S., Wackman, D., & Wartella, E. (1979). *How children learn to buy: The development of consumer information-processing skills.* Newbury Park, CA: Sage.

Wartella, E. (1979). The developmental perspective. In E. Wartella (Ed.), *Children communicating: Media and development of thought, speech, understanding* (pp. 7-21). Newbury Park, CA: Sage.

Watt, J. H., & Krull, R. (1974). A cognitive development study of children's attention to television commercials. *Communication Research, 1*(1).

Webster, F., & Wind, Y. (1972). *Organizational buying behavior.* Englewood Cliffs, NJ: Prentice-Hall.

Weitz, B. (1978). Relationship between salesperson performance and understanding of customer decision making. *Journal of Marketing Research, 15,* 502.

Weitz, B. (1981). Effectiveness in sales interactions: A contingency framework. *Journal of Marketing, 45,* 85-103.

Wilson, D. (1975). Dyadic interaction: an exchange process. In B. Anderson (Ed.), *Advances in consumer research* (pp. 384-397).

Wright, P. (1974). Analyzing media effects on advertising responses. *Public Opinion Quarterly, 38,* 192-205.

Zielske, H. A. (1959). The remembering and forgetting of advertising. *Journal of Marketing, 23,* 239-243.

22 The Health Care Context

LOYD S. PETTEGREW
University of South Florida

ROBERT LOGAN
University of Missouri, Columbia

HEALTH communication has no overarching theory from which to proceed, nor an exemplar of research. This lack of coherence is due to three conditions: the peculiar nature of the health care context, the vast range of communication phenomena to study, and the fact that communication has been studied from the points of view of other disciplines.

Health care is a microcosm of the larger social context. It offers intriguing theoretical, empirical, and practical challenges across all levels of communication. Yet it has developed *in spite of* advances in communication science; it has been dominated by the values and interests of medicine. Pragmatic problems such as medical malpractice, unhealthy life styles, and ineffective but costly health care delivery cry out for attention by the communication scholar.

But health care is also very different from the overarching social context. It is far more hierarchical and institutionalized (Goffman, 1961; Illich, 1976). While society's central issue is quality of life, life itself is of overriding concern in health care. The field also has an identity problem; the definition of *medical* versus *health* clouds our understanding.

This is accentuated when health communication is examined crossculturally. In many countries, particularly in the Third World, the issues of who delivers care, how, and where are addressed only marginally by our current models. The notion of health itself is linked to social, economic, and political conditions (Rosen, 1972). For example, the fact that Great Britain has far fewer malpractice suits than the United States may be due to expectations created by a socialized rather than capitalistic health care delivery system.

CONCEPTUALIZATIONS OF HEALTH
AND ITS CONTEXT

While many "medicalized" health care systems view health as the relative absence of disease, this definition is often criticized. The World Health Organization (WHO, 1968) offers a broader concept: "Health is a state of complete physical, mental, and social well being and not merely the absence of disease or infirmity" (p. 453). Antonovsky (1982, p. 55) suggests a continuum ranging from "ease to disease," so that we could regard someone with chronic illness (e.g., diabetes) as "relatively healthy" in the long term (Burish & Bradley, 1983).

The concept of health in the United States has been so dominated by medicine that the terms are almost synonymous (Illich, 1976). Arntson and Droge (1983) warn health communication researchers that their research has sociopolitical consequences, serving a regulative function for the medical establishment. McKnight (1985) argues that medicine and health can be antithetical; communication in a medical context can be very different from what is health promoting. He asserts (1985, p. 3) that "mislabelling may have contributed to the national commitment of . . . 11 percent of GNP for medical care in the mistaken belief that this huge investment will 'produce' health." Matarazzo (1982) suggests that the next major contribution to health will come not from advances in medical science but from having people behave in more healthy ways. The process of health promotion and disease prevention must, therefore, be pursued at all communication levels.

The WHO definition of health as including physical, mental, and even social well-being leaves one trying to think of a communication context in which none of those factors is at stake. A concept of health that includes virtually all interactions is no context at all, so we will limit our review here to *formalized* health care programs and settings and focus primarily on *physical* health, mindful of the interaction of physiological and psychological states and the psychosomatic etiology of some illnesses (Zegans, 1983).

There are a number of subcontexts within a health care delivery system. Interactions of an epileptic self-help group differ from those between a member and his or her physician (Arntson & Droge, 1983). We should also consider communication differences of various health professions. Private doctors on London's Harley Street interact with their wealthy patients in a different context from the bulk of doctors who serve Great Britain's masses.

Communication promotes health or illness within society, makes the system run at optimal or marginal effectiveness, and can facilitate efforts to treat illness and prevent its recurrence. Communication is also pervasively taken for granted (Pettegrew, 1982).

THE INTRAPERSONAL LEVEL

Psychological states and processes shape health communication, as they do all human interaction. A person's state of health, in turn, affects psychological processes. Behaviors related to health and illness are a function of a person's attitude and belief system and its effect on motivations to act in health-conscious ways (Seibold & Roper, 1979, p. 625).

Intrapersonal explorations of health communication concentrate almost exclusively on the patient or at-risk target population. Two areas dominate the individual-level literature: patient personality studies and research on patients' cognitive constructs. Both focus on individual predispositions and cognitive processing mechanisms.

Patient Personality Research

Individual personality characteristics are believed to *predispose* people to illness-promoting behaviors, unhealthy emotional states, or inadequate coping strategies (Cohen, 1979). Personal health appraisals and modes of coping depend on personality factors (Lazarus, 1966; Lazarus, Averill, & Opton, 1970). Cohen (1979, pp. 84-85) suggests that personality is linked to reporting of symptoms and the predisposition to seek medical treatment. He also associates personality with hypersensitivity to stressful aspects of life.

Personality types. Most personality research on health and behavior concerns the impatient, ambitious Type A or coronary-prone personality (Jenkins, 1971; Jenkins, Rosenman, & Friedman, 1968; Jenkins, Rosenman, & Zyzanski, 1974). Type B persons do not differ from Type A persons on physiological measures (Carver & Humphries, 1979); Type A behavior is risky to health, independent of traditional risk factors such as high blood pressure. Research suggests a link between the Type A personality, attentional focus, and information processing. Type A people are able to process a broader range of environmental stimuli (Carmody, Hollis, Matarazzo, Fey, & Connor, 1984) and may be more sensitive to interpersonal interactions. They may also be predisposed to uncooperative or noncompliant health behavior (DiMatteo & DiNicola, 1982, p. 119).

A second personality area is the "pain-prone patient" (Engel, 1959) or those with "pain-prone disorder" (Blumer & Heilbronn, 1981). Pain-prone individuals respond to stressful events with extreme emotional reactance. They tend to avoid physical activity, seek surgical intervention, and suffer from depression (Blumer, 1984). They also share some behaviors of the Type A personality. People with depressive personalities also utilize medical care at a higher rate than do other patients (Weissman et al., 1983). Personality may also affect rate of medication and how patients communicate about their illness (Pilowsky, 1978).

Provider research. Personality research on health care providers almost exclusively involves physicians. Ross (1971) identified defense mechanisms that account for physicians' denial of or failure to report personal problems. Jones (1977) found a higher proportion of affective psychological disorders among physicians than among hospitalized patients. Physicians may also have a cognitive orientation toward privacy that leads them to avoid contact with sick colleagues (Menninger, 1970).

Female medical students have attitudes and self-evaluations of their medical skills that are quite different from males' (Arntson, Zimmerman, Feinsod, & Speer, 1982). Women students recognized more psychosocial issues for patients while men saw themselves in greater control of communication with patients. During medical school, students gradually develop more depersonalized orientations toward people, contrary to the pattern among law and nursing students (Rosenberg, 1979). Male medical students integrate the role of physician more completely into their personality; female students maintain a personal identity separate from their medical role.

Personal constructs. Kobasa's (1982) work on "the hearty personality" adopts a constructivist view. She suggests that internal constructs about health and stress give rise to personal expectations and attributions, which in turn influence health-related behaviors. The hearty personality consists of high levels of commitment, control, and personal challenge, which enable people across a variety of professions to deal positively with stress (Johnson & Sarason, 1978; Kobasa, 1982).

Health locus of control research demonstrates links between high internal control, lower reporting of symptoms, greater adherence to medical regimens, and preventive health behaviors (Wallston & Wallston, 1982). Desire for control may be more situationally based than a personality construct (Dembroski, MacDougall, & Musante, 1984). The concept of "learned helplessness" has been used to describe the traditional passive role of the patient (Seligman, 1975; Wortman & Brehm, 1975). While generally those patients with more control or less helplessness fare better, Wortman and Dunkel-Schetter (1979) suggest that control is maladaptive for terminal cancer patients. Langer and Rodin (1976) found that giving nursing home residents more responsibility in day-to-day decision making had a dramatic positive effect on their health and mortality rate. Taylor and Levin (1977) tested a two-stage surgical procedure that permitted patients more opportunity for planning and control, with positive results. A follow-up study found both emotional and physical benefits with increased personal control (Rodin & Langer, 1977).

Health Campaigns

Researchers in heart disease prevention programs at Stanford University and the University of Minnesota have examined some individual predispositions toward mass mediated health campaigns. Chaffee and Roser (1986) found some support for the hypothesis that a person's involvement in a health issue increases consistency among that individual's health knowledge, attitudes, and behaviors. Media campaigns appear to influence knowledge more than behavior (Lee, Kline, Jacobs, & Hannan, 1985).

INTERPERSONAL LEVEL

Doctor-patient communication is viewed as the primary health care relationship, but research on it has been cast in the traditions of medicine, psychology, and sociology. If progress is to be made in health communication research at the interpersonal level, communication theories must be embraced more fully.

Dominant Research Traditions

Patients entering the health care context are confronted by a cadre of professionals, only a few of whom are physicians. Health care is increasingly an interdisciplinary activity carried out by a host of professionals (Leininger, 1978), but the doctor-patient relationship remains the focus of research. It is not necessarily the most important to the health of the patient; success of a medical intervention often depends on establishing multiple effective health care relationships. We have virtually no information on most of these. The dominant research traditions of medicine, psychology, and sociology have each brought special language, values, and variables to bear on doctor-patient communication.

Medicine. Research in the medical tradition has been guided by a "medical model" and more recently by a "bio-psycho-social model" (Engel, 1977). The medical model stresses cure, a dominant physician role, rather than prevention and the information functions of communication. The bio-psycho-social model expands the participative role of the patient and takes into account individual background factors. The physician remains the primary source of influence. This tradition focuses on the medical interview and physician behaviors, not on the total relationship or on patient behaviors (Pettegrew & Turkat, 1986).

Korsch and others have investigated the relationship between patient demographics, doctor communication characteristics, and evaluations of the interview (Francis, Korsch, & Morris, 1969; Freemon, Negrete, Davis, & Korsch, 1971; Korsch, Freemon, & Negrete, 1971; Korsch, Gozzi, & Francis, 1968; Korsch & Negrete, 1972). Communication is seen as information exchange, such as asking leading questions, using jargon, giving advice, and logically ordering questions (Werner & Korsch, 1979, p. 126). This research has been criticized for using the Bales system, which was originated for observation of task-oriented small group behavior (Arntson, Droge, & Fassl, 1978).

Stoeckle and colleagues have expanded the medical tradition's conception of communication (Stoeckle, 1982; Stoeckle, Zola, & Davidson, 1963; Waitzkin & Stoeckle, 1972). They include secondary gain, characteristics of the medical setting, and physician communication tasks. A related area of research uses an instrument called the Patient-Doctor Interaction Scale (PDIS) to examine patient perceptions of the process (Smith, Falvo, McKillip, & Pitz, 1984). Tate has also expanded the medical view, introducing such factors as physician presentation style, dress, seating position, time, and prescribing behavior. Cassell (1985) extends the medical tradition to include at least theoretical attention to the patient's value system, linguistic and paralinguistic cues, and conversational rules.

Psychology. By focusing on state and trait dynamics the patient brings to the medical interview, psychologists expand significantly on the provider-oriented value system. They are less concerned with diseases than with the unhealthy behaviors that cause them. They value patient behavior change more than advances in biomedical research. The role of the doctor and other providers is to modify unhealthy behavior and exact new responses (Matarazzo, 1980, 1982). A doctor can change patient behavior through conditioning and modeling techniques (Becker et al., 1977; Byrne & Long, 1976; Leventhal & Cleary, 1980).

Doctor-patient communication research in the psychological tradition adopts a cognitive framework (see reviews by Friedman, 1982; Hunt & MacLeod, 1979; Mentzer & Snyder, 1982; Pendleton, 1983). Byrne and Long (1976) conceptualize doctors' interaction styles on a continuum from physician-centered to patient-centered (see also Szasz & Hollender, 1956). Barsky et al. (1980) investigated the dominating managerial processes doctors use in their medical interviews.

Nonverbal behaviors (see Knapp, Cody, & Reardon, Chapter 13 in this volume) have been given considerable attention in psychological work on doctor-patient communication, including nonverbal behaviors of both parties (DiMatteo, Friedman, & Taranta, 1979; DeMatteo, Taranta, Friedman & Prince, 1980; Friedman, 1979a, 1982; Friedman & DiMatteo, 1982). Voice tone, eye contact, facial expression, posture, hand movements, and body lean all have effects on patient perception and management of pain, anxiety reduction, and the physician's ability to form an accurate impression of a patient. Friedman (1979b) examined both verbal and nonverbal channels, and found that patients expressed greater negative affect when the two channels were contradictory.

Roter (1984) found that composing a list of questions the patient had prior to the medical encounter led to increased feelings of patient participation and satisfaction. DiMatteo and DiNicola (1982) summarize evidence that patient compliance could be improved if physicians were more adept at establishing communication affect through verbal and nonverbal means. The amount of information a patient has about both his or her illness and medical regimen is related to compliance (Blackwell, 1973; Hulka, Cassel, Kupper, & Burdette, 1976; Roter, 1977). DiMatteo and DiNicola (1982, pp. 29-67) reviewed this literature and concluded that the amount of information does influence patient compliance. The optimal amount of information and manner of presentation is a question for future research.

Communication factors also affect the amount of information patients retain, as shown in research summarized by Ley (1983). He concludes that increased patient understanding will lead to increased recall; such techniques as simplification, categorization, repetition, and precision increase patient comprehension and recall of medical information.

Communication is also associated with patient satisfaction (Pendleton, 1983, pp. 34-40). Carroll and Monroe's (1979) meta-analysis of research on medical interviewing concluded that interpersonal communication was a strong predictor of patient satisfaction. Korsch's work *(supra)* also establishes this link.

The notion of communication process including mutual influence, simultaneity, and relationship development has not found its way into psychological research (Smith & Pettegrew, 1986). The physician's (or health care system's) value system is pervasively accepted; important health care outcomes are patient compliance and satisfaction. Reciprocal provider compliance and satisfaction have not been studied to any extent.

Sociology. The dominant theory and value system that sociology has contributed to the study of doctor-patient communication is the "health belief model" (Becker, 1974a, 1974b; Rosenstock, 1966) and its reformulations (Kasl, 1974). The health belief model holds that unhealthy behavior can be lessened and healthy behavior increased to the extent that a person believes he or she is susceptible to illness, the threat of illness is severe, and that the prescribed action will have direct benefit. These socially situated beliefs are mediated by individual motivational states and cues to take prescribed action (Seibold & Roper, 1979).

Sociologists have typically focused on attitudes, roles, beliefs, and linguistic rules and cues. Kasl (1974) reviewed the sociological doctor-patient communication research and offers several indictments. First, the patient is seen mainly in regard to socioeconomic setting rather than interpersonal setting. Second, there is little attention to the actual doctor-patient exchange. Third, the treatment of beliefs, attitudes, and values is external to the relationship rather than the product of doctor-patient talk.

Research by the sociolinguists is the major exception to Kasl's characterization. Cassell, Skopek, and Fraser (1977), Cicourel, (1983), and Skopek (1979) have examined the linguistic variations that emerge from cognitive and conceptual differences between provider and patient. They have not yet identified the degree to which patients or providers tend to change their linguistic patterns in response to each other. Cassell (1985, p. 8) has also looked at patient narratives as a tool for diagnosis and teaching, and urges scholars and practitioners to examine meanings of paralinguistic cues and conversational logic of patients.

Other sociolinguists have attempted to uncover structural rules embedded in doctor-patient communication (Frankel, 1980; Frankel & Beckman, 1982; Litton-Hawes, 1978; West, 1983). For these researchers, the key to understanding doctor-patient talk lies in the structure of language and rule-governing usage. In one study, researchers allowed patients and physicians to review their just completed interaction on videotape to test the assumptions each had made about the encounter and to review pertinent medical information (Frankel & Beckman, 1982).

The Communication Tradition

Ideally, communication scholars studying health communication at the interpersonal level would incorporate the theories and variables of our tradition. The results to date have been less than ideal. Costello (1977) and Cassata (1978) have referred to the communication "process" between doctors and patients and the importance of understanding how both parties in this relationship understand their worlds. Most research has been neither longitudinal nor comprehensive. In a review of doctor-patient communication Adler (1977, p. 186) suggests that communication scientists must keep abreast of theoretical development in the field. Adler only cites three sources in the communication tradition and these are reviews, not original studies. Communication's limited contributions to understanding doctor-patient interaction is due in part to its very recent and restricted entry into the health care setting and its initial interest in the therapist-client relationship (Costello, 1972; Pettegrew, 1977; Pettegrew & Thomas, 1978; Rossiter, 1975).

The first significant study of doctor-patient communication was performed by Arntson, Droge, and Fassl (1978). This followed Korsch's work on the interaction between pediatricians and the parents of their patients. In a follow-up study, Arntson and Phillipsborn (1982) found strong evidence of a superior-subordinate relationship in pediatrician-parent communication.

Pettegrew and Turkat (1986) argue for examining the patient's communication contributions to the doctor-patient relationship. In a series of studies on lower back pain patients, they found a strong relationship between how patients communicate about their illness and health care utilization factors. O'Hair, Behnke, and O'Hair (1983) found that patients prefer their doctors to have affective styles rather than information-oriented styles. This was especially pronounced for patients who were high on communication apprehension. Smith and Occhipinti (1984) showed that patients have very different expectations and experiences in the medical interview than do their physicians. Lane (1982, 1983) examined podiatrists' use of compliance-gaining tactics, which are typically task/informational and personal compliance-gaining strategies, and reliance on referent power. Patient satisfaction was not related to any one strategy. In most cases, research on doctor-patient communication does not do a thorough job of applying and testing theory from the communication tradition.

Other Health Care Relationships

Nurse-patient, allied health professionals-patient, and doctor-nurse communication are also studied. Generally neglected are peer relationships: doctor-doctor, nurse-nurse, even patient-patient.

Taylor (1970) suggests that nurses and doctors often act in voluntary isolation from one another, minimizing the opportunity for interaction. Bates and Chamberlin (1970) say nurses avoid interaction because of the dominant role physicians assume when communicating with them. Most research on the nurse-doctor relationship paints a picture of professional avoidance (Hoeckelman, 1978; Smoyak, 1978; Taylor, 1970; Weiss, 1983).

There is evidence, however, that physician dominance is giving way to more egalitarian behavior (Ford, 1982; Mauksch, 1983). Redland (1983) suggests that nurses' communication behavior may be more the result of a generalized way of interacting rather than a situationally based evaluation/action orientation. Fritz, Russell, Wilcox, and Shirk (1984) propose a detailed communication framework for more effective nurse interaction with physicians.

In the area of nurse-patient communication, research has focused on the nonverbal component of touch (Northouse & Northouse, 1985, pp. 152-162). Nurse nonverbal communication has a very positive effect on most patients. There is also some evidence to suggest that nurses communicate differently with patients than do physicians. Physicians rely more heavily on information giving and their dominant position, while nurses communicate more attentively and affectively with patients (Davitz & Davitz, 1980; Keenan, Aiken, & Cluff, 1981; Klinzing & Klinzing, 1985).

Allied health professionals (health care providers other than physicians or nurses) can also increase patient satisfaction (Caplan & Sussman, 1966). DelPolito and Barresi (1983) and Klinzing, Klinzing, and Schindler (1977) have outlined communication categories on allied health professional-patient communication.

A major influence on provider-patient interaction is the quality of interaction providers and patients have among themselves (Pettegrew, Arntson, Bush, & Zoppi, 1982). Albrecht (1982) and Kreps (1985) found that interpersonal communication among nurses was one of the primary and more effective methods of dealing with stress at work. Pettegrew, Wolf, and Ford (1982) found that open and expressive communication styles had a negative correlation with job-related stress.

Summary

Our understanding of other important interpersonal relationships in the health care context is fragmented. Evans and Clarke (1983) drew similar conclusions after reviewing the role of information in health communication at the interpersonal level. Which of the many health care providers has the most important or influential communication role? We have only a vague understanding of how patients and health care providers communicate among themselves.

NETWORK/ORGANIZATIONAL LEVEL

Health care networks can be viewed as components of health care organizations. For example, an organ transplant team consisting of surgeons, nurses, pathologists, hematologists, social workers, and radiological technicians may come from very different areas of a hospital yet unite their efforts as a team when an organ is located for a transplant recipient. Likewise, a social support group for medical residents may form to help its members deal with the intense stress during the residency program.

A group of diabetic patients under the care of the same doctor may also form to create a diabetic support group to share their ideas and experiences and to help each other cope more effectively with their long-term illness. In the same vein, a group of alcoholics may form from a local chapter of Alcoholics Anonymous. All these examples are instances of health communication at the network/organizational level. Of course, the operation of each group's parent organization must also be considered, whether it be a physician's private practice or a large urban medical center.

This section considers communication in health networks and health organizations. Health networks are divided into health care teams and self-help groups. In considering health care organizations, we begin with a previous review (Costello & Pettegrew, 1979) and evaluate recent developments in this area in light of recommendations in that review.

Health Care Teams

There are two types of health care teams. The most common is the interdisciplinary health care team (IHCT), comprising a variety of health care specialists from medicine, nursing, and the allied health professions (Leininger, 1971). The need for interdisciplinary health care teams has risen with increased specialization (Wise, 1972). Charns (1976) proposes that effective team functioning is essential to the overall quality of modern health care organizations. It should not be surprising that physicians are viewed as the leaders on IHCTs.

A second type of health care team is intradisciplinary, composed of members who are all from the same health-related discipline. The team nursing approach, for example, is intradisciplinary. Manthey (1980) cites the communication complexity of team nursing as a major drawback of the concept and argues for primary care nursing as an alternative. Most of our attention will focus on IHCTs because the vast majority of health care delivery is now done in this manner; there is very little research on intradisciplinary health care teams.

Interdisciplinary teams. Thornton (1978) suggests that the effective functioning of IHCTs depends on understanding the issues (power, mission, authority, etc.) that underlie the interactions of its various members. Geogropoulos and Cooke (1979) believe that teams must deal specifically with resource allocation, coordination, integration, maintenance, adaptation, and strain.

Kreps and Thornton (1984, pp. 143-144) suggest that IHCTs are very task-oriented, which frequently leads to their failure to understand important socioemotional needs. Yanda (1977) claims that the physician's leadership role on IHCTs is complicated by the inordinate amount of information (sometimes contradictory) available to the team members.

Frank (1961) and Nagi (1975) indicate that different disciplinary orientations are barriers to communication that hinder coordination and integration. IHCTs follow hierarchical leadership patterns and are reluctant to engage in the group processes necessary to support an emergent leader who is not a physician (Kane, 1965). Physicians are expected to be leaders although their training and the orientation of their colleagues leaves them ill prepared to assume managerial/leadership roles (Yanda, 1977: 10).

Self-Help Groups

Patient or provider self-help groups deal with social support. Droge (1982) indicates that nearly 20 million people participate in 500,000 mutual aid groups. The prevalence of these groups has vastly outstripped research on them.

Patient groups. The definitive work on patient self-help groups comes from the work of Droge and his colleagues (Arntson & Droge, 1983; Droge, 1982; Droge, Arntson, & Norton, 1981; Norton, Murray, & Arntson, 1982). There is good reason to believe that patient self-help groups form because patients feel stigmatized in their sick role (Edelman, 1977) and are powerless to deal effectively with the medical hierarchy (Langer, 1979). McKnight (1985) suggests that health action groups function to exert political pressure on decision makers they would be powerless to affect on an individual basis.

Droge (1982) finds that through this kind of network participation, patients can regain a sense of power, control, and personal competence. Norton et al. (1982) demonstrate that the dramatic communicator style variable has a close association to perceptions of health and the absence of depression among epileptics. Arntson (1980) found patient narratives or story telling to be both a major reason for attending epileptic self-help groups and a primary vehicle for help. King and Cushman (1982, 1983) found that communication in ethnic support groups plays a crucial role in reducing occupational stress. While communication in the form of social support lowered stress among various ethnic groups, each group had its distinctive communication patterns.

Provider groups. Provider self-help groups assist health care professionals in dealing with stress from working in the health care context. Two types have been dominant: nurse and medical resident social support groups; but there is little research on them. Theory suggests that provider groups serve primarily affective ends (Gottlieb, 1981). For newcomers (new nurses and medical residents), provider support groups also help socialization into the health care organization. Provider groups among medical residents are controversial. Physicians purposefully design medical residency programs to be stressful. Physicians also are socialized into *not* communicating openly about their feelings or stress (Pettegrew & Raney, 1982; Werner & Korsch, 1979). Nonetheless, the American Medical Association (AMA) has finally recognized the importance of support groups for medical residents and has begun doing research on their structure and function (Hugenin, 1977; Tokarz, Bremer, & Peters, 1979).

The nursing profession has recognized the need for support groups for nearly two decades. Kramer suggests that nurses are confronted with a very different reality from what they were trained to expect. When they begin working at a hospital they are poorly equipped to deal with its complexity and impersonality and must be socialized gradually or they will drop out of nursing (Kramer, 1966, 1974; Kramer & Schmalenberg, 1978). Communication research by Albrecht (1982) confirmed that withdrawal strategies are ineffective for coping with stress in nursing practice. She also discovered that support groups for nurses include alliances outside the hospital setting. Pettegrew, Wolf, and Ford (1982) found that openness and social support are key mediators of nursing stress. Vredenburgh and Trinkhaus (1981) found evidence of similar relationships between communication and stress in nursing.

Organizationwide Research

Health communication research at the organization level has lagged behind other levels. Hite and Hite (1977) found so little communication research on health organizations that their review was confined to theses and dissertations. There are several reasons for this. First, health care organizations are exceedingly complex. Second, it is much easier to gain entry into part of a health care organization than the entire organization. Third, organizationwide research is quite costly.

The work on communication in health care organizations by Georgopoulos (1974, 1975), Georgopoulos and Mann (1962), and Georgopoulos and Cooke (1979) is reviewed in Costello and Pettegrew (1979). There have also been some significant contributions from the communication field. Ray (1981, 1983) examined both a hospital and a human service organization, looking for the relationship between communication patterns and job-related stress. Frequency of communication was unrelated to job burnout (Ray, 1983, p. 853). Pettegrew et al. (1980) examined an entire medical center organization and found that social support and personal participation were strong mediators of job-related stress. Salem and Williams (1982) conceived of a small community as an information system using subscales from the ICA Communication Audit to examine the flow of information. They found that employees wanted more information in both group and interpersonal meetings with management. Hospital employees also wanted more written information (opposite to manufacturing organizations). Message certainty was also correlated with job satisfaction.

One study examined communication *across* several health care organizations. Woodlock (1983) examined 171 offices of the National Institute of Alcohol and Alcohol Abuse looking at communication patterns across several levels. She found that participation, trust, and absence of conflict were most closely associated with a less stressful working environment.

Evaluation

Typically, at the network/organization level communication is viewed as a moderator or mediator of illness or job-related stress. While this makes sense, other issues need to be addressed. For example, if the functioning of self-help groups alienates patients from their physicians, are the groups really being helpful? Job-related stress as a dependent measure is an important meta-health issue, but so are cost containment, efficient operation, and health care marketing.

THE MACRO LEVEL

Since 1978 the improvement of public health in the United States has been a benchmark for measuring social progress. Most states established physician licensing mechanisms between 1820 and 1840 and their own public health agencies in the late 19th century. Starr (1982) describes how community hospitals rapidly developed as an instrument of social welfare and gained municipal status after 1870. The diffusion of medical information and health tips to the public also has been a significant issue to governments and the health care delivery system for more than two centuries. In the 18th and 19th centuries a flourishing medical counterculture was frequently criticized by the established medical community in the United States (Starr, 1982). The practice and acceptance of folk medicine in the United States was seen by physicians as the principal source of misinformation about health and disease, which unnecessarily exacerbated public health problems (Starr, 1982).

Concern about public awareness of health and disease shifted in the 20th century to the mass media, which were seen as a new and influential source of medical information (Krieghbaum, 1967). The medical community's alarm about the public's ability to obtain accurate health/medicine information grew as opinion polls indicated in the 1970s that media were the principal source of information about health and medicine other than a personal physician (Simpkins & Brenner, 1984). Physicians also turn to the mass media to obtain medical news (O'Keefe, 1970). Bogart (1982) found that health/medical news accounts for about 3% of the news and entertainment space in most U.S. newspapers.

The medical community's interest in the widespread public exposure to health and medical news derives from the finding that mass media can influence people's awareness of social issues, their priorities in determining decisions, and perceptions of the world around them (Gerbner, 1981; McCombs & Shaw, 1972). If the public's agenda regarding health care is linked to the mass media's agenda, the results could directly affect that status of health care. To mass communication researchers, the study of mass media portrayals of health provides an opportunity to participate in a debate with public policy implications and to supply needed data.

Portrayal of Health in the Mass Media

Most research about the mass media's portrayal of health and its effects on behavioral patterns (Atkin, 1981) has been limited to news, entertainment programming, and advertising on television, magazines, or newspapers. Forms of mass media are thought of as publicly accessible while exposure to media channels is presumed to be voluntary. Readers viewed are thought to "converge" on health communications (Simpkins & Brenner, 1984); they are not forced to attend to the message as they might in a formal educational setting (a class) or in a physician's office. Analyses of mass media content have focused on the depiction of new diseases, alcohol, smoking, cancer, and images conveyed by television entertainment programming and advertising. Researchers have assessed the accuracy and comprehension of health information conveyed by the mass media to the public. Recently studies have begun to determine the linkage between media content and health knowledge, attitudes, uses, and behavioral changes in audiences (Gerbner, Gross, Morgan, & Signorielli, 1981; Chaffee & Roser, 1986).

In a broad review of the news media's coverage of health risks from new diseases, nuclear power accidents, and toxic spills, Nelkin (1984) reported "a reasonable degree of accuracy, comprehensiveness and impartiality" in most major U.S. newspapers, wire services, and television networks. Although a task force of scientists, physicians, and journalists found some evidence to the contrary and made recommendations for improvements in journalistic training, they said the primary sources of misinformation and partiality in the press were usually scientists, researchers, and government officials. The press's willingness to provide a context about the risks of new diseases, such as AIDS, the report concluded, was often accomplished in spite of scientists/physicians who either emphasized narrow perspectives or suppressed rival interpretations.

Social and ethical dimensions of the first human heart transplantation in 1967 paralleled the "hard news" aspects of the transplantation story throughout its duration as a major news topic, according to a content analysis of major news magazines (Oates, 1973). Finn and Strickland (1982) concluded that alcohol advertisements in television and popular magazines did not carry much objectionable or controversial content.

On the other hand, Whelen, Sheridan, Meister, and Mosher's analysis (1981) of 12 years of news reporting about health topics in popular women's magazines found only 12 of 548 articles that could be classified as anti-smoking. The authors suggested that "the reluctance of a large segment of the print media to inform the public about health hazards of smoking is a serious impediment to public health education" (p. 28). A study of cancer coverage in the large U.S. newspapers found they gave the impression that "everything causes cancer" (Freimuth, Greenberg, DeWitt, & Romano, 1984). While surveys "indicate the public is seriously misinformed about the incidence and prevalence of cancer," the authors concluded, "information to dispel such misconceptions and alleviate public fears is rarely found in newspaper coverage of cancer." Gerbner et al. (1981) investigated the health-related content of 10 years of televised entertainment programming and 3 years of commercials. Obesity, smoking, need for medical treatment and illness among health care professionals were rarely portrayed on television.

Although these studies reveal mixed evidence, it is clear that the public can be misinformed about health care as a result of routine exposure to news reporting in major newspapers or network television programming. It has become public policy in the United States and other nations to reverse adverse effects of the mass media's portrayal of health care by barring some forms of advertising or by campaigns set along more therapeutic lines. For example, most Western nations have banned the advertising of cigarettes on television, and advertising of food products for children on television has been heavily regulated in several European nations. To encourage more health-promoting behaviors, mass media research has turned to applied campaigns in three areas: the prevention of smoking, drug and alcohol abuse prevention, and cardiovascular disease.

Anti-smoking. Governmental and private sponsors, including the National Cancer Institute, the American Cancer Society, and the American Lung Association, have been involved in smoking cessation and prevention campaigns since a 1964 U.S. Surgeon General's report that linked cigarette smoking to lung cancer. In a review of smoking cessation research Farquhar, Mangus, and Maccoby (1981, p. 414) found "that the dramatic changes noted in adult smoking, particularly among middle-aged males and certain professional groups can be attributed largely to the effectiveness of information and educational campaigns." The most optimistic estimate of audience impact was calculated by Warner (1977) suggesting that anti-smoking publicity reduced cigarette consumption in the United States by 20 to 30%. In Finland, a television series that instructed people how to stop smoking resulted in a "moderately sustained cessation" of between 2 and 4% of Finland's smokers in the 1970s (McAlister, 1981). Farquhar et al. (1981) indicated that a

Norwegian campaign that combined a total ban on all forms of tobacco promotion, prohibition of sales to persons under 16, smoking bans in public and work places, public relations efforts by 300 to 400 health educators and anti-smoking advertising in all mass media resulted in an "important decline in tobacco use."

A challenge to researchers in smoking campaigns has been the assessment of the interaction between mass media, individual, and interpersonal influences in determining behavioral changes (Farquhar, 1983; Flay, DiTecco, & Schlegel, 1980; Simpkins & Brenner, 1984). McAlister (1981) found that anti-smoking campaigns increased public awareness of smoking's health consequences and shifted attitudes—without necessarily altering smoking behaviors. There was little evidence to indicate which factors influenced reported cognitive or attitude changes. Farquhar et al. (1981, p. 417) noted that despite the success of anti-smoking campaigns, it was difficult to determine the relative contribution of the mass media in conjunction with interpersonal communication variables (such as physician's advice, or support structure within a family or peer unit) to changes in intention, action, or behavior. The next generation of research, they emphasized, should attempt to track the relative contribution of intrapersonal, interpersonal, and mass communication components upon the cognitive, affective, and behavioral dimensions of smoking socialization patterns.

Alcohol and drug abuse campaigns. Research in this area focused on the effects of commercial advertising on alcohol and drug consumption and the utilization of the mass media to encourage healthier drug and alcohol practices (Hammond, 1980; Wallack, 1981). Several public service broadcast campaigns in the United States and Canada were unable to increase awareness or affect attitudes regarding drug or alcohol abuse (Feingold & Knapp, 1977; Goodstadt, 1977; Kinder, 1975; Morrison, Kline, & Miller, 1976). Campaigns to cease drug purchases (Hanneman et al., 1978) and promote more moderate alcohol use (Wallack, 1979) reported unsuccessful results. A media campaign sponsored by the National Institute on Drug Abuse (1978) reported some cognitive shifts, but attitudes about drug abuse and drug use failed to improve.

One difference between drug abuse and the smoking and cardiovascular campaigns was an initial failure to supplement mass media with interpersonal and intrapersonal reinforcement. Research on commercial advertising effects has reflected a broader approach. In contrast to Atkin and Block (1979), Rossiter and Robinson (1980) reported no correlation between exposure to television drug advertising and attitudes and utilization patterns among children. Similar findings in international settings were reported by Williams, Plant, and Grant (1982) and Duffy (1972). Strickland (1982) found that teenagers who were highly motivated to watch alcohol advertising for social utility reasons were influenced by repeated exposure. Interpersonal influences, such as direct incentives and social rewards for alcohol consumption, were more significant influences on teenage alcohol consumption than were mass media.

This work has moved the field closer to the research agenda advocated by Comstock (1976) by identifying research needs in the following drug and alcohol abuse areas: (1) the patterns and character of advertising portrayals, (2) the contribution of advertising portrayals to concepts about alcohol and drugs held by adults and teenagers, (3) the effect of advertising portrayals on consumption, and (4) the potential for television advertising and entertainment programs to alter consumption patterns.

Cardiovascular disease prevention. The most extensive field testing of the impact of mass media on health behaviors has been in the area of cardiovascular disease prevention. Major campaigns to reduce the risk of heart disease have occurred in four U.S. states (California, Minnesota, Rhode Island, and Massachusetts) and in Finland, Australia, Switzerland, South Africa, and the Federal Republic of Germany (see Farquhar, 1983b, for a review). The most complete data are from the Stanford Heart Disease Prevention Program (SHDPP) in California.

The initial heart disease prevention program at Stanford was conducted from 1972 to 1975 in three California communities. Its goals were to reduce heart risk by reducing weight, cigarette smoking, cholesterol levels, and blood pressure. Campaign results revealed a reduction in multifactor cardiovascular risk in the "media-only" town and in the town with "media plus intensive face-to-face instruction of a subgroup at a high risk" in contrast to the "no-treatment" community (Farquhar, Fortmann, Wood, & Haskell, 1983, p. 177). The campaign was effective when mass media communication was supplemented by interpersonal instruction, and "in many instances the mass media efforts were quite successful even in the absence of supplemental personal instruction." Farquhar et al. (1983) added,

> It now seems evident that certain kinds of behavior associated with risk reduction, e.g., eating pattern changes, can be rather readily learned through exposure to mass media . . . while others, e.g., cigarette smoking cessation, require the media to provide a larger proportion of skills training to be successful. However, if the educator has access to it, mass media can be designed to provide some of that training and to organize personal instruction systems to augment that training. (pp. 177-178)

Stanford's Five City Project expanded the previous study by evaluating effects of a similar program in larger communities, broadening the target audience to all age groups, monitoring change over a longer period

(8 years), and developing a model program to be adopted by other communities (Farquhar, Maccoby, & Solomon, 1984). The Minnesota Heart Health Project (MHHP) suggests cognitive complexity regarding cardiovascular risk factors can be expanded without the psychological involvement formerly thought to be associated with information seeking behavior (Pavlik et al., 1985). The authors note that the nature of cardiovascular campaigns (which emphasize increased physical activity) may be more salient than anti-smoking or other behavior cessation health campaigns. Pavlik et al. (1985) and Finnegan and Loken (1985) demonstrated the effectiveness of "little media" (inexpensive pamphlets, brochures, and specialized publications) in increasing knowledge regarding heart disease prevention.

In contrast with most anti-smoking and drug and alcohol abuse studies, these cardiovascular disease campaigns suggest that mass media can be unilaterally effective in influencing awareness, attitudes, and change regarding health behaviors. As Maccoby and Alexander concluded (1980, p. 369): "If mass media alone . . . can lead to results in behavior change, then there is far more hope for health campaigns than was previously suspected."

Theoretical Considerations

In a critique of campaign research in the 1970s, Simpkins and Brenner (1984) found an overemphasis on social learning theory and a preoccupation with mass media at the expense of other communication variables. Most campaign research, they noted, emphasized a linear model of mass communications effects which evaluated 12 response steps from audience exposure on through to reinforcement of learned behaviors. This model, Simpkins and Brenner (1984, p. 291) concluded, is a comprehensive description of the "conditions with which communication-for-change programs must contend in the planning and design stage for persuasion campaigns. However, the model is not an explanation of why the outcomes (outputs) occur as a result of the communication programs (inputs)." Similarly, Atkin (1981) found research about the utilization of mass media to improve the public knowledge about health was one-dimensionally centered on the utilization of channels (radio, television, newspapers, etc.) to create persuasive messages. Atkin criticized the dearth of research about how the public acquires health knowledge or is motivated to attend to public health campaigns. Simpkins and Brenner (1984) suggested that health communication research should encompass the interaction of interpersonal, intrapersonal, and mass media communication upon cognitive, affective, and conative states.

The recent studies of alcohol abuse by Strickland (1982) and cardio-vascular risk reduction (Farquhar et al., 1983; Farquhar et al., 1984; Kline, 1982) appear to reflect more holistic conceptual approaches along the lines suggested by Simpkins and Brenner and by Atkin. The Five City Studies monitored the role of opinion leaders, for example, and traced communication via network analysis (Rogers & Kincaid, 1981). In the Minnesota project, researchers evaluated the impact of different family and community types on motivations for health information (Lee et al., 1985). The Minnesota and Stanford projects have explored applications of the hierarchical model of effects proposed by Ray et al. (1973), McGuire's (1969) communication-persuasion model, Ajzen and Fish-bein's (1980) attitude change model, and Rogers and Shoemaker's (1971) diffusion of innovations theory (see Rogers & Storey, Chapter 26).

Simpkins and Brenner (1984) and Atkin (1981) note that in most previous studies of mass media health communication the audience's expectations of the mass media and the quality of news or programming presented to the public have not been independent variables. Another missing component in advertising research seems to be the behavioral context in which advertising messages are applied. There has been little systematic research about the consumer's willingness to be influenced by advertising for health- and beauty-related products in comparison with public service campaigns. As Simpkins and Brenner (1984) note, the *context* of the experience of attending to mass media, as well as the audience's expectations, needs to be better identified by health commu-nication researchers.

The ascertainment of how the public converges on mass media does not answer how the public converges on *health*. The degree that health care providers and public and governmental *values* regarding health coincide or conflict, which has been all but ignored in the literature, could be a significant issue in research evaluating mass media effects. Graham (1981) points out a false conception about the process of formu-lating scientific or health knowledge, one that has been widely advocated by scientists. The commonly held theory of scientific and technology transfer (which Graham terms "restrictionism") assumes that the forma-tion of scientific (biomedical) knowledge is determined within scientific paradigms that are immune from social values. Since scientific infor-mation is perceived as more "value free" than public opinion, the mass media have been seen as a delivery system to optimize the transfer of health and science information to the public. This has focused scientific attention on the mass media's ability to influence public education about data provided by scientists—with a minimum of information "loss" via inaccurate or incomplete reporting.

But Graham argues the formation of scientific theories and knowl-edge is influenced constantly by public values. He proposes that a theory of science and technology transfer should recognize the interaction

between social values and science, making extrascientific considerations both an integral part of biomedical science and a critical element
of its mass communication and public understanding. Yankelovich (1982)
further suggests that the mass media's role is to provide new channels
for the discussion of public and provider values about health issues and
practices.

Another significant omission in mass media health research has been
the effects of media on social institutions and society (see Ettema & Whitney, Chapter 24). In health communication, these issues include the
assumption that mass media, coupled with the agenda of health care providers, can produce public health care behaviors that are socially therapeutic and utilitarian. In contrast, Illich (1976), Reiser (1978), and
Friedson (1970) maintain that the mass media (in collusion with the
health care delivery system) glamorize the use of drugs and expensive
medical technology in American society and sanction an ideology that
positions physicians as society's only healers. The result may be an
overdependency on the health care delivery system to treat illness and
identify health, which Illich (1976) and Friedson (1970) argue is both
socially deleterious and inequitable. Overmedicalization, Illich (1976,
p. 39) concludes, "unleashes a social pathogenic process" that changes
a person's innate "adaptive ability into passive medical consumer discipline." Although these writers fail to provide alternatives, they raise
significant questions about the mass media's role in maintaining the
institutional privileges of the health care delivery system.

Diffusion of Medical Information Systems

The newest health communication research at the macro level is the
impact of medical information systems (MISs) on medical practitioners
and the health care delivery system. Researchers in this area accept the
arguments advanced by Schiller (1984) and others that information systems are a mass medium and the impact of computing on professions,
society, and social change merits serious scholarly attention in the communications sciences.

In contrast with other forms of mass media where the receiver is more
passive or the audience can be "inadvertent," a user of information systems participates intesively in the communication setting. A physician
must enter patient data, learn to manipulate patient data bases, and learn
sets of commands to identify medical problems, or ask for alternative
diagnoses in order to achieve clinical benefits from interaction with a
computer. This higher level of media participation also replaces routine
forms of archiving patient records or obtaining a secondary opinion for a
diagnosis, which have been established as norms in medical praxis and
communication patterns for more than a century. As Ruchinskas, Pease,
and Svenning (1983) note, "the computer may potentially redefine the

traditional communication process, though its acceptance and use are in part dependent on these processes as they operate today" (p. 2).

First generation of MISs. Research interest in MISs began in 1980 after the National Academy of Sciences (1979) reported that the slow acceptance of MISs was in striking contrast to the widespread use of other equipment-embodied technologies and the utilization of other computing applications in the health care delivery system. Since work in the area of the diffusion of medical information systems is interdisciplinary, the discussion of findings will not be confined to communication studies. The academy (1979) reported that medical information systems had not gained acceptance despite evidence accumulated over two decades that MISs were economically feasible, widely available, technologically sound, and of clinical value (see also Henley & Wiederhold, 1975; Hodge, 1977; Lindberg, 1979a). Hirel (1979) differentiated MISs from more medically related computer and microprocessing technologies. Manning (1983) outlined extensive applications of electronic data processing in billing and administrative accounting departments in most U.S. hospitals and in private medical practice.

Lindberg (1979b) defined MISs as "formal arrangements by which the facts concerning the health or health care of patients are stored and processed by computers." MISs are often seen as incorporating the following elements (Lindberg, 1979b): patient identification; care location; demographic patient information; past hospitalizations; diagnosis or diagnoses; linkage information (linking new information to the existing record); time qualifiers; laboratory test results; interpretive data, such as working diagnoses, treatment plans, and therapeutic orders; billing information; relevant information from patient interviewing; and diagnostic capability to help physicians analyze clinical data.

In explaining the relatively poor adoption of medical information systems, researchers originally cited four principal dimensions: technological problems (Blois, 1980; Giebink & Hurst, 1975), organizational questions (Henley & Wiederhold, 1975; Weed, 1970), sociopolitical effects (Lindberg, 1979a; Needleman & Lewin, 1979); and sociopsychological factors (Ball & Snelbecker, 1982; McDermott, 1979; Schwartz, 1979; Shannon, 1979). Brenner and Logan (1980) note that the technical, organizational, and sociopolitical deficiencies of MISs were not sufficient to explain why equipment embodied technologies with similar difficulties had been widely accepted within the medical community; these authors point to sociopsychological factors.

Second Generation of MIS Research

Unlike the first MIS studies, which were qualitative analyses of MISs' assets and liabilities, the second generation of MIS research sought to determine the relative structuring of physician attitudes toward the four dimensions that surround the arguments over MISs. Most of the second-generation studies analyzed the relative importance of technological, organizational, sociopolitical, and sociopsychological arguments that were raised among physicians in support and criticism of MISs.

Hodge (1977) first confirmed that sociopsychological factors were an impediment to physician acceptance of MISs. He found a 60:40 favorability/unfavorability ratio among physicians toward MISs and noted that resistance to MISs was centered among internists, psychiatrists, and practitioners in private medical practice with limited experience with computers or microprocessing equipment. Teach and Shortliffe (1981) asked physicians about acceptability, perceived demands, and overall expectations of computer-assisted diagnostic systems. They found five orientations toward computer-assisted diagnosis, which partially corroborated and partially challenged previous assumptions about physician priorities.

Two groups of physicians were concerned about the organizational and technological impact of computer-assisted diagnosis on the health care delivery system. These groups noted that computer-assisted diagnostic systems would not replace valued medical assistants and should be more portable, flexible, and reviewable to override computer and human errors in treatment planning and diagnostic proficiency. Both these groups were optimistic that computer diagnostic systems could be developed to alleviate organizational and technological concerns among physicians. The opinions of three other segments of physicians were along narrower lines. One group seemed to be concerned exclusively with application of computer-assisted diagnosis in their personal medical practice. Another group emphasized effects of the systems on the medical profession. A final group was concerned that computer-assisted diagnostic systems should display superior medical knowledge plus "commonsense" reasoning capabilities.

Logan and Brenner (1982) similarly found two groups of physicians who judged MISs vis-à-vis professional and personal practice orientations, but both of these groups had more reservations about MISs than the physicians Teach and Shortliffe surveyed. Although the physicians believed that MISs improved the availability of medical and patient knowledge, they were concerned about the inaccuracy of MIS-provided information. The professionally oriented physicians said they might be willing to adopt MISs to help *other* physicians improve health care delivery, but they were concerned that MISs forced physicians to standardize medical terms. A third group thought the standardization of medical logic might seriously jeopardize the availability of patient information and lead to the practice of "defensive medicine" by physicians.

In a study of physicians highly favorable toward MISs, Logan (1985) found that three groups believed that MISs' technological deficiencies were a deterrent to acceptance. The physicians in the study, who all were involved in the design of MIS hardware and software, were uncertain whether MISs conflicted with professional values or adversely affected communication within the health care delivery system. But they conceded that MISs were inaccurate and could provide an illusion of reliability. Few of the physicians surveyed were optimistic that the medical community was willing to utilize MISs to process patient information or as a diagnostic substitute for the opinions of another physician. Logan concluded, "MISs, it seems, may not be widely perceived as technically sound and without clinical deficiencies until its proponents are similarly convinced."

In a review of the second generation of MIS research Logan and Brenner (1983) reached the following conclusions:

(1) A perceived threat to professional autonomy is not an important consideration for most physicians in determining the acceptability of an innovation that may benefit the profession or improve private practice.
(2) Physicians who judge an innovation primarily by its potential contribution to the medical profession are the most willing to accept change and overlook an innovation's deficiencies.
(3) Physicians who judge an innovation primarily by its long range social impact are the least willing to accept change or overlook an innovation's deficiencies.
(4) Physician resistance to MISs is less linked to an inherent conservatism about change than to tangible technical, sociopsychological, and sociopolitical reservations.

Theoretical considerations. MIS research to date has focused on obstacles and gateways to diffusion and the role of innovators among physicians, mostly within the framework of the diffusion of innovations perspective (Rogers & Shoemaker, 1971). Research is only beginning on campaigns to change attitudes, utilize mass media, and adjust computer software/hardware to accelerate acceptance, learning, and use of MISs within applied clinical settings. MIS research can be differentiated from most mass media health communication studies because adopters' values have been assumed from the beginning to be more critical to adoption than either the characteristics of an innovation or the communication processes used to introduce an innovation. This assumption was based on evidence that physicians have not been receptive to MISs—in contrast to the diffusion of other equipment embodied technologies with similar technological, organizational, and sociopolitical deficiencies.

Besides providing new evidence about diffusion phenomena and the sociology of the medical profession, MIS research contributes to an understanding that computers are expected to become communication as well as information tools within the medical community. Some physicians expect MISs to reason (or display a tacit dimension) as well as to provide useful clinical data. This suggests that the medical profession is an appropriate venue to study how machines are humanized within the values of a profession.

The development of fifth-generation computers may enable MISs to assimilate medical knowledge within several specialities simultaneously and provide medical reasoning via advanced artificial intelligence techniques (Feigenbaum & McCorduck, 1983). As the technological barriers of MISs decline in the future, will sociopsychological and organizational barriers increase in importance to explain physician resistance? The adoption of MISs is within the entire health care delivery system and not just among physicians. The study of the organizational consequences and responses to medical information systems should extend beyond physicians' opinions.

NOTE

1. A more complete treatment of communication's potential contributions to understanding the doctor-patient relationship via persuasion can be found in Smith and Pettegrew (1986).

REFERENCES

Adler, K. (1977). Doctor-patient communication: A shift to problem-oriented research. *Human Communication Research, 3,* 170-190.

Ajzen, I., & Fishbein, M. (1980). *Understanding attitudes and predicting social behavior.* Englewood Cliffs, NJ: Prentice-Hall.

Albrecht, T. (1982). Coping with occupational stress: Relational and individual strategies of nurses in acute health care settings. In M. Burgoon (Ed.), *Communication yearbook 6.* Newbury Park, CA: Sage.

Antonovsky, A. (1982). *Health, stress, and coping.* San Francisco: Jossey-Bass.

Arntson, P. (1980). *Professional-client communication: The narrative response in self-help groups.* Paper presented to the Health Communication Division of the International Communication Association Convention, Acapulco, Mexico.

Arntson, P., & Droge, D. (1983). *The socio-political consequences of health communication research.* Paper presented to the Health Communication Division of the International Communication Association Convention, Dallas.

Arntson, P., Droge, D., & Fassl, H. E. (1978). Pediatrician-patient communication: Final report. In B. Ruben (Ed.), *Communication yearbook 2.* New Brunswick, NJ: Transaction.

Arntson, P., & Phillipsborn, H. F. (1982). Pediatrician-parent communication in a continuity of care setting. *Clinical Pediatrics, 21,* 302-307.

Arntson, P., Zimmerman, B., Feinsod, P., & Speer, M. (1982). Communicating with patients: The perceptions of medical students. In L. S. Pettegrew, P. Arntson, D. Bush, & K. Zoppi (Eds.), *Straight talk: Explorations in provider-patient communication.* Louisville, KY: Humana.

Atkin, C. K. (1981). Mass media information campaign effectiveness. In R. E. Rice & W. J. Paisley (Eds.), *Public communication campaigns*. Newbury Park, CA: Sage.

Atkin, C. K., & Block, M. (1979). *Content and effects of alcohol advertising: Report 1. Overview and summary of project.* Unpublished manuscript, Michigan State University, Department of Communication.

Ball, M., & Snelbecker, G. (1982, July/August). Overcoming resistance to telecommunications innovations in medicine and continuing medical education. *Computers in Hospitals,* pp. 40-45.

Barber, B. (1979). Patients' perspectives on hospital information systems. In R. H. Shannon (Ed.), *Hospital information systems: An international perspective and problems and prospects.* New York: North.

Barsky, A. J., Kazis, L. E., Freiden, R. B., Goroll, A. H., Hatem, C. J., & Lawrence, R. S. (1980). Evaluating the interview in primary care medicine. *Social Science and Medicine, 14A,* 653-658.

Bates, B., & Chamberlin, R. W. (1970). Physician leadership as perceived by nurses. *Nursing Research, 19,* 534-539.

Becker, M. H. (1974a). The health belief model and personal health behavior: Introduction. *Health Education Monographs, 2,* 326-327.

Becker, M. H. (1974b). The health belief model and sick role behavior. *Health Education Monographs, 2,* 409-419.

Becker, M. H., Haefner, D., Kasl, S. V., Kirscht, J. P., Maiman, L. A., & Rosenstock, I. M. (1977). Selected psychosocial models and correlates of health-related behaviours. *Medical Care, 15,* 27-46.

Blackwell, B. (1973). Drug therapy: Patient compliance. *New England Journal of Medicine, 289,* 249-253.

Blois, M. S. (1980). Clinical judgements and computers. *New England Journal of Medicine, 303,* 192-197.

Blumer, D. (1984). Chronic pain and depression: The pain-prone disorder. In C. Van Dyke, L. Temoshok, & L. S. Zegans (Eds.), *Emotions in health and illness: Applications to clinical practice.* Orlando, FL: Grune & Stratton.

Blumer, D., & Heilbronn, M. (1981). Second-year follow-up study on systematic treatment of chronic pain with antidepressants. *Henry Ford Hospital Medical Journal, 29,* 67-68.

Bogart, L. (1982). Newspapers in transition. *Wilson Quarterly, 6,* Special Edition.

Brenner, D. J., & Logan, R. (1980). Some considerations in the diffusion of medical technologies: Medical information systems. In D. Nimmo (Ed.), *Communication yearbook 4.* New Brunswick, NJ: Transaction.

Burrish, T. G., & Bradley, L. A. (Eds.). (1983). *Coping with chronic disease: Research and applications.* New York: Academic Press.

Byrne, P. S., & Long, B.E.L. (1976). *Doctors talking to patients.* London: HMSO.

Caplan, E., & Sussman, M. (1966). Rank-order of important variables for patient and staff satisfaction. *Journal of Health and Human Behavior, 7,* 133-138.

Carmody, T. P., Hollis, J. F., Matarazzo, J. D., Fey, S. G., & Connor, W. E. (1984). Type A behavior, attentional style, and symptom reporting among adult men and women. *Health Psychology, 3,* 45-62.

Carroll, G., & Monroe, J. (1979). Teaching clinical interviewing in the health professions: A critique of educational research and practice. *Journal of Medical Education, 54,* 489-500.

Carver, C. S., & Humphries, C. (1982). Social psychology of the type A coronary-prone behavior pattern. In G. S. Sanders & J. Suls (Eds.), *Social psychology of health and illness.* Hillsdale, NJ: Lawrence Erlbaum.

Cassata, D. M. (1978). Health communication theory and research: An overview of the communication specialist interface. In B. Ruben (Ed.), *Communication yearbook 2.* New Brunswick, NJ: Transaction.

Cassell, E. J. (1985). *Talking with patients: Volume 1. The theory of doctor-patient communication.* Cambridge: MIT Press.

Cassell, E. J., Skopek, L., & Fraser, B. (1977). A preliminary model for the examination of doctor-patient communication. *Language Science, 43.*

Chaffee, S. H., & Roser, C. (1986). Involvement and the consistency of knowledge, attitudes and behaviors. *Communication Research, 13,* 373-399.

Charns, M. (1976). Breaking the tradition barrier: Managing integration in health care facilities. *Health Care Management Review, 1,* 55-67.

Cicourel, A. V. (1983). Hearing is not believing: Language and the structure of belief in medical communication. In S. Fisher & A. D. Todd (Eds.), *The social organization of doctor-patient communication.* Washington, DC: Center for Applied Linguistics.

Cohen, F. (1979). Personality, stress, and the development of illness and patient care. In G. C. Stone, F. Cohen, & N. E. Adler (Eds.), *Health psychology.* San Francisco: Jossey-Bass.

Collen, M. (1971). Reasons for failures and factors making for success. *Symposium on the development of hospital computing systems.* Copenhagen: World Health Organization, Regional Office for Europe.

Comstock, G. (1976). *Television and alcohol consumption.* Santa Monica, CA: Rand.

Costello, D. E. (1972). Therapeutic transaction: An approach to human communication. In R. Budd & B. Ruben (Eds.), *Approaches to human communication.* New York: Spartan.

Costello, D. E. (1977). Health communication theory and research: An overview. In B. Ruben (Ed.), *Communication yearbook 1.* New Brunswick, NJ: Transaction.

Costello, D. E., & Pettegrew, L. S. (1979). Health communication theory and research: An overview of health organizations. In D. Nimmo (Ed.), *Communication yearbook 3.* New Brunswick, NJ: Transaction.

Cullen, D. J., & Teplick, R. (1979). The role of computers in the future of intensive care. *Proceedings of IEEE, 67,* 1307-1308.

Davitz, L., & Davitz, J. (1980). *Nurses' responses to patients' suffering.* New York: Springer.

DelPolito, C. M., & Barresi, J. (Eds.). (1983). *Alliances in health and education: Serving youngsters with special needs.* Washington, DC: American Society of Allied Health Professions.

Dembroski, T. M., MacDougall, J. M., & Musante, L. (1984). Desirability of control versus locus of control. *Health Psychology, 3,* 15-26.

DiMatteo, M. R., & DiNicola, D. D. (1982). *Achieving patient compliance: The psychology of the medical practitioner's role.* New York: Pergamon.

DiMatteo, M. R., Friedman, H. S., & Taranta, A. (1979). Sensitivity to bodily nonverbal communication as a factor in practitioner-patient rapport. *Journal of Nonverbal Behavior, 4,* 18-26.

DiMatteo, M. R., Taranta, A., Friedman, H. S., & Prince, L. M. (1980). Predicting patient satisfaction from physicians' nonverbal skills. *Medical Care, 18,* 376-387.

Droge, D. (1982). *Epilepsy self-help groups, stigma, and social support.* Unpublished doctoral dissertation, Northwestern University.

Droge, D., Arntson, P., & Norton, R. W. (1981). *The social support function in epilepsy self-help groups.* Paper presented to the Health Communication Division of the International Communication Association Convention, Minneapolis.

Duffy, M. (1972). The effect of advertising on the total consumption of alcohol drinks in the United Kingdom: Some econometric measures. *Journal of Advertising, The Quarterly Review of Marketing Communications, 1,* 105-117.

Edelman, M. (1977). *Political language: Words that succeed and policies that fail.* New York: Academic Press.

Engel, G. (1959). "Psychogenic" pain and the pain-prone patient. *American Journal of Medicine, 26,* 899-918.

Engel, G. (1977). The need for a new medical model. *Science, 196,* 129-136.

Evans, S. H., & Clarke, P. (1983). When cancer patients fail to get well: Flaws in health communication. In R. Bostrom (Ed.), *Communication yearbook 7.* Newbury Park, CA: Sage.

Farquhar, J. W. (1983). Changes in American lifestyle and health. In J. Hamner III & B. Jacobs (Eds.), *Marketing and managing health care: Health promotion and health disease prevention.* Memphis: University of Tennessee Center for the Health Sciences.

Farquhar, J. W., Fortmann, S., Wood, P., & Haskell, W. (1983). Community studies of cardiovascular disease prevention. In N. Kaplan & J. Stamler (Eds.), *Prevention of coronary heart disease: Practical management of risk factors.* Philadelphia: W. B. Saunders.

Farquhar, J. W., Maccoby, N., & Solomon, D. (1984). Community applications of behavioral medicine. In W. D. Gentry (Ed.), *Handbook of behavioral medicine.* New York: Guilford.

Farquhar, J. W., Mangus, P., & Maccoby, N. (1981). The role of public information and education in cigarette smoking control. *Canadian Journal of Public Health, 72,* 412-420.

Feigenbaum, E., & McCorduck, P. (1983). *The fifth generation, artificial intelligence and Japan's computer challenge to the world.* Reading, MA: Addison-Wesley.

Feingold, P., & Knapp, M. (1977). Anti-drug abuse commercials. *Journal of Communication, 27,* 2-28.

Finn, T., & Strickland, D. (1982). The advertising and alcohol abuse issue: A cross-media comparison of alcohol beverage advertising content. In M. Burgoon (Ed.), *Communication yearbook 6.* Newbury Park, CA: Sage.

Finnegan, J., & Loken, B. (1985). *The effects of direct mail on health awareness and knowledge in community heart health campaigns.* Paper presented to the Health Communication Division of the International Communication Association Convention, Honolulu.

Flay, B., DiTecco, D., & Schlegel, R. P. (1980). Mass media in health promotion: An analysis using an extended information-processing model. *Health Education Quarterly, 7,* 127-147.

Ford, L. (1982). Nurse practitioners: History of a new idea and predictions for the future. In L. Aiken (Ed.), *Nursing in the 1980's.* Philadelphia: Lippincott.

Francis, V., Korsch, B. M., & Morris, M. J. (1969). Gaps in doctor-patient communication: Patients' response to medical advice. *New England Journal of Medicine, 280,* 535-540.

Frank, L. (1961). Interprofessional communication. *American Journal of Public Health, 51,* 1798-1804.

Frankel, R. M. (1980). Microanalysis and the medical encounter: An exploratory study. In D. Anderson (Ed.), *Analytic Sociology.*

Frankel, R. M., & Beckman, H. B. (1982). Impact: An interaction-based method for preserving and analyzing clinical transactions. In L. S. Pettegrew (Ed.), *Straight talk: Explorations in provider and patient interaction.* Louisville, KY, Humana.

Freeman, B., Negrete, V. F., Davis, M., & Korsch, B. M. (1971). Gaps in doctor-patient communications: Doctor-patient interaction analysis. Pediatric Residency, *5,* 298-311.

Freimuth, V., Greenberg, R., DeWitt, J., & Romano, R. (1984). Covering cancer: Newspapers and the public interest. *Journal of Communication, 34,* 62-73.

Friedman, H. S. (1979a). Nonverbal communication between patients and medical practitioners. *Journal of Social Issues, 35,* 82-100.

Friedman, H. S. (1979b). The interactive effect of facial expressions of emotion and verbal messages on perceptions of affective meaning. *Journal of Experimental Social Psychology, 15,* 453-469.

Friedman, H. S. (1982). Nonverbal communication in medical interaction. In H. S. Friedman & M. R. DiMatteo (Eds.), *Interpersonal issues in health care.* New York: Academic Press.

Friedman, H. S., & DiMatteo, M. R. (Eds.). (1982). *Interpersonal issues in health care.* New York: Academic Press.

Friedson, E. (1970). *Profession of medicine.* New York: Dodd, Mead.

Fritz, P. A., Russell, C. G., Wilcox, E. M., & Shirk, F. I. (1984). *Interpersonal communication in nursing: An interactionist approach.* Norwalk, CT: Appleton-Century-Crofts.

Georgopoulos, B. S. (Ed.). (1974). *Organization research on health institutions.* Ann Arbor, MI: Institute for Social Research.

Georgopoulos, B. S. (1975). *Hospital organization research: Review and source book.* Philadelphia: W. B. Saunders.

Georgopoulos, B. S., & Cooke, R. A. (1979). *Conceptual-theoretical framework for the organizational study of hospital emergency services* (ISR Working Paper Series). Ann Arbor, MI: Institute for Social Research.

Georgopoulos, B. S., & Mann, F. C. (1962). *The community general hospital.* New York: Macmillan.

Gerbner, G., Gross, L., Morgan, M., & Signorielli, N. (1981). Health and medicine on television. *New England Journal of Medicine, 305,* 901-904.

Giebink, G., & Hurst, L. (1975). *Computer projects in health care.* Ann Arbor, MI: Health Administration Press.

Goffman, E. (1961). *Asylums.* Garden City, NY: Doubleday.

Goodstadt, M. (1977). *An evaluation of the Ontario (1975-1976) alcohol education program: T.V. and radio exposure and initial impact.* Toronto: Addiction Research Foundation.

Gottlieb, B. H. (Ed.). (1981). *Social networks and social support.* Newbury Park, CA: Sage.

Graham, L. (1981). *Between science and values.* New York: Columbia University Press.

Hammond, J. (1980). *The use and abuse of drug information: A fix on ten years of drug abuse prevention campaigns.* Washington, DC: National Institute on Drug Abuse.

Hanneman, G. J., Weinbeck, W. L., Goldman, R., Svenning, L., Nicol, J., Quatelbaum, C. T., & Sciredos, J. (1978). *The medicine man message* (Vol. 3). Los Angeles: University of Southern California, Center for Communication Policy Research.

Henley, R. & Wiederhold, S. (1975). *An analysis of automated ambulatory medical record systems.* San Francisco: University of California at San Francisco Medical Center.

Hirel, J. (1979). General impact of new technology on health care. In R. H. Shannon (Ed.), *Hospital information systems: An international perspective on problems and prospects.* New York: North.

Hite, R. W., & Hite, S. A. (1977). *Recent doctoral research in hospital organizational communication: A critique.* Paper presented to the Western Speech Communication Association Convention, Phoenix.

Hodge, M. (1977). *Medical information systems: A resource for hospitals.* Germantown: Aspen Systems Publishing.

Hoeckelman, R. A. (1978). Nurse-physician relationships: Problems and solutions. In N. L. Chaska (Ed.), *The nursing profession: Views through the mist.* New York: McGraw-Hill.

Hugenin, M. B. (Ed.). (1977). *Helping the impaired physician: Proceedings of the AMA conference on "The impaired physician: Answering the challenge."* Chicago: American Medical Association.

Hulka, B., Cassel, J., Kupper, L., & Burdette, J. (1976). Communication, compliance, and concordance between physicians and patients with prescribed medications. *American Journal of Public Health, 66,* 847-853.

Hunt, E. B., & MacLeod, C. M. (1979). Cognition and information processing in patient and physician. In G. C. Stone, F. Cogen, & N. E. Adler (Eds.), *Health Psychology.* San Francisco: Jossey-Bass.

Illich, I. (1976). *Medical nemesis.* New York: Pantheon.

Jenkins, C. D. (1971). Psychologic and social precursors of coronary disease. *New England Journal of Medicine, 284,* 244-255.

Jenkins, C. D., Rosenman, R. H., & Friedman, M. (1968). Replicability of rating the coronary-prone behavior pattern. *British Journal of Preventive and Social Medicine, 22,* 16-22.

Jenkins, C. D., Rosenman, R. H., & Zyzanski, S. J. (1974). Prediction of clinical heart disease by a test for the coronary-prone behavior pattern. *New England Journal of Medicine, 290,* 1271-1275.

Johnson, J. H., & Sarason, I. G. (1978). Life stress, depression, and anxiety. Internal-external control as a moderator variable. *Journal of Psychosomatic Research, 22,* 205-208.

Jones, R. E. (1977). A study of 100 physician psychiatric inpatients. *American Journal of Psychiatry, 134,* 1119-1123.

Kane, R. A. (1975). *Interprofessional teamwork* (Manpower Monograph No. 8). Syracuse, NY: Syracuse University, Division of Continuing Education and Manpower Development.

Kasl, S. V. (1974). The health belief model and behavior related to chronic illness. *Health Education Monographs, 2,* 433-455.

Keenan, T., Aiken, L., & Cluff, L. (1981). *Nurses and doctors: Their education and practice.* Cambridge, MA: Oelgeschlager, Gunn & Hain.

Kinder, B. (1975). Attitudes toward alcohol and drug abuse II: Experimental data, media research, and methodological considerations. *International Journal of the Addictions, 10,* 1035-1054.

King, S. S., & Cushman, D. P. (1982). *Ethnic support systems: An overview with some preliminary findings.* Paper presented to the Health Communication Division of the International Communication Association Convention, Boston.

King, S. S., & Cushman, D. P. (1983). *Behavior patterns among ethnic groups in response to occupational stress.* Paper presented to the Health Communication Division of the International Communication Association Convention, Dallas.

Kline, F. G. (1982). *The Minnesota heart health project: Field intervention in American communities.* Att Forandra Levnadssatt, Riksbankens Jubileumsfond Stockholm.

Klinzing, D., & Klinzing, D. (1985). *Communication for allied health professionals.* Dubuque, IA: Wm. C. Brown.

Klinzing, D. R., Klinzing, D. G., & Schindler, P. D. (1977). A preliminary report of a methodology to assess the communicative interaction between hospital personnel and hospitalized children. *American Journal of Public Health, 67,* 670-672.

Kobasa, S. (1982). Stressful life events, personality and health: An inquiry into hardiness. In M. R. DiMatteo & H. S. Friedman (Eds.), *Social psychology and medicene.* Cambridge, MA: Oelgeschlager, Gunn, & Hain.

Korsch, B. M., Freemon, B., & Negrete, V. F. (1971). Practical implications of doctor-patient interaction: Analysis for pediatric practice. *American Journal of Diseases of Children, 121,* 109-114.

Korsch, B. M., Gozzi, E. K., & Francis, V. (1968). Gaps in doctor-patient communication I: Doctor-patient interaction and patient satisfaction. *Pediatrics, 42,* 855-871.

Korsch, B. M., & Negrete, V. F. (1972). Doctor-patient communication. *Scientific American, 227,* 66-74.

Kramer, M. (1966). *Some effects of exposure to employing bureaucracies on the role conceptions and role deprivation of neophyte collegiate nurses.* Unpublished doctoral dissertation, Stanford University.

Kramer, M. (1974). *Reality shock: Why nurses leave nursing.* St. Louis, MO: C. V. Mosby.

Kramer, M., & Schmalenberg, C. E. (1978). Bicultural training and the new graduate role transformation. *Nursing Digest, 5,* 1-47.

Kreps, G. L. (1985). *A field research and development study of nurse turnover and retention in a large urban health care organization.* Paper presented to the Health Communication Division of the International Communication Association Convention, Honolulu.

Kreps, G. L., & Thornton, B. C. (1984). *Health communication.* New York: Longman.

Krieghbaum, H. (1967). *Science and the mass media.* New York: New York University Press.

Lane, S. D. (1982). Communication and patient compliance. In L. Pettegrew, P. Arntson, D. Bush, & K. Zoppi (Eds.), *Straight talk: Explorations in provider and patient interaction.* Louisville, KY: Humana.

Lane, S. D. (1983). Compliance, satisfaction, and physician-patient communication. In R. Bostrom (Ed.), *Communication yearbook 7.* Newbury Park, CA: Sage.

Langer, E. J. (1979). The illusion of incompetence. In L. Permutter & R. Monty (Eds.), *Choice and perceived control.* Hillsdale, NJ: Lawrence Erlbaum.

Langer, E. J., & Rodin, J. (1976). The effects of choice and enhanced personal responsibility for the aged: A field experiment in an institutional setting. *Journal of Personality and Social Psychology, 34,* 191-198.

Lazarus, R. S. (1966). *Psychological stress and the coping process.* New York: McGraw-Hill.

Lazarus, R. S., Averill, J. R., & Opton, E. M., Jr. (1970). Toward a cognitive theory of emotion. In M. B. Arnold (Ed.), *Feelings and emotions.* New York: Academic Press.

Lazarus, R. S., & Cohen, J. B. (1977). Environmental stress. In I. Altman & J. F. Wohlwill (Eds.), *Human behavior and the environment: Current theory and research.* New York: Plenum.

Lee, J., Kline, F. G., Jacobs, D., & Hannan, P. (1985). *Acquisition of health messages for different individual and family types in different communities.* Paper presented to the Health Communication Division of the International Communication Association Convention, Honolulu.

Leininger, M. (1971). This I believe . . . about interdisciplinary health education for the future. *Nursing Outlook, 19,* 787-791.

Leininger, M. (1978). Professional, political, and ethnocentric role behaviors and their influence in multidisciplinary health education. In M. Hardy & M. Conway (Eds.), *Role theory.* New York: Appleton-Century-Crofts.

Leventhal, H., & Cleary, P. D. (1980). The smoking problem: A review of the research and theory in behavioral risk reduction. *Psychological Bulletin, 88,* 370-405.

Ley, P. (1983). Patients' understanding and recall in clinical communication failure. In D. Pendleton & J. Hasler (Eds.), *Doctor-patient communication.* London: Academic Press.

Lindberg, D.A.B. (1979a). The development of diffusion of medical technology: Medical information systems. In *Medical technology and the health care delivery system: A study of the diffusion of equipment embodied technology.* Washington, DC: National Academy of Science.

Lindberg, D.A.B. (1979b). *Growth of medical information systems in the United States.* Lexington, KY: Lexington.

Litton-Hawes, E. (1978). A discourse analysis of topic co-selection in medical interviews. *Sociolinguistic Newsletter, 9,* 25-26.

Logan, R. (1985). Attitudes about medical information systems: A Q study of AAMSI members. In A. Levy & B. Williams (Eds.), *Proceedings of the 1985 AAMSI Congress*. Washington, DC: American Association for Medical Systems and Informatics.

Logan, R., & Brenner, D. (1982). The effects of physicians' values and role perceptions on the diffusion of medical information systems. In L. Pettegrew et al. (Eds.), *Straight talk: Explorations in provider and patient communication*. Louisville, KY: Humana.

Logan, R., & Brenner, D. (1983). *Inclinations to communicate: Integration of two generations of diffusion research in medical information systems*. Paper presented to the Health Communication Division of the International Communication Association Convention, Dallas.

Maccoby, N., & Alexander, J. (1980). Use of media in lifestyle programs. In P. Davidson & S. Davidson (Eds.), *Behavioral medicine: Changing health lifestyles*. New York: Brunner/Mazel.

Manning, P. (1983, February 25). Continuing medical education: The next step. *The Journal of the American Medical Association*, p. 249.

Manthey, M. (1980). *The practice of primary nursing*. Boston: Blackwell Scientific Publications.

Matarazzo, J. D. (1980). Behavioral health and behavioral medicine: Frontiers for a new health psychology. *American Psychologist, 35,* 807-817.

Matarazzo, J. D. (1982). Behavioral health's challenge to academic, scientific, and professional psychology. *American Psychologist, 37,* 1-14.

Mauksch, I. (1983). An analysis of some critical contemporary issues in nursing. *Journal of Continuing Education in Nursing, 14,* 4-6.

McAlister, A. (1981). Anti-smoking campaigns: Process in developing effective communications. In R. E. Rice & W. J. Paisley (Eds.), *Public communication campaigns*. Newbury Park, CA: Sage.

McCombs, M., & Shaw, D. (1972). The agenda-setting function of the mass media. *Public Opinion Quarterly, 36,* 176-187.

McDermott, W. (1979). Evaluating the physician and his technology. *Daedalus, 106,* 135-157.

McGuire, W. J. (1969). The nature of attitudes and attitude change. In G. Lindzey & E. Aronson (Eds.), *The handbook of social psychology*. Reading, MA: Addison-Wesley.

McKnight, J. L. (1985). *Where can health communication be found?* Paper presented to the Health Communication Division of the International Communication Association Convention, Honolulu.

Mentzer, S. J., & Snyder, M. L. (1982). The doctor and the patient: A psychological perspective. In G. S. Sanders & J. Suls (Eds.), *Social psychology of health and illness*. Hillsdale, NJ: Lawrence Erlbaum.

Morrison, A. J., Kline, F. G., & Miller, P. V. (1976). Aspects of adolescent information acquisition about drugs and alcohol topics. In R. Ostman (Ed.), *Communication research and drug education*. Newbury Park, CA: Sage.

Nagi, S. (1975). Teamwork in health care in the United States: A sociological perspective. *The Milbank Quarterly, 53,* 103-119.

National Academy of Sciences. (1979). *Medical technology and the health care system: A study of the diffusion of equipment-embodied technology*. Washington, DC: Author.

National Institute on Drug Abuse. (1978). *Evaluation of the 1978 drug abuse prevention campaign: Final Report*. Washington, DC: National Institute on Drug Abuse, Public Sector Research Group.

Needleman, J., & Lewin, L. (1979). The impact of state regulation on the adoption and diffusion of new medical technology. In *Medical technology and the health care system: A study of the diffusion of equipment-embodied technology*. Washington, DC: National Academy of Sciences.

Nelkin, D. (1984). Task force on communication of scientific risk. *Science in the streets.* New York: Priority Press.

Northouse, P. G., & Northouse, L. L. (1985). Health communication: A handbook for health professionals. Englewood Cliffs, NJ: Prentice-Hall.

Norton, R. W., Murray, E., & Arntson, P. (1982). *Communication links to health: Dramatic style covariates of health perceptions.* Paper presented to the Health Communication Division of the International Communication Association Convention, Boston.

Oates, W. (1973). Social and ethical content in science coverage by newsmagazines. *Journalism Quarterly, 50,* 680-684.

O'Hair, H. D., Behnke, R. R., & O'Hair, M. J. (1983). *Health beliefs and receiver apprehension as predictors of patient preferences for physician communicator style.* Paper presented to the Health Communication Division of the International Communication Association Convention, Dallas.

O'Keefe, M. (1970). The mass media as sources of medical information for doctors. *Journalism Quarterly, 47,* 95-100.

Palley, N., & Groner, G. (1975). Information processing needs and the practices of clinical investigators. In *Proceedings of national computer conference 1975.* New York: American Federation of Information Processing.

Pavlik, J., Wackman, D., Kline, F. G., Jacobs, D., Pechacek, T., & Pirie, P. (1985). *Cognitive structure and involvement in a health information campaign.* Paper presented to the Health Communication Division of the International Communication Association Convention, Honolulu.

Pendleton, D. A. (1982). Communicating in the doctor's office: A model and a strategy for health communication research. In L. S. Pettegrew et al. (Eds.), *Straight talk: Explorations in provider and patient communication.* Louisville, KY: Humana.

Pendleton, D. A. (1983). Doctor-patient communication: A review. In D. A. Pendleton & J. Hasler (Eds.), *Doctor-patient communication.* London: Academic Press.

Pettegrew, L. S. (1977). An investigation of therapeutic communicator style. In B. Ruben (Ed.), *Communication yearbook 1.* New Brunswick, NJ: Transaction.

Pettegrew, L. S. (1982). Some boundaries and assumptions in health communication. In L. S. Pettegrew et al. (Eds.), *Straight talk: Explorations in provider and patient communication.* Louisville, KY: Humana.

Pettegrew, L. S., Arntson, P., Bush, D., & Zoppi, K. (Eds.). (1982). *Straight talk: Explorations in provider and patient communication.* Louisville, KY: Humana.

Pettegrew, L. S., & Raney, D. C. (1982). *Job-related stress in the medical residency across two points in time.* Paper presented to the Health Care Administration Division of the Academy of Management Convention, New York.

Pettegrew, L. S., & Thomas, R. C. (1978). Communicator style differences in formal vs. informal therapeutic relationships. In B. Ruben (Ed.), *Communication yearbook 1.* New Brunswick, NJ: Transaction.

Pettegrew, L. S., Thomas, R. C., Costello, D. E., Wolf, G. E., Lennox, L. & Thomas, S. L. (1980). Job-related stress in a medical center organization: Management of communication issues. In D. Nimmo (Ed.), *Communication Yearbook 4.* New Brunswick, NJ: Transaction.

Pettegrew, L. S., & Turkat, I. D. (1986). How patients communicate about their illness. *Human Communication Research, 12,* 376-394.

Pettegrew, L. S., Wolf, G. E., & Ford, J. (1982). *Differentiating stress-related factors among three nursing services.* Paper presented to the Health Communication Division of the International Communication Association Convention, Boston.

Pilowsky, I. (1978). A general classification of abnormal illness behavior. *British Journal of Medical Psychology, 51,* 131-137.

Ray, E. B. (1981). *A communication perspective on burnout in a human service organization.* Unpublished doctoral dissertation, University of Washington.

Ray, E. B. (1983). Job burnout from a communication perspective. In R. Bostrom (Ed.) *Communication yearbook 7.* Newbury Park, CA: Sage.

Ray, M. L., Sawyer, A. G., Rothschild, M. L., Heeler, R. M., Strong, E. C., & Reed, J.B. (1973). Marketing communication and the hierarchy of effects. In P. Clarke (Ed.), *New models for mass communication research.* Newbury Park, CA: Sage.

Redland, A. (1983). *An investigation of nurses' interaction styles with physicians and suggested patient care interventions.* Paper presented to the Health Communication Division of the International Communication Association Convention, Dallas.

Reiser, S. (1978). *Medicine and the reign of technology.* New York: Cambridge University Press.

Rodin, J., & Langer, E. (1977). Long-term effects of a control-relevant intervention with the institutionalized aged. *Journal of Personality and Social Psychology, 35,* 897-902.

Rogers, E. M., & Kincaid, D. L. (1981). *Communication network analysis: A new paradigm for research.* New York: Free Press.

Rogers, E. M., & Shoemaker, F. (1971). *Communication of innovations: A cross cultural approach.* New York: Free Press.

Rosen, G. (1972). The evolution of social medicine. In H. E. Freeman, S. Levine, & L. G. Reeder (Eds.), *Handbook of medical sociology* (2nd ed.). Englewood Cliffs, NJ: Prentice-Hall.

Rosenberg, P. R. (1979). Catch-22—The medical model. In E. C. Shapiro & L. M. Lowenstein (Eds.), *Becoming a physician: Development of values and attitudes in medicine.* Cambridge, MA: Ballinger.

Rosenstock, I. M. (1966). Why people use health services. *Milbank Memorial Fund, 44,* 94-124.

Ross, J. L. (1971). The physician as a psychiatric patient. *Psychiatric Digest, 37,* 46.

Rossiter, C. (1975). Defining therapeutic communication. *Journal of Communication, 25,* 127-130.

Rossiter, J., & Robinson, T. (1980). Children's dispositions toward proprietary drugs and the role of television drug advertising. *Public Opinion Quarterly, 44,* 316-329.

Roter, D. (1977). Patient participation in the patient-provider interaction: The effects of patient question-asking on the quality of interaction, satisfaction, and compliance. *Health Education Monographs, 5,* 281-330.

Roter, D. (1984). Patient question asking in physician-patient interaction. *Health Psychology, 3,* 395-410.

Ruchinskas, J., Pease, P. & Svenning, L. (1983). *Health communications in transition: The impact of computing on private care practitioners.* Paper presented to the Health Communication Division of the International Communication Association, Dallas.

Salem, P., & Williams, M. L. (1982). *An analysis of uncertainty and satisfaction: A hospital case study.* Paper presented to the Health Communication Division of the International Communication Association Convention, Boston.

Schiller, H. (1984). *Information in the crisis economy.* Norwood, NJ: Ablex.

Schwartz, W. (1979). Decision analysis: A look at the chief complaints. *New England Journal of Medicine, 300,* 556-559.

Seibold, D. R., & Roper, R. E. (1979). Psychosocial determinants of health care intentions: Test of the Triandis and Fishbein models. In D. Nimmo (Ed.), *Communication yearbook 3.* New Brunswick, NJ: Transaction.

Seligman, M. E. (1975). *Helplessness.* San Francisco: W. H. Freeman.

Shannon, R. (1979). Human factors in hospital information systems. In R. Shannon (Ed.), *Hospital information systems—An international perspective on problems and prospects.* New York: North.

Shapiro, E. C., & Jones, A. B. (1979). Women physicians and the exercise of power and authority in health care. In E. C. Shapiro & L. M. Lowenstein (Eds.), *Becoming a physician: Development of values and attitudes in medicine.* New York: Ballinger.

Simpkins, J., & Brenner, D. (1984). Mass media communication and health. In M. Voight & B. Dervin (Eds.), *Progress in communication science* (Vol. 5). Norwood, NJ: Ablex.

Skopek, L. (1979). Doctor-patient conversation: A way of analyzing its linguisitic problems. *Semiotica, 25,* 301-311.

Smith, D. H., & Occhipinti, S. L. (1984). *Patient reactions to physician interviews.* Paper presented to the Health Communication Division of the International Communication Association Convention, San Francisco.

Smith, D. H., & Pettegrew, L. S. (1986). Mutual persuasion as a model for doctor-patient communication. *Theoretical Medicine, 7,* 127-146.

Smith, F. K., Falvo, D., McKillip, J., & Pitz, G. (1984). Measuring patient perceptions of the patient-doctor interaction. *Evaluation and the Health Professions, 7,* 77-94.

Smoyak, S. A. (1978). Problems in interprofessional relations. In N. L. Chaska (Ed.) *The nursing profession: Views through the mist.* New York: McGraw-Hill.

Starr, P. (1982). *The social transformation of American medicine.* New York: Basic Books.

Stoeckle, J. D. (1982). The improvement of communication between doctor and patient. In L. S. Pettegrew et al. (Eds.), *Straight talk: Explorations in provider and patient communication.* Louisville, KY: Humana.

Stoeckle, J. D., Zola, I. M., & Davidson, G. E. (1963). On going to see the doctor: The contributions of the patient to the decision to seek medical aid. *Journal of Chronic Disease, 16,* 975-989.

Strickland, D. (1982). Alcohol advertising: Orientations and influence. *Journal of Advertising: The Quarterly Review of Marketing Communications, 1,* 307-319.

Szasz, T. S., & Hollender, M. H. (1956). A contribution to the philosophy of medicine: The basic models of doctor-patient relationship. *Archives of Internal Medicine, 97,* 585-592.

Tate, P. (1983). Doctor's style. In D. Pendleton & J. Hasler (Eds.), *Doctor-patient communication.* London: Academic Press.

Taylor, C. (1970). *In horizontal orbit.* New York: Holt, Rinehart & Winston.

Taylor, S., & Levin, S. (1977). The psychological impact of breast cancer: Theory and practice. In A. J. Enelow & D. M. Panagis (Eds.), *Psychological aspects of breast cancer* (Tech. Bulletin No. 1). San Francisco: West Coast Cancer Foundation.

Teach, R., & Shortliffe, E. (1981). *An analysis of physician attitudes regarding computer based clinical consulting systems.* Unpublished manuscript, Stanford University, Departments of Medicine and Computer Science Heuristic Programming Project.

Thornton, B. C. (1978). Health care teams and multimethodological research. In B. Ruben (Ed.), *Communication yearbook 2.* New Brunswick, NJ: Transaction.

Tokarz, J. P., Bremer, W., & Peters, K. (1979). *Beyond survival.* Chicago: American Medical Association.

Vredenburgh, D. J., & Trinkaus, R. J. (1981). *Job stress among hospital nurses.* Paper presented to the Health Administration Division of the Academy of Management Convention, San Diego.

Waitzkin, H., & Stoeckle, J. D. (1972). The communication of information about illness: Clinical, social and methodological considerations. *Advances in Psychosomatic Medicine, 8,* 180-215.

Wallack, L. (1979). The California prevention demonstration program evaluation: Description, methods and findings. In *Report for California department of alcohol and drug abuse.* Berkeley: Social Research Group.

Wallack, L. (1981). Mass media campaigns: The odds against finding behavior change. *Health Education Quarterly, 8,* 209-260.

Wallston, K. A., & Wallston, B. S. (1982). Who is responsible for your health: The construct of locus of control. In G. S. Sanders & J. Suls (Eds.), *Social psychology of health and illness.* Hillsdale, NJ: Lawrence Erlbaum.

Warner, K. (1977). The effects of the anti-smoking campaign on cigarette consumption. *American Journal of Public Health, 67,* 645-650.

Weed, L. (1970, February). Technology is a link, not a barrier for doctor and patient. *Modern Hospital,* pp. 89-92.

Weiss, S. (1983). Role differentiation between nurse and physician: Implications for nursing. *Nursing Research, 32,* 133-139.

Weiss, S. M. (1983). Health and illness: The behavioral medicine perspective. In L. Temoshok, C. Van Dyke, & L. S. Zegans (Eds.), *Emotions in health and illness: Theoretical and research foundations.* Orlando, FL: Grune & Stratton.

Weissman, M. M., Myers, J. K., Tischler, G. L., Orvaschel, H., Holzer, C. E., & Leaf, P. J. (1983). Depression and perception of health in an urban community. In L. Temoshok, C. Van Dyke, & L. S. Zegans (Eds.), *Emotions in health and illness.* Orlando, FL: Grune & Stratton.

Werner, E. R., & Korsch, B. M. (1979). Professionalization during the pediatric internship: Attitudes, adaptation and interpersonal skills. In E. C. Shapiro & L. M. Lowenstein (Eds.), *Becoming a physician: Development of values and attitudes in medicine.* Cambridge, MA: Ballinger.

West, C. (1983). "Ask me no questions . . ." An analysis of queries and replies in physician-patient dialogues. In S. Fisher & A. D. Todd (Eds.), *The social organization of doctor-patient communication.* Washington, DC: Center for Applied Linguistics.

Whelen, E., Sheridan, J., Meister, K., & Mosher, B. (1981). Analysis of coverage of tobacco hazards in women's magazines. *Journal of Public Health Policy, 2,* 28-35.

Williams, A., Plant, M., & Grant, M. (Eds.). (1982). *Economics and alcohol: Consumption and controls.* London: Croom-Helm.

Wise, H. (1972). The primary health care team. *Archives of Internal Medicine, 130,* 438-444.

Woodlock, B. K. (1983). Levels of exchange and organizational communication. In R. Bostrom (Ed.), *Communication Yearbook 7.* Newbury Park, CA: Sage.

World Health Organization. (1958). *The first ten years of the World Health Organization.* Geneva, Switzerland: Author.

Wortman, C. B., & Brehm, J. W. (1975). Responses to uncontrollable outcomes: An integration of reactance theory and the learned helplessness model. In L. Berkowitz (Ed.), *Advances in experimental social psychology* (Vol. 8). New York: Academic Press.

Wortman, C. B., & Dunkel-Schetter, C. (1979). Interpersonal relationships and cancer: A theoretical analysis. *Journal of Social Issues, 35,* 120-155.

Yankelovich, D. (1982). Changing public attitudes to science and the quality of life. *Science, Technology and Human Values, 39,* 23-29.

Yanda, R. L. (1977). *Doctors as managers of health teams.* New York: AMACOM.

Zegans, L. S. (1983). Emotions in health and illness: An attempt at integration. In L. Temoshok, C. Van Dyke, & L. S. Zegans (Eds.), *Emotions in health and illness.* Orlando, FL: Grune & Stratton.

23 Organizational Assimilation

FREDRIC M. JABLIN
University of Texas, Austin

KATHLEEN J. KRONE
Ohio State University

T
HE notion that organizational communication can be viewed from various levels of analysis is not new (e.g., Farace & Mac-Donald, 1974). While researchers have long recognized the theoretical importance of organizing their research around such levels of analysis as individuals, dyads, small groups, intact organizations, and environments, they have had great difficulty accomplishing this task. As a consequence, it is not unusual to find researchers in the area admonishing one another against inadvertently intermixing levels of analysis in their studies and thereby confusing the meaning of their research results and/or failing to recognize the effects of higher or lower levels of analysis on the particular level being studied (Jablin, 1980a).

The virtual universal acceptance by scholars of the notion that organizations are "open systems" (Katz & Kahn, 1978) largely accounts for the ease with which they have embraced the importance of clearly specified levels of analysis in their research. As frequently noted in discussions of systems theory, a "system" (be it individual, group, or organization) is composed of suprasystems as well as subsystems that are in hierarchical-interactive relationship with one another (e.g., Kast & Rosenzweig, 1972). In essence, this principle suggests that in order for researchers to depict accurately communication activity in organizations, they must not only explore behaviors within isolated levels of analysis, but also consider how the simultaneous interaction among levels affects the phenomenon under observation. However, as Roberts, Hulin, and Rousseau (1978) observe, organizational researchers rarely concern themselves with activities taking place on several levels at once "because those processes are so complex" (p. 25). As a result,

> organizational theorists try to reduce this complexity by factoring problems they address into quasi-independent parts and treating each part separately. Decomposition of complex problems into components imposes

AUTHORS' NOTE: An earlier version of this chapter was presented as a "Top 3" paper in the Organizational Communication Division at the annual convention of the International Communication Association, Chicago, May 1986.

arbitrary structures on organizational activities—structures that generate
convenient paradigms and simplified models of organizational activity.
(Roberts et al., 1978, p. 26)

Researchers have not only had difficulty in exploring the interactive
levels of communication activity occurring in organizations, but also
have not been very successful in integrating the dimension of "time"
and the corresponding notion of "process" into their studies. Barnard
(1938) declared that "temporal relationships and continuity are primary
aspects of organizations" (p. 80); yet 46 years later Monge, Farace,
Eisenberg, Miller, and White (1984) stated, "If the empirical study of
process has been relatively rare in the social sciences, it has been virtually nonexistent in organizational communication" (p. 26).

While we could easily write pages explaining (and lamenting) the reasons for this failure to integrate the effects of time or process and multiple levels of analysis into studies of organizational communication, that
is not our purpose here. These general research dilemmas have already
been addressed in earlier chapters of this volume; and, as should be evident to readers by this point, these dilemmas are not limited to the field
of organizational communication. Rather, the goals of this chapter are to
(1) examine several basic levels at which it is possible to study communication in organizations, (2) suggest potential research questions and
issues that relate within *and* among each of these levels, and (3) present a
theoretical framework that we believe may be useful in enhancing our
understanding of the processual nature of organizational communication and the multiple levels at which it can be analyzed.

Our analysis of organizational communication will be focused at four
levels: (1) intraindividual, (2) interpersonal or interactive, (3) network
or organizational, and (4) macrosocietal. Attention will be paid to the
analysis of organizational communication both within and among the
various levels. The above issues will be developed within the framework
of the "organizational assimilation process," which is at once inherently
communicative, processual, and ubiquitous to all organizations (Jablin,
1982a, 1985a).

ORGANIZATIONAL ASSIMILATION

Organizational assimilation encompasses those ongoing behavioral
and cognitive processes by which individuals join, become integrated
into, and exit organizations (Jablin, 1982a, 1985a). In general, the assimilation process consists of both explicit and implicit attempts by organizations to influence their employees (socialization), and corresponding
attempts by employees to influence their organizations (individualiza-

tion). In many respects these two reciprocal processes—employee individualization and organizational socialization—characterize what is frequently referred to as organizational "role making" (e.g., Graen, 1976); and, as Katz and Kahn (1978) and others have observed, roles are the building blocks of social systems.

Most often studied from the perspective of the individual employee as a newcomer, organizational socialization has been described as the process by which individuals learn the values, norms, and required behaviors that allow them to participate as members of organizations (Van Maanen, 1975, p. 67). Or as Schein (1968, p. 2) suggests, socialization is the process of "learning the ropes," of being indoctrinated and trained, of being taught what is important in an organization. Several "stage models" of organizational socialization have been proposed in recent years (e.g., Feldman, 1976; Porter, Lawler, & Hackman, 1975; Van Maanen, 1975). The Van Maanen model is fairly representative of most of the models and identifies three basic stages in the organizational socialization process: (1) anticipatory socialization, (2) entry/encounter, and (3) metamorphosis.

Anticipatory socialization describes the degree to which individuals are prepared, prior to organizational entry, to occupy organizational positions (Van Maanen, 1975). More specifically, anticipatory socialization can be divided into two related phases, the first of which is concerned with the process of occupational choice and entry while the second involves the process of organizational choice and entry (Jablin, 1985b). In turn, the *encounter* phase of socialization occurs during the initial weeks or months of one's employment in an organization and typically "involves a pattern of day-to-day experiences in which the individual is subjected to the reinforcement policies and practices of the organization and its members" (Porter et al., 1975, p. 164). These early experiences in the organization are considered critical to the development of attitudes and behaviors consistent with organizational expectations (e.g., Dunnette, Arvey, & Banas, 1973; Jablin, 1984). Moreover, the encounter period can be very stressful and disorienting for new recruits, since they may have difficulty "making sense" (Louis, 1980) of their new work environments and/or must "detach" themselves from expectations, values, and behaviors that they discover are incongruous with their organizations' cultures (e.g., Gomersall & Myers, 1966; Schein, 1968). The final stage of organizational socialization is referred to as the *metamorphosis* period. During this stage the recruit begins to become an accepted, participating member of the organization by learning new behaviors and attitudes and or modifying existing ones. The encounter and metamorphosis stages of socialization are to some degree a constant feature of all employees' lives (regardless of tenure in the organization). Assuming that organizations are "open systems" (see Katz & Kahn,

1978), they and their component subsystems are in constant flux and change (Jablin, 1982a, p. 257).

Though more research has focused on organizational socialization than the companion process of "individualization," the latter process is considered equally important from an assimilation perspective. As Porter et al. (1975, p. 70) state, "At the same time an organization is attempting to put its distinctive stamp on the individual, he [or she] in turn is striving to influence the organization so that it can better satisfy his ideas about how it can be best operated." It is during the metamorphosis stage of socialization that the employee will typically initiate attempts to individualize his or her role in the organization (Jablin, 1982a). In addition, it appears as if the nature of the superior-subordinate relationship that develops prior to and during this period is critical to the success of the employee's individualization efforts since it is with one's supervisor that an individual must ultimately negotiate his or her organizational role (Graen, 1976; Jablin, 1984).

In the following sections we consider the functions and characteristics of communication at the intraindividual, interpersonal, network or organizational, and macrosocietal levels of analysis that occur during organizational assimilation.

THE INTRAINDIVIDUAL LEVEL OF ANALYSIS

We start learning about and processing information related to the nature of work and organizing activity very early in life. As Drucker (1973) states, "By the time a human being has reached the age of four or five he has been conditioned to work" (p. 184). Concurrent with an individual's general socialization to work is the process of vocational organizational communication socialization, which has been described as "the process whereby individuals learn about the communication characteristics of organizational/occupational roles and assess the degree to which their own self-concepts as communicators 'match' those they attribute to persons in occupations they wish to enter" (Jablin, 1985b, p. 266). As individuals progress from early childhood through adolescence, they learn about communication in work/task settings from a variety of sources (including the media, family, friends, school, and part-time jobs), and this information leads them to develop expectations of the communication characteristics of persons in various organizational/occupational roles (Jablin, 1985a). However, the particular manner in which communication-related vocational information affects individuals' career choices, and how individuals resolve conflicts and inconsistencies in the information they receive from different sources, are just two of the many questions that await exploration.

Subsequent to choosing deliberately or accidentally a career or occupation and being trained in that field, one usually attempts to obtain employment in that area. Anticipatory *organizational* socialization is concerned with the ways in which individuals seek and transmit information about jobs, make employment decisions, and develop expectations of what "life" will be like in the organizations in which they are considering working. Recruiting and employment interviewing, probably the most common methods of information exchange between applicants and organizations during this stage, are information processing events for *both* parties. However, to date, the great majority of studies have focused on how *interviewers* process information and make decisions about applicants and not on applicants' information-processing and decision-making behaviors (e.g., Arvey & Campion, 1982; Jablin & McComb, 1984). Yet, from the applicant's perspective, it is important to realize that the interview is not only a time for providing information about oneself but is also an opportunity to gather and process information about the (1) job or organization and (2) the recruiter (Rynes, Heneman, & Schwab, 1978).

With respect to information about the job or organization, Teigen (1983) reports that about 38% of the talk (i.e., words) in employment interviews is focused on information about organizational climate factors (e.g., duties, supervision, coworker relations, rewards). Ironically, however, one of the most distinguishing outcomes of the recruiting process is that new hires characteristically enter organizations with inflated expectations of what work will be like (Wanous, 1980). This is problematic because the more inflated the recruit's expectations of his or her organization's communication climate, for example, the lower the recruit's level of job satisfaction and the higher the probability of job turnover (Jablin, 1981). Wanous (1980) argues that if recruiters provide "realistic job previews" applicants are more likely to possess accurate expectations when they begin work and as a consequence have increased levels of job satisfaction and lower rates of turnover. At this time, however, we have limited knowledge of how applicants seek and respond to positive and negative information during the recruitment interview (Jablin, 1987; Popovich & Wanous, 1982).

As noted above, in making employment decisions recruits attend to characteristics of their recruiters as well as to information about jobs and organizations (Schmitt & Coyle, 1976). For example, recruits' decisions to accept employment in organizations are sometimes influenced by perceptions of their interviewers' preparation and knowledge of job characteristics, verbal fluency, personality, age, sex, and job titles (Rogers & Sincoff, 1978; Schmitt & Coyle, 1976). How individuals prioritize and interpret such information and how these data affect their work expectations are questions for future research.

Newcomers may experience a sense of information overload as they begin to learn the important values and behaviors of their organizations. Van Maanen (1977) states, newcomers must learn "how and what to see and hear . . . they must determine where they stand relative to the objects, events, relationships and types of people they encounter" (p. 22). Thus recruits must construct cognitive maps (Kaplan, 1972) or models of their new situations to render life in the organization comprehensible.

Personality factors may affect the ways in which newcomers create and organize cognitive maps of their communication environments (e.g., Jablin, 1982a). Among such factors are (1) self-perceptions of locus of control (Rotter, 1966), (2) cognitive complexity (Herman, 1974; Stabell, 1978), (3) predispositions toward high or low self-monitoring (Snyder, 1979), and newcomers' past job experiences. For example, since cognitively complex individuals often spontaneously structure their social worlds around the personalities and characteristics of those with whom they interact (Delia, Clark, & Switzer, 1979), it may be easier for complex newcomers to map cognitively the "reality" of their organizations. It is possible that individuals with previous work experience use latent cognitive scripts (Abelson, 1976) to interpret their new organizational environments and as a consequence experience less "reality shock" (Hughes, 1958).

If the encounter stage involves identifying those areas where newcomers need to change in order to "fit" with their organizations, the metamorphosis period consists of how those changes actually come about. The processes by which attitudes or behaviors change are indeed complex but as applied to organizational metamorphosis are usually explained by cognitive consistency theories (Festinger, 1957; Newcomb, 1958); that is, newcomers change their views to be consistent with those of persons who are already members of their organizations. Newcomers may receive role-related information from several different organizational sources: (1) "official" downward (typically media-related) sources, (2) immediate superiors and subordinates (if one is in a supervisory position), and (3) coworkers (Jablin, 1982a).

Unfortunately, very little research has examined the relationships between downward media-assisted communication and the ways in which it affects the development of employee roles and interpretive frameworks. Role-defining messages are conveyed to employees through official written publications such as organizational handbooks, manuals, memos, bulletin boards, and more recently though videotape programs, computer-assisted instruction, electronic mail, and teleconferences (e.g., Rice & Associates, 1984). With regard to written communication, research generally suggests that information by itself almost never changes attitudes or behaviors. What new information can do is (1) strengthen the attitudes that some people already hold toward a specific topic, and/or (2) provide advocates of a position with ways to verbalize their positive sentiments (Haskins, 1966; Klapper, 1960). More recently, Jablin (1982a) proposed that media-related communication in organizations might serve more to inform employees about what constitutes "acceptable" attitudes/behaviors than to change those attitudes/behaviors. However, as suggested above, the actual ways in which downward, media-related communications affect the role- and sense-making processes of workers in organizations remains a matter of speculation, though numerous hypotheses appear tenable.

Other sources of information that have potential influences on the development of roles and interpretive schemas are an individual's supervisor and subordinates and his or her coworkers. Among socialization theorists, it is widely held that formal role requirements ("pivotal" and to some degree "relevant" norms and behaviors; Schein, 1968) are transmitted by supervisors while informal expections ("relevant" and "peripheral" norms and behaviors) are acquired through interactions with coworkers (e.g., Graen, 1976; Van Maanen, 1977). Information from supervisors is generally considered more influential since supervisors have formal rewards and sanctions to use in their role-making negotiations with subordinates (Jablin, 1984). However, consistent with social learning theory (Bandura, 1977) predictions, when supervisors are frequently unavailable or inaccessible and when their directives are of questionable validity and competence, subordinates may attend more to information from coworkers than from superiors. In addition, attentional processes may be affected by subordinates information-processing capabilities and levels of tolerance for uncertainty (e.g., Schroder, Driver, & Streufert, 1967). If large quantities of complex role-related information are conveyed (formally and informally) to recruits, they may experience information overload. Moreover, in many situations formal (superiors) and informal (coworkers) sources of information may convey contradictory behavioral and attitudinal expectations and thus lead newcomers to experience role conflict (Kahn, Wolfe, Quinn, Snoek, & Rosenthal, 1964).

Recently researchers have explored the mediating effects of such personal characteristics as communication apprehension, locus of control, dogmatism, communicator competence, and managerial communication style (e.g., Jablin, 1979, 1985a) on the communication behavior and attitudes of superiors and subordinates. Particular attention has been focused on how attributional models and schemas affect superiors' perceptions of subordinates' communication and performance (e.g., Jablin, 1982a). However, similar attempts to explain how subordinates interpret supervisory and coworker behaviors have not occurred. Research along these lines might be extremely valuable since it could illuminate the types of sense-making frameworks subordinates develop to explain their communication environments.

Recent studies of "social information processing" in organizations (Caldwell & O'Reilly, 1982; Salancik & Pfeffer, 1978) provide clues about how communication between newcomers and their coworkers affect the development of newcomers' sense-making processes. As Jablin (1985a) observes,

> the social information processing framework proposes that a worker's job attitudes are socially constructed and are largely a result of normative and informational cues communicated to the worker by others in the work environment, particularly co-workers. Thus, this approach suggests that the job attitudes a recruit develops in part arise from the elements of the work environment that co-workers somewhat unconsciously call attention to in their 'everyday' talk. In other words, by frequently talking about and evaluating certain aspects of the work context group members cue one another about the importance and 'meaning' of elements in the work environment. (p. 633)

To summarize, through their "ambient" communication (Jablin, 1985a) coworkers provide new recruits with information relevant to newcomers' efforts to make sense of their work environments. How newcomers interpret such information should likely affect their individualization efforts, and in particular their tendencies to become "team-players" (accept group and organizational expectations), "isolates" (accept organizational but not group expectations), "warriors" (accept group but not organizational expectations), or "outsiders" (accept neither group nor organization expectations; Van Maanen, 1975).

Multilevel analysis. It is difficult to discuss an individual's experience in an organization without considering interpersonal, organizational and macrosocietal levels of analysis. In this section, we will briefly review and exemplify the ways in which dyadic, group, organizational, and macrosocietal variables influence the manner in which individuals search for and process information related to their organizational assimilation.

During the vocational organizational communication socialization process individuals seek and receive information from multiple information sources that affects their perceptions of how people communicate in various occupations and work settings (e.g., Jablin, 1987). Some of these sources are interpersonal in nature (e.g., family, friends), others organizational (e.g., school, organizations in which one has a part-time job), while still others are at the macrosocietal level (e.g., media). In turn, during the anticipatory organizational socialization process recruits' expectations of jobs and organizations are affected by multiple information sources, some of which are interpersonal contacts (e.g., the employment interview, interactions with teachers, friends, current employees), others of which are organizational in nature (e.g., organizational literature such as annual reports, advertisements, and training manuals), while still others are at the macrosocietal level (e.g., media reports of the economic "health" of different industries, demographic and geographic changes in the work population). In addition, there are a number of fairly distinct socialization strategies that organizations use to educate newcomers about situationally acceptable norms, values, and behaviors (Van Maanen, 1978). These methods vary with respect to several characteristics, including the extent to which they are (1)formal/informal strategies, (2) individual/collective strategies, and (3) serial/disjunctive strategies.

Formal socialization takes place away from the work setting and presents a set of experiences that are designed especially for newcomers. Since formal socialization usually involves classroom training, this strategy allows the organization to control who acts as a source of information for newcomers. Relatedly, a newcomer may be socialized in isolation from others or as a member of a group of newcomers. The group interaction present in the latter condition clearly affects a recruit's sensemaking processes, as Becker observes: "As the group shares problems, various members of the group experiment with possible solutions and report back to the group. In the course of collective discussions, the members arrive at a definition of their situation and develop a consensus" (cited in Van Maanen & Schein, 1979, p. 233). By contrast, in "serial" socialization "experienced" members of the organization serve as role models for newcomers, while in "disjunctive" socialization newcomers are more or less "left to their own devices," since there are no immediate job incumbents to inform them how to enact the new role. Thus while the sense-making process may be very anxiety producing and discovery-oriented for newcomers experiencing disjunctive socialization, serially socialized persons may be less mindful of their environments since they can count on others to "act as guides, passing on consensual solutions to the typical problems faced by a recruit" (Van Maanen & Schein, 1979, p. 249).

Depending upon the socialization strategy or combination of strategies organizations employ, newcomers will likely have different information-seeking and information-processing propensities. The effect of these organizational socialization strategies, in interaction with newcomers' anticipatory socialization experiences, as well as their communication contacts at the dyadic and work-group levels once they have entered their organizations, must all be considered when trying to understand how newcomers interpret and individualize their communication roles in organizations.

THE INTERPERSONAL LEVEL OF ANALYSIS

While intraindividual analyses of communication during organizational assimilation focus on how individuals seek and process work-related and social information, interpersonal-level analyses explore the nature of organizational members' relational communication. In part, analyses at this level consider the roles and functions of communication in the initiation, development, maintenance, and dissolution of various dyadic and small group relationships in organizations. The following discussion (1) describes the communication characteristics of specific interpersonal relationships relevant to the assimilation process, and (2) explores ways to study the communication attributes of those relationships.

Anticipatory socialization consists of two related phases: occupational anticipatory socialization and organizational anticipatory socialization. Relevant outcomes for both processes include (1) choosing among alternative courses of action, and (2) developing expectations. With regard to occupational anticipatory socialization, family members, peers, teachers, coworkers and supervisors from part-time jobs, and other nonfamilial adults are influential interpersonal sources. To what extent does the communication of information from each of these sources shape the occupational choices individuals make? How does information from each source affect individuals' perceptions and expectations of the communication characteristics of occupations in various career areas? Generalizable answers to these questions are not currently available, but relevant research is in progress (e.g., Brown, Brooks, & Associates, 1984; Jablin, 1985a; Osipow, 1983).

Future communication research in this area might best be facilitated by conceptualizing the ways in which each of the above sender-receiver relationships are at once similar and dissimilar. Numerous dimensions of communication relationships may be of importance. The amount (Laska & Micklin, 1981) and quality of information provided by socialization sources no doubt affects occupational choices, as well as the perceived credibility of these sources. At present very little is known about how sources of occupational information affect individuals' career choices and communication-related occupational expectations. Moreover, the relative influence of interpersonal as compared to mediated sources of occupational information on vocational expectations and decisions remains to be determined.

At some point after individuals have chosen, or in some cases "fallen into" occupations, the experience of anticipatory organizational socialization begins. During this time, individuals select specific organizations for potential employment and develop expectations of what the day-to-day experience of working in them will be like. Since the employment interview serves the dual functions of selecting prospective employees and providing information to applicants of what organizational membership entails, communication between interview participants plays a pivotal role in the anticipatory organizational socialization process (e.g., Jablin & McComb, 1984).

Traditionally the employment screening interview is a formally structured communication event, in which each party largely follows role-prescribed behavior (e.g., Herriot, 1984; Shaw, 1983). According to conventional rules, the interviewer, as the high-status participant, structures the interaction by managing the question-and-answer process. "Appropriate" interviewee behavior requires acknowledgment of interviewer-interviewee status differences, anticipating likely questions, and primarily speaking only in response to interviewers' questions.

One could argue, however, that remaining within the confines of role- or rule-governed interaction may be problematic, especially for the job applicant. In fact, researchers have recently begun to question the efficacy of job applicants' strict adherence to role-prescribed communication throughout the interview (e.g., Ragan, 1983; Shaw, 1983; Babbitt & Jablin, 1985). For example, Tengler and Jablin (1983) found that applicants who were offered on-site interviews spent less time in question-response interactions but more total time talking in their interviews than did applicants who were rejected following their screening interviews. Interviewees may be viewed more favorably by interviewers when they act more like conversational participants than respondents to interrogation.

In addition, given findings that indicate discrepancies between pre-interview expectations and postinterview perceptions of recruiters and applicants of their own and the other interview party's communication behaviors (e.g., Cheatham & McLaughlin, 1976; Herriot & Rothwell, 1981, 1983), research directed at determining the causes and effects of interviewer-interviewee perceptual incongruence is recommended. The failure of an interviewee to meet the conversational expectations of the interviewer may result in the interviewer attributing unfavorable personality characteristics to the interviewee (Herriot & Rothwell, 1983). Even though research findings suggest that applicants need to broaden their repertoires of "appropriate" communication behaviors, optimal levels of shared control in the interview process need specification.

Our knowledge of the interview communication process might also be enhanced by studies examining both the content (e.g., topicality, word choice) and noncontent aspects (e.g., speech rate, response latency, turn duration) of interview conversations (e.g., McLaughlin, 1984). With regard to noncontent dimensions of communication, for example, recent research on speech accommodation theory (see Cappella, Chapter 7 in this volume; Giles & Weimann, Chapter 12; Street & Giles, 1982) may be of relevance to the employment interview. This theory suggests that interactants influence one another's speech on dimensions such as turn duration, speech rate, and response latency. In employment interviews, interviewers and interviewees often converge on the dimensions of turn duration and response latency (Matarazzo & Wiens, 1973); that is, as interviews progress length of pauses between speaker turns and amount of time spent talking become similar for both participants. However, as Street and Giles (1982, p. 212) observe, while convergence is typically viewed favorably, in situations such as the job interview too much convergence by either party may be perceived as inappropriate, ingratiating, or condescending.

To date, speech accommodation theory has been studied to a greater extent in fact-finding interviews (e.g., Street, 1984; Putman & Street, 1984) than in employment interviews. Moreover, since the few investigations that have explored the relative impact of interactants' verbal as compared to nonverbal communication behaviors upon interview outcomes have produced mixed results (e.g., Jablin & McComb, 1984), future studies simultaneously examining the functions of verbal and nonverbal communication in the interview are warranted.

While general models of interpersonal relationship development are available in the literature (e.g., Altman & Taylor, 1973; Knapp, 1984), their applicability to relationships at work is questionable. As Berger and Bradac (1982) have argued, communicating in work- or role-defined ways limits the breadth and depth of interaction among individuals, thereby constraining the nature of relationship development. Thus most models of the encounter period of organizational assimilation have not focused on the stages newcomers' relationships with other progress through over time but rather on the content of what newcomers need to learn. Models of assimilation tend to focus on the need for newcomers to clarify their new roles, make sense of their environments, become initiated in their jobs and work groups, and begin to develop new self-images that are congruent with their new roles and organizations (Buchanan, 1974; Feldman, 1976; Porter et al., 1975; Schein, 1968; Wanous, 1980). Further, most models suggest that the primary means by which newcomers acquire this knowledge is either through reinforcements from those with whom they interact (e.g., Porter et al., 1975) or through forms of vicarious learning and modeling (Bandura, 1977). The communication strategies newcomers and oldtimers use to communicate information and share knowledge with one another during the initial stages of their relationships, however, remain relatively unexplored (with notable exceptions, e.g., Feldman & Brett, 1983; Jablin, 1984).

Our purpose here is not to present a well-developed communication-oriented conceptual model of relationship development processes during the encounter stage of organizational assimilation but rather to raise some questions that require attention before such a model can be developed. First, how do newcomers seek out information and feedback from others during the encounter period? Berger and his colleagues have explored strategies for acquiring social knowledge during initial (non-work) interactions suggestive of several "interactive," "active," and "passive" message strategies that newcomers may use (Berger & Bradac, 1982; Berger & Kellermann, 1983; Kellermann & Berger, 1984). Strategies include asking questions of others about "target" persons, asking questions of "target" persons directly, converting "floor possessions" during conversations into question-asking sequences, using self-disclosure to encourage the other party to talk about him- or herself, observing the "target" in his or her interactions with others, and putting the other party at ease during conversations (thus encouraging him or her to feel comfortable talking about him- or herself). Obviously, strategies that newcomers use to gather social and work-related information warrants investigation. A related issue requiring study concerns the message strategies oldtimers and newcomers use to *avoid* revealing work-related and social secrets to one another (e.g., Feldman, 1981; Jablin, 1987).

It is also possible that relationship formation between newcomers and members of their role sets are affected by whether coworkers and supervisors send conflicting or supporting role-defining messages. For example, Feldman (1977) has found that "when there is interpersonal and intergroup conflict in a work area, new employees are confused and hold back from making friends or being trusting until they can better understand the tension they see" (p. 986). Moreover, individuals attempt to reduce the psychological stress associated with role conflict by reducing their frequency of communication with one or the other of the parties sending conflicting messages (Kahn et al., 1964).

In turn, how work groups redevelop their communication patterns and roles to accommodate the entrance of new group members during the "encounter" and later during the metamorphosis periods of assimilation warrants investigation (e.g., Jablin & Sussman, 1983). As Wanous, Reichers, & Malik (1984) observe, most previous research has focused on how newcomers change after joining new groups (e.g., Coulter & Taft, 1973; Wicker & Mehler, 1971) and not on the "likelihood of *group* redevelopment as a result of the newcomer assimilation process" (p. 671).

Without doubt, the relationships newcomers form with their supervisors are of special importance during the encounter and metamorphosis stages of organizational assimilation (Graen, 1976; Jablin, 1984). Specifically, since in open superior-subordinate relationships each party feels the other is a receptive and responsive communicator (Jablin, 1979), it follows that in open as compared to closed relationships subordinates may have a greater probability of success in negotiating their roles with their superiors. Indirectly, this notion is supported by research exploring a vertical dyadic linkage (VDL) theory of leadership (Graen, 1976). VDL research suggests that superior-subordinate relationships are either characterized by "leadership" exchanges or "supervisory" exchanges (e.g., Dansereau, Graen, & Haga, 1975; Graen & Cashman, 1975). Subordinates in leadership exchanges act as informal assistants to their superiors, are more involved in communicating and administering activities, and seem to have more say about how their formal organizational positions evolve. Moreover, these employees tend to have considerable "negotiating latitude" (Graen, 1976) with their supervisors. On the other hand, subordinates in supervisory exchanges tend to have more formal relationships with their supervisors and perform fairly routine tasks in their work groups. Subordinates who eventually enter into leadership exchanges with their supervisors are more effective in individualizing their organizational roles.

With its emphasis on the significance of subordinate negotiating latitude, VDL theory provides an interactional view of the superior-subordinate relationship. However, the framework still requires considerably more study. For example, we know little about how the initial (encounter period) relationships formed between supervisors and subordinates affect the extent to which one or the other relational forms emerges. The theory also does not suggest how (if at all) individuals in leadership exchanges talk differently with each other than individuals in supervisory exchanges do. Furthermore, if differences in talk patterns do exist, the degree to which these communication patterns influence the level of negotiating latitude in the superior-subordinate relationship needs to be considered.

Multilevel analysis. Since the great majority of studies exploring interpersonal-level organizational communication processes have used the individual as the unit of analysis, this section stresses the important effects network or organizational and macrosocietal factors can have on interpersonal communication and assimilation processes in organizations. For purposes of brevity, our discussion will focus on only two types of interpersonal communication relationships: (1) the interviewer-interviewee, and (2) the superior-subordinate.

With respect to the interviewer-interviewee relationship, several types of organizational-level variables may affect the nature and effects of each party's communication. For example, interviewees—especially new college graduates—usually belong to applicant communication networks composed of friends and peers. Their communication patterns are likely to be similar to those of organizational grapevines (Davis, 1969). Though we are aware of no research that has actually examined applicant communication networks, related studies do suggest that applicants frequently talk among themselves about the companies and recruiters with whom they interview (Herriot, Ecob, & Hutchinson, 1980). As a consequence, most applicants probably enter their interview interactions with expectations derived, in part, from information provided by members of the applicant communication networks to which they belong.

The interviewers also belong to a number of intra- and interorganizational communication networks that will likely affect their interview communication behavior and perceptions. For example, interviewers who are members of their organizations' personnel departments are likely to belong to different organizational communication networks than are interviewers who are incumbents from the departments seeking new employees. Depending upon the networks in which they are members, the information interviewers provide applicants will vary in accuracy or realism and be affected by their own network experiences (e.g., Jablin, Tengler, & Teigen, 1985).

In turn, macrosocietal-level factors can also affect interviewer-interviewee communication relationships. For instance, changes in equal employment opportunity law often mandate changes in the kinds of questions interviewers can legally ask job applicants and can affect the manner in which interviewees respond to questions (Jablin & Tengler, 1982). Interview communication may further be influenced by prevalent economic conditions. As a consequence, during economic downturns interviewers may spend more time asking applicants questions (selecting) than trying to sell the company (recruiting).

The superior-subordinate relationship might also be sensitive to changes in organizational and macrosocietal variables. At the network or organizational level such structural variables as organizational size, hierarchical level, span of control, and centralization of authority may affect perceptions of openness in superior-subordinate communication and cause variation in subordinates' upward influence tactics (e.g., Jablin, 1982b; Krone, 1984, 1985). Relatedly, emergent structures in organizations may also affect superior-subordinate communication. For example, the extent to which supervisors and subordinates are linked not only in their organizations' authority networks but in task, social, or innovation networks may affect the nature of their communication behaviors and attitudes (Roberts & O'Reilly, 1978). Finally, such organizational characteristics as technology and environment have been found to affect the nature of communication between superiors and subordinates (e.g., Jablin, 1979, 1980b).

Though scant research exists directly exploring how macrosocietal factors affect superior-subordinate communication roles and relationships, changes in both societal and/or organizational demography (e.g., age, sex, educational level, length of service or residence, unionization) are likely to produce impacts. For example, if persons belong to a particularly large age cohort (e.g., "baby boomers"), during most of their working lives they will probably experience a greater degree of competition for advancement and promotion than will individuals who are members of smaller age cohorts (Easterlin, 1980). Since persons with high mobility aspirations tend to distort upward communication to their superiors (Jablin, 1979), this tendency may be exacerbated among persons who are members of large as compared to small age cohorts (Pfeffer, 1983).

Another macrosocietal factor having important effects on the nature of superior-subordinate communication is the development of new information technologies (e.g., Rice & Associates, 1984). In the future more than 50% of the American work force may perform their jobs at home and "telecommute" to work (e.g., Nilles, Carlson, Gray, & Hanneman, 1976). As a result, many employees will rarely visit their "official" offices and superiors, but rather pursue their job-related activities from their homes via computer terminals. Obviously, the geographic separation of subordinates from their superiors is likely to affect how members of the dyad communicate with one another. Computer-mediated communication may result in increased misunderstandings between superiors and subordinates (e.g., Uhlig, 1977).

THE ORGANIZATIONAL LEVEL OF ANALYSIS

From an organizational assimilation perspective the study of communication at the network or organizational level of analysis focuses on how formal and informal organizational communication structures affect and are affected by the organizational socialization and employee individualization processes. Studies of *formally* prescribed organizational structures typically view communication as a dependent variable, posing questions concerning the effects on employee communication attitudes and behaviors (e.g., Jablin, 1982b) of such variables as organizational size, shape of hierarchy (tall-flat), extent of job or task specialization, centralization of decision making, and span of control (number of subordinates directly reporting to a superior). Historically, studies of formal organizational structure have focused on structure as a mechanism by which management attempts to "control" and influence workers (e.g., Chandler, 1962; Ouchi & Maguire, 1975). In contrast, analyses of *informal* organizational structures examine the nature of emergent, "enacted" (Weick, 1969) patterns of person-to-person interaction in organizations, frequently considering these networks as independent variables. For example, research from this perspective has linked variation in network "content" and "connectedness" with outcomes such as organizational commitment (Eisenberg, Monge, & Miller, 1983) and group attitude uniformity (Danowski, 1980).

In this section we will discuss the role of communication in the organizational assimilation process from each of the above viewpoints: (1) as a process that may vary as a result of formal organizational structure, and (2) as an emergent structuring process that may promote variation in assimilation outcomes (including formal structures). Though in our presentation these functions will be frequently discussed in isolation from one another, formal and informal organizational structures or networks are interactively created over time (e.g., Giddens, 1976); and as "emergent interactions become recurring patterns of behavior, further structure is added to the organization" (Brass, 1984, p. 519).

Earlier it was suggested that anticipatory socialization is a two-part process consisting of occupational anticipatory socialization and organizational anticipatory socialization. In what ways, if any, do the formal structural properties of organizations affect individuals' career-related communication expectations and occupational choices? Regrettably, little research has directly explored these issues. However, if one views the notion of formal organizational structure from a broad perspective, a number of structural variables (e.g., organizational size, centralization, formalization, shape) and organizational contexts (e.g., family, school, team sports, religious groups) might be suitable candidates for future research in this area. Epstein (1983) suggests that the decision-making structures of schools may "affect the way students think about the kinds of jobs they seek, the ways they interact with authorities at work, and the skills they bring to the work setting" (p. 122).

Relatedly, informal organizational structures may affect the communication-related occupational expectations and career choices individuals make. Specifically, individuals' involvement in informal peer/friend networks, kinship networks, community networks, and school networks may influence the formation of expectations about their careers and ultimately their occupational choices. By assessing the degrees to which persons are involved in these types of networks, it might be possible to locate important sources of information and influence in the development of occupational self-concepts. Further, research along these lines might be able to identify early inclinations among individuals toward highly communicative network roles (e.g., bridges, liaisons, boundary spanners) that may later affect not only their occupational choices but satisfaction and commitment to careers as well (Jablin, 1987).

With respect to organizational anticipatory socialization, we have already discussed how informal organizational networks may affect the types, quality, and "realism" of information that job applicants obtain during the employment interviewing process. At the same time, formal structural properties of the organizations in which applicants are applying for positions may also affect their job or organizational expectations. For example, an applicant who discovers, as a result of background research and interviewing with a company, that the organization has a high degree of centralization, is "peaked" in shape, large in size, and prefers that supervisors have very large spans of control may develop a very distinct impression of the organization's communication environment. In this case an applicant may "assume" that the company does not generally involve subordinates in decision making and has formalized procedures for communication (especially upward communication), and that individuals do not have much direct, face-to-face communication with their bosses (e.g., Zey-Ferrell, 1979).

The organizational entry or encounter stage of assimilation can also be studied at the organizational level of analysis. Several *formal* structural properties of organizations may affect the duration of the encounter stage and the degree to which newcomers receive conflicting work-related messages from members of their role sets. For instance, time spent encountering and making sense of disparate messages from others in the new organization may systematically vary with the degree to which the organization is high or low in horizontal complexity (number of specialized functions at the same organizational level) and vertical complexity (number of levels in the hierarchy). Further, an organization's structural characteristics are usually reflected in the types of socialization tactics it employs during the encounter period. Formal socialization is "most likely to be associated with hierarchical and inclusionary boundary passages wherein a newcomer is expected to assume a new *status* or *rank* in the organization," while informal socialization (self-selection of socialization agents) is more typical of "functional" (departmental) boundary passages (Van Maanen & Schein, 1979, p. 239).

Our understanding of the organizational entry experience might also benefit from conceptualizing organizations as *emergent* communication networks and applying network analysis techniques. This approach may reveal how patterns of interaction might be affected by such variables as the work histories of recruits, organizational socialization practices, and newcomers' efforts to cope with and make sense of the uncertainty associated with their new work environments. With respect to the relationship between an individual's work history and his or her network involvement during the encounter period, a number of recent non-network studies (see Katz, 1980; Feldman & Brett, 1983) suggest an interesting contrast: the possibility that newcomers to *organizations* in general initially tend to seek integration into social networks, whereas newly transferred or promoted employees (veterans) initially seek to become integrated into task-related networks.

Certain characteristics of organizational socialization tactics might also affect the types of communication networks into which newcomers become integrated. Recruits experiencing formal socialization tactics may have more predictable patterns of network membership than newcomers experiencing informal socialization, since in this latter condition recruits have the freedom to select their own socialization agents. Similarly, newcomers experiencing serial socialization (experienced organizational members serve as role models) might be expected to have more predictable and stable patterns of network membership than recruits experiencing disjunctive socialization (no recent predecessor in the job to role model).

Finally, the potential ways newcomers' involvements in communication networks serve to help recruits cope with the uncertainty of their new work environments also would seem worthy of future research. The use of network analysis would permit researchers to identify patterns of communication during the early weeks of employment and reveal the extent to which newcomers interact with and rely upon both formal (e.g., supervisors) and informal (e.g., coworkers) socializing agents for sensemaking purposes (e.g., Jablin, 1984).

Communication processes associated with the metamorphosis-individualization phase of organizational assimilation may be influenced by properties of both formally prescribed and emergent organizational structures. In particular, as organizational task complexity or diversity decreases and centralization of authority increases, it is likely that employees will have greater difficulty individualizing their roles (Roos & Starke, 1981), since "tight" specification of jobs, restriction of the range of workers' activities, formalization of communication processes, close rule observance and supervision, and limited role and organizational innovation tend to be closely associated with high levels of organizational centralization and low levels of task complexity (Hage, 1974, 1980). By contrast, since high levels of organizational task complexity and low levels of centralization tend to augment the volume of communication in an organization, increase superiors' dependencies upon subordinates, and result in the use of feedback and "mutual adjustment" as mechanisms of coordination among organization members (Hage & Aiken, 1969; Hage, Aiken, & Marrett, 1971), under these circumstances a newcomer's coworkers may play extremely influential roles in the metamorphosis-individualization process.

Emergent organizational structures may also affect metamorphosis and individualization processes. If organizational newcomers are depicted as either nonparticipants or isolates in communication networks, longitudinal network analyses might permit us to determine how their roles evolve and/or stabilize during the encounter through metamorphosis stages of the assimilation process. Research along the above lines would also allow us to explore relationships between individuals' levels of network participation and superior-subordinate and coworker communication behaviors and attitudes. For example, since the liaison role is typified by high levels of status and influence (Reynolds & Johnson, 1982), newcomers who eventually emerge as liaisons will likely be more effective in their attempts at negotiating their organizational roles with their superiors. Relatedly, newcomers who work for supervisors who are liaisons (as compared to newcomers working for nonliaison supervisors) may be more successful in their individualization efforts with their supervisors since liaisons tend to be "more open in their communication relationships than are other organizational members" (Reynolds & Johnson, 1982, p. 554) and tend to serve as "socializing agents and network builders" for employees (Katz & Tushman, 1983, p. 453).

In conclusion, individuals who have been effectively assimilated into their organizations may assume "linker" roles in their organizations' communication networks while persons who are less effectively assimilated may assume "nonlinker" roles (Jablin, 1985a). This notion has received tentative support from recent studies showing that individuals' job or work identification (Albrecht, 1979, 1984), job satisfaction (Roberts & O'Reilly, 1979), and in some situations organizational commitment (Eisenberg et al., 1983), are positively related to their communication network involvement.

Multilevel analysis. In a sense, the study of communication phenomena at the network or organizational level is inherently a multilevel form of analysis. In other words, since communication networks are composed of individual communicators (nodes) interpersonally linked to other communicators, it is essentially impossible to examine organizational structures without also considering intrapersonal and interpersonal level communication factors.

At the same time, however, because organizational structures are embedded within societal supranetwork systems, organizational structures will affect and be affected by macrosocietal-level factors. Eisenberg et al. (1985) suggest organizational networks are typically integrated with their environments (including other organizations) via three basic types of communication linkages: (1) *institutional* linkages (information exchanges that do not involve specific individuals), (2) *representative* linkages (information exchanges in which individuals "officially" represent their organizations in communicating with official representatives of other organizations) and (3) *personal* linkages (information exchanges between persons in different organizations that occur in a private, nonrepresentative capacity). Persons who perform these latter two forms of organization-environment linkage are typically referred to as "boundary spanners" (e.g., Adams, 1976, 1980). The effectiveness of a boundary spanner to gather environmental information and disseminate it within the organization is, in part, a byproduct of the individual's involvement in *both* organizational and extraorganizational communication networks (Tushman & Scanlon, 1981).

Information, material, and personnel derived from an organization's interaction with its environment can have numerous impacts on organizational communication networks. If there are abundant employment opportunities in the environment or society, and this is sensed by workers through their interactions with persons external to the organization's boundaries, the organization may experience increased employee turnover. In turn, this increase in turnover will likely have a negative impact on the stability of the organization's communication networks, lead to an influx of new network members (new hires), and ultimately cause the organization to alter its socialization practices. Also, intra- and interorganizational networks may exert pressure on governments to change their business policies (e.g., Champagne, Neef, & Nagel, 1981).

In summary, the few studies in this area have focused more on identifying network roles that serve to integrate or link organizations with their environments rather than on how organizational networks influence and are influenced by their environments. Obviously, until such research is pursued our understanding of communication phenomenon associated with formal and emergent organizational networks and structures will remain constrained.

THE MACROSOCIETAL LEVEL OF ANALYSIS

Literally speaking, the study of organizational communication at the societal level of analysis is concerned with comparing the similarities and differences in the communication systems of organizations in various societies and cultures. Thus, for example, research in this area explores these questions: (1) What differences, if any, exist in the communication norms and values of organizations in American as compared to those in Asian, Latin American, and Western European societies? (2) How do differences in the economic systems of societies affect the communication practices of organizations and their members? and (3) How does migration and regional development within and among societies affect organizational communication systems?

Obviously, because organizations are not independent of their host societies, it is important to consider how communication and assimilation processes within organizations can be examined from the macrosocietal level of analysis. At this time, however, the exact nature of how macrosocietal factors are related to organizational communication and assimilation processes requires a considerable amount of reasoned speculation, since a paucity of research exists exploring these types of relationships. As a consequence, in this section we will consider a limited number of characteristics of societies that appear to be related to organizational communication and assimilation processes. The characteristics we will examine include (1) the task environments of organizations, (2) developments in new information technology, (3) demographic characteristics, and (4) population ecology and organizational life cycles.

Organizational task environments. Organizational task environments are embedded in larger macrocultural environments and consists of those external factors that directly influence the operations of a "focal" organization. In simple terms, an organization has a "general-macro" environment and a "specific-task" environment (e.g., Hall, 1972). Aspects of the general environment include those environmental components that potentially may affect the focal organization, such as legal, technological, economic, political, ecological, cultural, and demographic conditions. On the other hand, components of an organization's task environment (often termed its "organization set"; Evan, 1972) include environmental elements with which an organization is in direct interaction and which are relevant to organizational decision making. Typical elements of an organization's task environment include suppliers of materials and equipment, customers, regulatory agencies, competitors for resources and customers, and technological developments in the industry (Duncan, 1972). However, "the distinction between the general environment and the task environment is not always clear-cut and is continually changing. Forces in the general environment are continually 'breaking through' into the task environment of the specific organization" (Kast & Rosenzweig, 1974, p. 137).

Building upon the work of earlier organizational theorists (e.g., Emery & Trist, 1965; Terreberry, 1968; Thompson, 1967), Shortell (1977) identifies four critical dimensions of organizational environments: complexity, diversity, stability, and certainty. Environmental complexity refers to the number of external factors that an organization must manage, while diversity refers to the degree to which the external factors are different from one another. Environmental stability refers to the rate at which external factors change over time, while environmental certainty involves the degree of predictability among external factors (including predictability of change).

Dimensions of organizational task environments may influence organizational communication and assimilation processes in a wide variety of ways. Stable environmental conditions tend to be associated with increased use of vertical communication between supervisors and subordinates, while unstable conditions tend to be associated with increased lateral communication (Burns & Stalker, 1961; Lawrence & Lorsch, 1967). Given this relationship, as an organization's task environment becomes increasingly stable the organization may rely upon supervisory influence and formal socialization strategies in assimilating newcomers. In turn, as environmental stability decreases, the socializing influence of peers may become more pronounced.

Additionally, as the complexity, diversity, instability, and uncertainty of organizational environments increase, the longer it may take for newcomers to develop cognitive maps of their organizations, resolve discrepancies in conflicting role-related messages they may receive, and learn appropriate organizational communication norms. Further, the more newcomers are buffered (Thompson, 1967) from environmental turbulence (for instance, by their supervisors or boundary spanners) the easier it may be for them to learn and adapt to the communication requirements of their jobs. Relatedly, the information-processing demands environmental turbulence creates for work groups and the effects it has on their interaction patterns (Daft & Macintosh, 1981; Tushman, 1979; Tushman & Nadler, 1978) may also affect the relative influence of coworkers in the socialization of newcomers.

Information technology. Advances in technology have historically had a strong influence on the nature of communication systems in organizations (e.g., Aldrich & Mueller, 1982; Hulin & Roznowski, 1985; Jablin, 1980b). The "new media" that are part of recent advances in technology include teleconferencing (audio, video, and computer), the use of computers to perform organizational functions (e.g., word processing), and computer-mediated communication (e.g., electronic mail), among other technological developments (Rice & Associates, 1984).

Exactly how might these advances in information and communication technology affect organizational communication and assimilation processes? With regard to occupational anticipatory socialization, the use of interactive career guidance systems in schools may result in students developing more realistic expectations of the communication characteristics of occupations. On the other hand, rather than interview applicants in face-to-face settings, in the future more organizations may use mediated communication systems (e.g., telephone, teleconferencing; e.g., Opsata, 1984) to conduct employment interviews with job candidates. Computer-mediated communication systems (e.g., electronic bulletin boards, mail) may eventually replace written employee newspapers and magazines as methods of informing workers of organizationally appropriate attitudes and behaviors. As Steinfield (1984) and Wynn (1980) suggest, participation in "electronic communities performs a socializing function, helping to integrate individuals into the organization . . . [and] also helps to create communication networks" (Steinfield, 1984, p. 24).

Moreover, the decision to implement new communication systems calls for varying degrees of new learning and "resocialization" by all organizational members, regardless of organizational or job tenure. For example, the use of teleconferencing to conduct meetings may require organizational members to alter their existing patterns of relational communication and group interaction (Rice, 1984). Similarly, Hiltz,

Turoff, and Johnson (1984) report that the leadership and participation skills required for effective group decision making in face-to-face settings as compared to computerized conferences are not necessarily similar. In addition, when bargaining and negotiating via audio conferencing, outcomes appear to be more dependent on the substance and strength of arguments than on interpersonal dynamics (Morley & Stephenson, 1970; Short, 1973).

Newcomers to organizations with computerized communication systems may also need to acquire knowledge about the formal and informal rules regulating their use and the appropriateness of each mode of communication for specific tasks (e.g., Rice, 1983; Svenning & Ruchinskas, 1984). Further, the extent to which organizations regulate the use of new information technologies may dramatically affect the nature of organizational networks (Danowski & Edison-Swift, 1984; Steinfield, 1984) and formal organizational structures (Rice, 1980; Whisler, 1970). Beyond this, to the extent that workers are free to experiment with new uses, the adoption and implementation of computerized communication systems in organizations could also mean increased opportunities for role negotiation and role innovation (Johnson & Rice, 1984).

Demographic characteristics. The demography of a society or an organization refers to the composition of its members with respect to such attributes as sex, age, length of service or residence, educational level, race, and so on (e.g., Pfeffer, 1983). Since organizations are subsystems of the societies in which they exist, changes in societal demographic characteristics affect organizational demographic attributes. However, in addition to being affected by shifts in societal-level demographic attributes, organizational demographic characteristics are affected by other factors including (1) the rate of growth of employment in the organization and the industry of which it is a part, (2) organizational personnel policies (e.g., selection policies, socialization practices, retirement policies), (3) changes in technology, and (4) extent of unionization in the organization and industry (Pfeffer, 1983). Exactly how does variation in demographic attributes affect organizational communication and assimilation processes?

First, as suggested earlier, the overall size of the societal age cohort and the cohort size and ages of fellow workers may influence subsequent organizational assimilation and communication experiences because of the effects of cohort size on upward mobility potential. Second, organizations with high rates of turnover and large numbers of new employees may rely more on bureaucratic methods of communication and control (e.g., rules, hierarchy) than upon shared norms and beliefs (socialization) to influence members' behavior (e.g., Pfeffer, 1983). Third, the communication needs and preferences of younger and older workers in organizations may differ (e.g., Gusfield, 1957; Jurgensen, 1978). In addition, the proportions of men and women in organizations can also affect group processes, social interaction, psychological well-being, stress, and commitment (Kanter, 1977). Finally, the ethnic composition of a work force may have some very direct impacts on communication and assimilation processes since (1) ethnic differences are often accompanied by differences in spoken language, (2) ethnic diversity can result in culturally bound interpretations of organizational reality that are incongruent with those desired by the organization, and (3) ethnic or immigrant groups may resist commitment to the organizations in which they are employed because they believe they will eventually return to their "home" countries (Bonacich, 1973).

In summary, as Pfeffer (1983) argues,

> Although demography has been largely ignored in the literature on organizations, it has the benefit of being objectively measurable and, furthermore, being potentially able to account for a wide range of organizational behaviors and attitudes in a parsimonious and straightforward fashion. (p. 302)

Population ecology and organizational life cycles. In recent years the biological metaphor has regained popularity as a way of thinking about the dynamics of organizations (though certainly not without controversy; e.g., Kimberly, 1980; McKelvey, 1979; Van de Ven, 1979). In particular, the notions of "natural selection" processes as evidenced in organizational populations (population ecology) and organizational "life cycles" have been foci of attention. Natural selection "refers to the differential reproduction and survival of organizations depending on relative competitive advantage," whereas organizational life cycles refer to "the patterns over time through which new organizations come into being, change, and disappear" (Freeman, 1982, p. 2). In other words, population ecologists explore those political, economic, and social environmental factors that affect the *net* mortality of the population of organizations in various ecological or resource "niches" or industries (e.g., Hannan & Freeman, 1977; Zammuto & Cameron, 1985); their concern is not the individual organization but the survival of organizational forms. In turn, organizational life-cycle researchers are interested in the process of organizational development—the stages of emergence, growth, maturity, and decline of organizations (e.g., Kimberly, Miles, & Associates, 1980).

The notion of ecological niche and the related concept of population density are important for understanding the basic relationships between population ecology and organizational life cycles. With respect to population density,

The greater the extent to which a population's niche is realized by the organizations inhabiting it, the greater the density of the population. Population density reflects the extent to which the potential of the niche for the performance of the population is realized. Mature industries typically have high population densities. . . . In contrast, emerging industries usually have low population densities, which create opportunities for organizational growth, and for the creation of new organizations within the population. (Zammuto & Cameron, 1985, p. 228)

In other words, organizational "foundings" (life-cycle emergence) frequently appear in niches with low population densities. By contrast, if they are to survive and grow, organizations in densely populated niches must learn to adapt to the constraints that define their population's niche, enter new "organizational domains" (that part of the niche which is the primary focus of the organization, e.g., clientele, services or products; Meyer, 1975), enter new niches, and so on. As a consequence, the life cycles of organizations in "mature" industries are also directly affected by the ecological characteristics of their population's niche.

At present, research exploring relationships among natural selection processes in organizational populations and the life cycles of organizations is still in its infancy. Thus it is not surprising that almost no empirical research exists examining population ecology, organizational life cycles, and communication or assimilation processes in organizations (with notable exception, see Monge, Farace, Miller, & Eisenberg, 1983). However, this perspective certainly represents some exciting prospects for future communication research, especially in relation to the study of organizational life cycles.

For example, recruiting and socialization processes may be somewhat different in an organization's infancy than in later stages of organizational maturity, since organizational births are typically associated with a high degree of entrepreneurial activity, such as generating resources and creating an ideology (Miller, 1984). Moreover, during this initial period of the life cycle, the socialization of newcomers and communication of the organization's mission tends to be performed by the founder or members of the "dominant coalition." As the organization grows, socialization becomes the responsibility of the new employees' peers and other formal and informal communication contacts (e.g., Lodahl & Mitchell, 1980). Consequently, as an organization becomes more formalized, some degree of organizational "drift" emerges—a gap develops between the founder's ideals and intentions and the "enacted organization" (Lodahl & Mitchell, 1980), creating conflicting socialization messages for newcomers.

Organizations in decline are often organizations in crisis, and these conditions cause organizations to operate in a more centralized fashion (Whetton, 1980). Consequently, to the extent that individualization attempts occur at all in declining organizations, they are apt to be less successful than at other stages. Relatedly, organizations in decline typically face decreased employee morale, increased employee turnover (Whetton, 1980), heavy use of "grapevine" and rumor-related communication networks, and correspondingly high levels of dissatisfaction among employees with their organizations' communication systems. Recruiting new members to such organizations may be difficult and require different communication strategies than would be used under conditions of organizational growth.

Multilevel analysis. Since throughout this chapter we have provided numerous examples of the interrelationships among the intrapersonal, interpersonal, and organizational levels of analysis, and issues related to macrosocietal variables, we will not reiterate these relationships here. At this juncture, however, we would like to explain why the primary emphasis of our discussion has been on how macrosocietal-level variables affect communication processes at lower-order levels of analysis and not on the reciprocal process. In selecting this focus we did not intend to diminish the importance of considering how lower-order levels of analysis affect higher-order variables. Rather, we assumed this approach because of the frequent failure of organizational communication researchers to attend to the effects of higher-order levels of analysis when conducting research and interpreting findings. Clearly the design of organizations and their prescribed and enacted communication systems are not solely determined by the dynamics of their suprasystems but are also byproducts of organizational members' perceptions of their environments and related strategic choices, intra- and extraorganizational political activity and coalition formation, and other idiosyncratic purposive behaviors (e.g., Child, 1972, 1977).

CONCLUSION

The purpose of this chapter has been to demonstrate how the organizational assimilation perspective can enhance our understanding of two crucial dimensions of organizational communication that most scholars agree have been treated inadequately in extant studies: (1) the processual nature of organizational communication, and (2) the multiple levels at which communication phenomena in organizations may require analysis. Our presentation has focused on explicating a theoretical framework and suggesting related directions for research with respect to these issues, and has not emphasized the methodological difficulties associated with the study of organizational communication processes and the various levels at which they can be analyzed. While we certainly recognize that the study of communication processes and their multiple levels of analysis present numerous methodological problems for researchers, we have minimized our discussion of these issues since they have recently received detailed treatment by other scholars. In particular, the interested reader is directed to Monge et al. (1984) for an extended discussion of methodological issues associated with the study of communication processes in organizations, and to Dansereau, Alluto, and Yammarino (1984) and Dansereau et al. (1986) for a methodological framework for exploring the multiple levels at which organizational communication-related data can be analyzed.

REFERENCES

Abelson, R. (1976). Script processing in attitude formation and decision making. In J. Carroll & T. Payne (Eds.), *Cognition and social behavior* (pp. 33-45). Hillsdale, NJ: Lawrence Erlbaum.

Adams, J. S. (1976). The structure and dynamics of behavior in organization boundary roles. In M. D. Dunnette (Ed.), *Handbook of industrial and organizational psychology* (pp. 1175-1199). Chicago: Rand McNally.

Adams, J. S. (1980). Interorganizational processes and organizational boundary activities. In B. M. Staw & L. L. Cummings (Eds.), *Research in organizational behavior,* (Vol. 2, pp. 321-355). Greenwich, CT: JAI.

Albrecht, T. L. (1979). The role of communication in perceptions of organizational climate. In D. Nimmo (Ed.), *Communication yearbook 3* (pp. 343-357). New Brunswick, NJ: Transaction.

Albrecht, T. L. (1984). Managerial communication and work perception. In R. N. Bostrom (Ed.), *Communication yearbook 8* (pp. 538-557). Newbury Park, CA: Sage.

Aldrich, H., & Mueller, S. (1982). The evolution of organizational forms: Technology, coordination, and control. In B. M. Staw & L. L. Cummings (Eds.), *Research in organizational behavior* (Vol. 4, pp. 33-87). Greenwich, CT: JAI.

Altman, I., & Taylor, D. A. (1973). *Social penetration: The development of interpersonal relationships.* New York: Holt, Rinehart & Winston.

Arvey, R. D., & Campion, J. E. (1982). The employment interview: A summary and review of recent research. *Personnel Psychology, 35,* 281-322.

Babbitt, L. V. & Jablin, F. M. (1985). Characteristics of applicants' questions and employment screening interview outcomes. *Human Communication Research, 11,* 507-535.

Bandura, A. (1977). *Social learning theory.* Englewood Cliffs, NJ: Prentice-Hall.

Barnard, C. I. (1938). *The functions of the executive.* Cambridge, MA: Harvard University Press.

Becker, H. S. (1964). Personal change in adult life. *Sociometry, 27,* 40-53.

Berger, C. R., & Bradac, J. J. (1982). *Language and social knowledge: Uncertainty in interpersonal relationships.* London: Edward Arnold.

Berger, C. R., & Kellermann, K. A. (1983). To ask or not to ask: Is that a question? In R. N. Bostrom (Ed.), *Communication yearbook 7* (pp. 342-369). Newbury Park, CA: Sage.

Bonacich, E. (1973). A theory of middleman minorities. *American Sociological Review, 30,* 583-594.

Brass, D. J. (1984). Being in the right place: A structural analysis of individual influence in an organization. *Administrative Science Quarterly, 29,* 518-539.

Brown, D., Brooks, L. & Associates. (1984). *Career choice and development.* San Francisco: Jossey-Bass.

Buchanan, B. (1974). Building organizational commitment: The socialization of managers in work organizations. *Administrative Science Quarterly, 19,* 533-546.

Burns, T., & Stalker, G. M. (1961). *The management of innovation.* London: Tavistock.

Caldwell, D. F., & O'Reilly, C. A. (1982). Task perceptions and job satisfaction: A question of causality. *Journal of Applied Psychology, 19,* 51-76.

Champagne, A., Neef, M., & Nagel, S. (1981). Laws, organizations, and the judiciary. In P. C. Nystrom & W. H. Starbuck (Eds.), *Handbook of organizational design* (Vol. 1, pp. 187-209). Oxford: Oxford University Press.

Chandler, A. D. (1962). *Strategy and structure: Chapters in the history of American industrial enterprise.* Cambridge: MIT Press.

Cheatham, T. R., & McLaughlin, M. (1976). A comparison of co-participant perceptions of self and others in placement center interviews. *Communication Quarterly, 24,* 9-13.

Child, J. (1972). Organizational structure, environment and performance: The role of strategic choice. *Sociology, 6,* 1-22.

Child, J. (1977). *Organizations: A guide to problems and practice.* London: Harper & Row.

Coulter, R. D., & Taft, R. (1973). The professional socialization of schoolteachers as social assimilation. *Human Relations, 26,* 681-693.

Daft, R., & Macintosh, N. (1981). A tentative exploration into the amount and equivocality of information processing in organizational work units. *Administrative Science Quarterly, 26,* 207-224.

Danowski, J. A. (1980). Group attitude uniformity and connectivity of organizational communication networks for production, innovation, and maintenance content. *Human Communication Research, 6,* 299-308.

Danowski, J. A., & Edison-Swift, P. (1984). *Crisis effects on intraorganizational computer-based communication: A one-year time-series analysis of networks and message content.* Paper presented at the annual meeting of the International Communication Association, San Francisco.

Dansereau, F., Alutto, J. A., & Yammarino, F. J. (1984). *Theory testing in organizational behavior: The varient approach.* Englewood Cliffs, NJ: Prentice-Hall.

Dansereau, F., Chandrasekeran, G., Dumas, M., Coleman, D., Ehrlich, S., & Bagchi, D. (1986). *Data enquiry that tests entity and correlational/causal theories: DETECT application and user's guide.* Williamsville, NY: Institute for Theory Testing.

Dansereau, F., Graen, G., & Haga, W. J. (1975). A vertical dyad linkage approach to leadership within formal organizations: A longitudinal investigation of the role-making process. *Organizational Behavior and Human Performance, 13,* 46-78.

Davis, K. (1969). Grapevine communication among lower and middle managers. *Personnel Journal, 46,* 269-272.

Delia, J. G., Clark, R. A., & Switzer, D. E. (1979). The content of informed conversations as a function of interactants' interpersonal cognitive complexity. *Communication Monographs, 46,* 274-281.

Drucker, P. (1973). *Management: Tasks, responsibilities, practices.* New York: Harper & Row.

Duncan, R. (1972). Characteristics of organizational environments and perceived uncertainty. *Administrative Science Quarterly, 17,* 313-327.

Dunnette, M. D., Arvey, R., & Banas, P. (1973). Why do they leave? *Personnel, 50,* 23-39.

Easterlin, R. A. (1980). *Birth and fortune: The impact of numbers on personal welfare.* New York: Basic Books.

Eisenberg, E. M., Farace, R. V., Monge, P. R., Bettinghaus, E. P., Kurchner-Hawkins, R., Miller, K. I., & Rothman, L. (1985). Communication linkages in interorganizational systems: Review and synthesis. In B. Dervin & M. Voigt (Eds.), *Progress in communication sciences* (Vol. 6, pp. 231-261). NJ: Ablex.

Eisenberg, E. M., Monge, P. R., & Miller, K. I. (1983). Involvement in communication networks as a predictor of organizational commitment. *Human Communication Research, 10,* 179-201.

Emery, F. E., & Trist, E. L. (1965). The causal texture of organizational environments. *Human Relations, 18,* 21-32.

Epstein, J. L. (1983). Longitudinal effects of family-school-person interactions on student outcomes. In A. C. Kerckhoff (Ed.), *Research in sociology of education and socialization* (Vol. 4, pp. 101-127). Greenwich, CT: JAI.

Evan, W. M. (1972). An organizational set model of interorganizational relations. In M. Tuite, M. Rodnor, & R. Chisolm (Eds.), *Interorganizational decision making* (pp. 181-200). Chicago: Aldine.

Farace, R. V., & MacDonald, D. (1974). New directions in the study of organizational communication. *Personnel Psychology, 27,* 1-15.

Feldman, D. C. (1976). A contingency theory of socialization. *Administrative Science Quarterly, 21,* 433-452.

Feldman, D. C. (1977). The role of initiation activities in socialization. *Human Relations, 30,* 977-990.

Feldman, D. C. (1981). The multiple socialization of organizational members. *Academy of Management Review, 6,* 47-53.

Feldman, D. C., & Brett, J. M. (1983). Coping with new jobs: A comparative study of new hires and job changers. *Academy of Management Journal, 26,* 257-272.

Festinger, L. (1957). *A theory of cognitive dissonance.* Stanford: Stanford University Press.

Freeman, J. (1982). Organizational life cycles and natural selection processes. In B. M. Staw & L. L. Cummings (Eds.), *Research in organizational behavior* (Vol. 4, pp. 1-32). Greenwich, CT: JAI.

Giddens, A. (1976). *New rules of sociological method.* London: Hutchinson.

Gomersall, E. R., & Myers, M. S. (1966). Breakthrough in on-the-job training. *Harvard Business Review, 44,* 62-72.

Graen, G. (1976). Role-making processes within complex organizations. In M. D. Dunnette (Ed.), *Handbook of industrial and organizational psychology* (pp. 1455-1525). Chicago: Rand McNally.

Graen, G., & Cashman, J. (1975). A role-making model of leadership in formal organizations: A developmental approach. In J. G. Hunt & L. L. Larson (Eds.) *Leadership frontiers* (pp. 143-165). Kent, OH: Kent State University Press.

Gusfield, J. R. (1957). The problem of generations in an organizational structure. *Social Forces, 35,* 323-330.

Hage, J. (1974). *Communication and organizational control: Cybernetics in health and welfare settings.* New York: John Wiley.

Hage, J. (1980). *Theories of organizations: Form, process, & transformation.* New York: John Wiley.

Hage, J., & Aiken, M. (1969). Routine, technology, social structure, and organizational goals. *Administrative Science Quarterly, 14,* 366-377.

Hage, J., Aiken, M., & Marrett, C. B. (1971). Organization structure and communication. *American Sociological Review, 36,* 860-871.

Hall, R. H. (1972). *Organizations: Structure and process.* Englewood Cliffs, NJ: Prentice-Hall.

Hannan, M. T., & Freeman, J. (1977). The population ecology of organizations. *American Journal of Sociology, 82,* 929-964.

Haskins, J. (1966). Factual recall as a measure of advertising effectiveness. *Journal of Advertising Research, 6,* 2-8.

Herman, J. B. (1974). Cognitive processing of persuasive communication. *Organizational Behavior and Human Performance, 19,* 126-147.

Herriot, P. (1984). *Down from the Ivory Tower: Graduates and their jobs.* Chichester, England: John Wiley.

Herriot, P., & Rothwell, C. (1981). Organizational choice and decision theory: Effects of employers' literature and selection interview. *Journal of Occupational Psychology, 54,* 17-31.

Herriot, P., & Rothwell, C. (1983). Expectations and impressions in the graduate selection interview. *Journal of Occupational Psychology, 56,* 303-314.

Herriot, P., Ecob, R., & Hutchinson, M. (1980). Decision theory and occupational choice: Some longitudinal data. *Journal of Occupational Psychology, 53,* 223-236.

Hiltz, S. R., Turoff, M., & Johnson, K. (1984). *The effects of human leadership and computer feedback on the quality of group problem solving via computer.* Paper presented at the annual meeting of the International Communication Association, San Francisco.

Hughes, E. C. (1958). The study of occupations. In R. K. Merton, L. Broomand, & L. Cotrell (Eds.), *Sociology today.* New York: Basic Books.

Hulin, C. L., & Roznowski, M. (1985). Organizational technologies: Effects on organizations' characteristics and individuals' responses. In L. L. Cummings & B. M. Staw (Eds.), *Research in organizational behavior* (Vol. 7, pp. 39-85). Greenwich, CT: JAI.

Jablin, F. M. (1979). Superior-subordinate communication: The state of the art. *Psychological Bulletin, 63,* 1201-1222.

Jablin, F. M. (1980a). Organizational communication theory and research: An overview of communication climate and network research. In D. Nimmo (Ed.), *Communication yearbook 4* (pp. 327-347). New Brunswick, NJ: Transaction.

Jablin, F. M. (1980b). *Applying theory and research in superior-subordinate communication: Realizing the limits of wishful thinking.* Paper presented at the annual meeting of the Speech Communication Association, New York.

Jablin, F. M. (1981). *Organizational entry and organizational communication: Job retrospections, expectations, and turnover.* Paper presented at the annual meeting of the Academy of Management, San Diego.

Jablin, F. M. (1982a). Organizational communication: An assimilation approach. In M. E. Roloff & C. R. Berger (Eds.), *Social cognition and communication* (pp. 255-286). Newbury Park, CA: Sage.

Jablin, F. M. (1982b). Formal structural characteristics of organizations and superior-subordinate communication. *Human Communication Research, 8,* 338-347.

Jablin, F. M. (1984). Assimilating new members into organizations. In R. N. Bostrom (Ed.), *Communication yearbook 8* (pp. 594-626). Newbury Park, CA: Sage.

Jablin, F. M. (1985a). Task/work relationships: A life-span perspective. In M.L. Knapp & G.R. Miller (Eds.), *Handbook of interpersonal communication* (pp. 615-654). Newbury Park, CA: Sage.

Jablin, F. M. (1985b). An exploratory study of vocational organizational communication socialization. *Southern Speech Communication Journal, 50,* 261-282.

Jablin, F. M. (1987). Organizational entry, assimilation and exit. In F. M. Jablin, L. L. Putnam, K. H. Roberts, & L. W. Porter (Eds.), *Handbook of organizational communication.* Newbury Park, CA: Sage.

Jablin, F. M., & McComb, K. B. (1984). The employment screening interview: An organizational assimilation and communication perspective. In R. N. Bostrom (Ed.), *Communication yearbook 8* (pp. 137-163). Newbury Park, CA: Sage.

Jablin, F. M., & Sussman, L. (1983). Organizational group communication: A review of the literature and model of the process. In H. H. Greenbaum, R. L. Falcione, & S. A. Hellweg (Eds.), *Organizational communication: Abstracts, analysis and overview* (Vol. 8, pp. 11-50). Newbury Park, CA: Sage.

Jablin, F. M., & Tengler, C. D. (1982). Facing discrimination in on-campus interviews. *Journal of College Placement, 42,* 57-61.

Jablin, F. M., Tengler, C. D., & Teigen, C. W. (1985). *Applicant perceptions of job incumbents and personnel representatives as communication sources in the screening interview.* Paper presented at the annual convention of the Academy of Management, San Diego.

Johnson, B. M., & Rice, R. E. (1984). Reinvention of the innovation process: The case of word processing. In R. E. Rice & Associates (Eds.), *The new media: Communication, research, and technology* (pp. 157-183). Newbury Park, CA: Sage.

Jurgenson, C. E. (1978). Job preferences: What makes a job good or bad? *Journal of Applied Psychology, 63,* 267-276.

Kahn, R. L., Wolf, D. M., Quinn, R. P., Snoek, J. D., & Rosenthal, R. A. (1964). *Organizational stress: Studies in role conflict and ambiguity.* New York: John Wiley.

Kanter, R. M. (1977). *Men and women of the corporation.* New York: Basic Books.

Kaplan, S. (1972). Cognitive maps in perception and thought. In R. M. Downs & D. Stea (Eds.), *Cognitive mapping: Images of spatial environment* (63-78). Chicago: Aldine.

Kast, F. E., & Rosenzweig, J. E. (1972). General systems theory: Applications for organization and management. *Academy of Management Journal, 15,* 447-465.

Kast, F. E., & Rosenzweig, J. E. (1974). *Organization and management: A systems approach.* New York: McGraw-Hill.

Katz, D., & Kahn, R. (1978). *The social psychology of organizations* (2nd ed.). New York: John Wiley.

Katz, R. (1980). Time and work: Toward an integrative perspective. In B. M. Staw & L. L. Cummings (Eds.), *Research in organizational behavior* (Vol. 2, pp. 81-127). Greenwich, CT: JAI.

Katz, R., & Tushman, M. L. (1983). A longitudinal study of the effects of boundary spanning supervision on turnover and promotion in research and development. *Academy of Management Journal, 26,* 437-456.

Kellermann, K. A., & Berger, C. R. (1984). Affect and social information acquisition: Sit back, relax, and tell me about yourself. In R. N. Bostrom (Ed.), *Communication yearbook 8* (pp. 412-445). Newbury Park, CA: Sage.

Kimberly, J. R. (1980). The life cycle analogy and the study of organizations: Introduction. In J. R. Kimberly, R. H. Miles, & Associates (Eds.), *The organizational life cycle* (pp. 1-17). San Francisco: Jossey-Bass.

Kimberly, J. R., Miles, R. H., & Associates. (1980). *The organizational life cycle.* San Francisco: Jossey-Bass.

Klapper, J. T. (1960). *The effects of mass communication.* New York: Free Press.

Knapp, M. L. (1984). *Interpersonal communication and human relationships.* Boston: Allyn & Bacon.

Krone, K. J. (1984). *A framework for studying upward influence messages in decision making contexts.* Paper presented at the annual meeting of the International Communication Association, San Francisco.

Krone, K. J. (1985). *Subordinate influence in organizations: The differential use of upward influence messages in decision making contexts.* Unpublished doctoral dissertation, University of Texas at Austin.

Laska, S. B. & Micklin, M. (1981). Modernization, the family and work socialization: A comparative study of U.S. and Colombian youth. *Journal of Comparative Family Studies, 12,* 187-201.

Lawrence, P. R., & Lorsch, J. W. (1967). *Organization and environment.* Boston: Harvard University, Graduate School of Business Administration.

Lodahl, T. M., & Mitchell, S. M. (1980). Drift in the development of innovative organizations. In J. R. Kimberly, R. H. Miles, & Associates (Eds.), *The organizational life cycle* (pp. 184-207). San Francisco: Jossey-Bass.

Louis, M. R. (1980). Surprise and sensemaking: What newcomers experience in entering unfamiliar organizational settings. *Administrative Science Quarterly, 25,* 226-251.

Matarazzo, J. D., & Wiens, A. N. (1973). *The interview: Research on its anatomy and structure.* Chicago: Aldine.

McKelvey, B. (1979). Comment on the biological analogue in organizational science. *Administrative Science Quarterly, 24,* 488-493.

McLaughlin, M. L. (1984). *Conversation: How talk is organized.* Newbury Park, CA: Sage.

Meyer, M. W. (1975). Organizational domains. *American Sociological Review, 40,* 599-615.

Miller, V. D. (1984). *Ideology, communication, and the life cycle of organizations.* Paper presented at the annual convention of the Speech Communication Association, Chicago.

Monge, P. R., Farace, R. V., Eisenberg, E. M., Miller, K. I., & White, L. L. (1984). The process of studying process in organizational communication. *Journal of Communication, 34,* 22-43.

Monge, P. R., Farace, R. V., Miller, K. I., & Eisenberg, E. M. (1983). *Life cycle changes in interorganizational information networks.* Paper presented at the annual meeting of the International Communication Association, Dallas.

Morley, I. E., & Stephenson, G. M. (1970). Formality in experimental negotiations: A validation study. *British Journal of Psychology, 61,* 383-384.

Newcomb, T. M. (1958). Attitude development as a function of reference groups: The Bennington study. In E. E. Maccoby, T. M. Newcomb, & E. L. Hartley (Eds.), *Readings in social psychology* (3rd ed., pp. 265-275). New York: Holt, Rinehart & Winston.

Niles, J., Carlson, F., Gray, P., & Hanneman, G. (1976). *The telecommunication-transportation tradeoff.* New York: John Wiley.

Opsata, M. (1984). Winning strategies for telephone interviews. *Graduating Engineer, 5,* 12-15.

Osipow, S. H. (1983). *Theories of career development* (3rd ed.). Englewood Cliffs, NJ: Prentice-Hall.

Ouchi, W. G., & Maguire, M. A. (1975). Organizational control: Two functions. *Administrative Science Quarterly, 20,* 559-569.

Pfeffer, J. (1983). Organizational demography. In L. L. Cummings & B. M. Staw (Eds.), *Research in organizational behavior,* (Vol. 5, pp. 299-357). Greenwich, CT: JAI.

Popovich, P., & Wanous, J. P. (1982). The realistic job preview as a persuasive communication. *Academy of Management Review, 7,* 570-578.

Porter, L. W., Lawler, E. E., & Hackman, J. R. (1975). *Behavior in organizations.* New York: McGraw-Hill.

Putman, W. B., & Street, R. L. (1984). The conception and perception of noncontent speech performance: Implications for speech accommodation theory. *International Journal of the Sociology of Language, 46,* 97-114.

Ragan, S. L. (1983). A conversational analysis of alignment talk in job interviews. In R. N. Bostrom (Ed.), *Communication yearbook 7* (pp. 502-516). Newbury Park, CA: Sage.

Reynolds, E. V. & Johnson, J. D. (1982). Liaison emergence: Relating theoretical perspectives. *Academy of Management Review, 7,* 551-559.

Rice, R. E. (1980). Impacts of organizational and interpersonal computer-mediated communication. In M. Williams (Ed.), *Annual review of information science and technology* (Vol. 15, pp. 221-249). White Plains, NY: Knowledge Industry Publications.

Rice, R. E. (1983). *Media style and organizational use of computer-based communication systems.* Paper presented at the annual meeting of the International Communication Association, Dallas.

Rice, R. E. (1984). Mediated group communication. In R. E. Rice & Associates (Eds.), *The new media: Communication, research, and technology* (pp. 129-154). Newbury Park, CA: Sage.

Rice, R. E., & Associates (1984). *The new media: Communication, research, and technology.* Newbury Park, CA: Sage.

Roberts, K. H., Hulin, C. L., & Rousseau, D. M. (1978). *Developing an interdisciplinary science of organizations.* San Francisco: Jossey-Bass.

Roberts, K. H., & O'Reilly, C. A. (1978). Organizations as communication structures: An empirical approach. *Human Communication Research, 4,* 283-293.

Roberts, K. H., & O'Reilly, C. A. (1979). Some correlates of communication roles in organizations. *Academy of Management Journal, 22,* 42-57.

Rogers, D. P., & Sincoff, M. Z. (1978). Favorable impression characteristics of the recruitment interview. *Personnel Psychology, 31,* 495-503.

Roos, L. L., Jr., & Starke, F. A. (1981). Organizational roles. In P. C. Nystrom & W. H. Starbuck (Eds.), *Handbook of organizational design* (Vol. 1, pp. 290-308). Oxford: Oxford University Press.

Rotter, J. B. (1966). Generalized expectations for internal versus external control of reinforcement. *Psychological Monographs: General and Applied, 80*(1).

Rynes, S. L., Heneman, H. G., & Schwab, D. P. (1978). Individual reactions to organizational recruiting: A review. *Personnel Psychology, 31,* 495-503.

Salancik, G. R., & Pfeffer, J. (1978). A social information processing approach to job attitudes and task design. *Administrative Science Quarterly, 23,* 224-253.

Schein, E. H. (1968). Organizational socialization and the profession of management. *Industrial Management Review, 9,* 1-16.

Schmitt, N., & Coyle, B. W. (1976). Applicant decisions in the employment interview. *Journal of Applied Psychology, 61,* 184-192.

Schroder, H. M., Driver, M. H., & Streufert, S. (1967). *Human information processing.* New York: Holt, Rinehart & Winston.

Shaw, M. R. (1983). Taken-for-granted assumptions of applicants in simulated selection interviews. *Western Journal of Speech Communication, 47,* 138-156.

Short, J. A. (1973). *The effects of medium of communication on persuasion, bargaining, and perception of the other* (Communication Studies Group Report #E/73100/SH). London: University College.

Shortell, S. M. (1977). The role of environment in a configurational theory of organizations. *Human Relations, 30,* 275-302.

Snyder, M. (1979). Self-monitoring processes. In L. Berkowitz (Ed.), *Advances in experimental social psychology* (Vol. 12, pp. 85-128). New York: Academic Press.

Stabell, C. B. (1978). Integrative complexity of information environment perception and use. *Organizational Behavior and Human Performance, 22,* 116-142.

Steinfeld, C. (1984). *The nature of electronic mail usage in organizations: Purposes and dimensions of use.* Paper presented at the annual meeting of the International Communication Association, San Francisco.

Street, R. L. (1984). Speech convergence and speech evaluation in fact-finding interviews. *Human Communication Research, 11,* 139-169.

Street, R. L., & Giles, H. (1982). Speech accommodation theory: A social cognitive approach to language and speech behavior. In M. E. Roloff & C. R. Berger (Eds.), *Social cognition and communication* (pp. 193-226). Newbury Park, CA: Sage.

Svenning, L. L., & Ruchinskas, J. E. (1984). Organizational teleconferencing. In R. E. Rice & Associates (Eds.), *The new media: Communication, research, and technology* (pp. 217-248). Newbury Park, CA: Sage.

Teigen, C. W. (1983). *Communication of organizational climate during job screening interviews: A field study of interviewee perceptions, "actual" communication behavior and interview outcomes.* Unpublished doctoral dissertation, University of Texas at Austin.

Tengler, C. D., & Jablin, F. M. (1983). Effects of question type, orientation, and sequencing in the employment screening interview. *Communication Monographs, 50,* 245-262.

Terreberry, S. (1968). The evolution of organizational environments. *Administrative Science Quarterly, 12,* 590-613.

Thompson, J. D. (1967). *Organizations in action.* New York: McGraw-Hill.

Tushman, M. L. (1979). Impacts of perceived environmental variability on patterns of work related communication. *Academy of Management Journal, 22,* 482-500.

Tushman, M. L., & Nadler, D. (1978). Information processing as an integrating concept in organizational design. *Academy of Management Review, 3,* 613-624.

Tushman, M. L., & Scanlon, T. S. (1981). Boundary spanning individuals: Their roles in information transfer and their antecedents. *Academy of Management Journal, 24,* 289-305.

Uhlig, R. P. (1977). Human factors in computer message systems. *Datamation, 23,* 121-126.

Van de Ven, A. H. (1979). Book review of H. E. Aldrich, Organizations and environments. *Administrative Science Quarterly, 24,* 320-326.

Van Maanen, J. (1975). Breaking in: Socialization to work. In R. Dubin (Ed.), *Handbook of work, organization and society* (pp. 67-120). Chicago: Rand McNally.

Van Maanen, J. (1977). Experiencing organization: Notes on the meaning of careers and socialization. In J. Van Maanen (Ed.), *Organizational careers: Some new perspectives* (pp. 15-45). New York: John Wiley.

Van Maanen, J. (1978). People processing: Strategies of organizational socializing. *Organizational Dynamics, 7,* 18-36.

Van Maanen, J., & Schein, E. H. (1979). Toward a theory of organizational socialization. In B. M. Staw (Ed.), *Research in organizational behavior* (Vol. 1, pp. 209-264). Greenwich, CT: JAI.

Wanous, J. P. (1980). *Organizational entry: Recruitment, selection and socialization of newcomers.* Reading, MA: Addison-Wesley.

Wanous, J. P., Reichers, A. E., & Malik, S. D. (1984). Organizational socialization and group development: Toward an integrative perspective. *Academy of Management Review, 9,* 670-683.

Weick, K. E. (1969). *The social psychology of organizing.* Reading, MA: Addison-Wesley.

Whetton, D. A. (1980). Organization decline: A neglected topic in organizational science. *Academy of Management Review, 4,* 577-588.

Whisler, T. L. (1970). *The impact of computers on organizations.* New York: Praeger.

Wicker, A. W., & Mehler, A. (1971). Assimilation of new members in a large and a small church. *Journal of Applied Psychology, 53,* 151-156.

Wynn, E. (1980). *Computer message systems as a unique medium of communication.* Paper presented at the International Conference on Computer Communications, Atlanta, Georgia.

Zammuto, R. E., & Cameron, K. S. (1985). Environmental decline and organizational response. In L. L. Cummings & B. M. Staw (Eds.), *Research in organizational behavior* (Vol. 7, pp. 223-262). Greenwich, CT: JAI.

Zey-Ferrell, M. (1979). *Dimensions of organizations: Environment, context, structure, process, and performance.* Santa Monica, CA: Goodyear.

24 Professional Mass Communicators

JAMES S. ETTEMA
Northwestern University

D. CHARLES WHITNEY
University of Illinois, Urbana-Champaign

with DANIEL B. WACKMAN
University of Minnesota, Minneapolis

STUDIES of professional mass communicators that could be fairly termed "communication science" date back at least to Rosten's (1937) survey of Washington correspondents. Such studies have, however, been much enriched since the early 1970s by several developments. One is the infusion of ideas from cognate fields of study, particularly sociology. Sociology of knowledge, for example, while not new to mass communication (e.g., Park, 1940), has lately revitalized the critique of journalistic objectivity (e.g., Tuchman, 1972, 1973, 1978). Similarly, the sociology of complex organizations has reshaped the study of popular culture. In drawing up a prospectus for "production of culture" research, Peterson (1976) urged a focus on organizational structures and processes by which the "creation, manufacture, marketing, distribution, exhibiting, inculcation, evaluation and consumption" (p. 10) of symbol systems are accomplished.

Interest in professional mass communicators has also been intensified by the blossoming of cultural and critical perspectives within communication scholarship. While a variety of approaches—cultural anthropology, social history, political economy—are pursued under the cultural and critical banners, they share an interest in the meaning of mass media symbol systems and in the processes that yield those meanings. From a cultural perspective, for example, Newcomb and Alley (1983) emphasize the transformatory potential of television as ritual. Television, they argue, like the "in-between" phase of an initiation rite in tribal society, provides a release from sociocultural constraint and an opportunity to envision alternatives. The alternative visions are often unrealistic, and even monstrous, but this may make them all the more compelling as deconstructions of the commonsensical and the taken-for-granted (see Farrell, Chapter 4 in this volume). Television provides commentary on social reality by constructing *unreality.* Newcomb and Alley search for

the source of these visions in the work of the producer who often originates the TV series concept and who manages series production.

Those working from a critical perspective, on the other hand, emphasize the confirmatory potential of popular culture. Gitlin (1979), for
example, recognizes that television does confront social issues but in a
way that "domesticates" them. The issues of race, gender and class may
be raised on television but the prevailing arrangements of capitalist consumer society are typically confirmed as offering the solution to such
"social problems." This is Gitlin's interpretation of the concept of
"hegemony," finding on television not social commentary but social
control. Theorists in this tradition urge attention to how, for example,
occupational cultures of professional communicators mediate the relationship between "the ruling ideology" and media content (Murdock &
Golding, 1977).

These perspectives are at odds with an attempt to develop a sociology
of cultural production that is analytic rather than evaluative in goal.
Peterson's (1976) vision of such a sociology sets aside the idealist/mate-
rialist debate—whether culture creates social structure or vice versa—
to study the production and reproduction of culture. Such a sociology
would hold in abeyance the evaluation of cultural forms and focus on the
mechanisms that reproduce these forms. But this, argue the cultural and
critical theorists, is impossible. Writing from a materialist position,
Tuchman (1983) argues that much "production of culture" research is a
brand of organizational sociology that takes for granted contemporary
capitalism and thus "obscure[s] the historicity of cultural products" and
how such products are "implicated in the creation of ideology" (p. 332).
She urges attention to how ideology is "embedded" in organizational
process. Writing from an idealist position, Jensen (1984) argues that the
production of culture perspective fails to recognize cultural production
as a truly cultural enterprise—one "encompassing both the producers
and the audience for which they create" (p. 110). She urges viewing
popular culture not as "a container of messages processed along a line
from sender to receiver" but rather as "the means through which people
construct meaningful worlds in which to live" (p. 108). These critics are
unwilling to hold the study of meaning in abeyance, arguing that the
study of message formulation without a theory of meaning is, indeed,
meaningless.

There is substantial merit in these arguments. The social science
approach to the study of professional mass communicators has only
recently begun to come to terms with the critique of news as ideology
(see Hackett, 1984). It still does not emphasize the relationships between
production process and social setting that yield particular themes, songs,
stories, or images in popular entertainment. Instead it emphasizes more
global dimensions of media content such as degree of content diversity

within a medium. But the approach need not be "meaningless." For example, Peterson and Berger's (1975) analysis of the relationship between recording industry concentration and musical diversity is informed by an appreciation of the content of postwar popular music. Similarly, Schatz (1981) begins his history of film genre with a review of the organizational functions of genre in the old Hollywood studio system. These authors do not reduce the meaning of popular music and film genre to market structure or organizational routine but rather enumerate some conditions necessary for particular meanings to be formulated. Meaning cannot be reduced to economic, industrial, organizational, or psychological processes, and yet mass-mediated meaning cannot exist without these processes. Still, the social science approach is more attuned to how symbols are produced than to what they mean and more attuned to industrial and organizational context than to the text itself. In outlining a "communication science" of professional mass communicators that emphasizes structures and processes of message production we can, then, provide only part—albeit an important part—of what should be said about the form, content, and meaning of mass communication.

MASS COMMUNICATORS IN CONTEXT

Mass-mediated symbol systems—news, popular music, television, and film—are, at one level of analysis, the work of individual or small groups of media professionals. At another level of analysis, however, they are the products of complex organizations; and at still another, higher level they reflect the economic arrangements of media industries and institutions. The work of individual mass communicators cannot be understood outside these organizational, industrial, and institutional contexts (Dimmick & Coit, 1982; Whitney, 1982). For example, Hirsch's (1977) reanalysis of White's (1950) classic gatekeeper study, as well as data collected by Whitney and Becker (1982), suggest that influences on news selection that have been traced to individual or professional values must also be traced to organizational routines that partly cue news selection by wire editors. The analysis of symbol formulation and diffusion via the mass media must, then, be pursued on several levels of analysis; and yet the activities at each level so interpenetrate these other levels that it is difficult to disentangle them.

This chapter is organized into two essentially self-contained essays, each dealing with a key process in symbol formulation and diffusion: creating entertainment, and gathering news. We recognize, as Hirsch (1977) points out, that these processes have important similarities. Both are constrained by their markets, expedited by organizational routines, and subject to professional value systems. It may also be argued that the products of these processes are not so very different: News is now, more than ever, entertainment; and there is, at times, substantial social insight in the popular arts.

Nevertheless, we will review news and entertainment separately. They have been treated in relatively separate bodies of literature up to this point and, more important, we want to highlight different issues in each. We take seriously the idea that the production of popular culture can be a creative and meaningful activity despite the constraints of the market-place. And for journalism we wish to pay our respects—we trust not final respects—to the often maligned idea that its essential task is to find the truth despite strong economic, political, and organizational constraints. Our goal is not, then, to evaluate the creativity in particular materials of popular culture nor to critique the truth of particular news stories, but rather to assess the general prospects for creativity and for truth given what is known about these production processes.

CREATIVITY AND POPULAR CULTURE

"Cultural material," Jensen (1984) argues, "is symbolic material that both expresses and constitutes experience." For many of us there is still more than a little discomfiture in the realization that it is the material of popular culture, particularly television, that expresses and constitutes the experience of so many people so much of the time. If, however, we wish to take this experience seriously—and its ubiquity alone demands that we do so—then the sociocultural process behind that experience becomes crucial. How is it, for example, that the television experience can "ring changes on the themes of innocence and corruption, truth and deception, integrity and duplicity" (Newcomb & Alley, 1983, p. 27) or "enshrine, confirm, finally . . . soothe even acute psychological con-flicts" (Gitlin, 1983, p. 218)? And, most central to the question at hand, may we say that these experiences, like those of "higher" or "finer" cultural material, are in any sense "created"?

Industrial and Institutional Levels:
The Cultural Economy

The processes of cultural production occur within and are shaped by what DiMaggio (1977) calls "the cultural economy." Following Peter-son and Berger (1975), DiMaggio argues that degree of competition within a culture industry (e.g., broadcasting, recording, publishing) is related to degree of diversity and innovativeness of the products offered by that industry. In highly concentrated industries, a few firms often compete for shares of a single mass market with a few similar products.

When a small number of firms can retain control of their markets and thus avoid the risks of significant innovation, they can also control and routinize the work of their creative personnel. These creative staffs may wish to innovate but are not offered the opportunity by their organizations. In more competitive industries, on the other hand, firms may find it more profitable to serve specialized market segments with unique products. In this market setting firms cannot avoid the risks and uncertainties of innovation and often must delegate substantial freedom to their creative personnel. Peterson and Berger's (1975) research shows, for example, that concentration in the recording industry has fluctuated cyclically and that periods of concentration have been marked by homogeneity in recorded music while times of greater competition produce innovation and diversity. Further, a long period of concentration and homogeneity has been followed by "a brief burst of competition and creativity" (p. 170).

Nord (1980) finds this relationship between market dominance and media content in other industries as well:

> The greater the market power a producer has (the greater the opportunity to control risk) the tighter and more standardized will be the formulas. . . . The business history of book and magazine publishing, film making, song selling, comic stripping and radio and television broadcasting provides evidence in support of this hypothesis. (p. 215)

In the period before World War II when a few mass circulation magazines dominated their market through control of advertising, article formulas were highly standardized, imitative, inoffensive, and probably more reflective of publishers' and advertisers' tastes than those of the large and heterogeneous audience.

Television destroyed the advertising market dominance of national magazines such as *Life* and *Look*, but it inherited their market logic. Though threatened by independent broadcasters, cablecasters, and videocassette recorders, the television networks remain a powerful oligopoly. Further, the system of advertiser support makes the industry much more sensitive to audience size than to intensity of audience demand (Owen, 1975; Owen, Beebe, & Manning, 1974) and sensitive to the demands of advertisers for inoffensive vehicles to bear commercial messages (Barnow, 1978; Intintoli, 1984). Together these economic factors constrain commercial broadcasting to a few genres (Dominick & Pearce, 1976) and a range of themes that are emotionally and intellectually accessible to a very large portion of the possible audience. Programmers dare not stray very often or very far from the center of popular taste for fear of losing one sort of viewer or another. "The gravity of television," in actor Robin Williams's phrase, "keeps pulling you down to mediocre" (Goldman,

1982). The gravity metaphor is apt: Market structure pulls television content not toward the lowest taste but rather toward the average taste—the *center,* in a sense, of the audience's cultural world. Contrast this with the structure and content of book publishing, in which as many as 12,000 publishers (Powell, 1982), many of them very small and highly specialized, generate a vast array of content. Publishers are allowed, indeed forced, to specialize; and as if in a state of reduced gravity, they fly off in nearly every conceivable direction. But even in this most diverse of cultural industries there is concern about the impact of concentration among publishers (Coser, Kadushin, & Powell, 1981; Powell, 1982; Whiteside, 1981) and about constrictions within distribution channels (Turow, 1977, 1979).

It is clear that market structure may lead media industries to constrain their output. From the viewpoint of the industries' management, on the other hand, the issue is not *constraint* of content but rather *selection* of content. Network programmers must select producers and series, and publishers must select authors and titles, that fit their markets. However, the criteria for selection, even in concentrated and relatively noninnovative industries, are not well defined. It is unclear who can generate content that meets market requirements. Further,it is not even clear what those requirements will be; consumer tastes seem unstable, even unknowable. Organizational theorists characterize this situation as one of "uncertainty" (Perrow, 1979; Thompson, 1967) or "turbulence" (Emery & Trist, 1965; Hirsch, 1975) at both the input and output boundaries of the organization. Strategies to cope with these uncertainties have evolved, and these are the mechanisms by which content is at once selected and constrained.

A basic strategy is the segmentation of cultural industries into functional subsystems (Hirsch, 1972). Some workers are separated from the managerial subsystem (the network, the publisher, the recording company) and are accorded "artist" or "professional" status; they work on a temporary or freelance basis. These workers constitute the creative or technical subsystem. Some culture industries also have separate promotion and distribution subsystems such as book retailers or movie distributors and exhibitors (DiMaggio & Hirsch, 1976). These subsystems are coordinated by "boundary-spanning" agents such as record, movie, and television producers, who assemble the sort of creative talent that can meet market demands. This industry structure provides the managerial subsystem with flexibility to meet changing consumer tastes, spreads the risks of innovation to other organizations, and delegates substantial creative responsibility to those with a special talent for generating commercially viable content.

Hirsch (1972) likens this industry structure to the craft administrative system of the construction industry (Stinchcombe, 1959). DiMaggio

(1977) argues, however, that the arrangement is more adequately characterized as a "brokerage administration" system. He notes that craft administration is based on employer-employee relations structured by contracts and by clear standards of professional competence. In cultural industries, however, employer-employee relations are marked by informality and negotiation because standards for evaluation of finished products are vague. DiMaggio further specifies three types of brokerage administration systems: (1) pure brokerage, in which the broker (e.g., book editor) mediates between administrative decision makers and artists; (2) entrepreneurial brokerage, found in turbulent settings where managers abdicate decision making to the broker (e.g., record producer); and (3) centralized brokerage, found in much less turbulent settings in which the broker (e.g., television producer) represents the decision maker's views to artists but is also subject to close supervision.

Hirsch (1972) outlines several other strategies for coping with uncertainty. He argues that record companies, book publishers, and movie studios all deploy relatively many contact personnel at their output boundaries to link the organization to retailers, "surrogate consumers" (e.g., disk jockeys), relevant policymakers (Hirsch, 1975), and pressure groups (Cantor, 1979, 1980; Montgomery, 1981; Turow, 1984a, 1984b). Another strategy is the overproduction and differential promotion of products. Because the cost of producing a record or book is relatively low, many are produced and become available for promotion and distribution. However, only those that are judged by entrepreneurs to have commercial potential are promoted heavily; faltering products can be quickly replaced on store shelves. While the television industry differs from those studied by Hirsch in that its market environment has been less turbulent, networks still have created departments to look after their relationship with affiliated local stations. The networks also commission many more treatments, scripts and pilots than can become series, so that a faltering series can be quickly replaced.

The example of a faltering series points out another strategy for coping with uncertain consumer tastes—the use of ratings and other feedback research. By providing a widely accepted audience measurement system, ratings help regulate the interchanges among networks, affiliates, advertisers, and program suppliers. Ratings, even if methodologically imperfect and inconsistently used, enforce the economic rules of the television game as established by the industry. Indeed, ratings are a primary mechanism through which economically imposed constraints impinge upon selection of content. Pekurny (1982), however, argues that ratings and other coping strategies (e.g., adherence to tried-and-true formulas) cannot fully routinize the industry. Organizations within the industry must still take chances, individuals in them still find creative opportunities, and occasionally conditions are present for truly innovative work.

Turow (1982) has explored the industrial conditions from which innovative content may emerge on television. Drawing upon the substantial literature on industrial innovation, Turow argues that innovation on commercial television is often the result of "the coming together of an unestablished production firm with a network experiencing extraordinary problems or changes" (p. 125). A case in point is *All in the Family*. When Norman Lear conceived that series, he was producing feature films and only marginally involved in television production. He was, then, able to offer his idea to the networks on a take-it-or-leave-it basis, a powerful position from which to promote a departure from the conventional. Meanwhile, CBS was strong in overall ratings but felt that it was falling behind its competitors in the ratings race for the young urban adult market. The network was, then, willing to take a chance on something different.

The need to find new products continually tugs against the attempt to make business stable, predictable, and thus more manageable through routinization of the selection process. This is what DiMaggio and Hirsch (1976) refer to as the pervasive tension between innovation and control in cultural industries. For example, television networks, recognizing that their industry requires constant—if modest—innovation, contract out the tasks of series creation and production to independent brokers who may be given substantial autonomy. At the same time, the networks attempt to control creation and production through elaborate audience research requirements for pilots (Gitlin, 1983) and through close monitoring of productions to ensure adherence to broadcast standards and to successful formulas (Pekurny, 1982). It is also the networks that apply ratings data to the selection of series for continuation. It is from the pull and tug between innovation and control that television programs and other cultural products emerge that are at once new and old, endlessly varied and yet always the same.

Organizational Level:
Working Within, Around, and Through Constraints

The tension between innovation and control is a feature not only of the selection of content by the managerial subsystem but also the creation of content within the technical subsystem. Television provides the best-researched example of how this industrial fact of life penetrates organizational and, ultimately, individual life. In the centralized brokerage system of television, the producer is commissioned by the networks to generate programming. Schedules, budgets, and other creative controls imposed by the networks constrain producers and their organizations, but even within the closely controlled setting of ongoing series production a producer may be able to "work within, around and through"

(Newcomb & Alley, 1982, p. 69) the constraints to embody some personal visions and values in a show. Television is a producer's medium, Newcomb and Alley (1982, 1983) argue, because it is typically producers who figure out what networks and audiences will accept and who hire, coordinate, and regulate other creative personnel (writers, story editors, directors). Thus producers are powerful because they personally absorb much of the uncertainty of television production and because they are the central decision makers in an organization with a relatively clear division of labor. Uncertainty absorption and organizational centrality, along with nonsubstitutability or indispensability, have been identified by Hickson, Hinnings, Lee, and Schenck (1971) as important bases of individual and subunit power within organizations.

Creativity opportunity is, then, a matter of organizational power. Ettema (1980) found that the producer of a public television series held complete creative control despite the formal right of educational and scientific advisors to review and approve his work. It was, after all, the producer whose role was most central to the primary task of getting television shows "in the can" and who was left to cope with much of the uncertainty of that task when advisors could not provide unequivocal advice. Intintoli (1984) found, on the other hand, that in soap opera production head writers often have substantial creative control because they are difficult to replace. Similarly, star performers may enjoy creative control because of their perceived nonsubstitutability though, as Peters and Cantor (1982) point out, it is ease of substitution that renders most screen actors and actresses powerless.

While producers usually play the central creative role in their organizations, they too rely upon a variety of strategies to cope with the tasks of creation. The division of labor among creative personnel, for example, helps consolidate producer power, but it also facilitates the orderly flow of work through the production organization and thus helps routinize the "core technology" (Thompson, 1967) of television production.

Another coping strategy is to rely upon proven personnel to fill creative roles. Just as the producer may be chosen by the network based upon track record, so the producer may select creative personnel. Faulkner's (1982) study of track records in the film industry is instructive. An analysis of screen credits from 1964 to 1979 indicated that a majority of producers, directors, screen writers, and cinematographers worked on only one film during that period and just a tiny fraction worked on more than five or six films. Further, those who worked on relatively few films tended to work with others who had relatively few credits, while those with many credits worked with others of similar accomplishment. The most productive producers tend to hire creative personnel from an "inner circle," Faulkner argues, "to reduce uncertainty, . . . narrow the complexity of their choices, and . . . increase their confidence while boosting their perceived chances of securing control over a turbulent environment" (1982, p. 95). The use of track records, or "career portfolios" in Faulkner's more elegant phrase, is a rationalized if not always rational way to cope with uncertainties of innovation. According to one informant,

> You could shop around and see who's good but not expensive but if your picture goes down the drain, the people who are working with you, and the people in charge, say, of distribution at Disney, Universal, Fox— wherever—will scream, "Idiot, why didn't you hire the best?" So there's pressure to hire a name. (Faulkner, 1982, p. 96)

According to Pekurny (1982) the situation is much the same in television.

As managers of somewhat bureaucratized organizations, producers can exercise overt authority through such mechanisms as budgets, schedules, and, of course, explicit instructions, but they may also exercise control through less obtrusive mechanisms such as reliance upon production conventions (Sanders, 1982). Thus according to Turow (1978), criteria for casting minor television parts (e.g., credibility and visual balance) are well known and generally accepted among producers, casting directors, and agents. Series are typified according to casting needs (e.g., "beautiful people," "real people," "street people"). Similarly, potential talk show guests are typified to facilitate assembly of the show (Tuchman, 1974). These shared understandings of what must be done—that is, what the producer wants—control work by establishing the *premises* for worker's decision making (March & Simon, 1958; Perrow, 1979).

Sanders (1982) distinguishes these *production* conventions from *product* conventions, which are features of content that producers consistently employ and consumers come to expect. Product conventions include the standardized features of film and literary genres (Cawelti, 1969, 1976; Kaminsky, 1985; Schatz, 1981) and the formulas for television series (Brown, 1968; Pekurny, 1982). Such product conventions may contain substantial meaning—"define and express a world," as Jensen (1984) suggests—but they also serve to regulate and coordinate the tasks of production. Thus the distinction between production and product convention is often not clear. Becker (1982) sees conventions as features of artworks but also as shared understandings that unite artists and support personnel into "art worlds." Ryan and Peterson (1982) synthesize the distinction between production and product conventions with the argument that, in country music recording at least, it is not so much well-established conventions or formulas that regulate and coordinate the production process as "product images"—models or images continually shaped and reshaped by recently successful songs. In a variety of ways, then, culture-producing organizations struggle to bring their tasks under control.

Individual Level:
Creativity as Work

Ultimately, it is the individual worker who confronts the creative task. Even in settings of "corporate" creativity (DiMaggio & Hirsch, 1976) there is opportunity for individual creativity. And so it is that Newcomb and Alley (1983) find the meaning of television in work of individual producers just as a generation of critics and historians have found the meaning of film, or at least some films, in the work of directors (e.g., Nichols, 1976).

Creative skills can to some extent be taught, and yet the act of creation itself does not yield easily to either the inquiries of researchers or the introspection of practitioners themselves. When asked how poems are made, Amy Lowell replied, "What I do know about them is only a millionth part of what there must be to know. I meet them where they touch consciousness, and that is already a considerable distance along the road of evolution" (1930, p. 24). And so photographers and cinematographers are said simply to have "a good eye" while writers may have "an ear for dialog." Programmers may have a "golden gut" while successful producers have "instinct" or, best of all, "magic."

If generalizations about the act of creation remain elusive, it is at least possible to appreciate how industries and organizations structure not only the work of individual creators but also their artistic consciousness. Here again the television producer provides the best-researched case. The producers studied by Cantor (1971) and by Newcomb and Alley (1982, 1983) experience powerful constraints—the pull of the "gravity of television"—and yet many of them have found worthwhile opportunities for creative self-expression. Producer Quinn Martin takes obvious pride in detailing for Newcomb and Alley how he manages his production company to achieve as much creative control as possible and, in turn, to embody personal values in his productions. Martin's attitude is an example of the professional value system that, according to Cantor, is marked by a belief in the creative possibilities of television and the need to struggle for creative freedom—but also the need, finally, to bow to the authority of the network. While this professional value system is not the only one found by Cantor, it is the system that best characterizes the "self-conscious artistic producers" studied by Newcomb and Alley. This search for meaningful creative opportunity within industrial and organizational constraint is also a theme of Griff's (1960) study of commercial artists, Faulkner's (1971) study of studio musicians, and Peters and Cantor's (1982) study of aspiring screen actors.

It is ironic that constraints are often imposed upon creators in the name of the audience—the ratings, according to the networks, help give people what they want—and yet the creators' image of their audience is relatively undeveloped (Cantor, 1971). The industry provides creators with data about audience size and demographic composition, but this is an image not of the audience but of the market. Even so, some researchers (e.g., Gans, 1957) have argued that creators consciously strive to please their audience. Intintoli (1984) argues that soap opera staffers read and analyze letters from viewers and that letters have an impact on story development. Similarly, Espinosa (1982) argues that audience interests and needs were considered by the participants in the television story conference he studied, although the audience is rarely invoked explicitly. It is easy to imagine that, if asked, the participants in the story conference would have defended their ideas with generalizations about the audience, but we might doubt whether those generalizations would be based on study of or even systematic exposure to the television audience. Writers learn their craft not through an audience image but rather by learning a product image—an image that, as Ryan and Peterson (1982) argue, assures not so much acceptance by the audience as acceptance by superiors and coworkers in the production chain. Network executives and coworkers are, according to Pekurny (1982), the real audience for television creators.

Creativity and Constraint

If there is a dominant theme in this literature on the production of popular culture it is the tension between innovation and control, or creativity and constraint (Ettema & Whitney, 1982). Constraints are often imposed by culture-producing industries and organizations to cope with the uncertainties of profitably generating and marketing cultural products. Yet opportunities for creativity exist within these constraints for individuals or small groups of collaborators who acquire enough power to exercise creative control. It is, then, tempting to conclude simply that industries and organizations constrain while individuals create. This conclusion would, however, vastly oversimplify the nature of mass mediated creativity.

At the industrial level of analysis, mass marketing strategies do play a real, if limited, role in attuning media content to popular taste. Schatz (1981) and Kaminsky (1985) suggest that the form, content, and meaning of film genres have developed through a process of marketing trial and error. Many films, each somewhat different, have been produced; and those which have been most successful represent a product image to be learned, emulated, and eventually altered. And so a genre evolves.

Individual creators need not have a clear idea of who their audience is or what that audience wants to see. They need not even grasp the full meaning of their work; it is the industry system as a whole through box office receipts and track records that attunes content to audience and to critic. While individuals produce and direct specific films, the meaning of the genre need not be sought in the artistic vision of individuals. Similarly, long-running television series result from a process of marketing trial and error. Many series are created, but few survive to be critically analyzed. So media industry systems create, or at least participate in the creative process. Having said this, however, we hasten to add that cultural industries, particularly television, do not inevitably or necessarily give audiences what they want. More exactly, they inevitably and necessarily give markets what they will accept.

It is at this point that the study of production establishes contact with the study of meaning in popular entertainment. When we recognize that communicating with an audience *is,* for better or worse, tapping a market, then we also recognize as problematic the assumption that popular culture speaks clearly and compellingly to its audience or that it reflects the spirit of the times (Nord, 1980). There are powerful constraints upon the ability of this sort of material to express and constitute meaningful experience, although such meaning may perhaps be found in large and coherent bodies of popular material such as literary, film, and television genres or even long-running television series. It is also at this point that the study of production makes contact with media policy analysis by contributing to an understanding of what can and cannot be communicated within the constraints of market control or other systems of socioeconomic control.

At the organizational level, much as at the industrial level, it is tempting to focus on strategies and routines as inhibitors of individual creativity. Indeed the social psychology of creativity does indicate that such organizational givens as deadlines, evaluations, and extrinsic rewards ("doing it for the money") can inhibit creative output (Amabile, 1983). To be a media professional means, however, to deliver acceptable products—as Gitlin (1983) says, "to execute the standard formulas with high production values, seamlessly" (p. 155)—whatever the constraints may be. More than that, to be a media creator means not merely to work within and around the organizational facts of life but to work *through* them—to acquire power and harness the organization, as Newcomb and Alley's (1983) producers have done, to express one's visions and values. Organizations constrain the behavior of all who work within them, but they are also necessary instruments for mass-mediated creativity. Thus to be a creator means mastering the organization and directing it toward one's own creative goals.

It is at this point that the study of culture-producing organizations should make contact with the extensive literature on such organizational processes as the accrual of power and the conduct of politics (e.g., Bacharach & Lawler, 1980), the exercise of leadership (Bennis & Nanus, 1985), and the management of innovation (e.g., Blau & McKinley, 1979; Downs & Mohr, 1976). Kanter (1983), for example, concludes that innovation in any organization requires managers and professionals who can "move outside of the formal bonds of their job, maneuvering through and around the organization in sometimes risky, unique and novel ways" (p. 216), an assessment strikingly similar to Newcomb and Alley's (1982) conclusion that innovation in television requires producers who can skillfully work "within, around and through (organizational limits) to achieve their creative goals" (p. 69). Recognizing the political nature of organizational life, Kanter (1983) maintains that "organizational genius is 10 percent inspiration and 90 percent acquisition—acquisition of power to move beyond a formal job charter and to influence others" (p. 216).

Finally we come back to the individual media professionals who must get behind the camera, the sound mixer, or the word processor and *do* something. Even if we can never know much of what there must be to know, we can at least explore the conscious experience of life and work as a media creator. Much has been said about the paucity of creators' audience images and yet little is really understood of what creators actually do with whatever images they may have or what they could do with richer images. Similarly much has been said about the constraints on individual workers but more could be known about how these constraints are experienced and the degree to which they inhibit creativity as an intrapsychic process. A variety of constraints can inhibit creative output among adults and children (Amabile, 1983). It is not clear, however, how these results apply to media professionals who have been organizationally selected (and self-selected) for their ability to work under such conditions. Ettema (1982) argues that the constraints on the development of a public television series he studied—the goals of the funding agency, needs of educators, the findings of the formative evaluators—energized rather than inhibited the executive producer. The producer and some script writers experienced their work on the project as a puzzle to be solved in the most creative possible way:

> "I happen to believe that setting limits increases creativity," one of the writers said. "I think if you take a creative person and give him nothing to fight against, nothing to bump up against, he can't flex his muscles. He's flabby. I think that restrictions are very good creatively."

> Another of the writers strongly agreed. "Writing for the series," she said, "is like solving a puzzle." (Ettema, 1982, p. 104)

Constraints of some sort—whether the demands of a television network or a royal patron, whether the form of a film genre or an organ fugue—are and always have been present in the creative life. The issue is how individuals devise ways to work within, around, and through them to achieve their creative purposes.

Here the study of the creation of popular culture makes contact with research on psychosocial (Amabile, 1983) and intrapsychic (Perkins, 1981) processes of creative production. The study of the individual creator, however, stands at a crossroads. Down one route lies the study of creativity as an intensely personal experience; down the other lies the study of creativity as the interpretation of cultural heritage. Individual creators draw upon cultural traditions as creative resources and, in turn, become the interpreters of those traditions. Fussell (1975), a literary critic, traces the traditions that inform the modern understanding of warfare, a tradition with roots in the work of those who survived World War I to write of their experiences. Fussell concludes, "there seems to be one dominating form of modern understanding; that it is essentially ironic; and that it originates largely in the application of mind and memory to the events of the Great War" (p. 35). Just as Joseph Heller in *Catch-22* drew upon this understanding to interpret the great war of his own generation, so the creators of *M*A*S*H* drew upon it to interpret not so much the war in Korea as that in Vietnam. The tradition is thus updated and its power to render experience meaningful is renewed. Those who create for the mass media, argue Newcomb and Hirsch (1984) are "seeking and creating new meaning in the combination of cultural elements with embedded significance" (p. 60). To understand the creative act would be to understand the culturally universal resources and rituals as well as uniquely personal inspiration and insights at work in this process.

JOURNALISM AND TRUTH

If the search for creative opportunity is a central issue in the production of popular entertainment, knowing and telling the truth is the corresponding goal in journalism. Whether truth can be equated with fact or differentiated from value and how it can be known at all are old and enduring issues of the craft (e.g., Hutchins, 1947; Lippmann, 1922). Even so, practitioners and critics alike regularly affirm the *possibility* of truth through journalism (Epstein, 1975; *Harpers,* 1985). Gitlin (1979) acknowledges, if grudgingly, that journalism does seek "truth—partial, superficial, occasion—and celebrity-centered truth, but truth nevertheless" (p. 263). Our focus on truth in journalism does not, then, deny the ancient philosophical problems surrounding truth; but as we held in abeyance the materialist/idealist debate in the study of culture, we set aside this problem by assuming that *as a practical matter* there is truth to be known and told. In this section, then, we assess the prospects for knowing and telling that truth given what is known about how journalism works.

Industrial and Institutional Levels:
The Political Economy of Journalism

Analysis of the extent to which—or whether at all—journalism can approximate truth begins with the political economy of the craft. From a variety of (typically British) materialist (e.g., Murdock, 1982; Murdock & Golding, 1977) and cultural Marxist (e.g., Hall 1977, 1980, 1982) positions, mass communication is viewed as a means for legitimation and maintenance of socioeconomic stratification. These authors see more than simple deterministic between the prevailing economic order and the practice of journalism. Murdock and Golding (1977) maintain that while Marx "saw the basic economic relations of capitalism as structuring the overall framework and 'general process' of intellectual life, within these general limits he allowed a good deal of room for intellectual autonomy and innovation" (p. 16).

Authors in this critical tradition, like social historians and organizational theorists, argue that the relationship between capitalist ownership of the means of mass communication and the day-to-day practice of journalism is mediated by a journalistic "culture of objectivity." (On the rise of this culture and what Carey, 1969, calls "the purely commercial motives" behind it, see Roshco, 1975; Schiller, 1981; Schudson, 1978.) This culture of objectivity does allow—indeed it prizes—autonomy, as evidenced by occasional clashes with corporate and governmental authorities. But it also demands fairness and balance within the limits of the "consensus" (Schlesinger, 1978) or the "common sense" (Hartley, 1982) of liberal capitalism. The partisan bias of an earlier era is reduced considerably, but this culture is subject to biases of its own—biases not so much *in* the news as biases *of* the news. Gitlin (1980), for example, argues that journalistic devotion to hard fact and editorial balance led to coverage of the Vietnam-era antiwar movement that emphasized confrontation with authorities rather than analysis of issues and portrayed the movement as operating beyond the bounds of reasonable dissent.

If journalism is a tool of social control, and one need not be a Marxist to argue that it is, that tool is used with considerable subtlety and restraint. Dreier (1982) interrelated memberships on the boards of directors of the 25 largest U.S. newspaper-owning firms with other affiliations and argues that at this top corporate level, these media firms are intimately tied to the U.S. power structure. These firms, Dreier suggests, embody a "corporate liberal" perspective more concerned with stability of the entire system than with more conservative or parochial interests often identified with large corporations.

Few current political-economic approaches, then, suggest that big-industry news media work to stifle dissent entirely. Most, if not all, suggest instead that the primary effect is either to direct and shape political dialogue or to limit the diversity of opinion and information that is expressed. On diversity, we shall have more to say later. On shaping the news, we must add to Gitlin (1980) a variety of literature that suggests that corporate-capitalist ownership of news media predisposes news to routinely uncritical treatment of corporate and governmental power sources (e.g., Bennett, 1983). This is seen most clearly when ruptures in the normal webs of coverage, such as accidents, scandals, and disasters, occasion "repair work" by the powerful (Molotch & Lester, 1974) or by the news media themselves (Bennett, Gressett, & Haltom, 1985).

Across the news industry scarcity of resources promotes efficiency in news gathering, particularly in ways of conceptualizing newsworthiness that make for predictability and economy. The beat system, for example, disperses reporters to where news is most likely to occur—usually centers of institutional power (Tuchman, 1978). Television network news is geographically biased; that is, when news occurs in places where its production and distribution is cheaper, it is more "newsworthy" or at least more likely to be transmitted as news (Dominick, 1977; Epstein, 1974; Whitney, Fritzler, Jones, Mazzarella, & Rakow, 1985).

On diversity, scholars who argue that news media *are* diverse usually point to the number, variety, and competitiveness of media outlets either nationally or in particular markets (e.g., Compaine, 1982, 1985). Those who argue that they are not point instead to a lack of direct competition within a particular medium in a particular market. For example, only about 30 U.S. cities have two separately owned daily newspapers (Bagdikian, 1985). Competition in a media market may be related to organizational differentiation in news gathering by its daily newspapers (DuBick, 1978), but the evidence that direct newspaper competition is reflected in news or editorial diversity is far less compelling (Entman, 1985).

Studies comparing the content of competitive versus noncompetitive media rarely find significant differences. Why? It may be that the "logic" of news in a market economy is itself standardized, as suggested above. Or competition itself may breed standardization rather than diversity, as Dominick and Pearce (1976) have argued for prime-time television entertainment, and as Crouse (1973) and Dunwoody (1980) document for beat reporters. It may be that the news values of journalists overlap so much that "diversity" does not show up in content analysis categories. Finally, it may be that only a few news sources—the television networks, the wire services, and a few major newspapers—either supply the bulk of news or set the agenda for news production (Breed, 1959; Gold & Simmons, 1965; Hirsch, 1977; McCombs & Shaw, 1977; Whitney & Becker, 1982).

A number of noneconomic institutional factors are also related to journalistic performance. Two important categories are community or market structural differences and industry sector differences. Tichenor and his colleagues (Donohue, Olien, & Tichenor, 1985; Olien, Dono-hue, & Tichenor, 1968; Tichenor, Donohue, & Olien, 1980) have identified several predictors of the amount of coverage devoted to social conflict by smaller dailies. Such reporting is positively associated with community size, community pluralism, location of the newspaper publisher *outside* the community power structure, and absentee ownership. (In larger cities, newspapers whose publishers are *inside* the power structure report more conflict.) In regard to industry sector differences, how do newspapers, magazines, radio, and television differ in news content and process? In terms of content, the visual nature and more limited capacity of television as compared to the newspaper "news hole" may explain why Robinson (1976) found that television news is more devoted to conflict and negativity than newspaper news. Patterson (1980), however, was struck by the similarity across the two media (and news magazines as well) in how presidential campaign news is presented. In terms of process, Tuchman (1969) demonstrates that local television and local newspaper news production, while sharing a logic of "objectivity," differ markedly in news handling. Compared to newspaper reporters, television reporters have less autonomy in the selection of stories, but there is a greater likelihood that television reporters' stories will appear as the reporters have prepared them (see also Bantz, McCorkle, & Baade, 1980; Weaver & Wilhoit, 1986). Several surveys of American journalists (Becker, 1982; Johnstone, Slawski, & Bowman, 1976; Weaver & Wilhoit, 1986) reveal both structural and attitudinal differences between newspaper and broadcast journalists. Newspaper journalists are more likely to engage in beat reporting and to value interpretive and adversarial news; broadcast journalists are more mobile and experience greater job satisfaction.

Turow (1985) argues that an understanding of what becomes news requires an appreciation of the differences between "mainstream" and "peripheral" media and of the role served by "linking pin" organizations. The mainstream media's constant need for information and ideas that are new and "progressive" can lead them to adapt material from peripheral media that stands in "remedial opposition" to established interests. However, the linking pin activities of wire services, public relations firms, syndicators, and integrated media conglomerates "are counter-elements in the structure of mass communication that act as an ironic brake on the breadth, depth and diversity" of news (Turow, 1985,

p. 150). For Turow, then, news reflects a tension between journalism's historical definition of news and the counterelements in the structure of the industry.

In related research, Strodthoff, Hawkins, and Schoenfeld (1985) have shown via content analysis of general- and special-interest media coverage of one social movement—environmentalism in the 1960s and 1970s—that the "diffusion of ideology" is complex but patterned. News coverage of the issue begins in special-interest media and is early marked by "disambiguation," or establishment of the doctrinal tenets of various positions on the issue. This is followed by a period of "legitimation" in which gatekeepers come to recognize that information about the issue is valid news; and then a period of "routinization," in which regular allocations of time, budget, and space are devoted to news about the issue (see also Tichenor et al., 1980).

In sum, a considerable body of research supports the argument that interorganizational and institutional level forces, realized in a journalistic culture of "objectivity," fostered by, and in the service of, progressive liberal capitalism, constrain what journalists report. News thus exhibits an identifiable and widely shared form and a content broadly consonant with the social structures and values of its political-economic context. To understand these uniformities—but also the differences—we must move to the organizational level of analysis where the culture of journalism is enacted and news is made.

Organizational Level: Making News

News media, like entertainment firms, have devised organizational structures and processes to cope with uncertainties. Focusing on the organizational level highlights (1) the bureaucratic nature of news production, (2) the routines and conventions by which work is accomplished, and (3) the management of organizational conflict.

News is the product of bureaucratically structured organizations. The work of gathering, assembling, and selecting news is left primarily to workers who are relatively low in the hierarchy but who, in Western industrialized countries, are considered professionals and given substantial autonomy. Several observers have noted that remarkably little task-related discussion accompanies newswork (Schlesinger, 1978; Tuchman, 1972). Exceptions occur when news is truly nonroutine (Bailey & Lichty, 1972; Robinson, 1970) or is "close to home" (Bowers, 1967) and when the news has direct relevance to the organization's revenues (Donohew, 1967). In such situations, decision making may shift upward in the hierarchy. In larger newspapers there tends to be less "publisher power" in directing news decisions (Bowers, 1967; Olien et al., 1968).

The limited character of intraorganizational communication under normal conditions is evidence of the importance of routines in news organizations. But, as many researchers have pointed out (Dimmick, 1974; Gans, 1979; Tuchman, 1973, 1978), newsworkers see their environment as highly uncertain in several respects. Far more "news" is available at a given time than most organizations can reproduce as "their" news. Moreover, uncertainty underlies the generation of news: The organization must make a priori decisions about where news is likely to occur. When news breaks out in unexpected places (e.g., accidents, disasters, conflict) decisions about reallocating staff resources become necessary. Organizations deal with such uncertainties by routinization: typifications, reliance on routine sources, allocation of personnel to places where news is most likely, and adherence to organizational policy. We examine each of these in turn.

Tuchman (1973, 1978) has suggested that newsworkers employ "typifications" of potential news stories (e.g., spot news versus continuing news, hard news versus soft news) in an effort to routinize the unexpected features of events as news. These newsroom terms are applied to stories to define appropriate modes of coverage and scheduling. These terms, for example, help identify stories that demand the "rituals of objectivity"—covering "both sides," adducing supportive evidence, judiciously using quotation marks. In other words, the organization knows how to define unknown news in terms of known forms and modes of production.

Reliance on routine news sources shapes news in several ways. Almost all news media depend for the bulk of their news content on other news suppliers, selecting from among the offerings of wire services and syndicators (Breed, 1955a; Turow, 1985). This dependence leads to content standardization. But even for their own news product, media depend on other organizations as sources. According to Sigal (1973), such "pseudoevents" as press conferences and news releases account for about two-thirds of Washington Post and New York Times coverage of national and international news. Moreover, in developing their own news, organizations deploy their reporters on news beats. Tuchman (1978) likens a beat to a "news net" designed to "catch" information offered by some individuals and organizations—especially those in government—but to let other information slip through (see also Gans, 1979). Sigal (1973) found that almost four-fifths of New York Times and Washington Post news emanates from official sources. Not only do official and institutional sources predominate, but they are given favorable treatment, because journalists either consider them legitimate spokespersons (Paletz & Dunn, 1969; Paletz, Reichert, & McIntyre, 1971) or are accustomed to and accept administrative procedures routinely employed by official sources. Fishman (1980, 1982) suggests that government and police reporters become so tied to "bureaucratic phase structures" that public activities only become news "events" at times when formal action is taken. A crime only becomes a story, for example, at the time of initial police reports and at the times of arrest, arraignment, trial, and sentencing—and at no other.

Organizational policy provides an uncertain guide to understanding a news organization's behavior. As most studies following Breed's (1955b) lead have suggested, policy tends to be unwritten and informal, accessible to news workers only through organizational socialization—except for formal written policies concerning nonroutine occurrences that news organizations tend to adopt *after* experiencing major news events, such as serious accidents and natural disasters (Kueneman & Wright, 1975). However, as Siegelman (1973) has noted, socialization may be an informal process in which reporters and editors internalize "rules" inferred from the treatment of stories but policy is still sufficiently transparent that journalists are aware of it before they go to work in a news organization. Further, there are instances of newsroom policy that do make a substantial difference in content selection and play of news. Lester (1980), for example, notes that for policy reasons one newspaper does not employ the typifications identified by Tuchman (1973).

Despite typifications, routines, and socialization, organizational conflict still occurs (see Roloff, Chapter 16). Within news organizations, several kinds of conflict are apparent: conflict between business and professional norms, between partisan and ideological factions, and between neutral and participant news values. These disputes usually involve hierarchical role conflict, where management is more conservative (i.e., more oriented toward business and entertainment, conservative and neutral values) than are the journalists responsible for most newswork (Bantz, 1985). While management clearly has an upper hand in such disputes, newsworkers are not without informal power. Their major weapon is journalism's canons of professionalism, most especially objectivity. Objectivity becomes, in Tuchman's (1972) felicitous phrase, a "strategic ritual" by which a journalist questioned about a particular news story may defend it by demonstrating that the account is factually veridical, that it confines statements of opinion to legitimate news sources, or that it contains no "unjustified" adjectives and adverbs. Journalists may also attempt to negotiate questioned news reports by referring to their individual expertise, talent, or ability (Breed, 1955a; Roshco, 1975; Stark, 1962).

Another sort of conflict in news organizations is for "turf." Tuchman (1978) documents internal disputes between news desks, as between the city desk and the state government desk when a "state" story occurs within the city. She suggests that these issues are disputed with shared news values as the coin of the realm: Each desk attempts to claim high-value stories as its own while attempting to palm off low-value ones. Sigal (1973) documents an equal accommodation of international, national, and local news desks on the *New York Times* and *Washington Post,* whereby editorial management apportions almost identical space on the front news page to each desk over time. In other words, newsworthiness of international, national, and local news are defined by policy as equivalent, reducing endemic conflict.

In sum, news organizations' attempts to routinize the production of news provide the news with much of its character and content. Even so, there is still some validity to the notion that news is what journalists make it (Gieber, 1964). It is thus to the individual level of analysis that we turn.

Individual Level: News as Work

While more than one individual may be required to move a news story from inception to publication (particularly in television), the reporting and writing of news accounts usually falls to a single person or at most a few collaborators. The issue at this level of analysis is whether, or to what extent, individuals' attitudes, values, cognitions, demographic characteristics, and the like influence what they report and write. This has been studied in four somewhat overlapping streams of research: (1) perceptions of audiences and sources, (2) news values and news cognitions, (3) personal characteristics and ideological biases, and (4) objectivity as a personal value.

Do journalists "know their audience," and to what extent do images of that audience shape what they write or how they edit? From depth interviews of journalists and experiments with journalism students, Pool and Shulman (1959) argued that journalists' "fantasies" about their audiences did influence newswriting and, further, that when student journalists held views discrepant from those of the perceived audience, they tended to write less accurate or favorable stories. This study has been criticized on conceptual and methodological grounds (Darnton, 1975; Whitney, 1982, pp. 248-249), primarily because it ignores organizational and institutional reality. Routine organizational practice (editing) does tend to smooth out any deviation from "objective" copy, a point that Pool and Shulman (1959) acknowledge:

> The author's private fantasies are clearly not the only things that affect the character of what he writes. An experienced professional newsman will have acquired great facility in turning out a standard product for each of the many kinds of routine story of which so much of the news consists. (p. 150)

In other words, news is first and foremost an organizational product born of routines.

More recent investigators have expressed surprise at how little news-workers seem to know about their audiences (Burgoon, Burgoon, & Atkin, 1982; Gans, 1979; Schlesinger, 1978). Gans's (1979) observational study of national newsmagazine and network television journalists is illustrative:

> I . . . paid close attention to how the journalists conceived of and related to their audience. I was surprised to find, however, that they had little knowledge about their actual audience and rejected feedback from it. Although they had a vague image of the audience, they paid little attention to it; instead, they filmed and wrote for their superiors and for themselves, assuming . . . that what interested them would interest the audience. (p. 230)

Audience images seem to have minor influence on journalistic performance relative to other potential influence sources. Flegel and Chaffee (1971) found that among eight sources of perceived influence journalists ranked readers' opinions seventh. An unexamined premise in the research on journalists' perception of the audience is that professional mass communicators should have one; that it should be accurate; and that if it were, content would somehow change. There is little to support this premise, however, and the most compelling writing on the topic is still among the oldest. News, George Herbert Mead (1964) once wrote, could serve an "aesthetic function" if it could "interpret to the reader his experiences as the shared experiences of the community of which he feels he himself to be a part" (p. 302). Presumably this would indeed demand a keener sense of the reader and the community than journalists typically have.

Another stream of research on journalists concerns news values and news cognitions. Journalism textbooks characteristically begin by attempting to define news usually by reference to characteristics, elements, or values of news. The list of such values usually includes timeliness, consequence or significance, proximity, known principals, conflict, and human interest. Journalists are said to invoke such values in deciding whether stories are to be covered or selected for use. A number of studies (e.g., Buckalew, 1969; Dimmick, 1974) have examined this but generally they explain little selection variance among journalists, less than can be accounted for by organizational- or institutional-level variables.

The agenda-setting concept has been applied to journalists, to suggest that they are influenced by issue priorities in the media upon which they themselves rely. Fresh looks at the classic "Mr. Gates" study (White, 1950) by McCombs and Shaw (1977) and Hirsch (1977) for example, dispute White's original conclusion that the gatekeeper's personal bias in news selection was a principal news determinant. Both studies argued instead that wire services' priorities, as reflected by proportions of content in standard news categories, were an important news determinant. This result was confirmed experimentally by Whitney and Becker (1982). Fishman (1978, 1980) has shown that reporting on crimes against the elderly was generated more by other reporting on the topic than by any change in the rate of crime against older persons. Similarly Protess, Leff, Brooks, & Gordon (1985), in a study of one Chicago newspaper's extensive coverage of rape, found virtually no agenda-setting effect on the public, on the newspaper's audience, or on policymakers. Following the series on rape, however, the newspaper featuring the series gave more prominent attention to rape while neither the incidence of rape in the city nor coverage of the crime in other city newspapers changed.

Still another stream of research concerns the personal attributes of journalists. In the original gate keeper study, White (1950) concluded,

> Through studying his overt reasons for rejecting news stories from the press associations, we see how highly subjective, how based on the "gate-keeper's" own set of experiences, attitudes and expectations the communication of "news" really is. (p. 390)

Subsequent interpretations of the data from this study as we noted have undercut this conclusion but the notion that what becomes news is dependent upon the attitudes of individual journalists continues to have force in the literature. Lichter and Rothman (1981) describe individuals within U.S. "elite" news media organizations as more liberal politically and socially than a comparison sample of executives of major businesses. They also described them as of disproportionately high social and economic status, white, and not religiously observant. Most of these trends are also evident in more representative surveys of U.S. journalists (Associated Press Managing Editors, 1985; Lewis, 1985; Weaver & Wilhoit, 1986) but to a lesser degree, particularly in regard to political and social liberalism. Critics of the Lichter and Rothman study (Clancey & Robinson, 1985; Gans, 1985; Robinson, 1983, 1985; Schneider & Lewis, 1985), have noted the absence of any evidence that a liberal bias enters news presentations. Content analyses of the 1980 and 1984 presidential elections (Robinson, 1983, 1985) indicate biases in treatment against the incumbent and against minority parties in coverage, but no left/right or majority partisan bias at all in primary and election coverage. Clarke and Evans's (1983) analysis of congressional campaigns found a pronounced bias in favor of the incumbent but no partisan bias. There was much less tendency to endorse Republicans for Congress than is the case in presidential elections; local newspapers mostly endorse their local incumbent representatives in Washington. Mainstream news media bias is not so much toward one party as toward powerful individuals and institutions in general.

The final stream of research we consider here concerns journalistic objectivity as a personal value set. Clearly the set of values motivating journalistic performance is broader than the news values previously discussed. In an argument that crosses all three levels of analysis, Nord (1984) traces the development of a modern journalistic ethic emphasizing public service and public responsibility, community, consensus, and social order among major Chicago newspapers in the late 19th century—before such values emerged as important concepts in the Progressive Movement and despite the fact that, while sharing these values, the Chicago papers could hardly have differed more sharply in their news and editorial treatment of the great labor disputes of the day. Moreover, in discussions concerning the professional status of journalists (Singletary, 1982) a critical issue has been the proper role of the news media in society and of the journalist in gathering news. Researchers typically contrast conflicting values: participant versus neutral (Johnstone, Slawski, & Bowman, 1973), or gatekeeper versus advocate (Janowitz, 1975). However, in their survey of American journalists, Johnstone and colleagues (1976) found *both* the neutral and participant orientations were embraced by majorities of newsworkers; there were relatively few pure neutral or participant cases. Participant values were associated with working for elite media, being younger, and socializing with other journalists. A replication by Weaver and Wilhoit (1986) found less adherence to participant values and suggested that three roles (adversarial, interpretive, and disseminator) better characterize journalistic ideologies.

How do these values relate to actual practice? Ettema and Glasser (1985) argue that the more participant-oriented investigative journalists may employ an epistemology quite different from that of neutralists. Because truth claims by sources used in investigative reporting, unlike those by the representatives of established institutions used in daily reporting, are often problematic, the investigative reporter may be at great pains to justify the claims made in a story. Investigative reporters may, then, devise elaborate procedures—the "test of moral certainty" for example—to render the story credible to readers, to superiors, and to themselves. Levy (1981) suggests that there is an important interaction between journalists' personal views as to the worth of a news story, of competition for that story, and of competing journalists' assessment of their story. Where journalists see a story as important and also expect competition, Levy argues, they produce an "objective" story. Where they see competitive pressure as high *and* believe the story somehow *tainted,* the result, particularly if they believe other journalists share these assessments, is the "disdained" story, which is presented in such a

way as to distance reporters from what they are reporting. Truth operates for journalists at two levels: They can report the "objective" truth
about an event (for example, accurately reproduce what was said at a
news conference) while distancing themselves from the truth of what
was said (see also Hallin & Mancini, 1984). Journalists deal as best they
can with the fact that accurate and objective stories are not necessarily
true.

Truth and Constraint

What, then, can be said of the prospects for knowing and telling the
truth through journalism? If we are willing to stipulate that there is such
a thing as truth to be known and told—a key stipulation, we admit—then
we can formulate the issue of truth in journalism much as we formulated
the issue for creativity in popular entertainment and much as journalists
themselves sometimes formulate it (*Harper's*, 1985): as a tension between
the search for truth and the organizational and institutional constraints
upon that process.

According to the ethic of professional journalism, an ethic that blurs
truth and objectivity, constraints on the search for truth are *imposed on*
journalistic practice either by the power of other institutions (particularly government) or by the human limitations of individual journalists.
Normative journalistic ethics codes thus celebrate freedom of the press
and yet urge restraint on the part of the reporter. This formulation of the
threat to truth in journalism is reflected, for example, in White's (1950)
emphasis on the failure of Mr. Gates to be very vigilant against personal
bias.

More recent scholarship, however, has drastically reformulated the
issue as one of constraints imposed *by* journalistic practice rather than
on it. In this reformulation, the threats to truth are raised by organizational process and institutional arrangement, shifting research attention
to higher levels of analysis. Cognitions of individual journalists are still
of interest but they are now seen to reflect the "phase structures" of the
bureaucracies to be covered. Similarly, the value of objectivity itself is
seen as an organizational routine or ritual that serves the corporate drive
to make news an efficiently produced commodity. In this formulation,
then, it is not the attempt of individuals to make sense of their world that
threatens truth but rather the constraints upon that attempt imposed by
the social organization of journalism. Carey (1969) expresses this concern compellingly, though perhaps with a bit too much nostalgia for
19th-century journalism:

> With the rise of "objective reporting" in the latter part of the 19th cen-
> tury, the journalist went through a process that can be fairly termed a
> "conversion downwards," a process whereby a role is de-intellectualized
> and technicalized. . . . In this role he does not principally utilize an

> intellectual skill as critic, interpreter and contemporary historian but a technical skill at writing, a capacity to translate the specialized language and purposes of government, science, art, medicine and finance into an idiom that can be understood by a broader, more amorphous, less educated audience. (p. 32)

The finding that many journalists do express participant, adversarial, or interpretive values as part of their personal value systems suggests, however, that at the individual level there is at least the desire to utilize intellectual as well as technical skill and to find release from the constraints of objectivity. The prospects for truth in journalism, much like the prospects for creativity in popular entertainment, it seems, turn on the willingness and skill of individuals to work within, around, and through the organizational and institutional constraints to achieve their goals. The difference is that for popular entertainment we emphasize "through" while for journalism we may wish to emphasize "around" such constraints.

Lest our celebration of the individual journalist as truth teller get out of hand, we must acknowledge that, of course, journalists live and work within an encompassing social and cultural context that powerfully and implicitly informs their attempts to make sense of the world. Journalists have no alternative but to draw upon the intellectual tools—theory and concept, myth and metaphor—of their place and time in the world. Very much as memoirists drew upon the cultural resource of irony to interpret the great wars of their times, so, for example, journalists draw upon widely shared understandings of nuclear weapons and strategy to report on the great war that may yet come. William Dorman's (1985) critique of press performance in the nuclear age begins with the problem of establishing independence of journalistic vision and voice:

> Since Hiroshima, journalism, like most other aspects of society, has been held in nuclear thrall. The prospects of absolute warfare against the homeland (and species) created the national-security state, and journalism has proved no more independent of it than national government, education, the church or business. (p. 119)

Dorman concludes by asking the peace community to help reinvent journalism; but while some other journalism might be more critical of American nuclear policy, it is not at all clear that any other journalism could be independent of theory or interest. The knowledge-creating machinery of professional journalism reviewed here has a particular social location with particular political ramifications. But is it not so that *any* process of knowledge creation must have *some* location with political ramifications of its own? And if this is so, then should not media access and diversity be our goals? But do such goals imply that truth, after all, is not really a useful concept? We find ourselves back to the ancient questions that we attempted to set aside to study the sociology of journalism. Much as the research on the production of culture cannot ultimately resolve questions of the role and meaning of culture materials in human life, so the research on newsmaking cannot finally resolve questions of knowledge and truth. The social science of professional mass communicators, their organizations, and institutions can, however, help define the terms and enrich the vocabulary used in the ongoing discussion of these enduring questions.

REFERENCES

Amabile, T. M. (1983). *The social psychology of creativity.* New York: Springer-Verlag.
Associated Press Managing Editors. (1985). *Journalists and readers: Bridging the credibility gap.* San Francisco: APME Credibility Committee.
Bacharach, S. B., & Lawler, E. J. (1980). *Power and politics in organizations.* San Francisco: Jossey-Bass.
Bagdikian, B. H. (1985). The U.S. media: Supermarket or assembly line? *Journal of Communication, 35,* 97-109.
Bailey, G., & Lichty, L. W. (1972). Rough justice on a Saigon street. *Journalism Quarterly, 42,* 221-238.
Bantz, C. R. (1985). News organizations: Conflict as cultural norm. *Communication, 8,* 225-244.
Bantz, C. R., McCorkle, S., & Baade, R. C. (1980). The news factory. *Communication Research, 7,* 45-68.
Barnouw, E. (1978). *The sponsor: Notes on a modern potentate.* New York: Oxford University Press.
Becker, L. B. (1982). Print or broadcast: How the medium influences the reporter. In J. S. Ettema & D. C. Whitney (Eds.), *Individuals in mass media organizations: Creativity and constraint.* Newbury Park, CA: Sage.
Becker, H. S. (1982). *Art worlds.* Berkeley: University of California Press.
Bennett, W. L. (1983). *News: The politics of illusion.* New York: Longman.
Bennett, W. L., Gressett, L. A., & Haltom, W. (1985). Repairing the news: A case study of the news paradigm. *Journal of Communication, 35,* 50-68.
Bennis, W., & Nanus, B. (1985). *Leaders: The strategies for taking charge.* New York: Harper & Row.
Blau, J. R., & McKinley, W. (1979). Ideas, complexity and innovation. *Administrative Science Quarterly, 24,* 200-219.
Bowers, D. R. (1967). A report on activity by publishers in directing newsroom decisions. *Journalism Quarterly, 44,* 43-52.
Breed, W. (1955a). Newspaper 'opinion leaders' and the process of standardization. *Journalism Quarterly, 32,* 277-284.
Breed, W. (1955b). Social control in the newsroom: A functional analysis. *Social Forces, 33,* 326-335.
Brown, R. L. (1968). The creative process in the popular arts. *International Social Science Journal, 20,* 613-624.
Buckalew, J. K. (1969). A Q-analysis of TV news editors' decisions. *Journalism Quarterly, 46,* 135-137.
Burgoon, J. K., Burgoon, M. & Atkin, C. K. (1982). *The world of the working journalist.* New York: Newspaper Advertising Bureau.

Cantor, M. G. (1971). *The Hollywood television producer.* New York: Basic Books.
Cantor, M. G. (1979). The politics of popular drama. *Communication Research, 6,* 387-406.
Cantor, M. G. (1980). *Prime-time television: Content and control.* Newbury Park, CA: Sage.
Carey, J. W. (1969). The communications revolution and the professional communicator. In *The sociology of mass media communicators* (Sociological Review Monograph No. 13, pp. 23-38).
Cawelti, J. (1969). The concept of formula in the study of popular literature. *Journal of Popular Culture, 3,* 381-403.
Cawelti, J. (1976). *Adventure, mystery, and romance.* Chicago: University of Chicago Press.
Clancey, M., & Robinson, M. J. (1985, December/January). The media in Campaign '84: General election coverage. *Public Opinion,* pp. 49-54, 59.
Clarke, P., & Evans, S. H. (1983). *Covering campaigns.* Stanford: Stanford University Press.
Compaine, B. (1985). The expanding base of media competition. *Journal of Communication, 35,* 81-96.
Compaine, B. (Ed.). (1982). *Who owns the media?* White Plains, NY: Knowledge Industry Publications.
Coser, L. A., Kadushin, C., & Powell, W. (1981). *Books: The culture and commerce of publishing.* New York: Basic Books.
Crouse, T. (1973). *The boys on the bus.* New York: Random House.
Darnton, R. (1975). Writing news and telling stories. *Daedalus, 104,* 175-194.
DiMaggio, P. (1977). Market structure, the creative process and popular culture: Toward an organizational reinterpretation of mass culture theory. *Journal of Popular Culture, 11,* 436-452.
DiMaggio, P., & Hirsch, P. (1976). Production organization in the arts. *American Behavioral Scientist, 19,* 735-749.
Dimmick, J. (1974, November). The gate-keeper: an uncertainty theory. *Journalism Monographs 37.*
Dimmick, J., & Coit, P. (1982). Levels of analysis in mass media decision making. *Communication Research, 9,* 3-32.
Dominick, J. (1977). Geographic bias in network TV news. *Journal of Communication, 27,* 94-99.
Dominick, J., & Pearce, M. C. (1976). Trends in network prime time programming, 1953-1974. *Journal of Communication, 26,* 70-80.
Donohew, L. (1967). Newspaper gatekeepers and forces in the news channel. *Public Opinion Quarterly, 31,* 61-68.
Donohue, G. A., Olien, C. N., & Tichenor, P. J. (1985). Reporting conflict by pluralism, newspaper type and ownership. *Journalism Quarterly, 62,* 489-499.
Dorman, W. A. (1985, August). The media: Playing the government's game. *Bulletin of the Atomic Scientists,* pp. 118-124.
Downs, W. G. & Mohr, B. L. (1976). Conceptual issues in the study of innovations. *Administrative Science Quarterly, 21,* 700-714.
Dreier, P. (1982). The position of the press in the U.S. power structure. *Social Problems, 29,* 298-310.
DuBick, M. A. (1978). The organizational structure of newspapers in relation to their metropolitan environments. *Administrative Science Quarterly, 23,* 418-433.
Dunwoody, S. L. (1980). The science writing inner club. *Science, technology and human values, 5,* 14-22.
Emery, F. C., & Trist, E. L. (1965). The causal texture of organizational environment. *Human Relations, 18,* 21-31.

Epstein, E. J. (1974). *News from nowhere.* New York: Vintage.

Epstein, E. J. (1975). *Between fact and fiction.* New York: Vintage.

Entman, R. M. (1985). Newspaper competition and First Amendment ideals: Does monopoly matter? *Journal of Communication 35,* 147-165.

Espinosa, P. (1982). The audience in the text: Ethnographic observations of a Hollywood story conference. *Media, Culture and Society, 4,* 77-86.

Ettema, J. S. (1980). The role of educators and researchers in the production of educational television. *Journal of Broadcasting, 24,* 487-498.

Ettema, J. S. (1982). The organizational context of creativity: A case study from public television. In J. S. Ettema & D. C. Whitney (Eds.), *Individuals in mass media organizations: Creativity and constraint.* Newbury Park, CA: Sage.

Ettema, J. S., & Glasser, T. L. (1985). On the epistemology of investigative journalism. *Communication, 8,* 183-206.

Ettema, J. S., & Whitney, D. C. (1982). Introduction: Mass communicators in context. In J. S. Ettema & D. C. Whitney (Eds.), *Individuals in mass media organizations: Creativity and constraint.* Newbury Park, CA: Sage.

Faulkner, R. R. (1971). *Hollywood studio musicians.* Chicago: Aldine.

Faulkner, R. R. (1982). Improvising on a triad. In J. Van Maanen, J. M. Dabbs, Jr., & R. R. Faulkner, *Varieties of qualitative research.* Newbury Park, CA: Sage.

Fishman, M. (1978). Crime waves as ideology. *Social Problems, 25,* 531-543.

Fishman, M. (1980). *Manufacturing the news.* Austin: University of Texas Press.

Fishman, M. (1982). News and nonevents: making the visible invisible. In J. S. Ettema & D. C. Whitney (Eds.), *Individuals in mass media organizations: Creativity and constraint.* Newbury Park, CA: Sage.

Flegel, R. C., & Chaffee, S.H. (1971). Influences of editors, readers and personal opinions on reporters. *Journalism Quarterly, 48,* 645-51.

Fussell, P. (1975). *The great war and modern memory.* New York: Oxford University Press.

Gans, H. J. (1957). The creator-audience relationship in the mass media: An analysis of movie making. In B. Rosenberg & D. M. White (Eds.), *Mass culture: The popular arts in America.* New York: Free Press.

Gans, H. J. (1979). *Deciding what's news.* New York: Pantheon.

Gans, H. J. (1985, November/December). Are U.S. journalists dangerously liberal? *Columbia Journalism Review,* pp. 29-33.

Gieber, W. (1964). News is what newspapermen make it. In L. A. Dexter & D. M. White (Eds.), *People, society and mass communications.* New York: Free Press.

Gitlin, T. (1979). Prime-time ideology: The hegemonic process in television entertainment. *Social Problems, 26,* 251-266.

Gitlin, T. (1980). *The whole world is watching.* Berkeley: University of California Press.

Gitlin, T. (1983). *Inside prime time.* New York: Pantheon.

Gold, D., & Simmons, J. L. (1965). News selection patterns among Iowa dailies. *Public Opinion Quarterly, 29,* 425-430.

Goldman, R. (1982). Hegemony and managed critique in prime-time television. *Theory and Society, 11,* 363-388.

Griff, M. (1960). The commercial artist. In M. R. Stein, A. J. Vidich, & D. M. White (Eds.), *Identity and anxiety.* New York: Free Press.

Hackett, R. A. (1984). Decline of a paradigm? Bias and objectivity in news media studies. *Critical Studies in Mass Communication, 1,* 229-259.

Hall, S. (1977). Culture, the media and the "ideological" effect. In J. Curran, M. Gurevitch, & J. Woollacott (Eds.), *Mass communication and society.* London: Edward Arnold.

Hall, S. (1980). Encoding and decoding in the television discourse. In S. Hall et al. (Eds.), *Culture, media, language.* London: Hutchinson.

Hall, S. (1982). The rediscovery of "ideology": Return of the repressed in media studies. In M. Gurevitch, T. Bennett, J. Curran, & J. Woollacott (Eds.), *Culture, society and the media*. London: Methuen.

Hallin, D. C., & Mancini, P. (1984). Speaking of the president: Political structure and representational form in U.S. and Italian television news. *Theory and Society, 13,* 829-850.

Harper's (1985). Can the press tell the truth? (January): 37-51.

Hartley, J. (1982). *Understanding news*. London: Methuen.

Hickson, D. J., Hinings, C. R., Lee, C. A., & Schenck, R. E. (1971). A strategic contingencies theory of intra-organizational power. *Administrative Science Quarterly, 16,* 216-229.

Hirsch, P. M. (1972). Processing fads and fashions: An organization-set analysis of cultural industry systems. *American Journal of Sociology, 77,* 639-659.

Hirsch, P. M. (1975). Organizational effectiveness and the institutional environment. *Administrative Science Quarterly, 20,* 327-344.

Hirsch, P. M. (1977). Occupational, organizational and institutional models in mass media research: Toward an integrated framework. In P. M. Hirsch, P. V. Miller, & F. G. Kline (Eds.), *Strategies for communication research*. Newbury Park, CA: Sage.

Hutchins, R. M. (1947). *Commission on freedom of the press: Toward a free and responsible press*. Chicago: University of Chicago Press.

Intintoli, M. J. (1984). *Taking soaps seriously: The world of 'Guiding Light'*. New York: Praeger.

Janowitz, M. (1975). Professional models in journalism: The gatekeeper and the advocate. *Journalism Quarterly, 57,* 618-626, 662.

Jensen, J. (1984). An interpretive approach to culture production. In W. D. Rowland, Jr., & B. Watkins (Eds.), *Interpreting television: Current research perspectives*. Newbury Park, CA: Sage.

Johnstone, J.W.C., Slawski, E., & Bowman, W. (1973). The professional values of American newsmen. *Public Opinion Quarterly, 36,* 522-540.

Johnstone, J.W.C., Slawski, E., & Bowman, W. (1976). *The news people: A sociological portrait of American journalists and their work*. Urbana: University of Illinois Press.

Kaminsky, S. M. (1985). *American film genres*. Chicago: Nelson-Hall.

Kanter, R. M. (1983). The change masters: Innovations for productivity in the American corporation. New York: Simon & Schuster.

Kueneman, R. M., & Wright, J. E. (1975). News policies of broadcast stations for civil disturbances and disasters. *Journalism Quarterly, 52,* 670-677.

Lester, M. (1980). Generating newsworthiness: The interpretive construction of public events. *American Sociological Review, 45,* 984-994.

Levy, M. R. (1981). Disdaining the news. *Journal of Communication, 31,* 24-31.

Lewis, I. A. (1985). *The news media: Los Angeles Times Poll No. 94*. Los Angeles: Los Angeles Times.

Lichter, S. R., & Rothman, S. (1981, October/November). Media and business elites. *Public Opinion*, pp. 42-46, 59-60.

Lippman, W. (1922). *Public opinion*. New York: Macmillan.

Lowell, A. (1930). *Poetry and poets*. Boston: Houghton Mifflin.

March, J. G., & Simon, H. A. (1958). *Organizations*. New York: John Wiley.

McCombs, M. E., & Shaw, D. L. (1972). The agenda-setting function of the mass media. *Public Opinion Quarterly, 36,* 176-187.

McCombs, M. E., & Shaw, D. L. (1977). Structuring the "unseen environment." *Journal of communication, 27,* 18-22.

Mead, G. H. (1964). The nature of the aesthetic experience. In A. J. Peck (Ed.), *The selected writings of George Herbert Mead*. Indianapolis: Bobbs-Merrill.

Molotch, H., & Lester, M. (1974). News as purposive behavior: On the strategic use of routine events, accidents and scandals. *American Sociological Review, 39,* 101-112.

Montgomery, K. (1981). Gay activists and the networks, *Journal of Communication, 31,* 49-71.

Murdock, G. (1982). Large corporations and the control communications industries. In M. Gurevitch, T. Bennett, J. Curran, & J. Woollacott (Eds.), *Culture, society and the media.* London: Methuen.

Murdock, G., & Golding, P. (1977). Capitalism, communication and class relations. In J. Curran, M. Gurevitch, & J. Woollacott (Eds.), *Mass Communication and Society.* London: Edward Arnold.

Newcomb, H. M., & Alley, R. S. (1982). The producer as artist: Commercial television. In J. S. Ettema & D. C. Whitney (Eds.), *Individuals in mass media organizations: Creativity and constraint.* Newbury Park, CA: Sage.

Newcomb, H. M., & Alley, R. S. (1983). *The producer's medium.* New York: Oxford University Press.

Newcomb, H. M., & Hirsch, P. M. (1984). Television as a cultural forum: Implications for research. In W. R. Rowland, Jr., & B. Watkins (Eds.), *Interpreting television: Current research perspectives.* Newbury Park, CA: Sage.

Nichols, B. (1976). *Motives and methods.* Berkeley: University of California Press.

Nord, D. P. (1980). An economic perspective on formula in popular culture. *Journal of American Culture, 3,* 17-31.

Nord, D. P. (1984). The business values of American newspapers: The 19th century watershed in Chicago. *Journalism Quarterly, 61,* 265-273.

Olien, C. N., Donohue, G. A., & Tichenor, P. J. (1968). The community editor's power and the reporting of conflict. *Journalism Quarterly, 45,* 243-252.

Owen, B. M. (1975). *Economics and freedom of expression: Media structure and the First Amendment.* Cambridge, MA: Ballinger.

Owen, B. M., Beebe, J. H., & Manning, W. G., Jr. (1974). *Television economics.* Lexington, MA: Lexington Books.

Paletz, D., & Dunn, R. (1969). Press coverage of civil disorders: A case study of Winston-Salem, 1967. *Public Opinion Quarterly, 33,* 328-345.

Paletz, D., Reichert, P., & McIntyre, B. (1971). How the media support local government authority. *Public Opinion Quarterly, 35,* 80-92.

Park, R. E. (1940). News as a form of knowledge. *American Journal of Sociology, 45,* 669-686.

Patterson, T. (1980). *The mass media election.* New York: Praeger.

Pekurny, R. (1982). Coping with television production. In J. S. Ettema & D. C. Whitney (Eds.), *Individuals in mass media organizations: Creativity and constraint.* Newbury Park, CA: Sage.

Perkins, D. N. (1981). *The mind's best work.* Cambridge, MA: Harvard University Press.

Perrow, C. (1979). *Complex organizations: A critical essay* (2nd ed.). Glenview, IL: Scott Foresman.

Peters, S. K., & Cantor, M. G. (1982). Screen acting as work. In J. S. Ettema & D. C. Whitney (Eds.), *Individuals in mass media organizations: Creativity and constraint.* Newbury Park, CA: Sage.

Peterson, R. A. (1976). The production of culture: A prolegomenon. *American Behavioral Scientist, 19,* 7-22.

Peterson, R. A., & Berger, D. G. (1975). Cycles in symbol production: The case of popular music. *American Sociological Review, 40,* 158-173.

Pool, I., & Shulman, I. (1959). Newsmen's fantasies, audiences and newswriting. *Public Opinion Quarterly, 23,* 145-158.

Powell, W. W. (1982). From craft to corporation: The impact of outside ownership on book publishing. In J. S. Ettema & D. C. Whitney (Eds.), *Individuals in mass media organizations: Creativity and constraint.* Newbury Park, CA: Sage.

Protess, D. L., Leff, D. R., Brooks, S. C., & Gordon, M. T. (1985). Uncovering rape: The watchdog press and the limits of agenda setting. *Public Opinion Quarterly, 49,* 19-37.

Robinson, G. J. (1970). Foreign news selection is non-linear in Yugoslavia's Tanjug agency. *Journalism Quarterly, 47,* 340-351.

Robinson, M. J. (1976). Public affairs television and the growth of political malaise. *American Political Science Review, 70,* 409-432.

Robinson, M. J. (1983, February/March). Just how liberal is the news? 1980 revisited. *Public Opinion,* pp. 55-60.

Robinson, M. J. (1985, February/March). The media in Campaign '84, Part II: Wingless, toothless and hopeless. *Public Opinion,* pp. 43-48.

Roshco, B. (1975). *Newsmaking.* Chicago: University of Chicago Press.

Rosten, L. C. (1937). *The Washington correspondents* New York: Harcourt Brace Jovanovich.

Ryan, J., & Peterson, R. A. (1982). The product image: The fate of creativity in country music songwriting. In J. S. Ettema & D. C. Whitney (Eds.), *Individuals in mass media organizations: Creativity and constraint.* Newbury Park, CA: Sage.

Sanders, C. R. (1982). Structural and interactional features of popular culture production: An introduction to the production of culture perspective. *Journal of Popular Culture, 16,* 66-74.

Schatz, T. (1981). *Hollywood genres: Formulas, filmmaking and the studio system.* Philadelphia: Temple University Press.

Schiller, D. (1981). *Objectivity and the news.* Philadelphia: University of Pennsylvania Press.

Schlesinger, P. (1978). *Putting "reality" together: BBC news.* London: Constable.

Schneider, W., & Lewis, I. A. (1985, August/September). Views on the news. *Public Opinion,* pp. 6-11, 58-59.

Schudson, M. (1978). *Discovering the news.* New York: Basic Books.

Siegelman, L. (1973). Reporting the news: An organizational analysis. *American Journal of Sociology, 79,* 132-151.

Sigal, L. V. (1973). *Reporters and officials.* Lexington, MA: D.C. Heath.

Singletary, M. (1982). Commentary: Are journalists "professionals"? *Newspaper Research Journal, 3,* 75-78.

Stark, R. (1962). Policy and the pros: An organizational analysis of a metropolitan newspaper. *Berkeley Journal of Sociology, 7,* 11-31.

Stinchcombe, A. L. (1959). Bureaucratic and craft administration of production: A comparative study. *Administrative Science Quarterly, 4,* 168-187.

Strodthoff, G. G., Hawkins, R. P., & A. C. Schoenfeld (1985). Media roles in a social movement: A model of ideology diffusion. *Journal of Communication, 35,* 134-153.

Thompson, J. D. (1967). *Organizations in action.* New York: McGraw-Hill.

Tichenor, P. J., Donohue, G. A., & Olien, C. N. (1980). *Community conflict and the press.* Newbury Park, CA: Sage.

Tuchman, G. (1969). *News, the newsman's reality.* Ph.D. dissertation, Brandeis University.

Tuchman, G. (1972). Objectivity as strategic ritual. *American Journal of Sociology, 77,* 660-679.

Tuchman, G. (1973). Making news by doing work: Routinizing the unexpected. *American Journal of Sociology, 79,* 110-131.

Tuchman, G. (1974). Assembling a network talk-show. In G. Tuchman (Ed.), *The TV establishment: Programming for power and profit.* Englewood Cliffs, NJ: Prentice-Hall.

Tuchman, G. (1978). *Making news: A study in the construction of reality.* New York: Free Press.

Tuchman, G. (1983). Consciousness industries and the production of culture. *Journal of Communication, 33,* 330-341.

Turow, J. (1977). Client relationship and children's book publishing: A comparative study of mass media policy in two marketplaces. In P. M. Hirsch, P. V. Miller, & F. G. Kline (Eds.), *Strategies for communication research.* Newbury Park, CA: Sage.

Turow, J. (1978). Casting for television: The anatomy of social typing. *Journal of Communication, 28,* 18-24.

Turow, J. (1979). *Getting books to children.* Chicago: American Library Association.

Turow, J. (1982). Unconventional programs on commercial television: An organizational perspective. In J. S. Ettema & D. C. Whitney (Eds.), *Individuals in mass media organizations: Creativity and constraints.* Newbury Park, CA: Sage.

Turow, J. (1984a). *Media industries: The production of news and entertainment.* New York: Longman.

Turow, J. (1984b). Pressure groups and television entertainment: A Framework for analysis. In W. D. Rowland, Jr., & B. Watkins (Eds.), *Interpreting television: Current research perspectives.* Newbury Park, CA: Sage.

Turow, J. (1985). Cultural argumentation through the mass media: a framework for organizational research. *Communication, 8,* 139-164.

Weaver, D. H., & Wilhoit, G. C. (1986). *The American journalist: A portrait of U.S. news people and their work.* Bloomington: Indiana University Press.

White, D. M. (1950). The gatekeeper: A case study in the selection of news. *Journalism Quarterly, 27,* 383-396.

Whiteside, T. (1981). *The blockbuster complex.* Middletown, CT: Wesleyan University Press.

Whitney, D. C. (1982). Mass communicator studies: similarity, difference and level of analysis. In J. S. Ettema & D. C. Whitney (Eds.), *Individuals in mass media organizations: Creativity and constraint.* Newbury Park, CA: Sage.

Whitney, D. C., & Becker, L. B. (1982). "Keeping the gates" for gatekeepers: The effects of wire news. *Journalism Quarterly, 59,* 60-65.

Whitney, D. C., Fritzler, M., Jones, S., Mazzarella, S., & Rakow, L. (1985, August). *Geographic and source biases in network television news 1982-1984.* Paper presented at Association for Education in Journalism, Memphis.

25   Public Opinion Processes

VINCENT PRICE
University of Michigan

DONALD F. ROBERTS
Stanford University

FTER more than a half-century of scientific investigation, we find that "public opinion research, mass communication research, and public opinion theory have become disconnected" (Katz, 1983, p. 89). Although early conceptual formulations of public opinion heavily emphasized social organization, empirical public opinion research has not always reflected that early emphasis. Today readers might well expect, upon encountering a chapter on public opinion, to find detailed discussions of opinion polling, analyses of the public's support for the president, or examinations of one or another aspect of election campaigns. This is not so surprising. We often think of public opinion research as a matter of polling. To the industry pollster, public opinion is treated largely as the aggregation of individual-level traits (opinions) within a defined population (the public) at a particular point in time.

The direction we take in this chapter is quite different. Our discussion will instead focus on a theoretical approach to public opinion *as a social process*. Moreover, we regard it as a *communication* process. Whereas to the pollster the "public" in public opinion is a noun, we propose to treat it as an adjective.[1] Our plan is to consider public opinion as a complex of communication processes, involving inter-level relations over time, where people, groups, and organizations play differentiated roles. These opinion processes are *public* in the sense that they operate together, across levels, in shaping collective responses to social issues. Scientific understanding of public opinion will only come with a greater synthesis of communication theory and research at multiple levels of analysis. This chapter represents a step in that direction. We will focus mainly on conceptual issues, drawing together ideas from disparate bodies of literature. In depicting public opinion with such broad strokes, we may produce less detail than some might expect. Ours is not a comprehensive account of public opinion research. Rather, we hope that by taking a more global view of opinion phenomena, we will suggest fresh ideas for study.

AUTHORS' NOTE: The authors express their thanks to Steven Chaffee, David Ritchie, John Peters, Michael Slater, and Douglas Storey for extremely helpful comments and suggestions.

Our outline is threefold. First, we briefly discuss conceptual problems in defining public opinion, noting some contrasts between turn-of-the-century ("classical") formulations and subsequent public opinion research. Then we investigate in greater detail the nature of opinion processes at three levels of analysis: individual, group, and organization. Finally, we consider processes of public opinion formation and change in larger society, taking a new look at some old questions concerning the influence of mass media.

CONCEPTUALIZING PUBLIC OPINION

Opinions are the property of individuals but are also, in a less obvious but no less important way, the properties of social groups. Pre-empirical views of public opinion often framed it, not as a simple attribute of either people or publics, but as a dynamic process of social organization via discursive communication. Built upon an interactionist, social-psychological foundation laid by James (1890) and Baldwin (1893), the early theoretical model of public opinion (e.g., Cooley, 1909; Dewey, 1927) viewed the individual self, including attitudes and opinions, as a social entity formed through communication and social action. Public opinion was likewise thought to be a product of interactive influences, formed within "the larger mind," shaped by—but by no means reducible to—the many individual expressions that enter public discussion.

Such interactive influences were not to be the primary emphasis of subsequent empirical study, which focused instead on accurate scientific description of public opinion. To that end, early empirical researchers sought to exorcise the "daemon of the group mind" (Allport, 1937). The central proposition behind their work was that public opinion could be defined as "simply any collection of individual opinions designated" (Childs, 1939, p. 331). While empirical attention has since been directed toward a wide array of social (particularly interpersonal) influences on attitudes and beliefs, the frame of empirical analysis has been set squarely upon individual opinions. Higher-level "public" opinion has been for the most part equated with the product of a fairly straightforward aggregation of opinions.

Cognition versus communication. The fundamental conceptual problem in defining public opinion, as illustrated by these contrasting views, revolves around a differentiation of cognition and communication. "Groups don't have opinions," goes the old saw, "people do." If we equate opinions with cognition, this seems true enough, since human thought is only possible within individual minds. But *public* opinion is not a simple matter of cognition. It occurs within groups of communicating people, who together determine what the issue is, why it is a cause for public concern, and what can be done about it. While the process unquestionably involves private cognition, individuals' thoughts about a social issue are largely dependent for both form and content on public discussion. This is why communication is so often metaphorically equated with externalized cognition: Communication requires "thinking together." (It is just as common, we might point out, to equate cognition with internalized communication: People sometimes have "trouble hearing themselves think.") The main point here is that analytical focus on individual opinion will never result in theories of public opinion. We can study the way individual scientists work, for example, without learning much about how *science itself* works. So too we can study opinions without greatly advancing our understanding of how the larger process of public opinion works.

Viewing the Public as a Communicating Group

Pre-empirical approaches to public opinion sought, albeit through speculation, a general model of social opinion formation as it leads to collective action. Discursive public communication—analogous to a kind of mental organization—was seen as structuring collective opinion in response to an issue. This view was perhaps best expressed by Cooley (1909), who described public opinion as "no mere aggregate of separate individual opinions, but an organization, a cooperative product of communication and reciprocal influence."

> A group "makes up its mind" in very much the same manner that the individual makes up his. The latter must give time and attention to his question, search his consciousness for pertinent ideas and sentiments, and work them together into a whole, before he knows what his real thought about it is. In the case of a nation the same thing must take place, only on a larger scale. . . . Every one who has any fact, or thought, or feeling, which he thinks is unknown, and insufficiently regarded, tries to impart it; and thus not only one mind but all minds are searched for pertinent material, which is poured into the general stream of thought. (Cooley, 1909, p. 121)

This process of social organization through public communication was distinguished from spontaneous crowd behavior that was irrational and imitative. Much of the thinking behind nineteenth-century European crowd psychology focused not on the role of reasoned communication but on the power of contagion (Le Bon, 1960), a phenomenon whereby collective action spread through an almost physical impulse. Unlike the crowd, the public is marked by a cooperative organization and by discussion in response to an issue.

The mass and the public. Blumer (1946) later made much the same distinction in his differentiation of the mass and the public. The mass is an anonymous group, loosely organized and unable to act in concert; it is merely a composite of heterogeneous people who "participate in mass behavior, such as those who are excited by some national event, those who share in a land boom, [or] those who are interested in a murder trial" (1946, p. 186). People within the mass act according to their own needs, without regard for any collective concerns. It is under conditions of great excitement and physical unity that mass behavior becomes crowdlike. In contrast, the public is a "group of people (a) who are confronted by an issue, (b) who are divided in their ideas as to how to meet the issue, and (c) who engage in discussion over the issue" (1946, p. 188). The concepts of mass, crowd, and public—as ideal types—relate to collectives that are marked by unique forms of social organization. In rarefied form, the distinction is one of organization by *contiguity* (the mass), by *contagion* (the crowd), and by *conversation* (the public). Called upon to act in unison, the public lacks consensual response. It is thus characterized by conscious consideration of both individual desires and collective welfare, and by discussion aimed at some resolution of the issue.

Some Implications of the "Process" View

The concept of public opinion as a process of social organization through communication, while less than commonplace in our empirical research, is well worth considering (see Davison, 1958; Foote & Hart, 1953; Nimmo, 1978). It restores communication to a central role and suggests that the key to developing public opinion theory is to focus not on phenomena at any single level (e.g., individual opinions) but instead on reciprocal relationships between people and higher-level collectives. There are, in effect, interactions of individual and "public" opinion at each successive level; and what we normally describe as public opinion is an organization of these numerous personal, interpersonal, and institutional interactions. We should note several implications of this conception. First, a public is not organized in any fixed fashion until forced to communicate in resolving an issue. Second, public opinion is decidedly *not* the distribution of opinions within a public, but is instead a complex function of processes where disparate ideas are expressed, adjusted, and compromised en route to collective determination of a course of action.

The developing public. The issue and the discussion it evokes in the media and on the street together determine the shape of a public that will ultimately include lobbyists, interest groups, and relatively uninterested participants. In opinion research, however, the public is often equated with some defined population, compromising a finite number of people sharing certain demographic attributes. Perhaps in most practical applications there is nothing grossly defective in such a practice, but this is due more to fortunate accident than to conceptual rigor. Most of the groups so defined are in fact constituted of people faced by common issues. Yet their status as publics must be seen as quite independent of the demographic criteria used to demarcate them in research. Although the issue defines the public, common practice assumes that publics define their issues. Publics grow in size and change in composition as the issue moves through disputation. Once the issue is handled somehow, its public presumably shrinks back again due to attrition and reduced communication. Public opinion processes form around an issue over time. In contrast, polls and election studies imply that issue opinions exist within a public at any given time.

Interactive influences between levels. If public opinion is a complex function of interactive communication at multiple levels, then the "one-man-one-vote" model underlying many empirical procedures has little chance of representing it adequately (see Lemert, 1981, p. 2). Social compromise and adjustment, so central to the formation of public opinion, are completely leveled by this model, which not only implies equal sociopolitical status among opinions, but also assumes a sizable amount of individual independence from the normative influences of larger groups. The voting-style aggregation of opinions betrays a confusion across levels. Even the earliest empirical findings suggested that people's opinions, attitudes, and beliefs are dependent upon many interpersonal processes.

Normative Concerns in
Public Opinion Theory

The question of individual independence in opinion formation is a central problem in conceptualizing and researching public opinion. What are we measuring in our polls? Are opinions in fact thoughtful, personal responses to the issue, or are they in some way "determined" by higher-level processes? Given its genesis in democratic theory, the concept of public opinion seems naturally wedded to a one-man-one-vote model. Public opinion is considered vital to representative governments, performing a presumed linkage function, where the beliefs and proposals of private individuals are translated into policy choices made by government officials (Nimmo, 1978, p. 9). Political leaders are expected to respond to expressions of opinion that arise from popular origins. Publics (at least smaller, elite publics) doubtlessly exist in all political states. But the role of public opinion in democratic or republican states is presumed to be far greater: There is a tendency to "publicize" the opinion process, to invest partial or total authority in larger, communicating publics. The key question is whether public opinion processes in their natural operation are at all democratic in the sense implied by the model; in other words, whether "true" public opinion, or that which influences policy choices (Key, 1961), is in reality shaped by a bottom-up aggregation of independently rendered, individual opinions. Is public opinion subject to control by mass media coverage of political affairs? Are people capable of producing independent and thoughtful decisions about public affairs, or are they easily swayed by outside influences? Are state officials able to convince the public of its own desires? If officials do respond to public opinion, how do they gauge it? Normative interests are clearly at stake in resolving these questions—indeed, even in framing them for research.

The phantom public. Lippmann (1922, 1925) leveled an early and forceful attack on the populist model of public opinion. In his view, accurate knowledge of political events is unavailable to the ordinary citizen; the political world is "out of reach, out of sight, out of mind" (1922, p. 30). People form their ideas and opinions from indirect and incomplete accounts, resulting in shallow "stereotyped" images of the political world. Allowed no direct contact with political "reality," public opinion is inherently capricious, subject to whim and susceptible to demagoguery. The major thrust of Lippman's work was quite pragmatic: He argued that democratic theory had profoundly misplaced its trust in public decision making. Without some independent, expert organization to ensure that political "facts" are properly represented to people, democratic government would not work successfully. The press, considered a savior to many progressive democrats, in Lippmann's view merely intensified the inherent defects of public opinion, propagating simplistic political notions. Thus a major function of Lippmann's expert organization would be to guide the mass media in organizing public opinion.[2]

Administrative social science. There is little question that public opinion research, in its more administrative role (see Lazarsfeld, 1941), has sought as much to service democratic ideals as to drop a plumb line disinterestedly into public waters. Developments in attitude measurement (e.g., Thurstone, 1928) spawned not only volumes of empirical research aimed at detecting mass media effects on opinion change, but a burgeoning opinion-polling industry as well (see Delia, Chapter 2 in this volume). As a result public opinion research has become not only an academic pursuit but an institutional reality as well, offering the worrisome prospect of "government by empiricism." In point of fact, pollsters do far more than hover objectively outside the public opinion process, assembling statistical moments into composite measures of opinion. Publicized poll results may be powerfully intrusive as scientific measures, constituting mass-mediated expressions of opinion that can play a major role in the public communication process by influencing the bystander public as well as political actors. Candidates for office wield their own polls as readily as their own "positions on the issues." Public opinion research has become an institutional component of the very political process it seeks to understand.

INDIVIDUAL-LEVEL OPINION

Empirical communication and opinion research has generally aimed at explaining not so much how communication and social action unfold over time in response to social issues but how much influence particular (usually persuasive) mass media messages exert on individual "receivers'" opinions (Chaffee, 1977; McLeod & Reeves, 1980; Miller, 1980). The landmark scientific works in the growing field of mass communication research were just such studies of individual attitude and opinion change (e.g., Berelson, Lazarsfeld, & McPhee, 1954; Hovland, Lumsdaine, & Sheffield, 1949; Katz & Lazarsfeld, 1955; Lazarsfeld, Berelson, & Gaudet, 1948). Accordingly, our discussion of individual opinion processes begins with the relationship between attitudes and opinions. In keeping with the view of public opinion as a discursive process, however, we will suggest that individual opinions arise out of public communication, consisting mainly in a person's ongoing effort to organize both cognitive and behavioral responses to a public issue. Opinions are thus linked to their surrounding social environment, originating and developing within the context of public discussion.

Opinions and Attitudes

The growth of opinion research is inseparable from the history of attitude research, although attitude and opinion have often been conceptualized as distinct psychological and behavioral phenomena. They are thought to differ in two ways. First, opinions are generally considered to be verbal, or otherwise overt responses to a specific stimulus (an issue), while attitudes are more basic global tendencies to respond favorably or unfavorably to a general class of stimuli. While opinions are largely situational, attitudes are more enduring within a person across situations. Second, opinions are considered to be more cognitive and somewhat less affective in their makeup. As Wiebe (1953) suggests, an attitude is an immediate, intuitive orientation while an opinion is a thought-out, reasoned choice between alternatives for action in a social matrix.

Opinion as overt expression. The restriction of opinion to instances of overt behavior can easily be viewed as more a matter of methodological convenience than a clear conceptual distinction. But there are a number of reasons why such a restriction may be theoretically useful. The most compelling reason lies in the relationship of individual opinion to the larger public opinion process: Only expressed opinions will have much impact on the formation of opinion at higher levels. Covert or private opinions may indeed exist, but without political force if they are not expressed. The distinction, however, is still somewhat vague. What is a person's "private" opinion and what is a "public" opinion? The former may be usefully conceptualized as an abstract judgment, as the product of one person's thought on an issue. The latter presents a far stickier conceptual problem. Is an expressed opinion the property of an individual or of the interpreting party? If a husband says, "Let's go to the movies," and the wife gives no reply, she may have expressed an opinion against going. She may not have *intended* to express anything, and yet in the course of behaving socially people do provide others with indications of "opinions." Even simple expressions of opinion, it seems, are difficult to confine to the individual level of analysis. They may be individual behaviors; but to the extent that they are opinions, the interpretive context is public, or at least interpersonal.

Opinion as a cognitive product. What about the second distinction between attitudes and opinions, which frames opinions as more cognitive, more thoughtful. Opinions are often figured to be the end product of a reasoned thought process in which several relevant attitudes are brought to bear on a given social action or issue. In this context, opinion bears a remarkable resemblance to what Fishbein and Ajzen have termed "behavioral intention" (Fishbein, 1967; Fishbein & Ajzen, 1981). In their theory of reasoned action they posit that behavioral intention is a function of a defined set of context-relevant attitudes (beliefs and evaluations relevant to that particular behavior) and subjective norms (salient normative beliefs presumed held by significant others, and motivations to comply with them). Similarly, an opinion regarding an issue can be viewed as the combinatory judgment arrived at through the counterweighting of salient attitudes toward issues and perceptions of the opinions of significant others.

But there are at least two additional characteristics of opinions that are not expressed by the Fishbein and Ajzen model. First, an opinion is formed not simply out of consideration of personal attitudes and desires (which would presumably determine personal behavior) but also out of considerations of what is appropriate for a *public* undertaking. These latter elements of the "opinion equation" might simply be attitudes of a different kind, but they seem most consequential. People do in fact separate personal from public interests. Studies of voting on the basis of economic self-interest indicate that such political behavior is not very common (Meehl, 1977). Voters rely more upon their perceptions of the nation's economic well-being than of their own (Kinder & Kiewiet,

1979). Second, the behavioral intention model is purely intrapersonal and cognitive, taking place in somewhat of a social vacuum, where subjective norms stand in for those whose opinions are valued. In fact few of our judgments—at least few important ones—result from such isolated contemplation. We rarely know what we think about an issue until we talk it over with people. Others give us an idea of what range of opinions will be acceptable; they help us to rethink our own views. Discussion shapes not only evolving public opinion but private opinions as well.

A Developmental Model of Opinion

Opinions must be seen as developing over time. They are the ongoing product of discursive activity, whether that discussion is internal (i.e., intrapersonal) or external (i.e., social or public). Implicitly the character of this "debate," even if it is intrapersonal, is still social in the sense that other people and reference groups will undoubtedly play a role. Opinion processes from the perspective of the individual are fundamentally learning experiences. We learn from personal discussions, from our own thinking about the issue, and from information we encounter in the mass media. We learn what kind of issue is at stake and what people are saying about it, as well as what stance we might reasonably take in response to it.

A dialectic of cognition and behavior. Opinions are formed through a continuing dialectic between thought and behavior. In discussing an issue, people make increasingly thoughtful attempts to express their evolving views. Yet people also actively infer motives for their own behavior (Bem, 1970). So an expressed opinion may constitute a kind of test behavior. As Kelman (1974) suggested, action itself may be seen as a step in the attitude-change process, a step that reflects a move toward a new attitude that is as yet uncrystallized. Attitudes have a *range* of commitment and a *range* of actions that a person is willing to take. Someone may enact a behavior that is partially discrepant with internal attitudes as a vehicle for attitude change. Similarly, we can view expressions of opinion as one step in the developmental opinion process. In addition to searching within for relevant thoughts and feelings, one expresses them as part of an ongoing opinion-formation procedure.

Covert judgments and expressed opinions. We may speak separately of either (a) private or covert opinion, which is not a vague, purely sentimental state but a developing, organized judgment; or (b) expressed opinion, which is communicated verbally. The two are surely related as facets of the same individual opinion process, but they may be profitably distinguished. The relative degree of "publicness" of an expressed opinion is variable, depending upon the social context of the behavior. An opinion may be "mentioned" in casual conversation, "registered" with a supervisor on the job, or "cast" in the voting booth. Each expression plays a role in shaping opinion within a different public, exercising different forms of influence. Expressed opinions may simply sway a friend or they may influence an organization's position.

Opinions as epistemological tools. Perhaps the most interesting feature of expressed opinions is that they may not for any single person demonstrate much consistency across occasions. People who think their opinions are unpopular, for example, may be less willing to express them in conversation (Noelle-Neumann, 1974, 1977). But individuals may also simply be coming to terms with and rather unsure of a private judgment. Expressions of opinion are epistemological tools—efforts to define one's beliefs. A person might express a particular view simply to "try it on for size." Opinions may progress through relative states of infancy, adolescence, adulthood, or decline. The latter is socially determined. A "dead issue" is one that people are no longer talking about.

How "Well-Considered" are Most Opinions?

Following Lippmann's (1922, 1925) early attack on the idea of well-informed popular opinion, empirical researchers have amassed evidence that generally appears to support his argument. Converse (1964), for example, concluded that the American populace, with respect to any given issue, is composed only partly of people who hold genuine opinions reflecting developed systems of political beliefs. Well-formed opinions, Converse reasoned, should persist over time. Instead of expressing stable opinions on the same public policies between 1956 and 1960, though, most people flip-flopped on issues rather markedly, almost randomly. While Converse's argument that the majority of Americans are relatively "innocent" of developed political belief systems has been greeted by considerable debate (e.g., Nie, Verba, & Petrocik, 1976), it nonetheless concurs with empirical findings (Kinder & Sears, 1985). Generally people can express opinions when asked about an issue, regardless of whether they have thought about it at all and even when the issue is a pure fiction (Bishop, Oldendick, Tuchfarber, & Bennet, 1980). As Kinder and Sears (1985) suggest, political events are "for most of us, most of the time, peripheral curiosities." Along similar lines, the distinction is sometimes drawn between "valid" opinion and "pseudo-opinion." The former has some "informational" base and is generally equated with a judgment rendered by an individual who has thought about and publicly discussed the issue. In contrast, a pseudo-opinion is formed out of vague impressions and snap judgments made "off the top of the head" (Graber, 1982).

A developmental model of opinion largely circumvents the need to distinguish valid from false opinion since it assumes that for any given issue at a given time, sizable portions of the population are not active members of a communicating public. Because opinions are the products of ongoing public discussion, we have no reason to expect them to be equally developed across people. If we use Blumer's distinction between the mass as an unfocused, disconnected group and the public as an active, communicating group, we can classify most opinion measured by polls (what Graber has termed pseudo-opinion) as *mass,* not public, opinion. In other words, for many political issues, decidedly small communicating publics develop within a much larger population of mass observers who may be only minimally interested, if at all, in forming opinions. When issues do trigger large-scale public discussion, as for example in the case of racial integration or the Vietnam war, then we might reasonably expect more widely developed opinions.

The Nature of Thinking about Political Issues

Even in those cases where people think and talk about an issue and develop well-defined opinions, we should not necessarily expect them to be well informed by detailed knowledge of the issue. The communication of ideas certainly helps people sort through issues in an attempt to organize information logically. Although classically presented as a ratiocinative activity, however, the reciprocal communication that produces personal as well as public opinion is principally an *organizing* activity. Order is not necessarily rational.

Some recent research. Investigations into the varieties of "mental shorthand" that might be used in political cognition may help advance our understanding of individual opinion processes. Graber (1984), for example, has applied the notion of cognitive *schemas*—commonsense models about situations and people—to political information processing. From intensive interviews she finds that schemas about politics are hierarchically ordered, with memories of specific incidents bolstering more general political conclusions. Graber concludes from her work that political thinking is rarely organized into logically coherent patterns (Lane, 1962). Instead of drawing opinions from an overarching ideology or political model, people "morselize," thinking through separate issues and events in relative isolation from wider political affairs. Swanson (1981) has studied "personal constructs," conceptualized as fundamental cognitive dimensions (e.g., honest-dishonest, Republican-Democrat) along which people discriminate other actors, objects, and events. Cognitive complexity can be indexed by the number of dimensions used to judge stimuli within a given domain. The number of constructs used by people in political affairs, Swanson reports, is generally only about *half* the number used in interpersonal contexts.

A very small number of salient beliefs about an issue may determine people's opinions. For example, van der Plight, van der Linden, & Ester

(1982) asked people to select the three most important possible consequences of nuclear energy. Pro- and anti-nuclear-power groups showed clear differences: Supporters cited economic issues; opponents, safety issues. The correlation between selected consequences and a direct attitude measure was .83. Differences of opinion may actually reflect fundamental differences in beliefs about the issue itself. Is nuclear power an economic issue or a safety issue? Opposing sides in a public dispute may construe it in quite different ways.

Developmental questions. Social cognition research may be extended in other ways to help explain opinion processes. We would certainly expect changes in the structure and complexity of issue-related cognition, with increased discussion and exposure to issue information in the mass media. Fiske, Kinder, and Larter (1983) investigated differences in information processing that depend upon novice versus expert political knowledge. As with constructivists' research (O'Keefe, 1980; Swanson, 1981) this work indicates that more politically knowledgeable respondents are *less* likely to use simple heuristic strategies in responding to political issues. Close analyses of single issues over time might allow us to begin charting people's evolving knowledge of the issue. These cognitive changes could be investigated alongside various expressive behaviors (e.g., participation in discussion, flexibility in modifying stands) and patterns of issue-related media use (e.g., selective exposure, differential attention and comprehension). The degree to which a person has *decided* an opinion should be of great interest, given the voluminous body of research suggesting that the extremity or fixedness of an opinion has important perceptual and judgmental consequences (e.g., Eiser, 1973; Sherif & Hovland, 1961; Sherif, Sherif, & Nebergall, 1965). In the early stages of the opinion process, ideas and expressions may be largely exploratory. Once comfortable with an opinion, however, a person may become more interested in confirming and defending those ideas than in testing them.

Opinions should be investigated as *communicative* expressions. They may reflect a lengthy internal "dialogue," an impulsive response to a social situation, an adjustment to a perceived majority view, a desire to play devil's advocate, or simply random behavior. Whether these expressions are accepted as a valid opinion or pseudo-opinion often has less to do with the expression itself than with the interpreting party and the surrounding political context.

GROUP-LEVEL OPINION

Social cognition research can take us quite a bit further in understanding how reciprocal thought and behavior shape a person's beliefs and evolving opinion about a social issue. Current research in social cognition, however, generally "does not lend insight into how social knowledge is constructed and negotiated in actual communication" (Markus & Zajonc, 1985, p. 174). The public opinion process is social not merely because ideas and expressions of opinion are oriented toward some collective undertaking but also because it involves social compromise and adjustment through discussion. Group-level processes play an essential role in shaping public opinion. At the highest level, we have the public itself as a communicating group. Within this public we find subgroups: organizations, interest groups, social movements. At a lower level are primary groups of personal acquaintances. Let us now briefly explore some of the ways discussion organizes the public at each of these levels.

In What Sense Are Opinions Social?

Communication requires mutual cognitive "orientation toward a set of informational signs" (Schramm, 1971, p. 13) or what Boulding (1956) terms a "critical watershed" of shared images. These shared images become social conventions of meaning, objects of the "public domain." Social groups large and small develop their own cognitive systems over time—unique ways of representing information, of interpreting behavior, or of solving problems. Issues and opinions, in the context of group communication, are in this sense objects of the public domain. In the course of discussing a public issue, people create shared ways of understanding the problem and alternative solutions. Discussion provides a clearer impression of others' ideas—information to help form one's private views.

Lessons from group dynamics research. Empirical research has given us good reasons *not* to assume that group opinion processes are well described by any simple aggregation of individual opinions. Research on group decision making, for example, has produced a number of findings where group communication outcomes are clearly not the product of any averaging process. One prominent and early example was the "risky shift" finding (Ziller, 1957; later reinterpreted and expanded by Moscovici & Zavalloni, 1969), where discussion leads to more polarized or extreme group decisions than the distribution of initial individual opinions would have predicted. These early findings have been replicated in many subsequent group polarization studies (e.g., Doise, 1971; Fraser, 1971; Lamm & Myers, 1978). Likewise, the conformity perspective on group processes has focused on the susceptibility of group members to majority pressure (e.g., Allen, 1965; Allen & Crutchfield, 1963; Asch, 1956; Schachter, 1951). More recently, researchers have turned their attention to innovation as well as conformity in group settings. Just as a majority can force deviant members to conform, so can a persistent minority convert members of the majority to its view (Allen, 1975; Moscovici & Faucheux, 1972).

Negotiation. Moscovici (1985) views both innovation and conformity in group communication as two sides of the same general process: nego-tiation. "The whole question," he asserts, "must be seen in the context of interaction."

> In dealing with other persons or groups, each person or subgroup pre-sents its very own system of values and behaviors. It has some leeway in accepting or rejecting its antagonist's system . . . To avoid [tensions] each side is compelled to try to remodel its opinions and actions a little. As a result, a redefinition or reduction of the opposition takes place and stimulates concessions in turn. (1985, p. 357)

Continual flux, rather than normative stability, is the natural condition of social groups. After all, changes in group consensus must logically originate with eccentric (i.e., minority) opinions. Consistent opposi-tion to a majority view can force group members to undertake a serious reevaluation of the issue. ("Why are they so persistent?" people may wonder; "Maybe they have a legitimate concern"). In this case private conversions may occur, even while public concessions to the majority opinion continue. But conversion of the group as a whole may take more time. Unless they are confident enough to counter the perceived norm of the group, for example, people with deviant opinions may continue to make public concessions, even while holding fast to their private views.

Cognitive Processes in Group Communication

Cognition in group discussion is thus interactive, with each person's thoughts and actions influenced by the expressed or anticipated reac-tions of others. As communication unfolds and new information is re-vealed, group members' ideas about the issue and about other members' views are continually adjusted. People develop through discussion (a) their own covert ideas and opinions concerning the issue and (b) evolv-ing perceptions of the thoughts and feelings of other group members.

Group opinion is not a static relationship of ideas and opinions in a group but an unfolding of group-mediated perception and cognition. Discussion of an issue proceeds through at least three important phases: first, the disclosure of disagreements concerning the issue; second, the alignment of people who share similar views; and finally, some form of collective bargaining involving the eventual acquiescence or conversion of people and subgroups en route to a resolution. Members sort out mat-ters of agreement and differences of opinion, using new information to interpret relationships among members as they cluster into subgroups.

Each member eventually develops a perception of the way the group is *organized* with respect to the issue: what views have reasonable support, who stands for which positions, and how the group is divided. In effect, group members come to understand the issue in terms of the group itself. They are not simply deciding on their own opinions on the issue; they are also defining their social allegiances. The organization of the group with respect to the issue proceeds along two lines. On the one hand, discussion allows the sorting out of ideational differences, the organization of meanings and opinions. On the other, it allows the distillation of social differences, the organization of people and subgroups. Thus by social organization of a group we mean the development of both cognitive *and* social structure. In an important sense the two forms of organization, being interdependent, mirror each other.

Group Processes in the Context of Public Debate

We can conceptualize the larger process of public debate (in a national public, for example) as proceeding in the same way, only on a much greater scale. As with conversation in smaller groups, large-scale "conversation" via extensive mass media coverage and popular expression structures the public over time into opinion factions and social alliances. Interpersonal links among all members of such a large public are of course impossible. So when we speak of the public as a communicating group, we can only mean a large network of interpersonal groups made up of people who attend to mass media messages for news and information related to an issue and who in turn actively discuss the matter with local acquaintances. Thus each member of a national public experiences two kinds of communication: (1) interpersonal conversation within groups of personal acquaintances (the *inside* public) and (2) contact via the mass media with larger collective movements, organizations, and personalities beyond the confines of one's personal associations (the *outside* public). Exposure to media coverage and involvement in interpersonal discussions allows members of the public to sort out group differences at multiple levels. In other words, communicating members of the public are simultaneously adjusting their relationships to both (1) interpersonal groups and (2) broader social groups and movements that emerge in response to the public issue.

The inside public. The view that interpersonal relations (primary groups) have a strong influence on individual opinions has acquired nearly axiomatic status in empirical research on mass communication and public opinion (Lane & Sears, 1964, p. 34). Of the five factors influencing media effects in Klapper's landmark analysis (1960, p. 19), three pertain directly to interpersonal associations: shared group norms, interpersonal dissemination of mass media content, and opinion leadership from personal acquaintances. The traditional model of mass media effects rested on the view that primary group solidarity is a strong filter through which mass media messages must flow. Specifically, messages were thought to flow through opinion leaders to other less attentive members of the group (Katz & Lazarsfeld, 1955; Lazarsfeld et al., 1948). In thinking about and discussing public affairs, people were assumed to coorient primarily with personal acquaintances, notably local experts on the issues.

The outside public. The "limited effects" findings were produced by research in a different time and mass media setting (in the 1940s and 1950s) and by a tradition that framed interpersonal communication processes largely as *obstacles* to mass media influence (see Chaffee & Hochheimer, 1982). But there is an important resonance between exposure to mass communication and interpersonal discussion of public affairs (Chaffee, 1981). The media perform the key function of placing people in contact with the "world outside" (Lippmann, 1922), conveying important information about ideas, opinions, and larger social movements beyond the boundaries of personal experience. The mass media provide, as Graber (1982, p. 557) puts it, the symbolic "background" against which the public opinion process—including interpersonal debate—is played out. Group opinion processes cannot be limited to the inside public alone, to instances where group members look to personal opinion leadership or local opinion norms for guidance. When the focus of discussion is on matters of widespread public concern, social orientation may reach well beyond the bounds of personal association, as people perceive wider social movements and broad groups of people organizing on the issue.

Issues in Terms of Group Relations

The major effect of communication surrounding a social issue is a clearer perception in people's minds regarding agreements and disagreements, and a more extensive mapping of social groups. Members of a communicating public may come to perceive issues largely in terms of group associations, local and distal. One of the early findings from voting studies was that public debate crystallizes differences between sides of an issue—between political parties, for instance, in the context of an election (Berelson et al., 1954). Public discussion may also produce new and unique group divisions in response to specific issues. Social conflict over the issue of abortion, for example, not only elicits opinion stands from existing churches and political groups but also brings forth a new breed of issue-specific right-to-lifers. The military campaign analogies so often used in describing political events suggest that public debate may be less a war of ideas than a war of opposing factions and social groups. People often understand an issue in terms of their loyalties to one or another camp of opinion. They may stake out their position as a stand against the perceived opinion of a particularly disliked group or personality, as some theories of "balance" or "symmetry" would predict (Newcomb, 1953).

As with interpersonal group debate, widespread public discussion of an issue also involves (a) an organization of the communicating public along group lines, as well as (b) an organization of ideas and opinions in the minds of each participating member of the public. The two forms of organization, one *sociological* and the other *ideological,* are in a sense the same thing. In reading, thinking, and talking about an issue, each member of the public locates him- or herself within a complex network of social relations, and may define the issue largely in terms of those relations. Considering nuclear power, for example, a student might rely heavily on what "other students" appear to think. This is not to say that people invariably conform to perceived group norms, but that their perceptions of group opinion help them to understand public communication and guide them in making their own decisions. Thinking and discussion concerning nuclear power may revolve not so much around intricacies of the issue itself but around understood differences between environmentalists, big businesses, no-nukes activists, and perhaps key political personalities, such as "the liberal senator from California." The process of public communication translates ideas and opinions into social relationships.

Studying Group Processes in Public Debate

A useful approach to researching the cognitive structure of communicating groups along these lines has been developed by McLeod and Chaffee (1972, 1973). Following Newcomb's (1953) general model of cognitive coorientation, they begin by assuming that communication within a social system requires that members be simultaneously oriented toward the same object (in the present case, a public issue). To describe the communication system empirically, two types of measures are needed: each group member's own cognitions about the issue, as well as each member's perceptions of each other member's cognitions. In this way a researcher can determine (a) the extent of *understanding* or *agreement* between members (how much their personal ideas or opinions about the issue actually coincide); (b) the *accuracy* of people's perceptions (how close members come in estimating others' points of view); and (c) *congruency* (the extent to which people perceive agreement or understanding between themselves and other group members). With the exchange of ideas and the negotiation of opinions, these cognitive relations within the group develop and change. Our present concern is not with the static cognitive structure of a communicating group, but with its ongoing "structuration" or social organization. In these terms coorientation is not a state but a social process. Wackman (1973), for example, notes that interpersonal discussion over time tends to increase accuracy more than agreement: People do not necessarily end up seeing eye to eye on a controversial topic after debating it, but they come away from discussion with a better understanding of how other people think. A communicating group should be modeled not as a static structure of cognitive relations within a group but as a developing coorientational system.

Modeling public coorientation. Extension of the coorientation model beyond smaller interpersonal groups, as McLeod and Chaffee admit (1972, p. 65), is not without its complications. For larger groups, cognitive norms often become reified, that is, people may react to the group as a "generalized other" rather than a collection of individuals as the basic coorientation model assumes. In studying public opinion processes, reification becomes a central concern. Our conceptualization of public discussion suggests that developing perceptions of group opinions— both local and distal—function for people as important cognitive reference points in comprehending and discussing public issues.

Perceiving inside and outside opinion. Miller (1978) has drawn a conceptual distinction in a somewhat different context that may help to clarify the reification question. In his attempt to define interpersonal communication, Miller argues for a developmental concept of human relations. What makes a communication relationship interpersonal, he suggests, is the fact that participants use *psychological* (i.e., personal) information rather than *sociological* (i.e., impersonal or public) information. In an interpersonal encounter, people react to one another as unique individuals. In noninterpersonal situations, on the other hand, people respond to others more in terms of stereotypical social roles. We can adapt Miller's conceptualization to opinion perception. Within the inside public of interpersonal associations, group opinion is perceived by its members as a collection of individual opinions, just as the coorientation model assumes. In the case of larger impersonal groups in the outside public, however, collective opinion is perceived in more reified terms—as the "typical" opinion of a "typical" group member. Reification of group opinion, then, is variable (McLeod & Chaffee, 1972), decreasing with the "interpersonalness"—as Miller (1978) puts it—of social relationships in the communication setting.

Learning More About the Role of Groups

Conceptualizing the public as a communicating group focuses our attention on interactive social organization. The developmental model suggests that a key step in advancing public opinion theory is to learn more about the way opinions and the groups representing them are organized through public discussion. Over-time investigations of the ways people perceive the cognitive attributes of other people and subgroups can allow us to model, in coorientational terms, the progress of public communication. How are members of a public coming to understand different sides of the issue? What social group differences do they perceive? How does a person perceive him- or herself fitting into these groups?

Coorientation of groups. Some coorientation research has already investigated intergroup perceptions of opinion (e.g., Grunig & Stamm, 1973) and has produced some interesting questions. Does public discussion of an issue engender greater accuracy in people's perceptions of other groups' opinions? Although Wackman's (1973) investigation of interpersonal communication shows such increases in accuracy, larger public debate at an intergroup level may result in oversimplifications (i.e., distorted group stereotypes) and exaggerated perceptions. Pearce, Stamm, and Strentz (1971) studied intergroup coorientation during campus demonstrations in 1970, and their results illustrate how perceptions of group differences may polarize as a function of public interaction. Pearce et al. asked two groups of students, demonstrators and nondemonstrators, their views on the Vietnam war and their estimates of how the other student group felt. Results showed that while the two groups actually agreed on the issues, nondemonstrating students held exaggerated perceptions of intergroup opinion differences. Apparently the most visible demonstrators were more extreme in their views, and the entire group of demonstrating students was perceived in line with these few examples (see Grunig & Stamm, 1973). How do examples of group opinion provided by the mass media influence intergroup perceptions? Over-time analyses could certainly bring us closer to some answers. As polarization research in small group settings illustrates, the process is probably quite complex (see Giles & Wiemann, Chapter 12).

Construing group relations in the public. On an even more basic level, we need to learn more about how members of the public define an issue along group lines. Social-psychological theorizing and research in social categorization and intergroup relations may help point public opinion research in some useful directions. A person's self-concept includes many possible social selves. In different situations people may define themselves in any number of ways, "activating" one or another salient group membership role (Turner, 1985). Shibutani (1955) advocated using the reference group concept in a similar way to denote a psychological "perspective." A reference group, in this usage, is "that group whose outlook is used by the actor as the frame of reference in the organization of his perceptual field" (1955, p. 168). More recently, researchers of social categorization and intergroup behavior (e.g., Allen & Wilder, 1975; Doise, 1978; Tajfel & Turner, 1979; Turner, 1985; Wilder, 1986) have produced experimental evidence suggesting that when intergroup distinctions become salient, people behave less as individuals and more on the basis of their social identities. Self-identification with a particular group seems to prime people to impose schematic group categorizations on information they encounter, focusing on stereotypical differences between people "like me" (i.e., the salient *ingroup*) and people "not like me" in other groups (i.e., salient *outgroups*) (see Giles & Wiemann, Chapter 12).

Implications for opinion research. Differences in how people come to define the ingroup and outgroup with respect to a particular issue should have important implications for opinion formation and change. Sampled opinions, as we noted, often seem more like pseudo-opinion, failing to reflect logically coherent ideologies. They do not appear to be internalized, that is, adopted because they are congruent with a general system of values. Perhaps we are discovering that many people, in the course of deciding their stand on a public issue, are not so much deciding their own opinion (or *where* they stand on the matter) but instead deciding on their social loyalties (in other words, *with whom* they stand). Issue-related thinking and discussion focusing on particular intergroup differences may be a central feature of opinion formation. Kelman (1961) was one of the first researchers to investigate the adoption of opinions due to *social identification,* the process of accepting an opinion because it is associated with a "satisfying self-defining relationship" to a particular group (1961, p. 61). Opinions adopted due to social identification, in Kelman's view, are dependent upon a person's role as a member of the group and so will be expressed only when that role is somehow made salient. Social identification may serve as a mechanism of opinion formation or change through either (a) the assimilation of perceived ingroup opinion norms (e.g., Kelman, 1961; Mackie, 1986; Turner, 1985) or through (b) contrasts with perceived outgroup opinion norms (or "negative reference groups"; see for example Hyman & Singer, 1968; Newcomb, 1948). An appropriate focus for public opinion research would be on the way people process issue information in light of their perceptions of group relations.

ORGANIZATIONAL-LEVEL OPINION

While unique social alliances and groups can form naturally in response to specific issues, enduring social organizations—corporate bodies, churches, political action groups—also engage as collective voices for various positions on matters of public dispute. As Key (1961) observed and as Graber (1982) has recently reemphasized, public opinion is something that "governments find it prudent to heed." Organizations of many kinds doubtless have much to say in the determination of public policy. In spite of this fact, the role of organizational opinions is often overlooked in research (Namenwirth, Miller & Webber, 1981).

Defining organizations. Distinguishing organizations from the less formal groups we have already discussed is somewhat problematic. It may be best to think of social groups along a continuum of organized formality; at some point they become sufficiently formal to be called organizations. Here we will simply define organizations as *enduring systems of social policies*. The defining feature of a social institution or organization is its overall plan, including a set of goals and regulatory procedures drawn up with the aim of achieving them. These goals and procedures may vary greatly in scope and complexity: They may be economic, political, philosophical, or ethical in nature. Businesses, for example, usually exist for the straightforward purpose of producing or exchanging goods and services. Religious organizations, on the other hand, have more abstract ethical and spiritual goals. In either case, the social identity of the organization finds its expression in policy, in methods of collective behavior directed toward realizing the organization's goals.

Opinion Processes Within Organizations

When applied to public issues, an organization's policies often imply a certain stand. Namenwirth and others (1981) investigated this phenomenon empirically by attempting to sample "organizations' opinions." They found that representatives (often permanent public affairs officers) were quite willing to offer opinions on a number of issues on behalf of their organizations. Furthermore, these opinions were often at odds with the representatives' personal views. The respondents were apparently able to "think for the organization" as easily as for themselves when confronted with social issues and placed in their official roles.

A canonical process. What separates an organizational position on an issue from a personal opinion is the fact that the former is tied to a relatively objective canon of goals and policies. The process of generating an organizational stand on an issue involves, in balance, less consideration of private judgments and greater attention to collective concerns as they exist in codes and historical precedents. The overriding concern is with fidelity to policy and to the stated goals of the group. Organizational positions on public issues represent a judgment rendered by a person or a communicating group in service of a larger whole, aiming not merely at private satisfaction but at furthering collective interests. Different types of goals will generate different opinions. In the case of a corporation, commercial interests will have much, perhaps everything, to do with the organization's stand on a public issue. In the case of a religious institution, with its more complex social charter, the spiritual and ethical dimensions of the issue will presumably play a greater role in shaping a stated position. Goals and policies also imply whether a given public issue is of central importance to an establishment. Those organizations with very restricted goals may not become interested parties in the resolution of many public issues, while others with broad ideological goals (such as churches or civil rights groups) may actively respond to a variety of issues.

Organizational Voices in Public Debate

There is little doubt that organizations have a key role in shaping public opinion (see Graber, 1982). A great number of organizations, although not formally structured as part of the political system, nonetheless influence public debate and the resolution of issues. The relative sociopolitical force of an organizational position will vary greatly, depending upon institutional power or apparent popular support. Opinions rendered officially by such bodies as the National Rifle Association or the American Civil Liberties Union can affect the public opinion process in numerous ways: by influencing citizens who identify with or oppose the organizations, by initiating counteractivity from other groups that expound opposing views, or by influencing attentive politicians, for example.

Elite publics and organizational perspectives. The involvement of organizations in public debate can arise from a great many sources but usually begins with a relatively small core of more interested and active members. These are political elites, whose point of entry into public dispute is commonly from the vantage point of organizational, ideological concerns. We use the term "elites" here in a restricted sense, with reference only to the particular issues with which they and the organizations they represent are concerned. In this sense, a leader within the organization Mothers Against Drunk Driving would be a political elite. Countless institutions and organizations try to place their own issues on the public agenda, to inform the citizenry of their opinions, and to recruit supporters for their views. These exercises in public relations are fundamental to the larger opinion process, carried out by communicating groups of elites who are pursuing not so much personal interests as common causes.

Researching Organizational Roles

As Graber (1982) and Namenwirth et al. (1981) suggest, these elites and their organizations deserve greater empirical attention in public opinion research. Some recent studies along these lines have proven quite

promising. Granberg (1984), for example, has investigated two competing social movement organizations: the National Right to Life Committee (the largest anti-abortion group in the U.S.) and the National Abortion
Rights Action League (the largest U.S. pro-abortion-rights group). Of
primary interest to Granberg are the attributions of popular support made
by members of these interest groups. Each side tends to overestimate
support for its own views. The fact that interest group leaders perceive
false consensus in the larger population regarding their issue may be
related to a more general tendency for affectively involved people to make
exaggerated judgments about the extent of concern over the issue within
the wider population. Judd and Johnson (1984), for example, find that
women with intense affective ties to feminist issues perceive greater division over those issues in the general population: They estimate both larger
amounts of public support for their views and stronger opposition to them.

   Organizational strategies in public debate. Just as people's perceptions
of other's opinions influence small group decision making, so too elite
perceptions of popular and governmental support and opposition should
affect organizational strategies in public debate. Granberg (1984) has
proposed that organizational strategies in public debate are influenced
by two key factors: (1) leaders' perceptions of public support for their
cause and (2) perceptions of how well current policymakers are responding to their demands. In a case where interest group leaders perceive
extensive support in the wider population but find that policymakers are
not acting in accordance with their preferences, frustration with officials may lead to an unwillingness to compromise on the issue. In this
situation the interest group would be quite willing to have the issue put to
popular vote. On the other hand, if policymakers are viewed as responsive while the wider population is perceived to be *nonsupportive*, then
entirely different strategies (e.g., mass educational campaigns) are likely.

SOCIETAL-LEVEL OPINION

   When we speak of the national public as a communicating group we
refer in large part to an interacting network of collective bodies and their
representatives, "conversing" via widely publicized actions and statements of opinion. We have come nearly full circle at this point, to a consideration of public opinion processes at the societal level. In light of our
review across individual, group, and organizational levels, recall our
earlier argument that the public is no unitary thing but is instead a developing, organizing body of people—within groups, within organizations—
attempting through discursive means to resolve a common issue. At the
individual level of analysis, we find an intrapersonal "conversation"
between thought and behavior; at the group level, conversation between

individuals; at the organizational level, debate among internal groups. Finally we have at the societal level a developing, communicative response to public issues between formal organizations and emerging popular movements. Their political interaction is tied in a fundamental way to their ability to display power through demonstrations of support among people in the general population. The ultimate resolution of public issues in society, then, is a process of large-scale social organization: At this level, political countermoves are shadowed by a larger movement of popular support. When we speak of public opinion in everyday conversation we attempt to describe the public's "state of mind" with respect to some issue. But here we suggest that public opinion is perhaps better equated with the public's issue-specific "state of social organization."

Political Actors and the Interested Public

We suggested earlier that discussion of an issue involves three phases: the disclosure of disagreements or misunderstandings, the alignment of people who share similar views, and some kind of collective bargaining. In an interpersonal group, organization into opinion factions may be fairly natural and democratic as people expressing similar views tend to cluster into relatively homogeneous subgroups. In a larger society, however, the process of public organization is twofold. Certain interested and active individuals and groups first recognize and respond to the issue; only then does the issue and the developing public response to it diffuse throughout the larger society. So we should clearly distinguish *political actors,* who perform the general task of forming and representing political coalitions, from the *interested public* (Lippmann's "bystander" public), a larger body of people drawn into eventual alignment with one political faction or another. Political actors and members of the interested public enter the communicative public opinion process out of a much larger mass of disconnected people. In many cases the distillation of opinion factions has less to do with members of the interested public actively seeking alignment than with committed political actors recruiting popular support.

Political actors. Who are these political actors? Certainly this segment of a public extends well beyond the confines of formal political office. Most often, public issues first gain the attention of a small group of committed people who pursue the matter publicly for their own ideological purposes (see Davison, 1958, p. 93 for an illustration). Innovation in the political world, as anywhere, must originate with the actions of a minority, even a minority of one. But once the process of publicity is set in motion the circle of political actors must widen, perhaps first to established social and political organizations. Extremely interested members of the larger population may likewise begin to organize active responses to the issue, especially if institutional channels for expression of their views are limited. This process of growing institutional and public response may be very rapid, given the capability of the mass media to disseminate news and information instantaneously throughout society. But often the gestation period of public issues is an extended one. As Lang and Lang (1981b) observe, a problem that is personally experienced throughout an entire population and is thus widely relevant (e.g., a food shortage) may require a low threshold of mass media attention before it becomes a matter of widespread concern and discussion. High threshold issues such as Watergate, however, being remote from the experience of ordinary citizens, require sustained media attention and coverage to break into public debate.

The interested public. Although not highly active in the political arena, a large number of people nonetheless remain somewhat attentive to public events and unfolding social issues. As we noted, these members of the population may be relatively innocent of defined, overarching ideologies. Yet they are sufficiently capable, in everyday conversation as well as in the act of voting, to express their allegiance to one or another emerging coalition (Graber, 1984, p. 204). Members of the interested public play an important third-party role in the political process: "When mobilized and having aligned themselves, [they can] change the power relationship. Even when they do not intervene . . . their acquiescence is often essential for the success of any policy" (Lang & Lang, 1981a, p. 677). How is this political power exercised? It operates via the perceptions of political actors, who gauge their own efficacy in the changing political world by their perceptions of public response. Broad public support for their actions may not be necessary. But most political actors must believe at the very least that there is not insurmountable public opposition to their policies. So the political power of the interested public lies not so much in what it does but in political actors' perceptions of what it *might* do.

Perceptions of Public Alignment

We can see that true public opinion—that which has political force (Key, 1961)—is precisely the state of organization within the public that is perceived by the political actors who are responsible for policy. In discussing opinion processes in interpersonal groups we suggested that participants are increasingly able to perceive their own views of the issue, the opinions and ideas of other participants, and the developing organization of the group as a whole. Interacting parties in public debate at the societal level, whether political actors or members of the interested public, are also formulating impressions of overall public alignment. This evolving organization of contrasting views, expressed in representative social groups and political factions, is just as much the product of compromise and adjustment (albeit on a far greater scale) as we might find in smaller group opinion processes.

The dual role of the mass media. People come to develop impressions of "what is happening" in public debate that are both (1) based on mass mediated representations of political events and of developing, distal public response and (2) filtered through the social influences of their immediate personal surroundings. Juxtaposed as they are between political actors and the interested public, the mass media perform two key roles with respect to the public opinion process. First, they carry out what we may call their *reporting* function. By this we mean that they provide mediated representations of important events and political actions, by presenting both news and commentary. Second, they function as *polltakers,* by which we mean they provide mediated representations of the public's organizing response to issues. This latter function is sometimes exercised formally in the reporting of scientific opinion polls, but more generally through informal characterizations of broad trends in public reaction (e.g., "man on the street" interviews, letters to the editor, summaries in news reports, etc.).

A simplified model of the process is presented in Figure 25.1. The general cycle of mass mediated information is depicted as one in which, to start, the media (as "reporters") represent ongoing events and political actions to the interested public. The media also (as "polltakers") provide representations of public response to political actors, carrying out the "linkage" function of keeping political actors attuned to shifts in the alignment of the interested public with respect to an issue. This schematic representation is designed to highlight a central aspect of the public opinion process: a reciprocal exchange between political actors, on the one hand, and their supporters or opponents within the interested public, on the other. What we have, in essence, are two distinct publics: one actively attempting to shape the course of policy; the other somewhat interestedly watching events unfold, attempting to understand the political climate and adjusting its balance of support or opposition to the opinions of political actors and organizations. People on either side of this exchange behave on the basis of their unique perceptions of public affairs (i.e., important political events and actions) and their perceptions of the current and likely future alignment of opinion within the public. These impressions of events surrounding the issue ("perceived public affairs") and of the organization of the public ("perceived public opinion") are based upon media images but formed within the context of immediate personal influences.

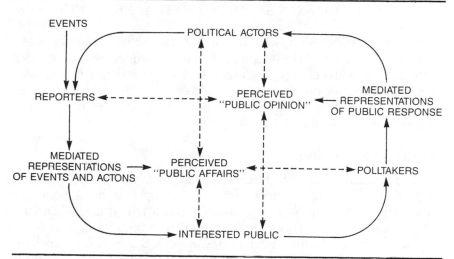

Figure 25.1. A simplified model of the public opinion process.

Media portrayals. The public opinion process, then, may be conceptualized largely as communication between political actors who are restlessly pursuing public recognition and support for their views and members of the interested public who are trying to understand the issue and decide whom to support. But they communicate principally via the language provided by the mass media, through intermediate representations. And the language of mass-mediated debate is a strange one indeed, because unlike face-to-face communication, the interlocutors have incomplete control over their expressions. Certainly in the case of political actors, quite a bit of energy is expended trying to use the media to express the desired message. And while it is far more passive about the whole affair, the interested public as well is dependent upon the media (including polling organizations) to relay their responses. On both sides, participants in the debate frequently express reservations about how well the mass media perform (see, for example, Vallone, Ross, & Lepper, 1985). Embittered authors of letters to the editor and politicians alike lay claim to silent majorities whose views are allegedly ignored by the press. Personnel in media organizations develop their own perceptions of public affairs and public opinion in precisely the same way as do political actors and members of the interested public. Just as other participants in the opinion process behave on the basis of those perceptions, so also do media agents. In reporting the news, for instance, they are not only performing a responsible social role, they are also responding to economic pressures.

DIRECTIONS IN STUDYING MEDIA INFLUENCE

By way of conclusion, we return to questions concerning the role of the media. We will briefly consider two current trends in empirical research on media effects. Both represent very profitable directions in the study of public opinion processes. In light of our review across levels, however, we will suggest that there is still considerable room for growth and expansion.

Media Setting the Stage

The first broad trend in research relates to what we have called the reporting function of the media—that is, the impact of mass media representations on people's perceptions of public affairs (the left-hand portion of Figure 25.1). This is best exemplified by empirical research on agenda setting by the mass media (McCombs & Shaw, 1972). Much like the "status conferral" function hypothesized by Lazarsfeld and Merton (1948), agenda setting refers to the ability of mass media coverage of a certain problem to grant it status (i.e., importance or salience) as a social issue. As Cohen (1963, p. 16) claimed, even if the media are not successful in telling people what to think, they are nevertheless "stunningly" successful in telling people "what to think about." Audience perceptions of the importance of various public issues, then, are expected to be a function of the emphasis accorded those issues by the mass media. The agenda-setting hypothesis has been extensively researched, usually in surveys that have produced mixed but generally supportive results (e.g., Shaw & McCombs, 1977; Weaver, Graber, McCombs, & Eyal, 1981; for a review see Roberts & Maccoby, 1985). More recently experiments have provided rather convincing evidence of the effect (e.g., Iyengar, Peters, & Kinder, 1982).

Cooperative influences. Agenda-setting research captures only part of the much wider concept of media "reporting" as it relates to the opinion process. First, it has focused almost entirely on mass media influence on the interested public, to the relative exclusion of political actors (Graber, 1982). How are elite perceptions of public affairs affected by mass media coverage? As Lang and Lang (1981b) point out, the usual concept of agenda setting fails to capture the reciprocal nature of influences in building a public issue. The research of Cook et al. (1983), for example, illustrates how government officials interested in drawing attention to a problem can work in tandem with investigative journalists to air public issues and propose policy changes.

Mass media and the public outside. Our model suggests that the mass media operate primarily to carry information about the outside public, about events, ideas, and social movements beyond the confines of personal association. We would expect media coverage, then, to alter not so much perceptions of how personally important an issue is but rather perceptions of its broader social implications (i.e., its public importance). McLeod and Becker have pursued this line of inquiry (Becker, McCombs, & McLeod, 1975; McLeod, Becker, & Byrnes, 1974), and their research findings seem to support our expectation. McLeod et al. (1974) investigated three types of issue saliences: the personal importance assigned to an issue; the importance a person thinks others have given the issue; and "community issue salience," indexed by how many respondents in a community report talking about an issue. Along similar lines, Tyler and Cook (1984) found that media reports have an "impersonal impact," affecting societal-level rather than personal-level judgments.

Beyond issue salience. The perceived world of public affairs includes quite a bit more than issue salience. In what symbolic terms is an issue defined? What social movements or personalities within the public champion particular stands on an issue? We suggested that public debate organizes perceptions of opposing groups, institutions, and personalities, and that group differences often define the issue under debate. How can these processes be researched? Clarke and Kline (1974) give us a start. They have argued that researchers too often use textbook measures to investigate people's knowledge of public affairs; more appropriate, they suggest, are measures of "information holding," where respondents are allowed to identify what *they* perceive to be the major problems facing a community, what solutions have been advanced, and what persons or groups are advocating different solutions. Benton and Frazier (1976) used this kind of measure to extend the concept of agenda setting beyond simple issue salience and include people's awareness of particular problems, their causes, and proposed solutions. Tichenor and Wackman (1973) studied community opinion concerning a suburb's controversial decision to dump treated sewage into a nearby river. Local newspapers supported the decision, while rival metropolitan papers attacked it. Answers to open-ended survey items showed that what people believed about the sewage issue depended on which papers they read.

Media Providing the Looking Glass

The second broad trend in empirical research of mass communication, equally important for the study of public opinion, involves the polltaking function of the media—that is, the impact of mass media representations on people's perceptions of public opinion (the right-hand portion of Figure 25.1). Leading examples of this research are commonly referred to as inquiries into "pluralistic ignorance" (e.g., O'Gorman, 1975; O'Gorman with Garry, 1976) or the "spiral of silence" (e.g., Noelle-Neumann, 1974, 1981).

Perceptions and misperceptions of opinion. Pluralistic ignorance usually refers to a situation where members of a public are ignorant of their broad covert agreement on an issue. In this event an impression of widespread public opposition to one's private view may prevent people from publicly expressing what is in fact a majority opinion. Publicity of the supposed minority view will then be met with surprising agreement, creating the impression of rapid public conversion to a new opinion. As Fields and Schuman (1976, p. 427) put it, pluralistic ignorance suggests "a situation where people appear to operate within a 'false' social world, or at least one quite different from that observed by the presumably objective social scientist." Noelle-Neumann's (1974) spiral of silence theory represents a broader conceptual foray into this false social world. According to her theory, people who perceive from media reports that trends of opinion are running against their views, fearing social isolation, will refrain from expressing their opinions (except to those who share them). So even if these persons constitute a numerical majority, the failure to communicate their views will lead to a strengthening of the opposition, creating the spiral of silence.

Communication influences across levels. We also need to account for the ways in which communication at different levels affects people's impressions of the surrounding climate of opinion. Perceptions of public opinion are based upon media representations, but interpersonal contacts are also a likely influence. Fields and Schuman (1976) found a general tendency among respondents to overestimate the extent to which other people agreed with their own views. What about occasions when mass media and interpersonal sources offer different pictures of the public? Perhaps people are informed by mass media sources that national opinion runs against them; they may nonetheless be encouraged by a perception of very strong local support. Or consider the case in which a citizen harbors views that are quite unpopular among local acquaintances. An impression that many other people "out there" share his or her views may be quite invigorating, supporting independence from perceived local norms.

Spirals of silence or spirals of change? A theoretical underpinning of the spiral of silence theory is conformity to perceived group norms, drawn from small group research of the 1950s (e.g., Asch, 1956). More recent group decision making research, as we noted, has revealed the considerable importance of innovation and change in group behavior. Even in Asch's experiments most subjects reported being fully aware of their conflict with the unanimous group; and most important, when given a single partner siding with them, they held their own course against the majority. As Katz (1983) points out, mass publicity of opinions may have either a silencing *or* a liberating effect on public expressions, given different social conditions. At the institutional level, standing traditions and policies may exercise great influence in maintaining societal-level opinion, even when individual-level consensus runs in an opposing direction.

Perceptions of policymakers. We also need to pay special attention to the ways perceived public opinion might influence the reciprocal exchange between political actors and the interested public. Noelle-Neumann's theorizing has been useful in probing the ways perceived opinion trends can influence interpersonal expression among the interested public. Yet these members of the public maintain a rather passive role in the larger debate over policy, at least in comparison to that played by political actors. Gitlin (1980), in portraying the relationship between the media and the fledgling Students for a Democratic Society movement, provides extensive anecdotal evidence that media portrayals influence political actors at least as much as they affect the bystander public. Davison (1983) draws attention to a third-person effect in mass communication: People generally say they are personally unaffected by media messages, even while they assume considerable impact on other people. Vallone et al. (1985) found a similar result. Opinionated TV viewers on both sides of a controversial issue found identical news reports biased against them; both sides estimated that the reports would sway neutral viewers against them. How often are the actions and expressions of political actors based upon overreactions to media coverage?

The dynamic properties of mass and interpersonal communication make public opinion difficult to conceptualize let alone research empirically. Widely divergent appraisals of mass media influence—many dire, some optimistic—will doubtless continue while variations on the theme of agenda setting and additional efforts to investigate spirals of silence and change slowly add to our knowledge of societal opinion processes. Our discussion here has aimed at exploring theoretical issues, focusing on the concept of the public as a communicating group and tracing that concept across levels of analysis. Public opinion processes are above all communication phenomena, involving inter-level relations over time, where people and groups play differentiated roles. Certainly more than a simple matter of polling, public opinion research richly deserves to be conducted as communication science.

NOTES

1. We owe this formulation to Steve Chaffee.
2. Lippmann planned to give social scientists a very consequential role in government. Heading up his expert organization would be "in the first instance the task of political science that has won its proper place as formulator, in advance of real decision, instead of apologist, critic, or reporter after the decision has been made" (1922, p. 33).

REFERENCES

Allen, V. L. (1965). Situational factors in conformity. In L. Berkowitz (Ed.), *Advances in experimental social psychology* (Vol. 2, pp. 133-176). New York: Academic Press.

Allen, V. L. (1975). Social support for non-conformity. In L. Berkowitz (Ed.), *Advances in experimental social psychology* (Vol. 8). New York: Academic Press.

Allen, V. L., & Crutchfield, R. S. (1963). Generalization of experimentally reinforced conformity. *Journal of Abnormal and Social Psychology, 67,* 326-333.

Allen, V. L., & Wilder, D. A. (1975). Categorization, belief similarity and inter-group discrimination. *Journal of Personality and Social Psychology, 32,* 971-977.

Allport, F. D. (1937). Toward a science of public opinion. *Public Opinion Quarterly, 1,* 7-23.

Asch, S. E. (1956). *Studies of independence and conformity: A minority of one against a unanimous majority* (Psychological Monographs 70: no. 9, whole no. 416).

Baldwin, J. M. (1893). *Elements of psychology.* New York: Holt, Rinehart & Winston.

Becker, L. B., McCombs, M. E., & McLeod, J. M. (1975). The development of political cognitions. In S. H. Chaffee (Ed.), *Political communication: Issues and strategies for research* (pp. 21-63). Newbury Park, CA: Sage.

Bem, D. J. (1970). *Beliefs, attitudes, and human affairs.* Belmont, CA: Brooks/Cole.

Benton, M., & Frazier, P. J. (1976). The agenda-setting function of mass media at three levels of information holding. *Communication Research, 3,* 261-274.

Berelson, B. P., Lazarsfeld, P., & McPhee, W. N. (1954). *Voting.* Chicago: University of Chicago Press.

Bishop, G. F., Oldendick, R. W., Tuchfarber, A. J., & Bennet, S. E. (1980). Pseudo-opinions on public affairs. *Public Opinion Quarterly, 44,* 198-209.

Blumer, H. (1946). Collective behavior. In A. M. Lee (Ed.), *New outlines of the principles of sociology* (pp. 167-222). New York: Barnes & Noble.

Boulding, K. E. (1956). *The image.* Ann Arbor: University of Michigan Press.

Chaffee, S. H. (1977). Mass media effects: New research perspectives. In D. Lerner & L. Nelson (Eds.), *Communication research: A half century appraisal* (pp. 210-241). Honolulu, HI: East-West Center.

Chaffee, S. H. (1981). Mass media in political campaigns: an expanding role. In R. E. Rice & W. J. Paisley (Eds.), *Public communication campaigns* (pp. 181-198). Newbury Park, CA: Sage.

Chaffee, S. H., & Hochheimer, J. L. (1982). The beginnings of political communication research in the United States: Origins of the "limited effects" model. In E. M. Rogers & F. Balle (Eds.), *The media revolution in America and Western Europe* (pp. 262-283). Norwood, NJ: Ablex.

Childs, H. (1939). By public opinion I mean . . . . *Public Opinion Quarterly, 4,* 53-69.

Clarke, P., & Kline, F. G. (1974). Media effects reconsidered: Some new strategies for communication research. *Communication Research, 1,* 224-240.

Cohen, B. (1963). *The press and foreign policy.* Princeton, NJ: Princeton University Press.

Converse, P. E. (1964). The nature of belief systems in mass publics. In D. E. Apter (Ed.), *Ideology and discontent* (pp. 206-261). New York: Free Press.

Cook, F. L., Tyler, T. R., Goetz, E. G., Gordon, M. T., Protess, D., Leff, D. R., & Molotch, H. L. (1983). Media and agenda setting: Effects on the public, interest group leaders, policy makers and policy. *Public Opinion Quarterly, 47,* 16-35.

Cooley, C. H. (1909). *Social organization: A study of the larger mind.* New York: Scribner's.

Davison, W. P. (1958). The public opinion process. *Public Opinion Quarterly, 21,* 91-106.

Davison, W. P. (1983). The third-person effect in communication. *Public Opinion Quarterly, 47,* 1-15.

Dewey, J. (1927). *The public and its problems.* New York: Holt, Rinehart & Winston.

Doise, W. (1971). An apparent exception to the extremization of collective judgments. *European Journal of Social Psychology, 12,* 511-518.

Doise, W. (1978). *Groups and individuals: Explanations in social psychology.* London: Cambridge University Press.

Eiser, J. R. (1973). Judgment of attitude statements as a function of judges' attitudes and the judgemental dimension. *British Journal of Social and Clinical Psychology, 15,* 51-60.

Fields, J. M., & Schuman, H. (1976). Public beliefs about the beliefs of the public. *Public Opinion Quarterly, 40,* 427-448.

Fishbein, M. (1967). A consideration of beliefs, and their role in attitude measurement. In M. Fishbein (Ed.), *Attitude theory and measurement.* New York: John Wiley.

Fishbein, M. & Ajzen, I. (1981). Acceptance, yielding and impact: Cognitive processes in persuasion. In R. E. Petty, T. M. Ostrom, & T. C. Brock (Eds.), *Cognitive responses in persuasion* (pp. 338-359). Hillsdale, NJ: Lawrence Erlbaum.

Fiske, S. T., Kinder, D. R., & Larter, W. M. (1983). The novice and the expert: Knowledge-based strategies in political cognition. *Journal of Experimental Social Psychology, 19,* 381-400.

Foote, N. N., & Hart, C. W. (1953). Public opinion and collective behavior. In M. Sherif & M. O. Wilson (Eds.), *Group relations at the crossroads* (pp. 308-331). New York: Harper & Row.

Fraser, C. (1971). Group risk taking and group polarization. *European Journal of Social Psychology, 1,* 490-510.

Gitlin, T. (1980). *The whole world is watching.* Berkeley: University of California Press.

Glynn, C. J., & McLeod, J. M. (1984). Public opinion du jour: An examination of the spiral of silence. *Public Opinion Quarterly, 48,* 731-740.

Graber, D. A. (1982). The impact of media research on public opinion studies. In D. C. Whitney, E. Wartella, & S. Windahl (Eds.), *Mass communication review yearbook 3* (pp. 555-564). Newbury Park, CA: Sage.

Graber, D. A. (1984). *Processing the news: How people tame the information tide.* New York: Longman.

Granberg, D. (1984). Attributing attitudes to members of groups. In J. R. Eiser (Ed.), *Attitudinal judgment* (pp. 85-108). New York: Springer-Verlag.

Grunig, J. E., & Stamm, K. R. (1973). Communication and coorientation of collectivities. *American Behavioral Scientist, 16,* 567-591.

Hennesy, B. (1972). A headnote on the existence of and study of political attitudes. In D. D. Nimmo & C. M. Bonjean (Eds.), *Political attitudes and public opinion* (pp. 27-40). New York: Daniel McKay.

Hovland, C. I., Lumsdaine, A. A., & Sheffield, F. D. (1949). *Experiments on mass communication.* Princeton: Princeton University Press.

Hyman, H. H., & Singer, E. (1968). Introduction. In H. H. Hyman & E. Singer (Eds.), *Readings in reference group theory and research* (pp. 3-21). New York: Free Press.

Iyengar, S., Peters, M. D., & Kinder, D. R. (1982). Experimental demonstration of the "not-so-minimal" consequences of television news programs. *American Political Science Review, 76,* 848-858.

James, W. (1890). *The principles of psychology.* New York: Holt, Rinehart & Winston.

Judd, C. M., & Johnson, J. T. (1984). The polarizing effects of affective intensity. In J. R. Eiser (Ed.), *Attitudinal judgment* (pp. 65-84). New York: Springer-Verlag.

Katz, E. (1983). Publicity and pluralistic ignorance: Notes on "the spiral of silence." In E. Wartella, D. C. Whitney, & S. Windahl (Eds.), *Mass communication review yearbook 4* (pp. 89-100). Newbury Park, CA: Sage.

Katz, E., & Lazarsfeld, P. F. (1955). *Personal influence*. New York: Free Press.

Kelman, H. C. (1961). Processes of opinion change. *Public Opinion Quarterly, 25,* 57-78.

Kelman, H. C. (1974). Attitudes are alive and well and gainfully employed in the sphere of action. *American Psychologist, 29,* 310-324.

Key, V. O., Jr. (1961). *Public opinion and American democracy.* New York: Knopf.

Kinder, D. R., & Kiewiet, D. R. (1979). Economic discontent and political behavior: The role of personal grievances and collective economic judgments in congressional voting. *American Journal of Political Science, 23,* 495-527.

Kinder, D. R., & Sears, D. O. (1985). Public opinion and political action. In G. Lindzey & E. Aronson (Eds.), *Handbook of Social Psychology* (3rd ed., Vol. 2, pp. 659-742). Random House.

Klapper, J. T. (1960). *The effects of mass communication.* New York: Free Press.

Lamm, H., & Meyers, D. G. (1978). Group-induced polarization of attitudes and behavior. In L. Berkowitz (Ed.), *Advances in experimental social psychology* (Vol. 11, pp. 145-195). New York: Academic Press.

Lane, R. E. (1962). *Political ideology.* New York: Free Press.

Lane, R. E., & Sears, D. O. (1964). *Public opinion.* Englewood Cliffs, NJ: Prentice-Hall.

Lang, G. E., & Lang, K. (1981a). Mass communication and public opinion: strategies for research. In M. Rosenberg & R. H. Turner (Eds.), *Social psychology: sociological perspectives* (pp. 653-682). New York: Basic Books.

Lang, G. E., & Lang, K. (1981b). Watergate: An exploration of the agenda-building process. In G. C. Wilhoit & H. deBock (Eds.), *Mass communication review yearbook 2* (pp. 2-16). Newbury Park, CA: Sage.

Lazarsfeld, P. F. (1941). Remarks on administrative and critical communications research. In *Studies in philosophy and social science 9.*

Lazarsfeld, P. F., & Merton, R. K. (1948). Mass communication, popular taste, and organized social action. In L. Bryson (Ed.), *The communication of ideas* (pp. 95-118). New York: Harper & Row.

Lazarsfeld, P. F., Berelson, B., & Gaudet, H. (1948). *The people's choice.* New York: Columbia University Press.

LeBon, G. (1960). *La psychologie des foules* [The Crowd] (R. K. Merton, Ed.). New York: Viking Press. (Original work published 1895)

Lemert, J. B. (1981). *Does mass communication change public opinion after all? A new approach to effects analysis.* Chicago: Nelson Hall.

Lippmann, W. (1922). *Public opinion.* New York: Harcourt Brace Jovanovich.

Lippmann, W. (1925). *The phantom public.* New York: Harcourt Brace Jovanovich.

Mackie, D. M. (1986). Social identification effects in group polarization. *Journal of Personality and Social Psychology, 50,* 720-728.

Markus, H., & Zajonc, R. B. (1985). The cognitive perspective in social psychology. In G. Lindzey & E. Aronson (Eds.), *The handbook of social psychology* (3rd ed., Vol. 1, pp. 137-230). New York: Random House.

McCombs, M. E., & Shaw, D. L. (1972). The agenda-setting function of the mass media. *Public Opinion Quarterly, 36,* 176-187.

McLeod, J. M., & Chaffee, S. H. (1972). The construction of social reality. In J. T. Tedeschi (Ed.), *The social influence processes* (pp. 50-99). Chicago: Aldine.

McLeod, J. M., & Chaffee, S. H. (1973). Interpersonal approaches to communication research. *American Behavioral Scientist, 16,* 469-500.

McLeod, J. M., Becker, L. B., & Byrnes, J. E. (1974). Another look at the agenda-setting function of the press. *Communication Research, 1,* 131-166.

McLeod, J. M., & Reeves, B. (1980). On the nature of mass media effects. In S. B. Withey & R. P. Abeles (Eds.), *Television and social behavior: Beyond violence and children* (pp. 17-54). Hillsdale, NJ: Lawrence Erlbaum.

Mead, G. H. (1934). *Mind, self, and society.* Chicago: University of Chicago Press.

Meehl, P. E. (1977). The selfish voter paradox and the throw-away vote argument. *American Political Science Review, 71,* 11-30.

Miller, G. R. (1978). The current status of theory and research in interpersonal communication. *Human Communication Research, 4,* 164-178.

Miller, G. R. (1980). On being persuaded: some basic distinctions. In M. E. Roloff & G. R. Miller (Eds.), *Persuasion: New directions in theory and research* (pp. 11-28). Newbury Park, CA: Sage.

Moscovici, S. (1985). Social influence and conformity. In G. Lindzey & E. Aronson (Eds.), *The handbook of social psychology* (3rd ed., Vol. 2, pp. 347-412). New York: Random House.

Moscovici, S., & Faucheux, C. (1972). Social influence, conformity bias, and the study of active minorities. In L. Berkowitz (Ed.), *Advances in experimental social psychology* (Vol. 6, pp. 150-202). New York: Academic Press.

Moscovici, S., & Zavalloni, M. (1969). The group as a polarizer of attitudes. *Journal of Personality and Social Psychology, 12,* 125-135.

Namenwirth, J. Z., Miller, R. L., & Weber, R. P. (1981). Organizations have opinions: a redefinition of publics. *Public Opinion Quarterly, 45,* 463-476.

Newcomb, T. M. (1948). Attitude development as a function of reference groups. In M. Sherif (Ed.), *An outline of social psychology.* New York: Harper & Row.

Newcomb, T. M. (1953). An approach to the study of communicative acts. *Psychological Review, 60,* 393-404.

Nie, N. H., Verba, S., & Petrocik, J. R. (1976). *The changing American voter.* Cambridge, MA: Harvard University Press.

Nimmo, D. (1978). *Political communication and public opinion in America.* Santa Monica, CA: Goodyear.

Noelle-Neumann, E. (1974). Spiral of silence: A theory of public opinion. *Journal of Communication, 24,* 43-51.

Noelle-Neumann, E. (1977). Turbulences in the climate of opinion: Methodological applications of the spiral of silence theory. *Public Opinion Quarterly, 41,* 143-158.

Noelle-Neumann, E. (1981). Mass media and social change in developed societies. In E. Katz & T. Szekso (Eds.), *Mass Media and Social Change* (pp. 137-165). Newbury Park, CA: Sage.

O'Gorman, H. J. (1975). Pluralistic ignorance and white estimates of white support for racial segregation. *Public Opinion Quarterly, 39,* 313-330.

O'Gorman, H. J., with Garry, S. L. (1976). Pluralistic ignorance—a replication and extension. *Public Opinion Quarterly, 40,* 449-458.

O'Keefe, D. J. (1980). The relationship of attitude and behavior: a constructivist analysis. In D. P. Cushman & R. D. McPhee (Eds.), *Message-attitude-behavior relationship* (pp. 117-148). New York: Academic Press.

Pearce, W. B., Stamm, K. R., & Strentz, H. (1971). Communication and polarization during a campus strike. *Public Opinion Quarterly, 35,* 228-236.

Roberts, D. F., & Maccoby, N. (1985). Effects of mass communication. In G. Lindzey & E. Aronson (Eds.), *The Handbook of Social Psychology* (3rd ed., Vol. 2, pp. 539-598). New York: Random House.

Schachter, S. (1951). Deviation, rejection and communication. *Journal of Abnormal and Social Psychology, 46,* 190-207.

Schramm, W. (1971). The nature of communication between humans. In W. Schramm & D. F. Roberts (Eds.), *The process and effects of mass communication* (pp. 3-54). Urbana: University of Illinois Press.

Shaw, D. L., & McCombs, M. E. (1977). *The emergence of American political issues.* St. Paul, MN: West Publishing.

Sherif, M., & Hovland, C. I. (1961). *Social judgment: Assimilation and contrast effects in communication and attitude change.* New Haven, CT: Yale University Press.

Sherif, C. W., Sherif, M., & Nebergall, R. E. (1965). *Attitudes and attitude change: The social-judgment-involvement approach.* Philadelphia: W. B. Sanders.

Shibutani, T. (1955). Reference groups as perspectives. *American Journal of Sociology, 60,* 562-569.

Swanson, D. L. (1981). A constructivist approach. In D. D. Nimmo & K. R. Sanders (Eds.), *Handbook of political communication* (pp. 169-271). Newbury Park, CA: Sage.

Tajfel, H., & Turner, J. C. (1979). An integrative theory of intergroup conflict. In W. G. Austin & S. Worchel (Eds.), *The social psychology of intergroup relations.* Monterey, CA: Brooks/Cole.

Thurstone, L. L. (1928). Attitudes can be measured. *Psychological Review, 33,* 529-554.

Tichenor, P. J., & Wackman, D. B. (1973). Mass media and community public opinion. *American Behavioral Scientist, 16,* 593-606.

Turner, J. C. (1982). Towards a cognitive redefinition of the social group. In H. Tajfel (Ed.), *Social identity and intergroup relations* (pp. 15-40). Cambridge: Cambridge University Press.

Turner, J. C. (1985). Social categorization and the self-concept: A social-cognitive theory of group behavior. In E. J. Lawler (Ed.), Advances in Group Processes (Vol. 2, pp. 77-122). Greenwich, CT: JAI.

Tyler, T. R., & Cook, F. L. (1984). The mass media and judgments of risk: Distinguishing impact on personal and societal level judgments. *Journal of Personality and Social Psychology, 47,* 693-708.

Vallone, R. P., Ross, L., & Lepper, M. R. (1985). The hostile media phenomenon: Biased perception and perceptions of media bias in coverage of the Beirut massacre. *Journal of Personality and Social Psychology, 49,* 577-585.

van der Plight, J., van der Linden, J., & Ester, P. (1982). Attitudes toward nuclear energy: Beliefs, values, and false consensus. *Journal of Environmental Psychology, 2,* 221-231.

Wackman, D. B. (1973). Interpersonal communication and coorientation. *American Behavioral Scientist, 16,* 537-550.

Weaver, D. H., Graber, D. A., McCombs, M. E., & Eyal, C. H. (1981). *Media agenda-setting in a presidential election: Issues, images, interest.* New York: Praeger.

Wiebe, G. D. (1953). Some implications of separating opinions from attitudes. *Public Opinion Quarterly, 17,* 328-352.

Wilder, D. A. (1986). Social categorization: Implications for creation and reduction of intergroup bias. In L. Berkowitz (Ed.), *Advances in experimental social psychology* (Vol. 19, pp. 293-355). New York: Academic Press.

Ziller, R. C. (1957). Four techniques of group decision making under uncertainty. *Journal of Applied Psychology, 41,* 384-388.

26 Communication Campaigns

EVERETT M. ROGERS
University of Southern California

J. DOUGLAS STOREY
Stanford University

THIS chapter synthesizes what has been learned about human communication behavior from research on communication campaigns. First we define campaigns. Then we discuss three eras in the study of campaigns that correspond roughly to the shifting paradigms[1] within communication research. Examples of campaigns that typify each era are provided. Finally, we generalize from past research on campaign experiences, and draw conclusions about the design and implementation of future communication campaigns that can enhance their success.

Even more than most subareas of communication science, campaign research has historically been driven by practical questions more than it has been driven by theoretical considerations. But in certain respects, campaigns provide ideal situations for the study of human communication behavior and for the development of communication theory. While paradigm shifts in the field have been felt by campaign practitioners and researchers, in several cases, reasons for change have been provided by the analysis of campaigns.

In the 1960s and 1970s, development campaigns in Third World countries sought such individual outcomes as gains in knowledge, attitude change, and decisions to adopt new ideas in health, agriculture, and family planning (Rogers, 1976). Political campaigns and advertising sought to create awareness of candidates or products and to influence voting or purchasing decisions. Research on these campaigns in the United States and elsewhere sought evidence that types of message structures and delivery systems could produce specific effects among audience members. In recent years, campaign research has tended to look for evidence of longer-term change produced by more individually tailored communication efforts.

The literature of campaign research is filled with failures, along with some qualified successes—evidence that campaigns *can* be effective under certain conditions. Campaign failures are not all from the formative years of communication research, nor are all the successes products

of the present era. A reexamination of some classic literature from earlier campaign research reveals important, and still relevant, principles
of campaign design. But little scholarly work has been devoted to identifying how a successful strategy in one campaign can be generalized to
other campaigns. A synthesis of lessons learned from past campaign
research might be a step toward drawing theoretical propositions out of
this area of highly applied communication research and practice.

DEFINING CAMPAIGNS

Campaigns have been defined in many ways by theorists and practitioners. These definitions differ in the general versus specific objectives
thought to be associated with a campaign, the duration of a campaign
and its intended effects, the units of analysis and locus of benefits of a
campaign, and the channels of communication that are used (Table 26.1).

Paisley (1981, p. 24) notes that definitions of campaign stress either (1)
the intention, or (2) the process, of the campaign. For example, campaigns in the People's Republic of China "aimed at transforming thought
patterns, class/power relationships and/or economic institutions" (Cell,
1977, Table 1) were clearly defined in terms of their intention. A "process" definition, on the other hand, focuses on campaign approaches and
the sequence of activities involved. An example is Rogers and others'
(1979, Table 1) concept of a "preplanned set of communication activities . . . using a particular type of message . . . for a short period . . .
[that] almost always use a multi-media approach."

Campaigns represent an enormous variety of purposes. They have
targeted urban and rural populations, females and males, adults and
children, in Third World as well as industrialized countries. Campaigns
have attempted to influence individuals (political lobbying to influence a
congress member's vote), small and large social groups (acceptance in a
community of a controversial manufacturing facility), and entire societies (national birth control campaigns). The effect sought (and effects
invariably are sought) range from creating literacy to getting votes, from
preventing drug abuse to advertising cosmetics, from changing nutritional intake to transforming the social structure. Given such diversity, a
minimal definition of a communication campaign would have to include
four characteristic features:

(1) *A campaign is purposive.* The military origin of the term "campaign" is reflected in this feature. Specific outcomes are intended to
result from the communication efforts of a campaign. The specific
effects of campaigns can be extremely varied, ranging from individual-
level cognitive effects to societal-level structural changes. Effects can
benefit either the sender or receiver of the campaign messages. Ulti-

TABLE 26.1
Selected Definitions of Campaigns

(1) Schramm (1964, p. 155)

"(1) We must base the whole campaign on an understanding of the life, beliefs, and attitudes of the villagers, and the social factors that help to determine how they live; (2) we must expect to provide face-to-face communication with field workers or other individuals . . .; and (3) we must use a combination of communication channels, employing each in such a way and at such a time as to contribute most to the total usefulness of the information."

(2) Rogers (1973, p. 277)

"A campaign is a preplanned set of communication activities designed by change agents to achieve certain changes in receiver behavior in a specified time period."

(3) Cell (1977, p. 7)

"Formally defined, the mass mobilization campaign in China is an organized mobilization of collective action aimed at transforming thought patterns, class/power relationships and/or economic institutions and productivity."

(4) Hall (1978, p. 5)

"Campaigns tend to be more concentrated and to focus on a small number of related topics. Mass campaigns often rely on political mobilization as a base for stimulating widespread reflection and action on education or health concerns. The communication strategy stresses mass media, including broadcast, print, billboards, and popular theater. The organizations that coordinate and bear these messages are temporary, but build upon the already existing personnel and resources of many permanent institutions."

(5) Rogers et al. (1979, p. 60)

"A communication campaign is preplanned set of communication activities designed to reach and motivate people using a particular type of message. Campaigns are conducted for a short period (usually from one week to three months) with specific attitudinal and behavioral objectives. [They] almost always use a multi-media approach."

(6) Atkin (1981, p. 265)

"Information campaigns usually involve a series of promotional messages in the public interest disseminated through mass media channels to target audiences."

(7) Chaffee (1981, p. 182)

"Political campaigns are aimed at the mobilization of support for one's cause or candidate."

(8) Flay & Cook (1981, p. 239)

"Increasingly, media-based campaigns are being designed to prevent behaviors that are seen as socially undesirable or harmful. . . . They include campaigns using various media, face-to-face interventions in school settings, and programs that occur in the home or the offices of professionals."

(continued)

TABLE 26.1 Continued

---

(9) Paisley (1981, p. 23)

"A public information campaign seems to represent someone's intention to influence someone else's beliefs or behavior, using communicated appeals."

(10) McQuail (1983, p. 180)

"[A campaign is] the situation in which a number of media are used to achieve a persuasive or informational purpose with a chosen population, the most common examples being found in politics, advertising, fund-raising, and public information for health and safety."

(11) McGuire (1984, p. 299)

"[A health communication campaign] involves convincing individuals to exercise personal responsibility for their health by altering their lifestyles in more healthful directions, [through the use of] mass media and other communication channels to inform the public about dangers, motivate them to reduce risks, or train them in skills that enable them to adopt more healthful lifestyles."

---

mately, campaigns seek to influence individuals, although the objectives of a campaign may be, and often are, stated in aggregate terms.

(2) *A campaign is aimed at a large audience.* The word "large" is used to distinguish a campaign from small-scale, interpersonal persuasive communication by one individual or a few seeking to influence only a few others—although most campaign strategies have a direct foundation in theories of interpersonal persuasion. The campaign audience is determined to a certain extent by campaign goals, but these usually include influencing enough people to make an organized expenditure of resources worthwhile. Campaigns are usually designed and implemented either by organizations created specifically for the campaign or by an existing institution (Hall, 1978). The expense and effort of a campaign can usually be justified only by a target population of some size. Nevertheless, target populations can range from the few hundred employees of a small business to the entire population of a huge country.

(3) *A campaign has a more or less specifically defined time limit.* The time span for campaigns is demarcated by the period between the initiation of the campaign intervention and the conclusion of evaluation efforts to assess the impacts of the campaign, in other words, by the span of activities in the field. For example, the length of an agricultural development campaign is defined from the launching of the communication effort (the first broadcast message or the first attempts by campaign workers to contact the target population) to the ultimate measurement of the effectiveness of campaign efforts. Some campaigns have ongoing objectives, such as commercial campaigns to sell a product (see Ward, Chapter 21 in this volume). Messages may be changed periodically—

when sales slump, for example—but the sales goal remains. Nevertheless, the introduction of a new message or series of messages is considered to initiate a new campaign.

The beginning or the end of a campaign can become blurred if extensive formative research and planning precede the intervention or if long-term effects on part of the target population are sought. For example, the Stanford Heart Disease Prevention Program (SHDPP) (see Pettegrew & Logan, Chapter 22) was launched in 1971 and is to continue until at least 1989, an 18-year span. Distal effects including long-term life-style changes are sought, and one ultimate goal of the program is to transfer responsibility for continuing conduct of the campaign from the university to local health organizations in the communities of study. This transfer and the ongoing nature of the program, defy specification of any clear conclusion of the campaign. Nevertheless, most communication campaigns last for a specified period, often only a few weeks or several months. In fact, the SHDPP is most accurately a series of related but distinct campaigns (Maccoby & Solomon, 1981).

(4) *A campaign involves an organized set of communication activities.* Usually these are temporarily established to reach an audience for which current channels and institutions are thought to be insufficient for meeting desired goals. Organized activity can be seen in all phases of a campaign, but it is particularly evident in message production and distribution. This is a natural result of the generally linear nature of most campaigns. In most cases, the campaign organization determines the form messages will take, if not their content. It also assumes major responsibility for selecting and creating or coordinating the channels through which the messages will be disseminated. Even campaigns that take an "emancipatory" approach—that is, campaigns that aim to increase grass roots participation (Kidd, 1982; Oepen, 1984)—still involve organizing message design and distribution, albeit from the bottom up rather than from the top down. While the logistics of campaign planning are quite different when working with an advertising agency versus a nonprofessional community environmental group, the success of the campaign will depend in great measure on how effectively coordinated the communication activities are.

To summarize, a minimal definition of "campaign" would have to state that (1) *a campaign intends to generate specific outcomes or effects* (2) *in a relatively large number of individuals,* (3) *usually within a specified period of time* and (4) *through an organized set of communication activities.* Of course this minimal definition of campaign has certain limitations, most notably an implicit linearity and effects orientation, and it is intended only as a framework for the present discussion of the ways in which mass communication campaigns have traditionally been conceptualized and of the ways in which the failures of past campaign efforts might be avoided.

DIMENSIONS OF CAMPAIGN OBJECTIVES AND EFFECTS

The objectives and effects of a campaign can be conceptualized along three dimensions, which should be considered as continua: (1) the level of objective, (2) the locus of the behavior change that is sought, and (3) the locus of the benefit derived from the campaign outcomes (Figure 26.1).

Level of Objective

The vast array of possible objectives and outcomes of a communication campaign can be arranged along a continuum that has three main loci: to inform, to persuade, and to mobilize overt behavior change. Numerous hierarchies of this sort have been proposed including the cognitive/affective/conative hierarchy of communication effects discussed by Ray (1973) in the context of marketing new commercial products; McGuire's (1968) attention/comprehension/yielding/retention/action model; Fishbein and Ajzen's (1975) belief/attitude/intention/behavior model; and the knowledge/persuasion/decision/confirmation stages of the innovation-decision process described by Rogers (1983). Campaigns typically select one level of objective, the lowest of which is to disseminate information to a target population. Higher-level objectives usually involve the prior activation of lower-level objectives, so that an effective smoking-cessation campaign presumably includes components intended to inform cigarette smokers about the consequences of their smoking behavior, to persuade them that they should discontinue smoking, and to mobilize them to stop smoking and to resist starting again (McAllister, 1981, p. 91).

Campaigns that intend to inform an audience usually seek to achieve a range of specific effects such as to increase individual levels of knowledge, to raise awareness of certain consequences, of options, or of support available, or to increase the salience of an idea. Persuasion campaigns might have these same objectives but also seek to generate new attitudes or behaviors or to change existing ones. Mobilization campaigns, at an even higher level of objective, build on the lower levels of communication effects to promote or prevent a particular behavioral change. Specific outcomes may include performance of a new behavior, participation in some group activity, or activation of interpersonal channels of communication. In all these cases overt behavior change is involved.

Not all campaigns with higher-order objectives have the time or financial resources to address the full range of potential prior objectives as well. Campaigns of this sort generally take pains to ensure that the target audience already possesses the prior levels of knowledge or motivation

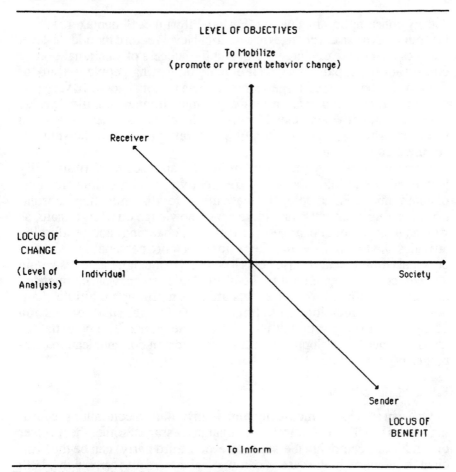

Figure 26.1. Dimensions of campaign objectives and effects.

that enable activation at the level being addressed. This is frequently done by defining the target audience as people who are, in a sense, already prepared for the campaign.

Locus of Change

Campaign effects can be sought at any level of analysis from the intrapersonal to the institutional. Often, individual effects are directly sought in a campaign, but the ultimate locus of intended effect may be broader in scope, ranging from perceptual changes to changes in the structure of a social system. For example, a communication campaign may intend to motivate individuals to use automobile seat belts (Robertson et al., 1974), to discourage smoking by others (Flay, 1985), or to lower the energy consumption in a nation (Farhar-Pilgrim & Shoemaker, 1981). Of course, even small changes at a national level require individual-level changes on a relatively large scale. But the success of a national energy conservation campaign may well depend on getting people to think of their own behaviors in a larger context of the national good. In very significant ways communication campaigns must frequently build a bridge between individual and social levels of objectives, so they provide an ideal opportunity to employ a multiple-level approach to the study of communication behavior.

Campaigns usually involve individual responses to institutionally generated communication. They frequently rely on multiple channels of communication including the mass media for disseminating information, creating awareness, and increasing knowledge on a large scale, as well as interpersonal channels for forming, changing, and reinforcing attitudes and to mobilize overt behavior on a more personal scale. Interpersonal communication also helps to ground campaign messages within a *social* context meaningful to the *individual* members of the intended audience. Multiple levels of effects are sought through multiple channels of communication, including the mass media, small discussion groups, and the activation of interpersonal networks. The potential for interlevel theory development through research on communication campaigns is great but largely unrealized.

Locus of Benefit

One can also locate most campaign efforts along a continuum according to who benefits from effective campaign messages. Either the receiver or sender of a campaign message (or even a third party) can be the principal beneficiary. In the case of commercial advertising campaigns, both sender and receiver might benefit from the consumer information that is conveyed. While the consumer may be able to make a better-informed purchase decision or to save some money, the primary *economic* benefit of effective advertising accrues to the advertiser. In contrast, the main beneficiaries of public health campaign effects are the individual receivers of the health promotion messages. Although work organizations and society may benefit from a higher general level of public health, it is mainly the individual audience members who gain benefits, not the health workers who generate and deliver the messages.

Often, persuasion campaigns can benefit sender or receiver, depending on the message. In social marketing,[2] for example, the emphasis is on a transaction "whereby something of value is exchanged among parties" to the communication activities (Kotler, 1972; Rogers & Flora, 1983). Political campaigns, as another example, usually benefit the candidate who has paid for a promotional advertisement, but voters can also benefit from their increased knowledge of the candidate's background or stand on political issues. A voter registration campaign may be sponsored by a candidate or political party, or by a population group with chronic low turnout, but it presumably benefits the public by virtue of increased citizen participation in the political process. (For descriptions of selected campaigns, see Table 26.2.)

ERAS IN RESEARCH ON CAMPAIGNS

The study of campaigns is one of the oldest traditions of communication research, and it has traditionally focused on linear models of communication and on investigating communication effects. Not surprisingly, campaign research has followed closely the ups-and-downs of alternating pessimism and optimism of the larger field of mass communication research regarding the strength of communication effects.

Era #1: Minimal Effects

The era of minimal effects reached its peak during the 1940s and 1950s in the United States through a series of investigations mounted by communication scientists at the Bureau of Applied Social Research, Columbia University, under the direction of Paul F. Lazarsfeld (see Delia, Chapter 2; McLeod & Blumler, Chapter 9; Schramm, 1985). Lazarsfeld and his colleagues described their research results on the limited effects of mass communication in counterpoint to a "hypodermic needle" model, which would hold that the mass media have direct, immediate, and powerful effects on an audience. Today it is difficult for contemporary scholars to find any statement of the hypodermic needle model by a responsible communication scholar prior to the minimal effects era, or any research that would have justified it. Apparently the Lazarsfeld group set up this ideal model to contrast with their more limited findings.

The prime example of early campaign research was the study by Lazarsfeld and others (1948) on the way voters made up their minds in the presidential election of 1940 in Erie County, Ohio. They found very few people who changed their minds once they had decided how to vote that year, so they concluded that the campaign had not made much difference. They did posit that interpersonal influence was fairly strong, and that media influence worked through opinion leaders who in turn influence other people. This "two-step flow" model was pursued in a study of women's consumer decisions in Decatur, Illinois (Katz & Lazarsfeld, 1955), which focused on personal influence and downplayed evidence of media impact. This research was synthesized by Klapper (1960)

TABLE 26.2
Characteristics and Dimensions of Selected Types of Communication Campaigns

Author	Type and Location of Campaign	Level of Analysis	Specific Outcomes Sought	Time Frame of Campaign Effects
(1) Schramm (1964)	National development (agriculture, health, literacy) in Third World nations	Individuals, groups, society	To inform, change attitudes, and overt behavior.	Short to long
(2) Cell (1977)	Mass mobilization for health, family planning, politics in the People's Republic of China	Social system	Reduce social inequalities, change attitudes, change institutions.	Short to long
(3) Hall (1978)	Public health in Tanzania	Individuals, groups, society	To inform, change attitudes and overt behavior; and to mobilize community action.	Moderate to long
(4) Rogers et al. (1979)	Family planning in Third World nations	Individuals	To inform, change attitudes, and overt behavior.	Short to long
(5) Atkin (1981)	Information in the United States	Individuals	To inform, create awareness, and change attitudes.	Short to long
(6) Chaffee (1981)	Political in the United States	Individuals, interpersonal links, groups	To arouse participation/support and attract voters.	Short to long
(7) Flay & Cook (1981)	Disease prevention in the United States	Individuals	To change issue salience or relevance, to increase audience sensitivity, and to change attitudes and overt behavior.	Moderate to long
(8) Paisley (1981)	Public information in the United States	Individuals	To inform, change attitudes, and overt behavior; to cause aggregate social change	Long
(9) Rogers (1983: pp. 1-5)	Preventive innovations in general	Individuals, interpersonal networks	To create knowledge, form and change attitudes, and overt behavior.	Short to long
(10) McGuire (1984)	Health in the United States	Individuals	To change attitudes and overt behavior.	Long

in a limited effects viewpoint that was interpreted as including all campaigns via mass media.

Two studies that dealt more specifically with campaigns put the stamp on the minimal effects era. One was Hyman and Sheatsley's (1947) synthesis, "Some Reasons Why Information Campaigns Fail." They reviewed survey evaluations from a variety of campaigns designed to increase public affairs knowledge and concluded that "those responsible for information campaigns cannot rely simply on 'increasing the flow' to spread their information directly." They identified a number of psychological barriers as limiting factors on campaign effectiveness, including three selectivity processes: *selective exposure*, the tendency to attend to messages that are consistent with the individual's prior attitudes and experience; *selective perception*, the tendency to interpret a message in terms of prior attitudes and experience; and *selective retention*, the tendency to remember messages that are consistent with prior attitudes and experience. Hyman and Sheatsley referred to the hard-to-reach audience as "chronic know-nothings," terminology that implied a procampaign bias and obvious disappointment with the prospect for communication campaigns.

The other landmark study of campaigns that fail was Star and Hughes's (1950) evaluation of a plan to build support for the United Nations in Cincinnati. The campaign was massive—60,000 pieces of literature distributed, 2,800 organizations addressed by speakers, radio stations airing up to 60 spots a week. It was targeted for groups that were poorly informed about the United Nations, which according to precampaign surveys were women, the elderly, the poor, and the less educated. Six months later, though, the campaign turned out to have reached the wrong audience (men, the younger, and the better educated) and to have had at best minor cognitive effects. For instance, those who knew anything about the main purpose of the United Nations changed from 70 to 72% according to evaluative surveys before and after the campaign.

Star and Hughes (1950) concluded, "Information grows interesting when it is functional, that is, when it is so presented that it is seen to impinge upon one's personal concerns." The campaign slogan, "Peace Begins with the United Nations—and the United Nations Begins with You," illustrates the abstract, general nature of the Cincinnati campaign; the hoped-for increase in knowledge was not tied to any specific behavior that would impinge on the individual's own affairs. A female respondent questioned about the campaign slogan replied, "Why, yes. I heard it over and over again. . . . But I never did find out what it means."

The Cincinnati campaign evaluation helped convince scholars that the mass media were not so powerful as previously hoped or feared.

These campaigns mainly depended upon mass media channels, with relatively little attention to the role of interpersonal networks in campaign effects. Nor were such networks appropriately investigated in the research designs and data-gathering methodologies utilized in the minimal effects era (Sheingold, 1973). Only belatedly was it recognized that the intended audience for a campaign was not just a passive target, waiting to be acted upon by the mass media—a notion reflected in Bauer's (1964) article, "The Obstinate Audience."

One useful product of the media-centered campaigns of the pre-1960s was a set of synthetic generalizations for the conduct of more successful mass campaigns in the future. Cartwright (1949, 1954) proposed several reasons for the disappointing results of media-centered campaigns and suggested a number of ways in which they might be improved, primarily by taking a receiver-centered, psychologically oriented approach. He argued that for campaigns to influence behavior, they had to activate a particular cognitive structure, a particular motivational structure, and a particular behavioral structure that were complementary and oriented toward the same promoted path of action. Cartwright was among the first to explore the complexity of the cognition-motivation-behavior relationship from a campaign perspective.

Era #2: Campaigns *Can* Succeed

The minimal effects era was followed by a period in which it was realized that campaigns could succeed if they were designed and conducted according to certain communication strategies. The key document expressing the central themes of the 1960s and 1970s campaign era is Mendelsohn's (1973) "Some Reasons Why Information Campaigns Can Succeed." The author drew on three successful communication campaign experiences to identify such campaign strategies as the following:

(1) Utilize *formative evaluation*[3] in designing a campaign, so that accumulated communication research-based knowledge is incorporated along with "feedforward" data about the campaign's audience. Such a formative evaluation approach puts communication scientists in league with communication campaign practitioners rather than creating a tension between them, as when communication scholars simply tell practitioners post hoc that their campaign failed. "Most evidence on the failures of information campaigns actually tells us more about flaws in the communicator—the originator of messages—than it does about shortcomings either in the content or in the audience" (Mendelsohn, 1973). The recommendation about formative evaluation by Mendelsohn fit with the increasing attention to formative research by mass communicators following the success of the Children's Television Workshop in producing *Sesame Street* (Palmer, 1981). While *Sesame Street* is not,

strictly speaking, a campaign by our definition, it did provide campaign researchers with valuable insights.

(2) Set *reasonable campaign goals* in light of the fact that few in a campaign audience will change their overt behavior. Such changed behavior is particularly unlikely on the part of subaudiences initially poorly informed about and uninterested in the topic of the campaign.

(3) Use *audience segmentation,* the strategy of dividing a heterogeneous mass audience into relatively homogeneous subaudiences. This strategy allows the design of messages aimed specifically at the particular needs and interests of a subaudience. An analogy is to use a rifle instead of a shotgun. The audience segmentation strategy is emphasized in social marketing (Kotler & Zaltman, 1971) and has long been a tool of the trade in commercial advertising. It is also clearly reflected in the diversity of specialized radio entertainment formats.

(4) Consider the role of *interpersonal channels* including networks triggered by mass media messages in a campaign. Building on the research of Lazarsfeld and others (1948) and Katz and Lazarsfeld (1955) in the Bureau of Applied Social Research tradition as well as on the results of diffusion research on how individuals adopt innovations (Rogers, 1983), campaign planners began to realize that they should utilize both mass and interpersonal channels, with the latter playing the crucial role of changing strongly held attitudes and clinching decisions for overt behavior change.

Overall, the second era of research on communication campaigns recognized that greater likelihood of success could be obtained if campaigns were carried out in a more strategic way. This change called for communication scientists not only to evaluate campaign effects but also to engage in formative evaluation in the early stages of a campaign's design. Thus communication scholars were being called upon to join in campaign planning and conduct rather than just playing the role of independent evaluators at a campaign's conclusion. The general result seemed to be a higher likelihood of campaign success. An illustration is provided by Salcedo and others' (1974) successful campaign concerning pesticide information; by serving as campaign insiders these communication scholars were able to help the campaign reach its objectives while enhancing their summative evaluation procedures through close contact with the campaign.

During the second era of campaign studies, an important change occurred in the conception of campaign failures: Instead of blaming a campaign's audience for not being affected by the campaign, communication scientists began to blame an ineffective campaign on such other factors as the campaign's planners, channels, or messages. In his criticism of Hyman and Sheatsley (1947), Mendelsohn (1973) pointed out that they used "public apathy . . . to describe a non-reaction to information stimuli in terms which suggest that somehow the targets of given messages are at fault for the absence of effect, rather than the creators or the content of the messages, or the media through which they were disseminated." To put it another way, when the communication hypodermic needle fails, is the patient to blame?

Era #3: Moderate Effects

Contemporary campaign research has reached a more balanced view of effects. Increasing attention is being given to investigation of the *intermediate* effects of campaigns, such as status-conferral or agenda setting. As research-based knowledge about communication campaigns accumulates, the trend toward use of behavior-related strategies continues. As in other fields of communication scholarship, researchers are turning toward new models of communication, different research methods, and to alternatives to measures of proximal effects on knowledge, attitude, and behavioral intention. More common these days is a focus on small but overt behavior change and distal consequences of such changes. An example is the SHDPP's attention to long-range decreases in mortality, as a result of shorter-term decreases in heart disease risk factor scores. The ultimate objective is fewer heart disease related deaths, but the campaign focuses on reducing an individual's obesity, level of stress, blood lipid content, and smoking, all of which are factors related to heightened risk of heart disease.

Campaigns still represent an operational equivalent to linear models of communication events. "Linear" refers to the notion that information flows primarily in one direction from people who originate a message to those who receive it. The direction of information flow may change—that is, a former receiver may generate a message directed back to the original message source ("feedback")—but the essential communication act is still unidirectional. Early communication campaigns and many contemporary ones, particularly commercial advertising campaigns, have an explicit linearity. A campaign organization determines what the messages will be and tries to deliver them to a target audience. While some audience response is usually desired by the information source (for example, purchasing behavior or changed attitudes toward a political candidate), there is very little that resembles dialog between the communication participants. Instead, many campaigns closely resemble a monolog by the campaign organization.

Attempts have been made over the years to improve on the linear conception of communication. One result has been a focus on dyads or pairs of communicators as the basic communicative unit rather than on individuals (Rogers & Kincaid, 1981). Such an approach conceptualizes the communication process as a reciprocal act of expression and interpretation or as a process of accommodation between pairs or within networks of communicators. It is quite difficult logistically to build reflexivity into a mass campaign. Instead, most campaigns resort to use of field-workers, extensive formative evaluation, and process evaluation during campaign implementation as ways of increasing audience input. Still, planners must accept the fact that in most campaigns that rely heavily on mass media for message dissemination, information will largely flow in one direction.

In the early eras of communication campaigns there was frequent reliance on mass media alone to accomplish campaign objectives. The shifting conceptualization of communication effects and of the communication process has led to recognition that communication operates within a complex social, political, and economic matrix, and that communication could not be expected to generate effects all by itself. Hornik's (1980) argument that communication could *complement* national development efforts, not necessarily drive them, reflects that thinking. Now more attention is given to the intermediate or indirect effects of communication that may cumulatively contribute to the sorts of major attitude changes or overt behavior changes that earlier campaigns sought and that contemporary campaign planners would still like to generate.

One of the more significant theoretical shifts has been recognition of the potential power of interpersonal network links (perhaps activated by the media) to influence attitudes and behavior. The importance of *multiple* channels of communication in achieving campaign objectives is also recognized. The effect of multiple communication channels is synergistic; changes in the behavior of audience members are greater than the sum of the effects of each separate channel (Rogers et al., 1979). Multiple channels tend to reinforce each other and are each capable of carrying different types of information. In general, mass media channels are more effective if the goal of the communication campaign is to reach and inform large numbers of people. Interpersonal channels serve to reinforce existing attitudes and overt behavior and to motivate behavior change. Bandura (1977; 1986) also points out the potential influence of interpersonal others as a source of behavioral modeling for the individual.

Campaigns are also more likely to be successful now simply because we know more about effective communication. For example, message production and distribution technologies are better than they were in mid-century. Research methodologies have also improved. The basic research design in campaign studies remains the pre/post field experiment (usually without a control) with data gathered by survey interviews. However, recent studies of campaigns supplement such data gathering with unobtrusive measurement; an example is the SHDPP, where grocery store sales are monitored to indicate nutritional change in certain food items, and where the response to particular campaign messages is determined by providing special post office box numbers or telephone numbers from which further information can be requested by audience members.

Although the probability of campaign success may be higher in recent years, many communication campaigns still seem to fail. For example:

• In one of three communities, radio and television ads urging seat belt use were used intensively, only moderately in a second community, and not at all in a third community. No significant change in seat belt use could be attributed to the broadcast advertising campaigns in the 5 weeks of the study (Fleisher, 1972).

• A 9-month safety belt use campaign was conducted on one channel of a dual cable television system. Observations of seat belt use, linked to the households by auto license tag numbers, were no more frequent in the households on the experimental cable than on the control cable or in the community at large. The ads were shown more than 100 times per month, and were directed by content to specific subaudiences, often during prime time, in contrast to most "public service" advertising (Robertson et al., 1974).

• An intensive advertising campaign promoting contraception in several U.S. cities increased awareness of contraceptive issues but failed to generate contraceptive behavior changes (Udry et al., 1974).

But some campaigns successfully combine multiple channels of mass communication with the activation of interpersonal networks, all coordinated with the activities of established institutions to convey well-designed, culturally appropriate messages. In other words, some campaigns manage to put it all together. One of the most striking examples is Tanzania's *Mtu ni Afya* ("Man Is Health") project of 1973. Using a radio study group strategy, the project had these aims: (1) to increase awareness of how health could be improved and to motivate people to take appropriate action to achieve these improvements; (2) to provide information about disease symptoms and preventive measures; and (3) to link the health campaign with a previous literacy campaign, thereby reinforcing reading skills among the newly literate (Hall, 1978).

A comprehensive formative evaluation of the health needs and circumstances of the potential participants in the campaign established a basis for planning. The target population for the Tanzania campaign numbered 1 million people, and 2 million were eventually involved in the campaign. A major effort was made to involve existing organizations and networks of individuals to take advantage of information distribution mechanisms already in place. Rather than aiming just to promote *individual* health behavior change, radio programs were used to promote *community* action. *Mtu ni Afya* was integrated with other development campaigns (especially the national literacy campaign) to take advantage of the existing infrastructure and incipient motivation for change within the target population.

Press releases announced each new phase of the campaign, and newspapers and magazines were used to build interest in it. Textile patterns were designed that incorporated the health campaign symbol and various campaign messages and were worn by Tanzanian women as garments. Small study groups (12 to 15 people) were organized to listen to and discuss weekly half-hour radio broadcasts. These groups were led by 75,000 trained discussion leaders. Each radio program (broadcast twice) included news of campaign progress in various parts of the country, commentary by health experts, and dramatizations of important health problems. Each program emphasized one important health practice (for example, malaria control). Study guides accompanying the radio programs included text and illustrations and were geared to the vocabulary level of the newly literate Tanzanian. And as a way of encouraging behavioral outcomes, each study group was responsible for putting the lessons into action, doing such things as building a latrine, spraying with insecticides, or taking malaria-preventing medicine. The methods used to evaluate campaign effectiveness were in some cases ingenious. Visible public demonstrations of campaign-induced change reinforced the knowledge gains brought about by the radio study groups and also constituted one type of summative evaluation. A year after the *Mtu ni Afya* campaign, an evaluation measured the campaign's effects in part by observing whether grass was growing on village paths leading to the latrines that had been constructed during the campaign.

Overview

The history of campaign research is the story of a mismatch between issues of mass media systems and issues of individual effects. Communication research in the last 25 years has gradually come to recognize the gulf between those two levels of analysis and to try to bridge it with analyses in the middle ground of interpersonal and social network levels of communication activities and effects. The multiple-level theme of this volume is perhaps nowhere as important historically as well as currently as it is in research on communication campaigns.

The earliest era of campaign research was characterized by studies that countered the notion that mass media could directly and consistently affect the behavior of individuals. Research continued to emphasize mass communication following the minimal effects era, but campaigns targeted somewhat smaller audiences, specifically individuals who were thought to be important links in an indirect chain of effects or were otherwise appropriate receivers of campaign messages. Essentially the same types of effects were sought—voting behavior, adoption of innovations, in short, changes in overt, individual behavior—but attempts were made to define more clearly the appropriate audiences to receive specific persuasive messages.

In recent years, communication research has turned more toward *intermediate* effects of communication. Campaign research in the current era, while not rejecting grander objectives such as social change, national development, the improvement of community or national health, or other large-scale aggregate behavior changes, has turned toward analysis of changes at both micro and macro levels that usually precede more distal objectives. But while communication scholars no longer view communication exclusively as a means of changing attitudes and shaping behaviors, many campaigns are still very much persuasion-oriented and still employ for the most part a top-down communication strategy in that they target a mass audience of individuals. The careful use of audience segmentation techniques, for example, is still relatively rare outside of marketing and advertising. Yet campaign research in the past 10 years has begun to recognize a greater diversity of objectives and sequential effects at multiple levels in which the interests promoted are as often those of the receivers of campaign messages as they are of the senders.

All levels of analysis are relevant in campaigns research. In fact, the opportunity for synthetic research bridging levels of analysis is perhaps greater in communication research on campaigns than in any other area. To overlook the fact that it is *individuals* within an organization who plan a campaign can be as misleading as to overlook the *institutional* factors that affect how those individuals approach their task. Similarly, individual cognition is necessarily involved in almost any campaign impact; but those cognitions occur within a matrix of social perceptions, and any behavioral consequences of those cognitive processes will be acted out within, and have an influence on, the framework of social roles, social institutions, and social relationships. Changes in individual behavior may affect not only one's own health but by example may affect the behaviors and subsequent health status of others. Someone who successfully quits smoking can be to acquaintances who still smoke a significant reminder that attitudes toward smoking are changing.

Ultimately, campaign effects occur at the individual level. Aggregated individual behavior change may turn out to be something greater than the sum of its parts but *is* made up of individuals whose attitudes and behaviors change. It is important both that normative attitudes change and that people perceive attitudes to have changed. There is a growing public belief (that is, more and more people express the belief) that smoking is an unacceptable practice. A perception of the norm can be a powerful inducement to change one's own behavior.

Campaigns also involve communication at both interpersonal and social network levels. A number of successful campaigns have specifically tried to stimulate interpersonal contact (e.g., help-seeking or information-seeking) and to activate interpersonal communication networks. Examples include the creation and/or promotion of group activities such as Neighborhood Watch (O'Keefe, 1985; O'Keefe et al., 1984), seminars and group discussions (Adhikarya & Posamentier, 1986), and various kinds of support groups (Farquhar et al., 1985). Network data can be useful in the evaluation of campaigns that are group-minded in their design. For example, the Korean National Family Planning campaign (Rogers & Kincaid, 1981) was organized around the formation of mothers' clubs through which information could be channeled and interpersonal influence and reinforcement could be brought to bear on potential family planning adopters. The Stanford heart project takes advantage of communication network links at the dyadic or clique level through its use of community leaders and support groups to disseminate information and to persuade by example (Kim, 1985).

At the institutional level, campaign research is concerned with the structure and functioning of the communities in which the campaign is conducted, particularly with regard to the accessibility of communication channels and constraints on information flow. Also important, particularly in the evaluation of information programs, are the organizations that plan, implement, and evaluate the campaign. Administrative histories can often reveal much about a message production and delivery system.

At the macro-system level, campaign research seeks to understand how political, economic, and social structures affect the processes and outcomes of campaign efforts (Bordenave, 1976; McAnany, 1980). In some societies, the risks of trying new practices may outweigh potential advantages. Subsistence farmers may be afraid to gamble on a new planting technique when they know that tried and true methods can keep their families from starving, if only barely. Lack of credit may prohibit the purchase of promoted agricultural hardware or supplies such as fertilizer or insecticide, even if one is willing to use them. In many societies unhealthy dietary practices are firmly entrenched and reflected in restaurant menus and aggressive marketing campaigns for "strengthgiving" red meat, "versatile" eggs, and "wholesomely rich" dairy products. In the United States, it took a long time to get seat belts into every car, to put health warnings on tobacco products, and to have ingredients listed on food packaging. Resistance to these protective measures came from manufacturers who wished to avoid the added expense and possible loss of sales.

Legislation is one way to change such economic structures, and campaigns that seek to affect individual attitudes or behaviors may also need to create an environment in which change is valued or at least possible. One strategy is to include system-level enabling change as a campaign objective. Mobilizing public support and pressure for an anti-public smoking ordinance, or establishing Third World rural credit unions are examples. It should be noted, however, that the macro-system is generally more conservative than the individuals in it, and that in some cases systemic change must accompany if not precede change at other levels.

Successful campaigns such as *Mtu ni Afya* (Hall, 1978), the Mass Media and Health Practices project in Honduras and the Gambia (Applied Communication Technology, 1985a, 1985b), and the SHDPP (Farquhar et al., 1985; Maccoby & Solomon, 1981) have components that involve multiple levels of communication activity. In fact, they frequently take advantage of interactions between levels that occur naturally or can be induced with a thoughtful design. As Chaffee and Berger (Chapter 3) note, there has been little research that has attempted to link theory and research across levels. Communication campaigns provide excellent opportunities to explore interlevel processes and effects.

GENERALIZATIONS FROM CAMPAIGN RESEARCH

Despite many failures, important lessons about successful campaigns have been learned. Here we draw a series of general propositions from the considerable body of communication research that has been conducted on a wide variety of campaigns. Our main focus is on factors that contribute to campaign success.

Generalization #1: Widespread exposure to campaign messages is a necessary ingredient in a communication campaign's effectiveness. Although exposure to campaign messages of a relatively high proportion of the audience certainly does not guarantee a campaign's success, a campaign will usually fail without it. Salcedo and others (1974) concluded that "the first prerequisite of an information campaign is that the message must reach the intended audience. Any hope for effects of the campaign must begin from there." Once wide exposure is reached, then other variables such as the effectiveness of campaign messages enter into the successful campaign equation. Evidence of this point was provided by the Star and Hughes (1950) evaluation of the United Nations campaign; even though considerable exposure occurred, campaign messages do not seem to have been appropriately constructed and the campaign's objective was overly optimistic.

Generalization #2: The mass media can play an important role in creating awareness-knowledge, in stimulating interpersonal communication, and in recruiting individuals to participate in campaign activities. Mass media communication is not a campaign panacea. Some messages communicated through some channels affect some people more than others under some conditions. Many campaigns may not so much fail as fall short of unrealistic objectives, perhaps by delivering their messages to the wrong audience. Strongly held opinions and ingrained behaviors are very difficult to change. In their evaluation of a family planning promotion campaign using national mass media advertising, Udry and others (1974) found that the campaign had substantially increased awareness of family planning in the selected communities of study, but it had only negligible effects on contraceptive use and birth rates. Depending on the effects sought, modest changes in audience behavior are frequently achievable. A health promotion campaign might be considered successful if 5% of the members of a large target audience make long-term changes in their overt health behavior. So one key to successful communication campaigns is the setting of reasonable campaign goals.

Generalization #3: Interpersonal communication through peer networks is very important in leading to and maintaining behavior change. While the mass media may be effective in disseminating information, interpersonal channels are more influential in motivating people to act on that information. Bandura (1977, 1986) argues that much individual behavior change is learned through observing (and modeling) the behavior of others like oneself.[4] The Stanford project tried to activate interpersonal networks through health promoters who acted as opinion leaders, behavioral models, and recruiters of new participants in the heart disease prevention campaign. The influence of lay leaders has been demonstrated in a number of other health-related campaigns, including the North Karelia health education project in Finland (Neittaanmaki et al., 1980; Puska and others, 1981), the *Mtu ni Afya* campaign in Tanzania, and the Isfahan family planning campaign in Iran (Gillespie, 1976).

Furthermore, Farquhar and others (1977), Maccoby and Solomon (1981) and McAlister and others (1980) have all shown that people act on information more readily when appropriate social and environmental support is present. The "Take a Bite Out of Crime" mass media campaign used the strategy of promoting household participation in neighborhood crime prevention groups (Neighborhood Watch) as a necessary precondition to effective mobilization of preventive crime behavior. This campaign's success was enhanced by interpersonal channels carrying information not only about a particular behavior but about its social acceptability and adoption by others. Thus a group approach at the local level is one means for a campaign to utilize interpersonal networks.

Generalization #4: The perceived credibility of a communication source or channel enhances the effectiveness of a communication campaign. Credibility is the degree to which a source or a channel of communication is considered knowledgeable or trustworthy. Peers are more likely to be considered trustworthy than are professionals or experts or others more socially distant from members of a campaign audience, but professionals or those perceived to be in positions of authority are more likely to be considered competent or knowledgeable (Rogers, 1983). In a controversial example, the Nestlé company was criticized for taking advantage of this tendency in Third World advertising campaigns by promoting infant formula (a health-threatening and uneconomical substitute for breast milk) using people dressed as nurses; appearances can be deceiving. Campaign success seems to depend in part on audience perceptions of a match between what the communication source is promoting and that source's motives. For example, commercial sources are often perceived as low in credibility because they are trying to sell a product. This perception is clearly an interlevel issue because audience perceptions of the communicator as well as of the institutional source of a communication may combine to affect the credibility of a particular message.

Generalization #5: Formative evaluation can improve the effectiveness of campaigns by producing messages that are specific to the desired behavior change. Planners of commercial media campaigns have long practiced formative research for message design: (1) market research to determine audience predispositions, and (2) pretesting messages for comprehensibility and response. Only since its successful and highly publicized use in producing *Sesame Street* has formative research been widely applied outside of the advertising industry. In the Bangladesh National Rat Control Campaign (Adhikarya & Posamentier, 1986), extensive pretesting went into the development of campaign materials; some logos were redesigned after tests revealed that people misunderstood campaign posters that showed "sleeping rats." The *Mtu ni Afya* project used formative evaluation to determine the health needs and circumstances of the potential audience in Tanzania, and then designed campaign materials and activities to suit the characteristics of those who would participate, including the newly literate.

Promoted behaviors must not only be targeted to appropriate audiences, but their adoption must be possible and ideally both easy and rewarding. The SHDPP was forced to modify its exercise promotion campaign when it was realized that California winters can be too rainy and jogging paths too muddy for the less than highly motivated runner. Consequently, vigorous walking (to and from work, for example) was promoted as a less constrained but equally effective rainy season exercise. In Honduras and the Gambia, a campaign promoting oral rehydration therapy for infant diarrhea provided instructions for mixing the rehydration solutions that had been carefully designed through formative research to use commonly available measuring containers (soft drink bottles and caps) and solution ingredients (water, sugar, and salt; Mass Media and Health Practices Project, 1981).

Generalization #6: Campaign appeals that are socially distant from the audience member are not effective. The use of patriotic appeals by national government leaders in the promotion of overt behavior change is rarely effective except in cases where the values and attitudes evoked by such appeals run parallel to other salient concerns of the individual. Family planning campaigns centering on patriotic appeals by a prime minister or president have been unsuccessful unless the direct impact of contraceptive practice on individual parents is understood by them. Appeals emphasizing population pressures, national food imports, and strains on the national educational system have little relevance to parents unless the effects of larger family size on their personal quality of life can also be conveyed. Mendelsohn and others (1981) and Baumer and Rosenbaum (1980) emphasize that successful United States campaigns for citizen involvement in crime prevention must relate such behavior to individual beliefs in personal vulnerability to victimization from crime. Similarly, a successful energy conservation campaign must hit audience members close to home, rather than just using statements by a national leader that the energy crisis is the "moral equivalent of war." Again, socially distant campaign appeals can be seen as an interlevel issue in that the goals of a national bureaucracy may not correspond to the personal goals of individual citizens.

Generalization #7: Campaigns promoting prevention are less likely to be successful than those with immediate positive consequences. A *preventive innovation* is a new idea that an individual adopts in order to avoid the possible occurrence of some unwanted event in the future (Rogers, 1983, p. 171). The undesired event may, or may not, occur if the innovation is not adopted. Thus the desired consequences of a preventive innovation are relatively uncertain. Examples of preventive ideas are the use of automobile seat belts, buying insurance, and making preparations for a possible disaster such as an earthquake or hurricane. The nature of preventive ideas means that rewards for their adoption and use are often delayed, uncertain, and weak; the locus of benefit may not be clearly perceived to be oneself. Campaigns promoting preventive ideas are not likely to be successful unless special communication strategies are utilized to reinforce or create a perception of more immediate rewards for adoption (Rogers, 1987). Such rewards might include material or symbolic reinforcement for taking little steps toward the larger, more distal objectives or learning to appreciate intermediate advantages of working toward a longer range objective. For example, having more energy as a result of regular exercise may be more obvious and a source of more immediate gratification than is the reduced risk of heart disease in the long run.

Generalization #8: Audience segmentation strategies can improve campaign effectiveness by targeting specific messages to particular audiences. Audience segmentation involves breaking down a mass audience into a number of subgroups, each one internally homogeneous yet different from each other subgroup (Frank et al., 1972). Like other aspects of the social marketing approach to communication campaigns (Kotler & Zaltman, 1971; Solomon, 1981), audience segmentation by definition improves the likelihood that an appropriate message will reach the intended audience. The alternative campaign strategy equivalent to "dropping messages from airplanes" reduces the control that campaign planners have over where and when their information is delivered. In a classic study that *did* involve dropping campaign messages from airplanes, DeFleur and Larsen (1958) found that saturating a town with leaflets (up to 32 per person were dropped) got the message to a large proportion of the population, but access to the information was limited among several important segments of the desired audience—older people, those with smaller families, and the less mobile.

Also, with audience segmentation campaign workers are more likely to know what to expect from each subaudience and it is easier to build into the campaign design homophily (that is, similarity) between campaign workers and campaign participants, a factor that improves response to the communicated information (Rogers, 1983). In the Isfahan family planning project (Gillespie, 1976) separate promotional strategies were used (1) to persuade national elites and medical professionals, (2) to persuade community opinion leaders, and (3) to approach segments of the population that had been identified as likely adopters of contraceptive practices. Audience segments were identified on the basis of demographic data, surveys that assessed attitudes toward family planning, and demographic media exposure profiles.

When campaign planners do not pay attention to a segmentation strategy, information gaps are likely to be created within the intended audience. An *information gap* is the widening difference in knowledge or other communication effects between the information-rich and the information-poor in an audience, as the result of an information campaign. Those individuals in an audience who are already better-informed about an issue and already have more favorable attitudes toward it, are most likely to be reached by campaign activities. Within any particular segment of the audience, gaps are more likely to close than to widen as a result of the campaign. Consequently, gap widening can be minimized or prevented if the information-poor are identified and then targeted for special campaign efforts.

Generalization #9: Timeliness and accessibility of media and interpersonal messages can contribute to campaign success. It has not always been obvious that people must have access to a particular medium of message delivery. Newspapers and television were the preferred media in most early communication campaigns. Levels of literacy and television ownership patterns, however, were soon discovered to constrain access to campaign information among those subaudiences most in need. Consequently, campaigns in the 1970s began to emphasize technologies such as radio listening groups, posters, or traditional folk media, and to rely more on interpersonal channels as means of overcoming social structural constraints on access to information (McAnany, 1980; Spain et al., 1977). Unless high-priority audience segments are reached by messages in appropriate channels, a campaign is unlikely to be successful.

The timeliness of communication activities can also contribute to the effectiveness of campaigns. Rogers (1983) noted the importance of "cues to action," events at critical times that crystallize favorable attitudes toward a promoted behavior. For example, a woman may be especially likely to adopt a contraceptive practice following a pregnancy scare or an abortion. Campaign planners may be able to create cues to action under some circumstances, such as by providing incentives for adoption of a behavior change. Campaign planners may also take advantage of naturally occurring cues to action. For example, the SHDPP mailed to 100,000 high-risk individuals cardiovascular health promotion materials emblazoned with a red heart logo—on Valentine's Day. Another illustration of timing is the advertising campaign for Miller High Life beer. Market research studies indicated that two-thirds of all beer in the United States is consumed at home between 4:00 p.m. and 8:00 p.m. (Schudson, 1984, p. 56). Hence the Miller High Life campaign theme: "It's Miller Time: When it's time to relax, one beer stands clear; if you've got the time, we've got the beer." Miller ads often featured a sunset, emphasizing the late afternoon hour.

CONCLUSIONS

All communication campaigns are not yet scientifically designed, nor is all research on campaigns conducted using scientific methods. But increasingly rigorous research is being undertaken and increasingly successful campaigns are being built on the foundations of that research. Campaign research has the advantages (and the pitfalls, of course) of being mostly field research. Particularly when it is formative, campaign research frequently employs elements of quasi-experimental design such as pre/post measures, time series analysis, and control groups or control communities.

A survey of the campaigns literature reveals a large body of research tenuously linked by a few general principles but without many overarching generalizations or theories. This lack of theoretical grounding can be attributed partly to the practical nature of most communication campaigns but also the fact that the context of campaigns varies so greatly from one to another. It is precisely this diversity that should stimulate us to look for generalizations in the *relationships* between elements of a campaign rather than just in the elements themselves. Communication campaigns almost invariably involve communication processes at all four levels of analysis—intrapersonal, interpersonal, social network, and institutional. The most successful campaigns appear to be successful because they are able to integrate these processes and produce communication effects across all levels. Communication research that approaches the study of campaigns from an integrated, multilevel perspective takes advantage of the unique opportunities that communication campaigns afford and will be more likely to contribute to the growth of a unified discipline of communication science.

NOTES

1. A *paradigm* is the predominant explanatory model that informs the perspectives and activities of researchers in a field of scientific inquiry (Kuhn, 1970).

2. *Social marketing* is "the design, implementation, and control of programs calculated to influence the acceptability of social ideas and involving considerations of product planning, pricing, communication, distribution, and marketing research" (Kotler & Zaltman, 1971). In other words, social marketing consists of the application of marketing strategies for commercial products to the "marketing" of noncommercial goods and services (for example, good health, better education, mass transportation).

3. *Formative evaluation* is a type of research that is conducted while an activity, process, or system is on-going, in order to improve its effectiveness. In contrast, *summative evaluation* is conducted near the end of an activity, process, or system in order to form judgments about its effectiveness.

4. Similarly, many other models or theories of behavior or attitude change include the notion of social comparison, such as beliefs about the social consequences of behavior (Bandura, 1977), attitudes about normative beliefs (Fishbein & Ajzen, 1975), attributions about observed behaviors (Petty & Cacioppo, 1981), and the strength of interpersonal ties in social networks (Rogers & Kincaid, 1981).

REFERENCES

Applied Communication Technology. (1985a). *The mass media and health practices evaluation in Honduras: Findings from the first two years* (Report to Stanford University and USAID). Menlo Park, CA: Author.

Applied Communication Technology (1985b). *The mass media and health practices evaluation in the Gambia: A report of the major findings* (Report to Stanford University and USAID). Menlo Park, CA: Author.

Adhikarya, R. (1983). *A planned communication support strategy for increasing BAVS' ligation acceptors* (Report to the Bangladesh Association of Voluntary Sterilization). Dhaka, Bangladesh: USAID.

Adhikarya, R., & Posamentier, H. (1986). *Motivating farmers for action: How a strategic multimedia campaign can help.* Frankfurt, West Germany: Deutsche Gesellschaft fur Technische Zusammenarbeit.

Atkin, C. K. (1981). Mass media information campaign effectiveness. In R. E. Rice and W. J. Paisley (Eds.), *Public communication campaigns.* Newbury Park, CA: Sage.

Atkin, C. K. (1979). Research evidence on mass mediated health communication campaigns. In D. Nimmo (Ed.), *Communication yearbook 3*. New Brunswick, NJ: Transaction.

Bandura, A. (1977). *Social learning theory*. Englewood Cliffs, NJ: Prentice-Hall.

Bandura, A. (1986). *Social foundations of thought and action*. Englewood Cliffs, NJ: Prentice-Hall.

Bauer, R. (1964). The obstinate audience: The influence process from the point of view of social communication. *American Psychologist, 19,* 319-328.

Baumer, T. L., & Rosenbaum, D. R. (1980). Measuring fear of crime. Paper presented to the Special Workshop on Research Methodology and Criminal Justice Program Evaluation, Baltimore, MD.

Bordenave, J. D. (1976). Communication of agricultural innovations in Latin America: The need for new models. In E. M. Rogers (Ed.), *Communication and development: Critical perspectives*. Newbury Park, CA: Sage.

Butler-Paisley, M., et al. (1975). *Public communication programs for cancer control*. Stanford: Stanford University, Institute for Communication Research.

Cartwright, D. (1949). Some principles of mass persuasion: Selected findings of research on the sale of United States War Bonds. *Human Relations, 2,* 253-267.

Cartwright, D. (1954). Achieving change in people: Some applications of group dynamics theory. *Human Relations, 4,* 381-392.

Cell, C. P. (1977). *Revolution at work*. New York: Academic Press.

Chaffee, S. H. (1981). Mass media in political campaigns: An expanding role. In R. E. Rice & W. J. Paisley (Eds.), *Public communication campaigns*. Newbury Park, CA: Sage.

Dervin, B., Harlock, S., Atwood, R., & Garzona, C. (1980). The human side of information: An exploration in a health communication context. In D. Nimmo (Ed.), *Communication yearbook 4*. New Brunswick, NJ: Transaction.

Douglas, D. F., Westley, B. H., & Chaffee, S. H. (1970). An information campaign that changed community attitudes. *Journalism Quarterly, 47,* 479-487.

Farhar-Pilgrim, B., & Shoemaker, F. (1981). Campaigns to affect energy behavior. In R. E. Rice & W. J. Paisley (Eds.), *Public communication campaigns*. Newbury Park, CA: Sage.

Farquhar, J. W., Maccoby, N., Wood, P. D., et al. (1977). Community education for Cardiovascular health. *Lancet, 1,* 1192-1195.

Farquhar, J. W., Flora, J. A., Good, L. T. & Fortmann, S. P. (1985). *Integrated comprehensive health promotion programs*. (Monograph prepared for the Kaiser Family Foundation). Stanford: Stanford Center for Research in Disease Prevention.

Fishbein, M., & Ajzen, I. (1975). *Belief, attitude, intention, and behavior: An introduction to theory and research*. Reading, MA: Addison-Wesley.

Flay, B. R. (1986). Mass media and smoking cessation. Paper presented at the Annual Conference of the International Communication Association, Chicago.

Flay, B. R., & Cook, T. D. (1981). Evaluation of mass media prevention campaigns. In R. E. Rice & W. J. Paisley (Eds.), *Public communication campaigns*. Beverly Hills, CA: Sage.

Fleischer, G. A. (1972). *An experiment in the use of broadcast media in highway safety*. Los Angeles: University of Southern California, Department of Industrial and Systems Engineering.

Frank, R. E., Massy, W. J., & Wind, Y. (1972). *Market segmentation*. Englewood Cliffs, NJ: Prentice-Hall.

Gillespie, R. (1976). The Isfahan experiment: Evaluation of a family planning communication campaign. In E. M. Rogers & R. Agarwala-Rogers (Eds.), *Evaluation research on family planning communication*. (Population Communication: Technical Documentation, 4). Paris: UNESCO.

Hall, B. (1978). *Mtu ni afya: Tanzania's health campaign.* Washington, DC: Academy for Educational Development.

Heinzelmann, F. (1987). Means of promoting citizen involvement in the prevention and control of crime. In N. Weinstein (Ed.), *Taking care: Why people take precautions.* New York: Cambridge University Press.

Hornik, R. (1980). Communication as complement in development. *Journal of Communication, 30,* 10-24.

Hornik, R. (1985). Nutrition Education: A State of the Art Review. ACC/SCN State of the Art Series, Nutrition Policy Discussion Paper No. 1. Rome: United Nations.

Hornik, R., Sankar, P., et al. (1986). *Communication for diarrheal disease control: Swaziland program evaluation 1984-1985.* Washington, DC: Academy for Educational Development.

Hyman, H. H., & Sheatsley, P. B. (1974). Some reasons why information campaigns fail. *Public Opinion Quarterly, 11,* 412-423.

Katz, E., & Lazarsfeld, P. F. (1955). *Personal influence: The part played by people in mass communication.* New York: Free Press.

Kidd, R. (1982). *The popular performing arts, non-formal education, and social change in the Third World.* The Hague: Centre for the Study of Education in Developing Countries.

Kidd, R., & Colletta, N. (1980). *Tradition for development: Indigenous structures and folk media in nonformal education* (Reports and Papers from the International Seminar on the Use of Indigenous Social Structures and Traditional Media in Nonformal Education and Development). Berlin: German Foundation for International Development and International Council for Adult Education.

Kim, Y. S. (1985). Opinion leadership in a preventive health campaign. Unpublished doctoral dissertation, Stanford University.

Klapper, J. (1960). *The effects of mass communication.* New York: Free Press.

Kotler, P. (1972). A generic concept of marketing. Journal of Marketing, 36, 46-54.

———& Zaltman, G. (1971). Social marketing: An approach to planned social change. *Journal of Marketing, 35,* 3-12.

Kuhn, T. S. (1970). *The structure of scientific revolutions* (2nd ed.). Chicago: University of Chicago Press.

Lazarsfeld, P. F., Berelson, B., & Gaudet, H. (1948). *The people's choice.* New York: Columbia University Press.

Maccoby, N., & Solomon, D. S. (1981). Heart disease prevention: Community studies. In R. E. Rice & W. J. Paisley (Eds.), *Public communication campaigns.* Newbury Park, CA: Sage.

Mass Media and Health Practices Project. (1981). *Field notes.* Washington, DC: Academy for Educational Development.

Mass Media and Health Practices Project. (1982). *Evaluation plan for the Gambia: Mass media and health practices.* Stanford: Institute for Communication Research, Stanford University.

Mass Media and Health Practices Project. (1983). The mass media and health practices evaluation in Honduras: Findings from the first year. Stanford: Institute for Communication Research, Stanford University.

McAlister, A. (1981). Antismoking campaigns: Progress in developing effective communications. In R. E. Rice & W. J. Paisley (Eds.), *Public communication campaigns.* Newbury Park, CA: Sage.

McAnany, E. G. (Ed.). (1980). *Communication in the rural Third World: The role of information in development.* New York: Praeger.

McGuire, W. J. (1968). The nature of attitudes and attitude change. In G. Lindzey & E. Aronson (Eds.), *Handbook of Social Psychology* (2nd ed., Vol. 3, pp. 136-314.) Reading, MA: Addison-Wesley.

McGuire, W. J. (1984). Public communication as a strategy for inducing health-promoting behavior change. *Preventive Medicine, 13,* 299-319.

McQuail, D. (1983). *Mass communication theory.* Newbury Park, CA: Sage.

Mendelsohn, H. (1973). Some reasons why information campaigns can succeed. *Public Opinion Quarterly, 39,* 50-61.

———& O'Keefe, G. (1981). *Social psychological grounding for effective public communication on behalf of crime prevention.* Paper presented to the American Psychological Association, Los Angeles.

Neittaanmaki, L., Koskela, K., Puska, P., & McAlister, A. (1980). The role of lay workers in community health education: Experiences of the North Karelia project. *Scandinavian Journal of Social Medicine, 8,* 1-7.

Oepen, M. (1984). *Development support communication in community development: The case of the integrated rural development program in Kabupaten Ciamis, West Java.* Bandung, Indonesia: PPLH-Institut Teknologi Bandung.

Oepen, M. (1985). *Development Support Communication By Not For the Rural Poor.* Bandung, Indonesia: PPLH-Institut Teknologi Bandung.

O'Keefe, G. (1985). "Taking a bite out of crime": The impact of a public information campaign. *Communication Research, 12,* 147-178.

O'Keefe, G., Mendelsohn, H., Reid-Nash, K., Henry, E., Rosenzweig, B., & Spetnagel, H. (1984). *Taking a bite out of crime: The impact of a mass media crime prevention campaign.* Washington, DC: National Institute of Justice.

Palmer, E. (1981). Shaping persuasive messages with formative research. In R. E. Rice & W. J. Paisley (Eds.), *Public communication campaigns.* Beverly Hills, CA: Sage.

Paisley, W. J. (1981). Public communication campaigns: The American experience. In R. E. Rice & W. J. Paisley (Eds.), *Public communication campaigns.* Newbury Park, CA: Sage.

Petty, R. E., & Cacioppo, J. T. (1981). *Attitudes and persuasion: Classic and contemporary approaches.* Dubuque, IA: Brown.

Puska, P., et al. (1981a). *The North Karelia project: Evaluation of a comprehensive programme for control of cardiovascular diseases in 1972-1977 in North Karelia, Finland* (WHO Monograph Series). Copenhagen: Public Health in Europe.

Puska, P., et al. (1981b). Television in health promotion: Evaluation of a national programme in Finland. *International Journal of Health Education, 24,* 4.

Ray, M. (1973). Marketing communication and the hierarchy of effects. In P. Clarke (Ed.), *New Models for Communication Research.* Newbury Park, CA: Sage.

Rice, R. E., & Associates. (1984). *The New Media.* Newbury Park, CA: Sage.

Robertson, L. S., Kelley, A. B., O'Neill, B., Wixom, C. W., Eiswirth, R. S., & Hadden, W., Jr., (1974). A controlled study of the effect of television messages on safety belt use. *American Journal of Public Health, 64,* 1071-1080.

Rogers, E. M. (1973). *Communication strategies for family planning.* New York: Free Press.

Rogers, E. M. (Ed.). (1976). *Communication and development: Critical perspectives.* Newbury Park, CA: Sage.

Rogers, E. M. (1983). *Diffusion of innovations.* New York: Free Press.

Rogers, E. M. (1987). The diffusion of innovations perspective. In N. Weinstein (Ed.), *Taking care: Why people take precautions.* New York: Cambridge University Press.

Rogers, E. M., & Flora, J. A. (1983). A revised plan for community organization. Unpublished manuscript, Stanford Heart Disease Prevention Program.

Rogers, E. M., & Kincaid, D. L. (1981). *Communication networks: Toward a new paradigm for research.* New York: Free Press.

Rogers, E. M., Solomon, D. S. & Adhikarya, R. (1979). Further directions for USAID's communication policies in population. Stanford: Stanford University Institute for Communication Research.

Salcedo, R. N., Read, H., Evans, J. F., & Kong, A. C. (1974). A successful information campaign on pesticides. *Journalism Quarterly, 51,* 91-95.

Schramm, W. (1964). *Mass media and national development.* Stanford: Stanford University Press.

Schramm, W. (1985). The beginnings of communication study in the United States. In E. M. Rogers & F. Balle (Eds.), *The media revolution in America and in Western Europe.* Norwood, NJ: Ablex.

Schudson, M. (1984). *Advertising: The uneasy persuasion.* New York: Basic Books.

Sheingold, C. A. (1973). Social networks and voting: The resurrection of a research agenda. *American Sociological Review, 38,* 712-720.

Shils, E., & Janowitz, M. (1975). Cohesion and disintegration in the Wehrmacht in World War II. In E. Shils, *Center and periphery: Essays in macrosociology.* Chicago: University of Chicago Press. (Original work published 1948)

Solomon, D. S. (1981). A social marketing perspective on campaigns. In R. E. Rice & W. J. Paisley (Eds.), *Public communication campaigns.* Newbury Park, CA: Sage.

Spain, P., Jamison, D., & McAnany, E. (Eds.). (1977). *Radio for education and development: Case studies* (Working Paper 266). Washington, DC: World Bank.

Star, S. A., & Hughes, H. G. (1950). Report on an educational campaign: The Cincinnati plan for the United Nations. *American Journal of Sociology, 55,* 389-400.

Udry, J. R., et al. (1974). *The media and family planning.* Cambridge, MA: Ballinger.

27 Cross-Cultural Comparisons

WILLIAM B. GUDYKUNST
Arizona State University

NUMEROUS definitions of culture exist (Kroeber & Kluckhohn, 1952; Schweder & LeVine, 1984), but no consensus definition has emerged within or across disciplines. Culture, for example, can be conceived as everything that is human made (Herskovitts, 1955) or as involving shared meanings (Geertz, 1973). Hall (1959) equates it with communication. Birdwhistell (1970) suggests that "culture and communication are terms which represent two different viewpoints or methods of representation of patterned and structured interconnectedness. As 'culture' the focus is on structure; as 'communication' it is on process" (p. 318).

Keesing's (1974) review of cultural theories concluded that two themes predominate: Culture is an adaptive system, and culture is an ideational system. To overcome dilemmas in both definitions (cognitive reductionism and a vision of the world of cultural symbols as spuriously uniform, respectively), Keesing (1974) borrowed the distinction between "competence" and "performance" from linguistics to explain culture:

> It is his [or her] *theory of what his [or her] fellows know, believe, and mean,* his [or her] theory of the code being followed, the game being played, in the society into which he [or she] was born. . . . It is this theory to which a native actor *refers* in interpreting the unfamiliar or the ambiguous, in interacting with strangers. . . . But note that the actor's "theory" . . . may be in large measure unconscious. Actors follow rules of which they are not consciously aware, and assume a world to be "out there" that they have in fact created with culturally shaped and shaded patterns of mind. . . . Even though no one native actor knows all the culture, and each has a variant version of the code, culture in this view is ordered not simply as a collection of symbols fitted together by the ana-

AUTHOR'S NOTE: The framework proffered in this chapter draws on the work of Harry Triandis. He graciously provided advice on the original outline and a draft of the chapter. Charles Berger, David Johnson, Felipe Korzenny, Tsukasa Nishida, and Stella Ting-Toomey also read an earlier version and made valuable suggestions for improvement. I am grateful to Gert Hofstede for permission to reprint a figure and to Michael Bond for providing numerous sources used in the chapter.

lyst but as a *system of knowledge,* shaped and constrained by the way the human brain acquires, organizes, and processes information and creates "internal models of reality." (p. 89)

Culture focuses on "competence," but sociocultural "performance" also must be studied, according to Keesing. Culture must, therefore, be distinguished from the social system (the behavior of people who share a common culture, including networks of social relations and patterns of social interaction; Geertz, 1973; Parsons, 1951) and society (the population of humans who share a common culture and social system; Parsons, 1951). Rohner (1984) argues that "an individual is a *member* of a society . . . individuals *participate* in social systems . . . and *share* cultures" (p. 132). Given that society, social system, and culture are all interrelated and have an impact upon communication, the focus of this chapter is on the sociocultural system, which is conceived as including all three.

The study of sociocultural systems and communication is not one unified area of research. Figure 27.1 shows two dimensions that differentiate the various areas of inquiry: interactive-comparative and mediated-interpersonal. Quadrant I represents intercultural communication research; that is, interpersonal communication *between* people from different sociocultural systems and/or communication between members of different subsystems (e.g., ethnic or racial groups) within the same sociocultural system. Quadrant II represents cross-cultural communication research; that is, interpersonal communication as in Quadrant I, but research is comparative. Quadrants III and IV differ in that the phenomenon studied is mediated communication. Research in Quadrant III focuses on mediated communication from one sociocultural system to another—research typically labeled international communication. Quadrant IV, in contrast, involves comparisons of media systems across sociocultural systems (comparative mass communication). A review of research in each quadrant is beyond the scope of this chapter. The remainder of the chapter, therefore, is devoted to outlining a theoretical framework for the study of sociocultural variability and communication that is applicable across the four quadrants.[1]

AN ORGANIZING FRAMEWORK

Sechrest (1977) argues that cross-cultural research constitutes "bits and pieces of knowledge that do not fit together in any particular way, that do not form any pattern and that more often than not fall far short of the aim of permitting a causal inference about the influence of culture on behavior and psychological processes" (p. 75). For previous findings to

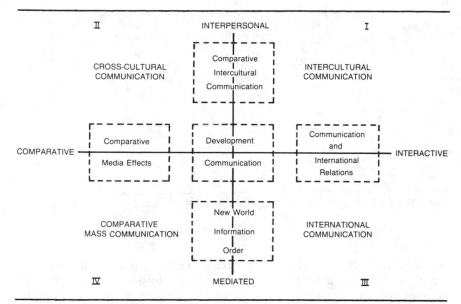

Figure 27.1. Areas of inquiry in the study of sociocultural variability and communication.

be integrated theory is necessary. If theories of communication are to be developed that are not ethnocentric and limited to specific sociocultural contexts, sociocultural variability must be considered. Foschi and Hales (1979) outline the issues involved in treating sociocultural differences as variables in theories: "culture X and culture Y serve to operationally define a characteristic *a*, which the two cultures exhibit to different degrees, and which is usually the independent variable in the study" (p. 246). Sociocultural differences per se, therefore, are not of interest in theory construction; however, treating sociocultural differences as operationalizations of dimensions of sociocultural variation is of interest.

Triandis's (1977, 1980a, 1984) model of behavior provides the starting point for the present framework. In order to create a communication focus, a social cognitive perspective on communication is integrated with his model. The framework depicted in Figure 27.2 is designed to provide a foundation for future research and theorizing.

The major premise underlying the framework is that sociocultural systems interact with the language or languages of a system (see Giles & Wiemann, Chapter 12 in this volume) to influence mediating processes (e.g., situational factors, social cognitive processes, habits) that affect communication processes. Sociocultural systems vary along several definable dimensions (e.g., individualism-collectivism). It is this variance that has an impact on the mediating processes. Sociocultural variability is influenced by two major factors: history and ecology (or

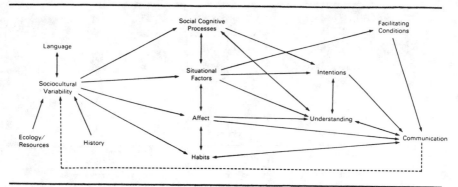

Figure 27.2. A framework for the study of sociocultural variability and communication.

resources). "Ecology refers to the relationship between organisms and the physical environment, including climate, physical terrain, prevailing fauna and flora, and the extent to which resources are limited or plentiful" (Triandis, 1980a, p. 212; see Berry, 1976). Resources include genetic and biological factors that affect particular populations.

The mediating processes affected by sociocultural variability include such social cognitive processes as categorization, patterns of thought, and the implicit theories individuals have regarding the motivational basis of behavior, human personalities, abnormal psychology, social relations, and self-perceptions, as well as affect (emotions and feelings) and habits (schemata, scripts). Sociocultural variability also has a major impact on situational factors; i.e., norms/rules, roles, language use, environmental settings, the difficulties individuals have in communicating with others, and the skills that facilitate effective communication (Argyle, Furnham, & Graham, 1981). The situational factors, social cognitive processes, affect, and habits interact; that is, each influences the other.

Social cognitive processes, situational factors, and affect, in turn, influence intentions and understanding, which reciprocally influence each other. Intentions are instructions individuals give themselves about how to communicate (Triandis, 1977, 1980a). Understanding involves the interpretation of incoming stimuli and the ability to describe, predict, or explain these stimuli, including others' behavior. Understanding, in turn, feeds back and influences social cognitive processes. Communication ultimately is based upon understanding *and* habits, intentions, *or* affect. The link between intentions and communication is influenced by facilitating conditions, the "ability of the person to carry out the act, the person's arousal to carry out the act . . . and the person's knowledge" (Triandis, 1977, p. 10), which are a function of the situation.

DIMENSIONS OF SOCIOCULTURAL VARIABILITY

Sociocultural variability has been studied along the dimensions of syntality (comparable to personality at the cultural level, Cattell & Brennan, 1984), nations (Rummel, 1972), national character (Inkeles & Levinson, 1969), and evolution (Naroll, 1970). These schemas are useful, but their relationship to communication processes has not been articulated.

Kluckhohn and Strodtbeck's Value Orientations

Value orientations are "complex but definitely patterned . . . principles . . . which give order and direction to the ever flowing stream of human acts and thoughts as these relate to the solution of common human problems" (Kluckhohn & Strodtbeck, 1961, p. 4). Kluckhohn and Strodtbeck argue that existential beliefs regarding five problems shared in all sociocultural systems influence concrete choices individuals make in their everyday interactions. First, the innate character of human nature can be assumed to be good, evil, or a mixture of good and evil, and to be mutable or immutable. Second, humans can master, be in harmony with, or be subjugated by nature. Third, the temporal focus of human life is concerned with conceptions of time. The past orientation places a high value on tradition; the present orientation pays relatively little attention to what has gone on in the past and what might happen in the future; and the future orientation highly values change. The fourth problem involves the way human activity is handled. Doing focuses on activities that have outcomes external to the individual, while being involves "a spontaneous expression of what is conceived to be 'given' in the human personality" (Kluckhohn & Strodtbeck, 1961, p. 16) and being-in-becoming is concerned with who humans are, not what they have accomplished. The final problem involves the ways in which humans define their relationships to other humans. Individualism is characterized by autonomy of the individual. Lineality focuses on the continuity of the group through time (the family), with group goals taking precedence over individual goals. Collaterality also focuses on the group, but the laterally extended group.

Parsons's Pattern Variables

Parsons's (1951) analysis of sociocultural variability centers around his concept of "pattern variables." A pattern variable is "a dichotomy, one side of which must be chosen by an actor before the meaning of a situation is determinant for him [or her], and thus before he [or she] can act with respect to that situation" (Parsons & Shils, 1951, p. 77). The *affectivity-affective neutrality* pattern variable is concerned with whether persons look for immediate gratification from the situation at hand (affectivity) or delay gratification into the future (affective neutrality). The *self-collective* pattern variable is similar to Kluckhohn and Strodtbeck's (1961) relational problem, with the lineal and collateral orientations collapsed into the collective orientation. The third pattern variable, *universalism-particularism* is concerned with modes of categorizing people or objects. Categorization of people or objects in terms of some universal or general frame of reference is universalistic, while the categorization of people or objects in specific categories is particularistic. In contrast to universalism-particularism, *diffuseness-specificity* is concerned with how individuals respond to people or objects. Wholistic responses indicate a diffuseness orientation, while a response to a particular aspect of a person or object suggests a specificity orientation. The *ascription-achievement* pattern variable addresses whether people are treated in terms of qualities ascribed to them or in terms of qualities they have achieved. Finally, the nature of goals sought in interactions with others defines the *instrumental-expressive* pattern variable.

Hall's High-Low Context Continuum

Hall (1976) contends that the way messages are encoded and decoded depends upon the context. Sociocultural systems vary in the importance they place upon context in communication. He asserts,

> A high-context (HC) communication or message is one in which most of the information is either in the physical context or internalized in the person, while very little is in the coded, explicit transmitted part of the message. A low-context (LC) communication is just the opposite; i.e., the mass of the message is vested in the explicit code. (p. 79)

Hall argues that high-context communication is a long-lived cohesive force that is slow to change and, therefore, unifies the sociocultural system. Low-context communication, in contrast, does not unify the sociocultural system. Both low- and high-context messages are used in every sociocultural system, but in each system one tends to predominate.

Structural Tightness

Witkin and Berry (1975, p. 11) view tightness as the "degree of hierarchical structure among sociocultural elements in a society." They conclude that tight sociocultural systems display lower levels of differentiation than do loose sociocultural systems. Boldt (1978) argues that role diversity and role relatedness must be distinguished when discussing structural tightness. Boldt and Roberts (1979) contend that role relatedness "bonds are defined by reciprocal role of expectations of individuals in a given social network, expectations which vary in the degree they are either 'imposed and received' or 'proposed and interpreted'" (pp. 225-226). Variation in role relatedness, not role diversity, defines a sociocultural system as relatively tight or loose.

Hofstede's Dimensions of Sociocultural Systems

Hofstede (1979, 1980, 1983) empirically derived four sociocultural dimensions from data gathered in over 40 countries: power distance, uncertainty avoidance, individualism-collectivism, and masculinity-feminity. Power distance involves the degree that power in organizations and institutions is distributed unequally. Uncertainty avoidance involves the lack of tolerance in a sociocultural system "for uncertainty and ambiguity, which expresses itself in higher levels of anxiety and energy release, greater need for formal rules and absolute truth, and less tolerance for people or groups with deviant ideas or behaviours" (Hofstede, 1979, p. 395). The individualism-collectivism dimension is similar to Parsons's (1951) self-collective pattern variable. High individualism emphasizes "I," individual achievement, autonomy, specific friendships, and emotional independence of individuals from the organizations for which they work. Collectivism, in contrast, is reflected in the pattern of values complementary to these. High masculinity, according to Hofstede, involves values on things, money, and assertiveness, while sociocultural systems where people, quality of life, and nurturance prevail are low on masculinity. Scores for the 40 sociocultural systems in Hofstede's (1980) sample are presented in Table 27.1.[2]

To summarize, the schemas of sociocultural variability presented can be used to reinterpret previous studies and suggest directions for future research. While they do not all have the same heuristic value, each of the schemas provide insight into the influence of sociocultural variability on communication processes.

SOCIAL COGNITIVE PROCESSES

"There is no evidence . . . that any [socio]cultural group wholly lacks a basic process such as abstraction, or inferential reasoning, or categorization" (Cole & Scribner, 1974, p. 193). Rather, it appears that sociocultural variations influence which of the alternative processes are evoked in particular situations. The focus of the present analysis is those areas that have been linked to sociocultural variations and that influence communication processes, including social categorization, patterns of thought, and implicit theories.

Social Categorization

Social categorization involves "the ordering of the social environment in terms of groupings of persons in a manner which makes sense to

TABLE 27.1
Values of Hofstede's Four Indices in 40 Countries

Country	PDI	UAI	IDV	MAS
Argentina	49	86	46	56
Australia	36	51	90	61
Austria	11	70	55	79
Belgium	65	94	75	54
Brazil	69	76	38	49
Canada	39	48	80	52
Chile	63	86	23	28
Colombia	67	80	13	64
Denmark	18	23	74	16
Finland	33	59	63	26
France	68	86	71	43
Great Britain	35	35	89	66
Germany (F.R.)	35	65	67	66
Greece	60	112	35	57
Hong Kong	68	29	25	57
India	77	40	48	56
Iran	58	59	41	43
Ireland	28	35	70	68
Israel	13	81	54	47
Italy	50	75	76	70
Japan	54	92	46	95
Mexico	81	82	30	69
Netherlands	38	53	80	14
Norway	31	50	69	8
New Zealand	22	49	79	58
Pakistan	55	70	14	50
Peru	64	87	16	42
Philippines	94	44	32	64
Portugal	63	104	27	31
South Africa	49	49	65	63
Singapore	74	8	20	48
Spain	57	86	51	42
Sweden	31	29	71	5
Switzerland	34	58	68	70
Taiwan	58	69	17	45
Thailand	64	64	20	34
Turkey	66	85	37	45
USA	40	46	91	62
Venezuela	81	76	12	73
Yugoslavia	76	88	27	21
Mean	52	64	50	50
Standard Deviation	20	24	25	20

SOURCE: Hofstede (1980, p. 315; Figure 7.1). Used by permission of the author and publisher. PDI = Power Distance; UAI = Uncertainty Avoidance; IDV = Individualism; MAS = Masculinity.

the individual" (Tajfel, 1978, p. 61)—for example, men and women, or blacks and whites (see Rosch, 1978, for a review of cross-cultural research). Once categories are formed, people have a tendency to exaggerate differences on critical dimensions between categories (i.e., social group memberships) and minimize these differences within categories when category membership is salient (Tajfel, 1981a). One of the the major categorizations individuals employ in all sociocultural systems is that of ingroup or outgroup membership (Brewer & Campbell, 1976).

Triandis's (1985) conceptualization of individualism-collectivism suggests there are sociocultural variations in the number, importance, and influence of ingroups. Individualistic cultures have many ingroups that tend to have narrow spheres of influence, while collectivistic cultures tend to have few (one or two) ingroups that have wide spheres of influence. Collectivistic cultures place emphasis on the goals and needs of the ingroup over those of individuals; the norms of duty toward the ingroup rather than individual pleasure; beliefs shared with the ingroup rather than individual beliefs; and a readiness to cooperate with ingroup members rather than maximizing individual outcomes.

Classifications of others into ingroups and outgroups produce differential attitudes toward the groups involved and discrimination toward the outgroup (Brewer, 1979a). Ingroup bias does not occur to the same extent in all sociocultural systems; for example, European New Zealanders display more ingroup bias than Polynesian New Zealanders (Wetherall, 1982). The difference appears to be related to individualism-collectivism; Europeans are more individualistic and Polynesians more collectivistic. Leung and Bond (1984) similarly found that members of collectivistic systems are more likely to follow the equity norm with outgroup members.

A major factor used by members of one group to categorize others into their ingroup or outgroup is the language or dialect spoken. Giles and Johnson's (1981) extensive review of research led them to these conclusions:

Individuals are more likely to define an encounter with an out-group person in interethnic terms and adopt strategies for positive linguistic distinctiveness when they:
(1) identify with their ethnic group which considers language an important dimension of its identity;
(2) make insecure interethnic comparisons (for example, are aware of cognitive alternatives to their own group's status position);
(3) perceive their in-group to have ethnolinguistic vitality;
(4) perceive their in-group boundaries as hard and closed;
(5) identify strongly with few other social categories;

(6) perceive little overlap with the out-group person in terms of other category memberships;

(7) consider that the social identities derived from other social category memberships are relatively inadequate;

(8) perceive their status within the ethnic group to be higher than their intragroup status in their other social category memberships. (p. 240)

Language spoken is only one dimension used to identify ingroup members. In systems that focus on ascription, for example, characteristics with which individuals are born tend to be used (sex, race, caste, age, family, tribe), while in systems that focus on achievement, individuals' accomplishments tend to be used (education, wealth, ideology, social class, occupation).

When individuals communicate with someone from a different sociocultural system, the relevant ingroups and outgroups are the sociocultural systems themselves. If, however, individuals communicate with members of different systems within their own sociocultural system (e.g., members of different ethnic or racial groups) the relevant ingroups and outgroups are the subsystems. These "forms" of communication often are given such labels as interracial or interethnic communication (see Kim, 1986a; Yu, 1982). When members of one group come into contact with members of another group who are unknown and unfamiliar, outgroup members are not treated as individuals, communication with them is based upon perceived group memberships. Intergroup communication based upon social categorization has been labeled "communicating with strangers" (see Gudykunst, 1985b; Gudykunst & Kim, 1984a).

Patterns of Thought

When knowledge is acquired through direct experience with the environment it is associative. "The codification of thought into precise meanings and well organized lexicons is carried out by abstraction" (Glenn, 1981, p. ii). Associative patterns tend to be diffuse, indefinite, and rigid, while abstract patterns tend to be discrete, articulated, definite, and flexible. Associative versus abstractive thought is related to deriving identity from ascription and achievement in that assessing achievement requires abstraction. It also is related to specificity-diffuseness, with associative thought related to a tendency for diffuse response patterns and abstract thought associated with specific patterns. Triandis (1984) argues that people with associative patterns of information processing depend on oral, face-to-face communication and find it difficult to follow written instructions.

Universalistic thought does not take into consideration experiences that make individuals different; it is abstract. Particularism, in contrast, recognizes specifics; it tends to be associative, reflecting personal lives (Glenn, 1981). Particularistic thought is inductive while universalistic thought is deductive. Universalism and abstraction tend to go together, while particularism and associative patterns of thought also coincide.

Universalism and abstraction are related to an axiomatic-deductive style of persuasion; that is, a style that goes from fundamental principles to their implications (this style predominates in the Soviet Union; Glenn, Witmeyer, & Stevenson, 1977). Particularism and associative thought, in contrast, are related to a factual-inductive style of persuasion; that is, they begin with the relevant facts and draw conclusions from them (used in the United States). Both of these styles involve an affective neutrality orientation (Parsons, 1951) toward persuasion. An affective orientation toward persuasion is related to Glenn et al.'s (1977) affective-intuitive style of persuasion; that is, it uses affective or emotional messages to persuade (used in Arab countries). Ting-Toomey (1985) argues that these styles also are related to Hall's (1976) high-low context continuum. Specifically, factual-inductive or axiomatic-deductive styles predominate in low-context sociocultural systems while the affective-intuitive styles predominate in high-context systems.

Triandis (1984) points out that particularism tends to be probabilistic, while universalism tends to be absolutistic. Wright et al. (1978), Wright, Phillips, and Wishuhda (1983), and Wright and Phillips (1980), for example, found that the British tend to view uncertainty in terms of well-calibrated degrees of probability, while people from Hong Kong, Malaysia, and Indonesia tend to view it dichotomously. Universalistic patterns should dominate in sociocultural systems high in uncertainty avoidance while particularistic patterns predominate in systems low in uncertainty avoidance (Hofstede, 1980).

Differentiation refers to the complexity of a system's structure. "A less differentiated system is a relatively homogeneous structural state; a more differentiated system is a relatively heterogeneous state" (Witkin, Dyk, Faterson, Goodenough, & Karp, 1962, p. 9). As differentiation increases, increased specialization and separation of psychological processes occurs (i.e., cognition is separated from affect and behavior). Thought based on increased differentiation is field independent, while thought based on lower levels of differentiation is field dependent. Field dependence is associated with forming impressions of people based on physical characteristics, conforming to authority, and showing relatively little interest in individual achievement (Witkin et al., 1962). Witkin and Berry (1975) also contend that field dependent people are more personal and more attentive in their dealings with others than are field independent. Field dependent thought tends to be associative while field independent thought tends to be abstractive. Witkin and Berry's (1975) description suggests that field dependence, in contrast to independence, is associated with tight social structure (Boldt, 1978) and high power distance (Hofstede, 1980).

Implicit Theories

Cultures provide individuals with implicit theories about the nature of the social world (Keesing, 1974). Implicit theories are not accessible to individuals' immediate awareness, but are important in their everyday interactions. Wegner and Vallacher (1977) isolate five types of implicit theories that influence behavior: implicit motivation, personality, abnormal psychology, social relations, and self-perception theories.

Implicit motivation theories involve explanations of the underlying causes of regularity in the behaviors of others (i.e., attributional processes). Attribution theory suggests that individuals confronted with others' behaviors attribute the cause of others' behavior to internal characteristics of the other person (i.e., his or her personality) or characteristics external to the individual (e.g., situational factors). However, Hewstone and Jaspars (1982a) contend that "an observer attributes the behavior of an actor, not simply on the basis of individual characteristics, but on the basis of the group or social category to which the actor belongs and to which the observer belongs" (p. 102). Observers tend to underestimate the influence of situational factors in explaining others' behaviors. In intergroup interactions, Pettigrew (1978) claims this is the "ultimate attribution error."

Sociocultural variations also influence the attributes on which individuals focus in making attributions. Bond (1979; Bond & Forgas, 1984), for example, found differences due to collectivism (Hong Kong) and individualism (Australia) in the attributes associated with conscientiousness. Similarly, Miller (1984) found that people in India (collectivistic) make greater reference to contextual factors and less reference to dispositional factors than do people in the United States (individualistic) when explaining others' behavior. Social attributions about people from other sociocultural systems are influenced by intergroup attitudes such as prejudice (Pettigrew, 1978), category width (Detweiler, 1975, 1978), and social representations (Hewstone, Jaspers, & Lalljee, 1982). There is conflicting evidence with respect to ethnocentrism. Taylor and Jaggi (1974) found that ethnocentrism influences attributions Hindus make about Muslims, but Hewstone and Ward (1985) suggest that this may not be a universal tendency.

Bond (1983) contends there is need for future research on sociocultural variability and attributional processes in three areas. First, the frequency with which attributions are made needs to be investigated. Bond suggests there should be variation along Kluckhohn and Strodtbeck's (1961) human-nature orientation, Boldt's (1978) tight versus loose social structure, and individualism-collectivism. Second, what causal categories are used? Finally, the issue of how sociocultural variations influence attributions should be investigated further.

Implicit personality theories determine how information about others is selected, organized, and combined to form a personality impression. Information is selected as a function of observers' cognitive structures and the situation in which the observations occur. As indicated in the preceding section, sociocultural variations influence the attributes to which individuals attune in observing others. People from high-context cultures, for example, focus on factors that give an indication of others' background and social status, while members of low-context cultures focus on individual attitudes, values, and beliefs (Gudykunst, Nishida, Koike, & Shiino, 1986).

Triandis (1977) argues that the situation influences the "weights" given selected factors (i.e., norms or rules, roles) in predicting behavior. Boyanowsky and Allen (1973) found that when whites' behavior toward blacks is known to other whites, responses are different from when the behavior is unknown to others in the ingroup. Such a response is to be expected given the ingroup-outgroup distinction, but sociocultural variation also should be expected. Bond (1983) suggests that collectivism-individualism variations influence the impact of responses that are public or private (i.e., those that are known and unknown to members of the ingroup, respectively). Public responses should be more affected in collectivistic sociocultural systems than in individualistic systems.

Information about others is generated by inferences based on observations. When dealing with a person from a different sociocultural system, there is limited information available and many gaps must be filled and, therefore, numerous inferences are necessary (Koltuv, 1982). Information generated originates in stereotypes that emerge from categorizations of people. The stereotypes individuals hold are related to such intergroup attitudes as prejudice and ethnocentrism (LeVine & Campbell, 1972) and, in turn, have an impact on discriminatory behavior toward members of outgroups (Rubovits & Maehr, 1973). Stereotypes also influence other aspects of the communication process. Drawing on Hewstone and Giles's (1986) analysis, at least four generalizations are warranted: Stereotyping is the result of cognitive biases stemming from illusory correlations between group membership and psychological attributes; stereotypes influence the way information is processed (i.e., more favorable information is remembered about ingroups and more unfavorable information is remembered about outgroups); stereotypes create expectancies about others and individuals try to confirm those expectancies; and stereotypes constrain others' patterns of communication and engender stereotype confirming communication (i.e., they create self-fulfilling prophecies).

Information gathered through stereotypes must be organized. While there is little research on variations across sociocultural systems, studies drawing on Norman's (1963) dimensions of personality structure are applicable. Norman found five dimensions of personality in the United States: extroversion, good-naturedness, conscientiousness, emotional stability, and culture (e.g., good manners, savoir faire). Guthrie and Bennett (1971) conducted comparable research in the Philippines, while Bond, Nakazato, and Shiraishi (1975) and Bond (1979) replicated the study in Japan and Hong Kong, respectively. The first three factors appear to be consistent across sociocultural systems, but the weights of the factors vary. Bond (1979) points out that these factors are associated with Osgood and his associates' (1975) three dimensions of affective meaning: Extroversion is similar to the activity dimension; good-naturedness and emotional stability are related to evaluation; and conscientiousness and "culture" are similar to potency.

Wegner and Vallacher (1977) argue that individuals go to extreme lengths to achieve consistency in combining information about others. Triandis (1968) reviewed several cross-cultural studies of cognitive consistency, concluding,

> People do utilize a number of judgment continua that are related to each other in roughly comparable ways across the cultures studied so far. People from different cultures combine simple stimuli to make complex judgments in roughly similar ways. On the other hand, they do utilize different weights for different characteristics. (p. 729)

Implicit abnormal psychology theories address how individuals evaluate whether someone or something is "good" or "bad." Sociocultural variations in the characteristics associated with good and bad are to be expected. High power distance systems value inequality between people, dependency, hierarchy, blaming the underdog, and mistrusting people who can be a threat. Inequality, for example, would be viewed as "good" or at least neutral in high power distance cultures.

Sources of evaluation include personal characteristics, perceived similarity, and labels. The majority of research on perceived similarity focuses on the similarity-attraction hypothesis. Rokeach and his associates (1960) argue that prejudice and social distance are a function of perceived dissimilarity of beliefs, not ethnic dissimilarity. This hypothesis is supported by cross-cultural data (Brewer, 1968; Murata, 1984; Ting-Toomey, 1981). Triandis (1961; Triandis & Davis, 1965), in contrast, found that ethnic dissimilarity is more important than belief similarity. Also, Triandis and Davis reported that prejudiced subjects are more likely to show race effects than belief effects. Insko, Nacoste, and Moe (1983) argue there is support only for "a weak version of belief congruence theory which states that in those contexts in which social pressure is nonexistent or ineffective, belief is more important than race as a determinant of racial or ethnic discrimination" (p. 153). This finding is consistent with Triandis's (1980a) integration of his own and Rokeach's research.

Implicit social relations theories involve the dimensions people use to evaluate similarities and differences in social relationships. Triandis (1977, 1978) isolated four dimensions of social relations that appear to be "universal" across sociocultural systems (see Lonner, 1980, for research supporting this claim): *association-dissociation* (associative behaviors include being helpful and cooperative); *superordination-subordination* (superordinate behaviors include criticizing, giving orders, etc.); *intimacy-formality* (intimate behaviors include self-disclosure and expressing emotions); and *overt-covert* (overt behaviors are visible to others, covert behaviors are not). The last dimension is closely associated with the loose-tight sociocultural variations; that is, more overt behavior occurs in loose than in tight sociocultural systems (Triandis, 1984).

Foa and Foa (1974) take a different approach to examining universal dimensions of behavior. Using an exchange framework, they argue that resources individuals exchange during interaction can be classified into six groups that are arranged on a clock face: love (12:00), services (2:00), goods (4:00), money (6:00), information (8:00), and status (10:00). These resources vary along two dimensions: particularism—the importance of the individual's (receiver and/or giver) identity in the exchange (runs vertically down the clock's face, with low particularism at 6:00, high at 12:00); and concreteness—the degree the resource has face versus symbolic value (runs horizontally across the clock's face, with low concreteness at 9:00, high at 3:00). Research suggests that the structure is applicable in Greece, Hawaii, India, Israel, and Senegal.

Triandis's dimensions and those isolated by Foa and Foa are related. The exchange of universalistic resources is associated with formal behavior, while exchange of particularistic resources is associated with intimate behaviors (Lonner, 1980). Formal attempts to integrate the two perspectives, however, are just beginning (Adamopolous, 1984). Also, the dimensions of personality structure isolated in the previous section are related to Triandis's dimensions of behavior (Bond, 1979).

An alternative approach to the study of social behavior is presented by Triandis and his associates (1984), who take an individualistic approach to examining sociocultural differences. Rather than using "nomothetic" data, these researchers used "ideothetic" data from 10 individuals with different sociocultural backgrounds. Their data revealed that the correlations across individuals drop as heterogeneity of sociocultural background increases, thereby revealing sociocultural differences.

The research on social relations discussed above is individually or interpersonally based. Intergroup theorists argue that interpersonal theories do not generalize directly to encounters that are mainly intergroup in nature (Gudykunst, 1986a, 1986b; Stehan, 1985). To illustrate, Sherif (1966) asserts that "whenever individuals belonging to one group interact collectively or individually, with another group or its members *in terms of their group identification,* we have an instance of intergroup behavior" (p. 12). Tajfel and Turner (1979) contend that behavior varies along a continuum from purely interpersonal to intergroup. Gudykunst and Lim (1986), however, argue that a single dimension oversimplifies the situation and that both interpersonal and intergroup factors may be salient in the same encounter. Two dimensions, therefore, are needed: low-high intergroup salience and low-high interpersonal salience (see Giles & Wiemann, Chapter 12).

Future research on social relations across sociocultural systems needs to take the salience of both "types" of communication into account. Issues for future research include the following: Does the interpersonal and intergroup salience of initial interactions vary across sociocultural systems? Are intergroup factors more salient in collectivistic than individualistic sociocultural systems? Are interpersonal factors more salient in particularistic than universalistic sociocultural systems? What group memberships affect intercultural communication?

Implicit self-perception theories focus on how the self is conceived. Individuals' self-concepts involve components that originate both within individuals and from memberships in social groups. Turner (1982) argues that "a social group can be defined as two or more individuals who share a common social identification of themselves or . . . perceive themselves to be members of the same social category" (p. 15). Social group membership, therefore, is based on individuals' social identifications. The total of all social identifications individuals use to define themselves is their social identity, part of their self-concept (Tajfel, 1978). Social identity refers to "that *part* of an individual's self-concept which derives from his memberships in a social group (or groups) together with the value and emotional significance attached to that membership" (Tajfel, 1978, p. 63). Zavalloni (1975) differentiates eight components of social identity: sex, nationality, political ideology, family, profession, age, social class, and religion.

Several areas of research are needed in the future. Sociocultural variations in the relative weights given to personal and social identities needs to be investigated. Driver and Driver's (1983) research suggests that there is more emphasis on social identity in collectivistic systems and more emphasis on personal identities in individualistic systems, but Bond and Leung's (1983) research does not reveal consistent findings. Since neither study focus on predicted theoretical variation based on sociocultural variability, future research based on sociocultural variability is necessary.

SITUATIONAL FACTORS

Norms and Rules

Triandis (1978) presents evidence to indicate that reciprocity, equality, and equity are universal norms, but some research (Kahn, Lamm, & Nelson, 1977; Mikula, 1974) reveals that people in the United States are more concerned with equity than are Europeans. Moscovici (1972) contends that the basic tenets of the equity principle are derived from the sociocultural system in the United States. However, the equity norm is applicable in collectivistic Asian systems and suggests that there are differences depending on whether the others involved are members of the ingroup or the outgroup (Leung & Bond, 1982, 1984). These findings are consistent with Triandis's (1985) conceptualization of collectivism.

Cross-cultural replications of Asch's (1956) study of individual reactions to pressures to conform to group norms suggest that similar processes occur across many sociocultural systems (Mann, 1980). Replications in Germany (Timaeus, 1968) and Japan (Frager, 1970) yielded less conformity than in the United States and other sociocultural systems, but the differences were not predicted. Future research is needed to examine conformity as a function of specific dimensions of sociocultural variability. Tight versus loose social structures, for example, should yield differences in conformity, but these differences may be mediated by variations in ingroup-outgroup relations.

Olsen (1978) contends that norms have an ethical or moral connotation that is lacking in rules. Rules, according to Olsen, are developed for reasons of expediency because they allow people to coordinate their activities. Rules vary along four dimensions: level of understanding, rule clarity, rule range, and rule homogeneity or consensus (Cushman & Whiting, 1972). Given Hall's (1976) description of low- and high-context sociocultural systems, it can be argued there is greater need for coordination of activity in high-context systems and, therefore, there should be a correspondingly greater degree of accuracy in the understanding of the rules in high-context systems. Rules may be more specific and have more range in high-context systems. Further, because of the homogeneity of their system, members of high-context systems are more likely to exhibit coordinated activity than are members of low-context systems.

Noesjirwan's (1977, 1978) research in Indonesia and Australia revealed little systematic variation within systems on 69 different rules, while there were many between-system variations in the same rules. To illustrate, dealing with people in waiting rooms and at bus stops differs in Indonesia and Australia. The rule in both situations in Indonesia requires individuals to talk to any other person present. In Australia, in contrast, both situations require individuals to ignore any other person present. These differences may be related to Hofstede's (1980) individualism-collectivism dimension of sociocultural variation. Hofstede (1983) reported that Australia's individualism score is 90 while Indonesia's score is 14. Since the two cultures were not selected because of variation along this dimension, this post hoc explanation needs to be tested in other sociocultural systems.

Argyle, Henderson, Bond, Iizuka, and Contarello (1986) present an alternative approach to the study of rules across sociocultural systems. These researchers examined the applicability of 33 general rules in 22 different relationships in four systems: England, Italy, Japan, and Hong Kong. Their research reveals that all relationships have rules; certain rules are endorsed highly for each relationship in each system; one rule, respecting privacy, applied to all relationships in each system; reward and control rules are found in each system, but there is variation across systems; the relationships cluster similarly across systems; and differences were observed along Hofstede's (1980) individualism dimension, though findings for the other dimensions did not support Hofstede's predictions.

Role Systems

Four interrelated dimensions of role relationships that differ across sociocultural systems can be isolated: the degree of personalness of the relationship, the degree of formality expected in the participants' behavior, the degree of hierarchy present in the relationship, and the degree of deviation allowed from the "ideal" role enactment (Gudykunst & Kim, 1984a). Research to date has not tied variations in role behavior to specific variations in sociocultural systems, but differences along the four dimensions appear to be related to the sociocultural variations elaborated earlier. Expectations of impersonalness stem from a specificity orientation, the tendency to respond to specific aspects of others (i.e., the role). Expectations of personalness, in contrast, stem from a diffuseness orientation, the tendency to respond to others as whole persons. This prediction appears to be supported by Cohen's (1969) findings that abstract and analytic thought are related to specialized roles, while associative and relational thought are related to nonspecialized roles. Higher power distance should produce higher formality, and more formality is expected in high-context than low-context systems. Finally, more deviation should be allowed in loose social structures than in tight structures.

Role systems in organizations. Barrett and Bass (1970) categorized cross-cultural studies of organizational processes into three schools of thought (for an alternative perspective, see Lammers, 1978). The universal school of thought assumes that major differences in managerial style do not exist across cultures (Koontz, 1969). The economic cluster school, in contrast, sees managerial style as the product of the sociocultural systems' industrial and economic development (Kerr, Dunlop, Harbison, & Meyers, 1964), while the cultural cluster school argues that it is culture that explains managerial style (Ajiferuke & Boddewyn, 1970; see Schoelhammer, 1969, for a critique).

Attitudes toward participative management have been studied widely (Drenth et al., 1979; Schaupp, 1978). Research also has been conducted on employee motivation/needs (Haire, Giselli, & Porter, 1966), job satisfaction (Simonetti & Weitz, 1972), hierarchy (Tannenbaum, Karvic, Rossner, Vianello, & Weiser, 1974), and managerial values (England, Neghandi, & Wilpert, 1979), to name only a few areas of research (see Gudykunst, Stewart, & Ting-Toomey, 1985; Tannenbaum, 1980 for reviews). While cultural differences have been isolated, these differences generally have not been linked to theory or sociocultural variations (Roberts, 1970), with the exception of Hofstede's (1980) analysis and the analysis by Koike, Gudykunst, Stewart, Ting-Toomey, & Nishida (1986) of Japanese organizations. Future studies and meta-analyses of cross-cultural research on organizational roles need to select sociocultural systems that are theoretically predicted to differ because of sociocultural variations, rather than selecting systems because of their availability.

Communication networks. There is extensive research on networks in various sociocultural systems; however, few studies have compared the structure of networks across systems. Early kinship studies by anthropologists (Evans-Pritchard, 1940) can be considered network analyses even though the term "network" was not used (Foster, 1979). More recently, comparisons of networks across ethnic groups have begun; for example, Garrison (1978) compared Puerto Rican and black networks, and Yum (1983) examined the network structure of ethnic groups in Hawaii. Communication networks also are a focus of much of the research on the diffusion of innovations and social change (Rogers & Kincaid, 1981). They also play a major role in the study of rural-urban migration (Mayer, 1961) and acculturation of immigrants (Kim, 1977b, 1978; Yum, 1982).

Blau and Schwartz (1984) argue that multiple group memberships exert "structural constraints to establish intergroup relations, for multiple intersection implies that many in-group associations in any one dimension involve intergroup associations in other dimensions" (p. 15). Two theorems from Blau and Schwartz's macrostructural theory of intergroup relations are applicable here. The first theorem states that as size of the ingroup increases, the likelihood of out-group contact decreases; the second theorem contends that the more heterogeneous the social structure, the more intergroup relations are promoted. Both the size of the ingroup and the heterogeniety of the social structure are influenced by dimensions of sociocultural variability, particularly individualism-collectivism. Research on personal networks further suggests that networks tend to exist within sociocultural groups rather than across groups. This finding is supported by research on black-white communication in the United States (Korte & Milgram, 1970; Lin, Dayton, & Greenwald 1977) and Oriental-Ashkenazi communication in Israel (Wiemann, 1983).

Kim (1986b) argues that the more heterogeneous and the more central outgroup members are, and the greater the tie strengths with outgroup members are in individuals' personal networks, the greater their competence in communicating with strangers. This contention is intuitively appealing, but it has not been tested to date. Other questions that need to be addressed include these: What is the relationship between dimensions of sociocultural variability and network structure? Are network structures similar or different in individualistic and collectivistic systems?

Situations and Language

Situations influence at least two major aspects of language use: language attitudes and code-switching. Ryan, Giles, and Sebastian (1982) isolated two major determinants of language attitudes: standardization of the language and language vitality. In addition, two dimensions (status-stressing/solidarity-stressing and person-centered/group-centered) are used in perceiving situations and evaluating the language used (Giles & Ryan, 1982). Ryan, Hewstone, and Giles (1984) extend this analysis to take into account intergroup dynamics, social attributional processes, and cognitive representations of forces operating in the society.

Scotton and Ury (1977) define code-switching as "the use of two or more linguistic varieties in the same conversation or interaction. . . . The varieties may be anything from genetically unrelated languages to two styles of the same language" (p. 5). Bourhis (1979) isolated three general categories of factors that influence code switching in encounters with strangers: micro-sociolinguistic, social psychological, and macro-sociolinguistic. An individual characteristic of particular interest in encounters with strangers is second language competence (Gardner et al., 1983; and Clement & Kruidenier, 1985). An individual's second language competence and the other's decoding skills account for over one-half of the code switches occurring in a conversation (diSciullo, Van Amerigen, Cedergren, & Pupier, 1976). The major social psychological factor influencing code-switching is speech accommodation (Street and Giles, 1982).

Macrosociolinguistic influences on code-switching stem from structural factors associated with ethnolinguistic vitality. Giles, Bourhis, and Taylor (1977) argue there are three categories of variables influencing ethnolinguistic vitality: status (economic, social, and language status), demographic (group size and its distribution), and institutional support (language use in social institutions). One group's evaluations of code-switching by members of another group is not consistent throughout a conversation. The evaluation of language choice is initially based on situational norms, but is based on interpersonal language accommodation later in conversations (Genese & Bourhis, 1982).

Environmental Setting

The environmental setting in general and the use of space in particular are tied closely to privacy regulation. Privacy is the "selective control of access to the self or to one's group" (Altman, 1975, p. 18). Privacy regulation, therefore, is a mechanism that allows individuals to control their interactions with others. Privacy is regulated through the use of personal space and territoriality, as well as through verbal and nonverbal behaviors. Altman and Chemers (1980a, 1980b) hypothesize that privacy regulation is universal across sociocultural systems. What differs across sociocultural systems is "the particular set of behavioral mechanisms used to regulate privacy . . . [socio-cultural systems] differ in how their members regulate contacts with one another. Some rely heavily on environmental mechanisms, others do not. Some use mixes of verbal and nonverbal behaviors, others use these plus environmental mechanisms" (Altman & Chemers, 1980a, p. 100).

There is extensive comparative research on the use of space, territoriality, and the verbal/nonverbal behaviors used to regulate privacy (Altman & Chemers, 1980a, 1980b). To date, however, this research has not been linked to dimensions of sociocultural variability. Rather, most research is still at the stage of documenting differences across sociocultural systems (LaFrance & Mayo, 1978a). Future research, therefore, needs to link variations in the use of privacy regulation mechanisms to dimensions of sociocultural variability. Do individualistic systems use environmental mechanisms more than collectivistic systems? Do collectivistic systems use psychological mechanisms of privacy regulation more than individualistic systems?

Difficulties and Skills

Research on sojourner adjustment to "foreign" sociocultural systems (see Church, 1982; Kim & Gudykunst, in press, for reviews) has examined the temporal pattern of adjustment (Gullahorn & Gullahorn, 1966), personality types (Cleveland, Mangone, & Adams, 1960), stages through which sojourners pass (e.g., culture shock; Furnham & Bochner, 1986), situational factors (Suddenfield, 1967), interaction with host nationals (Gudykunst, Wiseman, & Hammer, 1977), nature of the sojourn (Lambert, 1966), sojourners' reference groups (Herman & Schield, 1961), intercultural communication competence (Ruben & Kealey, 1979), and the difficulties strangers have in new sociocultural environments (Furnham & Bochner, 1982). In addition to the research on adjustment, extensive research on the communication acculturation of immigrants to new sociocultural environments exists (Kim, 1977a, 1977b, 1978, 1979; Yum, 1982; see also Kim, in press; Kim & Gudykunst, in press). Adjustment (short-term adaptation) and acculturation (long-term adaptation) tend to be treated as unique areas of research. Both, however, involve strangers' adaptation to new sociocultural environments; future work should integrate the two areas into one theoretical perspective. Previous research on intercultural adaptation also has not taken into consideration the strangers' sociocultural background and/or the sociocultural environment to which the strangers are adapting.

Because of strangers' problems in adapting to new sociocultural environments, it often is assumed that intercultural communication is less effective than intracultural communication. However, this is not necessarily the case (Taylor & Simard, 1975). Gudykunst and Kim (1984a) argue there are three components to intercultural effectiveness: cognitive, affective, and behavioral. The cognitive component involves the way information is processed, including such factors as language spoken, knowledge of other systems, category width (Detweiler, 1975), cognitive complexity (Hale, 1980), openness of stereotypes (Harvey et al., 1961), and attitudes, particularly prejudice (Milner, 1981; Van Dijk, 1984) and ethnocentrism (Brewer, 1979b, 1981; Burk, 1976; Lukens, 1978, 1979). The affective component involves the sentiment and emotion attached to the information processed. One aspect of this component examined cross-culturally is empathy (Hwang, Chase, & Kelly, 1980; Lindgran & Marrash, 1970). In a study of Chinese, Chinese-Americans, and Caucasians in the United States, Hwang et al. (1980) found empathy to be the only factor shared by all three groups. The behavioral component of effectiveness involves the ability to enact the proper behaviors. Hammer, Gudykunst, and Wiseman's (1978) research with North Americans revealed three dimensions: the ability to deal with psychological stress, the ability to communicate effectively, and the ability to establish interpersonal relationships. Partial cross-cultural support for these dimensions is provided by Abe and Wiseman's (1983) replication with Japanese.

AFFECT

In Triandis's (1977, 1980a) model of interpersonal behavior, affect is seen as influencing intentions but not behavior directly. Affect can also have a direct impact on behavior and is not always mediated through the cognitive process of forming intentions (Isen, 1984). Affect is important in the study of communication with strangers because a large part of individuals' responses to sociocultural differences is affective, not cognitive. While there is little research on affect in intercultural communication, there is some cross-cultural research (Izard, 1980; Leff, 1977; Scherer, 1984).

The expression of emotions is universal and innate to humans (Izard, 1980). The universality of emotion expression may, however, be limited to "fundamental" or "primary" emotions (interest-excitement, distress-anguish), but some combinations of emotions can be recognized across sociocultural systems. Differences in emotion communication may not be due to the emotions themselves but to attitude toward the emotions (Izard, 1971). Recent research by Scherer and his colleagues (Scherer, 1984; Scherer, Summerfield, & Wallbott, 1983) also indicates there may be consistency across sociocultural systems in antecedents of specific emotions (joy, sadness, fear, and anger) and in reactions to these emotions. Joy, for example, consistently is experienced in relationships with friends in six European cities. Similar patterns emerge for other emotions. Using Hofstede's (1980, 1983) data, only the individualism dimension yields similar scores for the six cities studied. Future research on affect, however, is needed to examine such questions as: Under what conditions does affect influence behavior directly? Do antecedents and reactions to emotions vary as a function of specific sociocultural variations?

HABITS

Habits "are situation-behavior sequences that are or have become automatic, so that they occur without self-instruction. The individual is not usually 'conscious' of these sequences" (Triandis, 1980a, p. 204). Habits, therefore, include schemata, scripts, social episodes, and prototypes (see Casson, 1983, for a discussion of cultural schemata). Unconscious behavior is guided by scripts, which are "a coherent sequence of events expected by the individual, involving him either as a participant or an observer (Abelson, 1976, p. 33). When individuals are first confronted with a situation they consciously seek cues to guide their behavior. Repeated experiences with the same event lessens the need to attune consciously to behavior and scripts or episodes emerge (Langer, 1978).

To date, only one study has examined how perceptions of episodes differ across sociocultural systems (Forgas & Bond, 1985). They found that Chinese in Hong Kong differentiate among episodes based on equal/unequal (Hofstede's power distance) and communal/individual (Hofstede's individualism). Australians also used equal/unequal to differentiate among episodes, but interpretations placed on the dimension were different from those of the Chinese and these differences are consistent with the two cultures' scores on power distance. Future research might examine the question: Do episodes representations differ as a function of specific sociocultural variations intraculturally and interculturally?

The degree of unconsciousness associated with scripted behavior is debatable. Some argue that it is relatively mindless, while others contend it involves higher levels of conscious involvement (Bargh, 1984). Nevertheless, individuals may be more conscious of their behavior when communicating with people from other sociocultural systems than when communicating with someone from their own system (Gudykunst & Kim, 1984a). While this contention is intuitively appealing, no research to date directly addresses this issue. Future research, therefore, should focus on two areas. First, to what extent do members of different sociocultural systems vary in the degree that they utilize scripted behavior? Second, to what extent are there differences in the degree of consciousness displayed in interacting with strangers from the same sociocultural system and those from other systems?

UNDERSTANDING

Understanding involves perceiving meaning, knowing, comprehending, interpreting, and/or obtaining information. Three levels of understanding can be differentiated: description, prediction, and explanation (Berger, Gardner, Parks, Schulman, & Miller, 1976). Description involves delineating what is observed in terms of physical attributes (i.e., to draw a picture in words). Prediction involves knowing what will happen in a particular situation. Explanation involves knowing why something occurred. Understanding, therefore, is the opposite of uncertainty—the inability to make accurate descriptions, predictions, and/or explanations.

Berger (1979) isolates three general strategies individuals use to obtain information about others: passive—strategies that involve unobtrusive observations of others; active—strategies that involve exerting effort to obtain information, but without direct contact with those being observed; and interactive—strategies that involve direct interaction with those about whom information is sought. Observing strangers, either personally or through mass media, is one way of gaining information. The mass media provide most of the information individuals have about strangers for those who do not have contact with other groups (Hartmann & Husband, 1972). Individuals who have little contact also tend to perceive the media's content to be "real" (Greenberg & Reeves, 1976; Murray & Kippax, 1979). The media, therefore, provide individuals with stereotypes that are perceived to be accurate. Stereotypes emerge from secondary sources (e.g., the media) rather than primary sources (e.g., contact), and contact is necessary to decrease stereotyping (Rothbart, Dawes, & Park, 1984).

Information also is obtained through active methods. Hamilton and Bishop (1976), for example, found that whites in an integrated housing area changed their racial attitudes independent of actual interaction with blacks. Change was attributed to indirect methods of collective information about blacks, such as discussion with other whites about blacks in the housing area. When contact takes place with strangers, information is obtained. Accurate information, however, can be obtained only if contact occurs under favorable conditions (i.e., conditions that do not increase prejudice and/or ethnocentrism; see Gudykunst, 1977; Miller & Brewer, 1984; Stephan & Brigham, 1985, for intercultural and intergroup reviews of this research). These conditions include equal status, supporting social climate, intimate rather than casual contact, pleasant or rewarding contact, and the presence of superordinate goals (Amir, 1969). Actual intergroup contact, however, is not likely to meet these "favorable" conditions. In fact, Rose (1981) argues that intergroup contact is a novel form of interaction. Because of its novelty, Thibaut and Kelley (1959) suggest there is greater uncertainty in communicating with strangers than in communicating with people who are familiar. Uncertainty is higher for at least three reasons: linguistic differences, lack of knowledge of socially appropriate actions, and perceived lack of shared similarities (Berger, 1986).

Members of high-context systems are more cautious in initial interactions, make more assumptions about strangers based on their background, and ask more demographic questions than members of low-context systems (Gudykunst, 1983d). Further, members of low-context systems tend to ask more questions about attitudes and feelings and self-disclose more about themselves than do members of high-context systems, while members of high-context systems display more nonverbal affiliative expressiveness and report greater confidence in predicting strangers' behavior based on background information than do members of low-context systems (Gudykunst & Nishida, 1984). It also appears that similar factors (e.g., interpersonal attraction, attitude similarity) contribute to uncertainty reduction processes in developed relationships (acquaintance, friend, and dating relationships) in high-context systems such as Japan and Korea just as much as they contribute in low-context systems such as the United States (Gudykunst, Yang, & Nishida, 1985). However, dimensions of sociocultural variability (power distance, individualism, uncertainty avoidance, and masculinity) influence the perceived intimacy of relationship terms and perceptions of communication behavior associated with those terms (Gudykunst & Nishida, 1986b).

Individuals make more assumptions about others based on their background, prefer to talk less, ask more questions about others' background, see conversations as developing less easily, and have less confidence in predicting strangers' behavior when communicating with someone from another system than when communicating with someone from their own system (Gudykunst, 1983c, 1985a; Gudykunst & Nishida, 1984). Uncertainty reduction processes in intercultural relationships, however, systematically vary as a function of the stage of relationship (Gudykunst, Nishida, & Chua, 1986). Uncertainty reduction about individuals from other cultures is a direct or indirect function of social identity, intergroup comparisons, experience in the other sociocultural system, the degree of cultural similarity, second language competence, intergroup attitudes, sociocultural knowledge, shared communication networks, interpersonal attraction, frequency of communication, the intimacy of the relationship, attitude similarity, and the use of uncertainty reduction strategies (Gudykunst, 1985c). Recent research (Gudykunst, Chua, & Gray, 1987) further indicates that these processes are influenced by interaction between cultural dissimilarity along Hofstede's (1980) four dimensions of sociocultural variability and the stage of relationship development.

Several areas remain to be addressed in the future. What, for example, constitutes uncertainty in different sociocultural systems? Does the nature of uncertainty covary with specific dimensions of sociocultural variability? In low-context systems the focus is on predictability of strangers' behavior, while in high-context systems the focus is on predicting whether strangers will follow the norms/rules of the situation (Gudykunst & Nishida, 1986a). What constitutes uncertainty also should be related to other dimensions, including uncertainty avoidance, individualism, and tight-loose structures. To what extent, for example, is uncertainty in individualistic and collectivistic systems a function of predicting individual behavior? Is the focus in collectivistic systems the same as in individualistic or is it on predicting the degree to which individuals will fit into the group or follow group norms? Do certain situations produce differential amounts of uncertainty across sociocultural systems? How and to what extent does the language spoken (i.e., native versus second language) influence what individuals learn about others? What is the role of the different uncertainty reduction strategies across systems? Are interactive strategies used more in individualistic systems than in collectivistic systems? How is engaging in habitual behavior related to understanding? Does the relationship differ as a function of sociocultural variability?

METHODOLOGICAL ISSUES

Doing research across sociocultural systems involves methodological issues that are unique to this area of study. All of the issues involved in doing cross-cultural and intercultural research cannot be addressed here (see Gudykunst & Kim, 1984b; Lonner & Berry, 1986; Triandis & Berry, 1980); but three major areas can be considered: level of analysis, emic versus etic research, and the issue of equivalence across sociocultural systems.

Level of Analysis

In examining sociocultural variations, researchers must attune to the level of analysis: Is the focus on individuals, organization, or sociocultural systems? If data are collected from individuals in several organizations across sociocultural systems it is possible to compare data for individuals globally across organizations and sociocultural systems, compare within-organization data, compare within-sociocultural system data, compare between-organization data, and compare between-sociocultural system data. If correlational data are being analyzed, the five different correlations are, in all likelihood, not equal. One concern is whether the within-organization correlations are equal across organizations or whether the within-sociocultural system correlations are equal across systems. If these correlations are not equal, useful information is obtained about the organizational and sociocultural system levels.

When correlations at the individual, within-organization, or within-sociocultural system are confused with ecological correlations, the ecological fallacy occurs (Robinson, 1950; Thorndike, 1939). Ecological data can be used to draw conclusions at the organizational or systems level, but care must be taken when drawing conclusions at individual level. Hofstede (1980) points out that cross-cultural researchers also must be careful not to commit the reverse ecological fallacy—that is, create dimensions within sociocultural systems and then use these dimensions to correlate ecological data.

The Emic-Etic Distinction

The distinction between the emic and etic approaches to cross-cultural research can be traced to Pike's (1966) discussion of phonetics (vocal utterances that are universal) and phonemics (culturally specific vocal utterances). The implications of the distinction for cross-cultural research have been discussed widely (Berry, 1969, 1980; Hall, 1985; Jahoda, 1983; Lonner, 1979), with the most succinct summary presented by Berry (1980, pp. 11-12):

Emic approach	*Etic approach*
studies behavior from within the system	studies behavior from a position outside the system
examines only one culture	examines many cultures, comparing them
structure discovered by the analyst	structure created by the analyst
criteria are relative to internal characteristics	criteria are considered absolute or universal

When the concepts tested using the etic method are assumed to exist across sociocultural systems, they are referred to as imposed etics (Berry, 1969) or pseudo-etics (Triandis, Malpass, & Davidson, 1973). Derived etics (Berry, 1969, in contrast, emerge from empirical data—the common features of the concept under examination in the sociocultural systems studied. Triandis (1972) recommends that researchers studying subjective culture utilize combined emic and etic measures. Specifically, attributes of concepts under study should be elicited in all cultures studied and both unique (emic) and common (etic) attributes should be included in the final instrument. Davidson, Jaccard, Triandis, Morales, and Diaz-Guerrero (1976) argue that etic models can be tested using emic operationalizations of variables. Triandis and Marin (1983), however, found that appropriate etic scales provide similar findings of cultural differences as emic scales.

Equivalence

"If comparisons are to be legitimately made across cultural boundaries, it is first necessary to establish equivalence based upon which to make comparisons" (Lonner, 1979, p. 27). Functional equivalence involves the relationship between specific observations and the inferences that are made from the observations. Goldschmidt (1966) argued that activities must have similar functions if they are to be used for purposes of comparison. As Berry (1969) elaborated,

> Functional equivalence of behavior exists when the behavior in question has developed in response to a problem shared by two or more societal/cultural groups, even though the behavior in one society does not appear to be related to its counterpart in another society. Functional equivalence involves equivalence at the macro level. (p. 122)

Conceptual equivalence, in contrast, "focuses upon the presence (or absence) of meanings that *individuals* attach to specific stimuli" (Lonner, 1979, p. 27). Linguistic (or transition) equivalence is similar to conceptual equivalence, but the focus is on the language used in questionnaires, interviews, or instructions used in research. Administration of research instruments in a language of one sociocultural system to people in another system, for whom this language is not the native language or who are not bilingual in the language, yields data that lack equivalence (see Brislin, 1976, for a complete discussion of translation).

Metric equivalence involves establishing that the score levels obtained on an instrument in one sociocultural system are equivalent to score levels obtained in another system. Poortinga (1975a, 1975b) argues that there are at least three alternative interpretations of differences in scores between two cultures: the differences exist and are real; the test measures qualitatively different aspects of the concept; and the test measures quantitatively different aspects of the concept. Without establishing metric equivalence, the second and third explanations cannot be ruled out and are, therefore, rival hypotheses to explain differences between samples.

The final form of equivalence involves the sample studied. Berry (1976) points out that choice of sociocultural systems represents a "quasi-manipulation by selection" of the independent variable. He argues that the sociocultural systems selected do not have to be representative of all systems, but they should represent values of the sociocultural variable under consideration if covariation is to be examined. Stated differently, samples should represent theoretically interesting dimensions of sociocultural variability. The same ideals apply in cross-cultural research as in intracultural research; that is, random samples are desirable. Random samples, however, are an ideal often not met. Most cross-cultural research uses "samples of convenience" rather than randomly selected samples (Brislin & Baumgardner, 1971). Since random sampling is almost impossible in cross-cultural research, steps should be taken to ensure that nonrandom samples lead to good research. Given that samples of convenience are the norm, researchers must demonstrate that samples from different sociocultural systems are equivalent and thereby rule out other explanatory variables (i.e., different sample compositions by education, age, sex, social class, etc.) that may be rival hypotheses to explain significant differences.

CONCLUSION

A framework for conceptualizing how sociocultural variability influences communication processes was proffered and discussed in light of previous cross-cultural and intercultural research. The framework and findings analyzed thereotically integrate sociocultural variability with a social cognitive view of communication. The model can be utilized in developing hypotheses for future studies, as well as reinterpreting previous research in literature reviews and meta-analyses. If it serves as a stimulant for either, the primary goal of this chapter will have been accomplished.

NOTES

1. Areas of research not directly discussed but reviewed elsewhere include the following (reviews and/or representative studies are cited): attitudes and beliefs (Davidson & Thompson, 1980), bargaining (Fisher, 1983; Harnet & Cummings, 1980; Stephenson, 1981), bilingualism (Davey, 1982; Hammers & Blanc, 1982; Lambert, 1967; Segalowitz, 1980), black-white communication (Ickes, 1984; Shuter, 1982), cognition (Enber, 1977; Okonji, 1980; Pick, 1980), communication and change (Schramm & Lerner, 1976), conflict (Glenn, Johnson, Kimmel, & Wedge, 1970; Hewstone & Giles, 1984; Kochman, 1982), cross-cultural psychological research (Brislin, 1983), diffusion of innovations (Roberts, 1983), diplomacy (Cioffi-Revilla, 1979; Fisher, 1979), discourse processes (Gumperz, 1982a, 1982b), foreigner talk (Varonis & Gass, 1985), gestures (Morris, Collett, Marsh, & O'Shaughnessy, 1979), intercultural friendships (Bochner, McCleod, & Lin, 1977), international media appraisal (Johnson, 1983), language development (Bowerman, 1981), minorities and the media (Greenberg, Burgoon, Burgoon, & Korzenny, 1983), new world information order (McBride et al., 1980; McPhail, 1981; Nordenstreng, 1984), nonverbal signals (Diabo, 1980; LaFrance & Mayo, 1976, 1978a, 1978b; Ramsey, 1979; Sussman & Rosenfeld, 1982; Watson, 1970), perception (Deregowski, 1980; Oddou & Mendenhall, 1984), satellite broadcasting (Wigand, 1982), second-language acquisition (Clement & Kruidenier, 1985; Gardner, LaLonde, & Pierson, 1983; Giles & Byrne, 1982), speech norms (McKirnan & Hamayan, 1984a, 1984b), subjective meaning (Szalay & Deese, 1978), tourism (Cohen, 1984), training (Brislin, Cushner, Cherrie, & Yong, 1986; Landis & Brislin, 1983), and values (Spates, 1983; Zavalloni, 1980).

2. Hofstede (1983) presents scores for 10 additional countries and three general regions, but these additions were made using smaller numbers of cases and therefore are omitted here.

REFERENCES

Abe, H., & Wiseman, R. (1983). A cross-cultural confirmation of the dimensions of intercultural effectiveness. *International Journal of Intercultural Relations, 7*, 53-68.

Abelson, R. (1976). Script processing in attitude formation and decision-making. In J. Carroll & T. Payne (Eds.), *Cognition and social behavior.* Hillsdale, NJ: Lawrence Erlbaum.

Adamopoulos, J. (1984). The differentiation of social behavior. *Journal of Cross-Cultural Psychology, 15*, 487-508.

Ajiferuke, M., & Boddewyn, J. (1970). Culture and other explanatory variables in comparative management studies. *Academy of Management Journal, 13*, 153-178.

Alba, R. (1978). Ethnic networks and tolerant attitudes. *Public Opinion Quarterly, 42*, 1-16.

Allen, V., & Wilder, D. (1975). Categorization, belief similarity, and group discrimination. *Journal of Personality and Social Psychology, 32,* 971-977.

Altman, I. (1975). *The environment and social behavior.* Monterey, CA: Brooks/Cole.

Altman, I., & Chemers, M. (1980a). *Culture and environment.* Monterey, CA: Brooks/Cole.

Altman, I., & Chemers, M. (1980b). Cultural aspects of environment-behavior relationships. In H. Triandis & R. Brislin (Eds.), *Handbook of cross-cultural psychology* (Vol. 5). Boston: Allyn & Bacon.

Amir, Y. (1969). The contact hypothesis in ethnic relations. *Psychological Bulletin, 71,* 319-342.

Argyle, M., Furnham, A., & Graham, J. (1981). *Social situations.* Cambridge: Cambridge University Press.

Argyle, M., Henderson, M., Bond, M., Iizuka, Y., & Contarello, A. (1986). Cross-cultural variations in relationship rules. *International Journal of Psychology, 21,* 287-315.

Asch, S. (1956). Studies of independence and conformity. *Psychological Monographs, 70*(9), Whole No. 46.

Bargh, J. (1984). Automatic and conscious processing of social information. In R. Wyler & T. Srull (Eds.), *Handbook of social cognition* (Vol. 3). Hillsdale, NJ: Lawrence Erlbaum.

Barrett, G., & Bass, B. (1970). *Comparative surveys of managerial attitudes and behavior* (Technical Report No. 36). Rochester, NY: University of Rochester, Management Research Center.

Berger, C. R. (1979). Beyond initial interactions: Uncertainty, understanding, and the development of interpersonal relationships. In H. Giles & R. St. Clair (Eds.), *Language and social psychology.* Oxford: Basil Blackwell.

Berger, C. R. (1986). Social cognition and intergroup communication. In W. Gudykunst (Ed.), *Intergroup communication.* London: Edward Arnold.

Berger, C. R., Gardner, R., Parks, M., Schulman, L., & Miller, G. (1976). Interpersonal epistemology and interpersonal understanding. In G. Miller (Ed.), *Explorations in interpersonal communication.* Newbury Park, CA: Sage.

Berger, J., & Zelditch, M. (1985). *Status, rewards, and influence.* San Francisco: Jossey-Bass.

Berry, J. (1969). On cross-cultural comparability. *International Journal of Psychology, 4,* 119-128.

Berry, J. (1976). *Human ecology and cognitive style: Comparative studies in cultural and psychological adaptation.* New York: John Wiley.

Berry, J. (1980). Introduction to methodology. In H. Triandis & J. Berry (Eds.), *Handbook of cross-cultural psychology* (Vol. 2). Boston: Allyn & Bacon.

Birdwhistell, R. (1970). *Kinesics and contexts.* New York: Ballentine.

Blau, P., & Schwartz, J. (1984). *Cross-cutting social circles: Testing a macro theory of intergroup relations.* New York: Academic Press.

Bochner, S., McCleod, B., & Lin, A. (1977). Friendship patterns of overseas students: A functional model. *International Journal of Psychology, 12,* 277-294.

Boldt, E. (1978). Structural tightness and cross-cultural research. *Journal of Cross-Cultural Psychology, 9,* 151-165.

Boldt, E., & Roberts, L. (1979). Structural tightness and social conformity. *Journal of Cross-Cultural Psychology, 10,* 221-230.

Bond, M. (1979). Dimensions of personality used in perceiving peers: Cross-cultural comparisons of Hong Kong, Japanese, American, and Filipino university students. *International Journal of Psychology, 14,* 47-56.

Bond, M. (1983). A proposal for cross-cultural studies of attribution. In M. Hewstone (Ed.), *Attribution theory.* Oxford: Basil Blackwell.

Bond, M., & Cheung, T. (1983). College students' spontaneous self-concept: The effects of culture among respondents in Hong Kong, Japan, and the United States. *Journal of Cross-Cultural Psychology, 14,* 153-171.

Bond, M., & Forgas, J. (1984). Linking person perception to behavior intention across cultures. *Journal of Cross-Cultural Psychology, 15,* 337-353.

Bond, M., Leung, K., & Wan, K. (1982). How does cultural collectivism operate? *Journal of Cross-Cultural Psychology, 13,* 186-200.

Bond, M., Nakazato, H., & Shiraishi, D. (1975). Universality and distinctiveness in dimensions of Japanese person perception. *Journal of Cross-Cultural Psychology, 6,* 346-357.

Bourhis, R. (1979). Language in ethnic interaction. In H. Giles & R. Saint-Jacques (Eds.), *Language and ethnic relations.* Elmsford, NY: Pergamon.

Bowerman, M. (1981). Language development. In H. Triandis & A. Heron (Eds.), *Handbook of cross-cultural psychology* (Vol. 4). Boston: Allyn & Bacon.

Boyanowsky, E., & Allen, V. (1973). In-group norms and self-identity as determinants of discriminatory behavior. *Journal of Personality and Social Psychology, 25,* 408-418.

Brewer, M. (1969). Determinants of social distance among East African tribal groups. *Journal of Personality and Social Psychology, 10,* 279-289.

Brewer, M. (1979a). In-group bias in the minimal group situation. *Psychological Bulletin, 56,* 307-324.

Brewer, M. (1979b). The role of ethnocentrism in intergroup conflict. In W. Austin & S. Worchel (Eds.), *The social psychology of intergroup relations.* Monterey, CA: Brooks/Cole.

Brewer, M. (1981). Ethnocentrism and its role in interpersonal trust. In M. Brewer & B. Collins (Eds.), *Scientific inquiry and the social sciences.* San Francisco: Jossey-Bass.

Brewer, M., & Campbell, D. (1976). *Ethnocentrism and intergroup attitudes.* New York: John Wiley.

Brislin, R. (1976). *Translation: Application and research.* New York: Garner.

Brislin, R. (1983). Cross-cultural research in psychology. *Annual Review of Psychology, 34,* 363-400.

Brislin, R., & Baumgardner, S. (1971). Non-random sampling of individuals in cross-cultural research. *Journal of Cross-Cultural Psychology, 2,* 397-400.

Brislin, R., Cushner, K., Cherrie, C., & Yong, M. (1986). *Intercultural interactions: A practical guide.* Newbury Park, CA: Sage.

Burk, J. (1976). The effects of ethnocentrism on intercultural communication. In F. Casmir (Ed.), *International and intercultural communication annual* (Vol. 3). Annandale, VA: Speech Communication Association.

Casson, R. (1983). Schemata in cognitive anthropology. *Annual Review of Psychology, 12,* 429-462.

Cattell, R., & Brennan, J. (1984). The cultural types of modern nations by two quantitative classification methods. *Sociology and Social Research, 86,* 208-235.

Church, A. (1982). Sojourner adjustment. *Psychological Bulletin, 91,* 540-572.

Cioffi-Revilla, C. (1979). Diplomatic communication theory. *International Interactions, 6,* 209-265.

Clement, R., & Kruidenier, B. (1985). Aptitude, attitude and motivation in second language competency: A test of Clement's model. *Journal of Language and Social Psychology, 4,* 21-37.

Cleveland, H., Mangone, G., & Adams, J. (1960). *The overseas Americans.* New York: McGraw-Hill.

Cohen, E. (1984). The sociology of tourism. *Annual Review of Sociology, 10,* 373-392.

Cohen, R. A. (1969). Conceptual styles, culture conflict and nonverbal tests of intelligence. *American Anthropologist, 71,* 828-856.

Cole, M., & Scribner, S. (1974). *Culture and thought.* New York: John Wiley.

Cushman, D., & Whiting, G. (1972). An approach to communication theory: Toward a consensus on rules. *Journal of Communication, 22,* 217-233.

D'Andrade, R. (1981). The cultural part of cognition. *Cognitive Science, 5,* 179-195.

Davidson, A., Jaccard, J., Triandis, H., Morales, M., & Diaz-Guerrero, R. (1976). Cross-cultural model testing. *International Journal of Psychology, 11,* 1-13.

Davidson, A., & Thomson, E. (1980). Cross-cultural studies of attitudes and beliefs. In H. Triandis & R. Brislin (Eds.), *Handbook of cross-cultural psychology* (Vol. 5). Boston: Allyn & Bacon.

Davey, W. (1982). The bilingual education movement: Critical issues for language planning. In N. Jain (Ed.), *International and intercultural communication annual* (Vol. 6). Annandale, VA: Speech Communication Association.

Deregowski, J. (1980). Perception. In H. Triandis & W. Lonner (Eds.), *Handbook of cross-cultural psychology* (Vol. 3). Boston: Allyn & Bacon.

DeSousa, M. (1982). The cultural impact of American television abroad. In N. Jain (Ed.), *International and intercultural communication annual* (Vol. 6). Annandale, VA: Speech Communication Association.

Detweiler, R. (1975). On inferring the intentions of a person from another culture. *Journal of Personality, 43,* 591-611.

Detweiler, R. (1978). Culture, category width, and attributions. *Journal of Cross-Cultural Psychology, 9,* 259-284.

diSciullo, A., Van Amerigen, A., Cedergren, H., & Pupier, P. (1976). E'tude d'interaction verbale chez des Montrealis d'origine Italienne. *Cashier de Linguistique: La Sociolinguistique arc Quebec, 6,* 127-153.

Drenth, P., Kooperman, P., Rus, V., Odar, M., Heller, F., & Brown, A. (1979). Participative decision-making: A comparative study. *Industrial Relations, 18,* 295-309.

Driver, E., & Driver, A. (1983). Gender, society and self-conceptions. *International Journal of Comparative Sociology, 24,* 200-217.

Enber, C. (1977). Cross-cultural cognitive studies. *Annual Review of Anthropology, 6,* 33-56.

England, G., Negandhi, A., & Wilpert, B. (Eds.). (1979). *Organizational functioning in a cross-cultural perspective.* Kent, OH: Kent State University Press.

Evans-Pritchard, E. (1940). *The nuer.* Oxford: Carledon.

Fisher, G. (1979). *American communication in a global society.* Norwood, NJ: Ablex.

Fisher, G. (1983). *International negotiation.* Chicago: Intercultural Press.

Foa, U., & Foa, E. (1974). *Societal structures of the mind.* Springfield, IL: Charles C Thomas.

Forgas, J. (1982). Episode cognition. In L. Berkowitz (Ed.), *Advances in experimental social psychology* (Vol. 15). New York: Academic Press.

Forgas, J. (Ed.). (1985). *Language and social situations.* New York: Springer-Verlag.

Forgas, J., & Bond, M. (1985). Cultural influences on the perception of interaction episodes. *Personality and Social Psychology Bulletin, 11,* 75-88.

Foschi, M., & Hales, W. (1979). The theoretical role of cross-cultural comparisons in experimental social psychology. In L. Eckensberger, W. Lonner, & Y. Poortinga (Eds.), *Cross-cultural contributions to psychology.* Lisse: Swets & Zeitlinger.

Foster, B. (1979). Formal network studies and the anthropological perspective. *Social Networks, 1,* 241-255.

Frager, R. (1970). Conformity and anti-conformity in Japan. *Journal of Personality and Social Psychology, 15,* 203-210.

Furnham, A., & Bochner, S. (1982). Social difficulty in a foreign culture. In S. Bochner (Ed.), *Cultures in contact.* New York: Pergamon.

Furnham, A., & Bochner, S. (1986). *Culture shock: Psychological reactions to unfamiliar environments.* London: Methuen.

Gardner, R., LaLonde, R., & Pierson, R. (1983). The socio-emotional model of second language acquisition. *Journal of Language and Social Psychology, 2,* 1-15.

Garrison, V. (1978). Support systems of schizophrenic and nonschizophrenic Puerto Rican migrant women in New York City. *Schizophrenic Bulletin, 4,* 591-596.

Geertz, C. (1973). *The interpretation of culture.* New York: Basic Books.

Genesee, F., & Bourhis, R. (1982). The social psychological significance of code switching in cross-cultural communication. *Journal of Language and Social Psychology, 1,* 1-27.

Gergen, K., Morse, S., & Gergen, M. (1980). Behavior exchange in cross-cultural perspective. In H. Triandis & R. Brislin (Eds.), *Handbook of cross-cultural psychology* (Vol. 5). Boston: Allyn & Bacon.

Giles, H., Bourhis, R., & Taylor, D. (1977). Towards a theory of language in ethnic group relations. In H. Giles (Ed.), *Language, ethnicity and intergroup relations.* London: Academic Press.

Giles, H., & Byrne, J. (1982). An intergroup approach to second language acquisition. *Journal of Multilingual and Multicultural Development, 3,* 17-40.

Giles, H., & Hewstone, M. (1982). Cognitive structures, speech, and social situations. *Language Sciences, 4,* 187-219.

Giles, H., & Johnson, P. (1981). The role of language in ethnic group relations. In J. Turner & H. Giles (Eds.), *Intergroup behavior.* Chicago: University of Chicago Press.

Giles, H., & Ryan, E. (1982). Prolegomena for developing a social psychological theory of language attitudes. In E. Ryan & H. Giles (Eds.), *Attitudes toward language variation.* London: Edward Arnold.

Glenn, E. (1981). *Man and mankind.* Norwood, NJ: Ablex.

Glenn, E., Johnson, R., Kimmel, P., & Wedge, B. (1970). A cognitive model to analyze culture conflict in international relations. *Journal of Conflict Resolution, 14,* 35-48.

Glenn, E., Witmeyer, D., & Stevenson, K. (1977). Cultural styles of persuasion. *International Journal of Intercultural Relations, 1,* 52-66.

Goldschmidt, W. (1966). *Comparative functionalism.* Berkeley: University of California Press.

Greenberg, B., Burgoon, M., Burgoon, J., & Korzenny, F. (1983). *Mexican Americans and the mass media.* Norwood, NJ: Ablex.

Greenberg, B., & Reeves, B. (1976). Children and the perceived reality of television. *Journal of Social Issues, 32*(4), 86-97.

Gudykunst, W. (1977). Intercultural contact and attitude change. In N. Jain (Ed.), *International and intercultural communication annual* (Vol. 4). Annandale, VA: Speech Communication Association.

Gudykunst, W. (Ed.). (1983a). *Intercultural communication theory.* Newbury Park, CA: Sage.

Gudykunst, W. (1983b). Theorizing in intercultural communication. In W. Gudykunst (Ed.), *Intercultural communication theory.* Newbury Park, CA: Sage.

Gudykunst, W. (1983c). Similarities and differences in perceptions of initial intracultural and intercultural encounters. *The Southern Speech Communication Journal, 49,* 49-65.

Gudykunst, W. (1983d). Uncertainty reduction and predictability of behavior in low and high context cultures. *Communication Quarterly, 31,* 49-55.

Gudykunst, W. (1985a). The influence of cultural similarity, type of relationship, and self-monitoring on uncertainty reduction processes. *Communication Monographs, 52,* 203-217.

Gudykunst, W. (1985b). Normative power and conflict potential in intergroup relationships. In W. Gudykunst, L. Stewart, & S. Ting-Toomey (Eds.), *Communication, culture, and organizational processes.* Newbury Park, CA: Sage.

Gudykunst, W. (1985c). A model of uncertainty reduction during intercultural encounters. *Journal of Language and Social Psychology, 4,* 79-98.

Gudykunst, W. (1986a). *Intergroup communication.* London: Edward Arnold.

Gudykunst, W. (1986b). Toward a theory of intergroup communication. In W. Gudykunst (Ed.), *Intergroup communication.* London: Edward Arnold.

Gudykunst, W., Chua, E., & Gray, A. (1987). Cultural dissimilarities and uncertainty reduction processes. In M. McLaughlin (Ed.), *Communication yearbook 10.* Newbury Park, CA: Sage.

Gudykunst, W., & Kim, Y. Y. (1984a). *Communicating with strangers.* Reading, MA: Addison-Wesley.

Gudykunst, W., & Kim, Y. Y. (Eds.). (1984b). *Methods for intercultural communication research.* Newbury Park, CA: Sage.

Gudykunst, W., & Lim, T. (1986). A perspective for the study of intergroup communication. In W. Gudykunst (Ed.), *Intergroup communication.* London: Edward Arnold.

Gudykunst, W., & Nishida, T. (1984). Individual and cultural influence on uncertainty reduction. *Communication Monographs, 51,* 23-36.

Gudykunst, W., & Nishida, T. (1986a). Attributional confidence in low and high context cultures. *Human Communication Research, 12,* 525-539.

Gudykunst, W., & Nishida, T. (1986b). The influence of cultural variability on perceptions of communication behavior associated with relationship terms. *Human Communication Research, 13,* 147-166.

Gudykunst, W., Nishida, T., & Chua, E. (1986). Uncertainty reduction processes in Japanese-North American dyads. *Communication Research Reports, 3,* 39-46.

Gudykunst, W., Nishida, T., Koike, H., & Shiino, N. (1986). The influence of language on uncertainty reduction: An exploratory study of Japanese-Japanese and Japanese-North American interactions. In M. McLaughlin (Ed.), *Communication yearbook 9.* Newbury Park, CA: Sage.

Gudykunst, W., Stewart, L., & Ting-Toomey, S. (Eds.). (1985). *Communication, culture and organizational processes.* Newbury Park, CA: Sage.

Gudykunst, W., Wiseman, R., & Hammer, M. (1977). Determinants of sojourners' attitudinal satisfaction. In B. Ruben (Ed.), *Communication yearbook 1.* New Brunswick, NJ: Transaction.

Gudykunst, W., Yang, S., & Nishida, T. (1985). A cross-cultural test of uncertainty reduction theory. *Human Communication Research, 11,* 407-454.

Gullahorn, J. E., & Gullahorn, J. T. (1966). American students abroad. *The Annals of the American Academy of Political and Social Science, 368,* 43-59.

Gumperz, J. (1982a). *Discourse strategies.* London: Cambridge University Press.

Gumperz, J. (Ed.). (1982b). *Language and social identity.* London: Cambridge University Press.

Guthrie, G., & Bennett, A. (1971). Cultural differences in implicit personality theory. *International Journal of Psychology, 6,* 305-312.

Haire, M., Ghiselli, E., & Porter, L. (1966). *Managerial thinking: An international study.* New York: John Wiley.

Hale, C. (1980). Cognitive complexity-simplicity as determinants of communication effectiveness. *Communication Monographs, 47,* 304-311.

Hall, E. P. (1985). The etic-emic distinction. In B. Dervin & M. Voigt (Eds.), *Progress in communication science* (Vol. 7). Norwood, NJ: Ablex.

Hall, E. T. (1959). *The silent language.* Garden City, NY: Doubleday.

Hall, E. T. (1976). *Beyond culture.* Garden City, NY: Doubleday.

Hamilton, D., & Bishop, G. (1976). Attitudinal and behavioral effects of initial integration of white suburban neighborhoods. *Journal of Social Issues, 32*(2), 47-67.

Hammer, M., Gudykunst, W., & Wiseman, R. (1978). Dimensions of intercultural effectiveness. *International Journal of Intercultural Relations, 2*, 382-393.

Hammers, J., & Blanc, M. (1982). Towards a social-psychological model of bilingual development. *Journal of Language and Social Psychology, 1*, 29-49.

Harnet, D., & Cumming, L. (1980). *Bargaining behavior: An international study.* Houston, TX: Dane Publications.

Hartman, P., & Husband, C. (1972). The mass media and racial conflict. In D. McPhail (Ed.), *Sociology of mass communication.* Harmondsworth, England: Penguin.

Harvey, Q., Hunt, D., & Schroder, H. (1961). *Conceptual systems and personality organization.* New York: John Wiley.

Herskovits, M. (1955). *Cultural anthropology.* New York: Knopf.

Herman, S., & Schield, E. (1961). The stranger group in a cross-cultural situation. *Sociometry, 24*, 165-176.

Hewstone, M., & Giles, H. (1984). Intergroup conflict. In A. Gale & A. Chapman (Eds.), *Psychology and social problems.* Chichester, England: John Wiley.

Hewstone, M., & Giles, H. (1986). Stereotypes and intergroup communications. In W. Gudykunst (Ed.), *Intergroup communication.* London: Edward Arnold.

Hewstone, M., & Jaspers, J. (1982a). Intergroup relations and attributional processes. In H. Tajfel (Ed.), *Social identity and intergroup relations.* London: Cambridge University Press.

Hewstone, M., & Jaspers, J. (1982b). Explanations for racial discrimination. *European Journal of Social Psychology, 12*, 1-16.

Hewstone, M., Jaspers, J., & Lalljee, M. (1982). Social representations, social attribution, and social identity. *European Journal of Social Psychology, 12*, 241-269.

Hewstone, M., & Ward, C. (1985). Ethnocentrism and causal attribution in Southeast Asia. *Journal of Personality and Social Psychology, 48*, 614-623.

Hofstede, G. (1979). Value systems in forty countries. In L. Eckensberger, W. Lonner, & Y. Poortinga (Eds.), *Cross-cultural contributions to psychology.* Lesse: Swets & Zeitlinger.

Hofstede, G. (1980). *Culture's consequences.* Newbury Park, CA: Sage.

Hofstede, G. (1983). Dimensions of national cultures in fifty countries and three regions. In J. Deregowski, S. Dzuirawiec, & R. Annis (Eds.), *Expications in cross-cultural psychology.* Lisse: Swets & Zeitlinger.

Hofstede, G., & Bond, M. (1984). Hofstede's culture dimensions: An independent validation using Rokeach's value survey. *Journal of Cross-Cultural Psychology, 15*, 417-433.

Hwang, J., Chase, L., & Kelly, C. (1980). An intercultural examination of communication competence. *Communication, 9*, 70-79.

Ickes, W. (1984). Compositions in black and white: Determinants of interaction in interracial dyads. *Journal of Personality and Social Psychology, 47*, 330-341.

Inkeles, A., & Levinson, D. (1969). National character and sociocultural systems. In G. Lindzey & E. Aronson, (Eds.), *Handbook of social psychology* (2nd ed., Vol 4). Reading, MA: Addison-Wesley.

Insko, C., Nacoste, R., & Moe, J. (1983). Belief congruence and racial discrimination. *European Journal of Social Psychology, 13*, 153-174.

Isen, A. (1984). Toward understanding the role of affect in cognition. In R. Wyler & T. Srull (Eds.), *Handbook of social cognition* (Vol. 3). Hillsdale, NJ: Lawrence Erlbaum.

Izard, C. (1971). *The face of emotion.* New York: Appleton-Century-Crofts.

Izard, C. (1980). Cross-cultural perspectives on emotion and emotion communication. In H. Triandis & W. Lonner (Eds.), *Handbook of cross-cultural psychology* (Vol. 3). Boston: Allyn & Bacon.

Jahoda, G. (1983). The cross-cultural emperor's conceptual clothes: The emic-etic issue revisited. In J. Deregowski, S. Dzuirawiec, & R. Annis (Eds.), *Expications in cross-cultural psychology.* Lisse: Swets & Zeitlinger.

Johnson, J. D. (1983). A test of a model of magazine exposure and appraisal in India. *Communication Monographs, 50,* 148-157.

Kahn, A., Lamm, H., & Nelson, R. (1977). Preferences for an equal or equitable allocation. *Journal of Personality and Social Psychology, 35,* 837-844.

Keesing, R. (1974). Theories of culture. *Annual Review of Anthropology, 3,* 73-97.

Kerr, C., Dunlop, R., Harbison, F., & Meyers, C. (1964). *Industrialism and industrial man* (2nd ed.). New York: Oxford University Press.

Kim, Y. Y. (1977a). Communication patterns of foreign immigrants in the process of acculturation. *Human Communication Research, 41,* 66-76.

Kim, Y. Y. (1977b). Inter-ethnic and intra-ethnic communication. In N. Jain (Ed.), *International and intercultural communication annual* (Vol. 4). Annandale, VA: Speech Communication Association.

Kim, Y. Y. (1978). A communication approach to the acculturation process. *International Journal of Intercultural Relations, 2,* 197-224.

Kim, Y. Y. (1979). Towards an interactive theory of communications acculturation. In D. Nimmo (Ed.), *Communication yearbook 3.* New Brunswick, NJ: Transaction.

Kim, Y. Y. (1986a). *Interethnic communication.* Newbury Park, CA: Sage.

Kim, Y. Y. (1986b). Social networks in intergroup communication. In W. Gudykunst (Ed.), *Intergroup communication.* London: Edward Arnold.

Kim, Y. Y. (in press). *Communication and cross-cultural adaptation.* Clevendon, England: Multilingual Matters.

Kim, Y. Y., & Gudykunst, W. (Eds.). (in press). *Cross-cultural adaptation.* Newbury Park, CA: Sage.

Kluckhohn, F., & Strodtbeck, F. (1961). *Variations in value orientations.* New York: Row, Peterson.

Kochman, T. (1982). *Black and white: Styles in conflict.* Chicago, IL: University of Chicago Press.

Koike, H., Gudykunst, W., Stewart, L., Ting-Toomey, S., & Nishida, T. (1986). *Communication openness, job satisfaction, and length of employment in Japanese organizations.* Paper presented at the International Communication Association convention, Chicago.

Koltuv, B. (1962). Some characteristics of intrajudge trait intercorrelations. *Psychological Monographs, 76*(33), Whole No. 552.

Koontz, H. (1969). A model for analyzing the university and transferability of management. *Academy of Management Journal, 12,* 415-429.

Korte, C., & Milgram, S. (1970). Acquaintance networks between racial groups. *Journal of Personality and Social Psychology, 15,* 101-108.

Kroeber, A., & Kluckhohn, C. (1952). *Culture: A critical review of concepts and definitions.* Cambridge, MA: Peabody Museum.

LaFrance, M., & Mayo, C. (1976). Racial differences in gaze behavior during conversations. *Journal of Personality and Social Psychology, 33,* 547-552.

LaFrance, M., & Mayo, C. (1978a). Cultural aspects of nonverbal communication. *International Journal of Intercultural Relations, 2,* 71-89.

LaFrance, M., & Mayo, C. (1978b). Gaze direction in interracial dyadic communication. *Ethnicity, 5,* 167-173.

Lambert, R. (Ed.). (1966). Americans abroad. *The Annals of the American Academy of Political and Social Science, 368.*

Lambert, W. (1967). The social psychology of bilingualism. *Journal of Social Issues, 23,* 91-109.

Lammers, C. (1978). The comparative sociology of organizations. *Annual Review of Sociology, 4,* 485-510.

Landis, D., & Brislin, R. (Eds.). (1983). *Handbook of intercultural training. Vol. 1: Issues in theory and design. Vol. 2: Issues in training methodology. Vol. 3: Area studies in intercultural training.* Elmsford, NY: Pergamon.

Langer, E. (1978). Rethinking the role of thought in social interaction. In J. Harvey et al. (Eds.), *New directions in attribution research* (Vol. 2). Hillsdale, NJ: Erlbaum.

Leung, K., & Bond, M. (1982). How Chinese and Americans reward task-related contributions. *Psychologia, 25,* 32-39.

Leung, K., & Bond, M. (1984). The impact of cultural collectivism on reward allocation. *Journal of Personality and Social Psychology, 47,* 793-904.

LeVine, R., & Campbell, D. (1972). *Ethnocentrism: Theories of conflict, ethnic attitudes, and group behavior.* New York: John Wiley.

Lin, N., Dayton, P., & Greenwald, P. (1977). The urban communication network and social stratification. In B. Ruben (Ed.), *Communication yearbook 1.* New Brunswick, NJ: Transaction Books.

Lindgren, H., & Marrash, J. (1970). A comparative study of intercultural insight and empathy. *Journal of Social Psychology, 80,* 135-141.

Lonner, W. (1979). Issues in cross-cultural psychology. In A. Marsell, A. Tharp, & T. Cibrowski (Eds.), *Perspectives in cross-cultural psychology.* New York: Academic Press.

Lonner, W. (1980). The search for psychological universals. In H. Triandis & W. Lambert (Eds.), *Handbook of cross-cultural psychology* (Vol. 1). Boston: Allyn & Bacon.

Lonner, W., & Berry, J. (1986). *Field methods in cross-cultural research.* Newbury Park, CA: Sage.

Lukens, J. (1978). Ethnocentric speech. *Ethnic groups, 2,* 35-53.

Lukens, J. (1979). Interethnic conflict and communicative distance. In H. Giles & R. Saint-Jacques (Eds.), *Language and ethnic relations.* Elmsford, NY: Pergamon.

Mahler, I., Greenberg, L., & Hayashi, H. (1981). A comparative study of rules of justice: Japanese versus Americans. *Psychologia, 24,* 1-8.

Malpass, R. S. (1977). Theory and method in cross-cultural psychology. *American Psychologist, 32,* 1069-1079.

Mann, L. (1980). Cross-cultural studies of small groups. In H. Triandis & R. Brislin (Eds.), *Handbook of cross-cultural psychology* (Vol. 5). Boston: Allyn & Bacon.

Marin, G. (1981). Perceiving justice across cultures. *International Journal of Psychology, 16,* 153-159.

Marsella, A. J., DeVos, G., & Hsu, F.L.K. (1985). *Culture and self: Asian and Western perspectives.* London: Tavistock Publications.

Mayer, P. (1961). *Townsmen and tribesmen.* Cape Town: Oxford University Press.

McBride, S., et al. (1980). *Many voices, one world.* Paris: UNESCO.

McKirnan, D. J., & Hamayan, E. (1984a). Speech norms and attitudes toward outgroup members. *Journal of Language and Social Psychology, 3,* 21-30.

McKirnan, D. J., & Hamayan, E. (1984b). Speech norms and perceptions of ethnolinguistic group differences. *European Journal of Social Psychology, 14,* 151-168.

McPhail, T. L. (1981). *Electronic colonialism: The future of international broadcasting and communication.* Newbury Park, CA: Sage.

Mikula, G. (1974). Nationality, performance, and sex as determinants of reward allocation. *Journal of Personality and Social Psychology, 29,* 435-440.

Miller, G. R., & Steinberg, M. (1975). *Between people.* Chicago: Science Research Associates.

Miller, J. G. (1984). Culture and the development of everyday social explanations. *Journal of Personality and Social Psychology, 46,* 961-978.

Miller, N., & Brewer, M. (Eds.). (1984). *Groups in contact: The psychology of deseg-regation.* New York: Academic Press.

Milner, D. (1981). Racial prejudice. In J. Turner & H. Giles (Eds.), *Intergroup behavior.* Chicago: University of Chicago Press.

Morris, D., Collett, P., Marsh, P., & O'Shaughnessy, M. (1979). *Gestures: Their origins and distribution.* New York: Stein & Day.

Moscovici, S. (1972). Society and theory in social psychology. In J. Israel & H. Tajfel (Eds.), *The context of social psychology.* London: Academic Press.

Murata, K. (1984). Formation of interpersonal attraction and causal attribution [in Japanese with English abstract]. *The Japanese Journal of Experimental Social Psychology, 24,* 13-22.

Murray, J. P., & Kippax, S. (1979). From the early window to the late night show: International trends in the study of television's impact on children and adults. In L. Berkowitz (Ed.), *Advances in experimental social psychology* (Vol. 12). New York: Academic Press.

Nakane, C. (1970). *Japanese society.* Berkeley: University of California Press.

Naroll, R. (1970). What have we learned from cross-cultural surveys? *American Anthropologist, 72,* 1227-1288.

Noesjirwan, J. (1977). Contrasting cultural patterns of interpersonal closeness in doctors' waiting rooms in Sydney and Jakarta. *Journal of Cross-Cultural Psychology, 8,* 357-368.

Noesjirwan, J. (1978). A rule-based analysis of cultural differences in social behavior: Indonesia and Australia. *International Journal of Psychology, 13,* 305-316.

Nordenstreng, G. K. (1984). *The mass media declaration of UNESCO.* Norwood, NJ: Ablex.

Norman, W. T. (1963). Toward an adequate taxonomy of personality attributes. *Journal of Abnormal and Social Psychology, 66,* 574-583.

Oddou, G., & Mendenhall, M. (1984). Person perception in cross-cultural settings. *International Journal of Intercultural Relations, 8,* 77-96.

Okonji, M. O. (1980). Cognitive styles across cultures. In N. Warren (Ed.), *Studies in cross-cultural psychology* (Vol. 2). London: Academic Press.

Olsen, M. (1978). *The process of social organization* (2nd ed.). New York: Holt, Rinehart & Winston.

Osgood, C., May, H., & Miron, S. (1975). *Cross-cultural universals of affective meaning.* Urbana: University of Illinois Press.

Parsons, T. (1951). *The social system.* New York: Free Press.

Parsons, T., & Shils, E. (1951). *Toward a general theory of action.* Cambridge, MA: Harvard University Press.

Pelto, P. J. (1968, April). The difference between 'tight' and 'loose' societies. *Transaction, 5,* 37-40.

Peterson, R. A. (1979). Revitalizing the culture concept. *Annual Review of Sociology, 5,* 137-166.

Pettigrew, T. F. (1978). Three issues in ethnicity. In Y. Yinger & S. Cutler (Eds.), *Major social issues.* New York: Free Press.

Philipsen, G. (1975). Speaking 'like a man' in Teamsterville. *Quarterly Journal of Speech, 61,* 13-22.

Pick, A. (1980). Cognition: Psychological perspectives. In H. Triandis & W. Lonner (Eds.), *Handbook of cross-cultural psychology* (Vol. 3). Boston: Allyn & Bacon.

Pike, K. (1966). *Language in relation to a unified theory of the structure of human behavior.* The Hague: Mouton.

Poortinga, Y. H. (1975a). Limitations on intercultural comparisons of psychological data. *Nederlands Tijdschrift voor de Psychologie, 30,* 23-39.

Poortinga, Y. H. (1975b). Some implications of three different approaches to intercultural comparisons. In J. Berry & W. Lonner (Eds.), *Applied cross-cultural psychology.* Amsterdam: Swets & Zeitlinger.

Ramsey, S. (1979). Nonverbal behavior: An intercultural perspective. In M. Asante, E. Newmark, & C. Blake (Eds.), *Handbook of international communication.* Newbury Park, CA: Sage.

Roberts, K. H. (1970). On looking at an elephant: An evaluation of cross-cultural research related to organizations. *Psychological Bulletin, 74,* 327-350.

Robinson, W. S. (1950). Ecological correlations and the behavior of individuals. *American Sociological Review, 15,* 351-357.

Rogers, E. M. (1983). *Diffusion of innovations* (3rd ed.). New York: Free Press.

Rogers, E. M., & Kincaid, D. L. (1981). *Communication networks.* New York: Free Press.

Rohner, R. P. (1984). Toward a conception of culture for cross-cultural psychology. *Journal of Cross-Cultural Psychology, 15,* 111-138.

Rokeach, M., Smith, P., & Evans, R. (1960). Two kinds of prejudice or one? In M. Rokeach (Ed.), *The open and closed mind.* New York: Basic Books.

Rosch, E. (1978). Human categorization. In N. Warren (Ed.), *Studies in cross-cultural psychology* (Vol. 1). London: Academic Press.

Rose, T. L. (1981). Cognitive and dyadic processes in intergroup contact. In D. Hamilton (Ed.), *Cognitive processes in stereotyping and intergroup behavior.* Hillsdale, NJ: Lawrence Erlbaum.

Rothbart, M., Dawes, R., & Park, B. (1984). Stereotyping and sampling biases in intergroup perception. In J. Eiser (Ed.), *Attitudinal judgement.* New York: Springer-Verlag.

Ruben, B., & Kealey, D. (1979). Behavioral assessment of communication competency and the prediction of cross-cultural adaptation. *International Journal of Intercultural Relations, 3,* 15-48.

Rubovits, P., & Maehr, M. (1973). Pygmalian in black and white. *Journal of Personality and Social Psychology, 25,* 210-218.

Rummel, R. J. (1972). *The dimensions of nations.* Newbury Park, CA: Sage.

Ryan, E., Giles, H., & Sebastian, R. (1982). An integrative perspective for the study of attitudes toward language. In E. Ryan & H. Giles (Eds.), *Attitudes toward language variation.* London: Edward Arnold.

Ryan, E., Hewstone, M., & Giles, H. (1984). Language and intergroup attitudes. In J. Eiser (Ed.), *Attitudinal judgment.* New York: Springer-Verlag.

Schaupp, D. (1978). *A cross-cultural study of a multinational company.* New York, NY: Praeger.

Scherer, K. (1984). Emotion as a multicomponent process: A model and some cross-cultural data. *Review of Personality and Social Psychology, 5,* 37-63.

Scherer, K., Summerfield, A., & Wallbott, H. (1983). Cross-national research on antecedents and components of emotion. *Social Science Information, 22,* 355-385.

Schollhammer, H. (1969). The comparative management theory jungle. *Academy of Management Journal, 13,* 81-97.

Schramm, W., & Lerner, C. (Eds.). (1976). *Communication and change.* Honolulu: University of Hawaii Press.

Scotton, C., & Ury, W. (1977). Bilingual strategies: The social functions of code switching. *International Journal of the Sociology of Language, 13,* 5-20.

Sears, R. (1961). Transcultural variables and conceptual equivalence. In B. Kaplan (Ed.), *Studying personality cross-culturally.* New York: Harper.

Sechrest, L. (1977). On the dearth of theory in cross-cultural psychology. In Y. Poortinga (Ed.), *Basic problems in cross-cultural psychology.* Amsterdam: Swets & Zeitlinger.

Segalowitz, N. (1980). Issues in cross-cultural study of bilingual development. In H. Triandis & A. Heron (Eds.), *Handbook of cross-cultural psychology* (Vol. 4). Boston: Allyn & Bacon.

Segall, M. H. (1983). On the search for the independent variable in cross-cultural psychology. In S. Irvine & J. Berry (Eds.), *Human assessment and cultural factors*. New York: Plenum Press.

Sherif, M. (1966). *Group conflict and cooperation*. London: Routledge & Kegan Paul.

Shuter, R. (1982). Initial interactions of American blacks and whites in interracial and intraracial dyads. *Journal of Social Psychology, 117,* 45-52.

Shweder, R., & LeVine, R. (Eds.). (1984). *Culture theory.* Cambridge: Cambridge University Press.

Simmel, G. (1950). The stranger. In K. Wolff (Ed. & Trans.). *The sociology of Georg Simmel.* New York: Free Press.

Simonetti, S., & Weitz, J. (1972). Job-satisfaction: Some cross-cultural effects. *Personnel Psychology, 25,* 107-118.

Smith, H. (1981). Territorial spacing on a beach revisited: A cross-national exploration. *Social Psychology Quarterly, 44,* 132-137.

Spates, J. L. (1983). The sociology of values. *Annual Review of Sociology, 9,* 27-49.

Stephan, W. (1985). Intergroup relations. In G. Lindzey & E. Aronson (Eds.), *Handbook of social psychology* (3rd ed.). New York: Random House.

Stephan, W., & Brigham, J. (Eds.). (1985). Intergroup contact [Special issue]. *Journal of Social Issues, 41*(3).

Stephenson, G. M. (1981). Intergroup bargaining and negotiation. In J. Turner & H. Giles (Eds.), *Intergroup behavior.* Chicago: University of Chicago Press.

Street, R., & Giles, H. (1982). Speech accommodation theory. In M. Roloff & C. Berger (Eds.), *Social cognition and communication.* Newbury Park, CA: Sage.

Suddenfield, P. (1967). Paternal absence and the overseas success of Peace Corp volunteers. *Journal of Consulting Psychology, 31,* 424-425.

Sussman, N., & Rosenfeld, H. (1982). Influence of culture, language and sex on conversational distance. *Journal of Personality and Social Psychology, 42,* 66-74.

Szalay, L., & Deese, J. (1978). *Subjective meaning and culture.* Hillsdale, NJ: Lawrence Erlbaum.

Tajfel, H. (1978). Social categorization, social identity, and social comparison. In H. Tajfel (Ed.), *Differentiation between social groups.* London: Academic Press.

Tajfel, H. (1981a). *Human categories and social groups.* Cambridge: Cambridge University Press.

Tajfel, H. (1981b). Social stereotypes and social groups. In J. Turner & H. Giles (Eds.), *Intergroup behavior.* Chicago: University of Chicago Press.

Tajfel, H. (Ed.). (1982). *Social identity and intergroup relations.* Cambridge: Cambridge University Press.

Tajfel, H., & Turner, J. (1979). An integrative theory of intergroup conflict. In W. Austin & S. Worchel (Eds.), *The social psychology of intergroup relations.* Monterey, CA: Brooks/Cole.

Tannenbaum, A. (1980). Organizational psychology. In H. Triandis & R. Brislin (Eds.), *Handbook of cross-cultural psychology* (Vol. 5). Boston: Allyn & Bacon.

Tannenbaum, A., Kavcic, B., Rossner, M., Vianello, M., & Weiser, G. (1974). *Hierarchy in organizations.* San Francisco: Jossey-Bass.

Taylor, D., & Guimond, S. (1978). The belief theory of prejudice in an inter-group context. *Journal of Social Psychology, 105,* 11-25.

Taylor, D., & Jaggi, V. (1974). Ethnocentrism and causal attribution in a South Indian context. *Journal of Cross-Cultural Psychology, 5,* 162-171.

Taylor, D., & Simard, L. (1975). Social interaction in a bilingual setting. *Canadian Psychological Review, 16,* 240-254.

Thibaut, J., & Kelley, H. (1959). *The social psychology of groups.* New York: John Wiley.

Thorndike, E. (1939). On the fallacy of inputting the correlations found for groups to the individual of smaller groups composing them. *American Journal of Psychology, 3,* 122-124.

Tiamaeus, E. (1968). Untersuchungen zum sogenannten konformen Verhatten. *Zeitschrift fur Experimentelle and Angewandte Psychologie, 15,* 176-194.

Ting-Toomey, S. (1981). Ethnic identity and close friendship in Chinese-American college students. *International Journal of Intercultural Relations, 5,* 383-406.

Ting-Toomey, S. (1985). Toward a theory of conflict and culture. In W. Gudykunst, L. Stewart, & S. Ting-Toomey (Eds.), *Communication, culture, and organizational processes.* Newbury Park, CA: Sage.

Triandis, H. C. (1961). A note on Rokeach's theory of prejudice. *Journal of Abnormal and Social Psychology, 62,* 184-186.

Triandis, H. C. (1967). Toward an analysis of components of interpersonal attitudes. In C. Sherif & M. Sherif (Eds.), *Attitude, ego-involvement, and change.* New York: John Wiley.

Triandis, H. C. (1968). Some cross-cultural studies of cognitive consistency. In R. Abelson et al. (Eds.), *Theories of cognitive consistency.* Chicago: Rand McNally.

Triandis, H. C. (1972). *The analysis of subjective culture.* New York: John Wiley.

Triandis, H. C. (1976). On the value of cross-cultural research in social psychology. *European Journal of Social Psychology, 6,* 331-341.

Triandis, H. C. (1977). *Interpersonal behavior.* Monterey, CA: Brooks/Cole.

Triandis, H. C. (1978). Some universals of social behavior. *Personality and Social Psychology Bulletin, 4,* 1-16.

Triandis, H. C. (1980a). Values, attitudes, and interpersonal behavior. In M. Page (Ed.), *Nebraska symposium on motivation 1979* (Vol. 27). Lincoln: University of Nebraska Press.

Triandis, H. C. (1980b). Introduction to handbook. In H. Triandis & W. Lambert (Eds.), *Handbook of cross-cultural psychology* (Vol. 1). Boston: Allyn & Bacon.

Triandis, H. C. (1984). A theoretical framework for the more efficient construction of culture assimilators. *International Journal of Intercultural Relations, 8,* 301-330.

Triandis, H. C. (1985). Collectivism vs. individualism. In C. Bagley & G. Verma (Eds.), *Personality, cognition and values.* London: Macmillan.

Triandis, H. C. (in press). Cross-cultural research in organization psychology. In M. Dunnette (Ed.), *Handbook of industrial and organization psychology* (2nd ed.). New York: John Wiley.

Triandis, H. C., & Berry, J. (Eds.). (1980). *Handbook of cross-cultural psychology. Vol 2: Methodology.* Boston: Allyn & Bacon.

Triandis, H. C., & Davis, E. (1965). Race and belief as determinants of behavioral intentions. *Journal of Personality and Social Psychology, 2,* 715-725.

Triandis, H. C., Hui, C., Albert, R., Leung, S., Lisansky, J., Betancourt, H., & Loyola-Cintron, C. (1984). Individual models of social behavior. *Journal of Personality and Social Psychology, 46,* 1389-1404.

Triandis, H. C., Malpass, R., & Davidson. (1973). Cross-cultural psychology. *Biennial Review of Anthropology, 24,* 1-84.

Triandis, H. C., & Marin, G. (1983). Etic plus emic versus pseudoetic. *Journal of Cross-Cultural Psychology, 14,* 489-500.

Turner, J. (1982). Towards a cognitive redefinition of the social group. In H. Tajfel (Ed.), *Social identity and intergroup relations.* Cambridge: Cambridge University Press.

Van Dijk, T. A. (1984). *Prejudice in discourse: An analysis of ethnic prejudice in cognition and conversation.* Amsterdam: John Benjamins.

Varonis, E. M., & Gass, S. M. (1985). Miscommunication in native/nonnative conversation. *Language in Society, 14,* 327-343.

Warr, P., & Haycock, V. (1970). Scales for a British personality differential. *British Journal of Social and Clinical Psychology, 9,* 328-337.

Watson, O. (1970). *Proxemic behavior: A cross-cultural study.* The Hague: Mouton.

Wegner, D., & Vallacher, P. (1977). *Implicit psychology.* New York: Oxford University Press.

Wiemann, G. (1983). The not-so-small world: Ethnicity and acquaintance networks in Israel. *Social Networks, 5,* 289-302.

Wetherall, M. (1982). Cross-cultural studies of minimal groups. In H. Tajfel (Ed.), *Social identity and intergroup relations.* Cambridge: Cambridge University Press.

Wigand, R. (1982). Direct satellite broadcasting. In M. Burgoon (Ed.), *Communication yearbook 6.* Newbury Park, CA: Sage.

Witkin, H. A., & Berry, J. W. (1975). Psychological differentiation in cross-cultural perspective. *Journal of Cross-Cultural Psychology, 6,* 4-87.

Witkin, H. S., Dyk, R., Faterson, H., Goodenough, D., & Karp, S. (1962). *Psychological differentiation.* New York: John Wiley.

Wright, G. N., & Phillips, L. (1980). Cultural variation in probabilistic thinking. *International Journal of Psychology, 15,* 239-257.

Wright, G. N., Phillips, L., Whalley, P., Choo, G., Ng, K., Tan, I., & Wisudha, A. (1978). Cultural differences in probabilistic thinking. *Journal of Cross-Cultural Psychology, 9,* 285-299.

Wright, G. N., Phillips, L., & Wisudha, A. (1983). Cultural comparisons on decision-making under uncertainty. In J. Deregowski, S. Dziurawiec, & R. Annis (Eds.), *Expications in cross-cultural psychology.* Lisse: Swets & Zeitlinger.

Wyer, R., & Srull, T. (1980). The processing of social stimulus information. In R. Hastie et al. (Eds.), *Person memory: The cognitive basis of social perception.* Hillsdale, NJ: Lawrence Erlbaum.

Yu, D. (Ed.). (1982). *Ethnicity and interpersonal interaction: A cross-cultural study.* Singapore: Maruzen Asia.

Yum, J. (1982). Communication diversity and information acquisition among Korean immigrants in Hawaii. *Human Communication Research, 8,* 154-169.

Yum, J. (1983). Social network patterns of five ethnic groups in Hawaii. In R. Bostrom (Ed.), *Communication yearbook 7.* Newbury Park, CA: Sage.

Zavalloni, M. (1975). Social identity and the recoding of reality. *International Journal of Psychology, 10,* 197-217.

Zavalloni, M. (1980). Values. In H. Triandis & R. Brislin (Eds.), *Handbook of cross-cultural psychology* (Vol. 5). Boston: Allyn & Bacon.

PART V
CONCLUSION

28 Epilogue

STEVEN H. CHAFFEE
Stanford University

CHARLES R. BERGER
Northwestern University

T HERE were a number of ways the chapters of this handbook could have been organized. By structuring it the way we did, and because of proverbial space limitations, some topics could not be included. For example, no specific chapter is devoted to the emerging communication technologies. Nevertheless, several chapters raise issues about these technologies within their areas of focus. Hewes and Planalp (Chapter 6) describe how conversations can be simulated with artificial intelligence programs. Giles and Wiemann (Chapter 12) indicate that new technologies perpetuate sexism by using male voices in important situations and female voices in less critical contexts. Pettegrew and Logan (Chapter 22) describe how doctors are adapting to computer-assisted medical information systems. Jablin and Krone (Chapter 23) speculate about the effects new technologies have on organizational socialization. So even though no particular chapter focuses upon new technologies, several chapters reflect the interest in technology that permeates the field.

Several of our authors consider technological impacts in their particular domains of inquiry. Perhaps this is as it should be for now. While it is obvious that new technologies will have considerable impact upon social behavior in general and communication in particular, this concern is currently devoid of a unique theoretical focus. It may be more useful to study these new technologies within contexts that already have well-developed theoretical bases. When a corpus of theory is developed in new technologies, the time will be right for that area's inclusion in this handbook.

This volume also has no chapter on communication policy. Still, policy is a pervasive concern. There is continued interest in the issue of television advertising directed toward children and how it should be regulated. The same is true for media violence. Giles and Wiemann (Chapter 12) discuss national language policies, and Roloff (Chapter 16) describes the efforts of various pressure groups to alter media content. Fitzpatrick (Chapter 19) mentions how government policy toward the family influences the funding of marital research. Ettema and Whitney with Wackman (Chapter 24) touch upon communication policy issues in their discussion of media professionals. These social issues are important and communication scientists are frequently asked for their opinions when policies are being formulated or modified.

Another omission, which we discussed at length while planning this book, is a chapter on communication research methods. Given the veritable explosion in data collection devices and methods, and the continuing development of statistical techniques to handle complex multivariate analysis of data, we felt no chapter could do justice to this topic. However, several of our authors discuss methodological issues. Cappella (Chapter 7) outlines techniques that might be used to answer different levels of questions on interpersonal communication. McLeod and Blumler (Chapter 9) point to several methodological issues in the study of macro-level communication systems. Knapp, Cody, and Reardon (Chapter 13) cite several problems encountered in experimental studies of deception. Fitzpatrick (Chapter 19) devotes considerable space to describing pitfalls in measuring marital quality. Gudykunst (Chapter 27) describes methodological decisions that intercultural communication researchers face. Integration of methodological issues and substantive theorical concerns is a welcome development. Too many times, researchers hop on the newest methodological bandwagon and fall prey to Kaplan's (1964) Law of the Instrument, using a favored technique to study all research questions even when its use is unjustified. Our authors have shown how thoughtful consideration of theoretical issues leads naturally to the choice of appropriate techniques, if available.

Even though we did not include a methods chapter in this volume, we feel that human communication presents researchers with *unique* methodological problems. For example, communication researchers at all levels are concerned with change over time. At the intrapersonal level we focus on changes in knowledge structures and memory processes as a function of communicative experience. At the interpersonal level, where mutual influence is the key phenomenon, the temporal dimension is of critical importance. How social networks evolve through time is crucial to prediction and explanation of organizational behavior. Finally, media as well as other institutions generally do not have dramatic effects on publics at one point in time. Rather, effects are accretive and require time to manifest themselves. The institutions themselves typically show slow rates of change.

Not only are communication scientists concerned with change through time, their unique focus on *message exchanges* and *message impacts* requires that they deal with the very complex problems associated with text and discourse analysis. Communication researchers have to deal with reliability and validity of message analysis schemes, and they must also be concerned with theoretical justifications for such schemes. Unfortunately, interaction coding schemes as well as systems for analyzing messages disseminated by media and other institutions are frequently ad hoc affairs with little or no underlying theoretical rationale. Worse, the validity of these schemes is almost never assessed. The manifold difficulties of analyses of written texts and discourse should not deter communication scientists. Indeed, message analysis is perhaps the single activity that sets communication scientists apart from other social science researchers.

In discussing the omission of chapters on new technologies, communication policy, and methodology, it is apparent that these concerns cut across all four levels of analysis dealt with in this volume. New technologies influence the ways that persons process information individually, the interactions they have in informal social situations, their work relationships and their dealings with institutions. Similarly, communication policy decisions by government agencies as well as other institutions can affect communication at all levels. And we have shown how methodological concerns cut across levels. These three areas show how our four levels of analysis can be integrated.

We see some additional commonalities across the levels of this volume. In Chapter 3, we point to the importance of providing definitions for key theoretical constructs. Several authors wrestle with this definitional process in their chapters. Cappella's (Chapter 7) exercise in "definitional minimalism" is a good case in point, but there are several others. Knapp et al. (Chapter 13) delineate several types of deception in communication transactions. Two chapters (O'Keefe & Reid-Nash, Chapter 14; Wartella & Reeves, Chapter 20) pay considerable attention to the construct of "communication competence," a term that is currently gaining popularity in a number of sectors of the discipline. Other authors provide definitions for such key constructs as conflict (Roloff, Chapter 16), optimally functioning families (Bochner & Eisenberg, Chapter 18), and public opinion (Price & Roberts, Chapter 25). These construct explications help us clarify the meanings of theoretical terms so they can be shared by members of the research community. This "diffusion of meaning" is essential for clarity in scientific communication and development of useful theories.

Several chapters raise the problem of meaningful aggregation of individuals into larger social entities. Cappella (Chapter 7) specifies conditions necessary for interpersonal communication to occur. One must demonstrate that a person behaves differently when confronted by another. Bochner and Eisenberg (Chapter 18) point out that individual measures of interaction behavior are not sufficient to make inferences about the relative power of individuals in a family. Message exchanges must be the unit of analysis to determine control. Fitzpatrick (Chapter 19) considers the problem of aggregating responses of husbands and wives to estimate marital happiness. Price and Roberts (Chapter 25) present cogent arguments to support the position that public opinion is not merely the sum of individual opinions. Instead, they suggest, public opinion is a process involving both mass media and interpersonal communication in which opinions emerge. Finally, Gudykunst (Chapter 27) discusses problems associated with ecological correlations to relate group characteristics to individuals. Although the substantive interests of these researchers are quite different, they face similar problems of data aggregation.

A final commonality among these chapters is their scholarly excellence. The authors worked long and hard to produce the chapters of this volume, in most cases going well beyond their usual areas of scholarship. While it was impossible for them to cover all aspects of their particular areas, they provide ample sources for interested readers to consult. We are especially impressed with their graciousness in the face of revisions. Their dedication to the craft accounts for their excellent contributions.

In Chapter 1 we described the excitement surrounding the "new discipline" of communication that Schramm wrote about some 25 years ago. We noted that the communication discipline then was seen as a crossroads where travelers from psychology, sociology, political science, and linguistics met to do research.

A look at our contributors' biographies reveals that most received their graduate education in departments of communication. Those who did not study in the discipline have made long-term commitments to communication, many through academic department affiliations. This book attests to the vitality and cohesion of communication science.

The commonalities across the work in this handbook suggest an increase in disciplinary integration. Despite different substantive backgrounds, we as editors have found it quite easy to collaborate on this volume. The lines between the studies of interpersonal, mass, organizational, political, and health communication are becoming blurred. This is a most positive trend, one that will encourage development of more general theories of communication. Whether there is to be *a* general theory of communication is a question we cannot answer. But we can say with confidence that the work presented in this volume portends a healthy and vital future for communication science.

REFERENCE

Kaplan, A. (1964). *The conduct of inquiry.* San Francisco: Chandler Publishing.

AUTHOR INDEX

Deese, J., 887
DeFleur, M. L., 21, 66, 89, 286, 293, 294, 310, 315, 316, 319, 453, 456, 457, 478, 840
DeGrazia, S., 29, 91
Delia, J., 129, 146, 147, 149, 150, 151, 157, 165, 174, 175, 176, 179, 192, 236, 240, 265, 441, 628, 646, 716, 739
Dell, P., 543, 544, 560
DelPolito, C. M., 684, 701
Dembroski, T. M., 678, 701
Dengerink, H. A., 493, 523
Denison, D. R., 388, 418
Dennis, H. S., 111, 120, 392, 399, 415
Dentch, G., 606
Denzin, N. K., 148, 175
DePaulo, B. M., 148, 183, 366, 375, 392, 393, 397, 398, 399, 400, 402, 403, 413, 414, 417, 418, 496, 530
Deregowski, J., 879
Derrida, J., 135, 136, 137, 138
Dervin, B., 843
Desmond, R. J., 33, 77, 89, 635, 646
de Sola Pool, I., 56, 251, 261, 265
DeSousa, M., 879
de Turck, M., 111, 121, 209, 231, 396, 414, 416
Detweiler, R., 858, 868, 879
Deutsch, K. W., 343, 348, 433, 441
Deutsch, M., 371, 485, 486, 520, 590, 611
DeVilliers, J. G., 166, 175
DeVilliers, P. A., 175
DeVos, G., 884
Dewey, J., 24, 25, 29, 31, 38, 66, 89, 281, 317, 782, 813
Dewey, M. E., 170, 180
DeWick, H. N., 50, 89
DeWitt, J., 588, 690, 702
Dewitt, K. N., 607
Diamond, E., 509, 520
Diaz-Guerrero, R., 874, 879
Dichter, E., 654, 673
Dickinson, R. L., 584, 606
Dickson, W. J., 42, 96
Dickson, W. P., 626, 627, 646
Diener, E., 504, 520
Diez, M. E., 419, 441, 462, 478
Dillard, J. P., 206, 207, 232, 240, 268, 469, 477, 587, 606
DiMaggio, P., 750, 752, 754, 757, 775
DiMatteo, M. R., 389, 414, 417, 677, 680, 681, 701, 702, 703
Dimmick, J., 749, 766, 769, 775
Dindia, K., 219, 233, 571, 585, 606, 607
DiNicola, D. D., 677, 681
Dion, K., 423, 441
diSciullo, A., 866, 879
DiTecco, D., 702
Dittmann, A. T., 196, 232, 414
Divine, C., 517

Doane, J., 548, 552, 553, 560
Dobb, L. W., 90
Dodd, S., 35, 293
Doelger, J. A., 153, 155, 156, 157, 165, 167, 168, 170, 172, 175, 177, 180, 366, 378
Doherty, W. J., 581, 606
Dohrenwend, B. P., 597, 606
Dohrenwend, B. S., 597, 606
Doise, W., 359, 375, 793, 800, 813
Domhoff, G. W., 259, 265
Dominick, J., 507, 520, 751, 763, 775
Donaldson, M., 624, 646
Donnerstein, E., 370, 379
Donohew, L., 765, 775
Donohue, G. A., 273, 286, 296, 317, 321, 764, 775, 778
Donohue, T. R., 462, 502, 505, 520
Donohue, W. A., 478, 520
Doob, A. N., 512, 520
Doob, L., 59
Dooling, D. J., 160, 175
Doolittle, J., 102, 119
Doran, N. E., 469, 477
Dorman, W. A., 773, 775
Dorr, A., 421, 429, 441
Douglas, D. F., 843
Douglas, J. D., 37, 90
Douglas, M., 131, 138
Douglas, W., 476
Downing, H., 608
Downs, A., 497, 498, 520
Downs, W. G., 760, 775
Drabman, R. S., 305, 520
Drake, G., 361, 375
Draper, P., 389, 414
Drecksel, G. L., 212, 233
Dreier, P., 762, 775
Drenth, P., 865, 879
Dreyer, A., 495, 530, 589, 616
Driver, A., 862, 879
Driver, E., 862, 879
Driver, M. H., 717, 744
Driver, M. J., 109, 121
Driver, R. E., 397, 400, 402, 418
Droba, D. D., 29, 38, 90
Droge, D., 676, 680, 682, 686, 699, 701
Drucker, P., 714, 739
Druckman, D., 462, 478
Dryden, C., 375
Dube-Simard, L., 362, 375
DuBick, M. A., 763, 775
Duby, G., 566, 606
Duchnowski, A., 397, 416
Duck, S., 355, 364, 375, 380, 431, 441
Duffy, M., 691, 701
Dulany, D. E., 154, 175
Dumas, M., 739
Duncan, H. D., 31, 90

SUBJECT INDEX

Actors, political, 804-805
Adaptation studies, 216-217
Advertising, 409-410, 640-641, 751, 841; level of effects research, 50, 656-658; growth, 46; scientific, 47-49
Advocacy, counterattitudinal, 448, 452, 459-462
Affect, 205, 207, 566-567, 583-586, 869
Affiliation, 336, 337, 339-340
Affiliativeness, 209
Age and communication, 422-423
Agenda-setting, 105-106, 277-278, 303, 309, 363, 808
Aggression and television, 103-104, 426-427, 506-508
Alienation and the media, 66-67
American Association for Opinion Research, 29
American Sociological Association, 31, 58
Anthropology and communication, 37, 131
Anxiety, 80
Army, Information and Education Division, 55
Arousal, 205, 354, 397, 640
Assimilation, organizational, 432-433, 711-738; definitions, 712-714; interpersonal, 720-726; intraindividual, 714-719; macro/social, 731-737; network/organizational, 726-731
Asymmetry, 355
Attitudes, 28, 103, 205, 453-457; assessment, 660; change, 43, 64, 284, 335, 453-457; scaling procedures, 38; Yale School, 60, 63-65
Attraction, 431, 462
Attributional processes, 454, 493, 581
Audiences, 50, 758, 768-769; atomistic, 66; social networks, 66-68, 146
Authority, 500
Avoidance, 187

Bargaining, 462, 501-502
Behavior modification, 451-452, 691-693
Behaviorism, 23, 77; in advertising, 48-49, 653-654; psychological, 48; social, 38
Behaviors, 196-200, 331, 492-495, 499-500, 789, 861
Being function of communication, 333, 334, 339, 341, 343
Bilingualism, 866
Boundaries, organizational, 253-254
Boundary conditions, 102
Boundary-spanners, 245, 254-256, 502-503, 752

Broadcasting, 311; commercialization, 47; regulation, 47

Campaigns, communication, 273, 278-279, 429, 679, 817-842; definitions, 818-821; effects, 690-693; future research, 841-842; history of research, 817-818, 825-836; locus of benefit, 824; locus of change, 823-824; objectives, 818-819, 822-823
Casting conventions, 852-853
Chicago School of Sociology, 30-37, 49
Child language, 621-623
Children and communication, 619-643; communicative competence, 625-642; future research, 642-643; language acquisition, 620-625; research trends, 42
Children and the media, 22-23, 292, 629-643, 667-669; attention, 633-634; consumption, 629-631; effects of message content, 639-642; inferences, 634-635; interpersonal factors, 637-638; message processing, 631-639; retention, 634, 635; social reality, 640-641
Choice in theory construction, 296-300
Class, 357, 434-435, 595-596; and media usage, 748; struggle, 596
Climate, organizational, 240
Cognition: and emotion, 158; and opinion, 782-783
Cognitive development, 625-629
Cognitive/interpretive approaches, 156-172; and complexity of the individual, 158; and communication processes, 157, 169-172; definition, 156-157; discourse processing, 159-163; and intersubjectivity, 159; and message impact, 169-170; social metacognition, 164-169
Cognitive processes, 161-163, 387, 794-795; definition, 157; implementation, 162-163; inference, 161, 163, 166, 859; integration, 161, 163, 166, 190; focusing, 161, 166; and prior knowledge, 794; retrieval, 161-162, 166; selection, 162-163; storage, 161-162, 166
Cognitive responses, 457-459, 661-663
Commercially focused research, 46-54
Communality, 292
Communication: and industrialization, 24; and literacy, 24; and urbanization, 24
Communication acts, 153

ABOUT THE AUTHORS

CHARLES R. BERGER (Ph.D., Michigan State University) is Professor of Communication Studies at Northwestern University. Author of numerous articles on the development of interpersonal relationships and social information gathering, his current publications include *Language and Social Knowledge* (with James Bradac) and *Social Cognition and Communication* (co-edited with Michael E. Roloff), the former having won the Speech Communication Association's Golden Book Award. In addition to his distinguished publishing record, he is currently on the editorial board of *Human Communication Research* which he also served as Editor from 1983-1986.

JAY G. BLUMLER is Professor of the Social and Political Aspects of Broadcasting and Director of the Centre for Television Research at the University of Leeds, and Associate Director of the Center for Research in Public Communication in the College of Journalism at the University of Maryland. He is a Founding Coeditor of the *European Journal of Communication,* and has taught at the Annenberg School of Communications of the University of Southern California, and the University of Wisconsin—Madison. His research interests include studies of media effects, especially on voting behavior. He is coauthor (with Denis McQuail) of *Television and Politics,* and coeditor (with Elihu Katz) of *The Uses of Mass Communication*. He headed the multinational research team that studied the first parliamentary elections of the European Community. He recently completed a report, "Television in the United States: Funding Sources and Programming Consequences," for the UK's Peacock Committee on Financing the BBC.

ARTHUR P. BOCHNER (Ph.D., Bowling Green State University) is Professor of Communication at the University of South Florida. He has contributed more than 25 articles to both national and international journals and has authored several monographs and chapters in books on interpersnal relationships. He is currently studying the effects of serious illness on marital and family communication.

JOSEPH N. CAPPELLA (Ph.D., Michigan State University) is Professor, Department of Communication Arts and Center for Communication Research at the University of Wisconsin—Madison. He currently serves as Editor of the journal *Human Communication Research*. He has also coedited two books, *Multivariate Techniques in Human Communication Research* with Peter R. Monge (Academic Press) and *Sequence and Pattern in Communicative Behavior* with Richard L. Street. His research interests include interaction patterns for adult and child-adult groups and the mathematical and statistical representation of these interactions.

STEVEN H. CHAFFEE (Ph.D., Stanford University), is Janet M. Peck Professor of International Communication and Chairman of the Department of Communication at Stanford University. Former Director of the School of Journalism and Mass Communication at the University of Wisconsin—Madison and Past-President of the International Communication Association, he is currently on the editorial board of the journal *Communication Research,* which he served as Editor of from 1985-1986, and four other editorial boards. His publications include *Using the Mass Media* (with Michael Petrick), *Political Communication,* and *Television and Human Behavior* (with George Comstock and others).

MICHAEL J. CODY (Ph.D. Michigan State University) is Associate Professor at the Department of Communication Arts, University of Southern California. He is coauthor of *Persuasive Communication* (with E. P. Bettinghaus) and publishes articles in nonverbal communication and social influence.

JESSE G. DELIA (Ph.D., University of Kansas) is Professor and Head, Department of Speech Communication, and Research Professor, Institute of Communications Research, at the University of Illinois. In 1981, he was a senior Fulbright Scholar in Australia. He has also lectured at virtually all major communication programs in American universities, primarily on issues in communication theory and research. His major research interests are in interpersonal communication processes. His publications include numerous journal articles, book chapters, and *The Nature of Human Communication* (Science Research Associates). He is currently working on a full-length book that will cover the history and development of the field of communication research in greater depth.

ERIC M. EISENBERG (Ph.D., Michigan State University) is Assistant Professor of Communication Arts and Sciences at the University of Southern California. His articles dealing with organizational communication have appeared in *Human Communication Research, Communication Monographs,* and the *Journal of Communication.* His paper "Ambiguity as Strategy in Organizational Communication" won the Speech Communication Association's Award for the Outstanding Publication in organizational communication, 1983-1984.

JAMES S. ETTEMA (Ph.D., University of Michigan) is Associate Professor of Communication Studies at Northwestern University. He previously taught in the School of Journalism and Mass Communication at the University of Minnesota. He conducts research on the social organization and impact of the mass media and new communication technology and is the author of *Working Together: A Study of Cooperation Among Producers, Educators and Researchers to Create Educational Television,* coauthor (with Jerome Johnston) of *Positive Images: Breaking Stereotypes with Children's Television* and coeditor (with D. Charles Whitney) of *Individuals in Mass Media Organizations: Creativity and Constraint.*

THOMAS B. FARRELL (Ph.D., University of Wisconsin—Madison) is Professor of Communication Studies at Northwestern University. He was educated at the universities of Chicago and Wisconsin, where he received his Ph.D. in 1974. He taught at the University of Southern California and UCLA before coming to Northwestern in 1976. Farrell's research focuses on the forms and practices of discourse formation in political and other public settings. He has published work on the limits of technical knowledge in public life, and the difference between narrative in conversation and rhetoric. Several of Farrell's studies of social knowledge and language action have received research awards. In 1980, Farrell's first dissertation advisee, James Aune, received an outstanding dissertation award. Farrell became chair of the Department of Communication Studies in 1983 and served in that capacity until 1986, when he received the Van Zelst chair of Communication Studies. He is working on a book uniting the rhetorical tradition with contemporary issues in ethical theory. Currently, Farrell serves on the editorial board of the journal *Philosophy and Rhetoric.*

MARY ANNE FITZPATRICK (Ph.D., Temple University) is Professor of Communication Arts and Director of the Center for Communication Research at the University of Wisconsin—Madison. She has published numerous articles and book chapters on interpersonal communication and relationships, with special interests in the marriage and family area. Fitzpatrick's current research interests include discourse processing and the connection between cognition, emotion, and marital interaction. Her books include *Perspectives on Marital Interaction* (coedited with Patricia Noller) and one in process on her marital typology.

HOWARD GILES (Ph.D., Bristol University) is Professor of Social Psychology and Director of the Centre for Communication and Social Relations at Bristol University. He has also taught at the University of California at Santa Barbara and at numerous universities in Europe, Canada, Japan, and the United States. He is the Founding Editor of the

Journal of Language and Social Psychology and has published widely in sociolinguistics, sociology, and communication. His research interests include interpersonal communication and intergroup communication (particularly intergenerational talk) and their relationships with health issues. He is the coauthor of *Speech Style and Social Evaluation* (Academic Press Ltd.) and editor of numerous books, including *Language, Ethnicity and Intergroup Relations* (Academic Press Ltd.); *Social Markers in Speech* (Cambridge University Press), with K. R. Scherer; *Intergroup Behavior* (Blackwell), with J. C. Turner; *Language: Social Psychological Perspectives* (Pergamon), with W. P. Robinson and P. M. Smith; *Language and Ethnic Relations* (Pergamon), with B. Saint-Jacques; *Recent Advances in Language, Communication and Social Psychology* (Lawrence Erlbaum), with R. N. St. Clair.

WILLIAM B. GUDYKUNST is Professor of Communication at Arizona State University. He previously taught at the State University of New York at Albany. He is the coauthor (with Y. Y. Kim) of *Communicating with Strangers* (Addison-Wesley), editor of *Intergroup Communication* (Edward Arnold Ltd.), and has served as Series Editor of the Intercultural and International Communication Annuals (published by Sage in cooperation with the Speech Communication Association), editing or coediting three volumes on theory, methods, and organizational communication in an intercultural context. He is currently coauthoring a book (with Elizabeth Chua) on the subject of intercultural communication at the interpersonal level, and coediting the forthcoming second edition of the *Handbook of Intercultural Communication* (with Molefi B. Asante), *Cross-Cultural Adaptation: Current Approaches,* and *Theoretical Perspectives on Intercultural Communication* (all from Sage).

DEAN E. HEWES (Ph.D., Florida State University) is Associate Professor of Speech Communication at the University of Illinois, Urbana-Champaign. He formerly taught at the University of Wisconsin—Madison. He has served as Associate Editor of *Communication Research* and has been a leader in the development of quantitative methods for the analysis of interpersonal interaction. He has published numerous articles and book chapters on a broad range of research interests including cognitive/interpretive approaches to interpersonal communication, small group communication, persuasion in message campaigns, rumor, interaction analysis, and research methodology.

FREDRIC M. JABLIN (Ph.D., Purdue University) is Associate Professor of Speech Communication at the University of Texas, Austin. His research has been published in a wide variety of communication, psychology, and management journals, and he is senior editor of the *Handbook of Organizational Communication* (Sage, 1987). He is a member of the editorial boards of the *Academy of Management Journal, Human*

Communication Research, and *Communication Research,* and has served as a consultant-researcher to a number of organizations. His current research interests are focused on exploring the nature of communication in the organizational assimilation process.

MARK L. KNAPP (Ph.D., Pennsylvania State University) is in the Department of Speech Communication at the University of Texas, Austin. He is past President of the International Communication Association and has served as Editor of *Human Communication Research.* He was the Founding Editor of the *Sage Series in Interpersonal Communication* and is coeditor (with Gerald R. Miller) of the recent *Handbook of Interpersonal Communication.* His research focuses mainly on nonverbal communication and communication in relationship development.

KATHLEEN J. KRONE (Ph.D., University of Texas, Austin) is Assistant Professor of Speech Communication at the Ohio State University. Her research interests include upward influence in organizations, communicative aspects of organizational assimilation, and interviewing.

ROBERT LOGAN (Ph.D., University of Iowa) is Director of the Science Journalism Center and an Associate Professor at the University of Missouri-Columbia School of Journalism. His recent articles and reviews have appeared in *Journal of Mass Media Ethics, Mass Comm. Review,* and *Proceedings of the American Association for Medical Systems and Informatics Congress* (1985, 1987). His research has focused on the diffusion of medical information systems and technologies.

JACK M. McLEOD (Ph.D., University of Michigan) is Maier-Bascom Professor of Journalism and Mass Communication and Chairman of the Mass Communications Research Center at the University of Wisconsin—Madison. He has published widely on media effects, with emphasis on political processes and socialization to media behaviors. His other research interests extend to professionalization of mass communicators, and interpersonal coorientation.

DENIS McQUAIL (Ph.D., University of Leeds) is Professor of Mass Communication at the University of Amsterdam. He has been affiliated to the television research unit, University of Leeds; the University of Southampton; and the Annenberg School of Communications, University of Pennsylvania. He is coauthor (with Jay Blumler) of *Television and Politics: Its Use and Influence* and author of the widely used textbook *Mass Communication Theory: An Introduction.* He is a Founding Coeditor of the *European Journal of Communication.* His other major publications include *Television and the Political Image* (with J. Trenaman); *Towards a Sociology of Mass Communications; Sociology of Mass Communications* (editor); *Communications; Review of Sociological Writ-*

ing on the Press; Analysis of Newspaper Content; and *Communication Models for the Study of Mass Communications.*

GERALD R. MILLER (Ph.D., University of Iowa) is Professor and Chairman of the Department of Communication at Michigan State University. He is a past President of the International Communication Association and has served as Founding Editor of *Human Communication Research* and as Editor of *Communication Monographs.* His recent books include *Videotape on Trial* (with Norman Fontes), which won the SCA's Golden Book Award, the coedited (with Mark L. Knapp) *Handbook of Interpersonal Communication, Interpersonal Processes: New Directions in Communication Research* (coedited with Michael E. Roloff), and *Persuasion: New Directions in Theory and Research* (coedited with Michael E. Roloff).

PETER R. MONGE (Ph.D., Michigan State University) is Professor of Communications in the Annenberg School of Communications, University of Southern California. He formerly taught at San Jose State University and Michigan State University. He is Editor of the journal *Communication Research,* coauthor of *Communicating and Organizing,* and coeditor (with Joseph N. Cappella) of *Multivariate Techniques in Human Communication Research.* He has published articles on applications of systems theory to communication, the role of emergent communication networks in organizations, the relationship of communication processes to organization participation, and research procedures for studying communication processes.

GARRETT J. O'KEEFE (Ph.D., University of Wisconsin—Madison) is Professor of Technical Journalism at Colorado State University, and was formerly Professor and Chair in the Department of Mass Communications at the University of Denver. He has published numerous articles and book chapters on mass media and politics, political socialization, and communication and socialization. His more recent research interests include the social and political effects of public information campaigns, as well as media impact on public perceptions of crime. He is currently conducting a long-term study of communication interventions to promote crime prevention among elderly persons.

LOYD S. PETTEGREW (Ph.D., University of Michigan) is an Associate Professor of Communication in the Department of Communication and is the Director of the Center for Organizational Communication Research and Service at the University of South Florida. He is the former Chair of the Health Communication Division of ICA and senior editor of the book *Straight Talk: Explorations in Provider and Patient Interaction* (Humana Inc., 1982). His research has focused largely on job-related stress, communication in health care organizations, and the relationship between health care providers and their patients.

SALLY PLANALP (Ph.D., University of Wisconsin—Madison) is Assistant Professor of Speech Communication at the University of Illinois. She previously taught at the University of Wisconsin—Madison. She studies relational communication, discourse processing, social cognition, and emotion. She has published both journal articles and book chapters growing out of her research in these areas.

VINCENT PRICE (Ph.D., Stanford University) is Assistant Professor of Communication at the University of Michigan. He was formerly an administrator and lectured in television production at the University of Santa Clara. His research interests center on social processes related to public opinion, and mass communication and persuasion.

BYRON REEVES (Ph.D., Michigan State University) is a Professor in the Institute for Communication Research at Stanford University. He was formerly Associate Chairman of the Mass Communications Research Center at the University of Wisconsin—Madison, and an Associate Editor of *Communication Research.* His research has focused on mass media effects, with particular emphasis on children and on advertising. He is currently conducting psychophysiological experiments (with Esther Thorson) on attentional processes in watching television.

KATHALEEN REID-NASH (Ph.D., University of Denver) is Assistant Professor of Language Arts at Lee College. She previously held faculty positions at the University of Denver and Colorado State University. Much of her work has focused on the uses and effects of public information campaigns, with particular emphasis on crime prevention campaigns and the elderly. Additional interests include rhetorical analysis and criticism, especially as applied to the visual arts and architecture.

KATHLEEN KELLEY REARDON (Ph.D., University of Massachusetts) is Associate Research Professor of Preventive Medicine at the Institute for Health Promotion and Disease Prevention, University of Southern California. She was previously an Associate Professor in the Department of Communication Sciences at the University of Connecticut. She was recently a Visiting Scholar at Stanford University. She currently serves as a lecturer for the Conference Board and has published a widely known study of international business gift giving customs. Her books include *Persuasion: Theory and Context* and *Where Minds Meet.* Her research interests include health communication, interpersonal communication, and persuasion.

DONALD F. ROBERTS (Ph.D., Stanford University) is Professor of Communication and Director of the Institute for Communication Research at Stanford University. He is coauthor (with George Comstock and others) of *Television and Social Behavior,* (Columbia University Press) and is conducting a long-term study of the impact of television on reading achievement by children. His recent publications include (with Nathan Maccoby) the chapter on mass media effects in the *Handbook of Social Psychology,* third edition, Volume 2 (Random House).

EVERETT M. ROGERS (Ph.D., Iowa State University) is Walter H. Annenberg Professor and Associate Dean in the Annenberg School of Communications, University of Southern California. A past President of the International Communication Association, he has taught at Ohio State University, Michigan State University, the University of Michigan, and Stanford University. His recent books include *Diffusion of Innovations* (Free Press), now in its third edition, *The Media Revolution in America and Western Europe* (Ablex), *Silicon Valley Fever* (Basic Books) and *Communication Technology* (Free Press). His research focuses on mass communication in national development, and diffusion and the impacts of new communication technologies.

MICHAEL E. ROLOFF (Ph.D., Michigan State University) is Professor of Communication Studies at Northwestern University. His research interests include bargaining and negotiation, conflict management, social exchange within intimate relationships, and persuasion. He wrote *Interpersonal Communication: The Social Exchange Approach,* and coedited *Persuasion: New Directions in Theory and Research* (with Gerald Miller), *New Developments in Interpersonal Communication* (with Gerald Miller), and *Social Cognition and Communication* (with Charles Berger). He has published articles in *Human Communication Research, Communication Monographs, Communication Quarterly,* and *Journal of Broadcasting* and served on the editorial boards of Human Communication Research and the *Central States Speech Communication Journal.*

J. DOUGLAS STOREY (M.A., University of Texas) is a doctoral candidate in the Institute for Communication Research at Stanford University. He has recently conducted research on the role of communication in development in Indonesia.

DANIEL B. WACKMAN (Ph.D., University of Wisconsin—Madison) is Professor of Journalism and Mass Communication at the University of Minnesota. His books include *How Children Learn to Buy* (with Scott Ward and Ellen Wartella), and *Working Together: Improving Communication on the Job.* He has recently coauthored *Managing Media Organizations.* (Longman, 1987). His current research focuses on relations between advertising agencies and their clients, and on the management of creative personnel.

SCOTT WARD (Ph.D., University of Wisconsin—Madison) is Professor of Marketing at the University of Pennsylvania's Wharton School. He formerly taught at the University of Washington and the Harvard Business School. His books include *How Children Learn to Buy* (with D. B.

Wackman and Ellen Wartella; Sage), *Problems in Marketing* (with E. R. Corey and C. Lovelock; McGraw-Hill) and *Consumer Behavior* (with T. S. Robertson and J. Zielinski; Scott-Foresman). His current research interests include cross-cultural issues in consumer socialization, marketing strategies in the deregulated environment, and customer behavior in large organizations.

ELLEN WARTELLA (Ph.D., University of Minnesota) is Associate Professor in the Institute of Communications Research at the University of Illinois. She formerly taught at Ohio State University and has been a Fellow of the Gannett Center for Media Studies at Columbia University. Her books include *Children Communicating* and (with Daniel Wackman and Scott Ward) *How Children Learn to Buy.* She was coeditor (with D. Charles Whitney) of Volumes 3 and 4 of the *Mass Communication Review Yearbook.* Her current research interests include the history of mass communication research and programming of television for children.

D. CHARLES WHITNEY (Ph.D., University of Minnesota) is Research Associate Professor in the Institute of Communications Research and Associate Professor of Journalism at the University of Illinois. He has also taught at Stanford University and Ohio State University, and was research coordinator at the Gannett Center for Media Studies at Columbia University from 1985 to 1986. He was coeditor (with Ellen Wartella) of Volumes 3 and 4 of the *Mass Communication Review Yearbook* and (with James Ettema) of *Individuals in Mass Media Organizations.* His research areas include the study of news media organizations, public opinion, and political communication.

JOHN M. WIEMANN (Ph.D., Purdue University) is Associate Professor of Communication Studies at the University of California, Santa Barbara. He is coeditor (with Robert Hawkins and Suzanne Pingree) of the Sage Annual Reviews of Communication Research for 1987-1991 and, with Hawkins and Pingree, is editing *Rethinking Communication Research,* Volume 16 of the series. He edited an earlier volume in that series, *Nonverbal Interaction* (with Randall Harrison); is coeditor (with John Daly) of *Communication Strategies* (Lawrence Erlbaum, in press), and coauthor (with James Bradac) of *Communicative Competence: A Theoretical Analysis* (Edward Arnold, in press). He is currently working (with Howard Giles) on a monograph on the subject of intergenerational communication. His research interests include communicative competence, nonverbal behavior, and conversation structure and strategy. He has been a W. K. Kellogg Foundation National Fellow (1980-1983) and Fulbright-Hayes Senior Research Scholar (1985) at the University of Bristol.

NOTES

NOTES

NOTES

NOTES

NOTES

NOTES